Collins
German
Dictionary

HarperCollins Publishers
Westerhill Road
Bishopbriggs
Glasgow
G64 2QT
Great Britain

First Edition 2005

© HarperCollins Publishers 2005

ISBN 0-00-720321-7

Collins® and Bank of English® are
registered trademarks of
HarperCollins Publishers Limited

www.collins.co.uk

A catalogue record for this book is
available from the British Library

HarperCollins Publishers, Inc.
10 East 53rd Street, New York,
NY 10022

ISBN 0-06-074901-6

Library of Congress Cataloging-in-
Publication Data has been applied for

www.harpercollins.com

HarperCollins books may be
purchased for educational, business,
or sales promotional use. For
information, please write to:
Special Markets Department,
HarperCollins Publishers Inc., 10 East
53rd Street, New York, NY 10022

Typeset by Morton Word Processing
Ltd, Scarborough

Printed in Italy by Amadeus S.r.l.

Acknowledgements
We would like to thank those authors
and publishers who kindly gave
permission for copyright material to
be used in the Collins Word Web. We
would also like to thank Times
Newspapers Ltd for providing
valuable data.

editors/Redaktion
Veronika Schnorr • Ute Nicol • Peter Terrell
Bob Grossmith • Helga Holtkamp • Horst Kopleck
Beate Wengel • John Whitlam

editorial staff/Manuskriptbearbeitung
Joyce Littlejohn • Elspeth Anderson
Christine Bahr • John Podbielski

series editor/Gesamtleitung
Lorna Sinclair Knight

William Collins' dream of knowledge for all began with the publication of his first book in 1819. A self-educated mill worker, he not only enriched millions of lives, but also founded a flourishing publishing house. Today, staying true to this spirit, Collins books are packed with inspiration, innovation, and practical expertise. They place you at the centre of a world of possibility and give you exactly what you need to explore it.

Language is the key to this exploration, and at the heart of Collins Dictionaries, is language as it is really used. New words, phrases, and meanings spring up every day, and all of them are captured and analysed by the Collins Word Web. Constantly updated, and with over 2.5 billion entries, this living language resource is unique to our dictionaries.

Words are tools for life. And a Collins Dictionary makes them work for you.

Collins. Do more.

INTRODUCTION

We are delighted you have decided to buy this Collins German Dictionary and hope you will enjoy and benefit from using it at home, at school, on holiday or at work.

The innovative use of colour guides you quickly and efficiently to the word you want, and the comprehensive wordlist provides a wealth of modern and idiomatic phrases not normally found in a dictionary this size.

In addition, the supplement provides you with guidance on using the dictionary, along with entertaining ways of improving your dictionary skills.

We hope that you will enjoy using it and that it will significantly enhance your language studies.

Zum Gebrauch Ihres Wörterbuchs	vi
Using your dictionary	viii
Abbreviations	x
Regular German noun endings	xiii
Phonetic symbols	xiv
Numbers	xv
Time	xvii
GERMAN-ENGLISH	1-274
VERB TABLES	1-52
ENGLISH-GERMAN	327-608
German verb forms	609-613
German spelling changes	614

ZUM GEBRAUCH IHRES COLLINS WÖRTERBUCHS

Das Wörterbuch enthält eine Fülle von Informationen, die mithilfe von unterschiedlichen Schriften und Schriftgrößen, Symbolen, Abkürzungen und Klammern vermittelt werden. Die dabei verwendeten Regeln und Symbole werden in den folgenden Abschnitten erklärt.

Stichwörter

Die Wörter, die Sie im Wörterbuch nachschlagen — „Stichwörter" — sind alphabetisch geordnet. Sie sind **in Farbe** gedruckt, damit man sie schnell erkennt. Die beiden Stichwörter oben links und rechts auf jeder Doppelseite geben das erste bzw. letzte Wort an, das auf den betreffenden Seiten behandelt wird.

Informationen zur Verwendung oder zur Form bestimmter Stichwörter stehen in Klammern hinter der Lautschrift. Sie erscheinen meist in abgekürzter Form und sind kursiv gedruckt (z. B. *(fam)*, *(COMM)*).

Wo es angebracht ist, werden mit dem Stichwort verwandte Wörter im selben Artikel behandelt (z. B. **accept, acceptance**). Sie sind wie das Stichwort fett, aber etwas kleiner gedruckt.

Häufig verwendete Ausdrücke, in denen das Stichwort vorkommt (z. B. **to be cold**), sind in einer anderen Schrift halbfett gedruckt.

Lautschrift

Die Lautschrift für jedes Stichwort (zur Angabe seiner Aussprache) steht in eckigen Klammern direkt hinter dem Stichwort (z. B. **Quark** [kvark]; **knead** [niːd]). Die Symbole der Lautschrift sind auf Seite xii erklärt.

Übersetzungen

Die Übersetzungen des Stichworts sind normal gedruckt. Wenn es mehr als eine Bedeutung oder Verwendung des Stichworts gibt, sind diese durch ein Semikolon voneinander getrennt. Vor den Übersetzungen stehen oft andere, kursiv gedruckte Wörter in Klammern. Sie geben an, in welchem Zusammenhang das Stichwort erscheinen könnte (z. B. **rough** *(voice)* oder *(weather)*), oder sie sind Synonyme (z. B. **rough** *(violent)*).

Schlüsselwörter

Besonders behandelt werden bestimmte deutsche und englische Wörter, die man als „Schlüsselwörter" der jeweiligen Sprache betrachten kann. Diese Wörter kommen beispielsweise sehr häufig vor oder werden unterschiedlich verwendet (z. B. **sein, auch; get, that**). Mithilfe von Rauten und Ziffern können Sie die verschiedenen Wortarten und Verwendungen unterscheiden. Weitere nützliche Hinweise finden Sie kursiv und in Klammern in der jeweiligen Sprache des Benutzers.

Grammatische Informationen

Wortarten stehen in abgekürzter Form kursiv gedruckt hinter der Aussprache des

Stichworts (z. B. *vt, adv, conj*).

Die unregelmäßigen Formen englischer Substantive und Verben stehen in Klammern vor der Wortart (z. B. **man** (*pl* **men**) *n*, **give** (*pt* **gave**, *pp* **given**) *vt*).

Die deutsche Rechtschreibreform

Dieses Wörterbuch folgt durchweg der reformierten deutschen Rechtschreibung. Alle Stichwörter auf der deutsch-englischen Seite, die von der Rechtschreibreform betroffen sind, sind mit ▲ gekennzeichnet. Alte Schreibungen, die sich wesentlich von der neuen Schreibung unterscheiden und an einem anderen alphabetischen Ort erscheinen, sind jedoch weiterhin aufgeführt und werden zur neuen Schreibung verwiesen. Diese alten Schreibungen sind mit △ gekennzeichnet.

USING YOUR COLLINS DICTIONARY

A wealth of information is presented in the dictionary, using various typefaces, sizes of type, symbols, abbreviations and brackets. The conventions and symbols used are explained in the following sections.

Headwords

The words you look up in a dictionary — "headwords" — are listed alphabetically. They are printed in colour for rapid identification. The two headwords appearing at the top left and top right of each double page indicate the first and last word dealt with on the pages in question.

Information about the usage or form of certain headwords is given in brackets after the phonetic spelling. This usually appears in abbreviated form and in italics (e.g. (*umg*), (*COMM*)).

Where appropriate, words related to headwords are grouped in the same entry (Glück, glücken) in a slightly smaller bold type than the headword.

Common expressions in which the headword appears are shown in a different bold roman type (e.g. **Glück haben**).

Phonetic spellings

The phonetic spelling of each headword (indicating its pronunciation) is given in square brackets immediately after the headword (e.g. Quark [kvark]). A list of these symbols is given on page xii.

Meanings

Headword translations are given in ordinary type and, where more than one meaning or usage exists, these are separated by a semi-colon. You will often find other words in italics in brackets before the translations. These offer suggested contexts in which the headword might appear (e.g. eng (*Kleidung*) or (*Freundschaft*)) or provide synonyms (e.g. eng (*fig: Horizont*)).

"Key" words

Special status is given to certain German and English words which are considered as "key" words in each language. They may, for example, occur very frequently or have several types of usage (e.g. **sein, auch; get, that**). A combination of lozenges and numbers helps you to distinguish different parts of speech and different meanings. Further helpful information is provided in brackets and in italics in the relevant language for the user.

Grammatical information

Parts of speech are given in abbreviated form in italics after the phonetic spellings of headwords (e.g. *vt, adv, konj*).

Genders of German nouns are indicated as follows: *m* for a masculine and *f* for a feminine and *nt* for a neuter noun. The genitive and plural forms of regular nouns are shown on the table on page xi. Nouns which do not follow these rules have the genitive and plural in brackets immediately preceding the gender (e.g. **Spaß**, (**-es, ⁻e**), *m*).

Adjectives are normally shown in their basic form (e.g. **groß** *adj*), but where they are only used attributively (i.e. before a noun) feminine and neuter endings follow in brackets (**hohe (r, s)** *adj attrib*).

German spelling reform

The German spelling reform has been fully implemented in this dictionary. All headwords on the German-English side which are affected by the spelling changes are marked with ▲, but old spellings which are markedly different from the new ones and have a different alphabetical position are still listed and are cross-referenced to the new spellings. The old spellings are marked with △.

ABKÜRZUNGEN

ABBREVIATIONS

Abkürzung	abk, abbr	abbreviation
Akkusativ	acc	accusative
Adjektiv	adj	adjective
Adverb	adv	adverb
Landwirtschaft	AGR	agriculture
Akkusativ	akk	accusative
Anatomie	ANAT	anatomy
Architektur	ARCHIT	architecture
Astrologie	ASTROL	astrology
Astronomie	ASTRON	astronomy
attributiv	attrib	attributive
Kraftfahrzeuge	AUT	automobiles
Hilfsverb	aux	auxiliary
Luftfahrt	AVIAT	aviation
besonders	bes	especially
Biologie	BIOL	biology
Botanik	BOT	botany
britisch	BRIT	British
Chemie	CHEM	chemistry
Film	CINE	cinema
Handel	COMM	commerce
Komparativ	compar	comparative
Computer	COMPUT	computing
Konjunktion	conj	conjunction
Kochen und Backen	COOK	cooking
zusammengesetztes Wort	cpd	compound
Dativ	dat	dative
bestimmter Artikel	def art	definite article
Diminutiv	dimin	diminutive
kirchlich	ECCL	ecclesiastical
Eisenbahn	EISENB	railways
Elektrizität	ELEK, ELEC	electricity
besonders	esp	especially
und so weiter	etc	et cetera
etwas	etw	something
Euphemismus, Hüllwort	euph	euphemism
Interjektion, Ausruf	excl	exclamation
Femininum	f	feminine
übertragen	fig	figurative
Finanzwesen	FIN	finance
nicht getrennt gebraucht	fus	(phrasal verb) inseparable
Genitiv	gen	genitive
Geografie	GEOG	geography
Geologie	GEOL	geology
Grammatik	GRAM	grammar

Geschichte	HIST	history
unpersönlich	impers	impersonal
unbestimmter Artikel	indef art	indefinite article
umgangssprachlich (! vulgär)	inf(!)	informal (! particularly offensive)
Infinitiv, Grundform	infin	infinitive
nicht getrennt gebraucht	insep	inseparable
unveränderlich	inv	invariable
unregelmäßig	irreg	irregular
jemand	jd	somebody
jemandem	jdm	(to) somebody
jemanden	jdn	somebody
jemandes	jds	somebody's
Rechtswesen	JUR	law
Kochen und Backen	KOCH	cooking
Komparativ	kompar	comparative
Konjunktion	konj	conjunction
Sprachwissenschaft	LING	linguistics
Literatur	LITER	of literature
Maskulinum	m	masculine
Mathematik	MATH	mathematics
Medizin	MED	medicine
Meteorologie	MET	meteorology
Militär	MIL	military
Bergbau	MIN	mining
Musik	MUS	music
Substantiv, Hauptwort	n	noun
nautisch, Seefahrt	NAUT	nautical, naval
Nominativ	nom	nominative
Neutrum	nt	neuter
Zahlwort	num	numeral
Objekt	obj	object
oder	od	or
sich	o.s.	oneself
Parlament	PARL	parliament
abschätzig	pej	pejorative
Fotografie	PHOT	photography
Physik	PHYS	physics
Plural	pl	plural
Politik	POL	politics
Präfix, Vorsilbe	pp	prefix
Präposition	präp, prep	preposition
Typografie	PRINT	printing
Pronomen, Fürwort	pron	pronoun
Psychologie	PSYCH	psychology
1. Vergangenheit, Imperfekt	pt	past tense
Radio	RAD	radio
Eisenbahn	RAIL	railways
Religion	REL	religion

jemand(-en, -em)	**sb**	someone, somebody
Schulwesen	**SCH**	school
Naturwissenschaft	**SCI**	science
Singular, Einzahl	**sg**	singular
etwas	**sth**	something
Konjunktiv	**sub**	subjunctive
Subjekt	**subj**	(grammatical) subject
Superlativ	**superl**	superlative
Technik	**TECH**	technology
Nachrichtentechnik	**TEL**	telecommunications
Theater	**THEAT**	theatre
Fernsehen	**TV**	television
Typografie	**TYP**	printing
umgangssprachlich (! vulgär)	**umg(!)**	informal (! particularly offensive)
Hochschulwesen	**UNIV**	university
unpersönlich	**unpers**	impersonal
unregelmäßig	**unreg**	irregular
(nord)amerikanisch	**US**	(North) America
gewöhnlich	**usu**	usually
Verb	**vb**	verb
intransitives Verb	**vi**	intransitive verb
reflexives Verb	**vr**	reflexive verb
transitives Verb	**vt**	transitive verb
Zoologie	**ZOOL**	zoology
zusammengesetztes Wort	**zW**	compound
zwischen zwei Sprechern	—	change of speaker
ungefähre Entsprechung	≈	cultural equivalent
eingetragenes Warenzeichen	®	registered trademark

Warenzeichen

Wörter, die unseres Wissens eingetragene
Warenzeichen darstellen, sind als solche
gekennzeichnet. Es ist jedoch zu
beachten, dass weder das
Vorhandensein noch das Fehlen
derartiger Kennzeichnungen die
Rechtslage hinsichtlich eingetragener
Warenzeichen berührt.

Note on trademarks

Words which we have reason to believe
constitute trademarks have been
designated as such. However, neither
the presence nor the absence of such
designation should be regarded as
affecting the legal status of any
trademark.

REGULAR GERMAN NOUN ENDINGS

nom		*gen*	*pl*
-ant	*m*	-anten	-anten
-anz	*f*	-anz	-anzen
-ar	*m*	-ar(e)s	-are
-chen	*nt*	-chens	-chen
-e	*f*	-	-n
-ei	*f*	-ei	-eien
-elle	*f*	-elle	-ellen
-ent	*m*	-enten	-enten
-enz	*f*	-enz	-enzen
-ette	*f*	-ette	-etten
-eur	*m*	-eurs	-eure
-euse	*f*	-euse	-eusen
-heit	*f*	-heit	-heiten
-ie	*f*	-ie	-ien
-ik	*f*	-ik	-iken
-in	*f*	-in	-innen
-ine	*f*	-ine	-inen
-ion	*f*	-ion	-ionen
-ist	*m*	-isten	-isten
-ium	*nt*	-iums	-ien
-ius	*m*	-ius	-iusse
-ive	*f*	-ive	-iven
-keit	*f*	-keit	-keiten
-lein	*nt*	-leins	-lein
-ling	*m*	-lings	-linge
-ment	*nt*	-ments	-mente
-mus	*m*	-mus	-men
-schaft	*f*	-schaft	-schaften
-tät	*f*	-tät	-täten
-tor	*m*	-tors	-toren
-ung	*f*	-ung	-ungen
-ur	*f*	-ur	-uren

PHONETIC SYMBOLS / LAUTSCHRIFT

[ː] *length mark/Längezeichen* ['] *stress mark/Betonung*
[|] *glottal stop/Knacklaut*

all vowel sounds are approximate only
alle Vokallaute sind nur ungefähre Entsprechungen

bet	[b]	**B**all		[e]	Metall
dim	[d]	**d**ann		[eː]	geben
face	[f]	**F**ass	set	[ɛ]	hässlich
go	[g]	**G**ast		[ɛ̃ː]	Cousin
hit	[h]	**H**err	pity	[ɪ]	Bischof
you	[j]	**j**a		[i]	vital
cat	[k]	**k**alt	green	[iː]	viel
lick	[l]	**L**ast	rot	[ɔ]	Post
must	[m]	**M**ast	board	[ɔː]	
nut	[n]	**N**uss		[o]	Moral
bang	[ŋ]	la**ng**		[oː]	oben
pepper	[p]	**P**akt		[õ]	Champign**on**
red	[r]	**R**egen		[ø]	ökonomisch
sit	[s]	**R**asse		[œ]	gönnen
shame	[ʃ]	**Sch**al	full	[u]	kulant
tell	[t]	**T**al	root	[uː]	Hut
chat	[tʃ]	**tsch**üs	come	[ʌ]	
vine	[v]	**w**as		[ʊ]	Pult
wine	[w]			[y]	physisch
loch	[x]	Ba**ch**		[yː]	für
	[ç]	i**ch**		[ʏ]	Müll
zero	[z]	**H**ase	above	[ə]	bitte
leisure	[ʒ]	**G**enie	girl	[əː]	
join	[dʒ]				
thin	[θ]		lie	[aɪ]	weit
this	[ð]		now	[au]	
	[a]	**H**ast		[aʊ]	Haut
hat	[æ]		day	[eɪ]	
	[ɑː]	**B**ahn	fair	[ɛə]	
farm	[ɑː]		beer	[ɪə]	
	[ã]	**En**semble	toy	[ɔɪ]	
fiancé	[ũː]			[ɔY]	Heu
			pure	[uə]	

[ʳ] r can be pronounced before a vowel; Bindungs-R

ZAHLEN

NUMBERS

ein(s)	1	one
zwei	2	two
drei	3	three
vier	4	four
fünf	5	five
sechs	6	six
sieben	7	seven
acht	8	eight
neun	9	nine
zehn	10	ten
elf	11	eleven
zwölf	12	twelve
dreizehn	13	thirteen
vierzehn	14	fourteen
fünfzehn	15	fifteen
sechzehn	16	sixteen
siebzehn	17	seventeen
achtzehn	18	eighteen
neunzehn	19	nineteen
zwanzig	20	twenty
einundzwanzig	21	twenty-one
zweiundzwanzig	22	twenty-two
dreißig	30	thirty
vierzig	40	forty
fünfzig	50	fifty
sechzig	60	sixty
siebzig	70	seventy
achtzig	80	eighty
neunzig	90	ninety
hundert	100	a hundred
hunderteins	101	a hundred and one
zweihundert	200	two hundred
zweihunderteins	201	two hundred and one
dreihundert	300	three hundred
dreihunderteins	301	three hundred and one
tausend	1000	a thousand
tausend(und)eins	1001	a thousand and one
fünftausend	5000	five thousand
eine Million	1000000	a million

erste(r, s)	1.	first	1st
zweite(r, s)	2.	second	2nd
dritte(r, s)	3.	third	3rd
vierte(r, s)	4.	fourth	4th
fünfte(r, s)	5.	fifth	5th
sechste(r, s)	6.	sixth	6th

siebte(r, s)	7.	seventh	7th
achte(r, s)	8.	eighth	8th
neunte(r, s)	9.	ninth	9th
zehnte(r, s)	10.	tenth	10th
elfte(r, s)	11.	eleventh	11th
zwölfte(r, s)	12.	twelfth	12th
dreizehnte(r, s)	13.	thirteenth	13th
vierzehnte(r, s)	14.	fourteenth	14th
fünfzehnte(r, s)	15.	fifteenth	15th
sechzehnte(r, s)	16.	sixteenth	16th
siebzehnte(r, s)	17.	seventeenth	17th
achtzehnte(r, s)	18.	eighteenth	18th
neunzehnte(r, s)	19.	nineteenth	19th
zwanzigste(r, s)	20.	twentieth	20th
einundzwanzigste(r, s)	21.	twenty-first	21st
dreißigste(r, s)	30.	thirtieth	30th
hundertste(r, s)	100.	hundredth	100th
hunderterste(r, s)	101.	hundred-and-first	101st
tausendste(r, s)	1000.	thousandth	1000th

Brüche usw.

Fractions etc.

ein Halb	$\frac{1}{2}$	a half	
ein Drittel	$\frac{1}{3}$	a third	
ein Viertel	$\frac{1}{4}$	a quarter	
ein Fünftel	$\frac{1}{5}$	a fifth	
null Komma fünf	0,5	(nought) point five	0.5
drei Komma vier	3,4	three point four	3.4
sechs Komma acht neun	6,89	six point eight nine	6.89
zehn Prozent	10%	ten per cent	
hundert Prozent	100%	a hundred per cent	

Beispiele

Examples

er wohnt in Nummer 10

he lives at number 10

es steht in Kapitel 7

it's in chapter 7

auf Seite 7

on page 7

er wohnt im 7. Stock

he lives on the 7th floor

er wurde 7.

he came in 7th

Maßstab eins zu zwanzigtausend

scale one to twenty thousand

wie viel Uhr ist es?, wie spät ist es?

what time is it?

es ist ...

it's ...

Mitternacht, zwölf Uhr nachts	midnight, twelve p.m.
ein Uhr (morgens *or* früh)	one o'clock (in the morning), one (a.m.)
fünf nach eins, ein Uhr fünf	five past one
zehn nach eins, ein Uhr zehn	ten past one
Viertel nach eins, ein Uhr fünfzehn	a quarter past one, one fifteen
fünf vor halb zwei, ein Uhr fünfundzwanzig	twenty-five past one, one twenty-five
halb zwei, ein Uhr dreißig	half past one, one thirty
fünf nach halb zwei, ein Uhr fünfunddreißig	twenty-five to two, one thirty-five
zwanzig vor zwei, ein Uhr vierzig	twenty to two, one forty
Viertel vor zwei, ein Uhr fünfundvierzig	a quarter to two, one forty-five
zehn vor zwei, ein Uhr fünfzig	ten to two, one fifty
zwölf Uhr (mittags), Mittag	twelve o'clock, midday, noon
halb eins (mittags *or* nachmittags), zwölf Uhr dreißig	half past twelve, twelve thirty (p.m.)
zwei Uhr (nachmittags)	two o'clock (in the afternoon), two (p.m.)
halb acht (abends)	half past seven (in the evening), seven thirty (p.m.)

um wie viel Uhr?

at what time?

um Mitternacht	at midnight
um sieben Uhr	at seven o'clock
in zwanzig Minuten	in twenty minutes
vor fünfzehn Minuten	fifteen minutes ago

DEUTSCH – ENGLISCH
GERMAN – ENGLISH

A, a

Aal [aːl] (-(e)s, -e) m eel

Aas [aːs] (-es, -e od **Äser**) nt carrion

ab [ap] präp +dat from; **Kinder ab 12 Jahren** children from the age of 12; **ab morgen** from tomorrow; **ab sofort** as of now
♦ adv **1** off; **links ab** to the left; **der Knopf ist ab** the button has come off; **ab nach Hause!** off you go home
2 (zeitlich): **von da ab** from then on; **von heute ab** from today, as of today
3 (auf Fahrplänen): **München ab 12.20** leaving Munich 12.20
4 : ab und zu od **an** now and then od again

Abänderung [ˈapˌɛndərʊŋ] f alteration

Abbau [ˈapbaʊ] (-(e)s) m (+gen) dismantling; (Verminderung) reduction (in); (Verfall) decline (in); (MIN) mining; quarrying; (CHEM) decomposition; **a~en** vt to dismantle; (MIN) to mine; to quarry; (verringern) to reduce; (CHEM) to break down

abbeißen [ˈapbaɪsən] (unreg) vt to bite off

abbekommen [ˈapbəkɔmən] (unreg) vt (Deckel, Schraube, Band) to loosen; **etwas ~** (beschädigt werden) to get damaged; (: Person) to get injured

abbestellen [ˈapbəʃtɛlən] vt to cancel

abbezahlen [ˈapbətsaːlən] vt to pay off

abbiegen [ˈapbiːgən] (unreg) vi to turn off; (Straße) to bend ♦ vt to bend; (verhindern) to ward off

abbilden [ˈapbɪldən] vt to portray; **Abbildung** f illustration

abblenden [ˈapblɛndən] vt, vi (AUT) to dip (BRIT), to dim (US)

Abblendlicht [ˈapblɛntlɪçt] nt dipped (BRIT) od dimmed (US) headlights pl

abbrechen [ˈapbrɛçən] (unreg) vt, vi to break off; (Gebäude) to pull down; (Zelt) to take down; (aufhören) to stop; (COMPUT) to abort

abbrennen [ˈapbrɛnən] (unreg) vt to burn off; (Feuerwerk) to let off ♦ vi (aux sein) to burn down

abbringen [ˈapbrɪŋən] (unreg) vt: **jdn von etw ~** to dissuade sb from sth; **jdn vom Weg ~** to divert sb

abbröckeln [ˈapbrœkəln] vt, vi to crumble off od away

Abbruch [ˈapbrʊx] m (von Verhandlungen etc) breaking off; (von Haus) demolition; **jdm/ etw ~ tun** to harm sb/sth; **a~reif** adj only fit for demolition

abbrühen [ˈapbryːən] vt to scald; **abgebrüht** (umg) hard-boiled

abbuchen [ˈapbuːxən] vt to debit

abdanken [ˈapdaŋkən] vi to resign; (König) to abdicate; **Abdankung** f resignation; abdication

abdecken [ˈapdɛkən] vt (Loch) to cover; (Tisch) to clear; (Plane) to uncover

abdichten [ˈapdɪçtən] vt to seal; (NAUT) to caulk

abdrehen [ˈapdreːən] vt (Gas) to turn off; (Licht) to switch off; (Film) to shoot ♦ vi (Schiff) to change course

Abdruck [ˈapdrʊk] m (Nachdrucken) reprinting; (Gedrucktes) reprint; (Gipsabdruck, Wachsabdruck) impression; (Fingerabdruck) print; **a~en** vt to print, to publish

abdrücken [ˈapdrʏkən] vt (Waffe) to fire; (Person) to hug, to squeeze

Abend [ˈaːbənt] (-s, -e) m evening; **guten ~** good evening; **zu ~ essen** to have dinner od supper; **heute ~** this evening; **~brot** nt supper; **~essen** nt supper; **~garderobe** f evening dress; **~kasse** f box office; **~kleid** nt evening dress; **~kurs** m evening classes pl; **~land** nt (Europa) West; **a~lich** adj evening; **~mahl** nt Holy Communion; **~rot** nt sunset; **a~s** adv in the evening

Abenteuer ['aːbəntɔyər] (**-s, -**) nt adventure; **~film** m adventure film; **a~lich** adj adventurous; **~urlaub** m adventure holiday

Abenteurer (**-s, -**) m adventurer; **~in** f adventuress

aber ['aːbər] konj but; (jedoch) however ♦ adv: **das ist ~ schön** that's really nice; **nun ist ~ Schluss!** now that's enough!; **vielen Dank – ~ bitte!** thanks a lot – you're welcome; **A~glaube** m superstition; **~gläubisch** adj superstitious

aberkennen ['ap|ɛrkɛnən] (unreg) vt (JUR): **jdm etw ~** to deprive sb of sth, to take sth (away) from sb

abermals ['aːbəmaːls] adv once again

Abertausend, abertausend ['aːbətauzənt] indef pron **tausend** od **Tausend und ~** thousands upon thousands

Abf. abk (= Abfahrt) dep.

abfahren ['apfaːrən] (unreg) vi to leave, to depart ♦ vt to take od cart away; (Strecke) to drive; (Reifen) to wear; (Fahrkarte) to use

Abfahrt ['apfaːrt] f departure; (SKI) descent; (Piste) run; **~zeit** f departure time

Abfall ['apfal] m waste; (von Speisen etc) rubbish (BRIT), garbage (US); (Neigung) slope; (Verschlechterung) decline; **~eimer** m rubbish bin (BRIT), garbage can (US); **a~en** (unreg) vi (auch fig) to fall od drop off; (sich neigen) to fall od drop away

abfällig ['apfɛlɪç] adj disparaging, deprecatory

abfangen ['apfaŋən] (unreg) vt to intercept; (Person) to catch; (unter Kontrolle bringen) to check

abfärben ['apfɛrbən] vi to lose its colour; (Wäsche) to run; (fig) to rub off

abfassen ['apfasən] vt to write, to draft

abfertigen ['apfɛrtɪgən] vt to prepare for dispatch, to process; (an der Grenze) to clear; (Kundschaft) to attend to

Abfertigungsschalter m (Flughafen)

check-in desk

abfeuern ['apfɔyərn] vt to fire

abfinden ['apfɪndən] (unreg) vt to pay off ♦ vr to come to terms; **sich mit jdm ~/ nicht ~** to put up with/not get on with sb

Abfindung f (von Gläubigern) payment; (Geld) sum in settlement

abflauen ['apflauən] vi (Wind, Erregung) to die away, to subside; (Nachfrage, Geschäft) to fall od drop off

abfliegen ['apfliːgən] (unreg) vi (Flugzeug) to take off; (Passagier auch) to fly ♦ vt (Gebiet) to fly over

abfließen ['apfliːsən] (unreg) vi to drain away

Abflug ['apfluːk] m departure; (Start) take-off; **~halle** f departure lounge; **~zeit** f departure time

Abfluss ▲ ['apflus] m draining away; (Öffnung) outlet; **~rohr** nt drain pipe; (von sanitären Anlagen auch) waste pipe

abfragen ['apfraːgən] vt (bes SCH) to test orally (on)

Abfuhr ['apfuːr] (**-, -en**) f removal; (fig) snub, rebuff

abführen ['apfyːrən] vt to lead away; (Gelder, Steuern) to pay ♦ vi (MED) to have a laxative effect

Abführmittel ['apfyːrmɪtəl] nt laxative

abfüllen ['apfʏlən] vt to draw off; (in Flaschen) to bottle

Abgabe ['apgaːbə] f handing in; (von Ball) pass; (Steuer) tax; (eines Amtes) giving up; (einer Erklärung) giving

Abgang ['apgaŋ] m (von Schule) leaving; (THEAT) exit; (Abfahrt) departure; (der Post, von Waren) dispatch

Abgas ['apgaːs] nt waste gas; (AUT) exhaust

abgeben ['apgeːbən] (unreg) vt (Gegenstand) to hand od give in; (Ball) to pass; (Wärme) to give off; (Amt) to hand over; (Schuss) to fire; (Erklärung, Urteil) to give; (darstellen, sein) to make ♦ vr: **sich mit jdm/etw ~** to associate with sb/bother with sth; **jdm etw ~** (überlassen) to let sb have sth

abgebrüht ['apgəbryːt] (umg) adj (skrupellos)

hard-boiled

abgehen ['apge:ən] (unreg) vi to go away, to leave; (THEAT) to exit; (Knopf etc) to come off; (Straße) to branch off ♦ vt (Strecke) to go od walk along; **etw geht jdm ab** (fehlt) sb lacks sth

abgelegen ['apgəle:gən] adj remote

abgemacht ['apgəmaxt] adj fixed; **~!** done!

abgeneigt ['apgənaikt] adj disinclined

abgenutzt ['apgənʊtst] adj worn

Abgeordnete(r) ['apgəʔɔrdnətə(r)] f(m) member of parliament; elected representative

abgeschlossen ['apgəʃlɔsən] adj attrib (Wohnung) self-contained

abgeschmackt ['apgəʃmakt] adj tasteless

abgesehen ['apgəze:ən] adj: **es auf jdn/ etw ~ haben** to be after sb/sth; **~ von ...** apart from ...

abgespannt ['apgəʃpant] adj tired out

abgestanden ['apgəʃtandən] adj stale; (Bier auch) flat

abgestorben ['apgəʃtɔrbən] adj numb; (BIOL, MED) dead

abgetragen ['apgətra:gən] adj shabby, worn out

abgewinnen ['apgəvinən] (unreg) vt: **einer Sache etw/Geschmack ~** to get sth/ pleasure from sth

abgewöhnen ['apgəvø:nən] vt: **jdm/sich etw ~** to cure sb of sth/give sth up

abgrenzen ['apgrɛntsən] vt (auch fig) to mark off; to fence off

Abgrund ['apgrʊnt] m (auch fig) abyss

abhacken ['aphakən] vt to chop off

abhaken ['apha:kən] vt (auf Papier) to tick off

abhalten ['aphaltən] (unreg) vt (Versammlung) to hold; **jdn von etw ~** (fern halten) to keep sb away from sth; (hindern) to keep sb from sth

abhanden [ap'handən] adj: **~ kommen** to get lost

Abhandlung ['aphandlʊŋ] f treatise, discourse

Abhang ['aphaŋ] m slope

abhängen ['aphɛŋən] vt (Bild) to take down; (Anhänger) to uncouple; (Verfolger) to shake off ♦ vi (unreg: Fleisch) to hang; **von jdm/ etw ~** to depend on sb/sth

abhängig ['aphɛŋɪç] adj: **~ (von)** dependent (on); **A~keit** f: **A~keit (von)** dependence (on)

abhärten ['aphɛrtən] vt, vr to toughen (o.s.) up; **sich gegen etw ~** to inure o.s. to sth

abhauen ['aphaʊən] (unreg) vt to cut off; (Baum) to cut down ♦ vi (umg) to clear off od out

abheben ['aphe:bən] (unreg) vt to lift (up); (Karten) to cut; (Geld) to withdraw, to take out ♦ vi (Flugzeug) to take off; (Rakete) to lift off ♦ vr to stand out

abheften ['aphɛftən] vt (Rechnungen etc) to file away

abhetzen ['aphɛtsən] vr to wear od tire o.s. out

Abhilfe ['aphɪlfə] f remedy; **~ schaffen** to put things right

abholen ['apho:lən] vt (Gegenstand) to fetch, to collect; (Person) to call for; (am Bahnhof etc) to pick up, to meet

abholzen ['aphɔltsən] vt (Wald) to clear

abhorchen ['aphɔrçən] vt (MED) to listen to a patient's chest

abhören ['aphø:rən] vt (Vokabeln) to test; (Telefongespräch) to tap; (Tonband etc) to listen to

Abhörgerät nt bug

Abitur [abi'tu:r] (-s, -e) nt German school-leaving examination; **~i'ent(in)** m(f) candidate for school-leaving certificate

---
Abitur

ⓘ The **Abitur** is the German school-leaving examination taken in four subjects by pupils at a **Gymnasium** at the age of 18 or 19. It is necessary for entry to university.

Abk. abk (= Abkürzung) abbr.

abkapseln ['apkapsəln] vr to shut od cut o.s. off

abkaufen ['apkaʊfən] vt: **jdm etw ~** (auch fig) to buy sth from sb

abkehren ['apkeːrən] *vt* (*Blick*) to avert, to turn away ♦ *vr* to turn away

abklingen ['apklɪŋən] (*unreg*) *vi* to die away; (*Radio*) to fade out

abknöpfen ['apknœpfən] *vt* to unbutton; **jdm etw ~** (*umg*) to get sth off sb

abkochen ['apkɔxən] *vt* to boil

abkommen ['apkɔmən] (*unreg*) *vi* to get away; **von der Straße/von einem Plan ~** to leave the road/give up a plan; **A~ (-s, -)** *nt* agreement

abkömmlich ['apkœmlɪç] *adj* available, free

abkratzen ['apkratsən] *vt* to scrape off ♦ *vi* (*umg*) to kick the bucket

abkühlen ['apkyːlən] *vt* to cool down ♦ *vr* (*Mensch*) to cool down *od* off; (*Wetter*) to get cool; (*Zuneigung*) to cool

abkürzen ['apkʏrtsən] *vt* to shorten; (*Wort auch*) to abbreviate; **den Weg ~** to take a short cut

Abkürzung *f* (*Wort*) abbreviation; (*Weg*) short cut

abladen ['aplaːdən] (*unreg*) *vt* to unload

Ablage ['aplaːgə] *f* (*für Akten*) tray; (*für Kleider*) cloakroom

ablassen ['aplasən] (*unreg*) *vt* (*Wasser, Dampf*) to let off; (*vom Preis*) to knock off ♦ *vi*: **von etw ~** to give sth up, to abandon sth

Ablauf ['aplauf] *m* (*Abfluss*) drain; (*von Ereignissen*) course; (*einer Frist, Zeit*) expiry (*BRIT*), expiration (*US*); **a~en** (*unreg*) *vi* (*abfließen*) to drain away; (*Ereignisse*) to happen; (*Frist, Zeit, Pass*) to expire ♦ *vt* (*Sohlen*) to wear (down *od* out)

ablegen ['apleːgən] *vt* to put *od* lay down; (*Kleider*) to take off; (*Gewohnheit*) to get rid of; (*Prüfung*) to take, to sit; (*Zeugnis*) to give

Ableger (-s, -) *m* layer; (*fig*) branch, offshoot

ablehnen ['apleːnən] *vt* to reject; (*Einladung*) to decline, to refuse ♦ *vi* to decline, to refuse

ablehnend *adj* (*Haltung, Antwort*) negative; (*Geste*) disapproving; **ein ~er Bescheid** a rejection

Ablehnung *f* rejection; refusal

ableiten ['aplaitən] *vt* (*Wasser*) to divert; (*deduzieren*) to deduce; (*Wort*) to derive; **Ableitung** *f* diversion; deduction; derivation; (*Wort*) derivative

ablenken ['aplɛŋkən] *vt* to turn away, to deflect; (*zerstreuen*) to distract ♦ *vi* to change the subject; **Ablenkung** *f* distraction

ablesen ['apleːzən] (*unreg*) *vt* to read out; (*Messgeräte*) to read

ablichten ['aplɪçtən] *vt* to photocopy

abliefern ['apliːfərn] *vt* to deliver; **etw bei jdm ~** to hand sth over to sb

Ablieferung *f* delivery

ablösen ['apløːzən] *vt* (*abtrennen*) to take off, to remove; (*in Amt*) to take over from; (*Wache*) to relieve

Ablösung *f* removal; relieving

abmachen ['apmaxən] *vt* to take off; (*vereinbaren*) to agree; **Abmachung** *f* agreement

abmagern ['apmaːgərn] *vi* to get thinner

Abmagerungskur *f* diet; **eine ~ machen** to go on a diet

abmarschieren ['apmarʃiːrən] *vi* to march off

abmelden ['apmɛldən] *vt* (*Zeitungen*) to cancel; (*Auto*) to take off the road ♦ *vr* to give notice of one's departure; (*im Hotel*) to check out; **jdn bei der Polizei ~** to register sb's departure with the police

abmessen ['apmɛsən] (*unreg*) *vt* to measure; **Abmessung** *f* measurement

abmontieren ['apmɔntiːrən] *vt* to take off

abmühen ['apmyːən] *vr* to wear o.s. out

Abnahme ['apnaːmə] *f* (*+gen*) removal; (*COMM*) buying; (*Verringerung*) decrease (in)

abnehmen ['apneːmən] (*unreg*) *vt* to take off, to remove; (*Führerschein*) to take away; (*Prüfung*) to hold; (*Maschen*) to decrease ♦ *vi* to decrease; (*schlanker werden*) to lose weight; **(jdm) etw ~** (*Geld*) to get sth (out of sb); (*kaufen, umg: glauben*) to buy sth (from sb); **jdm Arbeit ~** to take work off sb's shoulders

Abnehmer (-s, -) *m* purchaser, customer

Abneigung ['apnaigʊŋ] *f* aversion, dislike

abnorm [ap'nɔrm] *adj* abnormal

abnutzen ['apnʊtsən] *vt* to wear out;
Abnutzung *f* wear (and tear)

Abo ['abo] (*umg*) *nt abk* = **Abonnement**

Abonnement [abɔn(ə)'mãː] (**-s, -s**) *nt*
subscription; **Abonnent(in)** [abɔ'nɛnt(ɪn)]
m(f) subscriber; **abonnieren** *vt* to
subscribe to

Abordnung ['ap|ɔrdnʊŋ] *f* delegation

abpacken ['appakən] *vt* to pack

abpassen ['appasən] *vt* (*Person, Gelegenheit*)
to wait for

Abpfiff ['appfɪf] *m* final whistle

abplagen ['appla:gən] *vr* to wear o.s. out

abprallen ['appralən] *vi* to bounce off; to
ricochet

abraten ['apra:tən] (*unreg*) *vi*: **jdm von etw
~** to advise *or* warn sb against sth

abräumen ['aprɔymən] *vt* to clear up *od*
away

abreagieren ['apreagi:rən] *vt*: **seinen Zorn
(an jdm/etw) ~** to work one's anger off
(on sb/sth) ♦ *vr* to calm down

abrechnen ['apreçnən] *vt* to deduct, to take
off ♦ *vi* to settle up; (*fig*) to get even

Abrechnung *f* settlement; (*Rechnung*) bill

Abrede ['apre:də] *f*: **etw in ~ stellen** to
deny *od* dispute sth

Abreise ['apraɪzə] *f* departure; **a~n** *vi* to
leave, to set off

abreißen ['apraɪsən] (*unreg*) *vt* (*Haus*) to tear
down; (*Blatt*) to tear off

abrichten ['aprɪçtən] *vt* to train

abriegeln ['apri:gəln] *vt* (*Straße, Gebiet*) to
seal off

Abruf ['apru:f] *m*: **auf ~** on call; **a~en**
(*unreg*) *vt* (*Mensch*) to call away; (*COMM:
Ware*) to request delivery of

abrunden ['aprʊndən] *vt* to round off

abrupt [a'brʊpt] *adj* abrupt

abrüsten ['aprystən] *vi* to disarm;
Abrüstung *f* disarmament

abrutschen ['aprʊtʃən] *vi* to slip; (*AVIAT*) to
sideslip

Abs. *abk* (= *Absender*) sender, from

Absage ['apza:gə] *f* refusal; **a~n** *vt* to
cancel, to call off; (*Einladung*) to turn down

♦ *vi* to cry off; (*ablehnen*) to decline

absahnen ['apza:nən] *vt* to skim ♦ *vi* (*fig*) to
rake in

Absatz ['apzats] *m* (*COMM*) sales *pl*;
(*Bodensatz*) deposit; (*neuer Abschnitt*)
paragraph; (*Treppenabsatz*) landing;
(*Schuhabsatz*) heel; **~gebiet** *nt* (*COMM*)
market

abschaffen ['apʃafən] *vt* to abolish, to do
away with; **Abschaffung** *f* abolition

abschalten ['apʃaltən] *vt, vi* (*auch umg*) to
switch off

abschätzen ['apʃɛtsən] *vt* to estimate;
(*Lage*) to assess; (*Person*) to size up

abschätzig ['apʃɛtsɪç] *adj* disparaging,
derogatory

Abschaum ['apʃaʊm] (**-(e)s**) *m* scum

Abscheu ['apʃɔy] (**-(e)s**) *m* loathing,
repugnance; **~ erregend** repulsive,
loathsome; **a~lich** [ap'ʃɔylɪç] *adj*
abominable

abschicken ['apʃɪkən] *vt* to send off

abschieben ['apʃi:bən] (*unreg*) *vt* to push
away; (*Person*) to deport

Abschied ['apʃi:t] (**-(e)s, -e**) *m* parting; (*von
Armee*) discharge; (**von jdm) ~ nehmen** to
say goodbye (to sb), to take one's leave (of
sb); **seinen ~ nehmen** (*MIL*) to apply for
discharge; **~sbrief** *m* farewell letter;
~sfeier *f* farewell party

abschießen ['apʃi:sən] (*unreg*) *vt* (*Flugzeug*)
to shoot down; (*Geschoss*) to fire

abschirmen ['apʃɪrmən] *vt* to screen

abschlagen ['apʃla:gən] (*unreg*) *vt*
(*abhacken, COMM*) to knock off; (*ablehnen*)
to refuse; (*MIL*) to repel

abschlägig ['apʃlɛ:gɪç] *adj* negative

Abschlagszahlung *f* interim payment

Abschlepp- ['apʃlɛp] *zW*: **~dienst** *m* (*AUT*)
breakdown service (*BRIT*), towing company
(*US*); **a~en** *vt* to (take in) tow; **~seil** *nt*
towrope

abschließen ['apʃli:sən] (*unreg*) *vt* (*Tür*) to
lock; (*beenden*) to conclude, to finish;
(*Vertrag, Handel*) to conclude ♦ *vr* (*sich
isolieren*) to cut o.s. off; **~d** *adj* concluding

Abschluss ▲ ['apʃlʊs] *m* (*Beendigung*) close,

conclusion; (*COMM: Bilanz*) balancing; (*von Vertrag, Handel*) conclusion; **zum ~** in conclusion; **~feier** f (*SCH*) end of term party; **~prüfung** f final exam

abschneiden ['apʃnaɪdən] (*unreg*) vt to cut off ♦ vi to do, to come off

Abschnitt ['apʃnɪt] m section; (*MIL*) sector; (*Kontrollabschnitt*) counterfoil; (*MATH*) segment; (*Zeitabschnitt*) period

abschrauben ['apʃraubən] vt to unscrew

abschrecken ['apʃrɛkən] vt to deter, to put off; (*mit kaltem Wasser*) to plunge in cold water; **~d** adj deterrent; **~des Beispiel** warning

abschreiben ['apʃraibən] (*unreg*) vt to copy; (*verloren geben*) to write off; (*COMM*) to deduct

Abschrift ['apʃrɪft] f copy

Abschuss ▲ ['apʃʊs] m (*eines Geschützes*) firing; (*Herunterschießen*) shooting down; (*Tötung*) shooting

abschüssig ['apʃʏsɪç] adj steep

abschwächen ['apʃvɛçən] vt to lessen; (*Behauptung, Kritik*) to tone down ♦ vr to lessen

abschweifen ['apʃvaifən] vi to digress

abschwellen ['apʃvɛlən] (*unreg*) vi (*Geschwulst*) to go down; (*Lärm*) to die down

abschwören ['apʃvøːrən] vi (+*dat*) to renounce

absehbar ['apzeːbaːr] adj foreseeable; **in ~er Zeit** in the foreseeable future; **das Ende ist ~** the end is in sight

absehen ['apzeːən] (*unreg*) vt (*Ende, Folgen*) to foresee ♦ vi: **von etw ~** to refrain from sth; (*nicht berücksichtigen*) to leave sth out of consideration

abseilen ['apzailən] vr (*Bergsteiger*) to abseil (down)

abseits ['apzaits] adv out of the way ♦ präp +*gen* away from; **A~** nt (*SPORT*) offside

absenden ['apzɛndən] (*unreg*) vt to send off, to dispatch

Absender (-s, -) m sender

absetzen ['apzɛtsən] vt (*niederstellen, aussteigen lassen*) to put down; (*abnehmen*) to take off; (*COMM: verkaufen*) to sell; (*FIN: abziehen*) to deduct; (*entlassen*) to dismiss; (*König*) to depose; (*streichen*) to drop; (*hervorheben*) to pick out ♦ vr (*sich entfernen*) to clear off; (*sich ablagern*) to be deposited

Absetzung f (*FIN: Abzug*) deduction; (*Entlassung*) dismissal; (*von König*) deposing

absichern ['apzɪçərn] vt to make safe; (*schützen*) to safeguard ♦ vr to protect o.s.

Absicht ['apzɪçt] f intention; **mit ~** on purpose; **a~lich** adj intentional, deliberate

absinken ['apzɪŋkən] (*unreg*) vi to sink; (*Temperatur, Geschwindigkeit*) to decrease

absitzen ['apzɪtsən] (*unreg*) vi to dismount ♦ vt (*Strafe*) to serve

absolut [apzoˈluːt] adj absolute; **A~ismus** m absolutism

absolvieren [apzɔlˈviːrən] vt (*SCH*) to complete

absonder- ['apzɔndər] zW: **~lich** adj odd, strange; **~n** vt to separate; (*ausscheiden*) to give off, to secrete ♦ vr to cut o.s. off; **A~ung** f separation; (*MED*) secretion

abspalten ['apʃpaltən] vt to split off

abspannen ['apʃpanən] vt (*Pferde*) to unhitch; (*Wagen*) to uncouple

abspeisen ['apʃpaizən] vt (*fig*) to fob off

abspenstig ['apʃpɛnstɪç] adj: **(jdm) ~ machen** to lure away (from sb)

absperren ['apʃpɛrən] vt to block od close off; (*Tür*) to lock; **Absperrung** f (*Vorgang*) blocking od closing off; (*Sperre*) barricade

abspielen ['apʃpiːlən] vt (*Platte, Tonband*) to play; (*SPORT: Ball*) to pass ♦ vr to happen

Absprache ['apʃpraːxə] f arrangement

absprechen ['apʃprɛçən] (*unreg*) vt (*vereinbaren*) to arrange; **jdm etw ~** to deny sb sth

abspringen ['apʃprɪŋən] (*unreg*) vi to jump down/off; (*Farbe, Lack*) to flake off; (*AVIAT*) to bale out; (*sich distanzieren*) to back out

Absprung ['apʃprʊŋ] m jump

abspülen ['apʃpyːlən] vt to rinse; (*Geschirr*) to wash up

abstammen ['apʃtamən] vi to be descended; (*Wort*) to be derived; **Abstammung** f descent; derivation

Abstand ['apʃtant] *m* distance; (*zeitlich*) interval; **davon ~ nehmen, etw zu tun** to refrain from doing sth; **mit ~ der Beste** by far the best

abstatten ['apʃtatən] *vt* (*Dank*) to give; (*Besuch*) to pay

abstauben ['apʃtaʊbən] *vt, vi* to dust; (*umg: stehlen*) to pinch; (: *schnorren*) to scrounge

Abstecher ['apʃteçər] **(-s, -)** *m* detour

abstehen ['apʃteːən] (*unreg*) *vi* (*Ohren, Haare*) to stick out; (*entfernt sein*) to stand away

absteigen ['apʃtaɪgən] (*unreg*) *vi* (*vom Rad etc*) to get off, to dismount; **(in die zweite Liga) ~** to be relegated (to the second division)

abstellen ['apʃtɛlən] *vt* (*niederstellen*) to put down; (*entfernt stellen*) to pull out; (*hinstellen: Auto*) to park; (*ausschalten*) to turn *od* switch off; (*Missstand, Unsitte*) to stop

Abstellraum *m* storage room

abstempeln ['apʃtɛmpəln] *vt* to stamp

absterben ['apʃtɛrbən] (*unreg*) *vi* to die; (*Körperteil*) to go numb

Abstieg ['apʃtiːk] **(-(e)s, -e)** *m* descent; (*SPORT*) relegation; (*fig*) decline

abstimmen ['apʃtɪmən] *vi* to vote ♦ *vt*: **~ (auf** +*akk*) (*Instrument*) to tune (to); (*Interessen*) to match (with); (*Termine, Ziele*) to fit in (with) ♦ *vr* to agree

Abstimmung *f* vote

Abstinenz [apstiˈnɛnts] *f* abstinence; teetotalism; **~ler(in) (-s, -)** *m(f)* teetotaller

abstoßen ['apʃtoːsən] (*unreg*) *vt* to push off *od* away; (*verkaufen*) to unload; (*anekeln*) to repel, to repulse; **~d** *adj* repulsive

abstrakt [apˈstrakt] *adj* abstract ♦ *adv* abstractly, in the abstract

abstreiten ['apʃtraɪtən] (*unreg*) *vt* to deny

Abstrich ['apʃtrɪç] *m* (*Abzug*) cut; (*MED*) smear; **~e machen** to lower one's sights

abstufen ['apʃtuːfən] *vt* (*Hang*) to terrace; (*Farben*) to shade; (*Gehälter*) to grade

Absturz ['apʃtʊrts] *m* fall; (*AVIAT*) crash

abstürzen ['apʃtʏrtsən] *vi* to fall; (*AVIAT*) to crash

absuchen ['apzuːxən] *vt* to scour, to search

absurd [apˈzʊrt] *adj* absurd

Abszess ▲ [apsˈtsɛs] **(-es, -e)** *m* abscess

Abt [apt] **(-(e)s, ⁓e)** *m* abbot

Abt. *abk* (= *Abteilung*) dept.

abtasten ['aptastən] *vt* to feel, to probe

abtauen ['aptaʊən] *vt, vi* to thaw

Abtei [apˈtaɪ] **(-, -en)** *f* abbey

Abteil [apˈtaɪl] **(-(e)s, -e)** *nt* compartment; **'a~n** *vt* to divide up; (*abtrennen*) to divide off; **~ung** *f* (*in Firma, Kaufhaus*) department; (*in Krankenhaus*) section; (*MIL*) unit

abtippen ['aptɪpən] *vt* (*Text*) to type up

abtransportieren ['aptransˌpɔrtiːrən] *vt* to take away, to remove

abtreiben ['aptraɪbən] (*unreg*) *vt* (*Boot, Flugzeug*) to drive off course; (*Kind*) to abort ♦ *vi* to be driven off course; to abort

Abtreibung *f* abortion

abtrennen ['aptrɛnən] *vt* (*lostrennen*) to detach; (*entfernen*) to take off; (*abteilen*) to separate off

abtreten ['aptreːtən] (*unreg*) *vt* to wear out; (*überlassen*) to hand over, to cede ♦ *vi* to go off; (*zurücktreten*) to step down

Abtritt ['aptrɪt] *m* resignation

abtrocknen ['aptrɔknən] *vt, vi* to dry

abtun ['aptuːn] (*unreg*) *vt* (*fig*) to dismiss

abwägen ['apvɛːgən] (*unreg*) *vt* to weigh up

abwälzen ['apvɛltsən] *vt* (*Schuld, Verantwortung*): **~ (auf** +*akk*) to shift (onto)

abwandeln ['apvandəln] *vt* to adapt

abwandern ['apvandərn] *vi* to move away; (*FIN*) to be transferred

abwarten ['apvartən] *vt* to wait for ♦ *vi* to wait

abwärts ['apvɛrts] *adv* down

Abwasch ['apvaʃ] **(-(e)s)** *m* washing-up; **a~en** (*unreg*) *vt* (*Schmutz*) to wash off; (*Geschirr*) to wash (up)

Abwasser ['apvasər] **(-s, -wässer)** *nt* sewage

abwechseln ['apvɛksəln] *vi, vr* to alternate; (*Personen*) to take turns; **~d** *adj* alternate; **Abwechslung** *f* change; **abwechslungsreich** *adj* varied

abwegig ['apveːɡɪç] *adj* wrong

Abwehr ['apveːr] (-) *f* defence; (*Schutz*) protection; (*~dienst*) counterintelligence (service); **a~en** *vt* to ward off; (*Ball*) to stop

abweichen ['apvaiçən] (*unreg*) *vi* to deviate; (*Meinung*) to differ

abweisen ['apvaizən] (*unreg*) *vt* to turn away; (*Antrag*) to turn down; **~d** *adj* (*Haltung*) cold

abwenden ['apvɛndən] (*unreg*) *vt* to avert ♦ *vr* to turn away

abwerfen ['apvɛrfən] (*unreg*) *vt* to throw off; (*Profit*) to yield; (*aus Flugzeug*) to drop; (*Spielkarte*) to discard

abwerten ['apvɛrtən] *vt* (*FIN*) to devalue

abwertend *adj* (*Worte, Sinn*) pejorative

Abwertung *f* (*von Währung*) devaluation

abwesend ['apveːzənt] *adj* absent

Abwesenheit ['apveːzənhait] *f* absence

abwickeln ['apvikəln] *vt* to unwind; (*Geschäft*) to wind up

abwimmeln ['apvɪməln] (*umg*) *vt* (*Menschen*) to get shot of

abwischen ['apvɪʃən] *vt* to wipe off *od* away; (*putzen*) to wipe

Abwurf ['apvʊrf] *m* throwing off; (*von Bomben etc*) dropping; (*von Reiter, SPORT*) throw

abwürgen ['apvʏrgən] (*umg*) *vt* to scotch; (*Motor*) to stall

abzahlen ['aptsaːlən] *vt* to pay off

abzählen ['aptsɛːlən] *vt, vi* to count (up)

Abzahlung *f* repayment; **auf ~ kaufen** to buy on hire purchase

abzapfen ['aptsapfən] *vt* to draw off; **jdm Blut ~** to take blood from sb

abzäunen ['aptsɔʏnən] *vt* to fence off

Abzeichen ['aptsaiçən] *nt* badge; (*Orden*) decoration

abzeichnen ['aptsaiçnən] *vt* to draw, to copy; (*Dokument*) to initial ♦ *vr* to stand out; (*fig: bevorstehen*) to loom

abziehen ['aptsiːən] (*unreg*) *vt* to take off; (*Tier*) to skin; (*Bett*) to strip; (*Truppen*) to withdraw; (*subtrahieren*) to take away, to subtract; (*kopieren*) to run off ♦ *vi* to go away; (*Truppen*) to withdraw

abzielen ['aptsiːlən] *vi*: **~ auf** *+akk* to be aimed at

Abzug ['aptsuːk] *m* departure; (*von Truppen*) withdrawal; (*Kopie*) copy; (*Subtraktion*) subtraction; (*Betrag*) deduction; (*Rauchabzug*) flue; (*von Waffen*) trigger

abzüglich ['aptsyːklɪç] *präp +gen* less

abzweigen ['aptsvaigən] *vi* to branch off ♦ *vt* to set aside

Abzweigung *f* junction

ach [ax] *excl* oh; **~ ja!** (oh) yes; **~ so!** I see; **mit A~ und Krach** by the skin of one's teeth

Achse ['aksə] *f* axis; (*AUT*) axle

Achsel ['aksəl] (-, -n) *f* shoulder; **~höhle** *f* armpit

acht [axt] *num* eight; **~ Tage** a week; **A~**[1] (-, -en) *f* eight; (*beim Eislaufen etc*) figure eight

Acht[2] (-, -en) *f*: **~ geben (auf** *+akk*) to pay attention (to); **sich in ~ nehmen (vor** *+dat*) to be careful (of), to watch out (for); **etw außer ~ lassen** to disregard sth; **a~bar** *adj* worthy

acht- *zW*: **~e(r, s)** *adj* eighth; **A~el** *num* eighth; **~en** *vt* to respect ♦ *vi*: **~en (auf** *+akk*) to pay attention (to); **~en, dass ...** to be careful that ...

ächten ['ɛçtən] *vt* to outlaw, to ban

Achterbahn ['axtər-] *f* roller coaster

acht- *zW*: **~fach** *adj* eightfold; **~geben** △ (*unreg*) *vi siehe* **Acht**[2]; **~hundert** *num* eight hundred; **~los** *adj* careless; **~mal** *adv* eight times; **~sam** *adj* attentive

Achtung ['axtʊŋ] *f* attention; (*Ehrfurcht*) respect ♦ *excl* look out!; (*MIL*) attention!; **alle ~!** good for you/him *etc*

achtzehn *num* eighteen

achtzig *num* eighty

ächzen ['ɛçtsən] *vi* to groan

Acker ['akər] (-s, ⸚) *m* field; (*umg*) to plough; (*umg*) to slog away

ADAC [aːdeːʔaːˈtseː] *abk* (= *Allgemeiner Deutscher Automobil-Club*) ≃ AA, RAC

Adapter [aˈdaptər] (-s, -) *m* adapter

addieren [aˈdiːrən] *vt* to add (up); **Addition** [adiˈtsioːn] *f* addition

Adel ['aːdəl] (-s) *m* nobility; **a~ig** *adj* noble;

a~n vt to raise to the peerage
Ader ['aːdər] (-, -n) f vein
Adjektiv ['atjektiːf] (-s, -e) nt adjective
Adler ['aːdlər] (-s, -) m eagle
adlig adj noble
Adopt- zW: **a~ieren** [adɔp'tiːrən] vt to adopt; **~ion** [adɔptsi'oːn] f adoption; **~iveltern** pl adoptive parents; **~ivkind** nt adopted child
Adressbuch ▲ nt directory; (privat) address book
Adress- zW: **~e** [a'drɛsə] f address; **a~ieren** [adrɛ'siːrən] vt: **a~ieren (an** +akk) to address (to)
Adria ['aːdria] (-) f Adriatic
Advent [at'vɛnt] (-(e)s, -e) m Advent; **~skalender** m Advent calendar; **~skranz** m Advent wreath
Adverb [at'vɛrp] nt adverb
Aerobic [ae'roːbik] nt aerobics sg
Affäre [a'fɛːrə] f affair
Affe ['afə] (-n, -n) m monkey
Affekt [a'fɛkt] (-(e)s, -e) m: **im ~ handeln** to act in the heat of the moment; **a~iert** [afɛk'tiːrt] adj affected
Affen- zW: **a~artig** adj like a monkey; **mit a~artiger Geschwindigkeit** like a flash; **~hitze** (umg) f incredible heat
affig ['afɪç] adj affected
Afrika ['aːfrika] (-s) nt Africa; **~ner(in)** [-'kaːnər(ɪn)] (-s, -) m(f) African; **a~nisch** adj African
AG [aː'geː] abk (= Aktiengesellschaft) ≃ plc (BRIT), ≃ Inc. (US)
Agent [a'gɛnt] m agent; **~ur** f agency
Aggregat [agre'gaːt] (-(e)s, -e) nt aggregate; (TECH) unit
Aggress- zW: **~ion** [agrɛsi'oːn] f aggression; **a~iv** [agrɛ'siːf] adj aggressive; **~ivität** [agrɛsivi'tɛːt] f aggressiveness
Agrarpolitik [a'graːr-] f agricultural policy
Ägypten [ɛ'gʏptən] (-s) nt Egypt; **ägyptisch** adj Egyptian
aha [a'haː] excl aha
ähneln ['ɛːnəln] vi +dat to be like, to resemble ♦ vr to be alike od similar
ahnen ['aːnən] vt to suspect; (Tod, Gefahr) to have a presentiment of
ähnlich ['ɛːnlɪç] adj (+dat) similar (to); **Ä~keit** f similarity
Ahnung ['aːnʊŋ] f idea, suspicion; presentiment; **a~slos** adj unsuspecting
Ahorn ['aːhɔrn] (-s, -e) m maple
Ähre ['ɛːrə] f ear
Aids [eːdz] nt AIDS sg
Airbag ['ɛːəbɛk] (-s, -s) m airbag
Akademie [akade'miː] f academy; **Aka'demiker(in)** (-s, -) m(f) university graduate; **akademisch** adj academic
akklimatisieren [aklimati'ziːrən] vr to become acclimatized
Akkord [a'kɔrt] (-(e)s, -e) m (MUS) chord; **im ~ arbeiten** to do piecework
Akkordeon [a'kɔrdeɔn] (-s, -s) nt accordion
Akku ['aku] (-s, -s) m rechargeable battery
Akkusativ ['akuzatiːf] (-s, -e) m accusative
Akne ['aknə] f acne
Akrobat(in) [akro'baːt(ɪn)] (-en, -en) m(f) acrobat
Akt [akt] (-(e)s, -e) m act; (KUNST) nude
Akte ['aktə] f file
Akten- zW: **~koffer** m attaché case; **a~kundig** adj on the files; **~schrank** m filing cabinet; **~tasche** f briefcase
Aktie ['aktsiə] f share
Aktien- zW: **~gesellschaft** f public limited company; **~index** (-(es), -e od -indices) m share index; **~kurs** m share price
Aktion [aktsi'oːn] f campaign; (Polizeiaktion, Suchaktion) action
Aktionär [aktsio'nɛːr] (-s, -e) m shareholder
aktiv [ak'tiːf] adj active; (MIL) regular; **~ieren** [-'viːrən] vt to activate; **A~i'tät** f activity
Aktualität [aktuali'tɛːt] f topicality; (einer Mode) up-to-dateness
aktuell [aktu'ɛl] adj topical; up-to-date
Akupunktur [akupʊŋk'tuːər] f acupuncture
Akustik [a'kʊstɪk] f acoustics pl
akut [a'kuːt] adj acute
Akzent [ak'tsɛnt] m accent; (Betonung) stress
akzeptabel [aktsɛp'taːbl] adj acceptable
akzeptieren [aktsɛp'tiːrən] vt to accept
Alarm [a'larm] (-(e)s, -e) m alarm; **a~bereit** adj standing by; **~bereitschaft** f stand-by;

a~ieren [-'mi:rən] *vt* to alarm
Albanien [al'ba:niən] **(-s)** *nt* Albania
albanisch *adj* Albanian
albern ['albɐn] *adj* silly
Albtraum ▲ ['alptraʊm] *m* nightmare
Album ['album] **(-s, Alben)** *nt* album
Alge ['algə] *f* algae
Algebra ['algebra] **(-)** *f* algebra
Algerier(in) [al'ge:riːɐ(ɪn)] **(-s, -)** *m(f)* Algerian
algerisch *adj* Algerian
alias ['a:lias] *adv* alias
Alibi ['a:libi] **(-s, -s)** *nt* alibi
Alimente [ali'mɛntə] *pl* alimony *sg*
Alkohol ['alkohɔl] **(-s, -e)** *m* alcohol; **a~frei** *adj* non-alcoholic; **~iker(in)** [alko'ho:likɐ(ɪn)] **(-s, -)** *m(f)* alcoholic; **a~isch** *adj* alcoholic; **~verbot** *nt* ban on alcohol
All [al] **(-s)** *nt* universe
all'abendlich *adj* every evening
'allbekannt *adj* universally known

SCHLÜSSELWORT
---

alle(r, s) ['alə(r,s)] *adj* **1** *(sämtliche)* all; **wir alle** all of us; **alle Kinder waren da** all the children were there; **alle Kinder mögen ...** all children like ...; **alle beide** both of us/them; **sie kamen alle** they all came; **alles Gute** all the best; **alles in allem** all in all **2** *(mit Zeit- oder Maßangaben)* every; **alle vier Jahre** every four years; **alle fünf Meter** every five metres
♦ *pron* everything; **alles was er sagt** everything he says, all that he says
♦ *adv (zu Ende, aufgebraucht)* finished; **die Milch ist alle** the milk's all gone, there's no milk left; **etw alle machen** to finish sth up

---

Allee [a'le:] *f* avenue
allein [a'laɪn] *adv* alone; *(ohne Hilfe)* on one's own, by oneself ♦ *konj* but, only; **nicht ~** *(nicht nur)* not only; **~ stehend** single; **A~erziehende(r)** *f(m)* single parent; **A~gang** *m*: **im A~gang** on one's own
allemal ['alə'ma:l] *adv (jedes Mal)* always; *(ohne weiteres)* with no bother; *siehe* **Mal**

allenfalls ['alən'fals] *adv* at all events; *(höchstens)* at most
aller- ['alɐ] *zW*: **~beste(r, s)** *adj* very best; **~dings** *adv (zwar)* admittedly; *(gewiss)* certainly
Allergie [aler'gi:] *f* allergy; **al'lergisch** *adj* allergic
aller- *zW*: **~hand** *(umg)* *adj inv* all sorts of; **das ist doch ~hand!** that's a bit much; **~hand!** *(lobend)* good show!; **A~'heiligen** *nt* All Saints' Day; **~höchstens** *adv* at the very most; **~lei** *adj inv* all sorts of; **~letzte(r, s)** *adj* very last; **A~seelen** **(-s)** *nt* All Souls' Day; **~seits** *adv* on all sides; **prost ~seits!** cheers everyone!

Allerheiligen
---

i **Allerheiligen** *(All Saints' Day)* is celebrated on November 1st and is a public holiday in some parts of Germany and in Austria. **Allerseelen** *(All Souls' Day)* is celebrated on November 2nd in the Roman Catholic Church. It is customary to visit cemeteries and place lighted candles on the graves of relatives and friends.

Allerwelts- *in zW (Durchschnitts-)* common; *(nichts sagend)* commonplace
alles *pron* everything; **~ in allem** all in all; **~ Gute!** all the best!
Alleskleber **(-s, -)** *m* multi-purpose glue
allgemein ['algəmaɪn] *adj* general; **im A~en** in general; **~ gültig** generally accepted; **A~wissen** *nt* general knowledge
Alliierte(r) [ali'i:rtə(r)] *m* ally
all- *zW*: **~jährlich** *adj* annual; **~mächtig** *adj* almighty; **~mählich** *adj* gradual; **A~tag** *m* everyday life; **~täglich** *adj, adv* daily; *(gewöhnlich)* commonplace; **~tags** *adv* on weekdays; **~'wissend** *adj* omniscient; **~zu** *adv* all too; **~ oft** all too often; **~ viel** too much
Allzweck- ['altsvɛk-] *in zW* multi-purpose
Alm [alm] **(-, -en)** *f* alpine pasture
Almosen ['almo:zən] **(-s, -)** *nt* alms *pl*
Alpen ['alpən] *pl* Alps; **~vorland** *nt* foothills *pl* of the Alps

---

Rechtschreibreform: ▲ *neue Schreibung* △ *alte Schreibung (auslaufend)*

Alphabet [alfa'be:t] *(-(e)s, -e) nt* alphabet; **a~isch** *adj* alphabetical

Alptraum ['alptraʊm] = **Albtraum**

SCHLÜSSELWORT

als [als] *konj* **1** *(zeitlich)* when; *(gleichzeitig)* as; **damals, als ...** (in the days) when ...; **gerade, als ...** just as ...

2 *(in der Eigenschaft)* than; **als Antwort** as an answer; **als Kind** as a child

3 *(bei Vergleichen)* than; **ich kam später als er** I came later than he (did) *od* later than him; **lieber ... als ...** rather ... than ...; **nichts als Ärger** nothing but trouble

4: **als ob/wenn** as if

---

also ['alzo:] *konj* so; *(folglich)* therefore; **~ gut** *od* **schön!** okay then; **~, so was!** well really!; **na ~!** there you are then!

Alsterwasser ['alstər-] *nt* shandy *(BRIT)*, beer and lemonade

Alt [alt] *(-s, -e) m (MUS)* alto

alt *adj* old; **alles beim A~en lassen** to leave everything as it was

Altar [al'ta:r] *(-(e)s, -äre) m* altar

Alt- *zW:* **~bau** *m* old building; **a~bekannt** *adj* long-known; **~bier** *nt* top-fermented German dark beer; **~'eisen** *nt* scrap iron

Alten(wohn)heim *nt* old people's home

Alter ['altər] *(-s, -) nt* age; *(hohes)* old age; **im ~ von** at the age of; **a~n** *vi* to grow old, to age

Alternativ- [alterna'ti:f] *in zW* alternative; **~e** *f* alternative

Alters- *zW:* **~grenze** *f* age limit; **~heim** *nt* old people's home; **~rente** *f* old age pension; **a~schwach** *adj (Mensch)* frail; **~versorgung** *f* old age pension

Altertum ['altərtu:m] *nt* antiquity

alt- *zW:* **A~glas** *nt* glass for recycling; **A~glascontainer** *m* bottle bank; **~klug** *adj* precocious; **~modisch** *adj* old-fashioned; **A~papier** *nt* waste paper; **A~stadt** *f* old town

Alufolie ['a:lufo:liə] *f* aluminium foil

Aluminium [alu'mi:niʊm] *(-s) nt* aluminium, aluminum *(US)*

Alzheimerkrankheit ['altshaɪmər'kraŋkhaɪt] *f* Alzheimer's (disease)

am [am] = **an dem**; **~ Schlafen**; *(umg)* sleeping; **~ 15. März** on March 15th; **~ besten/schönsten** best/most beautiful

Amateur [ama'tø:r] *m* amateur

Amboss ▲ ['ambɔs] *(-es, -e) m* anvil

ambulant [ambu'lant] *adj* outpatient; **Ambulanz** *f* outpatients *sg*

Ameise ['a:maɪzə] *f* ant

Ameisenhaufen *m* ant hill

Amerika [a'me:rika] *(-s) nt* America; **~ner(in)** [-'ka:nər(ɪn)] *(-s, -) m(f)* American; **a~nisch** [-'ka:nɪʃ] *adj* American

Amnestie [amnɛs'ti:] *f* amnesty

Ampel ['ampəl] *(-, -n) f* traffic lights *pl*

amputieren [ampu'ti:rən] *vt* to amputate

Amsel ['amzəl] *(-, -n) f* blackbird

Amt [amt] *(-(e)s, -er) nt* office; *(Pflicht)* duty; *(TEL)* exchange; **a~ieren** [am'ti:rən] *vi* to hold office; **a~lich** *adj* official

Amts- *zW:* **~richter** *m* district judge; **~stunden** *pl* office hours; **~zeichen** *nt* dialling tone; **~zeit** *f* period of office

amüsant [amy'zant] *adj* amusing

amüsieren [amy'zi:rən] *vt* to amuse ♦ *vr* to enjoy o.s.

Amüsierviertel *nt* nightclub district

SCHLÜSSELWORT

an [an] *präp +dat* **1** *(räumlich: wo?)* at; *(auf, bei)* on; *(nahe bei)* near; **an diesem Ort** at this place; **an der Wand** on the wall; **zu nahe an etw** too near to sth; **unten am Fluss** down by the river; **Köln liegt am Rhein** Cologne is on the Rhine

2 *(zeitlich: wann?)* on; **an diesem Tag** on this day; **an Ostern** at Easter

3: **arm an Fett** low in fat; **an etw sterben** to die of sth; **an (und für) sich** actually

♦ *präp +akk* **1** *(räumlich: wohin?)* to; **er ging ans Fenster** he went (over) to the window; **etw an die Wand hängen/ schreiben** to hang/write sth on the wall

2 *(zeitlich: woran?)*: **an etw denken** to think of sth

3 *(gerichtet an)* to; **ein Gruß/eine Frage**

Spelling Reform: ▲ new spelling △ old spelling (to be phased out)

an dich greetings/a question to you
♦ *adv* **1** (*ungefähr*) about; **an die hundert** about a hundred
2 (*auf Fahrplänen*): **Frankfurt an 18.30** arriving Frankfurt 18.30
3 (*ab*): **von dort/heute an** from there/today onwards
4 (*angeschaltet, angezogen*) on; **das Licht ist an** the light is on; **ohne etwas an** with nothing on; *siehe auch* **am**

analog [ana'lo:k] *adj* analogous; **A~ie** [-'gi:] *f* analogy
Analphabet(in) [an|alfa'be:t(ɪn)] (**-en, -en**) *m(f)* illiterate (person)
Analyse [ana'ly:zə] *f* analysis
analysieren [analy'zi:rən] *vt* to analyse
Ananas ['ananas] (**-, -** *od* **-se**) *f* pineapple
Anarchie [anar'çi:] *f* anarchy
Anatomie [anato'mi:] *f* anatomy
anbahnen ['anba:nən] *vt, vr* to open up
Anbau ['anbau] *m* (*AGR*) cultivation; (*Gebäude*) extension; **a~en** *vt* (*AGR*) to cultivate; (*Gebäudeteil*) to build on
anbehalten ['anbəhaltən] (*unreg*) *vt* to keep on
anbei [an'bai] *adv* enclosed
anbeißen ['anbaisən] (*unreg*) *vt* to bite into ♦ *vi* to bite; (*fig*) to swallow the bait; **zum A~** (*umg*) good enough to eat
anbelangen ['anbəlaŋən] *vt* to concern; **was mich anbelangt** as far as I am concerned
anbeten ['anbe:tən] *vt* to worship
Anbetracht ['anbətraxt] *m*: **in ~** *+gen* in view of
anbieten ['anbi:tən] (*unreg*) *vt* to offer ♦ *vr* to volunteer
anbinden ['anbɪndən] (*unreg*) *vt* to tie up; **kurz angebunden** (*fig*) curt
Anblick ['anblɪk] *m* sight; **a~en** *vt* to look at
anbraten ['anbra:tən] *vt* to brown
anbrechen ['anbrɛçən] (*unreg*) *vt* to start; (*Vorräte*) to break into ♦ *vi* to start; (*Tag*) to break; (*Nacht*) to fall
anbrennen ['anbrɛnən] (*unreg*) *vi* to catch fire; (*KOCH*) to burn

anbringen ['anbrɪŋən] (*unreg*) *vt* to bring; (*Ware*) to sell; (*festmachen*) to fasten
Anbruch ['anbrʊx] *m* beginning; **~ des Tages/der Nacht** dawn/nightfall
anbrüllen ['anbrʏlən] *vt* to roar at
Andacht ['andaxt] (**-, -en**) *f* devotion; (*Gottesdienst*) prayers *pl*; **andächtig** *adj* ['andɛçtɪç] devout
andauern ['andauərn] *vi* to last, to go on; **~d** *adj* continual
Anden ['andən] *pl* Andes
Andenken ['andɛŋkən] (**-s, -**) *nt* memory; souvenir
andere(r, s) ['andərə(r, z)] *adj* other; (*verschieden*) different; **ein ~s Mal** another time; **kein ~r** nobody else; **von etw ~m sprechen** to talk about something else; **~rseits** *adv* on the other hand
andermal *adv*: **ein ~** some other time
ändern ['ɛndərn] *vt* to alter, to change ♦ *vr* to change
andernfalls ['andərnfals] *adv* otherwise
anders ['andərs] *adv*: **~ (als)** differently (from); **wer ~?** who else?; **jd/irgendwo ~** sb/somewhere else; **~ aussehen/klingen** to look/sound different; **~artig** *adj* different; **~herum** *adv* the other way round; **~wo** *adv* somewhere else; **~woher** *adv* from somewhere else
anderthalb ['andərt'halp] *adj* one and a half
Änderung ['ɛndərʊŋ] *f* alteration, change
Änderungsschneiderei *f* tailor (*who does alterations*)
anderweitig ['andər'vaitɪç] *adj* other ♦ *adv* otherwise; (*anderswo*) elsewhere
andeuten ['andɔytən] *vt* to indicate; (*Wink geben*) to hint at; **Andeutung** *f* indication; hint
Andrang ['andraŋ] *m* crush
andrehen ['andre:ən] *vt* to turn *od* switch on; **jdm etw ~** (*umg*) to unload sth onto sb
androhen ['andro:ən] *vt*: **jdm etw ~** to threaten sb with sth
aneignen ['an|aignən] *vt*: **sich** *dat* **etw ~** to acquire sth; (*widerrechtlich*) to appropriate sth

Rechtschreibreform: ▲ *neue Schreibung* △ *alte Schreibung (auslaufend)*

aneinander [an|aɪˈnandər] *adv* at/on/to *etc* one another *od* each other; **~ geraten** to clash

Anekdote [anɛkˈdoːtə] *f* anecdote

anekeln [ˈan|eːkəln] *vt* to disgust

anerkannt [ˈan|ɛrkant] *adj* recognized, acknowledged

anerkennen [ˈan|ɛrkɛnən] (*unreg*) *vt* to recognize, to acknowledge; (*würdigen*) to appreciate; **~d** *adj* appreciative

Anerkennung *f* recognition, acknowledgement; appreciation

anfachen [ˈanfaxən] *vt* to fan into flame; (*fig*) to kindle

anfahren [ˈanfaːrən] (*unreg*) *vt* to deliver; (*fahren gegen*) to hit; (*Hafen*) to put into; (*fig*) to bawl out ♦ *vi* to drive up; (*losfahren*) to drive off

Anfahrt [ˈanfaːrt] *f* (*~sweg*, *~szeit*) journey

Anfall [ˈanfal] *m* (*MED*) attack; **a~en** (*unreg*) *vt* to attack; (*fig*) to overcome ♦ *vi* (*Arbeit*) to come up; (*Produkt*) to be obtained

anfällig [ˈanfɛlɪç] *adj* delicate; **~ für etw** prone to sth

Anfang [ˈanfaŋ] **(-(e)s, -fänge)** *m* beginning, start; **von ~ an** right from the beginning; **zu ~** at the beginning; **~ Mai** at the beginning of May; **a~en** (*unreg*) *vt*, *vi* to begin, to start; (*machen*) to do

Anfänger(in) [ˈanfɛŋər(ɪn)] **(-s, -)** *m(f)* beginner

anfänglich [ˈanfɛŋlɪç] *adj* initial

anfangs *adv* at first; **A~buchstabe** *m* initial *od* first letter; **A~gehalt** *nt* starting salary

anfassen [ˈanfasən] *vt* to handle; (*berühren*) to touch ♦ *vi* to lend a hand ♦ *vr* to feel

anfechten [ˈanfɛçtən] (*unreg*) *vt* to dispute

anfertigen [ˈanfɛrtɪɡən] *vt* to make

anfeuern [ˈanfɔyərn] *vt* (*fig*) to spur on

anflehen [ˈanfleːən] *vt* to implore

anfliegen [ˈanfliːɡən] (*unreg*) *vt* to fly to

Anflug [ˈanfluːk] *m* (*AVIAT*) approach; (*Spur*) trace

anfordern [ˈanfɔrdərn] *vt* to demand; (*COMM*) to requisition

Anforderung *f* (*+gen*) demand (for)

Anfrage [ˈanfraːɡə] *f* inquiry; **a~n** *vi* to inquire

anfreunden [ˈanfrɔyndən] *vr* to make friends

anfügen [ˈanfyːɡən] *vt* to add; (*beifügen*) to enclose

anfühlen [ˈanfyːlən] *vt*, *vr* to feel

anführen [ˈanfyːrən] *vt* to lead; (*zitieren*) to quote; (*umg: betrügen*) to lead up the garden path

Anführer *m* leader

Anführungszeichen *pl* quotation marks, inverted commas

Angabe [ˈanɡaːbə] *f* statement; (*TECH*) specification; (*umg: Prahlerei*) boasting; (*SPORT*) service

angeben [ˈanɡeːbən] (*unreg*) *vt* to give; (*anzeigen*) to inform on; (*bestimmen*) to set ♦ *vi* (*umg*) to boast; (*SPORT*) to serve

Angeber (-s, -) (*umg*) *m* show-off; **Angebeˈrei** (*umg*) *f* showing off

angeblich [ˈanɡeːplɪç] *adj* alleged

angeboren [ˈanɡəboːrən] *adj* inborn, innate

Angebot [ˈanɡəboːt] *nt* offer; **~ (an** +*dat*) (*COMM*) supply (of)

angebracht [ˈanɡəbraxt] *adj* appropriate, in order

angegriffen [ˈanɡəɡrɪfən] *adj* exhausted

angeheitert [ˈanɡəhaɪtərt] *adj* tipsy

angehen [ˈanɡeːən] (*unreg*) *vt* to concern; (*angreifen*) to attack; (*bitten*): **jdn ~ (um)** to approach sb (for) ♦ *vi* (*Feuer*) to light; (*umg: beginnen*) to begin; **~d** *adj* prospective

angehören [ˈanɡəhøːrən] *vi* (+ *dat*) to belong to; (*Partei*) to be a member of

Angehörige(r) *f(m)* relative

Angeklagte(r) [ˈanɡəklaːktə(r)] *f(m)* accused

Angel [ˈaŋəl] **(-, -n)** *f* fishing rod; (*Türangel*) hinge

Angelegenheit [ˈanɡələːɡənhaɪt] *f* affair, matter

Angel- *zW*: **~haken** *m* fish hook; **a~n** *vt* to catch ♦ *vi* to fish; **~n (-s)** *nt* angling, fishing; **~rute** *f* fishing rod; **~schein** *m* fishing permit

angemessen [ˈanɡəmɛsən] *adj* appropriate, suitable

angenehm [ˈangəneːm] *adj* pleasant; **~!** (*bei Vorstellung*) pleased to meet you

angeregt [angəreːkt] *adj* animated, lively

angesehen [ˈangəzeːən] *adj* respected

angesichts [ˈangəzɪçts] *präp +gen* in view of, considering

angespannt [ˈangəʃpant] *adj* (*Aufmerksamkeit*) close; (*Arbeit*) hard

Angestellte(r) [ˈangəʃtɛltə(r)] *f(m)* employee

angestrengt [ˈangəʃtrɛnt] *adv* as hard as one can

angetan [ˈangətaːn] *adj*: **von jdm/etw ~ sein** to be impressed by sb/sth; **es jdm ~ haben** to appeal to sb

angetrunken [ˈangətrʊŋkən] *adj* tipsy

angewiesen [ˈangəviːzən] *adj*: **auf jdn/etw ~ sein** to be dependent on sb/sth

angewöhnen [ˈangəvøːnən] *vt*: **jdm/sich etw ~** to get sb/become accustomed to sth

Angewohnheit [ˈangəvoːnhaɪt] *f* habit

angleichen [ˈanglaɪçən] (*unreg*) *vt, vr* to adjust

Angler [ˈaŋlər] (**-s, -**) *m* angler

angreifen [ˈangraɪfən] (*unreg*) *vt* to attack; (*beschädigen*) to damage

Angreifer [ˈangraɪfər] *m* attacker

Angriff [ˈangrɪf] *m* attack; **etw in ~ nehmen** to make a start on sth

Angst (**-, ⁻e**) *f* fear; **jdm ist a~ig** sb is afraid *od* scared; **~ haben** (**vor** +*dat*) to be afraid *od* scared (**of**); **~ haben um jdn/etw** to be worried about sb/sth; **jdm ~ machen** to scare sb; **~hase** (*umg*) *m* chicken, scaredy-cat

ängst- [ˈɛŋst] *zW*: **~igen** *vt* to frighten ♦ *vr*: **sich ~igen** (**vor** +*dat od* **um**) to worry (o.s.) (about); **~lich** *adj* nervous; (*besorgt*) worried; **Ä~lichkeit** *f* nervousness

anhaben [ˈanhaːbən] (*unreg*) *vt* to have on; **er kann mir nichts ~** he can't hurt me

anhalt- [ˈanhalt] *zW*: **~en** (*unreg*) *vt* to stop ♦ *vi* to stop; (*andauern*) to persist; (**jdm**) **etw ~en** to hold sth up (against sb); **jdn zur Arbeit/Höflichkeit ~en** to make sb work/be polite; **~end** *adj* persistent;

A~er(in) (**-s, -**) *m(f)* hitch-hiker; **per A~er fahren** to hitch-hike; **A~spunkt** *m* clue

anhand [anˈhant] *präp +gen* with

Anhang [ˈanhaŋ] *m* appendix; (*Leute*) family; supporters *pl*

anhäng- [ˈanhɛŋ] *zW*: **~en** (*unreg*) *vt* to hang up; (*Wagen*) to couple up; (*Zusatz*) to add (on); **A~er** (**-s, -**) *m* supporter; (*AUT*) trailer; (*am Koffer*) tag; (*Schmuck*) pendant; **A~erschaft** *f* supporters *pl*; **~lich** *adj* devoted; **A~lichkeit** *f* devotion; **A~sel** (**-s, -**) *nt* appendage

Anhäufung [ˈanhɔyfʊŋ] *f* accumulation

anheben [ˈanheːbən] (*unreg*) *vt* to lift up; (*Preise*) to raise

anheizen [ˈanhaɪtsən] *vt* (*Stimmung*) to lift; (*Moral*) to boost

Anhieb [ˈanhiːb] *m*: **auf ~** at the very first go; (*kurz entschlossen*) on the spur of the moment

Anhöhe [ˈanhøːə] *f* hill

anhören [ˈanhøːrən] *vt* to listen to; (*anmerken*) to hear ♦ *vr* to sound

animieren [aniˈmiːrən] *vt* to encourage, to urge on

Anis [aˈniːs] (**-es, -e**) *m* aniseed

Ank. *abk* (= *Ankunft*) arr.

Ankauf [ˈankaʊf] *m* (*von Wertpapieren, Devisen, Waren*) purchase; **a~en** *vt* to purchase, to buy

Anker [ˈaŋkər] (**-s, -**) *m* anchor; **vor ~ gehen** to drop anchor

Anklage [ˈanklaːgə] *f* accusation; (*JUR*) charge; **~bank** *f* dock; **a~n** *vt* to accuse; **jdn (eines Verbrechens) a~n** (*JUR*) to charge sb (with a crime)

Ankläger [ˈanklɛːgər] *m* accuser

Anklang [ˈanklaŋ] *m*: **bei jdm ~ finden** to meet with sb's approval

Ankleidekabine *f* changing cubicle

ankleiden [ˈanklaɪdən] *vt, vr* to dress

anklicken [ˈanklɪkən] *vt* (*COMPUT*) to click on

anklopfen [ˈanklɔpfən] *vi* to knock

anknüpfen [ˈanknʏpfən] *vt* to fasten *od* tie on; (*fig*) to start ♦ *vi* (*anschließen*): **~ an** +*akk* to refer to

ankommen [ˈankɔmən] (*unreg*) *vi* to arrive;

(*näher kommen*) to approach; (*Anklang finden*): **bei jdm (gut) ~** to go down well with sb; (*hervorheben*) to highlight

ankreuzen ['ankrɔytsən] *vt* to mark with a cross; (*hervorheben*) to highlight

ankündigen ['ankʏndɪgən] *vt* to announce; **Ankündigung** *f* announcement

Ankunft ['ankʊnft] (-, **-künfte**) *f* arrival; **~szeit** *f* time of arrival

ankurbeln ['ankʊrbəln] *vt* (*fig*) to boost

Anlage ['anla:gə] *f* disposition; (*Begabung*) talent; (*Park*) gardens *pl*; (*Beilage*) enclosure; (*TECH*) plant; (*FIN*) investment; (*Entwurf*) layout

Anlass ▲ ['anlas] (**-es, -lässe**) *m*: **~ (zu)** cause (for); (*Ereignis*) occasion; **aus ~** +*gen* on the occasion of; **~ zu etw geben** to give rise to sth; **etw zum ~ nehmen** to take the opportunity of sth

anlassen (*unreg*) *vt* to leave on; (*Motor*) to start ♦ *vr* (*umg*) to start off

Anlasser (-s, -) *m* (*AUT*) starter

anlässlich ▲ ['anlɛslɪç] *präp* +*gen* on the occasion of

Anlauf ['anlauf] *m* run-up; **a~en** (*unreg*) *vi* to begin; (*neuer Film*) to show; (*SPORT*) to run up; (*Fenster*) to mist up; (*Metall*) to tarnish ♦ *vt* to call at; **rot a~en** to blush; **angelaufen kommen** to come running up

anlegen ['anle:gən] *vt* to put; (*anziehen*) to put on; (*gestalten*) to lay out; (*Geld*) to invest ♦ *vi* to dock; **etw an etw** *akk* **~** to put sth against *od* on sth; **ein Gewehr ~ (auf** +*akk*) to aim a weapon (at); **es auf etw** *akk* **~** to be out for sth/to do sth; **sich mit jdm ~** (*umg*) to quarrel with sb

Anlegestelle *f* landing place

anlehnen ['anle:nən] *vt* to lean; (*Tür*) to leave ajar; **(sich) an etw** *akk* **~** to lean on/against sth

Anleihe ['anlaiə] *f* (*FIN*) loan

anleiten ['anlaitən] *vt* to instruct;

Anleitung *f* instructions *pl*

anliegen ['anli:gən] (*unreg*) *vi* (*Kleidung*) to cling; **A~ (-s, -)** *nt* matter; (*Wunsch*) wish; **~d** *adj* adjacent; (*beigefügt*) enclosed

Anlieger (-s, -) *m* resident; „**~ frei"** "residents only"

anmachen ['anmaxən] *vt* to attach; (*ELEK*) to put on; (*Zigarette*) to light; (*Salat*) to dress

anmaßen ['anma:sən] *vt*: **sich** *dat* **etw ~** (*Recht*) to lay claim to sth; **~d** *adj* arrogant

Anmaßung *f* presumption

anmelden ['anmɛldən] *vt* to announce ♦ *vr* (*sich ankündigen*) to make an appointment; (*polizeilich, für Kurs etc*) to register

Anmeldung *f* announcement; appointment; registration

anmerken ['anmɛrkən] *vt* to observe; (*anstreichen*) to mark; **sich** *dat* **nichts ~ lassen** to not give anything away

Anmerkung *f* note

anmieten ['anmi:tən] *vt* to rent; (*auch Auto*) to hire

Anmut ['anmu:t] (-) *f* grace; **a~en** *vt* to give a feeling; **a~ig** *adj* charming

annähen ['annɛ:ən] *vt* to sew on

annähern ['annɛ:ərn] *vr* to get closer; **~d** *adj* approximate

Annäherung *f* approach

Annäherungsversuch *m* advances *pl*

Annahme ['anna:mə] *f* acceptance; (*Vermutung*) assumption

annehm- ['annɛ:m] *zW*: **~bar** *adj* acceptable; **~en** (*unreg*) *vt* to accept; (*Namen*) to take; (*Kind*) to adopt; (*vermuten*) to suppose, to assume ♦ *vr* (+*gen*) to take care (of); **A~lichkeit** *f* comfort

Annonce [a'nõ:sə] *f* advertisement

annoncieren [anõ'si:rən] *vt, vi* to advertise

annullieren [anʊ'li:rən] *vt* to annul

anonym [ano'ny:m] *adj* anonymous

Anorak ['anorak] (-s, -s) *m* anorak

anordnen ['anɔrdnən] *vt* to arrange; (*befehlen*) to order

Anordnung *f* arrangement; order

anorganisch ['anɔrga:nɪʃ] *adj* inorganic

anpacken ['anpakən] *vt* to grasp; (*fig*) to tackle; **mit ~** to lend a hand

Spelling Reform: ▲ *new spelling* △ *old spelling (to be phased out)*

anpassen ['anpasən] *vt*: **(jdm)** ~ to fit (on sb); (*fig*) to adapt ♦ *vr* to adapt

anpassungsfähig *adj* adaptable

Anpfiff ['anpfɪf] *m* (*SPORT*) (starting) whistle; kick-off; (*umg*) rocket

anprallen ['anpralən] *vi*: ~ **(gegen** *od* **an** +*akk*) to collide (with)

anprangern ['anpraŋərn] *vt* to denounce

anpreisen ['anpraɪzən] *vt* (*unreg*) to extol

Anprobe ['anproːbə] *f* trying on

anprobieren ['anprobiːrən] *vt* to try on

anrechnen ['anrɛçnən] *vt* to charge; (*fig*) to count; **jdm etw hoch** ~ to think highly of sb for sth

Anrecht ['anrɛçt] *nt*: ~ **(auf** +*akk*) right (to)

Anrede ['anreːdə] *f* form of address; **a~n** *vt* to address; (*belästigen*) to accost

anregen ['anreːgən] *vt* to stimulate; **angeregte Unterhaltung** lively discussion; **~d** *adj* stimulating

Anregung *f* stimulation; (*Vorschlag*) suggestion

anreichern ['anraɪçərn] *vt* to enrich

Anreise ['anraɪzə] *f* journey; **a~n** *vi* to arrive

Anreiz ['anraɪts] *m* incentive

Anrichte ['anrɪçtə] *f* sideboard; **a~n** *vt* to serve up; **Unheil a~n** to make mischief

anrüchig ['anryçɪç] *adj* dubious

anrücken ['anrʏkən] *vi* to approach; (*MIL*) to advance

Anruf ['anruːf] *m* call; ~**beantworter** [-bə-ˈlantvɔrtər] **(-s, -)** *m* answering machine; **a~en** (*unreg*) *vt* to call out to; (*bitten*) to call on; (*TEL*) to ring up, to phone, to call

ans [ans] = **an das**

Ansage ['anzaːgə] *f* announcement; **a~n** *vt* to announce ♦ *vr* to say one will come; ~**r(in)** **(-s, -)** *m(f)* announcer

ansammeln ['anzaməln] *vt* (*Reichtümer*) to amass ♦ *vr* (*Menschen*) to gather, to assemble; (*Wasser*) to collect; **Ansammlung** *f* collection; (*Leute*) crowd

ansässig ['anzɛsɪç] *adj* resident

Ansatz ['anzats] *m* start; (*Haaransatz*) hairline; (*Halsansatz*) base; (*Verlängerungsstück*) extension; (*Veranschlagung*) estimate; ~**punkt** *m* starting point

anschaffen ['anʃafən] *vt* to buy, to purchase; **Anschaffung** *f* purchase

anschalten ['anʃaltən] *vt* to switch on

anschau- ['anʃaʊ] *zW*: ~**en** *vt* to look at; ~**lich** *adj* illustrative; **A~ung** *f* (*Meinung*) view; **aus eigener A~ung** from one's own experience

Anschein ['anʃaɪn] *m* appearance; **allem ~ nach** to all appearances; **den ~ haben** to seem, to appear; **a~end** *adj* apparent

anschieben ['anʃiːbən] *vt* to push

Anschlag ['anʃlaːk] *m* notice; (*Attentat*) attack; (*COMM*) estimate; (*auf Klavier*) touch; (*Schreibmaschine*) character; **a~en** ['anʃlaːgən] (*unreg*) *vt* to put up; (*beschädigen*) to chip; (*Akkord*) to strike; (*Kosten*) to estimate ♦ *vi* to hit; (*wirken*) to have an effect; (*Glocke*) to ring; **an etw** *akk* **a~en** to hit against sth

anschließen ['anʃliːsən] (*unreg*) *vt* to connect up; (*Sender*) to link up ♦ *vi*: **an etw** *akk* ~ to adjoin sth; (*zeitlich*) to follow sth ♦ *vr*: **sich jdm/etw** ~ to join sb/sth; (*beipflichten*) to agree with sb/sth; **sich an etw** *akk* ~ to adjoin sth; **~d** *adj* adjacent; (*zeitlich*) subsequent ♦ *adv* afterwards

Anschluss ▲ ['anʃlʊs] *m* (*ELEK, EISENB*) connection; (*von Wasser etc*) supply; **im ~ an** +*akk* following; **~ finden** to make friends; **~flug** *m* connecting flight

anschmiegsam ['anʃmiːkzaːm] *adj* affectionate

anschnallen ['anʃnalən] *vt* to buckle on ♦ *vr* to fasten one's seat belt

anschneiden ['anʃnaɪdən] (*unreg*) *vt* to cut into; (*Thema*) to introduce

anschreiben ['anʃraɪbən] (*unreg*) *vt* to write (up); (*COMM*) to charge up; (*benachrichtigen*) to write to

anschreien ['anʃraɪən] (*unreg*) *vt* to shout at

Anschrift ['anʃrɪft] *f* address

Anschuldigung ['anʃʊldɪgʊŋ] *f* accusation

anschwellen ['anʃvelən] (*unreg*) *vi* to swell (up)

anschwindeln ['anʃvɪndəln] *vt* to lie to

ansehen ['anzeːən] (*unreg*) *vt* to look at;

jdm etw ~ to see sth (from sb's face);
jdn/etw als etw ~ to look on sb/sth as sth;
~ **für** to consider; **A~** (-s) nt respect; (Ruf)
reputation
ansehnlich ['anze:nlɪç] adj fine-looking;
(beträchtlich) considerable
ansetzen ['anzɛtsən] vt (festlegen) to fix;
(entwickeln) to develop; (Fett) to put on;
(Blätter) to grow; (zubereiten) to prepare
♦ vi (anfangen) to start, to begin;
(Entwicklung) to set in; (dick werden) to put
on weight ♦ vr (Rost etc) to start to
develop; ~ **an** +akk (anfügen) to fix on to;
(anlegen, an Mund etc) to put to
Ansicht ['anzɪçt] f (Anblick) sight; (Meinung)
view, opinion; **zur ~** on approval; **meiner ~
nach** in my opinion; ~**skarte** f picture
postcard; ~**ssache** f matter of opinion
ansonsten [an'zɔnstən] adv otherwise
anspannen ['anʃpanən] vt to harness;
(Muskel) to strain; **Anspannung** f strain
anspielen ['anʃpi:lən] vi (SPORT) to start
play; **auf etw** akk ~ to refer od allude to
sth
Anspielung f: ~ **(auf** +akk) reference (to),
allusion (to)
Anspitzer ['anʃpɪtsər] (-s, -) m pencil
sharpener
Ansporn ['anʃpɔrn] (-(e)s) m incentive
Ansprache ['anʃpra:xə] f address
ansprechen ['anʃprɛçən] (unreg) vt to speak
to; (bitten, gefallen) to appeal to ♦ vi: (auf
etw akk) ~ to react (to sth); **jdn auf etw**
akk **(hin)** ~ to ask sb about sth; ~**d** adj
attractive
anspringen ['anʃprɪŋən] (unreg) vi (AUT) to
start ♦ vt to jump at
Anspruch ['anʃprʊx] m (Recht): ~ **(auf** +akk)
claim (to); **hohe Ansprüche stellen/
haben** to demand/expect a lot; **jdn/etw in
~ nehmen** to occupy sb/take up sth;
a~slos adj undemanding; **a~svoll** adj
demanding
anstacheln ['anʃtaxəln] vt to spur on
Anstalt ['anʃtalt] (-, -en) f institution; ~**en
machen, etw zu tun** to prepare to do sth
Anstand ['anʃtant] m decency

anständig ['anʃtɛndɪç] adj decent; (umg)
proper; (groß) considerable
andstandslos adv without any ado
anstarren ['anʃtarən] vt to stare at
anstatt [an'ʃtat] präp +gen instead of ♦ konj:
~ **etw zu tun** instead of doing sth
Ansteck- ['anʃtek] zW: **a~en** vt to pin on;
(MED) to infect; (Pfeife) to light; (Haus) to
set fire to ♦ vr: **ich habe mich bei ihm
angesteckt** I caught it from him ♦ vi (fig)
to be infectious; **a~end** adj infectious;
~**ung** f infection
anstehen ['anʃte:ən] (unreg) vi to queue
(up) (BRIT), to line up (US)
ansteigen ['anʃtaɪɡən] vt (Straße) to climb;
(Gelände, Temperatur, Preise) to rise
anstelle, an Stelle [an'ʃtɛlə] präp +gen in
place of; ~**n** ['an-] vt (einschalten) to turn
on; (Arbeit geben) to employ; (machen) to
do ♦ vr to queue (up) (BRIT), to line up (US);
(umg) to act
Anstellung f employment; (Posten) post,
position
Anstieg ['anʃti:k] (-(e)s, -e) m (+gen) climb;
(fig: von Preisen etc) increase (in)
anstiften ['anʃtɪftən] vt (Unglück) to cause;
jdn zu etw ~ to put sb up to sth
anstimmen ['anʃtɪmən] vt (Lied) to strike up
with; (Geschrei) to set up
Anstoß ['anʃto:s] m impetus; (Ärgernis)
offence; (SPORT) kick-off; **der erste ~** the
initiative; ~ **nehmen an** +dat to take
offence at; **a~en** (unreg) vt to push; (mit
Fuß) to kick ♦ vi to knock, to bump; (mit der
Zunge) to lisp; (mit Gläsern): **a~en (auf**
+akk) to drink (to), to drink a toast (to)
anstößig ['anʃtø:sɪç] adj offensive, indecent
anstreichen ['anʃtraɪçən] (unreg) vt to paint
anstrengen ['anʃtrɛŋən] vt to strain; (JUR) to
bring ♦ vr to make an effort; ~**d** adj tiring
Anstrengung f effort
Anstrich ['anʃtrɪç] m coat of paint
Ansturm ['anʃtʊrm] m rush; (MIL) attack
Antarktis [ant'arktɪs] (-) f Antarctic
antasten ['antastən] vt to touch; (Recht) to
infringe upon; (Ehre) to question
Anteil ['antaɪl] (-s, -e) m share; (Mitgefühl)

Spelling Reform: ▲ *new spelling* △ *old spelling (to be phased out)*

sympathy; **~ nehmen (an** +*dat*) to share (in); (*sich interessieren*) to take an interest (in); **~nahme** (-) *f* sympathy

Antenne [an'tɛnə] *f* aerial

Anti- ['anti] *in zW* anti; **~alko'holiker** *m* teetotaller; **a~autori'tär** *adj* anti-authoritarian; **~babypille** *f* contraceptive pill; **~biotikum** [antibi'o:tikʊm] (-s, -ka) *nt* antibiotic

antik [an'ti:k] *adj* antique; **A~e** *f* (*Zeitalter*) ancient world

Antiquariat [antikvari'a:t] (-(e)s, -e) *nt* secondhand bookshop

Antiquitäten [antikvi'tɛːtən] *pl* antiques; **~händler** *m* antique dealer

Antrag ['antra:k] (-(e)s, -träge) *m* proposal; (*PARL*) motion; (*Gesuch*) application; **~steller(in)**(-s, -) *m(f)* claimant; (*für Kredit*) applicant

antreffen ['antrɛfən] (*unreg*) *vt* to meet

antreiben ['antraɪbən] (*unreg*) *vt* to drive on; (*Motor*) to drive

antreten ['antre:tən] (*unreg*) *vt* (*Amt*) to take up; (*Erbschaft*) to come into; (*Beweis*) to offer; (*Reise*) to start, to begin ♦ *vi* (*MIL*) to fall in; (*SPORT*) to line up; **gegen jdn ~** to play/fight (against) sb

Antrieb ['antri:p] *m* (*auch fig*) drive; **aus eigenem ~** of one's own accord

antrinken ['antrɪŋkən] (*unreg*) *vt* (*Flasche, Glas*) to start to drink from; **sich** *dat* **Mut/einen Rausch ~** to give o.s. Dutch courage/get drunk; **angetrunken sein** to be tipsy

Antritt ['antrɪt] *m* beginning, commencement; (*eines Amts*) taking up

antun ['antu:n] (*unreg*) *vt*: **jdm etw ~** to do sth to sb; **sich** *dat* **Zwang ~** to force o.s.; **sich** *dat* **etwas ~** to (try to) take one's own life

Antwort ['antvɔrt] (-, -en) *f* answer, reply; **a~en** *vi* to answer, to reply

anvertrauen ['anfertraʊən] *vt*: **jdm etw ~** to entrust sb with sth; **sich jdm ~** to confide in sb

anwachsen ['anvaksən] (*unreg*) *vi* to grow; (*Pflanze*) to take root

Anwalt ['anvalt] (-(e)s, -wälte) *m* solicitor; lawyer; (*fig*) champion

Anwältin ['anvɛltɪn] *f siehe* **Anwalt**

Anwärter ['anvɛrtər] *m* candidate

anweisen ['anvaɪzən] (*unreg*) *vt* to instruct; (*zuteilen*) to assign

Anweisung *f* instruction; (*COMM*) remittance; (*Postanweisung, Zahlungsanweisung*) money order

anwend- ['anvɛnd] *zW*: **~bar** ['anvɛnt-] *adj* practicable, applicable; **~en** (*unreg*) *vt* to use, to employ; (*Gesetz, Regel*) to apply; **A~ung** *f* use; application

anwesend ['anve:zənt] *adj* present; **die A~en** those present

Anwesenheit *f* presence

anwidern ['anvi:dərn] *vt* to disgust

Anwohner(in) ['anvo:nər(ɪn)] (-s, -) *m(f)* neighbour

Anzahl ['antsa:l] *f*: **~** (**an** +*dat*) number (of); **a~en** *vt* to pay on account; **~ung** *f* deposit, payment on account

Anzeichen ['antsaɪçən] *nt* sign, indication

Anzeige ['antsaɪgə] *f* (*Zeitungsanzeige*) announcement; (*Werbung*) advertisement; (*bei Polizei*) report; **~ erstatten gegen jdn** to report sb (to the police); **a~n** *vt* (*zu erkennen geben*) to show; (*bekannt geben*) to announce; (*bei Polizei*) to report

anziehen ['antsi:ən] (*unreg*) *vt* to attract; (*Kleidung*) to put on; (*Mensch*) to dress; (*Seil*) to pull tight; (*Schraube*) to tighten; (*Knie*) to draw up ♦ *vr* to get dressed; **~d** *adj* attractive

Anziehung *f* (*Reiz*) attraction; **~skraft** *f* power of attraction; (*PHYS*) force of gravitation

Anzug ['antsu:k] *m* suit; (*Herankommen*): **im ~ sein** to be approaching

anzüglich ['antsy:klɪç] *adj* personal; (*anstößig*) offensive; **A~keit** *f* offensiveness; (*Bemerkung*) personal remark

anzünden ['antsyndən] *vt* to light

anzweifeln ['antsvaɪfəln] *vt* to doubt

apathisch [a'pa:tɪʃ] *adj* apathetic

Apfel ['apfəl] (-s, ") *m* apple; **~saft** *m* apple juice; **~sine** [-'zi:nə] *f* orange; **~wein** *m* cider

Apostel [a'pɔstəl] **(-s, -)** *m* apostle

Apotheke [apo'te:kə] *f* chemist's (shop), drugstore (*US*); **a~npflichtig** [-pflɪçtɪç] *adj* available only at a chemist's shop (*BRIT*) or pharmacy; **~r(in) (-s, -)** *m(f)* chemist, druggist (*US*)

Apotheke

ⓘ *The Apotheke is a pharmacy selling medicines available only on prescription and toiletries. The pharmacist is qualified to give advice on medicines and treatments.*

Apparat [apa'ra:t] **(-(e)s, -e)** *m* piece of apparatus; camera; telephone; (*RADIO, TV*) set; **am ~!** speaking!; **~ur** [-'tu:r] *f* apparatus

Appartement [apart(ə)'mã:] **(-s, -s)** *nt* flat

appellieren [apɛ'li:rən] *vi*: **~ (an** +*akk*) to appeal (to)

Appetit [ape'ti:t] **(-(e)s, -e)** *m* appetite; **guten ~!** enjoy your meal; **a~lich** *adj* appetizing; **~losigkeit** *f* lack of appetite

Applaus [ap'laus] **(-es, -e)** *m* applause

Aprikose [apri'ko:zə] *f* apricot

April [a'prɪl] **(-(s), -e)** *m* April

Aquarell [akva'rɛl] **(-s, -e)** *nt* watercolour

Äquator [ɛ'kva:tɔr] **(-s, -)** *m* equator

Arab- ['arab] *zW*: **~er(in) (-s, -)** *m(f)* Arab; **~ien** [a'ra:biən] **(-s)** *nt* Arabia; **a~isch** [a'ra:bɪʃ] *adj* Arabian

Arbeit ['arbaɪt] **(-, -en)** *f* work *no art*; (*Stelle*) job; (*Erzeugnis*) piece of work; (*wissenschaftliche*) dissertation; (*Klassenarbeit*) test; **das war eine ~** that was a hard job; **a~en** *vi* to work ♦ *vt* to work, to make; **~er(in) (-s, -)** *m(f)* worker; (*ungelernt*) labourer; **~erschaft** *f* workers *pl*, labour force; **~geber (-s, -)** *m* employer; **~nehmer (-s, -)** *m* employee

Arbeits- *in zW* labour; **a~am** *adj* industrious; **~amt** *nt* employment exchange; **~erlaubnis** *f* work permit; **a~fähig** *adj* fit for work, able-bodied; **~gang** *m* operation; **~kräfte** *pl* (*Mitarbeiter*) workforce; **a~los** *adj*

unemployed, out-of-work; **~lose(r)** *f(m)* unemployed person; **~losigkeit** *f* unemployment; **~markt** *m* job market; **~platz** *m* job; place of work; **a~scheu** *adj* workshy; **~tag** *m* work(ing) day; **a~unfähig** *adj* unfit for work; **~zeit** *f* working hours *pl*; **~zimmer** *nt* study

Archäologe [arçɛo'lo:gə] **(-n, -n)** *m* archaeologist

Architekt(in) [arçi'tɛkt(ɪn)] **(-en, -en)** *m(f)* architect; **~ur** [-'tu:r] *f* architecture

Archiv [ar'çi:f] **(-s, -e)** *nt* archive

arg [ark] *adj* bad, awful ♦ *adv* awfully, very

Argentinien [argen'ti:niən] **(-s)** *nt* Argentina, the Argentine

argentinisch *adj* Argentinian

Ärger ['ɛrgər] **(-s)** *m* (*Wut*) anger; (*Unannehmlichkeit*) trouble; **ä~lich** *adj* (*zornig*) angry; (*lästig*) annoying, aggravating; **ä~n** *vt* to annoy ♦ *vr* to get annoyed

arg- *zW*: **~listig** *adj* cunning, insidious; **~los** *adj* guileless, innocent

Argument [argu'mɛnt] *nt* argument

argwöhnisch *adj* suspicious

Arie ['a:riə] *f* aria

Aristokrat [aristo'kra:t] **(-en, -en)** *m* aristocrat; **~ie** [-'ti:] *f* aristocracy

Arktis ['arktɪs] **(-)** *f* Arctic

Arm [arm] **(-(e)s, -e)** *m* arm; (*Flussarm*) branch

arm *adj* poor

Armatur [arma'tu:r] *f* (*ELEK*) armature; **~enbrett** *nt* instrument panel; (*AUT*) dashboard

Armband *nt* bracelet; **~uhr** *f* (wrist) watch

Arme(r) *f(m)* poor man (woman); **die ~n** the poor

Armee [ar'me:] *f* army

Ärmel ['ɛrməl] **(-s, -)** *m* sleeve; **etw aus dem ~ schütteln** (*fig*) to produce sth just like that; **~kanal** *m* English Channel

ärmlich ['ɛrmlɪç] *adj* poor

armselig *adj* wretched, miserable

Armut ['armu:t] **(-)** *f* poverty

Aroma [a'ro:ma] **(-s, Aromen)** *nt* aroma; **~therapie** *f* aromatherapy; **a~tisch**

[aro'ma:tɪʃ] *adj* aromatic

arrangieren [arãː'ʒiːrən] *vt* to arrange ♦ *vr* to come to an arrangement

Arrest [a'rɛst] (-(e)s, -e) *m* detention

arrogant [aro'gant] *adj* arrogant

Arsch [arʃ] (-es, ⁼e) (*umg!*) *m* arse (*BRIT!*), ass (*US!*)

Art [aːrt] (-, -en) *f* (*Weise*) way; (*Sorte*) kind, sort; (*BIOL*) species; **eine ~ (von) Frucht** a kind of fruit; **Häuser aller ~** houses of all kinds; **es ist nicht seine ~, das zu tun** it's not like him to do that; **ich mache das auf meine ~** I do that in my (own) way

Arterie [ar'te:riə] *f* artery; **~nverkalkung** *f* arteriosclerosis

artig ['aːrtɪç] *adj* good, well-behaved

Artikel [ar'tiːkəl] (-s, -) *m* article

Artillerie [artɪlə'riː] *f* artillery

Artischocke [artɪ'ʃɔkə] *f* artichoke

Artist(in) [ar'tɪst(ɪn)] (-en, -en) *m(f)* (circus/variety) artiste *od* performer

Arznei [aːrts'naɪ] *f* medicine; **~mittel** *nt* medicine, medicament

Arzt [aːrtst] (-es, ⁼e) *m* doctor; **~helferin** *f* (doctor's) receptionist

Ärztin ['ɛːrtstɪn] *f* doctor

ärztlich ['ɛːrtstlɪç] *adj* medical

As △ [as] (-ses, -se) *nt* = **Ass**

Asche ['aʃə] *f* (-, -n) ash, cinder

Aschen- *zW:* **~bahn** *f* cinder track; **~becher** *m* ashtray

Aschermittwoch *m* Ash Wednesday

Äser ['ɛːzər] *pl von* **Aas**

Asiat(in) [azi'aːt(ɪn)] (-en, -en) *m(f)* Asian; **asiatisch** [-'aːtɪʃ] *adj* Asian

Asien ['aːziən] (-s) *nt* Asia

asozial ['azotsiaːl] *adj* antisocial; (*Familien*) asocial

Aspekt [as'pɛkt] (-(e)s, -e) *m* aspect

Asphalt [as'falt] (-(e)s, -e) *m* asphalt

Ass ▲ [as] (-es, -e) *nt* ace

aß *etc* [aːs] *vb siehe* **essen**

Assistent(in) [asɪs'tɛnt(ɪn)] *m(f)* assistant

Assoziation [asotsiatsi'oːn] *f* association

Ast [ast] (-(e)s, ⁼e) *m* bough, branch

ästhetisch [ɛs'teːtɪʃ] *adj* aesthetic

Asthma ['astma] (-s) *nt* asthma; **~tiker(in)**

(-s, -) *m(f)* asthmatic

Astro- [astro] *zW:* **~loge** (-n, -n) *m* astrologer; **~lo'gie** *f* astrology; **~'naut** (-en, -en) *m* astronaut; **~'nom** (-en, -en) *m* astronomer; **~no'mie** *f* astronomy

Asyl [a'zyːl] (-s, -e) *nt* asylum; (*Heim*) home; (*Obdachlosenasyl*) shelter; **~ant(in)** [azy'lant(ɪn)] (-en, -en) *m(f)* asylum-seeker; **~bewerber(in)** *m(f)* asylum-seeker

Atelier [atəli'eː] (-s, -s) *nt* studio

Atem ['aːtəm] (-s) *m* breath; **den ~ anhalten** to hold one's breath; **außer ~** out of breath; **a~beraubend** *adj* breathtaking; **a~los** *adj* breathless; **~not** *f* difficulty in breathing; **~pause** *f* breather; **~zug** *m* breath

Atheismus [ate'ɪsmʊs] *m* atheism

Atheist *m* atheist; **a~isch** *adj* atheistic

Athen [a'teːn] (-s) *nt* Athens

Äthiopien [eti'oːpiən] (-s) *nt* Ethiopia

Athlet [at'leːt] (-en, -en) *m* athlete

Atlantik [at'lantɪk] (-s) *m* Atlantic (Ocean)

Atlas ['atlas] (- *od* -ses, -se *od* **Atlanten**) *m* atlas

atmen ['aːtmən] *vt, vi* to breathe

Atmosphäre [atmo'sfɛːrə] *f* atmosphere; **atmosphärisch** *adj* atmospheric

Atmung ['aːtmʊŋ] *f* respiration

Atom [a'toːm] (-s, -e) *nt* atom; **a~ar** *adj* atomic; **~bombe** *f* atom bomb; **~energie** *f* atomic *od* nuclear energy; **~kern** *m* atomic nucleus; **~kraftwerk** *nt* nuclear power station; **~krieg** *m* nuclear *od* atomic war; **~müll** *m* atomic waste; **~strom** *m* (electricity generated by) nuclear power; **~versuch** *m* atomic test; **~waffen** *pl* atomic weapons; **a~waffenfrei** *adj* nuclear-free; **~zeitalter** *nt* atomic age

Attentat [atɛn'taːt] (-(e)s, -e) *nt:* **~ (auf** +*akk*) (attempted) assassination (of)

Attentäter [atɛn'tɛːtər] *m* (would-be) assassin

Attest [a'tɛst] (-(e)s, -e) *nt* certificate

Attraktion [atraktsi'oːn] *f* (*Tourismus, Zirkus*) attraction

attraktiv [atrak'tiːf] *adj* attractive

Attrappe [a'trapə] *f* dummy

Rechtschreibreform: ▲ *neue Schreibung* △ *alte Schreibung (auslaufend)*

Attribut [atri'buːt] (-(e)s, -e) nt (GRAM)
attribute

ätzen ['ɛtsən] vi to be caustic; ~d adj (Säure)
corrosive; (fig: Spott) cutting

au [au] excl ouch!; ~ ja! oh yes!

Aubergine [obɛr'ʒiːnə] f aubergine,
eggplant

auch [aux] adv 1 (ebenfalls) also, too, as well;
das ist auch schön that's nice too od as
well; **er kommt - ich auch** he's coming -
so am I, me too; **auch nicht** not ... either;
ich auch nicht nor I, me neither; **oder
auch** or; **auch das noch!** not that as well!
2 (selbst, sogar) even; **auch wenn das
Wetter schlecht ist** even if the weather is
bad; **ohne auch nur zu fragen** without
even asking
3 (wirklich) really; **du siehst müde aus -
bin ich auch** you look tired - (so) I am; **so
sieht es auch aus** it looks like it too
4 (auch immer): **wer auch** whoever; **was
auch** whatever; **wie dem auch sei** be that
as it may; **wie sehr er sich auch bemühte**
however much he tried

auf [auf] präp +dat (wo?) on; **auf dem Tisch**
on the table; **auf der Reise** on the way;
auf der Post/dem Fest at the post office/
party; **auf der Straße** on the road; **auf
dem Land/der ganzen Welt** in the
country/the whole world
♦ präp +akk 1 (wohin?) on(to); **auf den
Tisch** on(to) the table; **auf die Post gehen**
go to the post office; **auf das Land** into
the country; **etw auf einen Zettel
schreiben** to write sth on a piece of paper
2 : **auf Deutsch** in German; **auf Lebenszeit**
for my/his lifetime; **bis auf ihn** except for
him; **auf einmal** at once; **auf seinen
Vorschlag (hin)** at his suggestion
♦ adv 1 (offen) open; **auf sein** (umg) (Tür,
Geschäft) to be open; **das Fenster ist auf**
the window is open

2 (hinauf) up; **auf und ab** up and down;
auf und davon up and away; **auf!** (los!)
come on!
3 (aufgestanden) up; **auf sein** to be up; **ist
er schon auf?** is he up yet?
♦ konj: **auf dass** (so) that

aufatmen ['aufˌaːtmən] vi to heave a sigh of
relief

aufbahren ['aufbaːrən] vt to lay out

Aufbau ['aufbau] m (Bauen) building,
construction; (Struktur) structure;
(aufgebautes Teil) superstructure; **a~en** vt to
erect, to build (up); (Existenz) to make;
(gestalten) to construct; **a~en (auf** +dat)
(gründen) to found od base (on)

aufbauschen ['aufbauʃən] vt to puff out;
(fig) to exaggerate

aufbekommen ['aufbəkɔmən] (unreg) vt
(öffnen) to get open; (Hausaufgaben) to be
given

aufbessern ['aufbɛsərn] vt (Gehalt) to
increase

aufbewahren ['aufbəvaːrən] vt to keep;
(Gepäck) to put in the left-luggage office
(BRIT) od baggage check (US)

Aufbewahrung f (safe)keeping;
(Gepäckaufbewahrung) left-luggage office
(BRIT), baggage check (US)

aufbieten ['aufbiːtən] (unreg) vt (Kraft) to
summon (up); (Armee, Polizei) to mobilize

aufblasen ['aufblaːzən] (unreg) vt to blow
up, to inflate ♦ vr (umg) to become
bigheaded

aufbleiben ['aufblaibən] (unreg) vi (Laden) to
remain open; (Person) to stay up

aufblenden ['aufblɛndən] vt (Scheinwerfer)
to switch on full beam ♦ vi (Fahrer) to have
the lights on full beam; (AUT: Scheinwerfer)
to be on full beam

aufblicken ['aufblɪkən] vi to look up; ~ **zu**
to look up at; (fig) to look up to

aufblühen ['aufblyːən] vi to blossom, to
flourish

aufbrauchen ['aufbrauxən] vt to use up

aufbrausen ['aufbrauzən] vi (fig) to flare up;
~d adj hot-tempered

aufbrechen ['aʊfbrɛçən] (*unreg*) *vt* to break *od* prise (BRIT) open ♦ *vi* to burst open; (*gehen*) to start, to set off

aufbringen ['aʊfbrɪŋən] (*unreg*) *vt* (*öffnen*) to open; (*in Mode*) to bring into fashion; (*beschaffen*) to procure; (FIN) to raise; (*ärgern*) to irritate; **Verständnis für etw ~** to be able to understand sth

Aufbruch ['aʊfbrʊx] *m* departure

aufbrühen ['aʊfbryːən] *vt* (*Tee*) to make

aufbürden ['aʊfbʏrdən] *vt*: **jdm etw ~** to burden sb with sth

aufdecken ['aʊfdɛkən] *vt* to uncover

aufdrängen ['aʊfdrɛŋən] *vt*: **jdm etw ~** to force sth on sb ♦ *vr* (*Mensch*): **sich jdm ~** to intrude on sb

aufdrehen ['aʊfdreːən] *vt* (*Wasserhahn etc*) to turn on; (*Ventil*) to open up

aufdringlich ['aʊfdrɪŋlɪç] *adj* pushy

aufeinander [aʊfaɪ'nandər] *adv* on top of each other; (*schießen*) at each other; (*vertrauen*) each other; **~ folgen** to follow one another; **~ folgend** consecutive; **~ prallen** to hit one another

Aufenthalt ['aʊfɛnthalt] *m* stay; (*Verzögerung*) delay; (EISENB: *Halten*) stop; (*Ort*) haunt

Aufenthaltserlaubnis *f* residence permit

auferlegen ['aʊfɛrleːgən] *vt*: **(jdm) ~** to impose (upon sb)

Auferstehung ['aʊfɛrʃteːʊŋ] *f* resurrection

aufessen ['aʊfɛsən] (*unreg*) *vt* to eat up

auffahr- ['aʊffaːr] *zW*: **~en** (*unreg*) *vi* (*herankommen*) to draw up; (*hochfahren*) to jump up; (*wütend werden*) to flare up; (*in den Himmel*) to ascend ♦ *vt* (*Kanonen, Geschütz*) to bring up; **~en auf** +*akk* (*Auto*) to run *od* crash into; **~end** *adj* hot-tempered; **~t** *f* (*Hausauffahrt*) drive; (*Autobahnauffahrt*) slip road (BRIT), (freeway) entrance (US); **A~unfall** *m* pile-up

auffallen ['aʊffalən] (*unreg*) *vi* to be noticeable; **jdm ~** to strike sb

auffällig ['aʊffɛlɪç] *adj* conspicuous, striking

auffangen ['aʊffaŋən] (*unreg*) *vt* to catch; (*Funkspruch*) to intercept; (*Preise*) to peg

auffassen ['aʊffasən] *vt* to understand, to comprehend; (*auslegen*) to see, to view

Auffassung *f* (*Meinung*) opinion; (*Auslegung*) view, concept; (*auch:* **~sgabe**) grasp

auffindbar ['aʊffɪntbaːr] *adj* to be found

auffordern ['aʊffɔrdərn] *vt* (*befehlen*) to call upon, to order; (*bitten*) to ask

Aufforderung *f* (*Befehl*) order; (*Einladung*) invitation

auffrischen ['aʊffrɪʃən] *vt* to freshen up; (*Kenntnisse*) to brush up; (*Erinnerungen*) to reawaken ♦ *vi* (*Wind*) to freshen

aufführen ['aʊffyːrən] *vt* (THEAT) to perform; (*in einem Verzeichnis*) to list, to specify ♦ *vr* (*sich benehmen*) to behave

Aufführung *f* (THEAT) performance; (*Liste*) specification

Aufgabe ['aʊfgaːbə] *f* task; (SCH) exercise; (*Hausaufgabe*) homework; (*Verzicht*) giving up; (*von Gepäck*) registration; (*von Post*) posting; (*von Inserat*) insertion

Aufgang ['aʊfgaŋ] *m* ascent; (*Sonnenaufgang*) rise; (*Treppe*) staircase

aufgeben ['aʊfgeːbən] (*unreg*) *vt* (*verzichten*) to give up; (*Paket*) to send, to post; (*Gepäck*) to register; (*Bestellung*) to give; (*Inserat*) to insert; (*Rätsel, Problem*) to set ♦ *vi* to give up

Aufgebot ['aʊfgaboːt] *nt* supply; (*Eheaufgebot*) banns *pl*

aufgedunsen ['aʊfgedʊnzən] *adj* swollen, puffed up

aufgehen ['aʊfgeːən] (*unreg*) *vi* (*Sonne, Teig*) to rise; (*sich öffnen*) to open; (*klar werden*) to become clear; (MATH) to come out exactly; **~ (in** +*dat*) (*sich widmen*) to be absorbed (in); **in Rauch/Flammen ~** to go up in smoke/flames

aufgelegt ['aʊfgeleːkt] *adj*: **gut/schlecht ~ sein** to be in a good/bad mood; **zu etw ~ sein** to be in the mood for sth

aufgeregt ['aʊfgəreːkt] *adj* excited

aufgeschlossen ['aʊfgəʃlɔsən] *adj* open, open-minded

aufgeweckt ['aʊfgəvɛkt] *adj* bright, intelligent

aufgießen ['aʊfgiːsən] (*unreg*) *vt* (*Wasser*) to

pour over; (*Tee*) to infuse

aufgreifen ['aʊfɡraɪfən] (*unreg*) *vt* (*Thema*) to take up; (*Verdächtige*) to pick up, to seize

aufgrund, auf Grund [aʊf'ɡrʊnt] *präp* +*gen* on the basis of; (*wegen*) because of

aufhaben ['aʊfhaːbən] (*unreg*) *vt* to have on; (*Arbeit*) to have to do

aufhalsen ['aʊfhalzən] (*umg*) *vt*: **jdm etw ~** to saddle *od* lumber sb with sth

aufhalten ['aʊfhaltən] (*unreg*) *vt* (*Person*) to detain; (*Entwicklung*) to check; (*Tür, Hand*) to hold open; (*Augen*) to keep open ♦ *vr* (*wohnen*) to live; (*bleiben*) to stay; **sich mit etw ~** to waste time over sth

aufhängen ['aʊfhɛŋən] (*unreg*) *vt* (*Wäsche*) to hang up; (*Menschen*) to hang ♦ *vr* to hang o.s.

Aufhänger (**-s, -**) *m* (*am Mantel*) loop; (*fig*) peg

aufheben ['aʊfheːbən] (*unreg*) *vt* (*hochheben*) to raise, to lift; (*Sitzung*) to wind up; (*Urteil*) to annul; (*Gesetz*) to repeal, to abolish; (*aufbewahren*) to keep ♦ *vr* to cancel itself out; **bei jdm gut aufgehoben sein** to be well looked after at sb's; **viel A~(s) machen (von)** to make a fuss (about)

aufheitern ['aʊfhaɪtərn] *vt, vr* (*Himmel, Miene*) to brighten; (*Mensch*) to cheer up

aufhellen ['aʊfhɛlən] *vt, vr* to clear up; (*Farbe, Haare*) to lighten

aufhetzen ['aʊfhɛtsən] *vt* to stir up

aufholen ['aʊfhoːlən] *vt* to make up ♦ *vi* to catch up

aufhorchen ['aʊfhɔrçən] *vi* to prick up one's ears

aufhören ['aʊfhøːrən] *vi* to stop; **~, etw zu tun** to stop doing sth

aufklappen ['aʊfklapən] *vt* to open

aufklären ['aʊfklɛːrən] *vt* (*Geheimnis etc*) to clear up; (*Person*) to enlighten; (*sexuell*) to tell the facts of life to; (*MIL*) to reconnoitre ♦ *vr* to clear up

Aufklärung *f* (*von Geheimnis*) clearing up; (*Unterrichtung, Zeitalter*) enlightenment; (*sexuell*) sex education; (*MIL, AVIAT*) reconnaissance

aufkleben ['aʊfkleːbən] *vt* to stick on;

Aufkleber (**-s, -**) *m* sticker

aufknöpfen ['aʊfknœpfən] *vt* to unbutton

aufkommen ['aʊfkɔmən] (*unreg*) *vi* (*Wind*) to come up; (*Zweifel, Gefühl*) to arise; (*Mode*) to start; **für jdn/etw ~** to be liable *od* responsible for sb/sth

aufladen ['aʊflaːdən] (*unreg*) *vt* to load

Auflage ['aʊflaːɡə] *f* edition; (*Zeitung*) circulation; (*Bedingung*) condition

auflassen ['aʊflasən] (*unreg*) *vt* (*offen*) to leave open; (*aufgesetzt*) to leave on

auflauern ['aʊflaʊərn] *vi*: **jdm ~** to lie in wait for sb

Auflauf ['aʊflaʊf] *m* (*KOCH*) pudding; (*Menschenauflauf*) crowd

aufleben ['aʊfleːbən] *vi* (*Mensch, Gespräch*) to liven up; (*Interesse*) to revive

auflegen ['aʊfleːɡən] *vt* to put on; (*Telefon*) to hang up; (*TYP*) to print

auflehnen ['aʊfleːnən] *vt* to lean on ♦ *vr* to rebel

Auflehnung *f* rebellion

auflesen ['aʊfleːzən] (*unreg*) *vt* to pick up

aufleuchten ['aʊflɔʏçtən] *vi* to light up

auflisten ['aʊflɪstən] *vt* to list

auflockern ['aʊflɔkərn] *vt* to loosen; (*fig: Eintönigkeit etc*) to liven up

auflösen ['aʊfløːzən] *vt* to dissolve; (*Haare etc*) to loosen; (*Missverständnis*) to sort out ♦ *vr* to dissolve; to come undone; to be resolved; **(in Tränen) aufgelöst sein** to be in tears

Auflösung *f* dissolving; (*fig*) solution

aufmachen ['aʊfmaxən] *vt* to open; (*Kleidung*) to undo; (*zurechtmachen*) to do up ♦ *vr* to set out

Aufmachung *f* (*Kleidung*) outfit, get-up; (*Gestaltung*) format

aufmerksam ['aʊfmɛrkzaːm] *adj* attentive; **jdn auf etw** *akk* **~ machen** to point sth out to sb; **A~keit** *f* attention, attentiveness

aufmuntern ['aʊfmʊntərn] *vt* (*ermutigen*) to encourage; (*erheitern*) to cheer up

Aufnahme ['aʊfnaːmə] *f* reception; (*Beginn*) beginning; (*in Verein etc*) admission; (*in Liste etc*) inclusion; (*Notieren*) taking down; (*PHOT*) shot; (*auf Tonband etc*) recording;

Spelling Reform: ▲ *new spelling* △ *old spelling (to be phased out)*

a~fähig *adj* receptive; **~prüfung** *f* entrance test

aufnehmen ['aʊfneːmən] (*unreg*) *vt* to receive; (*hochheben*) to pick up; (*beginnen*) to take up; (*in Verein etc*) to admit; (*in Liste etc*) to include; (*fassen*) to hold; (*notieren*) to take down; (*fotografieren*) to photograph; (*auf Tonband, Platte*) to record; (*FIN: leihen*) to take out; **es mit jdm ~ können** to be able to compete with sb

aufopfern ['aʊfʔɔpfərn] *vt, vr* to sacrifice; **~d** *adj* selfless

aufpassen ['aʊfpasən] *vi* (*aufmerksam sein*) to pay attention; **auf jdn/etw ~** to look after *od* watch sb/sth; **aufgepasst!** look out!

Aufprall ['aʊfpral] (**-s, -e**) *m* impact; **a~en** *vi* to hit, to strike

Aufpreis ['aʊfpraɪs] *m* extra charge

aufpumpen ['aʊfpʊmpən] *vt* to pump up

aufräumen ['aʊfrɔʏmən] *vt, vi* (*Dinge*) to clear away; (*Zimmer*) to tidy up

aufrecht ['aʊfrɛçt] *adj* (*auch fig*) upright; **~erhalten** (*unreg*) *vt* to maintain

aufreg- ['aʊfreːg] *zW:* **~en** *vt* to excite ♦ *vr* to get excited; **~end** *adj* exciting; **A~ung** *f* excitement

aufreibend ['aʊfraɪbənt] *adj* strenuous

aufreißen ['aʊfraɪsən] (*unreg*) *vt* (*Umschlag*) to tear open; (*Augen*) to open wide; (*Tür*) to throw open; (*Straße*) to take up

aufreizen ['aʊfraɪtsən] *vt* to incite, to stir up; **~d** *adj* exciting, stimulating

aufrichten ['aʊfrɪçtən] *vt* to put up, to erect; (*moralisch*) to console ♦ *vr* to rise; (*moralisch*): **sich ~ (an** +*dat*) to take heart (from)

aufrichtig ['aʊfrɪçtɪç] *adj* sincere, honest; **A~keit** *f* sincerity

aufrücken ['aʊfrʏkən] *vi* to move up; (*beruflich*) to be promoted

Aufruf ['aʊfruːf] *m* summons; (*zur Hilfe*) call; (*des Namens*) calling out; **a~en** (*unreg*) *vt* (*Namen*) to call out; (*auffordern*): **jdn a~en (zu)** to call upon sb (for)

Aufruhr ['aʊfruːr] (**-(e)s, -e**) *m* uprising, revolt

aufrührerisch ['aʊfryːrərɪʃ] *adj* rebellious

aufrunden ['aʊfrʊndən] *vt* (*Summe*) to round up

Aufrüstung ['aʊfrʏstʊŋ] *f* rearmament

aufrütteln ['aʊfrʏtəln] *vt* (*auch fig*) to shake up

aufs [aʊfs] = **auf das**

aufsagen ['aʊfzaːgən] *vt* (*Gedicht*) to recite

aufsässig ['aʊfzɛsɪç] *adj* rebellious

Aufsatz ['aʊfzats] *m* (*Geschriebenes*) essay; (*auf Schrank etc*) top

aufsaugen ['aʊfzaʊgən] (*unreg*) *vt* to soak up

aufschauen ['aʊfʃaʊən] *vi* to look up

aufscheuchen ['aʊfʃɔʏçən] *vt* to scare *od* frighten away

aufschieben ['aʊfʃiːbən] (*unreg*) *vt* to push open; (*verzögern*) to put off, to postpone

Aufschlag ['aʊfʃlaːk] *m* (*Ärmelaufschlag*) cuff; (*Jackenaufschlag*) lapel; (*Hosenaufschlag*) turn-up; (*Aufprall*) impact; (*Preisaufschlag*) surcharge; (*Tennis*) service; **a~en** [-gən] (*unreg*) *vt* (*öffnen*) to open; (*verwunden*) to cut; (*hochschlagen*) to turn up; (*aufbauen: Zelt, Lager*) to pitch, to erect; (*Wohnsitz*) to take up ♦ *vi* (*aufprallen*) to hit; (*teurer werden*) to go up; (*Tennis*) to serve

aufschließen ['aʊfʃliːsən] (*unreg*) *vt* to open up, to unlock ♦ *vi* (*aufrücken*) to close up

aufschlussreich ▲ *adj* informative, illuminating

aufschnappen ['aʊfʃnapən] *vt* (*umg*) to pick up ♦ *vi* to fly open

aufschneiden ['aʊfʃnaɪdən] (*unreg*) *vt* (*Brot*) to cut up; (*MED*) to lance ♦ *vi* to brag

Aufschneider (**-s, -**) *m* boaster, braggart

Aufschnitt ['aʊfʃnɪt] *m* (slices of) cold meat

aufschrauben ['aʊfʃraʊbən] *vt* (*festschrauben*) to screw on; (*lösen*) to unscrew

aufschrecken ['aʊfʃrɛkən] *vt* to startle ♦ *vi* (*unreg*) to start up

aufschreiben ['aʊfʃraɪbən] (*unreg*) *vt* to write down

aufschreien ['aʊfʃraɪən] (*unreg*) *vi* to cry out

Aufschrift ['aʊfʃrɪft] *f* (*Inschrift*) inscription; (*auf Etikett*) label

Rechtschreibreform: ▲ *neue Schreibung* △ *alte Schreibung (auslaufend)*

Aufschub ['aʊfʃuːp] (-(e)s, -schübe) m
delay, postponement

Aufschwung ['aʊfʃvʊŋ] m (Elan) boost;
(wirtschaftlich) upturn, boom; (SPORT) circle

aufsehen ['aʊfzeːən] (unreg) vi to look up; ~
zu to look up at; (fig) to look up to; **A~**
(-s) nt sensation, stir; ~ **erregend** sensational

Aufseher(in) (-s, -) m(f) guard; (im Betrieb)
supervisor; (Museumsaufseher) attendant;
(Parkaufseher) keeper

auf sein ▲ siehe auf

aufsetzen ['aʊfzɛtsən] vt to put on;
(Dokument) to draw up ♦ vr to sit up(right)
♦ vi (Flugzeug) to touch down

Aufsicht ['aʊfzɪçt] f supervision; **die ~**
haben to be in charge

Aufsichtsrat m (supervisory) board

aufsitzen ['aʊfzɪtsən] (unreg) vi (aufrecht
hinsitzen) to sit up; (aufs Pferd, Motorrad) to
mount, to get on; (Schiff) to run aground;
jdm ~ (umg) to be taken in by sb

aufsparen ['aʊfʃpaːrən] vt to save (up)

aufsperren ['aʊfʃpɛrən] vt to unlock; (Mund)
to open wide

aufspielen ['aʊfʃpiːlən] vr to show off

aufspießen ['aʊfʃpiːsən] vt to spear

aufspringen ['aʊfʃprɪŋən] (unreg) vi
(hochspringen) to jump up; (sich öffnen) to
spring open; (Hände, Lippen) to become
chapped; **auf etw** akk ~ to jump onto sth

aufspüren ['aʊfʃpyːrən] vt to track down, to
trace

aufstacheln ['aʊfʃtaxəln] vt to incite

Aufstand ['aʊfʃtant] m insurrection,
rebellion; **aufständisch** ['aʊfʃtɛndɪʃ] adj
rebellious, mutinous

aufstehen ['aʊfʃteːən] (unreg) vi to get up;
(Tür) to be open

aufsteigen ['aʊfʃtaɪɡən] (unreg) vi
(hochsteigen) to climb; (Rauch) to rise; **auf**
etw akk ~ to get onto sth

aufstellen ['aʊfʃtɛlən] vt (aufrecht stellen) to
put up; (aufreihen) to line up; (nominieren)
to nominate; (formulieren: Programm etc) to
draw up; (leisten: Rekord) to set up

Aufstellung f (SPORT) line-up; (Liste) list

Aufstieg ['aʊfʃtiːk] (-(e)s, -e) m (auf Berg)
ascent; (Fortschritt) rise; (beruflich, SPORT)
promotion

aufstocken ['aʊfʃtɔkən] vt (Kapital) to
increase

aufstoßen ['aʊfʃtoːsən] (unreg) vt to push
open ♦ vi to belch

aufstützen ['aʊfʃtʏtsən] vt (Körperteil) to
prop, to lean; (Person) to prop up ♦ vr: **sich**
auf etw akk ~ to lean on sth

aufsuchen ['aʊfzuːxən] vt (besuchen) to visit;
(konsultieren) to consult

Auftakt ['aʊftakt] m (MUS) upbeat; (fig)
prelude

auftanken ['aʊftaŋkən] vi to get petrol (BRIT)
od gas (US) ♦ vt to refuel

auftauchen ['aʊftaʊxən] vi to appear; (aus
Wasser etc) to emerge; (U-Boot) to surface;
(Zweifel) to arise

auftauen ['aʊftaʊən] vt to thaw ♦ vi to
thaw; (fig) to relax

aufteilen ['aʊftaɪlən] vt to divide up; (Raum)
to partition; **Aufteilung** f division;
partition

Auftrag ['aʊftraːk] (-(e)s, -träge) m order;
(Anweisung) commission; (Aufgabe) mission;
im ~ von on behalf of; **a~en** (-gən) (unreg)
vt (Essen) to serve; (Farbe) to put on;
(Kleidung) to wear out; **jdm etw a~en** to
tell sb sth; **dick a~en** (fig) to exaggerate;
~geber(-s, -) m (COMM) purchaser,
customer

auftreiben ['aʊftraɪbən] (unreg) vt (umg:
beschaffen) to raise

auftreten ['aʊftreːtən] (unreg) vt to kick open
♦ vi to appear; (mit Füßen) to tread; (sich
verhalten) to behave; **A~ (-s)** nt (Vorkommen) appearance; (Benehmen) behaviour

Auftrieb ['aʊftriːp] m (PHYS) buoyancy, lift;
(fig) impetus

Auftritt ['aʊftrɪt] m (des Schauspielers)
entrance; (Szene: auch fig) scene

aufwachen ['aʊfvaxən] vi to wake up

aufwachsen ['aʊfvaksən] (unreg) vi to grow
up

Aufwand ['aʊfvant] (-(e)s) m expenditure;
(Kosten auch) expense; (Luxus) show

Spelling Reform: ▲ new spelling △ old spelling (to be phased out)

aufwändig ▲ ['aʊfvɛndɪç] *adj* costly
aufwärmen ['aʊfvɛrmən] *vt* to warm up; (*alte Geschichten*) to rake up
aufwärts ['aʊfvɛrts] *adv* upwards; **A~entwicklung** *f* upward trend
Aufwasch ['aʊfvaʃ] *m* washing-up
aufwecken ['aʊfvɛkən] *vt* to wake up, to waken up
aufweisen ['aʊfvaɪzən] (*unreg*) *vt* to show
aufwenden ['aʊfvɛndən] (*unreg*) *vt* to expend; (*Geld*) to spend; (*Sorgfalt*) to devote
aufwendig *adj siehe* **aufwändig**
aufwerfen ['aʊfvɛrfən] (*unreg*) *vt* (*Fenster etc*) to throw open; (*Probleme*) to throw up, to raise
aufwerten ['aʊfvɛrtən] *vt* (*FIN*) to revalue; (*fig*) to raise in value
aufwickeln ['aʊfvɪkəln] *vt* (*aufrollen*) to roll up; (*umg: Haar*) to put in curlers
aufwiegen ['aʊfviːgən] (*unreg*) *vt* to make up for
Aufwind ['aʊfvɪnt] *m* up-current
aufwirbeln ['aʊfvɪrbəln] *vt* to whirl up; **Staub ~** (*fig*) to create a stir
aufwischen ['aʊfvɪʃən] *vt* to wipe up
aufzählen ['aʊftsɛːlən] *vt* to list
aufzeichnen ['aʊftsaɪçnən] *vt* to sketch; (*schriftlich*) to jot down; (*auf Band*) to record
Aufzeichnung *f* (*schriftlich*) note; (*Tonbandaufzeichnung*) recording; (*Filmaufzeichnung*) record
aufzeigen ['aʊftsaɪgən] *vt* to show, to demonstrate
aufziehen ['aʊftsiːən] (*unreg*) *vt* (*hochziehen*) to raise, to draw up; (*öffnen*) to pull open; (*Uhr*) to wind; (*umg: necken*) to tease; (*großziehen: Kinder*) to raise, to bring up; (*Tiere*) to rear
Aufzug ['aʊftsuːk] *m* (*Fahrstuhl*) lift, elevator; (*Aufmarsch*) procession, parade; (*Kleidung*) get-up; (*THEAT*) act
aufzwingen ['aʊftsvɪŋən] (*unreg*) *vt*: **jdm etw ~** to force sth upon sb
Augapfel ['aʊkʔapfəl] *m* eyeball; (*fig*) apple of one's eye
Auge ['aʊgə] (*-s, -n*) *nt* eye; (*Fettauge*)

globule of fat; **unter vier ~n** in private
Augen- *zW*: **~blick** *m* moment; **im ~blick** at the moment; **a~blicklich** *adj* (*sofort*) instantaneous; (*gegenwärtig*) present; **~braue** *f* eyebrow; **~optiker(in)** *m(f)* optician; **~weide** *f* sight for sore eyes; **~zeuge** *m* eye witness
August [aʊˈgʊst] (*-(e)s od -, -e*) *m* August
Auktion [aʊktsiˈoːn] *f* auction
Aula ['aʊla] (*-, Aulen od -s*) *f* assembly hall

SCHLÜSSELWORT

aus [aʊs] *präp +dat* **1** (*räumlich*) out of; (*von ... her*) from; **er ist aus Berlin** he's from Berlin; **aus dem Fenster** out of the window

2 (*gemacht/hergestellt aus*) made of; **ein Herz aus Stein** a heart of stone

3 (*auf Ursache deutend*) out of; **aus Mitleid** out of sympathy; **aus Erfahrung** from experience; **aus Spaß** for fun

4: **aus ihr wird nie etwas** she'll never get anywhere

♦ *adv* **1** (*zu Ende*) finished, over; **aus sein** to be over; **aus und vorbei** over and done with

2 (*ausgeschaltet, ausgezogen*) out; (*Aufschrift an Geräten*) off; **aus sein** (*nicht brennen*) to be out; (*abgeschaltet sein: Radio, Herd*) to be off; **Licht aus!** lights out!

3 (*nicht zu Hause*): **aus sein** to be out

4 (*in Verbindung mit von*): **von Rom aus** from Rome; **vom Fenster aus** out of the window; **von sich aus** (*selbstständig*) of one's own accord; **von ihm aus** as far as he's concerned

ausarbeiten ['aʊsʔarbaɪtən] *vt* to work out
ausarten ['aʊsʔartən] *vi* to degenerate
ausatmen ['aʊsʔaːtmən] *vi* to breathe out
ausbaden ['aʊsbaːdən] (*umg*) *vt*: **etw ~ müssen** to carry the can for sth
Ausbau ['aʊsbaʊ] *m* extension, expansion; removal; **a~en** *vt* to extend, to expand; (*herausnehmen*) to take out, to remove; **a~fähig** *adj* (*fig*) worth developing
ausbessern ['aʊsbɛsərn] *vt* to mend, to

repair

ausbeulen ['aʊsbɔʏlən] vt to beat out

Ausbeute ['aʊsbɔʏtə] f yield; (Fische) catch; **a~n** vt to exploit; (MIN) to work

ausbild- ['aʊsbɪld] zW: **~en** vt to educate; (Lehrling, Soldat) to instruct, to train; (Fähigkeiten) to develop; (Geschmack) to cultivate; **A~er (-s, -)** m instructor; **A~ung** f education; training, instruction; development; cultivation

ausbleiben ['aʊsblaɪbən] (unreg) vi (Personen) to stay away, not to come; (Ereignisse) to fail to happen, not to happen

Ausblick ['aʊsblɪk] m (auch fig) prospect, outlook, view

ausbrechen ['aʊsbrɛçən] (unreg) vi to break out ♦ vt to break off; **in Tränen/Gelächter ~** to burst into tears/out laughing

ausbreiten ['aʊsbraɪtən] vt to spread (out); (Arme) to stretch out ♦ vr to spread; **sich über ein Thema ~** to expand od enlarge on a topic

ausbrennen ['aʊsbrɛnən] (unreg) vt to scorch; (Wunde) to cauterize ♦ vi to burn out

Ausbruch ['aʊsbrʊx] m outbreak; (von Vulkan) eruption; (Gefühlsausbruch) outburst; (von Gefangenen) escape

ausbrüten ['aʊsbryːtən] vt (auch fig) to hatch

Ausdauer ['aʊsdaʊər] f perseverance, stamina; **a~nd** adj persevering

ausdehnen ['aʊsdeːnən] vt, vr (räumlich) to expand; (zeitlich, auch Gummi) to stretch; (Nebel, fig: Macht) to extend

ausdenken ['aʊsdɛŋkən] (unreg) vt: **sich dat etw ~** to think sth up

Ausdruck ['aʊsdrʊk] m expression, phrase; (Kundgabe, Gesichtsausdruck) expression; (COMPUT) print-out, hard copy; **a~en** vt (COMPUT) to print out

ausdrücken ['aʊsdrʏkən] vt (auch vr: formulieren, zeigen) to express; (Zigarette) to put out; (Zitrone) to squeeze

ausdrücklich adj express, explicit

ausdrucks- zW: **~los** adj expressionless, blank; **~voll** adj expressive; **A~weise** f mode of expression

auseinander [aʊsˌaɪˈnandər] adv (getrennt) apart; **~ schreiben** to write as separate words; **~ bringen** to separate; **~ fallen** to fall apart; **~ gehen** (Menschen) to separate; (Meinungen) to differ; (Gegenstand) to fall apart; **~ halten** to tell apart; **~ nehmen** to take to pieces, to dismantle; **~ setzen** (erklären) to set forth, to explain; **sich ~ setzen** (sich verständigen) to come to terms, to settle; (sich befassen) to concern o.s.; **A~setzung** f argument

ausfahren ['aʊsfaːrən] (unreg) vt (spazieren fahren: im Auto) to take for a drive; (: im Kinderwagen) to take for a walk; (liefern) to deliver

Ausfahrt f (des Zuges etc) leaving, departure; (Autobahnausfahrt) exit; (Garagenausfahrt etc) exit, way out; (Spazierfahrt) drive, excursion

Ausfall ['aʊsfal] m loss; (Nichtstattfinden) cancellation; (MIL) sortie; (radioaktiv) fall-out; **a~en** (unreg) vi (Zähne, Haare) to fall od come out; (nicht stattfinden) to be cancelled; (wegbleiben) to be omitted; (Person) to drop out; (Lohn) to be stopped; (nicht funktionieren) to break down; (Resultat haben) to turn out; **~straße** f arterial road

ausfertigen ['aʊsfɛrtɪgən] vt (förmlich: Urkunde, Pass) to draw up; (Rechnung) to make out

Ausfertigung ['aʊsfɛrtɪgʊŋ] f drawing up; making out; (Exemplar) copy

ausfindig ['aʊsfɪndɪç] adj: **~ machen** to discover

ausfließen ['aʊsfliːsən] (unreg) vt (her~): **~ (aus)** to flow out (of); (auslaufen: Öl etc): **~ (aus)** to leak (out of)

Ausflucht ['aʊsflʊxt] (-, **-flüchte**) f excuse

Ausflug ['aʊsfluːk] m excursion, outing; **Ausflügler** ['aʊsflyːklər] (-s, -) m tripper

Ausflugslokal nt tourist café

Ausfluss ▲ ['aʊsflʊs] m outlet; (MED) discharge

ausfragen ['aʊsfraːgən] vt to interrogate, to question

ausfressen ['aʊsfrɛsən] (unreg) vt to eat up;

(*aushöhlen*) to corrode; (*umg: anstellen*) to be up to

Ausfuhr ['aʊsfuːr] (-, -en) *f* export, exportation ♦ *in zW* export

ausführ- ['aʊsfyːr] *zW:* **~en** *vt* (*verwirklichen*) to carry out; (*Person*) to take out; (*Hund*) to take for a walk; (*COMM*) to export; (*erklären*) to give details of; **~lich** *adj* detailed ♦ *adv* in detail; **A~lichkeit** *f* detail; **A~ung** *f* execution, performance; (*Durchführung*) completion; (*Herstellungsart*) version; (*Erklärung*) explanation

ausfüllen ['aʊsfʏlən] *vt* to fill up; (*Fragebogen etc*) to fill in; (*Beruf*) to be fulfilling for

Ausgabe ['aʊsgaːbə] *f* (*Geld*) expenditure, outlay; (*Aushändigung*) giving out; (*Gepäckausgabe*) left-luggage office; (*Buch*) edition; (*Nummer*) issue; (*COMPUT*) output

Ausgang ['aʊsgaŋ] *m* way out, exit; (*Ende*) end; (*~spunkt*) starting point; (*Ergebnis*) result; (*Ausgehtag*) free time, time off; **kein ~** no exit

Ausgangs- *zW:* **~punkt** *m* starting point; **~sperre** *f* curfew

ausgeben ['aʊsgeːbən] (*unreg*) *vt* (*Geld*) to spend; (*austeilen*) to issue, to distribute ♦ *vr:* **sich für etw/jdn ~** to pass o.s. off as sth/sb

ausgebucht ['aʊsgəbuːxt] *adj* (*Vorstellung, Flug, Maschine*) fully booked

ausgedient ['aʊsgədiːnt] *adj* (*Soldat*) discharged; (*verbraucht*) no longer in use; **~ haben** to have done good service

ausgefallen ['aʊsgəfalən] *adj* (*ungewöhnlich*) exceptional

ausgeglichen ['aʊsgəglɪçən] *adj* (well-) balanced; **A~heit** *f* balance; (*von Mensch*) even-temperedness

ausgehen ['aʊsgeːən] (*unreg*) *vi* to go out; (*zu Ende gehen*) to come to an end; (*Benzin*) to run out; (*Haare, Zähne*) to fall *od* come out; (*Feuer, Ofen, Licht*) to go out; (*Strom*) to go off; (*Resultat haben*) to turn out; **mir ging das Benzin aus** I ran out of petrol (*BRIT*) *od* gas (*US*); **von etw ~** (*wegführen*) to lead away from sth; (*herrühren*) to come

from sth; (*zugrunde legen*) to proceed from sth; **wir können davon ~, dass ...** we can take as our starting point that ...; **leer ~** to get nothing

ausgelassen ['aʊsgəlasən] *adj* boisterous, high-spirited

ausgelastet ['aʊsgəlastət] *adj* fully occupied

ausgelernt ['aʊsgəlɛrnt] *adj* trained, qualified

ausgemacht ['aʊsgəmaxt] *adj* settled; (*umg: Dummkopf etc*) out-and-out, downright; **es war eine ~e Sache, dass ...** it was a foregone conclusion that ...

ausgenommen ['aʊsgənɔmən] *präp +gen* except ♦ *konj* except; **Anwesende sind ~** present company excepted

ausgeprägt ['aʊsgəprɛːkt] *adj* distinct

ausgerechnet ['aʊsgəreçnət] *adv* just, precisely; **~ du/heute** you of all people/ today of all days

ausgeschlossen ['aʊsgəʃlɔsən] *adj* (*unmöglich*) impossible, out of the question

ausgeschnitten ['aʊsgəʃnɪtən] *adj* (*Kleid*) low-necked

ausgesprochen ['aʊsgəʃprɔxən] *adj* (*Faulheit, Lüge etc*) out-and-out; (*unverkennbar*) marked ♦ *adv* decidedly

ausgezeichnet ['aʊsgətsaɪçnət] *adj* excellent

ausgiebig ['aʊsgiːbɪç] *adj* (*Gebrauch*) thorough, good; (*Essen*) generous, lavish; **~ schlafen** to have a good sleep

ausgießen ['aʊsgiːsən] *vt* to pour out; (*Behälter*) to empty

Ausgleich ['aʊsglaɪç] (-(e)s, -e) *m* balance; (*Vermittlung*) reconciliation; (*SPORT*) equalization; **zum ~ einer Sache** *gen* in order to offset sth; **a~en** (*unreg*) *vt* to balance (out); to reconcile; (*Höhe*) to even up ♦ *vi* (*SPORT*) to equalize

ausgraben ['aʊsgraːbən] (*unreg*) *vt* to dig up; (*Leichen*) to exhume; (*fig*) to unearth

Ausgrabung *f* excavation; (*Ausgraben auch*) digging up

Ausguss ▲ ['aʊsgʊs] *m* (*Spüle*) sink; (*Abfluss*) outlet; (*Tülle*) spout

aushalten ['aʊshaltən] (*unreg*) *vt* to bear, to

stand; (*Geliebte*) to keep ♦ *vi* to hold out;
das ist nicht zum A~ that is unbearable
aushandeln ['aʊshandəln] *vt* to negotiate
aushändigen ['aʊshɛndɪgən] *vt:* **jdm etw ~**
to hand sth over to sb
Aushang ['aʊshaŋ] *m* notice
aushängen ['aʊshɛŋən] (*unreg*) *vt* (*Meldung*)
to put up; (*Fenster*) to take off its hinges
♦ *vi* to be displayed
ausharren ['aʊsharən] *vi* to hold out
ausheben ['aʊshe:bən] (*unreg*) *vt* (*Erde*) to
lift out; (*Grube*) to hollow out; (*Tür*) to take
off its hinges; (*Diebesnest*) to clear out; (*MIL*)
to enlist
aushecken ['aʊshɛkən] (*umg*) *vt* to cook up
aushelfen ['aʊshɛlfən] (*unreg*) *vi:* **jdm ~** to
help sb out
Aushilfe ['aʊshɪlfə] *f* help, assistance;
(*Person*) (temporary) worker
Aushilfs- *zW:* **~kraft** *f* temporary worker;
a~weise *adv* temporarily, as a stopgap
ausholen ['aʊsho:lən] *vi* to swing one's arm
back; (*zur Ohrfeige*) to raise one's hand;
(*beim Gehen*) to take long strides
aushorchen ['aʊshɔrçən] *vt* to sound out,
to pump
auskennen ['aʊskɛnən] (*unreg*) *vr* to know a
lot; (*an einem Ort*) to know one's way
about; (*in Fragen etc*) to be knowledgeable
Ausklang ['aʊsklaŋ] *m* end
auskleiden ['aʊsklaɪdən] *vr* to undress ♦ *vt*
(*Wand*) to line
ausklingen ['aʊsklɪŋən] (*unreg*) *vi* (*Ton, Lied*)
to die away; (*Fest*) to peter out
ausklopfen ['aʊsklɔpfən] *vt* (*Teppich*) to
beat; (*Pfeife*) to knock out
auskochen ['aʊskɔxən] *vt* to boil; (*MED*) to
sterilize; **ausgekocht** (*fig*) out-and-out
Auskommen (**-s**) *nt:* **sein A~ haben** to
have a regular income; **a~** (*unreg*) *vi:* **mit
jdm a~** to get on with sb; **mit etw a~** to
get by with sth
auskosten ['aʊskɔstən] *vt* to enjoy to the
full
auskundschaften ['aʊskʊntʃaftən] *vt* to
spy out; (*Gebiet*) to reconnoitre
Auskunft ['aʊskʊnft] (**-, -künfte**) *f*

information; (*nähere*) details *pl*, particulars
pl; (*Stelle*) information office; (*TEL*) directory
inquiries *sg*
auslachen ['aʊslaxən] *vt* to laugh at, to
mock
ausladen ['aʊsla:dən] (*unreg*) *vt* to unload;
(*umg: Gäste*) to cancel an invitation to
Auslage ['aʊsla:gə] *f* shop window (display);
~n *pl* (*Ausgabe*) outlay *sg*
Ausland ['aʊslant] *nt* foreign countries *pl*;
im ~ abroad; **ins ~** abroad
Ausländer(in) ['aʊslɛndər(ɪn)] (**-s, -**) *m(f)*
foreigner
ausländisch *adj* foreign
Auslands- *zW:* **~gespräch** *nt*
international call; **~reise** *f* trip abroad;
~schutzbrief *m* international travel cover
auslassen ['aʊslasən] (*unreg*) *vt* to leave
out; (*Wort etc auch*) to omit; (*Fett*) to melt;
(*Kleidungsstück*) to let out ♦ *vr:* **sich über
etw** *akk* **~** to speak one's mind about sth;
seine Wut *etc* **an jdm ~** to vent one's rage
etc on sb
Auslassung *f* omission
Auslauf ['aʊslaʊf] *m* (*für Tiere*) run; (*Ausfluss*)
outflow, outlet; **a~en** (*unreg*) *vi* to run out;
(*Behälter*) to leak; (*NAUT*) to put out (to
sea); (*langsam aufhören*) to run down
Ausläufer ['aʊslɔʏfər] *m* (*von Gebirge*) spur;
(*Pflanze*) runner; (*MET: von Hoch*) ridge;
(*: von Tief*) trough
ausleeren ['aʊsle:rən] *vt* to empty
auslegen ['aʊsle:gən] *vt* (*Waren*) to lay out;
(*Köder*) to put down; (*Geld*) to lend;
(*bedecken*) to cover; (*Text etc*) to interpret
Auslegung *f* interpretation
ausleiern ['aʊslaɪərn] *vi* (*Gummi*) to wear
out
Ausleihe ['aʊslaɪə] *f* issuing; (*Stelle*) issue
desk; **a~n** (*unreg*) *vt* (*verleihen*) to lend; **sich**
dat **etw a~n** to borrow sth
Auslese ['aʊsle:zə] *f* selection; (*Elite*) elite;
(*Wein*) choice wine; **a~n** (*unreg*) *vt* to
select; (*umg: zu Ende lesen*) to finish
ausliefern ['aʊsli:fərn] *vt* to deliver (up), to
hand over; (*COMM*) to deliver; **jdm/etw
ausgeliefert sein** to be at the mercy of

sb/sth

ausloggen ['auslɔgən] *vi* (*COMPUT*) to log off

auslöschen ['auslœʃən] *vt* to extinguish; (*fig*) to wipe out, to obliterate

auslosen ['auslo:zən] *vt* to draw lots for

auslösen ['auslø:zən] *vt* (*Explosion, Schuss*) to set off; (*hervorrufen*) to cause, to produce; (*Gefangene*) to ransom; (*Pfand*) to redeem

ausmachen ['ausmaxən] *vt* (*Licht, Radio*) to turn off; (*Feuer*) to put out; (*entdecken*) to make out; (*vereinbaren*) to agree; (*beilegen*) to settle; (*Anteil darstellen, betragen*) to represent; (*bedeuten*) to matter; **macht es Ihnen etwas aus, wenn ...?** would you mind if ...?

ausmalen ['ausma:lən] *vt* to paint; (*fig*) to describe; **sich** *dat* **etw ~** to imagine sth

Ausmaß ['ausma:s] *nt* dimension; (*fig auch*) scale

ausmessen ['ausmesən] (*unreg*) *vt* to measure

Ausnahme ['ausna:mə] *f* exception; **~fall** *m* exceptional case; **~zustand** *m* state of emergency

ausnahms- *zW:* **~los** *adv* without exception; **~weise** *adv* by way of exception, for once

ausnehmen ['ausne:mən] (*unreg*) *vt* to take out, to remove; (*Tier*) to gut; (*Nest*) to rob; (*umg: Geld abnehmen*) to clean out; (*ausschließen*) to make an exception of ♦ *vr* to look, to appear; **~d** *adj* exceptional

ausnützen ['ausnʏtsən] *vt* (*Zeit, Gelegenheit*) to use, to turn to good account; (*Einfluss*) to use; (*Mensch, Gutmütigkeit*) to exploit

auspacken ['auspakən] *vt* to unpack

auspfeifen ['auspfaifən] (*unreg*) *vt* to hiss/boo at

ausplaudern ['ausplaudərn] *vt* to blab

ausprobieren ['ausprobi:rən] *vt* to try (out)

Auspuff ['auspuf] (**-(e)s, -e**) *m* (*TECH*) exhaust; **~rohr** *nt* exhaust (pipe)

ausradieren ['ausradi:rən] *vt* to erase, to rub out; (*fig*) to annihilate

ausrangieren ['ausrãʒi:rən] (*umg*) *vt* to chuck out

ausrauben ['ausraubən] *vt* to rob

ausräumen ['ausrɔʏmən] *vt* (*Dinge*) to clear away; (*Schrank, Zimmer*) to empty; (*Bedenken*) to dispel

ausrechnen ['ausrɛçnən] *vt* to calculate, to reckon

Ausrede ['ausre:də] *f* excuse; **a~n** *vi* to have one's say ♦ *vt:* **jdm etw a~n** to talk sb out of sth

ausreichen ['ausraiçən] *vi* to suffice, to be enough; **~d** *adj* sufficient, adequate; (*SCH*) adequate

Ausreise ['ausraizə] *f* departure; **bei der ~** when leaving the country; **~erlaubnis** *f* exit visa; **a~n** *vi* to leave the country

ausreißen ['ausraisən] (*unreg*) *vt* to tear *od* pull out ♦ *vi* (*Riss bekommen*) to tear; (*umg*) to make off, to scram

ausrenken ['ausrɛŋkən] *vt* to dislocate

ausrichten ['ausriçtən] *vt* (*Botschaft*) to deliver; (*Gruß*) to pass on; (*Hochzeit etc*) to arrange; (*in gerade Linie bringen*) to get in a straight line; (*angleichen*) to bring into line; (*TYP*) to justify; **ich werde es ihm ~** I'll tell him; **etwas/nichts bei jdm ~** to get somewhere/nowhere with sb

ausrotten ['ausrɔtən] *vt* to stamp out, to exterminate

Ausruf ['ausru:f] *m* (*Schrei*) cry, exclamation; (*Bekanntmachung*) proclamation; **a~en** (*unreg*) *vt* to cry out, to exclaim; to call out; **~ezeichen** *nt* exclamation mark

ausruhen ['ausru:ən] *vt, vr* to rest

ausrüsten ['ausrʏstən] *vt* to equip, to fit out

Ausrüstung *f* equipment

ausrutschen ['ausrutʃən] *vi* to slip

Aussage ['ausza:gə] *f* (*JUR*) statement; **a~n** *vt* to say, to state ♦ *vi* (*JUR*) to give evidence

ausschalten ['ausʃaltən] *vt* to switch off; (*fig*) to eliminate

Ausschank ['ausʃaŋk] (**-(e)s, -schänke**) *m* dispensing, giving out; (*COMM*) selling; (*Theke*) bar

Ausschau ['ausʃau] *f:* **~ halten (nach)** to look out (for), to watch (for); **a~en** *vi:* **a~en (nach)** to look out (for), to be on the look-out (for)

ausscheiden ['ausʃaidən] (*unreg*) *vt* to take

out; (MED) to secrete ♦ vi: ~ **(aus)** to leave; (SPORT) to be eliminated (from) od knocked out (of)

Ausscheidung f separation; secretion; elimination; (aus Amt) retirement

ausschenken ['ausʃɛŋkən] vt (Alkohol, Kaffee) to pour out; (COMM) to sell

ausschildern ['ausʃɪldərn] vt to signpost

ausschimpfen ['ausʃɪmpfən] vt to scold, to tell off

ausschlafen ['ausʃlaːfən] (unreg) vi, vr to have a good sleep ♦ vt to sleep off; **ich bin nicht ausgeschlafen** I didn't have od get enough sleep

Ausschlag ['ausʃlaːk] m (MED) rash; (Pendelausschlag) swing; (Nadelausschlag) deflection; **den ~ geben** (fig) to tip the balance; **a~en** [-gən] (unreg) vt to knock out; (auskleiden) to deck out; (verweigern) to decline ♦ vi (Pferd) to kick out; (BOT) to sprout; **a~gebend** adj decisive

ausschließen ['ausʃliːsən] (unreg) vt to shut od lock out; (fig) to exclude

ausschließlich adj exclusive ♦ adv exclusively ♦ präp +gen exclusive of, excluding

Ausschluss ▲ ['ausʃlʊs] m exclusion

ausschmücken ['ausʃmʏkən] vt to decorate; (fig) to embellish

ausschneiden ['ausʃnaidən] (unreg) vt to cut out; (Büsche) to trim

Ausschnitt ['ausʃnɪt] m (Teil) section; (von Kleid) neckline; (Zeitungsausschnitt) cutting; (aus Film etc) excerpt

ausschreiben ['ausʃraibən] (unreg) vt (ganz schreiben) to write out (in full); (ausstellen) to write (out); (Stelle, Wettbewerb etc) to announce, to advertise

Ausschreitung ['ausʃraitʊŋ] f (usu pl) riot

Ausschuss ▲ ['ausʃʊs] m committee, board; (Abfall) waste, scraps pl; (COMM: auch: ~ware) reject

ausschütten ['ausʃʏtən] vt to pour out; (Eimer) to empty; (Geld) to pay ♦ vr to shake (with laughter)

ausschweifend ['ausʃvaifənt] adj (Leben) dissipated, debauched; (Fantasie)

extravagant

aussehen ['ausze:ən] (unreg) vi to look; **es sieht nach Regen aus** it looks like rain; **es sieht schlecht aus** things look bad; **A~** (-s) nt appearance

aus sein ▲ siehe aus

außen ['ausən] adv outside; (nach ~) outwards; **~ ist es rot** it's red (on the) outside

Außen- zW: **~dienst** m: **im ~dienst sein** to work outside the office; **~handel** m foreign trade; **~minister** m foreign minister; **~ministerium** nt foreign office; **~politik** f foreign policy; **a~politisch** adj (Entwicklung, Lage) foreign; **~seite** f outside; **~seiter** (-s, -) m outsider; **~stände** pl outstanding debts; **~stehende(r)** f(m) outsider; **~welt** f outside world

außer ['ausər] präp +dat (räumlich) out of; (abgesehen von) except ♦ konj (ausgenommen) except; **~ Gefahr** out of danger; **~ Zweifel** beyond any doubt; **~ Betrieb** out of order; **~ Dienst** retired; **~ Landes** abroad; **~ sich** dat **sein** to be beside o.s.; **~ sich** akk **geraten** to go wild; **~ wenn** unless; **~ dass** except; **~dem** konj besides, in addition

äußere(r, s) ['ɔysərə(r,s)] adj outer, external

außergewöhnlich adj unusual

außerhalb präp +gen outside ♦ adv outside

äußerlich adj external

äußern vt to utter, to express; (zeigen) to show ♦ vr to give one's opinion; (Krankheit etc) to show itself

außerordentlich adj extraordinary

außerplanmäßig adj unscheduled

äußerst ['ɔysərst] adv extremely, most; **~e(r, s)** adj utmost; (räumlich) farthest; (Termin) last possible; (Preis) highest

Äußerung f remark, comment

aussetzen ['auszɛtsən] vt (Kind, Tier) to abandon; (Boote) to lower; (Belohnung) to offer; (Urteil, Verfahren) to postpone ♦ vi (aufhören) to stop; (Pause machen) to have a break; **jdm/etw ausgesetzt sein** to be exposed to sb/sth; **an jdm/etw etwas ~** to

Spelling Reform: ▲ *new spelling* △ *old spelling (to be phased out)*

find fault with sb/sth

Aussicht ['aʊszɪçt] *f* view; (*in Zukunft*) prospect; **etw in ~ haben** to have sth in view

Aussichts- *zW*: **a~los** *adj* hopeless; **~punkt** *m* viewpoint; **a~reich** *adj* promising; **~turm** *m* observation tower

aussöhnen ['aʊszøːnən] *vt* to reconcile ♦ *vr* to reconcile o.s., to become reconciled

aussondern ['aʊszɔndərn] *vt* to separate, to select

aussortieren ['aʊszɔrtiːrən] *vt* to sort out

ausspannen ['aʊsʃpanən] *vt* to spread *od* stretch out; (*Pferd*) to unharness; (*umg: Mädchen*): **(jdm) jdn ~** to steal sb (from sb) ♦ *vi* to relax

aussperren ['aʊsʃpɛrən] *vt* to lock out

ausspielen ['aʊsʃpiːlən] *vt* (*Karte*) to lead; (*Geldprämie*) to offer as a prize ♦ *vi* (*KARTEN*) to lead; **jdn gegen jdn ~** to play sb off against sb; **ausgespielt haben** to be finished

Aussprache ['aʊsʃpraːxə] *f* pronunciation; (*Unterredung*) (frank) discussion

aussprechen ['aʊsʃprɛçən] (*unreg*) *vt* to pronounce; (*äußern*) to say, to express ♦ *vr* (*sich äußern*): **sich ~ (über** +*akk*) to speak (about); (*sich anvertrauen*) to unburden o.s. (about *od* on); (*diskutieren*) to discuss ♦ *vi* (*zu Ende sprechen*) to finish speaking

Ausspruch ['aʊsʃprʊx] *m* saying, remark

ausspülen ['aʊsʃpyːlən] *vt* to wash out; (*Mund*) to rinse

Ausstand ['aʊsʃtant] *m* strike; **in den ~ treten** to go on strike

ausstatten ['aʊsʃtatən] *vt* (*Zimmer etc*) to furnish; (*Person*) to equip, to kit out

Ausstattung *f* (*Ausstatten*) provision; (*Kleidung*) outfit; (*Aufmachung*) make-up; (*Einrichtung*) furnishing

ausstechen ['aʊsʃtɛçən] (*unreg*) *vt* (*Augen, Rasen, Graben*) to dig out; (*Kekse*) to cut out; (*übertreffen*) to outshine

ausstehen ['aʊsʃteːən] (*unreg*) *vt* to stand, to endure ♦ *vi* (*noch nicht da sein*) to be outstanding

aussteigen ['aʊsʃtaɪgən] (*unreg*) *vi* to get

out, to alight

ausstellen ['aʊsʃtɛlən] *vt* to exhibit, to display; (*umg: ausschalten*) to switch off; (*Rechnung etc*) to make out; (*Pass, Zeugnis*) to issue

Ausstellung *f* exhibition; (*FIN*) drawing up; (*einer Rechnung*) making out; (*eines Passes etc*) issuing

aussterben ['aʊsʃtɛrbən] (*unreg*) *vi* to die out

Aussteuer ['aʊsʃtɔyər] *f* dowry

Ausstieg ['aʊsʃtiːk] (*-(e)s, -e*) *m* exit

ausstopfen ['aʊsʃtɔpfən] *vt* to stuff

ausstoßen ['aʊsʃtoːsən] (*unreg*) *vt* (*Luft, Rauch*) to give off, to emit; (*aus Verein etc*) to expel, to exclude; (*Auge*) to poke out

ausstrahlen ['aʊsʃtraːlən] *vt, vi* to radiate; (*RADIO*) to broadcast

Ausstrahlung *f* radiation; (*fig*) charisma

ausstrecken ['aʊsʃtrɛkən] *vt, vr* to stretch out

ausstreichen ['aʊsʃtraɪçən] (*unreg*) *vt* to cross out; (*glätten*) to smooth (out)

ausströmen ['aʊsʃtrøːmən] *vi* (*Gas*) to pour out, to escape ♦ *vt* to give off; (*fig*) to radiate

aussuchen ['aʊszuːxən] *vt* to select, to pick out

Austausch ['aʊstaʊʃ] *m* exchange; **a~bar** *adj* exchangeable; **a~en** *vt* to exchange, to swap

austeilen ['aʊstaɪlən] *vt* to distribute, to give out

Auster ['aʊstər] (*-, -n*) *f* oyster

austoben ['aʊstoːbən] *vr* (*Kind*) to run wild; (*Erwachsene*) to sow one's wild oats

austragen ['aʊstraːgən] (*unreg*) *vt* (*Post*) to deliver; (*Streit etc*) to decide; (*Wettkämpfe*) to hold

Australien [aʊsˈtraːliən] (*-s*) *nt* Australia; **Australier(in)** (*-s, -*) *m(f)* Australian; **australisch** *adj* Australian

austreiben ['aʊstraɪbən] (*unreg*) *vt* to drive out, to expel; (*Geister*) to exorcize

austreten ['aʊstreːtən] (*unreg*) *vi* (*zur Toilette*) to be excused ♦ *vt* (*Feuer*) to tread out, to trample; (*Schuhe*) to wear out; (*Treppe*) to wear down; **aus etw ~** to leave sth

austrinken ['austrɪŋkən] (*unreg*) *vt* (*Glas*) to drain; (*Getränk*) to drink up ♦ *vi* to finish one's drink, to drink up

Austritt ['austrɪt] *m* emission; (*aus Verein, Partei etc*) retirement, withdrawal

austrocknen ['austrɔknən] *vt*, *vi* to dry up

ausüben ['ausˌyːbən] *vt* (*Beruf*) to practise, to carry out; (*Funktion*) to perform; (*Einfluss*) to exert; **einen Reiz auf jdn ~** to hold an attraction for sb; **eine Wirkung auf jdn ~** to have an effect on sb

Ausverkauf ['ausferkauf] *m* sale; **a~en** *vt* to sell out; (*Geschäft*) to sell up; **a~t** *adj* (*Karten, Artikel*) sold out; (*THEAT: Haus*) full

Auswahl ['ausvaːl] *f*: **eine ~ (an** +*dat*) a selection (of), a choice (of)

auswählen ['ausvɛːlən] *vt* to select, to choose

Auswander- ['ausvandər] *zW*: **~er** *m* emigrant; **a~n** *vi* to emigrate; **~ung** *f* emigration

auswärtig ['ausvɛrtɪç] *adj* (*nicht am/vom Ort*) out-of-town; (*ausländisch*) foreign

auswärts ['ausvɛrts] *adv* outside; (*nach außen*) outwards; **~ essen** to eat out; **A~spiel** ['ausvɛrtsʃsiːl] *nt* away game

auswechseln ['ausvɛksəln] *vt* to change, to substitute

Ausweg ['ausveːk] *m* way out; **a~los** *adj* hopeless

ausweichen ['ausvaiçən] (*unreg*) *vi*: **jdm/ etw ~** to move aside *od* make way for sb/ sth; (*fig*) to side-step sb/sth; **~d** *adj* evasive

ausweinen ['ausvainən] *vr* to have a (good) cry

Ausweis ['ausvais] (**-es, -e**) *m* identity card; passport; (*Mitgliedsausweis, Bibliotheksausweis etc*) card; **a~en** [-zən] (*unreg*) *vt* to expel, to banish ♦ *vr* to prove one's identity; **~kontrolle** *f* identity check; **~papiere** *pl* identity papers; **~ung** *f* expulsion

ausweiten ['ausvaitən] *vt* to stretch

auswendig ['ausvɛndɪç] *adv* by heart

auswerten ['ausvɛrtən] *vt* to evaluate; **Auswertung** *f* evaluation, analysis; (*Nutzung*) utilization

auswirken ['ausvɪrkən] *vr* to have an effect; **Auswirkung** *f* effect

auswischen ['ausvɪʃən] *vt* to wipe out; **jdm eins ~** (*umg*) to put one over on sb

Auswuchs ['ausvuːks] *m* (out)growth; (*fig*) product

auszahlen ['austsaːlən] *vt* (*Lohn, Summe*) to pay out; (*Arbeiter*) to pay off; (*Miterbe*) to buy out ♦ *vr* (*sich lohnen*) to pay

auszählen ['austsɛːlən] *vt* (*Stimmen*) to count

auszeichnen ['austsaiçnən] *vt* to honour; (*MIL*) to decorate; (*COMM*) to price ♦ *vr* to distinguish o.s.

Auszeichnung *f* distinction; (*COMM*) pricing; (*Ehrung*) awarding of decoration; (*Ehre*) honour; (*Orden*) decoration; **mit ~** with distinction

ausziehen ['austsiːən] (*unreg*) *vt* (*Kleidung*) to take off; (*Haare, Zähne, Tisch etc*) to pull out; (*nachmalen*) to trace ♦ *vr* to undress ♦ *vi* (*aufbrechen*) to leave; (*aus Wohnung*) to move out

Auszubildende(r) ['austsubɪldəndə(r)] *f(m)* trainee

Auszug ['austsuːk] *m* (*aus Wohnung*) removal; (*aus Buch etc*) extract; (*Konto~*) statement; (*Ausmarsch*) departure

Auto ['auto] (**-s, -s**) *nt* (motor)car; **~ fahren** to drive; **~atlas** *m* road atlas; **~bahn** *f* motorway; **~bahndreieck** *nt* motorway junction; **~bahngebühr** *f* toll; **~bahnkreuz** *nt* motorway intersection; **~bus** *m* bus; **~fähre** *f* car ferry; **~fahrer(in)** *m(f)* motorist, driver; **~fahrt** *f* drive; **a~gen** [-ˈgeːn] *adj* autogenous; **~gramm** *nt* autograph

---
Autobahn
---

i *An* **Autobahn** *is a motorway. In former West Germany there is a widespread motorway network but in the former* **DDR** *the motorways are somewhat less extensive. There is no overall speed limit but a limit of 130 km/hour is recommended and there are lower mandatory limits on certain stretches of road. As yet there are no tolls payable on*

German Autobahnen. However, a yearly toll is payable in Switzerland and tolls have been introduced in Austria.

Auto- zW: **~'mat** (**-en, -en**) m machine; **~matik** [auto'ma:tɪk] f (AUT) automatic; **a~'matisch** adj automatic; **a~nom** [-'no:m] adj autonomous

Autor(in) ['autɔr(ɪn)] (**-s, -en**) m(f) author

Auto- zW: **~radio** nt car radio; **~reifen** m car tyre; **~reisezug** m motorail train; **~rennen** nt motor racing

autoritär [autori'tɛ:r] adj authoritarian

Autorität f authority

Auto- zW: **~telefon** nt car phone; **~unfall** m car od motor accident; **~vermietung** m car hire (BRIT) od rental (US); **~waschanlage** f car wash

Axt [akst] (**-, ⁻e**) f axe

B, b

Baby ['be:bi] (**-s, -s**) nt baby; **~nahrung** f baby food; **~sitter** (**-s, -**) m baby-sitter

Bach [bax] (**-(e)s, ⁻e**) m stream, brook

Backbord (**-(e)s, -e**) nt (NAUT) port

Backe ['bakə] f cheek

backen ['bakən] (unreg) vt, vi to bake

Backenzahn m molar

Bäcker ['bɛkər(ɪn)] (**-s, -**) m baker; **~ei** f bakery; (~eiladen) baker's (shop)

Back- zW: **~form** f baking tin; **~obst** nt dried fruit; **~ofen** m oven; **~pflaume** f prune; **~pulver** nt baking powder; **~stein** m brick

Bad [ba:t] (**-(e)s, ⁻er**) nt bath; (Schwimmen) bathe; (Ort) spa

Bade- ['ba:də] zW: **~anstalt** f (swimming) baths pl; **~anzug** m bathing suit; **~hose** f bathing od swimming trunks pl; **~kappe** f bathing cap; **~mantel** m bath(ing) robe; **~meister** m baths attendant; **b~n** vi to bathe, to have a bath ♦ vt to bath; **~ort** m spa; **~tuch** nt bath towel; **~wanne** f bath (tub); **~zimmer** nt bathroom

Bagatelle [baga'tɛlə] f trifle

Bagger ['bagər] (**-s, -**) m excavator; (NAUT) dredger; **b~n** vt, vi to excavate; to dredge

Bahn [ba:n] (**-, -en**) f railway, railroad (US); (Weg) road, way; (Spur) lane; (Rennbahn) track; (ASTRON) orbit; (Stoffbahn) length; **b~brechend** adj pioneering; **~Card** ['ba:nka:rd] ® f ≈ railcard; **~damm** m railway embankment; **b~en** vt: **sich/ jdm einen Weg b~en** to clear a way/a way for sb; **~fahrt** f railway journey; **~fracht** f rail freight; **~hof** (**-, -e**) m station; **auf dem ~hof** at the station; **~hofshalle** f station concourse; **~linie** f (railway) line; **~steig** m platform; **~übergang** m level crossing, grade crossing (US)

Bahre ['ba:rə] f stretcher

Bakterien [bak'te:riən] pl bacteria pl

Balance [ba'lā:sə] f balance, equilibrium

balan'cieren vt, vi to balance

bald [balt] adv (zeitlich) soon; (beinahe) almost; **~ig** ['baldɪç] adj early, speedy

Baldrian ['baldria:n] (**-s, -e**) m valerian

Balkan ['balka:n] (**-s**) m: **der ~** the Balkans pl

Balken ['balkən] (**-s, -**) m beam; (Tragbalken) girder; (Stützbalken) prop

Balkon [bal'kō:] (**-s, -s** od **-e**) m balcony; (THEAT) (dress) circle

Ball [bal] (**-(e)s, ⁻e**) m ball; (Tanz) dance, ball

Ballast ['balast] (**-(e)s, -e**) m ballast; (fig) weight, burden

Ballen ['balən] (**-s, -**) m bale; (ANAT) ball; **b~** vt (formen) to make into a ball; (Faust) to clench ♦ vr (Wolken etc) to build up; (Menschen) to gather

Ballett [ba'lɛt] (**-(e)s, -e**) nt ballet

Ballkleid nt evening dress

Ballon [ba'lō:] (**-s, -s** od **-e**) m balloon

Ballspiel nt ball game

Ballungsgebiet ['baluŋsgəbi:t] nt conurbation

Baltikum ['baltikum] (**-s**) nt: **das ~** the Baltic States

Banane [ba'na:nə] f banana

Band¹ [bant] (**-(e)s, ⁻e**) m (Buchband) volume

Band² (-(e)s, ¨er) nt (Stoffband) ribbon, tape; (Fließband) production line; (Tonband) tape; (ANAT) ligament; **etw auf ~ aufnehmen** to tape sth; **am laufenden ~** (umg) non-stop

Band³ (-(e)s, -e) nt (Freundschaftsband etc) bond

Band⁴ [bɛnt] (-, -s) f band, group

band etc vb siehe **binden**

Bandage [ban'da:ʒə] f bandage

banda'gieren vt to bandage

Bande ['bandə] f band; (Straßenbande) gang

bändigen ['bɛndɪgən] vt (Tier) to tame; (Trieb, Leidenschaft) to control, to restrain

Bandit [ban'di:t] (-en, -en) m bandit

Band- zW: **~nudel** f (KOCH: gew pl) ribbon noodles pl; **~scheibe** f (ANAT) disc; **~wurm** m tapeworm

bange ['baŋə] adj scared; (besorgt) anxious; **jdm wird es ~** sb is becoming scared; **jdm B~ machen** to scare sb; **~n** vi: **um jdn/ etw ~n** to be anxious od worried about sb/sth

Bank¹ [baŋk] (-, ¨e) f (Sitz~) bench; (Sand~ etc) (sand)bank, (sand)bar

Bank² [baŋk] (-, -en) f (Geldbank) bank; **~anweisung** f banker's order; **~einzug** m direct debit

Bankett [baŋ'kɛt] (-(e)s, -e) nt (Essen) banquet; (Straßenrand) verge (BRIT), shoulder (US)

Bankier [baŋki'e:] (-s, -s) m banker

Bank- zW: **~konto** m bank account; **~leitzahl** f bank sort code number; **~note** f banknote; **~raub** m bank robbery

Bankrott [baŋ'krɔt] (-(e)s, -e) m bankruptcy; **~ machen** to go bankrupt; **b~** adj bankrupt

Bankverbindung f banking arrangements pl; **geben Sie bitte Ihre ~ an** please give your account details

Bann [ban] (-(e)s, -e) m (HIST) ban; (Kirchenbann) excommunication; (fig: Zauber) spell; **b~en** vt (Geister) to exorcize; (Gefahr) to avert; (bezaubern) to enchant; (HIST) to banish

Banner (-s, -) nt banner, flag

Bar (-, -s) f bar

bar [ba:r] adj (+gen) (unbedeckt) bare; (frei von) lacking (in); (offenkundig) utter, sheer; **~e(s) Geld** cash; **etw (in) ~ bezahlen** to pay sth (in) cash; **etw für ~e Münze nehmen** (fig) to take sth at its face value

Bär [bɛ:r] (-en, -en) m bear

Baracke [ba'rakə] f hut

barbarisch [bar'ba:rɪʃ] adj barbaric, barbarous

Bar- zW: **b~fuß** adj barefoot; **~geld** nt cash, ready money; **b~geldlos** adj non-cash

Barkauf m cash purchase

Barkeeper ['ba:rki:pər] (-s, -) m barman, bartender

barmherzig [barm'hɛrtsɪç] adj merciful, compassionate

Baron [ba'ro:n] (-s, -e) m baron; **~in** f baroness

Barren ['barən] (-s, -) m parallel bars pl; (Goldbarren) ingot

Barriere [bari'e:rə] f barrier

Barrikade [bari'ka:də] f barricade

Barsch [barʃ] (-(e)s, -e) m perch

barsch [barʃ] adj brusque, gruff

Bar- zW: **~schaft** f ready money; **~scheck** m open od uncrossed cheque (BRIT), open check (US)

Bart [ba:rt] (-(e)s, ¨e) m beard; (Schlüsselbart) bit; **bärtig** ['bɛ:rtɪç] adj bearded

Barzahlung f cash payment

Base ['ba:zə] f (CHEM) base; (Kusine) cousin

Basel ['ba:zəl] nt Basle

Basen pl von **Base**; **Basis**

basieren [ba'zi:rən] vt to base ♦ vi to be based

Basis ['ba:zɪs] (-, Basen) f basis

Bass ▲ [bas] (-es, ¨e) m bass

Bassin [ba'sɛ̃:] (-s, -s) nt pool

basteln ['bastəln] vt to make ♦ vi to do handicrafts

bat etc [ba:t] vb siehe **bitten**

Bataillon [batal'jo:n] (-s, -e) nt battalion

Batik ['ba:tɪk] f (Verfahren) batik

Batterie [batə'ri:] f battery

Bau [bau] (-(e)s) m (~en) building,

Spelling Reform: ▲ new spelling △ old spelling (to be phased out)

construction; (*Aufbau*) structure; (*Körperbau*) frame; (*~stelle*) building site; (*pl ~e: Tierbau*) hole, burrow; (: *MIN*) working(s); (*pl ~ten: Gebäude*) building; **sich im ~ befinden** to be under construction; **~arbeiten** *pl* building *od* construction work *sg*; **~arbeiter** *m* building worker

Bauch [baʊx] **(-(e)s, Bäuche)** *m* belly; (*ANAT auch*) stomach, abdomen; **~fell** *nt* peritoneum; **b~ig** *adj* bulbous; **~nabel** *m* navel; **~redner** *m* ventriloquist; **~schmerzen** *pl* stomachache; **~weh** *nt* stomachache

Baudenkmal *nt* historical monument

bauen ['baʊən] *vt, vi* to build; (*TECH*) to construct; **auf jdn/etw ~** to depend *od* count upon sb/sth

Bauer¹ ['baʊər] **(-n** *od* **-s, -n)** *m* farmer; (*Schach*) pawn

Bauer² ['baʊər] **(-s, -)** *nt od m* (bird)cage

Bäuerin ['bɔʏərɪn] *f* farmer; (*Frau des Bauers*) farmer's wife

bäuerlich *adj* rustic

Bauern- *zW*: **~haus** *nt* farmhouse; **~hof** *m* farm(yard)

Bau- *zW*: **b~fällig** *adj* dilapidated; **~gelände** *f* building site; **~genehmigung** *f* building permit; **~gerüst** *nt* scaffolding; **~herr** *m* purchaser; **~kasten** *m* box of bricks; **~land** *nt* building land; **b~lich** *adj* structural

Baum [baʊm] **(-(e)s, Bäume)** *m* tree

baumeln ['baʊməln] *vi* to dangle

bäumen ['bɔʏmən] *vr* to rear (up)

Baum- *zW*: **~schule** *f* nursery; **~stamm** *m* tree trunk; **~stumpf** *m* tree stump; **~wolle** *f* cotton

Bau- *zW*: **~plan** *m* architect's plan; **~platz** *m* building site

bauspar- *zW*: **~en** *vi* to save with a building society; **B~kasse** *f* building society; **B~vertrag** *m* building society savings agreement

Bau- *zW*: **~stein** *m* building stone, freestone; **~stelle** *f* building site; **~teil** *nt* prefabricated part (of building); **~ten** *pl von* **Bau**; **~unternehmer** *m* building

contractor; **~weise** *f* (method of) construction; **~werk** *nt* building; **~zaun** *m* hoarding

Bayern ['baɪərn] *nt* Bavaria

bayrisch ['baɪrɪʃ] *adj* Bavarian

Bazillus [ba'tsɪlʊs] **(-, Bazillen)** *m* bacillus

beabsichtigen [bə'apzɪçtɪgən] *vt* to intend

beacht- [bə'axt] *zW*: **~en** *vt* to take note of; (*Vorschrift*) to obey; (*Vorfahrt*) to observe; **~lich** *adj* considerable; **B~ung** *f* notice, attention, observation

Beamte(r) [bə'amtə(r)] **(-n, -n)** *m* official; (*Staatsbeamte*) civil servant; (*Bankbeamte etc*) employee

Beamtin *f siehe* **Beamte(r)**

beängstigend [bə'ɛŋstɪgənt] *adj* alarming

beanspruchen [bə'anʃprʊxən] *vt* to claim; (*Zeit, Platz*) to take up, to occupy; **jdn ~** to take up sb's time

beanstanden [bə'anʃtandən] *vt* to complain about, to object to

beantragen [bə'antra:gən] *vt* to apply for, to ask for

beantworten [bə'antvɔrtən] *vt* to answer; **Beantwortung** *f* (*+gen*) reply (to)

bearbeiten [bə'arbaɪtən] *vt* to work; (*Material*) to process; (*Thema*) to deal with; (*Land*) to cultivate; (*CHEM*) to treat; (*Buch*) to revise; (*umg: beeinflussen wollen*) to work on

Bearbeitung *f* processing; cultivation; treatment; revision

Bearbeitungsgebühr *f* handling charge

Beatmung [bə'a:tmʊŋ] *f* respiration

beaufsichtigen [bə'aʊfzɪçtɪgən] *vt* to supervise; **Beaufsichtigung** *f* supervision

beauftragen [bə'aʊftra:gən] *vt* to instruct; **jdn mit etw ~** to entrust sb with sth

Beauftragte(r) *f(m)* representative

bebauen [bə'baʊən] *vt* to build on; (*AGR*) to cultivate

beben ['be:bən] *vi* to tremble, to shake; **B~ (-s, -)** *nt* earthquake

Becher ['bɛçər] **(-s, -)** *m* mug; (*ohne Henkel*) tumbler

Becken ['bɛkən] **(-s, -)** *nt* basin; (*MUS*) cymbal; (*ANAT*) pelvis

bedacht [bə'daxt] *adj* thoughtful, careful; **auf etw** *akk* ~ **sein** to be concerned about sth

bedächtig [bə'dɛçtɪç] *adj (umsichtig)* thoughtful, reflective; *(langsam)* slow, deliberate

bedanken [bə'daŋkən] *vr*: **sich (bei jdm)** ~ to say thank you (to sb)

Bedarf [bə'darf] *(-(e)s) m* need, requirement; *(COMM)* demand; **je nach** ~ according to demand; **bei** ~ if necessary; ~ **an etw** *dat* **haben** to be in need of sth

Bedarfs- *zW*: ~**fall** *m* case of need; ~**haltestelle** *f* request stop

bedauerlich [bə'dauərlɪç] *adj* regrettable

bedauern [bə'dauərn] *vt* to be sorry for; *(bemitleiden)* to pity; **B~** *(-s) nt* regret; ~**swert** *adj (Zustände)* regrettable; *(Mensch)* pitiable, unfortunate

bedecken [bə'dɛkən] *vt* to cover

bedeckt *adj* covered; *(Himmel)* overcast

bedenken [bə'dɛŋkən] *(unreg) vt* to think over, to consider

Bedenken *(-s, -) nt (Überlegen)* consideration; *(Zweifel)* doubt; *(Skrupel)* scruple

bedenklich *adj* doubtful; *(bedrohlich)* dangerous, risky

Bedenkzeit *f* time to think

bedeuten [bə'dɔytən] *vt* to mean; to signify; *(wichtig sein)* to be of importance; ~**d** *adj* important; *(beträchtlich)* considerable

bedeutsam *adj (wichtig)* significant

Bedeutung *f* meaning; significance; *(Wichtigkeit)* importance; **b~slos** *adj* insignificant, unimportant; **b~svoll** *adj* momentous, significant

bedienen [bə'di:nən] *vt* to serve; *(Maschine)* to work, to operate ♦ *vr (beim Essen)* to help o.s.; **sich jds / einer Sache** ~ to make use of sb/sth

Bedienung *f* service; *(Kellnerin)* waitress; *(Verkäuferin)* shop assistant; *(Zuschlag)* service (charge)

Bedienungsanleitung *f* operating instructions *pl*

bedingen [bə'dɪŋən] *vt (verursachen)* to cause

bedingt *adj (Richtigkeit, Tauglichkeit)* limited; *(Zusage, Annahme)* conditional

Bedingung *f* condition; *(Voraussetzung)* stipulation; **b~slos** *adj* unconditional

bedrängen [bə'drɛŋən] *vt* to pester, to harass

bedrohen [bə'dro:ən] *vt* to threaten; **Bedrohung** *f* threat, menace

bedrücken [bə'drykən] *vt* to oppress, to trouble

bedürf- [bə'dyrf] *zW*: ~**en** *(unreg) vi +gen* to need, to require; **B~nis** *(-ses, -se) nt* need; ~**tig** *adj* in need, poor, needy

beeilen [bə'|aɪlən] *vr* to hurry

beeindrucken [bə'|aɪndrʊkən] *vt* to impress, to make an impression on

beeinflussen [bə'|aɪnflʊsən] *vt* to influence

beeinträchtigen [bə'|aɪntrɛçtɪgən] *vt* to affect adversely; *(Freiheit)* to infringe upon

beend(ig)en [bə'|ɛnd(ɪg)ən] *vt* to end, to finish, to terminate

beengen [bə'|ɛŋən] *vt* to cramp; *(fig)* to hamper, to oppress

beerben [bə'|ɛrbən] *vt*: **jdn** ~ to inherit from sb

beerdigen [bə'|e:rdɪgən] *vt* to bury; **Beerdigung** *f* funeral, burial

Beere ['be:rə] *f* berry; *(Traubenbeere)* grape

Beet [be:t] *(-(e)s, -e) nt* bed

befähigen [bə'fɛ:ɪgən] *vt* to enable

befähigt *adj (begabt)* talented; ~ **(für)** *(fähig)* capable (of)

Befähigung *f* capability; *(Begabung)* talent, aptitude

befahrbar [bə'fa:rba:r] *adj* passable; *(NAUT)* navigable

befahren [bə'fa:rən] *(unreg) vt* to use, to drive over; *(NAUT)* to navigate ♦ *adj* used

befallen [bə'falən] *(unreg) vt* to come over

befangen [bə'faŋən] *adj (schüchtern)* shy, self-conscious; *(voreingenommen)* biased

befassen [bə'fasən] *vr* to concern o.s.

Befehl [bə'fe:l] *(-(e)s, -e) m* command, order; **b~en** *(unreg) vt* to order ♦ *vi* to give orders; **jdm etw b~en** to order sb to do sth; ~**sverweigerung** *f* insubordination

Spelling Reform: ▲ *new spelling* △ *old spelling (to be phased out)*

befestigen [bəˈfɛstɪgən] *vt* to fasten; (*stärken*) to strengthen; (*MIL*) to fortify; **~ an** +*dat* to fasten to

Befestigung *f* fastening; strengthening; (*MIL*) fortification

befeuchten [bəˈfɔʏçtən] *vt* to damp(en), to moisten

befinden [bəˈfɪndən] (*unreg*) *vr* to be; (*sich fühlen*) to feel ♦ *vt*: **jdn/etw für** *od* **als etw ~** to deem sb/sth to be sth ♦ *vi*: **~ (über** +*akk*) to decide (on), to adjudicate (on); **B~ (-s)** *nt* health, condition; (*Meinung*) view, opinion

befolgen [bəˈfɔlgən] *vt* to comply with, to follow

befördern [bəˈfœrdərn] *vt* (*senden*) to transport, to send; (*beruflich*) to promote; **Beförderung** *f* transport; promotion

befragen [bəˈfraːgən] *vt* to question

befreien [bəˈfraɪən] *vt* to set free; (*erlassen*) to exempt; **Befreiung** *f* liberation, release; (*Erlassen*) exemption

befreunden [bəˈfrɔʏndən] *vr* to make friends; (*mit Idee etc*) to acquaint o.s.

befreundet *adj* friendly

befriedigen [bəˈfriːdɪgən] *vt* to satisfy; **~d** *adj* satisfactory

Befriedigung *f* satisfaction, gratification

befristet [bəˈfrɪstət] *adj* limited

befruchten [bəˈfrʊxtən] *vt* to fertilize; (*fig*) to stimulate

Befruchtung *f*: **künstliche ~** artificial insemination

Befugnis [bəˈfuːknɪs] **(-, -se)** *f* authorization, powers *pl*

befugt *adj* authorized, entitled

Befund [bəˈfʊnt] **(-(e)s, -e)** *m* findings *pl*; (*MED*) diagnosis

befürchten [bəˈfʏrçtən] *vt* to fear; **Befürchtung** *f* fear, apprehension

befürworten [bəˈfyːrvɔrtən] *vt* to support, to speak in favour of; **Befürworter (-s, -)** *m* supporter, advocate

begabt [bəˈgaːpt] *adj* gifted

Begabung [bəˈgaːbʊŋ] *f* talent, gift

begann *etc* [bəˈgan] *vb siehe* **beginnen**

begeben [bəˈgeːbən] (*unreg*) *vr* (*gehen*) to

betake o.s.; (*geschehen*) to occur; **sich ~ nach** *od* **zu** to proceed to(wards); **B~heit** *f* occurrence

begegnen [bəˈgeːgnən] *vi*: **jdm ~** to meet sb; (*behandeln*) to treat sb; **einer Sache** *dat* **~** to meet with sth

Begegnung *f* meeting

begehen [bəˈgeːən] (*unreg*) *vt* (*Straftat*) to commit; (*abschreiten*) to cover; (*Straße etc*) to use, to negotiate; (*Feier*) to celebrate

begehren [bəˈgeːrən] *vt* to desire

begehrt *adj* in demand; (*Junggeselle*) eligible

begeistern [bəˈgaɪstərn] *vt* to fill with enthusiasm, to inspire ♦ *vr*: **sich für etw ~** to get enthusiastic about sth

begeistert *adj* enthusiastic

Begierde [bəˈgiːrdə] *f* desire, passion

begierig [bəˈgiːrɪç] *adj* eager, keen

begießen [bəˈgiːsən] (*unreg*) *vt* to water; (*mit Alkohol*) to drink to

Beginn [bəˈgɪn] **(-(e)s)** *m* beginning; **zu ~** at the beginning; **b~en** (*unreg*) *vt, vi* to start, to begin

beglaubigen [bəˈglaʊbɪgən] *vt* to countersign; **Beglaubigung** *f* countersignature

begleichen [bəˈglaɪçən] (*unreg*) *vt* to settle, to pay

Begleit- [bəˈglaɪt] *zW*: **b~en** *vt* to accompany; (*MIL*) to escort; **~er (-s, -)** *m* companion; (*Freund*) escort; (*MUS*) accompanist; **~schreiben** *nt* covering letter; **~umstände** *pl* concomitant circumstances; **~ung** *f* company; (*MIL*) escort; (*MUS*) accompaniment

beglücken [bəˈglʏkən] *vt* to make happy, to delight

beglückwünschen [bəˈglʏkvʏnʃən] *vt*: **~ (zu)** to congratulate (on)

begnadigen [bəˈgnaːdɪgən] *vt* to pardon; **Begnadigung** *f* pardon, amnesty

begnügen [bəˈgnyːgən] *vr* to be satisfied, to content o.s.

begonnen *etc* [bəˈgɔnən] *vb siehe* **beginnen**

begraben [bəˈgraːbən] (*unreg*) *vt* to bury; **Begräbnis (-ses, -se)** [bəˈgrɛːpnɪs] *nt* burial, funeral

egreifen [bə'graɪfən] (*unreg*) *vt* to understand, to comprehend

egreiflich [bə'graɪflɪç] *adj* understandable

egrenzen [bə'grɛntsən] *vt* (*beschränken*) to limit

egrenztheit [bə'grɛntshaɪt] *f* limitation, restriction; (*fig*) narrowness

egriff [bə'grɪf] **(-(e)s, -e)** *m* concept, idea; **im ~ sein, etw zu tun** to be about to do sth; **schwer von ~** (*umg*) slow, dense

egriffsstutzig *adj* slow, dense

egründ- [bə'grʏnd] *zW*: **~en** *vt* (*Gründe geben*) to justify; **~et** *adj* well-founded, justified; **B~ung** *f* justification, reason

egrüßen [bə'gry:sən] *vt* to greet, to welcome; **Begrüßung** *f* greeting, welcome

egünstigen [bə'gʏnstɪgən] *vt* (*Person*) to favour; (*Sache*) to further, to promote

egutachten [bə'gu:t|axtən] *vt* to assess

egütert [bə'gy:tərt] *adj* wealthy, well-to-do

ehaart [bə'ha:rt] *adj* hairy

ehagen [bə'ha:gən] *vi*: **das behagt ihm nicht** he does not like it

ehaglich [bə'ha:klɪç] *adj* comfortable, cosy; **B~keit** *f* comfort, cosiness

ehalten [bə'haltən] (*unreg*) *vt* to keep, to retain; (*im Gedächtnis*) to remember

ehälter [bə'hɛltər] **(-s, -)** *m* container, receptacle

ehandeln [bə'handəln] *vt* to treat; (*Thema*) to deal with; (*Maschine*) to handle

ehandlung *f* treatment; (*von Maschine*) handling

eharren [bə'harən] *vi*: **auf etw** *dat* **~** to stick *od* keep to sth

eharrlich [bə'harlɪç] *adj* (*ausdauernd*) steadfast, unwavering; (*hartnäckig*) tenacious, dogged; **B~keit** *f* steadfastness; tenacity

ehaupten [bə'haʊptən] *vt* to claim, to assert, to maintain; (*sein Recht*) to defend ♦ *vr* to assert o.s.

ehauptung *f* claim, assertion

eheben [bə'he:bən] (*unreg*) *vt* to remove

ehelfen [bə'hɛlfən] (*unreg*) *vr*: **sich mit etw ~** to make do with sth

ehelfsmäßig *adj* improvised, makeshift;

(*vorübergehend*) temporary

behelligen [bə'hɛlɪgən] *vt* to trouble, to bother

beherbergen [bə'hɛrbɛrgən] *vt* to put up, to house

beherrsch- [bə'hɛrʃ] *zW*: **~en** *vt* (*Volk*) to rule, to govern; (*Situation*) to control; (*Sprache, Gefühle*) to master ♦ *vr* to control o.s.; **~t** *adj* controlled; **B~ung** *f* rule; control; mastery

beherzigen [bə'hɛrtsɪgən] *vt* to take to heart

beherzt *adj* courageous, brave

behilflich [bə'hɪlflɪç] *adj* helpful; **jdm ~ sein (bei)** to help sb (with)

behindern [bə'hɪndərn] *vt* to hinder, to impede

Behinderte(r) *f(m)* disabled person

Behinderung *f* hindrance; (*Körperbehinderung*) handicap

Behörde [bə'hø:rdə] *f* (*auch pl*) authorities *pl*

behördlich [bə'hø:rtlɪç] *adj* official

behüten [bə'hy:tən] *vt* to guard; **jdn vor etw** *dat* **~** to preserve sb from sth

behutsam [bə'hu:tza:m] *adj* cautious, careful; **B~keit** *f* caution, carefulness

---

SCHLÜSSELWORT

bei [baɪ] *präp +dat* **1** (*nahe bei*) near; (*zum Aufenthalt*) at, with; (*unter, zwischen*) among; **bei München** near Munich; **bei uns** at our place; **beim Friseur** at the hairdresser's; **bei seinen Eltern wohnen** to live with one's parents; **bei einer Firma arbeiten** to work for a firm; **etw bei sich haben** to have sth on one; **jdn bei sich haben** to have sb with one; **bei Goethe** in Goethe; **beim Militär** in the army

2 (*zeitlich*) at, on; (*während*) during; (*Zustand, Umstand*) in; **bei Nacht** at night; **bei Nebel** in fog; **bei Regen** if it rains; **bei solcher Hitze** in such heat; **bei meiner Ankunft** on my arrival; **bei der Arbeit** when I'm *etc* working; **beim Fahren** while driving

---

beibehalten ['baɪbəhaltən] (*unreg*) *vt* to keep, to retain

beibringen ['baɪbrɪŋən] (*unreg*) *vt* (*Beweis, Zeugen*) to bring forward; (*Gründe*) to adduce; **jdm etw ~** (*lehren*) to teach sb sth; (*zu verstehen geben*) to make sb understand sth; (*zufügen*) to inflict sth on sb

Beichte ['baɪçtə] *f* confession; **b~n** *vt* to confess ♦ *vi* to go to confession

beide(s) ['baɪdə(s)] *pron, adj* both; **meine ~n Brüder** my two brothers, both my brothers; **die ersten ~n** the first two; **wir ~** we two; **einer von ~n** one of the two; **alles ~s** both (of them)

beider- ['baɪdər] *zW*: **~lei** *adj inv* of both; **~seitig** *adj* mutual, reciprocal; **~seits** *adv* mutually ♦ *präp +gen* on both sides of

beieinander [baɪaɪˈnandər] *adv* together

Beifahrer ['baɪfaːrər] *m* passenger

Beifall ['baɪfal] **(-(e)s)** *m* applause; (*Zustimmung*) approval

beifügen ['baɪfyːgən] *vt* to enclose

beige ['beːʒ] *adj* beige, fawn

beigeben ['baɪgeːbən] (*unreg*) *vt* (*zufügen*) to add; (*mitgeben*) to give ♦ *vi* (*nachgeben*) to give in

Beihilfe ['baɪhɪlfə] *f* aid, assistance; (*Studienbeihilfe*) grant; (*JUR*) aiding and abetting

beikommen ['baɪkɔmən] (*unreg*) *vi +dat* to get at; (*einem Problem*) to deal with

Beil [baɪl] **(-(e)s, -e)** *nt* axe, hatchet

Beilage ['baɪlaːgə] *f* (*Buchbeilage etc*) supplement; (*KOCH*) vegetables and potatoes *pl*

beiläufig ['baɪlɔʏfɪç] *adj* casual, incidental ♦ *adv* casually, by the way

beilegen ['baɪleːgən] *vt* (*hinzufügen*) to enclose, to add; (*beimessen*) to attribute, to ascribe; (*Streit*) to settle

Beileid ['baɪlaɪt] *nt* condolence, sympathy; **herzliches ~** deepest sympathy

beiliegend ['baɪliːgənt] *adj* (*COMM*) enclosed

beim [baɪm] = **bei dem**

beimessen ['baɪmɛsən] (*unreg*) *vt* (*+dat*) to attribute (to), to ascribe (to)

Bein [baɪn] **(-(e)s, -e)** *nt* leg

beinah(e) ['baɪnaː(ə)] *adv* almost, nearly

Beinbruch *m* fracture of the leg

beinhalten [bəˈlɪnhaltən] *vt* to contain

Beipackzettel ['baɪpaktsetəl] *m* instruction leaflet

beipflichten ['baɪpflɪçtən] *vi*: **jdm/etw ~** t← agree with sb/sth

beisammen [baɪˈzamən] *adv* together; **B~sein (-s)** *nt* get-together

Beischlaf ['baɪʃlaːf] *m* sexual intercourse

Beisein ['baɪzaɪn] **(-s)** *nt* presence

beiseite [baɪˈzaɪtə] *adv* to one side, aside; (*stehen*) on one side, aside; **etw ~ legen** (*sparen*) to put sth by

beisetzen ['baɪzetsən] *vt* to bury; **Beisetzung** *f* funeral

Beisitzer ['baɪzɪtsər] **(-s, -)** *m* (*bei Prüfung*) assessor

Beispiel ['baɪʃpiːl] **(-(e)s, -e)** *nt* example; **sich +dat an jdm ein ~ nehmen** to take s← as an example; **zum ~** for example; **b~haft** *adj* exemplary; **b~los** *adj* unprecedented; **b~sweise** *adv* for instan← *od* example

beißen ['baɪsən] (*unreg*) *vt, vi* to bite; (*stechen: Rauch, Säure*) to burn ♦ *vr* (*Farber←* to clash; **~d** *adj* biting, caustic; (*fig auch*) sarcastic

Beistand ['baɪʃtant] **(-(e)s, ⁺e)** *m* support, help; (*JUR*) adviser

beistehen ['baɪʃteːən] (*unreg*) *vi*: **jdm ~** to stand by sb

beisteuern ['baɪʃtɔʏərn] *vt* to contribute

Beitrag ['baɪtraːk] **(-(e)s, ⁺e)** *m* contributio← (*Zahlung*) fee, subscription; (*Versicherungsbeitrag*) premium; **b~en** ['baɪtraːgən] (*unreg*) *vt, vi*: **b~en (zu)** to contribute (to); (*mithelfen*) to help (with)

beitreten ['baɪtreːtən] (*unreg*) *vi +dat* to joi←

Beitritt ['baɪtrɪt] *m* joining, membership

Beiwagen ['baɪvaːgən] *m* (*Motorradbeiwage←* sidecar

beizeiten [baɪˈtsaɪtən] *adv* in time

bejahen [bəˈjaːən] *vt* (*Frage*) to say yes to, ← answer in the affirmative; (*gutheißen*) to agree with

bekämpfen [bəˈkɛmpfən] *vt* (*Gegner*) to fight; (*Seuche*) to combat ♦ *vr* to fight;

Bekämpfung f fight, struggle

ekannt [bə'kant] adj (well-)known; (nicht fremd) familiar; **~ geben** to announce publicly; **mit jdm ~ sein** to know sb; **~ machen** to announce; **jdn mit jdm ~ machen** to introduce sb to sb; **das ist mir ~** I know that; **es/sie kommt mir ~ vor** it/she seems familiar; **B~e(r)** f(m) acquaintance; friend; **B~enkreis** m circle of friends; **~lich** adv as is well known, as you know; **B~machung** f publication; announcement; **B~schaft** f acquaintance

ekehren [bə'ke:rən] vt to convert ♦ vr to be od become converted

ekennen [bə'kɛnən] (unreg) vt to confess; (Glauben) to profess; **Farbe ~** (umg) to show where one stands

ekenntnis [bə'kɛntnɪs] (-ses, -se) nt admission, confession; (Religion) confession, denomination

eklagen [bə'kla:gən] vt to deplore, to lament ♦ vr to complain

ekleiden [bə'klaɪdən] vt to clothe; (Amt) to occupy, to fill

ekleidung f clothing

eklemmen [bə'klɛmən] vt to oppress

eklommen [bə'klɔmən] adj anxious, uneasy

ekommen [bə'kɔmən] (unreg) vt to get, to receive; (Kind) to have; (Zug) to catch, to get ♦ vi: **jdm ~** to agree with sb

ekömmlich [bə'kœmlɪç] adj easily digestible

ekräftigen [bə'krɛftɪgən] vt to confirm, to corroborate

ekreuzigen [bə'krɔytsɪgən] vr to cross o.s.

ekunden [bə'kʊndən] vt (sagen) to state; (zeigen) to show

elächeln [bə'lɛçəln] vt to laugh at

eladen [bə'la:dən] (unreg) vt to load

elag [bə'la:k] (-(e)s, ⁻e) m covering, coating; (Brotbelag) spread; (Zahnbelag) tartar; (auf Zunge) fur; (Bremsbelag) lining

elagern [bə'la:gərn] vt to besiege; **Belagerung** f siege

elang [bə'laŋ] (-(e)s) m importance; **~e** pl (Interessen) interests, concerns; **b~los** adj

trivial, unimportant

belassen [bə'lasən] (unreg) vt (in Zustand, Glauben) to leave; (in Stellung) to retain

belasten [bə'lastən] vt to burden; (fig: bedrücken) to trouble, to worry; (COMM: Konto) to debit; (JUR) to incriminate ♦ vr to weigh o.s. down; (JUR) to incriminate o.s.; **~d** adj (JUR) incriminating

belästigen [bə'lɛstɪgən] vt to annoy, to pester; **Belästigung** f annoyance, pestering

Belastung [bə'lastʊŋ] f load; (fig: Sorge etc) weight; (COMM) charge, debit(ing); (JUR) incriminatory evidence

belaufen [bə'laʊfən] (unreg) vr: **sich ~ auf** +akk to amount to

beleben [bə'le:bən] vt (anregen) to liven up; (Konjunktur, jds Hoffnungen) to stimulate ♦ vr (Augen) to light up; (Stadt) to come to life

belebt [bə'le:pt] adj (Straße) busy

Beleg [bə'le:k] (-(e)s, -e) m (COMM) receipt; (Beweis) documentary evidence, proof; (Beispiel) example; **b~en** vt to cover; (Kuchen, Brot) to spread; (Platz) to reserve, to book; (Kurs, Vorlesung) to register for; (beweisen) to verify, to prove; (MIL: mit Bomben) to bomb; **~schaft** f personnel, staff; **b~t** adj: **b~tes Brot** open sandwich

belehren [bə'le:rən] vt to instruct, to teach; **Belehrung** f instruction

beleibt [bə'laɪpt] adj stout, corpulent

beleidigen [bə'laɪdɪgən] vt to insult, to offend; **Beleidigung** f insult; (JUR) slander, libel

beleuchten [bə'lɔyçtən] vt to light, to illuminate; (fig) to throw light on

Beleuchtung f lighting, illumination

Belgien ['bɛlgiən] nt Belgium; **Belgier(in)** m(f) Belgian; **belgisch** adj Belgian

belichten [bə'lɪçtən] vt to expose

Belichtung f exposure; **~smesser** m exposure meter

Belieben [bə'li:bən] nt: **(ganz) nach ~** (just) as you wish

beliebig [bə'li:bɪç] adj any you like ♦ adv as you like; **ein ~es Thema** any subject you like od want; **~ viel/viele** as much/many as you like

beliebt [bə'li:pt] *adj* popular; **sich bei jdm ~ machen** to make o.s. popular with sb; **B~heit** *f* popularity

beliefern [bə'li:fərn] *vt* to supply

bellen ['bɛlən] *vi* to bark

belohnen [bə'lo:nən] *vt* to reward; **Belohnung** *f* reward

Belüftung [bə'lʏftʊŋ] *f* ventilation

belügen [bə'ly:gən] (*unreg*) *vt* to lie to, to deceive

belustigen [bə'lʊstɪgən] *vt* to amuse; **Belustigung** *f* amusement

bemalen [bə'ma:lən] *vt* to paint

bemängeln [bə'mɛŋəln] *vt* to criticize

bemerk- [bə'mɛrk] *zW:* **~bar** *adj* perceptible, noticeable; **sich ~bar machen** (*Person*) to make *od* get o.s. noticed; (*Unruhe*) to become noticeable; **~en** *vt* (*wahrnehmen*) to notice, to observe; (*sagen*) to say, to mention; **~enswert** *adj* remarkable, noteworthy; **B~ung** *f* remark; (*schriftlich auch*) note

bemitleiden [bə'mɪtlaɪdən] *vt* to pity

bemühen [bə'my:ən] *vr* to take trouble *od* pains; **Bemühung** *f* trouble, pains *pl*, effort

benachbart [bə'naxba:rt] *adj* neighbouring

benachrichtigen [bə'na:xrɪçtɪgən] *vt* to inform; **Benachrichtigung** *f* notification, information

benachteiligen [bə'na:xtaɪlɪgən] *vt* to put at a disadvantage; to victimize

benehmen [bə'ne:mən] (*unreg*) *vr* to behave; **B~** (**-s**) *nt* behaviour

beneiden [bə'naɪdən] *vt* to envy; **~swert** *adj* enviable

benennen [bə'nɛnən] (*unreg*) *vt* to name

Bengel ['bɛŋəl] (**-s, -**) *m* (little) rascal *od* rogue

benommen [bə'nɔmən] *adj* dazed

benoten [bə'no:tən] *vt* to mark

benötigen [bə'nø:tɪgən] *vt* to need

benutzen [bə'nʊtsən] *vt* to use

Benutzer (**-s, -**) *m* user

Benutzung *f* utilization, use

Benzin [bɛnt'si:n] (**-s, -e**) *nt* (*AUT*) petrol

(*BRIT*), gas(oline) (*US*); **~kanister** *m* petro (*BRIT*) *od* gas (*US*) can; **~tank** *m* petrol tar (*BRIT*), gas tank (*US*); **~uhr** *f* petrol (*BRIT*) *o* gas (*US*) gauge

beobachten [bə'o:baxtən] *vt* to observe; **Beobachter** (**-s, -**) *m* observer; (*eines Unfalls*) witness; (*PRESSE, TV*) corresponden **Beobachtung** *f* observation

bepacken [bə'pakən] *vt* to load, to pack

bequem [bə'kve:m] *adj* comfortable; (*Ausrede*) convenient; (*Person*) lazy, indolent; **~en** *vr:* **sich ~en(, etw zu tun)** condescend (to do sth); **B~lichkeit** [-'lɪçkaɪt] *f* convenience, comfort; (*Faulheit*) laziness, indolence

beraten [bə'ra:tən] (*unreg*) *vt* to advise; (*besprechen*) to discuss, to debate ♦ *vr* to consult; **gut/schlecht ~ sein** to be well/i advised; **sich ~ lassen** to get advice

Berater (**-s, -**) *m* adviser

Beratung *f* advice; (*Besprechung*) consultation; **~sstelle** *f* advice centre

berauben [bə'raubən] *vt* to rob

berechenbar [bə'rɛçənba:r] *adj* calculable

berechnen [bə'rɛçnən] *vt* to calculate; (*COMM: anrechnen*) to charge; **~d** *adj* (*Mensch*) calculating, scheming

Berechnung *f* calculation; (*COMM*) charg

berechtigen [bə'rɛçtɪgən] *vt* to entitle; to authorize; (*fig*) to justify

berechtigt [bə'rɛçtɪçt] *adj* justifiable, justifi

Berechtigung *f* authorization; (*fig*) justification

bereden [bə're:dən] *vt* (*besprechen*) to discuss; (*überreden*) to persuade ♦ *vr* to discuss

Bereich [bə'raɪç] (**-(e)s, -e**) *m* (*Bezirk*) area, (*PHYS*) range; (*Ressort, Gebiet*) sphere

bereichern [bə'raɪçərn] *vt* to enrich ♦ *vr* to get rich

bereinigen [bə'raɪnɪgən] *vt* to settle

bereisen [bə'raɪzən] *vt* (*Land*) to travel through

bereit [bə'raɪt] *adj* ready, prepared; **zu etw sein** to be ready for sth; **sich ~ erklären** declare o.s. willing; **~en** *vt* to prepare, to make ready; (*Kummer, Freude*) to cause;

~halten (*unreg*) *vt* to keep in readiness; **~legen** *vt* to lay out; **~machen** *vt*, *vr* to prepare, to get ready; **~s** *adv* already; **B~schaft** *f* readiness; (*Polizei*) alert; **B~schaftsdienst** *m* emergency service; **~stehen** (*unreg*) *vi* (*Person*) to be prepared; (*Ding*) to be ready; **~stellen** *vt* (*Kisten, Pakete etc*) to put ready; (*Geld etc*) to make available; (*Truppen, Maschinen*) to put at the ready; **~willig** *adj* willing, ready; **B~willigkeit** *f* willingness, readiness

ereuen [bə'rɔyən] *vt* to regret

erg [bɛrk] (**-(e)s, -e**) *m* mountain; hill; **b~ab** *adv* downhill; **~arbeiter** *m* miner; **b~auf** *adv* uphill; **~bahn** *f* mountain railway; **~bau** *m* mining

ergen ['bɛrgən] (*unreg*) *vt* (*retten*) to rescue; (*Ladung*) to salvage; (*enthalten*) to contain

erg- *zW:* **~führer** *m* mountain guide; **~gipfel** *m* peak, summit; **b~ig** ['bɛrgɪç] *adj* mountainous; hilly; **~kette** *f* mountain range; **~mann** (*pl* **~leute**) *m* miner; **~rettungsdienst** *m* mountain rescue team; **~rutsch** *m* landslide; **~steigen** *nt* mountaineering; **~steiger(in)** (**-s, -**) *m(f)* mountaineer, climber; **~tour** *f* mountain climb

ergung ['bɛrgʊŋ] *f* (*von Menschen*) rescue; (*von Material*) recovery; (*NAUT*) salvage

erg- *zW:* **~wacht** *f* mountain rescue service; **~wanderung** *f* hike in the mountains; **~werk** *nt* mine

ericht [bə'rɪçt] (**-(e)s, -e**) *m* report, account; **b~en** *vt*, *vi* to report; **~erstatter** (**-s, -**) *m* reporter; (*newspaper*) correspondent

erichtigen [bə'rɪçtɪgən] *vt* to correct; **Berichtigung** *f* correction

ernstein ['bɛrnʃtaɪn] *m* amber

ersten ['bɛrstən] (*unreg*) *vi* to burst, to split

erüchtigt [bə'rʏçtɪçt] *adj* notorious, infamous

erücksichtigen [bə'rʏkzɪçtɪgən] *vt* to consider, to bear in mind; **Berücksichtigung** *f* consideration

eruf [bə'ru:f] (**-(e)s, -e**) *m* occupation, profession; (*Gewerbe*) trade; **b~en** (*unreg*)

vt: **b~en zu** to appoint to ♦ *vr*: **sich auf jdn/etw b~en** to refer *od* appeal to sb/sth ♦ *adj* competent, qualified; **b~lich** *adj* professional

Berufs- *zW:* **~ausbildung** *f* job training; **~berater** *m* careers adviser; **~beratung** *f* vocational guidance; **~geheimnis** *nt* professional secret; **~leben** *nt* professional life; **~schule** *f* vocational *od* trade school; **~sportler** [-ʃpɔrtlər] *m* professional (sportsman); **b~tätig** *adj* employed; **b~unfähig** *adj* unfit for work; **~verkehr** *m* rush-hour traffic

Berufung *f* vocation, calling; (*Ernennung*) appointment; (*JUR*) appeal; **~ einlegen** to appeal

beruhen [bə'ru:ən] *vi*: **auf etw** *dat* **~** to be based on sth; **etw auf sich ~ lassen** to leave sth at that

beruhigen [bə'ru:ɪgən] *vt* to calm, to pacify, to soothe ♦ *vr* (*Mensch*) to calm (o.s.) down; (*Situation*) to calm down

Beruhigung *f* soothing; (*der Nerven*) calming; **zu jds ~** (in order) to reassure sb; **~smittel** *nt* sedative

berühmt [bə'ry:mt] *adj* famous; **B~heit** *f* (*Ruf*) fame; (*Mensch*) celebrity

berühren [bə'ry:rən] *vt* to touch; (*gefühlsmäßig bewegen*) to affect; (*flüchtig erwähnen*) to mention, to touch on ♦ *vr* to meet, to touch

Berührung *f* contact

besagen [bə'za:gən] *vt* to mean

besänftigen [bə'zɛnftɪgən] *vt* to soothe, to calm

Besatz [bə'zats] (**-es, ⁺e**) *m* trimming, edging

Besatzung *f* garrison; (*NAUT, AVIAT*) crew

Besatzungsmacht *f* occupying power

beschädigen [bə'ʃe:dɪgən] *vt* to damage; **Beschädigung** *f* damage; (*Stelle*) damaged spot

beschaffen [bə'ʃafən] *vt* to get, to acquire ♦ *adj*: **das ist so ~, dass** that is such that; **B~heit** *f* (*von Mensch*) constitution, nature

Beschaffung *f* acquisition

beschäftigen [bə'ʃɛftɪgən] *vt* to occupy;

(*beruflich*) to employ ♦ *vr* to occupy *od* concern o.s.

beschäftigt *adj* busy, occupied

Beschäftigung *f* (*Beruf*) employment; (*Tätigkeit*) occupation; (*Befassen*) concern

beschämen [bəˈʃɛːmən] *vt* to put to shame; **~d** *adj* shameful; (*Hilfsbereitschaft*) shaming

beschämt *adj* ashamed

Bescheid [bəˈʃaɪt] (**-(e)s, -e**) *m* information; (*Weisung*) directions *pl*; **~ wissen (über** +*akk*) to be well-informed (about); **ich weiß ~** I know; **jdm ~ geben** *od* **sagen** to let sb know

bescheiden [bəˈʃaɪdən] (*unreg*) *vr* to content o.s. ♦ *adj* modest; **B~heit** *f* modesty

bescheinen [bəˈʃaɪnən] (*unreg*) *vt* to shine on

bescheinigen [bəˈʃaɪnɪgən] *vt* to certify; (*bestätigen*) to acknowledge

Bescheinigung *f* certificate; (*Quittung*) receipt

beschenken [bəˈʃɛŋkən] *vt*: **jdm mit etw ~** to give sb sth as a present

bescheren [bəˈʃeːrən] *vt*: **jdm etw ~** to give sb sth as a Christmas present; **jdn ~** to give Christmas presents to sb

Bescherung *f* giving of Christmas presents; (*umg*) mess

beschildern [bəˈʃɪldərn] *vt* to put signs/a sign on

beschimpfen [bəˈʃɪmpfən] *vt* to abuse; **Beschimpfung** *f* abuse; insult

Beschlag [bəˈʃlaːk] (**-(e)s, ²e**) *m* (*Metallband*) fitting; (*auf Fenster*) condensation; (*auf Metall*) tarnish; finish; (*Hufeisen*) horseshoe; **jdn/etw in ~ nehmen** *od* **mit ~ belegen** to monopolize sb/sth; **b~en** [bəˈʃlaːgən] (*unreg*) *vt* to cover; (*Pferd*) to shoe ♦ *vi, vr* (*Fenster etc*) to mist over; **b~en sein (in** *od* **auf** +*dat*) to be well versed (in); **b~nahmen** *vt* to seize, to confiscate; to requisition; **~nahmung** *f* confiscation, sequestration

beschleunigen [bəˈʃlɔʏnɪgən] *vt* to accelerate, to speed up ♦ *vi* (*AUT*) to accelerate; **Beschleunigung** *f* acceleration

beschließen [bəˈʃliːsən] (*unreg*) *vt* to decic on; (*beenden*) to end, to close

Beschluss ▲ [bəˈʃlʊs] (**-es, ²e**) *m* decisio. conclusion; (*Ende*) conclusion, end

beschmutzen [bəˈʃmʊtsən] *vt* to dirty, to soil

beschönigen [bəˈʃøːnɪgən] *vt* to gloss ove

beschränken [bəˈʃrɛŋkən] *vt, vr*: (**sich**) **~ (auf** +*akk*) to limit *od* restrict (o.s.) (to)

beschränk- *zW*: **~t** *adj* confined, restricted; (*Mensch*) limited, narrow-minded; **B~ung** *f* limitation

beschreiben [bəˈʃraɪbən] (*unreg*) *vt* to describe; (*Papier*) to write on

Beschreibung *f* description

beschriften [bəˈʃrɪftən] *vt* to mark, to labe **Beschriftung** *f* lettering

beschuldigen [bəˈʃʊldɪgən] *vt* to accuse; **Beschuldigung** *f* accusation

Beschuss ▲ [bəˈʃʊs] *m*: **jdn/etw unter ~ nehmen** (*MIL*) to open fire on sb/sth

beschützen [bəˈʃʏtsən] *vt*: **~ (vor** +*dat*) to protect (from); **Beschützer (-s, -)** *m* protector

Beschwerde [bəˈʃveːrdə] *f* complaint; (*Mühe*) hardship; **~n** *pl* (*Leiden*) trouble

beschweren [bəˈʃveːrən] *vt* to weight down; (*fig*) to burden ♦ *vr* to complain

beschwerlich *adj* tiring, exhausting

beschwichtigen [bəˈʃvɪçtɪgən] *vt* to sooth to pacify

beschwindeln [bəˈʃvɪndəln] *vt* (*betrügen*) cheat; (*belügen*) to fib to

beschwingt [bəˈʃvɪŋt] *adj* in high spirits

beschwipst [bəˈʃvɪpst] (*umg*) *adj* tipsy

beschwören [bəˈʃvøːrən] (*unreg*) *vt* (*Aussage*) to swear to; (*anflehen*) to implor (*Geister*) to conjure up

beseitigen [bəˈzaɪtɪgən] *vt* to remove; **Beseitigung** *f* removal

Besen [ˈbeːzən] (**-s, -**) *m* broom; **~stiel** *m* broomstick

besessen [bəˈzɛsən] *adj* possessed

besetz- [bəˈzɛts] *zW*: **~en** *vt* (*Haus, Land*) t occupy; (*Platz*) to take, to fill; (*Posten*) to fill; (*Rolle*) to cast; (*mit Edelsteinen*) to set; ◀ *adj* full; (*TEL*) engaged, busy; (*Platz*) taken;

(*WC*) engaged; **B~tzeichen** *nt* engaged tone; **B~ung** *f* occupation; filling; (*von Rolle*) casting; (*die Schauspieler*) cast

esichtigen [bəˈzɪçtɪgən] *vt* to visit, to have a look at; **Besichtigung** *f* visit

esiegen [bəˈziːgən] *vt* to defeat, to overcome

esinn- [bəˈzɪn] *zW*: **~en** (*unreg*) *vr* (*nachdenken*) to think, to reflect; (*erinnern*) to remember; **sich anders ~en** to change one's mind; **B~ung** *f* consciousness; **zur B~ung kommen** to recover consciousness; (*fig*) to come to one's senses; **~ungslos** *adj* unconscious

esitz [bəˈzɪts] (*-es*) *m* possession; (*Eigentum*) property; **b~en** (*unreg*) *vt* to possess, to own; (*Eigenschaft*) to have; **~er(in)** (*-s, -*) *m(f)* owner, proprietor; **~ergreifung** *f* occupation, seizure

esoffen [bəˈzɔfən] (*umg*) *adj* drunk, stoned

esohlen [bəˈzoːlən] *vt* to sole

esoldung [bəˈzɔldʊŋ] *f* salary, pay

esondere(r, s) [bəˈzɔndərə(r, s)] *adj* special; (*eigen*) particular; (*gesondert*) separate; (*eigentümlich*) peculiar

esonderheit [bəˈzɔndərhaɪt] *f* peculiarity

esonders [bəˈzɔndərs] *adv* especially, particularly; (*getrennt*) separately

esonnen [bəˈzɔnən] *adj* sensible, level-headed

esorg- [bəˈzɔrg] *zW*: **~en** *vt* (*beschaffen*) to acquire, (*kaufen auch*) to purchase; (*erledigen*: *Geschäfte*) to deal with; (*sich kümmern um*) to take care of; **B~nis** (*-, -se*) *f* anxiety, concern; **~t** [bəˈzɔrçt] *adj* anxious, worried; **B~ung** *f* acquisition; (*Kauf*) purchase

espielen [bəˈʃpiːlən] *vt* to record

espitzeln [bəˈʃpɪtsəln] *vt* to spy on

esprechen [bəˈʃprɛçən] (*unreg*) *vt* to discuss; (*Tonband etc*) to record, to speak onto; (*Buch*) to review ♦ *vr* to discuss, to consult; **Besprechung** *f* meeting, discussion; (*von Buch*) review

esser [ˈbɛsər] *adj* better; **es geht ihm ~** he is feeling better; **~n** *vt* to make better, to improve ♦ *vr* to improve; (*Menschen*) to

reform; **B~ung** *f* improvement; **gute B~ung!** get well soon!; **B~wisser** (*-s, -*) *m* know-all

Bestand [bəˈʃtant] (*-(e)s, ⁺e*) *m* (*Fortbestehen*) duration, stability; (*Kassenbestand*) amount, balance; (*Vorrat*) stock; **~ haben, von ~ sein** to last long, to endure

beständig [bəˈʃtɛndɪç] *adj* (*ausdauernd*: *auch fig*) constant; (*Wetter*) settled; (*Stoffe*) resistant; (*Klagen etc*) continual

Bestandsaufnahme [bəˈʃtantsaʊfnaːmə] *f* stocktaking

Bestandteil *m* part, component; (*Zutat*) ingredient

bestärken [bəˈʃtɛrkən] *vt*: **jdn in etw** *dat* **~** to strengthen *od* confirm sb in sth

bestätigen [bəˈʃtɛːtɪgən] *vt* to confirm; (*anerkennen, COMM*) to acknowledge; **Bestätigung** *f* confirmation; acknowledgement

bestatten [bəˈʃtatən] *vt* to bury

Bestattung *f* funeral

Bestattungsinstitut *nt* funeral director's

bestaunen [bəˈʃtaʊnən] *vt* to marvel at, gaze at in wonder

beste(r, s) [ˈbɛstə(r, s)] *adj* best; **so ist es am ~n** it's best that way; **am ~n gehst du gleich** you'd better go at once; **jdn zum B~n haben** to pull sb's leg; **einen Witz** *etc* **zum B~n geben** to tell a joke *etc*; **aufs B~** *od* **~** in the best possible way; **zu jds B~n** for the benefit of sb

bestechen [bəˈʃtɛçən] (*unreg*) *vt* to bribe; **bestechlich** *adj* corruptible; **Bestechung** *f* bribery, corruption

Besteck [bəˈʃtɛk] (*-(e)s, -e*) *nt* knife, fork and spoon, cutlery; (*MED*) set of instruments

bestehen [bəˈʃteːən] (*unreg*) *vi* to be; to exist; (*andauern*) to last ♦ *vt* (*Kampf, Probe, Prüfung*) to pass; **~ auf** +*dat* to insist on; **~ aus** to consist of

bestehlen [bəˈʃteːlən] (*unreg*) *vt*: **jdn (um etw) ~** to rob sb (of sth)

besteigen [bəˈʃtaɪgən] (*unreg*) *vt* to climb, to ascend; (*Pferd*) to mount; (*Thron*) to ascend

Spelling Reform: ▲ new spelling △ old spelling (to be phased out)

Bestell- [bə'ʃtɛl] zW: **~buch** nt order book;
b~en vt to order; (kommen lassen) to
arrange to see; (nominieren) to name;
(Acker) to cultivate; (Grüße, Auftrag) to pass
on; **~formular** nt order form; **~nummer** f
order code; **~ung** f (COMM) order; (~en)
ordering

bestenfalls ['bɛstən'fals] adv at best

bestens ['bɛstəns] adv very well

besteuern [bə'ʃtɔyərn] vt (jdn, Waren) to tax

Bestie ['bɛstiə] f (auch fig) beast

bestimm- [bə'ʃtɪm] zW: **~en** vt (Regeln) to
lay down; (Tag, Ort) to fix; (beherrschen) to
characterize; (vorsehen) to mean; (ernennen)
to appoint; (definieren) to define;
(veranlassen) to induce; **~t** adj (entschlossen)
firm; (gewiss) certain, definite; (Artikel)
definite ♦ adv (gewiss) definitely, for sure;
suchen Sie etwas B~tes? are you looking
for something in particular?; **B~theit** f
firmness; certainty; **B~ung** f (Verordnung)
regulation; (Festsetzen) determining;
(Verwendungszweck) purpose; (Schicksal)
fate; (Definition) definition; **B~ungsland** nt
(country of) destination; **B~ungsort** m
(place of) destination

Bestleistung f best performance

bestmöglich adj best possible

bestrafen [bə'ʃtraːfən] vt to punish;
Bestrafung f punishment

bestrahlen [bə'ʃtraːlən] vt to shine on;
(MED) to treat with X-rays

Bestrahlung f (MED) X-ray treatment,
radiotherapy

Bestreben [bə'ʃtreːbən] (-s) nt endeavour,
effort

bestreiten [bə'ʃtraɪtən] (unreg) vt (abstreiten)
to dispute; (finanzieren) to pay for, to
finance

bestreuen [bə'ʃtrɔyən] vt to sprinkle, to
dust; (Straße) to grit

bestürmen [bə'ʃtʏrmən] vt (mit Fragen,
Bitten etc) to overwhelm, to swamp

bestürzend [bə'ʃtʏrtsənd] adj (Nachrichten)
disturbing

bestürzt [bə'ʃtʏrtst] adj dismayed

Bestürzung f consternation

Besuch [bə'zuːx] (-(e)s, -e) m visit; (Person)
visitor; **einen ~ machen bei jdm** to pay
a visit od call; **~ haben** to have visitors; **b**
jdm auf od **zu ~ sein** to be visiting sb;
b~en vt to visit; (SCH etc) to attend; **gut**
b~t well-attended; **~er(in)** (-s, -) m(f)
visitor, guest; **~szeit** f visiting hours pl

betätigen [bə'tɛːtɪgən] vt (bedienen) to wol
to operate ♦ vr to involve o.s.; **sich als e**
~ to work as sth

Betätigung f activity; (beruflich)
occupation; (TECH) operation

betäuben [bə'tɔybən] vt to stun; (fig:
Gewissen) to still; (MED) to anaesthetize

Betäubung f (Narkose): **örtliche ~** local
anaesthetic

Betäubungsmittel nt anaesthetic

Bete ['beːtə] f: **Rote ~** beetroot (BRIT), beet
(US)

beteilig- [bə'taɪlɪg] zW: **~en** vr: **sich ~en**
(an +dat) to take part (in), to participate
(in), to share (in); (an Geschäft: finanziell)
have a share (in) ♦ vt: **jdn ~en (an** +dat) t
give sb a share od interest (in); **B~te(r)**
f(m) (Mitwirkender) partner; (finanziell)
shareholder; **B~ung** f participation; (Ante
share, interest; (Besucherzahl) attendance

beten ['beːtən] vt, vi to pray

beteuern [bə'tɔyərn] vt to assert; (Unschul
to protest

Beton [be'tɔ̃ː] (-s, -s) m concrete

betonen [be'toːnən] vt to stress

betonieren [beto'niːrən] vt to concrete

Betonung f stress, emphasis

betr. abk (= betrifft) re

Betracht [bə'traxt] m: **in ~ kommen** to be
considered od relevant; **etw in ~ ziehen** t
take sth into consideration; **außer ~**
bleiben not to be considered; **b~en** vt t
look at; (fig) to look at, to consider; **~er(**
(-s, -) m(f) observer

beträchtlich [bə'trɛçtlɪç] adj considerable

Betrachtung f (Ansehen) examination;
(Erwägung) consideration

Betrag [bə'traːk] (-(e)s, ⁻e) m amount;
b~en (unreg) vt to amount to ♦ vr to
behave; **~en** (-s) nt behaviour

Betreff *m*: ~ **ihr Schreiben vom ...** re your letter of ...

betreffen [bə'trɛfən] (*unreg*) *vt* to concern, to affect; **was mich betrifft** as for me; ~**d** *adj* relevant, in question

betreffs [bə'trɛfs] *präp +gen* concerning, regarding; (COMM) re

betreiben [bə'traɪbən] (*unreg*) *vt* (*ausüben*) to practise; (*Politik*) to follow; (*Studien*) to pursue; (*vorantreiben*) to push ahead; (TECH: *antreiben*) to drive

betreten [bə'tre:tən] (*unreg*) *vt* to enter; (*Bühne etc*) to step onto ♦ *adj* embarrassed; **B~ verboten** keep off/out

Betreuer(in) [bə'trɔyər(ın)] (**-s, -**) *m(f)* (*einer Person*) minder; (*eines Gebäudes, Arbeitsgebiets*) caretaker; (SPORT) coach

Betreuung *f* care

Betrieb [bə'tri:p] (**-(e)s, -e**) *m* (*Firma*) firm, concern; (*Anlage*) plant; (*Tätigkeit*) operation; (*Treiben*) traffic; **außer ~ sein** to be out of order; **in ~ sein** to be in operation

Betriebs- *zW*: ~**ausflug** *m* works outing; **b~bereit** *adj* operational; **b~fähig** *adj* in working order; ~**ferien** *pl* company holidays (BRIT), company vacation *sg* (US); ~**klima** *nt* (working) atmosphere; ~**kosten** *pl* running costs; ~**rat** *m* workers' council; **b~sicher** *adj* safe (to operate); ~**störung** *f* breakdown; ~**system** *nt* (COMPUT) operating system; ~**unfall** *m* industrial accident; ~**wirtschaft** *f* economics

betrinken [bə'trıŋkən] (*unreg*) *vr* to get drunk

betroffen [bə'trɔfən] *adj* (*bestürzt*) full of consternation; **von etw ~ werden** *od* **sein** to be affected by sth

betrüben [bə'try:bən] *vt* to grieve

betrübt [bə'try:pt] *adj* sorrowful, grieved

Betrug [bə'tru:k] (**-(e)s**) *m* deception; (JUR) fraud

betrügen [bə'try:gən] (*unreg*) *vt* to cheat; (JUR) to defraud; (*Ehepartner*) to be unfaithful to ♦ *vr* to deceive o.s.

Betrüger (**-s, -**) *m* cheat, deceiver; **b~isch** *adj* deceitful; (JUR) fraudulent

betrunken [bə'trʊŋkən] *adj* drunk

Bett [bɛt] (**-(e)s, -en**) *nt* bed; **ins** *od* **zu ~ gehen** to go to bed; ~**bezug** *m* duvet cover; ~**decke** *f* blanket; (*Daunenbett*) quilt; (*Überwurf*) bedspread

Bettel- ['bɛtəl] *zW*: **b~arm** *adj* very poor, destitute; ~**ei** [bɛtə'laɪ] *f* begging; **b~n** *vi* to beg

bettlägerig ['bɛtlɛ:gərıç] *adj* bedridden

Bettlaken *nt* sheet

Bettler(in) ['bɛtlər(ın)] (**-s, -**) *m(f)* beggar

Bett- *zW*: ~**tuch** ▲ *nt* sheet; ~**vorleger** *m* bedside rug; ~**wäsche** *f* bed linen; ~**zeug** *nt* bed linen *pl*

beugen ['bɔygən] *vt* to bend; (GRAM) to inflect ♦ *vr* (*sich fügen*) to bow

Beule ['bɔylə] *f* bump, swelling

beunruhigen [bə'ʊnru:ıgən] *vt* to disturb, to alarm ♦ *vr* to become worried

Beunruhigung *f* worry, alarm

beurlauben [bə'u:rlaubən] *vt* to give leave *od* a holiday to (BRIT), to grant vacation time to (US)

beurteilen [bə'ʊrtaılən] *vt* to judge; (*Buch etc*) to review

Beurteilung *f* judgement; review; (*Note*) mark

Beute ['bɔytə] (**-**) *f* booty, loot

Beutel (**-s, -**) *m* bag; (*Geldbeutel*) purse; (*Tabakbeutel*) pouch

Bevölkerung [bə'fœlkərʊŋ] *f* population

bevollmächtigen [bə'fɔlmɛçtıgən] *vt* to authorize

Bevollmächtigte(r) *f(m)* authorized agent

bevor [bə'fo:r] *konj* before; ~**munden** *vt insep* to treat like a child; ~**stehen** (*unreg*) *vi*: **(jdm) ~stehen** to be in store (for sb); ~**stehend** *adj* imminent, approaching; ~**zugen** *vt insep* to prefer

bewachen [bə'vaxən] *vt* to watch, to guard

Bewachung *f* (*Bewachen*) guarding; (*Leute*) guard, watch

bewaffnen [bə'vafnən] *vt* to arm

Bewaffnung *f* (*Vorgang*) arming; (*Ausrüstung*) armament, arms *pl*

bewahren [bə'va:rən] *vt* to keep; **jdn vor jdm/etw ~** to save sb from sb/sth

Spelling Reform: ▲ new spelling △ old spelling (to be phased out)

bewähren [bəˈvɛːrən] *vr* to prove o.s.; (*Maschine*) to prove its worth

bewahrheiten [bəˈvaːrhaɪtən] *vr* to come true

bewährt *adj* reliable

Bewährung *f* (*JUR*) probation

bewältigen [bəˈvɛltɪgən] *vt* to overcome; (*Arbeit*) to finish; (*Portion*) to manage

bewandert [bəˈvandərt] *adj* expert, knowledgeable

bewässern [bəˈvɛsərn] *vt* to irrigate

Bewässerung *f* irrigation

bewegen [bəˈveːgən] *vt, vr* to move; **jdn zu etw ~** to induce sb to do sth; **~d** *adj* touching, moving

Beweg- [bəˈveːk] *zW:* **~grund** *m* motive; **b~lich** *adj* movable, mobile; (*flink*) quick; **b~t** *adj* (*Leben*) eventful; (*Meer*) rough; (*ergriffen*) touched

Bewegung *f* movement, motion; (*innere*) emotion; (*körperlich*) exercise; **~sfreiheit** *f* freedom of movement; (*fig*) freedom of action; **b~ungslos** *adj* motionless

Beweis [bəˈvaɪs] (**-es, -e**) *m* proof; (*Zeichen*) sign; **b~en** [-zən] (*unreg*) *vt* to prove; (*zeigen*) to show; **~mittel** *nt* evidence

Bewerb- [bəˈverb] *zW:* **b~en** (*unreg*) *vr* to apply (for); **~er(in)** (**-s, -**) *m(f)* applicant; **~ung** *f* application

bewerkstelligen [bəˈvɛrkʃtɛlɪgən] *vt* to manage, to accomplish

bewerten [bəˈveːrtən] *vt* to assess

bewilligen [bəˈvɪlɪgən] *vt* to grant, to allow

Bewilligung *f* granting

bewirken [bəˈvɪrkən] *vt* to cause, to bring about

bewirten [bəˈvɪrtən] *vt* to feed, to entertain (to a meal)

bewirtschaften [bəˈvɪrtʃaftən] *vt* to manage

Bewirtung *f* hospitality

bewog *etc* [bəˈvoːk] *vb siehe* **bewegen**

bewohn- [bəˈvoːn] *zW:* **~bar** *adj* habitable; **~en** *vt* to inhabit, to live in; **B~er(in)** (**-s, -**) *m(f)* inhabitant; (*von Haus*) resident

bewölkt [bəˈvœlkt] *adj* cloudy, overcast

Bewölkung *f* clouds *pl*

Bewunder- [bəˈvʊndər] *zW:* **~er** (**-s, -**) *m* admirer; **b~n** *vt* to admire; **b~nswert** *adj* admirable, wonderful; **~ung** *f* admiration

bewusst ▲ [bəˈvʊst] *adj* conscious; (*absichtlich*) deliberate; **sich** *dat* **einer Sache** *gen* **~ sein** to be aware of sth; **~los** *adj* unconscious; **B~losigkeit** *f* unconsciousness; **B~sein** *nt* consciousness; **bei B~sein** conscious

bezahlen [bəˈtsaːlən] *vt* to pay for

Bezahlung *f* payment

bezaubern [bəˈtsaubərn] *vt* to enchant, to charm

bezeichnen [bəˈtsaɪçnən] *vt* (*kennzeichnen*) to mark; (*nennen*) to call; (*beschreiben*) to describe; (*zeigen*) to show, to indicate; **~d** *adj:* **~d (für)** characteristic (of), typical (of)

Bezeichnung *f* (*Zeichen*) mark, sign; (*Beschreibung*) description

bezeugen [bəˈtsɔʏgən] *vt* to testify to

Bezichtigung [bəˈtsɪçtɪgʊŋ] *f* accusation

beziehen [bəˈtsiːən] (*unreg*) *vt* (*mit Überzug*) to cover; (*Bett*) to make; (*Haus, Position*) to move into; (*Standpunkt*) to take up; (*erhalten*) to receive; (*Zeitung*) to subscribe to, to take ♦ *vr* (*Himmel*) to cloud over; **etw auf jdn/etw ~** to relate sth to sb/sth; **sich ~ auf** +*akk* to refer to

Beziehung *f* (*Verbindung*) connection; (*Zusammenhang*) relation; (*Verhältnis*) relationship; (*Hinsicht*) respect; **~en haben** (*vorteilhaft*) to have connections *od* contacts; **b~sweise** *adv* or; (*genauer gesagt auch*) that is, or rather

Bezirk [bəˈtsɪrk] (**-(e)s, -e**) *m* district

Bezug [bəˈtsuːk] (**-(e)s, ⁺e**) *m* (*Hülle*) covering; (*COMM*) ordering; (*Gehalt*) income, salary; (*Beziehung*): **~ (zu)** relation(ship) (to); **in ~ auf** +*akk* with reference to; **~ nehmen auf** +*akk* to refer to

bezüglich [bəˈtsyːklɪç] *präp* +*gen* concerning, referring to ♦ *adj* (*GRAM*) relative; **auf etw** *akk* **~** relating to sth

bezwecken [bəˈtsvɛkən] *vt* to aim at

bezweifeln [bəˈtsvaɪfəln] *vt* to doubt, to query

Rechtschreibreform: ▲ *neue Schreibung* △ *alte Schreibung (auslaufend)*

BH *m abk von* **Büstenhalter**

Bhf. *abk (= Bahnhof)* station

Bibel ['biːbəl] **(-, -n)** *f* Bible

Biber ['biːbər] **(-s, -)** *m* beaver

Biblio- [biːblio] *zW:* **~grafie** ▲ [-graˈfiː] *f* bibliography; **~thek** [-'teːk] **(-, -en)** *f* library; **~thekar(in)** [-teˈkaːr(ɪn)] **(-s, -e)** *m(f)* librarian

biblisch ['biːblɪʃ] *adj* biblical

bieder ['biːdər] *adj* upright, worthy; *(Kleid etc)* plain

bieg- ['biːg] *zW:* **~en** *(unreg) vt, vr* to bend ♦ *vi* to turn; **~sam** ['biːk-] *adj* flexible; **B~ung** *f* bend, curve

Biene ['biːnə] *f* bee

Bienenhonig *m* honey

Bienenwachs *nt* beeswax

Bier [biːr] **(-(e)s, -e)** *nt* beer; **~deckel** *m* beer mat; **~garten** *m* beer garden; **~krug** *m* beer mug; **~zelt** *nt* beer tent

Biest [biːst] **(-s, -er)** *(umg: pej) nt (Tier)* beast, creature; *(Mensch)* beast

bieten ['biːtən] *(unreg) vt* to offer; *(bei Versteigerung)* to bid ♦ *vr (Gelegenheit):* **sich jdm ~** to present itself to sb; **sich** *dat* **etw ~ lassen** to put up with sth

Bikini [biˈkiːni] **(-s, -s)** *m* bikini

Bilanz [biˈlants] *f* balance; *(fig)* outcome; **~ ziehen (aus)** to take stock (of)

Bild [bɪlt] **(-(e)s, -er)** *nt (auch fig)* picture; photo; *(Spiegelbild)* reflection; **~bericht** *m* photographic report

bilden ['bɪldən] *vt* to form; *(erziehen)* to educate; *(ausmachen)* to constitute ♦ *vr* to arise; *(erziehen)* to educate o.s.

Bilderbuch *nt* picture book

Bilderrahmen *m* picture frame

Bild- *zW:* **~fläche** *f* screen; *(fig)* scene; **~hauer** **(-s, -)** *m* sculptor; **b~hübsch** *adj* lovely, pretty as a picture; **b~lich** *adj* figurative; pictorial; **~schirm** *m* television screen; *(COMPUT)* monitor; **~schirmschoner** *m (COMPUT)* screen saver; **b~schön** *adj* lovely

Bildung [bɪldʊŋ] *f* formation; *(Wissen, Benehmen)* education

Billard ['bɪljart] **(-s, -e)** *nt* billiards *sg;*

~kugel *f* billiard ball

billig ['bɪlɪç] *adj* cheap; *(gerecht)* fair, reasonable; **~en** ['bɪlɪgən] *vt* to approve of

Binde ['bɪndə] *f* bandage; *(Armbinde)* band; *(MED)* sanitary towel; **~gewebe** *nt* connective tissue; **~glied** *nt* connecting link; **~hautentzündung** *f* conjunctivitis; **b~n** *(unreg) vt* to bind, to tie; **~strich** *m* hyphen

Bindfaden ['bɪnt-] *m* string

Bindung *f* bond, tie; *(Skibindung)* binding

binnen ['bɪnən] *präp (+dat od gen)* within; **B~hafen** *m* river port; **B~handel** *m* internal trade

Bio- [bio-] *in zW* bio-; **~chemie** *f* biochemistry; **~grafie** ▲ [-graˈfiː] *f* biography; **~laden** [-'loːgə] **(-n, -n)** *m* wholefood shop; **~loge** [-'loːgə] **(-n, -n)** *m* biologist; **~logie** [-lo'giː] *f* biology; **b~logisch** [-'loːgɪʃ] *adj* biological; **~top** *m od nt* biotope

---
Bioladen

ⓘ *A* **Bioladen** *is a shop specializing in environmentally-friendly products such as phosphate-free washing powders, recycled paper and organically-grown vegetables.*

Birke ['bɪrkə] *f* birch

Birne ['bɪrnə] *f* pear; *(ELEK)* (light) bulb

SCHLÜSSELWORT

bis [bɪs] *präp +akk, adv* **1** *(zeitlich)* till, until; *(bis spätestens)* by; **Sie haben bis Dienstag Zeit** you have until *od* till Tuesday; **bis Dienstag muss es fertig sein** it must be ready by Tuesday; **bis auf weiteres** until further notice; **bis in die Nacht** into the night; **bis bald/gleich** see you later/soon

2 *(räumlich)* (up) to; **ich fahre bis Köln** I'm going to *od* I'm going as far as Cologne; **bis an unser Grundstück** (right *od* up) to our plot; **bis hierher** this far

3 *(bei Zahlen)* up to; **bis zu** up to

4 : bis auf etw *akk (außer)* except sth; *(einschließlich)* including sth

♦ *konj* **1** *(mit Zahlen)* to; **10 bis 20** 10 to 20

2 *(zeitlich)* till, until; **bis es dunkel wird** till

---

od until it gets dark; **von ... bis ...** from ... to ...

Bischof ['bɪʃɔf] (**-s**, **ⁿe**) *m* bishop; **bischöflich** ['bɪʃøːflɪç] *adj* episcopal

bisher [bɪs'heːr] *adv* till now, hitherto; **~ig** *adj* till now

Biskuit [bɪs'kviːt] (**-(e)s**, **-s** *od* **-e**) *m od nt* (fatless) sponge

Biss ▲ [bɪs] (**-es**, **-e**) *m* bite

biss *etc vb siehe* **beißen**

bisschen ▲ ['bɪsçən] *adj*, *adv* bit

Bissen ['bɪsən] (**-s**, **-**) *m* bite, morsel

bissig ['bɪsɪç] *adj* (*Hund*) snappy; (*Bemerkung*) cutting, biting

bist [bɪst] *vb siehe* **sein**

bisweilen [bɪs'vaɪlən] *adv* at times, occasionally

Bitte ['bɪtə] *f* request; **b~** *excl* please; (*wie b~?*) (I beg your) pardon? ♦ *interj* (*als Antwort auf Dank*) you're welcome; **darf ich? – aber b~!** may I? – please do; **b~ schön!** it was a pleasure; **b~n** (*unreg*) *vt, vi*: **b~n (um)** to ask (for); **b~nd** *adj* pleading, imploring

bitter ['bɪtɐ] *adj* bitter; **~böse** *adj* very angry; **B~keit** *f* bitterness; **~lich** *adj* bitter

Blähungen ['blɛːʊŋən] *pl* (*MED*) wind *sg*

blamabel [bla'maːbəl] *adj* disgraceful

Blamage [bla'maːʒə] *f* disgrace

blamieren [bla'miːrən] *vr* to make a fool of o.s., to disgrace o.s. ♦ *vt* to let down, to disgrace

blank [blaŋk] *adj* bright; (*unbedeckt*) bare; (*sauber*) clean, polished; (*umg: ohne Geld*) broke; (*offensichtlich*) blatant

blanko ['blaŋko] *adv* blank; **B~scheck** *m* blank cheque

Blase ['blaːzə] *f* bubble; (*MED*) blister; (*ANAT*) bladder; **~balg(-(e)s, -bälge)** *m* bellows *pl*; **b~n** (*unreg*) *vt, vi* to blow; **~nentzündung** *f* cystitis

Blas- ['blaːs] *zW*: **~instrument** *nt* wind instrument; **~kapelle** *f* brass band

blass ▲ [blas] *adj* pale

Blässe ['blɛsə] (**-**) *f* paleness, pallor

Blatt [blat] (**-(e)s**, **ⁿer**) *nt* leaf; (*von Papier*)

sheet; (*Zeitung*) newspaper; (*KARTEN*) hand

blättern ['blɛtɐn] *vi*: **in etw** *dat* **~** to leaf through sth

Blätterteig *m* flaky *od* puff pastry

blau [blaʊ] *adj* blue; (*umg*) drunk, stoned; (*KOCH*) boiled; (*Auge*) black; **~er Fleck** bruise; **Fahrt ins B~e** mystery tour; **~äugig** *adj* blue-eyed

Blech [blɛç] (**-(e)s**, **-e**) *nt* tin, sheet metal; (*Backblech*) baking tray; **~büchse** *f* tin, can; **~dose** *f* tin, can; **b~en** (*umg*) *vt, vi* to fork out; **~schaden** *m* (*AUT*) damage to bodywork

Blei [blaɪ] (**-(e)s**, **-e**) *nt* lead

Bleibe ['blaɪbə] *f* roof over one's head; **b~n** (*unreg*) *vi* to stay, to remain; **~ lassen** to leave alone; **b~nd** *adj* (*Erinnerung*) lasting; (*Schaden*) permanent

bleich [blaɪç] *adj* faded, pale; **~en** *vt* to bleach

Blei- *zW*: **b~ern** *adj* leaden; **b~frei** *adj* (*Benzin*) lead-free; **~stift** *m* pencil

Blende ['blɛndə] *f* (*PHOT*) aperture; **b~n** *vt* to blind, to dazzle; (*fig*) to hoodwink; **b~nd** (*umg*) *adj* grand; **b~nd aussehen** to look smashing

Blick [blɪk] (**-(e)s**, **-e**) *m* (*kurz*) glance, glimpse; (*Anschauen*) look; (*Aussicht*) view; **b~en** *vi* to look; **sich b~en lassen** to put in an appearance; **~fang** *m* eye-catcher

blieb *etc* [bliːp] *vb siehe* **bleiben**

blind [blɪnt] *adj* blind; (*Glas etc*) dull; **~er Passagier** stowaway; **B~darm** *m* appendix; **B~darmentzündung** *f* appendicitis; **B~enschrift** ['blɪndən-] *f* Braille; **B~heit** *f* blindness; **~lings** *adv* blindly

blink- ['blɪŋk] *zW*: **~en** *vi* to twinkle, to sparkle; (*Licht*) to flash, to signal; (*AUT*) to indicate ♦ *vt* to flash, to signal; **B~er(-s, -)** *m* (*AUT*) indicator; **B~licht** *nt* (*AUT*) indicator; (*an Bahnübergängen usw*) flashing light

blinzeln ['blɪntsəln] *vi* to blink, to wink

Blitz [blɪts] (**-es**, **-e**) *m* (flash of) lightning; **~ableiter** *m* lightning conductor; **b~en** *vi* (*aufleuchten*) to flash, to sparkle; **es b~t**

Rechtschreibreform: ▲ *neue Schreibung* △ *alte Schreibung (auslaufend)*

(MET) there's a flash of lightning; **~licht** nt flashlight; **b~schnell** adj lightning ♦ adv (as) quick as a flash

Block [blɔk] (**-(e)s, ⁻e**) m block; (von Papier) pad; **~ade** [blɔˈkaːdə] f blockade; **~flöte** f recorder; **b~frei** adj (POL) unaligned; **~haus** nt log cabin; **b~ieren** [blɔˈkiːrən] vt to block ♦ vi (Räder) to jam; **~schrift** f block letters pl

blöd [bløːt] adj silly, stupid; **~eln** [ˈbløːdəln] (umg) vi to act the goat (fam), to fool around; **B~sinn** m nonsense; **~sinnig** adj silly, idiotic

blond [blɔnt] adj blond, fair-haired

SCHLÜSSELWORT
---

bloß [bloːs] adj **1** (unbedeckt) bare; (nackt) naked; **mit der bloßen Hand** with one's bare hand; **mit bloßem Auge** with the naked eye

2 (alleinig, nur) mere; **der bloße Gedanke** the very thought; **bloßer Neid** sheer envy ♦ adv only, merely; **lass das bloß!** just don't do that!; **wie ist das bloß passiert?** how on earth did that happen?

Blöße [ˈbløːsə] f bareness; nakedness; (fig) weakness

bloßstellen vt to show up

blühen [ˈblyːən] vi to bloom (lit), to be in bloom; (fig) to flourish; **~d** adj (Pflanze) blooming; (Aussehen) blooming, radiant; (Handel) thriving, booming

Blume [ˈbluːmə] f flower; (von Wein) bouquet

Blumen- zW: **~kohl** m cauliflower; **~topf** m flowerpot; **~zwiebel** f bulb

Bluse [ˈbluːzə] f blouse

Blut [bluːt] (**-(e)s**) nt blood; **b~arm** adj anaemic; (fig) penniless; **b~befleckt** adj bloodstained; **~bild** nt blood count; **~druck** m blood pressure

Blüte [ˈblyːtə] f blossom; (fig) prime

Blut- zW: **b~en** vi to bleed; **~er** m (MED) haemophiliac; **~erguss** ▲ m haemorrhage; (auf Haut) bruise

Blütezeit f flowering period; (fig) prime

Blut- zW: **~gruppe** f blood group; **b~ig** adj bloody; **b~jung** adj very young; **~probe** f blood test; **~spender** m blood donor; **~transfusion** f (MED) blood transfusion; **~ung** f bleeding, haemorrhage; **~vergiftung** f blood poisoning; **~wurst** f black pudding

Bö [bøː] (**-, -en**) f squall

Bock [bɔk] (**-(e)s, ⁻e**) m buck, ram; (Gestell) trestle, support; (SPORT) buck; **~wurst** f type of pork sausage

Boden [ˈboːdən] (**-s, ⁻**) m ground; (Fußboden) floor; (Meeresboden, Fassboden) bottom; (Speicher) attic; **b~los** adj bottomless; (umg) incredible; **~nebel** m ground mist; **~personal** nt (AVIAT) ground staff; **~schätze** pl mineral resources; **~see** m: **der ~see** Lake Constance; **~turnen** nt floor exercises pl

Böe [ˈbøːə] f squall

Bogen [ˈboːgən] (**-s, -**) m (Biegung) curve; (ARCHIT) arch; (Waffe, MUS) bow; (Papier) sheet

Bohne [ˈboːnə] f bean

bohnern vt to wax, to polish

Bohnerwachs nt floor polish

Bohr- [boːr] zW: **b~en** vt to bore; **~er** (**-s, -**) m drill; **~insel** f oil rig; **~maschine** f drill; **~turm** m derrick

Boiler [ˈbɔylər] (**-s, -**) m (hot-water) tank

Boje [ˈboːjə] f buoy

Bolzen [ˈbɔltsən] (**-s, -**) m bolt

bombardieren [bɔmbarˈdiːrən] vt to bombard; (aus der Luft) to bomb

Bombe [ˈbɔmbə] f bomb

Bombenangriff m bombing raid

Bombenerfolg (umg) m smash hit

Bon [bɔŋ] (**-s, -s**) m voucher, chit

Bonbon [bõˈbõː] (**-s, -s**) m od nt sweet

Boot [boːt] (**-(e)s, -e**) nt boat

Bord [bɔrt] (**-(e)s, -e**) m (AVIAT, NAUT) board ♦ nt (Brett) shelf; **an ~** on board

Bordell [bɔrˈdɛl] (**-s, -e**) nt brothel

Bordstein m kerb(stone)

borgen [ˈbɔrgən] vt to borrow; **jdm etw ~** to lend sb sth

borniert [bɔrˈniːrt] adj narrow-minded

Börse ['bœːrzə] f stock exchange; (*Geldbörse*) purse; **~nmakler** m stockbroker

Borte ['bɔrtə] f edging; (*Band*) trimming

bös [bøːs] *adj* = **böse**

bösartig ['bøːzˌartɪç] *adj* malicious

Böschung ['bœʃʊŋ] f slope; (*Uferböschung etc*) embankment

böse ['bøːzə] *adj* bad, evil; (*zornig*) angry

boshaft ['boːshaft] *adj* malicious, spiteful

Bosheit f malice, spite

Bosnien ['bɔsniən] (**-s**) *nt* Bosnia; **~ und Herzegowina** [-hɛrtsəˈgoːvina] *nt* Bosnia (and) Herzegovina

böswillig ['bøːsvɪlɪç] *adj* malicious

bot *etc* [boːt] *vb siehe* **bieten**

Botanik [boˈtaːnɪk] f botany; **botanisch** *adj* botanical

Bot- ['boːt] *zW:* **~e** (**-n, -n**) m messenger; **~schaft** f message, news; (*POL*) embassy; **~schafter** (**-s, -**) m ambassador

Bottich ['bɔtɪç] (**-(e)s, -e**) m vat, tub

Bouillon [buˈljõː] (**-, -s**) f consommé

Bowle ['boːlə] f punch

Box- ['bɔks] *zW:* **b~en** vi to box; **~er** (**-s, -**) m boxer; **~kampf** m boxing match

boykottieren [bɔykɔˈtiːrən] vt to boycott

brach *etc* [braːx] *vb siehe* **brechen**

brachte *etc* ['braxtə] *vb siehe* **bringen**

Branche ['brãːʃə] f line of business

Branchenverzeichnis *nt* Yellow Pages® pl

Brand [brant] (**-(e)s, ⁻e**) m fire; (*MED*) gangrene; **b~en** ['brandən] vi to surge; (*Meer*) to break; **b~marken** vt to brand; (*fig*) to stigmatize; **~salbe** f ointment for burns; **~stifter** [-ʃtɪftər] m arsonist, fire raiser; **~stiftung** f arson; **~ung** f surf

Branntwein ['brantvain] m brandy

Brasilien [braˈziːliən] *nt* Brazil

Brat- ['braːt] *zW:* **~apfel** m baked apple; **b~en** (*unreg*) vt to roast; to fry; **~en** (**-s, -**) m roast, joint; **~hähnchen** *nt* roast chicken; **~huhn** *nt* roast chicken; **~kartoffeln** pl fried od roast potatoes; **~pfanne** f frying pan

Bratsche ['braːtʃə] f viola

Bratspieß m spit

Bratwurst f grilled/fried sausage

Brauch [braux] (**-(e)s, Bräuche**) m custom; **b~bar** *adj* usable, serviceable; (*Person*) capable; **b~en** vt (*bedürfen*) to need; (*müssen*) to have to; (*umg: verwenden*) to use

Braue ['brauə] f brow

brauen ['brauən] vt to brew

Braue'rei f brewery

braun [braun] *adj* brown; (*von Sonne auch*) tanned; **~ gebrannt** tanned

Bräune ['brɔynə] (**-**) f brownness; (*Sonnenbräune*) tan; **b~n** vt to make brown; (*Sonne*) to tan

Brause ['brauzə] f shower bath; (*von Gießkanne*) rose; (*Getränk*) lemonade; **b~n** vi to roar; (*auch vr: duschen*) to take a shower

Braut [braut] (**-, Bräute**) f bride; (*Verlobte*) fiancée

Bräutigam ['brɔytɪgam] (**-s, -e**) m bridegroom; fiancé

Brautpaar *nt* bride and (bride)groom, bridal pair

brav [braːf] *adj* (*artig*) good; (*ehrenhaft*) worthy, honest

bravo ['braːvo] *excl* well done

BRD ['beːʔɛrˈdeː] (**-**) f *abk* = **Bundesrepublik Deutschland**

> BRD

⚫ *The* **BRD** (*Bundesrepublik Deutschland*) *is the official name for the Federal Republic of Germany. It comprises 16* **Länder** (*see* **Land**). *It was formerly the name given to West Germany as opposed to East Germany (the* **DDR**). *The two Germanies were reunited on 3rd October 1990.*

Brech- ['brɛç] *zW:* **~eisen** *nt* crowbar; **b~en** (*unreg*) vt, vi to break; (*Licht*) to refract; (*fig: Mensch*) to crush; (*speien*) to vomit; **~reiz** m nausea, retching

Brei [brai] (**-(e)s, -e**) m (*Masse*) pulp; (*KOCH*) gruel; (*Haferbrei*) porridge

breit [brait] *adj* wide, broad; **sich ~ machen** to spread o.s. out; **B~e** f width; (*bes bei*

Maßangaben) breadth; (*GEOG*) latitude; **~en**
vt: **etw über etw** *akk* **~en** to spread sth
over sth; **B~engrad** *m* degree of latitude;
~treten (*unreg*) (*umg*) *vt* to go on about

Brems- ['brɛms] *zW:* **~belag** *m* brake
lining; **~e** [-zə] *f* brake; (*ZOOL*) horsefly;
b~en [-zən] *vi* to brake ♦ *vt* (*Auto*) to brake;
(*fig*) to slow down; **~flüssigkeit** *f* brake
fluid; **~licht** *nt* brake light; **~pedal** *nt*
brake pedal; **~spur** *f* skid mark(s *pl*); **~weg**
m braking distance

Brenn- ['brɛn] *zW:* **b~bar** *adj* inflammable;
b~en (*unreg*) *vi* to burn, to be on fire;
(*Licht, Kerze etc*) to burn ♦ *vt* (*Holz etc*) to
burn; (*Ziegel, Ton*) to fire; (*Kaffee*) to roast;
darauf b~en, etw zu tun to be dying to
do sth; **~nessel** ▲ *f* stinging nettle;
~punkt *m* (*PHYS*) focal point; (*Mittelpunkt*)
focus; **~stoff** *m* fuel

brenzlig ['brɛntslɪç] *adj* precarious

Bretagne [brə'tanjə] *f:* **die ~** Brittany

Brett [brɛt] (*-(e)s, -er*) *nt* board, plank;
(*Bord*) shelf; (*Spielbrett*) board; **~er** *pl* (*SKI*)
skis; (*THEAT*) boards; **schwarzes ~** notice
board; **~erzaun** *m* wooden fence; **~spiel**
nt board game

Brezel ['bre:tsəl] (*-, -n*) *f* pretzel

brichst *etc* [brɪçst] *vb siehe* **brechen**

Brief [bri:f] (*-(e)s, -e*) *m* letter; **~freund** *m*
penfriend; **~kasten** *m* letterbox; **b~lich**
adj, adv by letter; **~marke** *f* (*postage*)
stamp; **~papier** *nt* notepaper; **~tasche** *f*
wallet; **~träger** *m* postman; **~umschlag**
m envelope; **~waage** *f* letter scales;
~wechsel *m* correspondence

briet *etc* [bri:t] *vb siehe* **braten**

Brikett [bri'kɛt] (*-s, -s*) *nt* briquette

brillant [brɪl'jant] *adj* (*fig*) brilliant; **B~** (*-en,
-en*) *m* brilliant, diamond

Brille ['brɪlə] *f* spectacles *pl*; (*Schutzbrille*)
goggles *pl*; (*Toilettenbrille*) (toilet) seat;
~ngestell *nt* (spectacle) frames

bringen ['brɪŋən] (*unreg*) *vt* to bring;
(*mitnehmen, begleiten*) to take; (*einbringen:
Profit*) to bring in; (*veröffentlichen*) to
publish; (*THEAT, CINE*) to show; (*RADIO, TV*) to
broadcast; (*in einen Zustand versetzen*) to

get; (*umg: tun können*) to manage; **jdn
dazu ~, etw zu tun** to make sb do sth; **jdn
nach Hause ~** to take sb home; **jdn um
etw ~** to make sb lose sth; **jdn auf eine
Idee ~** to give sb an idea

Brise ['bri:zə] *f* breeze

Brit- ['brɪt] *zW:* **~e** *m* Briton; **~in** *f* Briton;
b~isch *adj* British

bröckelig ['brœkəlɪç] *adj* crumbly

Brocken ['brɔkən] (*-s, -*) *m* piece, bit;
(*Felsbrocken*) lump of rock

brodeln ['bro:dəln] *vi* to bubble

Brokkoli ['brɔkoli] *pl* (*BOT*) broccoli

Brombeere ['brɔmbe:rə] *f* blackberry,
bramble (*BRIT*)

Bronchien ['brɔnçiən] *pl* bronchia(l tubes)
pl

Bronchitis [brɔn'çi:tis] (*-*) *f* bronchitis

Bronze ['brõ:sə] *f* bronze

Brosche ['brɔʃə] *f* brooch

Broschüre [brɔ'ʃy:rə] *f* pamphlet

Brot [bro:t] (*-(e)s, -e*) *nt* bread; (*Laib*) loaf

Brötchen ['brø:tçən] *nt* roll

Bruch [brʊx] (*-(e)s, ⁺e*) *m* breakage;
(*zerbrochene Stelle*) break; (*fig*) split, breach;
(*MED: Eingeweidebruch*) rupture, hernia;
(*Beinbruch etc*) fracture; (*MATH*) fraction

brüchig ['brʏçɪç] *adj* brittle, fragile; (*Haus*)
dilapidated

Bruch- *zW:* **~landung** *f* crash landing;
~strich *m* (*MATH*) line; **~stück** *nt*
fragment; **~teil** *m* fraction; **~zahl** [brʊxtsa:l]
f (*MATH*) fraction

Brücke ['brʏkə] *f* bridge; (*Teppich*) rug

Bruder ['bru:dər] (*-s, ⁺*) *m* brother;
brüderlich *adj* brotherly

Brühe ['bry:ə] *f* broth, stock; (*pej*) muck

brüllen ['brʏlən] *vi* to bellow, to roar

brummen ['brʊmən] *vi* (*Bär, Mensch etc*) to
growl; (*Insekt*) to buzz; (*Motoren*) to roar;
(*murren*) to grumble

brünett [bry'nɛt] *adj* brunette, dark-haired

Brunnen ['brʊnən] (*-s, -*) *m* fountain; (*tief*)
well; (*natürlich*) spring

Brust [brʊst] (*-, ⁺e*) *f* breast; (*Männerbrust*)
chest

brüsten ['brʏstən] *vr* to boast

Brust- *zW:* **~kasten** *m* chest;
~schwimmen *nt* breast-stroke
Brüstung ['brʏstʊŋ] *f* parapet
Brut [bruːt] (**-**, **-en**) *f* brood; (*Brüten*)
hatching
brutal [bru'taːl] *adj* brutal
Brutali'tät *f* brutality
brüten ['bryːtən] *vi* (*auch fig*) to brood
Brutkasten *m* incubator
brutto ['brʊto] *adv* gross; **B~einkommen** *nt*
gross salary; **B~gehalt** *nt* gross salary;
B~gewicht *nt* gross weight; **B~lohn** *m*
gross wages *pl*; **B~sozialprodukt** *nt* gross
national product
BSE *f abk* (= *Bovine Spongiforme
Enzephalopathie*) BSE
Bube ['buːbə] (**-n**, **-n**) *m* (*Schurke*) rogue;
(*KARTEN*) jack
Buch [buːx] (**-(e)s**, **ꞋꞋer**) *nt* book; (*COMM*)
account book; **~binder** *m* bookbinder;
~drucker *m* printer
Buche *f* beech tree
buchen *vt* to book; (*Betrag*) to enter
Bücher- ['byːçər] *zW:* **~brett** *nt* book-
helf; **~ei** [-'raɪ] *f* library; **~regal** *nt* book-
shelves *pl*, bookcase; **~schrank** *m* bookcase
Buch- *zW:* **~führung** *f* book-keeping,
accounting; **~halter(in)** (**-s**, **-**) *m(f)* book-
keeper; **~handel** *m* book trade;
~händler(in) *m(f)* bookseller; **~handlung**
f bookshop
Büchse ['bʏksə] *f* tin, can; (*Holzbüchse*) box;
(*Gewehr*) rifle; **~nfleisch** *nt* tinned meat;
~nmilch *f* (*KOCH*) evaporated milk, tinned
milk; **~nöffner** *m* tin *od* can opener
Buchstabe (**-ns**, **-n**) *m* letter (of the
alphabet)
buchstabieren [buːxʃta'biːrən] *vt* to spell
buchstäblich ['buːxʃtɛːplɪç] *adj* literal
Bucht ['bʊxt] (**-**, **-en**) *f* bay
Buchung ['buːxʊŋ] *f* booking; (*COMM*) entry
Buckel ['bʊkəl] (**-s**, **-**) *m* hump
bücken ['bʏkən] *vr* to bend
Bude ['buːdə] *f* booth, stall; (*umg*) digs *pl*
(*BRIT*)
Büfett [by'fɛt] (**-s**, **-s**) *nt* (*Anrichte*) sideboard;

(*Geschirrschrank*) dresser; **kaltes ~** cold
buffet
Büffel ['bʏfəl] (**-s**, **-**) *m* buffalo
Bug [buːk] (**-(e)s**, **-e**) *m* (*NAUT*) bow; (*AVIAT*)
nose
Bügel ['byːgəl] (**-s**, **-**) *m* (*Kleider~*) hanger;
(*Steig~*) stirrup; (*Brillen~*) arm; **~brett** *nt*
ironing board; **~eisen** *nt* iron; **~falte** *f*
crease; **b~frei** *adj* crease-resistant, noniron;
b~n *vt*, *vi* to iron
Bühne ['byːnə] *f* stage; **~nbild** *nt* set,
scenery
Buhruf ['buːruːf] *m* boo
buk *etc* [buːk] *vb siehe* **backen**
Bulgarien [bul'gaːriən] *nt* Bulgaria
Bull- ['bʊl] *zW:* **~auge** *nt* (*NAUT*) porthole;
~dogge *f* bulldog; **~dozer** ['bʊldoːzər] (**-s**,
-) *m* bulldozer; **~e** (**-n**, **-n**) *m* bull
Bumerang ['buːməraŋ] (**-s**, **-e**) *m*
boomerang
Bummel ['bʊməl] (**-s**, **-**) *m* stroll;
(*Schaufensterbummel*) window-shopping;
~ant [-'lant] *m* slowcoach; **~ei** [-'laɪ] *f*
wandering; dawdling; skiving; **b~n** *vi* to
wander, to stroll; (*trödeln*) to dawdle;
(*faulenzen*) to skive, to loaf around; **~streik**
['bʊməlʃtraɪk] *m* go-slow
Bund[1] [bʊnt] (**-(e)s**, **ꞋꞋe**) *m*
(*Freundschaftsbund etc*) bond; (*Organisation*)
union; (*POL*) confederacy; (*Hosenbund,
Rockbund*) waistband
Bund[2] (**-(e)s**, **-e**) *nt* bunch; (*Strohbund*)
bundle
Bündel ['bʏndəl] (**-s**, **-**) *nt* bundle, bale; **b~n**
vt to bundle
Bundes- ['bʊndəs] *in zW* Federal; **~bürger**
m German citizen; **~hauptstadt** *f* Federal
capital; **~kanzler** *m* Federal Chancellor;
~land *nt* Land; **~liga** *f* football league;
~präsident *m* Federal President; **~rat** *m*
upper house of German Parliament;
~regierung *f* Federal government;
~republik *f* Federal Republic (of
Germany); **~staat** *m* Federal state;
~straße *f* Federal road; **~tag** *m* German
Parliament; **~wehr** *f* German Armed Forces
pl; **b~weit** *adj* nationwide

ⓘ The **Bundespräsident** is the head of
state of the Federal Republic of
Germany. He is elected every 5 years - no-
one can be elected more than twice - by the
members of the **Bundesversammlung**, a
body formed especially for this purpose. His
role is to represent Germany at home and
abroad. In Switzerland the
Bundespräsident is the head of the
government, known as the **Bundesrat**.
The **Bundesrat** is the Upper House of the
German Parliament whose 68 members are
nominated by the parliaments of the
Länder. Its most important function is to
approve federal laws concerned with the
jurisdiction of the **Länder**; it can raise
objections to other laws, but can be
outvoted by the **Bundestag**. In Austria the
Länder are also represented in the
Bundesrat.

ⓘ The **Bundestag** is the Lower House of
the German Parliament and is elected by
the people by proportional representation.
There are 672 MPs, half of them elected
directly from the first vote (**Erststimme**),
and half from the regional list of
parliamentary candidates resulting from the
second vote (**Zweitstimme**). The
Bundestag exercises parliamentary control
over the government.

Bündnis ['byntnɪs] (**-ses, -se**) nt alliance
bunt [bʊnt] adj coloured; (gemischt) mixed;
jdm wird es zu ~ it's getting too much for
sb;**B~stift** m coloured pencil, crayon
Burg [bʊrk] (**-, -en**) f castle, fort
Bürge ['byrgə] (**-n, -n**) m guarantor;
b~n für vt to vouch for
Bürger(in) ['byrgər(ɪn)] (**-s, -**) m(f) citizen;
member of the middle class;**~krieg** m civil
war;**b~lich** adj (Rechte) civil; (Klasse)
middle-class; (pej) bourgeois;**~meister** m

mayor; **~recht** nt civil rights pl; **~schaft** f
(Vertretung) City Parliament; **~steig** m
pavement
Bürgschaft f surety; **~ leisten** to give
security
Büro [by'ro:] (**-s, -s**) nt office;
~angestellte(r) f(m) office worker;
~klammer f paper clip;**~kra'tie** f
bureaucracy; b~'kratisch adj bureaucratic;
~schluss ▲ m office closing time
Bursche ['bʊrʃə] (**-n, -n**) m lad, fellow;
(Diener) servant
Bürste ['byrstə] f brush;b~n vt to brush
Bus [bʊs] (**-ses, -se**) m bus;**~bahnhof** m
bus/coach (BRIT) station
Busch [bʊʃ] (**-(e)s, ⁼e**) m bush, shrub
Büschel ['byʃəl] (**-s, -**) nt tuft
buschig adj bushy
Busen ['bu:zən] (**-s, -**) m bosom;
(Meerbusen) inlet, bay
Bushaltestelle f bus stop
Buße ['bu:sə] f penance; (Geld) fine
büßen ['by:sən] vi to do penance, to atone
♦ vt to do penance for, to atone for
Bußgeld ['bu:sgelt] nt fine;**~bescheid** m
notice of payment due (for traffic offence
etc)
Büste ['bystə] f bust;**~nhalter** m bra
Butter ['bʊtər] (**-**) f butter;**~blume** f
buttercup;**~brot** nt (piece of) bread and
butter; (umg) sandwich;**~brotpapier** nt
greaseproof paper;**~dose** f butter dish;
~milch f buttermilk;b~weich ['bʊtərvaɪç]
adj soft as butter; (fig, umg) soft
b. w. abk (= bitte wenden) p.t.o.
bzgl. abk (= bezüglich) re
bzw. abk = **beziehungsweise**

C, c

ca. [ka] abk (= circa) approx.
Cabin Crew [kɛbɪnkru:] f cabin crew
Café [ka'fe:] (**-s, -s**) nt café
Cafeteria [kafete'ri:a] (**-, -s**) f cafeteria
Camcorder (**-s, -**) m camcorder
Camp- ['kɛmp] zW:c~en vi to camp;**~er**

(-s, -) *m* camper; **~ing (-s)** *nt* camping; **~ingführer** *m* camping guide (book); **~ingkocher** *m* camping stove; **~ingplatz** *m* camp(ing) site

CD-Spieler *m* CD (player)

Cello ['tʃɛlo] **(-s, -s** *od* **Celli)** *nt* cello

Celsius ['tsɛlziʊs] **(-)** *nt* centigrade

Cent [sɛnt] **(-s, -s)** *m* cent

Champagner [ʃamˈpanjər] **(-s, -)** *m* champagne

Champignon ['ʃampɪnjõ] **(-s, -s)** *m* button mushroom

Chance ['ʃã:s(ə)] *f* chance, opportunity

Chaos ['ka:ɔs] **(-, -)** *nt* chaos; **chaotisch** [kaˈo:tiʃ] *adj* chaotic

Charakter [kaˈraktər, *pl* karakˈteːrə] **(-s, -e)** *m* character; **c~fest** *adj* of firm character, strong; **c~i'sieren** *vt* to characterize; **c~istisch** [karakteˈrɪstɪʃ] *adj*: **c~istisch (für)** characteristic (of), typical (of); **c~los** *adj* unprincipled; **~losigkeit** *f* lack of principle; **~schwäche** *f* weakness of character; **~stärke** *f* strength of character; **~zug** *m* characteristic, trait

charmant [ʃarˈmant] *adj* charming

Charme [ʃarm] **(-s)** *m* charm

Charterflug ['tʃartərfluːk] *m* charter flight

Chauffeur [ʃɔˈføːr] *m* chauffeur

Chauvinist [ʃoviˈnɪst] *m* chauvinist, jingoist

Chef [ʃɛf] **(-s, -s)** *m* head; (*umg*) boss; **~arzt** *m* senior consultant; **~in** (*umg*) *f* boss

Chemie [çeˈmiː] **(-)** *f* chemistry; **~faser** *f* man-made fibre

Chemikalie [çemiˈkaːliə] *f* chemical

Chemiker ['çeːmikər] **(-s, -)** *m* (industrial) chemist

chemisch ['çeːmɪʃ] *adj* chemical; **~e Reinigung** dry cleaning

Chicorée ['ʃikoreː] **(-s)** *m od f* chicory

Chiffre ['ʃifrə] *f* (*Geheimzeichen*) cipher; (*in Zeitung*) box number

Chile ['tʃiːle] *nt* Chile

Chin- ['çiːn] *zW*: **~a** *nt* China; **~akohl** *m* Chinese leaves; **~ese** [-ˈneːzə] *m* Chinese; **~esin** *f* Chinese; **c~esisch** *adj* Chinese

Chip [tʃɪp] **(-s, -s)** *m* (*Kartoffelchips*) crisp (*BRIT*), chip (*US*); (*COMPUT*) chip; **~karte** *f* smart card

Chirurg [çiˈrʊrg] **(-en, -en)** *m* surgeon; **~ie** [-ˈgiː] *f* surgery; **c~isch** *adj* surgical

Chlor [kloːr] **(-s)** *nt* chlorine; **~o'form (-s)** *nt* chloroform

cholerisch [koˈleːrɪʃ] *adj* choleric

Chor [koːr] **(-(e)s, ⁿe)** *m* choir; (*Musikstück, THEAT*) chorus; **~al** [koˈraːl] **(-s, -äle)** *m* chorale

Choreograf ▲ [koreoˈgraːf] **(-en, -en)** *m* choreographer

Christ [krɪst] **(-en, -en)** *m* Christian; **~baum** *m* Christmas tree; **~entum** *nt* Christianity; **~in** *f* Christian; **~kind** *nt* ≃ Father Christmas; (*Jesus*) baby Jesus; **c~lich** *adj* Christian; **~us (-)** *m* Christ

Chrom [kroːm] **(-s)** *nt* chromium; chrome

Chron- ['kroːn] *zW*: **~ik** *f* chronicle; **c~isch** *adj* chronic; **c~ologisch** [-oˈloːgɪʃ] *adj* chronological

circa ['tsɪrka] *adv* about, approximately

Clown [klaʊn] **(-s, -s)** *m* clown

Cocktail ['kɔkteːl] **(-s, -s)** *m* cocktail

Cola ['koːla] **(-, -s)** *f* Coke ®

Computer [kɔmˈpjuːtər] **(-s, -)** *m* computer; **~spiel** *nt* computer game

Cord [kɔrt] **(-s)** *m* cord, corduroy

Couch [kaʊtʃ] **(-, -es** *od* **-en)** *f* couch

Coupon [kuˈpõː] **(-s, -s)** *m* = **Kupon**

Cousin [kuˈzɛ̃] **(-s, -s)** *m* cousin; **~e** [kuˈziːnə] *f* cousin

Creme [krɛːm] **(-, -s)** *f* cream; (*Schuhcreme*) polish; (*Zahncreme*) paste; (*KOCH*) mousse; **c~farben** *adj* cream(-coloured)

cremig ['kreːmɪç] *adj* creamy

Curry ['kari] **(-s)** *m od nt* curry powder; **~pulver** *nt* curry powder; **~wurst** *f* curried sausage

D, d

da [daː] *adv* **1** (*örtlich*) there; (*hier*) here; **da draußen** out there; **da sein** to be there; **da**

bin ich here I am; **da, wo** where; **ist noch Milch da?** is there any milk left?
2 (*zeitlich*) then; (*folglich*) so
3: da haben wir Glück gehabt we were lucky there; **da kann man nichts machen** nothing can be done about it
♦ *konj* (*weil*) as, since

dabehalten (*unreg*) *vt* to keep
dabei [da'baɪ] *adv* (*räumlich*) close to it; (*noch dazu*) besides; (*zusammen mit*) with them; (*zeitlich*) during this; (*obwohl doch*) but, however; **was ist schon ~?** what of it?; **es ist doch nichts ~, wenn ...** it doesn't matter if ...; **bleiben wir ~** let's leave it at that; **es bleibt ~** that's settled; **das Dumme/Schwierige ~** the stupid/difficult part of it; **er war gerade ~ zu gehen** he was just leaving; **~ sein** (*anwesend*) to be present; (*beteiligt*) to be involved; **~stehen** (*unreg*) *vi* to stand around

Dach [dax] (**-(e)s, ⁻er**) *nt* roof; **~boden** *m* attic, loft; **~decker** (**-s, -**) *m* slater, tiler; **~fenster** *nt* skylight; **~gepäckträger** *m* roof rack; **~luke** *f* skylight; **~pappe** *f* roofing felt; **~rinne** *f* gutter
Dachs [daks] (**-es, -e**) *m* badger
dachte *etc* ['daxtə] *vb siehe* **denken**
Dackel ['dakəl] (**-s, -**) *m* dachshund
dadurch [da'dʊrç] *adv* (*räumlich*) through it; (*durch diesen Umstand*) thereby, in that way; (*deshalb*) because of that, for that reason
♦ *konj*: **~, dass** because
dafür [da'fy:r] *adv* for it; (*anstatt*) instead; **er kann nichts ~** he can't help it; **er ist bekannt ~** he is well-known for that; **was bekomme ich ~?** what will I get for it?

dagegen [da'ge:gən] *adv* against it; (*im Vergleich damit*) in comparison with it; (*bei Tausch*) for it/them ♦ *konj* however; **ich habe nichts ~** I don't mind; **ich war ~** I was against it; **~ kann man nichts tun** one can't do anything about it; **~halten** (*unreg*) *vt* (*vergleichen*) to compare with it; (*entgegnen*) to object to it; **~sprechen** (*unreg*) *vi*: **es spricht nichts ~** there's no reason why not

daheim [da'haɪm] *adv* at home; **D~ (-s)** *nt* home
daher [da'he:r] *adv* (*räumlich*) from there; (*Ursache*) from that ♦ *konj* (*deshalb*) that's why
dahin [da'hɪn] *adv* (*räumlich*) there; (*zeitlich*) then; (*vergangen*) gone; **~ gehend** on this matter; **~'gegen** *konj* on the other hand; **~gestellt** *adv*: **~gestellt bleiben** to remain to be seen; **~gestellt sein lassen** to leave open *od* undecided
dahinten [da'hɪntən] *adv* over there
dahinter [da'hɪntər] *adv* behind it; **~ . kommen** to get to the bottom of it
dalli ['dali] (*umg*) *adv* chop chop
damalig ['da:ma:lɪç] *adj* of that time, then
damals ['da:ma:ls] *adv* at that time, then
Dame ['da:mə] *f* lady; (*SCHACH, KARTEN*) queen; (*Spiel*) draughts *sg*; **~nbinde** *f* sanitary towel *od* napkin (*US*); **d~nhaft** *adj* ladylike; **~ntoilette** *f* ladies' toilet *od* restroom (*US*); **~nwahl** *f* ladies' excuse-me
damit [da'mɪt] *adv* with it; (*begründend*) by that ♦ *konj* in order that, in order to; **was meint er ~?** what does he mean by that?; **genug ~!** that's enough!
dämlich ['dɛ:mlɪç] (*umg*) *adj* silly, stupid
Damm [dam] (**-(e)s, ⁻e**) *m* dyke; (*Staudamm*) dam; (*Hafendamm*) mole; (*Bahndamm, Straßendamm*) embankment
dämmen ['dɛmən] *vt* (*Wasser*) to dam up; (*Schmerzen*) to keep back
dämmer- *zW*: **~ig** *adj* dim, faint; **~n** *vi* (*Tag*) to dawn; (*Abend*) to fall; **D~ung** *f* twilight; (*Morgendämmerung*) dawn; (*Abenddämmerung*) dusk
Dampf [dampf] (**-(e)s, ⁻e**) *m* steam; (*Dunst*) vapour; **d~en** *vi* to steam
dämpfen ['dɛmpfən] *vt* (*KOCH*) to steam; (*bügeln*) to iron with a damp cloth; (*fig*) to dampen, to subdue
Dampf- *zW*: **~schiff** *nt* steamship; **~walze** *f* steamroller
danach [da'na:x] *adv* after that; (*zeitlich*) after that, afterwards; (*gemäß*) accordingly; according to which; according to that; **er sieht ~ aus** he looks it

Däne ['dɛːnə] (**-n, -n**) *m* Dane
daneben [da'neːbən] *adv* beside it; (*im Vergleich*) in comparison; **~benehmen** (*unreg*) *vr* to misbehave; **~gehen** (*unreg*) *vi* to miss; (*Plan*) to fail
Dänemark ['dɛːnəmark] *nt* Denmark; **Dänin** *f* Dane; **dänisch** *adj* Danish
Dank [daŋk] (**-(e)s**) *m* thanks *pl*; **vielen** *od* **schönen ~** many thanks; **jdm ~ sagen** to thank sb; **d~** *präp (+dat od gen)* thanks to; **d~bar** *adj* grateful; (*Aufgabe*) rewarding; **~barkeit** *f* gratitude; **d~e** *excl* thank you, thanks; **d~en** *vi +dat* to thank; **d~enswert** *adj* (*Arbeit*) worthwhile; rewarding; (*Bemühung*) kind; **d~sagen** *vi* to express one's thanks
dann [dan] *adv* then; **~ und wann** now and then
daran [da'ran] *adv* on it; (*stoßen*) against it; **es liegt ~, dass ...** the cause of it is that ...; **gut/schlecht ~ sein** to be well-/badly off; **das Beste/Dümmste ~** the best/stupidest thing about it; **ich war nahe ~ zu ...** I was on the point of ...; **er ist ~ gestorben** he died from it *od* of it; **~gehen** (*unreg*) *vi* to start; **~setzen** *vt* to stake
darauf [da'raʊf] *adv* (*räumlich*) on it; (*zielgerichtet*) towards it; (*danach*) afterwards; **es kommt ganz ~ an, ob ...** it depends whether ...; **die Tage ~** the days following *od* thereafter; **am Tag ~** the next day; **~ folgend** (*Tag, Jahr*) next, following; **~ legen** to lay *od* put on top
daraus [da'raʊs] *adv* from it; **was ist ~ geworden?** what became of it?; **~ geht hervor, dass ...** this means that ...
Darbietung ['daːrbiːtʊŋ] *f* performance
darf *etc* [darf] *vb siehe* **dürfen**
darin [da'rɪn] *adv* in (there), in it
darlegen ['daːrleːgən] *vt* to explain, to expound, to set forth; **Darlegung** *f* explanation
Darleh(e)n (**-s, -**) *nt* loan
Darm [darm] (**-(e)s, ¨e**) *m* intestine; (*Wurstdarm*) skin; **~grippe** *f* (*MED*) gastric influenza *od* flu
darstell- ['daːrʃtɛl] *zW*: **~en** *vt* (*abbilden, bedeuten*) to represent; (*THEAT*) to act; (*beschreiben*) to describe ♦ *vr* to appear to be; **D~er(in)** (**-s, -**) *m(f)* actor (actress); **D~ung** *f* portrayal, depiction
darüber [da'ryːbər] *adv* (*räumlich*) over it, above it; (*fahren*) over it; (*mehr*) more; (*währenddessen*) meanwhile; (*sprechen, streiten*) about it; **~ geht nichts** there's nothing like it
darum [da'rʊm] *adv* (*räumlich*) round it ♦ *konj* that's why; **er bittet ~** he is pleading for it; **es geht ~, dass ...** the thing is that ...; **er würde viel ~ geben, wenn ...** he would give a lot to ...; **ich tue es ~, weil ...** I am doing it because ...
darunter [da'rʊntər] *adv* (*räumlich*) under it; (*dazwischen*) among them; (*weniger*) less; **ein Stockwerk ~** one floor below (it); **was verstehen Sie ~?** what do you understand by that?
das [das] *def art* the ♦ *pron* that
Dasein ['daːzaɪn] (**-s**) *nt* (*Leben*) life; (*Anwesenheit*) presence; (*Bestehen*) existence
da sein ▲ *siehe* **da**
dass ▲ [das] *konj* that
dasselbe [das'zɛlbə] *art, pron* the same
dastehen ['daːʃteːən] (*unreg*) *vi* to stand there
Datei [da'taɪ] *f* file
Daten- ['daːtən] *zW*: **~bank** *f* data base; **~schutz** *m* data protection; **~verarbeitung** *f* data processing
datieren [da'tiːrən] *vt* to date
Dativ ['daːtiːf] (**-s, -e**) *m* dative (case)
Dattel ['datəl] (**-, -n**) *f* date
Datum ['daːtʊm] (**-s, Daten**) *nt* date; **Daten** *pl* (*Angaben*) data *pl*
Dauer ['daʊər] (**-, -n**) *f* duration; (*gewisse Zeitspanne*) length; (*Bestand, Fortbestehen*) permanence; **es war nur von kurzer ~** it didn't last long; **auf die ~** in the long run; (*auf längere Zeit*) indefinitely; **~auftrag** *m* standing order; **d~haft** *adj* lasting, durable; **~karte** *f* season ticket; **~lauf** *m* jog(ging); **d~n** *vi* to last; **es hat sehr lang gedauert, bis er ...** it took him a long time to ...;

d~nd *adj* constant; ~**parkplatz** *m* long-stay car park; ~**welle** *f* perm, permanent wave; ~**wurst** *f* German salami; ~**zustand** *m* permanent condition

Daumen ['daʊmən] (**-s, -**) *m* thumb

Daune ['daʊnə] *f* down; ~**ndecke** *f* down duvet, down quilt

davon [da'fɔn] *adv* of it; (*räumlich*) away; (*weg von*) from; (*Grund*) because of it; **das kommt ~!** that's what you get; **~ abgesehen** apart from that; **~ sprechen/ wissen** to talk/know of *od* about it; **was habe ich ~?** what's the point?; ~**kommen** (*unreg*) *vi* to escape; ~**laufen** (*unreg*) *vi* to run away

davor [da'foːr] *adv* (*räumlich*) in front of it; (*zeitlich*) before (that); **~ warnen** to warn about it

dazu [da'tsuː] *adv* (*legen, stellen*) by it; (*essen, singen*) with it; **und ~ noch** and in addition; **ein Beispiel/seine Gedanken ~** one example for/his thoughts on this; **wie komme ich denn ~?** why should I?; **~ fähig sein** to be capable of it; **sich ~ äußern** to say something on it; ~**gehören** *vi* to belong to it; ~**kommen** (*unreg*) *vi* (*Ereignisse*) to happen too; (*an einen Ort*) to come along

dazwischen [da'tsvɪʃən] *adv* in between; (*räumlich auch*) between (them); (*zusammen mit*) among them; ~**kommen** (*unreg*) *vi* (*hineingeraten*) to get caught in it; **es ist etwas ~gekommen** something cropped up; ~**reden** *vi* (*unterbrechen*) to interrupt; (*sich einmischen*) to interfere; ~**treten** (*unreg*) *vi* to intervene

---
DDR

ℹ️ The **DDR** (*Deutsche Demokratische Republik*) was the name by which the former Communist German Democratic Republic was known. It was founded in 1949 from the Soviet-occupied zone. After the Berlin Wall was built in 1961 it was virtually sealed off from the West. Mass demonstrations and demands for reform forced the opening of the borders in 1989

and the **DDR** merged in 1990 with the **BRD**.

Debatte [de'batə] *f* debate

Deck [dɛk] (**-(e)s, -s** *od* **-e**) *nt* deck; **an ~ gehen** to go on deck

Decke *f* cover; (*Bettdecke*) blanket; (*Tischdecke*) tablecloth; (*Zimmerdecke*) ceiling; **unter einer ~ stecken** to be hand in glove; ~**l** (**-s, -**) *m* lid; **d~n** *vt* to cover ♦ *vr* to coincide

Deckung *f* (*Schützen*) covering; (*Schutz*) cover; (*SPORT*) defence; (*Übereinstimmen*) agreement

Defekt [de'fɛkt] (**-(e)s, -e**) *m* fault, defect; **d~** *adj* faulty

defensiv [defen'siːf] *adj* defensive

definieren [defi'niːrən] *vt* to define; **Definition** [definitsi'oːn] *f* definition

Defizit ['deːfitsɪt] (**-s, -e**) *nt* deficit

deftig ['dɛftɪç] *adj* (*Essen*) large; (*Witz*) coarse

Degen ['deːgən] (**-s, -**) *m* sword

degenerieren [degene'riːrən] *vi* to degenerate

dehnbar ['deːnbaːr] *adj* elastic; (*fig: Begriff*) loose

dehnen *vt, vr* to stretch

Deich [daɪç] (**-(e)s, -e**) *m* dyke, dike

deichseln (*umg*) *vt* (*fig*) to wangle

dein(e) [daɪn(ə)] *adj* your; ~**e(r, s)** *pron* yours; ~**er** (*gen von du*) *pron* of you; ~**erseits** *adv* on your part; ~**esgleichen** *pron* people like you; ~**etwegen** *adv* (*für dich*) for your sake; (*wegen dir*) on your account; ~**etwillen** *adv*: **um ~etwillen = deinetwegen**; ~**ige** *pron*: **der/die/das ~ige** *od* **D~ige** yours

Deklination [deklinatsi'oːn] *f* declension

deklinieren [dekli'niːrən] *vt* to decline

Dekolleté, Dekolletee ▲ [dekɔl'teː] (**-s, -s**) *nt* low neckline

Deko- [deko] *zW*: ~**rateur** [-ra'tøːr] *m* window dresser; ~**ration** [-ratsi'oːn] *f* decoration; (*in Laden*) window dressing; **d~rativ** [-ra'tiːf] *adj* decorative; **d~rieren** [-'riːrən] *vt* to decorate; (*Schaufenster*) to dress

---
Spelling Reform: ▲ *new spelling* △ *old spelling (to be phased out)*

Delegation [delegatsi'o:n] *f* delegation
delegieren [dele'gi:rən] *vt*: ~ **an** +*akk* (*Aufgaben*) to delegate to
Delfin ▲ [dɛl'fi:n] **(-s, -e)** *m* dolphin
delikat [deli'ka:t] *adj* (*zart, heikel*) delicate; (*köstlich*) delicious
Delikatesse [delika'tɛsə] *f* delicacy; **~n** *pl* (*Feinkost*) delicatessen food; **~ngeschäft** *nt* delicatessen
Delikt [de'lɪkt] **(-(e)s, -e)** *nt* (*JUR*) offence
Delle ['dɛlə] (*umg*) *f* dent
Delphin △ [dɛl'fi:n] **(-s, -e)** *m* = **Delfin**
dem [de(:)m] *art dat von* **der**
Demagoge [dema'go:gə] **(-n, -n)** *m* demagogue
dementieren [demɛn'ti:rən] *vt* to deny
dem- *zW*: **~gemäß** *adv* accordingly; **~nach** *adv* accordingly; **~nächst** *adv* shortly
Demokrat [demo'kra:t] **(-en, -en)** *m* democrat; **~ie** [-'ti:] *f* democracy; **d~isch** *adj* democratic; **d~isieren** [-i'zi:rən] *vt* to democratize
demolieren [demo'li:rən] *vt* to demolish
Demon- [demon] *zW*: **~strant(in)** [-'strant(ɪn)] *m(f)* demonstrator; **~stration** [-stratsi'o:n] *f* demonstration; **d~strativ** [-stra'ti:f] *adj* demonstrative; (*Protest*) pointed; **d~strieren** [-'stri:rən] *vt, vi* to demonstrate
Demoskopie [demosko'pi:] *f* public opinion research
Demut ['de:mu:t] **(-)** *f* humility
demütig ['de:my:tɪç] *adj* humble; **~en** ['de:my:tɪgən] *vt* to humiliate; **D~ung** *f* humiliation
demzufolge ['de:mtsu'fɔlgə] *adv* accordingly
den [de(:)n] *art akk von* **der**
denen ['de:nən] *pron dat pl von* **der**; **die**; **das**
Denk- ['dɛŋk] *zW*: **d~bar** *adj* conceivable; **~en** **(-s)** *nt* thinking; **d~en** (*unreg*) *vt, vi* to think; **d~faul** *adj* lazy; **~fehler** *m* logical error; **~mal** **(-s, -¤er)** *nt* monument; **~malschutz** *m* protection of historical monuments; **unter ~malschutz stehen** to be classified as a historical monument; **d~würdig** *adj* memorable; **~zettel** *m*: **jdm**

einen ~zettel verpassen to teach sb a lesson
denn [dɛn] *konj* for ♦ *adv* then; (*nach Komparativ*) than; **warum ~?** why?
dennoch ['dɛnɔx] *konj* nevertheless
Denunziant [denʊntsi'ant(ɪn)] *m* informer
Deodorant [deodo'rant] **(-s, -s od -e)** *nt* deodorant
Deponie [depo'ni:] *f* dump
deponieren [depo'ni:rən] *vt* (*COMM*) to deposit
Depot [de'po:] **(-s, -s)** *nt* warehouse; (*Busdepot, EISENB*) depot; (*Bankdepot*) strongroom, safe (*US*)
Depression [depresi'o:n] *f* depression; **depres'siv** *adj* depressive
deprimieren [depri'mi:rən] *vt* to depress

┌─────────────────────────┐
│ *SCHLÜSSELWORT* │
└─────────────────────────┘

der [de(:)r] (*f* **die**, *nt* **das**, *gen* **des, der, des**, *dat* **dem, der, dem**, *akk* **den, die, das**, *pl* **die**) *def art* the; **der Rhein** the Rhine; **der Klaus** (*umg*) Klaus; **die Frau** (*im Allgemeinen*) women; **der Tod/das Leben** death/life; **der Fuß des Berges** the foot of the hill; **gib es der Frau** give it to the woman; **er hat sich die Hand verletzt** he has hurt his hand
♦ *relativ pron* (*bei Menschen*) who, that; (*bei Tieren, Sachen*) which, that; **der Mann, den ich gesehen habe** the man who *od* whom *od* that I saw
♦ *demonstrativ pron* he/she/it; (*jener, dieser*) that; (*pl*) those; **der/die war es** it was him/her; **der mit der Brille** the one with glasses; **ich will den (da)** I want that one

derart ['de:r|a:rt] *adv* so; (*solcher Art*) such; **~ig** *adj* such, this sort of
derb [dɛrp] *adj* sturdy; (*Kost*) solid; (*grob*) coarse
der- *zW*: '~'**gleichen** *pron* such; '~**jenige** *pron* he; she; it; the one (who); that (which); '~'**maßen** *adv* to such an extent, so; ~'**selbe** *art, pron* the same; '~'**weil(en)** *adv* in the meantime; '~'**zeitig** *adj* present, current; (*damalig*) then

Rechtschreibreform: ▲ *neue Schreibung* △ *alte Schreibung (auslaufend)*

des [dɛs] *art gen von* **der**

desertieren [dezɛr'tiːrən] *vi* to desert

desgleichen ['dɛs'glaɪçən] *adv* likewise, also

deshalb ['dɛs'halp] *adv* therefore, that's why

Desinfektion [dɛzɪnfɛktsi'oːn] *f* disinfection; **~smittel** *nt* disinfectant

desinfizieren [dɛzɪnfi'tsiːrən] *vt* to disinfect

dessen ['dɛsən] *pron gen von* **der**; **das**; **~ ungeachtet** nevertheless, regardless

Dessert [dɛ'seːr] **(-s, -s)** *nt* dessert

destillieren [dɛstɪ'liːrən] *vt* to distil

desto ['dɛsto] *adv* all the more, so much the; **~ besser** all the better

deswegen ['dɛs've:gən] *konj* therefore, hence

Detail [de'taɪ] **(-s, -s)** *nt* detail

Detektiv [detɛk'tiːf] **(-s, -e)** *m* detective

deut- ['dɔʏt] *zW*: **~en** *vt* to interpret, to explain ♦ *vi*: **~en (auf** +*akk***)** to point (to *od* at); **~lich** *adj* clear; (*Unterschied*) distinct; **D~lichkeit** *f* clarity; distinctness

Deutsch [dɔʏtʃ] *nt* German

deutsch *adj* German; **auf D~** in German; **D~e Demokratische Republik** (*HIST*) German Democratic Republic, East Germany; **~es Beefsteak** ≃ hamburger; **D~e(r)** *mf* German; **ich bin D~er** I am German; **D~land** *nt* Germany

Devise [de'viːzə] *f* motto, device; **~n** *pl* (*FIN*) foreign currency, foreign exchange

Dezember [de'tsɛmbər] **(-s, -)** *m* December

dezent [de'tsɛnt] *adj* discreet

dezimal [detsi'maːl] *adj* decimal; **D~system** *nt* decimal system

d. h. *abk* (= *das heißt*) i.e.

Dia ['diːa] **(-s, -s)** *nt* (*PHOT*) slide, transparency

Diabetes [dia'beːtɛs] **(-, -)** *m* (*MED*) diabetes

Diagnose [dia'gnoːzə] *f* diagnosis

diagonal [diago'naːl] *adj* diagonal

Dialekt [dia'lɛkt] **(-(e)s, -e)** *m* dialect; **d~isch** *adj* dialectal; (*Logik*) dialectical

Dialog [dia'loːk] **(-(e)s, -e)** *m* dialogue

Diamant [dia'mant] *m* diamond

Diaprojektor ['diːaprojɛktɔr] *m* slide projector

Diät [di'ɛːt] **(-, -en)** *f* diet

dich [dɪç] (*akk von du*) *pron* you; yourself

dicht [dɪçt] *adj* dense; (*Nebel*) thick; (*Gewebe*) close; (*undurchlässig*) (water)tight; (*fig*) concise ♦ *adv*: **~ an/bei** close to; **~ bevölkert** densely *od* heavily populated; **D~e** *f* density; thickness; closeness; (water)tightness; (*fig*) conciseness

dichten *vt* (*dicht machen*) to make watertight, to seal; (*NAUT*) to caulk; (*LITER*) to compose, to write ♦ *vi* to compose, to write

Dichter(in) **(-s, -)** *m(f)* poet; (*Autor*) writer; **d~isch** *adj* poetical

dichthalten (*unreg*) (*umg*) *vi* to keep one's mouth shut

Dichtung *f* (*TECH*) washer; (*AUT*) gasket; (*Gedichte*) poetry; (*Prosa*) (piece of) writing

dick [dɪk] *adj* thick; (*fett*) fat; **durch ~ und dünn** through thick and thin; **D~darm** *m* (*ANAT*) colon; **D~e** *f* thickness; fatness; **~flüssig** *adj* viscous; **D~icht** **(-s, -e)** *nt* thicket; **D~kopf** *m* mule; **D~milch** *f* soured milk

die [diː] *def art siehe* **der**

Dieb(in) [diːp, 'diːbɪn] **(-(e)s, -e)** *m(f)* thief; **d~isch** *adj* thieving; (*umg*) immense; **~stahl** **(-(e)s, ⁿe)** *m* theft; **~stahlversicherung** *f* insurance against theft

Diele ['diːlə] *f* (*Brett*) board; (*Flur*) hall, lobby

dienen ['diːnən] *vi*: **(jdm) ~** to serve (sb)

Diener **(-s, -)** *m* servant; **~in** *f* (maid)servant; **~schaft** *f* servants *pl*

Dienst [diːnst] **(-(e)s, -e)** *m* service; **außer ~** retired; **~ haben** to be on duty; **~ habend** (*Arzt*) on duty

Dienstag ['diːnstaːk] *m* Tuesday; **d~s** *adv* on Tuesdays

Dienst- *zW*: **~bote** *m* servant; **~geheimnis** *nt* official secret; **~gespräch** *nt* business call; **~leistung** *f* service; **d~lich** *adj* official; **~mädchen** *nt* (house)maid; **~reise** *f* business trip; **~stelle** *f* office; **~vorschrift** *f* official regulations *pl*; **~weg** *m* official channels *pl*; **~zeit** *f* working hours *pl*; (*MIL*) period of service

Spelling Reform: ▲ *new spelling* △ *old spelling (to be phased out)*

dies [di:s] *pron (demonstrativ: sg)* this; (: *pl*) these; **~bezüglich** *adj (Frage)* on this matter; **~e(r, s)** ['di:zə(r, s)] *pron* this (one)

Diesel ['di:zəl] *m (Kraftstoff)* diesel

dieselbe [di:'zɛlbə] *pron, art* the same

Dieselmotor *m* diesel engine

diesig ['di:zɪç] *adj* drizzly

dies- *zW:* **~jährig** *adj* this year's; **~mal** *adv* this time; **~seits** *präp +gen* on this side; **D~seits** (-) *nt* this life

Dietrich ['di:trɪç] (-s, -e) *m* picklock

diffamieren [dɪfa'mi:rən] *(pej) vt* to defame

Differenz [dɪfa'rɛnts] (-, -en) *f (Unterschied)* difference; **~en** *pl (Meinungsverschiedenheit)* difference (of opinion); **d~ieren** *vt* to make distinctions in; **d~iert** *adj (Mensch etc)* complex

differenzial ▲ [dɪferɛntsia:l] *adj* differential; **D~rechnung** *f* differential calculus

digital [digi'ta:l] *adj* digital; **D~fernsehen** *f* digital TV

Dikt- [dɪkt] *zW:* **~afon**, **~aphon** [-a'fo:n] *nt* dictaphone; **~at** [-'ta:t] (-(e)s, -e) *nt* dictation; **~ator** [-'ta:tɔr] *m* dictator; **d~atorisch** [-a'to:rɪʃ] *adj* dictatorial; **~atur** [-a'tu:r] *f* dictatorship; **d~ieren** [-'ti:rən] *vt* to dictate

Dilemma [di'lema] (-s, *od* -ta) *nt* dilemma

Dilettant [dile'tant] *m* dilettante, amateur; **d~isch** *adj* amateurish, dilettante

Dimension [dimɛnzi'o:n] *f* dimension

DIN *f abk (= Deutsche Industrie-Norm)* German Industrial Standard

Ding [dɪŋ] (-(e)s, -e) *nt* thing, object; **d~lich** *adj* real, concrete; **~s(bums)** ['dɪŋks(bums)] (-) *(umg) m* thingummybob

Diplom [di'plo:m] (-(e)s, -e) *nt* diploma, certificate; **~at** [-'ma:t] (-en, -en) *m* diplomat; **~atie** [-a'ti:] *f* diplomacy; **d~atisch** [-'ma:tɪʃ] *adj* diplomatic; **~ingenieur** *m* qualified engineer

dir [di:r] *(dat von* **du***) pron* (to) you

direkt [di'rɛkt] *adj* direct; **D~flug** *m* direct flight; **D~or** *m* director; *(SCH)* principal, headmaster; **D~übertragung** *f* live broadcast

Dirigent [diri'gɛnt(ɪn)] *m* conductor

dirigieren [diri'gi:rən] *vt* to direct; *(MUS)* to conduct

Diskette [dɪs'kɛtə] *f* diskette, floppy disk

Diskont [dɪs'kɔnt] (-s, -e) *m* discount; **~satz** *m* rate of discount

Diskothek [dɪsko'te:k] (-, -en) *f* disco(theque)

diskret [dɪs'kre:t] *adj* discreet; **D~ion** *f* discretion

diskriminieren [dɪskrimi'ni:rən] *vt* to discriminate against

Diskussion [dɪskusi'o:n] *f* discussion; debate; **zur ~ stehen** to be under discussion

diskutieren [dɪsku'ti:rən] *vt, vi* to discuss; to debate

Distanz [dɪs'tants] *f* distance; **distan'zieren** *vr:* **sich von jdm/etw d~ieren** to distance o.s. from sb/sth

Distel ['dɪstəl] (-, -n) *f* thistle

Disziplin [dɪstsi'pli:n] *f* discipline

Dividende [divi'dɛndə] *f* dividend

dividieren [divi'di:rən] *vt:* **(durch etw) ~** to divide (by sth)

DM [de:'|ɛm] *abk (HIST = Deutsche Mark)* German Mark

D-Mark ['de:mark] *f (HIST)* D Mark, German Mark

SCHLÜSSELWORT

doch [dɔx] *adv* 1 *(dennoch)* after all; *(sowieso)* anyway; **er kam doch noch** he came after all; **du weißt es ja doch besser** you know better than I do anyway; **und doch ...** and yet ...

2 *(als bejahende Antwort)* yes I do/it does *etc*; **das ist nicht wahr - doch!** that's not true - yes it is!

3 *(auffordernd):* **komm doch** do come; **lass ihn doch** just leave him; **nicht doch!** oh no!

4: **sie ist doch noch so jung** but she's still so young; **Sie wissen doch, wie das ist** you know how it is (, don't you?); **wenn doch** if only

♦ *konj (aber)* but; *(trotzdem)* all the same;

---

und doch hat er es getan but still he did it

Docht [dɔxt] **(-(e)s, -e)** *m* wick

Dock [dɔk] **(-s, -s** *od* **-e)** *nt* dock

Dogge ['dɔgə] *f* bulldog

Dogma ['dɔgma] **(-s, -men)** *nt* dogma; **d~tisch** *adj* dogmatic

Doktor ['dɔktɔr, *pl* -'to:rən] **(-s, -en)** *m* doctor

Dokument [doku'mɛnt] *nt* document

Dokumentar- [dokumɛn'ta:r] *zW:* **~bericht** *m* documentary; **~film** *m* documentary (film); **d~isch** *adj* documentary

Dolch [dɔlç] **(-(e)s, -e)** *m* dagger

dolmetschen ['dɔlmɛtʃən] *vt, vi* to interpret; **Dolmetscher(in)** **(-s, -)** *m(f)* interpreter

Dom [do:m] **(-(e)s, -e)** *m* cathedral

dominieren [domi'ni:rən] *vt* to dominate ♦ *vi* to predominate

Donau ['do:nau] *f* Danube

Donner ['dɔnər] **(-s, -)** *m* thunder; **d~n** *vi unpers* to thunder

Donnerstag ['dɔnərsta:k] *m* Thursday

doof [do:f] (*umg*) *adj* daft, stupid

Doppel ['dɔpəl] **(-s, -)** *nt* duplicate; (*SPORT*) doubles; **~bett** *nt* double bed; **d~deutig** *adj* ambiguous; **~fenster** *nt* double glazing; **~gänger** **(-s, -)** *m* double; **~punkt** *m* colon; **~stecker** *m* two-way adaptor; **d~t** *adj* double; **in d~ter Ausführung** in duplicate; **~verdiener** *m* person with two incomes; (*pl: Paar*) two-income family; **~zentner** *m* 100 kilograms; **~zimmer** *nt* double room

Dorf [dɔrf] **(-(e)s, ⸚er)** *nt* village; **~bewohner** *m* villager

Dorn [dɔrn] **(-(e)s, -en)** *m* (*BOT*) thorn; **d~ig** *adj* thorny

Dörrobst ['dœro:pst] *nt* dried fruit

Dorsch [dɔrʃ] **(-(e)s, -e)** *m* cod

dort [dɔrt] *adv* there; **~ drüben** over there; **~her** *adv* from there; **~hin** *adv* (to) there; **~ig** *adj* of that place; in that town

Dose ['do:zə] *f* box; (*Blechdose*) tin, can

Dosen *pl von* **Dose; Dosis**

Dosenöffner *m* tin *od* can opener

Dosis ['do:zis] **(-, Dosen)** *f* dose

Dotter ['dɔtər] **(-s, -)** *m* (egg) yolk

Drache ['draxə] **(-n, -n)** *m* (*Tier*) dragon

Drachen **(-s, -)** *m* kite; **~fliegen** **(-s)** *nt* hang-gliding

Draht [dra:t] **(-(e)s, ⸚e)** *m* wire; **auf ~ sein** to be on the ball; **d~ig** *adj* (*Mann*) wiry; **~seil** *nt* cable; **~seilbahn** *f* cable railway, funicular

Drama ['dra:ma] **(-s, Dramen)** *nt* drama, play; **~tiker** [-'ma:tikər] **(-s, -)** *m* dramatist; **d~tisch** [-'ma:tiʃ] *adj* dramatic

dran [dran] (*umg*) *adv:* **jetzt bin ich ~!** it's my turn now; *siehe* **daran**

Drang [draŋ] **(-(e)s, ⸚e)** *m* (*Trieb*): **~ (nach)** impulse (for), urge (for), desire (for); (*Druck*) pressure

drängeln ['drɛŋəln] *vt, vi* to push, to jostle

drängen ['drɛŋən] *vt* (*schieben*) to push, to press; (*antreiben*) to urge ♦ *vi* (*eilig sein*) to be urgent; (*Zeit*) to press; **auf etw** *akk* **~** to press for sth

drastisch ['drastiʃ] *adj* drastic

drauf [drauf] (*umg*) *adv* = **darauf;** **D~gänger** **(-s, -)** *m* daredevil

draußen ['drausən] *adv* outside

Dreck [drɛk] **(-(e)s)** *m* mud, dirt; **d~ig** *adj* dirty, filthy

Dreh- ['dre:] *zW:* **~arbeiten** *pl* (*CINE*) shooting *sg;* **~bank** *f* lathe; **~buch** *nt* (*CINE*) script; **d~en** *vt* to turn, to rotate; (*Zigaretten*) to roll; (*Film*) to shoot ♦ *vi* to turn, to rotate ♦ *vr* to turn; (*handeln von*): **es d~t sich um ...** it's about ...; **~orgel** *f* barrel organ; **~tür** *f* revolving door; **~ung** *f* (*Rotation*) rotation; (*Umdrehung, Wendung*) turn; **~zahl** *f* rate of revolutions; **~zahlmesser** *m* rev(olution) counter

drei [drai] *num* three; **~ viertel** three quarters; **D~eck** *nt* triangle; **~eckig** *adj* triangular; **~einhalb** *num* three and a half; **~erlei** *adj inv* of three kinds; **~fach** *adj* triple, treble ♦ *adv* three times; **~hundert** *num* three hundred; **D~'königsfest** *nt* Epiphany; **~mal** *adv* three times; **~malig** *adj* three times

dreinreden ['draɪnre:dən] *vi*: **jdm ~** (*dazwischenreden*) to interrupt sb; (*sich einmischen*) to interfere with sb

Dreirad *nt* tricycle

dreißig ['draɪsɪç] *num* thirty

dreist [draɪst] *adj* bold, audacious

drei- *zW*: **~viertel** △ *num siehe* **drei**; **D~viertelstunde** *f* three-quarters of an hour; **~zehn** *num* thirteen

dreschen ['drɛʃən] (*unreg*) *vt* (*Getreide*) to thresh; (*umg: verprügeln*) to beat up

dressieren [drɛ'si:rən] *vt* to train

drillen ['drɪlən] *vt* (*bohren*) to drill, to bore; (*MIL*) to drill; (*fig*) to train

Drilling *m* triplet

drin [drɪn] (*umg*) *adv* = **darin**

dringen ['drɪŋən] (*unreg*) *vi* (*Wasser, Licht, Kälte*): **~ (durch/in** +*akk*) to penetrate (through/into); **auf etw** *akk* **~** to insist on sth

dringend ['drɪŋənt] *adj* urgent

Dringlichkeit *f* urgency

drinnen ['drɪnən] *adv* inside, indoors

dritte(r, s) [drɪtə(r, s)] *adj* third; **D~ Welt** Third World; **D~s Reich** Third Reich; **D~l** (**-s, -**) *nt* third; **~ns** *adv* thirdly

DRK [de:ʔɛr'ka:] *nt abk* (= *Deutsches Rotes Kreuz*) German Red Cross

droben ['dro:bən] *adv* above, up there

Droge ['dro:gə] *f* drug

drogen *zW*: **~abhängig** *adj* addicted to drugs; **D~händler** *m* drug pedlar, pusher

Drogerie [drogə'ri:] *f* chemist's shop

Drogerie

ℹ️ The **Drogerie** as opposed to the **Apotheke** sells medicines not requiring a prescription. It tends to be cheaper and also sells cosmetics, perfume and toiletries.

Drogist [dro'gɪst] *m* pharmacist, chemist

drohen ['dro:ən] *vi*: (**jdm**) **~** to threaten (sb)

dröhnen ['drø:nən] *vi* (*Motor*) to roar; (*Stimme, Musik*) to ring, to resound

Drohung ['dro:ʊŋ] *f* threat

drollig ['drɔlɪç] *adj* droll

Drossel ['drɔsəl] (**-, -n**) *f* thrush

drüben ['dry:bən] *adv* over there, on the other side

drüber ['dry:bər] (*umg*) *adv* = **darüber**

Druck [drʊk] (**-(e)s, -e**) *m* (*PHYS: Zwang*) pressure; (*TYP: Vorgang*) printing; (: *Produkt*) print; (*fig: Belastung*) burden, weight; **~buchstabe** *m* block letter

drücken ['drʏkən] *vt* (*Knopf, Hand*) to press; (*zu eng sein*) to pinch; (*fig: Preise*) to keep down; (: *belasten*) to oppress, to weigh down ♦ *vi* to press; to pinch ♦ *vr*: **sich vor etw** *dat* **~** to get out of (doing) sth; **~d** *adj* oppressive

Drucker (**-s, -**) *m* printer

Drücker (**-s, -**) *m* button; (*Türdrücker*) handle; (*Gewehrdrücker*) trigger

Druck- *zW*: **~erei** *f* printing works, press; **~erschwärze** *f* printer's ink; **~fehler** *m* misprint; **~knopf** *m* press stud, snap fastener; **~sache** *f* printed matter; **~schrift** *f* block *od* printed letters *pl*

drum [drʊm] (*umg*) *adv* = **darum**

drunten ['drʊntən] *adv* below, down there

Drüse ['dry:zə] *f* gland

Dschungel ['dʒʊŋəl] (**-s, -**) *m* jungle

du [du:] (*nom*) *pron* you; **~ sagen** = **duzen**

Dübel ['dy:bəl] (**-s, -**) *m* Rawlplug ®

ducken ['dʊkən] *vt* (*Kopf, Person*) to duck; (*fig*) to take down a peg or two ♦ *vr* to duck

Duckmäuser ['dʊkmɔyzər] (**-s, -**) *m* yes man

Dudelsack ['du:dəlzak] *m* bagpipes *pl*

Duell [du'ɛl] (**-s, -e**) *nt* duel

Duft [dʊft] (**-(e)s, ⁺e**) *m* scent, odour; **d~en** *vi* to smell, to be fragrant; **d~ig** *adj* (*Stoff, Kleid*) delicate, diaphanous

dulden ['dʊldən] *vt* to suffer; (*zulassen*) to tolerate ♦ *vi* to suffer

dumm [dʊm] *adj* stupid; (*ärgerlich*) annoying; **der D~e sein** to be the loser; **~erweise** *adv* stupidly; **D~heit** *f* stupidity; (*Tat*) blunder, stupid mistake; **D~kopf** *m* blockhead

dumpf [dʊmpf] *adj* (*Ton*) hollow, dull; (*Luft*)

musty; (*Erinnerung, Schmerz*) vague

Düne ['dy:nə] *f* dune

düngen ['dyŋən] *vt* to manure

Dünger (**-s, -**) *m* dung, manure; (*künstlich*) fertilizer

dunkel ['dʊŋkəl] *adj* dark; (*Stimme*) deep; (*Ahnung*) vague; (*rätselhaft*) obscure; (*verdächtig*) dubious, shady; **im D~n tappen** (*fig*) to grope in the dark

Dunkel- *zW:* **~heit** *f* darkness; (*fig*) obscurity; **~kammer** *f* (*PHOT*) darkroom; **d~n** *vi unpers* to grow dark; **~ziffer** *f* estimated number of unreported cases

dünn [dyn] *adj* thin; **~flüssig** *adj* watery, thin

Dunst [dʊnst] (**-es, ⁺e**) *m* vapour; (*Wetter*) haze

dünsten ['dynstən] *vt* to steam

dunstig ['dʊnstɪç] *adj* vaporous; (*Wetter*) hazy, misty

Duplikat [dupli'ka:t] (**-(e)s, -e**) *nt* duplicate

Dur [du:r] (**-, -**) *nt* (*MUS*) major

SCHLÜSSELWORT

---

durch [dʊrç] *präp +akk* **1** (*hindurch*) through; **durch den Urwald** through the jungle; **durch die ganze Welt reisen** to travel all over the world

2 (*mittels*) through, by (means of); (*aufgrund*) due to, owing to; **Tod durch Herzschlag/den Strang** death from a heart attack/by hanging; **durch die Post** by post; **durch seine Bemühungen** through his efforts

♦ *adv* **1** (*hindurch*) through; **die ganze Nacht durch** all through the night; **den Sommer durch** during the summer; **8 Uhr durch** past 8 o'clock; **durch und durch** completely

2 (*durchgebraten etc*): (**gut**) **durch** well-done

---

durch- *zW:* **~arbeiten** *vt, vi* to work through ♦ *vr* to work one's way through; **~'aus** *adv* completely; (*unbedingt*) definitely; **~aus nicht** absolutely not

Durchblick ['dʊrçblɪk] *m* view; (*fig*) comprehension; **d~en** *vi* to look through;

(*umg: verstehen*): (**bei etw**) **d~en** to understand (sth); **etw d~en lassen** (*fig*) to hint at sth

durchbrechen ['dʊrçbrɛçən] (*unreg*) *vt, vi* to break

durch'brechen [dʊrç'brɛçən] (*unreg*) *vt insep* (*Schranken*) to break through; (*Schallmauer*) to break; (*Gewohnheit*) to break free from

durchbrennen ['dʊrçbrɛnən] (*unreg*) *vi* (*Draht, Sicherung*) to burn through; (*umg*) to run away

durchbringen (*unreg*) *vt* (*Kranken*) to pull through; (*umg: Familie*) to support; (*durchsetzen: Antrag, Kandidat*) to get through; (*vergeuden: Geld*) to get through, to squander

Durchbruch ['dʊrçbrʊx] *m* (*Öffnung*) opening; (*MIL*) breach; (*von Gefühlen etc*) eruption; (*der Zähne*) cutting; (*fig*) breakthrough; **zum ~ kommen** to break through

durch- *zW:* **~dacht** [-'daxt] *adj* well thought-out; **~'denken** (*unreg*) *vt* to think out; **~drehen** *vt* (*Fleisch*) to mince ♦ *vi* (*umg*) to crack up

durcheinander [dʊrçʔaɪ'nandər] *adv* in a mess, in confusion; (*umg: verwirrt*) confused; **~ bringen** to mess up; (*verwirren*) to confuse; **~ reden** to talk at the same time; **D~** (**-s**) *nt* (*Verwirrung*) confusion; (*Unordnung*) mess

durch- *zW:* **~fahren** (*unreg*) *vi* (*~ Tunnel usw*) to drive through; (*ohne Unterbrechung*) to drive straight through; (*ohne anzuhalten*): **der Zug fährt bis Hamburg ~** the train runs direct to Hamburg; (*ohne Umsteigen*): **können wir ~fahren?** can we go direct?, can we go non-stop?; **D~fahrt** *f* transit; (*Verkehr*) thoroughfare; **D~fall** *m* (*MED*) diarrhoea; **~fallen** (*unreg*) *vi* to fall through; (*in Prüfung*) to fail; **~finden** (*unreg*) *vr* to find one's way through; **~fragen** *vr* to find one's way by asking

durchführ- ['dʊrçfy:r] *zW:* **~bar** *adj* feasible, practicable; **~en** *vt* to carry out; **D~ung** *f* execution, performance

---

Spelling Reform: ▲ *new spelling* △ *old spelling (to be phased out)*

Durchgang ['dʊrçgaŋ] *m* passage(way); (*bei Produktion, Versuch*) run; (*SPORT*) round; (*bei Wahl*) ballot; **„~ verboten"** "no thoroughfare"

Durchgangsverkehr *m* through traffic

durchgefroren ['dʊrçgəfro:rən] *adj* (*Mensch*) frozen stiff

durchgehen ['dʊrçge:ən] (*unreg*) *vt* (*behandeln*) to go over ♦ *vi* to go through; (*ausreißen: Pferd*) to break loose; (*Mensch*) to run away; **mein Temperament ging mit mir durch** my temper got the better of me; **jdm etw ~ lassen** to let sb get away with sth; **~d** *adj* (*Zug*) through; (*Öffnungszeiten*) continuous

durch- *zW:* **~greifen** (*unreg*) *vi* to take strong action; **~halten** (*unreg*) *vi* to last out ♦ *vt* to keep up; **~kommen** (*unreg*) *vi* to get through; (*überleben*) to pull through; **~'kreuzen** *vt insep* to thwart, to frustrate; **~lassen** (*unreg*) *vt* (*Person*) to let through; (*Wasser*) to let in; **~lesen** (*unreg*) *vt* to read through; **~'leuchten** *vt insep* to X-ray; **~machen** *vt* to go through; **die Nacht ~machen** to make a night of it

Durchmesser (**-s, -**) *m* diameter

durch- *zW:* **~'nässen** *vt insep* to soak (through); **~nehmen** (*unreg*) *vt* to go over; **~nummerieren** ▲ *vt* to number consecutively; **~queren** [dʊrç'kve:rən] *vt insep* to cross; **D~reise** *f* transit; **auf der D~reise** passing through; (*Güter*) in transit; **~ringen** (*unreg*) *vr* to reach a decision after a long struggle

durchs [dʊrçs] = **durch das**

Durchsage ['dʊrçza:gə] *f* intercom *od* radio announcement

durchschauen ['dʊrçʃauən] *vi* to look *od* see through; (*Person, Lüge*) to see through

durchscheinen ['dʊrçʃaɪnən] (*unreg*) *vi* to shine through; **~d** *adj* translucent

Durchschlag ['dʊrçʃla:k] *m* (*Doppel*) carbon copy; (*Sieb*) strainer; **d~en** [-gən] (*unreg*) *vt* (*entzweischlagen*) to split (in two); (*sieben*) to sieve ♦ *vi* (*zum Vorschein kommen*) to emerge, to come out ♦ *vr* to

get by

durchschlagend *adj* resounding

durchschneiden ['dʊrçʃnaɪdən] (*unreg*) *vt* to cut through

Durchschnitt ['dʊrçʃnɪt] *m* (*Mittelwert*) average; **über/unter dem ~** above/below average; **im ~** on average; **d~lich** *adj* average ♦ *adv* on average

Durchschnittswert *m* average

durch- *zW:* **D~schrift** *f* copy; **~sehen** (*unreg*) *vt* to look through; **~setzen** *vt* to enforce ♦ *vr* (*Erfolg haben*) to succeed; (*sich behaupten*) to get one's way; **seinen Kopf ~setzen** to get one's way; **~'setzen** *vt insep* to mix

Durchsicht ['dʊrçzɪçt] *f* looking through, checking; **d~ig** *adj* transparent

durch- *zW:* **~sprechen** (*unreg*) *vt* to talk over; **'~stehen** (*unreg*) *vt* to live through; **~stellen** *vt* (*an Telefon*) to put through; **~stöbern** (*auch untr*) *vt* (*Kisten*) to rummage through, to rifle through; (*Haus, Wohnung*) to ransack; **'~streichen** (*unreg*) *vt* to cross out; **~'suchen** *vt insep* to search; **D~'suchung** *f* search; **~'wachsen** *adj* (*Speck*) streaky; (*fig: mittelmäßig*) so-so; **D~wahl** *f* (*TEL*) direct dialling; **~weg** *adv* throughout, completely; **~ziehen** (*unreg*) *vt* (*Faden*) to draw through ♦ *vi* to pass through; **D~zug** *m* (*Luft*) draught; (*von Truppen, Vögeln*) passage

---
SCHLÜSSELWORT
---

dürfen ['dʏrfən] (*unreg*) *vi* **1** (*Erlaubnis haben*) to be allowed to; **ich darf das** I'm allowed to (do that); **darf ich?** may I?; **darf ich ins Kino?** can *od* may I go to the cinema?; **es darf geraucht werden** you may smoke
2 (*in Verneinungen*): **er darf das nicht** he's not allowed to (do that); **das darf nicht geschehen** that must not happen; **da darf sie sich nicht wundern** that shouldn't surprise her
3 (*in Höflichkeitsformeln*): **darf ich Sie bitten, das zu tun?** may *od* could I ask you to do that?; **was darf es sein?** what can I do for you?

4 (*können*): **das dürfen Sie mir glauben**
you can believe me
5 (*Möglichkeit*): **das dürfte genug sein** that
should be enough; **es dürfte Ihnen
bekannt sein, dass ...** as you will
probably know ...

dürftig ['dʏrftɪç] *adj* (*ärmlich*) needy, poor;
(*unzulänglich*) inadequate
dürr [dʏr] *adj* dried-up; (*Land*) arid; (*mager*)
skinny, gaunt; **D~e** *f* aridity; (*Zeit*) drought;
(*Magerkeit*) skinniness
Durst [dʊrst] **(-(e)s)** *m* thirst; **~ haben** to be
thirsty; **d~ig** *adj* thirsty
Dusche ['duʃə] *f* shower; **d~en** *vi, vr* to
have a shower
Düse ['dyːzə] *f* nozzle; (*Flugzeugdüse*) jet
Düsen- *zW*: **~antrieb** *m* jet propulsion;
~flugzeug *nt* jet (plane); **~jäger** *m* jet
fighter
Dussel ['dʊsəl] **(-s, -)** (*umg*) *m* twit
düster ['dyːstər] *adj* dark; (*Gedanken,
Zukunft*) gloomy
Dutzend ['dʊtsənt] **(-s, -e)** *nt* dozen; **~(e)** *od*
d~(e) Mal(e) a dozen times
duzen ['duːtsən] *vt*: **(jdn) ~** to use the
familiar form of address "du" (to *od* with
sb)

┌─────────┐
│ **duzen** │
└─────────┘

*There are two different forms of address
in Germany: du and Sie. **Duzen** means
addressing someone as 'du' - used with
children, family and close friends - and
siezen means addressing someone as 'Sie' -
used for all grown-ups and older teenagers.
Students almost always use 'du' to each
other.*

Dynamik [dy'naːmɪk] *f* (*PHYS*) dynamics *sg*;
(*fig: Schwung*) momentum; (*von Mensch*)
dynamism; **dynamisch** *adj* (*auch fig*)
dynamic
Dynamit [dyna'miːt] **(-s)** *nt* dynamite
Dynamo [dy'naːmo] **(-s, -s)** *m* dynamo
DZ *nt abk* = **Doppelzimmer**
D-Zug ['deːtsuːk] *m* through train

E, e

Ebbe ['ɛbə] *f* low tide
eben ['eːbən] *adj* level, flat; (*glatt*) smooth
♦ *adv* just; (*bestätigend*) exactly; **~
deswegen** just because of that; **~bürtig**
adj: **jdm ~bürtig sein** to be sb's equal;
E~e *f* plain; (*fig*) level; **~falls** *adv* likewise;
~so *adv* just as
Eber ['eːbər] **(-s, -)** *m* boar
ebnen ['eːbnən] *vt* to level
Echo ['ɛço] **(-s, -s)** *nt* echo
echt [ɛçt] *adj* genuine; (*typisch*) typical;
E~heit *f* genuineness
Eck- ['ɛk] *zW*: **~ball** *m* corner (kick); **~e** *f*
corner; (*MATH*) angle; **e~ig** *adj* angular;
~zahn *m* eye tooth
ECU [e'kyː] **(-, -s)** *m* (*FIN*) ECU
edel ['eːdəl] *adj* noble; **E~metall** *nt* rare
metal; **E~stahl** *m* high-grade steel;
E~stein *m* precious stone
EDV [eːdeː'faʊ] **(-)** *f abk* (= *elektronische
Datenverarbeitung*) electronic data
processing
Efeu ['eːfɔy] **(-s)** *m* ivy
Effekt [ɛ'fɛkt] **(-s, -e)** *m* effect
Effekten [ɛ'fɛktən] *pl* stocks
effektiv [ɛfɛk'tiːf] *adj* effective, actual
EG ['eː'geː] *f abk* (= *Europäische Gemeinschaft*)
EC
egal [e'gaːl] *adj* all the same
Ego- [e:go] *zW*: **~ismus** [-'ɪsmʊs] *m*
selfishness, egoism; **~ist** [-'ɪst] *m* egoist;
e~istisch *adj* selfish, egoistic
Ehe ['eːə] *f* marriage
ehe *konj* before
Ehe- *zW*: **~beratung** *f* marriage guidance
(counselling); **~bruch** *m* adultery; **~frau** *f*
married woman; wife; **~leute** *pl* married
people; **e~lich** *adj* matrimonial; (*Kind*)
legitimate
ehemalig *adj* former
ehemals *adv* formerly
Ehe- *zW*: **~mann** *m* married man; husband;
~paar *nt* married couple

eher ['eːɐ] *adv (früher)* sooner; *(lieber)* rather, sooner; *(mehr)* more

Ehe- *zW:* **~ring** *m* wedding ring; **~schließung** *f* marriage ceremony

eheste(r, s) ['eːəstə(r, s)] *adj (früheste)* first, earliest; **am ~n** *(liebsten)* soonest; *(meist)* most; *(wahrscheinlichst)* most probably

Ehr- [eːr] *zW:* **e~bar** *adj* honourable, respectable; **~e** *f* honour; **e~en** *vt* to honour

Ehren- ['eːrən] *zW:* **e~amtlich** *adj* honorary; **~gast** *m* guest of honour; **e~haft** *adj* honourable; **~platz** *m* place of honour *od (US)* honor; **~runde** *f* lap of honour; **~sache** *f* point of honour; **e~voll** *adj* honourable; **~wort** *nt* word of honour

Ehr- *zW:* **~furcht** *f* awe, deep respect; **e~fürchtig** *adj* reverent; **~gefühl** *nt* sense of honour; **~geiz** *m* ambition; **e~geizig** *adj* ambitious; **e~lich** *adj* honest; **~lichkeit** *f* honesty; **e~los** *adj* dishonourable; **~ung** *f* honour(ing); **e~würdig** *adj* venerable

Ei [ai] *(-(e)s, -er)* *nt* egg

Eich- *zW:* **~e** ['aiçə] *f* oak (tree); **~l** *(-, -n)* *f* acorn; **~hörnchen** *nt* squirrel

Eichmaß *nt* standard

Eid [ait] *(-(e)s, -e)* *m* oath

Eidechse ['aidɛksə] *f* lizard

eidesstattlich *adj:* **~e Erklärung** affidavit

Eidgenosse *m* Swiss

Eier- *zW:* **~becher** *m* eggcup; **~kuchen** *m* omelette; pancake; **~likör** *m* advocaat; **~schale** *f* eggshell; **~stock** *m* ovary; **~uhr** *f* egg timer

Eifer ['aifər] *(-s)* *m* zeal, enthusiasm; **~sucht** *f* jealousy; **e~süchtig** *adj:* **e~süchtig (auf +akk)** jealous (of)

eifrig ['aifrɪç] *adj* zealous, enthusiastic

Eigelb ['aigɛlp] *(-(e)s, -)* *nt* egg yolk

eigen ['aigən] *adj* own; *(~artig)* peculiar; **mit der/dem ihm ~en ...** with that ... peculiar to him; **sich** *dat* **etw zu E~ machen** to make sth one's own; **E~art** *f* peculiarity; **~artig** *adj* peculiar; characteristic; **E~bedarf** *m:* **zum E~bedarf** for (one's own) personal use/domestic requirements; **der Vermieter machte E~bedarf geltend**

the landlord showed he needed the house/flat for himself; **~händig** *adj* with one's own hand; **E~heim** *nt* owner-occupied house; **E~heit** *f* peculiarity; **~mächtig** *adj* high-handed; **E~name** *m* proper name; **~s** *adv* expressly, on purpose; **E~schaft** *f* quality, property, attribute; **E~sinn** *m* obstinacy; **~sinnig** *adj* obstinate; **~tlich** *adj* actual, real ♦ *adv* actually, really; **E~tor** *nt* own goal; **E~tum** *nt* property; **E~tümer(in)** *(-s, -)* *m(f)* owner, proprietor; **~tümlich** *adj* peculiar; **E~tümlichkeit** *f* peculiarity; **E~tumswohnung** *f* freehold flat

eignen ['aignən] *vr* to be suited; **Eignung** *f* suitability

Eil- [ail] *zW:* **~bote** *m* courier; **~brief** *m* express letter; **~e** *f* haste; **es hat keine ~e** there's no hurry; **e~en** *vi (Mensch)* to hurry; *(dringend sein)* to be urgent; **e~ends** *adv* hastily, hurriedly; **~gut** *nt* express goods *pl*, fast freight *(US)*; **e~ig** *adj* hasty, hurried; *(dringlich)* urgent; **es e~ig haben** to be in a hurry; **~zug** *m* semi-fast train, limited stop train

Eimer ['aimər] *(-s, -)* *m* bucket, pail

ein [ain] *adv:* **nicht ~ noch aus wissen** not to know what to do

ein(e) ['ain(ə)] *num* one ♦ *indef art* a, an

einander [ai'nandər] *pron* one another, each other

einarbeiten ['ain|arbaitən] *vt* to train ♦ *vr:* **sich in etw** *akk* **~** to familiarize o.s. with sth

einatmen ['ain|aːtmən] *vt, vi* to inhale, to breathe in

Einbahnstraße ['ainbaːnʃtraːsə] *f* one-way street

Einband ['ainbant] *m* binding, cover

einbauen ['ainbauən] *vt* to build in; *(Motor)* to install, to fit

Einbaumöbel *pl* built-in furniture *sg*

einbegriffen ['ainbəgrifən] *adj* included

einberufen ['ainbəruːfən] *(unreg)* *vt* to convene; *(MIL)* to call up

Einbettzimmer *nt* single room

einbeziehen ['ainbətsiːən] *(unreg)* *vt* to

include

einbiegen ['aɪnbiːgən] (unreg) vi to turn

einbilden ['aɪnbɪldən] vt: **sich** dat **etw ~** to imagine sth

Einbildung f imagination; (Dünkel) conceit; **~skraft** f imagination

Einblick ['aɪnblɪk] m insight

einbrechen ['aɪnbrɛçən] (unreg) vi (in Haus) to break in; (Nacht) to fall; (Winter) to set in; (durchbrechen) to break; **~ in** +akk (MIL) to invade

Einbrecher (-s, -) m burglar

einbringen ['aɪnbrɪŋən] (unreg) vt to bring in; (Geld, Vorteil) to yield; (mitbringen) to contribute

Einbruch ['aɪnbrʊx] m (Hauseinbruch) break-in, burglary; (Eindringen) invasion; (des Winters) onset; (Durchbrechen) break; (MET) approach; (MIL) penetration; **(bei / vor) ~ der Nacht** at/before nightfall; **e~sicher** adj burglar-proof

einbürgern ['aɪnbʏrgərn] vt to naturalize ♦ vr to become adopted

einbüßen ['aɪnbyːsən] vt to lose, to forfeit

einchecken ['aɪntʃɛkən] vt, vi to check in

eincremen ['aɪnkreːmən] vt to put cream on

eindecken ['aɪndɛkən] vr: **sich (mit etw) ~** to lay in stocks (of sth); to stock up (with sth)

eindeutig ['aɪndɔʏtɪç] adj unequivocal

eindringen ['aɪndrɪŋən] (unreg) vi: **~ (in** +akk) to force one's way in(to); (in Haus) to break in(to); (in Land) to invade; (Gas, Wasser) to penetrate; **(auf jdn) ~** (mit Bitten) to pester (sb)

eindringlich adj forcible, urgent

Eindringling m intruder

Eindruck ['aɪndrʊk] m impression

eindrücken ['aɪndrʏkən] vt to press in

eindrucksvoll adj impressive

eine(r, s) pron one; (jemand) someone

eineiig ['aɪn|aɪɪç] adj (Zwillinge) identical

eineinhalb ['aɪn|aɪn'halp] num one and a half

einengen ['aɪn|ɛŋən] vt to confine, to restrict

einer- ['aɪnər] zW: **'E~'lei** (-s) nt sameness; **'~'lei** adj (gleichartig) the same kind of; **es ist mir ~lei** it is all the same to me; **~seits** adv on the one hand

einfach ['aɪnfax] adj simple; (nicht mehrfach) single ♦ adv simply; **E~heit** f simplicity

einfädeln ['aɪnfɛːdəln] vt (Nadel, Faden) to thread; (fig) to contrive

einfahren ['aɪnfaːrən] (unreg) vt to bring in; (Barriere) to knock down; (Auto) to run in ♦ vi to drive in; (Zug) to pull in; (MIN) to go down

Einfahrt f (Vorgang) driving in; pulling in; (MIN) descent; (Ort) entrance

Einfall ['aɪnfal] m (Idee) idea, notion; (Lichteinfall) incidence; (MIL) raid; **e~en** (unreg) vi (Licht) to fall; (MIL) to raid; (einstürzen) to fall in, to collapse; (einstimmen): **(in etw** akk) **e~en** to join in (with sth); **etw fällt jdm ein** sth occurs to sb; **das fällt mir gar nicht ein** I wouldn't dream of it; **sich** dat **etw e~en lassen** to have a good idea

einfältig ['aɪnfɛltɪç] adj simple(-minded)

Einfamilienhaus [aɪnfaˈmiːliənhaʊs] nt detached house

einfarbig ['aɪnfarbɪç] adj all one colour; (Stoff etc) self-coloured

einfetten ['aɪnfɛtən] vt to grease

einfließen ['aɪnfliːsən] (unreg) vi to flow in

einflößen ['aɪnfløːsən] vt: **jdm etw ~** to give sb sth; (fig) to instil sth in sb

Einfluss ▲ ['aɪnflʊs] m influence; **~bereich** m sphere of influence

einförmig ['aɪnfœrmɪç] adj uniform; **E~keit** f uniformity

einfrieren ['aɪnfriːrən] (unreg) vi to freeze (up) ♦ vt to freeze

einfügen ['aɪnfyːgən] vt to fit in; (zusätzlich) to add

Einfuhr ['aɪnfuːr] (-) f import; **~beschränkung** f import restrictions pl; **~bestimmungen** pl import regulations

einführen ['aɪnfyːrən] vt to bring in; (Mensch, Sitten) to introduce; (Ware) to import

Einführung f introduction

Eingabe ['aɪngaːbə] f petition; (*COMPUT*) input

Eingang ['aɪngaŋ] m entrance; (*COMM*: Ankunft) arrival; (*Erhalt*) receipt

eingeben ['aɪngeːbən] (*unreg*) vt (*Arznei*) to give; (*Daten etc*) to enter

eingebildet ['aɪngəbɪldət] adj imaginary; (*eitel*) conceited

Eingeborene(r) ['aɪngəboːrənə(r)] f(m) native

Eingebung f inspiration

eingefleischt ['aɪngəflaɪʃt] adj (*Gewohnheit, Vorurteile*) deep-rooted

eingehen ['aɪngeːən] (*unreg*) vi (*Aufnahme finden*) to come in; (*Sendung, Geld*) to be received; (*Tier, Pflanze*) to die; (*Firma*) to fold; (*schrumpfen*) to shrink ♦ vt to enter into; (*Wette*) to make; **auf etw** akk **~** to go into sth; **auf jdn ~** to respond to sb; **jdm ~** (*verständlich sein*) to be comprehensible to sb; **~d** adj exhaustive, thorough

Eingemachte(s) ['aɪngəma:xtə(s)] nt preserves pl

eingenommen ['aɪngənɔmən] adj: **~ (von)** fond (of), partial (to); **~ (gegen)** prejudiced (against)

eingeschrieben ['aɪngəʃriːbən] adj registered

eingespielt ['aɪngəʃpiːlt] adj: **aufeinander ~ sein** to be in tune with each other

Eingeständnis ['aɪngəʃtɛntnɪs] (**-ses, -se**) nt admission, confession

eingestehen ['aɪngəʃteːən] (*unreg*) vt to confess

eingestellt ['aɪngəʃtɛlt] adj: **auf etw ~ sein** to be prepared for sth

eingetragen ['aɪngətraːgən] adj (*COMM*) registered

Eingeweide ['aɪngəvaɪdə] (**-s, -**) nt innards pl, intestines pl

Eingeweihte(r) ['aɪngəvaɪtə(r)] f(m) initiate

eingewöhnen ['aɪngəvøːnən] vr: **sich ~ in** +akk to settle (down) in

eingleisig ['aɪnglaɪzɪç] adj single-track

eingreifen ['aɪngraɪfən] (*unreg*) vi to intervene, to interfere; (*Zahnrad*) to mesh

Eingriff ['aɪngrɪf] m intervention, interference; (*Operation*) operation

einhaken ['aɪnha:kən] vt to hook in ♦ vr: **sich bei jdm ~** to link arms with sb ♦ vi (*sich einmischen*) to intervene

Einhalt ['aɪnhalt] m: **~ gebieten** +dat to put a stop to; **e~en** (*unreg*) vt (*Regel*) to keep ♦ vi to stop

einhändigen ['aɪnhɛndɪgən] vt to hand in

einhängen ['aɪnhɛŋən] vt to hang; (*Telefon*) to hang up ♦ vi (*TEL*) to hang up; **sich bei jdm ~** to link arms with sb

einheimisch ['aɪnhaɪmɪʃ] adj native; **E~e(r)** f(m) local

Einheit ['aɪnhaɪt] f unity; (*Maß, MIL*) unit; **e~lich** adj uniform; **~spreis** m standard price

einholen ['aɪnhoːlən] vt (*Tau*) to haul in; (*Fahne, Segel*) to lower; (*Vorsprung aufholen*) to catch up with; (*Verspätung*) to make up; (*Rat, Erlaubnis*) to ask ♦ vi (*einkaufen*) to shop

einhüllen ['aɪnhYlən] vt to wrap up

einhundert ['aɪn'hʊndərt] num one hundred, a hundred

einig ['aɪnɪç] adj (*vereint*) united; **~ gehen** to agree; **sich** dat **~ sein** to be in agreement; **~ werden** to agree

einige(r, s) ['aɪnɪgə(r, s)] adj, pron some ♦ pl some; (*mehrere*) several; **~ Mal** a few times

einigen vt to unite ♦ vr: **sich ~ (auf** +akk**)** to agree (on)

einigermaßen adv somewhat; (*leidlich*) reasonably

einig- zW: **E~keit** f unity; (*Übereinstimmung*) agreement; **E~ung** f agreement; (*Vereinigung*) unification

einkalkulieren ['aɪnkalkuliːrən] vt to take into account, to allow for

Einkauf ['aɪnkaʊf] m purchase; **e~en** vt to buy ♦ vi to shop; **e~en gehen** to go shopping

Einkaufs- zW: **~bummel** m shopping spree; **~korb** m shopping basket; **~wagen** m shopping trolley; **~zentrum** nt shopping centre

einklammern ['aɪnklamərn] vt to put in brackets, to bracket

Einklang ['aɪnklaŋ] *m* harmony

einklemmen ['aɪnklɛmən] *vt* to jam

einkochen ['aɪnkɔxən] *vt* to boil down; (*Obst*) to preserve, to bottle

Einkommen ['aɪnkɔmən] (**-s, -**) *nt* income; ~(**s**)**steuer** *f* income tax

Einkünfte ['aɪnkʏnftə] *pl* income *sg*, revenue *sg*

einladen ['aɪnlaːdən] (*unreg*) *vt* (*Person*) to invite; (*Gegenstände*) to load; **jdn ins Kino** ~ to take sb to the cinema

Einladung *f* invitation

Einlage ['aɪnlaːɡə] *f* (*Programm~*) interlude; (*Spar~*) deposit; (*Schuh~*) insole; (*Fußstütze*) support; (*Zahn~*) temporary filling; (*KOCH*) noodles *pl*, vegetables *pl etc* in soup

einlagern ['aɪnlaːɡərn] *vt* to store

Einlass ▲ ['aɪnlas] (**-es, ⁻e**) *m* (*Zutritt*) admission

einlassen ['aɪnlasən] (*unreg*) *vt* to let in; (*einsetzen*) to set in ♦ *vr*: **sich mit jdm / auf etw** *akk* ~ to get involved with sb/sth

Einlauf ['aɪnlaʊf] *m* arrival; (*von Pferden*) finish; (*MED*) enema; **e~en** (*unreg*) *vi* to arrive, to come in; (*in Hafen*) to enter; (*SPORT*) to finish; (*Wasser*) to run in; (*Stoff*) to shrink ♦ *vt* (*Schuhe*) to break in ♦ *vr* (*SPORT*) to warm up; (*Motor, Maschine*) to run in; **jdm das Haus e~en** to invade sb's house

einleben ['aɪnleːbən] *vr* to settle down

einlegen ['aɪnleːɡən] *vt* (*einfügen: Blatt, Sohle*) to insert; (*KOCH*) to pickle; (*Pause*) to have; (*Protest*) to make; (*Veto*) to use; (*Berufung*) to lodge; (*AUT: Gang*) to engage

einleiten ['aɪnlaɪtən] *vt* to introduce, to start; (*Geburt*) to induce; **Einleitung** *f* introduction; induction

einleuchten ['aɪnlɔʏçtən] *vi*: (**jdm**) ~ to be clear *od* evident (to sb); ~**d** *adj* clear

einliefern ['aɪnliːfərn] *vt*: ~ (**in** +*akk*) to take (into)

Einlieferungsschein *m* certificate of posting

Einliegerwohnung ['aɪnliːɡərvoːnʊŋ] *f* self-contained flat; (*für Eltern, Großeltern*) granny flat

einloggen ['aɪnlɔɡən] *vi* (*COMPUT*) to log on

einlösen ['aɪnløːzən] *vt* (*Scheck*) to cash; (*Schuldschein, Pfand*) to redeem; (*Versprechen*) to keep

einmachen ['aɪnmaxən] *vt* to preserve

einmal ['aɪnmaːl] *adv* once; (*erstens*) first; (*zukünftig*) sometime; **nehmen wir ~ an** just let's suppose; **noch ~** once more; **nicht** ~ not even; **auf ~** all at once; **es war ~** once upon a time there was/were; **E~'eins** *nt* multiplication tables *pl*; ~**ig** *adj* unique; (*einmal erforderlich*) single; (*prima*) fantastic

Einmarsch ['aɪnmarʃ] *m* entry; (*MIL*) invasion; **e~ieren** *vi* to march in

einmischen ['aɪnmɪʃən] *vr*: **sich ~ (in** +*akk*) to interfere (with)

einmütig ['aɪnmyːtɪç] *adj* unanimous

Einnahme ['aɪnaːmə] *f* (*von Medizin*) taking; (*MIL*) capture, taking; ~**n** *pl* (*Geld*) takings, revenue *sg*; ~**quelle** *f* source of income

einnehmen ['aɪnneːmən] (*unreg*) *vt* to take; (*Stellung, Raum*) to take up; ~ **für/gegen** to persuade in favour of/against; ~**d** *adj* charming

einordnen ['aɪnɔrdnən] *vt* to arrange, to fit in ♦ *vr* to adapt; (*AUT*) to get into lane

einpacken ['aɪnpakən] *vt* to pack (up)

einparken ['aɪnparkən] *vt* to park

einpendeln ['aɪnpɛndəln] *vr* to even out

einpflanzen ['aɪnpflantsən] *vt* to plant; (*MED*) to implant

einplanen ['aɪnplaːnən] *vt* to plan for

einprägen ['aɪnprɛːɡən] *vt* to impress, to imprint; (*beibringen*): (**jdm**) ~ to impress (on sb); **sich** *dat* **etw** ~ to memorize sth

einrahmen ['aɪnraːmən] *vt* to frame

einräumen ['aɪnrɔʏmən] *vt* (*ordnend*) to put away; (*überlassen: Platz*) to give up; (*zugestehen*) to admit, to concede

einreden ['aɪnreːdən] *vt*: **jdm/sich etw** ~ to talk sb/o.s. into believing sth

einreiben ['aɪnraɪbən] (*unreg*) *vt* to rub in

einreichen ['aɪnraɪçən] *vt* to hand in; (*Antrag*) to submit

Einreise ['aɪnraɪzə] *f* entry;

Spelling Reform: ▲ *new spelling* △ *old spelling (to be phased out)*

~**bestimmungen** pl entry regulations;
~**erlaubnis** f entry permit;
~**genehmigung** f entry permit; e~**n** vi:
(in ein Land) e~n to enter (a country)
einrichten ['aɪnrɪçtən] vt (Haus) to furnish;
(schaffen) to establish, to set up;
(arrangieren) to arrange; (möglich machen)
to manage ♦ vr (in Haus) to furnish one's
house; **sich ~ (auf +akk)** (sich vorbereiten) to
prepare o.s. (for); (sich anpassen) to adapt
(to)
Einrichtung f (Wohnungseinrichtung)
furnishings pl; (öffentliche Anstalt)
organization; (Dienste) service
einrosten ['aɪnrɔstən] vi to get rusty
einrücken ['aɪnrʏkən] vi (MIL: in Land) to
move in
Eins [aɪns] (-, -en) f one; e~ num one; **es ist
mir alles e~** it's all one to me
einsam ['aɪnzaːm] adj lonely, solitary;
E~keit f loneliness, solitude
einsammeln ['aɪnzaməln] vt to collect
Einsatz ['aɪnzats] m (Teil) inset; (an Kleid)
insertion; (Verwendung) use, employment;
(Spieleinsatz) stake; (Risiko) risk; (MIL)
operation; (MUS) entry; **im ~** in action;
e~**bereit** adj ready for action
einschalten ['aɪnʃaltən] vt (einfügen) to
insert; (Pause) to make; (ELEK) to switch on;
(Anwalt) to bring in ♦ vr (dazwischentreten)
to intervene
einschärfen ['aɪnʃɛrfən] vt: **jdm etw ~** to
impress sth (up)on sb
einschätzen ['aɪnʃɛtsən] vt to estimate, to
assess ♦ vr to rate o.s.
einschenken ['aɪnʃɛŋkən] vt to pour out
einschicken ['aɪnʃɪkən] vt to send in
einschl. abk (= einschließlich) incl.
einschlafen ['aɪnʃlaːfən] (unreg) vi to fall
asleep, to go to sleep
einschläfernd ['aɪnʃlɛːfərnt] adj (MED)
soporific; (langweilig) boring; (Stimme)
lulling
Einschlag ['aɪnʃlaːk] m impact; (fig:
Beimischung) touch, hint; e~**en** [-gən]
(unreg) vt to knock in; (Fenster) to smash, to
break; (Zähne, Schädel) to smash in; (AUT:

Räder) to turn; (kürzer machen) to take up;
(Ware) to pack, to wrap up; (Weg, Richtung)
to take ♦ vi to hit; (sich einigen) to agree;
(Anklang finden) to work, to succeed; **in etw
akk/auf jdn e~en** to hit sth/sb
einschlägig ['aɪnʃlɛːgɪç] adj relevant
einschließen ['aɪnʃliːsən] (unreg) vt (Kind) to
lock in; (Häftling) to lock up; (Gegenstand)
to lock away; (Bergleute) to cut off;
(umgeben) to surround; (MIL) to encircle;
(fig) to include, to comprise ♦ vr to lock
o.s. in
einschließlich adv inclusive ♦ präp +gen
inclusive of, including
einschmeicheln ['aɪnʃmaɪçəln] vr: **sich ~
(bei)** to ingratiate o.s. (with)
einschnappen ['aɪnʃnapən] vi (Tür) to click
to; (fig) to be touchy; **eingeschnappt sein**
to be in a huff
einschneidend ['aɪnʃnaɪdənt] adj drastic
Einschnitt ['aɪnʃnɪt] m cutting; (MED)
incision; (Ereignis) decisive point
einschränken ['aɪnʃrɛŋkən] vt to limit, to
restrict; (Kosten) to cut down, to reduce
♦ vr to cut down (on expenditure);
Einschränkung f restriction, limitation;
reduction; (von Behauptung) qualification
Einschreib- ['aɪnʃraɪb] zW: ~(e)**brief** m
recorded delivery letter; e~**en** (unreg) vt to
write in; (Post) to send recorded delivery
♦ vr to register; (UNIV) to enrol; ~**en** nt
recorded delivery letter
einschreiten ['aɪnʃraɪtən] (unreg) vi to step
in, to intervene; **~ gegen** to take action
against
einschüchtern ['aɪnʃʏçtərn] vt to intimidate
einschulen ['aɪnʃuːlən] vt: **eingeschult
werden** (Kind) to start school
einsehen ['aɪnzeːən] (unreg) vt (hineinsehen
in) to realize; (Akten) to have a look at;
(verstehen) to see; E~ (-s) nt
understanding; **ein E~ haben** to show
understanding
einseitig ['aɪnzaɪtɪç] adj one-sided
Einsend- ['aɪnzɛnt] zW: e~**en** (unreg) vt to
send in; ~**er** (-s, -) m sender, contributor;
~**ung** f sending in

einsetzen ['aɪnzɛtsən] *vt* to put (in); (*in Amt*) to appoint, to install; (*Geld*) to stake; (*verwenden*) to use; (*MIL*) to employ ♦ *vi* (*beginnen*) to set in; (*MUS*) to enter, to come in ♦ *vr* to work hard; **sich für jdn/etw ~** to support sb/sth

Einsicht ['aɪnzɪçt] *f* insight; (*in Akten*) look, inspection; **zu der ~ kommen, dass ...** to come to the conclusion that ...; **e~ig** *adj* (*Mensch*) judicious; **e~slos** *adj* unreasonable; **e~svoll** *adj* understanding

einsilbig ['aɪnzɪlbɪç] *adj* (*auch fig*) monosyllabic; (*Mensch*) uncommunicative

einspannen ['aɪnʃpanən] *vt* (*Papier*) to insert; (*Pferde*) to harness; (*umg: Person*) to rope in

Einsparung ['aɪnʃpaːrʊŋ] *f* economy, saving

einsperren ['aɪnʃpɛrən] *vt* to lock up

einspielen ['aɪnʃpiːlən] *vr* (*SPORT*) to warm up ♦ *vt* (*Film: Geld*) to bring in; (*Instrument*) to play in; **sich aufeinander ~** to become attuned to each other; **gut eingespielt** running smoothly

einsprachig ['aɪnʃpraːxɪç] *adj* monolingual

einspringen ['aɪnʃprɪŋən] (*unreg*) *vi* (*aushelfen*) to help out, to step into the breach

Einspruch ['aɪnʃprʊx] *m* protest, objection; **~srecht** *nt* veto

einspurig ['aɪnʃpuːrɪç] *adj* (*EISENB*) single-track; (*AUT*) single-lane

einst [aɪnst] *adv* once; (*zukünftig*) one day, some day

einstecken ['aɪnʃtɛkən] *vt* to stick in, to insert; (*Brief*) to post; (*ELEK: Stecker*) to plug in; (*Geld*) to pocket; (*mitnehmen*) to take; (*überlegen sein*) to put in the shade; (*hinnehmen*) to swallow

einstehen ['aɪnʃteːən] (*unreg*) *vi*: **für jdn/etw ~** to guarantee sb/sth; (*verantworten*): **für etw ~** to answer for sth

einsteigen ['aɪnʃtaɪɡən] (*unreg*) *vi* to get in *od* on; (*in Schiff*) to go on board; (*sich beteiligen*) to come in; (*hineinklettern*) to climb in

einstellen ['aɪnʃtɛlən] *vt* (*aufhören*) to stop; (*Geräte*) to adjust; (*Kamera etc*) to focus;

(*Sender, Radio*) to tune in; (*unterstellen*) to put; (*in Firma*) to employ, to take on ♦ *vi* (*Firma*) to take on staff/workers ♦ *vr* (*anfangen*) to set in; (*kommen*) to arrive; **sich auf jdn ~** to adapt to sb; **sich auf etw** *akk* **~** to prepare o.s. for sth

Einstellung *f* (*Aufhören*) suspension; adjustment; focusing; (*von Arbeiter etc*) appointment; (*Haltung*) attitude

Einstieg ['aɪnʃtiːk] **(-(e)s, -e)** *m* entry; (*fig*) approach

einstig ['aɪnstɪç] *adj* former

einstimmig ['aɪnʃtɪmɪç] *adj* unanimous; (*MUS*) for one voice

einstmals *adv* once, formerly

einstöckig ['aɪnʃtœkɪç] *adj* two-storeyed

Einsturz ['aɪnʃtʊrts] *m* collapse

einstürzen ['aɪnʃtʏrtsən] *vi* to fall in, to collapse

einst- *zW*: **~weilen** *adv* meanwhile; (*vorläufig*) temporarily, for the time being; **~weilig** *adj* temporary

eintägig ['aɪntɛːɡɪç] *adj* one-day

eintauschen ['aɪntaʊʃən] *vt*: **~ (gegen** *od* **für)** to exchange (for)

eintausend ['aɪn'taʊzənt] *num* one thousand

einteilen ['aɪntaɪlən] *vt* (*in Teile*) to divide (up); (*Menschen*) to assign

einteilig *adj* one-piece

eintönig ['aɪntøːnɪç] *adj* monotonous

Eintopf ['aɪntɔpf] *m* stew

Eintracht ['aɪntraxt] **(-)** *f* concord, harmony; **einträchtig** ['aɪntrɛçtɪç] *adj* harmonious

Eintrag ['aɪntraːk] **(-(e)s, ⁈e)** *m* entry; **amtlicher ~** entry in the register; **e~en** [-ɡən] (*unreg*) *vt* (*in Buch*) to enter; (*Profit*) to yield ♦ *vr* to put one's name down

einträglich ['aɪntrɛːklɪç] *adj* profitable

eintreffen ['aɪntrɛfən] (*unreg*) *vi* to happen; (*ankommen*) to arrive

eintreten ['aɪntreːtən] (*unreg*) *vi* to occur; (*sich einsetzen*) to intercede ♦ *vt* (*Tür*) to kick open; **~ in** +*akk* to enter; (*in Klub, Partei*) to join

Eintritt ['aɪntrɪt] *m* (*Betreten*) entrance; (*Anfang*) commencement; (*in Klub etc*)

joining

Eintritts- *zW:* **~geld** *nt* admission charge; **~karte** *f* (admission) ticket; **~preis** *m* admission charge

einüben ['aɪn|yːbən] *vt* to practise

Einvernehmen ['aɪnfɛrneːmən] **(-s, -)** *nt* agreement, harmony

einverstanden ['aɪnfɛrʃtandən] *excl* agreed, okay ♦ *adj:* **~ sein** to agree, to be agreed

Einverständnis ['aɪnfɛrʃtɛntnɪs] *nt* understanding; (*gleiche Meinung*) agreement

Einwand ['aɪnvant] **(-(e)s, ⁺e)** *m* objection

Einwand- *zW:* **~erer** ['aɪnvandərər] *m* immigrant; **e~ern** *vi* to immigrate; **~erung** *f* immigration

einwandfrei *adj* perfect ♦ *adv* absolutely

Einweg- ['aɪveːg] *zW:* **~flasche** *f* no-deposit bottle; **~spritze** *f* disposable syringe

einweichen ['aɪnvaɪçən] *vt* to soak

einweihen ['aɪnvaɪən] *vt* (*Kirche*) to consecrate; (*Brücke*) to open; (*Gebäude*) to inaugurate; **~ (in** +*akk*) (*Person*) to initiate (in); **Einweihung** *f* consecration; opening; inauguration; initiation

einweisen ['aɪnvaɪzən] (*unreg*) *vt* (*in Amt*) to install; (*in Arbeit*) to introduce; (*in Anstalt*) to send

einwenden ['aɪnvɛndən] (*unreg*) *vt:* **etwas ~ gegen** to object to, to oppose

einwerfen ['aɪnvɛrfən] (*unreg*) *vt* to throw in; (*Brief*) to post; (*Geld*) to put in, to insert; (*Fenster*) to smash; (*äußern*) to interpose

einwickeln ['aɪnvɪkəln] *vt* to wrap up; (*fig: umg*) to outsmart

einwilligen ['aɪnvɪlɪɡən] *vi:* **~ (in** +*akk*) to consent (to), to agree (to); **Einwilligung** *f* consent

einwirken ['aɪnvɪrkən] *vi:* **auf jdn/etw ~** to influence sb/sth

Einwohner ['aɪnvoːnər] **(-s, -)** *m* inhabitant; **~'meldeamt** *nt* registration office; **~schaft** *f* population, inhabitants *pl*

Einwurf ['aɪnvurf] *m* (*Öffnung*) slot; (*von Münze*) insertion; (*von Brief*) posting; (*Einwand*) objection; (*SPORT*) throw-in

Einzahl ['aɪntsaːl] *f* singular; **e~en** *vt* to pay

in; **~ung** *f* paying in; **~ungsschein** *m* paying-in slip, deposit slip

einzäunen ['aɪntsɔʏnən] *vt* to fence in

Einzel ['aɪntsəl] **(-s, -)** *nt* (*TENNIS*) singles; **~fahrschein** *m* one-way ticket; **~fall** *m* single instance, individual case; **~handel** *m* retail trade; **~handelspreis** *m* retail price; **~heit** *f* particular, detail; **~kind** *nt* only child; **e~n** *adj* single; (*vereinzelt*) the odd ♦ *adv* singly; **e~n angeben** to specify; **der/die E~ne** the individual; **das E~ne** the particular; **ins E~ne gehen** to go into detail(s); **~teil** *nt* component (part); **~zimmer** *nt* single room; **~zimmerzuschlag** *m* single room supplement

einziehen ['aɪntsiːən] (*unreg*) *vt* to draw in, to take in; (*Kopf*) to duck; (*Fühler, Antenne, Fahrgestell*) to retract; (*Steuern, Erkundigungen*) to collect; (*MIL*) to draft, to call up; (*aus dem Verkehr ziehen*) to withdraw; (*konfiszieren*) to confiscate ♦ *vi* to move in; (*Friede, Ruhe*) to come; (*Flüssigkeit*) to penetrate

einzig ['aɪntsɪç] *adj* only; (*ohnegleichen*) unique; **das E~e** the only thing; **der/die E~e** the only one; **~artig** *adj* unique

Einzug ['aɪntsuːk] *m* entry, moving in

Eis [aɪs] **(-es, -)** *nt* ice; (*Speiseeis*) ice cream; **~bahn** *f* ice *od* skating rink; **~bär** *m* polar bear; **~becher** *m* sundae; **~bein** *nt* pig's trotters *pl*; **~berg** *m* iceberg; **~café** *nt* ice-cream parlour (*BRIT*) *od* parlor (*US*); **~decke** *f* sheet of ice; **~diele** *f* ice-cream parlour

Eisen ['aɪzən] **(-s, -)** *nt* iron

Eisenbahn *f* railway, railroad (*US*); **~er (-s, -)** *m* railwayman, railway employee, railroader (*US*); **~schaffner** *m* railway guard; **~wagen** *m* railway carriage

Eisenerz *nt* iron ore

eisern ['aɪzərn] *adj* iron; (*Gesundheit*) robust; (*Energie*) unrelenting; (*Reserve*) emergency

Eis- *zW:* **e~frei** *adj* clear of ice; **~hockey** *nt* ice hockey; **e~ig** ['aɪzɪç] *adj* icy; **e~kalt** *adj* icy cold; **~kunstlauf** *m* figure skating; **~laufen** *nt* ice skating; **~pickel** *m* ice axe; **~schrank** *m* fridge, icebox (*US*); **~würfel**

m ice cube; **~zapfen** *m* icicle; **~zeit** *f* ice age

eitel ['aɪtəl] *adj* vain; **E~keit** *f* vanity

Eiter ['aɪtər] (**-s**) *m* pus; **e~ig** *adj* suppurating; **e~n** *vi* to suppurate

Eiweiß ⟨**-es, -e**⟩ *nt* white of an egg; (*CHEM*) protein

Ekel[1] ['eːkəl] (**-s, -**) *nt* (*umg: Mensch*) nauseating person

Ekel[2] ['eːkəl] (**-s**) *m* nausea, disgust; **~ erregend** nauseating, disgusting; **e~haft** *adj* nauseating, disgusting; **e~ig** *adj* nauseating, disgusting; **e~n** *vt* to disgust ♦ *vr*: **sich e~n (vor** +*dat*) to loathe, to be disgusted (at); **es e~t jdn** *od* **jdm** sb is disgusted; **eklig** *adj* nauseating, disgusting

Ekstase [ɛk'staːzə] *f* ecstasy

Ekzem [ɛk'tseːm] (**-s, -e**) *nt* (*MED*) eczema

Elan [e'lãː] (**-s**) *m* elan

elastisch [e'lastɪʃ] *adj* elastic

Elastizität [elastitsi'tɛːt] *f* elasticity

Elch [ɛlç] ⟨**-(e)s, -e**⟩ *m* elk

Elefant [ele'fant] *m* elephant

elegant [ele'gant] *adj* elegant

Eleganz [ele'gants] *f* elegance

Elek- [e'lɛk] *zW*: **~triker** [-trɪkər] (**-s, -**) *m* electrician; **e~trisch** [-trɪʃ] *adj* electric; **e~trisieren** [-tri'ziːrən] *vt* (*auch fig*) to electrify; (*Mensch*) to give an electric shock to ♦ *vr* to get an electric shock; **~trizität** [tritsi'tɛːt] *f* electricity; **~trizitätswerk** *nt* power station; (*Gesellschaft*) electric power company

Elektro- [e'lɛktro] *zW*: **~de** [-'troːdə] *f* electrode; **~gerät** *nt* electrical appliance; **~herd** *m* electric cooker; **~n** (**-s, -en**) *nt* electron; **~nik** *f* electronics *sg*; **e~nisch** *adj* electronic; **~rasierer** *m* electric razor; **~technik** *f* electrical engineering

Element [ele'mɛnt] (**-s, -e**) *nt* element; (*ELEK*) cell, battery; **e~ar** [-'taːr] *adj* elementary; (*naturhaft*) elemental

Elend ['eːlɛnt] (**-(e)s**) *nt* misery; **e~** *adj* miserable; **~sviertel** *nt* slum

elf [ɛlf] *num* eleven; **E~** (**-, -en**) *f* (*SPORT*) eleven

Elfe *f* elf

Elfenbein *nt* ivory

Elfmeter *m* (*SPORT*) penalty (kick)

Elite [e'liːtə] *f* elite

Ell- *zW*: **~bogen** *m* elbow; **~e** ['ɛlə] *f* ell; (*Maß*) yard; **~enbogen** *m* elbow; **~(en)bogenfreiheit** *f* (*fig*) elbow room

Elsass ▲ ['ɛlzas] (**-** *od* **-es**) *nt*: **das ~** Alsace

Elster ['ɛlstər] (**-, -n**) *f* magpie

Eltern ['ɛltərn] *pl* parents; **~beirat** *m* (*SCH*) ≈ PTA (*BRIT*), parents' council; **~haus** *nt* home; **e~los** *adj* parentless

E-Mail ['iːmeːl] (**-, -s**) *f* E-mail; **~-Adresse** *f* e-mail address

Emaille [e'maljə] (**-s, -s**) *nt* enamel

emaillieren [ema'jiːrən] *vt* to enamel

Emanzipation [emantsipatsi'oːn] *f* emancipation

emanzipieren *vt* to emancipate

Embryo ['ɛmbryo] (**-s, -s** *od* **Embryonen**) *m* embryo

Emi- *zW*: **~grant(in)** *m(f)* emigrant; **~gration** *f* emigration; **e~grieren** *vi* to emigrate

Emissionen [emisi'oːnən] *fpl* emissions

Empfang [ɛm'pfaŋ] (**-(e)s, ⸚e**) *m* reception; (*Erhalten*) receipt; **in ~ nehmen** to receive; **e~en** (*unreg*) *vt* to receive ♦ *vi* (*schwanger werden*) to conceive

Empfäng- [ɛm'pfɛŋ] *zW*: **~er** (**-s, -**) *m* receiver; (*COMM*) addressee, consignee; **~erabschnitt** *m* receipt slip; **e~lich** *adj* receptive, susceptible; **~nis** (**-, -se**) *f* conception; **~nisverhütung** *f* contraception

Empfangs- *zW*: **~bestätigung** *f* acknowledgement; **~dame** *f* receptionist; **~schein** *m* receipt; **~zimmer** *nt* reception room

empfehlen [ɛm'pfeːlən] (*unreg*) *vt* to recommend ♦ *vr* to take one's leave; **~swert** *adj* recommendable

Empfehlung *f* recommendation

empfiehlst *etc* [ɛm'pfiːlst] *vb siehe* **empfehlen**

empfind- [ɛm'pfɪnt] *zW*: **~en** [-dən] (*unreg*) *vt* to feel; **~lich** *adj* sensitive; (*Stelle*) sore; (*reizbar*) touchy; **~sam** *adj* sentimental;

E~ung [-dʊŋ] *f* feeling, sentiment
empfohlen *etc* [ɛm'pfoːlən] *vb siehe* **empfehlen**
empor [ɛm'poːr] *adv* up, upwards
empören [ɛm'pøːrən] *vt* to make indignant; to shock ♦ *vr* to become indignant; **~d** *adj* outrageous
Emporkömmling [ɛm'poːrkœmlɪŋ] *m* upstart, parvenu
Empörung *f* indignation
emsig [' ɛmzɪç] *adj* diligent, busy
End- [' ɛnt] *in zW* final; **~e** (**-s, -n**) *nt* end; **am ~e** at the end; (*schließlich*) in the end; **am ~e sein** to be at the end of one's tether; **~e Dezember** at the end of December; **zu ~e sein** to be finished; **e~en** *vi* to end; **e~gültig** [' ɛnt-] *adj* final, definite
Endivie [ɛn'diːviə] *f* endive
End- *zW:* **e~lich** *adj* final; (*MATH*) finite ♦ *adv* finally; at last!; **komm e~lich!** come on!; **e~los** *adj* endless, infinite; **~spiel** *nt* final(s); **~spurt** *m* (*SPORT*) final spurt; **~station** *f* terminus; **~ung** *f* ending
Energie [enɛr'giː] *f* energy; **~bedarf** *m* energy requirement; **e~los** *adj* lacking in energy, weak; **~verbrauch** *m* energy consumption; **~versorgung** *f* supply of energy; **~wirtschaft** *f* energy industry
energisch [e'nɛrgɪʃ] *adj* energetic
eng [ɛŋ] *adj* narrow; (*Kleidung*) tight; (*fig: Horizont*) narrow, limited; (*Freundschaft, Verhältnis*) close; **~ an etw** *dat* close to sth
Engagement [āgaʒə'mãː] (**-s, -s**) *nt* engagement; (*Verpflichtung*) commitment
engagieren [āga'ʒiːrən] *vt* to engage ♦ *vr* to commit o.s.
Enge [' ɛŋə] *f* (*auch fig*) narrowness; (*Landenge*) defile; (*Meerenge*) straits *pl*; **jdn in die ~ treiben** to drive sb into a corner
Engel [' ɛŋəl] (**-s, -**) *m* angel; **e~haft** *adj* angelic
England [' ɛŋlant] *nt* England; **Engländer(in)** *m(f)* Englishman(-woman); **englisch** *adj* English
Engpass ▲ *m* defile, pass; (*fig, Verkehr*) bottleneck

en gros [ā'gro] *adv* wholesale
engstirnig [' ɛŋʃtɪrnɪç] *adj* narrow-minded
Enkel [' ɛŋkəl] (**-s, -**) *m* grandson; **~in** *f* granddaughter; **~kind** *nt* grandchild
enorm [e'nɔrm] *adj* enormous
Ensemble [ā'sābəl] (**-s, -s**) *nt* company, ensemble
entbehr- [ɛnt'beːr-] *zW:* **~en** *vt* to do without, to dispense with; **~lich** *adj* superfluous; **E~ung** *f* deprivation
entbinden [ɛnt'bɪndən] (*unreg*) *vt* (*+gen*) to release (from); (*MED*) to deliver ♦ *vi* (*MED*) to give birth; **Entbindung** *f* release; (*MED*) confinement; **Entbindungsheim** *nt* maternity hospital
entdeck- [ɛnt'dɛk] *zW:* **~en** *vt* to discover; **E~er** (**-s, -**) *m* discoverer; **E~ung** *f* discovery
Ente [' ɛntə] *f* duck; (*fig*) canard, false report
enteignen [ɛnt'aɪgnən] *vt* to expropriate; (*Besitzer*) to dispossess
enterben [ɛnt'ɛrbən] *vt* to disinherit
entfallen [ɛnt'falən] (*unreg*) *vi* to drop, to fall; (*wegfallen*) to be dropped; **jdm ~** (*vergessen*) to slip sb's memory; **auf jdn ~** to be allotted to sb
entfalten [ɛnt'faltən] *vt* to unfold; (*Talente*) to develop ♦ *vr* to open; (*Mensch*) to develop one's potential; **Entfaltung** *f* unfolding; (*von Talenten*) development
entfern- [ɛnt'fɛrn] *zW:* **~en** *vt* to remove; (*hinauswerfen*) to expel ♦ *vr* to go away, to withdraw; **~t** *adj* distant; **weit davon ~t sein, etw zu tun** to be far from doing sth; **E~ung** *f* distance; (*Wegschaffen*) removal
entfremden [ɛnt'frɛmdən] *vt* to estrange, to alienate; **Entfremdung** *f* alienation, estrangement
entfrosten [ɛnt'frɔstən] *vt* to defrost
Entfroster (**-s, -**) *m* (*AUT*) defroster
entführ- [ɛnt'fyːr] *zW:* **~en** *vt* to carry off, to abduct; to kidnap; **E~er** *m* kidnapper; **E~ung** *f* abduction; kidnapping
entgegen [ɛnt'geːgən] *präp* +*dat* contrary to, against ♦ *adv* towards; **~bringen** (*unreg*) *vt* to bring; **jdm etw ~bringen** (*fig*) to show sb sth; **~gehen** (*unreg*) *vi* +*dat* to go to

meet, to go towards; **~gesetzt** *adj* opposite; (*widersprechend*) opposed; **~halten** (*unreg*) *vt* (*fig*) to object; **E~kommen** *nt* obligingness; **~kommen** (*unreg*) *vi* +*dat* to approach; to meet; (*fig*) to accommodate; **~kommend** *adj* obliging; **~nehmen** (*unreg*) *vt* to receive, to accept; **~sehen** (*unreg*) *vi* +*dat* to await; **~setzen** *vt* to oppose; **~treten** (*unreg*) *vi* +*dat* to step up to; (*fig*) to oppose, to counter; **~wirken** *vi* +*dat* to counteract

entgegnen [ɛnt'geːgnən] *vt* to reply, to retort

entgehen [ɛnt'geːən] (*unreg*) *vi* (*fig*): **jdm ~** to escape sb's notice; **sich** *dat* **etw ~ lassen** to miss sth

Entgelt [ɛnt'gɛlt] **(-(e)s, -e)** *nt* compensation, remuneration

entgleisen [ɛnt'glaɪzən] *vi* (*EISENB*) to be derailed; (*fig: Person*) to misbehave; **~ lassen** to derail

entgräten [ɛnt'grɛːtən] *vt* to fillet, to bone

Enthaarungscreme [ɛnt'haːrʊŋs-] *f* hair-removing cream

enthalten [ɛnt'haltən] (*unreg*) *vt* to contain ♦ *vr*: **sich (von etw) ~** to abstain (from sth), to refrain (from sth)

enthaltsam [ɛnt'haltzaːm] *adj* abstinent, abstemious

enthemmen [ɛnt'hɛmən] *vt*: **jdn ~** to free sb from his inhibitions

enthüllen [ɛnt'hʏlən] *vt* to reveal, to unveil

Enthusiasmus [ɛntuzi'asmʊs] *m* enthusiasm

entkommen [ɛnt'kɔmən] (*unreg*) *vi*: **~ (aus** *od* +*dat*) to get away (from), to escape (from)

entkräften [ɛnt'krɛftən] *vt* to weaken, to exhaust; (*Argument*) to refute

entladen [ɛnt'laːdən] (*unreg*) *vt* to unload; (*ELEK*) to discharge ♦ *vr* (*ELEK: Gewehr*) to discharge; (*Ärger etc*) to vent itself

entlang [ɛnt'laŋ] *adv* along; **~ dem Fluss, den Fluss ~** along the river; **~gehen** (*unreg*) *vi* to walk along

entlarven [ɛnt'larfən] *vt* to unmask, to expose

entlassen [ɛnt'lasən] (*unreg*) *vt* to discharge; (*Arbeiter*) to dismiss; **Entlassung** *f* discharge; dismissal

entlasten [ɛnt'lastən] *vt* to relieve; (*Achse*) to relieve the load on; (*Angeklagten*) to exonerate; (*Konto*) to clear

Entlastung *f* relief; (*COMM*) crediting

Entlastungszug *m* relief train

entlegen [ɛnt'leːgən] *adj* remote

entlocken [ɛnt'lɔkən] *vt*: **(jdm etw) ~** to elicit (sth from sb)

entmutigen [ɛnt'muːtɪgən] *vt* to discourage

entnehmen [ɛnt'neːmən] (*unreg*) *vt* (+*dat*) to take out (of), to take (from); (*folgern*) to infer (from)

entreißen [ɛnt'raɪsən] (*unreg*) *vt*: **jdm etw ~** to snatch sth (away) from sb

entrichten [ɛnt'rɪçtən] *vt* to pay

entrosten [ɛnt'rɔstən] *vt* to remove rust from

entrümpeln [ɛnt'rʏmpəln] *vt* to clear out

entrüst- [ɛnt'rʏst] *zW*: **~en** *vt* to incense, to outrage ♦ *vr* to be filled with indignation; **~et** *adj* indignant, outraged; **E~ung** *f* indignation

entschädigen [ɛnt'ʃɛːdɪgən] *vt* to compensate; **Entschädigung** *f* compensation

entschärfen [ɛnt'ʃɛrfən] *vt* to defuse; (*Kritik*) to tone down

Entscheid [ɛnt'ʃaɪt] **(-(e)s, -e)** *m* decision; **e~en** [-dən] (*unreg*) *vt, vi, vr* to decide; **e~end** *adj* decisive; (*Stimme*) casting; **~ung** *f* decision

entschieden [ɛnt'ʃiːdən] *adj* decided; (*entschlossen*) resolute; **E~heit** *f* firmness, determination

entschließen [ɛnt'ʃliːsən] (*unreg*) *vr* to decide

entschlossen [ɛnt'ʃlɔsən] *adj* determined, resolute; **E~heit** *f* determination

Entschluss ▲ [ɛnt'ʃlʊs] *m* decision; **e~freudig** *adj* decisive; **~kraft** *f* determination, decisiveness

entschuldigen [ɛnt'ʃʊldɪgən] *vt* to excuse ♦ *vr* to apologize

Entschuldigung *f* apology; (*Grund*)

excuse; **jdn um ~ bitten** to apologize to sb;
~! excuse me; (*Verzeihung*) sorry

entsetz- [ɛnt'zɛts] *zW*: **~en** *vt* to horrify;
(*MIL*) to relieve ♦ *vr* to be horrified *od*
appalled; **E~en (-s)** *nt* horror, dismay;
~lich *adj* dreadful, appalling; **~t** *adj*
horrified

Entsorgung [ɛnt'zɔrɡʊŋ] *f* (*von Kraftwerken, Chemikalien*) (waste) disposal

entspannen [ɛnt'ʃpanən] *vt*, *vr* (*Körper*) to
relax; (*POL: Lage*) to ease

Entspannung *f* relaxation, rest; (*POL*)
détente; **~spolitik** *f* policy of détente

entsprechen [ɛnt'ʃprɛçən] (*unreg*) *vi +dat* to
correspond to; (*Anforderungen, Wünschen*) to
meet, to comply with; **~d** *adj* appropriate
♦ *adv* accordingly

entspringen [ɛnt'ʃprɪŋən] (*unreg*) *vi* (+*dat*)
to spring (from)

entstehen [ɛnt'ʃteːən] (*unreg*) *vi*: **~ (aus** *od*
durch) to arise (from), to result (from)

Entstehung *f* genesis, origin

entstellen [ɛnt'ʃtɛlən] *vt* to disfigure;
(*Wahrheit*) to distort

entstören [ɛnt'ʃtøːrən] *vt* (*RADIO*) to
eliminate interference from

enttäuschen [ɛnt'tɔʏʃən] *vt* to disappoint;
Enttäuschung *f* disappointment

entwaffnen [ɛnt'vafnən] *vt* (*lit, fig*) to
disarm

entwässern [ɛnt'vɛsərn] *vt* to drain;
Entwässerung *f* drainage

entweder [ɛnt'veːdər] *konj* either

entwenden [ɛnt'vɛndən] (*unreg*) *vt* to
purloin, to steal

entwerfen [ɛnt'vɛrfən] (*unreg*) *vt* (*Zeichnung*)
to sketch; (*Modell*) to design; (*Vortrag, Gesetz etc*) to draft

entwerten [ɛnt'veːrtən] *vt* to devalue;
(*stempeln*) to cancel

Entwerter (-s, -) *m* ticket punching
machine

entwickeln [ɛnt'vɪkəln] *vt*, *vr* (*auch PHOT*) to
develop; (*Mut, Energie*) to show (o.s.), to
display (o.s.)

Entwicklung [ɛnt'vɪklʊŋ] *f* development;
(*PHOT*) developing

Entwicklungs- *zW*: **~hilfe** *f* aid for
developing countries; **~land** *nt* developing
country

entwöhnen [ɛnt'vøːnən] *vt* to wean;
(*Süchtige*): (**einer Sache** *dat od* **von etw**) **~**
to cure (of sth)

Entwöhnung *f* weaning; cure, curing

entwürdigend [ɛnt'vʏrdɪɡənt] *adj*
degrading

Entwurf [ɛnt'vʊrf] *m* outline, design;
(*Vertragsentwurf, Konzept*) draft

entziehen [ɛnt'tsiːən] (*unreg*) *vt* (+*dat*) to
withdraw (from), to take away (from);
(*Flüssigkeit*) to draw (from), to extract
(from) ♦ *vr* (+*dat*) to escape (from); (*jds
Kenntnis*) to be outside *od* beyond; (*der
Pflicht*) to shirk (from)

Entziehung *f* withdrawal; **~sanstalt** *f*
drug addiction/alcoholism treatment
centre; **~skur** *f* treatment for drug
addiction/alcoholism

entziffern [ɛnt'tsɪfərn] *vt* to decipher; to
decode

entzücken [ɛnt'tsʏkən] *vt* to delight; **E~
(-s)** *nt* delight; **~d** *adj* delightful, charming

entzünden [ɛnt'tsʏndən] *vt* to light, to set
light to; (*fig, MED*) to inflame; (*Streit*) to
spark off ♦ *vr* (*auch fig*) to catch fire; (*Streit*)
to start; (*MED*) to become inflamed

Entzündung *f* (*MED*) inflammation

entzwei [ɛnt'tsvaɪ] *adv* broken; in two;
~brechen (*unreg*) *vt*, *vi* to break in two;
~en *vt* to set at odds ♦ *vr* to fall out;
~gehen (*unreg*) *vi* to break (in two)

Enzian ['ɛntsiaːn] (**-s, -e**) *m* gentian

Epidemie [epide'miː] *f* epidemic

Epilepsie [epilɛ'psiː] *f* epilepsy

Episode [epi'zoːdə] *f* episode

Epoche [e'pɔxə] *f* epoch; **~ machend**
epoch-making

Epos ['eːpɔs] (**-s, Epen**) *nt* epic (poem)

er [eːr] (*nom*) *pron* he; it

erarbeiten [ɛr|arbaɪtən] *vt* to work for, to
acquire; (*Theorie*) to work out

erbarmen [ɛr'barmən] *vr* (+*gen*) to have pity
od mercy (on); **E~ (-s)** *nt* pity

erbärmlich [ɛr'bɛrmlɪç] *adj* wretched,

pitiful; **E~keit** f wretchedness

erbarmungslos [ɛr'barmʊŋsloːs] *adj* pitiless, merciless

erbau- [ɛr'baʊ] *zW*: **~en** *vt* to build, to erect; (*fig*) to edify; **E~er** (**-s, -**) *m* builder; **~lich** *adj* edifying

Erbe[1] ['ɛrbə] (**-n, -n**) *m* heir

Erbe[2] ['ɛrbə] *nt* inheritance; (*fig*) heritage

erben *vt* to inherit

erbeuten [ɛr'bɔytən] *vt* to carry off; (*MIL*) to capture

Erb- [ɛrb] *zW*: **~faktor** *m* gene; **~folge** f (line of) succession; **~in** f heiress

erbittern [ɛr'bɪtərn] *vt* to embitter; (*erzürnen*) to incense

erbittert [ɛr'bɪtərt] *adj* (*Kampf*) fierce, bitter

erblassen [ɛr'blasən] *vi* to (turn) pale

erblich ['ɛrplɪç] *adj* hereditary

erblinden [ɛr'blɪndən] *vi* to go blind

erbrechen [ɛr'brɛçən] (*unreg*) *vt, vr* to vomit

Erbschaft f inheritance, legacy

Erbse ['ɛrpsə] f pea

Erbstück *nt* heirloom

Erd- ['ɛːrt] *zW*: **~achse** f earth's axis; **~atmosphäre** f earth's atmosphere; **~beben** *nt* earthquake; **~beere** f strawberry; **~boden** *m* ground; **~e** f earth; **zu ebener ~e** at ground level; **e~en** *vt* (*ELEK*) to earth

erdenklich [ɛr'dɛŋklɪç] *adj* conceivable

Erd- *zW*: **~gas** *nt* natural gas; **~geschoss** ▲ *nt* ground floor; **~kunde** f geography; **~nuss** ▲ f peanut; **~öl** *nt* (mineral) oil

erdrosseln [ɛr'drɔsəln] *vt* to strangle, to throttle

erdrücken [ɛr'drʏkən] *vt* to crush

Erd- *zW*: **~rutsch** *m* landslide; **~teil** *m* continent

erdulden [ɛr'dʊldən] *vt* to endure, to suffer

ereignen [ɛr'|aignən] *vr* to happen

Ereignis [ɛr'|aignɪs] (**-ses, -se**) *nt* event; **e~los** *adj* uneventful; **e~reich** *adj* eventful

ererbt [ɛr'|ɛrpt] *adj* (*Haus*) inherited; (*Krankheit*) hereditary

erfahren [ɛr'faːrən] (*unreg*) *vt* to learn, to find out; (*erleben*) to experience ♦ *adj* experienced

Erfahrung f experience; **e~sgemäß** *adv* according to experience

erfassen [ɛr'fasən] *vt* to seize; (*fig: einbeziehen*) to include, to register; (*verstehen*) to grasp

erfind- [ɛr'fɪnd] *zW*: **~en** (*unreg*) *vt* to invent; **E~er** (**-s, -**) *m* inventor; **~erisch** *adj* inventive; **E~ung** f invention

Erfolg [ɛr'fɔlk] (**-(e)s, -e**) *m* success; (*Folge*) result; **~ versprechend** promising; **e~en** [-gən] *vi* to follow; (*sich ergeben*) to result; (*stattfinden*) to take place; (*Zahlung*) to be effected; **e~los** *adj* unsuccessful; **~losigkeit** f lack of success; **e~reich** *adj* successful

erforderlich *adj* requisite, necessary

erfordern [ɛr'fɔrdərn] *vt* to require, to demand

erforschen [ɛr'fɔrʃən] *vt* (*Land*) to explore; (*Problem*) to investigate; (*Gewissen*) to search; **Erforschung** f exploration; investigation; searching

erfreuen [ɛr'frɔyən] *vr*: **sich ~ an** +*dat* to enjoy ♦ *vt* to delight; **sich einer Sache** *gen* **~** to enjoy sth

erfreulich [ɛr'frɔylɪç] *adj* pleasing, gratifying; **~erweise** *adv* happily, luckily

erfrieren [ɛr'friːrən] (*unreg*) *vi* to freeze (to death); (*Glieder*) to get frostbitten; (*Pflanzen*) to be killed by frost

erfrischen [ɛr'frɪʃən] *vt* to refresh; **Erfrischung** f refreshment

Erfrischungs- *zW*: **~getränk** *nt* (liquid) refreshment; **~raum** *m* snack bar, cafeteria

erfüllen [ɛr'fʏlən] *vt* (*Raum etc*) to fill; (*fig: Bitte etc*) to fulfil ♦ *vr* to come true

ergänzen [ɛr'gɛntsən] *vt* to supplement, to complete ♦ *vr* to complement one another; **Ergänzung** f completion; (*Zusatz*) supplement

ergeben [ɛr'geːbən] (*unreg*) *vt* to yield, to produce ♦ *vr* to surrender; (*folgen*) to result ♦ *adj* devoted, humble

Ergebnis [ɛr'geːpnɪs] (**-ses, -se**) *nt* result; **e~los** *adj* without result, fruitless

ergehen [ɛr'geːən] (*unreg*) *vi* to be issued, to go out ♦ *vi unpers*: **es ergeht ihm gut/**

schlecht he's faring *od* getting on well/badly ♦ *vr:* **sich in etw** *dat* ~ to indulge in sth; **etw über sich** ~ **lassen** to put up with sth

ergiebig [ɛr'giːbɪç] *adj* productive

Ergonomie [ɛrgono'miː] *f* ergonomics *sg*

Ergonomik [ɛrgo'noːmɪk] *f* = **Ergonomie**

ergreifen [ɛr'graɪfən] (*unreg*) *vt* (*auch fig*) to seize; (*Beruf*) to take up; (*Maßnahmen*) to resort to; (*rühren*) to move; ~**d** *adj* moving, touching

ergriffen [ɛr'grɪfən] *adj* deeply moved

Erguss ▲ [ɛr'gʊs] *m* discharge; (*fig*) outpouring, effusion

erhaben [ɛr'haːbən] *adj* raised, embossed; (*fig*) exalted, lofty; **über etw** *akk* ~ **sein** to be above sth

erhalten [ɛr'haltən] (*unreg*) *vt* to receive; (*bewahren*) to preserve, to maintain; **gut** ~ in good condition

erhältlich [ɛr'hɛltlɪç] *adj* obtainable, available

Erhaltung *f* maintenance, preservation

erhärten [ɛr'hɛrtən] *vt* to harden; (*These*) to substantiate, to corroborate

erheben [ɛr'heːbən] (*unreg*) *vt* to raise; (*Protest, Forderungen*) to make; (*Fakten*) to ascertain, to establish ♦ *vr* to rise (up)

erheblich [ɛr'heːplɪç] *adj* considerable

erheitern [ɛr'haɪtərn] *vt* to amuse, to cheer (up)

Erheiterung *f* exhilaration; **zur allgemeinen** ~ to everybody's amusement

erhitzen [ɛr'hɪtsən] *vt* to heat ♦ *vr* to heat up; (*fig*) to become heated

erhoffen [ɛr'hɔfən] *vt* to hope for

erhöhen [ɛr'høːən] *vt* to raise; (*verstärken*) to increase

erhol- [ɛr'hoːl] *zW:* ~**en** *vr* to recover; (*entspannen*) to have a rest; ~**sam** *adj* restful; **E~ung** *f* recovery; relaxation, rest; ~**ungsbedürftig** *adj* in need of a rest, run-down; **E~ungsgebiet** *nt* ≈ holiday area; **E~ungsheim** *nt* convalescent home

erhören [ɛr'høːrən] *vt* (*Gebet etc*) to hear; (*Bitte etc*) to yield to

erinnern [ɛr'|ɪnərn] *vt:* ~ **(an** *+akk*) to

remind (of) ♦ *vr:* **sich (an** *akk* **etw)** ~ to remember (sth)

Erinnerung *f* memory; (*Andenken*) reminder

erkältet [ɛr'kɛltət] *adj* with a cold; ~ **sein** to have a cold

Erkältung *f* cold

erkennbar *adj* recognizable

erkennen [ɛr'kɛnən] (*unreg*) *vt* to recognize; (*sehen, verstehen*) to see

erkennt- *zW:* ~**lich** *adj:* **sich** ~**lich zeigen** to show one's appreciation; **E~lichkeit** *f* gratitude; (*Geschenk*) token of one's gratitude; **E~nis** (-, -**se**) *f* knowledge; (*das Erkennen*) recognition; (*Einsicht*) insight; **zur E~nis kommen** to realize

Erkennung *f* recognition

Erkennungszeichen *nt* identification

Erker ['ɛrkər] (-**s**, -) *m* bay

erklär- [ɛr'klɛːr] *zW:* ~**bar** *adj* explicable; ~**en** *vt* to explain; ~**lich** *adj* explicable; (*verständlich*) understandable; **E~ung** *f* explanation; (*Aussage*) declaration

erkranken [ɛr'krankən] *vi* to fall ill; **Erkrankung** *f* illness

erkund- [ɛr'kʊnd] *zW:* ~**en** *vt* to find out, to ascertain; (*bes MIL*) to reconnoitre, to scout; ~**igen** *vr:* **sich** ~**igen (nach)** to inquire (about); **E~igung** *f* inquiry; **E~ung** *f* reconnaissance, scouting

erlahmen [ɛr'laːmən] *vi* to tire; (*nachlassen*) to flag, to wane

erlangen [ɛr'laŋən] *vt* to attain, to achieve

Erlass ▲ [ɛr'las] (-**es**, ⁻**e**) *m* decree; (*Aufhebung*) remission

erlassen (*unreg*) *vt* (*Verfügung*) to issue; (*Gesetz*) to enact; (*Strafe*) to remit; **jdm etw** ~ to release sb from sth

erlauben [ɛr'laʊbən] *vt:* **(jdm etw)** ~ to allow *od* permit (sb (to do) sth) ♦ *vr* to permit o.s., to venture

Erlaubnis [ɛr'laʊpnɪs] (-, -**se**) *f* permission; (*Schriftstück*) permit

erläutern [ɛr'lɔʏtərn] *vt* to explain; **Erläuterung** *f* explanation

erleben [ɛr'leːbən] *vt* to experience; (*Zeit*) to live through; (*miterleben*) to witness; (*noch* miterleben) to live to see

Erlebnis [ɛr'le:pnɪs] **(-ses, -se)** nt experience

erledigen [ɛr'le:dɪgən] vt to take care of, to deal with; (Antrag etc) to process; (umg: erschöpfen) to wear out; (: ruinieren) to finish; (: umbringen) to do in

erleichtern [ɛr'laɪçtərn] vt to make easier; (fig: Last) to lighten; (lindern, beruhigen) to relieve; **Erleichterung** f facilitation; lightening; relief

erleiden [ɛr'laɪdən] (unreg) vt to suffer, to endure

erlernen [ɛr'lɛrnən] vt to learn, to acquire

erlesen [ɛr'le:zən] adj select, choice

erleuchten [ɛr'lɔʏçtən] vt to illuminate; (fig) to inspire

Erleuchtung f (Einfall) inspiration

Erlös [ɛr'løːs] **(-es, -e)** m proceeds pl

erlösen [ɛr'løːzən] vt to redeem, to save; **Erlösung** f release; (REL) redemption

ermächtigen [ɛr'mɛçtɪgən] vt to authorize, to empower; **Ermächtigung** f authorization; authority

ermahnen [ɛr'ma:nən] vt to exhort, to admonish; **Ermahnung** f admonition, exhortation

ermäßigen [ɛr'mɛsɪgən] vt to reduce; **Ermäßigung** f reduction

ermessen [ɛr'mɛsən] (unreg) vt to estimate, to gauge; **E~ (-s)** nt estimation; discretion; **in jds E~ liegen** to lie within sb's discretion

ermitteln [ɛr'mɪtəln] vt to determine; (Täter) to trace ♦ vi: **gegen jdn ~** to investigate sb

Ermittlung [ɛr'mɪtlʊŋ] f determination; (Polizeiermittlung) investigation

ermöglichen [ɛr'møːklɪçən] vt (+dat) to make possible (for)

ermorden [ɛr'mɔrdən] vt to murder

ermüden [ɛr'myːdən] vt, vi to tire; (TECH) to fatigue; **~d** adj tiring; (fig) wearisome

Ermüdung f fatigue

ermutigen [ɛr'muːtɪgən] vt to encourage

ernähr- [ɛr'nɛːr] zW: **~en** vt to feed, to nourish; (Familie) to support ♦ vr to support o.s., to earn a living; **sich ~en von** to live

on; **E~er (-s, -)** m breadwinner; **E~ung** f nourishment; nutrition; (Unterhalt) maintenance

ernennen [ɛr'nɛnən] (unreg) vt to appoint; **Ernennung** f appointment

erneu- [ɛr'nɔʏ] zW: **~ern** vt to renew; to restore; to renovate; **E~erung** f renewal; restoration; renovation; **~t** adj renewed, fresh ♦ adv once more

ernst [ɛrnst] adj serious; **~ gemeint** meant in earnest, serious; **E~ (-es)** m seriousness; **das ist mein E~** I'm quite serious; **im E~** in earnest; **E~ machen mit etw** to put sth into practice; **E~fall** m emergency; **~haft** adj serious; **E~haftigkeit** f seriousness; **~lich** adj serious

Ernte ['ɛrntə] f harvest; **e~n** vt to harvest; (Lob etc) to earn

ernüchtern [ɛr'nʏçtərn] vt to sober up; (fig) to bring down to earth

Erober- [ɛr'oːbər] zW: **~er (-s, -)** m conqueror; **e~n** vt to conquer; **~ung** f conquest

eröffnen [ɛr'œfnən] vt to open ♦ vr to present itself; **jdm etw ~** to disclose sth to sb

Eröffnung f opening

erörtern [ɛr'œrtərn] vt to discuss

Erotik [e'roːtɪk] f eroticism; **erotisch** adj erotic

erpress- [ɛr'prɛs] zW: **~en** vt (Geld etc) to extort; (Mensch) to blackmail; **E~er (-s, -)** m blackmailer; **E~ung** f extortion; blackmail

erprobt [ɛr'proːpt] adj (Gerät, Medikamente) proven, tested

erraten [ɛr'raːtən] (unreg) vt to guess

erreg- [ɛr're:g] zW: **~en** vt to excite; (ärgern) to infuriate; (hervorrufen) to arouse, to provoke ♦ vr to get excited od worked up; **E~er (-s, -)** m causative agent; **E~ung** f excitement

erreichbar adj accessible, within reach

erreichen [ɛr'raɪçən] vt to reach; (Zweck) to achieve; (Zug) to catch

errichten [ɛr'rɪçtən] vt to erect, to put up; (gründen) to establish, to set up

erringen [ɛrˈrɪŋən] (*unreg*) *vt* to gain, to win
erröten [ɛrˈrøːtən] *vi* to blush, to flush
Errungenschaft [ɛrˈrʊŋənʃaft] *f* achievement; (*umg: Anschaffung*) acquisition
Ersatz [ɛrˈzats] (**-es**) *m* substitute; replacement; (*Schadenersatz*) compensation; (*MIL*) reinforcements *pl*; **~dienst** *m* (*MIL*) alternative service; **~reifen** *m* (*AUT*) spare tyre; **~teil** *nt* spare (part)
erschaffen [ɛrˈʃafən] (*unreg*) *vt* to create
erscheinen [ɛrˈʃaɪnən] (*unreg*) *vi* to appear; **Erscheinung** *f* appearance; (*Geist*) apparition; (*Gegebenheit*) phenomenon; (*Gestalt*) figure
erschießen [ɛrˈʃiːsən] (*unreg*) *vt* to shoot (dead)
erschlagen [ɛrˈʃlaːgən] (*unreg*) *vt* to strike dead
erschöpf- [ɛrˈʃœpf] *zW*: **~en** *vt* to exhaust; **~end** *adj* exhaustive, thorough; **E~ung** *f* exhaustion
erschrecken [ɛrˈʃrɛkən] *vt* to startle, to frighten ♦ *vi* to be frightened *od* startled; **~d** *adj* alarming, frightening
erschrocken [ɛrˈʃrɔkən] *adj* frightened, startled
erschüttern [ɛrˈʃʏtərn] *vt* to shake; (*fig*) to move deeply; **Erschütterung** *f* shaking; shock
erschweren [ɛrˈʃveːrən] *vt* to complicate
erschwinglich *adj* within one's means
ersetzen [ɛrˈzɛtsən] *vt* to replace; **jdm Unkosten** *etc* **~** to pay sb's expenses *etc*
ersichtlich [ɛrˈzɪçtlɪç] *adj* evident, obvious
ersparen [ɛrˈʃpaːrən] *vt* (*Ärger etc*) to spare; (*Geld*) to save
Ersparnis (**-, -se**) *f* saving

─── SCHLÜSSELWORT ───

erst [eːrst] *adv* **1** first; **mach erst mal die Arbeit fertig** finish your work first; **wenn du das erst mal hinter dir hast** once you've got that behind you
2 (*nicht früher als, nur*) only; (*nicht bis*) not till; **erst gestern** only yesterday; **erst morgen** not until tomorrow; **erst als** only when, not until; **wir fahren erst später**

we're not going until later; **er ist (gerade) erst angekommen** he's only just arrived
3: **wäre er doch erst zurück!** if only he were back!

└───

erstatten [ɛrˈʃtatən] *vt* (*Kosten*) to (re)pay; **Anzeige** *etc* **gegen jdn ~** to report sb; **Bericht ~** to make a report
Erstattung *f* (*von Kosten*) refund
Erstaufführung [ˈeːrstʔaʊffyːrʊŋ] *f* first performance
erstaunen [ɛrˈʃtaʊnən] *vt* to astonish ♦ *vi* to be astonished; **E~** (**-s**) *nt* astonishment
erstaunlich *adj* astonishing
erst- [ˈeːrst] *zW*: **E~ausgabe** *f* first edition; **~beste(r, s)** *adj* first that comes along; **~e(r, s)** *adj* first
erstechen [ɛrˈʃtɛçən] (*unreg*) *vt* to stab (to death)
erstehen [ɛrˈʃteːən] (*unreg*) *vt* to buy ♦ *vi* to (a)rise
erstens [ˈeːrstəns] *adv* firstly, in the first place
ersticken [ɛrˈʃtɪkən] *vt* (*auch fig*) to stifle; (*Mensch*) to suffocate; (*Flammen*) to smother ♦ *vi* (*Mensch*) to suffocate; (*Feuer*) to be smothered; **in Arbeit ~** to be snowed under with work
erst- *zW*: **~klassig** *adj* first-class; **~malig** *adj* first; **~mals** *adv* for the first time
erstrebenswert [ɛrˈʃtreːbənsveːrt] *adj* desirable, worthwhile
erstrecken [ɛrˈʃtrɛkən] *vr* to extend, to stretch
ersuchen [ɛrˈzuːxən] *vt* to request
ertappen [ɛrˈtapən] *vt* to catch, to detect
erteilen [ɛrˈtaɪlən] *vt* to give
Ertrag [ɛrˈtraːk] (**-(e)s, ⁻e**) *m* yield; (*Gewinn*) proceeds *pl*
ertragen [ɛrˈtraːgən] (*unreg*) *vt* to bear, to stand
erträglich [ɛrˈtrɛːklɪç] *adj* tolerable, bearable
ertrinken [ɛrˈtrɪŋkən] (*unreg*) *vi* to drown; **E~** (**-s**) *nt* drowning
erübrigen [ɛrˈyːbrɪgən] *vt* to spare ♦ *vr* to be unnecessary
erwachen [ɛrˈvaxən] *vi* to awake

erwachsen [ɛr'vaksən] *adj* grown-up; **E~e(r)** *f(m)* adult; **E~enbildung** *f* adult education

erwägen [ɛr've:gən] (*unreg*) *vt* to consider; **Erwägung** *f* consideration

erwähn- [ɛr've:n] *zW*: **~en** *vt* to mention; **~enswert** *adj* worth mentioning; **E~ung** *f* mention

erwärmen [ɛr'vɛrmən] *vt* to warm, to heat ♦ *vr* to get warm, to warm up; **sich ~ für** to warm to

Erwartung *nt*: **über meinen/unseren** *usw* **~** beyond my/our *etc* expectations; **wider ~** contrary to expectations

erwarten [ɛr'vartən] *vt* to expect; (*warten auf*) to wait for; **etw kaum ~ können** to be hardly able to wait for sth

Erwartung *f* expectation

erwartungsgemäß *adv* as expected

erwartungsvoll *adj* expectant

erwecken [ɛr'vɛkən] *vt* to rouse, to awake; **den Anschein ~** to give the impression

Erweis [ɛr'vaɪs] (**-es, -e**) *m* proof; **e~en** (*unreg*) *vt* to prove ♦ *vr*: **sich e~en (als)** to prove (to be); **jdm einen Gefallen/Dienst e~en** to do sb a favour/service

Erwerb [ɛr'vɛrp] (**-(e)s, -e**) *m* acquisition; (*Beruf*) trade; **e~en** [-bən] (*unreg*) *vt* to acquire

erwerbs- *zW*: **~los** *adj* unemployed; **E~quelle** *f* source of income; **~tätig** *adj* (gainfully) employed

erwidern [ɛr'vi:dərn] *vt* to reply; (*vergelten*) to return

erwischen [ɛr'vɪʃən] (*umg*) *vt* to catch, to get

erwünscht [ɛr'vʏnʃt] *adj* desired

erwürgen [ɛr'vʏrgən] *vt* to strangle

Erz [e:rts] (**-es, -e**) *nt* ore

erzähl- [ɛr'tsɛːl] *zW*: **~en** *vt* to tell ♦ *vi*: **sie kann gut ~en** she's a good story-teller; **E~er** (**-s, -**) *m* narrator; **E~ung** *f* story, tale

Erzbischof *m* archbishop

erzeug- [ɛr'tsɔʏg] *zW*: **~en** *vt* to produce; (*Strom*) to generate; **E~nis** (**-ses, -se**) *nt* product, produce; **E~ung** *f* production; generation

erziehen [ɛr'tsi:ən] (*unreg*) *vt* to bring up; (*bilden*) to educate, to train; **Erzieher(in)** (**-s, -**) *m(f)* (*Berufsbezeichnung*) teacher; **Erziehung** *f* bringing up; (*Bildung*) education; **Erziehungsbeihilfe** *f* educational grant; **Erziehungsberechtigte(r)** *f(m)* parent; guardian

erzielen [ɛr'tsi:lən] *vt* to achieve, to obtain; (*Tor*) to score

erzwingen [ɛr'tsvɪŋən] (*unreg*) *vt* to force, to obtain by force

es [ɛs] (*nom, akk*) *pron* it

Esel ['e:zəl] (**-s, -**) *m* donkey, ass

Eskalation [ɛskalatsi'o:n] *f* escalation

ess- ▲ ['ɛs] *zW*: **~bar** [ˈɛsbaːr] *adj* eatable, edible; **E~besteck** *nt* knife, fork and spoon; **E~ecke** *f* dining area

essen ['ɛsən] (*unreg*) *vt, vi* to eat; **E~** (**-s, -**) *nt* meal; food

Essig ['ɛsɪç] (**-s, -e**) *m* vinegar

Ess- ▲ *zW*: **~kastanie** *f* sweet chestnut; **~löffel** *m* tablespoon; **~tisch** *m* dining table; **~waren** *pl* foodstuffs, provisions; **~zimmer** *nt* dining room

etablieren [eta'bli:rən] *vr* to become established; to set up in business

Etage [e'ta:ʒə] *f* floor, storey; **~nbetten** *pl* bunk beds; **~nwohnung** *f* flat

Etappe [e'tapə] *f* stage

Etat [e'ta:] (**-s, -s**) *m* budget

etc *abk* (= *et cetera*) etc

Ethik ['e:tɪk] *f* ethics *sg*; **ethisch** *adj* ethical

Etikett [eti'kɛt] (**-(e)s, -e**) *nt* label; tag; **~e** *f* etiquette, manners *pl*

etliche ['ɛtlɪçə] *pron pl* some, quite a few; **~s** *pron* a thing or two

Etui [ɛt'viː] (**-s, -s**) *nt* case

etwa ['ɛtva] *adv* (*ungefähr*) about; (*vielleicht*) perhaps; (*beispielsweise*) for instance; **nicht ~** by no means; **~ig** ['ɛtvaɪç] *adj* possible

etwas *pron* something; anything; (*ein wenig*) a little ♦ *adv* a little

euch [ɔʏç] *pron* (*akk von* **ihr**) you; yourselves; (*dat von* **ihr**) (to) you

euer ['ɔʏər] *pron* (*gen von* **ihr**) of you ♦ *adj* your

Eule ['ɔʏlə] *f* owl

eure ['ɔʏrə] *adj f siehe* **euer**

eure(r, s) ['ɔʏrə(r, s)] *pron* yours; **~rseits**
adv on your part; **~s** *adj nt siehe* **euer**;
~sgleichen *pron* people like you;
~twegen (*für euch*) for your sakes;
(*wegen euch*) on your account; **~twillen**
adv: **um ~twillen** = **euretwegen**

eurige ['ɔʏrɪgə] *pron*: **der/die/das ~** *od* **E~**
yours

Euro ['ɔʏro:] **(-, -s)** *m* (*FIN*) euro

Euro- *zW*: **~pa** ['ɔʏro:pa] *nt* Europe;
~päer(in) [ɔʏro'pɛːər(ɪn)] *m(f)* European;
e~päisch *adj* European; **~pameister**
[ɔʏ'ro:pa-] *m* European champion;
~paparlament *nt* European Parliament;
~scheck *m* (*FIN*) eurocheque

Euter ['ɔʏtər] **(-s, -)** *nt* udder

ev. *abk* = **evangelisch**

evakuieren [evaku'iːrən] *vt* to evacuate

evangelisch [evan'ge:lɪʃ] *adj* Protestant

Evangelium [evan'ge:liʊm] *nt* gospel

eventuell [eventu'ɛl] *adj* possible ♦ *adv*
possibly, perhaps

evtl. *abk* = **eventuell**

EWG [e:ve:'ge:] **(-)** *f abk* (= *Europäische
Wirtschaftsgemeinschaft*) EEC, Common
Market

ewig ['e:vɪç] *adj* eternal; **E~keit** *f* eternity

EWU [e:ve:'uː] *f abk* (= *Europäische
Währungsunion*) EMU

exakt [ɛ'ksakt] *adj* exact

Examen [ɛ'ksaːmən] **(-s, -** *od* **Examina)** *nt*
examination

Exemplar [ɛksɛm'plaːr] **(-s, -e)** *nt* specimen;
(*Buchexemplar*) copy; **e~isch** *adj* exemplary

Exil [ɛ'ksiːl] **(-s, -e)** *nt* exile

Existenz [ɛksɪs'tɛnts] *f* existence; (*Unterhalt*)
livelihood, living; (*pej: Mensch*) character;
~minimum **(-s)** *nt* subsistence level

existieren [ɛksɪs'tiːrən] *vi* to exist

exklusiv [ɛksklu'ziːf] *adj* exclusive; **~e** *adv*
exclusive of, not including ♦ *präp +gen*
exclusive of, not including

exotisch [ɛ'ksoːtɪʃ] *adj* exotic

Expedition [ɛkspeditsi'oːn] *f* expedition

Experiment [ɛksperi'mɛnt] *nt* experiment;

e~ell [-'tɛl] *adj* experimental; **e~ieren**
[-'tiːrən] *vi* to experiment

Experte [ɛks'pɛrtə] **(-n, -n)** *m* expert,
specialist; **Expertin** *f* expert, specialist

explo- [ɛksplo] *zW*: **~dieren** [-'diːrən] *vi* to
explode; **E~sion** [-zi'oːn] *f* explosion; **~siv**
[-'ziːf] *adj* explosive

Export [ɛks'pɔrt] **(-(e)s, -e)** *m* export; **~eur**
[-'tøːr] *m* exporter; **~handel** *m* export
trade; **~ieren** [-'tiːrən] *vt* to export; **~land**
nt exporting country

Express- ▲ [ɛks'prɛs] *zW*: **~gut** *nt* express
goods *pl*, express freight; **~zug** *m* express
(train)

extra ['ɛkstra] *adj inv* (*umg: gesondert*)
separate; (*besondere*) extra ♦ *adv* (*gesondert*)
separately; (*speziell*) specially; (*absichtlich*)
on purpose; (*vor Adjektiven, zusätzlich*) extra;
E~ **(-s, -s)** *nt* extra; **E~ausgabe** *f* special
edition; **E~blatt** *nt* special edition

Extrakt [ɛks'trakt] **(-(e)s, -e)** *m* extract

extravagant [ɛkstrava'gant] *adj* extravagant

extrem [ɛks'treːm] *adj* extreme; **~istisch**
[-'mɪstɪʃ] *adj* (*POL*) extremist; **E~itäten**
[-mi'tɛːtən] *pl* extremities

exzentrisch [ɛks'tsɛntrɪʃ] *adj* eccentric

EZ *nt abk* = **Einzelzimmer**

EZB *f abk* (= *Europäische Zentralbank*) ECB

F, f

Fa. *abk* (= *Firma*) firm; (*in Briefen*) Messrs

Fabel ['faːbəl] **(-, -n)** *f* fable; **f~haft** *adj*
fabulous, marvellous

Fabrik [fa'briːk] *f* factory; **~ant** [-'kant] *m*
(*Hersteller*) manufacturer; (*Besitzer*)
industrialist; **~arbeiter** *m* factory worker;
~at [-'kaːt] **(-(e)s, -e)** *nt* manufacture,
product; **~gelände** *nt* factory site

Fach [fax] **(-(e)s, ¨er)** *nt* compartment;
(*Sachgebiet*) subject; **ein Mann vom ~** an
expert; **~arbeiter** *m* skilled worker; **~arzt**
m (medical) specialist; **~ausdruck** *m*
technical term

Fächer ['fɛçər] **(-s, -)** *m* fan

Fach- *zW*: **~geschäft** *nt* specialist shop;

~**hochschule** f technical college; ~**kraft** f skilled worker, trained employee; **f~kundig** adj expert, specialist; **f~lich** adj professional; expert; ~**mann** (pl -**leute**) m specialist; **f~männisch** adj professional; ~**schule** f technical college; **f~simpeln** vi to talk shop; ~**werk** nt timber frame

Fackel ['fakəl] (-, -n) f torch

fad(e) [fa:t, 'fa:də] adj insipid; (langweilig) dull

Faden ['fa:dən] (-s, ⸚) m thread; **f~scheinig** adj (auch fig) threadbare

fähig ['fɛ:ɪç] adj: ~ (**zu** od +gen) capable (of); able (to); **F~keit** f ability

fahnden ['fa:ndən] vi: ~ **nach** to search for; **Fahndung** f search

Fahndungsliste f list of wanted criminals, wanted list

Fahne ['fa:nə] f flag, standard; **eine ~ haben** (umg) to smell of drink; ~**nflucht** f desertion

Fahr- zW: ~**ausweis** m ticket; ~**bahn** f carriageway (BRIT), roadway

Fähre ['fɛ:rə] f ferry

fahren ['fa:rən] (unreg) vt to drive; (Rad) to ride; (befördern) to drive, to take; (Rennen) to drive in ♦ vi (sich bewegen) to go; (Schiff) to sail; (abfahren) to leave; **mit dem Auto/ Zug ~** to go od travel by car/train; **mit der Hand ~ über** +akk to pass one's hand over

Fahr- zW: ~**er(in)** (-s, -) m(f) driver; ~**erflucht** f hit-and-run; ~**gast** m passenger; ~**geld** nt fare; ~**karte** f ticket; ~**kartenausgabe** f ticket office; ~**kartenautomat** m ticket machine; ~**kartenschalter** m ticket office; **f~lässig** adj negligent; **f~lässige Tötung** manslaughter; ~**lehrer** m driving instructor; ~**plan** m timetable; **f~planmäßig** adj scheduled; ~**preis** m fare; ~**prüfung** f driving test; ~**rad** nt bicycle; ~**radweg** m cycle lane; ~**schein** m ticket; ~**scheinentwerter** m (automatic) ticket stamping machine

Fährschiff ['fɛ:rʃɪf] nt ferry(boat)

Fahr- zW: ~**schule** f driving school; ~**spur** f lane; ~**stuhl** m lift (BRIT), elevator (US)

Fahrt [fa:rt] (-, -en) f journey; (kurz) trip;

(AUT) drive; (Geschwindigkeit) speed; **gute ~!** have a good journey

Fährte ['fɛ:rtə] f track, trail

Fahrt- zW: ~**kosten** pl travelling expenses; ~**richtung** f course, direction

Fahrzeit f time for the journey

Fahrzeug nt vehicle; ~**brief** m log book; ~**papiere** pl vehicle documents

fair [fɛ:r] adj fair

Fakt [fakt] (-(e)s, -en) m fact

Faktor ['faktɔr] m factor

Fakultät [fakʊl'tɛ:t] f faculty

Falke ['falkə] (-n, -n) m falcon

Fall [fal] (-(e)s, ⸚e) m (Sturz) fall; (Sachverhalt, JUR, GRAM) case; **auf jeden ~, auf alle Fälle** in any case; (bestimmt) definitely; **auf keinen ~!** no way!

Falle f trap

fallen (unreg) vi to fall; **etw ~ lassen** to drop sth; (Bemerkung) to make sth; (Plan) to abandon sth, to drop sth

fällen ['fɛlən] vt (Baum) to fell; (Urteil) to pass

fällig ['fɛlɪç] adj due

falls [fals] adv in case, if

Fallschirm m parachute; ~**springer** m parachutist

falsch [falʃ] adj false; (unrichtig) wrong

fälschen ['fɛlʃən] vt to forge

fälsch- zW: ~**lich** adj false; ~**licherweise** adv mistakenly; **F~ung** f forgery

Falte ['faltə] f (Knick) fold, crease; (Hautfalte) wrinkle; (Rockfalte) pleat; **f~n** vt to fold; (Stirn) to wrinkle

faltig ['faltɪç] adj (Hände, Haut) wrinkled; (zerknittert: Rock) creased

familiär [famili'ɛ:r] adj familiar

Familie [fa'mi:liə] f family

Familien- zW: ~**betrieb** m family business; ~**kreis** m family circle; ~**mitglied** nt member of the family; ~**name** m surname; ~**stand** m marital status

Fanatiker [fa'na:tikər] (-s, -) m fanatic; **fanatisch** adj fanatical

fand etc [fant] vb siehe **finden**

Fang [faŋ] (-(e)s, ⸚e) m catch; (Jagen) hunting; (Kralle) talon, claw; **f~en** (unreg) vt to catch ♦ vr to get caught; (Flugzeug) to level out; (*Mensch: nicht fallen*) to steady o.s.; (*fig*) to compose o.s.; (*in Leistung*) to get back on form

Fantasie ▲ [fanta'zi:] *f* imagination; **f~los** *adj* unimaginative; **f~ren** *vi* to fantasize; **f~voll** *adj* imaginative

fantastisch ▲ [fan'tastɪʃ] *adj* fantastic

Farb- ['farb] *zW:* **~abzug** *m* colour print; **~aufnahme** *f* colour photograph; **~band** *m* typewriter ribbon; **~e** *f* colour; (*zum Malen etc*) paint; (*Stoffarbe*) dye; **f~echt** *adj* colourfast

färben ['ferbən] *vt* to colour; (*Stoff, Haar*) to dye

farben- ['farbən] *zW:* **~blind** *adj* colour-blind; **~freudig** *adj* colourful; **~froh** *adj* colourful, gay

Farb- *zW:* **~fernsehen** *nt* colour television; **~film** *m* colour film; **~foto** *nt* colour photograph; **f~ig** *adj* coloured; **~ige(r)** *f(m)* coloured (person); **~kasten** *m* paintbox; **f~lich** *adj* colour; **f~los** *adj* colourless; **~stift** *m* coloured pencil; **~stoff** *m* dye; **~ton** *m* hue, tone

Färbung ['ferbʊŋ] *f* colouring; (*Tendenz*) bias

Farn [farn] (**-(e)s, -e**) *m* fern; bracken

Fasan [fa'za:n] (**-(e)s, -e(n)**) *m* pheasant

Fasching ['faʃɪŋ] (**-s, -e** *od* **-s**) *m* carnival

Faschismus [fa'ʃɪsmʊs] *m* fascism

Faschist *m* fascist

Faser ['fa:zər] (**-, -n**) *f* fibre; **f~n** *vi* to fray

Fass ▲ [fas] (**-es, ⁻er** *od* **-s**) *nt* vat, barrel; (*für Öl*) drum; **Bier vom ~** draught beer

Fassade [fa'sa:də] *f* façade

fassen ['fasən] *vt* (*ergreifen*) to grasp, to take; (*inhaltlich*) to hold; (*Entschluss etc*) to take; (*verstehen*) to understand; (*Ring etc*) to set; (*formulieren*) to formulate, to phrase ♦ *vr* to calm down; **nicht zu ~** unbelievable

Fassung ['fasʊŋ] *f* (*Umrahmung*) mounting; (*Lampenfassung*) socket; (*Wortlaut*) version; (*Beherrschung*) composure; **jdn aus der ~ bringen** to upset sb; **f~slos** *adj* speechless

fast [fast] *adv* almost, nearly

fasten ['fastən] *vi* to fast; **F~zeit** *f* Lent

Fastnacht *f* Shrove Tuesday; carnival

faszinieren [fastsi'ni:rən] *vt* to fascinate

fatal [fa'ta:l] *adj* fatal; (*peinlich*) embarrassing

faul [faʊl] *adj* rotten; (*Person*) lazy; (*Ausreden*) lame; **daran ist etwas ~** there's something fishy about it; **~en** *vi* to rot; **~enzen** *vi* to idle; **F~enzer** (**-s, -**) *m* idler, loafer; **F~heit** *f* laziness; **~ig** *adj* putrid

Faust ['faʊst] (**-, Fäuste**) *f* fist; **auf eigene ~** off one's own bat; **~handschuh** *m* mitten

Favorit [favo'ri:t] (**-en, -en**) *m* favourite

Fax [faks] (**-, -(e)**) *nt* fax

faxen ['faksən] *vt* to fax; **jdm etw ~** to fax sth to sb

FCKW *m abk* (= *Fluorchlorkohlenwasserstoff*) CFC

Februar ['fe:brua:r] (**-(s), -e**) *m* February

fechten ['fɛçtən] (*unreg*) *vi* to fence

Feder ['fe:dər] (**-, -n**) *f* feather; (*Schreibfeder*) pen nib; (*TECH*) spring; **~ball** *m* shuttlecock; **~bett** *nt* continental quilt; **~halter** *m* penholder, pen; **f~leicht** *adj* light as a feather; **f~n** *vi* (*nachgeben*) to be springy; (*sich bewegen*) to bounce ♦ *vt* to spring; **~ung** *f* (*AUT*) suspension

Fee [fe:] *f* fairy

fegen ['fe:gən] *vt* to sweep

fehl [fe:l] *adj:* **~ am Platz** *od* **Ort** out of place; **F~betrag** *m* deficit; **~en** *vi* to be wanting *od* missing; (*abwesend sein*) to be absent; **etw ~t jdm** sb lacks sth; **du ~st mir** I miss you; **was ~t ihm?** what's wrong with him?; **F~er** (**-s, -**) *m* mistake, error; (*Mangel, Schwäche*) fault; **~erfrei** *adj* faultless, without any mistakes; **~erhaft** *adj* incorrect; faulty; **~erlos** *adj* flawless, perfect; **F~geburt** *f* miscarriage; **~gehen** (*unreg*) *vi* to go astray; **F~griff** *m* blunder; **F~konstruktion** *f* badly designed thing; **~schlagen** (*unreg*) *vi* to fail; **F~start** *m* (*SPORT*) false start; **F~zündung** *f* (*AUT*) misfire, backfire

Feier ['faɪər] (**-, -n**) *f* celebration; **~abend** *m* time to stop work; **~abend machen** to stop, to knock off; **jetzt ist ~abend!** that's enough!; **f~lich** *adj* solemn; **~lichkeit** *f* solemnity; **~lichkeiten** *pl* (*Veranstaltungen*) festivities; **f~n** *vt, vi* to celebrate; **~tag** *m* holiday

feig(e) [faɪk, 'faɪɡə] adj cowardly

Feige ['faɪɡə] f fig

Feigheit f cowardice

Feigling m coward

Feile ['faɪlə] f file

feilschen ['faɪlʃən] vi to haggle

fein [faɪn] adj fine; (vornehm) refined; (Gehör etc) keen; **~!** great!

Feind [faɪnt] **(-(e)s, -e)** m enemy; **f~lich** adj hostile; **~schaft** f enmity; **f~selig** adj hostile

Fein- zW: **f~fühlig** adj sensitive; **~gefühl** nt delicacy, tact; **~heit** f fineness; refinement; keenness; **~kostgeschäft** nt delicatessen (shop); **~schmecker (-s, -)** m gourmet; **~wäsche** f delicate clothing (when washing); **~waschmittel** nt mild detergent

Feld [fɛlt] **(-(e)s, -er)** nt field; (SCHACH) square; (SPORT) pitch; **~herr** m commander; **~stecher (-s, -)** m binoculars pl; **~weg** m path; **~zug** m (fig) campaign

Felge ['fɛlɡə] f (wheel) rim

Fell [fɛl] **(-(e)s, -e)** nt fur; coat; (von Schaf) fleece; (von toten Tieren) skin

Fels [fɛls] **(-en, -en)** m rock; (Klippe) cliff

Felsen ['fɛlzən] **(-s, -)** m = **Fels**; **f~fest** adj firm

feminin [femi'niːn] adj feminine

Fenster ['fɛnstɐ] **(-s, -)** nt window; **~bank** f windowsill; **~laden** m shutter; **~leder** nt chamois (leather); **~scheibe** f windowpane

Ferien ['feːriən] pl holidays, vacation sg (US); **~ haben** to be on holiday; **~bungalow** [-bʊŋɡalo] **(-s, -s)** m holiday bungalow; **~haus** nt holiday home; **~kurs** m holiday course; **~lager** nt holiday camp; **~reise** f holiday; **~wohnung** f holiday apartment

Ferkel ['fɛrkəl] **(-s, -)** nt piglet

fern [fɛrn] adj, adv far-off, distant; **~ von hier** a long way (away) from here; **der F~e Osten** the Far East; **~ halten** to keep away; **F~bedienung** f remote control; **F~e** f distance; **~er** adj further ♦ adv further; (weiterhin) in future; **F~gespräch** nt trunk call; **F~glas** nt binoculars pl; **F~licht** nt

(AUT) full beam; **F~rohr** nt telescope; **F~ruf** m (förmlich) telephone number; **F~schreiben** nt telex; **F~sehapparat** m television set; **F~sehen (-s)** nt television; **im F~sehen** on television; **~sehen** (unreg) vi to watch television; **F~seher** m television; **F~sehturm** m television tower; **F~sprecher** m telephone; **F~steuerung** f remote control; **F~straße** f ≈ 'A' road (BRIT), highway (US); **F~verkehr** m long-distance traffic

Ferse ['fɛrzə] f heel

fertig ['fɛrtɪç] adj (bereit) ready; (beendet) finished; (gebrauchsfertig) ready-made; **~ bringen** (fähig sein) to be capable of; **~ machen** (beenden) to finish; (umg: Person) to finish; (: körperlich) to exhaust; (: moralisch) to get down; **sich ~ machen** to get ready; **~ stellen** to complete; **F~gericht** nt precooked meal; **F~haus** nt kit house, prefab; **F~keit** f skill

Fessel ['fɛsəl] **(-, -n)** f fetter; **f~n** vt to bind; (mit ~n) to fetter; (fig) to spellbind; **f~nd** adj fascinating, captivating

Fest [fɛst] **(-(e)s, -e)** nt party; festival; **frohes ~!** Happy Christmas!

fest [fɛst] adj firm; (Nahrung) solid; (Gehalt) regular; **~e Kosten** fixed cost ♦ adv (schlafen) soundly; **~ angestellt** permanently employed; **~binden** (unreg) vt to tie, to fasten; **~bleiben** (unreg) vi to stand firm; **F~essen** nt banquet; **~halten** (unreg) vt to seize, to hold fast; (Ereignis) to record ♦ vr: **sich ~halten (an** +dat) to hold on (to); **~igen** vt to strengthen; **F~igkeit** f strength; **F~ival** ['fɛstival] **(-s, -s)** nt festival; **~land** nt mainland; **~legen** vt to fix ♦ vr to commit o.s.; **~lich** adj festive; **~liegen** (unreg) vi (~stehen: Termin) to be confirmed, be fixed; **~machen** vt to fasten; (Termin etc) to fix; **F~nahme** f arrest; **~nehmen** (unreg) vt to arrest; **F~preis** m (COMM) fixed price; **F~rede** f address; **~setzen** vt to fix, to settle; **F~spiele** pl (Veranstaltung) festival sg; **~stehen** (unreg) vi to be certain; **~stellen** vt to establish; (sagen) to remark; **F~tag** m

Spelling Reform: ▲ *new spelling* △ *old spelling (to be phased out)*

feast day, holiday; **F~ung** *f* fortress;
F~wochen *pl* festival *sg*

Fett [fɛt] **(-(e)s, -e)** *nt* fat, grease

fett *adj* fat; (*Essen etc*) greasy; (*TYP*) bold;
~arm *adj* low fat; **~en** *vt* to grease;
F~fleck *m* grease stain; **~ig** *adj* greasy,
fatty

Fetzen ['fɛtsən] **(-s, -)** *m* scrap

feucht [fɔʏçt] *adj* damp; (*Luft*) humid;
F~igkeit *f* dampness; humidity;
F~igkeitscreme *f* moisturizing cream

Feuer ['fɔʏər] **(-s, -)** *nt* fire; (*zum Rauchen*) a
light; (*fig: Schwung*) spirit; **~alarm** *nt* fire
alarm; **f~fest** *adj* fireproof; **~gefahr** *f*
danger of fire; **f~gefährlich** *adj*
inflammable; **~leiter** *f* fire escape ladder;
~löscher (-s, -) *m* fire extinguisher;
~melder (-s, -) *m* fire alarm; **f~n** *vt, vi*
(*auch fig*) to fire; **~stein** *m* flint; **~treppe** *f*
fire escape; **~wehr (-, -en)** *f* fire brigade;
~wehrauto *nt* fire engine; **~wehrfrau** *f*
firewoman; **~wehrmann** *m* fireman;
~werk *nt* fireworks *pl*; **~zeug** *nt*
(cigarette) lighter

Fichte ['fɪçtə] *f* spruce, pine

Fieber ['fiːbər] **(-s, -)** *nt* fever, temperature;
f~haft *adj* feverish; **~thermometer** *nt*
thermometer; **fiebrig** *adj* feverish

fiel *etc* [fiːl] *vb siehe* **fallen**

fies [fiːs] (*umg*) *adj* nasty

Figur [fiˈɡuːr] **(-, -en)** *f* figure; (*Schachfigur*)
chessman, chess piece

Filet [fiˈleː] **(-s, -s)** *nt* (*KOCH*) fillet

Filiale [filiˈaːlə] *f* (*COMM*) branch

Film [fɪlm] **(-(e)s, -e)** *m* film; **~aufnahme** *f*
shooting; **f~en** *vt, vi* to film; **~kamera** *f*
cine camera

Filter ['fɪltər] **(-s, -)** *m* filter; **f~n** *vt* to filter;
~papier *nt* filter paper; **~zigarette** *f*
tipped cigarette

Filz [fɪlts] **(-es, -e)** *m* felt; **f~en** *vt* (*umg*) to
frisk ♦ *vi* (*Wolle*) to mat; **~stift** *m* felt-tip
pen

Finale [fiˈnaːlə] **(-s, -(s))** *nt* finale; (*SPORT*)
final(s)

Finanz [fiˈnants] *f* finance; **~amt** *nt* Inland
Revenue office; **~beamte(r)** *m* revenue

officer, **f~iell** [-tsiˈɛl] *adj* financial; **f~ieren**
[-ˈtsiːrən] *vt* to finance; **f~kräftig** *adj*
financially strong; **~minister** *m* Chancellor
of the Exchequer (*BRIT*), Minister of Finance

Find- [fɪnd] *zW:* **f~en** (*unreg*) *vt* to find;
(*meinen*) to think ♦ *vr* to be (found); (*sich
fassen*) to compose o.s.; **ich f~e nichts
dabei, wenn ...** I don't see what's wrong if
...; **das wird sich f~en** things will work
out; **~er (-s, -)** *m* finder; **~erlohn** *m*
reward (*for sb who finds sth*); **f~ig** *adj*
resourceful

fing *etc* [fɪŋ] *vb siehe* **fangen**

Finger ['fɪŋər] **(-s, -)** *m* finger; **~abdruck** *m*
fingerprint; **~nagel** *m* fingernail; **~spitze** *f*
fingertip

fingiert *adj* made-up, fictitious

Fink ['fɪŋk] **(-en, -en)** *m* finch

Finn- [fɪn] *zW:* **~e (-n, -n)** *m* Finn; **~in** *f*
Finn; **f~isch** *adj* Finnish; **~land** *nt* Finland

finster ['fɪnstər] *adj* dark, gloomy;
(*verdächtig*) dubious; (*verdrossen*) grim;
(*Gedanke*) dark; **F~nis (-)** *f* darkness, gloom

Firma ['fɪrma] **(-, -men)** *f* firm

Firmen- ['fɪrmən] *zW:* **~inhaber** *m* owner
of firm; **~schild** *nt* (shop) sign; **~wagen**
m company car; **~zeichen** *nt* trademark

Fisch [fɪʃ] **(-(e)s, -e)** *m* fish; **~e** *pl* (*ASTROL*)
Pisces *sg*; **f~en** *vt, vi* to fish; **~er (-s, -)** *m*
fisherman; **~erei** *f* fishing, fishery; **~fang**
m fishing; **~geschäft** *nt* fishmonger's
(shop); **~gräte** *f* fishbone; **~stäbchen**
[-ˈstɛːpçən] *nt* fish finger (*BRIT*), fish stick (*US*)

fit [fɪt] *adj* fit; **'F~ness ▲ (-, -)** *f* (physical)
fitness

fix [fɪks] *adj* fixed; (*Person*) alert, smart; **~ und
fertig** finished; (*erschöpft*) done in;
F~er(in) *m(f)* (*umg*) junkie; **F~erstube** *f*
(*umg*) junkies centre; **~ieren** [fɪˈksiːrən] *vt*
to fix; (*anstarren*) to stare at

flach [flax] *adj* flat; (*Gefäß*) shallow

Fläche ['flɛçə] *f* area; (*Oberfläche*) surface

Flachland *nt* lowland

flackern ['flakərn] *vi* to flare, to flicker

Flagge ['flagə] *f* flag; **f~n** *vi* to fly a flag

flämisch ['flɛːmɪʃ] *adj* (*LING*) Flemish

Flamme ['flamə] *f* flame

Flandern ['flandərn] *nt* Flanders

Flanke ['flaŋkə] *f* flank; (*SPORT: Seite*) wing

Flasche ['flaʃə] *f* bottle; (*umg: Versager*) wash-out

Flaschen- *zW:* **~bier** *nt* bottled beer; **~öffner** *m* bottle opener; **~zug** *m* pulley

flatterhaft *adj* flighty, fickle

flattern ['flatərn] *vi* to flutter

flau [flau] *adj* weak, listless; (*Nachfrage*) slack; **jdm ist ~** sb feels queasy

Flaum [flaum] (**-(e)s**) *m* (*Feder*) down; (*Haare*) fluff

flauschig ['flauʃɪç] *adj* fluffy

Flaute ['flautə] *f* calm; (*COMM*) recession

Flechte ['flɛçtə] *f* plait; (*MED*) dry scab; (*BOT*) lichen; **f~n** (*unreg*) *vt* to plait; (*Kranz*) to twine

Fleck [flɛk] (**-(e)s, -e**) *m* spot; (*Schmutzfleck*) stain; (*Stofffleck*) patch; (*Makel*) blemish; **nicht vom ~ kommen** (*auch fig*) not to get any further; **vom ~ weg** straight away

Flecken (**-s, -**) *m* = **Fleck; f~los** *adj* spotless; **~mittel** *nt* stain remover; **~wasser** *nt* stain remover

fleckig *adj* spotted; stained

Fledermaus ['fle:dərmaus] *f* bat

Flegel ['fle:gəl] (**-s, -**) *m* (*Mensch*) lout; **f~haft** *adj* loutish, unmannerly; **~jahre** *pl* adolescence *sg*

flehen ['fle:ən] *vi* to implore; **~tlich** *adj* imploring

Fleisch [flaiʃ] (**-(e)s**) *nt* flesh; (*Essen*) meat; **~brühe** *f* beef tea, meat stock; **~er** (**-s, -**) *m* butcher; **~erei** *f* butcher's (shop); **f~ig** *adj* fleshy; **f~los** *adj* meatless, vegetarian

Fleiß ['flaɪs] (**-es**) *m* diligence, industry; **f~ig** *adj* diligent, industrious

fletschen ['flɛtʃən] *vt* (*Zähne*) to show

flexibel [flɛ'ksi:bəl] *adj* flexible

Flicken ['flɪkən] (**-s, -**) *m* patch; **f~** *vt* to mend

Flieder ['fli:dər] (**-s, -**) *m* lilac

Fliege ['fli:gə] *f* fly; (*Kleidung*) bow tie; **f~n** (*unreg*) *vt, vi* to fly; **auf jdn/etw f~n** (*umg*) to be mad about sb/sth; **~npilz** *m* toadstool; **~r** (**-s, -**) *m* flier, airman

fliehen ['fli:ən] (*unreg*) *vi* to flee

Fliese ['fli:zə] *f* tile

Fließ- ['fli:s] *zW:* **~band** *nt* production *od* assembly line; **f~en** (*unreg*) *vi* to flow; **f~end** *adj* flowing; (*Rede, Deutsch*) fluent; (*Übergänge*) smooth

flimmern ['flɪmərn] *vi* to glimmer

flink [flɪŋk] *adj* nimble, lively

Flinte ['flɪntə] *f* rifle; shotgun

Flitterwochen *pl* honeymoon *sg*

flitzen ['flɪtsən] *vi* to flit

Flocke ['flɔkə] *f* flake

flog *etc* [flo:k] *vb siehe* **fliegen**

Floh [flo:] (**-(e)s, ̈e**) *m* flea; **~markt** *m* flea market

florieren [flo'ri:rən] *vi* to flourish

Floskel ['flɔskəl] (**-, -n**) *f* set phrase

Floß [flɔs] (**-es, ̈e**) *nt* raft, float

floss ▲ *etc vb siehe* **fließen**

Flosse ['flɔsə] *f* fin

Flöte ['flø:tə] *f* flute; (*Blockflöte*) recorder

flott [flɔt] *adj* lively; (*elegant*) smart; (*NAUT*) afloat; **F~e** *f* fleet, navy

Fluch [flu:x] (**-(e)s, ̈e**) *m* curse; **f~en** *vi* to curse, to swear

Flucht [fluxt] (**-, -en**) *f* flight; (*Fensterflucht*) row; (*Zimmerflucht*) suite; **f~artig** *adj* hasty

flücht- ['flʏçt] *zW:* **~en** *vi, vr* to flee, to escape; **~ig** *adj* fugitive; (*vergänglich*) transitory; (*oberflächlich*) superficial; (*eilig*) fleeting; **F~igkeitsfehler** *m* careless slip; **F~ling** *m* fugitive, refugee

Flug [flu:k] (**-(e)s, ̈e**) *m* flight; **~blatt** *nt* pamphlet

Flügel ['fly:gəl] (**-s, -**) *m* wing; (*MUS*) grand piano

Fluggast *m* airline passenger

Flug- *zW:* **~gesellschaft** *f* airline (company); **~hafen** *m* airport; **~lärm** *m* aircraft noise; **~linie** *f* airline; **~plan** *m* flight schedule; **~platz** *m* airport; (*klein*) airfield; **~reise** *f* flight; **~schein** *m* (*Ticket*) plane ticket; (*Pilotenschein*) pilot's licence; **~steig** [-ʃtaɪk] (**-(e)s, -e**) *m* gate; **~verbindung** *f* air connection; **~verkehr** *m* air traffic; **~zeug** *nt* (aero)plane, airplane (*US*); **~zeugentführung** *f* hijacking of a plane; **~zeughalle** *f* hangar; **~zeugträger**

m aircraft carrier

Flunder ['flʊndər] (-, -n) *f* flounder

flunkern ['flʊŋkərn] *vi* to fib, to tell stories

Fluor ['fluːɔr] (-s) *nt* fluorine

Flur [fluːr] (-(e)s, -e) *m* hall; (*Treppenflur*) staircase

Fluss ▲ [flʊs] (-es, ⸚e) *m* river; (*Fließen*) flow

flüssig ['flʏsɪç] *adj* liquid; ~ **machen** (*Geld*) to make available; **F~keit** *f* liquid; (*Zustand*) liquidity

flüstern ['flʏstərn] *vt, vi* to whisper

Flut [fluːt] (-, -en) *f* (*auch fig*) flood; (*Gezeiten*) high tide; **f~en** *vi* to flood; ~**licht** *nt* floodlight

Fohlen ['foːlən] (-s, -) *nt* foal

Föhn[1] [føːn] (-(e)s, -e) *m* (*warmer Fallwind*) föhn

Föhn[2] (-(e)s, -e) ▲ (*Haartrockner*) hairdryer; **f~en** ▲ *vt* to (blow) dry; ~**frisur** ▲ *f* blow-dry hairstyle

Folge ['fɔlgə] *f* series, sequence; (*Fortsetzung*) instalment; (*Auswirkung*) result; **in rascher** ~ in quick succession; **etw zur** ~ **haben** to result in sth; ~**n haben** to have consequences; **einer Sache** *dat* ~ **leisten** to comply with sth; **f~n** *vi* +*dat* to follow; (*gehorchen*) to obey; **jdm f~n können** (*fig*) to follow *od* understand sb; **f~nd** *adj* following; **f~ndermaßen** *adv* as follows, in the following way; **f~rn** *vt*: **f~rn (aus)** to conclude (from); ~**rung** *f* conclusion

folglich ['fɔlklɪç] *adv* consequently

folgsam ['fɔlkzaːm] *adj* obedient

Folie ['foːliə] *f* foil

Folklore ['fɔlkloːər] *f* folklore

Folter ['fɔltər] (-, -n) *f* torture; (*Gerät*) rack; **f~n** *vt* to torture

Fön [føːn] (-(e)s, -e) ® *m* hair dryer

Fondue [fõdyː] (-s, -s *od* -, -s) *nt od f* (*KOCH*) fondue

fönen △ *vt siehe* **föhnen**

Fönfrisur △ *f siehe* **Föhnfrisur**

Fontäne [fɔn'tɛːnə] *f* fountain

Förder- ['fœrdər] *zW*: ~**band** *nt* conveyor belt; ~**korb** *m* pit cage; **f~lich** *adj* beneficial

fordern ['fɔrdərn] *vt* to demand

fördern ['fœrdərn] *vt* to promote; (*unterstützen*) to help; (*Kohle*) to extract

Forderung ['fɔrdərʊŋ] *f* demand

Förderung ['fœrdərʊŋ] *f* promotion; help; extraction

Forelle [fo'rɛlə] *f* trout

Form [fɔrm] (-, -en) *f* shape; (*Gestaltung*) form; (*Gussform*) mould; (*Backform*) baking tin; **in** ~ **sein** to be in good form *od* shape; **in** ~ **von** in the shape of

Formali'tät *f* formality

Format [fɔr'maːt] (-(e)s, -e) *nt* format; (*fig*) distinction

formbar *adj* malleable

Formblatt *nt* form

Formel (-, -n) *f* formula

formell [fɔr'mɛl] *adj* formal

formen *vt* to form, to shape

Formfehler *m* faux pas, gaffe; (*JUR*) irregularity

formieren [fɔr'miːrən] *vt* to form ♦ *vr* to form up

förmlich ['fœrmlɪç] *adj* formal; (*umg*) real; **F~keit** *f* formality

formlos *adj* shapeless; (*Benehmen etc*) informal

Formular [fɔrmu'laːr] (-s, -e) *nt* form

formulieren [fɔrmu'liːrən] *vt* to formulate

forsch [fɔrʃ] *adj* energetic, vigorous

forsch- *zW*: ~**en** *vi*: ~**en (nach)** to search (for); (*wissenschaftlich*) to (do) research; ~**end** *adj* searching; **F~er** (-s, -) *m* research scientist; (*Naturforscher*) explorer; **F~ung** *f* research

Forst [fɔrst] (-(e)s, -e) *m* forest

Förster ['fœrstər] (-s, -) *m* forester; (*für Wild*) gamekeeper

fort [fɔrt] *adv* away; (*verschwunden*) gone; (*vorwärts*) on; **und so** ~ and so on; **in einem** ~ on and on; ~**bestehen** (*unreg*) *vi* to survive; ~**bewegen** *vt, vr* to move away; ~**bilden** *vr* to continue one's education; ~**bleiben** (*unreg*) *vi* to stay away; **F~dauer** *f* continuance; ~**fahren** (*unreg*) *vi* to depart; (*~setzen*) to go on, to continue; ~**führen** *vt* to continue, to carry on; ~**gehen** (*unreg*) *vi* to go away;

~**geschritten** adj advanced; ~**pflanzen** vr to reproduce; **F~pflanzung** f reproduction

fort- zW: ~**schaffen** vt to remove; ~**schreiten** (unreg) vi to advance

Fortschritt ['fɔrtʃrɪt] m advance; ~**e machen** to make progress; **f~lich** adj progressive

fort- zW: ~**setzen** vt to continue; **F~setzung** f continuation; (folgender Teil) instalment; **F~setzung folgt** to be continued; ~**während** adj incessant, continual

Foto ['fo:to] nt (-s, -s) photo(graph); ~**apparat** m camera; ~'**graf** m photographer; ~**gra'fie** f photography; (Bild) photograph; **f~gra'fieren** vt to photograph ♦ vi to take photographs; ~**kopie** f photocopy

Fr. abk (= Frau) Mrs, Ms

Fracht [fraxt] f (-, -en) freight; (NAUT) cargo; (Preis) carriage; ~ **zahlt Empfänger** (COMM) carriage forward; ~**er** (-s, -) m freighter, cargo boat; ~**gut** nt freight

Frack [frak] (-(e)s, ⁿe) m tails pl

Frage ['fra:gə] f (-, -n) f question; **jdm eine ~ stellen** to ask sb a question, to put a question to sb; siehe **infrage**; ~**bogen** m questionnaire; **f~n** vt, vi to ask; ~**zeichen** nt question mark

fraglich adj questionable, doubtful

fraglos adv unquestionably

Fragment [fra'gment] nt fragment

fragwürdig ['fra:kvyrdɪç] adj questionable, dubious

Fraktion [fraktsi'o:n] f parliamentary party

frankieren [fraŋ'ki:rən] vt to stamp, to frank

franko ['fraŋko] adv post-paid; carriage paid

Frankreich ['fraŋkraɪç] (-s) nt France

Franzose [fran'tso:zə] m Frenchman; **Französin** [fran'tsø:zɪn] f Frenchwoman; **französisch** adj French

fraß etc [fras] vb siehe **fressen**

Fratze ['fratsə] f grimace

Frau [frau] (-, -en) f woman; (Ehefrau) wife; (Anrede) Mrs, Ms; ~ **Doktor** Doctor

Frauen- zW: ~**arzt** m gynaecologist; ~**bewegung** f feminist movement; ~**haus**

nt women's refuge; ~**zimmer** nt female, broad (US)

Fräulein ['frɔylaɪn] nt young lady; (Anrede) Miss, Ms

fraulich ['fraulɪç] adj womanly

frech [freç] adj cheeky, impudent; **F~heit** f cheek, impudence

frei [fraɪ] adj free; (Stelle, Sitzplatz) free, vacant; (Mitarbeiter) freelance; (unbekleidet) bare; **von etw ~ sein** to be free of sth; **im F~en** in the open air; ~ **sprechen** to talk without notes; ~ **Haus** (COMM) carriage paid; ~**er Wettbewerb** (COMM) fair/open competition; **F~bad** nt open-air swimming pool; ~**bekommen** (unreg) vt: **einen Tag ~bekommen** to get a day off; ~**beruflich** adj self-employed; ~**gebig** adj generous; ~**halten** (unreg) vt to keep free; ~**händig** adv (fahren) with no hands; **F~heit** f freedom; ~**heitlich** adj liberal; **F~heitsstrafe** f prison sentence; **F~karte** f free ticket; ~**lassen** (unreg) vt to (set) free; ~**legen** vt to expose; ~**lich** adv certainly, admittedly; **ja ~lich** yes of course; **F~lichtbühne** f open-air theatre; **F~lichtmuseum** nt open-air museum; ~**machen** vt (Post) to frank ♦ vr to arrange to be free; (entkleiden) to undress; **Tage ~machen** to take days off; ~**nehmen** ▲ (unreg) vt: **sich** dat **einen Tag ~nehmen** to take a day off; ~**sprechen** (unreg) vt: ~**sprechen (von)** to acquit (of); **F~spruch** m acquittal; ~**stehen** (unreg) vi: **es steht dir ~, das zu tun** you're free to do that; (leer stehen: Wohnung, Haus) to lie/stand empty; ~**stellen** vt: **jdm etw ~stellen** to leave sth (up) to sb; **F~stoß** m free kick

Freitag m Friday; ~**s** adv on Fridays

frei- zW: ~**willig** adj voluntary; **F~zeit** f spare od free time; **F~zeitpark** m amusement park; **F~zeitzentrum** nt leisure centre; ~**zügig** adj liberal, broad-minded; (mit Geld) generous

fremd [fremt] adj (unvertraut) strange; (ausländisch) foreign; (nicht eigen) someone else's; **etw ist jdm ~** sth is foreign to sb; ~**artig** adj strange; **F~enführer** ['fremdən-]

m (tourist) guide; **F~enverkehr** *m* tourism; **F~enverkehrsamt** *nt* tourist board; **F~enzimmer** *nt* guest room; **F~körper** *m* foreign body; **~ländisch** *adj* foreign; **F~sprache** *f* foreign language; **F~wort** *nt* foreign word

Frequenz [fre'kvɛnts] *f (RADIO)* frequency

fressen ['frɛsən] *(unreg) vt, vi* to eat

Freude ['frɔydə] *f* joy, delight

freudig *adj* joyful, happy

freuen ['frɔyən] *vt unpers* to make happy *od* pleased ♦ *vr* to be glad *od* happy; **freut mich!** pleased to meet you; **sich auf etw** *akk* ~ to look forward to sth; **sich über etw** *akk* ~ to be pleased about sth

Freund ['frɔynt] **(-(e)s, -e)** *m* friend; boyfriend; **~in** [-dɪn] *f* friend; girlfriend; **f~lich** *adj* kind, friendly; **f~licherweise** *adv* kindly; **~lichkeit** *f* friendliness, kindness; **~schaft** *f* friendship; **f~schaftlich** *adj* friendly

Frieden ['fri:dən] **(-s, -)** *m* peace; **im ~** in peacetime

Friedens- *zW:* **~schluss** ▲ *m* peace agreement; **~vertrag** *m* peace treaty; **~zeit** *f* peacetime

fried- ['fri:t] *zW:* **~fertig** *adj* peaceable; **F~hof** *m* cemetery; **~lich** *adj* peaceful

frieren ['fri:rən] *(unreg) vt, vi* to freeze; **ich friere, es friert mich** I'm freezing, I'm cold

Frikadelle [frika'dɛlə] *f* rissole

Frikassee [frika'se:] **(-s, -s)** *nt (KOCH)* fricassee

frisch [frɪʃ] *adj* fresh; *(lebhaft)* lively; **~ gestrichen!** wet paint!; **sich ~ machen** to freshen (o.s.) up; **F~e** *f* freshness; liveliness; **F~haltefolie** *f* cling film

Friseur [fri'zø:r] *m* hairdresser

Friseuse [fri'zø:zə] *f* hairdresser

frisieren [fri'zi:rən] *vt, vi* to do (one's hair); *(fig: Abrechnung)* to fiddle, to doctor ♦ *vr* to do one's hair

Frisiersalon *m* hairdressing salon

frisst ▲ [frɪst] *vb siehe* **fressen**

Frist [frɪst] **(-, -en)** *f* period; *(Termin)* deadline; **f~gerecht** *adj* within the stipulated time *od* period; **f~los** *adj*

(Entlassung) instant

Frisur [fri'zu:r] *f* hairdo, hairstyle

frivol [fri'vo:l] *adj* frivolous

froh [fro:] *adj* happy, cheerful; **ich bin ~, dass ...** I'm glad that ...

fröhlich ['frø:lɪç] *adj* merry, happy; **F~keit** *f* merriness, gaiety

fromm [frɔm] *adj* pious, good; *(Wunsch)* idle; **Frömmigkeit** ['frœmɪçkait] *f* piety

Fronleichnam [fro:n'laiçna:m] **(-(e)s)** *m* Corpus Christi

Front [frɔnt] **(-, -en)** *f* front; **f~al** [frɔn'ta:l] *adj* frontal

fror *etc* [fro:r] *vb siehe* **frieren**

Frosch [frɔʃ] **(-(e)s, ⁺e)** *m* frog; *(Feuerwerk)* squib; **~mann** *m* frogman; **~schenkel** *m* frog's leg

Frost [frɔst] **(-(e)s, ⁺e)** *m* frost; **~beule** *f* chilblain

frösteln ['frœstəln] *vi* to shiver

frostig *adj* frosty

Frostschutzmittel *nt* antifreeze

Frottier(hand)tuch [frɔ'ti:r(hant)tu:x] *nt* towel

Frucht [frʊxt] **(-, ⁺e)** *f (auch fig)* fruit; *(Getreide)* corn; **f~bar** *adj* fruitful, fertile; **~barkeit** *f* fertility; **f~ig** *adj (Geschmack)* fruity; **f~los** *adj* fruitless; **~saft** *m* fruit juice

früh [fry:] *adj, adv* early; **heute ~** this morning; **F~aufsteher (-s, -)** *m* early riser; **F~e** *f* early morning; **~er** *adj* earlier; *(ehemalig)* former ♦ *adv* formerly; **~er war das anders** that used to be different; **~estens** *adv* at the earliest; **F~jahr** *nt*, **F~ling** *m* spring; **~reif** *adj* precocious; **F~stück** *nt* breakfast; **~stücken** *vi* to (have) breakfast; **F~stücksbüfett** *nt* breakfast buffet; **~zeitig** *adj* early; *(pej)* untimely

frustrieren [frʊs'tri:rən] *vt* to frustrate

Fuchs [fʊks] **(-es, ⁺e)** *m* fox; **f~en** *(umg) vt* to rile, to annoy; **f~teufelswild** *adj* hopping mad

Fuge ['fu:gə] *f* joint; *(MUS)* fugue

fügen ['fy:gən] *vt* to place, to join ♦ *vr*: **sich ~ (in** *+dat)* to be obedient (to); *(anpassen)* to adapt oneself (to) ♦ *vr unpers* to happen

fühl- *zW:* **~bar** *adj* perceptible, noticeable;
~en *vt, vi, vr* to feel; **F~er (-s, -)** *m* feeler

fuhr *etc* [fuːr] *vb siehe* **fahren**

führen ['fyːrən] *vt* to lead; (*Geschäft*) to run;
(*Name*) to bear; (*Buch*) to keep ♦ *vi* to lead
♦ *vr* to behave

Führer ['fyːrər] **(-s, -)** *m* leader;
(*Fremdenführer*) guide; **~schein** *m* driving
licence

Führung ['fyːrʊŋ] *f* leadership; (*eines
Unternehmens*) management; (MIL)
command; (*Benehmen*) conduct;
(*Museumsführung*) conducted tour;
~szeugnis *nt* certificate of good conduct

Fülle ['fʏlə] *f* wealth, abundance; **f~n** *vt* to
fill; (KOCH) to stuff ♦ *vr* to fill (up)

Füll- *zW:* **~er (-s, -)** *m* fountain pen;
~federhalter *m* fountain pen; **~ung** *f*
filling; (*Holzfüllung*) panel

fummeln ['fʊməln] (*umg*) *vi* to fumble

Fund [fʊnt] **(-(e)s, -e)** *m* find

Fundament [fʊnda'mɛnt] *nt* foundation;
fundamen'tal *adj* fundamental

Fund- *zW:* **~büro** *nt* lost property office,
lost and found (US); **~grube** *f* (*fig*) treasure
trove

fundiert [fʊn'diːrt] *adj* sound

fünf [fʏnf] *num* five; **~hundert** *num* five
hundred; **~te(r, s)** *adj* fifth; **F~tel (-s, -)** *nt*
fifth; **~zehn** *num* fifteen; **~zig** *num* fifty

Funk [fʊŋk] **(-s)** *m* radio, wireless; **~e (-ns,
-n)** *m* (*auch fig*) spark; **f~eln** *vi* to sparkle;
~en (-s, -) *m* (*auch fig*) spark; **f~en** *vi*
(*durch Funk*) to signal, to radio; (*umg: richtig
funktionieren*) to work ♦ *vt* (*Funken sprühen*)
to shower with sparks; **~er (-s, -)** *m* radio
operator; **~gerät** *nt* radio set;
~rufempfänger *m* pager, paging device;
~streife *f* police radio patrol; **~telefon** *nt*
cellphone

Funktion [fʊŋktsi'oːn] *f* function; **f~ieren**
[-'niːrən] *vi* to work, to function

für [fyːr] *präp +akk* for; **was ~** what kind *od*
sort of; **das F~ und Wider** the pros and
cons *pl*; **Schritt ~ Schritt** step by step

Furche ['fʊrçə] *f* furrow

Furcht [fʊrçt] **(-)** *f* fear; **f~bar** *adj* terrible,

frightful

fürchten ['fʏrçtən] *vt* to be afraid of, to fear
♦ *vr:* **sich ~ (vor** +*dat*) to be afraid (of)

fürchterlich *adj* awful

furchtlos *adj* fearless

füreinander [fyːr|aı'nandər] *adv* for each
other

Furnier [fʊr'niːr] **(-s, -e)** *nt* veneer

fürs [fyːrs] = **für das**

Fürsorge ['fyːrzɔrgə] *f* care; (*Sozialfürsorge*)
welfare; **~r(in) (-s, -)** *m(f)* welfare worker;
~unterstützung *f* social security, welfare
benefit (US); **fürsorglich** *adj* attentive,
caring

Fürsprache *f* recommendation; (*um
Gnade*) intercession

Fürsprecher *m* advocate

Fürst [fʏrst] **(-en, -en)** *m* prince; **~entum** *nt*
principality; **~in** *f* princess; **f~lich** *adj*
princely

Fuß [fuːs] **(-es, ⁻e)** *m* foot; (*von Glas, Säule
etc*) base; (*von Möbel*) leg; **zu ~** on foot;
~ball *m* football; **~ballplatz** *m* football
pitch; **~ballspiel** *nt* football match;
~ballspieler *m* footballer; **~boden** *m*
floor; **~bremse** *f* (AUT) footbrake; **~ende**
nt foot; **~gänger(in) (-s, -)** *m(f)*
pedestrian; **~gängerzone** *f* pedestrian
precinct; **~nagel** *m* toenail; **~note** *f*
footnote; **~spur** *f* footprint; **~tritt** *m* kick;
(*Spur*) footstep; **~weg** *m* footpath

Futter ['fʊtər] **(-s, -)** *nt* fodder, feed; (*Stoff*)
lining; **~al** [-'raːl] **(-s, -e)** *nt* case

füttern ['fʏtərn] *vt* to feed; (*Kleidung*) to line

Futur [fu'tuːr] **(-s, -e)** *nt* future

G, g

g *abk* = **Gramm**

gab *etc* [gaːp] *vb siehe* **geben**

Gabe ['gaːbə] *f* gift

Gabel ['gaːbəl] **(-, -n)** *f* fork; **~ung** *f* fork

gackern ['gakərn] *vi* to cackle

gaffen ['gafən] *vi* to gape

Gage ['gaːʒə] *f* fee; salary

gähnen ['gɛːnən] *vi* to yawn

Galerie [galə'ri:] f gallery

Galgen ['galgən] (**-s, -**) m gallows sg; **~frist** f respite; **~humor** m macabre humour

Galle ['galə] f gall; (*Organ*) gall bladder; **~nstein** m gallstone

gammeln ['gaməln] (*umg*) vi to bum around; **Gammler(in)** (**-s, -**) (*pej*) m(f) layabout, loafer (*inf*)

Gämse ▲ ['gɛmzə] f chamois

Gang [gaŋ] (**-(e)s, ¨e**) m walk; (*Botengang*) errand; (*~art*) gait; (*Abschnitt eines Vorgangs*) operation; (*Essensgang, Ablauf*) course; (*Flur etc*) corridor; (*Durchgang*) passage; (*TECH*) gear; **in ~ bringen** to start up; (*fig*) to get off the ground; **in ~ sein** to be in operation; (*fig*) to be under way

gang adj: **~ und gäbe** usual, normal

gängig ['gɛŋɪç] adj common, current; (*Ware*) in demand, selling well

Gangschaltung f gears pl

Ganove [ga'no:və] (**-n, -n**) (*umg*) m crook

Gans [gans] (**-, ¨e**) f goose

Gänse- ['gɛnzə] zW: **~blümchen** nt daisy; **~füßchen** (*umg*) pl (*Anführungszeichen*) inverted commas; **~haut** f goose pimples pl; **~marsch** m: **im ~marsch** in single file; **~rich** (**-s, -e**) m gander

ganz [gants] adj whole; (*vollständig*) complete ♦ adv quite; (*völlig*) completely; **~ Europa** all Europe; **sein ~es Geld** all his money; **~ und gar nicht** not at all; **es sieht ~ so aus** it really looks like it; **aufs G~e gehen** to go for the lot

gänzlich ['gɛntslɪç] adj complete, entire ♦ adv completely, entirely

Ganztagsschule f all-day school

gar [ga:r] adj cooked, done ♦ adv quite; **~ nicht/nichts/keiner** not/nothing/nobody at all; **~ nicht schlecht** not bad at all

Garage [ga'ra:ʒə] f garage

Garantie [garan'ti:] f guarantee; **g~ren** vt to guarantee; **er kommt g~rt** he's guaranteed to come

Garbe ['garbə] f sheaf

Garde ['gardə] f guard

Garderobe [gardə'ro:bə] f wardrobe; (*Abgabe*) cloakroom; **~nfrau** f cloakroom attendant

Gardine [gar'di:nə] f curtain

garen ['ga:rən] vt, vi to cook

gären ['gɛ:rən] (*unreg*) vi to ferment

Garn [garn] (**-(e)s, -e**) nt thread; yarn (*auch fig*)

Garnele [gar'ne:lə] f shrimp, prawn

garnieren [gar'ni:rən] vt to decorate; (*Speisen, fig*) to garnish

Garnison [garni'zo:n] (**-, -en**) f garrison

Garnitur [garni'tu:r] f (*Satz*) set; (*Unterwäsche*) set of (matching) underwear; **erste ~** (*fig*) top rank; **zweite ~** (*fig*) second rate

garstig ['garstɪç] adj nasty, horrid

Garten ['gartən] (**-s, ¨**) m garden; **~arbeit** f gardening; **~gerät** nt gardening tool; **~lokal** nt beer garden; **~tür** f garden gate

Gärtner(in) ['gɛrtnər(ɪn)] (**-s, -**) m(f) gardener; **~ei** [-'raɪ] f nursery; (*Gemüsegärtnerei*) market garden (*BRIT*), truck farm (*US*)

Gärung ['gɛ:rʊŋ] f fermentation

Gas [ga:s] (**-es, -e**) nt gas; **~ geben** (*AUT*) to accelerate, to step on the gas; **~hahn** m gas tap; **~herd** m gas cooker; **~kocher** m gas cooker; **~leitung** f gas pipe; **~pedal** nt accelerator, gas pedal

Gasse ['gasə] f lane, alley

Gast [gast] (**-es, ¨e**) m guest; (*in Lokal*) patron; **bei jdm zu ~ sein** to be sb's guest; **~arbeiter(in)** m(f) foreign worker

Gäste- ['gɛstə] zW: **~buch** nt visitors' book, guest book; **~zimmer** nt guest od spare room

Gast- zW: **g~freundlich** adj hospitable; **~geber** (**-s, -**) m host; **~geberin** f hostess; **~haus** nt hotel, inn; **~hof** m hotel, inn; **g~ieren** [-'ti:rən] vi (*THEAT*) to (appear as a) guest; **g~lich** adj hospitable; **~rolle** f guest role; **~spiel** nt (*THEAT*) guest performance; **~stätte** f restaurant; pub; **~wirt** m innkeeper; **~wirtschaft** f hotel, inn

Gaswerk nt gasworks sg

Gaszähler m gas meter

Gatte ['gatə] (**-n, -n**) m husband, spouse

Gattin f wife, spouse

Rechtschreibreform: ▲ *neue Schreibung* △ *alte Schreibung (auslaufend)*

Gattung ['gatʊŋ] f genus; kind

Gaudi ['gaʊdi] (umg: SÜDD, ÖSTERR) nt od f fun

Gaul [gaʊl] (-(e)s, Gäule) m horse; nag

Gaumen ['gaʊmən] (-s, -) m palate

Gauner ['gaʊnər] (-s, -) m rogue; **~ei** [-'raɪ] f swindle

geb. abk = **geboren**

Gebäck [gə'bɛk] (-(e)s, -e) nt pastry

gebacken [gə'bakən] adj baked; (gebraten) fried

Gebälk [gə'bɛlk] (-(e)s) nt timberwork

Gebärde [gə'bɛːrdə] f gesture; **g~n** vr to behave

gebären [gə'bɛːrən] (unreg) vt to give birth to, to bear

Gebärmutter f uterus, womb

Gebäude [gə'bɔʏdə] (-s, -) nt building; **~komplex** m (building) complex

geben ['geːbən] (unreg) vt, vi to give; (Karten) to deal ♦ vb unpers: **es gibt** there is/are; there will be ♦ vr (sich verhalten) to behave, to act; (aufhören) to abate; **jdm etw ~** to give sb sth od sth to sb; **was gibts?** what's up?; **was gibt es im Kino?** what's on at the cinema?; **sich geschlagen ~** to admit defeat; **das wird sich schon ~** that'll soon sort itself out

Gebet [gə'beːt] (-(e)s, -e) nt prayer

gebeten [gə'beːtən] vb siehe **bitten**

Gebiet [gə'biːt] (-(e)s, -e) nt area; (Hoheitsgebiet) territory; (fig) field; **g~en** (unreg) vt to command, to demand; **g~erisch** adj imperious

Gebilde [gə'bɪldə] (-s, -) nt object

gebildet adj cultured, educated

Gebirge [gə'bɪrgə] (-s, -) nt mountain chain

Gebiss [gə'bɪs] (-es, -e) nt teeth pl; (künstlich) dentures pl

gebissen vb siehe **beißen**

geblieben [gə'bliːbən] vb siehe **bleiben**

geblümt [gə'blyːmt] adj (Kleid, Stoff, Tapete) floral

geboren [gə'boːrən] adj born; (Frau) née

geborgen [gə'bɔrgən] adj secure, safe

Gebot [gə'boːt] (-(e)s, -e) nt command; (REL) commandment; (bei Auktion) bid

geboten [gə'boːtən] vb siehe **bieten**

Gebr. abk (= Gebrüder) Bros.

gebracht [gə'braxt] vb siehe **bringen**

gebraten [gə'braːtən] adj fried

Gebrauch [gə'braʊx] (-(e)s, Gebräuche) m use; (Sitte) custom; **g~en** vt to use

gebräuchlich [gə'brɔʏçlɪç] adj usual, customary

Gebrauchs- zW: **~anweisung** f directions pl for use; **g~fertig** adj ready for use; **~gegenstand** m commodity

gebraucht [gə'braʊxt] adj used; **G~wagen** m secondhand od used car

gebrechlich [gə'brɛçlɪç] adj frail

Gebrüder [gə'bryːdər] pl brothers

Gebrüll [gə'brʏl] (-(e)s) nt roaring

Gebühr [gə'byːr] (-, -en) f charge, fee; **nach ~** fittingly; **über ~** unduly; **g~en** vi: **jdm g~en** to be sb's due od due to sb ♦ vr to be fitting; **g~end** adj fitting, appropriate ♦ adv fittingly, appropriately

Gebühren- zW: **~einheit** f (TEL) unit; **~erlass** ▲ m remission of fees; **~ermäßigung** f reduction of fees; **g~frei** adj free of charge; **~ordnung** f scale of charges, tariff; **g~pflichtig** adj subject to a charge

gebunden [gə'bʊndən] vb siehe **binden**

Geburt [gə'buːrt] (-, -en) f birth

Geburtenkontrolle f birth control

Geburtenregelung f birth control

gebürtig [gə'bʏrtɪç] adj born in, native of; **~e Schweizerin** native of Switzerland

Geburts- zW: **~anzeige** f birth notice; **~datum** nt date of birth; **~jahr** nt year of birth; **~ort** m birthplace; **~tag** m birthday; **~urkunde** f birth certificate

Gebüsch [gə'bʏʃ] (-(e)s, -e) nt bushes pl

gedacht [gə'daxt] vb siehe **denken**

Gedächtnis [gə'dɛçtnɪs] (-ses, -se) nt memory; **~feier** f commemoration

Gedanke [gə'daŋkə] (-ns, -n) m thought; **sich über etw** akk **~n machen** to think about sth

Gedanken- zW: **~austausch** m exchange of ideas; **g~los** adj thoughtless; **~strich** m dash; **~übertragung** f thought transference, telepathy

Gedeck [gə'dɛk] **(-(e)s, -e)** *nt* cover(ing); (*Speisenfolge*) menu; **ein ~ auflegen** to lay a place

gedeihen [gə'daɪən] (*unreg*) *vi* to thrive, to prosper

Gedenken *nt*: **zum ~ an jdn** in memory of sb

gedenken [gə'dɛŋkən] (*unreg*) *vi* +*gen* (*beabsichtigen*) to intend; (*sich erinnern*) to remember

Gedenk- *zW*: **~feier** *f* commemoration; **~minute** *f* minute's silence; **~stätte** *f* memorial; **~tag** *m* remembrance day

Gedicht [gə'dɪçt] **(-(e)s, -e)** *nt* poem

gediegen [gə'di:gən] *adj* (good) quality; (*Mensch*) reliable, honest

Gedränge [gə'drɛŋə] **(-s)** *nt* crush, crowd

gedrängt *adj* compressed; **~ voll** packed

gedrückt [gə'drʏkt] *adj* (*deprimiert*) low, depressed

gedrungen [gə'drʊŋən] *adj* thickset, stocky

Geduld [gə'dʊlt] *f* patience; **g~en** [gə'dʊldən] *vr* to be patient; **g~ig** *adj* patient, forbearing; **~sprobe** *f* trial of (one's) patience

gedurft [gə'dʊrft] *vb siehe* **dürfen**

geehrt [gə'|e:rt] *adj*: **Sehr ~e Frau X!** Dear Mrs X

geeignet [gə'|aɪgnət] *adj* suitable

Gefahr [gə'fa:r] **(-, -en)** *f* danger; **~ laufen, etw zu tun** to run the risk of doing sth; **auf eigene ~** at one's own risk

gefährden [gə'fɛ:rdən] *vt* to endanger

Gefahren- *zW*: **~quelle** *f* source of danger; **~zulage** *f* danger money

gefährlich [gə'fɛ:rlɪç] *adj* dangerous

Gefährte [gə'fɛ:rtə] **(-n, -n)** *m* companion; (*Lebenspartner*) partner

Gefährtin [gə'fɛ:rtɪn] *f* (female) companion; (*Lebenspartner*) (female) partner

Gefälle [gə'fɛlə] **(-s, -)** *nt* gradient, incline

Gefallen¹ [gə'falən] **(-s, -)** *m* favour

Gefallen² [gə'falən] **(-s)** *nt* pleasure; **an etw** *dat* **~ finden** to derive pleasure from sth

gefallen *pp von* **fallen** ♦ *vi*: **jdm ~** to please

sb; **er/es gefällt mir** I like him/it; **das gefällt mir an ihm** that's one thing I like about him; **sich** *dat* **etw ~ lassen** to put up with sth

gefällig [gə'fɛlɪç] *adj* (*hilfsbereit*) obliging; (*erfreulich*) pleasant; **G~keit** *f* favour; helpfulness; **etw aus G~keit tun** to do sth out of the goodness of one's heart

gefangen [gə'faŋən] *adj* captured; (*fig*) captivated; **~ halten** to keep prisoner; **~ nehmen** to take prisoner; **G~e(r)** *f(m)* prisoner, captive; **G~nahme** *f* capture; **G~schaft** *f* captivity

Gefängnis [gə'fɛŋnɪs] **(-ses, -se)** *nt* prison; **~strafe** *f* prison sentence; **~wärter** *m* prison warder; **~zelle** *f* prison cell

Gefäß [gə'fɛ:s] **(-es, -e)** *nt* vessel; (*auch ANAT*) container

gefasst ▲ [gə'fast] *adj* composed, calm; **auf etw** *akk* **~ sein** to be prepared *od* ready for sth

Gefecht [gə'fɛçt] **(-(e)s, -e)** *nt* fight; (*MIL*) engagement

Gefieder [gə'fi:dər] **(-s, -)** *nt* plumage, feathers *pl*

gefleckt [gə'flɛkt] *adj* spotted, mottled

geflogen [gə'flo:gən] *vb siehe* **fliegen**

geflossen [gə'flɔsən] *vb siehe* **fließen**

Geflügel [gə'fly:gəl] **(-s)** *nt* poultry

Gefolgschaft [gə'fɔlkʃaft] *f* following

gefragt [gə'fra:kt] *adj* in demand

gefräßig [gə'frɛ:sɪç] *adj* voracious

Gefreite(r) [gə'fraɪtə(r)] *m* lance corporal; (*NAUT*) able seaman; (*AVIAT*) aircraftman

Gefrierbeutel *m* freezer bag

gefrieren [gə'fri:rən] (*unreg*) *vi* to freeze

Gefrier- *zW*: **~fach** *nt* icebox; **~fleisch** *nt* frozen meat; **g~getrocknet** [-gətrɔknət] *adj* freeze-dried; **~punkt** *m* freezing point; **~schutzmittel** *nt* antifreeze; **~truhe** *f* deep-freeze

gefroren [gə'fro:rən] *vb siehe* **frieren**

Gefühl [gə'fy:l] **(-(e)s, -e)** *nt* feeling; **etw im ~ haben** to have a feel for sth; **g~los** *adj* unfeeling

gefühls- *zW*: **~betont** *adj* emotional; **G~duselei** [-du:zə'laɪ] *f* over-sentimentality;

~**mäßig** *adj* instinctive

gefüllt [gəˈfʏlt] *adj* (*KOCH*) stuffed

gefunden [gəˈfʊndən] *vb siehe* **finden**

gegangen [gəˈɡaŋən] *vb siehe* **gehen**

gegeben [gəˈɡeːbən] *vb siehe* **geben** ♦ *adj* given; **zu ~er Zeit** in good time

gegebenenfalls [gəˈɡeːbənənfals] *adv* if need be

gegen [ˈɡeːɡən] *präp +akk* **1** against; **nichts gegen jdn haben** to have nothing against sb; **X gegen Y** (*SPORT, JUR*) X versus Y; **ein Mittel gegen Schnupfen** something for colds

2 (*in Richtung auf*) towards; **gegen Osten** to(wards) the east; **gegen Abend** towards evening; **gegen einen Baum fahren** to drive into a tree

3 (*ungefähr*) round about; **gegen 3 Uhr** around 3 o'clock

4 (*gegenüber*) towards; (*ungefähr*) around; **gerecht gegen alle** fair to all

5 (*im Austausch für*) for; **gegen bar** for cash; **gegen Quittung** against a receipt

6 (*verglichen mit*) compared with

Gegenangriff *m* counter-attack

Gegenbeweis *m* counter-evidence

Gegend [ˈɡeːɡənt] (**-, -en**) *f* area, district

Gegen- *zW:* **g~ei'nander** *adv* against one another; ~**fahrbahn** *f* oncoming carriageway; ~**frage** *f* counter-question; ~**gewicht** *nt* counterbalance; ~**gift** *nt* antidote; ~**leistung** *f* service in return; ~**maßnahme** *f* countermeasure; ~**mittel** *nt* antidote, cure; ~**satz** *m* contrast; ~**sätze überbrücken** to overcome differences; **g~sätzlich** *adj* contrary, opposite; (*widersprüchlich*) contradictory; **g~seitig** *adj* mutual, reciprocal; **sich g~seitig helfen** to help each other; ~**spieler** *m* opponent; ~**sprechanlage** *f* (two-way) intercom; ~**stand** *m* object; ~**stimme** *f* vote against; ~**stoß** *m* counterblow; ~**stück** *nt* counterpart; ~**teil** *nt* opposite; **im ~teil** on the contrary; **g~teilig** *adj* opposite,

contrary

gegenüber [ɡeːɡənˈyːbər] *präp +dat* opposite; (*zu*) to(wards); (*angesichts*) in the face of ♦ *adv* opposite; **G~** (**-s, -**) *nt* person opposite; ~**liegen** (*unreg*) *vr* to face each other; ~**stehen** (*unreg*) *vr* to be opposed (to each other); ~**stellen** *vt* to confront; (*fig*) to contrast; **G~stellung** *f* confrontation; (*fig*) contrast; ~**treten** (*unreg*) *vi +dat* to face

Gegen- *zW:* ~**verkehr** *m* oncoming traffic; ~**vorschlag** *m* counterproposal; ~**wart** *f* present; **g~wärtig** *adj* present ♦ *adv* at present; **das ist mir nicht mehr g~wärtig** that has slipped my mind; ~**wert** *m* equivalent; ~**wind** *m* headwind; **g~zeichnen** *vt, vi* to countersign

gegessen [ɡəˈɡesən] *vb siehe* **essen**

Gegner [ˈɡeːɡnər] (**-s, -**) *m* opponent; **g~isch** *adj* opposing

gegr. *abk* (= *gegründet*) est.

gegrillt [ɡəˈɡrɪlt] *adj* grilled

Gehackte(s) [ɡəˈhaktə(s)] *nt* mince(d meat)

Gehalt¹ [ɡəˈhalt] (**-(e)s, -e**) *m* content

Gehalt² [ɡəˈhalt] (**-(e)s, ⁼er**) *nt* salary

Gehalts- *zW:* ~**empfänger** *m* salary earner; ~**erhöhung** *f* salary increase; ~**zulage** *f* salary increment

gehaltvoll [ɡəˈhaltfɔl] *adj* (*nahrhaft*) nutritious

gehässig [ɡəˈhɛsɪç] *adj* spiteful, nasty

Gehäuse [ɡəˈhɔʏzə] (**-s, -**) *nt* case; casing; (*von Apfel etc*) core

Gehege [ɡəˈheːɡə] (**-s, -**) *nt* reserve; (*im Zoo*) enclosure

geheim [ɡəˈhaɪm] *adj* secret; ~ **halten** to keep secret; **G~dienst** *m* secret service, intelligence service; **G~nis** (**-ses, -se**) *nt* secret; mystery; ~**nisvoll** *adj* mysterious; **G~polizei** *f* secret police

gehemmt [ɡəˈhɛmt] *adj* inhibited, self-conscious

gehen [ˈɡeːən] (*unreg*) *vt, vi* to go; (*zu Fuß ~*) to walk ♦ *vb unpers:* **wie geht es (dir)?** how are you *od* things?; ~ **nach** (*Fenster*) to face; **mir/ihm geht es gut** I'm/he's (doing) fine; **geht das?** is that possible?; **gehts**

noch? can you manage?; **es geht** not too bad, O.K.; **das geht nicht** that's not on; **es geht um etw** it has to do with sth, it's about sth; **sich ~ lassen** (*unbeherrscht sein*) to lose control (of o.s.); **jdn ~ lassen** to let/leave sb alone; **lass mich ~!** leave me alone!

geheuer [gə'hɔʏər] *adj*: **nicht ~** eerie; (*fragwürdig*) dubious

Gehilfe [gə'hɪlfə] (**-n, -n**) *m* assistant; **Gehilfin** *f* assistant

Gehirn [gə'hɪrn] (**-(e)s, -e**) *nt* brain; **~erschütterung** *f* concussion; **~hautentzündung** *f* meningitis

gehoben [gə'ho:bən] *pp von* **heben** ♦ *adj* (*Position*) elevated; high

geholfen [gə'hɔlfən] *vb siehe* **helfen**

Gehör [gə'hø:r] (**-(e)s**) *nt* hearing; **musikalisches ~** ear; **~ finden** to gain a hearing; **jdm ~ schenken** to give sb a hearing

gehorchen [gə'hɔrçən] *vi +dat* to obey

gehören [gə'hø:rən] *vi* to belong ♦ *vr unpers* to be right *od* proper

gehörig *adj* proper; **~ zu** *od +dat* belonging to; part of

gehörlos *adj* deaf

gehorsam [gə'ho:rza:m] *adj* obedient; **G~** (**-s**) *m* obedience

Geh- ['ge:-] *zW*: **~steig** *m* pavement, sidewalk (*US*); **~weg** *m* pavement, sidewalk (*US*)

Geier ['gaɪər] (**-s, -**) *m* vulture

Geige ['gaɪgə] *f* violin; **~r** (**-s, -**) *m* violinist

geil [gaɪl] *adj* randy (*BRIT*), horny (*US*)

Geisel ['gaɪzəl] (**-, -n**) *f* hostage

Geist [gaɪst] (**-(e)s, -er**) *m* spirit; (*Gespenst*) ghost; (*Verstand*) mind

geisterhaft *adj* ghostly

Geistes- *zW*: **g~abwesend** *adj* absent-minded; **~blitz** *m* brainwave; **~gegenwart** *f* presence of mind; **g~krank** *adj* mentally ill; **~kranke(r)** *f(m)* mentally ill person; **~krankheit** *f* mental illness; **~wissenschaften** *pl* the arts; **~zustand** *m* state of mind

geist- *zW*: **~ig** *adj* intellectual; mental;

(*Getränke*) alcoholic; **~ig behindert** mentally handicapped; **~lich** *adj* spiritual, religious; clerical; **G~liche(r)** *m* clergyman; **G~lichkeit** *f* clergy; **~los** *adj* uninspired, dull; **~reich** *adj* clever; witty; **~voll** *adj* intellectual; (*weise*) wise

Geiz [gaɪts] (**-es**) *m* miserliness, meanness; **g~en** *vi* to be miserly; **~hals** *m* miser; **g~ig** *adj* miserly, mean; **~kragen** *m* miser

gekannt [gə'kant] *vb siehe* **kennen**

gekonnt [gə'kɔnt] *adj* skilful ♦ *vb siehe* **können**

gekünstelt [ge'kʏnstəlt] *adj* artificial, affected

Gel [ge:l] (**-s, -e**) *nt* gel

Gelächter [gə'lɛçtər] (**-s, -**) *nt* laughter

geladen [gə'la:dən] *adj* loaded; (*ELEK*) live; (*fig*) furious

gelähmt [gə'lɛ:mt] *adj* paralysed

Gelände [gə'lɛndə] (**-s, -**) *nt* land, terrain; (*von Fabrik, Sportgelände*) grounds *pl*; (*Bau~*) site; **~lauf** *m* cross-country race

Geländer [gə'lɛndər] (**-s, -**) *nt* railing; (*Treppengeländer*) banister(s)

gelangen [gə'laŋən] *vi*: **~ (an +akk od zu)** to reach; (*erwerben*) to attain; **in jds Besitz** *akk* **~** to come into sb's possession

gelangweilt [gə'laŋvaɪlt] *adj* bored

gelassen [gə'lasən] *adj* calm, composed; **G~heit** *f* calmness, composure

Gelatine [ʒela'ti:nə] *f* gelatine

geläufig [gə'lɔʏfɪç] *adj* (*üblich*) common; **das ist mir nicht ~** I'm not familiar with that

gelaunt [gə'laʊnt] *adj*: **schlecht/gut ~** in a bad/good mood; **wie ist er ~?** what sort of mood is he in?

gelb [gɛlp] *adj* yellow; (*Ampellicht*) amber; **~lich** *adj* yellowish; **G~sucht** *f* jaundice

Geld [gɛlt] (**-(e)s, -er**) *nt* money; **etw zu ~ machen** to sell sth off; **~anlage** *f* investment; **~automat** *m* cash dispenser; **~beutel** *m* purse; **~börse** *f* purse; **~geber** (**-s, -**) *m* financial backer; **g~gierig** *adj* avaricious; **~schein** *m* banknote; **~schrank** *m* safe, strongbox; **~strafe** *f* fine; **~stück** *nt* coin; **~wechsel**

m exchange (of money)

Gelee [ʒe'le:] (**-s, -s**) *nt od m* jelly

gelegen [gə'le:gən] *adj* situated; (*passend*) convenient, opportune ♦ *vb siehe* **liegen**; **etw kommt jdm ~** sth is convenient for sb

Gelegenheit [gə'le:gənhaɪt] *f* opportunity; (*Anlaß*) occasion; **bei jeder ~** at every opportunity; **~sarbeit** *f* casual work; **~skauf** *m* bargain

gelegentlich [gə'le:gəntlɪç] *adj* occasional ♦ *adv* occasionally; (*bei Gelegenheit*) some time (or other) ♦ *präp +gen* on the occasion of

gelehrt [gə'le:rt] *adj* learned; **G~e(r)** *f(m)* scholar; **G~heit** *f* scholarliness

Geleise [gə'laɪzə] (**-s, -**) *nt* = **Gleis**

Geleit [gə'laɪt] (**-(e)s, -e**) *nt* escort; **g~en** *vt* to escort

Gelenk [gə'lɛŋk] (**-(e)s, -e**) *nt* joint; **g~ig** *adj* supple

gelernt [gə'lɛrnt] *adj* skilled

Geliebte(r) [gə'li:ptə(r)] *f(m)* sweetheart, beloved

geliehen [gə'li:ən] *vb siehe* **leihen**

gelind(e) [gə'lɪnd(ə)] *adj* mild, light; (*fig: Wut*) fierce; **~ gesagt** to put it mildly

gelingen [gə'lɪŋən] (*unreg*) *vi* to succeed; **es ist mir gelungen, etw zu tun** I succeeded in doing sth

geloben [gə'lo:bən] *vt, vi* to vow, to swear

gelten ['gɛltən] (*unreg*) *vt* (*wert sein*) to be worth ♦ *vi* (*gültig sein*) to be valid; (*erlaubt sein*) to be allowed ♦ *vb unpers*: **es gilt, etw zu tun** it is necessary to do sth; **jdm viel/ wenig ~** to mean a lot/not to mean much to sb; **was gilt die Wette?** what do you bet?; **etw ~ lassen** to accept sth; **als** *od* **für etw ~** to be considered to be sth; **jdm** *od* **für jdn ~** (*betreffen*) to apply to *od* for sb; **~d** *adj* prevailing; **etw ~d machen** to assert sth; **sich ~d machen** to make itself/ o.s. felt

Geltung ['gɛltʊŋ] *f*: **~ haben** to have validity; **sich/etw** *dat* **~ verschaffen** to establish one's position/the position of sth; **etw zur ~ bringen** to show sth to its best advantage; **zur ~ kommen** to be seen/ heard *etc* to its best advantage

Geltungsbedürfnis *nt* desire for admiration

Gelübde [gə'lʏpdə] (**-s, -**) *nt* vow

gelungen [gə'lʊŋən] *adj* successful

gemächlich [gə'mɛːçlɪç] *adj* leisurely

Gemahl [gə'ma:l] (**-(e)s, -e**) *m* husband; **~in** *f* wife

Gemälde [gə'mɛːldə] (**-s, -**) *nt* picture, painting

gemäß [gə'mɛːs] *präp +dat* in accordance with ♦ *adj* (*+dat*) appropriate (to)

gemäßigt [gə'mɛːsɪçt] *adj* moderate; (*Klima*) temperate

gemein [gə'maɪn] *adj* common; (*niederträchtig*) mean; **etw ~ haben (mit)** to have sth in common (with)

Gemeinde [gə'maɪndə] *f* district, community; (*Pfarrgemeinde*) parish; (*Kirchengemeinde*) congregation; **~steuer** *f* local rates *pl*; **~verwaltung** *f* local administration; **~wahl** *f* local election

Gemein- *zW*: **g~gefährlich** *adj* dangerous to the public; **~heit** *f* commonness; mean thing to do/to say; **g~nützig** *adj* charitable; **g~nütziger Verein** non-profit-making organization; **g~sam** *adj* joint, common (*AUCH MATH*) ♦ *adv* together, jointly; **g~same Sache mit jdm machen** to be in cahoots with sb; **etw g~sam haben** to have sth in common; **~samkeit** *f* community, having in common; **~schaft** *f* community; **in ~schaft mit** jointly *od* together with; **g~schaftlich** *adj* = **gemeinsam; ~schaftsarbeit** *f* teamwork; team effort; **~sinn** *m* public spirit

Gemenge [gə'mɛŋə] (**-s, -**) *nt* mixture; (*Handgemenge*) scuffle

gemessen [gə'mɛsən] *adj* measured

Gemetzel [gə'mɛtsəl] (**-s, -**) *nt* slaughter, carnage, butchery

Gemisch [gə'mɪʃ] (**-es, -e**) *nt* mixture; **g~t** *adj* mixed

gemocht [gə'mɔxt] *vb siehe* **mögen**

Gemse △ ['gɛmzə] *f siehe* **Gämse**

Gemurmel [gə'mʊrməl] (**-s**) *nt* murmur(ing)

Gemüse [gə'my:zə] (**-s, -**) *nt* vegetables *pl*; **~garten** *m* vegetable garden; **~händler** *m* greengrocer

gemusst ▲ [gə'mʊst] *vb siehe* **müssen**

gemustert [gə'mʊstərt] *adj* patterned

Gemüt [gə'my:t] (-(e)s, -er) *nt* disposition, nature; person; **sich** *dat* **etw zu ~e führen** (*umg*) to indulge in sth; **die ~er erregen** to arouse strong feelings; **g~lich** *adj* comfortable, cosy; (*Person*) good-natured; **~lichkeit** *f* comfortableness, cosiness; amiability

Gemüts- *zW:* **~mensch** *m* sentimental person; **~ruhe** *f* composure; **~zustand** *m* state of mind

Gen [ge:n] (-s, -e) *nt* gene

genannt [gə'nant] *vb siehe* **nennen**

genau [gə'nau] *adj* exact, precise ♦ *adv* exactly, precisely; **etw ~ nehmen** to take sth seriously; **~ genommen** strictly speaking; **G~igkeit** *f* exactness, accuracy; **~so** *adv* just the same; **~so gut** just as good

genehm [gə'ne:m] *adj* agreeable, acceptable; **~igen** *vt* to approve, to authorize; **sich** *dat* **etw ~igen** to indulge in sth; **G~igung** *f* approval, authorization, (*Schriftstück*) permit

General [gene'ra:l] (-s, -e *od* ⸚e) *m* general; **~direktor** *m* director general; **~konsulat** *nt* consulate general; **~probe** *f* dress rehearsal; **~streik** *m* general strike; **g~überholen** *vt* to overhaul thoroughly; **~versammlung** *f* general meeting

Generation [generatsi'o:n] *f* generation

Generator [gene'ra:tɔr] *m* generator, dynamo

generell [genə'rɛl] *adj* general

genesen [ge'ne:zən] (*unreg*) *vi* to convalesce, to recover; **Genesung** *f* recovery, convalescence

genetisch [ge'ne:tɪʃ] *adj* genetic

Genf ['gɛnf] *nt* Geneva; **der ~er See** Lake Geneva

genial [geni'a:l] *adj* brilliant

Genick [gə'nɪk] (-(e)s, -e) *nt* (back of the) neck

Genie [ʒe'ni:] (-s, -s) *nt* genius

genieren [ʒe'ni:rən] *vt* to bother ♦ *vr* to feel awkward *od* self-conscious

genieß- *zW:* **~bar** *adj* edible; drinkable; **~en** [gə'ni:sən] (*unreg*) *vt* to enjoy; to eat; to drink; **G~er** (-s, -) *m* epicure; pleasure lover; **~erisch** *adj* appreciative ♦ *adv* with relish

genmanipuliert ['ge:nmanipuli:rt] *adj* genetically modified

genommen [gə'nɔmən] *vb siehe* **nehmen**

Genosse [gə'nɔsə] (-n, -n) *m* (*bes POL*) comrade, companion; **~nschaft** *f* cooperative (association)

Genossin *f* (*bes POL*) comrade, companion

Gentechnik ['ge:ntɛçnɪk] *f* genetic engineering

genug [gə'nu:k] *adv* enough

Genüge [gə'ny:gə] *f:* **jdm/etw ~ tun** *od* **leisten** to satisfy sb/sth; **g~n** *vi* (+*dat*) to be enough (for); **g~nd** *adj* sufficient

genügsam [gə'ny:kza:m] *adj* modest, easily satisfied; **G~keit** *f* moderation

Genugtuung [gə'nu:ktu:ʊŋ] *f* satisfaction

Genuss ▲ [gə'nʊs] (-es, ⸚e) *m* pleasure; (*Zusichnehmen*) consumption; **in den ~ von etw kommen** to receive the benefit of sth

genüsslich ▲ [gə'nʏslɪç] *adv* with relish

Genussmittel ▲ *pl* (semi-)luxury items

geöffnet [gə'œfnət] *adj* open

Geograf ▲ [geo'gra:f] (-en, -en) *m* geographer; **Geogra'fie** ▲ *f* geography; **g~isch** *adj* geographical

Geologe [geo'lo:gə] (-n, -n) *m* geologist; **Geolo'gie** *f* geology

Geometrie [geome'tri:] *f* geometry

Gepäck [gə'pɛk] (-(e)s) *nt* luggage, baggage; **~abfertigung** *f* luggage office; **~annahme** *f* luggage office; **~aufbewahrung** *f* left-luggage office (*BRIT*), baggage check (*US*); **~aufgabe** *f* luggage office; **~ausgabe** *f* luggage office; (*AVIAT*) luggage reclaim; **~netz** *nt* luggage rack; **~träger** *m* porter; (*Fahrrad*) carrier; **~versicherung** *f* luggage insurance; **~wagen** *m* luggage van (*BRIT*), baggage car (*US*)

gepflegt [gə'pfle:kt] *adj* well-groomed; (*Park etc*) well looked after

---

Rechtschreibreform: ▲ *neue Schreibung* △ *alte Schreibung (auslaufend)*

Gerade [gəˈraːdə] f straight line; **g~'aus** adv straight ahead; **g~he'raus** adv straight out, bluntly; **g~stehen** (unreg) vi: **für jdn/etw g~stehen** to be answerable for sb('s actions)/sth; **g~wegs** adv direct, straight; **g~zu** adv (beinahe) virtually, almost

---
SCHLÜSSELWORT
---

gerade [gəˈraːdə] adj straight; (aufrecht) upright; **eine gerade Zahl** an even number

♦ adv 1 (genau) just, exactly; (speziell) especially; **gerade deshalb** that's just od exactly why; **das ist es ja gerade!** that's just it!; **gerade du** you especially; **warum gerade ich?** why me (of all people)?; **jetzt gerade nicht!** not now!; **gerade neben** right next to

2 (eben, soeben) just; **er wollte gerade aufstehen** he was just about to get up; **gerade erst** only just; **gerade noch** (only) just

---

gerannt [gəˈrant] vb siehe **rennen**
Gerät [gəˈrɛːt] (-(e)s, -e) nt device; (Werkzeug) tool; (SPORT) apparatus; (Zubehör) equipment no pl
geraten [gəˈraːtən] (unreg) vi (gedeihen) to thrive; (gelingen): **(jdm) ~** to turn out well (for sb); **gut/schlecht ~** to turn out well/badly; **an jdn ~** to come across sb; **in etw** akk **~** to get into sth; **nach jdm ~** to take after sb
Geratewohl [gəraːtəˈvoːl] nt: **aufs ~** on the off chance; (bei Wahl) at random
geräuchert [gəˈrɔʏçɐt] adj smoked
geräumig [gəˈrɔʏmɪç] adj roomy
Geräusch [gəˈrɔʏʃ] (-(e)s, -e) nt sound, noise; **g~los** adj silent
gerben [ˈɡɛrbən] vt to tan
gerecht [gəˈrɛçt] adj just, fair; **jdm/etw ~ werden** to do justice to sb/sth; **G~igkeit** f justice, fairness
Gerede [gəˈreːdə] (-s) nt talk, gossip
geregelt [gəˈreːɡəlt] adj (Arbeit) steady, regular; (Mahlzeiten) regular, set

gereizt [gəˈraɪtst] adj irritable; **G~heit** f irritation
Gericht [gəˈrɪçt] (-(e)s, -e) nt court; (Essen) dish; **mit jdm ins ~ gehen** (fig) to judge sb harshly; **das Jüngste ~** the Last Judgement; **g~lich** adj judicial, legal ♦ adv judicially, legally
Gerichts- zW: **~barkeit** f jurisdiction; **~hof** m court (of law); **~kosten** pl (legal) costs; **~medizin** f forensic medicine; **~saal** m courtroom; **~verfahren** nt legal proceedings pl; **~verhandlung** f trial; **~vollzieher** m bailiff
gerieben [gəˈriːbən] adj grated; (umg: schlau) smart, wily ♦ vb siehe **reiben**
gering [gəˈrɪŋ] adj slight, small; (niedrig) low; (Zeit) short; **~fügig** adj slight, trivial; **~schätzig** adj disparaging
geringste(r, s) adj slightest, least; **~nfalls** adv at the very least
gerinnen [gəˈrɪnən] (unreg) vi to congeal; (Blut) to clot; (Milch) to curdle
Gerippe [gəˈrɪpə] (-s, -) nt skeleton
gerissen [gəˈrɪsən] adj wily, smart
geritten [gəˈrɪtən] vb siehe **reiten**
gern(e) [ˈɡɛrn(ə)] adv willingly, gladly; **~ haben, ~ mögen** to like; **etwas ~ tun** to like doing something; **ich möchte ~ ...** I'd like ...; **ja, ~** yes, please; yes, I'd like to; **~ geschehen** it's a pleasure
gerochen [gəˈrɔxən] vb siehe **riechen**
Geröll [gəˈrœl] (-(e)s, -e) nt scree
Gerste [ˈɡɛrstə] f barley; **~nkorn** nt (im Auge) stye
Geruch [gəˈrux] (-(e)s, ⁔e) m smell, odour; **g~los** adj odourless
Gerücht [gəˈrʏçt] (-(e)s, -e) nt rumour
geruhsam [gəˈruːzaːm] adj (Leben) peaceful; (Nacht, Zeit) peaceful, restful; (langsam: Arbeitsweise, Spaziergang) leisurely
Gerümpel [gəˈrʏmpəl] (-s) nt junk
Gerüst [gəˈrʏst] (-(e)s, -e) nt (Baugerüst) scaffold(ing); frame
gesalzen [gəˈzaltsən] pp von **salzen** ♦ adj (umg: Preis, Rechnung) steep
gesamt [gəˈzamt] adj whole, entire; (Kosten) total; (Werke) complete; **im G~en** all in all;

Spelling Reform: ▲ *new spelling* △ *old spelling (to be phased out)*

~deutsch adj all-German; **G~eindruck** m general impression; **G~heit** f totality, whole; **G~schule** f ≈ comprehensive school

---

Gesamtschule

ⓘ The **Gesamtschule** is a comprehensive school for pupils of different abilities. Traditionally pupils go to either a **Gymnasium**, **Realschule** or **Hauptschule**, depending on ability. The **Gesamtschule** seeks to avoid the elitism of many **Gymnasien**. However, these schools are still very controversial, with many parents still preferring the traditional education system.

---

gesandt [gə'zant] vb siehe **senden**
Gesandte(r) [gə'zantə(r)] m envoy
Gesandtschaft [gə'zantʃaft] f legation
Gesang [gə'zaŋ] **(-(e)s, ⁻e)** m song; (Singen) singing; **~buch** nt (REL) hymn book
Gesäß [gə'zɛːs] **(-es, -e)** nt seat, bottom
Geschäft [gə'ʃɛft] **(-(e)s, -e)** nt business; (Laden) shop; (~sabschluß) deal; **g~ig** adj active, busy; (pej) officious; **g~lich** adj commercial ♦ adv on business
Geschäfts- zW: **~bedingungen** pl terms pl of business; **~bericht** m financial report; **~frau** f businesswoman; **~führer** m manager; (Klub) secretary; **~geheimnis** nt trade secret; **~jahr** nt financial year; **~lage** f business conditions pl; **~mann** m businessman; **g~mäßig** adj businesslike; **~partner** m business partner; **~reise** f business trip; **~schluss** ▲ m closing time; **~stelle** f office, place of business; **g~tüchtig** adj business-minded; **~viertel** nt business quarter; shopping centre; **~wagen** m company car; **~zeit** f business hours pl
geschehen [gə'ʃeːən] (unreg) vi to happen; **es war um ihn ~** that was the end of him
gescheit [gə'ʃaɪt] adj clever
Geschenk [gə'ʃɛŋk] **(-(e)s, -e)** nt present, gift
Geschichte [gə'ʃɪçtə] f story; (Sache) affair;

(Historie) history
geschichtlich adj historical
Geschick [gə'ʃɪk] **(-(e)s, -e)** nt aptitude; (Schicksal) fate; **~lichkeit** f skill, dexterity; **g~t** adj skilful
geschieden [gə'ʃiːdən] adj divorced
geschienen [gə'ʃiːnən] vb siehe **scheinen**
Geschirr [gə'ʃɪr] **(-(e)s, -e)** nt crockery; pots and pans pl; (Pferdegeschirr) harness; **~spülmaschine** f dishwasher; **~spülmittel** nt washing-up liquid; **~tuch** nt dish cloth
Geschlecht [gə'ʃlɛçt] **(-(e)s, -er)** nt sex; (GRAM) gender; (Gattung) race; family; **g~lich** adj sexual
Geschlechts- zW: **~krankheit** f venereal disease; **~teil** nt genitals pl; **~verkehr** m sexual intercourse
geschlossen [gə'ʃlɔsən] adj shut ♦ vb siehe **schließen**
Geschmack [gə'ʃmak] **(-(e)s, ⁻e)** m taste; **nach jds ~** to sb's taste; **~ finden an etw** dat to (come to) like sth; **g~los** adj tasteless; (fig) in bad taste; **~ssinn** m sense of taste; **g~voll** adj tasteful
geschmeidig [gə'ʃmaɪdɪç] adj supple; (formbar) malleable
Geschnetzelte(s) [gə'ʃnɛtsəltə(s)] nt (KOCH) strips of meat stewed to produce a thick sauce
geschnitten [gə'ʃnɪtən] vb siehe **schneiden**
Geschöpf [gə'ʃœpf] **(-(e)s, -e)** nt creature
Geschoss ▲ **(-es, -e)** nt (MIL) projectile, missile; (Stockwerk) floor
geschossen [gə'ʃɔsən] vb siehe **schießen**
geschraubt [gə'ʃraʊpt] adj stilted, artificial
Geschrei [gə'ʃraɪ] **(-s)** nt cries pl, shouting; (fig: Aufheben) noise, fuss
geschrieben [gə'ʃriːbən] vb siehe **schreiben**
Geschütz [gə'ʃʏts] **(-es, -e)** nt gun, cannon; **ein schweres ~ auffahren** (fig) to bring out the big guns
geschützt adj protected
Geschw. abk siehe **Geschwister**
Geschwätz [gə'ʃvɛts] **(-es)** nt chatter, gossip; **g~ig** adj talkative
geschweige [gə'ʃvaɪgə] adv: **~ (denn)** let

alone, not to mention

eschwind [gə'ʃvɪnt] *adj* quick, swift; **G~igkeit** [-dɪçkaɪt] *f* speed, velocity; **G~igkeitsbeschränkung** *f* speed limit; **G~igkeitsüberschreitung** *f* exceeding the speed limit

eschwister [gə'ʃvɪstər] *pl* brothers and sisters

eschwommen [gə'ʃvɔmən] *vb siehe* **schwimmen**

eschworene(r) [ge'ʃvoːrənə(r)] *f(m)* juror; **~n** *pl* jury

eschwulst [gə'ʃvʊlst] (-, ⁓e) *f* swelling; growth, tumour

eschwungen [gə'ʃvʊŋən] *pp von* **schwingen** ♦ *adj* curved, arched

eschwür [gə'ʃvyːr] (-(e)s, -e) *nt* ulcer

esell- [gə'zɛl] *zW:* **~e** (-(e)n, -(e)n) *m* fellow; (*Handwerkgeselle*) journeyman; **g~ig** *adj* sociable; **~igkeit** *f* sociability; **~schaft** *f* society; (*Begleitung, COMM*) company; (*Abendgesellschaft etc*) party; **g~schaftlich** *adj* social; **~schaftsordnung** *f* social structure; **~schaftsschicht** *f* social stratum

esessen [gə'zɛsən] *vb siehe* **sitzen**

esetz [gə'zɛts] (-es, -e) *nt* law; **~buch** *nt* statute book; **~entwurf** *m* (draft) bill; **~gebung** *f* legislation; **g~lich** *adj* legal, lawful; **g~licher Feiertag** statutory holiday; **g~los** *adj* lawless; **g~mäßig** *adj* lawful; **g~t** *adj* (*Mensch*) sedate; **g~widrig** *adj* illegal, unlawful

esicht [gə'zɪçt] (-(e)s, -er) *nt* face; **das zweite** ~ second sight; **das ist mir nie zu** ~ **gekommen** I've never laid eyes on that

esichts- *zW:* **~ausdruck** *m* (facial) expression; **~creme** *f* face cream; **~farbe** *f* complexion; **~punkt** *m* point of view; **~wasser** *nt* face lotion; **~züge** *pl* features

esindel [gə'zɪndəl] (-s) *nt* rabble

esinnt [gə'zɪnt] *adj* disposed, minded

esinnung [gə'zɪnʊŋ] *f* disposition; (*Ansicht*) views *pl*

esittet [gə'zɪtət] *adj* well-mannered

espann [gə'ʃpan] (-(e)s, -e) *nt* team; (*umg*) couple

gespannt *adj* tense, strained; (*begierig*) eager; **ich bin** ~, **ob** I wonder if *od* whether; **auf etw/jdn** ~ **sein** to look forward to sth/meeting sb

Gespenst [gə'ʃpɛnst] (-(e)s, -er) *nt* ghost, spectre

gesperrt [gə'ʃpɛrt] *adj* closed off

Gespött [gə'ʃpœt] (-(e)s) *nt* mockery; **zum** ~ **werden** to become a laughing stock

Gespräch [gə'ʃprɛːç] (-(e)s, -e) *nt* conversation; discussion(s); (*Anruf*) call; **g~ig** *adj* talkative

gesprochen [gə'ʃprɔxən] *vb siehe* **sprechen**

gesprungen [gə'ʃprʊŋən] *vb siehe* **springen**

Gespür [gə'ʃpyːr] (-s) *nt* feeling

Gestalt [gə'ʃtalt] (-, -en) *f* form, shape; (*Person*) figure; **in** ~ **von** in the form of; ~ **annehmen** to take shape; **g~en** *vt* (*formen*) to shape, to form; (*organisieren*) to arrange, to organize ♦ *vr:* **sich g~en** (*zu*) to turn out (to be); **~ung** *f* formation; organization

gestanden [gə'ʃtandən] *vb siehe* **stehen**

Geständnis [gə'ʃtɛntnɪs] (-ses, -se) *nt* confession

Gestank [gə'ʃtaŋk] (-(e)s) *m* stench

gestatten [gə'ʃtatən] *vt* to permit, to allow; ~ **Sie?** may I?; **sich dat** ~, **etw zu tun** to take the liberty of doing sth

Geste ['gɛstə] *f* gesture

gestehen [gə'ʃteːən] (*unreg*) *vt* to confess

Gestein [gə'ʃtaɪn] (-(e)s, -e) *nt* rock

Gestell [gə'ʃtɛl] (-(e)s, -e) *nt* frame; (*Regal*) rack, stand

gestern ['gɛstərn] *adv* yesterday; ~ **Abend/ Morgen** yesterday evening/morning

Gestirn [gə'ʃtɪrn] (-(e)s, -e) *nt* star; (*Sternbild*) constellation

gestohlen [gə'ʃtoːlən] *vb siehe* **stehlen**

gestorben [gə'ʃtɔrbən] *vb siehe* **sterben**

gestört [gə'ʃtøːrt] *adj* disturbed

gestreift [gə'ʃtraɪft] *adj* striped

gestrichen [gə'ʃtrɪçən] *adj* cancelled

gestrig ['gɛstrɪç] *adj* yesterday's

Gestrüpp [gə'ʃtrʏp] (-(e)s, -e) *nt* undergrowth

Gestüt [gə'ʃtyːt] (-(e)s, -e) *nt* stud farm

Gesuch [gə'zuːx] (-(e)s, -e) *nt* petition;

(*Antrag*) application; **g~t** *adj* (COMM) in demand; wanted; (*fig*) contrived

gesund [gə'zʊnt] *adj* healthy; **wieder ~ werden** to get better; **G~heit** *f* health(iness); **G~heit!** bless you!; **~heitlich** *adj* health attrib, physical ♦ *adv*: **wie geht es Ihnen ~heitlich?** how's your health?; **~heitsschädlich** *adj* unhealthy; **G~heitswesen** *nt* health service; **G~heitszustand** *m* state of health

gesungen [gə'zʊŋən] *vb siehe* **singen**

getan [gə'ta:n] *vb siehe* **tun**

Getöse [gə'tø:zə] (**-s**) *nt* din, racket

Getränk [gə'trɛŋk] (**-(e)s, -e**) *nt* drink; **~ekarte** *f* wine list

getrauen [gə'trauən] *vr* to dare, to venture

Getreide [gə'traidə] (**-s, -**) *nt* cereals *pl*, grain; **~speicher** *m* granary

getrennt [gə'trɛnt] *adj* separate

Getriebe [gə'tri:bə] (**-s, -**) *nt* (*Leute*) bustle; (AUT) gearbox

getrieben *vb siehe* **treiben**

getroffen [gə'trɔfən] *vb siehe* **treffen**

getrost [gə'tro:st] *adv* without any bother

getrunken [gə'trʊŋkən] *vb siehe* **trinken**

Getue [gə'tu:ə] (**-s**) *nt* fuss

geübt [gə'y:pt] *adj* experienced

Gewächs [gə'vɛks] (**-es, -e**) *nt* growth; (*Pflanze*) plant

gewachsen [gə'vaksən] *adj*: **jdm/etw ~ sein** to be sb's equal/equal to sth

Gewächshaus *nt* greenhouse

gewagt [gə'va:kt] *adj* daring, risky

gewählt [gə'vɛ:lt] *adj* (*Sprache*) refined, elegant

Gewähr [gə'vɛ:r] (**-**) *f* guarantee; **keine ~ übernehmen für** to accept no responsibility for; **g~en** *vt* to grant; (*geben*) to provide; **g~leisten** *vt* to guarantee

Gewahrsam [gə'va:rzam] (**-s, -e**) *m* safekeeping; (*Polizeigewahrsam*) custody

Gewalt [gə'valt] (**-, -en**) *f* power; (*große Kraft*) force; (*~taten*) violence; **mit aller ~** with all one's might; **~anwendung** *f* use of force; **g~ig** *adj* tremendous; (*Irrtum*) huge; **~marsch** *m* forced march; **g~sam** *adj* forcible; **g~tätig** *adj* violent

Gewand [gə'vant] (**-(e)s, ̈er**) *nt* gown, rol

gewandt [gə'vant] *adj* deft, skilful; (*erfahren* experienced; **G~heit** *f* dexterity, skill

gewann *etc* [gə'va:n] *vb siehe* **gewinnen**

Gewässer [gə'vɛsər] (**-s, -**) *nt* waters *pl*

Gewebe [gə've:bə] (**-s, -**) *nt* (*Stoff*) fabric; (BIOL) tissue

Gewehr [gə've:r] (**-(e)s, -e**) *nt* gun; rifle; **~lauf** *m* rifle barrel

Geweih [gə'vai] (**-(e)s, -e**) *nt* antlers *pl*

Gewerb- [gə'vɛrb] *zW*: **~e** (**-s, -**) *nt* trade, occupation; **Handel und ~e** trade and industry; **~eschule** *f* technical school; **~ezweig** *m* line of trade

Gewerkschaft [gə'vɛrkʃaft] *f* trade union; **~ler** (**-s, -**) *m* trade unionist; **~sbund** *m* trade unions federation

gewesen [gə've:zən] *pp von* **sein**

Gewicht [gə'vɪçt] (**-(e)s, -e**) *nt* weight; (*fig*) importance

gewieft [gə'vi:ft] *adj* shrewd, cunning

gewillt [gə'vɪlt] *adj* willing, prepared

Gewimmel [gə'vɪməl] (**-s**) *nt* swarm

Gewinde [gə'vɪndə] (**-s, -**) *nt* (*Kranz*) wreat (*von Schraube*) thread

Gewinn [gə'vɪn] (**-(e)s, -e**) *m* profit; (*bei Spiel*) winnings *pl*; **~ bringend** profitable; **etw mit ~ verkaufen** to sell sth at a profit **~ und Verlustrechnung** (COMM) profit ar loss account; **~beteiligung** *f* profit-sharing; **g~en** (*unreg*) *vt* to win; (*erwerben* to gain; (*Kohle, Öl*) to extract ♦ *vi* to win; (*profitieren*) to gain; **an etw** *dat* **g~en** to gain (in) sth; **g~end** *adj* (*Lächeln, Aussehen* winning, charming; **~er(in)** (**-s, -**) *m(f)* winner; **~spanne** *f* profit margin; **~ung** *f* winning; gaining; (*von Kohle etc*) extraction

Gewirr [gə'vɪr] (**-(e)s, -e**) *nt* tangle; (*von Straßen*) maze

gewiss ▲ [gə'vɪs] *adj* certain ♦ *adv* certain

Gewissen [gə'vɪsən] (**-s, -**) *nt* conscience; **g~haft** *adj* conscientious; **g~los** *adj* unscrupulous

Gewissens- *zW*: **~bisse** *pl* pangs of conscience, qualms; **~frage** *f* matter of conscience; **~konflikt** *m* moral conflict

gewissermaßen [gəvɪsər'ma:sən] *adv* somew

or less, in a way

ewissheit ▲ [gə'vɪshaɪt] f certainty

ewitter [gə'vɪtər] (**-s, -**) nt thunderstorm; **g~n** vi unpers: **es g~t** there's a thunderstorm

ewitzt [gə'vɪtst] adj shrewd, cunning

ewogen [gə'vo:gən] adj (+dat) well-disposed (towards)

ewöhnen [gə'vø:nən] vt: **jdn an etw** akk **~** to accustom sb to sth; (*erziehen zu*) to teach sb sth ♦ vr: **sich an etw** akk **~** to get used od accustomed to sth

ewohnheit [gə'vo:nhaɪt] f habit; (*Brauch*) custom; **aus ~** from habit; **zur ~ werden** to become a habit

ewohnheits- zW: **~mensch** m creature of habit; **~recht** nt common law

ewöhnlich [gə'vø:nlɪç] adj usual; ordinary; (*pej*) common; **wie ~** as usual

ewohnt [gə'vo:nt] adj usual; **etw ~ sein** to be used to sth

ewöhnung f: **~ (an** +akk**)** getting accustomed (to)

ewölbe [gə'vœlbə] (**-s, -**) nt vault

ewollt [gə'vɔlt] adj affected, artificial

ewonnen [gə'vɔnən] vb siehe **gewinnen**

eworden [gə'vɔrdən] vb siehe **werden**

eworfen [gə'vɔrfən] vb siehe **werfen**

ewühl [gə'vy:l] (**-(e)s**) nt throng

ewürz [gə'vʏrts] (**-es, -e**) nt spice, seasoning; **g~t** adj spiced

ewusst ▲ [gə'vʊst] vb siehe **wissen**

ezeiten [gə'tsaɪtən] pl tides

ezielt [gə'tsi:lt] adj with a particular aim in mind, purposeful; (*Kritik*) pointed

ezogen [gə'tso:gən] vb siehe **ziehen**

ezwitscher [gə'tsvɪtʃər] (**-s**) nt twitter(ing), chirping

ezwungen [gə'tsvʊŋən] adj forced; **~ermaßen** adv of necessity

gf. abk von **gegebenenfalls**

bst etc [gi:pst] vb siehe **geben**

icht [gɪçt] (**-**) f gout

iebel ['gi:bəl] (**-s, -**) m gable; **~dach** nt gable(d) roof; **~fenster** nt gable window

ier [gi:r] (**-**) f greed; **g~ig** adj greedy

ießen ['gi:sən] (*unreg*) vt to pour; (*Blumen*)

to water; (*Metall*) to cast; (*Wachs*) to mould

Gießkanne f watering can

Gift [gɪft] (**-(e)s, -e**) nt poison; **g~ig** adj poisonous; (*fig: boshaft*) venomous; **~müll** m toxic waste; **~stoff** m toxic substance; **~zahn** m fang

ging etc [gɪŋ] vb siehe **gehen**

Gipfel ['gɪpfəl] (**-s, -**) m summit, peak; (*fig: Höhepunkt*) height; **g~n** vi to culminate; **~treffen** nt summit (meeting)

Gips [gɪps] (**-es, -e**) m plaster; (*MED*) plaster (of Paris); **~abdruck** m plaster cast; **g~en** vt to plaster; **~verband** m plaster (cast)

Giraffe [gi'rafə] f giraffe

Girlande [gɪr'landə] f garland

Giro ['ʒi:ro] (**-s, -s**) nt giro; **~konto** nt current account

Gitarre [gi'tarə] f guitar

Gitter ['gɪtər] (**-s, -**) nt grating, bars pl; (*für Pflanzen*) trellis; (*Zaun*) railing(s); **~bett** nt cot; **~fenster** nt barred window; **~zaun** m railing(s)

Glanz [glants] (**-es**) m shine, lustre; (*fig*) splendour

glänzen ['glɛntsən] vi to shine (*also fig*), to gleam ♦ vt to polish; **~d** adj shining; (*fig*) brilliant

Glanz- zW: **~leistung** f brilliant achievement; **g~los** adj dull; **~zeit** f heyday

Glas [gla:s] (**-es, ⁺er**) nt glass; **~er** (**-s, -**) m glazier; **~faser** f fibreglass; **g~ieren** [gla'zi:rən] vt to glaze; **g~ig** adj glassy; **~scheibe** f pane; **~ur** [gla'zu:r] f glaze; (*KOCH*) icing

glatt [glat] adj smooth; (*rutschig*) slippery; (*Absage*) flat; (*Lüge*) downright; **Glätte** f smoothness; slipperiness

Glatteis nt (black) ice; **jdn aufs ~ führen** (*fig*) to take sb for a ride

glätten vt to smooth out

Glatze ['glatsə] f bald head; **eine ~ bekommen** to go bald

Glaube ['glaʊbə] (**-ns, -n**) m: **~ (an** +akk**)** faith (in); belief (in); **g~n** vt, vi to believe; to think; **jdm g~n** to believe sb; **an etw** akk **g~n** to believe in sth; **daran g~n müssen**

(umg) to be for it

glaubhaft ['glaʊbhaft] *adj* credible

gläubig ['glɔʏbɪç] *adj (REL)* devout; *(vertrauensvoll)* trustful; **G~e(r)** *f(m)* believer; **die G~en** the faithful; **G~er** (**-s, -**) *m* creditor

glaubwürdig ['glaʊbvʏrdɪç] *adj* credible; *(Mensch)* trustworthy; **G~keit** *f* credibility; trustworthiness

gleich [glaɪç] *adj* equal; *(identisch)* (the) same, identical ♦ *adv* equally; *(sofort)* straight away; *(bald)* in a minute; **es ist mir ~** it's all the same to me; **~ bleibend** constant; **~ gesinnt** like-minded; **2 mal 2 ~ 4** 2 times 2 is *od* equals 4; **~ groß** the same size; **~ nach/an** right after/at; **~altrig** *adj* of the same age; **~artig** *adj* similar; **~bedeutend** *adj* synonymous; **G~berechtigung** *f* equal rights *pl*; **~en** *(unreg) vi*: **jdm/etw ~en** to be like sb/sth ♦ *vr* to be alike; **~falls** *adv* likewise; **danke ~falls!** the same to you; **G~förmigkeit** *f* uniformity; **G~gewicht** *nt* equilibrium, balance; **~gültig** *adj* indifferent; *(unbedeutend)* unimportant; **G~gültigkeit** *f* indifference; **G~heit** *f* equality; **~kommen** *(unreg) vi +dat* to be equal to; **~mäßig** *adj* even, equal; **~sam** *adv* as it were; **G~schritt** *m*: **im G~schritt gehen** to walk in step; **~stellen** *vt (rechtlich etc)* to treat as (an) equal; **G~strom** *m (ELEK)* direct current; **~tun** *(unreg) vi*: **es jdm ~tun** to match sb; **G~ung** *f* equation; **~viel** *adv* no matter; **~wertig** *adj (Geld)* of the same value; *(Gegner)* evenly matched; **~zeitig** *adj* simultaneous

Gleis [glaɪs] (**-es, -e**) *nt* track, rails *pl*; *(Bahnsteig)* platform

gleiten ['glaɪtən] *(unreg) vi* to glide; *(rutschen)* to slide

Gleitzeit *f* flex(i)time

Gletscher ['glɛtʃər] (**-s, -**) *m* glacier; **~spalte** *f* crevasse

Glied [gliːt] (**-(e)s, -er**) *nt* member; *(Arm, Bein)* limb; *(von Kette)* link; *(MIL)* rank(s); **g~ern** [-dərn] *vt* to organize, to structure; **~erung** *f* structure, organization

glimmen ['glɪmən] *(unreg) vi* to glow, to gleam

glimpflich ['glɪmpflɪç] *adj* mild, lenient; **~ davonkommen** to get off lightly

glitschig ['glɪtʃɪç] *adj (Fisch, Weg)* slippery

glitzern ['glɪtsərn] *vi* to glitter; to twinkle

global [glo'baːl] *adj* global

Globus ['gloːbʊs] (**-** *od* **-ses, Globen** *od* **-s** *m* globe

Glocke ['glɔkə] *f* bell; **etw an die große ~ hängen** *(fig)* to shout sth from the rooft.

Glocken- *zW*: **~blume** *f* bellflower; **~geläut** *nt* peal of bells; **~spiel** *nt* chime(s); *(MUS)* glockenspiel; **~turm** *m* b tower

Glosse ['glɔsə] *f* comment

glotzen ['glɔtsən] *(umg) vi* to stare

Glück [glʏk] (**-(e)s**) *nt* luck, fortune; *(Freu* happiness; **~ haben** to be lucky; **viel ~!** good luck!; **zum ~** fortunately; **g~en** *vi* t succeed; **es g~te ihm, es zu bekomme** he succeeded in getting it

gluckern ['glʊkərn] *vi* to glug

glück- *zW*: **~lich** *adj* fortunate; *(froh)* happy; **~licherweise** *adv* fortunately; **~'selig** *adj* blissful

Glücks- *zW*: **~fall** *m* stroke of luck; **~kin** *nt* lucky person; **~sache** *f* matter of luck **~spiel** *nt* game of chance

Glückwunsch *m* congratulations *pl*, bes wishes *pl*

Glüh- [glyː] *zW*: **~birne** *f* light bulb; **g~e** *vi* to glow; **~wein** *m* mulled wine; **~würmchen** *nt* glow-worm

Glut [gluːt] (**-, -en**) *f (Röte)* glow; *(Feuersgl* fire; *(Hitze)* heat; *(fig)* ardour

GmbH [geːʔɛmbeːˈhaː] *f abk* (= *Gesellschaft beschränkter Haftung)* limited company, L

Gnade ['gnaːdə] *f (Gunst)* favour; *(Erbarme* mercy; *(Milde)* clemency

Gnaden- *zW*: **~frist** *f* reprieve, respite; **g~los** *adj* merciless; **~stoß** *m* coup de grâce

gnädig ['gnɛːdɪç] *adj* gracious; *(voll Erbarm* merciful

Gold [gɔlt] (**-(e)s**) *nt* gold; **g~en** *adj* golde **~fisch** *m* goldfish; **~grube** *f* goldmine;

g~ig ['gɔldɪç] (umg) adj (fig: allerliebst) sweet, adorable; **~regen** m laburnum; **~schmied** m goldsmith

olf¹ [gɔlf] (-(e)s, -e) m gulf

olf² [gɔlf] (-s) nt golf; **~platz** m golf course; **~schläger** m golf club

olfstrom m Gulf Stream

ondel ['gɔndəl] (-, -n) f gondola; (Seilbahn) cable car

önnen ['gœnən] vt: **jdm etw ~** not to begrudge sb sth; **sich** dat **etw ~** to allow o.s. sth

önner (-s, -) m patron; **g~haft** adj patronizing

osse ['gɔsə] f gutter

ott [gɔt] (-es, ꞔer) m god; **mein ~!** for heaven's sake!; **um ~es Willen!** for heaven's sake!; **grüß ~!** hello; **~ sei Dank!** thank God!; **~heit** f deity

öttin ['gœtɪn] f goddess

öttlich adj divine

ottlos adj godless

ötze ['gœtsə] (-n, -n) m idol

rab [gra:p] (-(e)s, ꞔer) nt grave; **g~en** ['gra:bən] (unreg) vt to dig; **~en** (-s, ꞔ) m ditch; (MIL) trench; **~stein** m gravestone

rad [gra:t] (-(e)s, -e) m degree

raf [gra:f] (-en, -en) m count, earl

rafiker(in) ▲ ['gra:fɪkər(ɪn)] (-s, -) m(f) graphic designer

rafisch ▲ ['gra:fɪʃ] adj graphic

ram [gra:m] (-(e)s) m grief, sorrow

rämen ['grɛ:mən] vr to grieve

ramm [gram] (-s, -e) nt gram(me)

rammatik [gra'matɪk] f grammar

ranat [gra'na:t] (-(e)s, -e) m (Stein) garnet

ranate f (MIL) shell; (Handgranate) grenade

ranit [gra'ni:t] (-s, -e) m granite

ras [gra:s] (-es, ꞔer) nt grass; **g~en** ['gra:zən] vi to graze; **~halm** m blade of grass

rassieren [gra'si:rən] vi to be rampant, to rage

rässlich ▲ ['grɛslɪç] adj horrible

rat [gra:t] (-(e)s, -e) m ridge

räte ['grɛ:tə] f fishbone

ratis ['gra:tɪs] adj, adv free (of charge);

G~probe f free sample

Gratulation [gratulatsi'o:n] f congratulation(s)

gratulieren [gratu'li:rən] vi: **jdm ~ (zu etw)** to congratulate sb (on sth); **(ich) gratuliere!** congratulations!

grau [grau] adj grey

Gräuel ▲ ['grɔyəl] (-s, -) m horror, revulsion; **etw ist jdm ein ~** sb loathes sth

Grauen (-s) nt horror; **g~** vi unpers: **es graut jdm vor etw** sb dreads sth, sb is afraid of sth ♦ vr: **sich g~ vor** to dread, to have a horror of; **g~haft** adj horrible

grauhaarig adj grey-haired

gräulich ▲ ['grɔylɪç] adj horrible

grausam ['grauza:m] adj cruel; **G~keit** f cruelty

Grausen ['grauzən] (-s) nt horror; **g~** vb = **grauen**

gravieren [gra'vi:rən] vt to engrave; **~d** adj grave

graziös [gratsi'ø:s] adj graceful

greifbar adj tangible, concrete; **in ~er Nähe** within reach

greifen ['graifən] (unreg) vt to seize; to grip; **nach etw ~** to reach for sth; **um sich ~** (fig) to spread; **zu etw ~** (fig) to turn to sth

Greis [grais] (-es, -e) m old man; **g~enhaft** adj senile; **~in** f old woman

grell [grɛl] adj harsh

Grenz- ['grɛnts] zW: **~beamte(r)** m frontier official; **~e** f boundary; (Staatsgrenze) frontier; (Schranke) limit; **g~en** vi: **g~en (an** +akk) to border (on); **g~enlos** adj boundless; **~fall** m borderline case; **~kontrolle** f border control; **~übergang** m frontier crossing

Greuel △ ['grɔyəl] (-s, -) m siehe **Gräuel**

greulich △ adj siehe **gräulich**

Griech- ['gri:ç] zW: **~e** (-n, -n) m Greek; **~enland** nt Greece; **~in** f Greek; **g~isch** adj Greek

griesgrämig ['gri:sgrɛ:mɪç] adj grumpy

Grieß [gri:s] (-es, -e) m (KOCH) semolina

Griff [grɪf] (-(e)s, -e) m grip; (Vorrichtung) handle; **g~bereit** adj handy

Grill [grɪl] m grill; **~e** f cricket; **g~en** vt to

grill; **~fest** *nt* barbecue party

Grimasse [gri'masə] *f* grimace

grimmig ['grɪmɪç] *adj* furious; (*heftig*) fierce, severe

grinsen ['grɪnzən] *vi* to grin

Grippe ['grɪpə] *f* influenza, flu

grob [groːp] *adj* coarse, gross; (*Fehler, Verstoß*) gross; **G~heit** *f* coarseness; coarse expression

grölen ['grøːlən] (*pej*) *vt* to bawl, to bellow

Groll [grɔl] **(-(e)s)** *m* resentment; **g~en** *vi* (*Donner*) to rumble; **g~en (mit** *od* **+dat)** to bear ill will (towards)

groß [groːs] *adj* big, large; (*hoch*) tall; (*fig*) great ♦ *adv* greatly; **im G~en und Ganzen** on the whole; **bei jdm ~ geschrieben werden** to be high on sb's list of priorities; **~artig** *adj* great, splendid; **G~aufnahme** *f* (*CINE*) close-up; **G~britannien** *nt* Great Britain

Größe ['grøːsə] *f* size; (*Höhe*) height; (*fig*) greatness

Groß- *zW*: **~einkauf** *m* bulk purchase; **~eltern** *pl* grandparents; **g~enteils** *adv* mostly; **g~format** *nt* large size; **~handel** *m* wholesale trade; **~händler** *m* wholesaler; **~macht** *f* great power; **~mutter** *f* grandmother; **~rechner** *m* mainframe (computer); **g~schreiben** (*unreg*) *vt* (*Wort*) to write in block capitals; *siehe* **groß**; **g~spurig** *adj* pompous; **~stadt** *f* city, large town

größte(r, s) [grøːstə(r, s)] *adj superl von* **groß**; **größtenteils** *adv* for the most part

Groß- *zW*: **g~tun** (*unreg*) *vi* to boast; **~vater** *m* grandfather; **g~ziehen** (*unreg*) *vt* to raise; **g~zügig** *adj* generous; (*Planung*) on a large scale

grotesk [gro'tɛsk] *adj* grotesque

Grotte ['grɔtə] *f* grotto

Grübchen ['gryːpçən] *nt* dimple

Grube ['gruːbə] *f* pit; mine

grübeln ['gryːbəln] *vi* to brood

Gruft [gruft] **(-, ˈˈe)** *f* tomb, vault

grün [gryːn] *adj* green; **der ~e Punkt** green spot symbol on recyclable packaging

---

grüner Punkt

ⓘ *The* **grüner Punkt** *is a green spot which appears on packaging that shou be kept separate from normal household refuse to be recycled through the recycling company,* **DSD** *(Duales System Deutschland). The recycling is financed by licences bought by the packaging manufacturer from* **DSD**. *These costs are often passed on to the consumer.*

Grünanlage *f* park

Grund [grʊnt] **(-(e)s, ˈˈe)** *m* ground; (*von See, Gefäß*) bottom; (*fig*) reason; **im ~e genommen** basically; *siehe* **aufgrund**; **~ausbildung** *f* basic training; **~besitz** *m* land(ed property), real estate; **~buch** *nt* land register

gründen ['grʏndən] *vt* to found ♦ *vr*: **sich (auf** *+dat*) to be based (on); **~ auf** *+akk* to base on; **Gründer (-s, -)** *m* founder

Grund- *zW*: **~gebühr** *f* basic charge; **~gesetz** *nt* constitution; **~lage** *f* foundation; **g~legend** *adj* fundamental

gründlich *adj* thorough

Grund- *zW*: **g~los** *adj* groundless; **~rege** basic rule; **~riss** ▲ *m* plan; (*fig*) outline; **~satz** *m* principle; **g~sätzlich** *adj* fundamental; (*Frage*) of principle ♦ *adv* fundamentally; (*prinzipiell*) on principle; **~schule** *f* elementary school; **~stein** *m* foundation stone; **~stück** *nt* estate; plot

Grundwasser *nt* ground water

Grundschule

ⓘ *The* **Grundschule** *is a primary schoo which children attend for 4 years from the age of 6 to 10. There are no formal examinations in the* **Grundschule** *but parents receive a report on their child's progress twice a year. Many children atten a* **Kindergarten** *from 3-6 years before going to the* **Grundschule**, *though no formal instruction takes place in the* **Kindergarten**.

---

rünstreifen m central reservation

runzen ['grʊntsən] vi to grunt

ruppe ['grʊpə] f group; **~nermäßigung** f group reduction; **g~nweise** adv in groups

ruppieren [grʊ'piːrən] vt, vr to group

ruselig adj creepy

ruseln ['gruːzəln] vi unpers: **es gruselt jdm vor etw** sth gives sb the creeps ♦ vr to have the creeps

ruß [gruːs] (**-es, ⁻e**) m greeting; (MIL) salute; **viele Grüße** best wishes; **mit freundlichen Grüßen** yours sincerely; **Grüße an** +akk regards to

⁻üßen ['gryːsən] vt to greet; (MIL) to salute; **jdn von jdm ~** to give sb sb's regards; **jdn ~ lassen** to send sb one's regards

ucken ['gʊkən] vi to look

iltig ['gʏltɪç] adj valid; **G~keit** f validity

ummi ['gʊmi] (**-s, -s**) nt od m rubber; (~harze) gum; **~band** nt elastic band; (Hosenband) elastic; **~bärchen** nt ≈ jelly baby (BRIT); **~baum** m rubber plant; **g~eren** [gʊ'miːrən] vt to gum; **~stiefel** m rubber boot

instig ['gʏnstɪç] adj convenient; (Gelegenheit) favourable; **das habe ich ~ bekommen** it was a bargain

urgel ['gʊrgəl] f throat; **g~n** vi to gurgle; (im Mund) to gargle

urke ['gʊrkə] f cucumber; **saure ~** pickled cucumber, gherkin

urt [gʊrt] (**-(e)s, -e**) m belt

ürtel ['gʏrtəl] (**-s, -**) m belt; (GEOG) zone; **~reifen** m radial tyre

US f abk (= Gemeinschaft unabhängiger Staaten) CIS

uss ▲ [gʊs] (**-es, ⁻e**) m casting; (Regenguss) downpour; (KOCH) glazing; **~eisen** nt cast iron

ut adj good; **alles Gute** all the best; **also gut** all right then
♦ adv well; **gut gehen** to work, to come off; **es geht jdm gut** sb's doing fine; **gut gemeint** well meant; **gut schmecken** to taste good; **jdm gut tun** to do sb good; **gut, aber ...** OK, but ...; **(na) gut, ich komme** all right, I'll come; **gut drei Stunden** a good three hours; **das kann gut sein** that may well be; **lass es gut sein** that'll do

Gut [guːt] (**-(e)s, ⁻er**) nt (Besitz) possession; **Güter** pl (Waren) goods; **~achten** (**-s, -**) nt (expert) opinion; **~achter** (**-s, -**) m expert; **g~artig** adj good-natured; (MED) benign; **g~bürgerlich** adj (Küche) (good) plain; **~dünken** nt: **nach ~dünken** at one's discretion

Güte ['gyːtə] f goodness, kindness; (Qualität) quality

Güter- zW: **~abfertigung** f (EISENB) goods office; **~bahnhof** m goods station; **~wagen** m goods waggon (BRIT), freight car (US); **~zug** m goods train (BRIT), freight train (US)

Gütezeichen nt quality mark; ≈ kite mark

gut- zW: **~gehen** △ (unreg) vi unpers siehe **gut**; **~gemeint** △ adj siehe **gut**; **~gläubig** adj trusting; **G~haben** (**-s**) nt credit; **~heißen** (unreg) vt to approve (of)

gütig ['gyːtɪç] adj kind

Gut- zW: **g~mütig** adj good-natured; **~schein** m voucher; **g~schreiben** (unreg) vt to credit; **~schrift** f (Betrag) credit; **g~tun** △ (unreg) vi siehe **gut**; **g~willig** adj willing

Gymnasium [gʏm'naːziʊm] nt grammar school (BRIT), high school (US)

Gymnasium

ⓘ The **Gymnasium** is a selective secondary school. After nine years of study pupils sit the **Abitur** so they can go on to higher education. Pupils who successfully complete six years at a **Gymnasium** automatically gain the mittlere **Reife**.

Gymnastik [gʏm'nastɪk] f exercises pl, keep fit

H, h

Haag [ha:k] *m*: **Den ~** the Hague

Haar [ha:r] (-(e)s, -e) *nt* hair; **um ein ~** nearly; **an den ~en herbeigezogen** (*umg*: *Vergleich*) very far-fetched; **~bürste** *f* hairbrush; **h~en** *vi*, *vr* to lose hair; **~esbreite** *f*: **um ~esbreite** by a hair's-breadth; **~festiger** (-s, -) *m* (hair) setting lotion; **h~genau** *adv* precisely; **h~ig** *adj* hairy; (*fig*) nasty; **~klammer** *f* hairgrip; **~nadel** *f* hairpin; **h~scharf** *adv* (*beobachten*) very sharply; (*daneben*) by a hair's breadth; **~schnitt** *m* haircut; **~spange** *f* hair slide; **h~sträubend** *adj* hair-raising; **~teil** *nt* hairpiece; **~waschmittel** *nt* shampoo

Habe ['ha:bə] (-) *f* property

haben ['ha:bən] (*unreg*) *vt*, *vb aux* to have; **Hunger/Angst ~** to be hungry/afraid; **woher hast du das?** where did you get that from?; **was hast du denn?** what's the matter (with you)?; **du hast zu schweigen** you're to be quiet; **ich hätte gern** I would like; **H~** (-s, -) *nt* credit

Habgier *f* avarice; **h~ig** *adj* avaricious

Habicht ['ha:bɪçt] (-s, -e) *m* hawk

Habseligkeiten ['ha:pze:lɪçkaɪtən] *pl* belongings

Hachse ['haksə] *f* (*KOCH*) knuckle

Hacke ['hakə] *f* hoe; (*Ferse*) heel; **h~n** *vt* to hack, to chop; (*Erde*) to hoe

Hackfleisch *nt* mince, minced meat

Hafen ['ha:fən] (-s, ¨) *m* harbour, port; **~arbeiter** *m* docker; **~rundfahrt** *f* boat trip round the harbour; **~stadt** *f* port

Hafer ['ha:fər] (-s, -) *m* oats *pl*; **~flocken** *pl* rolled oats; **~schleim** *m* gruel

Haft [haft] (-) *f* custody; **h~bar** *adj* liable, responsible; **~befehl** *m* warrant (for arrest); **h~en** *vi* to stick, to cling; **h~en für** to be liable *od* responsible for; **h~en bleiben (an** +*dat*) to stick (to); **Häftling** *m* prisoner; **~pflicht** *f* liability; **~pflichtversicherung** *f* (*AUT*) third party

insurance; **~schalen** *pl* contact lenses; **~ung** *f* liability; **~ungsbeschränkung** *f* limitation of liability

Hagebutte ['ha:gəbʊtə] *f* rose hip

Hagel ['ha:gəl] (-s) *m* hail; **h~n** *vi unpers* t hail

hager ['ha:gər] *adj* gaunt

Hahn [ha:n] (-(e)s, ¨e) *m* cock; (*Wasserhal* tap, faucet (*US*)

Hähnchen ['hɛ:nçən] *nt* cockerel; (*KOCH*) chicken

Hai(fisch) ['haɪ(fɪʃ)] (-(e)s, -e) *m* shark

häkeln ['hɛ:kəln] *vt* to crochet

Haken ['ha:kən] (-s, -) *m* hook; (*fig*) catch; **~kreuz** *nt* swastika; **~nase** *f* hooked nose

halb [halp] *adj* half; **~ eins** half past twelve **~ offen** half-open; **ein ~es Dutzend** half dozen; **H~dunkel** *nt* semi-darkness

halber ['halbər] *präp* +*gen* (*wegen*) on account of; (*für*) for the sake of

Halb- *zW*: **~heit** *f* half-measure; **h~ieren** to halve; **~insel** *f* peninsula; **~jahr** *nt* six months; (*auch*: *COMM*) half-year; **h~jährlich** *adj* half-yearly; **~kreis** *m* semicircle; **~leiter** *m* semiconductor; **~mond** *m* half-moon; (*fig*) crescent; **~pension** *f* half-board; **~schuh** *m* shoe; **h~tags** *adv*: **h~tags arbeiten** to work part-time, to work mornings/afternoons; **h~wegs** *adv* halfway; **h~wegs besser** more or less better; **~zeit** *f* (*SPORT*) half; (*Pause*) half-time

Halde ['haldə] *f* (*Kohlen*) heap

half [half] *vb siehe* **helfen**

Hälfte ['hɛlftə] *f* half

Halfter ['halftər] (-s, -) *m od nt* (*für Tiere*) halter

Halle ['halə] *f* hall; (*AVIAT*) hangar; **h~n** *vi* echo, to resound; **~nbad** *nt* indoor swimming pool

hallo [ha'lo:] *excl* hello

Halluzination [halutsinatsi'o:n] *f* hallucination

Halm ['halm] (-(e)s, -e) *m* blade; stalk

Halogenlampe [halo'ge:nlampə] *f* haloge lamp

Hals [hals] (**-es**, ⸚e) m neck; (*Kehle*) throat; ~ **über Kopf** in a rush; ~**band** nt (*von Hund*) collar; ~**kette** f necklace; ~-**Nasen-Ohren-Arzt** m ear, nose and throat specialist; ~**schmerzen** pl sore throat sg; ~**tuch** nt scarf

Halt [halt] (**-(e)s**, **-e**) m stop; (*fester ~*) hold; (*innerer ~*) stability; ~ **od h~!** stop!, halt!; ~ **machen** to stop; **h~bar** adj durable; (*Lebensmittel*) non-perishable; (*MIL, fig*) tenable; ~**barkeit** f durability; (non-) perishability

halten ['haltən] (*unreg*) vt to keep; (*festhalten*) to hold ♦ vi to hold; (*frisch bleiben*) to keep; (*stoppen*) to stop ♦ vr (*frisch bleiben*) to keep; (*sich behaupten*) to hold out; ~ **für** to regard as; ~ **von** to think of; **an sich** ~ to restrain o.s.; **sich rechts/links** ~ to keep to the right/left

Halte- zW: ~**stelle** f stop; ~**verbot** nt: **hier ist ~verbot** there's no waiting here

Halt- zW: **h~los** adj unstable; **h~machen** △ vi siehe **Halt**; ~**ung** f posture; (*fig*) attitude; (*Selbstbeherrschung*) composure

Halunke [ha'lʊŋkə] (**-n**, **-n**) m rascal

hämisch ['hɛːmɪʃ] adj malicious

Hammel ['haməl] (**-s**, ⸚ od **-**) m wether; ~**fleisch** nt mutton

Hammer ['hamər] (**-s**, ⸚) m hammer

hämmern ['hɛmərn] vt, vi to hammer

Hämor(rho)iden [hɛmɔroˈiːdən,hɛmɔˈriːdn] pl haemorrhoids

Hamster ['hamstər] (**-s**, **-**) m hamster; ~**ei** [-'raɪ] f hoarding; **h~n** vi to hoard

Hand [hant] (**-**, ⸚e) f hand; ~**arbeit** f manual work; (*Nadelarbeit*) needlework; ~**ball** m (*SPORT*) handball; ~**bremse** f handbrake; ~**buch** nt handbook, manual

Händedruck ['hɛndədrʊk] m handshake

Handel ['handəl] (**-s**) m trade; (*Geschäft*) transaction

Handeln ['handəln] (**-s**) nt action

handeln vi to trade; (*agieren*) to act ♦ vr unpers: **sich ~ um** to be a question of, to be about; ~ **von** to be about

Handels- zW: ~**bilanz** f balance of trade;

~**kammer** f chamber of commerce; ~**reisende(r)** m commercial traveller; ~**schule** f business school; **h~üblich** adj customary; (*Preis*) going attrib; ~**vertreter** m sales representative

Hand- zW: ~**feger** (**-s**, **-**) m hand brush; **h~fest** adj hefty; **h~gearbeitet** adj handmade; ~**gelenk** nt wrist; ~**gemenge** nt scuffle; ~**gepäck** nt hand luggage; **h~geschrieben** adj handwritten; **h~greiflich** adj palpable; **h~greiflich werden** to become violent; ~**griff** m flick of the wrist; **h~haben** vt insep to handle

Händler ['hɛndlər] (**-s**, **-**) m trader, dealer

handlich ['hantlɪç] adj handy

Handlung ['handlʊŋ] f act(ion); (*in Buch*) plot; (*Geschäft*) shop

Hand- zW: ~**schelle** f handcuff; ~**schrift** f handwriting; (*Text*) manuscript; ~**schuh** m glove; ~**stand** m (*SPORT*) handstand; ~**tasche** f handbag; ~**tuch** nt towel; ~**umdrehen** nt: **im ~umdrehen** in the twinkling of an eye; ~**werk** nt trade, craft; ~**werker** (**-s**, **-**) m craftsman, artisan; ~**werkzeug** nt tools pl

Handy ['hɛndi] (**-s**, **-s**) nt mobile (telephone)

Hanf [hanf] (**-(e)s**) m hemp

Hang [haŋ] (**-(e)s**, ⸚e) m inclination; (*Abhang*) slope

Hänge- ['hɛŋə] in zW hanging; ~**brücke** f suspension bridge; ~**matte** f hammock

hängen ['hɛŋən] (*unreg*) vi to hang ♦ vt: **etw (an etw** akk**) ~** to hang sth (on sth); ~ **an** +dat (*fig*) to be attached to; **sich ~ an** +akk to hang on to, to cling to; ~ **bleiben** to be caught; (*fig*) to remain, to stick; ~ **bleiben an** +dat to catch od get caught on; ~ **lassen** (*vergessen*) to leave; **den Kopf ~ lassen** to get downhearted

Hannover [ha'noːfar] (**-s**) nt Hanover

hänseln ['hɛnzəln] vt to tease

Hansestadt ['hanzəʃtat] f Hanse town

hantieren [han'tiːrən] vi to work, to be busy; **mit etw ~** to handle sth

hapern ['haːpərn] vi unpers: **es hapert an etw** dat there is a lack of sth

Happen ['hapən] **(-s, -)** *m* mouthful

Harfe ['harfə] *f* harp

Harke ['harkə] *f* rake; **h~n** *vt, vi* to rake

harmlos ['harmlo:s] *adj* harmless; **H~igkeit** *f* harmlessness

Harmonie [harmo'ni:] *f* harmony; **h~ren** *vi* to harmonize

harmonisch [har'mo:nɪʃ] *adj* harmonious

Harn ['harn] **(-(e)s, -e)** *m* urine; **~blase** *f* bladder

Harpune [har'pu:nə] *f* harpoon

harren ['harən] *vi:* **~ (auf** +*akk*) to wait (for)

hart [hart] *adj* hard; (*fig*) harsh; **~ gekocht** hard-boiled

Härte ['hertə] *f* hardness; (*fig*) harshness

hart- *zW:* **~herzig** *adj* hard-hearted; **~näckig** *adj* stubborn

Harz [ha:rts] **(-es, -e)** *nt* resin

Haschee [ha'ʃe:] **(-s, -s)** *nt* hash

Haschisch ['haʃɪʃ] **(-)** *nt* hashish

Hase ['ha:zə] **(-n, -n)** *m* hare

Haselnuss ▲ ['ha:zəlnʊs] *f* hazelnut

Hasenscharte *f* harelip

Hass ▲ [has] **(-es)** *m* hate, hatred

hassen ['hasən] *vt* to hate

hässlich ▲ ['hɛslɪç] *adj* ugly; (*gemein*) nasty; **H~keit** *f* ugliness; nastiness

Hast [hast] *f* haste

hast *vb siehe* **haben**

hasten *vi* to rush

hastig *adj* hasty

hat [hat] *vb siehe* **haben**

hatte *etc* ['hatə] *vb siehe* **haben**

Haube ['haubə] *f* hood; (*Mütze*) cap; (*AUT*) bonnet, hood (*US*)

Hauch [haux] **(-(e)s, -e)** *m* breath; (*Lufthauch*) breeze; (*fig*) trace; **h~dünn** *adj* extremely thin

Haue ['hauə] *f* hoe, pick; (*umg*) hiding; **h~n** (*unreg*) *vt* to hew, to cut; (*umg*) to thrash

Haufen ['haufən] **(-s, -)** *m* heap; (*Leute*) crowd; **ein ~ (x)** (*umg*) loads *od* a lot (of x); **auf einem ~** in one heap

häufen ['hɔyfən] *vt* to pile up ♦ *vr* to accumulate

haufenweise *adv* in heaps; in droves; **etw ~ haben** to have piles of sth

häufig ['hɔyfɪç] *adj* frequent ♦ *adv* frequently; **H~keit** *f* frequency

Haupt [haupt] **(-(e)s, Häupter)** *nt* head; (*Oberhaupt*) chief ♦ *in zW* main; **~bahnhof** *m* central station; **h~beruflich** *adv* as one's main occupation; **~darsteller(in)** *m(f)* leading actor (actress); **~fach** *nt* (*SCH, UNIV*) main subject, major (*US*); **~gericht** *nt* (*KOCH*) main course

Häuptling ['hɔyptlɪŋ] *m* chief(tain)

Haupt- *zW:* **~mann** (*pl* **-leute**) *m* (*MIL*) captain; **~person** *f* central figure; **~quartier** *nt* headquarters *pl*; **~rolle** *f* leading part; **~sache** *f* main thing; **h~sächlich** *adj* chief ♦ *adv* chiefly; **~saison** *f* high season, peak season; **~schule** *f* ≈ secondary school; **~stadt** *f* capital; **~straße** *f* main street; **~verkehrszeit** *f* rush-hour, peak traffic hours *pl*

Hauptschule

ⓘ The **Hauptschule** *is a non-selective school which pupils may attend after the* **Grundschule**. *They complete five years of study and most go on to do some vocational training.*

Haus [haus] **(-es, Häuser)** *nt* house; **~ halten** (*sparen*) to economize; **nach ~e** home; **zu ~e** at home; **~apotheke** *f* medicine cabinet; **~arbeit** *f* housework; (*SCH*) homework; **~arzt** *m* family doctor; **~aufgabe** *f* (*SCH*) homework; **~besitzer(in)** *m(f)* house owner; **~besuch** *m* (*von Arzt*) house call; **~durchsuchung** *f* police raid; **h~eigen** *adj* belonging to a/ the hotel/firm

Häuser- ['hɔyzər] *zW:* **~block** *m* block (of houses); **~makler** *m* estate agent (*BRIT*), real estate agent (*US*)

Haus- *zW:* **~flur** *m* hallway; **~frau** *f* housewife; **h~gemacht** *adj* home-made; **~halt** *m* household; (*POL*) budget; **h~halten** (*unreg*) *vi* △ *siehe* **Haus**; **~hälterin** *f* housekeeper; **~haltsgeld** *nt* housekeeping (money); **~haltsgerät** *nt*

domestic appliance; **~herr** m host; (*Vermieter*) landlord; **h~hoch** adv: **h~hoch verlieren** to lose by a mile

hausieren [hau'zi:rən] vi to peddle

Hausierer (-s, -) m pedlar (*BRIT*), peddler (*US*)

häuslich ['hɔyslɪç] adj domestic

Haus- zW: **~meister** m caretaker, janitor; **~nummer** f street number; **~ordnung** f house rules pl; **~putz** m house cleaning; **~schlüssel** m front door key; **~schuh** m slipper; **~tier** nt pet; **~tür** f front door; **~wirt** m landlord; **~wirtschaft** f domestic science; **~zelt** nt frame tent

Haut [haut] (-, Häute) f skin; (*Tierhaut*) hide; **~creme** f skin cream; **h~eng** adj skin-tight; **~farbe** f complexion; **~krebs** m skin cancer

Haxe ['haksə] f = **Hachse**

Hbf. abk = **Hauptbahnhof**

Hebamme ['he:p|amə] f midwife

Hebel ['he:bəl] (-s, -) m lever

heben ['he:bən] (*unreg*) vt to raise, to lift

Hecht [hɛçt] (-(e)s, -e) m pike

Heck [hɛk] (-(e)s, -e) nt stern; (*von Auto*) rear

Hecke ['hɛkə] f hedge

Heckenschütze m sniper

Heckscheibe f rear window

Heer [he:r] (-(e)s, -e) nt army

Hefe ['he:fə] f yeast

Heft ['hɛft] (-(e)s, -e) nt exercise book; (*Zeitschrift*) number; (*von Messer*) haft; **h~en** vt: **h~en (an** +akk) to fasten (to); (*nähen*) to tack ((on) to); **etw an etw** akk **h~en** to fasten sth to sth; **~er** (-s, -) m folder

heftig adj fierce, violent; **H~keit** f fierceness, violence

Heft- zW: **~klammer** f paper clip; **~pflaster** nt sticking plaster; **~zwecke** f drawing pin

hegen ['he:gən] vt (*Wild, Bäume*) to care for, to tend; (*fig, geh: empfinden: Wunsch*) to cherish; (: *Misstrauen*) to feel

Hehl [he:l] m od nt: **kein(en) ~ aus etw machen** to make no secret of sth; **~er** (-s,

-) m receiver (of stolen goods), fence

Heide[1] ['haidə] (-n, -n) m heathen, pagan

Heide[2] ['haidə] f heath, moor; **~kraut** nt heather

Heidelbeere f bilberry

Heidentum nt paganism

Heidin f heathen, pagan

heikel ['haikəl] adj awkward, thorny

Heil [hail] (-(e)s) nt well-being; (*Seelenheil*) salvation; **h~** adj in one piece, intact; **~and** (-(e)s, -e) m saviour; **h~bar** adj curable; **h~en** vt to cure ♦ vi to heal; **h~froh** adj very relieved

heilig ['hailɪç] adj holy; **~ sprechen** to canonize; **H~abend** m Christmas Eve; **H~e(r)** f(m) saint; **~en** vt to sanctify, to hallow; **H~enschein** m halo; **H~keit** f holiness; **H~tum** nt shrine; (*Gegenstand*) relic

Heil- zW: **h~los** adj unholy; (*fig*) hopeless; **~mittel** nt remedy; **~praktiker(in)** m(f) non-medical practitioner; **h~sam** adj (*fig*) salutary; **~sarmee** f Salvation Army; **~ung** f cure

Heim [haim] (-(e)s, -e) nt home; **h~** adv home

Heimat ['haima:t] (-, -en) f home (town/country etc); **~land** nt homeland; **h~lich** adj native, home attrib; (*Gefühle*) nostalgic; **h~los** adj homeless; **~ort** m home town/area

Heim- zW: **~computer** m home computer; **h~fahren** (*unreg*) vi to drive home; **~fahrt** f journey home; **h~gehen** (*unreg*) vi to go home; (*sterben*) to pass away; **h~isch** adj (*gebürtig*) native; **sich h~isch fühlen** to feel at home; **~kehr** (-, -en) f homecoming; **h~kehren** vi to return home; **h~lich** adj secret; **~lichkeit** f secrecy; **~reise** f journey home; **~spiel** nt (*SPORT*) home game; **h~suchen** vt to afflict; (*Geist*) to haunt; **~trainer** m exercise bike; **h~tückisch** adj malicious; **~weg** m way home; **~weh** nt homesickness; **~werker** (-s, -) m handyman; **h~zahlen** vt: **jdm etw h~zahlen** to pay sb back for sth

Heirat ['haira:t] (-, -en) f marriage; **h~en** vt

to marry ♦ *vi* to marry, to get married ♦ *vr*
to get married; **~santrag** *m* proposal

heiser ['haɪzər] *adj* hoarse; **H~keit** *f*
hoarseness

heiß [haɪs] *adj* hot; **~e(s) Eisen** (*umg*) hot
potato; **~blütig** *adj* hot-blooded

heißen ['haɪsən] (*unreg*) *vi* to be called;
(*bedeuten*) to mean ♦ *vt* to command;
(*nennen*) to name ♦ *vi unpers*: **es heißt** it
says; it is said; **das heißt** that is (to say)

Heiß- *zW*: **~hunger** *m* ravenous hunger;
h~laufen (*unreg*) *vi*, *vr* to overheat

heiter ['haɪtər] *adj* cheerful; (*Wetter*) bright;
H~keit *f* cheerfulness; (*Belustigung*)
amusement

Heiz- ['haɪts] *zW*: **h~bar** *adj* heated; (*Raum*)
with heating; **h~en** *vt* to heat; **~körper** *m*
radiator; **~öl** *nt* fuel oil; **~sonne** *f* electric
fire; **~ung** *f* heating

hektisch ['hɛktɪʃ] *adj* hectic

Held [hɛlt] (**-en, -en**) *m* hero; **h~enhaft** *adj*
heroic; **~in** *f* heroine

helfen ['hɛlfən] (*unreg*) *vi* to help; (*nützen*) to
be of use ♦ *vb unpers*: **es hilft nichts, du
musst ...** it's no use, you'll have to ...; **jdm
(bei etw)** ~ to help sb (with sth); **sich** *dat*
zu ~ wissen to be resourceful

Helfer (**-s, -**) *m* helper, assistant; **~shelfer**
m accomplice

hell [hɛl] *adj* clear, bright; (*Farbe, Bier*) light;
~blau *adj* light blue; **~blond** *adj* ash
blond; **H~e** (**-**) *f* clearness, brightness;
~hörig *adj* (*Wand*) paper-thin; **~hörig
werden** (*fig*) to prick up one's ears;
H~seher *m* clairvoyant; **~wach** *adj* wide-
awake

Helm [hɛlm] (**-(e)s, -e**) *m* (*auf Kopf*) helmet

Hemd [hɛmt] (**-(e)s, -en**) *nt* shirt;
(*Unterhemd*) vest; **~bluse** *f* blouse

hemmen ['hɛmən] *vt* to check, to hold up;
gehemmt sein to be inhibited;
Hemmung *f* check; (*PSYCH*) inhibition;
hemmungslos *adj* unrestrained, without
restraint

Hengst [hɛŋst] (**-es, -e**) *m* stallion

Henkel ['hɛŋkəl] (**-s, -**) *m* handle

Henker (**-s, -**) *m* hangman

Henne ['hɛnə] *f* hen

SCHLÜSSELWORT
---

her [heːr] *adv* **1** (*Richtung*): **komm her zu mir**
come here (to me); **von England her** from
England; **von weit her** from a long way
away; **her damit!** hand it over!; **wo hat er
das her?** where did he get that from?
2 (*Blickpunkt*): **von der Form her** as far as
the form is concerned
3 (*zeitlich*): **das ist 5 Jahre her** that was 5
years ago; **wo bist du her?** where do you
come from?; **ich kenne ihn von früher her**
I know him from before

---

herab [hɛˈrap] *adv* down(ward(s)); **~hängen**
(*unreg*) *vi* to hang down; **~lassen** (*unreg*)
vt to let down ♦ *vr* to condescend;
~lassend *adj* condescending; **~setzen** *vt*
to lower, to reduce; (*fig*) to belittle, to
disparage

heran [hɛˈran] *adv*: **näher ~!** come up
closer!; **~ zu mir!** come up to me!;
~bringen (*unreg*) *vt*: **~bringen (an** +*akk*) to
bring up to (to); **~fahren** (*unreg*) *vi*: **~fahren
(an** +*akk*) to drive up to (to); **~kommen**
(*unreg*) *vi*: **(an jdn/etw) ~kommen** to
approach (sb/sth), to come near (to sb/
sth); **~machen** *vr*: **sich an jdn ~machen**
to make up to sb; **~treten** (*unreg*) *vi*: **mit
etw an jdn ~treten** to approach sb with
sth; **~wachsen** (*unreg*) *vi* to grow up;
~ziehen (*unreg*) *vt* to pull nearer;
(*aufziehen*) to raise; (*ausbilden*) to train; **jdn
zu etw ~ziehen** to call upon sb to help in
sth

herauf [hɛˈrauf] *adv* up(ward(s)), up here;
~beschwören (*unreg*) *vt* to conjure up, to
evoke; **~bringen** (*unreg*) *vt* to bring up;
~setzen *vt* (*Preise, Miete*) to raise, put up

heraus [hɛˈraus] *adv* out; **~bekommen**
(*unreg*) *vt* to get out; (*fig*) to find *od* figure
out; **~bringen** (*unreg*) *vt* to bring out;
(*Geheimnis*) to elicit; **~finden** (*unreg*) *vt* to
find out; **~fordern** *vt* to challenge;
H~forderung *f* challenge; provocation;
~geben (*unreg*) *vt* to hand over, to

surrender; (*zurückgeben*) to give back; (*Buch*) to edit; (*veröffentlichen*) to publish; **H~geber** (**-s, -**) *m* editor; (*Verleger*) publisher; **~gehen** (*unreg*) *vi*: **aus sich ~gehen** to come out of one's shell; **~halten** (*unreg*) *vr*: **sich aus etw ~halten** to keep out of sth; **~hängen¹** *vt* to hang out; **~hängen²** (*unreg*) *vi* to hang out; **~holen** *vt*: **~holen (aus)** to get out (of); **~kommen** (*unreg*) *vi* to come out; **dabei kommt nichts ~** nothing will come of it; **~nehmen** (*unreg*) *vt* to remove (from), take out (of); **sich** *dat* **etw ~nehmen** to take liberties; **~reißen** (*unreg*) *vt* to tear out; to pull out; **~rücken** *vt* (*Geld*) to fork out, to hand over; **mit etw ~rücken** (*fig*) to come out with sth; **~stellen** *vr*: **sich ~stellen (als)** to turn out (to be); **~suchen** *vt*: **sich** *dat* **jdn/etw ~suchen** to pick sb/sth out; **~ziehen** (*unreg*) *vt* to pull out, to extract

herb [hɛrp] *adj* (slightly) bitter, acid; (*Wein*) dry; (*fig: schmerzlich*) bitter

herbei [hɛrˈbaɪ] *adv* (over) here; **~führen** *vt* to bring about; **~schaffen** *vt* to procure

herbemühen [ˈhɛːrbəmyːən] *vr* to take the trouble to come

Herberge [ˈhɛrbɛrɡə] *f* shelter; hostel, inn

Herbergsmutter *f* warden

Herbergsvater *m* warden

herbitten (*unreg*) *vt* to ask to come (here)

Herbst [hɛrpst] (**-(e)s, -e**) *m* autumn, fall (*US*); **h~lich** *adj* autumnal

Herd [heːrt] (**-(e)s, -e**) *m* cooker; (*fig, MED*) focus, centre

Herde [ˈheːrdə] *f* herd; (*Schafherde*) flock

herein [hɛˈraɪn] *adv* in (here); here; **~!** come in!; **~bitten** (*unreg*) *vt* to ask in; **~brechen** (*unreg*) *vi* to set in; **~bringen** (*unreg*) *vt* to bring in; **~fallen** (*unreg*) *vi* to be caught, to be taken in; **~fallen auf** +*akk* to fall for; **~kommen** (*unreg*) *vi* to come in; **~lassen** (*unreg*) *vt* to admit; **~legen** *vt*: **jdn ~legen** to take sb in; **~platzen** (*umg*) *vi* to burst in

Her- *zW*: **~fahrt** *f* journey here; **h~fallen** (*unreg*) *vi*: **h~fallen über** +*akk* to fall upon; **~gang** *m* course of events; **h~geben**

(*unreg*) *vt* to give, to hand (over); **sich zu etw h~geben** to lend one's name to sth; **h~gehen** (*unreg*) *vi*: **hinter jdm h~gehen** to follow sb; **es geht hoch h~** there are a lot of goings-on; **h~halten** (*unreg*) *vt* to hold out; **h~halten müssen** (*umg*) to have to suffer; **h~hören** *vi* to listen

Hering [ˈheːrɪŋ] (**-s, -e**) *m* herring

her- [hɛr] *zW*: **~kommen** (*unreg*) *vi* to come; **komm mal ~!** come here!; **~kömmlich** *adj* traditional; **H~kunft** (**-, -künfte**) *f* origin; **H~kunftsland** *nt* country of origin; **H~kunftsort** *m* place of origin; **~laufen** (*unreg*) *vi*: **~laufen hinter** +*dat* to run after

hermetisch [hɛrˈmeːtɪʃ] *adj* hermetic ♦ *adv* hermetically

herˈnach *adv* afterwards

Heroin [heroˈiːn] (**-s**) *nt* heroin

Herr [hɛr] (**-(e)n, -en**) *m* master; (*Mann*) gentleman; (*REL*) Lord; (*vor Namen*) Mr.; **mein ~!** sir!; **meine ~en!** gentlemen!

Herren- *zW*: **~haus** *nt* mansion; **~konfektion** *f* menswear; **h~los** *adj* ownerless; **~toilette** *f* men's toilet *od* restroom (*US*)

herrichten [ˈheːrrɪçtən] *vt* to prepare

Herr- *zW*: **~in** *f* mistress; **h~isch** *adj* domineering; **h~lich** *adj* marvellous, splendid; **~lichkeit** *f* splendour, magnificence; **~schaft** *f* power, rule; (*~ und ~in*) master and mistress; **meine ~schaften!** ladies and gentlemen!

herrschen [ˈhɛrʃən] *vi* to rule; (*bestehen*) to prevail, to be

Herrscher(in) (**-s, -**) *m(f)* ruler

her- *zW*: **~rühren** *vi* to arise, to originate; **~sagen** *vt* to recite; **~stellen** *vt* to make, to manufacture; **H~steller** (**-s, -**) *m* manufacturer; **H~stellung** *f* manufacture

herüber [hɛˈryːbar] *adv* over (here), across

herum [hɛˈrʊm] *adv* about, (a)round; **um etw ~** around sth; **~führen** *vt* to show around; **~gehen** (*unreg*) *vi* to walk about; **um etw ~gehen** to walk *od* go round sth; **~kommen** (*unreg*) *vi* (*um Kurve etc*) to come round, to turn (round); **~kriegen**

(*umg*) *vt* to bring *od* talk around; **~lungern** (*umg*) *vi* to hang about *od* around; **~sprechen** (*unreg*) *vr* to get around, to be spread; **~treiben** *vi*, *vr* to drift about; **~ziehen** *vi*, *vr* to wander about

herunter [hɛˈrʊntər] *adv* downward(s), down (there); **~gekommen** *adj* run-down; **~kommen** (*unreg*) *vi* to come down; (*fig*) to come down in the world; **~laden** *unreg vt* (*COMPUT*) to download; **~machen** *vt* to take down; (*schimpfen*) to have a go at

hervor [hɛrˈfoːr] *adv* out, forth; **~bringen** (*unreg*) *vt* to produce; (*Wort*) to utter; **~gehen** (*unreg*) *vi* to emerge, to result; **~heben** (*unreg*) *vt* to stress; (*als Kontrast*) to set off; **~ragend** *adj* (*fig*) excellent; **~rufen** (*unreg*) *vt* to cause, to give rise to; **~treten** (*unreg*) *vi* to come out (from behind/ between/below); (*Adern*) to be prominent

Herz [hɛrts] (**-ens, -en**) *nt* heart; (*KARTEN*) hearts *pl*; **~anfall** *m* heart attack; **~fehler** *m* heart defect; **h~haft** *adj* hearty

herziehen [ˈheːrtsiːən] (*unreg*) *vi*: **über jdn/ etw ~** (*umg*) to pull sb/sth to pieces (*inf*)

Herz- *zW*: **~infarkt** *m* heart attack; **~klopfen** *nt* palpitation; **h~lich** *adj* cordial; **h~lichen Glückwunsch** congratulations *pl*; **h~liche Grüße** best wishes; **h~los** *adj* heartless

Herzog [ˈhɛrtsoːk] (**-(e)s, ⸚e**) *m* duke; **~tum** *nt* duchy

Herz- *zW*: **~schlag** *m* heartbeat; (*MED*) heart attack; **~stillstand** *m* cardiac arrest; **h~zerreißend** *adj* heartrending

Hessen [ˈhɛsən] (**-s**) *nt* Hesse

hessisch *adj* Hessian

Hetze [ˈhɛtsə] *f* (*Eile*) rush; **h~n** *vt* to hunt; (*verfolgen*) to chase ♦ *vi* (*eilen*) to rush; **jdn/etw auf jdn/etw h~n** to set sb/sth on sb/sth; **h~n gegen** to stir up feeling against; **h~n zu** to agitate for

Heu [hɔy] (**-(e)s**) *nt* hay; **Geld wie ~** stacks of money

Heuch- [ˈhɔyç] *zW*: **~elei** [-əˈlaɪ] *f* hypocrisy; **h~eln** *vt* to pretend, to feign ♦ *vi* to be hypocritical; **~ler(in)** (**-s, -**) *m(f)* hypocrite; **h~lerisch** *adj* hypocritical

heulen [ˈhɔylən] *vi* to howl; to cry

Heurige(r) [ˈhɔyrɪgə(r)] *m* new wine

Heu- *zW*: **~schnupfen** *m* hay fever; **'~schrecke** *f* grasshopper; locust

heute [ˈhɔytə] *adv* today; **~ Abend/früh** this evening/morning

heutig [ˈhɔytɪç] *adj* today's

heutzutage [ˈhɔytsutaːgə] *adv* nowadays

Hexe [ˈhɛksə] *f* witch; **h~n** *vi* to practise witchcraft; **ich kann doch nicht h~n** I can't work miracles; **~nschuss** ▲ *m* lumbago; **~'rei** *f* witchcraft

Hieb [hiːp] (**-(e)s, -e**) *m* blow; (*Wunde*) cut, gash; (*Stichelei*) cutting remark; **~e bekommen** to get a thrashing

hielt *etc* [hiːlt] *vb siehe* **halten**

hier [hiːr] *adv* here; **~ behalten** to keep here; **~ bleiben** to stay here; **~ lassen** to leave here; **~auf** *adv* thereupon; (*danach*) after that; **~bei** *adv* herewith, enclosed; **~durch** *adv* by this means; (*örtlich*) through here; **~her** *adv* this way, here; **~hin** *adv* here; **~mit** *adv* hereby; **~nach** *adv* hereafter; **~von** *adv* about this, hereof; **~zulande, ~ zu Lande** *adv* in this country

hiesig [ˈhiːzɪç] *adj* of this place, local

hieß *etc* [hiːs] *vb siehe* **heißen**

Hilfe [ˈhɪlfə] *f* help; aid; **erste ~** first aid; **~!** help!

Hilf- *zW*: **h~los** *adj* helpless; **~losigkeit** *f* helplessness; **h~reich** *adj* helpful

Hilfs- *zW*: **~arbeiter** *m* labourer; **h~bedürftig** *adj* needy; **h~bereit** *adj* ready to help; **~kraft** *f* assistant, helper

hilfst [hɪlfst] *vb siehe* **helfen**

Himbeere [ˈhɪmbeːrə] *f* raspberry

Himmel [ˈhɪməl] (**-s, -**) *m* sky; (*REL, auch fig*) heaven; **~bett** *nt* four-poster bed; **h~blau** *adj* sky-blue; **~fahrt** *f* Ascension; **~srichtung** *f* direction

himmlisch [ˈhɪmlɪʃ] *adj* heavenly

SCHLÜSSELWORT

hin [hɪn] *adv* **1** (*Richtung*): **hin und zurück** there and back; **hin und her** to and fro; **bis zur Mauer hin** up to the wall; **wo ist**

er hin? where has he gone?; **Geld hin, Geld her** money or no money

2 (auf ... hin): **auf meine Bitte hin** at my request; **auf seinen Rat hin** on the basis of his advice

3 : **mein Glück ist hin** my happiness has gone

hinab [hɪˈnap] adv down;**~gehen** (unreg) vi to go down;**~sehen** (unreg) vi to look down

hinauf [hɪˈnaʊf] adv up;**~arbeiten** vr to work one's way up;**~steigen** (unreg) vi to climb

hinaus [hɪˈnaʊs] adv out;**~gehen** (unreg) vi to go out; **~gehen über** +akk to exceed; **~laufen** (unreg) vi to run out; **~laufen auf** +akk to come to, to amount to; **~schieben** (unreg) vt to put off, to postpone;**~werfen** (unreg) vt (Gegenstand, Person) to throw out;**~wollen** vi to want to go out;**~wollen auf** +akk to drive at, to get at

Hinblick [ˈhɪnblɪk] m: **in** od **im ~ auf** +akk in view of

hinder- [ˈhɪndər] zW:**~lich** adj: **~lich sein** to be a hindrance od nuisance;**~n** vt to hinder, to hamper; **jdn an etw** dat **~n** to prevent sb from doing sth;**H~nis** (-ses, -se) nt obstacle;**H~nisrennen** nt steeplechase

hindeuten [ˈhɪndɔʏtən] vi: **~ auf** +akk to point to

hindurch [hɪnˈdʊrç] adv through; across; (zeitlich) through(out)

hinein [hɪˈnaɪn] adv in;**~fallen** (unreg) vi to fall in; **~fallen in** +akk to fall into;**~gehen** (unreg) vi to go in; **~gehen in** +akk to go into, to enter;**~geraten** (unreg) vi: **~geraten in** +akk to get into;**~passen** vi to fit in; **~passen in** +akk to fit into; (fig) to fit in with;**~steigern** vr to get worked up; **~versetzen** vr: **sich ~versetzen in** +akk to put o.s. in the position of;**~ziehen** (unreg) vt to pull in ♦ vi to go in

hin- [ˈhɪn] zW:**~fahren** (unreg) vi to go; to drive ♦ vt to take; to drive;**H~fahrt** f

journey there;**~fallen** (unreg) vi to fall (down);**~fällig** adj frail; (fig: ungültig) invalid;**H~flug** m outward flight;**H~gabe** f devotion;**~geben** (unreg) vr +dat to give o.s. up to, to devote o.s. to;**~gehen** (unreg) vi to go; (Zeit) to pass;**~halten** (unreg) vt to hold out; (warten lassen) to put off, to stall

hinken [ˈhɪŋkən] vi to limp; (Vergleich) to be unconvincing

hinkommen (unreg) vi (an Ort) to arrive

hin- [ˈhɪn] zW:**~legen** vt to put down ♦ vr to lie down;**~nehmen** (unreg) vt (fig) to put up with, to take;**H~reise** f journey out;**~reißen** (unreg) vt to carry away, to enrapture; **sich ~reißen lassen, etw zu tun** get carried away and do sth; **~richten** vt to execute;**H~richtung** f execution;**~setzen** vt to put down ♦ vr to sit down;**~sichtlich** präp +gen with regard to;**~stellen** vt to put (down) ♦ vr to place o.s.

hinten [ˈhɪntən] adv at the back; behind; **~herum** adv round the back; (fig) secretly

hinter [ˈhɪntər] präp (+dat od akk) behind; (: nach) after; **~ jdm her sein** to be after sb;**H~achse** f rear axle;**H~bliebene(r)** f(m) surviving relative;**~e(r, s)** adj rear, back;**~einander** adv one after the other; **H~gedanke** m ulterior motive;**~gehen** (unreg) vt to deceive;**H~grund** m background;**H~halt** m ambush;**~hältig** adj underhand, sneaky;**~her** adv afterwards, after;**H~hof** m backyard; **H~kopf** m back of one's head;**~'lassen** (unreg) vt to leave;**~'legen** vt to deposit; **H~list** f cunning, trickery; (Handlung) trick, dodge;**~listig** adj cunning, crafty; **H~mann** m person behind;**H~rad** nt back wheel;**H~radantrieb** m (AUT) rear wheel drive;**~rücks** adv from behind; **H~tür** f back door; (fig: Ausweg) loophole; **~'ziehen** (unreg) vt (Steuern) to evade

hinüber [hɪˈnyːbər] adv across, over; **~gehen** (unreg) vi to go over od across

hinunter [hɪˈnʊntər] adv down;**~bringen** (unreg) vt to take down;**~schlucken** vt *(auch fig)* to swallow; **~steigen** *(unreg) vi* to descend

Hinweg ['hɪnveːk] *m* journey out

hinweghelfen [hɪn'veːk-] *(unreg) vi*: **jdm über etw** *akk* **~** to help sb to get over sth

hinwegsetzen [hɪn'veːk-] *vr*: **sich ~ über** +*akk* to disregard

hin- ['hɪn] *zW*: **H~weis** *(-es, -e) m (Andeutung)* hint; *(Anweisung)* instruction; *(Verweis)* reference; **~weisen** *(unreg) vi*: **~weisen auf** +*akk (anzeigen)* to point to; *(sagen)* to point out, to refer to; **~werfen** *(unreg) vt* to throw down; **~ziehen** *(unreg) vr (fig)* to drag on

hinzu [hɪn'tsuː] *adv* in addition; **~fügen** *vt* to add; **~kommen** *(unreg) vi (Mensch)* to arrive, to turn up; *(Umstand)* to ensue

Hirn [hɪrn] *(-(e)s, -e) nt* brain(s); **~gespinst** *(-(e)s, -e) nt* fantasy

Hirsch [hɪrʃ] *(-(e)s, -e) m* stag

Hirt ['hɪrt] *(-en, -en) m* herdsman; *(Schafhirt, fig)* shepherd

hissen ['hɪsən] *vt* to hoist

Historiker [hɪs'toːrikar] *(-s, -) m* historian

historisch [hɪs'toːrɪʃ] *adj* historical

Hitze ['hɪtsə] *(-) f* heat; **h~beständig** *adj* heat-resistant; **h~frei** *adj*: **h~frei haben** to have time off school because of excessively hot weather; **~welle** *f* heat wave

hitzig ['hɪtsɪç] *adj* hot-tempered; *(Debatte)* heated

Hitzkopf *m* hothead

Hitzschlag *m* heatstroke

hl. *abk von* **heilig**

H-Milch ['haːmɪlç] *f* long-life milk

Hobby ['hɔbi] *(-s, -s) nt* hobby

Hobel ['hoːbəl] *(-s, -) m* plane; **~bank** *f* carpenter's bench; **h~n** *vt, vi* to plane; **~späne** *pl* wood shavings

Hoch *(-s, -s) nt (Ruf)* cheer; *(MET)* anticyclone

hoch [hoːx] *(attrib* **hohe(r, s)** *) adj* high; ♦ *adv*: **~ achten** to respect; **~ begabt** extremely gifted; **~ dotiert** highly paid; **H~achtung** *f* respect, esteem; **~achtungsvoll** *adv* yours faithfully; **H~amt** *nt* high mass; **~arbeiten** *vr* to

work one's way up; **H~betrieb** *m* intense activity; *(COMM)* peak time; **H~burg** *f* stronghold; **H~deutsch** *nt* High German; **H~druck** *m* high pressure; **H~ebene** *f* plateau; **H~form** *f* top form; **H~gebirge** *nt* high mountains *pl*; **H~glanz** *m (PHOT)* high gloss print; **etw auf H~glanz bringen** to make sth sparkle like new; **~halten** *(unreg) vt* to hold up; *(fig)* to uphold, to cherish; **H~haus** *nt* multi-storey building; **~heben** *(unreg) vt* to lift (up); **H~konjunktur** *f* boom; **H~land** *nt* highlands *pl*; **~leben** *vi*: **jdn ~leben lassen** to give sb three cheers; **H~mut** *m* pride; **~mütig** *adj* proud, haughty; **~näsig** *adj* stuck-up, snooty; **H~ofen** *m* blast furnace; **~prozentig** *adj (Alkohol)* strong; **H~rechnung** *f* projection; **H~saison** *f* high season; **H~schule** *f* college; university; **H~sommer** *m* middle of summer; **H~spannung** *f* high tension; **H~sprung** *m* high jump

höchst [høːçst] *adv* highly, extremely

Hochstapler ['hoːxstaːplər] *(-s, -) m* swindler

höchste(r, s) *adj* highest; *(äußerste)* extreme

Höchst- *zW*: **h~ens** *adv* at the most; **~geschwindigkeit** *f* maximum speed; **h~persönlich** *adv* in person; **~preis** *m* maximum price; **h~wahrscheinlich** *adv* most probably

Hoch- *zW*: **~verrat** *m* high treason; **~wasser** *nt* high water; *(Überschwemmung)* floods *pl*

Hochzeit ['hɔxtsaɪt] *(-, -en) f* wedding; **~sreise** *f* honeymoon

hocken ['hɔkən] *vi, vr* to squat, to crouch

Hocker *(-s, -) m* stool

Höcker ['hœkər] *(-s, -) m* hump

Hoden ['hoːdən] *(-s, -) m* testicle

Hof [hoːf] *(-(e)s, ⁺e) m (Hinterhof)* yard; *(Bauernhof)* farm; *(Königshof)* court

hoff- ['hɔf] *zW*: **~en** *vi*: **~en (auf** +*akk)* to hope (for); **~entlich** *adv* I hope, hopefully; **H~nung** *f* hope

Hoffnungs- *zW*: **h~los** *adj* hopeless;

~**losigkeit** f hopelessness; **h~voll** adj hopeful

höflich ['hø:flɪç] adj polite, courteous; **H~keit** f courtesy, politeness

hohe(r, s) adj attrib siehe **hoch**

Höhe ['hø:ə] f height; (Anhöhe) hill

Hoheit ['ho:haɪt] f (POL) sovereignty; (Titel) Highness

Hoheits- zW: ~**gebiet** nt sovereign territory; ~**gewässer** nt territorial waters pl

Höhen- ['hø:ən] zW: ~**luft** f mountain air; ~**messer** (-s, -) m altimeter; ~**sonne** f sun lamp; ~**unterschied** m difference in altitude

Höhepunkt m climax

höher adj, adv higher

hohl [ho:l] adj hollow

Höhle ['hø:lə] f cave, hole; (Mundhöhle) cavity; (fig, ZOOL) den

Hohlmaß nt measure of volume

Hohn [ho:n] (-(e)s) m scorn

höhnisch adj scornful, taunting

holen ['ho:lən] vt to get, to fetch; (Atem) to take; **jdn/etw ~ lassen** to send for sb/sth

Holland ['hɔlant] nt Holland; **Holländer** ['hɔlɛndər] m Dutchman; **holländisch** adj Dutch

Hölle ['hœlə] f hell

höllisch ['hœlɪʃ] adj hellish, infernal

holperig ['hɔlpərɪç] adj rough, bumpy

Holunder [ho'lʊndər] (-s, -) m elder

Holz [hɔlts] (-es, ⁻er) nt wood

hölzern ['hœltsərn] adj (auch fig) wooden

Holz- zW: ~**fäller** (-s, -) m lumberjack, woodcutter; **h~ig** adj woody; ~**kohle** f charcoal; ~**schuh** m clog; ~**weg** m (fig) wrong track; ~**wolle** f fine wood shavings pl

Homöopathie [homøopa'ti:] f homeopathy

homosexuell [homozɛksu'ɛl] adj homosexual

Honig ['ho:nɪç] (-s, -e) m honey; ~**melone** f (BOT, KOCH) honeydew melon; ~**wabe** f honeycomb

Honorar [hono'ra:r] (-s, -e) nt fee

Hopfen ['hɔpfən] (-s, -) m hops pl

hopsen ['hɔpsən] vi to hop

Hörapparat m hearing aid

hörbar adj audible

horchen ['hɔrçən] vi to listen; (pej) to eavesdrop

Horde ['hɔrdə] f horde

hör- ['hø:r] zW: ~**en** vt, vi to hear; **Musik/ Radio ~en** to listen to music/the radio; **H~er** (-s, -) m hearer; (RADIO) listener; (UNIV) student; (Telefonhörer) receiver; **H~funk** (-s) m radio; ~**geschädigt** [-gəʃɛːdɪçt] adj hearing-impaired

Horizont [hori'tsɔnt] (-(e)s, -e) m horizon; **h~al** [-'ta:l] adj horizontal

Hormon [hɔr'mo:n] (-s, -e) nt hormone

Hörmuschel f (TEL) earpiece

Horn [hɔrn] (-(e)s, ⁻er) nt horn; ~**haut** f horny skin

Hornisse [hɔr'nɪsə] f hornet

Horoskop [horo'sko:p] (-s, -e) nt horoscope

Hörspiel nt radio play

Hort [hɔrt] (-(e)s, -e) m (SCH) day centre for schoolchildren whose parents are at work

horten ['hɔrtən] vt to hoard

Hose ['ho:zə] f trousers pl, pants pl (US)

Hosen- zW: ~**anzug** m trouser suit; ~**rock** m culottes pl; ~**tasche** f (trouser) pocket; ~**träger** m braces pl (BRIT), suspenders pl (US)

Hostie ['hɔstiə] f (REL) host

Hotel [ho'tɛl] (-s, -s) nt hotel; ~**ier** (-s, -s) [hoteli'e:] m hotelkeeper, hotelier; ~**verzeichnis** nt hotel register

Hubraum ['hu:p-] m (AUT) cubic capacity

hübsch [hypʃ] adj pretty, nice

Hubschrauber ['hu:pʃraubər] (-s, -) m helicopter

Huf ['hu:f] (-(e)s, -e) m hoof; ~**eisen** nt horseshoe

Hüft- ['hyft] zW: ~**e** f hip; ~**gürtel** m girdle; ~**halter** (-s, -) m girdle

Hügel ['hy:gəl] (-s, -) m hill; **h~ig** adj hilly

Huhn [hu:n] (-(e)s, ⁻er) nt hen; (KOCH) chicken

Hühner- ['hy:nər] zW: ~**auge** nt corn; ~**brühe** f chicken broth

Hülle ['hylə] f cover(ing); wrapping; **in ~**

und Fülle galore; **h~n** *vt*: **h~n (in** +*akk*) to cover (with); to wrap (in)

Hülse ['hʏlzə] *f* husk, shell; **~nfrucht** *f* pulse

human [hu'maːn] *adj* humane; **~i'tär** *adj* humanitarian; **H~i'tät** *f* humanity

Hummel ['hʊməl] (**-, -n**) *f* bumblebee

Hummer ['hʊmər] (**-s, -**) *m* lobster

Humor [hu'moːr] (**-s, -e**) *m* humour; **~ haben** to have a sense of humour; **~ist** [-'rɪst] *m* humorist; **h~voll** *adj* humorous

humpeln ['hʊmpəln] *vi* to hobble

Humpen ['hʊmpən] (**-s, -**) *m* tankard

Hund [hʊnt] (**-(e)s, -e**) *m* dog

Hunde- ['hʊndə] *zW*: **~hütte** *f* (dog) kennel; **h~müde** (*umg*) *adj* dog-tired

hundert ['hʊndərt] *num* hundred; **H~'jahrfeier** *f* centenary; **~prozentig** *adj, adv* one hundred per cent

Hundesteuer *f* dog licence fee

Hündin ['hʏndɪn] *f* bitch

Hunger ['hʊŋər] (**-s**) *m* hunger; **~ haben** to be hungry; **h~n** *vi* to starve; **~snot** *f* famine

hungrig ['hʊŋrɪç] *adj* hungry

Hupe ['huːpə] *f* horn; **h~n** *vi* to hoot, to sound one's horn

hüpfen ['hʏpfən] *vi* to hop; to jump

Hürde ['hʏrdə] *f* hurdle; (*für Schafe*) pen; **~nlauf** *m* hurdling

Hure ['huːrə] *f* whore

hurtig ['hʊrtɪç] *adj* brisk, quick ♦ *adv* briskly, quickly

huschen ['hʊʃən] *vi* to flit; to scurry

Husten ['huːstən] (**-s**) *m* cough; **h~** *vi* to cough; **~anfall** *m* coughing fit; **~bonbon** *m* od *nt* cough drop; **~saft** *m* cough mixture

Hut¹ [huːt] (**-(e)s, -̈e**) *m* hat

Hut² [huːt] (**-**) *f* care; **auf der ~ sein** to be on one's guard

hüten ['hyːtən] *vt* to guard ♦ *vr* to watch out; **sich ~, zu** to take care not to; **sich ~ (vor)** to beware (of), to be on one's guard (against)

Hütte ['hʏtə] *f* hut; cottage; (*Eisen~*) forge

Hütten- *zW*: **~käse** *m* (*KOCH*) cottage cheese; **~schuh** *m* slipper sock

Hydrant [hy'drant] *m* hydrant

hydraulisch [hy'draʊlɪʃ] *adj* hydraulic

Hygiene [hygi'eːnə] (**-**) *f* hygiene

hygienisch [hygi'eːnɪʃ] *adj* hygienic

Hymne ['hʏmnə] *f* hymn; anthem

Hypno- [hʏp'noː] *zW*: **~se** *f* hypnosis; **h~tisch** *adj* hypnotic; **~tiseur** [-ti'zøːr] *m* hypnotist; **h~ti'sieren** *vt* to hypnotize

Hypothek [hypo'teːk] (**-, -en**) *f* mortgage

Hypothese [hypo'teːzə] *f* hypothesis

Hysterie [hyste'riː] *f* hysteria

hysterisch [hys'teːrɪʃ] *adj* hysterical

I, i

ICE [iːtseː'eː] *m abk* = **Intercity-Expresszug**

Ich (**-(s), -(s)**) *nt* self; (*PSYCH*) ego

ich [ɪç] *pron* I; **~ bins!** it's me!

Icon ['aɪkɔn] (**-s, -s**) *nt* (*COMPUT*) icon

Ideal [ide'aːl] (**-s, -e**) *nt* ideal; **ideal** *adj* ideal; **idealistisch** [-'lɪstɪʃ] *adj* idealistic

Idee [i'deː, *pl* i'deːən] *f* idea

identifizieren [identifi'tsiːrən] *vt* to identify

identisch [i'dɛntɪʃ] *adj* identical

Identität [identi'tɛːt] *f* identity

Ideo- [ideo] *zW*: **~loge** [-'loːgə] (**-n, -n**) *m* ideologist; **~logie** [-lo'giː] *f* ideology; **ideologisch** [-'loːgɪʃ] *adj* ideological

Idiot [idi'oːt] (**-en, -en**) *m* idiot; **idiotisch** *adj* idiotic

idyllisch [i'dʏlɪʃ] *adj* idyllic

Igel ['iːgəl] (**-s, -**) *m* hedgehog

ignorieren [igno'riːrən] *vt* to ignore

ihm [iːm] (*dat von* **er, es**) *pron* (to) him; (to) it

ihn [iːn] (*akk von* **er, es**) *pron* him; it; **~en** (*dat von* **sie** *pl*) *pron* (to) them; **Ihnen** (*dat von* **Sie** *pl*) *pron* (to) you

SCHLÜSSELWORT

ihr [iːr] *pron* **1** (*nom pl*) you; **ihr seid es** it's you

2 (*dat von* **sie**) to her; **gib es ihr** give it to her; **er steht neben ihr** he is standing beside her

♦ *possessiv pron* **1** (*sg*) her; (: *bei Tieren,*

Dingen) its; **ihr Mann** her husband
2 (pl) their; **die Bäume und ihre Blätter**
the trees and their leaves

ihr(e) [iːr] adj (sg) her, its; (pl) their; **Ihr(e)**
adj your
ihre(r, s) pron (sg) hers, its; (pl) theirs;
Ihre(r, s) pron yours; **~r** (gen von **sie** sg/pl)
pron of her/them; **Ihrer** (gen von **Sie**) pron
of you; **~rseits** adv for her/their part;
~sgleichen pron people like her/them;
(von Dingen) others like it; **~twegen** adv
(für sie) for her/its/their sake; (wegen ihr) on
her/its/their account; **~twillen** adv: **um**
~twillen = **ihretwegen**
ihrige ['iːrɪgə] pron: **der/die/das ~** od **I~**
hers; its; theirs

illegal ['ɪlegaːl] adj illegal
Illusion [ɪluzi'oːn] f illusion
illusorisch [ɪlu'zoːrɪʃ] adj illusory
illustrieren [ɪlʊs'triːrən] vt to illustrate
Illustrierte f magazine
im [ɪm] = **in dem**
Imbiss ▲ ['ɪmbɪs] (-es, -e) m snack;
~stube f snack bar
imitieren [imi'tiːrən] vt to imitate
Imker ['ɪmkər] (-s, -) m beekeeper
immatrikulieren [ɪmatriku'liːrən] vi, vr to
register
immer ['ɪmər] adv always; **~ wieder** again
and again; **~ noch** still; **~ noch nicht** still
not; **für ~** forever; **~ wenn ich ...** every
time I ...; **~ schöner/trauriger** more and
more beautiful/sadder and sadder; **was/**
wer (auch) ~ whatever/whoever; **~zu** adv
all the time; **~hin** adv all the same; **~zu** adv all the time
Immobilien [ɪmo'biːliən] pl real estate sg;
~makler m estate agent (BRIT), realtor (US)
immun [ɪ'muːn] adj immune; **Immunität**
[-i'tɛːt] f immunity; **Immunsystem** nt
immune system
Imperfekt ['ɪmpɛrfɛkt] (-s, -e) nt imperfect
(tense)
Impf- ['ɪmpf] zW: **impfen** vt to vaccinate;
~stoff m vaccine, serum; **~ung** f
vaccination
imponieren [ɪmpo'niːrən] vi +dat to impress

Import [ɪm'pɔrt] (-(e)s, -e) m import; **~eur**
m importer; **importieren** vt to import
imposant [ɪmpo'zant] adj imposing
impotent ['ɪmpotɛnt] adj impotent
imprägnieren [ɪmprɛ'gniːrən] vt to
(water)proof
improvisieren [ɪmprovi'ziːrən] vt, vi to
improvise
Impuls [ɪm'pʊls] (-es, -e) m impulse;
impulsiv [-'ziːf] adj impulsive
imstande, im Stande [ɪm'ʃtandə] adj: **~**
sein to be in a position; (fähig) to be able

SCHLÜSSELWORT

in [ɪn] präp +akk 1 (räumlich: wohin?) in, into;
in die Stadt into town; **in die Schule**
gehen to go to school
2 (zeitlich): **bis ins 20. Jahrhundert** into od
up to the 20th century
♦ präp +dat 1 (räumlich: wo) in; **in der Stadt**
in town; **in der Schule sein** to be at
school
2 (zeitlich: wann): **in diesem Jahr** this year;
(in jenem Jahr) in that year; **heute in zwei**
Wochen two weeks today

Inanspruchnahme [ɪn'|anʃpruxnaːmə] f
(+gen) demands pl (on)
Inbegriff ['ɪnbəgrɪf] m embodiment,
personification; **inbegriffen** adv included
indem [ɪn'deːm] konj while; **~ man etw**
macht (dadurch) by doing sth
Inder(in) ['ɪndər(ɪn)] m(f) Indian
indes(sen) [ɪn'dɛs(ən)] adv however;
(inzwischen) meanwhile ♦ konj while
Indianer(in) [ɪndi'aːnər(ɪn)] (-s, -) m(f)
American Indian, native American;
indianisch adj Red Indian
Indien ['ɪndiən] nt India
indirekt ['ɪndirɛkt] adj indirect
indisch ['ɪndɪʃ] adj Indian
indiskret ['ɪndɪskreːt] adj indiscreet
indiskutabel ['ɪndɪskutaːbəl] adj out of the
question
individuell [ɪndividu'ɛl] adj individual
Individuum [ɪndi'viːduʊm] (-s, -en) nt
individual

Spelling Reform: ▲ *new spelling* △ *old spelling (to be phased out)*

Indiz [ɪnˈdiːts] (**-es, -ien**) nt (JUR) clue; **~ (für)** sign (of)

industrialisieren [ɪndʊstrialiˈziːrən] vt to industrialize

Industrie [ɪndʊsˈtriː] f industry ♦ in zW industrial; **~gebiet** nt industrial area; **~- und Handelskammer** f chamber of commerce; **~zweig** m branch of industry

ineinander [ɪnˈaɪˈnandər] adv in(to) one another od each other

Infarkt [ɪnˈfarkt] (**-(e)s, -e**) m coronary (thrombosis)

Infektion [ɪnfɛktsiˈoːn] f infection; **~skrankheit** f infectious disease

Infinitiv [ˈɪnfinitiːf] (**-s, -e**) m infinitive

infizieren [ɪnfiˈtsiːrən] vt to infect ♦ vr: **sich (bei jdm) ~** to be infected (by sb)

Inflation [ɪnflatsiˈoːn] f inflation

inflationär [ɪnflatsioˈnɛːr] adj inflationary

infolge [ɪnˈfɔlgə] präp +gen as a result of, owing to; **~dessen** [-ˈdɛsən] adv consequently

Informatik [ɪnfɔrˈmatɪk] f information studies pl

Information [ɪnfɔrmatsiˈoːn] f information no pl

informieren [ɪnfɔrˈmiːrən] vt to inform ♦ vr: **sich ~ (über** +akk**)** to find out (about)

infrage, in Frage adv: **~ stellen** to question sth; **nicht ~ kommen** to be out of the question

Ingenieur [ɪnʒeˈniˈøːr] m engineer; **~schule** f school of engineering

Ingwer [ˈɪŋvər] (**-s**) m ginger

Inh. abk (= Inhaber) prop.; (= Inhalt) contents

Inhaber(in) [ˈɪnhaːbər(ɪn)] (**-s, -**) m(f) owner; (Hausinhaber) occupier; (Lizenzinhaber) licensee, holder; (FIN) bearer

inhaftieren [ɪnhafˈtiːrən] vt to take into custody

inhalieren [ɪnhaˈliːrən] vt, vi to inhale

Inhalt [ˈɪnhalt] (**-(e)s, -e**) m contents pl; (eines Buchs etc) content; (MATH) area; volume; **inhaltlich** adj as regards content

Inhalts- zW: **~angabe** f summary; **~verzeichnis** nt table of contents

inhuman [ˈɪnhumaːn] adj inhuman

Initiative [initsiaˈtiːvə] f initiative

inklusive [ɪnkluˈziːvə] präp +gen inclusive of ♦ adv inclusive

In-Kraft-Treten [ɪnˈkrafttreːtən] (**-s**) nt coming into force

Inland [ˈɪnlant] (**-(e)s**) nt (GEOG) inland; (POL, COMM) home (country); **~flug** m domestic flight

inmitten [ɪnˈmɪtən] präp +gen in the middle of; **~ von** amongst

innehaben [ˈɪnəhaːbən] (unreg) vt to hold

innen [ˈɪnən] adv inside; **Innenarchitekt** m interior designer; **Inneneinrichtung** f (interior) furnishings pl; **Innenhof** m inner courtyard; **Innenminister** m minister of the interior, Home Secretary (BRIT); **Innenpolitik** f domestic policy; **~politisch** adj (Entwicklung, Lage) internal, domestic; **Innenstadt** f town/city centre

inner- [ˈɪnər] zW: **~e(r, s)** adj inner; (im Körper, inländisch) internal; **Innere(s)** nt inside; (Mitte) centre; (fig) heart; **Innereien** [-ˈraɪən] pl innards; **~halb** adv within; (räumlich) inside ♦ präp +gen within; inside; **~lich** adj internal; (geistig) inward; **~ste(r, s)** adj innermost; **Innerste(s)** nt heart

innig [ˈɪnɪç] adj (Freundschaft) close

inoffiziell [ˈɪn|ofitsiɛl] adj unofficial

ins [ɪns] = **in das**

Insasse [ˈɪnzasə] (**-n, -n**) m (Anstalt) inmate; (AUT) passenger

Insassenversicherung f passenger insurance

insbesondere [ɪnsbəˈzɔndərə] adv (e)specially

Inschrift [ˈɪnʃrɪft] f inscription

Insekt [ɪnˈzɛkt] (**-(e)s, -en**) nt insect

Insektenschutzmittel nt insect repellent

Insel [ˈɪnzəl] (**-, -n**) f island

Inser- zW: **~at** [ɪnzeˈraːt] (**-(e)s, -e**) nt advertisement; **~ent** [ɪnzeˈrɛnt] m advertiser; **inserieren** [ɪnzeˈriːrən] vt, vi to advertise

insgeheim [ɪnsgəˈhaɪm] adv secretly

insgesamt [ɪnsgəˈzamt] adv altogether, all in all!

insofern [ɪnzo'fɛrn] *adv* in this respect ♦ *konj* if; *(deshalb)* (and) so; ~ **als** in so far as

insoweit [ɪnzo'vaɪt] = **insofern**

Installateur [ɪnstala'tøːr] *m* electrician; plumber

Instandhaltung [ɪn'ʃtanthaltʊŋ] *f* maintenance

inständig [ɪn'ʃtɛndɪç] *adj* urgent

Instandsetzung [ɪn'stant-] *f* overhaul; *(eines Gebäudes)* restoration

Instanz [ɪn'stants] *f* authority; *(JUR)* court

Instinkt [ɪn'stɪŋkt] **(-(e)s, -e)** *m* instinct; **instinktiv** [-'tiːf] *adj* instinctive

Institut [ɪnsti'tuːt] **(-(e)s, -e)** *nt* institute

Instrument [ɪnstru'mɛnt] *nt* instrument

Intell- [ɪntɛl] *zW:* **intellektuell** [-ɛktu'ɛl] *adj* intellectual; **intelligent** [-i'gɛnt] *adj* intelligent; **intelligenz** [-i'gɛnts] *f* intelligence; *(Leute)* intelligentsia *pl*

Intendant [ɪntɛn'dant] *m* director

intensiv [ɪntɛn'ziːf] *adj* intensive; **Intensivstation** *f* intensive care unit

Intercity- [ɪntər'sɪti] *zW:* **~-Expresszug** ▲ *m* high-speed train; **~-Zug** *m* intercity (train); **~-Zuschlag** *m* intercity supplement

Interess- *zW:* **i~ant** [ɪntɛrɛ'sant] *adj* interesting; **i~anterweise** *adv* interestingly enough; **~e haben an** *+dat* to be interested in; **~ent** [ɪntɛre'sɛnt] *m* interested party; **i~ieren** [ɪntɛre'siːrən] *vt* to interest ♦ *vr:* **sich i~ieren für** to be interested in

intern [ɪn'tɛrn] *adj (Angelegenheiten, Regelung)* internal; *(Besprechung)* private

Internat [ɪntɛr'naːt] **(-(e)s, -e)** *nt* boarding school

inter- [ɪntɛr] *zW:* **~national** [-natsio'naːl] *adj* international; **I~net** ['ɪntərnɛt] **(-s)** *nt:* **das I~net** the Internet; **I~net-Anbieter** *m* Internet Service Provider, ISP; **I~net-Café** *nt* Internet café; **~pretieren** [-pre'tiːrən] *vt* to interpret; **I~vall** [-'val] **(-s, -e)** *nt* interval; **I~view** [-'vjuː] **(-s, -s)** *nt* interview; **~viewen** [-'vjuːən] *vt* to interview

intim [ɪn'tiːm] *adj* intimate; **Intimität** *f* intimacy

intolerant ['ɪntolerant] *adj* intolerant

Intrige [ɪn'triːgə] *f* intrigue, plot

Invasion [ɪnvazi'oːn] *f* invasion

Inventar [ɪnvɛn'taːr] **(-s, -e)** *nt* inventory

Inventur [ɪnvɛn'tuːr] *f* stocktaking; **~ machen** to stocktake

investieren [ɪnvɛsti'iːrən] *vt* to invest

inwie- [ɪnvi'] *zW:* **~fern** *adv* how far, to what extent; **~weit** *adv* how far, to what extent

inzwischen [ɪn'tsvɪʃən] *adv* meanwhile

Irak [i'raːk] **(-s)** *m:* **der ~** Iraq; **irakisch** *adj* Iraqi

Iran [i'raːn] **(-s)** *m:* **der ~** Iran; **iranisch** *adj* Iranian

irdisch ['ɪrdɪʃ] *adj* earthly

Ire ['iːrə] **(-n, -n)** *m* Irishman

irgend ['ɪrgɛnt] *adv* at all; **wann/was/wer ~** whenever/whatever/whoever; **~etwas** *pron* something/anything; **~jemand** *pron* somebody/anybody; **~ein(e, s)** *adj* some, any; **~einmal** *adv* sometime or other; *(fragend)* ever; **~wann** *adv* sometime; **~wie** *adv* somehow; **~wo** *adv* somewhere; anywhere; **~wohin** *adv* somewhere; anywhere

Irin ['iːrɪn] *f* Irishwoman

Irland ['ɪrlant] **(-s)** *nt* Ireland

Ironie [iro'niː] *f* irony; **ironisch** [i'roːnɪʃ] *adj* ironic(al)

irre ['ɪrə] *adj* crazy, mad; **Irre(r)** *f(m)* lunatic; **~führen** *vt* to mislead; **~machen** *vt* to confuse; **~n** *vi* to be mistaken; *(umherirren)* to wander, to stray ♦ *vr* to be mistaken; **Irrenanstalt** *f* lunatic asylum

Irr- *zW:* **~garten** *m* maze; **i~ig** ['ɪrɪç] *adj* incorrect, wrong; **i~itieren** [ɪri'tiːrən] *vt (verwirren)* to confuse; *(ärgern)* to irritate; *(stören)* to annoy; **irrsinnig** *adj* mad, crazy; *(umg)* terrific; **~tum** **(-s, -tümer)** *m* mistake, error; **irrtümlich** *adj* mistaken

Island ['iːslant] **(-s)** *nt* Iceland

Isolation [izolatsi'oːn] *f* isolation; *(ELEK)* insulation

Isolier- [izo'liːr] *zW:* **~band** *nt* insulating tape; **isolieren** *vt* to isolate; *(ELEK)* to insulate; **~station** *f* *(MED)* isolation ward;

Spelling Reform: ▲ *new spelling* △ *old spelling (to be phased out)*

~ung *f* isolation; (*ELEK*) insulation
Israel ['israe:l] **(-s)** *nt* Israel; **~i** **(-s, -s)** [-'e:li] *m* Israeli; **israelisch** *adj* Israeli
isst ▲ [ist] *vb siehe* **essen**
ist [ist] *vb siehe* **sein**
Italien [i'ta:liən] **(-s)** *nt* Italy; **~er(in)** **(-s)** *m(f)* Italian; **italienisch** *adj* Italian
i. V. *abk =* **in Vertretung**

J, j

ja [ja:] *adv* **1** yes; **haben Sie das gesehen? - ja** did you see it? - yes(, I did); **ich glaube ja** (yes) I think so
2 (*fragend*) really?; **ich habe gekündigt - ja?** I've quit - have you?; **du kommst, ja?** you're coming, aren't you?
3: sei ja vorsichtig do be careful; **Sie wissen ja, dass ...** as you know, ...; **tu das ja nicht!** don't do that!; **ich habe es ja gewusst** I just knew it; **ja, also ...** well you see ...

Jacht [jaxt] **(-, -en)** *f* yacht
Jacke ['jakə] *f* jacket; (*Wolljacke*) cardigan
Jackett [ʒa'kɛt] **(-s, -s** *od* **-e)** *nt* jacket
Jagd [ja:kt] **(-, -en)** *f* hunt; (*Jagen*) hunting; **~beute** *f* kill; **~flugzeug** *nt* fighter; **~hund** *m* hunting dog
jagen ['ja:gən] *vi* to hunt; (*eilen*) to race ♦ *vt* to hunt; (*wegjagen*) to drive (off); (*verfolgen*) to chase
Jäger ['je:gər] **(-s, -)** *m* hunter; **~schnitzel** *nt* (*KOCH*) pork in a spicy sauce with mushrooms
jäh [je:] *adj* sudden, abrupt; (*steil*) steep, precipitous
Jahr [ja:r] **(-(e)s, -e)** *nt* year; **j~elang** *adv* for years
Jahres- *zW:* **~abonnement** *nt* annual subscription; **~abschluss** ▲ *m* end of the year; (*COMM*) annual statement of account; **~beitrag** *m* annual subscription; **~karte** *f*

yearly season ticket; **~tag** *m* anniversary; **~wechsel** *m* turn of the year; **~zahl** *f* date; year; **~zeit** *f* season
Jahr- *zW:* **~gang** *m* age group; (*von Wein*) vintage; **~'hundert** **(-s, -e)** *nt* century; **jährlich** ['je:rlɪç] *adj, adv* yearly; **~markt** *m* fair; **~tausend** *nt* millennium; **~'zehnt** *nt* decade
Jähzorn ['je:tsɔrn] *m* sudden anger; hot temper; **j~ig** *adj* hot-tempered
Jalousie [ʒalu'zi:] *f* venetian blind
Jammer ['jamər] **(-s)** *m* misery; **es ist ein ~, dass ...** it is a crying shame that ...
jämmerlich ['jemərlɪç] *adj* wretched, pathetic
jammern *vi* to wail ♦ *vt unpers:* **es jammert jdn** it makes sb feel sorry
Januar ['janua:r] **(-(s), -e)** *m* January
Japan ['ja:pan] **(-s)** *nt* Japan; **~er(in)** [-'pa:nər(ın)] **(-s)** *m(f)* Japanese; **j~isch** *adj* Japanese
jäten ['je:tən] *vt:* **Unkraut ~** to weed
jauchzen ['jauxtsən] *vi* to rejoice
jaulen ['jaulən] *vi* to howl
jawohl [ja'vo:l] *adv* yes (of course)
Jawort ['ja:vɔrt] *nt* consent
Jazz [dʒæz] **(-)** *m* Jazz

je [je:] *adv* **1** (*jemals*) ever; **hast du so was je gesehen?** did you ever see anything like it?
2 (*jeweils*) every, each; **sie zahlten je 3 Mark** they paid 3 marks each
♦ *konj* **1: je nach** depending on; **je nachdem** it depends; **je nachdem, ob ...** depending on whether ...
2: je eher, desto *od* **umso besser** the sooner the better

Jeans [dʒi:nz] *pl* jeans
jede(r, s) ['je:də(r, s)] *adj* every, each ♦ *pron* everybody; (~ *Einzelne*) each; **~s Mal** every time, each time; **ohne ~ x** without any x
jedenfalls *adv* in any case
jedermann *pron* everyone
jederzeit *adv* at any time

jedoch [je'dɔx] *adv* however
jeher ['je:he:r] *adv*: **von/seit ~** always
jemals ['je:ma:ls] *adv* ever
jemand ['je:mant] *pron* somebody; anybody
jene(r, s) ['je:nə(r, s)] *adj* that ♦ *pron* that one
jenseits ['je:nzaɪts] *adv* on the other side ♦ *präp* +*gen* on the other side of, beyond
Jenseits *nt*: **das ~** the hereafter, the beyond
jetzig ['jɛtsɪç] *adj* present
jetzt [jɛtst] *adv* now
jeweilig *adj* respective
jeweils *adv*: **~ zwei zusammen** two at a time; **zu ~ 5 Euros** at 5 euros each; **~ das Erste** the first each time
Jh. *abk* = **Jahrhundert**
Job [dʒɔp] **(-s, -s)** *m* (*umg*) job; **j~ben** ['dʒɔbən] *vi* (*umg*) to work
Jockei ['dʒɔke] **(-s, -s)** *m* jockey
Jod [jo:t] **(-(e)s)** *nt* iodine
jodeln ['jo:dəln] *vi* to yodel
joggen ['dʒɔgən] *vi* to jog
Jog(h)urt ['jo:gʊrt] **(-s, -s)** *m od nt* yogurt
Johannisbeere [jo'hanɪsbe:rə] *f* redcurrant; **schwarze ~** blackcurrant
johlen ['jo:lən] *vi* to yell
jonglieren [ʒõ'gliːrən] *vi* to juggle
Journal- [ʒʊrnal] *zW*: **~ismus** [-'lɪsmʊs] *m* journalism; **~ist(in)** [-'lɪst(ɪn)] *m(f)* journalist; **journa'listisch** *adj* journalistic
Jubel ['ju:bəl] **(-s)** *m* rejoicing; **j~n** *vi* to rejoice
Jubiläum [jubi'lɛ:ʊm] **(-s, Jubiläen)** *nt* anniversary; jubilee
jucken ['jʊkən] *vi* to itch ♦ *vt*: **es juckt mich am Arm** my arm is itching
Juckreiz ['jʊkraɪts] *m* itch
Jude ['ju:də] **(-n, -n)** *m* Jew
Juden- *zW*: **~tum** (-s) *nt* Judaism; Jewry; **~verfolgung** *f* persecution of the Jews
Jüdin ['jy:dɪn] *f* Jewess
jüdisch ['jy:dɪʃ] *adj* Jewish
Jugend ['ju:gənt] (-) *f* youth; **j~frei** *adj* (*CINE*) U (*BRIT*), G (*US*), suitable for children; **~herberge** *f* youth hostel; **~herbergsausweis** *m* youth hostelling

card; **j~lich** *adj* youthful; **~liche(r)** *f(m)* teenager, young person
Jugoslaw- [jugo'sla:v] *zW*: **~ien** **(-s)** *nt* Yugoslavia; **j~isch** *adj* Yugoslavian
Juli ['ju:li] **(-(s), -s)** *m* July
jun. *abk* (= *junior*) jr.
jung [jʊŋ] *adj* young; **J~e** **(-n, -n)** *m* boy, lad ♦ *nt* young animal; **J~en** *pl* (*von Tier*) young *pl*
Jünger ['jyŋər] **(-s, -)** *m* disciple
jünger *adj* younger
Jung- *zW*: **~frau** *f* virgin; (*ASTROL*) Virgo; **~geselle** *m* bachelor; **~gesellin** *f* unmarried woman
jüngst [jyŋst] *adv* lately, recently; **~e(r, s)** *adj* youngest; (*neueste*) latest
Juni ['ju:ni] **(-(s), -s)** *m* June
Junior ['ju:niɔr] **(-s, -en)** *m* junior
Jurist [ju'rɪst] *m* jurist, lawyer; **j~isch** *adj* legal
Justiz [jʊs'ti:ts] (-) *f* justice; **~beamte(r)** *m* judicial officer; **~irrtum** *m* miscarriage of justice; **~minister** *m* ≃ Lord (High) Chancellor (*BRIT*), ≃ Attorney General (*US*)
Juwel [ju've:l] **(-s, -en)** *nt od m* jewel
Juwelier [juve'li:r] **(-s, -e)** *m* jeweller; **~geschäft** *nt* jeweller's (shop)
Jux [jʊks] **(-es, -e)** *m* joke, lark

K, k

Kabarett [kaba'rɛt] **(-s, -e od -s)** *nt* cabaret; **~ist** [-'tɪst] *m* cabaret artiste
Kabel ['ka:bəl] **(-s, -)** *nt* (*ELEK*) wire; (*stark*) cable; **~fernsehen** *nt* cable television
Kabeljau ['ka:bəljau] **(-s, -e od -s)** *m* cod
Kabine [ka'bi:nə] *f* cabin; (*Zelle*) cubicle
Kabinenbahn *f* cable railway
Kabinett [kabi'nɛt] **(-s, -e)** *nt* (*POL*) cabinet
Kachel ['kaxəl] **(-, -n)** *f* tile; **k~n** *vt* to tile; **~ofen** *m* tiled stove
Käfer ['kɛ:fər] **(-s, -)** *m* beetle
Kaffee ['kafe] **(-s, -s)** *m* coffee; **~haus** *nt* café; **~kanne** *f* coffeepot; **~löffel** *m* coffee spoon
Käfig ['kɛ:fɪç] **(-s, -e)** *m* cage

kahl [ka:l] *adj* bald; **~ geschoren** shaven, shorn; **~köpfig** *adj* bald-headed

Kahn [ka:n] (-(e)s, ⁼e) *m* boat, barge

Kai [kaɪ] (-s, -e *od* -s) *m* quay

Kaiser ['kaɪzər] (-s, -) *m* emperor; **~in** *f* empress; **k~lich** *adj* imperial; **~reich** *nt* empire; **~schnitt** *m* (MED) Caesarian (section)

Kakao [ka'ka:o] (-s, -s) *m* cocoa

Kaktee [kak'te:(ə)] (-, -n) *f* cactus

Kaktus ['kaktʊs] (-, -teen) *m* cactus

Kalb [kalp] (-(e)s, ⁼er) *nt* calf; **k~en** ['kalbən] *vi* to calve; **~fleisch** *nt* veal; **~sleder** *nt* calf(skin)

Kalender [ka'lɛndər] (-s, -) *m* calendar; (*Taschenkalender*) diary

Kaliber [ka'li:bər] (-s, -) *nt* (*auch fig*) calibre

Kalk [kalk] (-(e)s, -e) *m* lime; (*BIOL*) calcium; **~stein** *m* limestone

kalkulieren [kalku'li:rən] *vt* to calculate

Kalorie [kalo'ri:] *f* calorie

kalt [kalt] *adj* cold; **mir ist (es) ~** I am cold; **~ bleiben** (*fig*) to remain unmoved; **~ stellen** to chill; **~blütig** *adj* cold-blooded; (*ruhig*) cool

Kälte ['kɛltə] (-) *f* cold; coldness; **~grad** *m* degree of frost *od* below zero; **~welle** *f* cold spell

kalt- *zW:* **~herzig** *adj* cold-hearted; **~schnäuzig** *adj* cold, unfeeling; **~stellen** *vt* (*fig*) to leave out in the cold

kam *etc* [ka:m] *vb siehe* **kommen**

Kamel [ka'me:l] (-(e)s, -e) *nt* camel

Kamera ['kamera] (-, -s) *f* camera

Kamerad [kamə'ra:t] (-en, -en) *m* comrade, friend; **~schaft** *f* comradeship; **k~schaftlich** *adj* comradely

Kameramann (-(e)s, -männer) *m* cameraman

Kamille [ka'mɪlə] *f* camomile; **~ntee** *m* camomile tea

Kamin [ka'mi:n] (-s, -e) *m* (*außen*) chimney; (*innen*) fireside, fireplace; **~kehrer** (-s, -) *m* chimney sweep

Kamm [kam] (-(e)s, ⁼e) *m* comb; (*Bergkamm*) ridge; (*Hahnenkamm*) crest

kämmen ['kɛmən] *vt* to comb ♦ *vr* to comb one's hair

Kammer ['kamər] (-, -n) *f* chamber; small bedroom

Kammerdiener *m* valet

Kampagne [kam'panjə] *f* campaign

Kampf [kampf] (-(e)s, ⁼e) *m* fight, battle; (*Wettbewerb*) contest; (*fig: Anstrengung*) struggle; **k~bereit** *adj* ready for action

kämpfen ['kɛmpfən] *vi* to fight

Kämpfer (-s, -) *m* fighter, combatant

Kampf- *zW:* **~handlung** *f* action; **k~los** *adj* without a fight; **~richter** *m* (SPORT) referee; (TENNIS) umpire; **~stoff** *m:* **chemischer/biologischer ~stoff** chemical/biological weapon

Kanada ['kanada] (-s) *nt* Canada; **Kanadier(in)** (-s, -) [kə'na:diər(ɪn)] *m(f)* Canadian; **k~nadisch** *adj* Canadian

Kanal [ka'na:l] (-s, **Kanäle**) *m* (*Fluss*) canal; (*Rinne, Ärmelkanal*) channel; (*für Abfluss*) drain; **~inseln** *pl* Channel Islands; **~isation** [-izatsi'o:n] *f* sewage system; **~tunnel** *m:* **der ~tunnel** the Channel Tunnel

Kanarienvogel [ka'na:riənfo:gəl] *m* (ZOOL) canary

kanarisch [ka'na:rɪʃ] *adj:* **K~e Inseln** Canary Islands, Canaries

Kandi- [kandi] *zW:* **~dat** [-'da:t] (-en, -en) *m* candidate; **~datur** [-da'tu:r] *f* candidature, candidacy; **k~dieren** [-'di:rən] *vi* to stand, to run

Kandis(zucker) ['kandɪs(tsʊkər)] (-) *m* candy

Känguru ▲ ['kɛŋguru] (-s, -s) *nt* kangaroo

Kaninchen [ka'ni:nçən] *nt* rabbit

Kanister [ka'nɪstər] (-s, -) *m* can, canister

Kännchen ['kɛnçən] *nt* pot

Kanne ['kanə] *f* (*Krug*) jug; (*Kaffeekanne*) pot; (*Milchkanne*) churn; (*Gießkanne*) can

kannst *etc* [kanst] *vb siehe* **können**

Kanone [ka'no:nə] *f* gun; (HIST) cannon; (*fig: Mensch*) ace

Kantate [kan'ta:tə] *f* cantaga

Kante ['kantə] *f* edge

Kantine [kan'ti:nə] *f* canteen

Kanton [kan'to:n] (-s, -e) *m* canton

Kanton

i **Kanton** *is the term for a state or region of Switzerland. Under the Swiss constitution the* **Kantone** *enjoy considerable autonomy. The Swiss* **Kantone** *are Aargau, Appenzell, Basel, Bern, Fribourg, Geneva, Glarus, Graubünden, Luzern, Neuchâtel, St. Gallen, Schaffhausen, Schwyz, Solothurn, Ticino, Thurgau, Unterwalden, Uri, Valais, Vaud, Zug and Zürich.*

Kanu ['ka:nu] (-s, -s) *nt* canoe
Kanzel ['kantsəl] (-, -n) *f* pulpit
Kanzler ['kantslər] (-s, -) *m* chancellor
Kap [kap] (-s, -s) *nt* cape (GEOG)
Kapazität [kapatsi'tɛ:t] *f* capacity; (*Fachmann*) authority
Kapelle [ka'pɛlə] *f* (*Gebäude*) chapel; (MUS) band
kapieren [ka'pi:rən] (*umg*) *vt, vi* to get, to understand
Kapital [kapi'ta:l] (-s, -e *od* -ien) *nt* capital; ~**anlage** *f* investment; ~**ismus** [-'lɪsmʊs] *m* capitalism; ~**ist** [-'lɪst] *m* capitalist; **k~istisch** *adj* capitalist
Kapitän [kapi'tɛ:n] (-s, -e) *m* captain
Kapitel [ka'pɪtəl] (-s, -) *nt* chapter
Kapitulation [kapitulatsi'o:n] *f* capitulation
kapitulieren [kapitu'li:rən] *vi* to capitulate
Kappe ['kapə] *f* cap; (*Kapuze*) hood
kappen *vt* to cut
Kapsel ['kapsəl] (-, -n) *f* capsule
kaputt [ka'pʊt] (*umg*) *adj* kaput, broken; (*Person*) exhausted, finished; **am Auto ist etwas ~** there's something wrong with the car; ~**gehen** (*unreg*) *vi* to break; (*Schuhe*) to fall apart; (*Firma*) to go bust; (*Stoff*) to wear out; (*sterben*) to cop it (*umg*); ~**machen** *vt* to break; (*Mensch*) to exhaust, to wear out
Kapuze [ka'pu:tsə] *f* hood
Karamell ▲ [kara'mɛl] (-s) *m* caramel; ~**bonbon** *m od nt* toffee
Karate [ka'ra:tə] (-s) *nt* karate
Karawane [kara'va:nə] *f* caravan

Kardinal [kardi'na:l] (-s, **Kardinäle**) *m* cardinal; ~**zahl** *f* cardinal number
Karfreitag [ka:r'fraita:k] *m* Good Friday
karg [kark] *adj* (*Landschaft, Boden*) barren; (*Lohn*) meagre
kärglich ['kɛrklɪç] *adj* poor, scanty
Karibik [ka'ri:bɪk] (-) *f:* **die ~** the Caribbean
karibisch [ka'ri:bɪʃ] *adj:* **K~e Inseln** Caribbean Islands
kariert [ka'ri:rt] *adj* (*Stoff*) checked; (*Papier*) squared
Karies ['ka:ries] (-) *f* caries
Karikatur [karika'tu:r] *f* caricature; ~**ist** [-'rɪst] *m* cartoonist
Karneval ['karnəval] (-s, -e *od* -s) *m* carnival

Karneval

i **Karneval** *is the time immediately before Lent when people gather to eat, drink and generally have fun before the fasting begins.* **Rosenmontag**, *the day before Shrove Tuesday, is the most important day of* **Karneval** *on the Rhine. Most firms take a day's holiday on that day to enjoy the celebrations. In South Germany and Austria* **Karneval** *is called* **Fasching**.

Karo ['ka:ro] (-s, -s) *nt* square; (KARTEN) diamonds
Karosserie [karɔsə'ri:] *f* (AUT) body(work)
Karotte [ka'rɔtə] *f* carrot
Karpfen ['karpfən] (-s, -) *m* carp
Karre ['karə] *f* cart, barrow
Karren (-s, -) *m* cart, barrow
Karriere [kari'e:rə] *f* career; **~ machen** to get on, to get to the top; ~**macher** (-s, -) *m* careerist
Karte ['kartə] *f* card; (*Landkarte*) map; (*Speisekarte*) menu; (*Eintrittskarte, Fahrkarte*) ticket; **alles auf eine ~ setzen** to put all one's eggs in one basket
Kartei [kar'tai] *f* card index; ~**karte** *f* index card
Kartell [kar'tɛl] (-s, -e) *nt* cartel
Karten- *zW:* ~**spiel** *nt* card game; pack of cards; ~**telefon** *nt* cardphone;

Spelling Reform: ▲ *new spelling* △ *old spelling (to be phased out)*

~vorverkauf m advance booking office

Kartoffel [kar'tɔfəl] (-, -n) f potato; **~brei** m mashed potatoes pl; **~mus** nt mashed potatoes pl; **~püree** nt mashed potatoes pl; **~salat** m potato salad

Karton [kar'tõ] (-s, -s) m cardboard; (Schachtel) cardboard box; **k~iert** [karto'niːrt] adj hardback

Karussell [karʊ'sɛl] (-s, -s) nt roundabout (BRIT), merry-go-round

Karwoche ['kaːrvɔxə] f Holy Week

Käse ['kɛːzə] (-s, -) m cheese; **~glocke** f cheese (plate) cover; **~kuchen** m cheesecake

Kaserne [ka'zɛrnə] f barracks pl; **~nhof** m parade ground

Kasino [ka'ziːno] (-s, -s) nt club; (MIL) officers' mess; (Spielkasino) casino

Kaskoversicherung ['kasko-] f (Teilkasko) ≈ third party, fire and theft insurance; (Vollkasko) ≈ fully comprehensive insurance

Kasse ['kasə] f (Geldkasten) cashbox; (in Geschäft) till, cash register; cash desk, checkout; (Kinokasse, Theaterkasse etc) box office; ticket office; (Krankenkasse) health insurance; (Sparkasse) savings bank; **~ machen** to count the money; **getrennte ~ führen** to pay separately; **an der ~** (in Geschäft) at the desk; **gut bei ~ sein** to be in the money

Kassen- zW: **~arzt** m panel doctor (BRIT); **~bestand** m cash balance; **~patient** m panel patient (BRIT); **~prüfung** f audit; **~sturz** m: **~sturz machen** to check one's money; **~zettel** m receipt

Kassette [ka'sɛtə] f small box; (Tonband, PHOT) cassette; (Bücherkassette) case

Kassettenrekorder (-s, -) m cassette recorder

kassieren [ka'siːrən] vt to take ♦ vi: **darf ich ~?** would you like to pay now?

Kassierer [ka'siːrər] (-s, -) m cashier; (von Klub) treasurer

Kastanie [kas'taːniə] f chestnut; (Baum) chestnut tree

Kasten ['kastən] (-s, ∸) m (auch SPORT) box; case; (Truhe) chest

kastrieren [kas'triːrən] vt to castrate

Katalog [kata'loːk] (-(e)s, -e) m catalogue

Katalysator [kataly'zaːtɔr] m catalyst; (AUT) catalytic converter

katastrophal [katastro'faːl] adj catastrophic

Katastrophe [kata'stroːfə] f catastrophe, disaster

Kat-Auto ['kat|aʊto] nt car fitted with a catalytic converter

Kategorie [katego'riː] f category

kategorisch [kate'goːrɪʃ] adj categorical

Kater ['kaːtər] (-s, -) m tomcat; (umg) hangover

kath. abk (= katholisch) Cath.

Kathedrale [kate'draːlə] f cathedral

Katholik [kato'liːk] (-en, -en) m Catholic

katholisch [ka'toːlɪʃ] adj Catholic

Kätzchen ['kɛtsçən] nt kitten

Katze ['katsə] f cat; **für die Katz** (umg) in vain, for nothing

Katzen- zW: **~auge** nt cat's eye; (Fahrrad) rear light; **~sprung** (umg) m stone's throw; short journey

Kauderwelsch ['kaʊdərvɛlʃ] (-(s)) nt jargon; (umg) double Dutch

kauen ['kaʊən] vt, vi to chew

kauern ['kaʊərn] vi to crouch down; (furchtsam) to cower

Kauf [kaʊf] (-(e)s, Käufe) m purchase, buy; (~en) buying; **ein guter ~** a bargain; **etw in ~ nehmen** to put up with sth; **k~en** vt to buy

Käufer(in) ['kɔyfər(ɪn)] (-s, -) m(f) buyer

Kauf- zW: **~frau** f businesswoman; **~haus** nt department store; **~kraft** f purchasing power

käuflich ['kɔyflɪç] adj purchasable, for sale; (pej) venal ♦ adv: **~ erwerben** to purchase

Kauf- zW: **k~lustig** adj interested in buying; **~mann** (pl -leute) m businessman; shopkeeper; **k~männisch** adj commercial; **k~männischer Angestellter** office worker; **~preis** m purchase price; **~vertrag** m bill of sale

Kaugummi ['kaʊgʊmi] m chewing gum

Kaulquappe ['kaʊlkvapə] f tadpole

kaum [kaʊm] adv hardly, scarcely

Kaution [kauˈtsɪoːn] f deposit; (JUR) bail

Kauz [kauts] (-es, Käuze) m owl; (fig) queer fellow

Kavalier [kavaˈliːr] (-s, -e) m gentleman, cavalier; **~sdelikt** nt peccadillo

Kaviar [ˈkaːviar] m caviar

keck [kɛk] adj daring, bold

Kegel [ˈkeːgəl] (-s, -) m skittle; (MATH) cone; **~bahn** f skittle alley; bowling alley; **k~n** vi to play skittles

Kehle [ˈkeːlə] f throat

Kehlkopf m larynx

Kehre [ˈkeːrə] f turn(ing), bend; **k~n** vt, vi (wenden) to turn; (mit Besen) to sweep; **sich an etw** dat **nicht k~n** not to heed sth

Kehricht [ˈkeːrɪçt] (-s) m sweepings pl

Kehrseite f reverse, other side; wrong side; bad side

kehrtmachen vi to turn about, to about-turn

keifen [ˈkaɪfən] vi to scold, to nag

Keil [kaɪl] (-(e)s, -e) m wedge; (MIL) arrowhead; **~riemen** m (AUT) fan belt

Keim [kaɪm] (-(e)s, -e) m bud; (MED, fig) germ; **k~en** vi to germinate; **k~frei** adj sterile; **~zelle** f (fig) nucleus

kein [kaɪn] adj no, not ... any; **~e(r, s)** pron no one, nobody; none; **~erlei** adj attrib no ... whatsoever

keinesfalls adv on no account

keineswegs adv by no means

keinmal adv not once

Keks [keːks] (-es, -e) m od nt biscuit

Kelch [kɛlç] (-(e)s, -e) m cup, goblet, chalice

Kelle [ˈkɛlə] f (Suppenkelle) ladle; (Maurerkelle) trowel

Keller [ˈkɛlər] (-s, -) m cellar

Kellner(in) [ˈkɛlnər(ɪn)] (-s, -) m(f) waiter (-tress)

keltern [ˈkɛltərn] vt to press

kennen [ˈkɛnən] (unreg) vt to know; **~lernen** ▲ to get to know; **sich ~ lernen** to get to know each other; (zum ersten Mal) to meet

Kenner (-s, -) m connoisseur

kenntlich adj distinguishable, discernible;

etw ~ machen to mark sth

Kenntnis (-, -se) f knowledge no pl; **etw zur ~ nehmen** to note sth; **von etw ~ nehmen** to take notice of sth; **jdn in ~ setzen** to inform sb

Kenn- zW: **~zeichen** nt mark, characteristic; **k~zeichnen** vt insep to characterize; **~ziffer** f reference number

kentern [ˈkɛntərn] vi to capsize

Keramik [keˈraːmɪk] (-, -en) f ceramics pl, pottery

Kerbe [ˈkɛrbə] f notch, groove

Kerker [ˈkɛrkər] (-s, -) m prison

Kerl [kɛrl] (-s, -e) m chap, bloke (BRIT), guy

Kern [kɛrn] (-(e)s, -e) m (Obstkern) pip, stone; (Nusskern) kernel; (Atomkern) nucleus; (fig) heart, core; **~energie** f nuclear energy; **~forschung** f nuclear research; **~frage** f central issue; **k~gesund** adj thoroughly healthy, fit as a fiddle; **k~ig** adj (kraftvoll) robust; (Ausspruch) pithy; **~kraftwerk** nt nuclear power station; **k~los** adj seedless, without pips; **~physik** f nuclear physics sg; **~spaltung** f nuclear fission; **~waffen** pl nuclear weapons

Kerze [ˈkɛrtsə] f candle; (Zündkerze) plug; **k~ngerade** adj straight as a die; **~nständer** m candle holder

kess ▲ [kɛs] adj saucy

Kessel [ˈkɛsəl] (-s, -) m kettle; (von Lokomotive etc) boiler; (GEOG) depression; (MIL) encirclement

Kette [ˈkɛtə] f chain; **k~n** vt to chain; **~nrauchen** (-s) nt chain smoking; **~nreaktion** f chain reaction

Ketzer [ˈkɛtsər] (-s, -) m heretic

keuchen [ˈkɔyçən] vi to pant, to gasp

Keuchhusten m whooping cough

Keule [ˈkɔylə] f club; (KOCH) leg

keusch [kɔyʃ] adj chaste; **K~heit** f chastity

kfm. abk = **kaufmännisch**

Kfz [kaːˈɛfˈtsɛt] nt abk = **Kraftfahrzeug**

KG [kaːˈgeː] (-, -s) f abk (= Kommanditgesellschaft) limited partnership

kg abk = **Kilogramm**

kichern [ˈkɪçərn] vi to giggle

kidnappen ['kɪtnɛpən] *vt* to kidnap

Kiefer¹ ['kiːfər] (**-s, -**) *m* jaw

Kiefer² ['kiːfər] (**-, -n**) *f* pine; **~nzapfen** *m* pine cone

Kiel [kiːl] (**-(e)s, -e**) *m* (*Federkiel*) quill; (*NAUT*) keel

Kieme ['kiːmə] *f* gill

Kies [kiːs] (**-es, -e**) *m* gravel

Kilo ['kiːlo] *nt* kilo; **~gramm** [kilo'gram] *nt* kilogram; **~meter** [kilo'meːtər] *m* kilometre; **~meterzähler** *m* milometer

Kind [kɪnt] (**-(e)s, -er**) *nt* child; **von ~ auf** from childhood

Kinder- ['kɪndər] *zW:* **~betreuung** *f* crèche; **~ei** [-'raɪ] *f* childishness; **~garten** *m* nursery school, playgroup; **~gärtnerin** *f* nursery school teacher; **~geld** *nt* child benefit (*BRIT*); **~heim** *nt* children's home; **~krippe** *f* crèche; **~lähmung** *f* poliomyelitis; **k~leicht** *adj* childishly easy; **k~los** *adj* childless; **~mädchen** *nt* nursemaid; **k~reich** *adj* with a lot of children; **~sendung** *f* (*RADIO, TV*) children's programme; **~sicherung** *f* (*AUT*) childproof safety catch; **~spiel** *nt* (*fig*) child's play; **~tagesstätte** *f* day nursery; **~wagen** *m* pram, baby carriage (*US*); **~zimmer** *nt* (*für ~*) children's room; (*für Säugling*) nursery

---
Kindergarten

ℹ️ A **Kindergarten** is a nursery school for children aged between 3 and 6 years. The children sing and play but do not receive any formal instruction. Most *Kindergärten* are financed by the town or the church with parents paying a monthly contribution towards the cost.

Kind- *zW:* **~heit** *f* childhood; **k~isch** *adj* childish; **k~lich** *adj* childlike

Kinn [kɪn] (**-(e)s, -e**) *nt* chin; **~haken** *m* (*BOXEN*) uppercut

Kino ['kiːno] (**-s, -s**) *nt* cinema; **~besucher** *m* cinema-goer; **~programm** *nt* film programme

Kiosk [ki'ɔsk] (**-(e)s, -e**) *m* kiosk

Kippe ['kɪpə] *f* cigarette end; (*umg*) fag; **auf der ~ stehen** (*fig*) to be touch and go

kippen *vi* to topple over, to overturn ♦ *vt* to tilt

Kirch- [kɪrç] *zW:* **~e** *f* church; **~enlied** *nt* hymn; **~ensteuer** *f* church tax; **~gänger** (**-s, -**) *m* churchgoer; **~hof** *m* churchyard; **k~lich** *adj* ecclesiastical

Kirmes ['kɪrmɛs] (**-, -sen**) *f* fair

Kirsche ['kɪrʃə] *f* cherry

Kissen ['kɪsən] (**-s, -**) *nt* cushion; (*Kopfkissen*) pillow; **~bezug** *m* pillowslip

Kiste ['kɪstə] *f* box; chest

Kitsch [kɪtʃ] (**-(e)s**) *m* kitsch; **k~ig** *adj* kitschy

Kitt [kɪt] (**-(e)s, -e**) *m* putty

Kittel (**-s, -**) *m* overall, smock

kitten *vt* to putty; (*fig: Ehe etc*) to cement

kitzelig ['kɪtsəlɪç] *adj* (*auch fig*) ticklish

kitzeln *vi* to tickle

Kiwi ['kiːvi] (**-, -s**) *f* (*BOT, KOCH*) kiwi fruit

KKW [kaːkaː'veː] *nt abk* = **Kernkraftwerk**

Klage ['klaːgə] *f* complaint; (*JUR*) action; **k~n** *vi* (*wehklagen*) to lament, to wail; (*sich beschweren*) to complain; (*JUR*) to take legal action

Kläger(in) ['klɛːgər(ɪn)] (**-s, -**) *m(f)* plaintiff

kläglich ['klɛːklɪç] *adj* wretched

klamm [klam] *adj* (*Finger*) numb; (*feucht*) damp

Klammer ['klamər] (**-, -n**) *f* clamp; (*in Text*) bracket; (*Büro~*) clip; (*Wäsche~*) peg; (*Zahn~*) brace; **k~n** *vr:* **sich k~n an** +*akk* to cling to

Klang [klaŋ] (**-(e)s, ⁸e**) *m* sound; **k~voll** *adj* sonorous

Klappe ['klapə] *f* valve; (*Ofen~*) damper; (*umg: Mund*) trap; **k~n** *vi* (*Geräusch*) to click; (*Sitz etc*) to tip ♦ *vt* to tip ♦ *vb unpers* to work

Klapper ['klapər] (**-, -n**) *f* rattle; **k~ig** *adj* run-down, worn-out; **k~n** *vi* to clatter, to rattle; **~schlange** *f* rattlesnake; **~storch** *m* stork

Klapp- *zW:* **~messer** *nt* jackknife; **~rad** *nt* collapsible bicycle; **~stuhl** *m* folding chair; **~tisch** *m* folding table

Klaps [klaps] (**-es, -e**) *m* slap

klar [klaːr] *adj* clear; (*NAUT*) ready for sea; (*MIL*) ready for action; **sich** *dat* (**über etw** *akk*) **~ werden** to get (sth) clear in one's mind; **sich** *dat* **im K~en sein über** +*akk* to be clear about; **ins K~e kommen** to get clear; (**na**) **~!** of course!; **~ sehen** to see clearly

Kläranlage *f* purification plant

klären ['klɛːrən] *vt* (*Flüssigkeit*) to purify; (*Probleme*) to clarify ♦ *vr* to clear (itself) up

Klarheit *f* clarity

Klarinette [klari'nɛtə] *f* clarinet

klar- *zW:* **~legen** *vt* to clear up, to explain; **~machen** *vt* (*Schiff*) to get ready for sea; **jdm etw ~machen** to make sth clear to sb; **~sehen** △ (*unreg*) *vi siehe* **klar**; **K~sichtfolie** *f* transparent film; **~stellen** *vt* to clarify

Klärung ['klɛːrʊŋ] *f* (*von Flüssigkeit*) purification; (*von Probleme*) clarification

klarwerden △ (*unreg*) *vi siehe* **klar**

Klasse ['klasə] *f* class; (*SCH*) class, form

klasse (*umg*) *adj* smashing

Klassen- *zW:* **~arbeit** *f* test; **~gesellschaft** *f* class society; **~lehrer** *m* form master; **k~los** *adj* classless; **~sprecher(in)** *m(f)* form prefect; **~zimmer** *nt* classroom

klassifizieren [klasifi'tsiːrən] *vt* to classify

Klassik ['klasɪk] *f* (*Zeit*) classical period; (*Stil*) classicism; **~er** (**-s, -**) *m* classic

klassisch *adj* (*auch fig*) classical

Klatsch [klatʃ] (**-(e)s, -e**) *m* smack, crack; (*Gerede*) gossip; **~base** *f* gossip, scandalmonger; **~e** (*umg*) *f* crib; **k~en** *vi* (*Geräusch*) to clash; (*reden*) to gossip; (*applaudieren*) to applaud, to clap ♦ *vt*: **jdm Beifall k~en** to applaud sb; **~mohn** *m* (corn) poppy; **k~nass** ▲ *adj* soaking wet

Klaue ['klaʊə] *f* claw; (*umg: Schrift*) scrawl; **k~n** (*umg*) *vt* to pinch

Klausel ['klaʊzəl] (**-, -n**) *f* clause

Klausur [klaʊ'zuːr] *f* seclusion; **~arbeit** *f* examination paper

Klavier [kla'viːr] (**-s, -e**) *nt* piano

Kleb- ['kleːb] *zW:* **k~en** ['kleːbən] *vt, vi:* **k~en (an** +*akk*) to stick (to); **k~rig** *adj*

sticky; **~stoff** *m* glue; **~streifen** *m* adhesive tape

kleckern ['klɛkərn] *vi* to make a mess ♦ *vt* to spill

Klecks [klɛks] (**-es, -e**) *m* blot, stain

Klee [kleː] (**-s**) *m* clover; **~blatt** *nt* cloverleaf; (*fig*) trio

Kleid [klaɪt] (**-(e)s, -er**) *nt* garment; (*Frauenkleid*) dress; **~er** *pl* (~*ung*) clothes; **k~en** ['klaɪdən] *vt* to clothe, to dress; to suit ♦ *vr* to dress

Kleider- ['klaɪdər] *zW:* **~bügel** *m* coat hanger; **~bürste** *f* clothes brush; **~schrank** *m* wardrobe

Kleid- *zW:* **k~sam** *adj* flattering; **~ung** *f* clothing; **~ungsstück** *nt* garment

klein [klaɪn] *adj* little, small; **~ hacken** to chop, to mince; **~ schneiden** to chop up; **K~e(r, s)** *mf* little one; **K~format** *nt* small size; **im K~format** small-scale; **K~geld** *nt* small change; **K~igkeit** *f* trifle; **K~kind** *nt* infant; **K~kram** *m* details *pl*; **~laut** *adj* dejected, quiet; **~lich** *adj* petty, paltry; **K~od** ['klaɪnoːt] (**-s, -odien**) *nt* gem, jewel; treasure; **K~stadt** *f* small town; **~städtisch** *adj* provincial; **~stmöglich** *adj* smallest possible

Kleister ['klaɪstər] (**-s, -**) *m* paste

Klemme ['klɛmə] *f* clip; (*MED*) clamp; (*fig*) jam; **k~n** *vt* (*festhalten*) to jam; (*quetschen*) to pinch, to nip ♦ *vr* to catch o.s.; (*sich hineinzwängen*) to squeeze o.s. ♦ *vi* (*Tür*) to stick, to jam; **sich hinter jdn / etw k~n** to get on to sb / down to sth

Klempner ['klɛmpnər] (**-s, -**) *m* plumber

Klerus ['kleːrʊs] (**-**) *m* clergy

Klette ['klɛtə] *f* burr

Kletter- ['klɛtər] *zW:* **~er** (**-s, -**) *m* climber; **k~n** *vi* to climb; **~pflanze** *f* creeper

klicken ['klɪkən] *vi* (*COMPUT*) to click

Klient(in) [kli'ɛnt(ɪn)] *m(f)* client

Klima ['kliːma] (**-s, -s** *od* **-te**) *nt* climate; **~anlage** *f* air conditioning; **~wechsel** *m* change of air

klimpern ['klɪmpərn] (*umg*) *vi* (*mit Münzen, Schlüsseln*) to jingle; (*auf Klavier*) to plonk (away)

Spelling Reform: ▲ *new spelling* △ *old spelling (to be phased out)*

Klinge ['klɪŋə] f blade; sword

Klingel ['klɪŋəl] (-, -n) f bell; **~beutel** m collection bag; **k~n** vi to ring

klingen ['klɪŋən] (*unreg*) vi to sound; (*Gläser*) to clink

Klinik ['kliːnɪk] f hospital, clinic

Klinke ['klɪŋkə] f handle

Klippe ['klɪpə] f cliff; (*im Meer*) reef; (*fig*) hurdle

klipp und klar ['klɪp|ʊntklaːr] adj clear and concise

klirren ['klɪrən] vi to clank, to jangle; (*Gläser*) to clink; **~de Kälte** biting cold

Klischee [klɪ'ʃeː] (-s, -s) nt (*Druckplatte*) plate, block; (*fig*) cliché; **~vorstellung** f stereotyped idea

Klo [kloː] (-s, -s) (*umg*) nt loo (*BRIT*), john (*US*)

Kloake [klo'aːkə] f sewer

klobig ['kloːbɪç] adj clumsy

Klon [kloːn] (-s, -e) m clone

klonen ['kloːnən] vti to clone

Klopapier (*umg*) nt loo paper (*BRIT*)

klopfen ['klɔpfən] vi to knock; (*Herz*) to thump ♦ vt to beat; **es klopft** somebody's knocking; **jdm auf die Schulter ~** to tap sb on the shoulder

Klopfer (-s, -) m (*Teppichklopfer*) beater; (*Türklopfer*) knocker

Klops [klɔps] (-es, -e) m meatball

Klosett [klo'zɛt] (-s, -e *od* -s) nt lavatory, toilet; **~papier** nt toilet paper

Kloß [kloːs] (-es, ᵉe) m (*im Hals*) lump; (*KOCH*) dumpling

Kloster ['kloːstər] (-s, ᵛ) nt (*Männerkloster*) monastery; (*Frauenkloster*) convent; **klösterlich** ['kløːstərlɪç] adj monastic; convent *cpd*

Klotz [klɔts] (-es, ᵛe) m log; (*Hackklotz*) block; **ein ~ am Bein** (*fig*) a drag, a millstone round (sb's) neck

Klub [klʊp] (-s, -s) m club; **~sessel** m easy chair

Kluft [klʊft] (-, ᵛe) f cleft, gap; (*GEOG*) gorge, chasm

klug [kluːk] adj clever, intelligent; **K~heit** f cleverness, intelligence

Klumpen ['klʊmpən] (-s, -) m (*Erd~*) clod;

(*Blut~*) clot; (*Gold~*) nugget; (*KOCH*) lump

km *abk* = **Kilometer**

knabbern ['knabərn] vt, vi to nibble

Knabe ['knaːbə] (-n, -n) m boy

Knäckebrot ['knɛkəbroːt] nt crispbread

knacken ['knakən] vt, vi (*auch fig*) to crack

Knacks [knaks] (-es, -e) m crack; (*fig*) defect

Knall [knal] (-(e)s, -e) m bang; (*Peitschenknall*) crack; **~ und Fall** (*umg*) unexpectedly; **~bonbon** nt cracker; **k~en** vi to bang; to crack; **k~rot** adj bright red

knapp [knap] adj tight; (*Geld*) scarce; (*Sprache*) concise; **eine ~e Stunde** just under an hour; **~ unter/neben** just under/by; **K~heit** f tightness; scarcity; conciseness

knarren ['knarən] vi to creak

Knast [knast] (-(e)s) (*umg*) m (*Haftstrafe*) porridge (*inf*), time (*inf*); (*Gefängnis*) slammer (*inf*), clink (*inf*)

knattern ['knatərn] vi to rattle; (*Maschinengewehr*) to chatter

Knäuel ['knɔyəl] (-s, -) m *od* nt (*Wollknäuel*) ball; (*Menschenknäuel*) knot

Knauf [knauf] (-(e)s, **Knäufe**) m knob; (*Schwertknauf*) pommel

Knebel ['kneːbəl] (-s, -) m gag

kneifen ['knaɪfən] (*unreg*) vt to pinch ♦ vi to pinch; (*sich drücken*) to back out; **vor etw ~** to dodge sth

Kneipe ['knaɪpə] (*umg*) f pub

kneten ['kneːtən] vt to knead; (*Wachs*) to mould

Knick [knɪk] (-(e)s, -e) m (*Sprung*) crack; (*Kurve*) bend; (*Falte*) fold; **k~en** vt, vi (*springen*) to crack; (*brechen*) to break; (*Papier*) to fold; **geknickt sein** to be downcast

Knicks [knɪks] (-es, -e) m curtsey

Knie [kniː] (-s, -) nt knee; **~beuge** f knee bend; **~bundhose** m knee breeches; **~gelenk** nt knee joint; **~kehle** f back of the knee; **k~n** vi to kneel; **~scheibe** f kneecap; **~strumpf** m knee-length sock

Kniff [knɪf] (-(e)s, -e) m (*fig*) trick, knack; **k~elig** adj tricky

knipsen ['knɪpsən] vt (Fahrkarte) to punch; (PHOT) to take a snap of, to snap ♦ vi to take a snap od snaps

Knirps [knɪrps] (-es, -e) m little chap; ((R): Schirm) telescopic umbrella

knirschen ['knɪrʃən] vi to crunch; **mit den Zähnen ~** to grind one's teeth

knistern ['knɪstərn] vi to crackle

Knitter- ['knɪtər] zW: **~falte** f crease; **k~frei** adj non-crease; **k~n** vi to crease

Knoblauch ['kno:plaʊx] (-(e)s) m garlic; **~zehe** f (KOCH) clove of garlic

Knöchel ['knœçəl] (-s, -) m knuckle; (Fußknöchel) ankle

Knochen ['knɔxən] (-s, -) m bone; **~bruch** m fracture; **~gerüst** nt skeleton; **~mark** nt bone marrow

knöchern ['knœçərn] adj bone

knochig ['knɔxɪç] adj bony

Knödel ['knø:dəl] (-s, -) m dumpling

Knolle ['knɔlə] f tuber

Knopf [knɔpf] (-(e)s, ⁻e) m button; (Kragenknopf) stud

knöpfen ['knœpfən] vt to button

Knopfloch nt buttonhole

Knorpel ['knɔrpəl] (-s, -) m cartilage, gristle; **k~ig** adj gristly

Knospe ['knɔspə] f bud

Knoten ['kno:tən] (-s, -) m knot; (BOT) node; (MED) lump; **k~** vt to knot; **~punkt** m junction

Knüller ['knʏlər] (-s, -) (umg) m hit; (Reportage) scoop

knüpfen ['knʏpfən] vt to tie; (Teppich) to knot; (Freundschaft) to form

Knüppel ['knʏpəl] (-s, -) m cudgel; (Polizeiknüppel) baton, truncheon; (AVIAT) (joy)stick

knurren ['knʊrən] vi (Hund) to snarl, to growl; (Magen) to rumble; (Mensch) to mutter

knusperig ['knʊspərɪç] adj crisp; (Keks) crunchy

k. o. [ka:'o:] adj knocked out; (fig) done in

Koalition [koalitsi'o:n] f coalition

Kobold ['ko:bɔlt] (-(e)s, -e) m goblin, imp

Koch [kɔx] (-(e)s, ⁻e) m cook; **~buch** nt

cook(ery) book; **k~en** vt, vi to cook; (Wasser) to boil; **~er** (-s, -) m stove, cooker; **~gelegenheit** f cooking facilities pl

Köchin ['kœçɪn] f cook

Koch- zW: **~löffel** m kitchen spoon; **~nische** f kitchenette; **~platte** f hotplate; **~salz** nt cooking salt; **~topf** m saucepan, pot

Köder ['kø:dər] (-s, -) m bait, lure

ködern vt (Tier) to trap with bait; (Person) to entice, to tempt

Koexistenz [koɛksɪs'tɛnts] f coexistence

Koffein [kɔfe'i:n] (-s) nt caffeine; **k~frei** adj decaffeinated

Koffer ['kɔfər] (-s, -) m suitcase; (Schrankkoffer) trunk; **~kuli** m (luggage) trolley; **~radio** nt portable radio; **~raum** m (AUT) boot (BRIT), trunk (US)

Kognak ['kɔnjak] (-s, -s) m brandy, cognac

Kohl [ko:l] (-(e)s, -e) m cabbage

Kohle ['ko:lə] f coal; (Holzkohle) charcoal; (CHEM) carbon; **~hydrat** (-(e)s, -e) nt carbohydrate

Kohlen- zW: **~dioxid** (-(e)s, -e) nt carbon dioxide; **~händler** m coal merchant, coalman; **~säure** f carbon dioxide; **~stoff** m carbon

Kohlepapier nt carbon paper

Koje ['ko:jə] f cabin; (Bett) bunk

Kokain [koka'i:n] (-s) nt cocaine

kokett [ko'kɛt] adj coquettish, flirtatious

Kokosnuss ▲ ['ko:kɔsnʊs] f coconut

Koks [ko:ks] (-es, -e) m coke

Kolben ['kɔlbən] (-s, -) m (Gewehrkolben) rifle butt; (Keule) club; (CHEM) flask; (TECH) piston; (Maiskolben) cob

Kolik ['ko:lɪk] f colic, the gripes pl

Kollaps ['kɔlaps] (-es, -e) m collapse

Kolleg [kɔl'e:k] (-s, -s od -ien) nt lecture course; **~e** [kɔl'e:gə] (-n, -n) m colleague; **~in** f colleague; **~ium** nt working party; (SCH) staff

Kollekte [kɔ'lɛktə] f (REL) collection

kollektiv [kɔlɛk'ti:f] adj collective

Köln [kœln] (-s) nt Cologne

Kolonie [kolo'ni:] f colony

kolonisieren [koloniˈtsiːrən] *vt* to colonize
Kolonne [koˈlɔnə] *f* column; *(von Fahrzeugen)* convoy
Koloss ▲ [koˈlɔs] (**-es, -e**) *m* colossus; **kolosˈsal** *adj* colossal
Kölsch [kœlʃ] (**-, -**) *nt (Bier)* ≈ (strong) lager
Kombi- [ˈkɔmbi] *zW:* **~nation** [-natsiˈoːn] *f* combination; *(Vermutung)* conjecture; *(Hemdhose)* combinations *pl*; **k~nieren** [-ˈniːrən] *vt* to combine ♦ *vi* to deduce, to work out; *(vermuten)* to guess; **~wagen** *m* station wagon; **~zange** *f* (pair of) pliers *pl*
Komet [koˈmeːt] (**-en, -en**) *m* comet
Komfort [kɔmˈfoːr] (**-s**) *m* luxury
Komik [ˈkoːmɪk] *f* humour, comedy; **~er** (**-s, -**) *m* comedian
komisch [ˈkoːmɪʃ] *adj* funny
Komitee [komiˈteː] (**-s, -s**) *nt* committee
Komma [ˈkɔma] (**-s, -s** *od* **-ta**) *nt* comma; **2 ~ 3** 2 point 3
Kommand- [koˈmand] *zW:* **~ant** [-ˈdant] *m* commander, commanding officer; **k~ieren** [-ˈdiːrən] *vt, vi* to command; **~o** (**-s, -s**) *nt* command, order; *(Truppe)* detachment, squad; **auf ~o** to order
kommen [ˈkɔmən] *(unreg) vi* to come; *(näher kommen)* to approach; *(passieren)* to happen; *(gelangen, geraten)* to get; *(Blumen, Zähne, Tränen etc)* to appear; *(in die Schule, das Zuchthaus etc)* to go; **~ lassen** to send for; **das kommt in den Schrank** that goes in the cupboard; **zu sich ~** to come round *od* to; **zu etw ~** to acquire sth; **um etw ~** to lose sth; **nichts auf jdn/etw ~ lassen** to have nothing said against sb/sth; **jdm frech ~** to get cheeky with sb; **auf jeden vierten kommt ein Platz** there's one place for every fourth person; **wer kommt zuerst?** who's first?; **unter ein Auto ~** to be run over by a car; **wie hoch kommt das?** what does that cost?; **komm gut nach Hause!** safe journey (home); **~den Sonntag** next Sunday; **K~** (**-s**) *nt* coming
Kommentar [kɔmɛnˈtaːr] *m* commentary; **kein ~** no comment; **k~los** *adj* without comment
Kommentator [kɔmɛnˈtaːtɔr] *m (TV)* commentator
kommentieren [kɔmɛnˈtiːrən] *vt* to comment on
kommerziell [kɔmɛrtsiˈɛl] *adj* commercial
Kommilitone [kɔmiliˈtoːnə] (**-n, -n**) *m* fellow student
Kommissar [kɔmɪˈsaːr] *m* police inspector
Kommission [kɔmɪsiˈoːn] *f (COMM)* commission; *(Ausschuss)* committee
Kommode [kɔˈmoːdə] *f (chest of)* drawers
kommunal [kɔmuˈnaːl] *adj* local; *(von Stadt auch)* municipal
Kommune [kɔˈmuːnə] *f* commune
Kommunikation [kɔmunikatsiˈoːn] *f* communication
Kommunion [kɔmuniˈoːn] *f* communion
Kommuniqué, Kommunikee ▲ [kɔmyniˈkeː] (**-s, -s**) *nt* communiqué
Kommunismus [kɔmuˈnɪsmʊs] *m* communism
Kommunist(in) [kɔmuˈnɪst(ɪn)] *m(f)* communist; **k~isch** *adj* communist
kommunizieren [kɔmuniˈtsiːrən] *vi* to communicate
Komödie [koˈmøːdiə] *f* comedy
Kompagnon [kɔmpanˈjöː] (**-s, -s**) *m (COMM)* partner
kompakt [kɔmˈpakt] *adj* compact
Kompanie [kɔmpaˈniː] *f* company
Kompass ▲ [ˈkɔmpas] (**-es, -e**) *m* compass
kompatibel [kɔmpaˈtiːbəl] *adj* compatible
kompetent [kɔmpeˈtɛnt] *adj* competent
Kompetenz *f* competence, authority
komplett [kɔmˈplɛt] *adj* complete
Komplex [kɔmˈpleks] (**-es, -e**) *m (Gebäudekomplex)* complex
Komplikation [kɔmplikatsiˈoːn] *f* complication
Kompliment [kɔmpliˈmɛnt] *nt* compliment
Komplize [kɔmˈpliːtsə] (**-n, -n**) *m* accomplice
kompliziert [kɔmpliˈtsiːrt] *adj* complicated
komponieren [kɔmpoˈniːrən] *vt* to compose
Komponist [kɔmpoˈnɪst(ɪn)] *m* composer
Komposition [kɔmpozitsiˈoːn] *f* composition
Kompost [kɔmˈpɔst] (**-(e)s, -e**) *m* compost

Kompott [kɔmˈpɔt] *(-(e)s, -e)* nt stewed fruit
Kompromiss ▲ [kɔmproˈmɪs] *(-es, -e)* m compromise; **k~bereit** adj willing to compromise
Kondens- [kɔnˈdɛns] zW: **~ation** [kɔndɛnzatsiˈoːn] f condensation; **k~ieren** [kɔndɛnˈziːrən] vt to condense; **~milch** f condensed milk
Kondition [kɔndɪtsiˈoːn] f (COMM, FIN) condition; (Durchhaltevermögen) stamina; (körperliche Verfassung) physical condition, state of health
Konditionstraining [kɔndɪtsiˈoːnstrɛːnɪŋ] nt fitness training
Konditor [kɔnˈdiːtɔr] m pastry cook; **~ei** [-ˈraɪ] f café; cake shop
Kondom [kɔnˈdoːm] *(-s, -e)* nt condom
Konferenz [kɔnfeˈrɛnts] f conference, meeting
Konfession [kɔnfɛsiˈoːn] f (religious) denomination; **k~ell** [-ˈnɛl] adj denominational; **k~slos** adj non-denominational
Konfirmand [kɔnfɪrˈmant] m candidate for confirmation
Konfirmation [kɔnfɪrmatsiˈoːn] f (REL) confirmation
konfirmieren [kɔnfɪrˈmiːrən] vt to confirm
konfiszieren [kɔnfɪsˈtsiːrən] vt to confiscate
Konfitüre [kɔnfiˈtyːrə] f jam
Konflikt [kɔnˈflɪkt] *(-(e)s, -e)* m conflict
konfrontieren [kɔnfrɔnˈtiːrən] vt to confront
konfus [kɔnˈfuːs] adj confused
Kongress ▲ [kɔnˈgrɛs] *(-es, -e)* m congress; **~zentrum** nt conference centre
Kongruenz [kɔngruˈɛnts] f agreement, congruence
König [ˈkøːnɪç] *(-s, -e)* m king; **~in** [ˈkøːnɪgɪn] f queen; **k~lich** adj royal; **~reich** nt kingdom
Konjugation [kɔnjugatsiˈoːn] f conjugation
konjugieren [kɔnjuˈgiːrən] vt to conjugate
Konjunktion [kɔnjʊŋktsiˈoːn] f conjunction
Konjunktiv [ˈkɔnjʊŋktiːf] *(-s, -e)* m subjunctive
Konjunktur [kɔnjʊŋkˈtuːr] f economic

situation; (Hochkonjunktur) boom
konkret [kɔnˈkreːt] adj concrete
Konkurrent(in) [kɔnkʊˈrɛnt(ɪn)] m(f) competitor
Konkurrenz [kɔnkʊˈrɛnts] f competition; **k~fähig** adj competitive; **~kampf** m competition; rivalry, competitive situation
konkurrieren [kɔnkʊˈriːrən] vi to compete
Konkurs [kɔnˈkʊrs] *(-es, -e)* m bankruptcy
Können *(-s)* nt ability

| SCHLÜSSELWORT |

können [ˈkœnən] *(pt konnte, pp gekonnt od (als Hilfsverb) können)* vt, vi 1 to be able to; **ich kann es machen** I can do it, I am able to do it; **ich kann es nicht machen** I can't do it, I'm not able to do it; **ich kann nicht ...** I can't ..., I cannot ...; **ich kann nicht mehr** I can't go on
2 (wissen, beherrschen) to know; **können Sie Deutsch?** can you speak German?; **er kann gut Englisch** he speaks English well; **sie kann keine Mathematik** she can't do mathematics
3 (dürfen) to be allowed to; **kann ich gehen?** can I go?; **könnte ich ...?** could I ...?; **kann ich mit?** (umg) can I come with you?
4 (möglich sein): **Sie könnten Recht haben** you may be right; **das kann sein** that's possible; **kann sein** maybe

Könner m expert
konnte etc [ˈkɔntə] vb siehe **können**
konsequent [kɔnzeˈkvɛnt] adj consistent
Konsequenz [kɔnzeˈkvɛnts] f consistency; (Folgerung) conclusion
Konserv- [kɔnˈzɛrv] zW: **k~ativ** [-aˈtiːf] adj conservative; **~ative(r)** [-aˈtiːvə(r)] f(m) (POL) conservative; **~e** f tinned food; **~enbüchse** f tin, can; **k~ieren** [-ˈviːrən] vt to preserve; **~ierung** f preservation; **~ierungsstoff** m preservatives
Konsonant [kɔnzoˈnant] m consonant
konstant [kɔnˈstant] adj constant
konstru- zW: **~ieren** [kɔnstruˈiːrən] vt to construct; **K~kteur** [kɔnstrʊkˈtøːr] m

designer; **K~ktion** [kanstrʊktsi'oːn] f construction; **~ktiv** [kɔnstrʊk'tiːf] *adj* constructive

Konsul ['kɔnzʊl] **(-s, -n)** *m* consul; **~at** [-'laːt] *nt* consulate

konsultieren [kɔnzʊl'tiːrən] *vt* to consult

Konsum [kɔn'zuːm] **(-s)** *m* consumption; **~artikel** *m* consumer article; **~ent** [-'mɛnt] *m* consumer; **k~ieren** [-'miːrən] *vt* to consume

Kontakt [kɔn'takt] **(-(e)s, -e)** *m* contact; **k~arm** *adj* unsociable; **k~freudig** *adj* sociable; **~linsen** *pl* contact lenses

kontern ['kɔntərn] *vt, vi* to counter

Kontinent [kɔnti'nɛnt] *m* continent

Kontingent [kɔntɪŋ'gɛnt] **(-(e)s, -e)** *nt* quota; *(Truppenkontingent)* contingent

kontinuierlich [kɔntinu'iːrlɪç] *adj* continuous

Konto ['kɔnto] **(-s, Konten)** *nt* account; **~auszug** *m* statement (of account); **~inhaber(in)** *m(f)* account holder; **~stand** *m* balance

Kontra ['kɔntra] **(-s, -s)** *nt (KARTEN)* double; **jdm ~ geben** *(fig)* to contradict sb; **~bass** ▲ *m* double bass; **~hent** *m (COMM)* contracting party; **~punkt** *m* counterpoint

Kontrast [kɔn'trast] **(-(e)s, -e)** *m* contrast

Kontroll- [kɔn'trɔl] *zW:* **~e** f control, supervision; *(Passkontrolle)* passport control; **~eur** [-'løːr] *m* inspector; **k~ieren** [-'liːrən] *vt* to control, to supervise; *(nachprüfen)* to check

Konvention [kɔnvɛntsi'oːn] f convention; **k~ell** [-'nɛl] *adj* conventional

Konversation [kɔnvɛrzatsi'oːn] f conversation; **~slexikon** *nt* encyclop(a)edia

Konvoi ['kɔnvɔy] **(-s, -s)** *m* convoy

Konzentration [kɔntsɛntratsi'oːn] f concentration

Konzentrationslager *nt* concentration camp

konzentrieren [kɔntsɛn'triːrən] *vt, vr* to concentrate

konzentriert *adj* concentrated ♦ *adv* (zuhören, arbeiten) intently

Konzern [kɔn'tsɛrn] **(-s, -e)** *m* combine

Konzert [kɔn'tsɛrt] **(-(e)s, -e)** *nt* concert; *(Stück)* concerto; **~saal** *m* concert hall

Konzession [kɔntsesi'oːn] f licence; *(Zugeständnis)* concession

Konzil [kɔn'tsiːl] **(-s, -e** *od* **-ien)** *nt* council

kooperativ [ko|opera'tiːf] *adj* cooperative

koordinieren [ko|ɔrdi'niːrən] *vt* to coordinate

Kopf [kɔpf] **(-(e)s, ⁿe)** *m* head; **~haut** f scalp; **~hörer** *m* headphones *pl*; **~kissen** *nt* pillow; **k~los** *adj* panic-stricken; **k~rechnen** *vi* to do mental arithmetic; **~salat** *m* lettuce; **~schmerzen** *pl* headache *sg*; **~sprung** *m* header, dive; **~stand** *m* headstand; **~stütze** f *(im Auto etc)* headrest, head restraint; **~tuch** *nt* headscarf; **~weh** *nt* headache; **~zerbrechen** *nt*: **jdm ~zerbrechen machen** to be a headache for sb

Kopie [ko'piː] f copy; **k~ren** *vt* to copy

Kopiergerät *nt* photocopier

Koppel[1] ['kɔpəl] **(-, -n)** f *(Weide)* enclosure

Koppel[2] ['kɔpəl] **(-s, -)** *nt (Gürtel)* belt

koppeln *vt* to couple

Koppelung f coupling

Koralle [ko'ralə] f coral

Korb [kɔrp] **(-(e)s, ⁿe)** *m* basket; **jdm einen ~ geben** *(fig)* to turn sb down; **~ball** *m* basketball; **~stuhl** *m* wicker chair

Kord [kɔrt] **(-(e)s, -e)** *m* cord, corduroy

Kordel ['kɔrdəl] **(-, -n)** f cord, string

Kork [kɔrk] **(-(e)s, -e)** *m* cork; **~en (-s, -)** *m* stopper, cork; **~enzieher (-s, -)** *m* corkscrew

Korn [kɔrn] **(-(e)s, ⁿer)** *nt* corn, grain; *(Gewehr)* sight

Körper ['kœrper] **(-s, -)** *m* body; **~bau** *m* build; **k~behindert** *adj* disabled; **~geruch** *m* body odour; **~gewicht** *nt* weight; **~größe** f height; **k~lich** *adj* physical; **~pflege** f personal hygiene; **~schaft** f corporation; **~schaftssteuer** f corporation tax; **~teil** *m* part of the body; **~verletzung** f bodily *od* physical injury

korpulent [kɔrpu'lɛnt] *adj* corpulent

korrekt [kɔ'rɛkt] *adj* correct; **K~ur** [-'tuːr] f

(*eines Textes*) proofreading; (*Text*) proof; (*SCH*) marking, correction

Korrespond- [kɔrɛspɔnd] *zW:* **~ent(in)** [-'dɛnt(ɪn)] *m(f)* correspondent; **~enz** [-'dɛnts] *f* correspondence; **k~ieren** [-'diːrən] *vi* to correspond

Korridor ['kɔridoːr] **(-s, -e)** *m* corridor

korrigieren [kɔri'giːrən] *vt* to correct

Korruption [kɔrʊptsi'oːn] *f* corruption

Kose- ['koːzə] *zW:* **~form** *f* pet form; **~name** *m* pet name; **~wort** *nt* term of endearment

Kosmetik [kɔs'meːtɪk] *f* cosmetics *pl;* **~erin** *f* beautician

kosmetisch *adj* cosmetic; (*Chirurgie*) plastic

kosmisch ['kɔsmɪʃ] *adj* cosmic

Kosmo- ['kɔsmo] *zW:* **~naut** [-'naʊt] **(-en, -en)** *m* cosmonaut; **k~politisch** *adj* cosmopolitan; **~s (-)** *m* cosmos

Kost [kɔst] **(-)** *f* (*Nahrung*) food; (*Verpflegung*) board; **k~bar** *adj* precious; (*teuer*) expensive; **~barkeit** *f* preciousness; costliness, expensiveness; (*Wertstück*) valuable

Kosten *pl* cost(s); (*Ausgaben*) expenses; **auf ~ von** at the expense of; **k~** *vt* to cost; (*versuchen*) to taste ♦ *vi* to taste; **was kostet ...?** what does ... cost?, how much is ...?; **~anschlag** *m* estimate; **k~los** *adj* free (of charge)

köstlich ['kœstlɪç] *adj* precious; (*Einfall*) delightful; (*Essen*) delicious; **sich ~ amüsieren** to have a marvellous time

Kostprobe *f* taste; (*fig*) sample

kostspielig *adj* expensive

Kostüm [kɔs'tyːm] **(-s, -e)** *nt* costume; (*Damenkostüm*) suit; **~fest** *nt* fancy-dress party; **k~ieren** [kɔsty'miːrən] *vt, vr* to dress up; **~verleih** *m* costume agency

Kot [koːt] **(-(e)s)** *m* excrement

Kotelett [kɔtə'lɛt] **(-(e)s, -e** *od* **-s)** *nt* cutlet, chop; **~en** *pl* (*Bart*) sideboards

Köter ['køːtər] **(-s, -)** *m* cur

Kotflügel *m* (*AUT*) wing

kotzen ['kɔtsən] (*umg!*) *vi* to puke (*umg*), to throw up (*umg*)

Krabbe ['krabə] *f* shrimp; **k~ln** *vi* to crawl

Krach [krax] **(-(e)s, -s** *od* **-e)** *m* crash; (*andauernd*) noise; (*umg: Streit*) quarrel, argument; **k~en** *vi* to crash; (*beim Brechen*) to crack ♦ *vr* (*umg*) to argue, to quarrel

krächzen ['krɛçtsən] *vi* to croak

Kraft [kraft] **(-, ⁺e)** *f* strength; power; force; (*Arbeitskraft*) worker; **in ~ treten** to come into force; **k~** *präp +gen* by virtue of; **~fahrer** *m* (motor) driver; **~fahrzeug** *nt* motor vehicle; **~fahrzeugbrief** *m* logbook; **~fahrzeugsteuer** *f* ≃ road tax; **~fahrzeugversicherung** *f* car insurance

kräftig ['krɛftɪç] *adj* strong; **~en** *vt* to strengthen

Kraft- *zW:* **k~los** *adj* weak; powerless; (*JUR*) invalid; **~probe** *f* trial of strength; **~stoff** *m* fuel; **k~voll** *adj* vigorous; **~werk** *nt* power station

Kragen ['kraːgən] **(-s, -)** *m* collar; **~weite** *f* collar size

Krähe ['krɛːə] *f* crow; **k~n** *vi* to crow

Kralle ['kralə] *f* claw; (*Vogelkralle*) talon; **k~n** *vt* to clutch; (*krampfhaft*) to claw

Kram [kraːm] **(-(e)s)** *m* stuff, rubbish; **k~en** *vi* to rummage; **~laden** *m* (*pej*) small shop

Krampf [krampf] **(-(e)s, ⁺e)** *m* cramp; (*zuckend*) spasm; **~ader** *f* varicose vein; **k~haft** *adj* convulsive; (*fig: Versuche*) desperate

Kran [kraːn] **(-(e)s, ⁺e)** *m* crane; (*Wasserkran*) tap, faucet (*US*)

krank [kraŋk] *adj* ill, sick; **K~e(r)** *f(m)* sick person, invalid; patient; **~en** *vi:* **an etw** *dat* **~en** (*fig*) to suffer from sth

kränken ['krɛŋkən] *vt* to hurt

Kranken- *zW:* **~geld** *nt* sick pay; **~gymnastik** *f* physiotherapy; **~haus** *nt* hospital; **~kasse** *f* health insurance; **~pfleger** *m* nursing orderly; **~schein** *m* health insurance card; **~schwester** *f* nurse; **~versicherung** *f* health insurance; **~wagen** *m* ambulance

Krank- *zW:* **k~haft** *adj* diseased; (*Angst etc*) morbid; **~heit** *f* illness; disease; **~heitserreger** *m* disease-causing agent

kränklich ['krɛŋklɪç] *adj* sickly

Kränkung *f* insult, offence

Spelling Reform: ▲ *new spelling* △ *old spelling (to be phased out)*

Kranz [krants] (**-es,** ⁼**e**) *m* wreath, garland

krass ▲ [kras] *adj* crass

Krater ['krɑːtər] (**-s, -**) *m* crater

Kratz- ['krats] *zW:* ~**bürste** *f* (*fig*) crosspatch; **k~en** *vt, vi* to scratch; ~**er** (**-s, -**) *m* scratch (*Werkzeug*) scraper

Kraul [kraʊl] (**-s**) *nt* crawl; ~ **schwimmen** to do the crawl; **k~en** *vi* (*schwimmen*) to do the crawl ♦ *vt* (*streicheln*) to fondle

kraus [kraʊs] *adj* crinkly; (*Haar*) frizzy; (*Stirn*) wrinkled

Kraut [kraʊt] (**-(e)s, Kräuter**) *nt* plant; (*Gewürz*) herb; (*Gemüse*) cabbage

Krawall [kra'val] (**-s, -e**) *m* row, uproar

Krawatte [kra'vatə] *f* tie

kreativ [krea'tiːf] *adj* creative

Krebs [kreːps] (**-es, -e**) *m* crab; (*MED, ASTROL*) cancer; **k~krank** *adj* suffering from cancer

Kredit [kre'diːt] (**-(e)s, -e**) *m* credit; ~**institut** *nt* bank; ~**karte** *f* credit card

Kreide ['kraɪdə] *f* chalk; **k~bleich** *adj* as white as a sheet

Kreis [kraɪs] (**-es, -e**) *m* circle; (*Stadtkreis etc*) district; **im ~ gehen** (*auch fig*) to go round in circles

kreischen ['kraɪʃən] *vi* to shriek, to screech

Kreis- *zW:* ~**el** ['kraɪzəl] (**-s, -**) *m* top; (*~verkehr*) roundabout (*BRIT*), traffic circle (*US*); **k~en** [kraɪzən] *vi* to spin; ~**lauf** *m* (*MED*) circulation; (*fig: der Natur etc*) cycle; ~**säge** *f* circular saw; ~**stadt** *f* county town; ~**verkehr** *m* roundabout traffic

Krematorium [krema'toːriʊm] *nt* crematorium

Kreml ['kreml] (**-s**) *m* Kremlin

krepieren [kre'piːrən] (*umg*) *vi* (*sterben*) to die, to kick the bucket

Krepp [krep] (**-s, -s** *od* **-e**) *m* crepe; ~**papier** ▲ *nt* crepe paper

Kresse ['kresə] *f* cress

Kreta ['kreːta] (**-s**) *nt* Crete

Kreuz [krɔʏts] (**-es, -e**) *nt* cross; (*ANAT*) small of the back; (*KARTEN*) clubs; **k~en** *vt, vr* to cross ♦ *vi* (*NAUT*) to cruise; **~en** *m* (*Schiff*) cruiser; ~**fahrt** *f* cruise; ~**feuer** *nt* (*fig*): **ins ~feuer geraten** to be under fire from all sides; ~**gang** *m* cloisters *pl*;

k~igen *vt* to crucify; ~**igung** *f* crucifixion; ~**ung** *f* (*Verkehrskreuzung*) crossing, junction; (*Züchten*) cross; ~**verhör** *nt* cross-examination; ~**weg** *m* crossroads; (*REL*) Way of the Cross; ~**worträtsel** *nt* crossword puzzle; ~**zug** *m* crusade

Kriech- ['kriːç] *zW:* **k~en** *vi* (*unreg*) to crawl, to creep; (*pej*) to grovel, to crawl; ~**er** (**-s, -**) *m* crawler; ~**spur** *f* crawler lane; ~**tier** *nt* reptile

Krieg [kriːk] (**-(e)s, -e**) *m* war

kriegen ['kriːgən] (*umg*) *vt* to get

Kriegs- *zW:* ~**erklärung** *f* declaration of war; ~**fuß** *m*: **mit jdm/etw auf ~fuß stehen** to be at loggerheads with sb/to have difficulties with sth; ~**gefangene(r)** *m* prisoner of war; ~**gefangenschaft** *f* captivity; ~**gericht** *nt* court-martial; ~**schiff** *nt* warship; ~**verbrecher** *m* war criminal; ~**versehrte(r)** *m* person disabled in the war; ~**zustand** *m* state of war

Krim [krɪm] (**-**) *f* Crimea

Krimi ['krɪmi] (**-s, -s**) (*umg*) *m* thriller

Kriminal- [krimi'naːl] *zW:* ~**beamte(r)** *m* detective; ~**i'tät** *f* criminality; ~**polizei** *f* ≈ Criminal Investigation Department (*BRIT*), Federal Bureau of Investigation (*US*); ~**ro'man** *m* detective story

kriminell [krimi'nel] *adj* criminal; **K~e(r)** *m* criminal

Krippe ['krɪpə] *f* crib; (*Kinderkrippe*) crèche

Krise ['kriːzə] *f* crisis; **k~ln** *vi*: **es k~lt** there's a crisis

Kristall [krɪs'tal] (**-s, -e**) *m* crystal ♦ *nt* (*Glas*) crystal

Kriterium [kri'teːriʊm] *nt* criterion

Kritik [kri'tiːk] *f* criticism; (*Zeitungskritik*) review, write-up; ~**er** ['kriːtikər] (**-s, -**) *m* critic; **k~los** *adj* uncritical

kritisch ['kriːtɪʃ] *adj* critical

kritisieren [kriti'ziːrən] *vt, vi* to criticize

kritzeln ['krɪtsəln] *vt, vi* to scribble, to scrawl

Kroatien [kro'aːtsiən] *nt* Croatia

Krokodil [kroko'diːl] (**-s, -e**) *nt* crocodile

Krokus ['kroːkʊs] (**-, -** *od* **-se**) *m* crocus

Krone ['kroːnə] *f* crown; (*Baumkrone*) top

krönen ['krøːnən] *vt* to crown

Kron- *zW:* **~korken** *m* bottle top;
~leuchter *m* chandelier; **~prinz** *m* crown
prince

Krönung ['krø:nʊŋ] *f* coronation

Kropf [krɔpf] (-(e)s, ⁼e) *m* (*MED*) goitre; (*von
Vogel*) crop

Kröte ['krø:tə] *f* toad

Krücke ['krʏkə] *f* crutch

Krug [kru:k] (-(e)s, ⁼e) *m* jug; (*Bierkrug*) mug

Krümel ['kry:məl] (-s, -) *m* crumb; **k~n** *vt, vi*
to crumble

krumm [krʊm] *adj* (*auch fig*) crooked;
(*kurvig*) curved; **jdm etw ~ nehmen** to take
sth amiss; **~beinig** *adj* bandy-legged;
~lachen (*umg*) *vr* to laugh o.s. silly

Krümmung ['krʏmʊŋ] *f* bend, curve

Krüppel ['krʏpəl] (-s, -) *m* cripple

Kruste ['krʊstə] *f* crust

Kruzifix [krutsi'fɪks] (-es, -e) *nt* crucifix

Kübel ['ky:bəl] (-s, -) *m* tub; (*Eimer*) pail

Kubikmeter [ku'bi:kme:tər] *m* cubic metre

Küche ['kʏçə] *f* kitchen; (*Kochen*) cooking,
cuisine

Kuchen ['ku:xən] (-s, -) *m* cake; **~form** *f*
baking tin; **~gabel** *f* pastry fork

Küchen- *zW:* **~herd** *m* cooker, stove;
~schabe *f* cockroach; **~schrank** *m*
kitchen cabinet

Kuckuck ['kʊkʊk] (-s, -e) *m* cuckoo; **~suhr**
f cuckoo clock

Kugel ['ku:gəl] (-, -n) *f* ball; (*MATH*) sphere;
(*MIL*) bullet; (*Erdkugel*) globe; (*SPORT*) shot;
k~förmig *adj* spherical; **~lager** *nt* ball
bearing; **k~rund** *adj* (*Gegenstand*) round;
(*umg: Person*) tubby; **~schreiber** *m* ballpoint (pen), Biro ®; **k~sicher** *adj*
bulletproof; **~stoßen** (-s) *nt* shot put

Kuh [ku:] (-, ⁼e) *f* cow

kühl [ky:l] *adj* (*auch fig*) cool; **K~anlage** *f*
refrigeration plant; **K~e** (-) *f* coolness; **~en**
vt to cool; **K~er** (-s, -) *m* (*AUT*) radiator;
K~erhaube *f* (*AUT*) bonnet (*BRIT*), hood
(*US*); **K~raum** *m* cold storage chamber;
K~schrank *m* refrigerator; **K~truhe** *f*
freezer; **K~ung** *f* cooling; **K~wasser** *nt*
radiator water

kühn [ky:n] *adj* bold, daring; **K~heit** *f*

boldness

Kuhstall *m* byre, cattle shed

Küken ['ky:kən] (-s, -) *nt* chicken

kulant [ku'lant] *adj* obliging

Kuli ['ku:li] (-s, -s) *m* coolie; (*umg:
Kugelschreiber*) Biro ®

Kulisse [ku'lɪsə] *f* scenery

kullern ['kʊlərn] *vi* to roll

Kult [kʊlt] (-(e)s, -e) *m* worship, cult; **mit
etw einen ~ treiben** to make a cult out of
sth

kultivieren [kʊlti'vi:rən] *vt* to cultivate

kultiviert *adj* cultivated, refined

Kultur [kʊl'tu:r] *f* culture; civilization; (*des
Bodens*) cultivation; **~banause** (*umg*) *m*
philistine, low-brow; **~beutel** *m* toilet bag;
k~ell [-u'rɛl] *adj* cultural; **~ministerium** *nt*
ministry of education and the arts

Kümmel ['kʏməl] (-s, -) *m* caraway seed;
(*Branntwein*) kümmel

Kummer ['kʊmər] (-s) *m* grief, sorrow

kümmerlich ['kʏmərlɪç] *adj* miserable,
wretched

kümmern ['kʏmərn] *vt* to concern ♦ *vr:* **sich
um jdn ~** to look after sb; **jdm kümmert
mich nicht** that doesn't worry me; **sich
um etw ~** to see to sth

Kumpel ['kʊmpəl] (-s, -) (*umg*) *m* mate

kündbar ['kʏntba:r] *adj* redeemable,
recallable; (*Vertrag*) terminable

Kunde¹ ['kʊndə] (-n, -n) *m* customer

Kunde² ['kʊndə] *f* (*Botschaft*) news

Kunden- *zW:* **~dienst** *m* after-sales service;
~konto *nt* charge account; **~nummer** *f*
customer number

Kund- *zW:* **k~geben** (*unreg*) *vt* to
announce; **~gebung** *f* announcement;
(*Versammlung*) rally

Künd- ['kʏnd] *zW:* **k~igen** *vi* to give in
one's notice ♦ *vt* to cancel; **jdm k~igen** to
give sb his/her notice; **die Stellung/Wohnung
k~igen** to give notice that one is leaving
one's job/house; **jdm die Stellung/
Wohnung k~igen** to give sb notice to
leave his/her job/house; **~igung** *f* notice;
~igungsfrist *f* period of notice;
~igungsschutz *m* protection against

wrongful dismissal

Kundin f customer

Kundschaft f customers pl, clientele

künftig ['kʏnftɪç] adj future ♦ adv in future

Kunst [kʊnst] (-, ⁻e) f art; (Können) skill; **das ist doch keine ~** it's easy; **~dünger** m artificial manure; **~faser** f synthetic fibre; **~fertigkeit** f skilfulness; **~gegenstand** m art object; **~gerecht** adj skilful; **~geschichte** f history of art; **~gewerbe** nt arts and crafts pl; **~griff** m trick, knack; **~händler** m art dealer

Künstler(in) ['kʏnstlər(ɪn)] (-s, -) m(f) artist; **k~isch** adj artistic; **~name** m pseudonym

künstlich ['kʏnstlɪç] adj artificial

Kunst- zW: **~sammler** (-s, -) m art collector; **~seide** f artificial silk; **~stoff** m synthetic material; **~stück** nt trick; **~turnen** nt gymnastics sg; **k~voll** adj artistic; **~werk** nt work of art

kunterbunt ['kʊntərbʊnt] adj higgledy-piggledy

Kupee ▲ [ku'pe:] (-s, -s) nt coupé

Kupfer ['kʊpfər] (-s) nt copper; **k~n** adj copper

Kupon [ku'põ:, ku'põŋ] (-s, -s) m coupon; (Stoff~) length of cloth

Kuppe ['kʊpə] f (Bergkuppe) top; (Fingerkuppe) tip

Kuppel (-, -n) f dome; **k~n** vi (JUR) to procure; (AUT) to declutch ♦ vt to join

Kupplung f coupling; (AUT) clutch

Kur [ku:r] (-, -en) f cure, treatment

Kür [ky:r] (-, -en) f (SPORT) free exercises pl

Kurbel ['kʊrbəl] (-, -n) f crank, winder; (AUT) starting handle; **~welle** f crankshaft

Kürbis ['kʏrbɪs] (-ses, -se) m pumpkin; (exotisch) gourd

Kurgast m visitor (to a health resort)

kurieren [ku'ri:rən] vt to cure

kurios [kuri'o:s] adj curious, odd; **K~i'tät** f curiosity

Kurort m health resort

Kurs [kʊrs] (-es, -e) m course; (FIN) rate; **~buch** nt timetable; **k~ieren** [kʊr'zi:rən] vi to circulate; **k~iv** [kʊr'zi:f] adv in italics; **~us** ['kʊrzʊs] (-, Kurse) m course; **~wagen**

m (EISENB) through carriage

Kurtaxe [-taksə] (-, -n) f visitors' tax (at health resort or spa)

Kurve ['kʊrvə] f curve; (Straßenkurve) curve, bend; **kurvig** adj (Straße) bendy

kurz [kʊrts] adj short; **~ gesagt** in short; **~ halten** to keep short; **zu ~ kommen** to come off badly; **den Kürzeren ziehen** to get the worst of it; **K~arbeit** f short-time work; **~ärm(e)lig** adj short-sleeved

Kürze ['kʏrtsə] f shortness, brevity; **k~n** vt to cut short; (in der Länge) to shorten; (Gehalt) to reduce

kurz- zW: **~erhand** adv on the spot; **~fristig** adj short-term; **K~geschichte** f short story; **~halten** △ (unreg) vt siehe **kurz**; **~lebig** adj short-lived

kürzlich ['kʏrtslɪç] adv lately, recently

Kurz- zW: **~schluss** ▲ m (ELEK) short circuit; **k~sichtig** adj short-sighted

Kürzung f (eines Textes) abridgement; (eines Theaterstück, des Gehalts) cut

Kurzwelle f short wave

kuscheln ['kʊʃəln] vr to snuggle up

Kusine [ku'zi:nə] f cousin

Kuss ▲ [kʊs] (-es, ⁻e) m kiss

küssen ['kʏsən] vt, vr to kiss

Küste ['kʏstə] f coast, shore

Küstenwache f coastguard

Küster ['kʏstər] (-s, -) m sexton, verger

Kutsche ['kʊtʃə] f coach, carriage; **~r** (-s, -) m coachman

Kutte ['kʊtə] f habit

Kuvert [ku'vɛrt] (-s, -e od -s) nt envelope; cover

KZ nt abk von **Konzentrationslager**

L, l

l abk = **Liter**

labil [la'bi:l] adj (MED: Konstitution) delicate

Labor [la'bo:r] (-s, -e od -s) nt lab; **~ant(in)** m(f) lab(oratory) assistant

Labyrinth [laby'rɪnt] (-s, -e) nt labyrinth

Lache ['laxə] f (Flüssigkeit) puddle; (von Blut, Benzin etc) pool

lächeln ['lɛçəln] vi to smile; **L~** (**-s**) nt smile
lachen ['laxən] vi to laugh
lächerlich ['lɛçərlɪç] adj ridiculous
Lachgas nt laughing gas
lachhaft adj laughable
Lachs [laks] (**-es, -e**) m salmon
Lack [lak] (**-(e)s, -e**) m lacquer, varnish; (von Auto) paint; **l~ieren** [la'ki:rən] vt to varnish; (Auto) to spray; **~ierer** [la'ki:rər] (**-s, -**) m varnisher
Laden ['la:dən] (**-s, ⁻**) m shop; (Fensterladen) shutter
laden ['la:dən] (unreg) vt (Lasten) to load; (JUR) to summon; (einladen) to invite
Laden- zW: **~dieb** m shoplifter; **~diebstahl** m shoplifting; **~schluss** ▲ m closing time; **~tisch** m counter
Laderaum m freight space; (AVIAT, NAUT) hold
Ladung ['la:duŋ] f (Last) cargo, load; (Beladen) loading; (JUR) summons; (Einladung) invitation; (Sprengladung) charge
Lage ['la:gə] f position, situation; (Schicht) layer; **in der ~ sein** to be in a position
Lageplan m ground plan
Lager ['la:gər] (**-s, -**) nt camp; (COMM) warehouse; (Schlaflager) bed; (von Tier) lair; (TECH) bearing; **~bestand** m stocks pl; **~feuer** nt campfire; **~haus** nt warehouse, store
lagern ['la:gərn] vi (Dinge) to be stored; (Menschen) to camp ♦ vt to store; (betten) to lay down; (Maschine) to bed
Lagune [la'gu:nə] f lagoon
lahm [la:m] adj lame; **~ legen** to paralyse; **~en** vi to be lame
Lähmung f paralysis
Laib [laɪp] (**-s, -e**) m loaf
Laie ['laɪə] (**-n, -n**) m layman; **l~nhaft** adj amateurish
Laken ['la:kən] (**-s, -**) nt sheet
Lakritze [la'krɪtsə] f liquorice
lallen ['lalən] vt, vi to slur; (Baby) to babble
Lamelle [la'mɛlə] f lamella; (ELEK) lamina; (TECH) plate
Lametta [la'mɛta] (**-s**) nt tinsel

Lamm [lam] (**-(e)s, ⁻er**) nt lamb
Lampe ['lampə] f lamp
Lampen- zW: **~fieber** nt stage fright; **~schirm** m lampshade
Lampion [lampi'ö:] (**-s, -s**) m Chinese lantern
Land [lant] (**-(e)s, ⁻er**) nt land; (Nation, nicht Stadt) country; (Bundesland) state; **auf dem ~(e)** in the country; siehe hierzulande; **~besitz** m landed property; **~ebahn** f runway; **l~en** ['landən] vt, vi to land

---

Land

i A **Land** (plural **Länder**) is a member state of the **BRD** and of Austria. There are 16 **Länder** in Germany, namely Baden-Württemberg, Bayern, Berlin, Brandenburg, Bremen, Hamburg, Hessen, Mecklenburg-Vorpommern, Niedersachsen, Nordrhein-Westfalen, Rheinland-Pfalz, Saarland, Sachsen, Sachsen-Anhalt, Schleswig-Holstein and Thüringen. Each **Land** has its own parliament and constitution. The 9 **Länder** of Austria are Vorarlberg, Tirol, Salzburg, Oberösterreich, Niederösterreich, Kärnten, Steiermark, Burgenland and Wien.

Landes- ['landəs] zW: **~farben** pl national colours; **~innere(s)** nt inland region; **~sprache** f national language; **l~üblich** adj customary; **~verrat** m high treason; **~währung** f national currency; **l~weit** adj nationwide
Land- zW: **~haus** nt country house; **~karte** f map; **~kreis** m administrative region; **l~läufig** adj customary
ländlich ['lɛntlɪç] adj rural
Land- zW: **~schaft** f countryside; (KUNST) landscape; **~schaftsschutzgebiet** nt nature reserve; **~sitz** m country seat; **~straße** f country road; **~streicher** (**-s, -**) m tramp; **~strich** m region
Landung ['landuŋ] f landing; **~sbrücke** f jetty, pier
Land- zW: **~weg** m: **etw auf dem ~weg befördern** to transport sth by land; **~wirt**

---

m farmer; **~wirtschaft** *f* agriculture; **~zunge** *f* spit

lang [laŋ] *adj* long; *(Mensch)* tall; **~atmig** *adj* long-winded; **~e** *adv* for a long time; *(dauern, brauchen)* a long time

Länge ['lɛŋə] *f* length; *(GEOG)* longitude

langen ['laŋən] *vi (ausreichen)* to do, to suffice; *(fassen)*: **~ (nach)** to reach (for) ♦ *vt*: **jdm etw ~** to hand *od* pass sb sth; **es langt mir** I've had enough

Längengrad *m* longitude

Längenmaß *nt* linear measure

lang- *zW*: **L~eweile** *f* boredom; **~fristig** *adj* long-term; **~jährig** *adj (Freundschaft, Gewohnheit)* long-standing; **L~lauf** *m (SKI)* cross-country skiing

länglich *adj* longish

längs [lɛŋs] *präp (+gen od dat)* along ♦ *adv* lengthwise

lang- *zW*: **~sam** *adj* slow; **L~samkeit** *f* slowness; **L~schläfer(in)** *m(f)* late riser

längst [lɛŋst] *adv*: **das ist ~ fertig** that was finished a long time ago, that has been finished for a long time; **~e(r, s)** *adj* longest

lang- *zW*: **~weilen** *vt* to bore ♦ *vr* to be bored; **~weilig** *adj* boring, tedious; **L~welle** *f* long wave; **~wierig** *adj* lengthy, long-drawn-out

Lanze ['lantsə] *f* lance

Lappalie [la'pa:liə] *f* trifle

Lappen ['lapən] **(-s, -)** *m* cloth, rag; *(ANAT)* lobe

läppisch ['lɛpɪʃ] *adj* foolish

Lapsus ['lapsʊs] **(-, -)** *m* slip

Laptop ['lɛptɔp] **(-s, -s)** *m* laptop (computer)

Lärche ['lɛrçə] *f* larch

Lärm [lɛrm] **(-(e)s)** *m* noise; **l~en** *vi* to be noisy, to make a noise

Larve ['larfə] *f (BIOL)* larva

lasch [laʃ] *adj* slack

Laser ['le:zər] **(-s, -)** *m* laser

─── SCHLÜSSELWORT ───

lassen ['lasən] *(pt* **ließ,** *pp* **gelassen** *od (als Hilfsverb)* **lassen)** *vt* **1** *(unterlassen)* to stop;

(momentan) to leave; **lass das (sein)!** don't (do it)!; *(hör auf)* stop it!; **lass wir das!** let's leave it; **lass mich!** leave me alone; **lassen wir das!** let's leave it; **er kann das Trinken nicht lassen** he can't stop drinking

2 *(zurücklassen)* to leave; **etw lassen, wie es ist** to leave sth (just) as it is

3 *(überlassen)*: **jdn ins Haus lassen** to let sb into the house

♦ *vi*: **lass mal, ich mache das schon** leave it, I'll do it

♦ *Hilfsverb* **1** *(veranlassen)*: **etw machen lassen** to have *od* get sth done; **sich** *dat* **etw schicken lassen** to have sth sent (to one)

2 *(zulassen)*: **jdn etw wissen lassen** to let sb know sth; **das Licht brennen lassen** to leave the light on; **jdn warten lassen** to keep sb waiting; **das lässt sich machen** that can be done

3: **lass uns gehen** let's go

lässig ['lɛsɪç] *adj* casual; **L~keit** *f* casualness

Last [last] **(-, -en)** *f* load, burden; *(NAUT, AVIAT)* cargo; *(meist pl: Gebühr)* charge; **jdm zur ~ fallen** to be a burden to sb; **~auto** *nt* lorry, truck; **l~en** *vi*: **l~en auf** +*dat* to weigh on; **~enaufzug** *m* goods lift *od* elevator *(US)*

Laster ['lastər] **(-s, -)** *nt* vice

lästern ['lɛstərn] *vt, vi (Gott)* to blaspheme; *(schlecht sprechen)* to mock

Lästerung *f* jibe; *(Gotteslästerung)* blasphemy

lästig ['lɛstɪç] *adj* troublesome, tiresome

Last- *zW*: **~kahn** *m* barge; **~kraftwagen** *m* heavy goods vehicle; **~schrift** *f* debit; **~wagen** *m* lorry, truck; **~zug** *m* articulated lorry

Latein [la'taɪn] **(-s)** *nt* Latin; **~amerika** *nt* Latin America

latent [la'tɛnt] *adj* latent

Laterne [la'tɛrnə] *f* lantern; *(Straßenlaterne)* lamp, light; **~npfahl** *m* lamppost

latschen ['la:tʃən] *(umg) vi (gehen)* to wander, to go; *(lässig)* to slouch

Latte ['latə] *f* lath; *(SPORT)* goalpost; *(quer)*

crossbar

Latzhose ['latsho:zə] f dungarees pl

lau [laʊ] adj (Nacht) balmy; (Wasser) lukewarm

Laub [laʊp] (-(e)s) nt foliage; ~baum m deciduous tree; ~frosch m tree frog; ~säge f fretsaw

Lauch [laʊx] (-(e)s, -e) m leek

Lauer ['laʊər] f: auf der ~ sein od liegen to lie in wait; l~n vi to lie in wait; (Gefahr) to lurk

Lauf [laʊf] (-(e)s, Läufe) m run; (Wettlauf) race; (Entwicklung, ASTRON) course; (Gewehrlauf) barrel; **einer Sache** dat **ihren ~ lassen** to let sth take its course; ~bahn f career

laufen ['laʊfən] (unreg) vt, vi to run; (umg: gehen) to walk; ~d adj running; (Monat, Ausgaben) current; **auf dem ~den sein/ halten** to be/keep up to date; **am ~den Band** (fig) continuously

Läufer ['lɔyfər] (-s, -) m (Teppich, SPORT) runner; (Fußball) half-back; (Schach) bishop

Lauf- zW: ~masche f run, ladder (BRIT); ~pass ▲ m: jdm den ~pass geben (umg) to send sb packing (inf); ~stall m playpen; ~steg m catwalk; ~werk nt (COMPUT) disk drive

Lauge ['laʊgə] f soapy water; (CHEM) alkaline solution

Laune ['laʊnə] f mood, humour; (Einfall) caprice; (schlechte) temper; l~nhaft adj capricious, changeable

launisch adj moody; bad-tempered

Laus [laʊs] (-, Läuse) f louse

lauschen ['laʊʃən] vi to eavesdrop, to listen in

lauschig ['laʊʃɪç] adj snug

lausig ['laʊzɪç] (umg: pej) adj measly; (Kälte) perishing

laut [laʊt] adj loud ♦ adv loudly; (lesen) aloud ♦ präp (+gen od dat) according to; **L~** (-(e)s, -e) m sound

Laute ['laʊtə] f flute

lauten ['laʊtən] vi to say; (Urteil) to be

läuten ['lɔytən] vt, vi to ring, to sound

lauter ['laʊtər] adj (Wasser) clear, pure; (Wahrheit, Charakter) honest ♦ adj inv (Freude, Dummheit etc) sheer ♦ adv nothing but, only

laut- zW: ~hals adv at the top of one's voice; ~los adj noiseless, silent; **L~schrift** f phonetics pl; **L~sprecher** m loudspeaker; ~stark adj vociferous; **L~stärke** f (RADIO) volume

lauwarm ['laʊvarm] adj (auch fig) lukewarm

Lavendel [la'vɛndəl] (-s, -) m lavender

Lawine [la'vi:nə] f avalanche; ~ngefahr f danger of avalanches

lax [laks] adj lax

Lazarett [latsa'rɛt] (-(e)s, -e) nt (MIL) hospital, infirmary

leasen ['li:zən] vt to lease

Leben (-s, -) nt life

leben ['le:bən] vt, vi to live; ~d adj living; ~dig [le'bɛndɪç] adj living, alive; (lebhaft) lively; **L~digkeit** f liveliness

Lebens- zW: ~art f way of life; ~erwartung f life expectancy; l~fähig adj able to live; ~freude f zest for life; ~gefahr f: **in ~gefahr** dangerously ill; l~gefährlich adj dangerous; (Verletzung) critical; ~haltungskosten pl cost of living sg; ~jahr nt year of life; l~länglich (Strafe) for life; ~lauf m curriculum vitae; ~mittel pl food sg; ~mittelgeschäft nt grocer's (shop); ~mittelvergiftung f (MED) food poisoning; l~müde adj tired of life; ~retter m lifesaver; ~standard m standard of living; ~unterhalt m livelihood; ~versicherung f life insurance; ~wandel m way of life; ~weise f lifestyle, way of life; l~wichtig adj vital, essential; ~zeichen nt sign of life

Leber ['le:bər] (-, -n) f liver; ~fleck m mole; ~tran m cod-liver oil; ~wurst f liver sausage

Lebewesen nt creature

leb- ['le:p] zW: ~haft adj lively, vivacious; **L~kuchen** m gingerbread; ~los adj lifeless

Leck [lɛk] (-(e)s, -e) nt leak; l~ adj leaky, leaking; l~en vi (Loch haben) to leak; (schlecken) to lick ♦ vt to lick

lecker ['lɛkər] *adj* delicious, tasty; **L~bissen** *m* dainty morsel

Leder ['le:dər] (**-s, -**) *nt* leather; **~hose** *f* lederhosen; **l~n** *adj* leather; **~waren** *pl* leather goods

ledig ['le:dɪç] *adj* single; **einer Sache** *gen* **~ sein** to be free of sth; **~lich** *adv* merely, solely

leer [le:r] *adj* empty; vacant; **~ machen** to empty; **~ stehend** empty; **L~e** (**-**) *f* emptiness; **~en** *vt, vr* to empty; **L~gewicht** *nt* weight when empty; **L~gut** *nt* empties *pl*; **L~lauf** *m* neutral; **L~ung** *f* emptying; (*Post*) collection

legal [le'ga:l] *adj* legal, lawful; **~i'sieren** *vt* to legalize

legen ['le:gən] *vt* to lay, to put, to place; (*Ei*) to lay ♦ *vr* to lie down; (*fig*) to subside

Legende [le'gɛndə] *f* legend

leger [le'ʒe:r] *adj* casual

Legierung [le'gi:rʊŋ] *f* alloy

Legislative [legɪsla'ti:və] *f* legislature

legitim [legi'ti:m] *adj* legitimate

legitimieren [legiti'mi:rən] *vt* to legitimate ♦ *vr* to prove one's identity

Lehm [le:m] (**-(e)s, -e**) *m* loam; **l~ig** *adj* loamy

Lehne ['le:nə] *f* arm; back; **l~n** *vt, vr* to lean

Lehnstuhl *m* armchair

Lehr- *zW*: **~amt** *nt* teaching profession; **~buch** *nt* textbook

Lehre ['le:rə] *f* teaching, doctrine; (*beruflich*) apprenticeship; (*moralisch*) lesson; (*TECH*) gauge; **l~n** *vt* to teach

Lehrer(in) (**-s, -**) *m(f)* teacher; **~zimmer** *nt* staff room

Lehr- *zW*: **~gang** *m* course; **~jahre** *pl* apprenticeship *sg*; **~kraft** *f* (*förmlich*) teacher; **~ling** *m* apprentice; **~plan** *m* syllabus; **l~reich** *adj* instructive; **~stelle** *f* apprenticeship; **~zeit** *f* apprenticeship

Leib [laɪp] (**-(e)s, -er**) *m* body; **halt ihn mir vom ~!** keep him away from me!; **l~haftig** *adj* personified; (*Teufel*) incarnate; **l~lich** *adj* bodily; (*Vater etc*) own; **~schmerzen** *pl* stomach pains; **~wache** *f* bodyguard

Leiche ['laɪçə] *f* corpse; **~nhalle** *f* mortuary;

~nwagen *m* hearse

Leichnam ['laɪçna:m] (**-(e)s, -e**) *m* corpse

leicht [laɪçt] *adj* light; (*einfach*) easy; **jdm ~ fallen** to be easy for sb; **es sich** *dat* **~ machen** to make things easy for o.s.; **L~athletik** *f* athletics *sg*; **~fertig** *adj* frivolous; **~gläubig** *adj* gullible, credulous; **~hin** *adv* lightly; **L~igkeit** *f* easiness; **mit L~igkeit** with ease; **L~sinn** *m* carelessness; **~sinnig** *adj* careless

Leid [laɪt] (**-(e)s**) *nt* grief, sorrow; **es tut mir/ihm ~** I am/he is sorry; **er/das tut mir ~** I am sorry for him/it; **l~** *adj*: **etw l~ haben** od **sein** to be tired of sth; **l~en** (*unreg*) *vt* to suffer; (*erlauben*) to permit ♦ *vi* to suffer; **jdn/etw nicht l~en können** not to be able to stand sb/sth; **~en** ['laɪdən] (**-s, -**) *nt* suffering; (*Krankheit*) complaint; **~enschaft** *f* passion; **l~enschaftlich** *adj* passionate

leider ['laɪdər] *adv* unfortunately; **ja, ~** yes, I'm afraid so; **~ nicht** I'm afraid not

leidig ['laɪdɪç] *adj* worrying, troublesome

leidlich ['laɪtlɪç] *adj* tolerable ♦ *adv* tolerably

Leid- *zW*: **~tragende(r)** *f(m)* bereaved; (*Benachteiligter*) one who suffers; **~wesen** *nt*: **zu jds ~wesen** to sb's disappointment

Leier ['laɪər] (**-, -n**) *f* lyre; (*fig*) old story; **~kasten** *m* barrel organ

Leihbibliothek *f* lending library

Leihbücherei *f* lending library

leihen ['laɪən] (*unreg*) *vt* to lend; **sich** *dat* **etw ~** to borrow sth

Leih- *zW*: **~gebühr** *f* hire charge; **~haus** *nt* pawnshop; **~wagen** *m* hired car

Leim [laɪm] (**-(e)s, -e**) *m* glue; **l~en** *vt* to glue

Leine ['laɪnə] *f* line, cord; (*Hundeleine*) leash, lead

Leinen *nt* linen; **l~** *adj* linen

Leinwand *f* (*KUNST*) canvas; (*CINE*) screen

leise ['laɪzə] *adj* quiet; (*sanft*) soft, gentle

Leiste ['laɪstə] *f* ledge; (*Zierleiste*) strip; (*ANAT*) groin

leisten ['laɪstən] *vt* (*Arbeit*) to do; (*Gesellschaft*) to keep; (*Ersatz*) to supply; (*vollbringen*) to achieve; **sich** *dat* **etw ~**

können to be able to afford sth
Leistung f performance; (*gute*) achievement; **~sdruck** m pressure; **l~sfähig** adj efficient
Leitartikel m leading article
Leitbild nt model
leiten ['laɪtn] vt to lead; (*Firma*) to manage; (*in eine Richtung*) to direct; (*ELEK*) to conduct
Leiter¹ ['laɪtər] (**-s, -**) m leader, head; (*ELEK*) conductor
Leiter² ['laɪtər] (**-, -n**) f ladder
Leitfaden m guide
Leitplanke f crash barrier
Leitung f (*Führung*) direction; (*CINE, THEAT etc*) production; (*von Firma*) management; directors pl; (*Wasserleitung*) pipe; (*Kabel*) cable; **eine lange ~ haben** to be slow on the uptake
Leitungs- zW: **~draht** m wire; **~rohr** nt pipe; **~wasser** nt tap water
Lektion [lɛktsi'oːn] f lesson
Lektüre [lɛk'tyːrə] f (*Lesen*) reading; (*Lesestoff*) reading matter
Lende ['lɛndə] f loin; **~nstück** nt fillet
lenk- ['lɛŋk] zW: **~bar** adj (*Fahrzeug*) steerable; (*Kind*) manageable; **~en** vt to steer; (*Kind*) to guide; (*Blick, Aufmerksamkeit*): **~en (auf** +*akk*) to direct (at); **L~rad** nt steering wheel; **L~radschloss** ▲ nt steering (wheel) lock; **L~stange** f handlebars pl; **L~ung** f steering
Lepra ['leːpra] (**-**) f leprosy
Lerche ['lɛrçə] f lark
lernbegierig adj eager to learn
lernen ['lɛrnən] vt to learn
lesbar ['leːsbaːr] adj legible
Lesbierin ['lɛsbiərɪn] f lesbian
lesbisch ['lɛsbɪʃ] adj lesbian
Lese ['leːzə] f (*Wein*) harvest
Lesebrille f reading glasses
Lesebuch nt reading book, reader
lesen (*unreg*) vt, vi to read; (*ernten*) to gather, to pick
Leser(in) (**-s, -**) m(f) reader; **~brief** m reader's letter; **l~lich** adj legible
Lesezeichen nt bookmark

Lesung ['leːzʊŋ] f (*PARL*) reading
letzte(r, s) ['lɛtstə(r, s)] adj last; (*neueste*) latest; **zum ~n Mal** for the last time; **~ns** adv lately; **~re(r, s)** adj latter
Leuchte ['lɔʏçtə] f lamp, light; **l~n** vi to shine, to gleam; **~r** (**-s, -**) m candlestick
Leucht- zW: **~farbe** f fluorescent colour; **~rakete** f flare; **~reklame** f neon sign; **~röhre** f strip light; **~turm** m lighthouse
leugnen ['lɔʏɡnən] vt to deny
Leukämie [lɔʏkɛ'miː] f leukaemia
Leukoplast [lɔʏko'plast] (®) (**-(e)s, -e**) nt Elastoplast ®
Leumund ['lɔʏmʊnt] (**-(e)s, -e**) m reputation
Leumundszeugnis nt character reference
Leute ['lɔʏtə] pl people pl
Leutnant ['lɔʏtnant] (**-s, -s** od **-e**) m lieutenant
leutselig ['lɔʏtzeːlɪç] adj amiable
Lexikon ['lɛksikɔn] (**-s, Lexiken** od **Lexika**) nt encyclop(a)edia
Libelle [li'bɛlə] f dragonfly; (*TECH*) spirit level
liberal [libe'raːl] adj liberal; **L~e(r)** f(m) liberal
Licht [lɪçt] (**-(e)s, -er**) nt light; **~bild** nt photograph; (*Dia*) slide; **~blick** m cheering prospect; **l~empfindlich** adj sensitive to light; **l~en** vt to clear; (*Anker*) to weigh ♦ vr to clear up; (*Haar*) to thin; **l~erloh** adv: **l~erloh brennen** to be ablaze; **~hupe** f flashing of headlights; **~jahr** nt light year; **~maschine** f dynamo; **~schalter** m light switch; **~schutzfaktor** m protection factor
Lichtung f clearing, glade
Lid [liːt] (**-(e)s, -er**) nt eyelid; **~schatten** m eyeshadow
lieb [liːp] adj dear; **das ist ~ von dir** that's kind of you; **~ gewinnen** to get fond of; **~ haben** to be fond of; **~äugeln** ['liːbɔʏɡəln] vi insep: **mit etw ~äugeln** to have one's eye on sth; **mit dem Gedanken ~äugeln, etw zu tun** to toy with the idea of doing sth
Liebe ['liːbə] f love; **l~bedürftig** adj: **l~bedürftig sein** to need love; **l~n** vt to love; to like

liebens- *zW:* **~wert** *adj* loveable; **~würdig** *adj* kind; **~würdigerweise** *adv* kindly; **L~würdigkeit** *f* kindness

lieber ['liːbər] *adv* rather, preferably; **ich gehe ~ nicht** I'd rather not go; *siehe auch* **gern; lieb**

Liebes- *zW:* **~brief** *m* love letter; **~kummer** *m:* **~kummer haben** to be lovesick; **~paar** *nt* courting couple, lovers *pl*

liebevoll *adj* loving

lieb- [liːp] *zW:* **~gewinnen** △ *(unreg) vt siehe* **lieb**; **~haben** △ *(unreg) vt siehe* **lieb**; **L~haber (-s, -)** *m* lover; **L~habe'rei** *f* hobby; **~kosen** ['liːpkoːzən] *vt insep* to caress; **~lich** *adj* lovely, charming; **L~ling** *m* darling; **L~lings-** *in zW* favourite; **~los** *adj* unloving; **L~schaft** *f* love affair

Lied [liːt] **(-(e)s, -er)** *nt* song; *(REL)* hymn; **~erbuch** ['liːdər-] *nt* songbook; hymn book

liederlich ['liːdərlɪç] *adj* slovenly; *(Lebenswandel)* loose, immoral; **L~keit** *f* slovenliness; immorality

lief *etc* [liːf] *vb siehe* **laufen**

Lieferant [liːfə'rant] *m* supplier

Lieferbedingungen *pl* terms of delivery

liefern ['liːfərn] *vt* to deliver; *(versorgen mit)* to supply; *(Beweis)* to produce

Liefer- *zW:* **~schein** *m* delivery note; **~termin** *m* delivery date; **~ung** *f* delivery; supply; **~wagen** *m* van; **~zeit** *f* delivery period

Liege ['liːgə] *f* bed

liegen ['liːgən] *(unreg) vi* to lie; *(sich befinden)* to be; **mir liegt nichts/viel daran** it doesn't matter to me/it matters a lot to me; **es liegt bei Ihnen, ob ...** it's up to you whether ...; **Sprachen ~ mir nicht** languages are not my line; **woran liegt es?** what's the cause?; **~ bleiben** *(im Bett)* to stay in bed; *(nicht aufstehen)* to stay lying down; *(vergessen werden)* to be left (behind); **~ lassen** *(vergessen)* to leave behind

Liege- *zW:* **~sitz** *m (AUT)* reclining seat; **~stuhl** *m* deck chair; **~wagen** *m (EISENB)* couchette

Lift [lɪft] **(-(e)s, -e** *od* **-s)** *m* lift

Likör [li'køːr] **(-s, -e)** *m* liqueur

lila ['liːla] *adj inv* purple, lilac; **L~ (-s, -s)** *nt (Farbe)* purple, lilac

Lilie ['liːliə] *f* lily

Limonade [limo'naːdə] *f* lemonade

Limone [li'moːnə] *f* lime

Linde ['lɪndə] *f* lime tree, linden

lindern ['lɪndərn] *vt* to alleviate, to soothe; **Linderung** *f* alleviation

Lineal [line'aːl] **(-s, -e)** *nt* ruler

Linie ['liːniə] *f* line

Linien- *zW:* **~blatt** *nt* ruled sheet; **~flug** *m* scheduled flight; **~richter** *m* linesman

linieren [li'niːrən] *vt* to line

Linke ['lɪŋkə] *f* left side; left hand; *(POL)* left

linkisch *adj* awkward, gauche

links [lɪŋks] *adv* left; to *od* on the left; **~ von mir** on *od* to my left; **L~händer(in) (-s, -)** *m(f)* left-handed person; **L~kurve** *f* left-hand bend; **L~verkehr** *m* driving on the left

Linoleum [li'noːleʊm] **(-s)** *nt* lino(leum)

Linse ['lɪnzə] *f* lentil; *(optisch)* lens *sg*

Lippe ['lɪpə] *f* lip; **~nstift** *m* lipstick

lispeln ['lɪspəln] *vi* to lisp

Lissabon ['lɪsabɔn] **(-s)** *nt* Lisbon

List [lɪst] **(-, -en)** *f* cunning; trick, ruse

Liste ['lɪstə] *f* list

listig ['lɪstɪç] *adj* cunning, sly

Liter ['liːtər] **(-s, -)** *nt od m* litre

literarisch [lɪte'raːrɪʃ] *adj* literary

Literatur [lɪtera'tuːr] *f* literature

Litfaßsäule ['lɪtfaszɔyla] *f* advertising pillar

Liturgie [lɪtʊr'giː] *f* liturgy

liturgisch [li'tʊrgɪʃ] *adj* liturgical

Litze ['lɪtsə] *f* braid; *(ELEK)* flex

Lizenz [li'tsɛnts] *f* licence

Lkw [ɛlkaː've:] **(-(s), -(s))** *m abk =* **Lastkraftwagen**

Lob [loːp] **(-(e)s)** *nt* praise

Lobby ['lɔbi] *f* lobby

loben ['loːbən] *vt* to praise; **~swert** *adj* praiseworthy

löblich ['løːplɪç] *adj* praiseworthy, laudable

Loch [lɔx] **(-(e)s, -̈er)** *nt* hole; **l~en** *vt* to punch holes in; **~er (-s, -)** *m* punch

löcherig ['lϸçəriç] *adj* full of holes

Lochkarte *f* punch card

Lochstreifen *m* punch tape

Locke ['lϸkə] *f* lock, curl; **l~n** *vt* to entice; (*Haare*) to curl; **~nwickler (-s, -)** *m* curler

locker ['lϸkər] *adj* loose; **~lassen** (*unreg*) *vi*: **nicht ~lassen** not to let up; **~n** *vt* to loosen

lockig ['lϸkɪç] *adj* curly

lodern ['loːdərn] *vi* to blaze

Löffel ['lϸfəl] **(-s, -)** *m* spoon

löffeln *vt* to spoon

Loge ['loːʒə] *f* (THEAT) box; (*Freimaurer*) (masonic) lodge; (*Pförtnerloge*) office

Logik ['loːɡɪk] *f* logic

logisch ['loːɡɪʃ] *adj* logical

Logopäde [loɡo'pɛːdə] **(-n, -n)** *m* speech therapist

Lohn [loːn] **(-(e)s, ⁺e)** *m* reward; (*Arbeitslohn*) pay, wages *pl*; **~büro** *nt* wages office; **~empfänger** *m* wage earner

lohnen ['loːnən] *vr unpers* to be worth it ♦ *vt*: (*jdm etw*) **~** to reward (sb for sth); **~d** *adj* worthwhile

Lohn- *zW*: **~erhöhung** *f* pay rise; **~steuer** *f* income tax; **~steuerkarte** *f* (income) tax card; **~streifen** *m* pay slip; **~tüte** *f* pay packet

Lokal [lo'kaːl] **(-(e)s, -e)** *nt* pub(lic house)

lokal *adj* local; **~isieren** *vt* to localize

Lokomotive [lokomo'tiːvə] *f* locomotive

Lokomotivführer *m* engine driver

Lorbeer ['lϸrbeːr] **(-s, -en)** *m* (*auch fig*) laurel; **~blatt** *nt* (KOCH) bay leaf

Los [loːs] **(-es, -e)** *nt* (*Schicksal*) lot, fate; (*Lotterielos*) lottery ticket

los [loːs] *adj* (*locker*) loose; **~!** go on!; **etw ~ sein** to be rid of sth; **was ist ~?** what's the matter?; **dort ist nichts/viel ~** there's nothing/a lot going on there; **~binden** (*unreg*) *vt* to untie

Löschblatt ['lϸʃblat] *nt* sheet of blotting paper

löschen ['lϸʃən] *vt* (*Feuer, Licht*) to put out, to extinguish; (*Durst*) to quench; (COMM) to cancel; (COMPUT) to delete; (*Tonband*) to erase; (*Fracht*) to unload ♦ *vi* (*Feuerwehr*) to

put out a fire; (*Tinte*) to blot

Lösch- *zW*: **~fahrzeug** *nt* fire engine; fire boat; **~gerät** *nt* fire extinguisher; **~papier** *nt* blotting paper

lose ['loːzə] *adj* loose

Lösegeld *nt* ransom

losen ['loːzən] *vi* to draw lots

lösen ['løːzən] *vt* to loosen; (*Rätsel etc*) to solve; (*Verlobung*) to call off; (CHEM) to dissolve; (*Partnerschaft*) to break up; (*Fahrkarte*) to buy ♦ *vr* (*aufgehen*) to come loose; (*Zucker etc*) to dissolve; (*Problem, Schwierigkeit*) to (re)solve itself

los- *zW*: **~fahren** (*unreg*) *vi* to leave; **~gehen** (*unreg*) *vi* to set out; (*anfangen*) to start; (*Bombe*) to go off; **auf jdn ~gehen** to go for sb; **~kaufen** *vt* (*Gefangene, Geißeln*) to pay ransom for; **~kommen** (*unreg*) *vi*: **von etw ~kommen** to get away from sth; **~lassen** (*unreg*) *vt* (*Seil*) to let go of; (*Schimpfe*) to let loose; **~laufen** (*unreg*) *vi* to run off

löslich ['løːslɪç] *adj* soluble; **L~keit** *f* solubility

los- *zW*: **~lösen** *vt*: **(sich) ~lösen** to free (o.s.); **~machen** *vt* to loosen; (*Boot*) to unmoor *vr* to get away; **~schrauben** *vt* to unscrew

Losung ['loːzʊŋ] *f* watchword, slogan

Lösung ['løːzʊŋ] *f* (*Lockermachen*) loosening; (*eines Rätsels, CHEM*) solution; **~smittel** *nt* solvent

los- *zW*: **~werden** (*unreg*) *vt* to get rid of; **~ziehen** (*unreg*) (*umg*) *vi* (*sich aufmachen*) to set off

Lot [loːt] **(-(e)s, -e)** *nt* plumbline; **im ~** vertical; (*fig*) on an even keel

löten ['løːtən] *vt* to solder

Lothringen ['loːtrɪŋən] **(-s)** *nt* Lorraine

Lotse ['loːtsə] **(-n, -n)** *m* pilot; (AVIAT) air traffic controller; **l~n** *vt* to pilot; (*umg*) to lure

Lotterie [lϸtə'riː] *f* lottery

Lotto ['lϸto] **(-s, -s)** *nt* national lottery; **~zahlen** *pl* winning lottery numbers

Löwe ['løːvə] **(-n, -n)** *m* lion; (ASTROL) Leo; **~nanteil** *m* lion's share; **~nzahn** *m*

dandelion

loyal [loaˈjaːl] *adj* loyal; **L~ität** *f* loyalty

Luchs [lʊks] **(-es, -e)** *m* lynx

Lücke [ˈlʏkə] *f* gap

Lücken- *zW*: **~büßer (-s, -)** *m* stopgap; **l~haft** *adj* full of gaps; *(Versorgung, Vorräte etc)* inadequate; **l~los** *adj* complete

Luft [lʊft] **(-, ⁼e)** *f* air; *(Atem)* breath; **in der ~ liegen** to be in the air; **jdn wie ~ behandeln** to ignore sb; **~angriff** *m* air raid; **~ballon** *m* balloon; **~blase** *f* air bubble; **l~dicht** *adj* airtight; **~druck** *m* atmospheric pressure

lüften [ˈlʏftən] *vt* to air; *(Hut)* to lift, to raise ♦ *vi* to let some air in

Luft- *zW*: **~fahrt** *f* aviation; **~fracht** *f* air freight; **l~gekühlt** *adj* air-cooled; **~gewehr** *nt* air rifle, airgun; **l~ig** *adj (Ort)* breezy; *(Raum)* airy; *(Kleider)* summery; **~kissenfahrzeug** *nt* hovercraft; **~kurort** *m* health resort; **l~leer** *adj*: **l~leerer Raum** vacuum; **~linie** *f*: **in der ~linie** as the crow flies; **~loch** *nt* air hole; *(AVIAT)* air pocket; **~matratze** *f* Lilo ® *(BRIT)* air mattress; **~pirat** *m* hijacker; **~post** *f* airmail; **~pumpe** *f* air pump; **~röhre** *f (ANAT)* windpipe; **~schlange** *f* streamer; **~schutzkeller** *m* air-raid shelter; **~verkehr** *m* air traffic; **~verschmutzung** *f* air pollution; **~waffe** *f* air force; **~zug** *m* draught

Lüge [ˈlyːgə] *f* lie; **jdn/etw ~n strafen** to give the lie to sb/sth; **l~n** *(unreg) vi* to lie

Lügner(in) (-s, -) *m(f)* liar

Luke [ˈluːkə] *f* dormer window; hatch

Lump [lʊmp] **(-en, -en)** *m* scamp, rascal

Lumpen [ˈlʊmpən] **(-s, -)** *m* rag

lumpen [ˈlʊmpən] *vi*: **sich nicht ~ lassen** not to be mean

lumpig [ˈlʊmpɪç] *adj* shabby

Lupe [ˈluːpə] *f* magnifying glass; **unter die ~ nehmen** *(fig)* to scrutinize

Lust [lʊst] **(-, ⁼e)** *f* joy, delight; *(Neigung)* desire; **~ haben zu** *od* **auf etw** *akk***/etw zu tun** to feel like sth/doing sth

lüstern [ˈlʏstərn] *adj* lustful, lecherous

lustig [ˈlʊstɪç] *adj (komisch)* amusing, funny;

(fröhlich) cheerful

Lust- *zW*: **l~los** *adj* unenthusiastic; **~mord** *m* sex(ual) murder; **~spiel** *nt* comedy

lutschen [ˈlʊtʃən] *vt, vi* to suck; **am Daumen ~** to suck one's thumb

Lutscher [ˈlʊtʃər] **(-s, -)** *m* lollipop

luxuriös [lʊksuriˈøːs] *adj* luxurious

Luxus [ˈlʊksʊs] **(-)** *m* luxury; **~artikel** *pl* luxury goods; **~hotel** *nt* luxury hotel

Luzern [luˈtsɛrn] **(-s)** *nt* Lucerne

Lymphe [ˈlʏmfə] *f* lymph

lynchen [ˈlʏnçən] *vt* to lynch

Lyrik [ˈlyːrɪk] *f* lyric poetry; **~er (-s, -)** *m* lyric poet

lyrisch [ˈlyːrɪʃ] *adj* lyrical

M, m

m *abk* = **Meter**

Machart *f* make

machbar *adj* feasible

SCHLÜSSELWORT

machen [ˈmaxən] *vt* **1** to do; *(herstellen, zubereiten)* to make; **was machst du da?** what are you doing (there)?; **das ist nicht zu machen** that can't be done; **das Radio leiser machen** to turn the radio down; **aus Holz gemacht** made of wood

2 *(verursachen, bewirken)* to make; **jdm Angst machen** to make sb afraid; **das macht die Kälte** it's the cold that does that

3 *(ausmachen)* to matter; **das macht nichts** that doesn't matter; **die Kälte macht mir nichts** I don't mind the cold

4 *(kosten, ergeben)* to be; **3 und 5 macht 8** 3 and 5 is *od* are 8; **was** *od* **wie viel macht das?** how much does that make?

5 was macht die Arbeit? how's the work going?; **was macht dein Bruder?** how is your brother doing?; **das Auto machen lassen** to have the car done; **machs gut!** take care!; *(viel Glück)* good luck!

♦ *vi*: **mach schnell!** hurry up!; **Schluss machen** to finish (off); **mach schon!** come on!; **das macht müde** it makes you tired; **in etw** *dat* **machen** to be *od* deal in sth ♦ *vr* to come along (nicely); **sich an etw** *akk* **machen** to set about sth; **sich verständlich machen** to make o.s. understood; **sich** *dat* **viel aus jdm/etw machen** to like sb/sth

Macht [maxt] (-, ⁻e) *f* power; ~**haber** (-s, -) *m* ruler

mächtig ['mɛçtɪç] *adj* powerful, mighty; (*umg: ungeheuer*) enormous

Macht- *zW*: **m~los** *adj* powerless; ~**probe** *f* trial of strength; ~**wort** *nt*: **ein ~wort sprechen** to exercise one's authority

Mädchen ['mɛːtçən] *nt* girl; **m~haft** *adj* girlish; ~**name** *m* maiden name

Made ['maːdə] *f* maggot

madig ['maːdɪç] *adj* maggoty; **jdm etw ~ machen** to spoil sth for sb

mag *etc* [maːk] *vb siehe* **mögen**

Magazin [maga'tsiːn] (-s, -e) *nt* magazine

Magen ['maːgən] (-s, -od ⁻) *m* stomach; ~**geschwür** *nt* (*MED*) stomach ulcer; ~**schmerzen** *pl* stomachache *sg*

mager ['maːgər] *adj* lean; (*dünn*) thin; **M~keit** *f* leanness; thinness

Magie [ma'giː] *f* magic

magisch ['maːgɪʃ] *adj* magical

Magnet [ma'gneːt] (-s *od* -en, -en) *m* magnet; **m~isch** *adj* magnetic; ~**nadel** *f* magnetic needle

mähen ['mɛːən] *vt, vi* to mow

Mahl [maːl] (-(e)s, -e) *nt* meal; **m~en** (*unreg*) *vt* to grind; ~**zeit** *f* meal ♦ *excl* enjoy your meal

Mahnbrief *m* reminder

Mähne ['mɛːnə] *f* mane

mahn- ['maːn] *zW*: ~**en** *vt* to remind; (*warnend*) to warn; (*wegen Schuld*) to demand payment from; **M~mal** *nt* memorial; **M~ung** *f* reminder; admonition, warning

Mai [maɪ] (-(e)s, -e) *m* May; ~**glöckchen** *nt* lily of the valley

Mailand ['maɪlant] *nt* Milan

mailändisch *adj* Milanese

mailen ['meːlən] *vti* to e-mail

Mais [maɪs] (-es, -e) *m* maize, corn (*US*); ~**kolben** *m* corncob; ~**mehl** *nt* (*KOCH*) corn meal

Majestät [majɛs'tɛːt] *f* majesty; **m~isch** *adj* majestic

Majonäse ▲ [majo'nɛːzə] *f* mayonnaise

Major [ma'joːr] (-s, -e) *m* (*MIL*) major; (*AVIAT*) squadron leader

Majoran [majo'raːn] (-s, -e) *m* marjoram

makaber [ma'kaːbər] *adj* macabre

Makel ['maːkəl] (-s, -) *m* blemish; (*moralisch*) stain; **m~los** *adj* immaculate, spotless

mäkeln ['mɛːkəln] *vi* to find fault

Makler(in) ['maːklər(ɪn)] (-s, -) *m(f)* broker

Makrele [ma'kreːlə] *f* mackerel

Mal [maːl] (-(e)s, -e) *nt* mark, sign; (*Zeitpunkt*) time; **ein für alle ~** once and for all; **m~** *adv* times; (*umg*) *siehe* **einmal** ♦ *suffix*: **-m~** -times

malen *vt, vi* to paint

Maler (-s, -) *m* painter; **Male'rei** *f* painting; **m~isch** *adj* picturesque

Malkasten *m* paintbox

Mallorca [ma'jɔrka, ma'lɔrka] (-s) *nt* Majorca

malnehmen (*unreg*) *vt, vi* to multiply

Malz [malts] (-es) *nt* malt; ~**bier** *nt* (*KOCH*) malt beer; ~**bonbon** *nt* cough drop; ~**kaffee** *m* malt coffee

Mama ['mamaː] (-, -s) (*umg*) *f* mum(my) (*BRIT*), mom(my) (*US*)

Mami ['mami] (-, -s) = **Mama**

Mammut ['mamʊt] (-s, -e *od* -s) *nt* mammoth

man [man] *pron* one, you; **~ sagt, ...** they *od* people say ...; **wie schreibt ~ das?** how do you write it?, how is it written?

Manager(in) ['mɛnɪdʒər(ɪn)] (-s, -) *m(f)* manager

manch [manç] (*unver*) *pron* many a

manche(r, s) ['mançə(r, s)] *adj* many a; (*pl: einige*) a number of ♦ *pron* some

mancherlei [mançər'laɪ] *adj inv* various ♦ *pron inv* a variety of things

manchmal *adv* sometimes

Mandant(in) [man'dant(ɪn)] *m(f)* (*JUR*) client

Mandarine [manda'riːnə] *f* mandarin,

tangerine

Mandat [man'da:t] **(-(e)s, -e)** *nt* mandate

Mandel ['mandəl] **(-, -n)** *f* almond; (ANAT) tonsil; **~entzündung** *f* (MED) tonsillitis

Manege [ma'ne:ʒə] *f* ring, arena

Mangel ['maŋəl] **(-s, ᵘ)** *m* lack; (Knappheit) shortage; (Fehler) defect, fault; **~ an** +*dat* shortage of; **~erscheinung** *f* deficiency symptom; **m~haft** *adj* poor; (fehlerhaft) defective, faulty; **m~n** *vi unpers*: **es m~t jdm an etw** *dat* sb lacks sth ♦ *vt* (Wäsche) to mangle

mangels *präp* +*gen* for lack of

Manie [ma'ni:] *f* mania

Manier [ma'ni:r] **(-)** *f* manner; style; (pej) mannerism; **~en** *pl* (Umgangsformen) manners; **m~lich** *adj* well-mannered

Manifest [mani'fɛst] **(-es, -e)** *nt* manifesto

Maniküre [mani'ky:rə] *f* manicure

manipulieren [manipu'li:rən] *vt* to manipulate

Manko ['maŋko] **(-s, -s)** *nt* deficiency; (COMM) deficit

Mann [man] **(-(e)s, ᵘer)** *m* man; (Ehemann) husband; (NAUT) hand; **seinen ~ stehen** to hold one's own

Männchen ['mɛnçən] *nt* little man; (Tier) male

Mannequin [manə'kɛ̃:] **(-s, -s)** *nt* fashion model

männlich ['mɛnlɪç] *adj* (BIOL) male; (fig, GRAM) masculine

Mannschaft *f* (SPORT, fig) team; (AVIAT, NAUT) crew; (MIL) other ranks *pl*

Manöver [ma'nø:vər] **(-s, -)** *nt* manoeuvre

manövrieren [manø'vri:rən] *vt, vi* to manoeuvre

Mansarde [man'zardə] *f* attic

Manschette [man'ʃɛtə] *f* cuff; (TECH) collar; sleeve; **~nknopf** *m* cufflink

Mantel ['mantəl] **(-s, ᵘ)** *m* coat; (TECH) casing, jacket

Manuskript [manu'skrɪpt] **(-(e)s, -e)** *nt* manuscript

Mappe ['mapə] *f* briefcase; (Aktenmappe) folder

Märchen ['mɛːrçən] *nt* fairy tale; **m~haft** *adj* fabulous; **~prinz** *m* Prince Charming

Margarine [marga'ri:nə] *f* margarine

Margerite [margə'ri:tə] *f* (BOT) marguerite

Marienkäfer [ma'ri:ɔnkɛːfər] *m* ladybird

Marine [ma'ri:nə] *f* navy; **m~blau** *adj* navy blue

marinieren [mari'ni:rən] *vt* to marinate

Marionette [mario'nɛtə] *f* puppet

Mark¹ [mark] **(-, -)** *f* (Münze) mark

Mark² [mark] **(-(e)s)** *nt* (Knochenmark) marrow; **jdm durch ~ und Bein gehen** to go right through sb

markant [mar'kant] *adj* striking

Marke ['markə] *f* mark; (Warensorte) brand; (Fabrikat) make; (Rabatt~, Brief~) stamp; (Essen~) ticket; (aus Metall etc) token, disc

Markenartikel *m* proprietary article

markieren [mar'ki:rən] *vt* to mark; (umg) to act ♦ *vi* (umg) to act it

Markierung *f* marking

Markise [mar'ki:zə] *f* awning

Markstück *nt* one-mark piece

Markt [markt] **(-(e)s, ᵘe)** *m* market; **~forschung** *f* market research; **~lücke** *f* (COMM) opening, gap in the market; **~platz** *m* market place; **m~üblich** *adj* (Preise, Mieten) standard, usual; **~wert** *m* (COMM) market value; **~wirtschaft** *f* market economy

Marmelade [marmə'la:də] *f* jam

Marmor ['marmɔr] **(-s, -e)** *m* marble; **m~ieren** [-'ri:rən] *vt* to marble

Marokko [ma'rɔko] **(-s)** *nt* Morocco

Marone [ma'ro:nə] **(-, -n od Maroni)** *f* chestnut

Marotte [ma'rɔtə] *f* fad, quirk

Marsch¹ [marʃ] **(-, -en)** *f* marsh

Marsch² [marʃ] **(-(e)s, ᵘe)** *m* march ♦ *excl* march!; **~befehl** *m* marching orders *pl*; **m~bereit** *adj* ready to move; **m~ieren** [mar'ʃi:rən] *vi* to march

Märtyrer(in) ['mɛrtyrər(ɪn)] **(-s, -)** *m(f)* martyr

März [mɛrts] **(-(es), -e)** *m* March

Marzipan [martsi'pa:n] **(-s, -e)** *nt* marzipan

Masche ['maʃə] *f* mesh; (Strickmasche) stitch; **das ist die neueste ~** that's the

latest thing; **~ndraht** m wire mesh;
m~nfest adj run-resistant

Maschine [ma'ʃiːnə] f machine; (*Motor*)
engine; (*Schreibmaschine*) typewriter; **~
schreiben** to type; **m~ll** [maʃi'nɛl] adj
machine(-); mechanical

Maschinen- zW: **~bauer** m mechanical
engineer; **~gewehr** nt machine gun;
~pistole f submachine gun; **~schaden** m
mechanical fault; **~schlosser** m fitter;
~schrift f typescript

Maschinist [maʃi'nɪst] m engineer

Maser ['maːzər] (**-, -n**) f (*von Holz*) grain; **~n**
pl (*MED*) measles sg

Maske ['maskə] f mask; **~nball** m fancy-
dress ball

maskieren [mas'kiːrən] vt to mask;
(*verkleiden*) to dress up ♦ vr to disguise o.s.;
to dress up

Maskottchen [mas'kɔtçən] nt (lucky)
mascot

Maß¹ [maːs] (**-es, -e**) nt measure;
(*Mäßigung*) moderation; (*Grad*) degree,
extent; **~ halten** to exercise moderation

Maß² [maːs] (**-, -(e)**) f litre of beer

Massage [ma'saːʒə] f massage

Maßanzug m made-to-measure suit

Maßarbeit f (*fig*) neat piece of work

Masse ['masə] f mass

Maßeinheit f unit of measurement

Massen- zW: **~artikel** m mass-produced
article; **~grab** nt mass grave; **m~haft** adj
loads of; **~medien** pl mass media pl;
~veranstaltung f mass meeting;
m~weise adv on a large scale

Masseur [ma'søːr] m masseur; **~in** f
masseuse

maßgebend adj authoritative

maßhalten △ (*unreg*) vi siehe **Maß¹**

massieren [ma'siːrən] vt to massage; (*MIL*)
to mass

massig ['masɪç] adj massive; (*umg*) massive
amount of

mäßig ['mɛːsɪç] adj moderate; **~en**
['mɛːsɪgən] vt to restrain, to moderate;
M~keit f moderation

Massiv (**-s, -e**) nt massif

massiv [ma'siːf] adj solid; (*fig*) heavy, rough

Maß- zW: **~krug** m tankard; **m~los** adj
extreme; **~nahme** f measure, step; **~stab**
m rule, measure; (*fig*) standard; (*GEOG*)
scale; **m~voll** adj moderate

Mast [mast] (**-(e)s, -e(n)**) m mast; (*ELEK*)
pylon

mästen ['mɛstən] vt to fatten

Material [materi'aːl] (**-s, -ien**) nt material(s);
~fehler m material defect; **~ismus** [-
'lɪsmʊs] m materialism; **m~istisch** [-'lɪstɪʃ]
adj materialistic

Materie [ma'teːriə] f matter, substance

materiell [materi'ɛl] adj material

Mathematik [matema'tiːk] f mathematics
sg; **~er(in)** [mate'maːtikər(ɪn)] (**-s, -**) m(f)
mathematician

mathematisch [mate'maːtɪʃ] adj
mathematical

Matjeshering ['matjəsheːrɪŋ] m (*KOCH*)
young herring

Matratze [ma'tratsə] f mattress

Matrixdrucker ['maːtrɪks-] m dot-matrix
printer

Matrose [ma'troːzə] (**-n, -n**) m sailor

Matsch [matʃ] (**-(e)s**) m mud;
(*Schneematsch*) slush; **m~ig** adj muddy;
slushy

matt [mat] adj weak; (*glanzlos*) dull; (*PHOT*)
matt; (*SCHACH*) mate

Matte ['matə] f mat

Mattscheibe f (*TV*) screen

Mauer ['mauər] (**-, -n**) f wall; **m~n** vi to
build; to lay bricks ♦ vt to build

Maul [maul] (**-(e)s, Mäuler**) nt mouth;
m~en (*umg*) vi to grumble; **~esel** m mule;
~korb m muzzle; **~sperre** f lockjaw;
~tasche f (*KOCH*) pasta envelopes stuffed
and used in soup; **~tier** nt mule; **~wurf** m
mole

Maurer ['maurər] (**-s, -**) m bricklayer

Maus [maus] (**-, Mäuse**) f (*auch COMPUT*)
mouse

Mause- ['mauzə] zW: **~falle** f mousetrap;
m~n vi to catch mice ♦ vt (*umg*) to pinch;
m~tot adj stone dead

Maut- [maut] zW: **~gebühr** f toll (charge);

~**straße** f toll road

maximal [maksi'maːl] *adj* maximum ♦ *adv* at most

Mayonnaise [majɔ'nɛːzə] f mayonnaise

Mechan- [me'çaːn] *zW:* ~**ik** f mechanics *sg;* *(Getriebe)* mechanics *pl;* ~**iker (-s, -)** *m* mechanic, engineer; **m~isch** *adj* mechanical; ~**ismus** *m* mechanism

meckern ['mɛkərn] *vi* to bleat; *(umg)* to moan

Medaille [me'daljə] f medal

Medaillon [medal'jõː] **(-s, -s)** *nt (Schmuck)* locket

Medikament [medika'mɛnt] *nt* medicine

Meditation [meditatsi'oːn] f meditation

meditieren [medi'tiːrən] *vi* to meditate

Medizin [medi'tsiːn] **(-, -en)** f medicine; **m~isch** *adj* medical

Meer [meːr] **(-(e)s, -e)** *nt* sea; ~**enge** f straits *pl;* ~**esfrüchte** *pl* seafood *sg;* ~**esspiegel** *m* sea level; ~**rettich** *m* horseradish; ~**schweinchen** *nt* guinea-pig

Mehl [meːl] **(-(e)s, -e)** *nt* flour; **m~ig** *adj* floury; **m~schwitze** f *(KOCH)* roux; ~**speise** f *(KOCH)* flummery

mehr [meːr] *adj, adv* more; ~**deutig** *adj* ambiguous; ~**ere** *adj* several; ~**eres** *pron* several things; ~**fach** *adj* multiple; *(wiederholt)* repeated; **M~fahrtenkarte** f multi-journey ticket; **M~heit** f majority; ~**malig** *adj* repeated; ~**mals** *adv* repeatedly; ~**stimmig** *adj* for several voices; ~**stimmig singen** to harmonize; **M~wertsteuer** f value added tax; **M~zahl** f majority; *(GRAM)* plural

Mehrzweck- *in zW* multipurpose

meiden ['maɪdən] *(unreg) vt* to avoid

Meile ['maɪlə] f mile; ~**nstein** *m* milestone; **m~nweit** *adj* for miles

mein(e) [maɪn] *adj* my; ~**e(r, s)** *pron* mine

Meineid ['maɪnʔaɪt] *m* perjury

meinen ['maɪnən] *vi* to think ♦ *vt* to think; *(sagen)* to say; *(sagen wollen)* to mean; **das will ich ~** I should think so

mein- *zW:* ~**erseits** *adv* for my part; ~**etwegen** *adv (für mich)* for my sake; *(wegen mir)* on my account; *(von mir aus)* as

far as I'm concerned; I don't care *od* mind; ~**etwillen** *adv:* **um ~etwillen** for my sake, on my account

Meinung ['maɪnʊŋ] f opinion; **ganz meine ~** I quite agree; **jdm die ~ sagen** to give sb a piece of one's mind

Meinungs- *zW:* ~**austausch** *m* exchange of views; ~**umfrage** f opinion poll; ~**verschiedenheit** f difference of opinion

Meise ['maɪzə] f tit(mouse)

Meißel ['maɪsəl] **(-s, -)** *m* chisel

meist [maɪst] *adj* most ♦ *adv* mostly; **am ~en** the most; ~**ens** *adv* generally, usually

Meister ['maɪstər] **(-s, -)** *m* master; *(SPORT)* champion; **m~haft** *adj* masterly; **m~n** *vt (Schwierigkeiten etc)* to overcome, conquer; ~**schaft** f mastery; *(SPORT)* championship; ~**stück** *nt* masterpiece; ~**werk** *nt* masterpiece

Melancholie [melaŋko'liː] f melancholy; **melancholisch** [melaŋ'koːlɪʃ] *adj* melancholy

Melde- ['mɛldə] *zW:* ~**frist** f registration period; **m~n** *vt* to report ♦ *vr* to report; *(SCH)* to put one's hand up; *(freiwillig)* to volunteer; *(auf etw, am Telefon)* to answer; **sich m~n bei** to report to; to register with; **sich zu Wort m~n** to ask to speak; ~**pflicht** f obligation to register with the police; ~**schluss** ▲ *m* closing date; ~**stelle** f registration office

Meldung ['mɛldʊŋ] f announcement; *(Bericht)* report

meliert [me'liːrt] *adj (Haar)* greying; *(Wolle)* flecked

melken ['mɛlkən] *(unreg) vt* to milk

Melodie [melo'diː] f melody, tune

melodisch [me'loːdɪʃ] *adj* melodious, tuneful

Melone [me'loːnə] f melon; *(Hut)* bowler (hat)

Membran [mɛm'braːn] **(-, -en)** f *(TECH)* diaphragm

Memoiren [memo'aːrən] *pl* memoirs

Menge ['mɛŋə] f quantity; *(Menschenmenge)* crowd; *(große Anzahl)* lot (of); **m~n** *vt* to mix ♦ *vr:* **sich m~n in** +*akk* to meddle

with; ~**nlehre** f (MATH) set theory;
~**nrabatt** m bulk discount

Mensch [mɛnʃ] (-**en**, -**en**) m human being,
man; person ♦ excl hey!; **kein ~** nobody

Menschen- zW: ~**affe** m (ZOOL) ape;
m~**freundlich** adj philanthropical;
~**kenner** m judge of human nature;
m~**leer** adj deserted; m~**möglich** adj
humanly possible; ~**rechte** pl human
rights; m~**unwürdig** adj beneath human
dignity; ~**verstand** m: **gesunder**
~**verstand** common sense

Mensch- zW: ~**heit** f humanity, mankind;
m~**lich** adj human; (human) humane;
~**lichkeit** f humanity

Menstruation [mɛnstruatsi'o:n] f
menstruation

Mentalität [mɛntali'tɛ:t] f mentality

Menü [me'ny:] (-**s**, -**s**) nt (auch COMPUT)
menu

Merk- [merk] zW: ~**blatt** nt instruction
sheet od leaflet; m~**en** vt to notice; **sich**
dat **etw** m~**en** to remember sth; m~**lich**
adj noticeable; ~**mal** nt sign, characteristic;
m~**würdig** adj odd

messbar ▲ ['mesba:r] adj measurable

Messbecher ▲ m measuring jug

Messe ['mesə] f fair; (ECCL) mass; ~**gelände**
nt exhibition centre; ~**halle** f pavilion at a
fair

messen (unreg) vt to measure ♦ vr to
compete

Messer (-**s**, -) nt knife; ~**spitze** f knife
point; (in Rezept) pinch

Messestand m stall at a fair

Messgerät ▲ nt measuring device, gauge

Messing ['mesɪŋ] (-**s**) nt brass

Metall [me'tal] (-**s**, -**e**) nt metal; m~**isch** adj
metallic

Meter ['me:tər] (-**s**, -) nt od m metre; ~**maß**
nt tape measure

Methode [me'to:də] f method;
methodisch adj methodical

Metropole [metro'po:lə] f metropolis

Metzger ['metsgər] (-**s**, -) m butcher; ~**ei**
[-'raɪ] f butcher's (shop)

Meute ['mɔytə] f pack; ~'**rei** f mutiny;

m~**rn** vi to mutiny

miauen [mi'auən] vi to miaow

mich [mɪç] (akk von **ich**) pron me; myself

Miene ['mi:nə] f look, expression

mies [mi:s] (umg) adj lousy

Miet- ['mi:t] zW: ~**auto** nt hired car; ~**e** f
rent; **zur ~e wohnen** to live in rented
accommodation; m~**en** vt to rent; (Auto)
to hire; ~**er(in)** (-**s**, -) m(f) tenant; ~**shaus**
nt tenement, block of (rented) flats;
~**vertrag** m lease

Migräne [mi'grɛ:nə] f migraine

Mikro- ['mikro] zW: ~**fon**, ~**phon**
[-'fo:n] (-**s**, -**e**) nt microphone; ~**skop**
[-'sko:p] (-**s**, -**e**) nt microscope;
m~**skopisch** adj microscopic;
~**wellenherd** m microwave (oven)

Milch [mɪlç] (-) f milk; ~**glas** nt frosted
glass; m~**ig** adj milky; ~**kaffee** m white
coffee; ~**mann** (pl -**männer**) m milkman;
~**mixgetränk** nt (KOCH) milkshake;
~**pulver** nt powdered milk; ~**straße** f
Milky Way; ~**zahn** m milk tooth

mild [mɪlt] adj mild; (Richter) lenient;
(freundlich) kind, charitable; **M~e** f
mildness; leniency; ~**ern** vt to mitigate, to
soften; (Schmerz) to alleviate; ~**ernde**
Umstände extenuating circumstances

Milieu [mili'ø:] (-**s**, -**s**) nt background,
environment; m~**geschädigt** adj
maladjusted

Mili- [mili] zW: m~**tant** [-'tant] adj militant;
~**tär** [-'tɛ:r] (-**s**) nt military, army;
~'**tärgericht** nt military court; m~'**tärisch**
adj military

Milli- ['mili] zW: ~**ardär** [-ar'dɛ:r] m
multimillionaire; ~**arde** [-'ardə] f milliard,
billion (BES US); ~**meter** m millimetre;
~**meterpapier** nt graph paper

Million [mɪli'o:n] (-, -**en**) f million; ~**är**
[-o'nɛ:r] m millionaire

Milz [mɪlts] (-, -**en**) f spleen

Mimik ['mi:mɪk] f mime

Mimose [mi'mo:zə] f mimosa, (fig) sensitive
person

minder ['mɪndər] adj inferior ♦ adv less;
M~heit f minority; ~**jährig** adj minor;

M~jährige(r) f(m) minor; **~n** vt, vr to decrease, to diminish; **M~ung** f decrease; **~wertig** adj inferior; **M~wertigkeitskomplex** m inferiority complex

Mindest- ['mɪndəst] zW: **~alter** nt minimum age; **~betrag** m minimum amount; **m~e(r, s)** adj least; **zum ~en** od **m~en** at least; **m~ens** adv at least; **~haltbarkeitsdatum** nt best-before date; **~lohn** m minimum wage; **~maß** nt minimum

Mine ['mi:nə] f mine; (Bleistiftmine) lead; (Kugelschreibermine) refill

Mineral [mine'ra:l] (**-s, -e** od **-ien**) nt mineral; **m~isch** adj mineral; **~wasser** nt mineral water

Miniatur [minia'tu:r] f miniature

Mini- zW: **~golf** ['mɪnɪɡɔlf] nt miniature golf, crazy golf; **m~mal** [mini'ma:l] adj minimal; **~mum** ['mɪnimum] nt minimum; **~rock** m miniskirt

Minister [mi'nɪstər] (**-s, -**) m minister; **m~iell** adj ministerial; **~ium** nt ministry; **~präsident** m prime minister

Minus ['mi:nʊs] (**-, -**) nt deficit

minus adv minus; **M~zeichen** nt minus sign

Minute [mi'nu:tə] f minute

Minze ['mɪntsə] f mint

mir [mi:r] (dat von **ich**) pron (to) me; **~ nichts, dir nichts** just like that

Misch- ['mɪʃ] zW: **~brot** nt bread made from more than one kind of flour; **~ehe** f mixed marriage; **m~en** vt to mix; **~ling** m half-caste; **~ung** f mixture

miserabel [mizə'ra:bəl] (umg) adj (Essen, Film) dreadful

Miss- ▲ ['mɪs] zW: **~behagen** nt discomfort, uneasiness; **~bildung** f deformity; **m~'billigen** vt insep to disapprove of; **~brauch** m abuse; (falscher Gebrauch) misuse; **m~'brauchen** vt insep to abuse; **jdn zu** od **für etw m~brauchen** to use sb for od to do sth; **~erfolg** m failure; **~fallen** (**-s**) nt displeasure; **m~'fallen** (unreg) vi insep: **jdm m~fallen**

to displease sb; **~geschick** nt misfortune; **m~glücken** [mɪs'ɡlʏkən] vi insep to fail; **jdm m~glückt etw** sb does not succeed with sth; **~griff** m mistake; **~gunst** f envy; **m~günstig** adj envious; **m~'handeln** vt insep to ill-treat; **~'handlung** f ill-treatment

Mission [mɪsi'o:n] f mission; **~ar(in)** m(f) missionary

Miss- ▲ zW: **~klang** m discord; **~kredit** m discredit; **m~lingen** [mɪs'lɪŋən] (unreg) vi insep to fail; **~mut** m sullenness; **m~mutig** adj sullen; **m~'raten** (unreg) vi insep to turn out badly ♦ adj ill-bred; **~stand** m bad state of affairs; abuse; **m~'trauen** vi insep to mistrust; **~trauen** (**-s**) nt distrust, suspicion; **~trauensantrag** m (POL) motion of no confidence; **m~trauisch** adj distrustful, suspicious; **~verhältnis** nt disproportion; **~verständnis** nt misunderstanding; **m~verstehen** (unreg) vt insep to misunderstand; **~wirtschaft** f mismanagement

Mist [mɪst] (**-(e)s**) m dung; dirt; (umg) rubbish

Mistel (**-, -n**) f mistletoe

Misthaufen m dungheap

mit [mɪt] präp +dat with; (~tels) by ♦ adv along, too; **~ der Bahn** by train; **~ 10 Jahren** at the age of 10; **wollen Sie ~?** do you want to come along?

Mitarbeit ['mɪtarbaɪt] f cooperation; **m~en** vi to cooperate, to collaborate; **~er(in)** m(f) collaborator; co-worker ♦ pl (Personal) staff

Mit- zW: **~bestimmung** f participation in decision-making; **m~bringen** (unreg) vt to bring along

miteinander [mɪtaɪ'nandər] adv together, with one another

miterleben vt to see, to witness

Mitesser ['mɪtɛsər] (**-s, -**) m blackhead

mitfahr- zW: **~en** vi to accompany; (auf Reise auch) to travel with; **M~gelegenheit** f lift; **M~zentrale** f agency for arranging lifts

mitfühlend adj sympathetic, compassionate

Mit- zW: **m~geben** (*unreg*) vt to give; **~gefühl** nt sympathy; **m~gehen** (*unreg*) vi to go/come along; **m~genommen** adj done in, in a bad way; **~gift** f dowry

Mitglied ['mɪtgliːt] nt member; **~sbeitrag** m membership fee; **~schaft** f membership

Mit- zW: **m~halten** (*unreg*) vt to keep up; **m~helfen** (*unreg*) vi to help; **~hilfe** f help, assistance; **m~hören** vt to listen in to; **m~kommen** (*unreg*) vi to come along; (*verstehen*) to keep up, to follow; **~läufer** m hanger-on; (*POL*) fellow traveller

Mitleid nt sympathy; (*Erbarmen*) compassion; **m~ig** adj sympathetic; **m~slos** adj pitiless, merciless

Mit- zW: **m~machen** vt to join in, to take part in; **~mensch** m fellow man; **m~nehmen** (*unreg*) vt to take along/away; (*anstrengen*) to wear out, to exhaust; **zum ~nehmen** to take away; **m~reden** vi: **bei etw ~reden** to have a say in sth; **m~reißen** (*unreg*) vt to carry away/along; (*fig*) to thrill, captivate

mitsamt [mɪt'zamt] präp +dat together with

Mitschuld f complicity; **m~ig** adj: **m~ig (an** +dat) implicated (in); (*an Unfall*) partly responsible (for)

Mit- zW: **~schüler(in)** m(f) schoolmate; **m~spielen** vi to join in, to take part; **~spieler(in)** m(f) partner

Mittag ['mɪtaːk] (-(e)s, -e) m midday, lunchtime; (*zu*) **~ essen** to have lunch; **heute/morgen ~** today/tomorrow at lunchtime *od* noon; **~essen** nt lunch, dinner

mittags adv at lunchtime *od* noon; **M~pause** f lunch break; **M~schlaf** m early afternoon nap, siesta

Mittäter(in) ['mɪttɛːtər(ɪn)] m(f) accomplice

Mitte ['mɪtə] f middle; (*POL*) centre; **aus unserer ~** from our midst

mitteilen ['mɪttaɪlən] vt: **jdm etw ~** to inform sb of sth, to communicate sth to sb

Mitteilung f communication

Mittel ['mɪtəl] (-s -) nt means; method; (*MATH*) average; (*MED*) medicine; **ein ~ zum Zweck** a means to an end; **~alter** nt

Middle Ages pl; **m~alterlich** adj mediaeval; **~ding** nt cross; **~europa** nt Central Europe; **~gebirge** nt low mountain range; **m~mäßig** adj mediocre, middling; **~mäßigkeit** f mediocrity; **~meer** nt Mediterranean; **~ohrentzündung** f inflammation of the middle ear; **~punkt** m centre; **~stand** m middle class; **~streifen** m central reservation; **~stürmer** m centre-forward; **~weg** m middle course; **~welle** f (*RADIO*) medium wave

mitten ['mɪtən] adv in the middle; **~ auf der Straße/in der Nacht** in the middle of the street/night

Mitternacht ['mɪtərnaxt] f midnight

mittlere(r, s) ['mɪtlərə(r, s)] adj middle; (*durchschnittlich*) medium, average; **~ Reife** ≃ O-levels

---
mittlere Reife
---

i *The* **mittlere Reife** *is the standard certificate gained at a* **Realschule** *or* **Gymnasium** *on successful completion of 6 years' education there. If a pupil at a* **Realschule** *attains good results in several subjects he is allowed to enter the 11th class of a* **Gymnasium** *to study for the* **Abitur.**

---

mittlerweile ['mɪtlər'vaɪlə] adv meanwhile

Mittwoch ['mɪtvɔx] (-(e)s, -e) m Wednesday; **m~s** adv on Wednesdays

mitunter [mɪt'ʊntər] adv occasionally, sometimes

Mit- zW: **m~verantwortlich** adj jointly responsible; **m~wirken** vi: **m~wirken (bei)** to contribute (to); (*THEAT*) to take part (in); **~wirkung** f contribution; participation

Mobbing ['mɔbɪŋ] (-s) nt workplace bullying

Möbel ['møːbəl] pl furniture sg; **~wagen** m furniture *od* removal van

mobil [mo'biːl] adj mobile; (*MIL*) mobilized; **M~iar** [mobi'aːr] (-s, -e) nt furnishings pl; **M~machung** f mobilization; **M~telefon** nt mobile phone

möblieren [mø'bliːrən] vt to furnish;

möbliert wohnen to live in furnished accommodation

möchte etc ['mœçtə] vb siehe **mögen**

Mode ['mo:də] f fashion

Modell [mo'del] (-s, -e) nt model; **m~ieren** [-'li:rən] vt to model

Modenschau f fashion show

moderig ['mo:dərɪç] adj (Keller) musty; (Luft) stale

modern [mo'dɛrn] adj modern; (modisch) fashionable; **~i'sieren** vt to modernize

Mode- zW: **~schau** f fashion show; **~schmuck** m fashion jewellery; **~schöpfer(in)** m(f) fashion designer; **~wort** nt fashionable word, buzz word

modisch ['mo:dɪʃ] adj fashionable

Mofa ['mo:fa] (-s, -s) nt small moped

mogeln ['mo:gəln] (umg) vi to cheat

SCHLÜSSELWORT

mögen ['mø:gən] (pt mochte, pp gemocht od (als Hilfsverb) mögen) vt, vi to like; **magst du/mögen Sie ihn?** do you like him?; **ich möchte ...** I would like ..., I'd like ...; **er möchte in die Stadt** he'd like to go into town; **ich möchte nicht, dass du ...** I wouldn't like you to ...; **ich mag nicht mehr** I've had enough

♦ Hilfsverb to like to; (wollen) to want; **möchtest du etwas essen?** would you like something to eat?; **sie mag nicht bleiben** she doesn't want to stay; **das mag wohl sein** that may well be; **was mag das heißen?** what might that mean?; **Sie möchten zu Hause anrufen** could you please call home?

---

möglich ['mø:klɪç] adj possible; **~erweise** adv possibly; **M~keit** f possibility; **nach M~keit** if possible; **~st** adv as ... as possible

Mohn [mo:n] (-(e)s, -e) m (~blume) poppy; (~samen) poppy seed

Möhre ['mø:rə] f carrot

Mohrrübe ['mo:rry:bə] f carrot

mokieren [mo'ki:rən] vr: **sich ~ über** +akk to make fun of

Mole ['mo:lə] f (harbour) mole

Molekül [mole'ky:l] (-s, -e) nt molecule

Molkerei [mɔlkə'raɪ] f dairy

Moll [mɔl] (-, -) nt (MUS) minor (key)

mollig adj cosy; (dicklich) plump

Moment [mo'mɛnt] (-(e)s, -e) m moment ♦ nt factor; **im ~** at the moment; **~ (mal)!** just a moment; **m~an** [-'ta:n] adj momentary ♦ adv at the moment

Monarch [mo'narç] (-en, -en) m monarch; **~ie** [monar'çi:] f monarchy

Monat ['mo:nat] (-(e)s, -e) m month; **m~elang** adv for months; **m~lich** adj monthly

Monats- zW: **~gehalt** nt: **das dreizehnte ~gehalt** Christmas bonus (of one month's salary); **~karte** f monthly ticket

Mönch [mœnç] (-(e)s, -e) m monk

Mond [mo:nt] (-(e)s, -e) m moon; **~finsternis** f eclipse of the moon; **m~hell** adj moonlit; **~landung** f moon landing; **~schein** m moonlight

Mono- [mono] in zW mono; **~log** [-'lo:k] (-s, -e) m monologue; **~pol** [-'po:l] (-s, -e) nt monopoly; **m~polisieren** [-poli'zi:rən] vt to monopolize; **m~ton** [-'to:n] adj monotonous; **~tonie** [-to'ni:] f monotony

Montag ['mo:nta:k] (-(e)s, -e) m Monday

Montage [mɔn'ta:ʒə] f (PHOT etc) montage; (TECH) assembly; (Einbauen) fitting

Monteur [mɔn'tø:r] m fitter

montieren [mɔn'ti:rən] vt to assemble

Monument [monu'mɛnt] nt monument; **m~al** [-'ta:l] adj monumental

Moor [mo:r] (-(e)s, -e) nt moor

Moos [mo:s] (-es, -e) nt moss

Moped ['mo:pɛt] (-s, -s) nt moped

Moral [mo'ra:l] (-, -en) f morality; (einer Geschichte) moral; **m~isch** adj moral

Morast [mo'rast] (-(e)s, -e) m morass, mire; **m~ig** adj boggy

Mord [mɔrt] (-(e)s, -e) m murder; **~anschlag** m murder attempt

Mörder(in) ['mœrdər(ɪn)] (-s, -) m(f) murderer (murderess)

mörderisch adj (fig: schrecklich) terrible, dreadful ♦ adv (umg: entsetzlich) terribly, dreadfully

Mord- *zW:* **~kommission** *f* murder squad; **~sglück** (*umg*) *nt* amazing luck; **m~smäßig** (*umg*) *adj* terrific, enormous; **~verdacht** *m* suspicion of murder; **~waffe** *f* murder weapon

morgen ['mɔrgən] *adv* tomorrow; **~ früh** tomorrow morning; **M~ (-s, -)** *m* morning; **M~mantel** *m* dressing gown; **M~rock** *m* dressing gown; **M~röte** *f* dawn; **~s** *adv* in the morning

morgig ['mɔrgɪç] *adj* tomorrow's; **der ~e Tag** tomorrow

Morphium ['mɔrfiʊm] *nt* morphine

morsch [mɔrʃ] *adj* rotten

Morsealphabet ['mɔrzəalfabeːt] *nt* Morse code

morsen *vi* to send a message by Morse code

Mörtel ['mœrtəl] **(-s, -)** *m* mortar

Mosaik [moza'iːk] **(-s, -en** *od* **-e)** *nt* mosaic

Moschee [mɔ'ʃeː] **(-, -n)** *f* mosque

Moskito [mɔs'kiːto] **(-s, -s)** *m* mosquito

Most [mɔst] **(-(e)s, -e)** *m* (unfermented) fruit juice; (*Apfelwein*) cider

Motel [mo'tel] **(-s, -s)** *nt* motel

Motiv [mo'tiːf] **(-s, -e)** *nt* motive; (*MUS*) theme; **~ation** [-vatsi'oːn] *f* motivation; **m~ieren** [moti'viːrən] *vt* to motivate

Motor ['moːtɔr, *pl* mo'toːrən] **(-s, -en)** *m* engine; (*bes ELEK*) motor; **~boot** *nt* motorboat; **~haube** *f* (*von Auto*) bonnet (*BRIT*), hood (*US*); **m~isieren** *vt* to motorize; **~öl** *nt* engine oil; **~rad** *nt* motorcycle; **~roller** *m* (motor) scooter; **~schaden** *m* engine trouble *od* failure

Motte ['mɔtə] *f* moth; **~nkugel** *f* mothball(s)

Motto ['mɔto] **(-s, -s)** *nt* motto

Möwe ['møːvə] *f* seagull

Mücke ['mʏkə] *f* midge, gnat; **~nstich** *m* midge *od* gnat bite

müde ['myːdə] *adj* tired

Müdigkeit ['myːdɪçkait] *f* tiredness

Muffel (-s, -) (*umg*) *m* killjoy, sourpuss

muffig *adj* (*Luft*) musty

Mühe ['myːə] *f* trouble, pains *pl*; **mit Müh und Not** with great difficulty; **sich** *dat* ~

geben to go to a lot of trouble; **m~los** *adj* without trouble, easy; **m~voll** *adj* laborious, arduous

Mühle ['myːlə] *f* mill; (*Kaffeemühle*) grinder

Müh- *zW:* **~sal (-, -e)** *f* tribulation; **m~sam** *adj* arduous, troublesome; **m~selig** *adj* arduous, laborious

Mulde ['mʊldə] *f* hollow, depression

Mull [mʊl] **(-(e)s, -e)** *m* thin muslin

Müll [mʏl] **(-(e)s)** *m* rubbish disposal; (*Leute*) dustmen *pl*; **~abladeplatz** *m* rubbish dump; **~binde** *f* gauze bandage; **~eimer** *m* dustbin, garbage can (*US*); **~haufen** *m* rubbish heap; **~schlucker (-s, -)** *m* garbage disposal unit; **~tonne** *f* dustbin; **~verbrennungsanlage** *f* incinerator

mulmig ['mʊlmɪç] *adj* rotten; (*umg*) dodgy; **jdm ist ~** sb feels funny

multiplizieren [mʊltipli'tsiːrən] *vt* to multiply

Mumie ['muːmiə] *f* mummy

Mumm [mʊm] **(-s)** (*umg*) *m* gumption, nerve

Mumps [mʊmps] **(-)** *m od f* (*MED*) mumps

München ['mʏnçən] **(-s)** *nt* Munich

Mund [mʊnt] **(-(e)s, ⁺er)** *m* mouth; **~art** *f* dialect

münden ['mʏndən] *vi:* **~ in** +*akk* to flow into

Mund- *zW:* **m~faul** *adj* taciturn; **~geruch** *m* bad breath; **~harmonika** *f* mouth organ

mündig ['mʏndɪç] *adj* of age; **M~keit** *f* majority

mündlich ['mʏntlɪç] *adj* oral

Mundstück *nt* mouthpiece; (*Zigarettenmundstück*) tip

Mündung ['mʏndʊŋ] *f* (*von Fluss*) mouth; (*Gewehr*) muzzle

Mund- *zW:* **~wasser** *nt* mouthwash; **~werk** *nt:* **ein großes ~werk haben** to have a big mouth; **~winkel** *m* corner of the mouth

Munition [munitsi'oːn] *f* ammunition; **~slager** *nt* ammunition dump

munkeln ['mʊŋkəln] *vi* to whisper, to

mutter

Münster ['mʏnstər] **(-s, -)** nt minster

munter ['mʊntər] adj lively

Münze ['mʏntsə] f coin; **m~n** vt to coin, to mint; **auf jdn gemünzt sein** to be aimed at sb

Münzfernsprecher ['mʏntsfɛrnʃpreçər] m callbox (BRIT), pay phone

mürb(e) ['mʏrb(ə)] adj (Gestein) crumbly; (Holz) rotten; (Gebäck) crisp; **jdn ~ machen** to wear sb down; **M~eteig** ['mʏrbətaɪç] m shortcrust pastry

murmeln ['mʊrməln] vt, vi to murmur, to mutter

murren ['mʊrən] vi to grumble, to grouse

mürrisch ['mʏrɪʃ] adj sullen

Mus [muːs] **(-es, -e)** nt purée

Muschel ['mʊʃəl] **(-, -n)** f mussel; (~schale) shell; (Telefonmuschel) receiver

Muse ['muːzə] f muse

Museum [mu'zeːʊm] **(-s, Museen)** nt museum

Musik [mu'ziːk] f music; (Kapelle) band; **m~alisch** [-ka:lɪʃ] adj musical; **~ant(in)** [-'kant(ɪn)] m(f) musician; **~box** f jukebox; **~er (-s, -)** m musician; **~hochschule** f college of music; **~instrument** nt musical instrument

musisch ['muːzɪʃ] adj (Mensch) artistic

musizieren [muzi'tsiːrən] vi to make music

Muskat [mʊs'kaːt] **(-(e)s, -e)** m nutmeg

Muskel ['mʊskəl] **(-s, -n)** m muscle; **~kater** m: **~kater haben** to be stiff

Muskulatur [mʊskula'tuːr] f muscular system

muskulös [mʊsku'løːs] adj muscular

Müsli ['mʏsli] **(-s, -)** nt (KOCH) muesli

Muss ▲ [mʊs] **(-)** nt necessity, must

Muße ['muːsə] **(-)** f leisure

SCHLÜSSELWORT

müssen ['mʏsən] (pt **musste**, pp **gemusst** od (als Hilfsverb) **müssen**) vi **1** (Zwang) must (nur im Präsens), to have to; **ich muss es tun** I must do it, I have to do it; **ich musste es tun** I had to do it; **er muss es**

nicht tun he doesn't have to do it; **muss ich?** must I?, do I have to?; **wann müsst ihr zur Schule?** when do you have to go to school?; **er hat gehen müssen** he (has) had to go; **muss das sein?** is that really necessary?; **ich muss mal** (umg) I need the toilet

2 (sollen): **das musst du nicht tun!** you oughtn't to od shouldn't do that; **Sie hätten ihn fragen müssen** you should have asked him

3: **es muss geregnet haben** it must have rained; **es muss nicht wahr sein** it needn't be true

müßig ['myːsɪç] adj idle

Muster ['mʊstər] **(-s, -)** nt model; (Dessin) pattern; (Probe) sample; **m~gültig** adj exemplary; **m~n** vt (Tapete) to pattern; (fig, MIL) to examine; (Truppen) to inspect; **~ung** f (von Stoff) pattern; (MIL) inspection

Mut [muːt] m courage; **nur ~!** cheer up!; **jdm ~ machen** to encourage sb; **m~ig** adj courageous; **m~los** adj discouraged, despondent

mutmaßlich ['muːtmaːslɪç] adj presumed
♦ adv probably

Mutprobe f test od trial of courage

Mutter¹ ['mʊtər] **(-, ¨)** f mother

Mutter² ['mʊtər] **(-, -n)** f (Schraubenmutter) nut

mütterlich ['mʏtərlɪç] adj motherly; **~erseits** adv on the mother's side

Mutter- zW: **~liebe** f motherly love; **~mal** nt birthmark; **~milch** f mother's milk; **~schaft** f motherhood, maternity; **~schutz** m maternity regulations; **'~'seelena|llein** adj all alone; **~sprache** f native language; **~tag** m Mother's Day

Mutti ['mʊti] **(-, -s)** f mum(my) (BRIT), mom(my) (US)

mutwillig ['muːtvɪlɪç] adj malicious, deliberate

Mütze ['mʏtsə] f cap

MwSt abk (= Mehrwertsteuer) VAT

mysteriös [mʏsteri'øːs] adj mysterious

Mythos ['myːtɔs] **(-, Mythen)** m myth

N, n

na [na] *excl* well; **~ gut** okay then
Nabel ['na:bəl] (**-s, -**) *m* navel; **~schnur** *f* umbilical cord

SCHLÜSSELWORT

nach [na:x] *präp +dat* **1** (*örtlich*) to; **nach Berlin** to Berlin; **nach links/rechts** (to the) left/right; **nach oben/hinten** up/back
2 (*zeitlich*) after; **einer nach dem anderen** one after the other; **nach Ihnen!** after you!; **zehn (Minuten) nach drei** ten (minutes) past three
3 (*gemäß*) according to; **nach dem Gesetz** according to the law; **dem Namen nach** judging by his/her name; **nach allem, was ich weiß** as far as I know
♦ *adv*: **ihm nach!** after him!; **nach und nach** gradually, little by little; **nach wie vor** still

nachahmen ['na:xʔa:mən] *vt* to imitate
Nachbar(in) ['naxbaːr(ɪn)] (**-s, -n**) *m(f)* neighbour; **~haus** *nt*: **im ~haus** next door; **n~lich** *adj* neighbourly; **~schaft** *f* neighbourhood; **~staat** *m* neighbouring state
nach- *zW*: **~bestellen** *vt*: **50 Stück ~bestellen** to order another 50; **N~bestellung** *f* (*COMM*) repeat order; **N~bildung** *f* imitation, copy; **~blicken** *vi* to gaze after; **~datieren** *vt* to postdate
nachdem [na:x'de:m] *konj* after; (*weil*) since; **je ~ (ob)** it depends (whether)
nachdenken (*unreg*) *vi*: **~ über** *+akk* to think about; **N~** (**-s**) *nt* reflection, meditation
nachdenklich *adj* thoughtful, pensive
Nachdruck ['na:xdrʊk] *m* emphasis; (*TYP*) reprint, reproduction
nachdrücklich ['na:xdrʏklɪç] *adj* emphatic
nacheinander [na:xʔaɪ'nandər] *adv* one after the other
nachempfinden ['na:xʔɛmpfɪndən] (*unreg*)

vt: **jdm etw ~** to feel sth with sb
Nacherzählung ['na:xʔɛrtse:lʊŋ] *f* reproduction (of a story)
Nachfahr ['na:xfa:r] (**-s, -en**) *m* descendant
Nachfolge ['na:xfɔlgə] *f* succession; **n~n** *vi +dat* to follow; **~r(in)** (**-s, -**) *m(f)* successor
nachforschen *vt, vi* to investigate
Nachforschung *f* investigation
Nachfrage ['na:xfra:gə] *f* inquiry; (*COMM*) demand; **n~n** *vi* to inquire
nach- *zW*: **~füllen** *vt* to refill; **~geben** (*unreg*) *vi* to give way, to yield; **N~gebühr** *f* (*POST*) excess postage
nachgehen ['na:xge:ən] (*unreg*) *vi* (*+dat*) to follow; (*erforschen*) to inquire (into); (*Uhr*) to be slow
Nachgeschmack ['na:xgəʃmak] *m* aftertaste
nachgiebig ['na:xgi:bɪç] *adj* soft, accommodating; **N~keit** *f* softness
nachhaltig ['na:xhaltɪç] *adj* lasting; (*Widerstand*) persistent
nachhause *adv* (österreichisch, schweizerisch) home
nachhelfen ['na:xhɛlfən] (*unreg*) *vi +dat* to assist, to help
nachher [na:x'he:r] *adv* afterwards
Nachhilfeunterricht ['na:xhɪlfəʔʊntərrɪçt] *m* extra tuition
nachholen ['na:xho:lən] *vt* to catch up with; (*Versäumtes*) to make up for
Nachkomme ['na:xkɔmə] (**-, -n**) *m* descendant
nachkommen (*unreg*) *vi* to follow; (*einer Verpflichtung*) to fulfil; **N~schaft** *f* descendants *pl*
Nachkriegszeit *f* postwar period
Nach- *zW*: **~lass** ▲ (**-es, -lässe**) *m* (*COMM*) discount, rebate; (*Erbe*) estate; **n~lassen** (*unreg*) *vt* (*Strafe*) to remit; (*Summe*) to take off; (*Schulden*) to cancel ♦ *vi* to decrease, to ease off; (*Sturm*) to die down, to ease off; (*schlechter werden*) to deteriorate; **er hat n~gelassen** he has got worse; **n~lässig** *adj* negligent, careless
nachlaufen ['na:xlaʊfən] (*unreg*) *vi +dat* to run after, to chase

nachlösen ['naːxløːzən] *vi (Zuschlag)* to pay on the train, pay at the other end; *(zur Weiterfahrt)* to pay the supplement

nachmachen ['naːxmaxən] *vt* to imitate, to copy; *(fälschen)* to counterfeit

Nachmittag ['naːxmɪtaːk] *m* afternoon; **am ~** in the afternoon; **n~s** *adv* in the afternoon

Nach- *zW:* **~nahme** *f* cash on delivery; **per ~nahme** C.O.D.; **~name** *m* surname; **~porto** *nt* excess postage

nachprüfen ['naːxpryːfən] *vt* to check, to verify

nachrechnen ['naːxrɛçnən] *vt* to check

nachreichen ['naːxraɪçən] *vt (Unterlagen)* to hand in later

Nachricht ['naːxrɪçt] *(-, -en) f (piece of) news; (Mitteilung)* message; **~en** *pl (Neuigkeiten)* news

Nachrichten- *zW:* **~agentur** *f* news agency; **~dienst** *m (MIL)* intelligence service; **~sprecher(in)** *m(f)* newsreader; **~technik** *f* telecommunications *sg*

Nachruf ['naːxruːf] *m* obituary

nachsagen ['naːxzaːgən] *vt* to repeat; **jdm etw ~** to say sth of sb

Nachsaison ['naːxzɛzõ:] *f* off-season

nachschicken ['naːxʃɪkən] *vt* to forward

nachschlagen ['naːxʃlaːgən] *(unreg) vt* to look up

Nachschlagewerk *nt* reference book

Nachschlüssel *m* duplicate key

Nachschub ['naːxʃuːp] *m* supplies *pl*; *(Truppen)* reinforcements *pl*

nachsehen ['naːxzeːən] *(unreg) vt (prüfen)* to check ♦ *vi (erforschen)* to look and see; **jdm etw ~** to forgive sb sth; **das N~ haben** to come off worst

Nachsendeantrag *m* application to have one's mail forwarded

nachsenden ['naːxzɛndən] *(unreg) vt* to send on, to forward

nachsichtig *adj* indulgent, lenient

nachsitzen ['naːxzɪtsən] *(unreg) vi:* **~ (müssen)** *(SCH)* to be kept in

Nachspeise ['naːxʃpaɪzə] *f* dessert, sweet, pudding

Nachspiel ['naːxʃpiːl] *nt* epilogue; *(fig)* sequel

nachsprechen ['naːxʃprɛçən] *(unreg) vt:* **(jdm) ~** to repeat (after sb)

nächst [nɛːçst] *präp +dat (räumlich)* next to; *(außer)* apart from; **~beste(r, s)** *adj* first that comes along; *(zweitbeste)* next best; **N~e(r)** *f(m)* neighbour; **~e(r, s)** *adj* next; *(~gelegen)* nearest

nachstellen ['naːxʃtɛlən] *vt (TECH: neu einstellen)* to adjust

nächst *zW:* **N~enliebe** *f* love for one's fellow men; **~ens** *adv* shortly, soon; **~liegend** *adj* nearest; *(fig)* obvious; **~möglich** *adj* next possible

Nacht [naxt] *(-, ̈e) f* night; **~dienst** *m* night shift

Nachteil ['naːxtaɪl] *m* disadvantage; **n~ig** *adj* disadvantageous

Nachthemd *nt (Herrennachthemd)* nightshirt; *(Damennachthemd)* nightdress

Nachtigall ['naxtɪgal] *(-, -en) f* nightingale

Nachtisch ['naːxtɪʃ] *m* = **Nachspeise**

Nachtklub *m* night club

Nachtleben *nt* nightlife

nächtlich ['nɛçtlɪç] *adj* nightly

Nachtlokal *nt* night club

Nach- *zW:* **~trag** *(-(e)s, -träge) m* supplement; **n~tragen** *(unreg) vt* to carry; *(zufügen)* to add; **jdm etw n~tragen** to hold sth against sb; **n~träglich** *adj* later, subsequent; additional ♦ *adv* later, subsequently; additionally; **n~trauern** *vi:* **jdm/etw n~trauern** to mourn the loss of sb/sth

Nacht- *zW:* **n~s** *adv* at *od* by night; **~schicht** *f* nightshift; **~schwester** *f* night nurse; **~tarif** *m* off-peak tariff; **~tisch** *m* bedside table; **~wächter** *m* night watchman

Nach- *zW:* **~untersuchung** *f* checkup; **n~wachsen** *(unreg) vi* to grow again; **~wahl** *f (POL)* ≃ by-election

Nachweis ['naːxvaɪs] *(-es, -e) m* proof; **n~bar** *adj* provable, demonstrable; **n~en** *(unreg) vt* to prove; **jdm etw n~en** to point sth out to sb; **n~lich** *adj* evident, demonstrable

nach- *zW:* **~wirken** *vi* to have after-effects; **N~wirkung** *f* aftereffect; **N~wort** *nt* epilogue; **N~wuchs** *m* offspring; (*beruflich etc*) new recruits *pl;* **~zahlen** *vt, vi* to pay extra; **N~zahlung** *f* additional payment; (*zurückdatiert*) back pay; **~ziehen** (*unreg*) *vt* (*hinter sich herziehen: Bein*) to drag; **N~zügler (-s, -)** *m* straggler

Nacken ['nakən] **(-s, -)** *m* nape of the neck

nackt [nakt] *adj* naked; (*Tatsachen*) plain, bare; **N~badestrand** *m* nudist beach; **N~heit** *f* nakedness

Nadel ['naːdəl] **(-, -n)** *f* needle; (*Stecknadel*) pin; **~öhr** *nt* eye of a needle; **~wald** *m* coniferous forest

Nagel ['naːgəl] **(-s, ")** *m* nail; **~bürste** *f* nailbrush; **~feile** *f* nailfile; **~lack** *m* nail varnish *od* polish (*BRIT*); **n~n** *vt, vi* to nail; **n~neu** *adj* brand-new; **~schere** *f* nail scissors *pl*

nagen ['naːgən] *vt, vi* to gnaw

Nagetier ['naːgətiːr] *nt* rodent

nah(e) ['naː(ə)] *adj* (*räumlich*) near(by); (*Verwandte*) close; (*zeitlich*) near, close ♦ *adv* near(by); near, close; (*verwandt*) closely ♦ *präp* (+*dat*) near (to), close to; **der Nahe Osten** the Near East; **~ gehen** (+*dat*) to grieve; **~ kommen** (+*dat*) to get closer (to); **jdm etw ~ legen** to suggest sth to sb; **~ liegen** to be obvious; **~ liegend** obvious; **~ stehen** (+*dat*) to be close to; **einer Sache ~ stehen** to sympathize with sth; **~ stehend** *adj;* **jdm (zu) ~ treten** to offend sb

Nahaufnahme *f* close-up

Nähe ['nɛːə] **(-)** *f* nearness, proximity; (*Umgebung*) vicinity; **in der ~** close by; at hand; **aus der ~** from close to

nah(e)bei *adv* nearby

nahen *vi, vr* to approach, to draw near

nähen ['nɛːən] *vt, vi* to sew

näher *adj, adv* nearer; (*Erklärung, Erkundigung*) more detailed; **(sich) ~ kommen** to get closer; **N~e(s)** *nt* details *pl,* particulars *pl*

Naherholungsgebiet *nt* recreational area

(*close to a town*)

nähern *vr* to approach

nahezu *adv* nearly

Nähgarn *nt* thread

Nahkampf *m* hand-to-hand fighting

Nähkasten *m* sewing basket, workbox

nahm *etc* [naːm] *vb siehe* **nehmen**

Nähmaschine *f* sewing machine

Nähnadel *f* needle

nähren ['nɛːrən] *vt* to feed ♦ *vr* (*Person*) to feed o.s.; (*Tier*) to feed

nahrhaft ['naːrhaft] *adj* nourishing, nutritious

Nahrung ['naːrʊŋ] *f* food; (*fig auch*) sustenance

Nahrungs- *zW:* **~mittel** *nt* foodstuffs *pl;* **~mittelindustrie** *f* food industry; **~suche** *f* search for food

Nährwert *m* nutritional value

Naht [naːt] **(-, "e)** *f* seam; (*MED*) suture; (*TECH*) join; **n~los** *adj* seamless; **n~los ineinander übergehen** to follow without a gap

Nah- *zW:* **~verkehr** *m* local traffic; **~verkehrszug** *m* local train; **~ziel** *nt* immediate objective

Name ['naːmə] **(-ns, -n)** *m* name; **im ~n von** on behalf of; **n~ns** *adv* by the name of; **~nstag** *m* name day, saint's day; **n~ntlich** *adj* by name ♦ *adv* particularly, especially

---

Namenstag

ⓘ In Catholic areas of Germany the **Namenstag** is often a more important celebration than a birthday. This is the day dedicated to the saint after whom a person is called, and on that day the person receives presents and invites relatives and friends round to celebrate.

---

namhaft ['naːmhaft] *adj* (*berühmt*) famed, renowned; (*beträchtlich*) considerable; **~ machen** to name

nämlich ['nɛːmlɪç] *adv* that is to say, namely; (*denn*) since

nannte *etc* ['nantə] *vb siehe* **nennen**

Napf [napf] **(-(e)s, "e)** *m* bowl, dish

Narbe ['narbə] f scar; **narbig** adj scarred
Narkose [nar'ko:zə] f anaesthetic
Narr [nar] (-en, -en) m fool; **n~en** vt to fool; **Närrin** ['nɛrɪn] f fool; **närrisch** adj foolish, crazy
Narzisse [nar'tsɪsə] f narcissus; daffodil
naschen ['naʃən] vt, vi to nibble; (heimlich kosten) to pinch a bit
naschhaft adj sweet-toothed
Nase ['na:zə] f nose
Nasen- zW: **~bluten** (-s) nt nosebleed; **~loch** nt nostril; **~tropfen** pl nose drops
naseweis adj pert, cheeky; (neugierig) nosey
Nashorn ['na:shɔrn] nt rhinoceros
nass ▲ [nas] adj wet
Nässe ['nɛsə] (-) f wetness; **n~n** vt to wet
nasskalt ▲ adj wet and cold
Nassrasur ▲ f wet shave
Nation [natsi'o:n] f nation
national [natsio'na:l] adj national; **N~feiertag** m national holiday; **N~hymne** f national anthem; **~isieren** [-i'zi:rən] vt to nationalize; **N~ismus** [-'lɪsmʊs] m nationalism; **~istisch** [-'lɪstɪʃ] adj nationalistic; **N~i'tät** f nationality; **N~mannschaft** f national team; **N~sozialismus** m national socialism
Natron ['na:trɔn] (-s) nt soda
Natter ['natər] (-, -n) f adder
Natur [na'tu:r] f nature; (körperlich) constitution; **~ell** (-es, -e) nt disposition; **~erscheinung** f natural phenomenon od event; **n~farben** adj natural coloured; **n~gemäß** adj natural; **~gesetz** nt law of nature; **n~getreu** adj true to life; **~katastrophe** f natural disaster
natürlich [na'ty:rlɪç] adj natural ♦ adv naturally; **ja, ~!** yes, of course; **N~keit** f naturalness
Natur- zW: **~park** m ≈ national park; **~produkt** nt natural product; **n~rein** adj natural, pure; **~schutz** m nature conservation; **unter ~schutz stehen** to be legally protected; **~schutzgebiet** nt nature reserve; **~wissenschaft** f natural science; **~wissenschaftler(in)** m(f)

scientist
nautisch ['nautɪʃ] adj nautical
Nazi ['na:tsi] (-s, -s) m Nazi
NB abk (= nota bene) nb
n. Chr. abk (= nach Christus) A.D.
Nebel ['ne:bəl] (-s, -) m fog, mist; **n~ig** adj foggy, misty; **~scheinwerfer** m fog lamp
neben ['ne:bən] präp (+akk od dat) next to; (+dat: außer) apart from, besides; **~an** [ne:bən'an] adv next door; **N~anschluss** ▲ m (TEL) extension; **N~ausgang** m side exit; **~bei** [ne:bən'bai] adv at the same time; (außerdem) additionally; (beiläufig) incidentally; **N~beruf** m second job; **N~beschäftigung** f second job; **N~buhler(in)** (-s, -) m(f) rival; **~einander** [ne:bən|ai'nandər] adv side by side; **~einander legen** to put next to each other; **N~eingang** m side entrance; **N~fach** nt subsidiary subject; **N~fluss** ▲ m tributary; **N~gebäude** nt annexe; **N~geräusch** nt (RADIO) atmospherics pl, interference; **~her** [ne:bən'he:r] adv (zusätzlich) besides; (gleichzeitig) at the same time; (daneben) alongside; **N~kosten** pl extra charges, extras; **N~produkt** nt by-product; **N~sache** f trifle, side issue; **~sächlich** adj minor, peripheral; **N~saison** f low season; **N~straße** f side street; **N~verdienst** m secondary income; **N~wirkung** f side effect; **N~zimmer** nt adjoining room
neblig ['ne:blɪç] adj foggy, misty
Necessaire [nese'sɛ:r] (-s, -s) nt (Nähnecessaire) needlework box; (Nagelnecessaire) manicure case
necken ['nɛkən] vt to tease
Neckerei [nɛkə'rai] f teasing
Neffe ['nɛfə] (-n, -n) m nephew
negativ ['ne:gati:f] adj negative; **N~** (-s, -e) nt (PHOT) negative
Neger ['ne:gər] (-s, -) m negro; **~in** f negress
nehmen ['ne:mən] (unreg) vt to take; **jdn zu sich ~** to take sb in; **sich ernst ~** to take o.s. seriously; **nimm dir doch bitte** please help yourself

Neid [naɪt] (-(e)s) m envy; ~**er** (-s, -) m envier; **n~isch** ['naɪdɪʃ] adj envious, jealous

neigen ['naɪgən] vt to incline, to lean; (Kopf) to bow ♦ vi: **zu etw ~** to tend to sth

Neigung f (des Geländes) slope; (Tendenz) tendency, inclination; (Vorliebe) liking; (Zuneigung) affection

nein [naɪn] adv no

Nektarine [nɛkta'riːnə] f (Frucht) nectarine

Nelke ['nɛlkə] f carnation, pink; (Gewürz) clove

Nenn- ['nɛn] zW: **n~en** (unreg) vt to name; (mit Namen) to call; **wie n~t man ...?** what do you call ...?; **n~enswert** adj worth mentioning; **~er** (-s, -) m denominator; **~wert** m nominal value; (COMM) par

Neon ['neːɔn] (-s) nt neon; **~licht** nt neon light; **~röhre** f neon tube

Nerv [nɛrf] (-s, -en) m nerve; **jdm auf die ~en gehen** to get on sb's nerves; **n~enaufreibend** adj nerve-racking; **~enbündel** nt bundle of nerves; **~enheilanstalt** f mental home; **n~enkrank** adj mentally ill; **~ensäge** (umg) f pain (in the neck) (umg); **~ensystem** nt nervous system; **~enzusammenbruch** m nervous breakdown; **n~lich** adj (Belastung) affecting the nerves; **n~ös** [nɛr'vøːs] adj nervous; **~osi'tät** f nervousness; **n~tötend** adj nerve-racking; (Arbeit) soul-destroying

Nerz [nɛrts] (-es, -e) m mink

Nessel ['nɛsəl] (-, -n) f nettle

Nessessär ▲ [nese'sɛːr] (-s, -s) nt = **Necessaire**

Nest [nɛst] (-(e)s, -er) nt nest; (umg: Ort) dump

nett [nɛt] adj nice; (freundlich) nice, kind; **~erweise** adv kindly

netto ['nɛto] adv net

Netz [nɛts] (-es, -e) nt net; (Gepäcknetz) rack; (Einkaufsnetz) string bag; (Spinnennetz) web; (System) network; **jdm ins ~ gehen** (fig) to fall into sb's trap; **~anschluss** ▲ m mains connection

Netzhaut f retina

neu [nɔy] adj new; (Sprache, Geschichte)

modern; **seit ~estem** (since) recently; **die ~esten Nachrichten** the latest news; **~ schreiben** to rewrite, to write again; **N~anschaffung** f new purchase od acquisition; **~artig** adj new kind of; **N~bau** m new building; **N~e(r)** f(m) the new man/woman; **~erdings** adv (kürzlich) (since) recently; (von ~em) again; **N~erscheinung** f (Buch) new publication; (Schallplatte) new release; **N~erung** f innovation, new departure; **N~gier** f curiosity; **~gierig** adj curious; **N~heit** f newness; novelty; **N~igkeit** f news sg; **N~jahr** nt New Year; **~lich** adv recently, the other day; **N~ling** m novice; **N~mond** m new moon

neun [nɔyn] num nine; **~zehn** num nineteen; **~zig** num ninety

neureich adj nouveau riche; **N~e(r)** f(m) nouveau riche

neurotisch adj neurotic

Neuseeland [nɔy'zeːlant] nt New Zealand; **Neuseeländer(in)** [nɔy'zeːlɛndər(ɪn)] m(f) New Zealander

neutral [nɔy'traːl] adj neutral; **~i'sieren** vt to neutralize

Neutrum ['nɔytrʊm] (-s, -a od -en) nt neuter

Neu- zW: **~wert** m purchase price; **n~wertig** adj (as) new, not used; **~zeit** f modern age; **n~zeitlich** adj modern, recent

| SCHLÜSSELWORT |

nicht [nɪçt] adv 1 (Verneinung) not; **er ist es nicht** it's not him, it isn't him; **er raucht nicht** (gerade) he isn't smoking; (gewöhnlich) he doesn't smoke; **ich kann das nicht - ich auch nicht** I can't do it - neither od nor can I; **es regnet nicht mehr** it's not raining any more; **nicht rostend** stainless

2 (Bitte, Verbot): **nicht!** don't!, no!; **nicht berühren!** do not touch!; **nicht doch!** don't!

3 (rhetorisch): **du bist müde, nicht (wahr)?** you're tired, aren't you?; **das ist schön,**

nicht (wahr)? it's nice, isn't it?
4: was du nicht sagst! the things you say!

Nichtangriffspakt [nɪçt'|angrɪfspakt] *m* non-aggression pact
Nichte [nɪçtə] *f* niece
nichtig [nɪçtɪç] *adj (ungültig)* null, void; *(wertlos)* futile
Nichtraucher(in) *m(f)* non-smoker
nichts [nɪçts] *pron* nothing; **für ~ und wieder ~** for nothing at all; **~ sagend** meaningless; **N~ (-)** *nt* nothingness; *(pej: Person)* nonentity
Nichtschwimmer *m* non-swimmer
nichts- *zW:* **~desto'weniger** *adv* nevertheless; **N~nutz (-es, -e)** *m* good-for-nothing; **~nutzig** *adj* worthless, useless; **N~tun (-s)** *nt* idleness
Nichtzutreffende(s) *nt:* **~s** *od* **nicht Zutreffendes (bitte) streichen!** (please) delete where appropriate
Nickel [nɪkəl] **(-s)** *nt* nickel
nicken [nɪkən] *vi* to nod
Nickerchen [nɪkərçən] *nt* nap
nie [niː] *adv* never; **~ wieder** *od* **mehr** never again; **~ und nimmer** never ever
nieder [niːdər] *adj* low; *(gering)* inferior
♦ *adv* down; **N~gang** *m* decline; **~gedrückt** *adj (deprimiert)* dejected, depressed; **~gehen** *(unreg) vi* to descend; *(AVIAT)* to come down; *(Regen)* to fall; *(Boxer)* to go down; **~geschlagen** *adj* depressed, dejected; **N~lage** *f* defeat; **N~lande** *pl* Netherlands; **N~länder(in)** *m(f)* Dutchman(-woman); **~ländisch** *adj* Dutch; **~lassen** *(unreg) vr (sich setzen)* to sit down; *(an Ort)* to settle (down); *(Arzt, Rechtsanwalt)* to set up a practice; **N~lassung** *f* settlement; *(COMM)* branch; **~legen** *vt* to lay down; *(Arbeit)* to stop; *(Amt)* to resign; **N~sachsen** *nt* Lower Saxony; **N~schlag** *m (MET)* precipitation; rainfall; **~schlagen** *(unreg) vt (Gegner)* to beat down; *(Gegenstand)* to knock down; *(Augen)* to lower; *(Aufstand)* to put down
♦ *vr (CHEM)* to precipitate; **~trächtig** *adj* base, mean; **N~trächtigkeit** *f* meanness,

baseness; outrage; **N~ung** *f (GEOG)* depression; *(Mündungsgebiet)* flats *pl*
niedlich [niːtlɪç] *adj* sweet, cute
niedrig [niːdrɪç] *adj* low; *(Stand)* lowly, humble; *(Gesinnung)* mean
niemals [niːmaːls] *adv* never
niemand [niːmant] *pron* nobody, no-one
Niemandsland [niːmantslant] *nt* no-man's-land
Niere [niːrə] *f* kidney
nieseln [niːzəln] *vi* to drizzle
niesen [niːzən] *vi* to sneeze
Niete [niːtə] *f (TECH)* rivet; *(Los)* blank; *(Reinfall)* flop; *(Mensch)* failure; **n~n** *vt* to rivet

---

St. Nikolaus

On December 6th, **St. Nikolaus** *visits German children to reward those who have been good by filling shoes they have left out with sweets and small presents.*

Nikotin [niko'tiːn] **(-s)** *nt* nicotine
Nilpferd [niːl-] *nt* hippopotamus
Nimmersatt [nɪmərzat] **(-(e)s, -e)** *m* glutton
nimmst *etc* [nɪmst] *vb siehe* **nehmen**
nippen [nɪpən] *vt, vi* to sip
nirgend- [nɪrgənt] *zW:* **~s** *adv* nowhere; **~wo** *adv* nowhere; **~wohin** *adv* nowhere
Nische [niːʃə] *f* niche
nisten [nɪstən] *vi* to nest
Niveau [ni'voː] **(-s, -s)** *nt* level
Nixe [nɪksə] *f* water nymph
nobel [noːbəl] *adj (großzügig)* generous; *(elegant)* posh *(inf)*

SCHLÜSSELWORT

noch [nɔx] *adv* **1** *(weiterhin)* still; **noch nicht** not yet; **noch nie** never (yet); **noch immer** *od* **immer noch** still; **bleiben Sie doch noch** stay a bit longer
2 *(in Zukunft)* still, yet; **das kann noch passieren** that might still happen; **er wird noch kommen** he'll come (yet)
3 *(nicht später als)*: **noch vor einer Woche** only a week ago; **noch am selben Tag** the

very same day; **noch im 19. Jahrhundert** as late as the 19th century; **noch heute** today

4 (*zusätzlich*): **wer war noch da?** who else was there?; **noch einmal** once more, again; **noch dreimal** three more times; **noch einer** another one

5 (*bei Vergleichen*): **noch größer** even bigger; **das ist noch besser** that's better still; **und wenn es noch so schwer ist** however hard it is

6: Geld noch und noch heaps (and heaps) of money; **sie hat noch und noch versucht, ...** she tried again and again to ...

♦ *konj*: **weder A noch B** neither A nor B

noch- *zW*: **~mal** ['nɔxmaːl] *adv* again, once more; **~malig** ['nɔxmaːlɪç] *adj* repeated; **~mals** *adv* again, once more

Nominativ ['noːminatiːf] (**-s, -e**) *m* nominative

nominell [nomi'nɛl] *adj* nominal

Nonne ['nɔnə] *f* nun

Nord(en) ['nɔrd(ən)] (**-s**) *m* north

Nord'irland *nt* Northern Ireland

nordisch *adj* northern

nördlich ['nœrtlɪç] *adj* northerly, northern ♦ *präp +gen* (to the) north of; **~ von** (to the) north of

Nord- *zW*: **~pol** *m* North Pole; **~rhein-Westfalen** *nt* North Rhine-Westphalia; **~see** *f* North Sea; **n~wärts** *adv* northwards

nörgeln ['nœrgəln] *vi* to grumble; **Nörgler** (**-s, -**) *m* grumbler

Norm [nɔrm] (**-, -en**) *f* norm; (*Größenvorschrift*) standard; **n~al** [nɔr'maːl] *adj* normal; **~al(benzin)** *nt* ≈ 2-star petrol (*BRIT*), regular petrol (*US*); **n~alerweise** *adv* normally; **n~ali'sieren** *vt* to normalize ♦ *vr* to return to normal

normen *vt* to standardize

Norwegen ['nɔrveːgən] *nt* Norway; **norwegisch** *adj* Norwegian

Nostalgie [nɔstal'giː] *f* nostalgia

Not [noːt] (**-, ⁺e**) *f* need; (*Mangel*) want; (*Mühe*) trouble; (*Zwang*) necessity; **~leidend** needy; **zur ~** if necessary; (*gerade noch*) just about

Notar [no'taːr] (**-s, -e**) *m* notary; **n~i'ell** *adj* notarial

Not- *zW*: **~arzt** *m* emergency doctor; **~ausgang** *m* emergency exit; **~behelf** (**-s, -e**) *m* makeshift; **~bremse** *f* emergency brake; **~dienst** *m* (*Bereitschaftsdienst*) emergency service; **n~dürftig** *adj* scanty; (*behelfsmäßig*) makeshift

Note ['noːtə] *f* note; (*SCH*) mark (*BRIT*), grade (*US*)

Noten- *zW*: **~blatt** *nt* sheet of music; **~schlüssel** *m* clef; **~ständer** *m* music stand

Not- *zW*: **~fall** *m* (case of) emergency; **n~falls** *adv* if need be; **n~gedrungen** *adj* necessary, unavoidable; **etw n~gedrungen machen** to be forced to do sth

notieren [no'tiːrən] *vt* to note; (*COMM*) to quote

Notierung *f* (*COMM*) quotation

nötig ['nøːtɪç] *adj* necessary; **etw ~ haben** to need sth; **~en** [-gən] *vt* to compel, to force; **~enfalls** *adv* if necessary

Notiz [no'tiːts] (**-, -en**) *f* note; (*Zeitungsnotiz*) item; **~ nehmen** to take notice; **~block** *m* notepad; **~buch** *nt* notebook

Not- *zW*: **~lage** *f* crisis, emergency; **n~landen** *vi* to make a forced *od* emergency landing; **n~leidend** △ *adj* siehe **Not**; **~lösung** *f* temporary solution; **~lüge** *f* white lie

notorisch [no'toːrɪʃ] *adj* notorious

Not- *zW*: **~ruf** *m* emergency call; **~rufsäule** *f* emergency telephone; **~stand** *m* state of emergency; **~unterkunft** *f* emergency accommodation; **~verband** *m* emergency dressing; **~wehr** (**-**) *f* self-defence; **n~wendig** *adj* necessary; **~wendigkeit** *f* necessity

Novelle [no'vɛlə] *f* short novel; (*JUR*) amendment

November [no'vɛmbər] (**-s, -**) *m* November

Nu [nuː] *m*: **im ~** in an instant

Spelling Reform: ▲ *new spelling* △ *old spelling (to be phased out)*

Nuance [ny'ã:sə] f nuance
nüchtern ['nʏçtərn] adj sober; (*Magen*) empty; (*Urteil*) prudent; **N~heit** f sobriety
Nudel ['nu:dəl] (-, -n) f noodle; ~**n** pl (*Teigwaren*) pasta sg; (*in Suppe*) noodles
Null [nʊl] (-, -en) f nought, zero; (*pej: Mensch*) washout; **n~** num zero; (*Fehler*) no; **n~ Uhr** midnight; **n~ und nichtig** null and void; ~**punkt** m zero; **auf dem ~punkt** at zero
numerisch [nu'me:rɪʃ] adj numerical
Nummer ['nʊmər] (-, -n) f number; (*Größe*) size; **n~ieren** ▲ vt to number; ~**nschild** nt (*AUT*) number od license (*US*) plate
nun [nu:n] adv now ♦ excl well; **das ist ~ mal so** that's the way it is
nur [nu:r] adv just, only; **wo bleibt er ~?** (just) where is he?
Nürnberg ['nʏrnbɛrk] (-s) nt Nuremberg
Nuss ▲ [nʊs] (-, ⸚e) f nut; ~**baum** m walnut tree; ~**knacker** (-s, -) m nutcracker
nutz [nʊts] adj: **zu nichts ~ sein** to be no use for anything; ~**bringend** adj (*Verwendung*) profitable
nütze ['nʏtsə] adj = **nutz**
Nutzen (-s) m usefulness; (*Gewinn*) profit; **von ~** useful; **n~ von** to be of use ♦ vt: **etw zu etw ~** to use sth for sth; **was nutzt es?** what's the use?, what use is it?
nützen vi, vt = **nutzen**
nützlich ['nʏtslɪç] adj useful; **N~keit** f usefulness
Nutz- zW: **n~los** adj useless; ~**losigkeit** f uselessness; ~**nießer** (-s, -) m beneficiary
Nylon ['naɪlɔn] (-(s)) nt nylon

O, o

Oase [o'a:zə] f oasis
ob [ɔp] konj if, whether; **~ das wohl wahr ist?** can that be true?; **und ~!** you bet!
obdachlos adj homeless
Obdachlose(r) f(m) homeless person; ~**nasyl** nt shelter for the homeless
Obduktion [ɔpdʊktsi'o:n] f post-mortem
obduzieren [ɔpdu'tsi:rən] vt to do a post-

mortem on
O-Beine ['o:baɪnə] pl bow od bandy legs
oben ['o:bən] adv above; (*in Haus*) upstairs; ~ **erwähnt, ~ gennant** above-mentioned; **nach ~** up; **von ~** down; **~ ohne** topless; **jdn von ~ bis unten ansehen** to look sb up and down; ~**an** adv at the top; ~**auf** adv up above, on the top ♦ adj (*munter*) in form; ~**drein** adv into the bargain
Ober ['o:bər] (-s, -) m waiter; **die ~en** pl (*umg*) the bosses; (*ECCL*) the superiors; ~**arm** m upper arm; ~**arzt** m senior physician; ~**aufsicht** f supervision; ~**bayern** nt Upper Bavaria; ~**befehl** m supreme command; ~**befehlshaber** m commander-in-chief; ~**bekleidung** f outer clothing; ~**bürgermeister** m lord mayor; ~**deck** nt upper od top deck; **o~e(r, s)** adj upper; ~**fläche** f surface; **o~flächlich** adj superficial; ~**geschoss** ▲ nt upper storey; **o~halb** adv above ♦ präp +gen above; ~**haupt** nt head, chief; ~**haus** nt (*POL*) upper house, House of Lords (*BRIT*); ~**hemd** nt shirt; ~**herrschaft** f supremacy, sovereignty; ~**in** f matron; (*ECCL*) Mother Superior; ~**kellner** m head waiter; ~**kiefer** m upper jaw; ~**körper** m upper part of body; ~**leitung** f direction; (*ELEK*) overhead cable; ~**licht** nt skylight; ~**lippe** f upper lip; ~**schenkel** m thigh; ~**schicht** f upper classes pl; ~**schule** f grammar school (*BRIT*), high school (*US*); ~**schwester** f (*MED*) matron
Oberst ['o:bərst] (-en od -s, -en od -e) m colonel; **o~e(r, s)** adj very top, top-most
Ober- zW: ~**stufe** f upper school; ~**teil** nt upper part; ~**weite** f bust/chest measurement
obgleich [ɔp'glaɪç] konj although
Obhut ['ɔphu:t] (-) f care, protection; **in jds ~ sein** to be in sb's care
obig ['o:bɪç] adj above
Objekt [ɔp'jɛkt] (-(e)s, -e) nt object; ~**iv** [-'ti:f] (-s, -e) nt lens; **o~iv** adj objective; ~**ivi'tät** f objectivity
Oblate [o'bla:tə] f (*Gebäck*) wafer; (*ECCL*) host

bligatorisch [obliga'to:rɪʃ] *adj* compulsory, obligatory

brigkeit ['ɔːbrɪçkaɪt] *f* (*Behörden*) authorities *pl*, administration; (*Regierung*) government

bschon [ɔp'ʃoːn] *konj* although

bservatorium [ɔpzɛrva'to:rɪʊm] *nt* observatory

bskur [ɔps'ku:r] *adj* obscure; (*verdächtig*) dubious

bst [o:pst] (**-(e)s**) *nt* fruit; **~baum** *m* fruit tree; **~garten** *m* orchard; **~händler** *m* fruiterer, fruit merchant; **~kuchen** *m* fruit tart

bszön [ɔps'tsø:n] *adj* obscene; **O~i'tät** *f* obscenity

bwohl [ɔp'vo:l] *konj* although

chse ['ɔksə] (**-n, -n**) *m* ox; **o~n** (*umg*) *vt, vi* to cram, to swot (*BRIT*)

chsenschwanzsuppe *f* oxtail soup

chsenzunge *f* oxtongue

d(e) ['øːd(ə)] *adj* (*Land*) waste, barren; (*fig*) dull; **Ö~** *f* desert, waste(land); (*fig*) tedium

der ['o:dər] *konj* or; **das stimmt, ~?** that's right, isn't it?

fen ['o:fən] (**-s, ¨**) *m* oven; (*Heizofen*) fire, heater; (*Kohlenofen*) stove; (*Hochofen*) furnace; (*Herd*) cooker, stove; **~rohr** *nt* stovepipe

ffen ['ɔfən] *adj* open; (*aufrichtig*) frank; (*Stelle*) vacant; **~ bleiben** (*Fenster*) to stay open; (*Frage, Entscheidung*) to remain open; **~ halten** to keep open; **~ lassen** to leave open; **~ stehen** to be open; (*Rechnung*) to be unpaid; **es steht Ihnen ~, es zu tun** you are at liberty to do it; **~ gesagt** to be honest; **~bar** *adj* obvious; **~baren** [ɔfən'ba:rən] *vt* to reveal, to manifest; **O~'barung** *f* (*REL*) revelation; **O~heit** *f* candour, frankness; **~herzig** *adj* candid, frank; (*Kleid*) revealing; **~kundig** *adj* well-known; (*klar*) evident; **~sichtlich** *adj* evident, obvious

ffensiv [ɔfɛn'ziːf] *adj* offensive; **O~e** [-'zi:və] *f* offensive

ffentlich ['œfəntlɪç] *adj* public; **Ö~keit** *f* (*Leute*) public; (*einer Versammlung etc*) public nature; **in aller Ö~keit** in public; **an die Ö~keit dringen** to reach the public ear

offiziell [ɔfitsi'ɛl] *adj* official

Offizier [ɔfi'tsiːr] (**-s, -e**) *m* officer; **~skasino** *nt* officers' mess

öffnen ['œfnən] *vt, vr* to open; **jdm die Tür ~** to open the door for sb

Öffner ['œfnər] (**-s, -**) *m* opener

Öffnung ['œfnʊŋ] *f* opening; **~szeiten** *pl* opening times

oft [ɔft] *adv* often

öfter ['œftər] *adv* more often *od* frequently; **~s** *adv* often, frequently

oh [o:] *excl* oh; **~ je!** oh dear

OHG *abk* (= *Offene Handelsgesellschaft*) general partnership

ohne ['o:nə] *präp +akk* without ♦ *konj* without; **das ist nicht ~** (*umg*) it's not bad; **~ weiteres** without a second thought; (*sofort*) immediately; **~ zu fragen** without asking; **~ dass er es wusste** without him knowing it; **~dies** [o:nə'di:s] *adv* anyway; **~gleichen** [o:nə'glaɪçən] *adj* unsurpassed, without equal; **~hin** [o:nə'hɪn] *adv* anyway, in any case

Ohnmacht ['o:nmaxt] *f* faint; (*fig*) impotence; **in ~ fallen** to faint

ohnmächtig ['o:nmɛçtɪç] *adj* in a faint, unconscious; (*fig*) weak, impotent; **sie ist ~** she has fainted

Ohr [o:r] (**-(e)s, -en**) *nt* ear

Öhr [ø:r] (**-(e)s, -e**) *nt* eye

Ohren- *zW:* **~arzt** *m* ear specialist; **o~betäubend** *adj* deafening; **~schmalz** *nt* earwax; **~schmerzen** *pl* earache *sg*

Ohr- *zW:* **~feige** *f* slap on the face; box on the ears; **o~feigen** *vt:* **jdn o~feigen** to slap sb's face; to box sb's ears; **~läppchen** *nt* ear lobe; **~ring** *m* earring; **~wurm** *m* earwig; (*MUS*) catchy tune

Öko- [øko] *zW:* **~laden** *m* wholefood shop; **ö~logisch** [-'lo:gɪʃ] *adj* ecological; **ö~nomisch** [-'no:mɪʃ] *adj* economical

Oktober [ɔk'to:bər] (**-s, -**) *m* October; **~fest** *nt* Munich beer festival

---

Oktoberfest

i *The annual beer festival, the* **Oktoberfest**, *takes place in Munich at the end of September in a huge area where beer tents and various amusements are set up. People sit at long wooden tables, drink beer from enormous beer mugs, eat pretzels and listen to brass bands. It is a great attraction for tourists and locals alike.*

ökumenisch [øku'me:nɪʃ] *adj* ecumenical

Öl [øːl] **(-(e)s, -e)** *nt* oil; **~baum** *m* olive tree; **ö~en** *vt* to oil; *(TECH)* to lubricate; **~farbe** *f* oil paint; **~feld** *nt* oilfield; **~film** *m* film of oil; **~heizung** *f* oil-fired central heating; **ö~ig** *adj* oily; **~industrie** *f* oil industry

oliv [o'liːf] *adj* olive-green; **O~e** *f* olive

Öl- *zW:* **~messstab** ▲ *m* dipstick; **~sardine** *f* sardine; **~stand** *m* oil level; **~standanzeiger** *m* (*AUT*) oil gauge; **~tanker** *m* oil tanker; **~ung** *f* lubrication; oiling; (*ECCL*) anointment; **die Letzte ~ung** Extreme Unction; **~wechsel** *m* oil change

Olymp- [o'lʏmp] *zW:* **~iade** [olʏmpi'aːdə] *f* Olympic Games *pl;* **~iasieger(in)** [-iaziˈgɐr(ɪn)] *m(f)* Olympic champion; **~iateilnehmer(in)** *m(f)* Olympic competitor; **o~isch** *adj* Olympic

Ölzeug *nt* oilskins *pl*

Oma ['oːma] **(-, -s)** (*umg*) *f* granny

Omelett [ɔm(ə)'lɛt] **(-(e)s, -s)** *nt* omelet(te)

ominös [omi'nøːs] *adj* (*unheilvoll*) ominous

Onanie [ona'niː] *f* masturbation; **o~ren** *vi* to masturbate

Onkel ['ɔŋkəl] **(-s, -)** *m* uncle

Opa ['oːpa] **(-s, -s)** (*umg*) *m* grandpa

Oper ['oːpɐr] **(-, -n)** *f* opera; opera house

Operation [operatsi'oːn] *f* operation; **~ssaal** *m* operating theatre

Operette [ope'rɛtə] *f* operetta

operieren [ope'riːrən] *vt* to operate ♦ *vi* to operate

Opern- *zW:* **~glas** *nt* opera glasses *pl;* **~haus** *nt* opera house

Opfer ['ɔpfɐr] **(-s, -)** *nt* sacrifice; (*Mensch*) victim; **o~n** *vt* to sacrifice; **~ung** *f* sacrifice

opponieren [ɔpo'niːrən] *vi:* **gegen jdn/etw ~** to oppose sb/sth

Opportunist [ɔpɔrtu'nɪst] *m* opportunist

Opposition [ɔpozitsi'oːn] *f* opposition; **o~ell** *adj* opposing

Optik ['ɔptɪk] *f* optics *sg;* **~er (-s, -)** *m* optician

optimal [ɔpti'maːl] *adj* optimal, optimum

Optimismus [ɔpti'mɪsmʊs] *m* optimism

Optimist [ɔpti'mɪst] *m* optimist; **o~isch** *adj* optimistic

optisch ['ɔptɪʃ] *adj* optical

Orakel [o'raːkəl] **(-s, -)** *nt* oracle

oral [o'raːl] *adj* (*MED*) oral

Orange [o'rãːʒə] *f* orange; **o~** *adj* orange; **~ade** [orã'ʒaːdə] *f* orangeade; **~at** [orã'ʒaːt] **(-s, -e)** *nt* candied peel

Orchester [ɔr'kɛstɐr] **(-s, -)** *nt* orchestra

Orchidee [ɔrçi'deːə] *f* orchid

Orden ['ɔrdən] **(-s, -)** *m* (*ECCL*) order; (*MIL*) decoration; **~sschwester** *f* nun

ordentlich ['ɔrdəntlɪç] *adj* (*anständig*) decent, respectable; (*geordnet*) tidy, neat; (*umg: annehmbar*) not bad; (: *tüchtig*) real, proper ♦ *adv* properly; **~er Professor** (full) professor; **O~keit** *f* respectability; tidiness, neatness

ordinär [ɔrdi'nɛːr] *adj* common, vulgar

ordnen ['ɔrdnən] *vt* to order, to put in order

Ordner (-s, -) *m* steward; (*COMM*) file

Ordnung *f* order; (*Ordnen*) ordering; (*Geordnetsein*) tidiness; **~ machen** to tidy up; **in ~!** okay!

Ordnungs- *zW:* **o~gemäß** *adj* proper, according to the rules; **o~liebend** *adj* orderly, methodical; **~strafe** *f* fine; **o~widrig** *adj* contrary to the rules, irregular; **~widrigkeit** [-vɪdrɪçkaɪt] *f* infringement (*of law or rule*); **~zahl** *f* ordinal number

Organ [ɔr'gaːn] **(-s, -e)** *nt* organ; (*Stimme*) voice; **~isation** [-izatsi'oːn] *f* organization; **~isator** [i'zaːtɔr] *m* organizer; **o~isch** *adj* organic; **o~isieren** [-i'ziːrən] *vt* to organize, to arrange; (*umg: beschaffen*) to acquire ♦ to organize; **~ismus** [-'nɪsmʊs] *m*

Rechtschreibreform: ▲ *neue Schreibung* △ *alte Schreibung (auslaufend)*

organism; **~ist** [-'nɪst] *m* organist;
~spende *f* organ donation;
~spenderausweis *m* donor card

Orgasmus [ɔr'gasmʊs] *m* orgasm

Orgel ['ɔrgəl] **(-, -n)** *f* organ

Orgie ['ɔrgiə] *f* orgy

Orient ['o:riɛnt] **(-s)** *m* Orient, east;
o~alisch [-'ta:lɪʃ] *adj* oriental

rientier- *zW:* **~en** [-'ti:rən] *vt* (*örtlich*) to
locate; (*fig*) to inform ♦ *vr* to find one's way
od bearings; to inform o.s.; **O~ung** [-'ti:rʊŋ]
f orientation; (*fig*) information;
O~ungssinn *m* sense of direction;
O~ungsstufe *f* period during which pupils
are selected for different schools

Orientierungsstufe

i The **Orientierungsstufe** *is the name
given to the first two years spent in a
Realschule or Gymnasium, during which
a child is assessed as to his or her
suitability for that type of school. At the
end of two years it may be decided to
transfer the child to a school more suited to
his or her ability.*

riginal [origi'na:l] *adj* original; **O~ (-s, -e)**
nt original; **O~fassung** *f* original version;
O~i'tät *f* originality

riginell [origi'nɛl] *adj* original

rkan [ɔr'ka:n] **(-(e)s, -e)** *m* hurricane;
o~artig *adj* (*Wind*) gale-force; (*Beifall*)
thunderous

rnament [ɔrna'mɛnt] *nt* decoration,
ornament; **o~al** [-'ta:l] *adj* decorative,
ornamental

rt [ɔrt] **(-(e)s, -e** *od* **¨er)** *m* place; **an ~ und
Stelle** on the spot; **o~en** *vt* to locate

tho- [ɔrto] *zW:* **~dox** [-'dɔks] *adj* orthodox;
O~grafie ▲ [-gra:'fi:] *f* spelling,
orthography; **~'grafisch** ▲ *adj*
orthographic; **O~päde** [-'pɛ:də] **(-n, -n)** *m*
orthopaedist; **O~pädie** [-pɛ'di:] *f*
orthopaedics *sg*; **~'pädisch** *adj*
orthopaedic

tlich ['œrtlɪç] *adj* local; **Ö~keit** *f* locality

tsansässig *adj* local

Ortschaft *f* village, small town

Orts- *zW:* **o~fremd** *adj* non-local;
~gespräch *nt* local (phone)call; **~name**
m place name; **~netz** *nt* (*TEL*) local
telephone exchange area; **~tarif** *m* (*TEL*)
tariff for local calls; **~zeit** *f* local time

Ortung *f* locating

Öse ['ø:zə] *f* loop, eye

Ostasien [ɔst'ta:ziən] *nt* Eastern Asia

Osten ['ɔstən] **(-s)** *m* east

Oster- ['o:stər] *zW:* **~ei** *nt* Easter egg; **~fest**
nt Easter; **~glocke** *f* daffodil; **~hase** *m*
Easter bunny; **~montag** *m* Easter Monday;
~n (-s, -) *nt* Easter

Österreich ['ø:stəraɪç] **(-s)** *nt* Austria;
~er(in) (-s, -) *m(f)* Austrian; **ö~isch** *adj*
Austrian

Ostküste *f* east coast

östlich ['œstlɪç] *adj* eastern, easterly

Ostsee *f:* **die ~** the Baltic (Sea)

Ouvertüre [uver'ty:rə] *f* overture

oval [o'va:l] *adj* oval

Ovation [ovatsi'o:n] *f* ovation

Oxid, Oxyd [ɔ'ksy:t] **(-(e)s, -e)** *nt* oxide;
o~ieren *vt, vi* to oxidize; **~ierung** *f*
oxidization

Ozean ['o:tsea:n] **(-s, -e)** *m* ocean;
~dampfer *m* (ocean-going) liner

Ozon [o'tso:n] **(-s)** *nt* ozone; **~loch** *nt* ozone
hole; **~schicht** *f* ozone layer

P, p

Paar [pa:r] **(-(e)s, -e)** *nt* pair; (*Ehepaar*)
couple; **ein p~** a few; **ein p~ Mal** a few
times; **p~en** *vt, vr* to couple; (*Tiere*) to
mate; **~lauf** *m* pair skating; **~ung** *f*
combination; mating; **p~weise** *adv* in
pairs; in couples

Pacht [paxt] **(-, -en)** *f* lease; **p~en** *vt* to
lease

Pächter ['pɛçtər] **(-s, -)** *m* leaseholder,
tenant

Pack[1] [pak] **(-(e)s, -e** *od* **¨e)** *m* bundle,
pack

Pack[2] [pak] **(-(e)s)** *nt* (*pej*) mob, rabble

Spelling Reform: ▲ *new spelling* △ *old spelling (to be phased out)*

Päckchen ['pɛkçən] *nt* small package; (*Zigaretten*) packet; (*Postpäckchen*) small parcel

Pack- *zW:* **p~en** *vt* to pack; (*fassen*) to grasp, to seize; (*umg: schaffen*) to manage; (*fig: fesseln*) to grip; **~en** (**-s, -**) *m* bundle; (*fig: Menge*) heaps of; **~esel** *m* (*auch fig*) packhorse; **~papier** *nt* brown paper, wrapping paper; **~ung** *f* packet; (*Pralinenpackung*) box; (*MED*) compress; **~ungsbeilage** *f* enclosed instructions *pl* for use

Pädagog- [pɛda'goːg] *zW:* **~e** (**-n, -n**) *m* teacher; **~ik** *f* education; **p~isch** *adj* educational, pedagogical

Paddel ['padəl] (**-s, -**) *nt* paddle; **~boot** *nt* canoe; **p~n** *vi* to paddle

Page ['paːʒə] (**-n, -n**) *m* page

Paket [pa'keːt] (**-(e)s, -e**) *nt* packet; (*Postpaket*) parcel; **~karte** *f* dispatch note; **~post** *f* parcel post; **~schalter** *m* parcels counter

Pakt [pakt] (**-(e)s, -e**) *m* pact

Palast [pa'last] (**-es, Paläste**) *m* palace

Palästina [palɛ'stiːna] (**-s**) *nt* Palestine

Palme ['palmə] *f* palm (tree)

Pampelmuse ['pampəlmuːzə] *f* grapefruit

panieren [pa'niːrən] *vt* (*KOCH*) to bread

Paniermehl [pa'niːrmeːl] *nt* breadcrumbs *pl*

Panik ['paːnɪk] *f* panic

panisch ['paːnɪʃ] *adj* panic-stricken

Panne ['panə] *f* (*AUT etc*) breakdown; (*Missgeschick*) slip; **~nhilfe** *f* breakdown service

panschen ['panʃən] *vi* to splash about ♦ *vt* to water down

Pantoffel [pan'tɔfəl] (**-s, -n**) *m* slipper

Pantomime [panto'miːmə] *f* mime

Panzer ['pantsər] (**-s, -**) *m* armour; (*Platte*) armour plate; (*Fahrzeug*) tank; **~glas** *nt* bulletproof glass; **p~n** *vt* to armour ♦ *vr* (*fig*) to arm o.s.

Papa [pa'paː] (**-s, -s**) *m* (*umg*) dad, daddy

Papagei [papa'gaɪ] (**-s, -en**) *m* parrot

Papier [pa'piːr] (**-s, -e**) *nt* paper; (*Wertpapier*) security; **~fabrik** *f* paper mill; **~geld** *nt* paper money; **~korb** *m* wastepaper basket;

~taschentuch *nt* tissue

Papp- ['pap] *zW:* **~deckel** *m* cardboard; ~ *f* cardboard; **~el** (**-, -n**) *f* poplar; **p~en** (*umg*) *vt, vi* to stick; **p~ig** *adj* sticky

Paprika ['paprika] (**-s, -s**) *m* (*Gewürz*) paprika; (*~schote*) pepper

Papst [paːpst] (**-(e)s, ⁼e**) *m* pope

päpstlich ['pɛːpstlɪç] *adj* papal

Parabel [pa'raːbəl] (**-, -n**) *f* parable; (*MATH*) parabola

Parabolantenne [para'boːlantɛnə] *f* satelli dish

Parade [pa'raːdə] *f* (*MIL*) parade, review; (*SPORT*) parry

Paradies [para'diːs] (**-es, -e**) *nt* paradise; **p~isch** *adj* heavenly

Paradox [para'dɔks] (**-es, -e**) *nt* paradox; *p adj* paradoxical

Paragraf ▲ [para'graːf] (**-en, -en**) *m* paragraph; (*JUR*) section

parallel [para'leːl] *adj* parallel; **P~e** *f* paralle

Parasit [para'ziːt] (**-en, -en**) *m* (*auch fig*) parasite

parat [pa'raːt] *adj* ready

Pärchen ['pɛːrçən] *nt* couple

Parfüm [par'fyːm] (**-s, -s** *od* **-e**) *nt* perfume **~erie** [-ə'riː] *f* perfumery; **p~frei** *adj* non-perfumed; **p~ieren** *vt* to scent, to perfum

parieren [pa'riːrən] *vt* to parry ♦ *vi* (*umg*) t obey

Paris [pa'riːs] (**-**) *nt* Paris; **~er** *adj* Parisian ♦ *m* Parisian; **~erin** *f* Parisian

Park [park] (**-s, -s**) *m* park; **~anlage** *f* park (*um Gebäude*) grounds *pl*; **p~en** *vt, vi* to park; **~ett** (**-(e)s, -e**) *nt* parquet (floor); (*THEAT*) stalls *pl*; **~gebühr** *f* parking fee; **~haus** *nt* multi-storey car park; **~lücke** *f* parking space; **~platz** *m* parking place; ca park, parking lot (*US*); **~scheibe** *f* parking disc; **~schein** *m* car park ticket; **~uhr** *f* parking meter; **~verbot** *nt* parking ban

Parlament [parla'mɛnt] *nt* parliament; **~arier** [-'taːriər] (**-s, -**) *m* parliamentarian; **p~arisch** [-'taːrɪʃ] *adj* parliamentary

Parlaments- *zW:* **~beschluss** ▲ *m* vote of parliament; **~mitglied** *nt* member of parliament; **~sitzung** *f* sitting (of parliament)

arodie [paro'di:] f parody; **p~ren** vt to parody

arole [pa'ro:lə] f password; (Wahlspruch) motto

artei [par'tai] f party; **~ ergreifen für jdn** to take sb's side; **p~isch** adj partial, bias(s)ed; **p~los** adj neutral, impartial; **~mitglied** nt party member; **~programm** nt (party) manifesto; **~tag** m party conference

arterre [par'ter] (-s, -s) nt ground floor; (THEAT) stalls pl

artie [par'ti:] f part; (Spiel) game; (Ausflug) outing; (Mann, Frau) catch; (COMM) lot; **mit von der ~ sein** to join in

artizip [parti'tsi:p] (-s, -ien) nt participle

artner(in) ['partnər(ɪn)] (-s, -) m(f) partner; **~schaft** f partnership; (von Städten) twinning; **p~schaftlich** adj as partners; **~stadt** f twin town

arty ['pa:rti] (-, -s) f party

ass ▲ [pas] (-es, ⸚e) m pass; (Ausweis) passport

assabel [pa'sa:bəl] adj passable, reasonable

assage [pa'sa:ʒə] f passage

assagier [pasa'ʒi:r] (-s, -e) m passenger; **~flugzeug** nt airliner

assamt ▲ nt passport office

assant [pa'sant] m passer-by

assbild ▲ nt passport photograph

assen ['pasən] vi to fit; (Farbe) to go; (auf Frage, KARTEN, SPORT) to pass; **das passt mir nicht** that doesn't suit me; **~ zu** (Farbe, Kleider) to go with; **er passt nicht zu dir** he's not right for you; **~d** adj suitable; (zusammenpassend) matching; (angebracht) fitting; (Zeit) convenient

assier- [pa'si:r] zW: **~bar** adj passable; **~en** vt to pass; (durch Sieb) to strain ♦ vi to happen; **P~schein** m pass, permit

assion [pasi'o:n] f passion; **p~iert** [-'ni:rt] adj enthusiastic, passionate; **~sspiel** nt Passion Play

assiv ['pasi:f] adj passive; **P~** (-s, -e) nt passive; **P~a** pl (COMM) liabilities; **P~i'tät** f passiveness; **P~rauchen** nt passive smoking

Pass- ▲ zW: **~kontrolle** f passport control; **~stelle** f passport office; **~straße** f (mountain) pass

Paste ['pastə] f paste

Pastete [pas'te:tə] f pie

pasteurisieren [pastøri'zi:rən] vt to pasteurize

Pastor ['pastɔr] m vicar; pastor, minister

Pate ['pa:tə] (-n, -n) m godfather; **~nkind** nt godchild

Patent [pa'tent] (-(e)s, -e) nt patent; (MIL) commission; **p~** adj clever; **~amt** nt patent office

Patentante f godmother

patentieren [paten'ti:rən] vt to patent

Patentinhaber m patentee

pathetisch [pa'te:tɪʃ] adj emotional; bombastic

Pathologe [pato'lo:gə] (-n, -n) m pathologist

pathologisch adj pathological

Pathos ['pa:tɔs] (-) nt emotiveness, emotionalism

Patient(in) [patsi'ent(ɪn)] m(f) patient

Patin ['pa:tɪn] f godmother

Patriot [patri'o:t] (-en, -en) m patriot; **p~isch** adj patriotic; **~ismus** [-'tɪsmʊs] m patriotism

Patrone [pa'tro:nə] f cartridge

Patrouille [pa'truljə] f patrol

patrouillieren [patrul'ji:rən] vi to patrol

patsch [patʃ] excl splash; **P~e** (umg) f (Bedrängnis) mess, jam; **~en** vi to smack, to slap; (im Wasser) to splash; **~nass** ▲ adj soaking wet

patzig ['patsɪç] (umg) adj cheeky, saucy

Pauke ['paukə] f kettledrum; **auf die ~ hauen** to live it up

pauken vt (intensiv lernen) to swot up (inf) ♦ vi to swot (inf), cram (inf)

pausbäckig ['pausbekɪç] adj chubby-cheeked

pauschal [pau'ʃa:l] adj (Kosten) inclusive; (Urteil) sweeping; **P~e** f flat rate; **P~gebühr** f flat rate; **P~preis** m all-in price; **P~reise** *f* package tour; **P~summe** *f* lump sum

Pause ['pauzə] *f* break; (*THEAT*) interval; (*Innehalten*) pause; (*Kopie*) tracing

pausen *vt* to trace; **~los** *adj* non-stop; **P~zeichen** *nt* call sign; (*MUS*) rest

Pauspapier ['pauspapiːr] *nt* tracing paper

Pavillon ['paviljõ] (**-s, -s**) *m* pavilion

Pazif- [pa'tsiːf] *zW:* **~ik** (**-s**) *m* Pacific; **p~istisch** *adj* pacifist

Pech [peç] (**-s, -e**) *nt* pitch; (*fig*) bad luck; **~ haben** to be unlucky; **p~schwarz** *adj* pitch-black; **~strähne** (*umg*) *m* unlucky patch; **~vogel** (*umg*) *m* unlucky person

Pedal [pe'daːl] (**-s, -e**) *nt* pedal

Pedant [pe'dant] *m* pedant; **~e'rie** *f* pedantry; **p~isch** *adj* pedantic

Pediküre [pedi'kyːrə] *f* (*Fußpflege*) pedicure

Pegel ['peːgəl] (**-s, -**) *m* water gauge; **~stand** *m* water level

peilen ['pailən] *vt* to get a fix on

Pein [pain] (**-**) *f* agony, pain; **p~igen** *vt* to torture; (*plagen*) to torment; **p~lich** *adj* (*unangenehm*) embarrassing, awkward, painful; (*genau*) painstaking

Peitsche ['paitʃə] *f* whip; **p~n** *vt* to whip; (*Regen*) to lash

Pelle ['pelə] *f* skin; **p~n** *vt* to skin, to peel

Pellkartoffeln *pl* jacket potatoes

Pelz [pelts] (**-es, -e**) *m* fur

Pendel ['pendəl] (**-s, -**) *nt* pendulum; **p~n** *vi* (*Zug, Fähre etc*) to operate a shuttle service; (*Mensch*) to commute; **~verkehr** *m* shuttle traffic; (*für Pendler*) commuter traffic

Pendler ['pendlər] (**-s, -**) *m* commuter

penetrant [pene'trant] *adj* sharp; (*Person*) pushing

Penis ['peːnɪs] (**-, -se**) *m* penis

pennen ['penən] (*umg*) *vi* to kip

Penner (*umg*: *pej*) *m* (*Landstreicher*) tramp

Pension [penzi'oːn] *f* (*Geld*) pension; (*Ruhestand*) retirement; (*für Gäste*) boarding *od* guesthouse; **~är(in)** [-'nɛːr(ɪn)] (**-s, -e**) *m(f)* pensioner; **p~ieren** *vt* to pension off; **p~iert** *adj* retired; **~ierung** *f* retirement; **~sgast** *m* boarder, paying guest

Pensum ['penzʊm] (**-s, Pensen**) *nt* quota;

(*SCH*) curriculum

per [pɛr] *präp +akk* by, per; (*pro*) per; (*bis*) b

Perfekt ['pɛrfɛkt] (**-(e)s, -e**) *nt* perfect; **p~** *adj* perfect

perforieren [pɛrfo'riːrən] *vt* to perforate

Pergament [pɛrga'mɛnt] *nt* parchment; **~papier** *nt* greaseproof paper

Periode [peri'oːdə] *f* period; **periodisch** *a* periodic; (*dezimal*) recurring

Perle ['pɛrlə] *f* (*auch fig*) pearl; **p~n** *vi* to sparkle; (*Tropfen*) to trickle

Perl- ['pɛrl] *zW:* **~mutt** (**-s**) *nt* mother-of-pearl; **~wein** *m* sparkling wine

perplex [pɛr'plɛks] *adj* dumbfounded

Person [pɛr'zoːn] (**-, -en**) *f* person; **ich für meine ~ ...** personally I ...

Personal [pɛrzo'naːl] (**-s**) *nt* personnel; (*Bedienung*) servants *pl*; **~ausweis** *m* identity card; **~computer** *m* personal computer; **~ien** [-iən] *pl* particulars; **~mangel** *m* undermanning; **~pronomer** *nt* personal pronoun

personell [pɛrzo'nɛl] *adj* (*Veränderungen*) personnel

Personen- *zW:* **~aufzug** *m* lift, elevator (*US*); **~kraftwagen** *m* private motorcar; **~schaden** *m* injury to persons; **~zug** *m* stopping train; passenger train

personifizieren [pɛrzonifi'tsiːrən] *vt* to personify

persönlich [pɛr'zøːnlɪç] *adj* personal ♦ *adv* in person; personally; **P~keit** *f* personality

Perspektive [pɛrspɛk'tiːvə] *f* perspective

Perücke [pe'rʏkə] *f* wig

pervers [pɛr'vɛrs] *adj* perverse

Pessimismus [pɛsi'mɪsmʊs] *m* pessimism

Pessimist [pɛsi'mɪst] *m* pessimist; **p~isch** *adj* pessimistic

Pest [pɛst] (**-**) *f* plague

Petersilie [petər'ziːliə] *f* parsley

Petroleum [pe'troːleʊm] (**-s**) *nt* paraffin, kerosene (*US*)

Pfad [pfaːt] (**-(e)s, -e**) *m* path; **~finder** (**-s, -**) *m* boy scout; **~finderin** *f* girl guide

Pfahl [pfaːl] (**-(e)s, ⁼e**) *m* post, stake

Pfand [pfant] (**-(e)s, ⁼er**) *nt* pledge, security (*Flaschenpfand*) deposit; (*im Spiel*) forfeit;

~brief m bond

~änden ['pfɛndən] vt to seize, to distrain

~änderspiel nt game of forfeits

~andflasche f returnable bottle

~andschein m pawn ticket

~ändung ['pfɛndʊŋ] f seizure, distraint

~anne ['pfanə] f (frying) pan

~annkuchen m pancake; (Berliner) doughnut

~arr- ['pfar] zW: ~ei f parish; ~er (-s, -) m priest; (evangelisch) vicar; minister; ~haus nt vicarage; manse

~au [pfaʊ] (-(e)s), -en f peacock; ~enauge nt peacock butterfly

~effer ['pfɛfər] (-s, -) m pepper; ~kuchen m gingerbread; ~minz (-es, -e) nt peppermint; ~mühle f pepper mill; p~n vt to pepper; (umg: werfen) to fling; **gepfefferte Preise/Witze** steep prices/spicy jokes

~eife ['pfaɪfə] f whistle; (Tabakpfeife, Orgelpfeife) pipe; p~n (unreg) vt, vi to whistle; ~r (-s, -) m piper

~eil [pfaɪl] (-(e)s, -e) m arrow

~eiler ['pfaɪlər] (-s, -) m pillar, prop; (Brückenpfeiler) pier

~ennig ['pfɛnɪç] (-(e)s, -e) m (HIST) pfennig (hundredth part of a mark)

~erd [pfeːrt] (-(e)s, -e) nt horse

~erde- ['pfeːrdə] zW: ~rennen nt horse race; horse racing; ~schwanz m (Frisur) ponytail; ~stall m stable

~iff [pfɪf] (-(e)s, -e) m whistle

~ifferling ['pfɪfɐlɪŋ] m yellow chanterelle (mushroom); **keinen ~ wert** not worth a thing

~iffig adj sly, sharp

~ingsten ['pfɪŋstən] (-, -) nt Whitsun (BRIT), Pentecost

~irsich ['pfɪrzɪç] (-s, -e) m peach

~lanz- ['pflants] zW: ~e f plant; p~en vt to plant; ~enfett nt vegetable fat; p~lich adj vegetable; ~ung f plantation

~laster ['pflastər] (-s, -) nt plaster; (Straße) pavement; p~n vt to pave; ~stein m paving stone

~laume ['pflaʊmə] f plum

Pflege ['pfleːgə] f care; (von Idee) cultivation; (Krankenpflege) nursing; **in ~ sein** (Kind) to be fostered out; p~bedürftig adj needing care; ~eltern pl foster parents; ~heim nt nursing home; ~kind nt foster child; p~leicht adj easy-care; ~mutter f foster mother; p~n vt to look after; (Kranke) to nurse; (Beziehungen) to foster; ~r (-s, -) m orderly; male nurse; ~rin f nurse, attendant; ~vater m foster father

Pflicht [pflɪçt] (-, -en) f duty; (SPORT) compulsory section; p~bewusst ▲ adj conscientious; ~fach nt (SCH) compulsory subject; ~gefühl nt sense of duty; p~gemäß adj dutiful ♦ adv as in duty bound; ~versicherung f compulsory insurance

pflücken ['pflʏkən] vt to pick; (Blumen) to pick, to pluck

Pflug [pfluːk] (-(e)s, ⁺e) m plough

pflügen ['pflyːgən] vt to plough

Pforte ['pfɔrtə] f gate; door

Pförtner ['pfœrtnər] (-s, -) m porter, doorkeeper, doorman

Pfosten ['pfɔstən] (-s, -) m post

Pfote ['pfoːtə] f paw; (umg: Schrift) scrawl

Pfropfen (-s, -) m (Flaschenpfropfen) stopper; (Blutpfropfen) clot

pfui [pfʊɪ] excl ugh!

Pfund [pfʊnt] (-(e)s, -e) nt pound

pfuschen ['pfʊʃən] (umg) vi to be sloppy; **jdm ins Handwerk ~** to interfere in sb's business

Pfuscher ['pfʊʃər] (-s, -) (umg) m sloppy worker; (Kurpfuscher) quack; ~ei (umg) f sloppy work; quackery

Pfütze ['pfʏtsə] f puddle

Phänomen [feno'meːn] (-s, -e) nt phenomenon

phänomenal [-'naːl] adj phenomenal

Phantasie etc [fanta'ziː] f = **Fantasie** etc

phantastisch [fan'tastɪʃ] adj = **fantastisch**

Phase ['faːzə] f phase

Philologie [filolo'giː] f philology

Philosoph [filo'zoːf] (-en, -en) m philosopher; ~ie [-'fiː] f philosophy; p~isch adj philosophical

Spelling Reform: ▲ new spelling △ old spelling (to be phased out)

phlegmatisch [fle'gma:tɪʃ] *adj* lethargic
Phonetik [fo'ne:tɪk] *f* phonetics *sg*
phonetisch *adj* phonetic
Phosphor ['fɔsfɔr] (**-s**) *m* phosphorus
Photo *etc* ['fo:to] (**-s, -s**) *nt* = **Foto** *etc*
Phrase ['fra:zə] *f* phrase; (*pej*) hollow phrase
pH-Wert [pe:'ha:vert] *m* pH-value
Physik [fy'zi:k] *f* physics *sg*; **p~alisch**
[-'ka:lɪʃ] *adj* of physics; **~er(in)** ['fy:zɪkər(ɪn)]
(**-s, -**) *m(f)* physicist
Physiologie [fyziolo'gi:] *f* physiology
physisch ['fy:zɪʃ] *adj* physical
Pianist(in) [pia'nɪst(ɪn)] *m(f)* pianist
Pickel ['pɪkəl] (**-s, -**) *m* pimple; (*Werkzeug*)
pickaxe; (*Bergpickel*) ice axe; **p~ig** *adj*
pimply, spotty
picken ['pɪkən] *vi* to pick, to peck
Picknick ['pɪknɪk] (**-s, -e** *od* **-s**) *nt* picnic; **~**
machen to have a picnic
piepen ['pi:pən] *vi* to chirp
piepsen ['pi:psən] *vi* to chirp
Piepser (*umg*) *m* pager, paging device
Pier [pi:ər] (**-s, -s** *od* **-e**) *m od f* pier
Pietät [pie'tɛ:t] *f* piety, reverence; **p~los** *adj*
impious, irreverent
Pigment [pɪg'mɛnt] *nt* pigment
Pik [pi:k] (**-s, -s**) *nt* (*KARTEN*) spades
pikant [pi'kant] *adj* spicy, piquant;
(*anzüglich*) suggestive
Pilger ['pɪlgər] (**-s, -**) *m* pilgrim; **~fahrt** *f*
pilgrimage
Pille ['pɪlə] *f* pill
Pilot [pi'lo:t] (**-en, -en**) *m* pilot
Pilz [pɪlts] (**-es, -e**) *m* fungus; (*essbar*)
mushroom; (*giftig*) toadstool; **~krankheit** *f*
fungal disease
Pinguin ['pɪngui:n] (**-s, -e**) *m* penguin
Pinie ['pi:niə] *f* pine
pinkeln ['pɪŋkəln] (*umg*) *vi* to pee
Pinnwand ['pɪnvant] *f* noticeboard
Pinsel ['pɪnzəl] (**-s, -**) *m* paintbrush
Pinzette [pɪn'tsɛtə] *f* tweezers *pl*
Pionier [pio'ni:r] (**-s, -e**) *m* pioneer; (*MIL*)
sapper, engineer
Pirat [pi'ra:t] (**-en, -en**) *m* pirate
Piste ['pɪstə] *f* (*SKI*) run, piste; (*AVIAT*) runway
Pistole [pɪs'to:lə] *f* pistol

Pizza ['pɪtsa] (**-, -s**) *f* pizza
Pkw [pe:ka:'ve:] (**-(s), -(s)**) *m abk* =
Personenkraftwagen
plädieren [plɛ'di:rən] *vi* to plead
Plädoyer [plɛdoa'je:] (**-s, -s**) *nt* speech for
the defence; (*fig*) plea
Plage ['pla:gə] *f* plague; (*Mühe*) nuisance;
~geist *m* pest, nuisance; **p~n** *vt* to
torment ♦ *vr* to toil, to slave
Plakat [pla'ka:t] (**-(e)s, -e**) *nt* placard; pos
Plan [pla:n] (**-(e)s, ᵘe**) *m* plan; (*Karte*) map
Plane *f* tarpaulin
planen *vt* to plan; (*Mord etc*) to plot
Planer (**-s, -**) *m* planner
Planet [pla'ne:t] (**-en, -en**) *m* planet
planieren [pla'ni:rən] *vt* to plane, to level
Planke ['plaŋkə] *f* plank
plan- [pla:n] *zW*: **~los** *adj* (*Vorgehen*)
unsystematic; (*Umherlaufen*) aimless;
~mäßig *adj* according to plan; systemati
(*EISENB*) scheduled
Plansoll (**-s**) *nt* output target
Plantage [plan'ta:ʒə] *f* plantation
Plan(t)schbecken ['plan(t)ʃbɛkən] *nt*
paddling pool
plan(t)schen ['plan(t)ʃən] *vi* to splash
Planung *f* planning
Planwirtschaft *f* planned economy
plappern ['plapərn] *vi* to chatter
plärren ['plɛrən] *vi* (*Mensch*) to cry, to
whine; (*Radio*) to blare
Plasma ['plasma] (**-s, Plasmen**) *nt* plasma
Plastik[1] ['plastɪk] *f* sculpture
Plastik[2] ['plastɪk] (**-s**) *nt* (*Kunststoff*) plasti
~beutel *m* plastic bag, carrier bag; **~foli**
f plastic film
plastisch ['plastɪʃ] *adj* plastic; **stell dir das**
~ vor! just picture it!
Platane [pla'ta:nə] *f* plane (tree)
Platin ['pla:tin] (**-s**) *nt* platinum
platonisch [pla'to:nɪʃ] *adj* platonic
platsch [platʃ] *excl* splash; **~en** *vi* to splash
plätschern ['plɛtʃərn] *vi* to babble
platschnass ▲ *adj* drenched
platt [plat] *adj* flat; (*umg: überrascht*)
flabbergasted; (*fig: geistlos*) flat, boring;
~deutsch *adj* low German; **P~e** *f*

(*Speisenplatte*, PHOT, TECH) plate; (*Steinplatte*) flag; (*Kachel*) tile; (*Schallplatte*) record; **P~enspieler** *m* record player; **P~enteller** *m* turntable

Platz [plats] (**-es**, **ᵉe**) *m* place; (*Sitzplatz*) seat; (*Raum*) space, room; (*in Stadt*) square; (*Sportplatz*) playing field; **~ nehmen** to take a seat; **jdm ~ machen** to make room for sb; **~angst** *f* claustrophobia; **~anweiser(in)** (**-s**, **-**) *m(f)* usher(ette)

Plätzchen ['pletsçən] *nt* spot; (*Gebäck*) biscuit

platzen *vi* to burst; (*Bombe*) to explode; **vor Wut p~en** (*umg*) to be bursting with anger

platzieren ▲ [pla'tsiːrən] *vt* to place ♦ *vr* (SPORT) to be placed; (TENNIS) to be seeded

Platz- *zW*: **~karte** *f* seat reservation; **~mangel** *m* lack of space; **~patrone** *f* blank cartridge; **~regen** *m* downpour; **~reservierung** [-rezɛrviːruŋ] *f* seat reservation; **~wunde** *f* cut

Plauderei [plaudə'raɪ] *f* chat, conversation; (RADIO) talk

plaudern ['plaudərn] *vi* to chat, to talk

plausibel [plau'ziːbəl] *adj* plausible

plazieren △ [pla'tsiːrən] *vt*, *vr siehe* **platzieren**

Pleite ['plaɪtə] *f* bankruptcy; (*umg: Reinfall*) flop; **~ machen** to go bust; **p~** (*umg*) *adj* broke

Plenum ['pleːnʊm] (**-s**) *nt* plenum

Plombe ['plɔmbə] *f* lead seal; (*Zahnplombe*) filling

plombieren [plɔm'biːrən] *vt* to seal; (*Zahn*) to fill

plötzlich ['plœtslɪç] *adj* sudden ♦ *adv* suddenly

plump [plʊmp] *adj* clumsy; (*Hände*) coarse; (*Körper*) shapeless; **~sen** (*umg*) *vi* to plump down, to fall

Plunder ['plʊndər] (**-s**) *m* rubbish

plündern ['plʏndərn] *vt* to plunder; (*Stadt*) to sack ♦ *vi* to plunder; **Plünderung** *f* plundering, sack, pillage

Plural ['pluːraːl] (**-s**, **-e**) *m* plural; **p~istisch** *adj* pluralistic

Plus [plʊs] (**-**, **-**) *nt* plus; (FIN) profit; (*Vorteil*) advantage; **p~** *adv* plus

Plüsch [plyːʃ] (**-(e)s**, **-e**) *m* plush

Plus- [plʊs] *zW*: **~pol** *m* (ELEK) positive pole; **~punkt** *m* point; (*fig*) point in sb's favour

Plutonium [plu'toːniʊm] (**-s**) *nt* plutonium

PLZ *abk* = **Postleitzahl**

Po [poː] (**-s**, **-s**) (*umg*) *m* bottom, bum

Pöbel ['pøːbəl] (**-s**) *m* mob, rabble; **~ei** *f* vulgarity; **p~haft** *adj* low, vulgar

pochen ['pɔxən] *vi* to knock; (*Herz*) to pound; **auf etw** *akk* **~** (*fig*) to insist on sth

Pocken ['pɔkən] *pl* smallpox *sg*

Podium ['poːdiʊm] *nt* podium; **~sdiskussion** *f* panel discussion

Poesie [poe'ziː] *f* poetry

Poet [po'eːt] (**-en**, **-en**) *m* poet; **p~isch** *adj* poetic

Pointe ['poɛ̃ːtə] *f* point

Pokal [po'kaːl] (**-s**, **-e**) *m* goblet; (SPORT) cup; **~spiel** *nt* cup tie

pökeln ['pøːkəln] *vt* to pickle, to salt

Poker ['poːkər] (**-s**) *nt od m* poker

Pol [poːl] (**-s**, **-e**) *m* pole; **p~ar** *adj* polar; **~arkreis** *m* Arctic circle

Pole ['poːlə] (**-n**, **-n**) *m* Pole

polemisch [po'leːmɪʃ] *adj* polemical

Polen ['poːlən] (**-s**) *nt* Poland

Police [po'liːs(ə)] *f* insurance policy

Polier [po'liːr] (**-s**, **-e**) *m* foreman

polieren *vt* to polish

Poliklinik [poli'kliːnɪk] *f* outpatients (department) *sg*

Polin *f* Pole

Politik [poli'tiːk] *f* politics *sg*; (*eine bestimmte*) policy; **~er(in)** [po'liːtɪkər(ɪn)] (**-s**, **-**) *m(f)* politician

politisch [po'liːtɪʃ] *adj* political

Politur [poli'tuːr] *f* polish

Polizei [poli'tsaɪ] *f* police; **~beamte(r)** *m* police officer; **p~lich** *adj* police; **sich p~lich melden** to register with the police; **~revier** *nt* police station; **~staat** *m* police state; **~streife** *f* police patrol; **~stunde** *f* closing time; **~wache** *f* police station

Polizist(in) [poli'tsɪst(ɪn)] (**-en**, **-en**) *m(f)* policeman(-woman)

Pollen ['pɔlən] (**-s, -**) *m* pollen; **~flug** *m* pollen count

polnisch ['pɔlnɪʃ] *adj* Polish

Polohemd ['po:lohɛmt] *nt* polo shirt

Polster ['pɔlstər] (**-s, -**) *nt* cushion; (**~ung**) upholstery; (*in Kleidung*) padding; (*fig: Geld*) reserves *pl*; **~er** (**-s, -**) *m* upholsterer; **~möbel** *pl* upholstered furniture *sg*; **p~n** *vt* to upholster; to pad

Polterabend ['pɔltəra:bənt] *m* party on eve of wedding

poltern *vi* (*Krach machen*) to crash; (*schimpfen*) to rant

Polyp [po'ly:p] (**-en, -en**) *m* polyp; (*umg*) cop; **~en** *pl* (*MED*) adenoids

Pomade [po'ma:də] *f* pomade

Pommes frites [pɔm'frɪt] *pl* chips, French fried potatoes

Pomp [pɔmp] (**-(e)s**) *m* pomp; **p~ös** [pɔm'pø:s] *adj* (*Auftritt, Fest, Haus*) ostentatious, showy

Pony ['pɔni] (**-s, -s**) *nt* (*Pferd*) pony ♦ *m* (*Frisur*) fringe

Popmusik ['pɔpmuzi:k] *f* pop music

Popo [po'po:] (**-s, -s**) *m* bottom, bum

poppig ['pɔpɪç] *adj* (*Farbe etc*) gaudy

populär [popu'lɛ:r] *adj* popular

Popularität [populari'tɛ:t] *f* popularity

Pore ['po:rə] *f* pore

Pornografie ▲ [pɔrnogra'fi:] *f* pornography; **pornografisch** ▲ [pɔrno'gra:fɪʃ] *adj* pornographic

porös [po'rø:s] *adj* porous

Porree ['pɔre] (**-s, -s**) *m* leek

Portefeuille [pɔrt(ə)'fø:j] *nt* (*POL, FIN*) portfolio

Portemonnaie [pɔrtmɔ'ne:] (**-s, -s**) *nt* purse

Portier [pɔrti'e:] (**-s, -s**) *m* porter

Portion [pɔrtsi'o:n] *f* portion, helping; (*umg: Anteil*) amount

Portmonee ▲ [pɔrtmɔ'ne:] (**-s, -s**) *nt* = **Portemonnaie**

Porto ['pɔrto] (**-s, -s**) *nt* postage; **p~frei** *adj* post-free, (postage) prepaid

Portrait [pɔr'trɛ:] (**-s, -s**) *nt* = **Porträt**; **p~ieren** *vt* = **porträtieren**

Porträt [pɔr'trɛ:] (**-s, -s**) *nt* portrait; **p~ieren** *vt* to paint, to portray

Portugal ['pɔrtugal] (**-s**) *nt* Portugal; **Portugiese** [pɔrtu'gi:zə] (**-n, -n**) *m* Portuguese; **Portu'giesin** *f* Portuguese; **portu'giesisch** *adj* Portuguese

Porzellan [pɔrtse'la:n] (**-s, -e**) *nt* china, porcelain; (*Geschirr*) china

Posaune [po'zaunə] *f* trombone

Pose ['po:zə] *f* pose

Position [pozitsi'o:n] *f* position

positiv ['po:ziti:f] *adj* positive; **P~** (**-s, -e**) *nt* (*PHOT*) positive

possessiv ['pɔsesi:f] *adj* possessive; **P~pronomen** (**-s, -e**) *nt* possessive pronoun

possierlich [pɔ'si:rlɪç] *adj* funny

Post [pɔst] (**-, -en**) *f* post (office); (*Briefe*) mail; **~amt** *nt* post office; **~anweisung** *f* postal order, money order; **~bote** *m* postman; **~en** (**-s, -**) *m* post, position; (*COMM*) item (*auf Liste*) entry; (*MIL*) sentry; (*Streikposten*) picket; **~er** (**-s, -(s)**) *nt* poster; **~fach** *nt* post office box; **~karte** *f* postcard; **p~lagernd** *adv* poste restante (*BRIT*), general delivery (*US*); **~leitzahl** *f* postal code; **~scheckkonto** *nt* postal giro account; **~sparbuch** *nt* post office savings book; **~sparkasse** *f* post office savings bank; **~stempel** *m* postmark; **p~wendend** *adv* by return of post; **~wertzeichen** *nt* postage stamp

potent [po'tent] *adj* potent

Potential △ [potentsi'a:l] (**-s, -e**) *nt siehe* **Potenzial**

potentiell △ [potentsi'ɛl] *adj siehe* **potenziell**

Potenz [po'tents] *f* power; (*eines Mannes*) potency

Potenzial ▲ [poten'tsia:l] (**-s, -e**) *nt* potential

potenziell ▲ [poten'tsiɛl] *adj* potential

Pracht [praxt] (**-**) *f* splendour, magnificence; **prächtig** ['prɛçtɪç] *adj* splendid

Prachtstück *nt* showpiece

prachtvoll *adj* splendid, magnificent

Prädikat [predi'ka:t] (**-(e)s, -e**) *nt* title;

(*GRAM*) predicate; (*Zensur*) distinction

prägen ['pre:gən] *vt* to stamp; (*Münze*) to mint; (*Ausdruck*) to coin; (*Charakter*) to form

prägnant [pre'gnant] *adj* precise, terse

Prägung ['pre:gʊŋ] *f* minting; forming; (*Eigenart*) character, stamp

prahlen ['pra:lən] *vi* to boast, to brag; **Prahle'rei** *f* boasting

Praktik ['praktɪk] *f* practice; **p~abel** [-'ka:bəl] *adj* practicable; **~ant(in)** [-'kant(ɪn)] *m(f)* trainee; **~um** (**-s, Praktika** *od* **Praktiken**) *nt* practical training

praktisch ['praktɪʃ] *adj* practical, handy; **~er Arzt** general practitioner

praktizieren [praktɪ'tsi:rən] *vt, vi* to practise

Praline [pra'li:nə] *f* chocolate

prall [pral] *adj* firmly rounded; (*Segel*) taut; (*Arme*) plump; (*Sonne*) blazing; **~en** *vi* to bounce, to rebound; (*Sonne*) to blaze

Prämie ['pre:miə] *f* premium; (*Belohnung*) award, prize; **p~ren** *vt* to give an award to

Präparat [prepa'ra:t] (**-(e)s, -e**) *nt* (*BIOL*) preparation; (*MED*) medicine

Präposition [prepozitsi'o:n] *f* preposition

Prärie [pre'ri:] *f* prairie

Präsens ['pre:zens] (**-**) *nt* present tense

präsentieren [prezen'ti:rən] *vt* to present

Präservativ [prezerva'ti:f] (**-s, -e**) *nt* contraceptive

Präsident(in) [prezi'dent(ɪn)] *m(f)* president; **~schaft** *f* presidency

Präsidium [pre'zi:diʊm] *nt* presidency, chair(manship); (*Polizeipräsidium*) police headquarters *pl*

prasseln ['prasəln] *vi* (*Feuer*) to crackle; (*Hagel*) to drum; (*Wörter*) to rain down

Praxis ['praksɪs] (**-, Praxen**) *f* practice; (*Behandlungsraum*) surgery; (*von Anwalt*) office

Präzedenzfall [pretse'dents-] *m* precedent

präzis [pre'tsi:s] *adj* precise; **P~ion** [pretsizi'o:n] *f* precision

predigen ['pre:dɪgən] *vt, vi* to preach; **Prediger** (**-s, -**) *m* preacher

Predigt ['pre:dɪçt] (**-, -en**) *f* sermon

Preis [prais] (**-es, -e**) *m* price; (*Siegespreis*) prize; **um keinen ~** not at any price;

p~bewusst ▲ *adj* price-conscious

Preiselbeere *f* cranberry

preis- ['prais] *zW:* **~en** (*unreg*) *vi* to praise; **~geben** (*unreg*) *vt* to abandon; (*opfern*) to sacrifice; (*zeigen*) to expose; **~gekrönt** *adj* prizewinning; **P~lage** *f* price range; **~lich** *adj* (*Lage, Unterschied*) price, in price; **P~liste** *f* price list; **P~richter** *m* judge (*in a competition*); **P~schild** *nt* price tag; **P~träger(in)** *m(f)* prizewinner; **~wert** *adj* inexpensive

Prell- [prel] *zW:* **~bock** *m* buffers *pl*; **p~en** *vt* to bump; (*fig*) to cheat, to swindle; **~ung** *f* bruise

Premiere [prəmi'e:rə] *f* premiere

Premierminister [prəmi'e:mɪnɪstər] *m* prime minister, premier

Presse ['presə] *f* press; **~agentur** *f* press agency; **~freiheit** *f* freedom of the press; **p~n** *vt* to press

Pressluft ▲ ['presluft] *f* compressed air; **~bohrer** *m* pneumatic drill

Prestige [pres'ti:ʒə] (**-s**) *nt* prestige

prickeln ['prɪkəln] *vt, vi* to tingle; to tickle

Priester ['pri:stər] (**-s, -**) *m* priest

prima *adj inv* first-class, excellent

primär [pri'me:r] *adj* primary

Primel ['pri:məl] (**-, -n**) *f* primrose

primitiv [primi'ti:f] *adj* primitive

Prinz [prɪnts] (**-en, -en**) *m* prince; **~essin** *f* princess

Prinzip [prɪn'tsi:p] (**-s, -ien**) *nt* principle; **p~iell** [-i'el] *adj, adv* on principle; **p~ienlos** *adj* unprincipled

Priorität [priori'te:t] *f* priority

Prise ['pri:zə] *f* pinch

Prisma ['prɪsma] (**-s, Prismen**) *nt* prism

privat [pri'va:t] *adj* private; **P~besitz** *m* private property; **P~fernsehen** *nt* commercial television; **P~patient(in)** *m(f)* private patient; **P~schule** *f* public school

Privileg [privi'le:k] (**-(e)s, -ien**) *nt* privilege

Pro [pro:] (**-**) *nt* pro

pro *präp +akk* per

Probe ['pro:bə] *f* test; (*Teststück*) sample; (*THEAT*) rehearsal; **jdn auf die ~ stellen** to put sb to the test; **~exemplar** *nt* specimen copy; **~fahrt** *f* test drive; **p~n** *vt* to try; (*THEAT*) to rehearse; **p~weise** *adv* on approval; **~zeit** *f* probation period

probieren [proˈbiːrən] *vt* to try; (*Wein, Speise*) to taste, to sample ♦ *vi* to try; to taste

Problem [proˈbleːm] **(-s, -e)** *nt* problem; **~atik** [-ˈmaːtɪk] *f* problem; **p~atisch** [-ˈmaːtɪʃ] *adj* problematic; **p~los** *adj* problem-free

Produkt [proˈdʊkt] **(-(e)s, -e)** *nt* product; (*AGR*) produce *no pl*; **~ion** [prodʊktsiˈoːn] *f* production; output; **p~iv** [-ˈtiːf] *adj* productive; **~ivität** *f* productivity

Produzent [produˈtsɛnt] *m* manufacturer; (*Film*) producer

produzieren [produˈtsiːrən] *vt* to produce

Professor [proˈfɛsɔr] *m* professor

Profi [ˈproːfi] **(-s, -s)** *m* (*umg, SPORT*) pro

Profil [proˈfiːl] **(-s, -e)** *nt* profile; (*fig*) image

Profit [proˈfiːt] **(-(e)s, -e)** *m* profit; **p~ieren** *vi*: **p~ieren (von)** to profit (from)

Prognose [proˈɡnoːzə] *f* prediction, prognosis

Programm [proˈɡram] **(-s, -e)** *nt* programme; (*COMPUT*) program; **p~ieren** [-ˈmiːrən] *vt* to programme; (*COMPUT*) to program; **~ierer(in)** **(-s, -)** *m(f)* programmer

progressiv [proɡrɛˈsiːf] *adj* progressive

Projekt [proˈjɛkt] **(-(e)s, -e)** *nt* project; **~or** [proˈjɛktɔr] *m* projector

proklamieren [proklaˈmiːrən] *vt* to proclaim

Prokurist(in) [prokuˈrɪst(ɪn)] *m(f)* ≃ company secretary

Prolet [proˈleːt] **(-en, -en)** *m* prole, pleb; **~arier** [-ˈtaːriər] **(-s, -)** *m* proletarian

Prolog [proˈloːk] **(-(e)s, -e)** *m* prologue

Promenade [proməˈnaːdə] *f* promenade

Promille [proˈmɪlə] **(-(s), -)** *nt* alcohol level

prominent [promiˈnɛnt] *adj* prominent

Prominenz [promiˈnɛnts] *f* VIPs *pl*

Promotion [promotsiˈoːn] *f* doctorate, Ph.D.

promovieren [promoˈviːrən] *vi* to do a doctorate *od* Ph.D.

prompt [prɔmpt] *adj* prompt

Pronomen [proˈnoːmɛn] **(-s, -)** *nt* pronoun

Propaganda [propaˈɡanda] **(-)** *f* propaganda

Propeller [proˈpɛlər] **(-s, -)** *m* propeller

Prophet [proˈfeːt] **(-en, -en)** *m* prophet

prophezeien [profeˈtsaɪən] *vt* to prophesy; **Prophezeiung** *f* prophecy

Proportion [propɔrtsiˈoːn] *f* proportion; **p~al** [-ˈnaːl] *adj* proportional

proportioniert [propɔrtsioˈniːrt] *adj*: **gut/schlecht ~** well-/badly-proportioned

Prosa [ˈproːza] **(-)** *f* prose; **p~isch** [proˈzaːɪʃ] *adj* prosaic

prosit [ˈproːzɪt] *excl* cheers

Prospekt [proˈspɛkt] **(-(e)s, -e)** *m* leaflet, brochure

prost [proːst] *excl* cheers

Prostituierte [prostituˈiːrtə] *f* prostitute

Prostitution [prostitutsiˈoːn] *f* prostitution

Protest [proˈtɛst] **(-(e)s, -e)** *m* protest; **~ant(in)** [protɛsˈtant(ɪn)] *m(f)* Protestant; **p~antisch** [protɛsˈtantɪʃ] *adj* Protestant; **p~ieren** [protɛsˈtiːrən] *vi* to protest

Prothese [proˈteːzə] *f* artificial limb; (*Zahnprothese*) dentures *pl*

Protokoll [protoˈkɔl] **(-s, -e)** *nt* register; (*von Sitzung*) minutes *pl*; (*diplomatisch*) protocol; (*Polizeiprotokoll*) statement; **p~ieren** [-ˈliːrən] *vt* to take down in the minutes

protzen [ˈprɔtsən] *vi* to show off

Proviant [proviˈant] **(-s, -e)** *m* provisions *pl*, supplies *pl*

Provinz [proˈvɪnts] **(-, -en)** *f* province; **p~iell** *adj* provincial

Provision [proviziˈoːn] *f* (*COMM*) commission

provisorisch [proviˈzoːrɪʃ] *adj* provisional

Provokation [provokatsiˈoːn] *f* provocation

provozieren [provoˈtsiːrən] *vt* to provoke

Prozedur [protseˈduːr] *f* procedure; (*pej*) carry-on

Prozent [proˈtsɛnt] **(-(e)s, -e)** *nt* per cent, percentage; **~satz** *m* percentage; **p~ual** [-uˈaːl] *adj* percentage *cpd*; as a percentage

Prozess ▲ [proˈtsɛs] **(-es, -e)** *m* trial, case

Prozession [protsɛsiˈoːn] *f* procession

prüde [ˈpryːdə] *adj* prudish; **P~rie** [-ˈriː] *f* prudery

Prüf- ['pry:f] *zW:* **p~en** *vt* to examine, to test; (*nachprüfen*) to check; **~er (-s, -)** *m* examiner; **~ling** *m* examinee; **~ung** *f* examination; checking; **~ungsausschuss** ▲ *m* examining board

Prügel ['pry:gəl] **(-s, -)** *m* cudgel ♦ *pl* (*Schläge*) beating; **~ei** [-'laɪ] *f* fight; **p~n** *vt* to beat ♦ *vr* to fight; **~strafe** *f* corporal punishment

Prunk [prʊŋk] **(-(e)s)** *m* pomp, show; **p~voll** *adj* splendid, magnificent

PS [pe:'ʔɛs] *abk* (= *Pferdestärke*) H.P.

Psych- ['psyç] *zW:* **~iater** [-i'a:tər] **(-s, -)** *m* psychiatrist; **p~iatrisch** *adj* (*MED*) psychiatric; **p~isch** *adj* psychological; **~oanalyse** [-o|ana'ly:zə] *f* psychoanalysis; **~ologe (-n, -n)** *m* psychologist; **~olo'gie** *f* psychology; **p~ologisch** *adj* psychological; **~otherapeut(in) (-en, -en)** *m(f)* psychotherapist

Pubertät [puber'tɛ:t] *f* puberty

Publikum ['pu:blikʊm] **(-s)** *nt* audience; (*SPORT*) crowd

publizieren [publi'tsi:rən] *vt* to publish, to publicize

Pudding ['pʊdɪŋ] **(-s, -e** *od* **-s)** *m* blancmange

Pudel ['pu:dəl] **(-s, -)** *m* poodle

Puder ['pu:dər] **(-s, -)** *m* powder; **~dose** *f* powder compact; **p~n** *vt* to powder; **~zucker** *m* icing sugar

Puff¹ [pʊf] **(-s, -e)** *m* (*Wäschepuff*) linen basket; (*Sitzpuff*) pouf

Puff² [pʊf] **(-s, ⁺e)** (*umg*) *m* (*Stoß*) push

Puff³ [pʊf] **(-s, -)** (*umg*) *m od nt* (*Bordell*) brothel

Puffer (-s, -) *m* buffer

Pullover [pʊ'lo:vər] **(-s, -)** *m* pullover, jumper

Puls [pʊls] **(-es, -e)** *m* pulse; **~ader** *f* artery; **p~ieren** *vi* to throb, to pulsate

Pult [pʊlt] **(-(e)s, -e)** *nt* desk

Pulver ['pʊlfər] **(-s, -)** *nt* powder; **p~ig** *adj* powdery; **~schnee** *m* powdery snow

pummelig ['pʊməlɪç] *adj* chubby

Pumpe ['pʊmpə] *f* pump; **p~n** *vt* to pump; (*umg*) to lend; to borrow

Punkt [pʊŋkt] **(-(e)s, -e)** *m* point; (*bei Muster*) dot; (*Satzzeichen*) full stop; **p~ieren** [-'ti:rən] *vt* to dot; (*MED*) to aspirate

pünktlich ['pʏŋktlɪç] *adj* punctual; **P~keit** *f* punctuality

Punktsieg *m* victory on points

Punktzahl *f* score

Punsch [pʊnʃ] **(-(e)s, -e)** *m* punch

Pupille [pu'pɪlə] *f* pupil

Puppe ['pʊpə] *f* doll; (*Marionette*) puppet; (*Insektenpuppe*) pupa, chrysalis

Puppen- *zW:* **~spieler** *m* puppeteer; **~stube** *f* doll's house; **~theater** *nt* puppet theatre

pur [pu:r] *adj* pure; (*völlig*) sheer; (*Whisky*) neat

Püree [py're:] **(-s, -s)** *nt* mashed potatoes *pl*

Purzelbaum ['pʊrtsəlbaʊm] *m* somersault

purzeln ['pʊrtsəln] *vi* to tumble

Puste ['pu:stə] **(-)** (*umg*) *f* puff; (*fig*) steam; **p~n** *vi* to puff, to blow

Pute ['pu:tə] *f* turkey hen; **~r (-s, -)** *m* turkey cock

Putsch [pʊtʃ] **(-(e)s, -e)** *m* revolt, putsch

Putz [pʊts] **(-es)** *m* (*Mörtel*) plaster, roughcast

putzen *vt* to clean; (*Nase*) to wipe, to blow ♦ *vr* to clean o.s.; to dress o.s. up

Putz- *zW:* **~frau** *f* charwoman; **p~ig** *adj* quaint, funny; **~lappen** *m* cloth

Puzzle ['pasəl] **(-s, -s)** *nt* jigsaw

PVC *nt abk* PVC

Pyjama [pi'dʒa:ma] **(-s, -s)** *m* pyjamas *pl*

Pyramide [pyra'mi:də] *f* pyramid

Pyrenäen [pyre'nɛ:ən] *pl* Pyrenees

Q, q

Quacksalber ['kvakzalbər] **(-s, -)** *m* quack (doctor)

Quader ['kva:dər] **(-s, -)** *m* square stone; (*MATH*) cuboid

Quadrat [kva'dra:t] **(-(e)s, -e)** *nt* square; **q~isch** *adj* square; **~meter** *m* square metre

quaken ['kva:kən] *vi* to croak; (*Ente*) to

quack

quäken ['kvɛːkən] *vi* to screech

Qual [kvaːl] (-, -en) *f* pain, agony; *(seelisch)* anguish; **q~en** *vt* to torment ♦ *vr* to struggle; *(geistig)* to torment o.s.; **~erei** *f* torture, torment

Qualifikation [kvalifikatsi'oːn] *f* qualification

qualifizieren [kvalifi'tsiːrən] *vt* to qualify; *(einstufen)* to label ♦ *vr* to qualify

Qualität [kvali'tɛːt] *f* quality; **~sware** *f* article of high quality

Qualle ['kvalə] *f* jellyfish

Qualm [kvalm] (-(e)s) *m* thick smoke; **q~en** *vt, vi* to smoke

qualvoll ['kvaːlfɔl] *adj* excruciating, painful, agonizing

Quant- ['kvant] *zW*: **~ität** [-i'tɛːt] *f* quantity; **q~itativ** [-ita'tiːf] *adj* quantitative; **~um** (-s) *nt* quantity, amount

Quarantäne [karan'tɛːnə] *f* quarantine

Quark [kvark] (-s) *m* curd cheese

Quartal [kvar'taːl] (-s, -e) *nt* quarter (year)

Quartier [kvar'tiːr] (-s, -e) *nt* accommodation; *(MIL)* quarters *pl*; *(Stadtquartier)* district

Quarz [kvaːrts] (-es, -e) *m* quartz

quasseln ['kvasəln] *(umg) vi* to natter

Quatsch [kvatʃ] (-es) *m* rubbish; **q~en** *vi* to chat, to natter

Quecksilber ['kvɛkzɪlbər] *nt* mercury

Quelle ['kvɛlə] *f* spring; *(eines Flusses)* source; **q~n** *(unreg) vi (hervorquellen)* to pour od gush forth; *(schwellen)* to swell

quer [kveːr] *adv* crossways, diagonally; *(rechtwinklig)* at right angles; **~ auf dem Bett** across the bed; **Q~balken** *m* crossbeam; **Q~flöte** *f* flute; **Q~format** *nt* *(PHOT)* oblong format; **Q~schnitt** *m* cross-section; **~schnittsgelähmt** *adj* paralysed below the waist; **Q~straße** *f* intersecting road

quetschen ['kvɛtʃən] *vt* to squash, to crush; *(MED)* to bruise

Quetschung *f* bruise, contusion

quieken ['kviːkən] *vi* to squeak

quietschen ['kviːtʃən] *vi* to squeak

Quintessenz ['kvɪntesɛnts] *f* quintessence

Quirl [kvɪrl] (-(e)s, -e) *m* whisk

quitt [kvɪt] *adj* quits, even

Quitte *f* quince

quittieren [kvɪ'tiːrən] *vt* to give a receipt for; *(Dienst)* to leave

Quittung *f* receipt

Quiz [kvɪs] (-, -) *nt* quiz

quoll *etc* [kvɔl] *vb siehe* **quellen**

Quote ['kvoːtə] *f* number, rate

R, r

Rabatt [ra'bat] (-(e)s, -e) *m* discount

Rabattmarke *f* trading stamp

Rabe ['raːbə] (-n, -n) *m* raven

rabiat [rabi'aːt] *adj* furious

Rache ['raxə] (-) *f* revenge, vengeance

Rachen (-s, -) *m* throat

rächen ['rɛçən] *vt* to avenge, to revenge ♦ *vr* to take (one's) revenge; **das wird sich ~** you'll pay for that

Rad [raːt] (-(e)s, ~er) *nt* wheel; *(Fahrrad)* bike; **~ fahren** to cycle

Radar ['raːdaːr] (-s) *m od nt* radar; **~falle** *f* speed trap; **~kontrolle** *f* radar-controlled speed trap

Radau [ra'dau] (-s) *(umg) m* row

radeln ['raːdəln] *(umg) vi* to cycle

Radfahr- *zW*: **r~en** △ *(unreg) vi siehe* **Rad**; **~er(in)** *m(f)* cyclist; **~weg** *m* cycle track *od* path

Radier- [ra'diːr] *zW*: **r~en** *vt* to rub out, to erase; *(KUNST)* to etch; **~gummi** *m* rubber, eraser; **~ung** *f* etching

Radieschen [ra'diːsçən] *nt* radish

radikal [radi'kaːl] *adj* radical

Radio ['raːdio] (-s, -s) *nt* radio, wireless; **r~ak'tiv** *adj* radioactive; **~aktivi'tät** *f* radioactivity; **~apparat** *m* radio, wireless set

Radius ['raːdius] (-, **Radien**) *m* radius

Rad- *zW*: **~kappe** *f (AUT)* hub cap; **~ler(in)** *(umg) m(f)* cyclist; **~rennen** *nt* cycle race; cycle racing; **~sport** *m* cycling; **~weg** *m* cycleway

raffen ['rafən] *vt* to snatch, to pick up; *(Stoff)*

to gather (up); (*Geld*) to pile up, to rake in
raffi'niert *adj* crafty, cunning
ragen ['ra:gən] *vi* to tower, to rise
Rahm [ra:m] **(-s)** *m* cream
Rahmen **(-s, -)** *m* frame(work); **im ~ des Möglichen** within the bounds of possibility; **r~** *vt* to frame
räkeln ['rɛ:kln] *vr* = **rekeln**
Rakete [ra'ke:tə] *f* rocket; **~nstützpunkt** *m* missile base
rammen ['ramən] *vt* to ram
Rampe ['rampə] *f* ramp; **~nlicht** *nt* (*THEAT*) footlights *pl*
ramponieren [rampo'ni:rən] (*umg*) *vt* to damage
Ramsch [ramʃ] **(-(e)s, -e)** *m* junk
ran [ran] (*umg*) *adv* = **heran**
Rand [rant] **(-(e)s, ⁻er)** *m* edge; (*von Brille, Tasse etc*) rim; (*Hutrand*) brim; (*auf Papier*) margin; (*Schmutzrand, unter Augen*) ring; (*fig*) verge, brink; **außer ~ und Band** wild; **am ~e bemerkt** mentioned in passing
randalieren [randa'li:rən] *vi* to (go on the) rampage
Rang [raŋ] **(-(e)s, ⁻e)** *m* rank; (*Stand*) standing; (*Wert*) quality; (*THEAT*) circle
Rangier- [rãʒi:r] *zW*: **~bahnhof** *m* marshalling yard; **r~en** *vt* (*EISENB*) to shunt, to switch (*US*) ♦ *vi* to rank, to be classed; **~gleis** *nt* siding
Ranke ['raŋkə] *f* tendril, shoot
ranzig ['rantsɪç] *adj* rancid
Rappen ['rapən] *m* (*FIN*) rappen, centime
rar [ra:r] *adj* rare; **sich ~ machen** (*umg*) to keep o.s. to o.s.; **R~i'tät** *f* rarity; (*Sammelobjekt*) curio
rasant [ra'zant] *adj* quick, rapid
rasch [raʃ] *adj* quick
rascheln *vi* to rustle
Rasen ['ra:zən] **(-s, -)** *m* lawn; grass
rasen *vi* to rave; (*schnell*) to race; **~d** *adj* furious; **~de Kopfschmerzen** a splitting headache
Rasenmäher **(-s, -)** *m* lawnmower
Rasier- [ra'zi:r] *zW*: **~apparat** *m* shaver; **~creme** *f* shaving cream; **r~en** *vt, vr* to shave; **~klinge** *f* razor blade; **~messer** *nt*

razor; **~pinsel** *m* shaving brush; **~schaum** *m* shaving foam; **~seife** *f* shaving soap *od* stick; **~wasser** *nt* shaving lotion
Rasse ['rasə] *f* race; (*Tierrasse*) breed; **~hund** *m* thoroughbred dog
Rassen- *zW*: **~hass** ▲ *m* race *od* racial hatred; **~trennung** *f* racial segregation
Rassismus [ra'sɪsmʊs] *m* racism
Rast [rast] **(-, -en)** *f* rest; **r~en** *vi* to rest; **~hof** *m* (*AUT*) service station; **r~los** *adj* tireless; (*unruhig*) restless; **~platz** *m* (*AUT*) layby; **~stätte** *f* (*AUT*) service station
Rasur [ra'zu:r] *f* shaving
Rat [ra:t] **(-(e)s, -schläge)** *m* advice *no pl*; **ein ~** a piece of advice; **keinen ~ wissen** not to know what to do; **siehe zurate**
Rate *f* instalment
raten (*unreg*) *vt, vi* to guess; (*empfehlen*): **jdm ~** to advise sb
Ratenzahlung *f* hire purchase
Ratgeber **(-s, -)** *m* adviser
Rathaus *nt* town hall
ratifizieren [ratifi'tsi:rən] *vt* to ratify
Ration [ratsi'o:n] *f* ration; **r~al** [-'na:l] *adj* rational; **r~ali'sieren** *vt* to rationalize; **r~ell** [-'nɛl] *adj* efficient; **r~ieren** [-'ni:rən] *vt* to ration
Rat- *zW*: **r~los** *adj* at a loss, helpless; **r~sam** *adj* advisable; **~schlag** *m* (piece of) advice
Rätsel ['rɛ:tsəl] **(-s, -)** *nt* puzzle; (*Worträtsel*) riddle; **r~haft** *adj* mysterious; **es ist mir r~haft** it's a mystery to me
Ratte ['ratə] *f* rat; **~nfänger** **(-s, -)** *m* ratcatcher
rattern ['ratərn] *vi* to rattle, to clatter
rau ▲ [rau] *adj* rough, coarse; (*Wetter*) harsh
Raub [raup] **(-(e)s)** *m* robbery; (*Beute*) loot, booty; **~bau** *m* ruthless exploitation; **r~en** ['raubən] *vt* to rob; (*Mensch*) to kidnap, to abduct
Räuber ['rɔybər] **(-s, -)** *m* robber
Raub- *zW*: **~mord** *m* robbery with murder; **~tier** *nt* predator; **~überfall** *m* robbery with violence; **~vogel** *m* bird of prey
Rauch [raux] **(-(e)s)** *m* smoke; **r~en** *vt, vi* to

smoke; **~er(in)** (-s, -) *m(f)* smoker;
~erabteil *nt* (EISENB) smoker; **räuchern** *vt*
to smoke, to cure; **~fleisch** *nt* smoked
meat; **r~ig** *adj* smoky

rauf [rauf] (umg) adv = **herauf; hinauf**

raufen *vt* (Haare) to pull out ♦ *vi, vr* to fight;
Raufe'rei *f* brawl, fight

rauh △ etc [rau] adj siehe **rau** etc

Raum [raum] (-(e)s, **Räume**) *m* space;
(Zimmer, Platz) room; (Gebiet) area

räumen ['rɔymən] *vt* to clear; (Wohnung,
Platz) to vacate; (wegbringen) to shift, to
move; (in Schrank etc) to put away

Raum- zW: **~fähre** *f* space shuttle; **~fahrt** *f*
space travel; **~inhalt** *m* cubic capacity,
volume

räumlich ['rɔymlɪç] adj spatial; **R~keiten** *pl*
premises

Raum- zW: **~pflegerin** *f* cleaner; **~schiff**
nt spaceship; **~schifffahrt** ▲ *f* space
travel

Räumung ['rɔymuŋ] *f* vacating, evacuation;
clearing (away)

Räumungs- zW: **~arbeiten** *pl* clearance
operations; **~verkauf** *m* clearance sale; (bei
Geschäftsaufgabe) closing down sale

raunen ['raunən] *vt, vi* to whisper

Raupe ['raupə] *f* caterpillar; (~nkette)
(caterpillar) track

Raureif ▲ ['rauraif] *m* hoarfrost

raus [raus] (umg) adv = **heraus; hinaus**

Rausch [rauʃ] (-(e)s, **Räusche**) *m*
intoxication

rauschen *vi* (Wasser) to rush; (Baum) to
rustle; (Radio etc) to hiss; (Mensch) to
sweep, to sail; **~d** adj (Beifall) thunderous;
(Fest) sumptuous

Rauschgift *nt* drug; **~süchtige(r)** *f(m)*
drug addict

räuspern ['rɔyspərn] *vr* to clear one's throat

Razzia ['ratsia] (-, **Razzien**) *f* raid

Reagenzglas [rea'gɛntsglaːs] *nt* test tube

reagieren [rea'giːrən] *vi:* **~ (auf** +akk) to
react (to)

Reakt- zW: **~ion** [reaktsi'oːn] *f* reaction;
r~io'när adj reactionary; **~or** [re'aktɔr] *m*
reactor

real [re'aːl] adj real, material

reali'sieren *vt* (verwirklichen: Pläne) to carry
out

Realismus [rea'lɪsmʊs] *m* realism

rea'listisch adj realistic

Realschule *f* secondary school

Rebe ['reːbə] *f* vine

rebellieren [rebɛ'liːrən] *vi* to rebel;
Rebelli'on *f* rebellion; **re'bellisch** adj
rebellious

Rebhuhn ['rɛphuːn] *nt* (KOCH, ZOOL)
partridge

Rechen ['rɛçən] (-s, -) *m* rake

Rechen- zW: **~fehler** *m* miscalculation;
~maschine *f* calculating machine;
~schaft *f* account; **für etw ~schaft
ablegen** to account for sth; **~schieber** *m*
slide rule

Rech- ['rɛç] zW: **r~nen** *vt, vi* to calculate;
jdn/etw r~nen zu to count sb/sth among;
r~nen mit to reckon with; **r~nen auf** +akk
to count on; **~ner** *nt* arithmetic; **~ner** (-s,
-) *m* calculator; (COMPUT) computer; **~nung**
f calculation(s); (COMM) bill, check (US);
jdm/etw in ~nung tragen to take sb/sth into
account; **~nungsbetrag** *m* total amount
of a bill/invoice; **~nungsjahr** *nt* financial
year; **~nungsprüfer** *m* auditor

Recht [rɛçt] (-(e)s, -e) *nt* right; (JUR) law;
mit ~ rightly, justly; **R~ haben** to be right;
jdm R~ geben to agree with sb; **von ~s
wegen** by rights

recht adj right ♦ adv (vor Adjektiv) really,
quite; **das ist mir ~** that suits me; **jetzt
erst ~** now more than ever

Rechte *f* right (hand); (POL) Right; **r~(r, s)**
adj right; (POL) right-wing; **ein ~r** a right-

winger; **~(s)** *nt* right thing; **etwas/nichts ~s** something/nothing proper

recht- *zW:* **~eckig** *adj* rectangular; **~fertigen** *vt insep* to justify ♦ *vr insep* to justify o.s.; **R~fertigung** *f* justification; **~haberisch** *(pej) adj (Mensch)* opinionated; **~lich** *adj (gesetzlich: Gleichstellung, Anspruch)* legal; **~los** *adj* with no rights; **~mäßig** *adj* legal, lawful

rechts [reçts] *adv* on/to the right; **R~anwalt** *m* lawyer, barrister; **R~anwältin** *f* lawyer, barrister

Rechtschreibung *f* spelling

Rechts- *zW:* **~fall** *m* (law) case; **~händer** **(-s, -)** *m* right-handed person; **r~kräftig** *adj* valid, legal; **~kurve** *f* right-hand bend; **r~verbindlich** *adj* legally binding; **~verkehr** *m* driving on the right; **r~widrig** *adj* illegal; **~wissenschaft** *f* jurisprudence

rechtwinklig *adj* right-angled

rechtzeitig *adj* timely ♦ *adv* in time

Reck [rɛk] **(-(e)s, -e)** *nt* horizontal bar; **r~en** *vt, vr* to stretch

recyceln [riːˈsaɪkəln] *vt* to recycle; **Recycling** [riːˈsaɪklɪŋ] **(-s)** *nt* recycling

Redakteur [redakˈtøːr] *m* editor

Redaktion [redaktsiˈoːn] *f* editing; *(Leute)* editorial staff; *(Büro)* editorial office(s)

Rede [ˈreːdə] *f* speech; *(Gespräch)* talk; **jdn zur ~ stellen** to take sb to task; **~freiheit** *f* freedom of speech; **r~gewandt** *adj* eloquent; **r~n** *vi* to talk, to speak ♦ *vt* to say; *(Unsinn etc)* to talk; **~nsart** *f* set phrase

redlich [ˈreːtlɪç] *adj* honest

Redner **(-s, -)** *m* speaker, orator

redselig [ˈreːtzeːlɪç] *adj* talkative, loquacious

reduzieren [reduˈtsiːrən] *vt* to reduce

Reede [ˈreːdə] *f* protected anchorage; **~r** **(-s, -)** *m* shipowner; **~'rei** *f* shipping line *od* firm

reell [reˈɛl] *adj* fair, honest; *(MATH)* real

Refer- *zW:* **~at** [refeˈraːt] **(-(e)s, -e)** *nt* report; *(Vortrag)* paper; *(Gebiet)* section; **~ent** [refeˈrɛnt] *m* speaker; *(Berichterstatter)* reporter; *(Sachbearbeiter)* expert; **r~ieren** [refeˈriːrən] *vi:* **r~ieren über** *+akk* to speak

od talk on

reflektieren [reflɛkˈtiːrən] *vt (Licht)* to reflect

Reflex [reˈflɛks] **(-es, -e)** *m* reflex; **r~iv** [-ˈksiːf] *adj (GRAM)* reflexive

Reform [reˈfɔrm] **(-, -en)** *f* reform; **~ation** *f* reformation; **~ationstag** *m* Reformation Day; **~haus** *nt* health food shop; **r~ieren** [-ˈmiːrən] *vt* to reform

Regal [reˈgaːl] **(-s, -e)** *nt* (book)shelves *pl*, bookcase; stand, rack

rege [ˈreːgə] *adj (lebhaft: Treiben)* lively; *(wach, lebendig: Geist)* keen

Regel [ˈreːgəl] **(-, -n)** *f* rule; *(MED)* period; **r~mäßig** *adj* regular; **~mäßigkeit** *f* regularity; **~n** *vt* to regulate, to control; *(Angelegenheit)* to settle ♦ *vr:* **sich von selbst r~n** to take care of itself; **r~recht** *adj* regular, proper, thorough; **~ung** *f* regulation; settlement; **r~widrig** *adj* irregular, against the rules

Regen [ˈreːgən] **(-s, -)** *m* rain; **~bogen** *m* rainbow; **~bogenpresse** *f* tabloids *pl*

regenerierbar [regeneˈriːrbaːr] *adj* renewable

Regen- *zW:* **~mantel** *m* raincoat, mac(kintosh); **~schauer** *m* shower (of rain); **~schirm** *m* umbrella; **~wald** *m* (GEOG) rainforest; **~wurm** *m* earthworm; **~zeit** *f* rainy season

Regie [reˈʒiː] *f (Film etc)* direction; *(THEAT)* production

Regier- [reˈgiːr] *zW:* **r~en** *vt, vi* to govern, to rule; **~ung** *f* government; *(Monarchie)* reign; **~ungssitz** *m* seat of government; **~ungswechsel** *m* change of government; **~ungszeit** *f* period in government; *(von König)* reign

Regiment [regiˈmɛnt] **(-s, -er)** *nt* regiment

Region [regiˈoːn] *f* region

Regisseur [reʒɪˈsøːr] *m* director; *(THEAT)* (stage) producer

Register [reˈgɪstər] **(-s, -)** *nt* register; *(in Buch)* table of contents, index

registrieren [regɪsˈtriːrən] *vt* to register

Regler [ˈreːglər] **(-s, -)** *m* regulator, governor

reglos [ˈreːkloːs] *adj* motionless

regnen [ˈreːgnən] *vi unpers* to rain

Spelling Reform: ▲ *new spelling* △ *old spelling (to be phased out)*

regnerisch *adj* rainy

regulär [regu'lɛ:r] *adj* regular

regulieren [regu'li:rən] *vt* to regulate; (*COMM*) to settle

Regung ['re:gʊŋ] *f* motion; (*Gefühl*) feeling, impulse; **r~slos** *adj* motionless

Reh [re:] (-(e)s, -e) *nt* deer, roe; **~bock** *m* roebuck; **~kitz** *nt* fawn

Reib- ['raib] *zW:* **~e** *f* grater; **~eisen** *nt* grater; **r~en** (*unreg*) *vt* to rub; (*KOCH*) to grate; **~fläche** *f* rough surface; **~ung** *f* friction; **r~ungslos** *adj* smooth

Reich (-(e)s, -e) *nt* empire, kingdom; (*fig*) realm; **das Dritte R~** the Third Reich

reich [raiç] *adj* rich

reichen *vi* to reach; (*genügen*) to be enough *od* sufficient ♦ *vt* to hold out; (*geben*) to pass, to hand; (*anbieten*) to offer; **jdm ~** to be enough *od* sufficient for sb

reich- *zW:* **~haltig** *adj* ample, rich; **~lich** *adj* ample, plenty of; **R~tum** (-s) *m* wealth; **R~weite** *f* range

Reif (-(e)s, -e) *m* (*Ring*) ring, hoop

reif [raif] *adj* ripe; (*Mensch, Urteil*) mature

Reife (-) *f* ripeness; maturity; **r~n** *vi* to mature; to ripen

Reifen (-s, -) *m* ring, hoop; (*Fahrzeugreifen*) tyre; **~druck** *m* tyre pressure; **~panne** *f* puncture

Reihe ['raiə] *f* row; (*von Tagen etc, umg: Anzahl*) series *sg;* **der ~ nach** in turn; **er ist an der ~** it's his turn; **an die ~ kommen** to have one's turn

Reihen- *zW:* **~folge** *f* sequence; **alphabetische ~folge** alphabetical order; **~haus** *nt* terraced house

reihum [rai'ʊm] *adv:* **es geht/wir machen das ~** we take turns

Reim [raim] (-(e)s, -e) *m* rhyme; **r~en** *vt* to rhyme

rein¹ [rain] (*umg*) *adv* = **herein; hinein**

rein² [rain] *adj* pure; (*sauber*) clean ♦ *adv* purely; **etw ins R~e schreiben** to make a fair copy of sth; **etw ins R~e bringen** to clear up sth; **R~fall** (*umg*) *m* let-down; **R~gewinn** *m* net profit; **R~heit** *f* purity; cleanness; **~igen** *vt* to clean; (*Wasser*) to

purify; **R~igung** *f* cleaning; purification; (*Geschäft*) cleaner's; **chemische R~igung** dry cleaning; dry cleaner's; **R~igungsmittel** *nt* cleansing agent; **~rassig** *adj* pedigree; **R~schrift** *f* fair copy

Reis [rais] (-es, -e) *m* rice

Reise ['raizə] *f* journey; (*Schiffsreise*) voyage; **~n** *pl* (*Herumreisen*) travels; **gute ~!** have a good journey; **~apotheke** *f* first-aid kit; **~büro** *nt* travel agency; **r~fertig** *adj* ready to start; **~führer** *m* guide(book); (*Mensch*) travel guide; **~gepäck** *nt* luggage; **~gesellschaft** *f* party of travellers; **~kosten** *pl* travelling expenses; **~leiter** *m* courier; **~lektüre** *f* reading matter for the journey; **r~n** *vi* to travel; **r~n nach** to go to; **~nde(r)** *f(m)* traveller; **~pass** ▲ *m* passport; **~proviant** *m* food and drink for the journey; **~route** *f* route, itinerary; **~ruf** *m* personal message; **~scheck** *m* traveller's cheque; **~veranstalter** *m* tour operator; **~versicherung** *f* travel insurance; **~ziel** *nt* destination

Reißbrett *nt* drawing board

reißen ['raisən] (*unreg*) *vt* to tear; (*ziehen*) to pull, to drag; (*Witz*) to crack ♦ *vi* to tear; to pull, to drag; **etw an sich ~** to snatch sth up; (*fig*) to take over sth; **sich um etw ~** to scramble for sth; **~d** *adj* (*Fluss*) raging; (*WIRTS: Verkauf*) rapid

Reiß- *zW:* **~verschluss** ▲ *m* zip(per), zip fastener; **~zwecke** *m* drawing pin (*BRIT*), thumbtack (*US*)

Reit- ['rait] *zW:* **r~en** (*unreg*) *vt, vi* to ride; **~er** (-s, -) *m* rider; (*MIL*) cavalryman, trooper; **~erin** *f* rider; **~hose** *f* riding breeches *pl;* **~pferd** *nt* saddle horse; **~stiefel** *m* riding boot; **~weg** *m* bridle path; **~zeug** *nt* riding outfit

Reiz [raits] (-es, -e) *m* stimulus; (*angenehm*) charm; (*Verlockung*) attraction; **r~bar** *adj* irritable; **~barkeit** *f* irritability; **r~en** *vt* to stimulate; (*unangenehm*) to irritate; (*verlocken*) to appeal to, to attract; **r~end** *adj* charming; **r~voll** *adj* attractive

rekeln ['re:kəln] *vr* to stretch out; (*lümmeln*)

to lounge *od* loll about

Reklamation [reklama'tsi:on] *f* complaint

Reklame [re'kla:mə] *f* advertising; advertisement; ~ **machen für etw** to advertise sth

rekonstruieren [rekɔnstru'i:rən] *vt* to reconstruct

Rekord [re'kɔrt] **(-(e)s, -e)** *m* record; ~**leistung** *f* record performance

Rektor ['rektɔr] *m* (*UNIV*) rector, vice-chancellor; (*SCH*) headteacher (*BRIT*), principal (*US*); ~**at** [-'ra:t] **(-(e)s, -e)** *nt* rectorate, vice-chancellorship; headship; (*Zimmer*) rector's *etc* office

Relais [rə'le:] **(-, -)** *nt* relay

relativ [rela'ti:f] *adj* relative; **R~ität** [relativi'tɛ:t] *f* relativity

relevant [rele'vant] *adj* relevant

Relief [reli'ɛf] **(-s, -s)** *nt* relief

Religion [religi'o:n] *f* religion

religiös [religi'ø:s] *adj* religious

Reling ['re:lɪŋ] **(-, -s)** *f* (*NAUT*) rail

Remoulade [remu'la:də] *f* remoulade

Rendezvous [rãde'vu:] **(-, -)** *nt* rendezvous

Renn- ['ren] *zW:* ~**bahn** *f* racecourse; (*AUT*) circuit, race track; **r~en** (*unreg*) *vt, vi* to run, to race; ~**en (-s, -)** *nt* running; (*Wettbewerb*) race; ~**fahrer** *m* racing driver; ~**pferd** *nt* racehorse; ~**wagen** *m* racing car

renommiert [renɔ'mi:rt] *adj* renowned

renovieren [reno'vi:rən] *vt* to renovate; **Renovierung** *f* renovation

rentabel [ren'ta:bəl] *adj* profitable, lucrative

Rentabilität [rentabili'tɛ:t] *f* profitability

Rente ['rentə] *f* pension

Rentenversicherung *f* pension scheme

rentieren [ren'ti:rən] *vr* to pay, to be profitable

Rentner(in) ['rentnər(ɪn)] **(-s, -)** *m(f)* pensioner

Reparatur [repara'tu:r] *f* repairing; repair; ~**werkstatt** *f* repair shop; (*AUT*) garage

reparieren [repa'ri:rən] *vt* to repair

Reportage [repɔr'ta:ʒə] *f* (on-the-spot) report; (*TV, RADIO*) live commentary *od* coverage

Reporter [re'pɔrtər] **(-s, -)** *m* reporter, commentator

repräsentativ [reprezenta'ti:f] *adj* (*stellvertretend, typisch: Menge, Gruppe*) representative; (*beeindruckend: Haus, Auto etc*) impressive

repräsentieren [reprezen'ti:rən] *vt* (*Staat, Firma*) to represent; (*darstellen: Wert*) to constitute ♦ *vi* (*gesellschaftlich*) to perform official duties

Repressalie [repre'sa:liə] *f* reprisal

Reprivatisierung [reprivati'zi:rʊŋ] *f* denationalization

Reproduktion [reprodʊktsi'o:n] *f* reproduction

reproduzieren [reprodu'tsi:rən] *vt* to reproduce

Reptil [rep'ti:l] **(-s, -ien)** *nt* reptile

Republik [repu'bli:k] *f* republic; **r~anisch** *adj* republican

Reservat [rezer'va:t] **(-(e)s, -e)** *nt* reservation

Reserve [re'zervə] *f* reserve; ~**rad** *nt* (*AUT*) spare wheel; ~**spieler** *m* reserve; ~**tank** *m* reserve tank

reservieren [rezer'vi:rən] *vt* to reserve

Reservoir [rezervo'a:r] **(-s, -e)** *nt* reservoir

Residenz [rezi'dents] *f* residence, seat

resignieren [rezi'gni:rən] *vi* to resign

resolut [rezo'lu:t] *adj* resolute

Resonanz [rezo'nants] *f* resonance; (*fig*) response

Resozialisierung [rezotsiali'zi:rʊŋ] *f* rehabilitation

Respekt [re'spekt] **(-(e)s)** *m* respect; **r~ieren** [-'ti:rən] *vt* to respect; **r~los** *adj* disrespectful; **r~voll** *adj* respectful

Ressort [re'so:r] **(-s, -s)** *nt* department

Rest [rest] **(-(e)s, -e)** *m* remainder, rest; (*Überrest*) remains *pl*

Restaurant [resto'rã:] **(-s, -s)** *nt* restaurant

restaurieren [restau'ri:rən] *vt* to restore

Rest- *zW:* ~**betrag** *m* remainder, outstanding sum; **r~lich** *adj* remaining; **r~los** *adj* complete

Resultat [rezʊl'ta:t] **(-(e)s, -e)** *nt* result

Retorte [re'tɔrtə] *f* retort

Retouren [re'tu:rən] *pl* (*COMM*) returns

retten ['rɛtən] *vt* to save, to rescue

Retter(in) *m(f)* rescuer

Rettich ['rɛtɪç] **(-s, -e)** *m* radish

Rettung *f* rescue; (*Hilfe*) help; **seine letzte ~** his last hope

Rettungs- *zW*: **~boot** *nt* lifeboat; **~dienst** *m* rescue service; **r~los** *adj* hopeless; **~ring** *m* lifebelt, life preserver (*US*); **~wagen** *m* ambulance

retuschieren [retu'ʃi:rən] *vt* (*PHOT*) to retouch

Reue ['rɔʏə] **(-)** *f* remorse; (*Bedauern*) regret; **r~n** *vt*: **es reut ihn** he regrets (it) *od* is sorry (about it)

Revanche [re'vã:ʃə] *f* revenge; (*SPORT*) return match

revanchieren [revã'ʃi:rən] *vr* (*sich rächen*) to get one's own back, to have one's revenge; (*erwidern*) to reciprocate, to return the compliment

Revier [re'vi:r] **(-s, -e)** *nt* district; (*Jagdrevier*) preserve; (*Polizeirevier*) police station; beat

Revolte [re'vɔltə] *f* revolt

revol'tieren *vi* (*gegen jdn/etw*) to rebel

Revolution [revolutsi'o:n] *f* revolution; **~är** [-'nɛ:r] **(-s, -e)** *m* revolutionary; **r~ieren** [-'ni:rən] *vt* to revolutionize

Rezept [re'tsɛpt] **(-(e)s, -e)** *nt* recipe; (*MED*) prescription; **r~frei** *adj* available without prescription; **~ion** *f* reception; **r~pflichtig** *adj* available only on prescription

R-Gespräch ['ɛrgəʃprɛːç] *nt* reverse charge call (*BRIT*), collect call (*US*)

Rhabarber [ra'barbər] **(-s)** *m* rhubarb

Rhein [raɪn] **(-s)** *m* Rhine; **r~isch** *adj* Rhenish

Rheinland-Pfalz *nt* (*GEOG*) Rheinland-Pfalz, Rhineland-Palatinate

Rhesusfaktor ['re:zusfaktor] *m* rhesus factor

rhetorisch [re'to:rɪʃ] *adj* rhetorical

Rheuma ['rɔʏma] **(-s)** *nt* rheumatism; **r~tisch** [-'ma:tɪʃ] *adj* rheumatic

rhythmisch ['rʏtmɪʃ] *adj* rhythmical

Rhythmus ['rʏtmʊs] *m* rhythm

richt- ['rɪçt] *zW*: **~en** *vt* to direct; (*Waffe*) to aim; (*einstellen*) to adjust; (*instandsetzen*) to

repair; (*zurechtmachen*) to prepare; (*bestrafen*) to pass judgement on ♦ *vr*: **sich ~en nach** to go by; **~en an** +*akk* to direct at; (*fig*) to direct to; **~en auf** +*akk* to aim at; **R~er(in)** **(-s, -)** *m(f)* judge; **~erlich** *adj* judicial; **R~geschwindigkeit** *f* recommended speed

richtig *adj* right, correct; (*echt*) proper ♦ *adv* (*umg*: *sehr*) really; **bin ich hier ~?** am I in the right place?; **der/die R~e** the right one/person; **das R~e** the right thing; **etw ~ stellen** to correct sth; **R~keit** *f* correctness

Richt- *zW*: **~linie** *f* guideline; **~preis** *m* recommended price

Richtung *f* direction; tendency, orientation

rieb *etc* [ri:p] *vb siehe* **reiben**

riechen ['ri:çən] (*unreg*) *vt, vi* to smell; **an etw** *dat* **~** to smell sth; **nach etw ~** to smell of sth; **ich kann das/ihn nicht ~** (*umg*) I can't stand it/him

rief *etc* [ri:f] *vb siehe* **rufen**

Riegel ['ri:gəl] **(-s, -)** *m* bolt; (*Schokolade usw*) bar

Riemen ['ri:mən] **(-s, -)** *m* strap; (*Gürtel, TECH*) belt; (*NAUT*) oar

Riese ['ri:zə] **(-n, -n)** *m* giant

rieseln *vi* to trickle; (*Schnee*) to fall gently

Riesen- *zW*: **~erfolg** *m* enormous success; **r~groß** *adj* colossal, gigantic, huge; **~rad** *nt* big wheel

riesig ['ri:zɪç] *adj* enormous, huge, vast

riet *etc* [ri:t] *vb siehe* **raten**

Riff [rɪf] **(-(e)s, -e)** *nt* reef

Rille ['rɪlə] *f* groove

Rind [rɪnt] **(-(e)s, -er)** *nt* ox; cow; cattle *pl*; (*KOCH*) beef

Rinde ['rɪndə] *f* rind; (*Baumrinde*) bark; (*Brotrinde*) crust

Rind- ['rɪnt] *zW*: **~fleisch** *nt* beef; **~vieh** *nt* cattle *pl*; (*umg*) blockhead, stupid oaf

Ring [rɪŋ] **(-(e)s, -e)** *m* ring; **~buch** *nt* ring binder; **r~en** (*unreg*) *vi* to wrestle; **~en (-s)** *nt* wrestling; **~finger** *m* ring finger; **~kampf** *m* wrestling bout; **~richter** *m* referee; **r~s** *adv*: **r~s um** round; **r~sherum** *adv* round about; **~straße** *f* ring road; **r~sum** *adv* (*rundherum*) round about; (*überall*) all round; **r~sumher =** **ringsum**

Rinn- ['rɪn] *zW:* **~e** *f* gutter, drain; **r~en** (*unreg*) *vi* to run, to trickle; **~stein** *m* gutter

Rippchen ['rɪpçən] *nt* small rib; cutlet

Rippe ['rɪpə] *f* rib

Risiko ['riːziko] (**-s, -s** *od* **Risiken**) *nt* risk

riskant [rɪs'kant] *adj* risky, hazardous

riskieren [rɪs'kiːrən] *vt* to risk

Riss ▲ [rɪs] (**-es, -e**) *m* tear; (*in Mauer, Tasse etc*) crack; (*in Haut*) scratch; (*TECH*) design

rissig ['rɪsɪç] *adj* torn; cracked; scratched

Ritt [rɪt] (**-(e)s, -e**) *m* ride

ritt *etc vb siehe* **reiten**

Ritter (**-s, -**) *m* knight; **r~lich** *adj* chivalrous

Ritze ['rɪtsə] *f* crack, chink

Rivale [ri'vaːlə] (**-n, -n**) *m* rival

Rivalität [rivali'tɛːt] *f* rivalry

Robbe ['rɔbə] *f* seal

Roboter ['rɔbɔtər] (**-s, -**) *m* robot

robust [ro'bʊst] *adj* (*kräftig: Mensch, Gesundheit*) robust

roch *etc* [rɔx] *vb siehe* **riechen**

Rock [rɔk] (**-(e)s, ᵉe**) *m* skirt; (*Jackett*) jacket; (*Uniformrock*) tunic

Rodel ['roːdəl] (**-s, -**) *m* toboggan; **~bahn** *f* toboggan run; **r~n** *vi* to toboggan

Rogen ['roːgən] (**-s, -**) *m* roe, spawn

Roggen ['rɔgən] (**-s, -**) *m* rye; **~brot** *nt* (*KOCH*) rye bread

roh [roː] *adj* raw; (*Mensch*) coarse, crude; **R~bau** *m* shell of a building; **R~material** *nt* raw material; **R~öl** *nt* crude oil

Rohr [roːr] (**-(e)s, -e**) *nt* pipe, tube; (*BOT*) cane; (*Schilf*) reed; (*Gewehrrohr*) barrel; **~bruch** *m* burst pipe

Röhre ['røːrə] *f* tube, pipe; (*RADIO etc*) valve; (*Backröhre*) oven

Rohr- *zW:* **~leitung** *f* pipeline; **~zucker** *m* cane sugar

Rohstoff *m* raw material

Rokoko ['rɔkoko] (**-s**) *nt* rococo

Rolladen △ *m siehe* **Rollladen**

Rollbahn ['rɔlbaːn] *f* (*AVIAT*) runway

Rolle ['rɔlə] *f* roll; (*THEAT, soziologisch*) role; (*Garnrolle etc*) reel, spool; (*Walze*) roller; (*Wäscherolle*) mangle; **keine ~ spielen** not to matter; **eine (wichtige) ~ spielen bei** to play a (major) part *od* role in; **r~n** *vt, vi* to roll; (*AVIAT*) to taxi; **~r (-s, -)** *m* scooter; (*Welle*) roller

Roll- *zW:* **~kragen** *m* rollneck; polo neck; **~laden** ▲ *m* shutter; **~mops** *m* pickled herring; **~schuh** *m* roller skate; **~stuhl** *m* wheelchair; **~stuhlfahrer(in)** *m(f)* wheelchair user; **~treppe** *f* escalator

Rom [roːm] (**-s**) *nt* Rome

Roman [ro'maːn] (**-s, -e**) *m* novel; **~tik** *f* romanticism; **~tiker** [ro'mantɪkər] (**-s, -**) *m* romanticist; **r~tisch** [ro'mantɪʃ] *adj* romantic; **~ze** [ro'mantsə] *f* romance

Römer ['røːmər] (**-s, -**) *m* wineglass; (*Mensch*) Roman

römisch ['røːmɪʃ] *adj* Roman; **~-katholisch** *adj* (*REL*) Roman Catholic

röntgen ['rœntgən] *vt* to X-ray; **R~bild** *nt* X-ray; **R~strahlen** *pl* X-rays

rosa ['roːza] *adj inv* pink, rose(-coloured)

Rose ['roːzə] *f* rose

Rosen- *zW:* **~kohl** *m* Brussels sprouts *pl;* **~kranz** *m* rosary; **~montag** *m* Monday before Ash Wednesday

rosig ['roːzɪç] *adj* rosy

Rosine [ro'ziːnə] *f* raisin, currant

Ross ▲ [rɔs] (**-es, -e**) *nt* horse, steed; **~kastanie** *f* horse chestnut

Rost [rɔst] (**-(e)s, -e**) *m* rust; (*Gitter*) grill, gridiron; (*Bettrost*) springs *pl;* **~braten** *m* roast(ed) meat, roast; **r~en** *vi* to rust

rösten ['rœstən] *vt* to roast; to toast; to grill

Rost- *zW:* **r~frei** *adj* rust-free; rustproof; stainless; **r~ig** *adj* rusty; **~schutz** *m* rust-proofing

rot [roːt] *adj* red; **in den ~en Zahlen** in the red

Röte ['røːtə] (**-**) *f* redness; **~ln** *pl* German measles *sg;* **r~n** *vt, vr* to redden

rothaarig *adj* red-haired

rotieren [ro'tiːrən] *vi* to rotate

Rot- *zW:* **~kehlchen** *nt* robin; **~stift** *m* red pencil; **~wein** *m* red wine

Rouge [ruːʒ] *nt* blusher

Roulade [ru'laːdə] *f* (*KOCH*) beef olive

Spelling Reform: ▲ *new spelling* △ *old spelling (to be phased out)*

Route ['ruːtə] f route

Routine [ru'tiːnə] f experience; routine

Rübe ['ryːbə] f turnip; **Gelbe ~** carrot; **Rote ~** beetroot (*BRIT*), beet (*US*)

rüber ['ryːbər] (*umg*) adv = **herüber; hinüber**

Rubrik [ru'briːk] f heading; (*Spalte*) column

Ruck [ruk] (**-(e)s, -e**) m jerk, jolt

Rück- ['rʏk] zW: **~antwort** f reply, answer; **r~bezüglich** adj reflexive

Rücken ['rʏkən] (**-s, -**) m back; (*Bergrücken*) ridge

rücken vt, vi to move

Rücken- zW: **~mark** nt spinal cord; **~schwimmen** nt backstroke

Rück- zW: **~erstattung** f return, restitution; **~fahrkarte** f return (ticket); **~fahrt** f return journey; **~fall** m relapse; **r~fällig** adj relapsing; **r~fällig werden** to relapse; **~flug** m return flight; **~frage** f question; **r~fragen** vi to check, to inquire (further); **~gabe** f return; **~gaberecht** nt right of return; **~gang** m decline, fall; **r~gängig** adj: **etw r~gängig machen** to cancel sth; **~grat** (**-(e)s, -e**) nt spine, backbone; **~halt** m (*Unterstützung*) backing, support; **~kehr** (**-, -en**) f return; **~licht** nt back light; **r~lings** adv from behind; backwards; **~nahme** f taking back; **~porto** nt return postage; **~reise** f return journey; (*NAUT*) home voyage; **~reiseverkehr** m homebound traffic; **~ruf** m recall

Rucksack ['rukzak] m rucksack; **~tourist(in)** m(f) backpacker

Rück- zW: **~schau** f reflection; **~schlag** m (*plötzliche Verschlechterung*) setback; **~schluss** ▲ m conclusion; **~schritt** m retrogression; **r~schrittlich** adj reactionary; retrograde; **~seite** f back; (*von Münze etc*) reverse; **~sicht** f consideration; **~sicht nehmen auf** +akk to show consideration for; **~sichtslos** adj inconsiderate; (*Fahren*) reckless; (*unbarmherzig*) ruthless; **r~sichtsvoll** adj considerate; **~sitz** m back seat; **~spiegel** m (*AUT*) rear-view mirror; **~spiel** nt return match; **~sprache** f further discussion od talk; **~stand** m arrears pl; **r~ständig** adj

backward, out-of-date; (*Zahlungen*) in arrears; **~strahler** (**-s, -**) m rear reflector; **~tritt** m resignation; **~trittbremse** f pedal brake; **~vergütung** f repayment; (*COMM*) refund; **~versicherung** f reinsurance; **r~wärtig** adj rear; **r~wärts** adv backward(s), back; **~wärtsgang** m (*AUT*) reverse gear; **~weg** m return journey, way back; **r~wirkend** adj retroactive; **~wirkung** f reaction; retrospective effect; **~zahlung** f repayment; **~zug** m retreat

Rudel ['ruːdəl] (**-s, -**) nt pack; herd

Ruder ['ruːdər] (**-s, -**) nt oar; (*Steuer*) rudder; **~boot** nt rowing boat; **r~n** vt, vi to row

Ruf [ruːf] (**-(e)s, -e**) m call, cry; (*Ansehen*) reputation; **r~en** (*unreg*) vt, vi to call; to cry; **~name** m usual (first) name; **~nummer** f (tele)phone number; **~säule** f (*an Autobahn*) emergency telephone; **~zeichen** nt (*RADIO*) call sign; (*TEL*) ringing tone

rügen ['ryːgən] vt to rebuke

Ruhe ['ruːə] (**-**) f rest; (*Ungestörtheit*) peace, quiet; (*Gelassenheit, Stille*) calm; (*Schweigen*) silence; **jdn in ~ lassen** to leave sb alone; **sich zur ~ setzen** to retire; **~!** be quiet!, silence!; **r~n** vi to rest; **~pause** f break; **~stand** m retirement; **~stätte** f: **letzte ~stätte** final resting place; **~störung** f breach of the peace; **~tag** m (*von Geschäft*) closing day

ruhig ['ruːɪç] adj quiet; (*bewegungslos*) still; (*Hand*) steady; (*gelassen, friedlich*) calm; (*Gewissen*) clear; **kommen Sie ~ herein** just come on in; **tu das ~** feel free to do that

Ruhm [ruːm] (**-(e)s**) m fame, glory

rühmen ['ryːmən] vt to praise ♦ vr to boast

Rühr- [ryːr] zW: **~ei** nt scrambled egg; **r~en** vt, vr (*auch fig*) to move, to stir ♦ vi: **r~en von** to come od stem from; **r~en an** +akk to touch; (*fig*) to touch on; **r~end** adj touching, moving; **r~selig** adj sentimental, emotional; **~ung** f emotion

Ruin [ru'iːn] (**-s, -e**) m ruin; **~e** f ruin; **r~ieren** [-'niːrən] vt to ruin

rülpsen ['rʏlpsən] vi to burp, to belch

Rum [rum] (**-s, -s**) m rum

Rumän- [ru'mɛːn] zW: ~**ien** (**-s**) nt Ro(u)mania; r~**isch** adj Ro(u)manian

Rummel ['rʊməl] (**-s**) (umg) m hubbub; (Jahrmarkt) fair; ~**platz** m fairground, fair

Rumpf [rʊmpf] (**-(e)s, ⁓e**) m trunk, torso; (AVIAT) fuselage; (NAUT) hull

rümpfen ['rʏmpfən] vt (Nase) to turn up

rund [rʊnt] adj round ♦ adv (etwa) around; ~ **um etw** round sth; **R~brief** m circular; **R~e** ['rʊndə] f round; (in Rennen) lap; (Gesellschaft) circle; **R~fahrt** f (round) trip

Rundfunk ['rʊntfʊŋk] (**-(e)s**) m broadcasting; **im ~** on the radio; ~**gerät** nt wireless set; ~**sendung** f broadcast, radio programme

Rund- zW: r~**heraus** adv straight out, bluntly; r~**herum** adv round about; all round; r~**lich** adj plump, rounded; ~**reise** f round trip; ~**schreiben** nt (COMM) circular; ~**(wander)weg** m circular path od route

runter ['rʊntər] (umg) adv = **herunter; hinunter**

Runzel ['rʊntsəl] (**-, -n**) f wrinkle; r~**ig** adj wrinkled; r~**n** vt to wrinkle; **die Stirn r~n** to frown

rupfen ['rʊpfən] vt to pluck

ruppig ['rʊpɪç] adj rough, gruff

Rüsche ['ryːʃə] f frill

Ruß [ruːs] (**-es**) m soot

Russe ['rʊsə] (**-n, -n**) m Russian

Rüssel ['rʏsəl] (**-s, -**) m snout; (Elefantenrüssel) trunk

rußig ['ruːsɪç] adj sooty

Russin ['rʊsɪn] f Russian

russisch adj Russian

Russland ▲ ['rʊslant] (**-s**) nt Russia

rüsten ['rʏstən] vt to prepare ♦ vi to prepare; (MIL) to arm ♦ vr to prepare (o.s.); to arm o.s.

rüstig ['rʏstɪç] adj sprightly, vigorous

Rüstung ['rʏstʊŋ] f preparation; arming; (Ritterrüstung) armour; (Waffen etc) armaments pl; ~**skontrolle** f arms control

Rute ['ruːtə] f rod

Rutsch [rʊtʃ] (**-(e)s, -e**) m slide; (Erdrutsch) landslide; ~**bahn** f slide; r~**en** vi to slide;

(ausrutschen) to slip; r~**ig** adj slippery

rütteln ['rʏtəln] vt, vi to shake, to jolt

S, s

S. abk (= Seite) p.; = **Schilling**

s. abk (= siehe) see

Saal [zaːl] (**-(e)s, Säle**) m hall; room

Saarland ['zaːrlant] nt: **das ~** the Saar(land)

Saat [zaːt] (**-, -en**) f seed; (Pflanzen) crop; (Säen) sowing

Säbel ['zɛːbəl] (**-s, -**) m sabre, sword

Sabotage [zabo'taːʒə] f sabotage

Sach- [zax] zW: ~**bearbeiter** m specialist; s~**dienlich** adj relevant, helpful; ~**e** f thing; (Angelegenheit) affair, business; (Frage) matter; (Pflicht) task; **zur ~e** to the point; s~**kundig** adj expert; s~**lich** adj matter-of-fact; objective; (Irrtum, Angabe) factual

sächlich ['zɛxlɪç] adj neuter

Sachschaden m material damage

Sachsen ['zaksən] (**-s**) nt Saxony

sächsisch ['zɛksɪʃ] adj Saxon

sacht(e) ['zaxt(ə)] adv softly, gently

Sachverständige(r) f(m) expert

Sack [zak] (**-(e)s, ⁓e**) m sack; ~**gasse** f cul-de-sac, dead-end street (US)

Sadismus [za'dɪsmʊs] m sadism

Sadist [za'dɪst] m sadist

säen ['zɛːən] vt, vi to sow

Safersex ▲, **Safer Sex** m safe sex

Saft [zaft] (**-(e)s, ⁓e**) m juice; (BOT) sap; s~**ig** adj juicy; s~**los** adj dry

Sage ['zaːgə] f saga

Säge ['zɛːgə] f saw; ~**mehl** nt sawdust

sagen ['zaːgən] vt, vi to say; (mitteilen): **jdm ~** to tell sb; ~ **Sie ihm, dass ...** tell him ...

sägen vt, vi to saw

sagenhaft adj legendary; (umg) great, smashing

sah etc [zaː] vb siehe **sehen**

Sahne ['zaːnə] (**-**) f cream

Saison [zɛ'zõ] (**-, -s**) f season

Saite ['zaɪtə] f string

Sakko ['zako] (**-s, -s**) *m od nt* jacket

Sakrament [zakra'mɛnt] *nt* sacrament

Sakristei [zakrɪs'taɪ] *f* sacristy

Salat [za'la:t] (**-(e)s, -e**) *m* salad; (*Kopfsalat*) lettuce; **~soße** *f* salad dressing

Salbe ['zalbə] *f* ointment

Salbei ['zalbaɪ] (**-s** *od* **-**) *m od f* sage

Saldo ['zaldo] (**-s, Salden**) *m* balance

Salmiak [zalmi'ak] (**-s**) *m* sal ammoniac; **~geist** *m* liquid ammonia

Salmonellenvergiftung [zalmo'nɛlən-] *f* salmonella (poisoning)

salopp [za'lɔp] *adj* casual

Salpeter [zal'pe:tər] (**-s**) *m* saltpetre; **~säure** *f* nitric acid

Salz [zalts] (**-es, -e**) *nt* salt; **s~en** (*unreg*) *vt* to salt; **s~ig** *adj* salty; **~kartoffeln** *pl* boiled potatoes; **~säure** *f* hydrochloric acid; **~streuer** *m* salt cellar; **~wasser** *nt* (*Meerwasser*) salt water

Samen ['za:mən] (**-s, -**) *m* seed; (*ANAT*) sperm

Sammel- ['zaməl] *zW:* **~band** *m* anthology; **~fahrschein** *m* multi-journey ticket; (*für mehrere Personen*) group ticket

sammeln ['zaməln] *vt* to collect ♦ *vr* to assemble, to gather; (*konzentrieren*) to concentrate

Sammlung ['zamlʊŋ] *f* collection; assembly, gathering; concentration

Samstag ['zamsta:k] *m* Saturday; **s~s** *adv* (on) Saturdays

Samt [zamt] (**-(e)s, -e**) *m* velvet; **s~** *präp* +*dat* (along) with, together with; **s~ und sonders** each and every one (of them)

sämtlich ['zɛmtlɪç] *adj* all (the), entire

Sand [zant] (**-(e)s, -e**) *m* sand

Sandale [zan'da:lə] *f* sandal

Sand- *zW:* **~bank** *f* sandbank; **s~ig** ['zandɪç] *adj* sandy; **~kasten** *m* sandpit; **~kuchen** *m* Madeira cake; **~papier** *nt* sandpaper; **~stein** *m* sandstone; **s~strahlen** *vt, vi insep* to sandblast; **~strand** *m* sandy beach

sandte *etc* ['zantə] *vb siehe* **senden**

sanft [zanft] *adj* soft, gentle; **~mütig** *adj* gentle, meek

sang *etc* [zaŋ] *vb siehe* **singen**

Sänger(in) ['zɛŋər(ɪn)] (**-s, -**) *m(f)* singer

Sani- *zW:* **s~eren** [za'ni:rən] *vt* to redevelop; (*Betrieb*) to make financially sound ♦ *vr* to line one's pockets; to become financially sound; **s~tär** [zani'tɛ:r] *adj* sanitary; **s~täre Anlagen** sanitation *sg*; **~täter** [zani'tɛ:tər] (**-s, -**) *m* first-aid attendant; (*MIL*) (medical) orderly

sanktionieren [zaŋktsio'ni:rən] *vt* to sanction

Sardelle [zar'dɛlə] *f* anchovy

Sardine [zar'di:nə] *f* sardine

Sarg [zark] (**-(e)s, ⁻e**) *m* coffin

Sarkasmus [zar'kasmʊs] *m* sarcasm

saß *etc* [za:s] *vb siehe* **sitzen**

Satan ['za:tan] (**-s, -e**) *m* Satan; devil

Satellit [zate'li:t] (**-en, -en**) *m* satellite; **~enfernsehen** *nt* satellite television

Satire [za'ti:rə] *f* satire; **satirisch** *adj* satirical

satt [zat] *adj* full; (*Farbe*) rich, deep; **jdn/etw ~ sein** *od* **haben** to be fed up with sb/sth; **sich ~ hören/sehen an** +*dat* to hear/see enough of; **sich ~ essen** to eat one's fill; **~ machen** to be filling

Sattel ['zatəl] (**-s, ⁻**) *m* saddle; (*Berg*) ridge; **s~n** *vt* to saddle; **~schlepper** *m* articulated lorry

sättigen ['zɛtɪgən] *vt* to satisfy; (*CHEM*) to saturate

Satz [zats] (**-es, ⁻e**) *m* (*GRAM*) sentence; (*Nebensatz, Adverbialsatz*) clause; (*Theorem*) theorem; (*MUS*) movement; (*TENNIS: Briefmarken etc*) set; (*Kaffee*) grounds *pl*; (*COMM*) rate; (*Sprung*) jump; **~teil** *m* part of a sentence; **~ung** *f* (*Statut*) statute, rule; **~zeichen** *nt* punctuation mark

Sau [zaʊ] (**-, Säue**) *f* sow; (*umg*) dirty pig

sauber ['zaʊbər] *adj* clean; (*ironisch*) fine; **~ halten** to keep clean; **S~keit** *f* cleanness; (*einer Person*) cleanliness

säuberlich ['zɔybərlɪç] *adv* neatly

säubern *vt* to clean; (*POL etc*) to purge; **Säuberung** *f* cleaning; purge

Sauce ['zo:sə] *f* sauce, gravy

sauer ['zaʊər] *adj* sour; (*CHEM*) acid; (*umg*)

cross; **saurer Regen** acid rain; S~**braten** *m* braised beef marinated in vinegar

Sauerei [zaʊəˈraɪ] (*umg*) *f* rotten state of affairs, scandal; (*Schmutz etc*) mess; (*Unanständigkeit*) obscenity

Sauerkraut *nt* sauerkraut, pickled cabbage

säuerlich [ˈzɔʏɐlɪç] *adj* (*Geschmack*) sour; (*missvergnügt: Gesicht*) dour

Sauer- *zW*: ~**milch** *f* sour milk; ~**rahm** *m* (*KOCH*) sour cream; ~**stoff** *m* oxygen; ~**teig** *m* leaven

saufen [ˈzaʊfən] (*unreg*) (*umg*) *vt, vi* to drink, to booze; **Säufer** [ˈzɔʏfɐ] (*-s, -*) (*umg*) *m* boozer

saugen [ˈzaʊɡən] (*unreg*) *vt, vi* to suck

säugen [ˈzɔʏɡən] *vt* to suckle

Sauger [ˈzaʊɡɐ] (*-s, -*) *m* dummy, comforter (*US*); (*auf Flasche*) teat

Säugetier [ˈzɔʏɡə-] *nt* mammal

Säugling *m* infant, baby

Säule [ˈzɔʏlə] *f* column, pillar

Saum [zaʊm] (*-(e)s, Säume*) *m* hem; (*Naht*) seam

säumen [ˈzɔʏmən] *vt* to hem; to seam ♦ *vi* to delay, to hesitate

Sauna [ˈzaʊna] (*-, -s*) *f* sauna

Säure [ˈzɔʏrə] *f* acid

sausen [ˈzaʊzən] *vi* to blow; (*umg: eilen*) to rush; (*Ohren*) to buzz; **etw ~ lassen** (*umg*) not to bother with sth

Saxofon, Saxophon [zakso'fo:n] (*-s, -e*) *nt* saxophone

SB *abk* = **Selbstbedienung**

S-Bahn *f abk* (= *Schnellbahn*) high speed railway; (= *Stadtbahn*) suburban railway

schaben [ˈʃaːbən] *vt* to scrape

schäbig [ˈʃɛːbɪç] *adj* shabby

Schablone [ʃaˈbloːnə] *f* stencil; (*Muster*) pattern; (*fig*) convention

Schach [ʃax] (*-s, -s*) *nt* chess; (*Stellung*) check; ~**brett** *nt* chessboard; ~**figur** *f* chessman; **~'matt** *adj* checkmate; ~**spiel** *nt* game of chess

Schacht [ʃaxt] (*-(e)s, ⁿe*) *m* shaft

Schachtel (*-, -n*) *f* box

schade [ˈʃaːdə] *adj* a pity *od* shame ♦ *excl*: **(wie) ~!** (what a) pity *od* shame; **sich** *dat*

zu ~ sein für etw to consider o.s. too good for sth

Schädel [ˈʃɛdəl] (*-s, -*) *m* skull; ~**bruch** *m* fractured skull

Schaden [ˈʃaːdən] (*-s, ⁿ*) *m* damage; (*Verletzung*) injury; (*Nachteil*) disadvantage; **s~** *vi +dat* to hurt; **einer Sache s~** to damage sth; ~**ersatz** *m* compensation, damages *pl*; ~**freude** *f* malicious glee; **s~froh** *adj* (*Mensch, Lachen*) gloating; ~**sfall** *m*: **im ~sfall** in the event of a claim

schadhaft [ˈʃaːthaft] *adj* faulty, damaged

schäd- [ˈʃɛːt] *zW*: ~**igen** [ˈʃɛdɪɡən] *vt* to damage; (*Person*) to do harm to, to harm; ~**lich** *adj*: ~**lich (für)** harmful (to); **S~lichkeit** *f* harmfulness; **S~ling** *m* pest

Schadstoff [ˈʃaːtʃtɔf] *m* harmful substance; **s~arm** *adj*: **s~arm sein** to contain a low level of harmful substances

Schaf [ʃaːf] (*-(e)s, -e*) *nt* sheep

Schäfer [ˈʃɛːfɐ] (*-s, -*) *m* shepherd; ~**hund** *m* Alsatian (dog) (*BRIT*), German shepherd (dog) (*US*)

Schaffen [ˈʃafən] (*-s*) *nt* (creative) activity

schaffen¹ [ˈʃafən] (*unreg*) *vt* to create; (*Platz*) to make

schaffen² [ˈʃafən] *vt* (*erreichen*) to manage, to do; (*erledigen*) to finish; (*Prüfung*) to pass; (*transportieren*) to take ♦ *vi* (*umg: arbeiten*) to work; **sich** *dat* **etw ~** to get o.s. sth; **sich an etw** *dat* **zu ~ machen** to busy o.s. with sth

Schaffner(in) [ˈʃafnɐ(ɪn)] (*-s, -*) *m(f)* (*Busschaffner*) conductor(-tress); (*EISENB*) guard

Schaft [ʃaft] (*-(e)s, ⁿe*) *m* shaft; (*von Gewehr*) stock; (*von Stiefel*) leg; (*BOT*) stalk; tree trunk

Schal [ʃaːl] (*-s, -e od -s*) *m* scarf

schal *adj* flat; (*fig*) insipid

Schälchen [ˈʃɛːlçən] *nt* cup, bowl

Schale [ˈʃaːlə] *f* skin; (*abgeschält*) peel; (*Nussschale, Muschelschale, Eischale*) shell; (*Geschirr*) dish, bowl

schälen [ˈʃɛːlən] *vt* to peel; to shell ♦ *vr* to peel

Schall [ʃal] (*-(e)s, -e*) *m* sound; ~**dämpfer** (*-s, -*) *m* (*AUT*) silencer; **s~dicht** *adj* soundproof; **s~en** vi to (re)sound; **s~end** adj resounding, loud; **~mauer** f sound barrier; **~platte** f (gramophone) record

Schalt- ['ʃalt] zW: **~bild** nt circuit diagram; **~brett** nt switchboard; **s~en** vt to switch, to turn ♦ vi (AUT) to change (gear); (umg: begreifen) to catch on; **~er** (**-s, -**) m counter; (an Gerät) switch; **~erbeamte(r)** m counter clerk; **~erstunden** pl hours of business; **~hebel** m switch; (AUT) gear lever; **~jahr** nt leap year; **~ung** f switching; (ELEK) circuit; (AUT) gear change

Scham [ʃaːm] (**-**) f shame; (~gefühl) modesty; (Organe) private parts pl

schämen ['ʃɛːmən] vr to be ashamed

schamlos adj shameless

Schande ['ʃandə] (**-**) f disgrace

schändlich ['ʃɛntlɪç] adj disgraceful, shameful

Schändung ['ʃɛnduŋ] f violation, defilement

Schanze ['ʃantsə] f (Sprungschanze) ski jump

Schar [ʃaːr] (**-, -en**) f band, company; (Vögel) flock; (Menge) crowd; **in ~en** in droves; **s~en** vr to assemble, to rally

scharf [ʃarf] adj sharp; (Essen) hot, spicy; (Munition) live; **~ nachdenken** to think hard; **auf etw** akk **~ sein** (umg) to be keen on sth

Schärfe ['ʃɛrfə] f sharpness; (Strenge) rigour; **s~n** vt to sharpen

Scharf- zW: **s~machen** (umg) vt to stir up; **~richter** m executioner; **~schütze** m marksman, sharpshooter; **s~sinnig** adj astute, shrewd

Scharlach ['ʃarlax] (**-s, -e**) m (~fieber) scarlet fever

Scharnier [ʃar'niːr] (**-s, -e**) nt hinge

scharren ['ʃarən] vt, vi to scrape, to scratch

Schaschlik ['ʃaʃlɪk] (**-s, -s**) m od nt (shish) kebab

Schatten ['ʃatən] (**-s, -**) m shadow; **~riss** ▲ m silhouette; **~seite** f shady side, dark side

schattieren [ʃa'tiːrən] vt, vi to shade

schattig ['ʃatɪç] adj shady

Schatulle [ʃa'tʊlə] f casket; (Geldschatulle) coffer

Schatz [ʃats] (**-es, ⁓e**) m treasure; (Person) darling

schätz- [ʃɛts] zW: **~bar** adj assessable; **S~chen** nt darling, love; **~en** vt (abschätzen) to estimate; (Gegenstand) to value; (würdigen) to value, to esteem; (vermuten) to reckon; **S~ung** f estimate; estimation; valuation; **nach meiner S~ung ...** I reckon that ...

Schau [ʃau] (**-**) f show; (Ausstellung) display, exhibition; **etw zur ~ stellen** to make a show of sth, to show sth off; **~bild** nt diagram

Schauder ['ʃaudər] (**-s, -s**) m shudder; (wegen Kälte) shiver; **s~haft** adj horrible; **s~n** vi to shudder; to shiver

schauen ['ʃauən] vi to look

Schauer ['ʃauər] (**-s, -**) m (Regenschauer) shower; (Schreck) shudder; **~geschichte** f horror story; **s~lich** adj horrific, spine-chilling

Schaufel ['ʃaufəl] (**-, -n**) f shovel; (NAUT) paddle; (TECH) scoop; **s~n** vt to shovel, to scoop

Schau- zW: **~fenster** nt shop window; **~fensterbummel** m window shopping (expedition); **~kasten** m showcase

Schaukel ['ʃaukəl] (**-, -n**) f swing; **s~n** vi to swing, to rock; **~pferd** nt rocking horse; **~stuhl** m rocking chair

Schaulustige(r) ['ʃaulʊstɪɡə(r)] f(m) onlooker

Schaum [ʃaum] (**-(e)s, Schäume**) m foam; (Seifenschaum) lather; **~bad** nt bubble bath

schäumen ['ʃɔymən] vi to foam

Schaum- zW: **~festiger** (**-s, -**) m mousse; **~gummi** m foam (rubber); **s~ig** adj frothy, foamy; **~stoff** m foam material; **~wein** m sparkling wine

Schauplatz m scene

schaurig ['ʃaurɪç] adj horrific, dreadful

Schauspiel nt spectacle; (THEAT) play; **~er(in)** m(f) actor (actress); **s~ern** vi insep to act; **Schauspielhaus** nt theatre

Scheck [ʃɛk] (**-s, -s**) m cheque; **~gebühr** f encashment fee; **~heft** nt cheque book; **~karte** f cheque card

scheffeln ['ʃɛfəln] vt to amass

Scheibe ['ʃaɪbə] f disc; (Brot etc) slice; (Glasscheibe) pane; (MIL) target

Scheiben- zW: **~bremse** f (AUT) disc brake; **~wischer** m (AUT) windscreen wiper

Scheide ['ʃaɪdə] f sheath; (Grenze) boundary; (ANAT) vagina; s~n (unreg) vt to separate; (Ehe) to dissolve ♦ vi to depart; to part; **sich s~n lassen** to get a divorce

Scheidung f (Ehescheidung) divorce

Schein [ʃaɪn] (-(e)s, -e) m light; (Anschein) appearance; (Geld) (bank)note; (Bescheinigung) certificate; **zum ~** in pretence; s~bar adj apparent; s~en (unreg) vi to shine; (Anschein haben) to seem; s~heilig adj hypocritical; ~werfer (-s, -) m floodlight; spotlight; (Suchscheinwerfer) searchlight; (AUT) headlamp

Scheiß- ['ʃaɪs] (umg) in zW bloody

Scheiße ['ʃaɪsə] (-) (umg) f shit

Scheitel ['ʃaɪtəl] (-s, -) m top; (Haarscheitel) parting; s~n vt to part

scheitern ['ʃaɪtərn] vi to fail

Schelle ['ʃɛlə] f small bell; s~n vi to ring

Schellfisch ['ʃɛlfɪʃ] m haddock

Schelm [ʃɛlm] (-(e)s, -e) m rogue; s~isch adj mischievous, roguish

Schelte ['ʃɛltə] f scolding; s~n (unreg) vt to scold

Schema ['ʃeːma] (-s, -s od -ta) nt scheme, plan; (Darstellung) schema; **nach ~** quite mechanically; s~tisch [ʃeˈmaːtɪʃ] adj schematic; (pej) mechanical

Schemel ['ʃeːməl] (-s, -) m (foot)stool

Schenkel ['ʃɛŋkəl] (-s, -) m thigh

schenken ['ʃɛŋkən] vt (auch fig) to give; (Getränk) to pour; **sich** dat **etw ~** (umg) to skip sth; **das ist geschenkt!** (billig) that's a giveaway!; (nichts wert) that's worthless!

Scherbe ['ʃɛrbə] f broken piece, fragment; (archäologisch) potsherd

Schere ['ʃeːrə] f scissors pl; (groß) shears pl; s~n (unreg) vt to cut; (Schaf) to shear; (kümmern) to bother ♦ vr to care; **scher dich zum Teufel!** get lost!; ~'rei (umg) f bother, trouble

Scherz [ʃɛrts] (-es, -e) m joke; fun; ~frage f conundrum; s~haft adj joking, jocular

Scheu [ʃɔy] (-) f shyness; (Angst) fear; (Ehrfurcht) awe; s~ adj shy; s~en vr: **sich s~en vor** +dat to be afraid of, to shrink from ♦ vt to shun ♦ vi (Pferd) to shy

scheuern ['ʃɔyərn] vt to scour, to scrub

Scheune ['ʃɔynə] f barn

Scheusal ['ʃɔyzaːl] (-s, -e) nt monster

scheußlich ['ʃɔyslɪç] adj dreadful, frightful

Schi [ʃiː] m = **Ski**

Schicht [ʃɪçt] (-, -en) f layer; (Klasse) class, level; (in Fabrik etc) shift; ~arbeit f shift work; s~en vt to layer, to stack

schick [ʃɪk] adj stylish, chic

schicken vt to send ♦ vr: **sich ~ (in** +akk) to resign o.s. (to) ♦ vb unpers (anständig sein) to be fitting

schicklich adj proper, fitting

Schicksal (-s, -e) nt fate; ~sschlag m great misfortune, blow

Schieb- ['ʃiːb] zW: **~edach** nt (AUT) sun roof; **s~en** (unreg) vt (auch Drogen) to push; (Schuld) to put ♦ vi to push; **~etür** f sliding door; **~ung** f fiddle

Schieds- ['ʃiːts] zW: **~gericht** nt court of arbitration; **~richter** m referee; umpire; (Schlichter) arbitrator

schief [ʃiːf] adj crooked; (Ebene) sloping; (Turm) leaning; (Winkel) oblique; (Blick) funny; (Vergleich) distorted ♦ adv crooked(ly); (ansehen) askance; **etw ~ stellen** to slope sth; **~ gehen** (umg) to go wrong

Schiefer ['ʃiːfər] (-s, -) m slate

schielen ['ʃiːlən] vi to squint; **nach etw ~** (fig) to eye sth

schien etc [ʃiːn] vb siehe **scheinen**

Schienbein nt shinbone

Schiene ['ʃiːnə] f rail; (MED) splint; s~n vt to put in splints

schier [ʃiːr] adj (fig) sheer ♦ adv nearly, almost

Schieß- ['ʃiːs] zW: **~bude** f shooting gallery; s~en (unreg) vt to shoot; (Ball) to kick; (Geschoss) to fire ♦ vi to shoot; (Salat etc) to run to seed; s~en auf +akk to shoot at; ~e'rei f shooting incident, shoot-out; ~pulver nt gunpowder; ~scharte f embrasure

Schiff [ʃɪf] (-(e)s, -e) nt ship, vessel; (Kirchenschiff) nave; s~bar adj (Fluss) navigable; ~bruch m shipwreck; s~brüchig adj shipwrecked; ~chen nt small boat; (Weben) shuttle; (Mütze) forage cap; ~er (-s, -) m bargeman, boatman; ~fahrt ▲ f shipping; (Reise) voyage

Schikane [ʃi'ka:nə] f harassment; dirty trick; **mit allen ~n** with all the trimmings

schikanieren [ʃika'ni:rən] vt to harass, to torment

Schikoree ▲ ['ʃikore:] (-s) m od f = **Chicorée**

Schild[1] [ʃɪlt] (-(e)s, -e) m shield; **etw im ~e führen** to be up to sth

Schild[2] [ʃɪlt] (-(e)s, -er) nt sign; nameplate; (Etikett) label

Schilddrüse f thyroid gland

schildern ['ʃɪldərn] vt to depict, to portray

Schildkröte f tortoise; (Wasserschildkröte) turtle

Schilf [ʃɪlf] (-(e)s, -e) nt (Pflanze) reed; (Material) reeds pl, rushes pl; ~rohr nt (Pflanze) reed

schillern ['ʃɪlərn] vi to shimmer; ~d adj iridescent

Schilling ['ʃɪlɪŋ] m schilling

Schimmel ['ʃɪməl] (-s, -) m mould; (Pferd) white horse; s~ig adj mouldy; s~n vi to get mouldy

Schimmer ['ʃɪmər] (-s) m (Lichtsein) glimmer; (Glanz) shimmer; s~n vi to glimmer, to shimmer

Schimpanse [ʃɪm'panzə] (-n, -n) m chimpanzee

schimpfen ['ʃɪmpfən] vt to scold ♦ vi to curse, to complain; to scold

Schimpfwort nt term of abuse

schinden ['ʃɪndən] (unreg) vt to maltreat, to drive too hard ♦ vr: **sich ~ (mit)** to sweat and strain (at), to toil away (at); **Eindruck ~** (umg) to create an impression

Schinde'rei f grind, drudgery

Schinken ['ʃɪŋkən] (-s, -) m ham

Schirm [ʃɪrm] (-(e)s, -e) m (Regenschirm) umbrella; (Sonnenschirm) parasol, sunshade; (Wandschirm, Bildschirm) screen; (Lampenschirm) (lamp)shade; (Mützenschirm) peak; (Pilzschirm) cap; ~mütze f peaked cap; ~ständer m umbrella stand

schizophren [ʃitso'fre:n] adj schizophrenic

Schlacht [ʃlaxt] (-, -en) f battle; s~en vt to slaughter, to kill; ~er (-s, -) m butcher; ~feld nt battlefield; ~hof m slaughterhouse, abattoir; ~schiff nt battleship; ~vieh nt animals kept for meat; beef cattle

Schlaf [ʃla:f] (-(e)s) m sleep; ~anzug m pyjamas pl

Schläfe f (ANAT) temple

schlafen ['ʃla:fən] (unreg) vi to sleep; ~ **gehen** to go to bed; **S~szeit** f bedtime

Schlaf- zW: ~gelegenheit f sleeping accommodation; ~lied nt lullaby; s~los adj sleepless; ~losigkeit f sleeplessness, insomnia; ~mittel nt sleeping pill

schläfrig ['ʃle:frɪç] adj sleepy

Schlaf- zW: ~saal m dormitory; ~sack m sleeping bag; ~tablette f sleeping pill; ~wagen m sleeping car, sleeper; s~wandeln vi insep to sleepwalk; ~zimmer nt bedroom

Schlag [ʃla:k] (-(e)s, ᵉe) m (auch fig) blow; (auch MED) stroke; (Pulsschlag, Herzschlag) beat; (ELEK) shock; (Blitzschlag) bolt, stroke; (Autotür) car door; (umg: Portion) helping; (Art) kind, type; **Schläge** pl (Tracht Prügel) beating sg; **mit einem ~** all at once; **~ auf ~** in rapid succession; ~ader f artery; ~anfall m stroke; s~artig adj sudden, without warning; ~baum m barrier

Schlägel ['ʃle:gəl] (-s, -) m (drum)stick; (Hammer) mallet, hammer

schlagen ['ʃla:gən] (unreg) vt, vi to strike, to hit; (wiederholt ~, besiegen) to beat; (Glocke) to ring; (Stunde) to strike; (Sahne) to whip; (Schlacht) to fight ♦ vr to fight; **nach jdm ~** (fig) to take after sb; **sich gut ~** (fig) to do well; **Schlager** ['ʃla:gər] (-s, -

m (auch fig) hit

Schläger ['ʃlɛːɡər] *m* brawler; (*SPORT*) bat; (*TENNIS etc*) racket; (*GOLF*) club; hockey stick; (*Waffe*) rapier; **Schläge'rei** *f* fight, punch-up

Schlagersänger(in) *m(f)* pop singer

Schlag- *zW:* **s~fertig** *adj* quick-witted; **~fertigkeit** *f* ready wit, quickness of repartee; **~loch** *nt* pothole; **~obers** (*ÖSTERR*) *nt* = **Schlagsahne**; **~sahne** *f* (whipped) cream; **~seite** *f* (*NAUT*) list; **~wort** *nt* slogan, catch phrase; **~zeile** *f* headline; **~zeug** *nt* percussion; drums *pl*; **~zeuger** (**-s, -**) *m* drummer

Schlamassel [ʃlaˈmasəl] (**-s, -**) (*umg*) *m* mess

Schlamm [ʃlam] (**-(e)s, -e**) *m* mud; **s~ig** *adj* muddy

Schlamp- ['ʃlamp] *zW:* **~e** (*umg*) *f* slut; **s~en** (*umg*) *vi* to be sloppy; **~e'rei** (*umg*) *f* disorder, untidiness; sloppy work; **s~ig** (*umg*) *adj* (*Mensch, Arbeit*) sloppy, messy

Schlange ['ʃlaŋə] *f* snake; (*Menschenschlange*) queue (*BRIT*), line-up (*US*); **~ stehen** to (form a) queue, to line up

schlängeln ['ʃlɛŋəln] *vr* (*Schlange*) to wind; (*Weg*) to wind, twist; (*Fluss*) to meander

Schlangen- *zW:* **~biss** ▲ *m* snake bite; **~gift** *nt* snake venom; **~linie** *f* wavy line

schlank [ʃlaŋk] *adj* slim, slender; **S~heit** *f* slimness, slenderness; **S~heitskur** *f* diet

schlapp [ʃlap] *adj* limp; (*locker*) slack; **S~e** (*umg*) *f* setback

Schlaraffenland [ʃlaˈrafənlant] *nt* land of milk and honey

schlau [ʃlau] *adj* crafty, cunning

Schlauch [ʃlaux] (**-(e)s, Schläuche**) *m* hose; (*in Reifen*) inner tube; (*umg: Anstrengung*) grind; **~boot** *nt* rubber dinghy; **s~en** (*umg*) *vt* to tell on, to exhaust

Schläue ['ʃlɔyə] (**-**) *f* cunning

Schlaufe ['ʃlaufə] *f* loop; (*Aufhänger*) hanger

Schlauheit *f* cunning

schlecht [ʃlɛçt] *adj* bad ♦ *adv* badly; **~ gelaunt** in a bad mood; **~ und recht** after

a fashion; **jdm ist ~** sb feels sick *od* bad; **jdm geht es ~** sb is in a bad way; **~ machen** to run down; **S~igkeit** *f* badness; bad deed

schlecken ['ʃlɛkən] *vt, vi* to lick

Schlegel ['ʃleːɡəl] (**-s, -**) *m* (*KOCH*) leg; *siehe* **Schlägel**

schleichen ['ʃlaiçən] (*unreg*) *vi* to creep, to crawl; **~d** *adj* gradual; creeping

Schleichwerbung *f* (*COMM*) plug

Schleier ['ʃlaiər] (**-s, -**) *m* veil; **s~haft** (*umg*) *adj*: **jdm s~haft sein** to be a mystery to sb

Schleif- [ʃlaif] *zW:* **~e** *f* loop; (*Band*) bow; **s~en¹** *vt, vi* to drag; **s~en²** (*unreg*) *vt* to grind; (*Edelstein*) to cut; **~stein** *m* grindstone

Schleim [ʃlaim] (**-(e)s, -e**) *m* slime; (*MED*) mucus; (*KOCH*) gruel; **~haut** *f* (*ANAT*) mucous membrane; **s~ig** *adj* slimy

Schlemm- ['ʃlɛm] *zW:* **s~en** *vi* to feast; **~er** (**-s, -**) *m* gourmet; **~e'rei** *f* gluttony, feasting

schlendern ['ʃlɛndərn] *vi* to stroll

schlenkern ['ʃlɛŋkərn] *vt, vi* to swing, to dangle

Schlepp- [ʃlɛp] *zW:* **~e** *f* train; **s~en** *vt* to drag; (*Auto, Schiff*) to tow; (*tragen*) to lug; **s~end** *adj* dragging, slow; **~er** (**-s, -**) *m* tractor; (*Schiff*) tug

Schlesien ['ʃleːziən] (**-s**) *nt* Silesia

Schleuder ['ʃlɔydər] (**-, -n**) *f* catapult; (*Wäscheschleuder*) spin-drier; (*Butterschleuder etc*) centrifuge; **~gefahr** *f* risk of skidding; **„Achtung ~gefahr"** "slippery road ahead"; **s~n** *vt* to hurl; (*Wäsche*) to spin-dry ♦ *vi* (*AUT*) to skid; (*fig*) hot seat; **~preis** *m* give-away price; **~sitz** *m* (*AVIAT*) ejector seat; (*fig*) hot seat; **~ware** *f* cheap *od* cut-price goods *pl*

schleunigst ['ʃlɔynɪçst] *adv* straight away

Schleuse ['ʃlɔyzə] *f* lock; (*~ntor*) sluice

schlicht [ʃlɪçt] *adj* simple, plain; **~en** *vt* (*glätten*) to smooth, to dress; (*Streit*) to settle; **S~er** (**-s, -**) *m* mediator, arbitrator; **S~ung** *f* settlement; arbitration

Schlick [ʃlɪk] (**-(e)s, -e**) *m* mud; (*Ölschlick*) slick

schlief *etc* [ʃliːf] *vb siehe* **schlafen**

Spelling Reform: ▲ new spelling △ old spelling (to be phased out)

Schließ- ['ʃliːs] zW: **s~en** (unreg) vt to close, to shut; (beenden) to close; (Freundschaft, Bündnis, Ehe) to enter into; (folgern): **s~en (aus)** to infer (from) ♦ vi, vr to close, to shut; **etw in sich s~en** to include sth; **~fach** nt locker; **s~lich** adv finally; **s~lich doch** after all

Schliff [ʃlɪf] **(-(e)s, -e)** m cut(ting); (fig) polish

schlimm [ʃlɪm] adj bad; **~er** adj worse; **~ste(r, s)** adj worst; **~stenfalls** adv at (the) worst

Schlinge ['ʃlɪŋə] f loop; (bes Henkersschlinge) noose; (Falle) snare; (MED) sling; **s~n** (unreg) vt to wind; (essen) to bolt, to gobble ♦ vi (essen) to bolt one's food, to gobble

schlingern vi to roll

Schlips [ʃlɪps] **(-es, -e)** m tie

Schlitten ['ʃlɪtən] **(-s, -)** m sledge, sleigh; **~fahren** (-s) nt tobogganing

schlittern ['ʃlɪtərn] vi to slide

Schlittschuh ['ʃlɪtʃuː] m skate; **~ laufen** to skate; **~bahn** f skating rink; **~läufer(in)** m(f) skater

Schlitz [ʃlɪts] **(-es, -e)** m slit; (für Münze) slot; (Hosenschlitz) flies pl; **s~äugig** adj slant-eyed

Schloss ▲ [ʃlɔs] **(-es, ¨er)** nt lock; (an Schmuck etc) clasp; (Bau) castle; chateau

schloss ▲ etc vb siehe **schließen**

Schlosser ['ʃlɔsər] **(-s, -)** m (Autoschlosser) fitter; (für Schlüssel etc) locksmith

Schlosserei [-'raɪ] f metal (working) shop

Schlot [ʃloːt] **(-(e)s, -e)** m chimney; (NAUT) funnel

schlottern ['ʃlɔtərn] vi to shake, to tremble; (Kleidung) to be baggy

Schlucht [ʃlʊxt] **(-, -en)** f gorge, ravine

schluchzen ['ʃlʊxtsən] vi to sob

Schluck [ʃlʊk] **(-(e)s, -e)** m swallow; (Menge) drop; **~auf (-s, -s)** m hiccups pl; **s~en** vt, vi to swallow

schludern ['ʃluːdərn] vi to skimp, to do sloppy work

schlug etc [ʃluːk] vb siehe **schlagen**

Schlummer ['ʃlʊmər] **(-s)** m slumber; **s~n** vi to slumber

Schlund [ʃlʊnt] **(-(e)s, ¨e)** m gullet; (fig) jaw

schlüpfen ['ʃlʏpfən] vi to slip; (Vogel etc) to hatch (out)

Schlüpfer ['ʃlʏpfər] **(-s, -)** m panties pl, knickers pl

schlüpfrig ['ʃlʏpfrɪç] adj slippery; (fig) lewd; **S~keit** f slipperiness; (fig) lewdness

schlurfen ['ʃlʊrfən] vi to shuffle

schlürfen ['ʃlʏrfən] vt, vi to slurp

Schluss ▲ [ʃlʊs] **(-es, ¨e)** m end; (~folgerung) conclusion; **am ~** at the end; **~ machen mit** to finish with

Schlüssel ['ʃlʏsəl] **(-s, -)** m (auch fig) key; (Schraubenschlüssel) spanner, wrench; (MUS) clef; **~bein** nt collarbone; **~blume** f cowslip, primrose; **~bund** m bunch of keys; **~dienst** m key cutting service; **~loch** nt keyhole; **~position** f key position; **~wort** nt keyword

schlüssig ['ʃlʏsɪç] adj conclusive

Schluss- ▲ zW: **~licht** nt taillight; (fig) tailender; **~strich** m (fig) final stroke; **~verkauf** m clearance sale

schmächtig ['ʃmɛçtɪç] adj slight

schmackhaft ['ʃmakhaft] adj tasty

schmal [ʃmaːl] adj narrow; (Person, Buch etc) slender, slim; (karg) meagre

schmälern ['ʃmɛːlərn] vt to diminish; (fig) to belittle

Schmalfilm m cine film

Schmalz [ʃmalts] **(-es, -e)** nt dripping, lard; (fig) sentiment, schmaltz; **s~ig** adj (fig) schmaltzy

schmarotzen [ʃma'rɔtsən] vi to sponge; (BOT) to be parasitic; **Schmarotzer (-s, -)** m parasite; sponger

Schmarren ['ʃmarən] **(-s, -)** m (ÖSTERR) small piece of pancake; (fig) rubbish, tripe

schmatzen ['ʃmatsən] vi to smack one's lips; to eat noisily

schmecken ['ʃmɛkən] vt, vi to taste; **es schmeckt ihm** he likes it

Schmeichel- ['ʃmaɪçəl] zW: **~ei** [-'laɪ] f flattery; **s~haft** adj flattering; **s~n** vi to flatter

schmeißen ['ʃmaɪsən] (unreg) (umg) vt to

throw, to chuck

Schmelz [ʃmɛlts] **(-es, -e)** m enamel; (*Glasur*) glaze; (*von Stimme*) melodiousness; **s~en** (*unreg*) vt to melt; (*Erz*) to smelt ♦ vi to melt; **~punkt** m melting point; **~wasser** nt melted snow

Schmerz [ʃmɛrts] **(-es, -en)** m pain; (*Trauer*) grief; **s~empfindlich** adj sensitive to pain; **s~en** vt, vi to hurt; **~ensgeld** nt compensation; **s~haft** adj painful; **s~lich** adj painful; **s~los** adj painless; **~mittel** nt painkiller; **~tablette** f painkiller

Schmetterling [ˈʃmɛtɐlɪŋ] m butterfly

schmettern [ˈʃmɛtɐn] vt (*werfen*) to hurl; (*TENNIS: Ball*) to smash; (*singen*) to belt out (*inf*)

Schmied [ʃmiːt] **(-(e)s, -e)** m blacksmith; **~e** [ˈʃmiːdə] f smithy, forge; **~eeisen** nt wrought iron; **s~en** vt to forge; (*Pläne*) to devise, to concoct

schmiegen [ˈʃmiːɡən] vt to press, to nestle ♦ vr: **sich ~ (an** +akk) to cuddle up (to), to nestle (up to)

Schmier- [ˈʃmiːr] zW: **~e** f grease; (*THEAT*) greasepaint, make-up; **s~en** vt to smear; (*ölen*) to lubricate, to grease; (*bestechen*) to bribe; (*schreiben*) to scrawl ♦ vi (*schreiben*) to scrawl; **~fett** nt grease; **~geld** nt bribe; **s~ig** adj greasy; **~seife** f soft soap

Schminke [ˈʃmɪŋkə] f make-up; **s~n** vt, vr to make up

schmirgeln [ˈʃmɪrɡəln] vt to sand (down)

Schmirgelpapier nt emery paper

schmollen [ˈʃmɔlən] vi to sulk, to pout

Schmorbraten m stewed od braised meat

schmoren [ˈʃmoːrən] vt to stew, to braise

Schmuck [ʃmʊk] **(-(e)s, -e)** m jewellery; (*Verzierung*) decoration

schmücken [ˈʃmʏkən] vt to decorate

Schmuck- zW: **s~los** adj unadorned, plain; **~sachen** pl jewels, jewellery sg

Schmuggel [ˈʃmʊɡəl] **(-s)** m smuggling; **s~n** vt, vi to smuggle

Schmuggler **(-s, -)** m smuggler

schmunzeln [ˈʃmʊntsəln] vi to smile benignly

schmusen [ˈʃmuːzən] (*umg*) vi (*zärtlich sein*) to cuddle, to canoodle (*inf*)

Schmutz [ʃmʊts] **(-es)** m dirt, filth; **~fink** m filthy creature; **~fleck** m stain; **s~ig** adj dirty

Schnabel [ˈʃnaːbəl] **(-s, ⸚)** m beak, bill; (*Ausguss*) spout

Schnalle [ˈʃnalə] f buckle, clasp; **s~n** vt to buckle

Schnapp- [ʃnap] zW: **s~en** vt to grab, to catch ♦ vi to snap; **~schloss** ▲ nt spring lock; **~schuss** ▲ m (*PHOT*) snapshot

Schnaps [ʃnaps] **(-es, ⸚e)** m spirits pl; schnapps

schnarchen [ˈʃnarçən] vi to snore

schnattern [ˈʃnatərn] vi (*Gänse*) to gabble; (*Ente*) to quack

schnauben [ˈʃnaʊbən] vi to snort ♦ vr to blow one's nose

schnaufen [ˈʃnaʊfən] vi to puff, to pant

Schnauze [ˈʃnaʊtsə] f snout, muzzle; (*Ausguss*) spout; (*umg*) gob

schnäuzen ▲ [ˈʃnɔʏtsən] vr to blow one's nose

Schnecke [ˈʃnɛkə] f snail; **~nhaus** nt snail's shell

Schnee [ʃneː] **(-s)** m snow; (*Eischnee*) beaten egg white; **~ball** m snowball; **~flocke** f snowflake; **s~frei** adj free of snow; **~gestöber** nt snowstorm; **~glöckchen** nt snowdrop; **~grenze** f snow line; **~kette** f (*AUT*) snow chain; **~mann** m snowman; **~pflug** m snowplough; **~regen** m sleet; **~schmelze** f thaw; **~wehe** f snowdrift

Schneide [ˈʃnaɪdə] f edge; (*Klinge*) blade; **s~n** (*unreg*) vt to cut; (*kreuzen*) to cross, to intersect with ♦ vr to cut o.s.; to cross, to intersect; **s~nd** adj cutting; **~r (-s, -)** m tailor; **~rei** f (*Geschäft*) tailor's; **~rin** f dressmaker; **s~rn** vt to make ♦ vi to be a tailor; **~zahn** m incisor

schneien [ˈʃnaɪən] vi unpers to snow

Schneise [ˈʃnaɪzə] f clearing

schnell [ʃnɛl] adj quick, fast ♦ adv quick, quickly, fast; **S~hefter (-s, -)** m loose-leaf binder; **S~igkeit** f speed; **S~imbiss** ▲ m (*Lokal*) snack bar; **S~kochtopf** m

(*Dampfkochtopf*) pressure cooker;
S~reinigung *f* dry cleaner's; ~stens *adv*
as quickly as possible; S~straße *f*
expressway; S~zug *m* fast *od* express train

schneuzen △ ['ʃnɔytsən] *vr siehe*
schnäuzen

schnippeln ['ʃnɪpəln] (*umg*) *vt*: ~ (**an** +*dat*)
to snip (at)

schnippisch ['ʃnɪpɪʃ] *adj* sharp-tongued

Schnitt (**-(e)s, -e**) *m* cut(ting); (~*punkt*)
intersection; (*Querschnitt*) (cross) section;
(*Durchschnitt*) average; (~*muster*) pattern;
(*an Buch*) edge; (*umg*: *Gewinn*) profit

schnitt *etc vb siehe* **schneiden**

Schnitt- *zW*: ~blumen *pl* cut flowers; ~e *f*
slice; (*belegt*) sandwich; ~fläche *f* section;
~lauch *m* chive; ~punkt *m* (point of)
intersection; ~stelle *f* (COMPUT) interface;
~wunde *f* cut

Schnitz- ['ʃnɪts] *zW*: ~arbeit *f* wood
carving; ~el (**-s, -**) *nt* chip; (KOCH)
escalope; s~en *vt* to carve; ~er (**-s, -**) *m*
carver; (*umg*) blunder; ~e'rei *f* carving;
carved woodwork

schnodderig ['ʃnɔdərɪç] (*umg*) *adj* snotty

Schnorchel ['ʃnɔrçəl] (**-s, -**) *m* snorkel

Schnörkel ['ʃnœrkəl] (**-s, -**) *m* flourish;
(ARCHIT) scroll

schnorren ['ʃnɔrən] *vt, vi* to cadge

schnüffeln ['ʃnʏfəln] *vi* to sniff

Schnüffler (**-s, -**) *m* snooper

Schnuller ['ʃnʊlər] (**-s, -**) *m* dummy,
comforter (*US*)

Schnupfen ['ʃnʊpfən] (**-s, -**) *m* cold

schnuppern ['ʃnʊpərn] *vi* to sniff

Schnur [ʃnuːr] (**-, ⁻e**) *f* string, cord; (ELEK)
flex

schnüren ['ʃnyːrən] *vt* to tie

schnurgerade *adj* straight (as a die)

Schnurrbart ['ʃnʊrbaːrt] *m* moustache

schnurren ['ʃnʊrən] *vi* to purr; (*Kreisel*) to
hum

Schnürschuh *m* lace-up (shoe)

Schnürsenkel *m* shoelace

schnurstracks *adv* straight (away)

Schock [ʃɔk] (**-(e)s, -e**) *m* shock; s~ieren
[ʃɔ'kiːrən] *vt* to shock, to outrage

Schöffe ['ʃœfə] (**-n, -n**) *m* lay magistrate;
Schöffin *f* lay magistrate

Schokolade [ʃoko'laːdə] *f* chocolate

Scholle ['ʃɔlə] *f* clod; (*Eisscholle*) ice floe;
(*Fisch*) plaice

SCHLÜSSELWORT

schon [ʃoːn] *adv* **1** (*bereits*) already; **er ist
schon da** he's there already, he's already
there; **ist er schon da?** is he there yet?;
warst du schon einmal da? have you ever
been there?; **ich war schon einmal da** I've
been there before; **das war schon immer
so** that has always been the case; **schon
oft** often; **hast du schon gehört?** have
you heard?

2 (*bestimmt*) all right; **du wirst schon
sehen** you'll see (all right); **das wird
schon noch gut** that'll be OK

3 (*bloß*) just; **allein schon das Gefühl ...**
just the very feeling ...; **schon der
Gedanke** the very thought; **wenn ich das
schon höre** I only have to hear that

4 (*einschränkend*): **ja schon, aber ...** yes
(well), but ...

5: schon möglich possible; **schon gut!**
OK!; **du weißt schon** you know; **komm
schon!** come on!

---

schön [ʃøːn] *adj* beautiful; (*nett*) nice; ~e
Grüße best wishes; ~e Ferien have a nice
holiday; ~en Dank (many) thanks; sich ~
machen to make o.s. look nice

schonen ['ʃoːnən] *vt* to look after ♦ *vr* to
take it easy; ~d *adj* careful, gentle

Schön- *zW*: ~heit *f* beauty; ~heitsfehler
m blemish, flaw; ~heitsoperation *f*
cosmetic surgery

Schonkost (**-**) *f* light diet; (*Spezialdiät*)
special diet

Schon- *zW*: ~ung *f* good care; (*Nachsicht*)
consideration; (*Forst*) plantation of young
trees; s~ungslos *adj* unsparing, harsh;
~zeit *f* close season

Schöpf- ['ʃœpf] *zW*: s~en *vt* to scoop, to
ladle; (*Mut*) to summon up; (*Luft*) to
breathe in; ~er (**-s, -**) *m* creator; s~erisch

adj creative; **~kelle** *f* ladle; **~ung** *f* creation

Schorf [ʃɔrf] **(-(e)s, -e)** *m* scab

Schornstein ['ʃɔrnʃtain] *m* chimney; (*NAUT*) funnel; **~feger (-s, -)** *m* chimney sweep

Schoß [ʃoːs] **(-es, ⸚e)** *m* lap

schoss ▲ *etc vb siehe* **schießen**

Schoßhund *m* pet dog, lapdog

Schote ['ʃoːtə] *f* pod

Schotte ['ʃɔtə] *m* Scot, Scotsman

Schotter ['ʃɔtər] **(-s)** *m* broken stone, road metal; (*EISENB*) ballast

Schott- [ʃɔt] *zW:* **~in** *f* Scot, Scotswoman; **s~isch** *adj* Scottish, Scots; **~land** *nt* Scotland

schraffieren [ʃra'fiːrən] *vt* to hatch

schräg [ʃrɛːk] *adj* slanting, not straight; **etw ~ stellen** to put sth at an angle; **~ gegenüber** diagonally opposite; **S~e** ['ʃrɛːgə] *f* slant; **S~strich** *m* oblique stroke

Schramme ['ʃramə] *f* scratch; **s~n** *vt* to scratch

Schrank [ʃraŋk] **(-(e)s, ⸚e)** *m* cupboard; (*Kleiderschrank*) wardrobe; **~e** *f* barrier; **~koffer** *m* trunk

Schraube ['ʃraubə] *f* screw; **s~n** *vt* to screw; **~nschlüssel** *m* spanner; **~nzieher (-s, -)** *m* screwdriver

Schraubstock ['ʃraupʃtɔk] *m* (*TECH*) vice

Schreck [ʃrɛk] **(-(e)s, -e)** *m* terror; fright; **~en (-s, -)** *m* terror; fright; **s~en** *vt* to frighten; to scare; **~gespenst** *nt* spectre, nightmare; **s~haft** *adj* jumpy, easily frightened; **s~lich** *adj* terrible, dreadful

Schrei [ʃrai] **(-(e)s, -e)** *m* scream; (*Ruf*) shout

Schreib- [ʃraib] *zW:* **~block** *m* writing pad; **s~en** (*unreg*) *vt, vi* to write; (*buchstabieren*) to spell; **~en (-s, -)** *nt* letter, communication; **s~faul** *adj* bad about writing letters; **~kraft** *f* typist; **~maschine** *f* typewriter; **~papier** *nt* notepaper; **~tisch** *m* desk; **~ung** *f* spelling; **~waren** *pl* stationery *sg*; **~weise** *f* spelling; way of writing; **~zentrale** *f* typing pool; **~zeug** *nt* writing materials *pl*

schreien ['ʃraiən] (*unreg*) *vt, vi* to scream; (*rufen*) to shout; **~d** *adj* (*fig*) glaring; (*Farbe*)

loud

Schrein [ʃrain] **(-(e)s, -e)** *m* shrine

Schreiner ['ʃrainər] **(-s, -)** *m* joiner; (*Zimmermann*) carpenter; (*Möbelschreiner*) cabinetmaker; **~ei** [-'rai] *f* joiner's workshop

schreiten ['ʃraitən] (*unreg*) *vi* to stride

schrieb *etc* [ʃriːp] *vb siehe* **schreiben**

Schrift [ʃrift] **(-, -en)** *f* writing; handwriting; (*~art*) script; (*Gedrucktes*) pamphlet, work; **~deutsch** *nt* written German; **~führer** *m* secretary; **s~lich** *adj* written ♦ *adv* in writing; **~sprache** *f* written language; **~steller(in)** *m(f)* writer; **~stück** *nt* document; **~wechsel** *m* correspondence

schrill [ʃril] *adj* shrill

Schritt [ʃrit] **(-(e)s, -e)** *m* step; (*Gangart*) walk; (*Tempo*) pace; (*von Hose*) crutch; **~ fahren** to drive at walking pace; **~macher (-s, -)** *m* pacemaker; **~tempo** ▲ *nt:* **im ~tempo** at a walking pace

schroff [ʃrɔf] *adj* steep; (*zackig*) jagged; (*fig*) brusque

schröpfen ['ʃrœpfən] *vt* (*fig*) to fleece

Schrot [ʃroːt] **(-(e)s, -e)** *m od nt* (*Blei*) (small) shot; (*Getreide*) coarsely ground grain, groats *pl*; **~flinte** *f* shotgun

Schrott [ʃrɔt] **(-(e)s, -e)** *m* scrap metal; **~haufen** *m* scrap heap; **s~reif** *adj* ready for the scrap heap

schrubben ['ʃrubən] *vt* to scrub

Schrubber (-s, -) *m* scrubbing brush

schrumpfen ['ʃrumpfən] *vi* to shrink; (*Apfel*) to shrivel

Schub- ['ʃuːb] *zW:* **~fach** *nt* drawer; **~karren** *m* wheelbarrow; **~lade** *f* drawer

Schubs [ʃuːps] **(-es, -e)** (*umg*) *m* shove (*inf*), push

schüchtern ['ʃʏçtərn] *adj* shy; **S~heit** *f* shyness

Schuft [ʃuft] **(-(e)s, -e)** *m* scoundrel

schuften (*umg*) *vi* to graft, to slave away

Schuh [ʃuː] **(-(e)s, -e)** *m* shoe; **~band** *nt* shoelace; **~creme** *f* shoe polish; **~größe** *f* shoe size; **~löffel** *m* shoehorn; **~macher (-s, -)** *m* shoemaker

Schul- *zW:* **~arbeit** *f* homework (*no pl*); **~aufgaben** *pl* homework *sg*; **~besuch** *m*

school attendance;~**buch** nt school book

Schuld [ʃʊlt] (-, -en) f guilt; (FIN) debt; (*Verschulden*) fault; ~ **haben** (an +dat) to be to blame (for); **er hat** ~ it's his fault; **jdm** ~ **geben** to blame sb; *siehe* **zuschulden;~** adj: **s~ sein** (an +dat) to be to blame (for); **er ist s~** it's his fault;s~**en** [ˈʃʊldən] vt to owe;s~**enfrei** adj free from debt;~**gefühl** nt feeling of guilt;s~**ig** adj guilty; (*gebührend*) due; **s~ig an etw** dat **sein** to be guilty of sth; **jdm etw s~ig sein** to owe sb sth; **jdm etw s~ig bleiben** not to provide sb with sth;s~**los** adj innocent, without guilt;~**ner** (-s, -) m debtor; ~**schein** m promissory note, IOU

Schule [ˈʃuːlə] f school;s~**n** vt to train, to school

Schüler(in) [ˈʃyːlər(ɪn)] (-s, -) m(f) pupil; ~**austausch** m school od student exchange;~**ausweis** m (school) student card

Schul- zW:~**ferien** pl school holidays; s~**frei** adj: **s~freier Tag** holiday; **s~frei sein** to be a holiday;~**hof** m playground; ~**jahr** nt school year;~**kind** nt schoolchild; s~**pflichtig** adj of school age;~**schiff** nt (NAUT) training ship;~**stunde** f period, lesson;~**tasche** f school bag

Schulter [ˈʃʊltər] (-, -n) f shoulder;~**blatt** nt shoulder blade;s~**n** vt to shoulder

Schulung f education, schooling

Schulzeugnis nt school report

Schund [ʃʊnt] (-(e)s) m trash, garbage

Schuppe [ˈʃʊpə] f scale; ~**n** pl (*Haarschuppen*) dandruff sg

Schuppen (-s, -) m shed

schuppig [ˈʃʊpɪç] adj scaly

Schur [ʃuːr] (-, -en) f shearing

schüren [ˈʃyːrən] vt to rake; (*fig*) to stir up

schürfen [ˈʃʏrfən] vt, vi to scrape, to scratch; (MIN) to prospect

Schurke [ˈʃʊrkə] (-n, -n) m rogue

Schurwolle f: **"reine ~"** "pure new wool"

Schürze [ˈʃʏrtsə] f apron

Schuss ▲ [ʃʊs] (-es, -̈e) m shot; (WEBEN) woof;~**bereich** m effective range

Schüssel [ˈʃʏsəl] (-, -n) f bowl

Schuss- ▲ zW:~**linie** f line of fire; ~**verletzung** f bullet wound;~**waffe** f firearm

Schuster [ˈʃuːstər] (-s, -) m cobbler, shoemaker

Schutt [ʃʊt] (-(e)s) m rubbish; (*Bauschutt*) rubble

Schüttelfrost m shivering

schütteln [ˈʃʏtəln] vt, vr to shake

schütten [ˈʃʏtən] vt to pour; (*Zucker, Kies etc*) to tip; (*verschütten*) to spill ♦ vi unpers to pour (down)

Schutthalde f dump

Schutthaufen m heap of rubble

Schutz [ʃʊts] (-es) m protection; (*Unterschlupf*) shelter; **jdn in ~ nehmen** to stand up for sb;~**anzug** m overalls pl; ~**blech** nt mudguard

Schütze [ˈʃʏtsə] (-n, -n) m gunman; (*Gewehrschütze*) rifleman; (*Scharfschütze, Sportschütze*) marksman; (ASTROL) Sagittarius

schützen [ˈʃʏtsən] vt to protect; ~ **vor** +dat od **gegen** to protect from

Schützenfest nt fair featuring shooting matches

Schutz- zW:~**engel** m guardian angel; ~**gebiet** nt protectorate; (*Naturschutzgebiet*) reserve;~**hütte** f shelter, refuge;~**impfung** f immunisation

Schützling [ˈʃʏtslɪŋ] m protégé(e); (*bes Kind*) charge

Schutz- zW:s~**los** adj defenceless;~**mann** m policeman;~**patron** m patron saint

Schwaben [ˈʃvaːbən] nt Swabia; **schwäbisch** adj Swabian

schwach [ʃvax] adj weak, feeble

Schwäche [ˈʃvɛçə] f weakness;s~**n** vt to weaken

Schwachheit f weakness

schwächlich adj weakly, delicate

Schwächling m weakling

Schwach- zW:~**sinn** m imbecility; s~**sinnig** adj mentally deficient; (*Idee*) idiotic;~**strom** m weak current

Schwächung [ˈʃvɛçʊŋ] f weakening

Schwager [ˈʃvaːgər] (-s, -̈) m brother-in-law

Schwägerin [ˈʃvɛːgərɪn] f sister-in-law

Schwalbe ['ʃvalbə] f swallow

Schwall [ʃval] **(-(e)s, -e)** m surge; (Worte) flood, torrent

Schwamm [ʃvam] **(-(e)s, "e)** m sponge; (Pilz) fungus

schwamm etc vb siehe **schwimmen**

schwammig adj spongy; (Gesicht) puffy

Schwan [ʃvaːn] **(-(e)s, "e)** m swan

schwanger ['ʃvaŋər] adj pregnant; **S~schaft** f pregnancy

schwanken vi to sway; (taumeln) to stagger, to reel; (Preise, Zahlen) to fluctuate; (zögern) to hesitate, to vacillate

Schwankung f fluctuation

Schwanz [ʃvants] **(-es, "e)** m tail

schwänzen ['ʃvɛntsən] (umg) vt to skip, to cut ♦ vi to play truant

Schwarm [ʃvarm] **(-(e)s, "e)** m swarm; (umg) heart-throb, idol

schwärm- ['ʃvɛrm] zW: **~en** vi to swarm; **~en für** to be mad od wild about; **S~erei** [-ə'raɪ] f enthusiasm; **~erisch** adj impassioned, effusive

Schwarte ['ʃvartə] f hard skin; (Speckschwarte) rind

schwarz [ʃvarts] adj black; **~es Brett** notice board; **ins S~e treffen** (auch fig) to hit the bull's eye; **in den ~en Zahlen** in the black; **~ sehen** (umg) to see the gloomy side of things; **S~arbeit** f illicit work, moonlighting; **S~brot** nt black bread; **S~e(r)** f(m) black (man/woman)

Schwärze ['ʃvɛrtsə] f blackness; (Farbe) blacking; (Druckerschwärze) printer's ink; **s~n** vt to blacken

Schwarz- zW: **s~fahren** (unreg) vi to travel without paying; to drive without a licence; **~handel** m black market (trade); **~markt** m black market; **~wald** m Black Forest; **s~weiß, s~-weiß** adj black and white

schwatzen ['ʃvatsən] vi to chatter

schwätzen ['ʃvɛtsən] vi to chatter

Schwätzer ['ʃvɛtsər] **(-s, -)** m gasbag

schwatzhaft adj talkative, gossipy

Schwebe ['ʃveːbə] f: **in der ~** (fig) in abeyance; **~bahn** f overhead railway; **s~n** vi to drift, to float; (hoch) to soar

Schwed- ['ʃveːd] zW: **~e** m Swede; **~en** nt Sweden; **~in** f Swede; **s~isch** adj Swedish

Schwefel ['ʃveːfəl] **(-s)** m sulphur; **s~ig** adj sulphurous; **~säure** f sulphuric acid

Schweig- ['ʃvaɪg] zW: **~egeld** nt hush money; **~en (-s)** nt silence; **s~en** (unreg) vi to be silent; to stop talking; **~epflicht** f pledge of secrecy; (von Anwalt) requirement of confidentiality; **s~sam** ['ʃvaɪkzaːm] adj silent, taciturn; **~samkeit** f taciturnity, quietness

Schwein [ʃvaɪn] **(-(e)s, -e)** nt pig; (umg) (good) luck

Schweine- zW: **~fleisch** nt pork; **~'rei** f mess; (Gemeinheit) dirty trick; **~stall** m pigsty

schweinisch adj filthy

Schweinsleder nt pigskin

Schweiß [ʃvaɪs] **(-es)** m sweat, perspiration; **s~en** vt, vi to weld; **~er (-s, -)** m welder; **~füße** pl sweaty feet; **~naht** f weld

Schweiz [ʃvaɪts] f Switzerland; **~er(in)** m(f) Swiss; **s~erisch** adj Swiss

schwelgen ['ʃvɛlgən] vi to indulge

Schwelle ['ʃvɛlə] f (auch fig) threshold; doorstep; (EISENB) sleeper (BRIT), tie (US)

schwellen (unreg) vi to swell

Schwellung f swelling

Schwemme ['ʃvɛmə] f (WIRTS: Überangebot) surplus

Schwenk- ['ʃvɛŋk] zW: **s~bar** adj swivel-mounted; **s~en** vt to swing; (Fahne) to wave; (abspülen) to rinse ♦ vi to turn, to swivel; (MIL) to wheel; **~ung** f turn; wheel

schwer [ʃveːr] adj heavy; (schwierig) difficult, hard; (schlimm) serious, bad ♦ adv (sehr) very (much); (verletzt etc) seriously, badly; **~ erziehbar** difficult (to bring up); **jdm ~ fallen** to be difficult for sb; **jdm/sich etw ~ machen** to make sth difficult for sb/o.s.; **~ nehmen** to take to heart; **sich dat od akk ~ tun** to have difficulties; **~ verdaulich** indigestible, heavy; **~ wiegend** weighty, important; **S~arbeiter** m manual worker, labourer; **S~behinderte(r)** f(m) seriously handicapped person; **S~e** f weight, heaviness; (PHYS) gravity; **~elos** adj weightless; (Kammer) zero-G; **~fällig** adj ponderous; **S~gewicht** nt heavyweight; (fig) emphasis; **~hörig** adj hard of hearing; **S~industrie** f heavy industry; **S~kraft** f gravity; **S~kranke(r)** f(m) person who is seriously ill; **~lich** adv hardly; **~mütig** adj melancholy; **S~punkt** m centre of gravity; (fig) emphasis, crucial point

Schwert [ʃveːrt] (-(e)s, -er) nt sword; **~lilie** f iris

schwer- zW: **S~verbrecher(in)** m(f) criminal, serious offender; **S~verletzte(r)** f(m) serious casualty; (bei Unfall usw auch) seriously injured person

Schwester [ʃvestər] (-, -n) f sister; (MED) nurse; **s~lich** adj sisterly

Schwieger- [ʃviːɡər] zW: **~eltern** pl parents-in-law; **~mutter** f mother-in-law; **~sohn** m son-in-law; **~tochter** f daughter-in-law; **~vater** m father-in-law

schwierig [ʃviːrɪç] adj difficult, hard; **S~keit** f difficulty

Schwimm- [ʃvɪm] zW: **~bad** nt swimming baths pl; **~becken** nt swimming pool; **s~en** (unreg) vi to swim; (treiben, nicht sinken) to float; (fig: unsicher sein) to be all at sea; **~er** (-s, -) m swimmer; (Angeln) float; **~erin** f (female) swimmer; **~lehrer** m swimming instructor; **~weste** f life jacket

Schwindel [ʃvɪndəl] (-s) m giddiness; dizzy spell; (Betrug) swindle, fraud; (Zeug) stuff; **s~frei** adj: **s~frei sein** to have a good head for heights; **s~n** (umg) vi (lügen) to fib; **jdm s~t es** sb feels dizzy

schwinden [ʃvɪndən] (unreg) vi to disappear; (sich verringern) to decrease; (Kräfte) to decline

Schwindler [ʃvɪndlər] m swindler; (Lügner) liar

schwindlig adj dizzy; **mir ist ~** I feel dizzy

Schwing- [ʃvɪŋ] zW: **s~en** (unreg) vt to swing; (Waffe etc) to brandish ♦ vi to swing; (vibrieren) to vibrate; (klingen) to sound; **~tür** f swing door(s); **~ung** f vibration;

(PHYS) oscillation

Schwips [ʃvɪps] (-es, -e) m: **einen ~ haben** to be tipsy

schwirren [ʃvɪrən] vi to buzz

schwitzen [ʃvɪtsən] vi to sweat, to perspire

schwören [ʃvøːrən] (unreg) vt, vi to swear

schwul [ʃvuːl] (umg) adj gay, queer

schwül [ʃvyːl] adj sultry, close; **S~e** (-) f sultriness

Schwule(r) (umg) f(m) gay (man/woman)

Schwung [ʃvʊŋ] (-(e)s, ⁻e) m swing; (Triebkraft) momentum; (fig: Energie) verve, energy; (umg: Menge) batch; **s~haft** adj brisk, lively; **s~voll** adj vigorous

Schwur [ʃvuːr] (-(e)s, ⁻e) m oath; **~gericht** nt court with a jury

sechs [zɛks] num six; **~hundert** num six hundred; **~te(r, s)** adj sixth; **S~tel** (-s, -) nt sixth

sechzehn [ʃvɛçtseːn] num sixteen

sechzig [zɛçtsɪç] num sixty

See¹ [zeː] (-, -n) f sea

See² [zeː] (-s, -n) m lake

See- [zeː] zW: **~bad** nt seaside resort; **~hund** m seal; **~igel** [zeːˈʔiːɡəl] m sea urchin; **s~krank** adj seasick; **~krankheit** f seasickness; **~lachs** m rock salmon

Seele [zeːlə] f soul; **s~nruhig** adv calmly

Seeleute [zeːlɔʏtə] pl seamen

Seel- zW: **s~isch** adj mental; **~sorge** f pastoral duties pl; **~sorger** (-s, -) m clergyman

See- zW: **~macht** f naval power; **~mann** (pl **-leute**) m seaman, sailor; **~meile** f nautical mile; **~möwe** f (ZOOL) seagull; **~not** f distress; **~räuber** m pirate; **~rose** f water lily; **~stern** m starfish; **s~tüchtig** adj seaworthy; **~weg** m sea route; **auf dem ~weg** by sea; **~zunge** f sole

Segel [zeːɡəl] (-s, -) nt sail; **~boot** nt yacht; **~fliegen** (-s) nt gliding; **~flieger** m glider pilot; **~flugzeug** nt glider; **s~n** vt, vi to sail; **~schiff** nt sailing vessel; **~sport** m sailing; **~tuch** nt canvas

Segen [zeːɡən] (-s, -) m blessing

Segler [zeːɡlər] (-s, -) m sailor, yachtsman

segnen [zeːɡnən] vt to bless

Seh- ['ze:] zW: **s~behindert** adj partially sighted; **s~en** (unreg) vt, vi to see; (in bestimmte Richtung) to look; **mal s~en(, ob ...)** let's see (if ...); **siehe Seite 5** see page 5; **s~enswert** adj worth seeing; **~enswürdigkeiten** pl sights (of a town); **~fehler** m sight defect

Sehne ['ze:nə] f sinew; (an Bogen) string

sehnen vr: **sich ~ nach** to long od yearn for

sehnig adj sinewy

Sehn- zW: **s~lich** adj ardent; **~sucht** f longing; **s~süchtig** adj longing

sehr ['ze:r] adv very; (mit Verben) a lot, (very) much; **zu ~** too much; **~ geehrte(r) ...** dear ...

seicht [zaiçt] adj (auch fig) shallow

Seide ['zaidə] f silk; **s~n** adj silk; **~npapier** nt tissue paper

seidig ['zaidiç] adj silky

Seife ['zaifə] f soap

Seifen- zW: **~lauge** f soapsuds pl; **~schale** f soap dish; **~schaum** m lather

seihen ['zaiən] vt to strain, to filter

Seil [zail] (-(e)s, -e) nt rope; cable; **~bahn** f cable railway; **~hüpfen** (-s) nt skipping; **~springen** (-s) nt skipping; **~tänzer(in)** m(f) tightrope walker

---

SCHLÜSSELWORT

sein [zain] (pt war, pp gewesen) vi 1 to be; **ich bin** I am; **du bist** you are; **er/sie/es ist** he/she/it is; **wir sind/ihr seid/sie sind** we/you/they are; **wir waren** we were; **wir sind gewesen** we have been

2: **seien Sie nicht böse** don't be angry; **sei so gut und ...** be so kind as to ...; **das wäre gut** that would od that'd be a good thing; **wenn ich Sie wäre** if I were od was you; **das wärs** that's all, that's it; **morgen bin ich in Rom** tomorrow I'll od I will od I shall be in Rome; **waren Sie mal in Rom?** have you ever been to Rome?

3: **wie ist das zu verstehen?** how is that to be understood?; **er ist nicht zu ersetzen** he cannot be replaced; **mit ihr ist nicht zu reden** you can't talk to her

---

4: **mir ist kalt** I'm cold; **was ist?** what's the matter?, what is it?; **ist was?** is something the matter?; **es sei denn, dass ...** unless ...; **wie dem auch sei** be that as it may; **wie wäre es mit ...?** how od what about ...?; **lass das sein!** stop that!

---

sein(e) ['zain(ə)] adj his; its; **~e(r, s)** pron his; its; **~er** (gen von er) pron of him; **~erseits** adv for his part; **~erzeit** adv in those days, formerly; **~esgleichen** pron people like him; **~etwegen** adv (für ihn) for his sake; (wegen ihm) on his account; (von ihm aus) as far as he is concerned; **~etwillen** adv: **um ~etwillen** = **seinetwegen**; **~ige** pron: **der/die/das ~ige** od **S~ige** his

seit [zait] präp +dat since ♦ konj since; **er ist ~ einer Woche hier** he has been here for a week; **~ langem** for a long time; **~dem** [zait'de:m] adv, konj since

Seite ['zaitə] f side; (Buch~) page; (MIL) flank

Seiten- zW: **~airbag** m side-impact airbag; **~ansicht** f side view; **~hieb** m (fig) passing shot, dig; **~s** präp +gen on the part of; **~schiff** nt aisle; **~sprung** m extramarital escapade; **~stechen** nt (a) stitch; **~straße** f side road; **~streifen** m verge; (der Autobahn) hard shoulder

seither [zait'he:r] adv, konj since (then)

seit- zW: **~lich** adj on one od the side; side cpd; **~wärts** adv sideways

Sekretär [zekre'tɛ:r] m secretary; (Möbel) bureau

Sekretariat [zekretari'a:t] (-(e)s, -e) nt secretary's office, secretariat

Sekretärin [zekre'tɛ:rin] f secretary

Sekt [zɛkt] (-(e)s, -e) m champagne

Sekte ['zɛktə] f sect

Sekunde [ze'kundə] f second

selber ['zɛlbər] = selbst

Selbst [zɛlpst] (-) nt self

SCHLÜSSELWORT

selbst [zɛlpst] pron 1: **ich/er/wir selbst** I myself/he himself/we ourselves; **sie ist die Tugend selbst** she's virtue itself; **er braut**

---

sein Bier selbst he brews his own beer;
wie gehts? - gut, und selbst? how are
things? - fine, and yourself?
2 *(ohne Hilfe)* alone, on my/his/one's *etc*
own; **von selbst** by itself; **er kam von
selbst** he came of his own accord; **selbst
gemacht** home-made
♦ *adv* even; **selbst wenn** even if; **selbst
Gott** even God (himself)

selbständig *etc* ['zɛlpʃtɛndɪç] = **selbstständig** *etc*
Selbst- *zW:* ~**auslöser** *m (PHOT)* delayed-
action shutter release; ~**bedienung** *f* self-
service; ~**befriedigung** *f* masturbation;
~**beherrschung** *f* self-control;
~**bestimmung** *f (POL)* self-determination;
~**beteiligung** *f (VERSICHERUNG: bei Kosten)*
(voluntary) excess; **s~bewusst** ▲ *adj*
(self-)confident; ~**bewusstsein** ▲ *nt* self-
confidence; ~**erhaltung** *f* self-preservation;
~**erkenntnis** *f* self-knowledge; **s~gefällig**
adj smug, self-satisfied; ~**gespräch** *nt*
conversation with o.s.; ~**kostenpreis** *m*
cost price; **s~los** *adj* unselfish, selfless;
~**mord** *m* suicide; ~**mörder(in)** *m(f)*
suicide; **s~mörderisch** *adj* suicidal;
s~sicher *adj* self-assured; **s~ständig** ▲
adj independent; ~**ständigkeit** ▲ *f*
independence; **s~süchtig** *adj (Mensch)*
selfish; ~**versorger** **(-s, -)** *m (im Urlaub etc)*
self-caterer; **s~verständlich**
['zɛlpstfɛrʃtɛntlɪç] *adj* obvious ♦ *adv* naturally;
ich halte das für s~verständlich I take
that for granted; ~**verteidigung** *f* self-
defence; ~**vertrauen** *nt* self-confidence;
~**verwaltung** *f* autonomy, self-
government
selig ['ze:lɪç] *adj* happy, blissful; *(REL)*
blessed; *(tot)* late; **S~keit** *f* bliss
Sellerie ['zɛləri:] **(-s, -(s)** *od* **-, -)** *m od f*
celery
selten ['zɛltən] *adj* rare ♦ *adv* seldom, rarely;
S~heit *f* rarity
Selterswasser ['zɛltərsvasər] *nt* soda water
seltsam ['zɛltza:m] *adj* strange, curious;
S~keit *f* strangeness

Semester [ze'mɛstər] **(-s, -)** *nt* semester;
~**ferien** *pl* vacation *sg*
Semi- [zemi] *in zW* semi-; ~**kolon** [-'ko:lɔn]
(-s, -s) *nt* semicolon
Seminar [zemi'na:r] **(-s, -e)** *nt* seminary;
(Kurs) seminar; *(UNIV: Ort)* department
building
Semmel ['zɛməl] **(-, -n)** *f* roll
Senat [ze'na:t] **(-(e)s, -e)** *m* senate, council
Sende- ['zɛndə] *zW:* ~**bereich** *m*
transmission range; ~**folge** *f (Serie)* series;
s~n *(unreg)* *vt* to send; *(RADIO, TV)* to
transmit, to broadcast ♦ *vi* to transmit, to
broadcast; ~**r** **(-s, -)** *m* station; *(Anlage)*
transmitter; ~**reihe** *f* series (of broadcasts)
Sendung ['zɛndʊŋ] *f* consignment;
(Aufgabe) mission; *(RADIO, TV)* transmission;
(Programm) programme
Senf [zɛnf] **(-(e)s, -e)** *m* mustard
senil [ze'ni:l] *(pej)* *adj* senile
Senior(in) ['ze:niɔr(ɪn)] **(-s, -en)** *m(f)*
(Mensch im Rentenalter) (old age) pensioner
Seniorenheim [zeni'o:rənhaɪm] *nt* old
people's home
Senk- ['zɛŋk] *zW:* ~**blei** *nt* plumb; ~**e** *f*
depression; **s~en** *vt* to lower ♦ *vr* to sink,
to drop gradually; **s~recht** *adj* vertical,
perpendicular; ~**rechte** *f* perpendicular;
~**rechtstarter** *m (AVIAT)* vertical take-off
plane; *(fig)* high-flyer
Sensation [zɛnzatsi'o:n] *f* sensation; **s~ell**
[-'nɛl] *adj* sensational
sensibel [zɛn'zi:bəl] *adj* sensitive
sentimental [zɛntimɛn'ta:l] *adj* sentimental;
S~i'tät *f* sentimentality
separat [zepa'ra:t] *adj* separate
September [zɛp'tɛmbər] **(-(s), -)** *m*
September
Serie ['ze:riə] *f* series
serien- *zW:* ~**mäßig** *adj* standard;
S~mörder(in) *m(f)* serial killer; ~**weise**
adv in series
seriös [zeri'ø:s] *adj* serious, bona fide
Service¹ [zɛr'vi:s] **(-(s), -)** *nt (Geschirr)* set,
service
Service² **(-, -s)** *m* service
servieren [zɛr'vi:rən] *vt, vi* to serve

Serviererin [zɛr'viːrərɪn] f waitress
Serviette [zɛrvi'ɛtə] f napkin, serviette
Servo- ['zɛrvo] zW: **~bremse** f (AUT) servo(-assisted) brake; **~lenkung** f (AUT) power steering
Sessel ['zɛsəl] (-s, -) m armchair; **~lift** m chairlift
sesshaft ▲ ['zɛshaft] adj settled; (ansässig) resident
setzen ['zɛtsən] vt to put, to set; (Baum etc) to plant; (Segel, TYP) to set ♦ vr to settle; (Person) to sit down ♦ vi (springen) to leap; (wetten) to bet
Setz- ['zɛts] zW: **~er** (-s, -) m (TYP) compositor; **~ling** m young plant
Seuche ['zɔʏçə] f epidemic; **~ngebiet** nt infected area
seufzen ['zɔʏftsən] vt, vi to sigh
Seufzer ['zɔʏftsər] (-s, -) m sigh
Sex [zɛks] (-(es)) m sex; **~ualität** [-uali'tɛt] f sex, sexuality; **~ualkunde** [zɛksu'aːl-] f (SCH) sex education; **s~uell** [-u'ɛl] adj sexual
Shampoo [ʃam'puː] (-s, -s) nt shampoo
Sibirien [zi'biːriən] nt Siberia

sich [zɪç] pron 1 (akk): **er/sie/es ... sich** he/she/it ... himself/herself/itself; **sie** pl/ **man ... sich** they/one ... themselves/ oneself; **Sie ... sich** you ... yourself/ yourselves pl; **sich wiederholen** to repeat oneself/itself
2 (dat): **er/sie/es ... sich** he/she/it ... to himself/herself/itself; **sie** pl/**man ... sich** they/one ... to themselves/oneself; **Sie ... sich** you ... to yourself/yourselves pl; **sie hat sich einen Pullover gekauft** she bought herself a jumper; **sich die Haare waschen** to wash one's hair
3 (mit Präposition): **haben Sie Ihren Ausweis bei sich?** do you have your pass on you?; **er hat nichts bei sich** he's got nothing on him; **sie bleiben gern unter sich** they keep themselves to themselves
4 (einander) each other, one another; **sie bekämpfen sich** they fight each other od

one another
5: **dieses Auto fährt sich gut** this car drives well; **hier sitzt es sich gut** it's good to sit here

Sichel ['zɪçəl] (-, -n) f sickle; (Mondsichel) crescent
sicher ['zɪçər] adj safe; (gewiss) certain; (zuverlässig) secure, reliable; (selbstsicher) confident; **vor jdm/etw ~ sein** to be safe from sb/sth; **ich bin nicht ~** I'm not sure od certain; **~ nicht** surely not; **aber ~!** of course!; **~gehen** (unreg) vi to make sure
Sicherheit ['zɪçərhait] f safety; (auch FIN) security; (Gewissheit) certainty; (Selbstsicherheit) confidence
Sicherheits- ['zɪçərhaits] zW: **~abstand** m safe distance; **~glas** nt safety glass; **~gurt** m safety belt; **s~halber** adv for safety; to be on the safe side; **~nadel** f safety pin; **~schloss** ▲ nt safety lock; **~vorkehrung** f safety precaution
sicher- zW: **~lich** adv certainly, surely; **~n** vt to secure; (schützen) to protect; (Waffe) to put the safety catch on; **jdm etw ~n** to secure sth for sb; **sich** dat **etw ~n** to secure sth (for o.s.); **~stellen** vt to impound; (COMPUT) to save; **S~ung** f (S~n) securing; (Vorrichtung) safety device; (an Waffen) safety catch; (ELEK) fuse; **S~ungskopie** f back-up copy
Sicht [zɪçt] (-) f sight; (Aussicht) view; **auf** od **nach ~** (FIN) at sight; **auf lange ~** on a long-term basis; **s~bar** adj visible; **s~en** vt to sight; (auswählen) to sort out; **s~lich** adj evident, obvious; **~verhältnisse** pl visibility sg; **~vermerk** m visa; **~weite** f visibility
sickern ['zɪkərn] vi to trickle, to seep
Sie [ziː] (nom, akk) pron you
sie [ziː] pron (sg: nom) she, it; (: akk) her, it; (pl: nom) they; (: akk) them
Sieb [ziːp] (-(e)s, -e) nt sieve; (KOCH) strainer; **s~en**[1] ['ziːbən] vt to sift; (Flüssigkeit) to strain
sieben[2] num seven; **~hundert** num seven hundred; **S~sachen** pl belongings

siebte(r, s) ['zi:ptə(r, s)] adj seventh; **S~l (-s, -)** nt seventh

siebzehn ['zi:ptse:n] num seventeen

siebzig ['zi:ptsɪç] num seventy

siedeln ['zi:dəln] vi to settle

sieden ['zi:dən] vt, vi to boil, to simmer

Siedepunkt m boiling point

Siedler (-s, -) m settler

Siedlung f settlement; (Häusersiedlung) housing estate

Sieg [zi:k] **(-(e)s, -e)** m victory

Siegel ['zi:gəl] **(-s, -)** nt seal; **~ring** m signet ring

Sieg- zW: **s~en** vi to be victorious; (SPORT) to win; **~er (-s, -)** m victor; (SPORT etc) winner; **s~reich** adj victorious

siehe etc ['zi:ə] vb siehe **sehen**

siezen ['zi:tsən] vt to address as "Sie"

Signal [zɪ'gna:l] **(-s, -e)** nt signal

Silbe ['zɪlbə] f syllable

Silber ['zɪlbər] **(-s)** nt silver; **~hochzeit** f silver wedding (anniversary); **s~n** adj silver; **~papier** nt silver paper

Silvester [zɪl'vɛstər] **(-s, -)** nt New Year's Eve, Hogmanay (SCOTTISH); **~abend** m = **Silvester**

Silvester

ⓘ Silvester is the German word for New Year's Eve. Although not an official holiday most businesses close early and shops shut at midday. Most Germans celebrate in the evening, and at midnight they let off fireworks and rockets; the revelry usually lasts until the early hours of the morning.

---

simpel ['zɪmpəl] adj simple

Sims [zɪms] **(-es, -e)** nt od m (Kaminsims) mantelpiece; (Fenstersims) (window)sill

simsen ['zɪmzn] vti to text

simulieren [zimu'li:rən] vt to simulate; (vortäuschen) to feign ♦ vi to feign illness

simultan [zimʊl'ta:n] adj simultaneous

Sinfonie [zɪnfo'ni:] f symphony

singen ['zɪŋən] (unreg) vt, vi to sing

Singular ['zɪŋgula:r] m singular

Singvogel ['zɪŋfo:gəl] m songbird

sinken ['zɪŋkən] (unreg) vi to sink; (Preise etc) to fall, to go down

Sinn [zɪn] **(-(e)s, -e)** m mind; (Wahrnehmungssinn) sense; (Bedeutung) sense, meaning; **~ für etw** sense of sth; **von ~en sein** to be out of one's mind; **es hat keinen ~** there's no point; **~bild** nt symbol; **s~en** (unreg) vi to ponder; **auf etw** akk **s~en** to contemplate sth; **~estäuschung** f illusion; **s~gemäß** adj faithful; (Wiedergabe) in one's own words; **s~ig** adj clever; **s~lich** adj sensual, sensuous; (Wahrnehmung) sensory; **~lichkeit** f sensuality; **s~los** adj senseless; meaningless; **~losigkeit** f senselessness; meaninglessness; **s~voll** adj meaningful; (vernünftig) sensible

Sintflut ['zɪntflu:t] f Flood

Sippe ['zɪpə] f clan, kin

Sippschaft ['zɪpʃaft] (pej) f relations pl, tribe; (Bande) gang

Sirene [zi're:nə] f siren

Sirup ['zi:rʊp] **(-s, -e)** m syrup

Sitt- ['zɪt] zW: **~e** f custom; **~en** pl (~lichkeit) morals; **~enpolizei** f vice squad; **s~sam** adj modest, demure

Situation [zituatsi'o:n] f situation

Sitz [zɪts] **(-es, -e)** m seat; **der Anzug hat einen guten ~** the suit is a good fit; **s~en** (unreg) vi to sit; (Bemerkung, Schlag) to strike home, to tell; (Gelerntes) to have sunk in; **s~en bleiben** to remain seated; (SCH) to have to repeat a year; **auf etw** dat **s~en bleiben** to be lumbered with sth; **s~en lassen** (SCH) to make (sb) repeat a year; (Mädchen) to jilt; (Wartenden) to stand up; **etw auf sich** dat **s~en lassen** to take sth lying down; **s~end** adj (Tätigkeit) sedentary; **~gelegenheit** f place to sit down; **~platz** m seat; **~streik** m sit-down strike; **~ung** f meeting

Sizilien [zi'tsi:liən] nt Sicily

Skala ['ska:la] **(-, Skalen)** f scale

Skalpell [skal'pɛl] **(-s, -e)** nt scalpel

Skandal [skan'da:l] **(-s, -e)** m scandal; **s~ös** [-'lø:s] adj scandalous

---

Skandinav- [skandi'na:v] *zW:* **~ien** *nt* Scandinavia; **~ier(in)** *m(f)* Scandinavian; **s~isch** *adj* Scandinavian

Skelett [ske'lɛt] **(-(e)s, -e)** *nt* skeleton

Skepsis ['skɛpsɪs] **(-)** *f* scepticism

skeptisch ['skɛptɪʃ] *adj* sceptical

Ski [ʃiː] **(-s, -er)** *m* ski; **~ laufen** *od* **fahren** to ski; **~fahrer** *m* skier; **~gebiet** *nt* ski(ing) area; **~läufer** *m* skier; **~lehrer** *m* ski instructor; **~lift** *m* ski-lift; **~springen** *nt* ski-jumping; **~stock** *m* ski-pole

Skizze ['skɪtsə] *f* sketch

skizzieren [skɪ'tsiːrən] *vt, vi* to sketch

Sklave ['skla:və] **(-n, -n)** *m* slave; **~'rei** *f* slavery; **Sklavin** *f* slave

Skorpion [skɔrpi'oːn] **(-s, -e)** *m* scorpion; (*ASTROL*) Scorpio

Skrupel ['skruːpəl] **(-s, -)** *m* scruple; **s~los** *adj* unscrupulous

Skulptur [skʊlp'tuːr] *f* (*Gegenstand*) sculpture

Slip [slɪp] **(-s, -s)** *m* (under)pants; **~einlage** *f* panty liner

Slowakei [slova'kaɪ] *f:* **die ~** Slovakia

Slowenien [slo've:niən] *nt* Slovenia

Smaragd [sma'rakt] **(-(e)s, -e)** *m* emerald

Smoking ['smo:kɪŋ] **(-s, -s)** *m* dinner jacket

SMS *abbr* (= *Short Message Service*) text message

Snowboarding ['sno:bɔ:bdɪŋ] *nt* snowboarding

so [zo:] *adv* 1 (*so sehr*) so; **so groß/schön** *etc* so big/nice *etc*; **so groß/schön wie ...** as big/nice as ...; **so viel (wie)** as much as; **rede nicht so viel** don't talk so much; **so weit sein** to be ready; **so weit wie** *od* **als möglich** as far as possible; **ich bin so weit zufrieden** by and large I'm quite satisfied; **so wenig (wie)** as little (as); **das hat ihn so geärgert, dass ...** that annoyed him so much that ...; **so einer wie ich** somebody like me; **na so was!** well, well!

2 (*auf diese Weise*) like this; **mach es nicht so** don't do it like that; **so oder so** in one way or the other; **und so weiter** and so on; **... oder so was** ... or something like

that; **das ist gut so** that's fine; **so genannt** so-called

3 (*umg: umsonst*): **ich habe es so bekommen** I got it for nothing

♦ *konj:* **so dass, sodass** so that; **so wie es jetzt ist** as things are at the moment

♦ *excl:* **so?** really?; **so, das wärs** so, that's it then

s. o. *abk* = **siehe oben**

Socke ['zɔkə] *f* sock

Sockel ['zɔkəl] **(-s, -)** *m* pedestal, base

sodass ▲ [zo'das] *konj* so that

Sodawasser ['zo:davasər] *nt* soda water

Sodbrennen ['zo:tbrɛnən] **(-s, -)** *nt* heartburn

soeben [zo'|e:bən] *adv* just (now)

Sofa ['zo:fa] **(-s, -s)** *nt* sofa

sofern [zo'fɛrn] *konj* if, provided (that)

sofort [zo'fɔrt] *adv* immediately, at once; **~ig** *adj* immediate

Sog [zo:k] **(-(e)s, -e)** *m* (*Strömung*) undertow

sogar [zo'ga:r] *adv* even

sogleich [zo'glaɪç] *adv* straight away, at once

Sohle ['zo:lə] *f* sole; (*Talsohle etc*) bottom; (*MIN*) level

Sohn [zo:n] **(-(e)s, ⁼e)** *m* son

Solar- [zo'la:r] *in zW* solar; **~zelle** *f* solar cell

solch [zɔlç] *pron* such; **ein ~e(r, s) ...** such a ...

Soldat [zɔl'da:t] **(-en, -en)** *m* soldier

Söldner ['zœldnər] **(-s, -)** *m* mercenary

solidarisch [zoli'da:rɪʃ] *adj* in *od* with solidarity; **sich ~ erklären** to declare one's solidarity

Solidari'tät *f* solidarity

solid(e) [zo'li:d(ə)] *adj* solid; (*Leben, Person*) respectable

Solist(in) [zo'lɪst(ɪn)] *m(f)* soloist

Soll [zɔl] **(-(s), -(s))** *nt* (*FIN*) debit (side); (*Arbeitsmenge*) quota, target

sollen ['zɔlən] (*pt* **sollte**, *pp* **gesollt** *od* (*als Hilfsverb*) **sollen**) *Hilfsverb* 1 (*Pflicht, Befehl*) to be supposed to; **du hättest nicht gehen**

sollen you shouldn't have gone, you oughtn't to have gone; **soll ich?** shall I?; **soll ich dir helfen?** shall I help you?; **sag ihm, er soll warten** tell him he's to wait; **was soll ich machen?** what should I do? 2 (*Vermutung*): **sie soll verheiratet sein** she's said to be married; **was soll das heißen?** what's that supposed to mean?; **man sollte glauben, dass ...** you would think that ...; **sollte das passieren, ...** if that should happen ...

♦ *vt, vi:* **was soll das?** what's all this?; **das sollst du nicht** you shouldn't do that; **was solls?** what the hell!

Solo ['zo:lo] (**-s, -s** *od* **Soli**) *nt* solo
somit [zo'mɪt] *konj* and so, therefore
Sommer ['zɔmər] (**-s, -**) *m* summer; **s~lich** *adj* summery; **~reifen** *m* normal tyre; **~schlussverkauf** ▲ *m* summer sale; **~sprossen** *pl* freckles
Sonde ['zɔndə] *f* probe
Sonder- ['zɔndər] *in zW* special; **~angebot** *nt* special offer; **s~bar** *adj* strange, odd; **~fahrt** *f* special trip; **~fall** *m* special case; **s~lich** *adj* particular; (*außergewöhnlich*) remarkable; (*eigenartig*) peculiar; **~marke** *f* special issue stamp; **s~n** *konj* but ♦ *vt* to separate; **nicht nur ..., s~n auch** not only ..., but also; **~preis** *m* special reduced price; **~zug** *m* special train
Sonnabend ['zɔn|a:bənt] *m* Saturday
Sonne ['zɔnə] *f* sun; **s~n** *vr* to sun o.s.
Sonnen- *zW*: **~aufgang** *m* sunrise; **s~baden** *vi* to sunbathe; **~brand** *m* sunburn; **~brille** *f* sunglasses *pl*; **~creme** *f* suntan lotion; **~energie** *f* solar energy, solar power; **~finsternis** *f* solar eclipse; **~kollektor** *m* solar panel; **~schein** *m* sunshine; **~schirm** *m* parasol, sunshade; **~schutzfaktor** *m* protection factor; **~stich** *m* sunstroke; **~uhr** *f* sundial; **~untergang** *m* sunset; **~wende** *f* solstice
sonnig ['zɔnɪç] *adj* sunny
Sonntag ['zɔnta:k] *m* Sunday
sonst [zɔnst] *adv* otherwise; (*mit pron, in Fragen*) else; (*zu anderer Zeit*) at other times,

normally ♦ *konj* otherwise; **~ noch etwas?** anything else?; **~ nichts** nothing else; **~ jemand** anybody (at all); **~ wo** somewhere else; **~ woher** from somewhere else; **~ wohin** somewhere else; **~ig** *adj* other
sooft [zo'|ɔft] *konj* whenever
Sopran [zo'pra:n] (**-s, -e**) *m* soprano
Sorge ['zɔrgə] *f* care, worry
sorgen *vi:* **für jdn ~** to look after sb ♦ *vr:* **sich ~ (um)** to worry (about); **für etw ~** to take care of *od* see to sth; **~frei** *adj* carefree; **~voll** *adj* troubled, worried
Sorgerecht *nt* custody (of a child)
Sorg- [zɔrk] *zW:* **~falt** (**-**) *f* care(fulness); **s~fältig** *adj* careful; **s~los** *adj* careless; (*ohne ~en*) carefree; **s~sam** *adj* careful
Sorte ['zɔrtə] *f* sort; (*Warensorte*) brand; **~n** *pl* (FIN) foreign currency *sg*
sortieren [zɔr'ti:rən] *vt* to sort (out)
Sortiment [zɔrti'mɛnt] *nt* assortment
sosehr [zo'ze:r] *konj* as much as
Soße ['zo:sə] *f* sauce; (*Bratensoße*) gravy
soufflieren [zu'fli:rən] *vt, vi* to prompt
Souterrain [zute'rɛ̃:] (**-s, -s**) *nt* basement
souverän [zuvə'rɛ:n] *adj* sovereign; (*überlegen*) superior
so- *zW:* **~viel** [zo'fi:l] *konj:* **~viel ich weiß** as far as I know; *siehe* **so**; **~weit** [zo'vait] *konj* as far as; *siehe* **so**; **~wenig** [zo've:nɪç] *konj* little as; *siehe* **so**; **~wie** [zo'vi:] *konj* (*~bald*) as soon as; (*ebenso*) as well as; **~wieso** [zovi'zo:] *adv* anyway
sowjetisch [zɔ'vjɛtɪʃ] *adj* Soviet
Sowjetunion *f* Soviet Union
sowohl [zo'vo:l] *konj:* **~ ... als** *od* **wie auch** both ... and
sozial [zotsi'a:l] *adj* social; **S~abgaben** *pl* national insurance contributions; **S~arbeiter(in)** *m(f)* social worker; **S~demokrat** *m* social democrat; **~demokratisch** *adj* social democratic; **S~hilfe** *f* income support (BRIT), welfare (aid) (US); **~i'sieren** *vt* to socialize; **S~ismus** [-'lɪsmʊs] *m* socialism; **S~ist** [-'lɪst] *m* socialist; **~istisch** *adj* socialist; **S~politik** *f* social welfare policy; **S~produkt** *nt* (net) national product;

S~staat *m* welfare state;
S~versicherung *f* national insurance (*BRIT*), social security (*US*); S~wohnung *f* council flat

soziologisch [zotsio'lo:gɪʃ] *adj* sociological

sozusagen [zotsu'za:gən] *adv* so to speak

Spachtel ['ʃpaxtəl] (-s, -) *m* spatula

spähen ['ʃpe:ən] *vi* to peep, to peek

Spalier [ʃpa'li:r] (-s, -e) *nt* (*Gerüst*) trellis; (*Leute*) guard of honour

Spalt [ʃpalt] (-(e)s, -e) *m* crack; (*Türspalt*) chink; (*fig: Kluft*) split; ~e *f* crack, fissure; (*Gletscherspalte*) crevasse; (*in Text*) column; s~en *vt, vr* (*auch fig*) to split; ~ung *f* splitting

Span [ʃpa:n] (-(e)s, ̈e) *m* shaving

Spanferkel *nt* sucking pig

Spange ['ʃpaŋə] *f* clasp; (*Haarspange*) hair slide; (*Schnalle*) buckle

Spanien ['ʃpa:niən] *nt* Spain; Spanier(in) *m(f)* Spaniard; spanisch *adj* Spanish

Spann- ['ʃpan] *zW:* ~beton *m* prestressed concrete; ~betttuch ▲ *nt* fitted sheet; ~e *f* (*Zeitspanne*) space; (*Differenz*) gap; s~en *vt* (*straffen*) to tighten, to tauten; (*befestigen*) to brace ♦ *vi* to be tight; s~end *adj* exciting, gripping; ~ung *f* tension; (*ELEK*) voltage; (*fig*) suspense; (*unangenehm*) tension

Spar- ['ʃpa:r] *zW:* ~buch *nt* savings book; ~büchse *f* money box; s~en *vt, vi* to save; sich *dat* etw s~en to save o.s. sth; (*Bemerkung*) to keep sth to o.s.; mit etw s~en to be sparing with sth; an etw *dat* s~en to economize on sth; ~er (-s, -) *m* saver

Spargel ['ʃpargəl] (-s, -) *m* asparagus

Sparkasse *f* savings bank

Sparkonto *nt* savings account

spärlich ['ʃpe:rlɪç] *adj* meagre; (*Bekleidung*) scanty

Spar- *zW:* ~preis *m* economy price; s~sam *adj* economical, thrifty; ~samkeit *f* thrift, economizing; ~schwein *nt* piggy bank

Sparte ['ʃpartə] *f* field; line of business; (*PRESSE*) column

Spaß [ʃpa:s] (-es, ̈e) *m* joke; (*Freude*) fun; jdm ~ machen to be fun (for sb); viel ~! have fun!; s~en *vi* to joke; mit ihm ist nicht zu s~en you can't take liberties with him; s~haft *adj* funny, droll; s~ig *adj* funny, droll

spät [ʃpe:t] *adj, adv* late; wie ~ ist es? what's the time?

Spaten ['ʃpa:tən] (-s, -) *m* spade

später *adj, adv* later

spätestens *adv* at the latest

Spätvorstellung *f* late show

Spatz [ʃpats] (-en, -en) *m* sparrow

spazier- [ʃpa'tsi:r] *zW:* ~en *vi* to stroll, to walk; ~en fahren to go for a drive; ~en gehen to go for a walk; S~gang *m* walk; S~stock *m* walking stick; S~weg *m* path, walk

Specht [ʃpeçt] (-(e)s, -e) *m* woodpecker

Speck [ʃpek] (-(e)s, -e) *m* bacon

Spediteur [ʃpedi'tø:r] *m* carrier; (*Möbelspediteur*) furniture remover

Spedition [ʃpediʦi'o:n] *f* carriage; (*~sfirma*) road haulage contractor; removal firm

Speer [ʃpe:r] (-(e)s, -e) *m* spear; (*SPORT*) javelin

Speiche ['ʃpaiçə] *f* spoke

Speichel ['ʃpaiçəl] (-s) *m* saliva, spit(tle)

Speicher ['ʃpaiçər] (-s, -) *m* storehouse; (*Dachspeicher*) attic, loft; (*Kornspeicher*) granary; (*Wasserspeicher*) tank; (*TECH*) store; (*COMPUT*) memory; s~n *vt* to store; (*COMPUT*) to save

speien ['ʃpaiən] (*unreg*) *vt, vi* to spit; (*erbrechen*) to vomit; (*Vulkan*) to spew

Speise ['ʃpaizə] *f* food; ~eis [-|ais] *nt* ice-cream; ~kammer *f* larder, pantry; ~karte *f* menu; s~n *vt* to feed; to eat ♦ *vi* to dine; ~röhre *f* gullet, oesophagus; ~saal *m* dining room; ~wagen *m* dining car

Speku- [ʃpeku] *zW:* ~lant *m* speculator; ~lation [-latsi'o:n] *f* speculation; s~lieren [-'li:rən] *vi* (*fig*) to speculate; auf etw *akk* s~lieren to have hopes of sth

Spelunke [ʃpe'luŋkə] *f* dive

Spende ['ʃpendə] *f* donation; s~n *vt* to donate, to give; ~r (-s, -) *m* donor,

---

Spelling Reform: ▲ *new spelling* △ *old spelling (to be phased out)*

donator

spendieren [ʃpɛnˈdiːrən] *vt* to pay for, to buy; **jdm etw ~** to treat sb to sth, to stand sb sth

Sperling [ˈʃpɛrlɪŋ] *m* sparrow

Sperma [ˈʃpɛrma] (**-s, Spermen**) *nt* sperm

Sperr- [ˈʃpɛr] *zW:* **~e** *f* barrier; (*Verbot*) ban; **s~en** *vt* to block; (*SPORT*) to suspend, to bar; (*vom Ball*) to obstruct; (*einschließen*) to lock; (*verbieten*) to ban ♦ *vr* to baulk, to jib(e); **~gebiet** *nt* prohibited area; **~holz** *nt* plywood; **s~ig** *adj* bulky; **~müll** *m* bulky refuse; **~sitz** *m* (*THEAT*) stalls *pl*; **~stunde** *f* closing time

Spesen [ˈʃpeːzən] *pl* expenses

Spezial- [ʃpetsiˈaːl] *in zW* special; **~gebiet** *nt* specialist field; **s~i'sieren** *vr* to specialize; **~i'sierung** *f* specialization; **~ist** [-ˈlɪst] *m* specialist; **~i'tät** *f* speciality

speziell [ʃpetsiˈɛl] *adj* special

spezifisch [ʃpeˈtsiːfɪʃ] *adj* specific

Sphäre [ˈsfɛːrə] *f* sphere

Spiegel [ˈʃpiːgəl] (**-s, -**) *m* mirror; (*Wasserspiegel*) level; (*MIL*) tab; **~bild** *nt* reflection; **s~bildlich** *adj* reversed; **~ei** *nt* fried egg; **s~n** *vt* to mirror, to reflect ♦ *vr* to be reflected ♦ *vi* to gleam; (*widerspiegeln*) to be reflective; **~ung** *f* reflection

Spiel [ʃpiːl] (**-(e)s, -e**) *nt* game; (*Schauspiel*) play; (*Tätigkeit*) play(ing); (*KARTEN*) deck; (*TECH*) (free) play; **s~en** *vt, vi* to play; (*um Geld*) to gamble; (*THEAT*) to perform, to act; **s~end** *adv* easily; **~er (-s, -)** *m* player; (*um Geld*) gambler; **~e'rei** *f* trifling pastime; **~feld** *nt* pitch, field; **~film** *m* feature film; **~kasino** *nt* casino; **~plan** *m* (*THEAT*) programme; **~platz** *m* playground; **~raum** *m* room to manoeuvre, scope; **~regel** *f* rule; **~sachen** *pl* toys; **~uhr** *f* musical box; **~verderber (-s, -)** *m* spoilsport; **~waren** *pl* toys; **~zeug** *nt* toy(s)

Spieß [ʃpiːs] (**-es, -e**) *m* spear; (*Bratspieß*) spit; **~bürger** *m* bourgeois; **~er (-s, -)** (*umg*) *m* bourgeois; **s~ig** (*pej*) *adj* (petit) bourgeois

Spinat [ʃpiˈnaːt] (**-(e)s, -e**) *m* spinach

Spind [ʃpɪnt] (**-(e)s, -e**) *m od nt* locker

Spinn- [ˈʃpɪn] *zW:* **~e** *f* spider; **s~en** (*unreg*) *vt, vi* to spin; (*umg*) to talk rubbish; (*verrückt sein*) to be crazy *od* mad; **~e'rei** *f* spinning mill; **~rad** *nt* spinning wheel; **~webe** *f* cobweb

Spion [ʃpiˈoːn] (**-s, -e**) *m* spy; (*in Tür*) spyhole; **~age** [ʃpioˈnaːʒə] *f* espionage; **s~ieren** [ʃpioˈniːrən] *vi* to spy; **~in** *f* (female) spy

Spirale [ʃpiˈraːlə] *f* spiral

Spirituosen [ʃpirituˈoːzən] *pl* spirits

Spiritus [ˈʃpiːritʊs] (**-, -se**) *m* (methylated) spirit

Spital [ʃpiˈtaːl] (**-s, ⁺er**) *nt* hospital

spitz [ʃpɪts] *adj* pointed; (*Winkel*) acute; (*fig: Zunge*) sharp; (: *Bemerkung*) caustic

Spitze *f* point, tip; (*Bergspitze*) peak; (*Bemerkung*) taunt, dig; (*erster Platz*) lead, top; (*meist pl: Gewebe*) lace

Spitzel (-s, -) *m* police informer

spitzen *vt* to sharpen

Spitzenmarke *f* brand leader

spitzfindig *adj* (over)subtle

Spitzname *m* nickname

Splitter [ˈʃplɪtər] (**-s, -**) *m* splinter

sponsern [ˈʃpɔnzərn] *vt* to sponsor

spontan [ʃpɔnˈtaːn] *adj* spontaneous

Sport [ʃpɔrt] (**-(e)s, -e**) *m* sport; (*fig*) hobby; **~lehrer(in)** *m(f)* games *od* P.E. teacher; **~ler(in) (-s, -)** *m(f)* sportsman(-woman); **s~lich** *adj* sporting; (*Mensch*) sporty; **~platz** *m* playing *od* sports field; **~schuh** *m* (*Turnschuh*) training shoe, trainer; **~stadion** *nt* sports stadium; **~verein** *m* sports club; **~wagen** *m* sports car

Spott [ʃpɔt] (**-(e)s**) *m* mockery, ridicule; **s~billig** *adj* dirt-cheap; **s~en** *vi* to mock; **s~en (über +akk)** to mock (at), to ridicule

spöttisch [ˈʃpœtɪʃ] *adj* mocking

sprach *etc* [ʃpraːx] *vb siehe* **sprechen**

Sprach- *zW:* **s~begabt** *adj* good at languages; **~e** *f* language; **~enschule** *f* language school; **~fehler** *m* speech defect; **~führer** *m* phrasebook; **~gefühl** *nt* feeling for language; **~kenntnisse** *pl* linguistic proficiency *sg*; **~kurs** *m* language course; **~labor** *nt* language laboratory; **s~lich** *adj* linguistic; s~los adj speechless

sprang etc [ʃpraŋ] vb siehe springen

Spray [spreː] (-s, -s) m od nt spray

Sprech- ['ʃprɛç] zW: ~anlage f intercom; s~en (unreg) vi to speak, to talk ♦ vt to say; (Sprache) to speak; (Person) to speak to; mit jdm s~en to speak to sb; das spricht für ihn that's a point in his favour; ~er(in) (-s, -) m(f) speaker; (für Gruppe) spokesman(-woman); (RADIO, TV) announcer; ~stunde f consultation (hour); (doctor's) surgery; ~stundenhilfe f (doctor's) receptionist; ~zimmer nt consulting room, surgery, office (US)

spreizen ['ʃpraitsən] vt (Beine) to open, to spread; (Finger, Flügel) to spread

Spreng- ['ʃprɛŋ] zW: s~en vt to sprinkle; (mit ~stoff) to blow up; (Gestein) to blast; (Versammlung) to break up; ~stoff m explosive(s)

sprichst etc [ʃprɪçst] vb siehe sprechen

Sprichwort nt proverb; sprichwörtlich adj proverbial

Spring- ['ʃprɪŋ] zW: ~brunnen m fountain; s~en (unreg) vi to jump; (Glas) to crack; (mit Kopfsprung) to dive; ~er (-s, -) m jumper; (Schach) knight

Sprit [ʃprɪt] (-(e)s, -e) (umg) m juice, gas

Spritz- ['ʃprɪts] zW: ~e f syringe; injection; (an Schlauch) nozzle; s~en vt to spray; (MED) to inject ♦ vi to splash; (herausspritzen) to spurt; (MED) to give injections; ~pistole f spray gun; ~tour f (umg) spin

spröde ['ʃprøːdə] adj brittle; (Person) reserved, coy

Sprosse ['ʃprɔsə] f rung

Sprössling ▲ ['ʃprœslɪŋ] (umg) m (Kind) offspring (pl inv)

Spruch [ʃprʊx] (-(e)s, ⸚e) m saying, maxim; (JUR) judgement

Sprudel ['ʃpruːdəl] (-s, -) m mineral water; lemonade; s~n vi to bubble; ~wasser nt (KOCH) sparkling od fizzy mineral water

Sprüh- ['ʃpryː] zW: ~dose f aerosol (can); s~en vi to spray; (fig) to sparkle ♦ vt to spray; ~regen m drizzle

Sprung [ʃprʊŋ] (-(e)s, ⸚e) m jump; (Riss) crack; ~brett nt springboard; s~haft adj erratic; (Aufstieg) rapid; ~schanze f ski jump

Spucke ['ʃpʊkə] (-) f spit; s~n vt, vi to spit

Spuk [ʃpuːk] (-(e)s, -e) m haunting; (fig) nightmare; s~en vi (Geist) to walk; hier s~t es this place is haunted

Spülbecken ['ʃpyːlbɛkən] nt (in Küche) sink

Spule ['ʃpuːlə] f spool; (ELEK) coil

Spül- ['ʃpyːl] zW: ~e f (kitchen) sink; s~en vt, vi to rinse; (Geschirr) to wash up; (Toilette) to flush; ~maschine f dishwasher; ~mittel nt washing-up liquid; ~stein m sink; ~ung f rinsing; flush; (MED) irrigation

Spur [ʃpuːr] (-, -en) f trace; (Fußspur, Radspur, Tonbandspur) track; (Fährte) trail; (Fahrspur) lane

spürbar adj noticeable, perceptible

spüren ['ʃpyːrən] vt to feel

spurlos adv without (a) trace

Spurt [ʃpʊrt] (-(e)s, -s od -e) m spurt; s~en vi to spurt

sputen ['ʃpuːtən] vr to make haste

St. abk = Stück; (= Sankt) St.

Staat [ʃtaːt] (-(e)s, -en) m state; (Prunk) show; (Kleidung) finery; s~enlos adj stateless; s~lich adj state(-); state-run

Staats- zW: ~angehörige(r) f(m) national; ~angehörigkeit f nationality; ~anwalt m public prosecutor; ~bürger m citizen; ~dienst m civil service; ~examen nt (UNIV) state exam(ination); s~feindlich adj subversive; ~mann (pl -männer) m statesman; ~oberhaupt nt head of state

Stab [ʃtaːp] (-(e)s, ⸚e) m rod; (Gitterstab) bar; (Menschen) staff; ~hochsprung m pole vault

stabil [ʃtaˈbiːl] adj stable; (Möbel) sturdy; ~i'sieren vt to stabilize

Stachel ['ʃtaxəl] (-s, -n) m spike; (von Tier) spine; (von Insekten) sting; ~beere f gooseberry; ~draht m barbed wire; s~ig adj prickly; ~schwein nt porcupine

Stadion ['ʃtaːdiɔn] (-s, Stadien) nt stadium

Stadium ['ʃtaːdiʊm] nt stage, phase

Stadt [ʃtat] (-, ⸚e) *f* town; **~autobahn** *f* urban motorway; **~bahn** *f* suburban railway; **~bücherei** *f* municipal library

Städt- [ʃtɛːt] *zW:* **~ebau** *m* town planning; **~epartnerschaft** *f* town twinning; **~er(in)** (-s, -) *m(f)* town dweller; **s~isch** *adj* municipal; (*nicht ländlich*) urban

Stadt- *zW:* **~kern** *m* town centre, city centre; **~mauer** *f* city wall(s); **~mitte** *f* town centre; **~plan** *m* street map; **~rand** *m* outskirts *pl*; **~rat** (*Behörde*) town council, city council; **~rundfahrt** *f* tour of a/the city; **~teil** *m* district, part of town; **~zentrum** *nt* town centre

Staffel [ʃtafəl] (-, -n) *f* rung; (*SPORT*) relay (team); (*AVIAT*) squadron; **~lauf** *m* (*SPORT*) relay (race); **s~n** *vt* to graduate

Stahl [ʃtaːl] (-(e)s, ⸚e) *m* steel

stahl *etc vb siehe* **stehlen**

stak *etc* [ʃtaːk] *vb siehe* **stecken**

Stall [ʃtal] (-(e)s, ⸚e) *m* stable; (*Kaninchenstall*) hutch; (*Schweinestall*) sty; (*Hühnerstall*) henhouse

Stamm [ʃtam] (-(e)s, ⸚e) *m* (*Baumstamm*) trunk; (*Menschenstamm*) tribe; (*GRAM*) stem; **~baum** *m* family tree; (*von Tier*) pedigree; **s~eln** *vt, vi* to stammer; **s~en** *vi:* **s~en von** *od* **aus** to come from; **~gast** *m* regular (customer)

stämmig [ʃtɛmɪç] *adj* sturdy; (*Mensch*) stocky

Stammtisch [ʃtamtɪʃ] *m* table for the regulars

stampfen [ʃtampfən] *vt, vi* to stamp; (*stapfen*) to tramp; (*mit Werkzeug*) to pound

Stand [ʃtant] (-(e)s, ⸚e) *m* position; (*Wasserstand, Benzinstand etc*) level; (*Stehen*) standing position; (*Zustand*) state; (*Spielstand*) score; (*Messestand etc*) stand; (*Klasse*) class; (*Beruf*) profession; *siehe* **imstande, zustande**

stand *etc vb siehe* **stehen**

Standard [ʃtandart] (-s, -s) *m* standard

Ständer [ʃtɛndər] (-s, -) *m* stand

Standes- [ʃtandəs] *zW:* **~amt** *nt* registry office; **~beamte(r)** *m* registrar; **s~gemäß** *adj, adv* according to one's social position;

~unterschied *m* social difference

Stand- *zW:* **s~haft** *adj* steadfast; **s~halten** (*unreg*) *vi:* **(jdm/etw) s~halten** to stand firm (against sb/sth), to resist (sb/sth)

ständig [ʃtɛndɪç] *adj* permanent; (*ununterbrochen*) constant, continual

Stand- *zW:* **~licht** *nt* sidelights *pl*, parking lights *pl* (*US*); **~ort** *m* location; (*MIL*) garrison; **~punkt** *m* standpoint; **~spur** *f* hard shoulder

Stange [ʃtaŋə] *f* stick; (*Stab*) pole, bar; rod; (*Zigaretten*) carton; **von der ~** (*COMM*) off the peg; **eine ~ Geld** (*umg*) quite a packet

Stängel ▲ [ʃtɛŋəl] (-s, -) *m* stalk

Stapel [ʃtaːpəl] (-s, -) *m* pile; (*NAUT*) stocks *pl*; **~lauf** *m* launch; **s~n** *vt* to pile (up)

Star[1] [ʃtaːr] (-(e)s, -e) *m* starling; (*MED*) cataract

Star[2] [ʃtaːr] (-s, -s) *m* (*Filmstar etc*) star

starb *etc* [ʃtarp] *vb siehe* **sterben**

stark [ʃtark] *adj* strong; (*heftig, groß*) heavy; (*Maßangabe*) thick

Stärke [ʃtɛrkə] *f* strength; heaviness; thickness; (*KOCH: Wäschestärke*) starch; **s~n** *vt* to strengthen; (*Wäsche*) to starch

Starkstrom *m* heavy current

Stärkung [ʃtɛrkʊŋ] *f* strengthening; (*Essen*) refreshment

starr [ʃtar] *adj* stiff; (*unnachgiebig*) rigid; (*Blick*) staring; **~en** *vi* to stare; **~en vor** *od* **von** to be covered in; (*Waffen*) to be bristling with; **S~heit** *f* rigidity; **~köpfig** *adj* stubborn; **S~sinn** *m* obstinacy

Start [ʃtart] (-(e)s, -e) *m* start; (*AVIAT*) takeoff; **~automatik** *f* (*AUT*) automatic choke; **~bahn** *f* runway; **s~en** *vt* to start ◆ *vi* to start; to take off; **~er** (-s, -) *m* starter; **~erlaubnis** *f* takeoff clearance; **~hilfekabel** *nt* jump leads *pl*

Station [ʃtatsioːn] *f* station; hospital ward; **s~är** [ʃtatsioˈnɛːr] *adj* (*MED*) in-patient *attr*; **s~ieren** [-ˈniːrən] *vt* to station

Statist [ʃtaˈtɪst] *m* extra, supernumerary

Statistik *f* statistics *sg*; **~er** (-s, -) *m* statistician

statistisch *adj* statistical

Stativ [ʃtaˈtiːf] (-s, -e) *nt* tripod

statt [ʃtat] *konj* instead of ♦ *präp* (+gen od dat) instead of

Stätte ['ʃtɛtə] *f* place

statt- *zW:* **~finden** (*unreg*) *vi* to take place; **~haft** *adj* admissible; **~lich** *adj* imposing, handsome

Statue ['ʃtaːtuə] *f* statue

Status ['ʃtaːtʊs] (-, -) *m* status

Stau [ʃtaʊ] **(-(e)s, -e)** *m* blockage; (*Verkehrsstau*) (traffic) jam

Staub [ʃtaʊp] **(-(e)s)** *m* dust; **~ saugen** to vacuum, to hoover®; **s~en** ['ʃtaʊbən] *vi* to be dusty; **s~ig** *adj* dusty; **s~saugen** *vi* to vacuum, to hoover ®; **~sauger** *m* vacuum cleaner; **~tuch** *nt* duster

Staudamm *m* dam

Staude ['ʃtaʊdə] *f* shrub

stauen ['ʃtaʊən] *vt* (*Wasser*) to dam up; (*Blut*) to stop the flow of ♦ *vr* (*Wasser*) to become dammed up; (*MED*: *Verkehr*) to become congested; (*Menschen*) to collect; (*Gefühle*) to build up

staunen ['ʃtaʊnən] *vi* to be astonished; **S~** **(-s)** *nt* amazement

Stausee ['ʃtaʊzeː] **(-s, -n)** *m* reservoir, man-made lake

Stauung ['ʃtaʊʊŋ] *f* (*von Wasser*) damming-up; (*von Blut, Verkehr*) congestion

Std. *abk* (= *Stunde*) hr.

Steak [ʃteːk] *nt* steak

Stech- ['ʃtɛç] *zW:* **s~en** (*unreg*) *vt* (*mit Nadel etc*) to prick; (*mit Messer*) to stab; (*mit Finger*) to poke; (*Biene etc*) to sting; (*Mücke*) to bite; (*Sonne*) to burn; (*KARTEN*) to take; (*ART*) to engrave; (*Torf, Spargel*) to cut; **in See s~en** to put to sea; **~en (-s, -)** *nt* (*SPORT*) play-off; jump-off; **s~end** *adj* piercing, stabbing; (*Geruch*) pungent; **~palme** *f* holly; **~uhr** *f* time clock

Steck- ['ʃtɛk] *zW:* **~brief** *m* "wanted" poster; **~dose** *f* (wall) socket; **s~en** *vt* to put, to insert; (*Nadel*) to stick; (*Pflanzen*) to plant; (*beim Nähen*) to pin ♦ *vi* (*auch unreg*) to be; (*festsitzen*) to be stuck; (*Nadeln*) to stick; **s~en bleiben** to get stuck; **s~en lassen** to leave in; **~enpferd** *nt* hobby-horse; **~er (-s, -)** *m* plug; **~nadel** *f* pin

Steg [ʃteːk] **(-(e)s, -e)** *m* small bridge; (*Anlegesteg*) landing stage; **~reif** *m:* **aus dem ~reif** just like that

stehen ['ʃteːən] (*unreg*) *vi* to stand; (*sich befinden*) to be; (*in Zeitung*) to say; (*stillstehen*) to have stopped ♦ *vi unpers:* **es steht schlecht um jdn/etw** things are bad for sb/sth; **zu jdm/etw ~** to stand by sb/sth; **jdm ~** to suit sb; **wie stehts?** how are things?; (*SPORT*) what's the score?; **~ bleiben** to remain standing; (*Uhr*) to stop; (*Fehler*) to stay as it is; **~ lassen** to leave; (*Bart*) to grow

Stehlampe ['ʃteːlampə] *f* standard lamp

stehlen ['ʃteːlən] (*unreg*) *vt* to steal

Stehplatz ['ʃteːplats] *m* standing place

steif [ʃtaɪf] *adj* stiff; **S~heit** *f* stiffness

Steig- [ʃtaɪk] *zW:* **~bügel** *m* stirrup; **s~en** ['ʃtaɪgən] (*unreg*) *vi* to rise; (*klettern*) to climb; **s~en in** *+akk*/**auf** *+akk* to get in/on; **s~ern** *vt* to raise; (*GRAM*) to compare ♦ *vi* (*Auktion*) to bid ♦ *vr* to increase; **~erung** *f* raising; (*GRAM*) comparison; **~ung** *f* incline, gradient, rise

steil [ʃtaɪl] *adj* steep; **S~küste** *f* steep coast; (*Klippen*) cliffs *pl*

Stein [ʃtaɪn] **(-(e)s, -e)** *m* stone; (*in Uhr*) jewel; **~bock** *m* (*ASTROL*) Capricorn; **~bruch** *m* quarry; **s~ern** *adj* (made of) stone; (*fig*) stony; **~gut** *nt* stoneware; **s~ig** ['ʃtaɪnɪç] *adj* stony; **s~igen** *vt* to stone; **~kohle** *f* mineral coal; **~zeit** *f* Stone Age

Stelle ['ʃtɛlə] *f* place; (*Arbeit*) post, job; (*Amt*) office; **an Ihrer/meiner ~** in your/my place; *siehe* **anstelle**

stellen *vt* to put; (*Uhr etc*) to set; (*zur Verfügung ~*) to supply; (*fassen: Dieb*) to apprehend ♦ *vr* (*sich aufstellen*) to stand; (*sich einfinden*) to present o.s.; (*bei Polizei*) to give o.s. up; (*vorgeben*) to pretend (to be); **sich zu etw ~** to have an opinion of sth

Stellen- *zW:* **~angebot** *nt* offer of a post; (*in Zeitung*) "vacancies"; **~anzeige** *f* job advertisement; **~gesuch** *nt* application for a post; **~vermittlung** *f* employment agency

Stell- zW: **~ung** f position; (MIL) line; **~ung nehmen zu** to comment on; **~ungnahme** f comment; **s~vertretend** adj deputy, acting; **~vertreter** m deputy

Stelze ['ʃtɛltsə] f stilt

stemmen ['ʃtɛmən] vt to lift (up); (drücken) to press; **sich ~ gegen** (fig) to resist, to oppose

Stempel ['ʃtɛmpəl] (-s, -) m stamp; (BOT) pistil; **~kissen** nt ink pad; **s~n** vt to stamp; (Briefmarke) to cancel; **s~n gehen** (umg) to be od go on the dole

Stengel △ ['ʃtɛŋəl] (-s, -) m = **Stängel**

Steno- [ʃteno] zW: **~gramm** [-'gram] nt shorthand report; **~grafie** ▲ [-gra'fiː] f shorthand; **s~grafieren** ▲ [-gra'fiːrən] vt, vi to write (in) shorthand; **~typist(in)** [-ty'pɪst(ɪn)] m(f) shorthand typist

Stepp- ['ʃtɛp] zW: **~decke** f quilt; **~e** f prairie; steppe; **s~en** vt to stitch ♦ vi to tap-dance

Sterb- ['ʃtɛrb] zW: **~efall** m death; **~ehilfe** f euthanasia; **s~en** (unreg) vi to die; **s~lich** ['ʃtɛrplɪç] adj mortal; **~lichkeit** f mortality; **~lichkeitsziffer** f death rate

stereo- ['steːreo] in zW stereo(-); **S~anlage** f stereo (system); **~typ** [ʃtereo'tyːp] adj stereotype

steril [ʃte'riːl] adj sterile; **~i'sieren** vt to sterilize; **S~i'sierung** f sterilization

Stern [ʃtɛrn] (-(e)s, -e) m star; **~bild** nt constellation; **~schnuppe** f meteor, falling star; **~stunde** f historic moment; **~zeichen** nt sign of the zodiac

stet [ʃteːt] adj steady; **~ig** adj constant, continual; **~s** adv continually, always

Steuer¹ ['ʃtɔʏər] (-s, -) nt (NAUT) helm; (~ruder) rudder; (AUT) steering wheel

Steuer² ['ʃtɔʏər] (-, -n) f tax; **~berater(in)** m(f) tax consultant

Steuerbord nt (NAUT, AVIAT) starboard

Steuer- ['ʃtɔʏər] zW: **~erklärung** f tax return; **s~frei** adj tax-free; **~freibetrag** m tax allowance; **~klasse** f tax group; **~knüppel** m control column; (AVIAT, COMPUT) joystick; **~mann** (pl -**männer** od -**leute**) m helmsman; **s~n** vt, vi to steer;

(Flugzeug) to pilot; (Entwicklung, Tonstärke) to control; **s~pflichtig** [-pflɪçtɪç] adj taxable; **~rad** nt steering wheel; **~ung** f (auch AUT) steering; piloting; control; (Vorrichtung) controls pl; **~zahler** (-s, -) m taxpayer

Steward ['stjuːərt] (-s, -s) m steward; **~ess** ▲ ['stjuːərdɛs] (-, -en) f stewardess; air hostess

Stich [ʃtɪç] (-(e)s, -e) m (Insektenstich) sting; (Messerstich) stab; (beim Nähen) stitch; (Färbung) tinge; (KARTEN) trick; (ART) engraving; **jdn im ~ lassen** to leave sb in the lurch; **s~eln** vi (fig) to jibe; **s~haltig** adj sound, tenable; **~probe** f spot check; **~straße** f cul-de-sac; **~wahl** f final ballot; **~wort** nt cue; (in Wörterbuch) headword; (für Vortrag) note

sticken ['ʃtɪkən] vt, vi to embroider

Sticke'rei f embroidery

stickig adj stuffy, close

Stickstoff m nitrogen

Stief- ['ʃtiːf] in zW step

Stiefel ['ʃtiːfəl] (-s, -) m boot

Stief- zW: **~kind** nt stepchild; (fig) Cinderella; **~mutter** f stepmother; **~mütterlich** nt pansy; **s~mütterlich** adj (fig): **jdn/etw s~mütterlich behandeln** to pay little attention to sb/sth; **~vater** m stepfather

stiehlst etc [ʃtiːlst] vb siehe **stehlen**

Stiel [ʃtiːl] (-(e)s, -e) m handle; (BOT) stalk

Stier (-(e)s, -e) m bull; (ASTROL) Taurus

stieren vi to stare

Stierkampf etc m bullfight

Stierkämpfer m bullfighter

Stift [ʃtɪft] (-(e)s, -e) m peg; (Nagel) tack; (Farbstift) crayon; (Bleistift) pencil ♦ nt (charitable) foundation; (ECCL) religious institution; **s~en** vt to found; (Unruhe) to cause; (spenden) to contribute; **~er(in)** (-s, -) m(f) founder; **~ung** f donation; (Organisation) foundation; **~zahn** m post crown

Stil [ʃtiːl] (-(e)s, -e) m style

still [ʃtɪl] adj quiet; (unbewegt) still; (heimlich) secret; **S~er Ozean** Pacific; **~ halten** to keep still; **~ stehen** to stand still; **S~e** f

stillness, quietness; **in aller S~e** quietly;
~en vt to stop; (*befriedigen*) to satisfy;
(*Säugling*) to breast-feed; **~legen** ▲ vt to
close down; **~schweigen** (*unreg*) vi to be
silent; **S~schweigen** nt silence;
~schweigend adj silent; (*Einverständnis*)
tacit ♦ adv silently; tacitly; **S~stand** m
standstill

Stimm- [ʃtɪm] zW: **~bänder** pl vocal cords;
s~berechtigt adj entitled to vote; **~e** f
voice; (*Wahlstimme*) vote; **s~en** vt (*MUS*) to
tune ♦ vi to be right; **das s~te ihn traurig**
that made him feel sad; **s~en für/gegen**
to vote for/against; **s~t so!** that's right;
~enmehrheit f majority (of votes);
~enthaltung f abstention; **~gabel** f
tuning fork; **~recht** nt right to vote; **~ung**
f mood; atmosphere; **s~ungsvoll** adj
enjoyable; full of atmosphere; **~zettel** m
ballot paper

stinken [ʃtɪŋkən] (*unreg*) vi to stink
Stipendium [ʃtiˈpɛndiʊm] nt grant
stirbst etc [ʃtɪrpst] vb siehe **sterben**
Stirn [ʃtɪrn] (-, -en) f forehead, brow;
(*Frechheit*) impudence; **~band** nt
headband; **~höhle** f sinus
stöbern [ʃtøːbərn] vi to rummage
stochern [ʃtɔxərn] vi to poke (about)
Stock¹ [ʃtɔk] (-(e)s, ⁻e) m stick; (*BOT*) stock
Stock² [ʃtɔk] (-(e)s, - od **Stockwerke**) m
storey
stocken vi to stop, to pause; **~d** adj halting
Stockung f stoppage
Stockwerk nt storey, floor
Stoff [ʃtɔf] (-(e)s, -e) m (*Gewebe*) material,
cloth; (*Materie*) matter; (*von Buch etc*)
subject (matter); **s~lich** adj material; **~tier**
nt soft toy; **~wechsel** m metabolism
stöhnen [ʃtøːnən] vi to groan
Stollen [ʃtɔlən] (-s, -) m (*MIN*) gallery;
(*KOCH*) cake eaten at Christmas; (*von
Schuhen*) stud
stolpern [ʃtɔlpərn] vi to stumble, to trip
Stolz [ʃtɔlts] (-es) m pride; **s~** adj proud;
s~ieren [ʃtɔlˈtsiːrən] vi to strut
stopfen [ʃtɔpfən] vt (*hineinstopfen*) to stuff;
(*voll stopfen*) to fill (up); (*nähen*) to darn ♦ vi

(*MED*) to cause constipation
Stopfgarn nt darning thread
Stoppel [ʃtɔpəl] (-, -n) f stubble
Stopp- [ʃtɔp] zW: **s~en** vt to stop; (*mit Uhr*)
to time ♦ vi to stop; **~schild** nt stop sign;
~uhr f stopwatch
Stöpsel [ʃtœpsəl] (-s, -) m plug; (*für
Flaschen*) stopper
Storch [ʃtɔrç] (-(e)s, ⁻e) m stork
Stör- [ʃtøːr] zW: **s~en** vt to disturb;
(*behindern, RADIO*) to interfere with ♦ vr:
sich an etw dat **s~en** to let sth bother
one; **s~end** adj disturbing, annoying;
~enfried (-(e)s, -e) m troublemaker
stornieren [ʃtɔrˈniːrən] vt (*Auftrag*) to
cancel; (*Buchung*) to reverse
Stornogebühr [ʃtɔrno-] f cancellation fee
störrisch [ʃtœrɪʃ] adj stubborn, perverse
Störung f disturbance; interference
Stoß [ʃtoːs] (-es, ⁻e) m (*Schub etc*) push; (*Schlag*)
blow; knock; (*mit Schwert*) thrust; (*mit Fuß*)
kick; (*Erdstoß*) shock; (*Haufen*) pile;
~dämpfer (-s, -) m shock absorber; **s~en**
(*unreg*) vt (*mit Druck*) to shove, to push; (*mit
Schlag*) to knock, to bump; (*mit Fuß*) to
kick; (*Schwert etc*) to thrust; (*anstoßen: Kopf
etc*) to bump ♦ vr to get a knock ♦ vi: **s~en
an** od **auf** +akk to bump into; (*finden*) to
come across; (*angrenzen*) to be next to;
sich s~en an +dat (*fig*) to take exception
to; **~stange** f (*AUT*) bumper
stottern [ʃtɔtərn] vt, vi to stutter
Str. abk (= *Straße*) St.
Straf- [ʃtraːf] zW: **~anstalt** f penal
institution; **~arbeit** f (*SCH*) punishment;
lines pl; **s~bar** adj punishable; **~e** f
punishment; (*JUR*) penalty; (*Gefängnisstrafe*)
sentence; (*Geldstrafe*) fine; **s~en** vt to
punish
straff [ʃtraf] adj tight; (*streng*) strict; (*Stil etc*)
concise; (*Haltung*) erect; **~en** vt to tighten,
to tauten
Strafgefangene(r) f(m) prisoner, convict
Strafgesetzbuch nt penal code
sträflich [ʃtrɛːflɪç] adj criminal
Sträfling m convict
Straf- zW: **~porto** nt excess postage

Spelling Reform: ▲ *new spelling* △ *old spelling (to be phased out)*

(charge); ~**predigt** f telling-off; ~**raum** m (SPORT) penalty area; ~**recht** nt criminal law; ~**stoß** m (SPORT) penalty (kick); ~**tat** f punishable act; ~**zettel** m ticket

Strahl [ʃtraːl] (**-s, -en**) m ray, beam; (*Wasserstrahl*) jet; **s~en** vi to radiate; (*fig*) to beam; ~**ung** f radiation

Strähne [ˈʃtrɛːnə] f strand

stramm [ʃtram] adj tight; (*Haltung*) erect; (*Mensch*) robust

strampeln [ˈʃtrampəln] vi to kick (about), to fidget

Strand [ʃtrant] (**-(e)s, ⁻e**) m shore; (*mit Sand*) beach; ~**bad** nt open-air swimming pool, lido; **s~en** [ˈʃtrandən] vi to run aground; (*fig: Mensch*) to fail; ~**gut** nt flotsam; ~**korb** m beach chair

Strang [ʃtraŋ] (**-(e)s, ⁻e**) m cord, rope; (*Bündel*) skein

Strapaz- zW: ~**e** [ʃtraˈpaːtsə] f strain, exertion; **s~ieren** [ʃtrapaˈtsiːrən] vt (*Material*) to treat roughly, to punish; (*Mensch, Kräfte*) to wear out, to exhaust; **s~ierfähig** adj hard-wearing; **s~iös** [ʃtrapaˈtsiˈøːs] adj exhausting, tough

Straße [ˈʃtraːsə] f street, road

Straßen- zW: ~**bahn** f tram, streetcar (US); ~**glätte** f slippery road surface; ~**karte** f road map; ~**kehrer** (**-s, -**) m roadsweeper; ~**sperre** f roadblock; ~**verkehr** m (road) traffic; ~**verkehrsordnung** f highway code

Strateg- [ʃtraˈteːg] zW: ~**e** (**-n, -n**) m strategist; ~**ie** [ʃtrateˈɡiː] f strategy; **s~isch** adj strategic

sträuben [ˈʃtrɔybən] vt to ruffle ♦ vr to bristle; (*Mensch*) **sich (gegen etw)** ~ to resist (sth)

Strauch [ʃtraux] (**-(e)s, Sträucher**) m bush, shrub

Strauß¹ [ʃtraus] (**-es, Sträuße**) m bunch; bouquet

Strauß² [ʃtraus] (**-es, -e**) m ostrich

Streb- [ˈʃtreːb] zW: **s~en** vi to strive to, to endeavour; **s~en nach** to strive for; ~**er** (**-s, -**) (*pej*) m pusher, climber; (*SCH*) swot (*BRIT*)

Strecke [ˈʃtrɛkə] f stretch; (*Entfernung*) distance; (*EISENB, MATH*) line; **s~n** vt to stretch; (*Waffen*) to lay down; (*KOCH*) to eke out ♦ vr to stretch (o.s.)

Streich [ʃtraɪç] (**-(e)s, -e**) m trick, prank; (*Hieb*) blow; **s~eln** vt to stroke; **s~en** (*unreg*) vt (*berühren*) to stroke; (*auftragen*) to spread; (*anmalen*) to paint; (*durchstreichen*) to delete; (*nicht genehmigen*) to cancel ♦ vi (*berühren*) to brush; (*schleichen*) to prowl; ~**holz** nt match; ~**instrument** nt string instrument

Streif- [ˈʃtraɪf] zW: ~**e** f patrol; **s~en** vt (*leicht berühren*) to brush against, to graze; (*Blick*) to skim over; (*Thema, Problem*) to touch on; (*abstreifen*) to take off ♦ vi (*gehen*) to roam; ~**en** (**-s, -**) m (*Linie*) stripe; (*Stück*) strip; (*Film*) film; ~**enwagen** m patrol car; ~**schuss** ▲ m graze, grazing shot; ~**zug** m scouting trip

Streik [ʃtraɪk] (**-(e)s, -s**) m strike; ~**brecher** (**-s, -**) m blackleg, strikebreaker; **s~en** vi to strike; ~**posten** m (strike) picket

Streit [ʃtraɪt] (**-(e)s, -e**) m argument; dispute; **s~en** (*unreg*) vi, vr to argue; to dispute; ~**frage** f point at issue; **s~ig** adj: **jdm etw s~ig machen** to dispute sb's right to sth; ~**igkeiten** pl quarrel sg, dispute sg; ~**kräfte** pl (MIL) armed forces

streng [ʃtrɛŋ] adj severe; (*Lehrer, Maßnahme*) strict; (*Geruch etc*) sharp; ~ **genommen** strictly speaking; **S~e** (**-**) f severity, strictness, sharpness; ~**gläubig** adj orthodox, strict; ~**stens** adv strictly

Stress ▲ [ʃtrɛs] (**-es, -e**) m stress

stressen vt to put under stress

streuen [ˈʃtrɔyən] vt to strew, to scatter, to spread

Strich [ʃtrɪç] (**-(e)s, -e**) m (*Linie*) line; (*Federstrich, Pinselstrich*) stroke; (*von Geweben*) nap; (*von Fell*) pile; **auf den ~ gehen** (*umg*) to walk the streets; **jdm gegen den ~ gehen** to rub sb up the wrong way; **einen ~ machen durch** to cross out; (*fig*) to foil; ~**kode** m (*auf Waren*) bar code; ~**mädchen** nt streetwalker; **s~weise** adv here and there

Strick [ʃtrɪk] (**-(e)s, -e**) *m* rope; **s~en** *vt, vi* to knit; **~jacke** *f* cardigan; **~leiter** *f* rope ladder; **~nadel** *f* knitting needle; **~waren** *pl* knitwear *sg*

strikt [strɪkt] *adj* strict

strittig [ʃtrɪtɪç] *adj* disputed, in dispute

Stroh [ʃtroː] (**-(e)s**) *nt* straw; **~blume** *f* everlasting flower; **~dach** *nt* thatched roof; **~halm** *m* (drinking) straw

Strom [ʃtroːm] (**-(e)s, ̈e**) *m* river; (*fig*) stream; (*ELEK*) current; **s~abwärts** *adv* downstream; **s~aufwärts** *adv* upstream; **~ausfall** *m* power failure

strömen [ʃtrøːmən] *vi* to stream, to pour

Strom- *zW*: **~kreis** *m* circuit; **s~linienförmig** *adj* streamlined; **~sperre** *f* power cut

Strömung [ʃtrøːmʊŋ] *f* current

Strophe [ʃtroːfə] *f* verse

strotzen [ʃtrɔtsən] *vi*: **~ vor** *od* **von** to abound in, to be full of

Strudel [ʃtruːdəl] (**-s, -**) *m* whirlpool, vortex; (*KOCH*) strudel

Struktur [ʃtrʊkˈtuːr] *f* structure

Strumpf [ʃtrʊmpf] (**-(e)s, ̈e**) *m* stocking; **~band** *nt* garter; **~hose** *f* (pair of) tights

Stube [ʃtuːbə] *f* room

Stuben- *zW*: **~arrest** *m* confinement to one's room; (*MIL*) confinement to quarters; **~hocker** (*umg*) *m* stay-at-home; **s~rein** *adj* house-trained

Stuck [ʃtʊk] (**-(e)s**) *m* stucco

Stück [ʃtʏk] (**-(e)s, -e**) *nt* piece; (*etwas*) bit; (*THEAT*) play; **~chen** *nt* little piece; **~lohn** *m* piecework wages *pl*; **s~weise** *adv* bit by bit, piecemeal; (*COMM*) individually

Student(in) [ʃtuˈdɛnt(ɪn)] *m(f)* student; **s~isch** *adj* student, academic

Studie [ʃtuːdiə] *f* study

Studienfahrt *f* study trip

studieren [ʃtuˈdiːrən] *vt, vi* to study

Studio [ʃtuːdio] (**-s, -s**) *nt* studio

Studium [ʃtuːdiʊm] *nt* studies *pl*

Stufe [ʃtuːfə] *f* step; (*Entwicklungsstufe*) stage; **s~nweise** *adv* gradually

Stuhl [ʃtuːl] (**-(e)s, ̈e**) *m* chair; **~gang** *m* bowel movement

stülpen [ʃtʏlpən] *vt* (*umdrehen*) to turn upside down; (*bedecken*) to put

stumm [ʃtʊm] *adj* silent; (*MED*) dumb

Stummel [ʃtʊməl] (**-s, -**) *m* stump; (*Zigarettenstummel*) stub

Stummfilm *m* silent film

Stümper [ʃtʏmpər] (**-s, -**) *m* incompetent, duffer; **s~haft** *adj* bungling, incompetent; **s~n** *vi* to bungle

Stumpf [ʃtʊmpf] (**-(e)s, ̈e**) *m* stump; **s~** *adj* blunt; (*teilnahmslos, glanzlos*) dull; (*Winkel*) obtuse; **~sinn** *m* tediousness; **s~sinnig** *adj* dull

Stunde [ʃtʊndə] *f* hour; (*SCH*) lesson

stunden *vt*: **jdm etw ~** to give sb time to pay sth; **S~geschwindigkeit** *f* average speed per hour; **S~kilometer** *pl* kilometres per hour; **~lang** *adj* for hours; **S~lohn** *m* hourly wage; **S~plan** *m* timetable; **~weise** *adj* by the hour; every hour

stündlich [ʃtʏntlɪç] *adj* hourly

Stups [ʃtʊps] (**-es, -e**) (*umg*) *m* push; **~nase** *f* snub nose

stur [ʃtuːr] *adj* obstinate, pigheaded

Sturm [ʃtʊrm] (**-(e)s, ̈e**) *m* storm, gale; (*MIL etc*) attack, assault

stürm- [ʃtʏrm] *zW*: **~en** *vi* (*Wind*) to blow hard, to rage; (*rennen*) to storm ♦ *vt* (*MIL, fig*) to storm ♦ *vb unpers*: **es ~t** there's a gale blowing; **S~er** (**-s, -**) *m* (*SPORT*) forward, striker; **~isch** *adj* stormy

Sturmwarnung *f* gale warning

Sturz [ʃtʊrts] (**-es, ̈e**) *m* fall; (*POL*) overthrow

stürzen [ʃtʏrtsən] *vt* (*werfen*) to hurl; (*POL*) to overthrow; (*umkehren*) to overturn ♦ *vr* to rush; (*hineinstürzen*) to plunge ♦ *vi* to fall; (*AVIAT*) to dive; (*rennen*) to dash

Sturzflug *m* nose dive

Sturzhelm *m* crash helmet

Stute [ʃtuːtə] *f* mare

Stützbalken *m* brace, joist

Stütze [ʃtʏtsə] *f* support; help

stutzen [ʃtʊtsən] *vt* to trim; (*Ohr, Schwanz*) to dock; (*Flügel*) to clip ♦ *vi* to hesitate; to become suspicious

stützen *vt* (*auch fig*) to support; (*Ellbogen*

etc) to prop up

stutzig *adj* perplexed, puzzled; *(misstrauisch)* suspicious

Stützpunkt *m* point of support; *(von Hebel)* fulcrum; *(MIL, fig)* base

Styropor [ʃtyroˈpoːr] (®, **-s**) *nt* polystyrene

s. u. *abk* = **siehe unten**

Subjekt [zʊpˈjɛkt] (**-(e)s, -e**) *nt* subject; **s~iv** [-ˈtiːf] *adj* subjective; **~iviˈtät** *f* subjectivity

Subsidiarität *f* subsidiary

Substantiv [zʊpstanˈtiːf] (**-s, -e**) *nt* noun

Substanz [zʊpˈstants] *f* substance

subtil [zʊpˈtiːl] *adj* subtle

subtrahieren [zʊptraˈhiːrən] *vt* to subtract

subtropisch [ˈzʊptroːpɪʃ] *adj* subtropical

Subvention [zʊpvɛntsiˈoːn] *f* subsidy; **s~ieren** *vt* to subsidize

Such- [ˈzuːx] *zW*: **~aktion** *f* search; **~e** *f* search; **s~en** *vt* to look (for), to seek; *(versuchen)* to try ♦ *vi* to seek, to search; **~er** (**-s, -**) *m* seeker, searcher; *(PHOT)* viewfinder; **~maschine** *f* (COMPUT) search engine

Sucht [zʊxt] (**-, ⁼e**) *f* mania; *(MED)* addiction, craving

süchtig [ˈzʏçtɪç] *adj* addicted; **S~e(r)** *f(m)* addict

Süd- [ˈzyːt] *zW*: **~en** [ˈzyːdən] (**-s**) *m* south; **~früchte** *pl* Mediterranean fruit *sg*; **s~lich** *adj* southern; **s~lich von** (to the) south of; **~pol** *m* South Pole; **s~wärts** *adv* southwards

süffig [ˈzʏfɪç] *adj* (Wein) pleasant to the taste

süffisant [zʏfiˈzant] *adj* smug

suggerieren [zʊɡeˈriːrən] *vt* to suggest

Sühne [ˈzyːnə] *f* atonement, expiation; **s~n** *vt* to atone for, to expiate

Sultan [ˈzʊltan] (**-s, -e**) *m* sultan; **~ine** [zʊltaˈniːnə] *f* sultana

Sülze [ˈzʏltsə] *f* brawn

Summe [ˈzʊmə] *f* sum, total

summen *vt, vi* to buzz; *(Lied)* to hum

Sumpf [zʊmpf] (**-(e)s, ⁼e**) *m* swamp, marsh; **s~ig** *adj* marshy

Sünde [ˈzʏndə] *f* sin; **~nbock** *(umg)* *m* scapegoat; **~r(in)** (**-s, -**) *m(f)* sinner; **sündigen** *vi* to sin

Super [ˈzuːpər] (**-s**) *nt* (Benzin) four star (petrol) (BRIT), premium (US); **~lativ** [-latiːf] (**-s, -e**) *m* superlative; **~macht** *f* superpower; **~markt** *m* supermarket

Suppe [ˈzʊpə] *f* soup; **~nteller** *m* soup plate

süß [zyːs] *adj* sweet; **S~e** (**-**) *f* sweetness; **~en** *vt* to sweeten; **S~igkeit** *f* sweetness; *(Bonbon etc)* sweet (BRIT), candy (US); **~lich** *adj* sweetish; *(fig)* sugary; **~sauer** *adj* (Gurke) pickled; *(Sauce etc)* sweet-and-sour; **S~speise** *f* pudding, sweet; **S~stoff** *m* sweetener; **S~waren** *pl* confectionery *(sing)*; **S~wasser** *nt* fresh water

Symbol [zʏmˈboːl] (**-s, -e**) *nt* symbol; **s~isch** *adj* symbolic(al)

Symmetrie [zʏmeˈtriː] *f* symmetry

symmetrisch [zʏˈmeːtrɪʃ] *adj* symmetrical

Sympathie [zʏmpaˈtiː] *f* liking, sympathy; **sympathisch** [zʏmˈpaːtɪʃ] *adj* likeable; **er ist mir sympathisch** I like him; **sympathi'sieren** *vi* to sympathize

Symphonie [zʏmfoˈniː] *f* (MUS) symphony

Symptom [zʏmpˈtoːm] (**-s, -e**) *nt* symptom; **s~atisch** [zʏmptoˈmaːtɪʃ] *adj* symptomatic

Synagoge [zynaˈɡoːɡə] *f* synagogue

synchron [zʏnˈkroːn] *adj* synchronous; **~i'sieren** *vt* to synchronize; *(Film)* to dub

Synonym [zynoˈnyːm] (**-s, -e**) *nt* synonym; **s~** *adj* synonymous

Synthese [zʏnˈteːzə] *f* synthesis

synthetisch *adj* synthetic

System [zʏsˈteːm] (**-s, -e**) *nt* system; **s~atisch** *adj* systematic; **s~ati'sieren** *vt* to systematize

Szene [ˈstseːnə] *f* scene; **~rie** [stsenəˈriː] *f* scenery

T, t

t *abk* (= *Tonne*) t

Tabak [ˈtaːbak] (**-s, -e**) *m* tobacco

Tabell- [taˈbɛl] *zW*: **t~arisch** [tabɛˈlaːrɪʃ] *adj* tabular; **~e** *f* table

Tablett [taˈblɛt] *nt* tray; **~e** *f* tablet, pill

Tabu [taˈbuː] *nt* taboo; **t~** *adj* taboo

Tachometer [taxoˈmeːtər] (**-s, -**) *m* (AUT)

speedometer

Tadel ['ta:dəl] **(-s, -)** m censure; scolding; (Fehler) fault, blemish; **t~los** adj faultless, irreproachable; **t~n** vt to scold

Tafel ['ta:fəl] **(-, -n)** f (auch MATH) table; (Anschlag~) board; (Wand~) blackboard; (Schiefer~) slate; (Gedenk~) plaque; (Illustration) plate; (Schalt~) panel; (Schokolade etc) bar

Tag [ta:k] **(-(e)s, -e)** m day; daylight; **unter/über ~e** (MIN) underground/on the surface; **an den ~ kommen** to come to light; **guten ~!** good morning/afternoon!; siehe **zutage**; **t~aus** adv: **t~aus, ~ein** day in, day out; **t~dienst** m day duty

Tage- ['ta:gə] zW: **~buch** ['ta:gəbu:x] nt diary, journal; **~geld** nt daily allowance; **t~lang** adv for days; **t~n** vi to sit, to meet ♦ vb unpers: **es tagt** dawn is breaking

Tages- zW: **~ablauf** m course of the day; **~anbruch** m dawn; **~fahrt** f day trip; **~karte** f menu of the day; (Fahrkarte) day ticket; **~licht** nt daylight; **~ordnung** f agenda; **~zeit** f time of day; **~zeitung** f daily (paper)

täglich ['tɛːklɪç] adj, adv daily

tagsüber ['ta:ksly:bər] adv during the day

Tagung f conference

Taille ['taljə] f waist

Takt [takt] **(-(e)s, -e)** m tact; (MUS) time; **~gefühl** nt tact

Taktik f tactics pl; **taktisch** adj tactical

Takt- zW: **t~los** adj tactless; **~losigkeit** f tactlessness; **~stock** m (conductor's) baton; **t~voll** adj tactful

Tal [ta:l] **(-(e)s, ⁷er)** nt valley

Talent [ta'lɛnt] **(-(e)s, -e)** nt talent; **t~iert** [talɛn'ti:rt] adj talented, gifted

Talisman ['ta:lɪsman] **(-s, -e)** m talisman

Talkshow ['tɔ:kʃo:] f chat show

Talsohle f bottom of a valley

Talsperre f dam

Tampon ['tampɔn] **(-s, -s)** m tampon

Tang [taŋ] **(-(e)s, -e)** m seaweed

Tank [taŋk] **(-s, -e)** m tank; **~anzeige** f fuel gauge; **t~en** vi to fill up with petrol (BRIT) od gas (US); (AVIAT) to (re)fuel; **~er (-s, -)** m tanker; **~schiff** nt tanker; **~stelle** f petrol (BRIT) od gas (US) station; **~wart** m petrol pump (BRIT) od gas station (US) attendant

Tanne ['tanə] f fir

Tannen- zW: **~baum** m fir tree; **~zapfen** m fir cone

Tante ['tantə] f aunt

Tanz [tants] **(-es, ⁷e)** m dance; **t~en** vt, vi to dance

Tänzer(in) ['tɛntsər(ɪn)] **(-s, -)** m(f) dancer

Tanzfläche f (dance) floor

Tanzschule f dancing school

Tapete [ta'pe:tə] f wallpaper; **~nwechsel** m (fig) change of scenery

tapezieren [tape'tsi:rən] vt to (wall)paper; **Tapezierer** [tape'tsi:rər] **(-s, -)** m (interior) decorator

tapfer ['tapfər] adj brave; **T~keit** f courage, bravery

Tarif [ta'ri:f] **(-s, -e)** m tariff, (scale of) fares od charges; **~lohn** m standard wage rate; **~verhandlungen** pl wage negotiations; **~zone** f fare zone

Tarn- ['tarn] zW: **t~en** vt to camouflage; (Person, Absicht) to disguise; **~ung** f camouflaging; disguising

Tasche ['taʃə] f pocket; handbag

Taschen- in zW pocket; **~buch** nt paperback; **~dieb** m pickpocket; **~geld** nt pocket money; **~lampe** f (electric) torch, flashlight (US); **~messer** nt penknife; **~tuch** nt handkerchief

Tasse ['tasə] f cup

Tastatur [tasta'tu:r] f keyboard

Taste ['tastə] f push-button control; (an Schreibmaschine) key; **t~n** vt to feel, to touch ♦ vi to feel, to grope ♦ vr to feel one's way

Tat [ta:t] **(-, -en)** f act, deed, action; **in der ~** indeed, as a matter of fact; **t~** etc vb siehe **tun**; **~bestand** m facts pl of the case; **t~enlos** adj inactive

Tät- ['tɛ:t] zW: **~er(in) (-s, -)** m(f) perpetrator, culprit; **t~ig** adj active; **in einer Firma t~ig sein** to work for a firm; **~igkeit** f activity; (Beruf) occupation; **t~lich** adj violent; **~lichkeit** f violence; **~lichkeiten** pl (Schläge) blows

tätowieren [tɛto'viːrən] *vt* to tattoo
Tatsache *f* fact
tatsächlich *adj* actual ♦ *adv* really
Tau¹ [tau] (**-(e)s, -e**) *nt* rope
Tau² [tau] (**-(e)s**) *m* dew
taub [taup] *adj* deaf; (*Nuss*) hollow
Taube ['taubə] *f* dove; pigeon; **~nschlag** *m* dovecote; **hier geht es zu wie in einem ~nschlag** it's a hive of activity here
taub- *zW:* **T~heit** *f* deafness; **~stumm** *adj* deaf-and-dumb
Tauch- [taux] *zW:* **t~en** *vt* to dip ♦ *vi* to dive; (*NAUT*) to submerge; **~er** (**-s, -**) *m* diver; **~eranzug** *m* diving suit; **~erbrille** *f* diving goggles *pl*; **~sieder** (**-s, -**) *m* immersion coil (*for boiling water*)
tauen ['tauən] *vt, vi* to thaw ♦ *vb unpers:* **es taut** it's thawing
Tauf- ['tauf] *zW:* **~becken** *nt* font; **~e** *f* baptism; **t~en** *vt* to christen, to baptize; **~pate** *m* godfather; **~patin** *f* godmother; **~schein** *m* certificate of baptism
taug- ['taug] *zW:* **~en** *vi* to be of use; **~en für** to do for; to be good for; **nicht ~en** to be no good *od* useless; **T~enichts** (**-es, -e**) *m* good-for-nothing; **~lich** ['taukliç] *adj* suitable; (*MIL*) fit (for service)
Taumel ['tauməl] (**-s**) *m* dizziness; (*fig*) frenzy; **t~n** *vi* to reel, to stagger
Tausch [tauʃ] (**-(e)s, -e**) *m* exchange; **t~en** *vt* to exchange, to swap
täuschen ['tɔyʃən] *vt* to deceive ♦ *vi* to be deceptive ♦ *vr* to be wrong; **~d** *adj* deceptive
Tauschhandel *m* barter
Täuschung *f* deception; (*optisch*) illusion
tausend ['tauzənt] *num* (a) thousand
Tauwetter *nt* thaw
Taxi ['taksi] (**-(s), -(s)**) *nt* taxi; **~fahrer** *m* taxi driver; **~stand** *m* taxi rank
Tech- [tɛç] *zW:* **~nik** *f* technology; (*Methode, Kunstfertigkeit*) technique; **~niker** (**-s, -**) *m* technician; **t~nisch** *adj* technical; **~nolo'gie** *f* technology; **t~no'logisch** *adj* technological
Tee [teː] (**-s, -s**) *m* tea; **~beutel** *m* tea bag; **~kanne** *f* teapot; **~löffel** *m* teaspoon

Teer [teːr] (**-(e)s, -e**) *m* tar; **t~en** *vt* to tar
Teesieb *nt* tea strainer
Teich [taiç] (**-(e)s, -e**) *m* pond
Teig [taik] (**-(e)s, -e**) *m* dough; **t~ig** ['taigiç] *adj* doughy; **~waren** *pl* pasta *sg*
Teil [tail] (**-(e)s, -e**) *m od nt* part; (*Anteil*) share; (*Bestandteil*) component; **zum ~** partly; **t~bar** *adj* divisible; **~betrag** *m* instalment; **~chen** *nt* (atomic) particle; **t~en** *vt, vr* to divide; (*mit jdm*) to share; **t~haben** (*unreg*) *vi:* **t~haben an** +*dat* to share in; **~haber** (**-s, -**) *m* partner; **~kaskoversicherung** *f* third party, fire and theft insurance; **t~möbliert** *adj* partially furnished; **~nahme** *f* participation; (*Mitleid*) sympathy; **t~nahmslos** *adj* disinterested, apathetic; **t~nehmen** (*unreg*) *vi:* **t~nehmen an** +*dat* to take part in; **~nehmer** (**-s, -**) *m* participant; **t~s** *adv* partly; **~ung** *f* division; **t~weise** *adv* partially, in part; **~zahlung** *f* payment by instalments; **~zeitarbeit** *f* part-time work
Teint [tɛ̃ː] (**-s, -s**) *m* complexion
Telearbeit ['teːleˌarbait] *f* teleworking
Telefax ['teːlefaks] *nt* fax
Telefon [tele'foːn] (**-s, -e**) *nt* telephone; **~anruf** *m* (tele)phone call; **~at** [telefo'naːt] (**-(e)s, -e**) *nt* (tele)phone call; **~buch** *nt* telephone directory; **~hörer** *m* (telephone) receiver; **t~ieren** *vi* to telephone; **t~isch** [-ɪʃ] *adj* telephone; (*Benachrichtigung*) by telephone; **~ist(in)** [telefo'nɪst(ɪn)] *m(f)* telephonist; **~karte** *f* phonecard; **~nummer** *f* (tele)phone number; **~zelle** *f* telephone kiosk, callbox; **~zentrale** *f* telephone exchange
Telegraf [tele'graːf] (**-en, -en**) *m* telegraph; **~enmast** *m* telegraph pole; **~ie** [-'fiː] *f* telegraphy; **t~ieren** [-'fiːrən] *vt, vi* to telegraph, to wire
Telegramm [tele'gram] (**-s, -e**) *nt* telegram, cable; **~adresse** *f* telegraphic address
Tele- *zW:* **~objektiv** ['teːleˌɔpjɛktiːf] *nt* telephoto lens; **t~pathisch** [tele'paːtɪʃ] *adj* telepathic; **~skop** [tele'skoːp] (**-s, -e**) *nt* telescope

Teller ['tɛlər] (**-s, -**) m plate; **~gericht** nt (KOCH) one-course meal
Tempel ['tɛmpəl] (**-s, -**) m temple
Temperament [tɛmpera'mɛnt] nt temperament; (Schwung) vivacity, liveliness; **t~voll** adj high-spirited, lively
Temperatur [tɛmpera'tu:r] f temperature
Tempo[1] ['tɛmpo] (**-s, Tempi**) nt (MUS) tempo
Tempo[2] ['tɛmpo] (**-s, -s**) nt speed, pace; **~!** get a move on!; **~limit** [-lɪmɪt] (**-s, -s**) nt speed limit; **~taschentuch** ® nt tissue
Tendenz [tɛn'dɛnts] f tendency; (Absicht) intention; **t~iös** [-i'ø:s] adj biased, tendentious
tendieren [tɛn'di:rən] vi: **~ zu** to show a tendency to, to incline towards
Tennis ['tɛnɪs] (**-**) nt tennis; **~ball** m tennis ball; **~platz** m tennis court; **~schläger** m tennis racket; **~schuh** m tennis shoe; **~spieler(in)** m(f) tennis player
Tenor [te'no:r] (**-s, ⁼e**) m tenor
Teppich ['tɛpɪç] (**-s, -e**) m carpet; **~boden** m wall-to-wall carpeting
Termin [tɛr'mi:n] (**-s, -e**) m (Zeitpunkt) date; (Frist) time limit, deadline; (Arzttermin etc) appointment; **~kalender** m diary, appointments book; **~planer** m personal organizer
Terrasse [tɛ'rasə] f terrace
Terrine [tɛ'ri:nə] f tureen
territorial [tɛritori'a:l] adj territorial
Territorium [tɛri'to:riʊm] nt territory
Terror ['tɛrɔr] (**-s**) m terror; reign of terror; **t~isieren** [tɛrori'zi:rən] vt to terrorize; **~ismus** [-'rɪsmʊs] m terrorism; **~ist** [-'rɪst] m terrorist
Tesafilm ['te:zafɪlm] ® m Sellotape ® (BRIT), Scotch tape ® (US)
Tessin [tɛ'si:n] (**-s**) nt: **das ~** Ticino
Test [tɛst] (**-s, -s**) m test
Testament [tɛsta'mɛnt] nt will, testament; (REL) Testament; **t~arisch** [-'ta:rɪʃ] adj testamentary
Testamentsvollstrecker m executor (of a will)
testen vt to test

Tetanus ['te:tanʊs] (**-**) m tetanus; **~impfung** f (anti-)tetanus injection
teuer ['tɔyər] adj dear, expensive; **T~ung** f increase in prices; **T~ungszulage** f cost of living bonus
Teufel ['tɔyfəl] (**-s, -**) m devil; **teuflisch** ['tɔyflɪʃ] adj fiendish, diabolical
Text [tɛkst] (**-(e)s, -e**) m text; (Liedertext) words pl; **t~en** vi to write the words
textil [tɛks'ti:l] adj textile; **T~ien** pl textiles; **T~industrie** f textile industry; **T~waren** pl textiles
Textverarbeitung f word processing
Theater [te'a:tər] (**-s, -**) nt theatre; (umg) fuss; **~ spielen** (auch fig) to playact; **~besucher** m playgoer; **~kasse** f box office; **~stück** nt (stage) play
Theke ['te:kə] f (Schanktisch) bar; (Ladentisch) counter
Thema ['te:ma] (**-s, Themen** od **-ta**) nt theme, topic, subject
Themse ['tɛmzə] f Thames
Theo- [teo] zW: **~loge** [-'lo:gə] (**-n, -n**) m theologian; **~logie** [-lo'gi:] f theology; **t~logisch** [-'lo:gɪʃ] adj theological; **~retiker** [-'re:tikər] (**-s, -**) m theorist; **t~retisch** [-'re:tɪʃ] adj theoretical; **~rie** [-'ri:] f theory
Thera- [tera] zW: **~peut** [-'pɔyt] (**-en, -en**) m therapist; **t~peutisch** [-'pɔytɪʃ] adj therapeutic; **~pie** [-'pi:] f therapy
Therm- zW: **~albad** [tɛr'ma:lba:t] nt thermal bath; thermal spa; **~odrucker** [tɛrmo-] m thermal printer; **~ometer** [tɛrmo'me:tər] (**-s, -**) nt thermometer; **~osflasche** ['tɛrmɔsflaʃə] ® f Thermos ® flask
These ['te:zə] f thesis
Thrombose [trɔm'bo:zə] f thrombosis
Thron [tro:n] (**-(e)s, -e**) m throne; **t~en** vi to sit enthroned; (fig) to sit in state; **~folge** f succession (to the throne); **~folger(in)** (**-s, -**) m(f) heir to the throne
Thunfisch ['tu:nfɪʃ] m tuna
Thüringen ['ty:rɪŋən] (**-s**) nt Thuringia
Thymian ['ty:mia:n] (**-s, -e**) m thyme
Tick [tɪk] (**-(e)s, -s**) m tic; (Eigenart) quirk;

(*Fimmel*) craze

ticken vi to tick

tief [ti:f] adj deep; (~*sinnig*) profound; (*Ausschnitt, Preis, Ton*) low; ~ **greifend** far-reaching; ~ **schürfend** profound; **T~ (-s, -s)** nt (MET) depression; **T~druck** m low pressure; **T~e** f depth; **T~ebene** f plain; **T~enschärfe** f (PHOT) depth of focus; **T~garage** f underground garage; ~**gekühlt** adj frozen; **T~kühlfach** nt deepfreeze compartment; **T~kühlkost** f (deep) frozen food; **T~kühltruhe** f deepfreeze, freezer; **T~punkt** m low point; (fig) low ebb; **T~schlag** m (BOXEN, fig) blow below the belt; **T~see** f deep sea; ~**sinnig** adj profound; melancholy; **T~stand** m low level; **T~stwert** m minimum od lowest value

Tier [ti:r] **(-(e)s, -e)** nt animal; ~**arzt** m vet(erinary surgeon); ~**garten** m zoo(logical gardens pl); ~**heim** nt cat/dog home; **t~isch** adj animal; (*auch fig*) brutish; (fig: *Ernst etc*) deadly; ~**kreis** m zodiac; ~**kunde** f zoology; **t~liebend** adj fond of animals; ~**park** m zoo; ~**quälerei** [-kvɛ:lə'raɪ] f cruelty to animals; ~**schutzverein** m society for the prevention of cruelty to animals

Tiger(in) ['ti:gər(ɪn)] **(-s, -)** m(f) tiger(-gress)

tilgen ['tɪlɡən] vt to erase; (*Sünden*) to expiate; (*Schulden*) to pay off

Tinte ['tɪntə] f ink

Tintenfisch m cuttlefish

Tipp ▲ [tɪp] m tip; **t~en** vt, vi to tap, to touch; (umg: *schreiben*) to type; (im *Lotto etc*) to bet (on); **auf jdn t~en** (umg: *raten*) to tip sb, to put one's money on sb (Brit)

Tipp- ['tɪp] zW: ~**fehler** (umg) m typing error; **t~topp** (umg) adj tip-top; ~**zettel** m (pools) coupon

Tirol [ti'ro:l] nt the Tyrol; ~**er(in)** m(f) Tyrolean; **t~isch** adj Tyrolean

Tisch [tɪʃ] **(-(e)s, -e)** m table; **bei ~** at table; **vor/nach ~** before/after eating; **unter den ~ fallen** (fig) to be dropped; ~**decke** f tablecloth; ~**ler (-s, -)** m carpenter, joiner; ~**le'rei** f joiner's workshop; (*Arbeit*)

carpentry, joinery; **t~lern** vi to do carpentry etc; ~**rede** f after-dinner speech; ~**tennis** nt table tennis; ~**tuch** nt tablecloth

Titel ['ti:tal] **(-s, -)** m title; ~**bild** nt cover (picture); (*von Buch*) frontispiece; ~**rolle** f title role; ~**seite** f cover; (*Buchtitelseite*) title page; ~**verteidiger** m defending champion, title holder

Toast [to:st] **(-(e)s, -s** od **-e)** m toast; ~**brot** nt bread for toasting; ~**er (-s, -)** m toaster

tob- ['to:b] zW: ~**en** vi to rage; (*Kinder*) to romp about; ~**süchtig** adj maniacal

Tochter ['tɔxtər] **(-, ⁿ)** f daughter; ~**gesellschaft** f subsidiary (company)

Tod [to:t] **(-(e)s, -e)** m death; **t~ernst** adj deadly serious ♦ adv in dead earnest

Todes- ['to:dəs] zW: ~**angst** [-aŋst] f mortal fear; ~**anzeige** f obituary (notice); ~**fall** m death; ~**strafe** f death penalty; ~**ursache** f cause of death; ~**urteil** nt death sentence; ~**verachtung** f utter disgust

todkrank adj dangerously ill

tödlich ['tø:tlɪç] adj deadly, fatal

tod- zW: ~**müde** adj dead tired; ~**schick** (umg) adj smart, classy; ~**sicher** (umg) adj absolutely od dead certain; **T~sünde** f deadly sin

Toilette [toa'lɛtə] f toilet, lavatory; (*Frisiertisch*) dressing table

Toiletten- zW: ~**artikel** pl toiletries, toilet articles; ~**papier** nt toilet paper; ~**tisch** m dressing table

toi, toi, toi ['tɔy'tɔy'tɔy] excl touch wood

tolerant [tole'rant] adj tolerant

Toleranz [tole'rants] f tolerance

tolerieren [tole'ri:rən] vt to tolerate

toll [tɔl] adj mad; (*Treiben*) wild; (umg) terrific; ~**en** vi to romp; **T~kirsche** f deadly nightshade; ~**kühn** adj daring; **T~wut** f rabies

Tomate [to'ma:tə] f tomato; ~**nmark** nt tomato purée

Ton¹ [to:n] **(-(e)s, -e)** m (*Erde*) clay

Ton² [to:n] **(-(e)s, ⁿe)** m (*Laut*) sound; (MUS) note; (*Redeweise*) tone; (*Farbton, Nuance*) shade; (*Betonung*) stress;

t~angebend *adj* leading; ~art *f* (musical) key; ~band *nt* tape; ~bandgerät *nt* tape recorder

tönen ['tø:nən] *vi* to sound ♦ *vt* to shade; (*Haare*) to tint

tönern ['tø:nərn] *adj* clay

Ton- *zW:* ~fall *m* intonation; ~film *m* sound film; ~leiter *f* (*MUS*) scale; t~los *adj* soundless

Tonne ['tɔnə] *f* barrel; (*Maß*) ton

Ton- *zW:* ~taube *f* clay pigeon; ~waren *pl* pottery *sg*, earthenware *sg*

Topf [tɔpf] (-(e)s, ⁿe) *m* pot; ~blume *f* pot plant

Töpfer ['tœpfər] (-s, -) *m* potter; ~ei [-'raɪ] *f* piece of pottery; potter's workshop; ~scheibe *f* potter's wheel

topografisch ▲ [topo'gra:fɪʃ] *adj* topographic

Tor¹ [to:r] (-en, -en) *m* fool

Tor² [to:r] (-(e)s, -e) *nt* gate; (*SPORT*) goal; ~bogen *m* archway

Torf [tɔrf] (-(e)s) *m* peat

Torheit *f* foolishness; foolish deed

töricht ['tø:rɪçt] *adj* foolish

torkeln ['tɔrkəln] *vi* to stagger, to reel

Torte ['tɔrtə] *f* cake; (*Obsttorte*) flan, tart

Tortur [tɔr'tu:r] *f* ordeal

Torwart ['to:rvart] (-(e)s, -e) *m* goalkeeper

tosen ['to:zən] *vi* to roar

tot [to:t] *adj* dead; ~ geboren stillborn; sich ~ stellen to pretend to be dead

total [to'ta:l] *adj* total; ~itär [totali'tɛ:r] *adj* totalitarian; T~schaden *m* (*AUT*) complete write-off

Tote(r) *f(m)* dead person

töten ['tø:tən] *vt, vi* to kill

Toten- *zW:* ~bett *nt* death bed; t~-blass ▲ *adj* deathly pale, white as a sheet; ~kopf *m* skull; ~schein *m* death certificate; ~stille *f* deathly silence

tot- *zW:* ~fahren (*unreg*) *vt* to run over; ~geboren △ *adj siehe* tot; ~lachen (*umg*) *vr* to laugh one's head off

Toto ['to:to] (-s, -s) *m od nt* pools *pl*; ~schein *m* pools coupon

tot- *zW:* T~schlag *m* manslaughter;

~schlagen (*unreg*) *vt* (*auch fig*) to kill; ~schweigen (*unreg*) *vt* to hush up; ~stellen △ *vr siehe* tot

Tötung ['tø:tʊŋ] *f* killing

Toupet [tu'pe:] (-s, -s) *nt* toupee

toupieren [tu'pi:rən] *vt* to backcomb

Tour [tu:r] (-, -en) *f* tour, trip; (*Umdrehung*) revolution; (*Verhaltensart*) way; in einer ~ incessantly; ~enzähler *m* rev counter; ~ismus [tu'rɪsmʊs] *m* tourism; ~ist [tu'rɪst] *m* tourist; ~istenklasse *f* tourist class; ~nee [tʊr'ne:] (-, -n) *f* (*THEAT etc*) tour; auf ~nee gehen to go on tour

Trab [tra:p] (-(e)s) *m* trot

Trabantenstadt *f* satellite town

traben ['tra:bən] *vi* to trot

Tracht [traxt] (-, -en) *f* (*Kleidung*) costume, dress; eine ~ Prügel a sound thrashing; t~en *vi*: t~en (nach) to strive (for); jdm nach dem Leben t~en to seek to kill sb; danach t~en, etw zu tun to strive *od* endeavour to do sth

trächtig ['trɛçtɪç] *adj* (*Tier*) pregnant

Tradition [traditsi'o:n] *f* tradition; t~ell [-'nɛl] *adj* traditional

traf *etc* [tra:f] *vb siehe* treffen

Tragbahre *f* stretcher

tragbar *adj* (*Gerät*) portable; (*Kleidung*) wearable; (*erträglich*) bearable

träge ['trɛ:gə] *adj* sluggish, slow; (*PHYS*) inert

tragen ['tra:gən] (*unreg*) *vt* to carry; (*Kleidung, Brille*) to wear; (*Namen, Früchte*) to bear; (*erdulden*) to endure ♦ *vi* (*schwanger sein*) to be pregnant; (*Eis*) to hold; sich mit einem Gedanken ~ to have an idea in mind; zum T~ kommen to have an effect

Träger ['trɛ:gər] (-s, -) *m* carrier; wearer; bearer; (*Ordensträger*) holder; (*an Kleidung*) (shoulder) strap; (*Körperschaft etc*) sponsor

Tragetasche *f* carrier bag

Tragfläche *f* (*AVIAT*) wing

Tragflügelboot *nt* hydrofoil

Trägheit ['trɛ:khaɪt] *f* laziness; (*PHYS*) inertia

Tragik ['tra:gɪk] *f* tragedy; tragisch *adj* tragic

Tragödie [tra'gø:diə] *f* tragedy

Tragweite *f* range; (*fig*) scope

Spelling Reform: ▲ new spelling △ old spelling (to be phased out)

Train- [trɛːn] zW: **~er** (-s, -) m (SPORT) trainer, coach; (Fußball) manager; **t~ieren** [trɛˈniːrən] vt, vi to train, to coach; (Mensch) to train, to coach; (Übung) to practise; **~ing** (-s, -s) nt training; **~ingsanzug** m track suit

Traktor [ˈtraktɔr] m tractor; (von Drucker) tractor feed

trällern [ˈtrɛlɐn] vt, vi to trill, to sing

Tram [tram] (-, -s) f tram

trampeln [ˈtrampəln] vt, vi to trample, to stamp

trampen [ˈtrɛmpən] vi to hitch-hike

Tramper(in) [trɛmpər(ɪn)] (-s, -) m(f) hitch-hiker

Tran [traːn] (-(e)s, -e) m train oil, blubber

tranchieren [trãˈʃiːrən] vt to carve

Träne [ˈtrɛːnə] f tear; **t~n** vi to water; **~ngas** nt teargas

trank etc [traŋk] vb siehe **trinken**

tränken [ˈtrɛŋkən] vt (Tiere) to water

transchieren ▲ [tranˈʃiːrən] vt to carve

Trans- zW: **~formator** [transfɔrˈmaːtɔr] m transformer; **~istor** [tranˈzɪstɔr] m transistor; **~itverkehr** [tranˈziːtfɛrkeːr] m transit traffic; **~itvisum** nt transit visa; **t~parent** adj transparent; **~parent** (-(e)s, -e) nt (Bild) transparency; (Spruchband) banner; **~plantation** [transplantatsiˈoːn] f transplantation; (Hauttransplantation) graft(ing)

Transport [transˈpɔrt] (-(e)s, -e) m transport; **t~ieren** [transpɔrˈtiːrən] vt to transport; **~kosten** pl transport charges, carriage sg; **~mittel** nt means sg of transportation; **~unternehmen** nt carrier

Traube [ˈtraubə] f grape; bunch (of grapes); **~nzucker** m glucose

trauen [ˈtrauən] vi: **jdm/etw ~** to trust sb/ sth ♦ vr to dare ♦ vt to marry

Trauer [ˈtrauɐr] (-) f sorrow; (für Verstorbenen) mourning; **~fall** m death, bereavement; **~feier** f funeral service; **~kleidung** f mourning; **t~n** vi to mourn; **um jdn t~n** to mourn (for) sb; **~rand** m black border; **~spiel** nt tragedy

traulich [ˈtraulɪç] adj cosy, intimate

Traum [traum] (-(e)s, Träume) m dream

Trauma (-s, -men) nt trauma

träum- [ˈtrɔym] zW: **~en** vt, vi to dream; **T~er** (-s, -) m dreamer; **T~erei** f dreaming; **~erisch** adj dreamy

traumhaft adj dreamlike; (fig) wonderful

traurig [ˈtraurɪç] adj sad; **T~keit** f sadness

Trau- [ˈtrau] zW: **~ring** m wedding ring; **~schein** m marriage certificate; **~ung** f wedding ceremony; **~zeuge** m witness (to a marriage); **~zeugin** f witness (to a marriage)

treffen [ˈtrɛfən] (unreg) vt to strike, to hit; (Bemerkung) to hurt; (begegnen) to meet; (Entscheidung etc) to make; (Maßnahmen) to take ♦ vi to hit ♦ vr to meet; **er hat es gut getroffen** he did well; **~ auf** +akk to come across, to meet with; **es traf sich, dass ...** it so happened that ...; **es trifft sich gut** it's convenient; **wie es so trifft** as these things happen; **T~** (-s, -) nt meeting; **~d** adj pertinent, apposite

Treffer (-s, -) m hit; (Tor) goal; (Los) winner

Treffpunkt m meeting place

Treib- [ˈtraib] zW: **~eis** nt drift ice; **t~en** (unreg) vt to drive; (Studien etc) to pursue; (Sport) to do, to go in for ♦ vi (Schiff etc) to drift; (Pflanzen) to sprout; (KOCH: aufgehen) to rise; (Tee, Kaffee) to be diuretic; **~haus** nt greenhouse; **~hauseffekt** m greenhouse effect; **~hausgas** nt greenhouse gas; **~stoff** m fuel

trenn- [trɛn] zW: **~bar** adj separable; **~en** vt to separate; (teilen) to divide ♦ vr to separate; **sich ~en von** to part with; **T~ung** f separation; **T~wand** f partition (wall)

Trepp- [ˈtrɛp] zW: **t~ab** adv downstairs; **t~auf** adv upstairs; **~e** f stair(case); **~engeländer** nt banister; **~enhaus** nt staircase

Tresor [treˈzoːr] (-s, -e) m safe

Tretboot nt pedalo, pedal boat

treten [ˈtreːtən] (unreg) vi to step; (Tränen, Schweiß) to appear ♦ vt (mit Fußtritt) to kick; (niedertreten) to tread, to trample; **~ nach** to kick at; **~ in** +akk to step in(to); **in Verbindung ~** to get in contact; **in**

Erscheinung ~ to appear

treu [trɔy] *adj* faithful, true; **T~e** (-) *f* loyalty, faithfulness; **T~händer** (-s, -) *m* trustee; **T~handanstalt** *f* trustee organization; **T~handgesellschaft** *f* trust company; **~herzig** *adj* innocent; **~los** *adj* faithless

Treuhandanstalt

*The **Treuhandanstalt** was the organization set up in 1990 to take over the nationally-owned companies of the former **DDR**, break them down into smaller units and privatize them. It was based in Berlin and had nine branches. Many companies were closed down by the **Treuhandanstalt** because of their outdated equipment and inability to compete with Western firms which resulted in rising unemployment. Having completed its initial task, the **Treuhandanstalt** was closed down in 1995.*

Tribüne [tri'byːnə] *f* grandstand; (*Rednertribüne*) platform

Trichter ['trɪçtər] (-s, -) *m* funnel; (*in Boden*) crater

Trick [trɪk] (-s, -e *od* -s) *m* trick; **~film** *m* cartoon

Trieb [triːp] (-(e)s, -e) *m* urge, drive; (*Neigung*) inclination; (*an Baum etc*) shoot; **t~** *etc vb siehe* **treiben**; **~kraft** *f* (*fig*) drive; **~täter** *m* sex offender; **~werk** *nt* engine

triefen ['triːfən] *vi* to drip

triffst *etc* [trɪfst] *vb siehe* **treffen**

triftig ['trɪftɪç] *adj* good, convincing

Trikot [tri'koː] (-s, -s) *nt* vest; (*SPORT*) shirt

Trimester [tri'mɛstər] (-s, -) *nt* term

trimmen ['trɪmən] *vr* to do keep fit exercises

trink- ['trɪŋk] *zW:* **~bar** *adj* drinkable; **~en** (*unreg*) *vt, vi* to drink; **T~er** (-s, -) *m* drinker; **T~geld** *nt* tip; **T~halle** *f* refreshment kiosk; **T~wasser** *nt* drinking water

Tripper ['trɪpər] (-s, -) *m* gonorrhoea

Tritt [trɪt] (-(e)s, -e) *m* step; (*Fußtritt*) kick; **~brett** *nt* (*EISENB*) step; (*AUT*) running board

Triumph [tri'ʊmf] (-(e)s, -e) *m* triumph; **~bogen** *m* triumphal arch; **t~ieren** [triʊm'fiːrən] *vi* to triumph; (*jubeln*) to exult

trocken ['trɔkən] *adj* dry; **T~element** *nt* dry cell; **T~haube** *f* hair dryer; **T~heit** *f* dryness; **~legen** *vt* (*Sumpf*) to drain; (*Kind*) to put a clean nappy on; **T~milch** *f* dried milk; **T~rasur** *f* dry shave, electric shave

trocknen ['trɔknən] *vt, vi* to dry

Trödel ['trøːdəl] (-s) (*umg*) *m* junk; **~markt** *m* flea market; **t~n** (*umg*) *vi* to dawdle

Trommel ['trɔməl] (-, -n) *f* drum; **~fell** *nt* eardrum; **t~n** *vt, vi* to drum

Trompete [trɔm'peːtə] *f* trumpet; **~r** (-s, -) *m* trumpeter

Tropen ['troːpən] *pl* tropics; **~helm** *m* sun helmet

tröpfeln ['trœpfəln] *vi* to drop, to trickle

Tropfen ['trɔpfən] (-s, -) *m* drop; **t~** *vt, vi* to drip ♦ *vb unpers*: **es tropft** a few raindrops are falling; **t~weise** *adv* in drops

Tropfsteinhöhle *f* stalactite cave

tropisch ['troːpɪʃ] *adj* tropical

Trost [troːst] (-es) *m* consolation, comfort

trösten ['trøːstən] *vt* to console, to comfort

trost- *zW:* **~los** *adj* bleak; (*Verhältnisse*) wretched; **T~preis** *m* consolation prize; **~reich** *adj* comforting

Trott [trɔt] (-(e)s, -e) *m* trot; (*Routine*) routine; **~el** (-s, -) (*umg*) *m* fool, dope; **t~en** *vi* to trot

Trotz [trɔts] (-es) *m* pigheadedness; **etw aus ~ tun** to do sth just to show them; **jdm zum ~** in defiance of sb; **t~** *präp* (+*gen od dat*) in spite of sb; **t~dem** *adv* nevertheless, all the same ♦ *konj* although; **t~en** *vi* (+*dat*) to defy; (*der Kälte, Klima etc*) to withstand; (*der Gefahr*) to brave; (*t~ig sein*) to be awkward; **t~ig** *adj* defiant, pig-headed; **~kopf** *m* obstinate child

trüb [tryːp] *adj* dull; (*Flüssigkeit, Glas*) cloudy; (*fig*) gloomy

Trubel ['truːbəl] (-s) *m* hurly-burly

trüb- *zW:* **~en** ['tryːbən] *vt* to cloud ♦ *vr* to become clouded; **T~heit** *f* dullness; cloudiness; gloom; **T~sal** (-, -e) *f* distress; **~selig** *adj* sad, melancholy; **T~sinn** *m* depression; ~sinnig *adj* depressed, gloomy

Trüffel ['trʏfəl] (-, -n) *f* truffle

trug *etc* ['tru:k] *vb siehe* **tragen**

trügen ['try:gən] (*unreg*) *vt* to deceive ♦ *vi* to be deceptive

trügerisch *adj* deceptive

Trugschluss ▲ ['tru:gʃlʊs] *m* false conclusion

Truhe ['tru:ə] *f* chest

Trümmer ['trʏmər] *pl* wreckage *sg*; (*Bautrümmer*) ruins; ~haufen *m* heap of rubble

Trumpf [trʊmpf] (-(e)s, ᵉe) *m* (*auch fig*) trump; t~en *vt*, *vi* to trump

Trunk [trʊŋk] (-(e)s, ᵉe) *m* drink; t~en *adj* intoxicated; ~enheit *f* intoxication; ~enheit am Steuer drunken driving; ~sucht *f* alcoholism

Trupp [trʊp] (-s, -s) *m* troop; ~e *f* troop; (*Waffengattung*) force; (*Schauspieltruppe*) troupe; ~en *pl* (*MIL*) troops; ~enübungsplatz *m* training area

Truthahn ['tru:tha:n] *m* turkey

Tschech- ['tʃɛç] *zW:* ~e *m* Czech; ~ien (-s) *nt* the Czech Republic; ~in *f* Czech; t~isch *adj* Czech; ~oslowakei [-oslova'kaɪ] *f:* **die ~oslowakei** Czechoslovakia; t~oslowakisch [-oslo'va:kɪʃ] *adj* Czechoslovak(ian)

tschüs(s) [tʃʏs] *excl* cheerio

T-Shirt ['ti:ʃə:t] *nt* T-shirt

Tube ['tu:bə] *f* tube

Tuberkulose [tuberku'lo:zə] *f* tuberculosis

Tuch [tu:x] (-(e)s, ᵉer) *nt* cloth; (*Halstuch*) scarf; (*Kopftuch*) headscarf; (*Handtuch*) towel

tüchtig ['tʏçtɪç] *adj* efficient, (cap)able; (*umg*: *kräftig*) good, sound; **T~keit** *f* efficiency, ability

Tücke ['tʏkə] *f* (*Arglist*) malice; (*Trick*) trick; (*Schwierigkeit*) difficulty, problem

tückisch ['tʏkɪʃ] *adj* treacherous; (*böswillig*) malicious

Tugend ['tu:gənt] (-, -en) *f* virtue; t~haft *adj* virtuous

Tülle *f* spout

Tulpe ['tʊlpə] *f* tulip

Tumor ['tu:mɔr] (-s, -e) *m* tumour

Tümpel ['tʏmpəl] (-s, -) *m* pool, pond

Tumult [tu'mʊlt] (-(e)s, -e) *m* tumult

tun [tu:n] (*unreg*) *vt* (*machen*) to do; (*legen*) to put ♦ *vi* to act ♦ *vr:* **es tut sich etwas/ viel** something/a lot is happening; **jdm etw ~** (*antun*) to do sth to sb; **etw tut es auch** sth will do; **das tut nichts** that doesn't matter; **das tut nichts zur Sache** that's neither here nor there; **so ~ als ob** to act as if

tünchen ['tʏnçən] *vt* to whitewash

Tunfisch ▲ ['tu:nfɪʃ] *m* = **Thunfisch**

Tunke ['tʊŋkə] *f* sauce; t~n *vt* to dip, to dunk

tunlichst ['tu:nlɪçst] *adv* if at all possible; ~ **bald** as soon as possible

Tunnel ['tʊnəl] (-s, -s *od* -) *m* tunnel

Tupfen ['tʊpfən] (-s, -) *m* dot, spot; t~ *vt*, *vi* to dab; (*mit Farbe*) to dot

Tür [ty:r] (-, -en) *f* door

Turbine [tʊr'bi:nə] *f* turbine

Türk- [tʏrk] *zW:* ~e *m* Turk; ~ei [tʏr'kaɪ] *f:* **die ~ei** Turkey; ~in *f* Turk

Türkis [tʏr'ki:s] (-es, -e) *m* turquoise; t~ *adj* turquoise

türkisch ['tʏrkɪʃ] *adj* Turkish

Türklinke *f* doorknob, door handle

Turm [tʊrm] (-(e)s, ᵉe) *m* tower; (*Kirchturm*) steeple; (*Sprungturm*) diving platform; (*SCHACH*) castle, rook

türmen ['tʏrmən] *vr* to tower up ♦ *vt* to heap up ♦ *vi* (*umg*) to scarper, to bolt

Turn- ['tʊrn] *zW:* t~en *vi* to do gymnastic exercises ♦ *vt* to perform; ~en (-s) *nt* gymnastics; (*SCH*) physical education, P.E.; ~er(in) (-s, -) *m(f)* gymnast; ~halle *f* gym(nasium); ~hose *f* gym shorts *pl*

Turnier [tʊr'ni:r] (-s, -e) *nt* tournament

Turn- *zW:* ~schuh *m* gym shoe; ~verein *m* gymnastics club; ~zeug *nt* gym things *pl*

Tusche ['tʊʃə] *f* Indian ink

tuscheln ['tʊʃəln] *vt*, *vi* to whisper

Tuschkasten *m* paintbox

Tüte ['ty:tə] *f* bag

tuten ['tu:tən] *vi* (*AUT*) to hoot (*BRIT*), to honk (*US*)

TÜV [tʏf] **(-s, -s)** *m abk* (= *Technischer Überwachungs-Verein*) ≈ MOT

Typ [ty:p] **(-s, -en)** *m* type; **~e** *f* (*TYP*) type

Typhus ['ty:fʊs] **(-)** *m* typhoid (fever)

typisch ['ty:pɪʃ] *adj:* **~ (für)** typical (of)

Tyrann [ty'ran] **(-en, -en)** *m* tyrant; **~ei** [-'naɪ] *f* tyranny; **t~isch** *adj* tyrannical; **t~i'sieren** *vt* to tyrannize

U, u

u. a. *abk* = **unter anderem**

U-Bahn ['u:ba:n] *f* underground, tube

übel ['y:bəl] *adj* bad; (*moralisch*) bad, wicked; **jdm ist ~** sb feels sick; **~ gelaunt** bad-tempered; **jdm eine Bemerkung etc ~ nehmen** to be offended at sb's remark *etc*; **Ü~ (-s, -)** *nt* evil; (*Krankheit*) disease; **Ü~keit** *f* nausea

üben ['y:bən] *vt, vi* to exercise, to practise

SCHLÜSSELWORT

über ['y:bər] *präp +dat* 1 (*räumlich*) over, above; **zwei Grad über null** two degrees above zero

2 (*zeitlich*) over; **über der Arbeit einschlafen** to fall asleep over one's work
♦ *präp +akk* 1 (*räumlich*) over; (*hoch über auch*) above; (*quer über auch*) across
2 (*zeitlich*) over; **über Weihnachten** over Christmas; **über kurz oder lang** sooner or later

3 (*mit Zahlen*): **Kinder über 12 Jahren** children over *od* above 12 years of age; **ein Scheck über 200 Mark** a cheque for 200 marks

4 (*auf dem Wege*) via; **nach Köln über Aachen** to Cologne via Aachen; **ich habe es über die Auskunft erfahren** I found out from information

5 (*betreffend*) about; **ein Buch über ...** a book about *od* on ...; **über jdn/etw lachen** to laugh at sb/sth

6: **Macht über jdn haben** to have power over sb; **sie liebt ihn über alles** she loves him more than everything

♦ *adv* over; **über und über** over and over; **den ganzen Tag über** all day long; **jdm in etw** *dat* **über sein** to be superior to sb in sth

überall [y:bər'al] *adv* everywhere; **~'hin** *adv* everywhere

überanstrengen [y:bər'|anʃtrɛŋən] *vt insep* to overexert ♦ *vr* insep to overexert o.s.

überarbeiten [y:bər'|arbaɪtən] *vt insep* to revise, to rework ♦ *vr insep* to overwork (o.s.)

überaus ['y:bər|aus] *adv* exceedingly

überbelichten ['y:bərbəlɪçtən] *vt* (*PHOT*) to overexpose

über'bieten (*unreg*) *vt insep* to outbid; (*übertreffen*) to surpass; (*Rekord*) to break

Überbleibsel ['y:bərblaɪpsəl] **(-s, -)** *nt* residue, remainder

Überblick ['y:bərblɪk] *m* view; (*fig: Darstellung*) survey, overview; (*Fähigkeit*): **~ (über +akk)** grasp (of), overall view (of); **ü~en** [-'blɪkən] *vt insep* to survey

überbring- [y:bər'brɪŋ] *zW:* **~en** (*unreg*) *vt insep* to deliver, to hand over; **Ü~er (-s, -)** *m* bearer

überbrücken [y:bər'brʏkən] *vt insep* to bridge (over)

überbuchen ['y:bərbu:xən] *vt insep* to overbook

über'dauern *vt insep* to outlast

über'denken (*unreg*) *vt insep* to think over

überdies [y:bər'di:s] *adv* besides

überdimensional ['y:bərdimenziona:l] *adj* oversize

Überdruss ▲ ['y:bərdrʊs] **(-es)** *m* weariness; **bis zum ~** ad nauseam

überdurchschnittlich ['y:bərdʊrçʃnɪtlɪç] *adj* above-average ♦ *adv* exceptionally

übereifrig ['y:bər|aɪfrɪç] *adj* over-keen

übereilt [y:bər'|aɪlt] *adj* (over)hasty, premature

überein- [y:bər'|aɪn] *zW:* **~ander** [y:bər|aɪ'|nandər] *adv* one upon the other; (*sprechen*) about each other; **~kommen** (*unreg*) *vi* to agree; **Ü~kunft (-, -künfte)** *f* agreement; **~stimmen** *vi* to agree;

Ü~stimmung *f* agreement

überempfindlich ['y:bər|ɛmpfɪntlɪç] *adj* hypersensitive

überfahren [y:bər'fa:rən] (*unreg*) *vt insep* (*AUT*) to run over; (*fig*) to walk all over

Überfahrt ['y:bərfa:rt] *f* crossing

Überfall ['y:bərfal] *m* (*Banküberfall, MIL*) raid; (*auf jdn*) assault; ü~en [-'falən] (*unreg*) *vt insep* to attack; (*Bank*) to raid; (*besuchen*) to drop in on, to descend on

überfällig ['y:bərfɛlɪç] *adj* overdue

überfliegen (*unreg*) *vt insep* to fly over, to overfly; (*Buch*) to skim through

Überfluss ▲ ['y:bərflʊs] *m:* ~ (**an** +*dat*) (super)abundance (of), excess (of)

überflüssig ['y:bərflʏsɪç] *adj* superfluous

überfordern *vt insep* (*Leiche etc*) to demand too much of; (*Kräfte etc*) to overtax

überführen *vt insep* (*Leiche etc*) to transport; (*Täter*) to have convicted

Überführung *f* transport; conviction; (*Brücke*) bridge, overpass

überfüllt ['y:bərfʏlt] *adj* (*Schulen, Straßen*) overcrowded; (*Kurs*) oversubscribed

Übergabe ['y:bərga:bə] *f* handing over; (*MIL*) surrender

Übergang ['y:bərgaŋ] *m* crossing; (*Wandel, Überleitung*) transition

Übergangs- *zW:* ~lösung *f* provisional solution, stopgap; ~zeit *f* transitional period

übergeben (*unreg*) *vt insep* to hand over; (*MIL*) to surrender ♦ *vr insep* to be sick

übergehen ['y:bərge:ən] (*unreg*) *vi* (*Besitz*) to pass; (*zum Feind etc*) to go over, to defect; ~ **in** +*akk* to turn into; **über'gehen** (*unreg*) *vt insep* to pass over, to omit

Übergewicht ['y:bərgəvɪçt] *nt* excess weight; (*fig*) preponderance

überglücklich ['y:bərglʏklɪç] *adj* overjoyed

Übergröße ['y:bərgrø:sə] *f* oversize

überhaupt [y:bər'haupt] *adv* at all; (*im Allgemeinen*) in general; (*besonders*) especially; ~ **nicht/keine** not/none at all

überheblich [y:bər'he:plɪç] *adj* arrogant; Ü~keit *f* arrogance

über'holen *vt insep* to overtake; (*TECH*) to

overhaul

über'holt *adj* out-of-date, obsolete

Überholverbot [y:bər'ho:lfɛrbo:t] *nt* restriction on overtaking

über'hören *vt insep* not to hear; (*absichtlich*) to ignore

überirdisch ['y:bər|ɪrdɪʃ] *adj* supernatural, unearthly

über'laden (*unreg*) *vt insep* to overload ♦ *adj* (*fig*) cluttered

über'lassen (*unreg*) *vt insep:* **jdm etw** ~ to leave sth to sb ♦ *vr insep:* **sich einer Sache** *dat* ~ to give o.s. over to sth

über'lasten *vt insep* to overload; (*Mensch*) to overtax

überlaufen ['y:bərlaufən] (*unreg*) *vi* (*Flüssigkeit*) to flow over; (*zum Feind etc*) to go over, to defect; ~ **sein** to be inundated *od* besieged; **über'laufen** (*unreg*) *vt insep* (*Schauer etc*) to come over

über'leben *vt insep* to survive; **Über'lebende(r)** *f(m)* survivor

über'legen *vt insep* to consider ♦ *adj* superior; **ich muss es mir** ~ I'll have to think about it; **Über'legenheit** *f* superiority

Über'legung *f* consideration, deliberation

über'liefern *vt insep* to hand down, to transmit

Überlieferung *f* tradition

überlisten [y:bər'lɪstən] *vt insep* to outwit

überm ['y:bərm] = **über dem**

Übermacht ['y:bərmaxt] *f* superior force, superiority; **übermächtig** ['y:bərmɛçtɪç] *adj* superior (in strength); (*Gefühl etc*) overwhelming

übermäßig ['y:bərmɛːsɪç] *adj* excessive

Übermensch ['y:bərmɛnʃ] *m* superman; ü~lich *adj* superhuman

übermitteln [y:bər'mɪtəln] *vt insep* to convey

übermorgen ['y:bərmɔrgən] *adv* the day after tomorrow

Übermüdung [y:bər'my:dʊŋ] *f* fatigue, overtiredness

Übermut ['y:bərmu:t] *m* exuberance

übermütig ['y:bərmy:tɪç] *adj* exuberant,

high-spirited; **~ werden** to get overconfident

übernächste(r, s) ['y:bərnɛːçstə(r, s)] *adj* (*Jahr*) next but one

übernacht- [y:bər'naxt] *zW:* **~en** *vi insep:* **(bei jdm) ~en** to spend the night (at sb's place); **Ü~ung** *f* overnight stay; **Ü~ung mit Frühstück** bed and breakfast; **Ü~ungsmöglichkeit** *f* overnight accommodation *no pl*

Übernahme ['y:bərnaːmə] *f* taking over *od* on, acceptance

über'nehmen (*unreg*) *vt insep* to take on, to accept; (*Amt, Geschäft*) to take over ♦ *vr insep* to take on too much

über'prüfen *vt insep* to examine, to check

überqueren [y:bər'kveːrən] *vt insep* to cross

überragen [y:bər'raːgən] *vt insep* to tower above; (*fig*) to surpass

überraschen [y:bər'raʃən] *vt insep* to surprise

Überraschung *f* surprise

überreden [y:bər're:dən] *vt insep* to persuade

überreichen [y:bər'raiçən] *vt insep* to present, to hand over

'Überrest *m* remains, remnants

überrumpeln [y:bər'rumpəln] *vt insep* to take by surprise

überrunden [y:bər'rundən] *vt insep* to lap

übers ['y:bərs] = **über das**

Überschall- [y:bər'ʃal] *zW:* **~flugzeug** *nt* supersonic jet; **~geschwindigkeit** *f* supersonic speed

über'schätzen *vt insep* to overestimate

'überschäumen *vi* (*Bier*) to foam over, bubble over; (*Temperament*) to boil over

Überschlag ['y:bərʃla:k] *m* (*FIN*) estimate; (*SPORT*) somersault; **ü~en** [-'ʃla:gən] (*unreg*) *vt insep* (*berechnen*) to estimate; (*auslassen: Seite*) to omit ♦ *vr insep* to somersault; (*Stimme*) to crack; (*AVIAT*) to loop the loop; **'überschlagen** (*unreg*) *vt* (*Beine*) to cross ♦ *vi* (*Wellen*) to break; (*Funken*) to flash

überschnappen ['y:bərʃnapən] *vi* (*Stimme*) to crack; (*umg: Mensch*) to flip one's lid

über'schneiden (*unreg*) *vr insep* (*auch fig*) to overlap; (*Linien*) to intersect

über'schreiben (*unreg*) *vt insep* to provide with a heading; **jdm etw ~** to transfer *od* make over sth to sb

über'schreiten (*unreg*) *vt insep* to cross over; (*fig*) to exceed; (*verletzen*) to transgress

Überschrift ['y:bərʃrɪft] *f* heading, title

Überschuss ▲ ['y:bərʃʊs] *m:* **~ (an +dat)** surplus (of); **überschüssig** ['y:bərʃʏsɪç] *adj* surplus, excess

über'schütten *vt insep:* **jdn/etw mit etw ~** to pour sth over sb/sth; **jdn mit etw ~** (*fig*) to shower sb with sth

überschwänglich ▲ ['y:bərʃvɛŋlɪç] *adj* effusive

überschwemmen [y:bər'ʃvɛmən] *vt insep* to flood

Überschwemmung *f* flood

Übersee ['y:bərze:] *f:* **nach/in ~** overseas; **ü~isch** *adj* overseas

über'sehen (*unreg*) *vt insep* to look (out) over; (*fig: Folgen*) to see, to get an overall view of; (: *nicht beachten*) to overlook

über'senden (*unreg*) *vt insep* to send, to forward

übersetz- *zW:* **~en** [y:bər'zɛtsən] *vt insep* to translate; **'übersetzen** *vi* to cross; **Ü~er(in)** [-'zɛtsər(ɪn)] (**-s, -**) *m(f)* translator; **Ü~ung** [-'zɛtsʊŋ] *f* translation; (*TECH*) gear ratio

Übersicht ['y:bərzɪçt] *f* overall view; (*Darstellung*) survey; **ü~lich** *adj* clear; (*Gelände*) open; **~lichkeit** *f* clarity, lucidity

übersiedeln [y:bər'zi:dəln] *vi sep* to move; **über'siedeln** *vi* to move

über'spannt *adj* eccentric; (*Idee*) wild, crazy

überspitzt [y:bər'ʃpɪtst] *adj* exaggerated

über'springen (*unreg*) *vt insep* to jump over; (*fig*) to skip

überstehen [y:bər'ʃte:ən] (*unreg*) *vt insep* to overcome, to get over; (*Winter etc*) to survive, to get through; **'überstehen** (*unreg*) *vi* to project

über'steigen (*unreg*) *vt insep* to climb over; (*fig*) to exceed

Spelling Reform: ▲ *new spelling* △ *old spelling (to be phased out)*

über'stimmen vt insep to outvote

Überstunden ['y:bərʃtʊndən] pl overtime sg

über'stürzen vt insep to rush ♦ vr insep to follow (one another) in rapid succession

überstürzt adj (over)hasty

Übertrag ['y:bərtra:k] (-(e)s, -träge) m (COMM) amount brought forward; **ü~bar** [-'tra:kba:r] adj transferable; (MED) infectious; **ü~en** [-'tra:gən] (unreg) vt insep to transfer; (RADIO) to broadcast; (übersetzen) to render; (Krankheit) to transmit ♦ vr insep to spread ♦ adj figurative; **ü~en auf** +akk to transfer to; **jdm etw ü~en** to assign sth to sb; **sich ü~en auf** +akk to spread to; **~ung** [-'tra:gʊŋ] f transfer(ence); (RADIO) broadcast; rendering; transmission

über'treffen (unreg) vt insep to surpass

über'treiben (unreg) vt insep to exaggerate; **Übertreibung** f exaggeration

übertreten [y:bər'tre:tən] (unreg) vt insep to cross; (Gebot etc) to break; **'übertreten** (unreg) vi (über Linie, Gebiet) to step (over); (SPORT) to overstep; (zu anderem Glauben) to be converted; **übertreten (in** +akk) (POL) to go over (to)

Über'tretung f violation, transgression

übertrieben [y:bər'tri:bən] adj exaggerated, excessive

übervölkert [y:bər'fœlkərt] adj overpopulated

übervoll ['y:bərfɔl] adj overfull

übervorteilen [y:bər'fɔrtaɪlən] vt insep to dupe, to cheat

über'wachen vt insep to supervise; (Verdächtigen) to keep under surveillance; **Überwachung** f supervision; surveillance

überwältigen [y:bər'vɛltɪgən] vt insep to overpower; **~d** adj overwhelming

überweisen [y:bər'vaɪzən] (unreg) vt insep to transfer

Überweisung f transfer; **~sauftrag** m (credit) transfer order

über'wiegen (unreg) vi insep to predominate; **~d** adj predominant

über'winden (unreg) vt insep to overcome ♦ vr insep to make an effort, to bring o.s. (to do sth)

Überwindung f effort, strength of mind

Überzahl ['y:bərtsa:l] f superiority, superior numbers pl; **in der ~ sein** to be numerically superior

überzählig ['y:bərtsɛ:lɪç] adj surplus

über'zeugen vt insep to convince; **~d** adj convincing

Überzeugung f conviction

überziehen ['y:bərtsi:ən] (unreg) vt to put on; **über'ziehen** (unreg) vt insep to cover; (Konto) to overdraw

Überziehungskredit m overdraft provision

Überzug ['y:bərtsu:k] m cover; (Belag) coating

üblich ['y:plɪç] adj usual

U-Boot ['u:bo:t] nt submarine

übrig ['y:brɪç] adj remaining; **für jdn etwas ~ haben** (umg) to be fond of sb; **die Ü~en** the others; **das Ü~e** the rest; **im Ü~en** besides; **~ bleiben** to remain, to be left (over); **~ lassen** to leave (over); **~ens** ['y:brɪgəns] adv besides; (nebenbei bemerkt) by the way

Übung ['y:bʊŋ] f practice; (Turnübung, Aufgabe etc) exercise; **~ macht den Meister** practice makes perfect

Ufer ['u:fər] (-s, -) nt bank; (Meeresufer) shore

Uhr [u:r] (-, -en) f clock; (Armbanduhr) watch; **wie viel ~ ist es?** what time is it?; **1 ~** 1 o'clock; **20 ~** 8 o'clock, 20.00 (twenty hundred) hours; **~(arm)band** nt watch strap; **~band** nt watch strap; **~macher** (-s, -) m watchmaker; **~werk** nt clockwork; works of a watch; **~zeiger** m hand; **~zeigersinn** m: **im ~zeigersinn** clockwise; **entgegen dem ~zeigersinn** anticlockwise; **~zeit** f time (of day)

Uhu ['u:hu] (-s, -s) m eagle owl

UKW [u:ka:'ve:] abk (= Ultrakurzwelle) VHF

ulkig ['ʊlkɪç] adj funny

Ulme ['ʊlmə] f elm

Ultimatum [ʊlti'ma:tʊm] (-s, Ultimaten) nt ultimatum

Ultra- ['ʊltra] zW: **~schall** m (PHYS) ultrasound; **u~violett** adj ultraviolet

m [ʊm] *präp +akk* 1 (*um herum*) (a)round;
um Weihnachten around Christmas; **er
schlug um sich** he hit about him
2 (*mit Zeitangabe*) at; **um acht (Uhr)** at
eight (o'clock)
3 (*mit Größenangabe*) by; **etw um 4 cm
kürzen** to shorten sth by 4 cm; **um 10%
teurer** 10% more expensive; **um vieles
besser** better by far; **um nichts besser**
not in the least bit better
4: **der Kampf um den Titel** the battle for
the title; **um Geld spielen** to play for
money; **Stunde um Stunde** hour after
hour; **Auge um Auge** an eye for an eye
♦ *präp +gen*: **um ... willen** for the sake of
...; **um Gottes willen** for goodness' *od*
(*stärker*) God's sake
♦ *konj*: **um zu** (in order) to ...; **zu klug,
um zu ...** too clever to ...; *siehe* **umso**
♦ *adv* 1 (*ungefähr*) about; **um (die) 30
Leute** about *od* around 30 people
2 (*vorbei*): **die 2 Stunden sind um** the two
hours are up

mändern ['ʊm|ɛndərn] *vt* to alter
mänderung *f* alteration
marbeiten ['ʊm|arbaɪtən] *vt* to remodel;
(*Buch etc*) to revise, to rework
marmen ['ʊm|armən] *vt insep* to embrace
mbau ['ʊmbaʊ] (**-(e)s, -e** *od* **-ten**) *m*
reconstruction, alteration(s); **u~en** *vt* to
rebuild, to reconstruct
mbilden ['ʊmbɪldən] *vt* to reorganize; (*POL:
Kabinett*) to reshuffle
mbinden ['ʊmbɪndən] (*unreg*) *vt* (*Krawatte
etc*) to put on
mblättern ['ʊmblɛtərn] *vt* to turn over
mblicken ['ʊmblɪkən] *vr* to look around
mbringen ['ʊmbrɪŋən] (*unreg*) *vt* to kill
mbuchen ['ʊmbuːxən] *vi* to change one's
reservation/flight ♦ *vt* to change
mdenken ['ʊmdɛŋkən] (*unreg*) *vi* to adjust
one's views
mdrehen ['ʊmdreːən] *vt* to turn (round);
(*Hals*) to wring ♦ *vr* to turn (round)

Um'**drehung** *f* revolution; rotation
umeinander [ʊm|aɪˈnandər] *adv* round one
another; (*füreinander*) for one another
umfahren ['ʊmfaːrən] (*unreg*) *vt* to run over;
um'**fahren** (*unreg*) *vt insep* to drive round;
to sail round
umfallen ['ʊmfalən] (*unreg*) *vi* to fall down
od over
Umfang ['ʊmfaŋ] *m* extent; (*von Buch*) size;
(*Reichweite*) range; (*Fläche*) area; (*MATH*)
circumference; **u~reich** *adj* extensive;
(*Buch etc*) voluminous
um'**fassen** *vt insep* to embrace; (*umgeben*)
to surround; (*enthalten*) to include;
um'**fassend** *adj* comprehensive, extensive
umformen ['ʊmfɔrmən] *vt* to transform
Umfrage ['ʊmfraːgə] *f* poll
umfüllen ['ʊmfʏlən] *vt* to transfer; (*Wein*) to
decant
umfunktionieren ['ʊmfʊŋktsioniːrən] *vt* to
convert, to transform
Umgang ['ʊmgaŋ] *m* company; (*mit jdm*)
dealings *pl*; (*Behandlung*) way of behaving
umgänglich ['ʊmgɛŋlɪç] *adj* sociable
Umgangs- *zW*: **~formen** *pl* manners;
~sprache *f* colloquial language
umgeben [ʊmˈgeːbən] (*unreg*) *vt insep* to
surround
Umgebung *f* surroundings *pl*; (*Milieu*)
environment; (*Personen*) people in one's
circle
umgehen ['ʊmgeːən] (*unreg*) *vi* to go
(a)round; **im Schlosse ~** to haunt the
castle; **mit jdm grob** *etc* **~** to treat sb
roughly *etc*; **mit Geld sparsam ~** to be
careful with one's money; um'**gehen** *vt
insep* to bypass; (*MIL*) to outflank; (*Gesetz
etc*) to circumvent; (*vermeiden*) to avoid;
'**umgehend** *adj* immediate
Um'**gehung** *f* bypassing; outflanking;
circumvention; avoidance; **~sstraße** *f*
bypass
umgekehrt ['ʊmgəkeːrt] *adj* reverse(d);
(*gegenteilig*) opposite ♦ *adv* the other way
around; **und ~** and vice versa
umgraben ['ʊmgraːbən] (*unreg*) *vt* to dig up
Umhang ['ʊmhaŋ] *m* wrap, cape

Spelling Reform: ▲ *new spelling* △ *old spelling (to be phased out)*

umhauen ['ʊmhaʊən] vt to fell; (fig) to bowl over

umher [ʊm'heːr] adv about, around; **~gehen** (unreg) vi to walk about; **~ziehen** (unreg) vi to wander from place to place

umhinkönnen [ʊm'hɪnkœnən] (unreg) vi: **ich kann nicht umhin, das zu tun** I can't help doing it

umhören ['ʊmhøːrən] vr to ask around

Umkehr ['ʊmkeːr] (-) f turning back; (Änderung) change; **u~en** vi to turn back ♦ vt to turn round, to reverse; (Tasche etc) to turn inside out; (Gefäß etc) to turn upside down

umkippen ['ʊmkɪpən] vt to tip over ♦ vi to overturn; (umg: Mensch) to keel over; (fig: Meinung ändern) to change one's mind

Umkleide- ['ʊmklaɪdə] zW: **~kabine** f (im Schwimmbad) (changing) cubicle; **~raum** m changing od dressing room

umkommen ['ʊmkɔmən] (unreg) vi to die, to perish; (Lebensmittel) to go bad

Umkreis ['ʊmkraɪs] m neighbourhood; **im ~ von** within a radius of

Umlage ['ʊmlaːgə] f share of the costs

Umlauf ['ʊmlaʊf] m (Geldumlauf) circulation; (von Gestirn) revolution; **~bahn** f orbit

Umlaut ['ʊmlaʊt] m umlaut

umlegen ['ʊmleːgən] vt to put on; (verlegen) to move, to shift; (Kosten) to share out; (umkippen) to tip over; (umg: töten) to bump off

umleiten ['ʊmlaɪtən] vt to divert

Umleitung f diversion

umliegend ['ʊmliːgənt] adj surrounding

um'randen vt insep to border, to edge

umrechnen ['ʊmreçnən] vt to convert

Umrechnung f conversion; **~skurs** m rate of exchange

um'reißen (unreg) vt insep to outline, to sketch

Umriss ▲ ['ʊmrɪs] m outline

umrühren ['ʊmryːrən] vt, vi to stir

ums [ʊms] = **um das**

Umsatz ['ʊmzats] m turnover; **~steuer** f sales tax

umschalten ['ʊmʃaltən] vt to switch

umschauen vr to look round

Umschlag ['ʊmʃlaːk] m cover; (Buchumschl auch) jacket; (MED) compress; (Briefumschlag) envelope; (Wechsel) chang (von Hose) turn-up; **u~en** [-gən] (unreg) vi to change; (NAUT) to capsize ♦ vt to knoc over; (Ärmel) to turn up; (Seite) to turn over; (Waren) to transfer; **~platz** m (COMM distribution centre

umschreiben ['ʊmʃraɪbən] (unreg) vt (neu schreiben) to rewrite; (übertragen) to transfer; **~ auf** +akk to transfer to; **um'schreiben** (unreg) vt insep to paraphrase; (abgrenzen) to define

umschulen ['ʊmʃuːlən] vt to retrain; (Kind to send to another school

Umschweife ['ʊmʃvaɪfə] pl: **ohne ~** witho beating about the bush, straight out

Umschwung ['ʊmʃvʊŋ] m change (around), revolution

umsehen ['ʊmzeːən] (unreg) vr to look around od about; (suchen): **sich ~ (nach)** look out (for)

umseitig ['ʊmzaɪtɪç] adv overleaf

umsichtig ['ʊmzɪçtɪç] adj cautious, pruden

umso ▲ ['ʊmzo] konj: **~ besser/schlimm** so much the better/worse

umsonst [ʊm'zɔnst] adv in vain; (gratis) fo nothing

umspringen ['ʊmʃprɪŋən] (unreg) vi to change; (Wind auch) to veer; **mit jdm ~** t treat sb badly

Umstand ['ʊmʃtant] m circumstance; **Umstände** pl (fig: Schwierigkeiten) fuss; **in anderen Umständen sein** to be pregnan **Umstände machen** to go to a lot of trouble; **unter Umständen** possibly

umständlich ['ʊmʃtɛntlɪç] adj (Methode) cumbersome, complicated; (Ausdrucksweis Erklärung) long-winded; (Mensch) ponderous

Umstandskleid nt maternity dress

Umstehende(n) ['ʊmʃteːəndə(n)] pl bystanders

umsteigen ['ʊmʃtaɪgən] (unreg) vi (EISENB) change

umstellen ['ʊmʃtɛlən] vt (an anderen Ort) t

change round, to rearrange; (*TECH*) to convert ♦ *vr* to adapt (o.s.); **sich auf etw** *akk* ~ to adapt to sth; **um'stellen** *vt insep* to surround

mstellung ['ʊmʃtɛlʊŋ] *f* change; (*Umgewöhnung*) adjustment; (*TECH*) conversion

mstimmen ['ʊmʃtɪmən] *vt* (*MUS*) to retune; **jdn** ~ to make sb change his mind

mstoßen ['ʊmʃtoːsən] (*unreg*) *vt* to overturn; (*Plan etc*) to change, to upset

mstritten [ʊm'ʃtrɪtn] *adj* disputed

msturz ['ʊmʃtʊrts] *m* overthrow

mstürzen ['ʊmʃtʏrtsən] *vt* (*umwerfen*) to overturn ♦ *vi* to collapse, to fall down; (*Wagen*) to overturn

mtausch ['ʊmtaʊʃ] *m* exchange; **u~en** *vt* to exchange

mverpackung ['ʊmfɛrpakʊŋ] *f* packaging

mwandeln ['ʊmvandəln] *vt* to change, to convert; (*ELEK*) to transform

mwechseln ['ʊmvɛksəln] *vt* to change

mweg ['ʊmveːk] *m* detour, roundabout way

mwelt ['ʊmvɛlt] *f* environment; **u~freundlich** *adj* not harmful to the environment, environment-friendly; **u~schädlich** *adj* ecologically harmful; **~schutz** *m* environmental protection; **~schützer** *m* environmentalist; **~verschmutzung** *f* environmental pollution

mwenden ['ʊmvɛndən] (*unreg*) *vt, vr* to turn (round)

mwerfen ['ʊmvɛrfən] (*unreg*) *vt* to upset, to overturn; (*fig: erschüttern*) to upset, to throw; **~d** (*umg*) *adj* fantastic

mziehen ['ʊmtsiːən] (*unreg*) *vt, vr* to change ♦ *vi* to move

mzug ['ʊmtsuːk] *m* procession; (*Wohnungsumzug*) move, removal

nab- ['ʊn|ap] *zW:* **~änderlich** *adj* irreversible, unalterable; **~hängig** *adj* independent; **U~hängigkeit** *f* independence; **~kömmlich** *adj* indispensable; **zur Zeit ~kömmlich** not free at the moment; **~lässig** *adj* incessant,

constant; **~sehbar** *adj* immeasurable; (*Folgen*) unforeseeable; (*Kosten*) incalculable; **~sichtlich** *adj* unintentional; **~'wendbar** *adj* inevitable

unachtsam ['ʊn|axtzaːm] *adj* careless; **U~keit** *f* carelessness

unan- ['ʊn|an] *zW:* **~'fechtbar** *adj* indisputable; **~gebracht** *adj* uncalled-for; **~gemessen** *adj* inadequate; **~genehm** *adj* unpleasant; **U~nehmlichkeit** *f* inconvenience; **U~nehmlichkeiten** *pl* (*Ärger*) trouble *sg*; **~sehnlich** *adj* unsightly; **~ständig** *adj* indecent, improper

unappetitlich ['ʊn|apeti:tlɪç] *adj* unsavoury

Unart ['ʊn|aːrt] *f* bad manners *pl*; (*Angewohnheit*) bad habit; **u~ig** *adj* naughty, badly behaved

unauf- ['ʊn|aʊf] *zW:* **~fällig** *adj* unobtrusive; (*Kleidung*) inconspicuous; **~'findbar** *adj* not to be found; **~gefordert** *adj* unasked ♦ *adv* spontaneously; **~haltsam** *adj* irresistible; **~'hörlich** *adj* incessant, continuous; **~merksam** *adj* inattentive; **~richtig** *adj* insincere

unaus- ['ʊn|aʊs] *zW:* **~geglichen** *adj* unbalanced; **~'sprechlich** *adj* inexpressible; **~'stehlich** *adj* intolerable

unbarmherzig ['ʊnbarmhɛrtsɪç] *adj* pitiless, merciless

unbeabsichtigt ['ʊnbə|apzɪçtɪçt] *adj* unintentional

unbeachtet ['ʊnbə|axtət] *adj* unnoticed, ignored

unbedenklich ['ʊnbədɛŋklɪç] *adj* (*Plan*) unobjectionable

unbedeutend ['ʊnbədɔʏtənt] *adj* insignificant, unimportant; (*Fehler*) slight

unbedingt ['ʊnbədɪŋt] *adj* unconditional ♦ *adv* absolutely; **musst du ~ gehen?** do you really have to go?

unbefangen ['ʊnbəfaŋən] *adj* impartial, unprejudiced; (*ohne Hemmungen*) uninhibited; **U~heit** *f* impartiality; uninhibitedness

unbefriedigend ['ʊnbəfriːdɪgənd] *adj* unsatisfactory

unbefriedigt ['ʊnbəfriːdɪçt] *adj* unsatisfied,

Spelling Reform: ▲ *new spelling* △ *old spelling (to be phased out)*

dissatisfied

unbefugt ['ʊnbəfuːkt] *adj* unauthorized

unbegreiflich [ʊnbə'graɪflɪç] *adj* inconceivable

unbegrenzt ['ʊnbəgrɛntst] *adj* unlimited

unbegründet ['ʊnbəgrʏndət] *adj* unfounded

Unbehagen ['ʊnbəhaːgən] *nt* discomfort; **unbehaglich** ['ʊnbəhaːklɪç] *adj* uncomfortable; (*Gefühl*) uneasy

unbeholfen ['ʊnbəhɔlfən] *adj* awkward, clumsy

unbekannt ['ʊnbəkant] *adj* unknown

unbekümmert ['ʊnbəkʏmərt] *adj* unconcerned

unbeliebt ['ʊnbəliːpt] *adj* unpopular

unbequem ['ʊnbəkveːm] *adj* (*Stuhl*) uncomfortable; (*Mensch*) bothersome; (*Regelung*) inconvenient

unberechenbar [ʊnbə'rɛçənbaːr] *adj* incalculable; (*Mensch, Verhalten*) unpredictable

unberechtigt ['ʊnbərɛçtɪçt] *adj* unjustified; (*nicht erlaubt*) unauthorized

unberührt ['ʊnbərʏːrt] *adj* untouched, intact; **sie ist noch ~** she is still a virgin

unbescheiden ['ʊnbəʃaɪdən] *adj* presumptuous

unbeschreiblich [ʊnbə'ʃraɪplɪç] *adj* indescribable

unbeständig ['ʊnbəʃtɛndɪç] *adj* (*Mensch*) inconstant; (*Wetter*) unsettled; (*Lage*) unstable

unbestechlich [ʊnbə'ʃtɛçlɪç] *adj* incorruptible

unbestimmt ['ʊnbəʃtɪmt] *adj* indefinite; (*Zukunft auch*) uncertain

unbeteiligt [ʊnbə'taɪlɪçt] *adj* unconcerned, indifferent

unbeweglich ['ʊnbəveːklɪç] *adj* immovable

unbewohnt ['ʊnbəvoːnt] *adj* uninhabited; (*Wohnung*) unoccupied

unbewusst ▲ ['ʊnbəvʊst] *adj* unconscious

unbezahlt ['ʊnbətsaːlt] *adj* (*Rechnung*) outstanding, unsettled; (*Urlaub*) unpaid

unbrauchbar ['ʊnbrauxbaːr] *adj* (*Arbeit*) useless; (*Gerät auch*) unusable

und [ʊnt] *konj* and; **~ so weiter** and so on

Undank ['ʊndaŋk] *m* ingratitude; **u~bar** *a* ungrateful

undefinierbar [ʊndefi'niːrbaːr] *adj* indefinable

undenkbar [ʊn'dɛŋkbaːr] *adj* inconceivable

undeutlich ['ʊndɔ̌ytlɪç] *adj* indistinct

undicht ['ʊndɪçt] *adj* leaky

Unding ['ʊndɪŋ] *nt* absurdity

undurch- ['ʊndʊrç] *zW:* **~führbar** [-'fyːrba] *adj* impracticable; **~lässig** [-'lɛsɪç] *adj* waterproof, impermeable; **~sichtig** [-'zɪç] *adj* opaque; (*fig*) obscure

uneben ['ʊn|eːbən] *adj* uneven

unecht ['ʊn|ɛçt] *adj* (*Schmuck*) fake; (*vorgetäuscht: Freundlichkeit*) false

unehelich ['ʊn|eːəlɪç] *adj* illegitimate

uneinig ['ʊn|aɪnɪç] *adj* divided; **~ sein** to disagree; **U~keit** *f* discord, dissension

uneins ['ʊn|aɪns] *adj* at variance, at odds

unempfindlich ['ʊn|ɛmpfɪntlɪç] *adj* insensitive; (*Stoff*) practical

unendlich [ʊn'|ɛntlɪç] *adj* infinite

unent- [ʊn'|ɛnt] *zW:* **~behrlich** [-'beːrlɪç] *a* indispensable; **~geltlich** [-gɛltlɪç] *adj* free (of charge); **~schieden** [-'ʃiːdən] *adj* undecided; **~schieden enden** (*SPORT*) to end in a draw; **~schlossen** [-'ʃlɔsən] *adj* undecided; irresolute; **~wegt** [-'veːkt] *adj* unswerving; (*unaufhörlich*) incessant

uner- [ʊn'|ɛr] *zW:* **~bittlich** [-'bɪtlɪç] *adj* unyielding, inexorable; **~fahren** [-faːrən] *adj* inexperienced; **~freulich** [-frɔ̌ylɪç] *adj* unpleasant; **~gründlich** *adj* unfathomable **~hört** [-høːrt] *adj* unheard-of; (*Bitte*) outrageous; **~lässlich** ▲ [-'lɛslɪç] *adj* indispensable; **~laubt** *adj* unauthorized; **~messlich** ▲ *adj* immeasurable, immense; **~reichbar** *adj* (*Ziel*) unattainable; (*Ort*) inaccessible; (*telefonisch*) unobtainable; **~schöpflich** [-'ʃœpflɪç] *adj* inexhaustible; **~schwinglich** [-'ʃvɪŋlɪç] *adj* (*Preis*) exorbitant; too expensive; **~träglich** [-'trɛːklɪç] *adj* unbearable; (*Frechheit*) insufferable; **~wartet** *adj* unexpected; **~wünscht** *adj* undesirable, unwelcome

unfähig ['ʊnfɛːɪç] *adj* incapable, incompetent; **zu etw ~ sein** to be

incapable of sth; **U~keit** f incapacity;
incompetence

nfair ['unfɛ:r] adj unfair

nfall ['unfal] m accident; **~flucht** f hit-
and-run (driving); **~schaden** m damages
ol; **~station** f emergency ward; **~stelle** f
scene of the accident; **~versicherung** f
accident insurance

nfassbar ▲ [un'fasba:r] adj inconceivable

nfehlbar [un'fe:lba:r] adj infallible ♦ adv
inevitably; **U~keit** f infallibility

nförmig ['unfœrmiç] adj (formlos) shapeless

nfrei ['unfrai] adj not free, unfree; (Paket)
unfranked; **~willig** adj involuntary, against
one's will

nfreundlich ['unfrɔyntlıç] adj unfriendly;
U~keit f unfriendliness

nfriede(n) ['unfri:də(n)] m dissension,
strife

nfruchtbar ['unfruxtba:r] adj infertile;
(Gespräche) unfruitful; **U~keit** f infertility;
unfruitfulness

nfug ['unfu:k] (**-s**) m (Benehmen) mischief;
(Unsinn) nonsense; **grober ~** (JUR) gross
misconduct; malicious damage

ngar(in) ['ungar(ın)] m(f) Hungarian;
u~isch adj Hungarian; **~n** nt Hungary

ngeachtet ['ungəʔaxtət] präp +gen
notwithstanding

ngeahnt ['ungəʔa:nt] adj unsuspected,
undreamt-of

ngebeten ['ungəbe:tən] adj uninvited

ngebildet ['ungəbıldət] adj uneducated;
uncultured

ngedeckt ['ungədɛkt] adj (Scheck)
uncovered

ngeduld ['ungədult] f impatience; **u~ig**
[-dıç] adj impatient

ngeeignet ['ungəʔaignət] adj unsuitable

ngefähr ['ungəfɛ:r] adj rough,
approximate; **das kommt nicht von ~**
that's hardly surprising

ngefährlich ['ungəfɛ:rlıç] adj not
dangerous, harmless

ngehalten ['ungəhaltən] adj indignant

ngeheuer ['ungəhɔyər] adj huge ♦ adv
(umg) enormously; **U~** (**-s, -**) nt monster;

~lich [-'hɔyərlıç] adj monstrous

ungehörig ['ungəhø:rıç] adj impertinent,
improper

ungehorsam ['ungəho:rza:m] adj
disobedient; **U~** m disobedience

ungeklärt ['ungəklɛ:rt] adj not cleared up;
(Rätsel) unsolved

ungeladen ['ungəla:dən] adj not loaded;
(Gast) uninvited

ungelegen ['ungəle:gən] adj inconvenient

ungelernt ['ungəlɛrnt] adj unskilled

ungelogen ['ungəlo:gən] adv really,
honestly

ungemein ['ungəmain] adj uncommon

ungemütlich ['ungəmy:tlıç] adj
uncomfortable; (Person) disagreeable

ungenau ['ungənau] adj inaccurate;
U~igkeit f inaccuracy

ungenießbar ['ungəni:sba:r] adj inedible;
undrinkable; (umg) unbearable

ungenügend ['ungəny:gənt] adj insufficient,
inadequate

ungepflegt ['ungəpfle:kt] adj (Garten etc)
untended; (Person) unkempt; (Hände)
neglected

ungerade ['ungəra:də] adj uneven, odd

ungerecht ['ungərɛçt] adj unjust; **~fertigt**
adj unjustified; **U~igkeit** f injustice,
unfairness

ungern ['ungɛrn] adv unwillingly, reluctantly

ungeschehen ['ungəfe:ən] adj: **~ machen**
to undo

Ungeschicklichkeit ['ungəfıklıçkait] f
clumsiness

ungeschickt adj awkward, clumsy

ungeschminkt ['ungəfmıŋkt] adj without
make-up; (fig) unvarnished

ungesetzlich ['ungəzɛtslıç] adj illegal

ungestört ['ungəftø:rt] adj undisturbed

ungestraft ['ungəftra:ft] adv with impunity

ungestüm ['ungəfty:m] adj impetuous;
tempestuous

ungesund ['ungəzunt] adj unhealthy

ungetrübt ['ungətry:pt] adj clear; (fig)
untroubled; (Freude) unalloyed

Ungetüm ['ungəty:m] (**-(e)s, -e**) nt monster

ungewiss ▲ ['ungəvıs] adj uncertain;

U~heit *f* uncertainty
ungewöhnlich ['ungəvø:nlıç] *adj* unusual
ungewohnt ['ungəvo:nt] *adj* unaccustomed
Ungeziefer ['ungətsi:far] (**-s**) *nt* vermin
ungezogen ['ungətso:gən] *adj* rude,
impertinent; U~heit *f* rudeness,
impertinence
ungezwungen ['ungətsvuŋən] *adj* natural,
unconstrained
unglaublich [un'glauplıç] *adj* incredible
ungleich ['unglaıç] *adj* dissimilar; unequal
♦ *adv* incomparably; ~artig *adj* different;
U~heit *f* dissimilarity; inequality; ~mäßig
adj irregular, uneven
Unglück ['unglyk] (**-(e)s, -e**) *nt* misfortune;
(*Pech*) bad luck; (~*sfall*) calamity, disaster;
(*Verkehrsunglück*) accident; u~lich *adj*
unhappy; (*erfolglos*) unlucky; (*unerfreulich*)
unfortunate; u~licherweise [-'vaɪzə] *adv*
unfortunately; ~sfall *m* accident, calamity
ungültig ['ungyltıç] *adj* invalid; U~keit *f*
invalidity
ungünstig ['ungynstıç] *adj* unfavourable
ungut ['ungu:t] *adj* (*Gefühl*) uneasy; **nichts
für** ~ no offence
unhaltbar ['unhaltba:r] *adj* untenable
Unheil ['unhaıl] *nt* evil; (*Unglück*) misfortune;
~ **anrichten** to cause mischief; u~bar *adj*
incurable
unheimlich ['unhaɪmlıç] *adj* weird, uncanny
♦ *adv* (*umg*) tremendously
unhöflich ['unhø:flıç] *adj* impolite; U~keit *f*
impoliteness
unhygienisch ['unhygie:nıʃ] *adj* unhygienic
Uni ['uni] (**-, -s**) (*umg*) *f* university
Uniform [uni'fɔrm] *f* uniform; u~iert
[-'mi:rt] *adj* uniformed
uninteressant ['un|ınteresant] *adj*
uninteresting
Uni- *zW*: ~versität [univerzi'te:t] *f* university;
~versum [uni'verzum] (**-s**) *nt* universe
unkenntlich ['unkɛntlıç] *adj* unrecognizable
Unkenntnis ['unkɛntnıs] *f* ignorance
unklar ['unkla:r] *adj* unclear; **im U~en sein
über** +*akk* to be in the dark about; U~heit
f unclarity; (*Unentschiedenheit*) uncertainty
unklug ['unklu:k] *adj* unwise

Unkosten ['unkɔstən] *pl* expense(s);
~beitrag *m* contribution to costs *od*
expenses
Unkraut ['unkraut] *nt* weed; weeds *pl*
unkündbar ['unkyntba:r] *adj* (*Stelle*)
permanent; (*Vertrag*) binding
unlauter ['unlautar] *adj* unfair
unleserlich ['unle:zərlıç] *adj* illegible
unlogisch ['unlo:gıʃ] *adj* illogical
unlösbar ['unlø:sbar] *adj* insoluble
Unlust ['unlust] *f* lack of enthusiasm
Unmenge ['unmɛŋə] *f* tremendous number
hundreds *pl*
Unmensch ['unmɛnʃ] *m* ogre, brute;
u~lich *adj* inhuman, brutal; (*ungeheuer*)
awful
unmerklich [un'mɛrklıç] *adj* imperceptible
unmissverständlich ▲ ['unmısfɛrʃtɛntlıç]
adj unmistakable
unmittelbar ['unmıtəlba:r] *adj* immediate
unmodern ['unmodɛrn] *adj* old-fashioned
unmöglich ['unmø:klıç] *adj* impossible;
U~keit *f* impossibility
unmoralisch ['unmora:lıʃ] *adj* immoral
Unmut ['unmu:t] *m* ill humour
unnachgiebig ['unna:xgi:bıç] *adj* unyieldi
unnahbar [un'na:ba:r] *adj* unapproachable
unnötig ['unnø:tıç] *adj* unnecessary
unnütz ['unnyts] *adj* useless
unordentlich ['un|ɔrdəntlıç] *adj* untidy
Unordnung ['un|ɔrdnuŋ] *f* disorder
unparteiisch ['unpartaıʃ] *adj* impartial;
U~e(r) *f(m)* umpire; (*FUSSBALL*) referee
unpassend ['unpasənt] *adj* inappropriate;
(*Zeit*) inopportune
unpässlich ▲ ['unpɛslıç] *adj* unwell
unpersönlich ['unperzø:nlıç] *adj* impersor
unpolitisch ['unpoli:tıʃ] *adj* apolitical
unpraktisch ['unpraktıʃ] *adj* unpractical
unpünktlich ['unpyŋktlıç] *adj* unpunctual
unrationell ['unratsionɛl] *adj* inefficient
unrealistisch ['unrealıstıʃ] *adj* unrealistic
unrecht ['unrɛçt] *adj* wrong; U~ *nt* wrong,
zu U~ wrongly; U~ **haben** to be wrong;
~mäßig *adj* unlawful, illegal
unregelmäßig ['unre:gəlmɛ:sıç] *adj*
irregular; U~keit *f* irregularity

hreif ['unraɪf] adj (Obst) unripe; (fig) immature

hrentabel ['unrenta:bəl] adj unprofitable

hrichtig ['unrɪçtɪç] adj incorrect, wrong

hruhe ['unru:ə] f unrest; ~stifter m troublemaker

hruhig ['unru:ɪç] adj restless

hs [uns] (akk, dat von wir) pron us; ourselves

hsachlich ['unzaxlɪç] adj not to the point, irrelevant

hsagbar [un'za:kba:r] adj indescribable

hsanft ['unzanft] adj rough

hsauber ['unzaubər] adj unclean, dirty; (fig) crooked; (MUS) fuzzy

hschädlich ['unʃɛ:tlɪç] adj harmless; **jdn/ etw ~ machen** to render sb/sth harmless

hscharf ['unʃarf] adj indistinct; (Bild etc) out of focus, blurred

hscheinbar ['unʃaɪnba:r] adj insignificant; (Aussehen, Haus etc) unprepossessing

hschlagbar [un'ʃla:kba:r] adj invincible

hschön ['unʃø:n] adj (hässlich: Anblick) ugly, unattractive; (unfreundlich: Benehmen) unpleasant, ugly

hschuld ['unʃult] f innocence; u~ig [-dɪç] adj innocent

hselbst(st)ändig ['unzɛlpstʃtɛndɪç] adj dependent, over-reliant on others

hser(e) ['unzər(ə)] adj our; ~e(r, s) pron ours; ~einer pron people like us; ~eins pron = unsereiner; ~erseits adv on our part; ~twegen adv (für uns) for our sake; (wegen uns) on our account; ~twillen adv: um ~twillen = unsertwegen

hsicher ['unzɪçər] adj uncertain; (Mensch) insecure; **U~heit** f uncertainty; insecurity

hsichtbar ['unzɪçtba:r] adj invisible

hsinn ['unzɪn] m nonsense; **u~ig** adj nonsensical

hsitte ['unzɪtə] f deplorable habit

hsozial ['unzotsia:l] adj (Verhalten) antisocial

hsportlich ['unʃpɔrtlɪç] adj not sporty; unfit; (Verhalten) unsporting

hsre ['unzrə] = unsere

hsterblich ['unʃtɛrplɪç] adj immortal

Unstimmigkeit ['unʃtɪmɪçkaɪt] f inconsistency; (Streit) disagreement

unsympathisch ['unzʏmpa:tɪʃ] adj unpleasant; **er ist mir ~** I don't like him

untätig ['untɛ:tɪç] adj idle

untauglich ['untauklɪç] adj unsuitable; (MIL) unfit

unteilbar [un'taɪlba:r] adj indivisible

unten ['untən] adv below; (im Haus) downstairs; (an der Treppe etc) at the bottom; **nach ~** down; **~ am Berg** etc at the bottom of the mountain etc; **ich bin bei ihm ~ durch** (umg) he's through with me

---

SCHLÜSSELWORT

---

unter ['untər] präp +dat 1 (räumlich, mit Zahlen) under; (drunter) underneath, below; **unter 18 Jahren** under 18 years 2 (zwischen) among(st); **sie waren unter sich** they were by themselves; **einer unter ihnen** one of them; **unter anderem** among other things
♦ präp +akk under, below

Unterarm ['untər|arm] m forearm

unter- zW: **~belichten** vt (PHOT) to underexpose; **U~bewusstsein** ▲ nt subconscious; **~bezahlt** adj underpaid

unterbieten [untər'bi:tən] (unreg) vt insep (COMM) to undercut; (Rekord) to lower

unterbrechen [untər'brɛçən] (unreg) vt insep to interrupt

Unterbrechung f interruption

unterbringen ['untərbrɪŋən] (unreg) vt (in Koffer) to stow; (in Zeitung) to place; (Person: in Hotel etc) to accommodate, to put up

unterdessen [untər'dɛsən] adv meanwhile

Unterdruck ['untərdrʊk] m low pressure

unterdrücken [untər'drʏkən] vt insep to suppress; (Leute) to oppress

untere(r, s) ['untərə(r, s)] adj lower

untereinander [untər|aɪ'nandər] adv with each other; among themselves etc

unterentwickelt ['untər|ɛntvɪkəlt] adj underdeveloped

unterernährt ['ʊntərˌɛrnɛːrt] *adj* undernourished, underfed

Unterernährung *f* malnutrition

Unter'führung *f* subway, underpass

Untergang ['ʊntərɡaŋ] *m* (down)fall, decline; (*NAUT*) sinking; (*von Gestirn*) setting

unter'geben *adj* subordinate

untergehen ['ʊntərɡeːən] (*unreg*) *vi* to go down; (*Sonne auch*) to set; (*Staat*) to fall; (*Volk*) to perish; (*Welt*) to come to an end; (*im Lärm*) to be drowned

Untergeschoss ▲ ['ʊntərɡəʃɔs] *nt* basement

'Untergewicht *nt* underweight

unter'gliedern *vt insep* to subdivide

Untergrund ['ʊntərɡrʊnt] *m* foundation; (*POL*) underground; **~bahn** *f* underground, tube, subway (*US*)

unterhalb ['ʊntərhalp] *präp +gen* below ♦ *adv* below; **~ von** below

Unterhalt ['ʊntərhalt] *m* maintenance; **u~en** (*unreg*) *vt insep* to maintain; (*belustigen*) to entertain ♦ *vr insep* to talk; (*sich belustigen*) to enjoy o.s.; **u~sam** *adj* (*Abend, Person*) entertaining, amusing; **~ung** *f* maintenance; (*Belustigung*) entertainment, amusement; (*Gespräch*) talk

Unterhändler ['ʊntərhɛntlər] *m* negotiator

Unter- *zW:* **~hemd** *nt* vest, undershirt (*US*); **~hose** *f* underpants *pl*; **~kiefer** *m* lower jaw

unterkommen ['ʊntərkɔmən] (*unreg*) *vi* to find shelter; to find work; **das ist mir noch nie untergekommen** I've never met with that

unterkühlt [ʊntərˈkyːlt] *adj* (*Körper*) affected by hypothermia

Unterkunft ['ʊntərkʊnft] (**-, -künfte**) *f* accommodation

Unterlage ['ʊntərlaːɡə] *f* foundation; (*Beleg*) document; (*Schreibunterlage etc*) pad

unter'lassen (*unreg*) *vt insep* (*versäumen*) to fail to do; (*sich enthalten*) to refrain from

unterlaufen [ʊntərˈlaʊfən] (*unreg*) *vi insep* to happen ♦ *adj*: **mit Blut ~** suffused with blood; (*Augen*) bloodshot

unterlegen ['ʊntərleːɡən] *vt* to lay *od* put under; **unter'legen** *adj* inferior; (*besiegt*) defeated

Unterleib ['ʊntərlaɪp] *m* abdomen

unter'liegen (*unreg*) *vi insep* (+*dat*) to be defeated *od* overcome (by); (*unterworfen sein*) to be subject (to)

Untermiete ['ʊntərmiːtə] *f*: **zur ~ wohnen** to be a subtenant *od* lodger; **~r(in)** *m(f)* subtenant, lodger

unter'nehmen (*unreg*) *vt insep* to undertake; **Unter'nehmen** (**-s, -**) *nt* undertaking, enterprise (*auch COMM*)

Unternehmer [ʊntərˈneːmər] (**-s, -**) *m* entrepreneur, businessman

'unterordnen ['ʊntərɔrdnən] *vr* +*dat* to submit o.s. (to), to give o.s. second place to

Unterredung [ʊntərˈreːdʊŋ] *f* discussion, talk

Unterricht ['ʊntərɪçt] (**-(e)s, -e**) *m* instruction, lessons *pl*; **u~en** [ʊntərˈrɪçtən] *insep* to teach ♦ *vr insep*: **sich u~en (über** +*akk*) to inform o.s. (about), to obtain information (about); **~sfach** *nt* subject (on school *etc* curriculum)

Unterrock ['ʊntərɔk] *m* petticoat, slip

unter'sagen *vt insep* to forbid; **jdm etw ~** to forbid sb to do sth

Untersatz ['ʊntərzats] *m* coaster, saucer

unter'schätzen *vt insep* to underestimate

unter'scheiden (*unreg*) *vt insep* to distinguish ♦ *vr insep* to differ

Unter'scheidung *f* (*Unterschied*) distinction; (*Unterscheiden*) differentiation

Unterschied ['ʊntərʃiːt] (**-(e)s, -e**) *m* difference, distinction; **im ~ zu** as distinct from; **u~lich** *adj* varying, differing; (*diskriminierend*) discriminatory

unterschiedslos *adv* indiscriminately

unter'schlagen (*unreg*) *vt insep* to embezzle; (*verheimlichen*) to suppress

Unter'schlagung *f* embezzlement

Unterschlupf ['ʊntərʃlʊpf] (**-(e)s, -schlüpfe**) *m* refuge

unter'schreiben (*unreg*) *vt insep* to sign

Unterschrift ['ʊntərʃrɪft] *f* signature

Unterseeboot ['untərzeːboːt] *nt* submarine
Untersetzer ['untərzɛtsər] *m* tablemat; (*für Gläser*) coaster
untersetzt [untər'zɛtst] *adj* stocky
unterste(r, s) ['untərstə(r, s)] *adj* lowest, bottom
unterstehen [untər'ʃteːən] (*unreg*) *vi insep* (*+dat*) to be under ♦ *vr insep* to dare; '**unterstehen** (*unreg*) *vi* to shelter
unterstellen [untər'ʃtɛlən] *vt insep* to subordinate; (*fig*) to impute ♦ *vt* (*Auto*) to garage, to park ♦ *vr* to take shelter
unter'streichen (*unreg*) *vt insep* (*auch fig*) to underline
Unterstufe ['untərʃtuːfə] *f* lower grade
unter'stützen *vt insep* to support
Unter'stützung *f* support, assistance
unter'suchen *vt insep* (*MED*) to examine; (*Polizei*) to investigate
Unter'suchung *f* examination; investigation, inquiry; **~sausschuss** ▲ *m* committee of inquiry; **~shaft** *f* imprisonment on remand
Untertasse ['untərtasə] *f* saucer
untertauchen ['untərtauxən] *vi* to dive; (*fig*) to disappear, to go underground
Unterteil ['untərtaıl] *nt od m* lower part, bottom; **u~en** [untər'taılən] *vt insep* to divide up
Untertitel ['untərtiːtəl] *m* subtitle
Unterwäsche ['untərvɛʃə] *f* underwear
unterwegs [untər'veːks] *adv* on the way
unter'werfen (*unreg*) *vt insep* to subject; (*Volk*) to subjugate ♦ *vr insep* (*+dat*) to submit (to)
unter'zeichnen *vt insep* to sign
unter'ziehen (*unreg*) *vt insep* to subject ♦ *vr insep* (*+dat*) to undergo; (*einer Prüfung*) to take
untragbar [un'traːkbaːr] *adj* unbearable, intolerable
untreu ['untrɔy] *adj* unfaithful; **U~e** *f* unfaithfulness
untröstlich [un'trøːstlıç] *adj* inconsolable
unüberlegt ['unyːbərleːkt] *adj* ill-considered ♦ *adv* without thinking
unübersichtlich *adj* (*Gelände*) broken;

(*Kurve*) blind
unumgänglich [un|um'gɛŋlıç] *adj* indispensable, vital; absolutely necessary
ununterbrochen ['un|untərbrɔxən] *adj* uninterrupted
unver- [unfɛr] *zW:* **~änderlich** [-'ɛndərlıç] *adj* unchangeable; **~antwortlich** [-'antvɔrtlıç] *adj* irresponsible; (*unentschuldbar*) inexcusable; **~besserlich** *adj* incorrigible; **~bindlich** *adj* not binding; (*Antwort*) curt ♦ *adv* (*COMM*) without obligation; **~bleit** *adj* (*Benzin usw*) unleaded; **ich fahre ~bleit** I use unleaded; **~blümt** [-'blyːmt] *adj* plain, blunt ♦ *adv* plainly, bluntly; **~daulich** *adj* indigestible; **~einbar** *adj* incompatible; **~fänglich** [-'fɛŋlıç] *adj* harmless; **~froren** *adj* impudent; **~gesslich** ▲ *adj* (*Tag, Erlebnis*) unforgettable; **~hofft** [-'hɔft] *adj* unexpected; **~meidlich** [-'maıtlıç] *adj* unavoidable; **~mutet** *adj* unexpected; **~nünftig** [-'nynftıç] *adj* foolish; **~schämt** *adj* impudent; **U~schämtheit** *f* impudence, insolence; **~sehrt** *adj* uninjured; **~söhnlich** [-'zøːnlıç] *adj* irreconcilable; **~ständlich** [-'ʃtɛntlıç] *adj* unintelligible; **~träglich** *adj* quarrelsome; (*Meinungen, MED*) incompatible; **~zeihlich** *adj* unpardonable; **~züglich** [-'tsyːklıç] *adj* immediate
unvollkommen ['unfɔlkɔmən] *adj* imperfect
unvollständig *adj* incomplete
unvor- ['unfoːr] *zW:* **~bereitet** *adj* unprepared; **~eingenommen** *adj* unbiased; **~hergesehen** [-heːrgezeːən] *adj* unforeseen; **~sichtig** [-zıçtıç] *adj* careless, imprudent; **~stellbar** [-'ʃtɛlbaːr] *adj* inconceivable; **~teilhaft** *adj* disadvantageous
unwahr ['unvaːr] *adj* untrue; **~scheinlich** *adj* improbable, unlikely ♦ *adv* (*umg*) incredibly
unweigerlich [un'vaıgərlıç] *adj* unquestioning ♦ *adv* without fail
Unwesen ['unveːzən] *nt* nuisance; (*Unfug*) mischief; **sein ~ treiben** to wreak havoc
unwesentlich *adj* inessential, unimportant; **~ besser** marginally better

---

Spelling Reform: ▲ *new spelling* △ *old spelling (to be phased out)*

Unwetter ['ʊnvɛtər] *nt* thunderstorm
unwichtig ['ʊnvɪçtɪç] *adj* unimportant
unwider- ['ʊnviːdər] *zW*: **~legbar** *adj*
irrefutable; **~ruflich** *adj* irrevocable;
~stehlich *adj* irresistible
unwill- ['ʊnvɪl] *zW*: **U~e(n)** *m* indignation;
~ig *adj* indignant; (*widerwillig*) reluctant;
~kürlich [-kyːrlɪç] *adj* involuntary ♦ *adv*
instinctively; (*lachen*) involuntarily
unwirklich ['ʊnvɪrklɪç] *adj* unreal
unwirksam ['ʊnvɪrkzaːm] *adj* (*Mittel,
Methode*) ineffective
unwirtschaftlich ['ʊnvɪrtʃaftlɪç] *adj*
uneconomical
unwissen- ['ʊnvɪsən] *zW*: **~d** *adj* ignorant;
U~heit *f* ignorance; **~tlich** *adv*
unknowingly, unwittingly
unwohl ['ʊnvoːl] *adj* unwell, ill; **U~sein (-s)**
nt indisposition
unwürdig ['ʊnvʏrdɪç] *adj* unworthy
unzählig [ʊn'tsɛːlɪç] *adj* innumerable,
countless
unzer- [ʊntsɛr] *zW*: **~brechlich** *adj*
unbreakable; **~störbar** *adj* indestructible;
~trennlich *adj* inseparable
Unzucht ['ʊntsʊxt] *f* sexual offence
unzüchtig ['ʊntsʏçtɪç] *adj* immoral; lewd
unzu- ['ʊntsu] *zW*: **~frieden** *adj* dissatisfied;
U~friedenheit *f* discontent; **~länglich** *adj*
inadequate; **~lässig** *adj* inadmissible;
~rechnungsfähig *adj* irresponsible;
~treffend *adj* incorrect; **~verlässig** *adj*
unreliable
unzweideutig ['ʊntsvaɪdɔʏtɪç] *adj*
unambiguous
üppig ['ʏpɪç] *adj* (*Frau*) curvaceous; (*Busen*)
full, ample; (*Essen*) sumptuous; (*Vegetation*)
luxuriant, lush
Ur- ['uːr] *in zW* original
uralt ['uːr|alt] *adj* ancient, very old
Uran [u'raːn] **(-s)** *nt* uranium
Ur- *zW*: **~aufführung** *f* first performance;
~einwohner *m* original inhabitant;
~eltern *pl* ancestors; **~enkel(in)** *m(f)*
great-grandchild, great-grandson
(-daughter); **~großeltern** *pl* great-
grandparents; **~heber (-s, -)** *m* originator;

(*Autor*) author; **~heberrecht** *nt* copyright
Urin [u'riːn] **(-s, -e)** *m* urine
Urkunde ['uːrkʊndə] *f* document, deed
Urlaub ['uːrlaʊp] **(-(e)s, -e)** *m* holiday(s *pl*)
(*BRIT*), vacation (*US*); (*MIL etc*) leave; **~er**
[-'laʊbər] **(-s, -)** *m* holiday-maker (*BRIT*),
vacationer (*US*); **~sort** *m* holiday resort;
~szeit *f* holiday season
Urne ['ʊrnə] *f* urn
Ursache ['uːrzaxə] *f* cause; **keine ~** that's all
right
Ursprung ['uːrʃprʊŋ] *m* origin, source; (*von
Fluss*) source
ursprünglich ['uːrʃprʏŋlɪç] *adj* original ♦ *adv*
originally
Ursprungsland *nt* country of origin
Urteil ['ʊrtaɪl] **(-s, -e)** *nt* opinion; (*JUR*)
sentence, judgement; **u~en** *vi* to judge;
~sspruch *m* sentence, verdict
Urwald *m* jungle
Urzeit *f* prehistoric times *pl*
USA [uːˈɛsˈʔaː] *pl abk* (= *Vereinigte Staaten von
Amerika*) USA
usw. *abk* (= *und so weiter*) etc
Utensilien [utɛnˈziːliən] *pl* utensils
Utopie [uto'piː] *f* pipe dream
utopisch [u'toːpɪʃ] *adj* utopian

V, v

vag(e) [vaːk, 'vaːgə] *adj* vague
Vagina [va'giːna] **(-, Vaginen)** *f* vagina
Vakuum ['vaːkuʊm] **(-s, Vakua *od* Vakuen)**
nt vacuum
Vampir [vam'piːr] **(-s, -e)** *m* vampire
Vanille [va'nɪljə] **(-)** *f* vanilla
Variation [variatsi'oːn] *f* variation
variieren [vari'iːrən] *vt, vi* to vary
Vase ['vaːzə] *f* vase
Vater ['faːtər] **(-s, ")** *m* father; **~land** *nt*
native country; Fatherland
väterlich ['fɛːtərlɪç] *adj* fatherly
Vaterschaft *f* paternity
Vaterunser (-s, -) *nt* Lord's prayer
Vati ['faːti] *m* daddy
v. Chr. *abk* (= *vor Christus*) B.C.

Vegetarier(in) [vege'taːriər(ɪn)] **(-s, -)** *m(f)* vegetarian

vegetarisch [vege'taːrɪʃ] *adj* vegetarian

Veilchen ['faɪlçən] *nt* violet

Vene ['veːnə] *f* vein

Ventil [vɛn'tiːl] **(-s, -e)** *nt* valve

Ventilator [vɛntila'toːr] *m* ventilator

verab- [fɛr'ʔap] *zW:* **~reden** *vt* to agree, to arrange ♦ *vr:* **sich mit jdm ~reden** to arrange to meet sb; **mit jdm ~redet sein** to have arranged to meet sb; **V~redung** *f* arrangement; (*Treffen*) appointment; **~scheuen** *vt* to abhor; **~schieden** *vt* (*Gäste*) to say goodbye to; (*entlassen*) to discharge; (*Gesetz*) to pass ♦ *vr* to take one's leave; **V~schiedung** *f* leave-taking; discharge; passing

ver- [fɛr] *zW:* **~achten** *vt* to despise; **~ächtlich** [-'ʔɛçtlɪç] *adj* contemptuous; (*~achtenswert*) contemptible; **jdn ~ächtlich machen** to run sb down; **V~achtung** *f* contempt

verallgemeinern [fɛrʔalgə'maɪnərn] *vt* to generalize; **Verallgemeinerung** *f* generalization

veralten [fɛr'ʔaltən] *vi* to become obsolete *od* out-of-date

Veranda [ve'randa] **(-, Veranden)** *f* veranda

veränder- [fɛr'ʔɛndər] *zW:* **~lich** *adj* changeable; **~n** *vt, vr* to change, to alter; **V~ung** *f* change, alteration

veran- [fɛr'ʔan] *zW:* **~lagt** *adj* with a ... nature; **V~lagung** *f* disposition; **~lassen** *vt* to cause; **Maßnahmen ~lassen** to take measures; **sich ~lasst sehen** to feel prompted; **~schaulichen** *vt* to illustrate; **~schlagen** *vt* to estimate; **~stalten** *vt* to organize, to arrange; **V~stalter (-s, -)** *m* organizer; **V~staltung** *f* (*V~stalten*) organizing; (*Konzert etc*) event, function

verantwort- [fɛr'ʔantvɔrt] *zW:* **~en** *vt* to answer for ♦ *vr* to justify o.s.; **~lich** *adj* responsible; **V~ung** *f* responsibility; **~ungsbewusst** ▲ *adj* responsible; **~ungslos** *adj* irresponsible

verarbeiten [fɛr'ʔarbaɪtən] *vt* to process; (*geistig*) to assimilate; **etw zu etw ~** to make sth into sth; **Verarbeitung** *f* processing; assimilation

verärgern [fɛr'ʔɛrgərn] *vt* to annoy

verausgaben [fɛr'ʔausgaːbən] *vr* to run out of money; (*fig*) to exhaust o.s.

Verb [vɛrp] **(-s, -en)** *nt* verb

Verband [fɛr'bant] **(-(e)s, ⁻e)** *m* (*MED*) bandage, dressing; (*Bund*) association, society; (*MIL*) unit; **~kasten** *m* medicine chest, first-aid box; **~zeug** *nt* bandage

verbannen [fɛr'banən] *vt* to banish

verbergen [fɛr'bɛrgən] (*unreg*) *vt, vr:* **(sich) ~ (vor +dat)** to hide (from)

verbessern [fɛr'bɛsərn] *vt, vr* to improve; (*berichtigen*) to correct (o.s.)

Verbesserung *f* improvement; correction

verbeugen [fɛr'bɔygən] *vr* to bow

Verbeugung *f* bow

ver'biegen (*unreg*) *vi* to bend

ver'bieten (*unreg*) *vt* to forbid; **jdm etw ~** to forbid sb to do sth

verbilligen [fɛr'bɪlɪgən] *vt* to reduce the cost of; (*Preis*) to reduce

ver'binden (*unreg*) *vt* to connect; (*kombinieren*) to combine; (*MED*) to bandage ♦ *vr* (*auch CHEM*) to combine, to join; **jdm die Augen ~** to blindfold sb

verbindlich [fɛr'bɪntlɪç] *adj* binding; (*freundlich*) friendly

Ver'bindung *f* connection; (*Zusammensetzung*) combination; (*CHEM*) compound; (*UNIV*) club

verbissen [fɛr'bɪsən] *adj* (*Kampf*) bitter; (*Gesichtsausdruck*) grim

ver'bitten (*unreg*) *vt:* **sich** *dat* **etw ~** not to tolerate sth, not to stand for sth

Verbleib [fɛr'blaɪp] **(-(e)s)** *m* whereabouts; **v~en** (*unreg*) *vi* to remain

verbleit [fɛr'blaɪt] *adj* (*Benzin*) leaded

verblüffen [fɛr'blʏfən] *vt* to stagger, to amaze; **Verblüffung** *f* stupefaction

ver'blühen *vi* to wither, to fade

ver'bluten *vi* to bleed to death

verborgen [fɛr'bɔrgən] *adj* hidden

Verbot [fɛr'boːt] **(-(e)s, -e)** *nt* prohibition, ban; **v~en** *adj* forbidden; **Rauchen v~en!** no smoking; **~sschild** *nt* prohibitory sign

Verbrauch [fɛr'braux] (-(e)s) m
consumption; **v~en** vt to use up; **~er(-s,
-)** m consumer; **v~t** adj used up, finished;
(*Luft*) stale; (*Mensch*) worn-out

Verbrechen [fɛr'brɛçən] (-s, -) nt crime

Verbrecher [fɛr'brɛçər] (-s, -) m criminal;
v~isch adj criminal

ver'breiten vt, vr to spread; **sich über etw**
akk ~ to expound on sth

verbreitern [fɛr'braitərn] vt to broaden

Verbreitung f spread(ing), propagation

verbrenn- [fɛr'brɛn] zW: **~bar** adj
combustible; **~en** (unreg) vt to burn;
(*Leiche*) to cremate; **V~ung** f burning; (*in
Motor*) combustion; (*von Leiche*) cremation;
V~ungsmotor m internal combustion
engine

verbringen [fɛr'brɪŋən] (unreg) vt to spend

verbrühen [fɛr'bryːən] vt to scald

verbuchen [fɛr'buːxən] vt (*FIN*) to register;
(*Erfolg*) to enjoy; (*Misserfolg*) to suffer

verbunden [fɛr'bundən] adj connected; **jdm**
~ sein to be obliged od indebted to sb;
„falsch ~" (*TEL*) "wrong number"

verbünden [fɛr'byndən] vr to ally o.s.;
Verbündete(r) f(m) ally

ver'bürgen vr: **sich ~ für** to vouch for

ver'büßen vt: **eine Strafe ~** to serve a
sentence

Verdacht [fɛr'daxt] (-(e)s) m suspicion

verdächtig [fɛr'dɛçtɪç] adj suspicious,
suspect; **~en** [fɛr'dɛçtɪgən] vt to suspect

verdammen [fɛr'damən] vt to damn, to
condemn; **verdammt!** damn!

verdammt (umg) adj, adv damned; **~ noch**
mal! dammit!, dammit!

ver'dampfen vi to vaporize, to evaporate

ver'danken vt: **jdm etw ~** to owe sb sth

verdau- [fɛr'dau] zW: **~en** vt (auch fig) to
digest; **~lich** adj digestible; **das ist schwer**
~lich that is hard to digest; **V~ung** f
digestion

Verdeck [fɛr'dɛk] (-(e)s, -e) nt (*AUT*) hood;
(*NAUT*) deck; **v~en** vt to cover (up);
(*verbergen*) to hide

Verderb- [fɛr'dɛrp] zW: **~en** [-'dɛrbən] (-s)
nt ruin; **v~en** (unreg) vt to spoil; (*schädigen*)

to ruin; (*moralisch*) to corrupt ♦ vi (*Essen*) to
spoil, to rot; (*Mensch*) to go to the bad; **es**
mit jdm v~en to get into sb's bad books;
v~lich adj (*Einfluss*) pernicious;
(*Lebensmittel*) perishable

verdeutlichen [fɛr'dɔytlɪçən] vt to make
clear

ver'dichten vt, vr to condense

ver'dienen vt to earn; (*moralisch*) to
deserve

Ver'dienst (-(e)s, -e) m earnings pl ♦ nt
merit; (*Leistung*): **~ (um)** service (to)

verdient [fɛr'diːnt] adj well-earned; (*Person*)
deserving of esteem; **sich um etw ~**
machen to do a lot for sth

verdoppeln [fɛr'dɔpəln] vt to double

verdorben [fɛr'dɔrbən] adj spoilt;
(*geschädigt*) ruined; (*moralisch*) corrupt

verdrängen [fɛr'drɛŋən] vt to oust, to
displace (*auch PHYS*); (*PSYCH*) to repress

ver'drehen vt (auch fig) to twist; (*Augen*) to
roll; **jdm den Kopf ~** (fig) to turn sb's
head

verdrießlich [fɛr'driːslɪç] adj peevish,
annoyed

Verdruss ▲ [fɛr'drʊs] (-es, -e) m
annoyance, worry

verdummen [fɛr'dumən] vt to make stupid
♦ vi to grow stupid

verdunkeln [fɛr'duŋkəln] vt to darken; (fig)
to obscure ♦ vr to darken

Verdunk(e)lung f blackout; (fig) obscuring

verdünnen [fɛr'dynən] vt to dilute

verdunsten [fɛr'dunstən] vi to evaporate

verdursten [fɛr'dʊrstən] vi to die of thirst

verdutzt [fɛr'dutst] adj nonplussed, taken
aback

verehr- [fɛr'eːr] zW: **~en** vt to venerate, to
worship (*auch REL*); **jdm etw ~en** to present
sb with sth; **V~er(in)** (-s, -) m(f) admirer,
worshipper (*auch REL*); **~t** adj esteemed;
V~ung f respect; (*REL*) worship

Verein [fɛr'|ain] (-(e)s, -e) m club,
association; **v~bar** adj compatible;
v~baren vt to agree upon; **~barung** f
agreement; **v~en** vt (*Menschen, Länder*) to
unite; (*Prinzipien*) to reconcile; **mit v~ten**

Kräften having pooled resources, having joined forces; **~te Nationen** United Nations; **v~fachen** vt to simplify; **v~heitlichen** [-haɪtlɪçən] vt to standardize; **v~igen** vt, vr to unite; **~igung** f union; (*Verein*) association; **v~t** adj united; **v~zelt** adj isolated

ver'eitern vi to suppurate, to fester

verengen [fɛr'ɛŋən] vr to narrow

vererb- [fɛr'ɛrb] zW: **~en** vt (*BIOL*) to transmit ♦ vr to be hereditary; **V~ung** f bequeathing; (*BIOL*) transmission; (*Lehre*) heredity

verewigen [fɛr'e:vɪgən] vt to immortalize ♦ vr (*umg*) to immortalize o.s.

ver'fahren (*unreg*) vi to act ♦ vr to get lost ♦ adj tangled; **Ver'fahren** (**-s, -**) nt procedure; (*TECH*) process; (*JUR*) proceedings pl

Verfall [fɛr'fal] (**-(e)s**) m decline; (*von Haus*) dilapidation; (*FIN*) expiry; **v~en** vi to decline; (*Haus*) to be falling down; (*FIN*) to lapse; **v~en in** +akk to lapse into; **v~en auf** +akk to hit upon; **einem Laster v~en sein** to be addicted to a vice; **~sdatum** nt expiry date; (*der Haltbarkeit*) sell-by date

ver'färben vr to change colour

verfassen [fɛr'fasən] vt (*Rede*) to prepare, work out

Verfasser(in) [fɛr'fasər(ɪn)] (**-s, -**) m(f) author, writer

Verfassung f (*auch POL*) constitution

Verfassungs- zW: **~gericht** nt constitutional court; **v~widrig** adj unconstitutional

ver'faulen vi to rot

ver'fehlen vt to miss; **etw für verfehlt halten** to regard sth as mistaken

verfeinern [fɛr'faɪnərn] vt to refine

ver'filmen vt to film

verflixt [fɛr'flɪkst] (*umg*) adj damned, damn

ver'fluchen vt to curse

verfolg- [fɛr'fɔlg] zW: **~en** vt to pursue; (*gerichtlich*) to prosecute; (*grausam, bes POL*) to persecute; **V~er** (**-s, -**) m pursuer; **V~ung** f pursuit; prosecution; persecution

verfrüht [fɛr'fry:t] adj premature

verfüg- [fɛr'fy:g] zW: **~bar** adj available; **~en** vt to direct, to order ♦ vr to proceed ♦ vi: **~en über** +akk to have at one's disposal; **V~ung** f direction, order; **zur V~ung** at one's disposal; **jdm zur V~ung stehen** to be available to sb

verführ- [fɛr'fy:r] zW: **~en** vt to tempt; (*sexuell*) to seduce; **V~er** m tempter; seducer; **~erisch** adj seductive; **V~ung** f seduction; (*Versuchung*) temptation

ver'gammeln (*umg*) vi to go to seed; (*Nahrung*) to go off

vergangen [fɛr'gaŋən] adj past; **V~heit** f past

vergänglich [fɛr'gɛŋlɪç] adj transitory

vergasen [fɛr'ga:zən] vt (*töten*) to gas

Vergaser (**-s, -**) m (*AUT*) carburettor

vergaß etc [fɛr'ga:s] vb siehe **vergessen**

vergeb- [fɛr'ge:b] zW: **~en** (*unreg*) vt (*verzeihen*) to forgive; (*weggeben*) to give away; **jdm etw ~en** to forgive sb (for) sth; **~ens** adv in vain; **~lich** [fɛr'ge:plɪç] adv in vain ♦ adj vain, futile; **V~ung** f forgiveness

ver'gehen (*unreg*) vi to pass by od away ♦ vr to commit an offence; **jdm vergeht etw** sb loses sth; **sich an jdm ~** to (sexually) assault sb; **Ver'gehen** (**-s, -**) nt offence

ver'gelten (*unreg*) vt: **jdm etw ~** to pay sb back for sth, to repay sb for sth

Ver'geltung f retaliation, reprisal

vergessen [fɛr'gɛsən] (*unreg*) vt to forget; **V~heit** f oblivion

vergesslich ▲ [fɛr'gɛslɪç] adj forgetful; **V~keit** f forgetfulness

vergeuden [fɛr'gɔydən] vt to squander, to waste

vergewaltigen [fɛrgə'valtɪgən] vt to rape; (*fig*) to violate

Vergewaltigung f rape

vergewissern [fɛrgə'vɪsərn] vr to make sure

ver'gießen (*unreg*) vt to shed

vergiften [fɛr'gɪftən] vt to poison

Vergiftung f poisoning

Vergissmeinnicht ▲ [fɛr'gɪsmaɪnnɪçt] (**-(e)s, -e**) nt forget-me-not

vergisst ▲ etc [fɛr'gɪst] vb siehe **vergessen**

Vergleich [fɛrˈglaɪç] **(-(e)s, -e)** *m* comparison; (*JUR*) settlement; **im ~ mit** *od* **zu** compared with *od* to; **v~bar** *adj* comparable; **v~en** (*unreg*) *vt* to compare ♦ *vr* to reach a settlement

vergnügen [fɛrˈɡnyːɡən] *vr* to enjoy *od* amuse o.s.; **V~ (-s, -)** *nt* pleasure; **viel V~!** enjoy yourself!

vergnügt [fɛrˈɡnyːkt] *adj* cheerful

Vergnügung *f* pleasure, amusement; **~spark** *m* amusement park

vergolden [fɛrˈɡɔldən] *vt* to gild

ver'graben *vt* to bury

ver'greifen (*unreg*) *vr*: **sich an jdm ~** to lay hands on sb; **sich an etw ~** to misappropriate sth; **sich im Ton ~** to say the wrong thing

vergriffen [fɛrˈɡrɪfən] *adj* (*Buch*) out of print; (*Ware*) out of stock

vergrößern [fɛrˈɡrøːsərn] *vt* to enlarge; (*mengenmäßig*) to increase; (*Lupe*) to magnify

Vergrößerung *f* enlargement; increase; magnification; **~sglas** *nt* magnifying glass

Vergünstigung [fɛrˈɡynstɪɡʊŋ] *f* concession, privilege

Vergütung *f* compensation

verhaften [fɛrˈhaftən] *vt* to arrest

Verhaftung *f* arrest

ver'halten (*unreg*) *vr* to be, to stand; (*sich benehmen*) to behave ♦ *vt* to hold *od* keep back; (*Schritt*) to check; **sich ~ (zu)** (*MATH*) to be in proportion (to); **Ver'halten (-s)** *nt* behaviour

Verhältnis [fɛrˈhɛltnɪs] **(-ses, -se)** *nt* relationship; (*MATH*) proportion, ratio; **~se** *pl* (*Umstände*) conditions; **über seine ~se leben** to live beyond one's means; **v~mäßig** *adj* relative, comparative ♦ *adv* relatively, comparatively

verhandeln [fɛrˈhandəln] *vi* to negotiate; (*JUR*) to hold proceedings ♦ *vt* to discuss; (*JUR*) to hear; **über etw** *akk* **~** to negotiate sth *od* about sth

Verhandlung *f* negotiation; (*JUR*) proceedings *pl*; **~sbasis** *f* (*FIN*) basis for negotiations

ver'hängen *vt* (*fig*) to impose, to inflict

Verhängnis [fɛrˈhɛŋnɪs] **(-ses, -se)** *nt* fate, doom; **jdm zum ~ werden** to be sb's undoing; **v~voll** *adj* fatal, disastrous

verharmlosen [fɛrˈharmloːzən] *vt* to make light of, to play down

verhärten [fɛrˈhɛrtən] *vr* to harden

verhasst ▲ [fɛrˈhast] *adj* odious, hateful

verhauen [fɛrˈhaʊən] (*unreg; umg*) *vt* (*verprügeln*) to beat up

verheerend [fɛrˈheːrənt] *adj* disastrous, devastating

verheimlichen [fɛrˈhaɪmlɪçən] *vt*: **jdm etw ~** to keep sth secret from sb

verheiratet [fɛrˈhaɪraːtət] *adj* married

ver'helfen (*unreg*) *vi*: **jdm ~ zu** to help sb to get

ver'hindern *vt* to prevent; **verhindert sein** to be unable to make it

verhöhnen [fɛrˈhøːnən] *vt* to mock, to sneer at

Verhör [fɛrˈhøːr] **(-(e)s, -e)** *nt* interrogation; (*gerichtlich*) (cross-)examination; **v~en** *vt* to interrogate; to (cross-)examine ♦ *vr* to misunderstand, to mishear

ver'hungern *vi* to starve, to die of hunger

ver'hüten *vt* to prevent, to avert

Ver'hütung *f* prevention; **~smittel** *nt* contraceptive

verirren [fɛrˈɪrən] *vr* to go astray

ver'jagen *vt* to drive away *od* out

verkalken [fɛrˈkalkən] *vi* to calcify; (*umg*) to become senile

Verkauf [fɛrˈkaʊf] *m* sale; **v~en** *vt* to sell

Verkäufer(in) [fɛrˈkɔʏfər(ɪn)] **(-s, -)** *m(f)* seller; salesman(-woman); (*in Laden*) shop assistant

verkaufsoffen *adj*: **~er Samstag** *Saturday when the shops stay open all day*

Verkehr [fɛrˈkeːr] **(-s, -e)** *m* traffic; (*Umgang, bes sexuell*) intercourse; (*Umlauf*) circulation; **v~en** *vi* (*Fahrzeug*) to ply, to run ♦ *vt, vr* to turn, to transform; **v~en mit** to associate with; **bei jdm v~en** (*besuchen*) to visit sb regularly

Verkehrs- *zW*: **~ampel** *f* traffic lights *pl*; **~aufkommen** *nt* volume of traffic;

~beruhigung f traffic calming; ~delikt nt traffic offence; ~funk m radio traffic service; v~günstig adj convenient; ~mittel nt means of transport; ~schild nt road sign; ~stau m traffic jam, stoppage; ~unfall m traffic accident; ~verein m tourist information office; ~zeichen nt traffic sign

verkehrt adj wrong; (umgekehrt) the wrong way round

ver'kennen (unreg) vt to misjudge, not to appreciate

ver'klagen vt to take to court

verkleiden [fɛr'klaɪdən] vr to disguise (o.s.); (sich kostümieren) to get dressed up ♦ vt (Wand) to cover

Verkleidung f disguise; (ARCHIT) wainscoting

verkleinern [fɛr'klaɪnərn] vt to make smaller, to reduce in size

ver'kneifen (umg) vt: sich dat etw ~ (Lachen) to stifle sth; (Schmerz) to hide sth; (sich versagen) to do without sth

verknüpfen [fɛr'knʏpfən] vt to tie (up), to knot; (fig) to connect

ver'kommen (unreg) vi to deteriorate, to decay; (Mensch) to go downhill, to come down in the world ♦ adj (moralisch) dissolute, depraved

ver'körpern [fɛr'kœrpərn] vt to embody, to personify

verkraften [fɛr'kraftən] vt to cope with

ver'kriechen (unreg) vr to creep away, to creep into a corner

verkrüppelt [fɛr'krʏpəlt] adj crippled

ver'kühlen vr to get a chill

ver'kümmern vi to waste away

verkünden [fɛr'kʏndən] vt to proclaim; (Urteil) to pronounce

verkürzen [fɛr'kʏrtsən] vt to shorten; (Wort) to abbreviate; sich dat die Zeit ~ to while away the time

Verkürzung f shortening; abbreviation

verladen [fɛr'la:dən] (unreg) vt (Waren, Vieh) to load; (Truppen: auf Schiff) to embark, (auf Zug) to entrain, (auf Flugzeug) to enplane

Verlag [fɛr'la:k] (-(e)s, -e) m publishing firm

verlangen [fɛr'laŋən] vt to demand; to desire ♦ vi: ~ nach to ask for, to desire; ~ Sie Herrn X ask for Mr X; V~ (-s, -) nt: V~ (nach) desire (for); auf jds V~ (hin) at sb's request

verlängern [fɛr'lɛŋərn] vt to extend; (länger machen) to lengthen

Verlängerung f extension; (SPORT) extra time; ~sschnur f extension cable

verlangsamen [fɛr'laŋza:mən] vt, vr to decelerate, to slow down

Verlass ▲ [fɛr'las] m: auf ihn/das ist kein ~ he/it cannot be relied upon

ver'lassen (unreg) vt to leave ♦ vr: sich ~ auf +akk to depend on ♦ adj desolate; (Mensch) abandoned

verlässlich ▲ [fɛr'lɛslɪç] adj reliable

Verlauf [fɛr'laʊf] m course; v~en (unreg) vi (zeitlich) to pass; (Farben) to run ♦ vr to get lost; (Menschenmenge) to disperse

ver'lauten vi: etw ~ lassen to disclose sth; wie verlautet as reported

ver'legen vt to move; (verlieren) to mislay; (Buch) to publish ♦ vr: sich auf etw akk ~ to take up od to sth ♦ adj embarrassed; nicht ~ um never at a loss for; Ver'legenheit f embarrassment; (Situation) difficulty, scrape

Verleger [fɛr'le:gər] (-s, -) m publisher

Verleih [fɛr'laɪ] (-(e)s, -e) m hire service; v~en (unreg) vt to lend; (Kraft, Anschein) to confer, to bestow; (Preis, Medaille) to award; ~ung f lending; bestowal; award

ver'leiten vt to lead astray; ~ zu to talk into, to tempt into

ver'lernen vt to forget, to unlearn

ver'lesen (unreg) vt to read out; (aussondern) to sort out ♦ vr to make a mistake in reading

verletz- [fɛr'lɛts] zW: ~en vt (auch fig) to injure, to hurt; (Gesetz etc) to violate; ~end adj (fig: Worte) hurtful; ~lich adj vulnerable, sensitive; V~te(r) f(m) injured person; V~ung f injury; (Verstoß) violation, infringement

verleugnen [fɛr'lɔʏgnən] vt (Herkunft, Glauben) to belie; (Menschen) to disown

Spelling Reform: ▲ new spelling △ old spelling (to be phased out)

verleumden [fɛr'lɔʏmdən] *vt* to slander; **Verleumdung** *f* slander, libel

ver'lieben *vr*: **sich ~ (in** +*akk*) to fall in love (with)

verliebt [fɛr'li:pt] *adj* in love

verlieren [fɛr'li:rən] (*unreg*) *vt, vi* to lose ♦ *vr* to get lost

Verlierer *m* loser

verlob- [fɛr'lo:b] *zW*: **~en** *vr*: **sich ~en (mit)** to get engaged (to); **V~te(r)** [fɛr'lo:ptə(r)] *f(m)* fiancé *m*, fiancée *f*; **V~ung** *f* engagement

ver'locken *vt* to entice, to lure

Ver'lockung *f* temptation, attraction

verlogen [fɛr'lo:gən] *adj* untruthful

verlor *etc vb siehe* **verlieren**

verloren [fɛr'lo:rən] *adj* lost; (*Eier*) poached ♦ *vb siehe* **verlieren**; **etw ~ geben** to give sth up for lost; **~ gehen** to get lost

verlosen [fɛr'lo:zən] *vt* to raffle, to draw lots for; **Verlosung** *f* raffle, lottery

Verlust [fɛr'lʊst] **(-(e)s, -e)** *m* loss; (*MIL*) casualty

ver'machen *vt* to bequeath, to leave

Vermächtnis [fɛr'mɛçtnɪs] **(-ses, -se)** *nt* legacy

Vermählung [fɛr'mɛ:lʊŋ] *f* wedding, marriage

vermarkten [fɛr'marktən] *vt* (*COMM: Artikel*) to market

vermehren [fɛr'me:rən] *vt, vr* to multiply; (*Menge*) to increase

Vermehrung *f* multiplying; increase

ver'meiden (*unreg*) *vt* to avoid

vermeintlich [fɛr'maɪntlɪç] *adj* supposed

Vermerk [fɛr'mɛrk] **(-(e)s, -e)** *m* note; (*in Ausweis*) endorsement; **v~en** *vt* to note

ver'messen (*unreg*) *vt* to survey ♦ *adj* presumptuous, bold; **Ver'messenheit** *f* presumptuousness; recklessness

Ver'messung *f* survey(ing)

vermiet- [fɛr'mi:t] *zW*: **ver'mieten** *vt* to let, to rent (out); (*Auto*) to hire out, to rent; **Ver'mieter(in) (-s, -)** *m(f)* landlord(-lady); **Ver'mietung** *f* letting, renting (out); (*von Autos*) hiring (out)

vermindern [fɛr'mɪndərn] *vt, vr* to lessen, to decrease; (*Preise*) to reduce

Verminderung *f* reduction

ver'mischen *vt, vr* to mix, to blend

vermissen [fɛr'mɪsən] *vt* to miss

vermitt- [fɛr'mɪt] *zW*: **~eln** *vi* to mediate ♦ *vt* (*Gespräch*) to connect; **jdm etw ~eln** to help sb to obtain sth; **V~ler (-s, -)** *m* (*Schlichter*) agent, mediator; **V~lung** *f* procurement; (*Stellenvermittlung*) agency; (*TEL*) exchange; (*Schlichtung*) mediation; **V~lungsgebühr** *f* commission

ver'mögen (*unreg*) *vt* to be capable of; **~ zu** to be able to; **Ver'mögen (-s, -)** *nt* wealth; (*Fähigkeit*) ability; **ein V~ kosten** to cost a fortune; **ver'mögend** *adj* wealthy

vermuten [fɛr'mu:tən] *vt* to suppose, to guess; (*argwöhnen*) to suspect

vermutlich *adj* supposed, presumed ♦ *adv* probably

Vermutung *f* supposition; suspicion

vernachlässigen [fɛr'na:xlɛsɪgən] *vt* to neglect

ver'nehmen (*unreg*) *vt* to perceive, to hear; (*erfahren*) to learn; (*JUR*) to (cross-)examine; **dem V~ nach** from what I/we *etc* hear

Vernehmung *f* (cross-)examination

verneigen [fɛr'naɪgən] *vr* to bow

verneinen [fɛr'naɪnən] *vt* (*Frage*) to answer in the negative; (*ablehnen*) to deny; (*GRAM*) to negate; **~d** *adj* negative

Verneinung *f* negation

vernichten [fɛr'nɪçtən] *vt* to annihilate, to destroy; **~d** *adj* (*fig*) crushing; (*Blick*) withering; (*Kritik*) scathing

Vernunft [fɛr'nʊnft] **(-)** *f* reason, understanding

vernünftig [fɛr'nʏnftɪç] *adj* sensible, reasonable

veröffentlichen [fɛr'œfəntlɪçən] *vt* to publish; **Veröffentlichung** *f* publication

verordnen [fɛr'ɔrdnən] *vt* (*MED*) to prescribe

Verordnung *f* order, decree; (*MED*) prescription

ver'pachten *vt* to lease (out)

ver'packen *vt* to pack

Ver'packung *f* packing, wrapping;

~smaterial *nt* packing, wrapping

ver'passen *vt* to miss; **jdm eine Ohrfeige ~** (*umg*) to give sb a clip round the ear

verpfänden [fɛr'pfɛndən] *vt* (*Besitz*) to mortgage

ver'pflanzen *vt* to transplant

ver'pflegen *vt* to feed, to cater for

Ver'pflegung *f* feeding, catering; (*Kost*) food; (*in Hotel*) board

verpflichten [fɛr'pflɪçtən] *vt* to oblige, to bind; (*anstellen*) to engage ♦ *vr* to undertake; (*MIL*) to sign on ♦ *vi* to carry obligations; **jdm zu Dank verpflichtet sein** to be obliged to sb

Verpflichtung *f* obligation, duty

verpönt [fɛr'pø:nt] *adj* disapproved (of), taboo

ver'prügeln (*umg*) *vt* to beat up, to do over

Verputz [fɛr'pʊts] *m* plaster, roughcast; **v~en** *vt* to plaster; (*umg: Essen*) to put away

Verrat [fɛr'ra:t] **(-(e)s)** *m* treachery; (*POL*) treason; **v~en** (*unreg*) *vt* to betray; (*Geheimnis*) to divulge ♦ *vr* to give o.s. away

Verräter [fɛr'rɛ:tər] **(-s, -)** *m* traitor(-tress); **v~isch** *adj* treacherous

ver'rechnen *vt*: **~ mit** to set off against ♦ *vr* to miscalculate

Verrechnungsscheck [fɛr'rɛçnʊŋsʃɛk] *m* crossed cheque

verregnet [fɛr're:gnət] *adj* spoilt by rain, rainy

ver'reisen *vi* to go away (on a journey)

verrenken [fɛr'rɛŋkən] *vt* to contort; (*MED*) to dislocate; **sich** *dat* **den Knöchel ~** to sprain one's ankle

ver'richten *vt* to do, to perform

verriegeln [fɛr'ri:gəln] *vt* to bolt up, to lock

verringern [fɛr'rɪŋərn] *vt* to reduce ♦ *vr* to diminish

Verringerung *f* reduction; lessening

ver'rinnen (*unreg*) *vi* to run out *od* away; (*Zeit*) to elapse

ver'rosten *vi* to rust

verrotten [fɛr'rɔtən] *vi* to rot

ver'rücken *vt* to move, to shift

verrückt [fɛr'rʏkt] *adj* crazy, mad; **V~e(r)** *f(m)* lunatic; **V~heit** *f* madness, lunacy

Verruf [fɛr'ru:f] *m*: **in ~ geraten/bringen** to fall/bring into disrepute; **v~en** *adj* notorious, disreputable

Vers [fɛrs] **(-es, -e)** *m* verse

ver'sagen *vt*: **jdm/sich etw ~** to deny sb/ o.s. sth ♦ *vi* to fail; **Ver'sagen (-s)** *nt* failure

ver'salzen (*unreg*) *vt* to put too much salt in; (*fig*) to spoil

ver'sammeln *vt, vr* to assemble, to gather

Ver'sammlung *f* meeting, gathering

Versand [fɛr'zant] **(-(e)s)** *m* forwarding; dispatch; (*~abteilung*) dispatch department; **~haus** *nt* mail-order firm

versäumen [fɛr'zɔʏmən] *vt* to miss; (*unterlassen*) to neglect, to fail

ver'schaffen *vt*: **jdm/sich etw ~** to get *od* procure sth for sb/o.s.

verschämt [fɛr'ʃɛ:mt] *adj* bashful

verschandeln [fɛr'ʃandəln] (*umg*) *vt* to spoil

verschärfen [fɛr'ʃɛrfən] *vt* to intensify; (*Lage*) to aggravate ♦ *vr* to intensify; to become aggravated

ver'schätzen *vr* to be out in one's reckoning

ver'schenken *vt* to give away

verscheuchen [fɛr'ʃɔʏçən] *vt* (*Tiere*) to chase off *od* away

ver'schicken *vt* to send off

ver'schieben (*unreg*) *vt* to shift; (*EISENB*) to shunt; (*Termin*) to postpone

verschieden [fɛr'ʃi:dən] *adj* different; (*pl: mehrere*) various; **sie sind ~ groß** they are of different sizes; **~tlich** *adv* several times

verschimmeln [fɛr'ʃɪməln] *vi* (*Nahrungsmittel*) to go mouldy

verschlafen [fɛr'ʃla:fən] (*unreg*) *vt* to sleep through; (*fig: versäumen*) to miss ♦ *vi, vr* to oversleep ♦ *adj* sleepy

Verschlag [fɛr'ʃla:k] *m* shed; **v~en** [-gən] (*unreg*) *vt* to board up ♦ *adj* cunning; **jdm den Atem v~en** to take sb's breath away; **an einen Ort v~en werden** to wind up in a place

Spelling Reform: ▲ new spelling △ old spelling (to be phased out)

verschlechtern [fɛrˈʃlɛçtərn] vt to make worse ♦ vr to deteriorate, to get worse; **Verschlechterung** f deterioration

Verschleiß [fɛrˈʃlaɪs] (**-es, -e**) m wear and tear; **v~en** (unreg) vt to wear out

ver'schleppen vt to carry off, to abduct; (Krankheit) to protract; (zeitlich) to drag out

ver'schleudern vt to squander; (COMM) to sell dirt-cheap

verschließbar adj lockable

verschließen [fɛrˈʃliːsən] (unreg) vt to close; to lock ♦ vr: **sich einer Sache** dat ~ to close one's mind to sth

verschlimmern [fɛrˈʃlɪmərn] vt to make worse, to aggravate ♦ vr to get worse, to deteriorate

verschlingen [fɛrˈʃlɪŋən] (unreg) vt to devour, to swallow up; (Fäden) to twist

verschlossen [fɛrˈʃlɔsən] adj locked; (fig) reserved; **v~heit** f reserve

ver'schlucken vt to swallow ♦ vr to choke

Verschluss ▲ [fɛrˈʃlʊs] m lock; (von Kleid etc) fastener; (PHOT) shutter; (Stöpsel) plug

verschlüsseln [fɛrˈʃlʏsəln] vt to encode

ver'schmieren vt (verstreichen: Gips, Mörtel) to apply, spread on; (schmutzig machen: Wand etc) to smear

verschmutzen [fɛrˈʃmʊtsən] vt to soil; (Umwelt) to pollute

verschneit [fɛrˈʃnaɪt] adj snowed up, covered in snow

verschollen [fɛrˈʃɔlən] adj lost, missing

ver'schonen vt: **jdn mit etw** ~ to spare sb sth

verschönern [fɛrˈʃøːnərn] vt to decorate; (verbessern) to improve

ver'schreiben (unreg) vt (MED) to prescribe ♦ vr to make a mistake (in writing); **sich einer Sache** dat ~ to devote o.s. to sth

verschreibungspflichtig adj (Medikament) available on prescription only

verschrotten [fɛrˈʃrɔtən] vt to scrap

verschuld- [fɛrˈʃʊld] zW: **~en** vt to be guilty of; **V~en** (**-s**) nt fault, guilt; **~et** adj in debt; **V~ung** f fault; (Geld) debts pl

ver'schütten vt to spill; (zuschütten) to fill; (unter Trümmern) to bury

ver'schweigen (unreg) vt to keep secret; **jdm etw** ~ to keep sth from sb

verschwend- [fɛrˈʃvɛnd] zW: **~en** vt to squander; **V~er** (**-s, -**) m spendthrift; **~erisch** adj wasteful, extravagant; **V~ung** f waste; extravagance

verschwiegen [fɛrˈʃviːɡən] adj discreet; (Ort) secluded; **V~heit** f discretion; seclusion

ver'schwimmen (unreg) vi to grow hazy, to become blurred

ver'schwinden (unreg) vi to disappear, to vanish; **Verschwinden** (**-s**) nt disappearance

verschwitzt [fɛrˈʃvɪtst] adj (Mensch) sweaty

verschwommen [fɛrˈʃvɔmən] adj hazy, vague

verschwör- [fɛrˈʃvøːr] zW: **~en** (unreg) vr to plot, to conspire; **V~ung** f conspiracy, plot

ver'sehen (unreg) vt to supply, to provide; (Pflicht) to carry out; (Amt) to fill; (Haushalt) to keep ♦ vr (fig) to make a mistake; **ehe er (es) sich** ~ **hatte ...** before he knew it ...; **Ver'sehen** (**-s, -**) nt oversight; **aus V~** by mistake; **~tlich** adv by mistake

Versehrte(r) [fɛrˈzeːrtə(r)] f(m) disabled person

ver'senden (unreg) vt to forward, to dispatch

ver'senken vt to sink ♦ vr: **sich** ~ **in** +akk to become engrossed in

versessen [fɛrˈzɛsən] adj: ~ **auf** +akk mad about

ver'setzen vt to transfer; (verpfänden) to pawn; (umg) to stand up ♦ vr: **sich in jds Lage** od **in jds Lage** ~ to put o.s. in sb's place; **jdm einen Tritt/Schlag** ~ to kick/hit sb; **etw mit etw** ~ to mix sth with sth; **jdn in gute Laune** ~ to put sb in a good mood

Ver'setzung f transfer

verseuchen [fɛrˈzɔʏçən] vt to contaminate

versichern [fɛrˈzɪçərn] vt to assure; (mit Geld) to insure

Versicherung f assurance; insurance

Versicherungs- zW: **~gesellschaft** f insurance company; **~karte** f insurance card; **die grüne ~karte** the green card;

~**police** f insurance policy

ver'**sinken** (unreg) vi to sink

ver**söhnen** [fɛr'zøːnən] vt to reconcile ♦ vr to become reconciled

Ver**söhnung** f reconciliation

ver**sorgen** vt to provide, to supply; (Familie etc) to look after

Ver**sorgung** f provision; (Unterhalt) maintenance; (Altersversorgung etc) benefit, assistance

ver**späten** [fɛr'ʃpɛːtən] vr to be late

ver**spätet** adj (Zug, Abflug, Ankunft) late; (Glückwünsche) belated

Ver**spätung** f delay; ~ **haben** to be late

ver'**sperren** vt to bar, to obstruct

ver**spielt** [fɛr'ʃpiːlt] adj (Kind, Tier) playful

ver'**spotten** vt to ridicule, to scoff at

ver**sprechen** (unreg) vt to promise; **sich** dat **etw von etw** ~ to expect sth from sth; Ver'**sprechen** (-s, -) nt promise

ver**staatlichen** [fɛr'ʃtaːtlɪçən] vt to nationalize

Ver**stand** [fɛr'ʃtant] m intelligence; mind; **den** ~ **verlieren** to go out of one's mind; **über jds** ~ **gehen** to go beyond sb

ver**ständig** [fɛr'ʃtɛndɪç] adj sensible; ~**en** [fɛr'ʃtɛndɪɡən] vt to inform ♦ vr to communicate; (sich einigen) to come to an understanding; V~**ung** f communication; (Benachrichtigung) informing; (Einigung) agreement

ver**ständ-** [fɛr'ʃtɛnt] zW: ~**lich** adj understandable, comprehensible; V~**lichkeit** f clarity, intelligibility; V~**nis** (-ses, -se) nt understanding; ~**nislos** adj uncomprehending; ~**nisvoll** adj understanding, sympathetic

ver**stärk-** [fɛr'ʃtɛrk] zW: ~**en** vt to strengthen; (Ton) to amplify; (erhöhen) to intensify ♦ vr to intensify; V~**er** (-s, -) m amplifier; V~**ung** f strengthening; (Hilfe) reinforcements pl; (von Ton) amplification

ver**stauchen** [fɛr'ʃtauxən] vt to sprain

ver**stauen** [fɛr'ʃtauən] vt to stow away

Ver**steck** [fɛr'ʃtɛk] (-(e)s, -e) nt hiding (place); v~**en** vt, vr to hide; v~**t** adj hidden

ver'**stehen** (unreg) vt to understand ♦ vr to get on; **das versteht sich (von selbst)** that goes without saying

ver**steigern** [fɛr'ʃtaɪɡərn] vt to auction; Ver**steigerung** f auction

ver**stell-** [fɛr'ʃtɛl] zW: ~**bar** adj adjustable, variable; ~**en** vt to move, to shift; (Uhr) to adjust; (versperren) to block; (fig) to disguise ♦ vr to pretend, to put on an act; V~**ung** f pretence

ver**steuern** [fɛr'ʃtɔɪərn] vt to pay tax on

ver**stimmt** [fɛr'ʃtɪmt] adj out of tune; (fig) cross, put out; (Magen) upset

ver'**stopfen** vt to block, to stop up; (MED) to constipate

Ver**stopfung** f obstruction; (MED) constipation

ver**storben** [fɛr'ʃtɔrbən] adj deceased, late

ver**stört** [fɛr'ʃtøːrt] adj (Mensch) distraught

Ver**stoß** [fɛr'ʃtoːs] m: ~ **(gegen)** infringement (of), violation (of); v~**en** (unreg) vt to disown, to reject ♦ vi: v~**en gegen** to offend against

ver**streichen** (unreg) vt to spread ♦ vi to elapse

ver**streuen** vt to scatter (about)

ver**stümmeln** [fɛr'ʃtʏməln] vt to maim, to mutilate (auch fig)

ver**stummen** [fɛr'ʃtʊmən] vi to go silent; (Lärm) to die away

Ver**such** [fɛr'zuːx] (-(e)s, -e) m attempt; (SCI) experiment; v~**en** vt to try; (verlocken) to tempt ♦ vr: **sich an etw** dat v~**en** to try one's hand at sth; ~**skaninchen** nt (fig) guinea-pig; ~**ung** f temptation

ver**tagen** [fɛr'taːɡən] vt, vi to adjourn

ver**tauschen** vt to exchange; (versehentlich) to mix up

ver**teidig-** [fɛr'taɪdɪç] zW: ~**en** vt to defend; V~**er** (-s, -) m defender; (JUR) defence counsel; V~**ung** f defence

ver**teilen** vt to distribute; (Rollen) to assign; (Salbe) to spread

Ver**teilung** f distribution, allotment

ver**tiefen** [fɛr'tiːfən] vt to deepen ♦ vr: **sich in etw** akk ~ to become engrossed od absorbed in sth

Ver**tiefung** f depression

vertikal [vɛrti'kaːl] *adj* vertical

vertilgen [fɛr'tɪlgən] *vt* to exterminate; (*umg*) to eat up, to consume

vertonen [fɛr'toːnən] *vt* to set to music

Vertrag [fɛr'traːk] **(-(e)s, ⁓e)** *m* contract, agreement; (*POL*) treaty; **v~en** [-gən] (*unreg*) *vt* to tolerate, to stand ♦ *vr* to get along; (*sich aussöhnen*) to become reconciled; **v~lich** *adj* contractual

verträglich [fɛr'trɛːklɪç] *adj* good-natured, sociable; (*Speisen*) easily digested; (*MED*) easily tolerated; **V~keit** *f* sociability; good nature; digestibility

Vertrags- *zW*: **~bruch** *m* breach of contract; **~händler** *m* appointed retailer; **~partner** *m* party to a contract; **~werkstatt** *f* appointed repair shop; **v~widrig** *adj* contrary to contract

vertrauen [fɛr'travən] *vi*: **jdm ~** to trust sb; **~ auf** +*akk* to rely on; **V~ (-s)** *nt* confidence; **V~ erweckend** inspiring trust; **~svoll** *adj* trustful; **~swürdig** *adj* trustworthy

vertraulich [fɛr'travlɪç] *adj* familiar; (*geheim*) confidential

vertraut [fɛr'travt] *adj* familiar; **V~heit** *f* familiarity

ver'treiben (*unreg*) *vt* to drive away; (*aus Land*) to expel; (*COMM*) to sell; (*Zeit*) to pass

vertret- [fɛr'treːt] *zW*: **~en** (*unreg*) *vt* to represent; (*Ansicht*) to hold, to advocate; **sich** *dat* **die Beine ~en** to stretch one's legs; **V~er (-s, -)** *m* representative; (*Verfechter*) advocate; **V~ung** *f* representation; advocacy

Vertrieb [fɛr'triːp] **(-(e)s, -e)** *m* marketing (department)

ver'trocknen *vi* to dry up

ver'trösten *vt* to put off

vertun [fɛr'tuːn] (*unreg*) *vt* to waste ♦ *vr* (*umg*) to make a mistake

vertuschen [fɛr'tʊʃən] *vt* to hush *od* cover up

verübeln [fɛr'|yːbəln] *vt*: **jdm etw ~** to be cross *od* offended with sb on account of sth

verüben [fɛr'|yːbən] *vt* to commit

verun- [fɛr'|ʊn] *zW*: **~glimpfen** *vt* to disparage; **~glücken** *vi* to have an accident; **tödlich ~glücken** to be killed in an accident; **~reinigen** *vt* to soil; (*Umwelt*) to pollute; **~sichern** *vt* to rattle; **~treuen** [-trɔyən] *vt* to embezzle

verur- [fɛr'|uːr] *zW*: **~sachen** *vt* to cause; **~teilen** [-taɪlən] *vt* to condemn; **V~teilung** *f* condemnation; (*JUR*) sentence

verviel- [fɛr'fiːl] *zW*: **~fachen** *vt* to multiply; **~fältigen** [-fɛltɪgən] *vt* to duplicate, to copy; **V~fältigung** *f* duplication, copying

vervollkommnen [fɛr'fɔlkɔmnən] *vt* to perfect

vervollständigen [fɛr'fɔlʃtɛndɪgən] *vt* to complete

ver'wackeln *vt* (*Foto*) to blur

ver'wählen *vr* (*TEL*) to dial the wrong number

verwahren [fɛr'vaːrən] *vt* to keep, to lock away ♦ *vr* to protest

verwalt- [fɛr'valt] *zW*: **~en** *vt* to manage; to administer; **V~er (-s, -)** *m* manager; (*Vermögensverwalter*) trustee; **V~ung** *f* administration; management

ver'wandeln *vt* to change, to transform ♦ *vr* to change; to be transformed; **Ver'wandlung** *f* change, transformation

verwandt [fɛr'vant] *adj*: **~ (mit)** related (to); **V~e(r)** *f(m)* relative, relation; **V~schaft** *f* relationship; (*Menschen*) relations *pl*

ver'warnen *vt* to caution

Ver'warnung *f* caution

ver'wechseln *vt*: **~ mit** to confuse with; to mistake for; **zum V~ ähnlich** as like as two peas

Ver'wechslung *f* confusion, mixing up

Verwehung [fɛr'veːʊŋ] *f* snowdrift; sand drift

verweichlicht [fɛr'vaɪçlɪçt] *adj* effeminate, soft

ver'weigern *vt*: **jdm etw ~** to refuse sb sth; **den Gehorsam/die Aussage ~** to refuse to obey/testify

Ver'weigerung *f* refusal

Verweis [fɛr'vaɪs] **(-es, -e)** *m* reprimand,

rebuke; (Hinweis) reference; **v~en** (unreg) vt to refer; **jdn von der Schule v~en** to expel sb (from school); **jdn des Landes v~en** to deport od expel sb

ver'welken vi to fade

verwend- [fɛr'vɛnd] zW: **~bar** [-'vɛntbaːr] adj usable; **ver'wenden** (unreg) vt to use; (Mühe, Zeit, Arbeit) to spend ♦ vr to intercede; **Ver'wendung** f use

ver'werfen (unreg) vt to reject

verwerflich [fɛr'vɛrflɪç] adj reprehensible

ver'werten vt to utilize

Ver'wertung f utilization

verwesen [fɛr've:zən] vi to decay

ver'wickeln vt to tangle (up); (fig) to involve ♦ vr to get tangled (up); **jdn in etw** akk ~ to involve sb in sth; **sich in etw** akk ~ to get involved in sth

verwickelt [fɛr'vɪkəlt] adj (Situation, Fall) difficult, complicated

verwildern [fɛr'vɪldərn] vi to run wild

verwirklichen [fɛr'vɪrklɪçən] vt to realize, to put into effect

Verwirklichung f realization

verwirren [fɛr'vɪrən] vt to tangle (up); (fig) to confuse

Verwirrung f confusion

verwittern [fɛr'vɪtərn] vi to weather

verwitwet [fɛr'vɪtvət] adj widowed

verwöhnen [fɛr'vø:nən] vt to spoil

verworren [fɛr'vɔrən] adj confused

verwundbar [fɛr'vʊntbaːr] adj vulnerable

verwunden [fɛr'vʊndən] vt to wound

verwunder- [fɛr'vʊndər] zW: **~lich** adj surprising; **V~ung** f astonishment

Verwundete(r) f(m) injured person

Verwundung f wound, injury

ver'wünschen vt to curse

verwüsten [fɛr'vy:stən] vt to devastate

verzagen [fɛr'tsa:gən] vi to despair

ver'zählen vr to miscount

verzehren [fɛr'tse:rən] vt to consume

ver'zeichnen vt to list; (Niederlage, Verlust) to register

Verzeichnis [fɛr'tsaɪçnɪs] (-ses, -se) nt list, catalogue; (in Buch) index

verzeih- [fɛr'tsaɪ] zW: **~en** (unreg) vt, vi to forgive; **jdm etw ~en** to forgive sb for sth; **~lich** adj pardonable; **V~ung** f forgiveness, pardon; **V~ung!** sorry!, excuse me!

verzichten [fɛr'tsɪçtən] vi: ~ **auf** +akk to forgo, to give up

ver'ziehen (unreg) vi to move ♦ vt to put out of shape; (Kind) to spoil; (Pflanzen) to thin out ♦ vr to go out of shape; (Gesicht) to contort; (verschwinden) to disappear; **das Gesicht ~** to pull a face

verzieren [fɛr'tsi:rən] vt to decorate, to ornament

Verzierung f decoration

verzinsen [fɛr'tsɪnzən] vt to pay interest on

ver'zögern vt to delay

Ver'zögerung f delay, time lag; **~staktik** f delaying tactics pl

verzollen [fɛr'tsɔlən] vt to pay duty on

Verzug [fɛr'tsu:k] m delay

verzweif- [fɛr'tsvaɪf] zW: **~eln** vi to despair; **~elt** adj desperate; **V~lung** f despair

Veto ['ve:to] (-s, -s) nt veto

Vetter ['fɛtər] (-s, -n) m cousin

vgl. abk (= vergleiche) cf.

v. H. abk (= vom Hundert) p.c.

vibrieren [vi'bri:rən] vi to vibrate

Video ['vi:deo] nt video; **~gerät** nt video recorder; **~rekorder** m video recorder

Vieh [fi:] (-(e)s) nt cattle pl; **v~isch** adj bestial

viel [fi:l] adj a lot of, much ♦ adv a lot; much; ~ **sagend** significant; ~ **versprechend** promising; **~e** pron pl a lot of, many; ~ **zu wenig** much too little; **~erlei** adj a great variety of; **~es** pron a lot; **~fach** adj, adv many times; **auf ~fachen Wunsch** at the request of many people; **V~falt** (-) f variety; **~fältig** adj varied, many-sided

vielleicht [fi'laɪçt] adv perhaps

viel- zW: **~mal(s)** adv many times; **danke ~mals** many thanks; **~mehr** adv rather, on the contrary; **~seitig** adj many-sided

vier [fi:r] num four; **V~eck** (-(e)s, -e) nt four-sided figure; (gleichseitig) square; **~eckig** adj four-sided; square; **V~takt-motor** m four-stroke engine; **~te(r, s)**

['fi:rtə(r, s)] *adj* fourth; **V~tel** ['fɪrtəl] **(-s, -)** *nt* quarter; **V~teljahr** *nt* quarter; **~teljährlich** *adj* quarterly; **~teln** *vt* to divide into four; (*Kuchen usw*) to divide into quarters; **V~telstunde** *f* quarter of an hour; **~zehn** ['fɪrtse:n] *num* fourteen; **in ~zehn Tagen** in a fortnight; **~zehntägig** *adj* fortnightly; **~zig** ['fɪrtsɪç] *num* forty

Villa ['vɪla] **(-, Villen)** *f* villa

violett [vio'lɛt] *adj* violet

Violin- [vio'li:n] *zW:* **~e** *f* violin; **~schlüssel** *m* treble clef

virtuell [vɪrtu'ɛl] *adj* (*COMPUT*) virtual; **~e Realität** virtual reality

Virus ['vi:rʊs] **(-, Viren)** *m od nt* (*auch COMPUT*) virus

Visa ['vi:za] *pl von* **Visum**

vis-a-vis ▲, **vis-à-vis** [viza'vi:] *adv* opposite

Visen ['vi:zən] *pl von* **Visum**

Visier [vi'zi:r] **(-s, -e)** *nt* gunsight; (*am Helm*) visor

Visite [vi'zi:tə] *f* (*MED*) visit; **~nkarte** *f* visiting card

Visum ['vi:zʊm] **(-s, Visa od Visen)** *nt* visa

vital [vi'ta:l] *adj* lively, full of life, vital

Vitamin [vita'mi:n] **(-s, -e)** *nt* vitamin

Vogel ['fo:gəl] **(-s, ¨)** *m* bird; **einen ~ haben** (*umg*) to have bats in the belfry; **jdm den ~ zeigen** (*umg*) to tap one's forehead (*meaning that one thinks sb stupid*); **~bauer** *nt* birdcage; **~perspektive** *f* bird's-eye view; **~scheuche** *f* scarecrow

Vokabel [vo'ka:bəl] **(-, -n)** *f* word

Vokabular [vokabu'la:r] **(-s, -e)** *nt* vocabulary

Vokal [vo'ka:l] **(-s, -e)** *m* vowel

Volk [fɔlk] **(-(e)s, ¨er)** *nt* people; nation

Völker- ['fœlkər] *zW:* **~recht** *nt* international law; **v~rechtlich** *adj* according to international law; **~verständigung** *f* international understanding

Volkshochschule

ⓘ *The Volkshochschule (VHS) is an institution which offers Adult Education classes. No set qualifications are necessary*

to attend. For a small fee adults can attend both vocational and non-vocational classes in the day-time or evening.

Volks- *zW:* **~entscheid** *m* referendum; **~fest** *nt* fair; **~hochschule** *f* adult education classes *pl*; **~lied** *nt* folksong; **~republik** *f* people's republic; **~schule** *f* elementary school; **~tanz** *m* folk dance; **~vertreter(in)** *m(f)* people's representative; **~wirtschaft** *f* economics *sg*

voll [fɔl] *adj* full; **etw ~ machen** to fill sth up; **~ tanken** to fill up; **~ und ganz** completely; **jdn für ~ nehmen** (*umg*) to take sb seriously; **~auf** *adv* amply; **V~bart** *m* full beard; **V~beschäftigung** *f* full employment; **~'bringen** (*unreg*) *vt insep* to accomplish; **~'enden** *vt insep* to finish, to complete; **~endet** *adj* (*~kommen*) completed; **~ends** ['fɔlɛnts] *adv* completely; **V~'endung** *f* completion

Volleyball ['vɔlibal] *m* volleyball

Vollgas *nt:* **mit ~** at full throttle; **~ geben** to step on it

völlig ['fœlɪç] *adj* complete ♦ *adv* completely

voll- *zW:* **~jährig** *adj* of age; **V~kaskoversicherung** ['fɔlkaskoferziçarʊŋ] *f* fully comprehensive insurance; **~'kommen** *adj* perfect; **V~'kommenheit** *f* perfection; **V~kornbrot** *nt* wholemeal bread; **V~macht (-, -en)** *f* authority, full powers *pl*; **V~milch** *f* (*KOCH*) full-cream milk; **V~mond** *m* full moon; **V~pension** *f* full board; **~ständig** ['fɔlʃtɛndɪç] *adj* complete; **~'strecken** *vt insep* to execute; **~tanken** △ *vt, vi siehe* **voll**; **V~waschmittel** *nt* detergent; **V~wertkost** *f* wholefood; **~zählig** ['fɔltse:lɪç] *adj* complete; in full number; **~'ziehen** (*unreg*) *vt insep* to carry out ♦ *vr insep* to happen; **V~zug** *m* execution

Volumen [vo'lu:mən] **(-s, - od Volumina)** *nt* volume

vom [fɔm] = **von dem**

SCHLÜSSELWORT

von [fɔn] *präp +dat* **1** (*Ausgangspunkt*) from;

von from ... to; **von morgens bis abends** from morning till night; **von ... nach ...** from ... to ...; **von ... an** from ...; **von ... aus** from ...; **von dort aus** from there; **etw von sich aus tun** to do sth of one's own accord; **von mir aus** (*umg*) if you like, I don't mind; **von wo/wann ...?** where/ when ... from?

2 (*Ursache, im Passiv*) by; **ein Gedicht von Schiller** a poem by Schiller; **von etw müde** tired from sth

3 (*als Genitiv*) of; **ein Freund von mir** a friend of mine; **nett von dir** nice of you; **jeweils zwei von zehn** two out of every ten

4 (*über*) about; **er erzählte vom Urlaub** he talked about his holiday

5: **von wegen!** (*umg*) no way!

voneinander *adv* from each other

SCHLÜSSELWORT
---

vor [foːr] *präp +dat* 1 (*räumlich*) in front of; **vor der Kirche links abbiegen** turn left before the church

2 (*zeitlich*) before; **ich war vor ihm da** I was there before him; **vor 2 Tagen** 2 days ago; **5 (Minuten) vor 4** 5 (minutes) to 4; **vor kurzem** a little while ago

3 (*Ursache*) with; **vor Wut/Liebe** with rage/love; **vor Hunger sterben** to die of hunger; **vor lauter Arbeit** because of work

4: **vor allem, vor allen Dingen** most of all
♦ *präp +akk* (*räumlich*) in front of
♦ *adv*: **vor und zurück** backwards and forwards

Vorabend ['foːrʔaːbənt] *m* evening before, eve

voran [fo'ran] *adv* before, ahead; **mach ~!** get on with it!; **~gehen** (*unreg*) *vi* to go ahead; **einer Sache** *dat* **~gehen** to precede sth; **~kommen** (*unreg*) *vi* to come along, to make progress

Voranschlag ['foːrʔanʃlaːk] *m* estimate

Vorarbeiter ['foːrʔarbaɪtər] *m* foreman

voraus [fo'raus] *adv* ahead; (*zeitlich*) in advance; **jdm ~ sein** to be ahead of sb; **im V~** in advance; **~gehen** (*unreg*) *vi* to go (on) ahead; (*fig*) to precede; **~haben** (*unreg*) *vt*: **jdm etw ~haben** to have the edge on sb in sth; **V~sage** *f* prediction; **~sagen** *vt* to predict; **~sehen** (*unreg*) *vt* to foresee; **~setzen** *vt* to assume; **~gesetzt, dass ...** provided that ...; **V~setzung** *f* requirement, prerequisite; **V~sicht** *f* foresight; **aller V~sicht nach** in all probability; **~sichtlich** *adv* probably

Vorbehalt ['foːrbəhalt] (**-(e)s, -e**) *m* reservation, proviso; **v~en** (*unreg*) *vt*: **sich/jdm etw v~en** to reserve sth (for o.s.)/for sb; **v~los** *adj* unconditional ♦ *adv* unconditionally

vorbei [fɔr'baɪ] *adv* by, past; **das ist ~** that's over; **~gehen** (*unreg*) *vi* to pass by, to go past; **~kommen** (*unreg*) *vi*: **bei jdm ~kommen** to drop in on *od* call in on sb

vor- *zW*: **~belastet** ['foːrbəlastət] *adj* (*fig*) handicapped; **~bereiten** *vt* to prepare; **V~bereitung** *f* preparation; **V~bestellung** *f* advance order; (*von Platz, Tisch etc*) advance booking; **~bestraft** ['foːrbəʃtraːft] *adj* previously convicted, with a record

vorbeugen ['foːrbɔʏɡən] *vt, vr* to lean forward ♦ *vi +dat* to prevent; **~d** *adj* preventive

Vorbeugung *f* prevention; **zur ~ gegen** for the prevention of

Vorbild ['foːrbɪlt] *nt* model; **sich** *dat* **jdn zum ~ nehmen** to model o.s. on sb; **v~lich** *adj* model, ideal

vorbringen ['foːrbrɪŋən] (*unreg*) *vt* to advance, to state

Vorder- ['fɔrdər] *zW*: **~achse** *f* front axle; **v~e(r, s)** *adj* front; **~grund** *m* foreground; **~mann** (*pl* **-männer**) *m* man in front; **jdn auf ~mann bringen** (*umg*) to get sb to shape up; **~seite** *f* front (side); **v~ste(r, s)** *adj* front

vordrängen ['foːrdrɛŋən] *vr* to push to the front

voreilig ['foːrʔaɪlɪç] *adj* hasty, rash

voreinander [foːrʔaɪ'nandər] *adv* (*räumlich*)

in front of each other

voreingenommen ['foːr|aɪngənɔmən] *adj* biased; **V~heit** *f* bias

vorenthalten ['foːr|ɛnthaltən] (*unreg*) *vt*: **jdm etw ~** to withhold sth from sb

vorerst ['foːrˈeːrst] *adv* for the moment *od* present

Vorfahr ['foːrfaːr] (**-en, -en**) *m* ancestor

vorfahren (*unreg*) *vi* to drive (on) ahead; (*vors Haus etc*) to drive up

Vorfahrt *f* (*AUT*) right of way; **~ achten!** give way!

Vorfahrts- *zW*: **~regel** *f* right of way; **~schild** *nt* give way sign; **~straße** *f* major road

Vorfall ['foːrfal] *m* incident; **v~en** (*unreg*) *vi* to occur

vorfinden ['foːrfɪndən] (*unreg*) *vt* to find

Vorfreude ['foːrfrɔʏdə] *f* (joyful) anticipation

vorführen ['foːrfyːrən] *vt* to show, to display; **dem Gericht ~** to bring before the court

Vorgabe ['foːrgaːbə] *f* (*SPORT*) start, handicap ♦ *in zW* (*COMPUT*) default

Vorgang ['foːrgaŋ] *m* course of events; (*bes SCI*) process

Vorgänger(in) ['foːrgɛŋər(ɪn)] (**-s, -**) *m(f)* predecessor

vorgeben ['foːrgeːbən] (*unreg*) *vt* to pretend, to use as a pretext; (*SPORT*) to give an advantage *od* a start of

vorgefertigt ['foːrgəfɛrtɪçt] *adj* prefabricated

vorgehen ['foːrgeːən] (*unreg*) *vi* (*voraus*) to go (on) ahead; (*nach vorn*) to go up front; (*handeln*) to act, to proceed; (*Uhr*) to be fast; (*Vorrang haben*) to take precedence; (*passieren*) to go on

Vorgehen (**-s**) *nt* action

Vorgeschichte ['foːrgəʃɪçtə] *f* past history

Vorgeschmack ['foːrgəʃmak] *m* foretaste

Vorgesetzte(r) ['foːrgəzɛtstə(r)] *f(m)* superior

vorgestern ['foːrgɛstərn] *adv* the day before yesterday

vorhaben ['foːrhaːbən] (*unreg*) *vt* to intend; **hast du schon was vor?** have you got anything on?; **V~** (**-s, -**) *nt* intention

vorhalten ['foːrhaltən] (*unreg*) *vt* to hold *od* put up ♦ *vi* to last; **jdm etw ~** (*fig*) to reproach sb for sth

vorhanden [foːrˈhandən] *adj* existing; (*erhältlich*) available

Vorhang ['foːrhaŋ] *m* curtain

Vorhängeschloss ▲ ['foːrhɛŋəʃlɔs] *nt* padlock

vorher [foːrˈheːr] *adv* before(hand); **~bestimmen** *vt* (*Schicksal*) to preordain; **~gehen** (*unreg*) *vi* to precede; **~ig** *adj* previous

Vorherrschaft ['foːrhɛrʃaft] *f* predominance, supremacy

vorherrschen ['foːrhɛrʃən] *vi* to predominate

vorher- [foːrˈheːr] *zW*: **V~sage** *f* forecast; **~sagen** *vt* to forecast, to predict; **~sehbar** *adj* predictable; **~sehen** (*unreg*) *vt* to foresee

vorhin [foːrˈhɪn] *adv* not long ago, just now; **V~ein** ▲ *adv*: **im V~ein** beforehand

vorig ['foːrɪç] *adj* previous, last

Vorkämpfer(in) ['foːrkɛmpfər(ɪn)] *m(f)* pioneer

Vorkaufsrecht ['foːrkaʊfsrɛçt] *nt* option to buy

Vorkehrung ['foːrkeːruŋ] *f* precaution

vorkommen ['foːrkɔmən] (*unreg*) *vi* to come forward; (*geschehen, sich finden*) to occur; (*scheinen*) to seem (to be); **sich** *dat* **dumm** *etc* **~** to feel stupid *etc*; **V~** (**-s, -**) *nt* occurrence

Vorkriegs- ['foːrkriːks] *in zW* prewar

Vorladung ['foːrlaːduŋ] *f* summons *sg*

Vorlage ['foːrlaːgə] *f* model, pattern; (*Gesetzesvorlage*) bill; (*SPORT*) pass

vorlassen ['foːrlasən] (*unreg*) *vt* to admit; (*vorgehen lassen*) to allow to go in front

vorläufig ['foːrlɔʏfɪç] *adj* temporary, provisional

vorlaut ['foːrlaʊt] *adj* impertinent, cheeky

vorlesen ['foːrleːzən] (*unreg*) *vt* to read (out)

Vorlesung *f* (*UNIV*) lecture

vorletzte(r, s) ['foːrlɛtstə(r, s)] *adj* last but one

vorlieb [foːrˈliːp] *adv*: **~ nehmen mit** to

make do with

Vorliebe ['foːrliːbə] f preference, partiality

vorliegen ['foːrliːgən] (unreg) vi to be (here); **etw liegt jdm vor** sb has sth; **~d** adj present, at issue

vormachen ['foːrmaxən] vt: **jdm etw ~** to show sb how to do sth; (fig) to fool sb; to have sb on

Vormachtstellung ['foːrmaxtʃtɛlʊŋ] f supremacy, hegemony

Vormarsch ['foːrmarʃ] m advance

vormerken ['foːrmɛrkən] vt to book

Vormittag ['foːrmɪtaːk] m morning; **v~s** adv in the morning, before noon

vorn [fɔrn] adv in front; **von ~ anfangen** to start at the beginning; **nach ~** to the front

Vorname ['foːrnaːmə] m first name, Christian name

vorne ['fɔrnə] adv = **vorn**

vornehm ['foːrneːm] adj distinguished; refined; elegant

vornehmen (unreg) vt (fig) to carry out; **sich** dat **etw ~** to start on sth; (beschließen) to decide to do sth; **sich** dat **jdn ~** to tell sb off

vornherein ['fɔrnhɛraɪn] adv: **von ~** from the start

Vorort ['foːrʔɔrt] m suburb

Vorrang ['foːrraŋ] m precedence, priority; **v~ig** adj of prime importance, primary

Vorrat ['foːrraːt] m stock, supply

vorrätig ['foːrreːtɪç] adj in stock

Vorratskammer f pantry

Vorrecht ['foːrreçt] nt privilege

Vorrichtung ['foːrrɪçtʊŋ] f device, contrivance

vorrücken ['foːrrʏkən] vi to advance ♦ vt to move forward

Vorsaison ['foːrzɛzõː] f early season

Vorsatz ['foːrzats] m intention; (JUR) intent; **einen ~ fassen** to make a resolution

vorsätzlich ['foːrzɛtslɪç] adj intentional; (JUR) premeditated ♦ adv intentionally

Vorschau ['foːrʃaʊ] f (RADIO, TV) (programme) preview; (Film) trailer

Vorschlag ['foːrʃlaːk] m suggestion, proposal; **v~en** (unreg) vt to suggest, to propose

vorschreiben ['foːrʃraɪbən] (unreg) vt to prescribe, to specify

Vorschrift ['foːrʃrɪft] f regulation(s); rule(s); (Anweisungen) instruction(s); **Dienst nach ~** work-to-rule; **v~smäßig** adj as per regulations/instructions

Vorschuss ▲ ['foːrʃʊs] m advance

vorsehen ['foːrzeːən] (unreg) vt to provide for, to plan ♦ vr to take care, to be careful ♦ vi to be visible

Vorsehung f providence

Vorsicht ['foːrzɪçt] f caution, care; **~!** look out!, take care!; (auf Schildern) caution!, danger!; **~, Stufe!** mind the step!; **v~ig** adj cautious, careful; **v~shalber** adv just in case

Vorsilbe ['foːrzɪlbə] f prefix

vorsingen ['foːrzɪŋən] vt (vor Zuhörern) to sing (to); (in Prüfung, für Theater etc) to audition (for) ♦ vi to sing

Vorsitz ['foːrzɪts] m chair(manship); **~ende(r)** f(m) chairman(-woman)

Vorsorge ['foːrzɔrgə] f precaution(s), provision(s); **v~n** vi: **v~n für** to make provision(s) for; **~untersuchung** f check-up

vorsorglich ['foːrzɔrklɪç] adv as a precaution

Vorspeise ['foːrʃpaɪzə] f hors d'oeuvre, appetizer

Vorspiel ['foːrʃpiːl] nt prelude

vorspielen vt: **jdm etw ~** (MUS) to play sth for od to sb ♦ vi (zur Prüfung etc) to play for od to sb

vorsprechen ['foːrʃprɛçən] (unreg) vt to say out loud, to recite ♦ vi: **bei jdm ~** to call on sb

Vorsprung ['foːrʃprʊŋ] m projection, ledge; (fig) advantage, start

Vorstadt ['foːrʃtat] f suburbs pl

Vorstand ['foːrʃtant] m executive committee; (COMM) board (of directors); (Person) director, head

vorstehen ['foːrʃteːən] (unreg) vi to project; **einer Sache** dat **~** (fig) to be the head of sth

vorstell- ['foːrʃtɛl] zW: **~bar** adj

conceivable; **~en** *vt* to put forward; (*bekannt machen*) to introduce; (*darstellen*) to represent; **~en vor** +*akk* to put in front of; **sich** *dat* **etw ~en** to imagine sth; **V~ung** *f* (*Bekanntmachen*) introduction; (*THEAT etc*) performance; (*Gedanke*) idea, thought

vorstoßen ['foːrʃtoːsən] (*unreg*) *vi* (*ins Unbekannte*) to venture (forth)

Vorstrafe ['foːrʃtraːfə] *f* previous conviction

Vortag ['foːrtaːk] *m*: **am ~ einer Sache** *gen* on the day before sth

vortäuschen ['foːrtɔʏʃən] *vt* to feign, to pretend

Vorteil ['foːrtaɪl] **(-s, -e)** *m*: **~ (gegenüber)** advantage (over); **im ~ sein** to have the advantage; **v~haft** *adj* advantageous

Vortrag ['foːrtraːk] **(-(e)s, Vorträge)** *m* talk, lecture; **v~en** [-gən] (*unreg*) *vt* to carry forward; (*fig*) to recite; (*Rede*) to deliver; (*Lied*) to perform; (*Meinung etc*) to express

vortreten ['foːrtreːtən] (*unreg*) *vi* to step forward; (*Augen etc*) to protrude

vorüber [foˈryːbər] *adv* past, over; **~gehen** (*unreg*) *vi* to pass (by); **~gehen an** +*dat* (*fig*) to pass over; **~gehend** *adj* temporary, passing

Vorurteil ['foːrʔʊrtaɪl] *nt* prejudice

Vorverkauf ['foːrfɛrkaʊf] *m* advance booking

Vorwahl ['foːrvaːl] *f* preliminary election; (*TEL*) dialling code

Vorwand ['foːrvant] **(-(e)s, Vorwände)** *m* pretext

vorwärts ['foːrvɛrts] *adv* forward; **~ gehen** to progress; **V~gang** *m* (*AUT etc*) forward gear; **~ kommen** to get on, to make progress

Vorwäsche *f* prewash

vorweg [foːrˈvɛk] *adv* in advance; **~nehmen** (*unreg*) *vt* to anticipate

vorweisen ['foːrvaɪzən] (*unreg*) *vt* to show, to produce

vorwerfen ['foːrvɛrfən] (*unreg*) *vt*: **jdm etw ~** to reproach sb for sth, to accuse sb of sth; **sich** *dat* **nichts vorzuwerfen haben** to have nothing to reproach o.s. with

vorwiegend ['foːrviːgənt] *adj* predominant ♦ *adv* predominantly

vorwitzig ['foːrvɪtsɪç] *adj* (*Mensch, Bemerkung*) cheeky

Vorwort ['foːrvɔrt] **(-(e)s, -e)** *nt* preface

Vorwurf ['foːrvʊrf] *m* reproach; **jdm/sich Vorwürfe machen** to reproach sb/o.s.; **v~svoll** *adj* reproachful

vorzeigen ['foːrtsaɪgən] *vt* to show, to produce

vorzeitig ['foːrtsaɪtɪç] *adj* premature

vorziehen ['foːrtsiːən] (*unreg*) *vt* to pull forward; (*Gardinen*) to draw; (*lieber haben*) to prefer

Vorzimmer ['foːrtsɪmər] *nt* (*Büro*) outer office

Vorzug ['foːrtsuːk] *m* preference; (*gute Eigenschaft*) merit, good quality; (*Vorteil*) advantage

vorzüglich [foːrˈtsyːklɪç] *adj* excellent

Vorzugspreis *m* special discount price

vulgär [vʊlˈgɛːr] *adj* vulgar

Vulkan [vʊlˈkaːn] **(-s, -e)** *m* volcano

W, w

Waage ['vaːgə] *f* scales *pl*; (*ASTROL*) Libra; **w~recht** *adj* horizontal

Wabe ['vaːbə] *f* honeycomb

wach [vax] *adj* awake; (*fig*) alert; **W~e** *f* guard, watch; **W~e halten** to keep watch; **W~e stehen** to stand guard; **~en** *vi* to be awake; (*Wache halten*) to guard

Wachs [vaks] **(-es, -e)** *nt* wax

wachsam ['vaxzaːm] *adj* watchful, vigilant, alert

wachsen (*unreg*) *vi* to grow

Wachstuch ['vakstuːx] *nt* oilcloth

Wachstum ['vakstuːm] **(-s)** *nt* growth

Wächter ['vɛçtər] **(-s, -)** *m* guard, warden, keeper; (*Parkplatzwächter*) attendant

wackel- ['vakəl] *zW*: **~ig** *adj* shaky, wobbly; **W~kontakt** *m* loose connection; **~n** *vi* to shake; (*fig: Position*) to be shaky

wacker ['vakər] *adj* valiant, stout ♦ *adv* well, bravely

Wade ['vaːdə] f (ANAT) calf

Waffe ['vafə] f weapon

Waffel ['vafəl] (-, -n) f waffle; wafer

Waffen- zW: **~schein** m gun licence; **~stillstand** m armistice, truce

Wagemut ['vaːgəmuːt] m daring

wagen ['vaːgən] vt to venture, to dare

Wagen ['vaːgən] (-s, -) m vehicle; (Auto) car; (EISENB) carriage; (Pferdewagen) cart; **~heber** m jack

Waggon [va'gõː] (-s, -s) m carriage; (Güterwaggon) goods van, freight truck (US)

Wagnis ['vaːknɪs] (-ses, -se) nt risk

Wagon ▲ [va'gõː, va'goːn] (-s, -s) m = **Waggon**

Wahl [vaːl] (-, -en) f choice; (POL) election; **zweite ~** (COMM) seconds pl

wähl- ['vɛːl] zW: **~bar** adj eligible; **~en** vt, vi to choose; (POL) to elect, to vote (for); (TEL) to dial; **W~er(in)** (-s, -) m(f) voter; **~erisch** adj fastidious, particular

Wahl- zW: **~fach** nt optional subject; **~gang** m ballot; **~kabine** f polling booth; **~kampf** m election campaign; **~kreis** m constituency; **~lokal** nt polling station; **w~los** adv at random; **~recht** nt franchise; **~spruch** m motto; **~urne** f ballot box

Wahn [vaːn] (-(e)s) m delusion; folly; **~sinn** m madness; **w~sinnig** adj insane, mad ♦ adv (umg) incredibly

wahr [vaːr] adj true

wahren vt to maintain, to keep

während ['vɛːrənt] präp +gen during ♦ konj while; **~dessen** adv meanwhile

wahr- zW: **~haben** (unreg) vt: **etw nicht ~haben wollen** to refuse to admit sth; **~haft** adv (tatsächlich) truly; **~haftig** [vaːr'haftɪç] adj true, real ♦ adv really; **W~heit** f truth; **~nehmen** (unreg) vt to perceive, to observe; **W~nehmung** f perception; **~sagen** vi to prophesy, to tell fortunes; **W~sager(in)** (-s, -) m(f) fortune teller; **~scheinlich** [vaːr'ʃaɪnlɪç] adj probable ♦ adv probably; **W~'scheinlichkeit** f probability; **aller W~scheinlichkeit nach** in all probability

Währung ['vɛːrʊŋ] f currency

Wahrzeichen nt symbol

Waise ['vaɪzə] f orphan; **~nhaus** nt orphanage

Wald [valt] (-(e)s, ⁓er) m wood(s); (groß) forest; **~brand** m forest fire; **~sterben** nt trees dying due to pollution

Wales [weɪlz] (-) nt Wales

Wal(fisch) ['vaːl(fɪʃ)] (-(e)s, -e) m whale

Waliser [va'liːzər] (-s, -) m Welshman; **Waliserin** [va'liːzərɪn] f Welshwoman; **walisisch** [va'liːzɪʃ] adj Welsh

Walkman ['wɔːkman] ®; **-s, Walkmen**) m Walkman ®, personal stereo

Wall [val] (-(e)s, ⁓e) m embankment; (Bollwerk) rampart

Wallfahr- zW: **~er(in)** m(f) pilgrim; **~t** f pilgrimage

Walnuss ▲ ['valnʊs] f walnut

Walross ▲ ['valrɔs] nt walrus

Walze ['valtsə] f (Gerät) cylinder; (Fahrzeug) roller; **w~n** vt to roll (out)

wälzen ['vɛltsən] vt to roll (over); (Bücher) to hunt through; (Probleme) to deliberate on ♦ vr to wallow; (vor Schmerzen) to roll about; (im Bett) to toss and turn

Walzer ['valtsər] (-s, -) m waltz

Wand [vant] (-, ⁓e) f wall; (Trennwand) partition; (Bergwand) precipice

Wandel ['vandəl] (-s) m change; **w~bar** adj changeable, variable; **w~n** vt, vr to change ♦ vi (gehen) to walk

Wander- ['vandər] zW: **~er** (-s, -) m hiker, rambler; **~karte** f map of country walks; **w~n** vi to hike; (Blick) to wander; (Gedanken) to stray; **~schaft** f travelling; **~ung** f walk, hike; **~weg** m trail, walk

Wandlung f change, transformation

Wange ['vaŋə] f cheek

wanken ['vaŋkən] vi to stagger; (fig) to waver

wann [van] adv when

Wanne ['vanə] f tub

Wanze ['vantsə] f bug

Wappen ['vapən] (-s, -) nt coat of arms, crest; **~kunde** f heraldry

war etc [vaːr] vb siehe **sein**

Ware ['vaːrə] f ware

Spelling Reform: ▲ *new spelling* △ *old spelling (to be phased out)*

Waren- zW: **~haus** nt department store; **~lager** nt stock, store; **~muster** nt trade sample; **~probe** f sample; **~sendung** f trade sample (sent by post); **~zeichen** nt: **(eingetragenes) ~zeichen** (registered) trademark

warf etc [vaːrf] vb siehe **werfen**

warm [varm] adj warm; (Essen) hot

Wärm- [vɛrm] zW: **~e** f warmth; **w~en** vt, vr to warm (up), to heat (up); **~flasche** f hot-water bottle

Warn- [ˈvarn] zW: **~blinkanlage** f (AUT) hazard warning lights pl; **~dreieck** nt warning triangle; **w~en** vt to warn; **~ung** f warning

warten [ˈvartən] vi: **~ (auf** +akk) to wait (for); **auf sich ~ lassen** to take a long time

Wärter(in) [ˈvɛrtər(ın)] (-s, -) m(f) attendant

Warte- [ˈvartə] zW: **~saal** m (EISENB) waiting room; **~zimmer** nt waiting room

Wartung f servicing; service; **~ und Instandhaltung** maintenance

warum [vaˈrʊm] adv why

Warze [ˈvartsə] f wart

was [vas] pron what; (umg: etwas) something; **~ für (ein) ...** what sort of ...

waschbar adj washable

Waschbecken nt washbasin

Wäsche [ˈvɛʃə] f wash(ing); (Bettwäsche) linen; (Unterwäsche) underclothing

waschecht adj colourfast; (fig) genuine

Wäsche- zW: **~klammer** f clothes peg (BRIT), clothespin (US); **~leine** f washing line (BRIT)

waschen [ˈvaʃən] (unreg) vt, vi to wash ♦ vr to (have a) wash; **sich** dat **die Hände ~** to wash one's hands

Wäsche'rei f laundry

Wasch- zW: **~gelegenheit** f washing facilities; **~küche** f laundry room; **~lappen** m face flannel, washcloth (US); (umg) sissy; **~maschine** f washing machine; **~mittel** nt detergent, washing powder; **~pulver** nt detergent, washing powder; **~raum** m washroom; **~salon** m Launderette ®

Wasser [ˈvasər] (-s, -) nt water; **~ball** m

water polo; **w~dicht** adj waterproof; **~fall** m waterfall; **~farbe** f watercolour; **~hahn** m tap, faucet (US); **~kraftwerk** nt hydroelectric power station; **~leitung** f water pipe; **~mann** n (ASTROL) Aquarius

wässern [ˈvɛsərn] vt, vi to water

Wasser- zW: **w~scheu** adj afraid of (the) water; **~ski** [ˈvasərʃiː] nt water-skiing; **~stoff** m hydrogen; **~waage** f spirit level; **~zeichen** nt watermark

wässrig ▲ [ˈvɛsrıç] adj watery

Watt [vat] (-(e)s, -en) nt mud flats pl

Watte f cotton wool, absorbent cotton (US)

WC [ˈveːˈtseː] (-s, -s) nt abk W.C.

Web [vɛb] (-s) nt (COMPUT) **das ~** the Web

Web- [ˈveːb] zW: **w~en** (unreg) vt to weave; **~er** (-s, -) m weaver; **~e'rei** f (Betrieb) weaving mill

Website [ˈvɛbsait] f (COMPUT) website

Webstuhl [ˈveːpʃtuːl] m loom

Wechsel [ˈvɛksəl] (-s, -) m change; (COMM) bill of exchange; **~geld** nt change; **w~haft** adj (Wetter) variable; **~jahre** pl change of life sg; **~kurs** m rate of exchange; **w~n** vt to change; (Blicke) to exchange ♦ vi to change; to vary; (Geldwechseln) to have change; **~strom** m alternating current; **~stube** f bureau de change; **~wirkung** f interaction

Weck- [ˈvɛk] zW: **~dienst** m alarm call service; **w~en** vt to wake (up); to call; **~er** (-s, -) m alarm clock

wedeln [ˈveːdəln] vi (mit Schwanz) to wag; (mit Fächer etc) to wave

weder [ˈveːdər] konj neither; **~ ... noch ...** neither ... nor ...

Weg [veːk] (-(e)s, -e) m way; (Pfad) path; (Route) route; **sich auf den ~ machen** to be on one's way; **jdm aus dem ~ gehen** to keep out of sb's way; siehe **zuwege**

weg [vɛk] adv away, off; **über etw** akk **~ sein** to be over sth; **er war schon ~** he had already left; **Finger ~!** hands off!

wegbleiben (unreg) vi to stay away

wegen [ˈveːgən] präp +gen (umg: +dat) because of

weg- [ˈvɛk] zW: **~fallen** (unreg) vi to be left

out; (*Ferien, Bezahlung*) to be cancelled; (*aufhören*) to cease; ~gehen (*unreg*) *vi* to go away; to leave; ~lassen (*unreg*) *vt* to leave out; ~laufen (*unreg*) *vi* to run away *od* off; ~legen *vt* to put aside; ~machen (*umg*) *vt* to get rid of; ~müssen (*unreg*, *umg*) *vt* to have to go; ~nehmen (*unreg*) *vt* to take away; ~tun (*unreg*) *vt* to put away; W~weiser (-s, -) *m* road sign, signpost; ~werfen (*unreg*) *vt* to throw away

weh [ve:] *adj* sore; ~(e) *excl*: ~(e), wenn du ... woe betide you if ...; o ~! oh dear!; ~e! just you dare!

wehen *vt, vi* to blow; (*Fahnen*) to flutter

weh- *zW*: ~leidig *adj* whiny, whining; ~mütig *adj* melancholy

Wehr [ve:r] (-, -en) *f*: sich zur ~ setzen to defend o.s.; ~dienst *m* military service; ~dienstverweigerer *m* ≈ conscientious objector; w~en *vr* to defend o.s.; w~los *adj* defenceless; ~pflicht *f* compulsory military service; w~pflichtig *adj* liable for military service

Wehrdienst

i **Wehrdienst** *is military service which is still compulsory in Germany. All young men receive their call-up papers at 18 and all those pronounced physically fit are required to spend 10 months in the* **Bundeswehr**. *Conscientious objectors are allowed to do* **Zivildienst** *as an alternative, after presenting their case.*

wehtun ▲ ['ve:tu:n] (*unreg*) *vt* to hurt, to be sore; jdm/sich ~ to hurt sb/o.s.

Weib [vaip] (-(e)s, -er) *nt* woman, female; wife; ~chen *nt* female; w~lich *adj* feminine

weich [vaiç] *adj* soft; W~e *f* points *pl*; ~en (*unreg*) *vi* to yield, to give way; W~heit *f* softness; ~lich *adj* soft, namby-pamby

Weide ['vaidə] *f* (*Baum*) willow; (*Gras*) pasture; w~n *vi* to graze ♦ *vr*: sich an etw *dat* w~n to delight in sth

weigern ['vaigərn] *vr* to refuse

Weigerung ['vaigərʊŋ] *f* refusal

Weihe ['vaiə] *f* consecration; (*Priesterweihe*) ordination; w~n *vt* to consecrate; to ordain

Weihnacht- *zW*: ~en (-) *nt* Christmas; w~lich *adj* Christmas *cpd*

Weihnachts- *zW*: ~abend *m* Christmas Eve; ~lied *nt* Christmas carol; ~mann *m* Father Christmas, Santa Claus; ~markt *m* Christmas fair; ~tag *m* Christmas Day; zweiter ~tag Boxing Day

Weihnachtsmarkt

i *The* **Weihnachtsmarkt** *is a market held in most large towns in Germany in the weeks prior to Christmas. People visit it to buy presents, toys and Christmas decorations, and to enjoy the festive atmosphere. Traditional Christmas food and drink can also be consumed there, for example,* **Lebkuchen** *and* **Glühwein.**

Weihwasser *nt* holy water

weil [vail] *konj* because

Weile ['vailə] (-) *f* while, short time

Wein [vain] (-(e)s, -e) *m* wine; (*Pflanze*) vine; ~bau *m* cultivation of vines; ~berg *m* vineyard; ~bergschnecke *f* snail; ~brand *m* brandy

weinen *vt, vi* to cry; das ist zum W~ it's enough to make you cry *od* weep

Wein- *zW*: ~glas *nt* wine glass; ~karte *f* wine list; ~lese *f* vintage; ~probe *f* wine-tasting; ~rebe *f* vine; w~rot *adj* burgundy, claret, wine-red; ~stock *m* vine; ~stube *f* wine bar; ~traube *f* grape

weise ['vaizə] *adj* wise

Weise *f* manner, way; (*Lied*) tune; auf diese ~ in this way

weisen (*unreg*) *vt* to show

Weisheit ['vaishait] *f* wisdom; ~szahn *m* wisdom tooth

weiß [vais] *adj* white ♦ *vb siehe* wissen; W~bier *nt* weissbier (*light, fizzy beer made using top-fermentation yeast*); W~brot *nt* white bread; ~en *vt* to whitewash; W~glut *f* (*TECH*) incandescence; jdn bis zur W~glut bringen (*fig*) to make sb see red; W~kohl *m* (white) cabbage; **W~wein** *m* white wine; **W~wurst** *f* veal sausage

weit [vaɪt] *adj* wide; (*Begriff*) broad; (*Reise, Wurf*) long ♦ *adv* far; **wie ~ ist es ...?** how far is it ...?; **in ~er Ferne** in the far distance; **~ blickend** far-seeing; **~ reichend** long-range; (*fig*) far-reaching; **~ verbreitet** widespread; **das geht zu ~** that's going too far; **~aus** *adv* by far; **~blickend** *adj* far-seeing; **W~e** *f* width; (*Raum*) space; (*von Entfernung*) distance; **~en** *vt, vr* to widen

weiter ['vaɪtər] *adj* wider; broader; farther (away); (*zusätzlich*) further ♦ *adv* further; **ohne ~es** without further ado; just like that; **~ nichts/niemand** nothing/nobody else; **~arbeiten** *vi* to go on working; **~bilden** *vr* to continue one's education; **~empfehlen** (*unreg*) *vt* to recommend (to others); **W~fahrt** *f* continuation of the journey; **~führen** *vi* (*Straße*) to lead on (to) ♦ *vt* (*fortsetzen*) to continue, carry on; **~gehen** (*unreg*) *vi* to go on; **~hin** *adv*: **etw ~hin tun** to go on doing sth; **~kommen** (*unreg*) *vi* (*fig: mit Arbeit*) to make progress; **~leiten** *vt* to pass on; **~machen** *vt, vi* to continue

weit- *zW*: **~gehend** *adj* considerable ♦ *adv* largely; **~läufig** *adj* (*Gebäude*) spacious; (*Erklärung*) lengthy; (*Verwandter*) distant; **~reichend** *adj* long-range; (*fig*) far-reaching; **~schweifig** *adj* long-winded; **~sichtig** *adj* (*MED*) long-sighted; (*fig*) far-sighted; **W~sprung** *m* long jump; **~verbreitet** *adj* widespread

Weizen ['vaɪtsən] (**-s, -**) *m* wheat

welche(r, s) *interrogativ pron* which; **welcher von beiden?** which (one) of the two?; **welchen hast du genommen?** which (one) did you take?; **welche eine ...!** what a ...!; **welche Freude!** what joy! ♦ *indef pron* some; (*in Fragen*) any; **ich habe welche** I have some; **haben Sie welche?** do you have any?

♦ *relativ pron* (*bei Menschen*) who; (*bei* *Sachen*) which, that; **welche(r, s) auch immer** whoever/whichever/whatever

welk [vɛlk] *adj* withered; **~en** *vi* to wither

Welle ['vɛlə] *f* wave; (*TECH*) shaft

Wellen- *zW*: **~bereich** *m* waveband; **~länge** *f* (*auch fig*) wavelength; **~linie** *f* wavy line; **~sittich** *m* budgerigar

Welt [vɛlt] (**-, -en**) *f* world; **~all** *nt* universe; **~anschauung** *f* philosophy of life; **w~berühmt** *adj* world-famous; **~krieg** *m* world war; **w~lich** *adj* worldly; (*nicht kirchlich*) secular; **~macht** *f* world power; **~meister** *m* world champion; **~raum** *m* space; **~reise** *f* trip round the world; **~stadt** *f* metropolis; **w~weit** *adj* world-wide

wem [veːm] (*dat von* **wer**) *pron* to whom

wen [veːn] (*akk von* **wer**) *pron* whom

Wende ['vɛndə] *f* turn; (*Veränderung*) change; **~kreis** *m* (*GEOG*) tropic; (*AUT*) turning circle; **~ltreppe** *f* spiral staircase; **w~n** (*unreg*) *vt, vi, vr* to turn; **sich an jdn w~n** to go/come to sb

wendig ['vɛndɪç] *adj* (*Auto etc*) manœuvrable; (*fig*) agile

Wendung *f* turn; (*Redewendung*) idiom

wenig ['veːnɪç] *adj, adv* little; **~e** *pron pl* few *pl*; **~er** *adj* less; (*mit pl*) fewer ♦ *adv* less; **~ste(r, s)** *adj* least; **am ~sten** least; **~stens** *adv* at least

wenn [vɛn] *konj* **1** (*falls, bei Wünschen*) if; **wenn auch ..., selbst wenn ...** even if ...; **wenn ich doch ...** if only I ...

2 (*zeitlich*) when; **immer wenn** whenever

wennschon ['vɛnʃoːn] *adv*: **na ~** so what?; **~, dennschon!** in for a penny, in for a pound

wer [veːr] *pron* who

Werbe- ['vɛrbə] *zW*: **~fernsehen** *nt* commercial television; **~geschenk** *nt* gift (*from company*); (*zu Gekauftem*) free gift; **w~n** (*unreg*) *vt* to win; (*Mitglied*) to recruit ♦ *vi* to advertise; **um jdn/etw w~n** to try to win sb/sth; **für jdn/etw w~n** to promote sb/sth

Werbung f advertising; *(von Mitgliedern)* recruitment; **~ um jdn/etw** promotion of sb/sth

Werdegang ['veːrdəɡaŋ] m *(Laufbahn)* development; *(beruflich)* career

SCHLÜSSELWORT

werden ['veːrdən] *(pt* **wurde,** *pp* **geworden** *od (bei Passiv)* **worden)** *vi* to become; **was ist aus ihm/aus der Sache geworden?** what became of him/it?; **es ist nichts/gut geworden** it came to nothing/turned out well; **es wird Nacht/Tag** it's getting dark/light; **mir wird kalt** I'm getting cold; **mir wird schlecht** I feel ill; **Erster werden** to come *od* be first; **das muss anders werden** that'll have to change; **rot/zu Eis werden** to turn red/to ice; **was willst du (mal) werden?** what do you want to be?; **die Fotos sind gut geworden** the photos have come out nicely

♦ *als Hilfsverb* **1** *(bei Futur):* **er wird es tun** he will *od* he'll do it; **er wird das nicht tun** he will not *od* he won't do it; **es wird gleich regnen** it's going to rain

2 *(bei Konjunktiv):* **ich würde ...** I would ...; **er würde gern ...** he would *od* he'd like to ...; **ich würde lieber ...** I would *od* I'd rather ...

3 *(bei Vermutung):* **sie wird in der Küche sein** she will be in the kitchen

4 *(bei Passiv):* **gebraucht werden** to be used; **er ist erschossen worden** he has *od* he's been shot; **mir wurde gesagt, dass ...** I was told that ...

werfen ['vɛrfən] *(unreg) vt* to throw
Werft [vɛrft] *(-, -en)* f shipyard, dockyard
Werk [vɛrk] *(-(e)s, -e)* nt work; *(Tätigkeit)* job; *(Fabrik, Mechanismus)* works *pl*; **ans ~ gehen** to set to work; **~statt(-, -stätten)** f workshop; *(AUT)* garage; **~tag** m working day; **w~tags** adv on working days; **w~tätig** adj working; **~zeug** nt tool
Wermut ['veːrmuːt] *(-(e)s)* m wormwood;

(Wein) vermouth

Wert [veːrt] *(-(e)s, -e)* m worth; *(FIN)* value; **~ legen auf** +akk to attach importance to; **es hat doch keinen ~** it's useless; **w~** adj worth; *(geschätzt)* dear; worthy; **das ist nichts/viel w~** it's not worth anything/it's worth a lot; **das ist es/er mir w~** it's/he's worth that to me; **~angabe** f declaration of value; **~brief** m registered letter *(containing sth of value)*; **w~en** vt to rate; **~gegenstände** mpl valuables; **w~los** adj worthless; **~papier** nt security; **w~voll** adj valuable

Wesen ['veːzən] *(-s, -)* nt *(Geschöpf)* being; *(Natur, Charakter)* nature; **w~tlich** adj significant; *(beträchtlich)* considerable

weshalb [vɛs'halp] adv why

Wespe ['vɛspə] f wasp

wessen ['vɛsən] *(gen von* wer*)* pron whose

Weste ['vɛstə] f waistcoat, vest *(US)*; *(Wollweste)* cardigan

West- zW: **~en** *(-s)* m west; **~europa** nt Western Europe; **w~lich** adj western ♦ adv to the west

weswegen [vɛs'veːɡən] adv why

wett [vɛt] adj even; **W~bewerb** m competition; **W~e** f bet, wager; **~en** vt, vi to bet

Wetter ['vɛtər] *(-s, -)* nt weather; **~bericht** m weather report; **~dienst** m meteorological service; **~lage** f (weather) situation; **~vorhersage** f weather forecast; **~warte** f weather station

Wett- zW: **~kampf** m contest; **~lauf** m race; **w~machen** vt to make good

wichtig ['vɪçtɪç] adj important; **W~keit** f importance

wickeln ['vɪkəln] vt to wind; *(Haare)* to set; *(Kind)* to change; **jdn/etw in etw** akk **~** to wrap sb/sth in sth

Wickelraum m mothers' (and babies') room

Widder ['vɪdər] *(-s, -)* m ram; *(ASTROL)* Aries

wider ['viːdər] präp +akk against; **~'fahren** *(unreg) vi* to happen; **~'legen** vt to refute

widerlich ['viːdərlɪç] adj disgusting, repulsive

wider- ['viːdər] *zW:* **~rechtlich** *adj*
unlawful; **W~rede** *f* contradiction; **~'rufen**
(*unreg*) *vt insep* to retract; (*Anordnung*) to
revoke; (*Befehl*) to countermand; **~'setzen**
vr insep: **sich jdm/etw ~setzen** to oppose
sb/sth

widerspenstig ['viːdərʃpɛnstɪç] *adj* wilful

wider- ['viːdər] *zW:* **~spiegeln** *vt*
(*Entwicklung, Erscheinung*) to mirror, reflect
♦ *vr* to be reflected; **~'sprechen** (*unreg*) *vi
insep:* **jdm ~sprechen** to contradict sb

Widerspruch ['viːdərʃprʊx] *m*
contradiction; **w~slos** *adv* without arguing

Widerstand ['viːdərʃtant] *m* resistance

Widerstands- *zW:* **~bewegung** *f*
resistance (movement); **w~fähig** *adj*
resistant, tough; **w~los** *adj* unresisting

wider'stehen (*unreg*) *vi insep:* **jdm/etw ~**
to withstand sb/sth

wider- ['viːdər] *zW:* **~wärtig** *adj* nasty,
horrid; **W~wille** *m:* **W~wille (gegen)**
aversion (to); **~willig** *adj* unwilling,
reluctant

widmen ['vɪtmən] *vt* to dedicate; to devote
♦ *vr* to devote o.s.

widrig ['viːdrɪç] *adj* (*Umstände*) adverse

SCHLÜSSELWORT

wie [viː] *adv* how; **wie groß/schnell?** how
big/fast?; **wie wärs?** how about it?; **wie ist
er?** what's he like?; **wie gut du das
kannst!** you're very good at it; **wie bitte?**
pardon?; (*entrüstet*) I beg your pardon!;
und wie! and how!; **wie viel** how much;
wie viel Menschen how many people;
wie weit to what extent

♦ *konj* **1** (*bei Vergleichen*): **so schön wie ...**
as beautiful as ...; **wie ich schon sagte** as I
said; **wie du** like you; **singen wie ein ...** to
sing like a ...; **wie (zum Beispiel)** such as
(for example)

2 (*zeitlich*): **wie er das hörte, ging er**
when he heard that he left; **er hörte, wie
der Regen fiel** he heard the rain falling

---

wieder ['viːdər] *adv* again; **~ da sein** to be
back (again); **~ aufbereiten** to recycle; **~**

aufnehmen to resume; **~ erkennen** to
recognize; **~ gutmachen** to make up for;
(*Fehler*) to put right; **~ herstellen** (*Ruhe,
Frieden etc*) to restore; **~ vereinigen** to
reunite; (*POL*) to reunify; **~ verwerten** to
recycle; **gehst du schon ~?** are you off
again?; **~ ein(e) ...** another ...; **W~aufbau**
m rebuilding; **~bekommen** (*unreg*) *vt* to
get back; **W~gabe** *f* reproduction;
~geben (*unreg*) *vt* (*zurückgeben*) to return;
(*Erzählung etc*) to repeat; (*Gefühle etc*) to
convey; **W~'gutmachung** *f* reparation;
~'herstellen (*Gesundheit, Gebäude*) to
restore; **~'holen** *vt insep* to repeat;
W~'holung *f* repetition; **W~hören** *nt:* **auf
W~hören** (*TEL*) goodbye; **W~kehr** (-) *f*
return; (*von Vorfall*) repetition, recurrence;
~sehen (*unreg*) *vt* to see again; **auf
W~sehen** goodbye; **~um** *adv* again;
(*andererseits*) on the other hand;
W~vereinigung *f* (*POL*) reunification;
W~wahl *f* re-election

Wiege ['viːgə] *f* cradle; **w~n¹** *vt* (*schaukeln*)
to rock

wiegen² (*unreg*) *vt, vi* (*Gewicht*) to weigh

Wien [viːn] *nt* Vienna

Wiese ['viːzə] *f* meadow

Wiesel ['viːzəl] (-s, -) *nt* weasel

wieso [viː'zoː] *adv* why

wieviel △ [viː'fiːl] *adj siehe* **wie**

wievielmal [viː'fiːlmaːl] *adv* how often

wievielte(r, s) *adj:* **zum ~n Mal?** how
many times?; **den W~n haben wir?** what's
the date?; **an ~r Stelle?** in what place?;
der ~ Besucher war er? how many
visitors were there before him?

wild [vɪlt] *adj* wild; **W~** (-(e)s) *nt* game;
W~e(r) ['vɪldə(r)] *f(m)* savage; **~ern** *vi* to
poach; **~'fremd** (*umg*) *adj* quite strange *od*
unknown; **W~heit** *f* wildness; **W~leder** *nt*
suede; **W~nis** (-, -se) *f* wilderness;
W~schwein *nt* (wild) boar

will *etc* [vɪl] *vb siehe* **wollen**

Wille ['vɪlə] (-ns, -n) *m* will; **w~n** *präp +gen:*
um ... w~n for the sake of ...; **w~nsstark**
adj strong-willed

will- *zW:* **~ig** *adj* willing; **W~kommen**

Rechtschreibreform: ▲ *neue Schreibung* △ *alte Schreibung (auslaufend)*

[vɪl'kɔmən] **(-s, -)** nt welcome; **~kommen** adj welcome; **jdn ~kommen heißen** to welcome sb; **~kürlich** adj arbitrary; (Bewegung) voluntary

wimmeln ['vɪməln] vi: **~ (von)** to swarm (with)

wimmern ['vɪmərn] vi to whimper

Wimper ['vɪmpər] **(-, -n)** f eyelash

Wimperntusche f mascara

Wind [vɪnt] **(-(e)s, -e)** m wind; **~beutel** m cream puff; (fig) rake; **~e** f (TECH) winch, windlass; (BOT) bindweed; **~el** ['vɪndəl] **(-, -n)** f nappy, diaper (US); **w~en** vi unpers to be windy ♦ vt (unreg) to wind; (Kranz) to weave; (entwinden) to twist ♦ vr (unreg) to wind; (Person) to writhe; **~energie** f wind energy; **w~ig** ['vɪndɪç] adj windy; (fig) dubious; **~jacke** f windcheater; **~mühle** f windmill; **~pocken** pl chickenpox sg; **~schutzscheibe** f (AUT) windscreen (BRIT), windshield (US); **~stärke** f wind force; **w~still** adj (Tag) still, windless; (Platz) sheltered; **~stille** f calm; **~stoß** m gust of wind

Wink [vɪŋk] **(-(e)s, -e)** m (mit Hand) wave; (mit Kopf) nod; (Hinweis) hint

Winkel ['vɪŋkəl] **(-s, -)** m (MATH) angle; (Gerät) set square; (in Raum) corner

winken ['vɪŋkən] vt, vi to wave

winseln ['vɪnzəln] vi to whine

Winter ['vɪntər] **(-s, -)** m winter; **w~fest** adj (Pflanze) hardy; **~garten** m conservatory; **w~lich** adj wintry; **~reifen** m winter tyre; **~sport** m winter sports pl

Winzer ['vɪntsər] **(-s, -)** m vine grower

winzig ['vɪntsɪç] adj tiny

Wipfel ['vɪpfəl] **(-s, -)** m treetop

wir [viːr] pron we; **~ alle** all of us, we all

Wirbel ['vɪrbəl] **(-s, -)** m whirl, swirl; (Trubel) hurly-burly; (Aufsehen) fuss; (ANAT) vertebra; **w~n** vi to whirl, to swirl; **~säule** f spine

wird [vɪrt] vb siehe **werden**

wirfst etc [vɪrfst] vb siehe **werfen**

wirken ['vɪrkən] vi to have an effect; (erfolgreich sein) to work; (scheinen) to seem ♦ vt (Wunder) to work

wirklich ['vɪrklɪç] adj real ♦ adv really;

W~keit f reality

wirksam ['vɪrkzaːm] adj effective

Wirkstoff m (biologisch, chemisch, pflanzlich) active substance

Wirkung ['vɪrkʊŋ] f effect; **w~slos** adj ineffective; **w~slos bleiben** to have no effect; **w~svoll** adj effective

wirr [vɪr] adj confused, wild; **W~warr** **(-s)** m disorder, chaos

wirst [vɪrst] vb siehe **werden**

Wirt(in) [vɪrt(ɪn)] **(-(e)s, -e)** m(f) landlord(lady); **~schaft** f (Gaststätte) pub; (Haushalt) housekeeping; (eines Landes) economy; (umg: Durcheinander) mess; **w~schaftlich** adj economical; (POL) economic

Wirtschafts- zW: **~krise** f economic crisis; **~politik** f economic policy; **~prüfer** m chartered accountant; **~wunder** nt economic miracle

Wirtshaus nt inn

wischen ['vɪʃən] vt to wipe

Wischer **(-s, -)** m (AUT) wiper

Wissbegier(de) ▲ ['vɪsbəgiːr(də)] f thirst for knowledge; **wissbegierig** ▲ adj inquisitive, eager for knowledge

wissen ['vɪsən] (unreg) vt to know; **was weiß ich!** I don't know!; **W~ (-s)** nt knowledge; **W~schaft** f science; **W~schaftler(in)** **(-s, -)** m(f) scientist; **~schaftlich** adj scientific; **~swert** adj worth knowing

wittern ['vɪtərn] vt to scent; (fig) to suspect

Witterung f weather; (Geruch) scent

Witwe ['vɪtvə] f widow; **~r (-s, -)** m widower

Witz [vɪts] **(-(e)s, -e)** m joke; **~bold** **(-(e)s, -e)** m joker, wit; **w~ig** adj funny

wo [voː] adv where; (umg: irgendwo) somewhere; **im Augenblick, ~ ...** the moment (that) ...; **die Zeit, ~ ...** the time when ...; **~anders** [voːˈandərs] adv elsewhere; **~bei** [-ˈbai] adv (relativ) by/with which; (interrogativ) what ... in/by/with

Woche ['vɔxə] f week

Wochen- zW: **~ende** nt weekend; **w~lang** adj, adv for weeks; **~markt** m weekly market; **~schau** f newsreel

Spelling Reform: ▲ new spelling △ old spelling (to be phased out)

wöchentlich ['vϵçəntlɪç] *adj, adv* weekly
wodurch [vo'dʊrç] *adv (relativ)* through which; *(interrogativ)* what ... through
wofür [vo'fy:r] *adv (relativ)* for which; *(interrogativ)* what ... for
wog *etc* [vo:k] *vb siehe* **wiegen**
wo- [vo:] *zW:* **~'gegen** *adv (relativ)* against which; *(interrogativ)* what ... against; **~her** [-'he:r] *adv* where ... from; **~hin** [-'hɪn] *adv* where ... to

---
SCHLÜSSELWORT
---

wohl [vo:l] *adv* 1: **sich wohl fühlen** *(zufrieden)* to feel happy; *(gesundheitlich)* to feel well; **jdm wohl tun** to do sb good; **wohl oder übel** whether one likes it or not 2 *(wahrscheinlich)* probably; *(gewiss)* certainly; *(vielleicht)* perhaps; **sie ist wohl zu Hause** she's probably at home; **das ist doch wohl nicht dein Ernst!** surely you're not serious!; **das mag wohl sein** that may well be; **ob das wohl stimmt?** I wonder if that's true; **er weiß das sehr wohl** he knows that perfectly well

Wohl [vo:l] *(-(e)s) nt* welfare; **zum ~!** cheers!; **w~auf** *adv* well; **~behagen** *nt* comfort; **~fahrt** *f* welfare; **~fahrtsstaat** *m* welfare state; **w~habend** *adj* wealthy; **w~ig** *adj* contented, comfortable; **w~schmeckend** *adj* delicious; **~stand** *m* prosperity; **~standsgesellschaft** *f* affluent society; **~tat** *f* relief; act of charity; **~täter(in)** *m(f)* benefactor; **w~tätig** *adj* charitable; **~tätigkeits-** *zW* charity, charitable; **w~tun** *(unreg) vi △ siehe* **wohl**; **w~verdient** *adj* well-earned, well-deserved; **w~weislich** *adv* prudently; **~wollen** *(-s) nt* good will; **w~wollend** *adj* benevolent

wohn- ['vo:n] *zW:* **~en** *vi* to live; **W~gemeinschaft** *f (Menschen)* people sharing a flat; **~haft** *adj* resident; **W~heim** *nt (für Studenten)* hall of residence; *(für Senioren)* home; *(bes für Arbeiter)* hostel; **~lich** *adj* comfortable; **W~mobil** *(-s, -e) nt* camper; **W~ort** *m* domicile; **W~sitz** *m* place of residence; **W~ung** *f* house; *(Etagenwohnung)* flat, apartment *(US)*; **W~wagen** *m* caravan; **W~zimmer** *nt* living room
wölben ['vœlbən] *vt, vr* to curve
Wolf [vɔlf] *(-(e)s, ⁼e) m* wolf
Wolke ['vɔlkə] *f* cloud; **~nkratzer** *m* skyscraper; **wolkig** ['vɔlkɪç] *adj* cloudy
Wolle ['vɔlə] *f* wool; **w~n¹** *adj* woollen

SCHLÜSSELWORT
---

wollen² ['vɔlən] *(pt* **wollte**, *pp* **gewollt** *od (als Hilfsverb)* **wollen)** *vt, vi* to want; **ich will nach Hause** I want to go home; **er will nicht** he doesn't want to; **er wollte das nicht** he didn't want it; **wenn du willst** if you like; **ich will, dass du mir zuhörst** I want you to listen to me
♦ *Hilfsverb:* **er will ein Haus kaufen** he wants to buy a house; **ich wollte, ich wäre ...** I wish I were ...; **etw gerade tun wollen** to be going to do sth

wollüstig ['vɔlystɪç] *adj* lusty, sensual
wo- *zW:* **~mit** *adv (relativ)* with which; *(interrogativ)* what ... with; **~möglich** *adv* probably, I suppose; **~nach** *adv (relativ)* after/for which; *(interrogativ)* what ... for/after; **~ran** *adv (relativ)* on/at which; *(interrogativ)* what ... on/at; **~rauf** *adv (relativ)* on which; *(interrogativ)* what ... on; **~raus** *adv (relativ)* from/out of which; *(interrogativ)* what ... from/out of; **~rin** *adv (relativ)* in which; *(interrogativ)* what ... in
Wort [vɔrt] *(-(e)s, ⁼er od -e) nt* word; **jdn beim ~ nehmen** to take sb at his word; **mit anderen ~en** in other words; **w~brüchig** *adj* not true to one's word
Wörterbuch ['vœrtərbu:x] *nt* dictionary
Wort- *zW:* **~führer** *m* spokesman; **w~karg** *adj* taciturn; **~laut** *m* wording
wörtlich ['vœrtlɪç] *adj* literal
Wort- *zW:* **~los** *adj* mute; **w~reich** *adj* wordy, verbose; **~schatz** *m* vocabulary; **~spiel** *nt* play on words, pun
wo- *zW:* **~rüber** *adv (relativ)* over/about which; *(interrogativ)* what ... over/about;

Rechtschreibreform: ▲ *neue Schreibung* △ *alte Schreibung (auslaufend)*

~rum adv (relativ) about/round which; (interrogativ) what ... about/round; ~runter adv (relativ) under which; (interrogativ) what ... under; ~von adv (relativ) from which; (interrogativ) what ... from; ~vor adv (relativ) in front of/before which; (interrogativ) in front of/before what; of what; ~zu adv (relativ) to/for which; (interrogativ) what ... for/to; (warum) why

Wrack [vrak] (-(e)s, -s) nt wreck

Wucher ['vuːxər] (-s) m profiteering; ~er (-s, -) m profiteer; w~isoh adj profiteering; w~n vi (Pflanzen) to grow wild; ~ung f (MED) growth, tumour

Wuchs [vuːks] (-es) m (Wachstum) growth; (Statur) build

Wucht [vʊxt] (-) f force

wühlen ['vyːlən] vi to scrabble; (Tier) to root; (Maulwurf) to burrow; (umg: arbeiten) to slave away ♦ vt to dig

Wulst [vʊlst] (-es, ⁺e) m bulge; (an Wunde) swelling

wund [vʊnt] adj sore, raw; W~e f wound

Wunder ['vʊndər] (-s, -) nt miracle; es ist kein ~ it's no wonder; w~bar adj wonderful, marvellous; ~kerze f sparkler; ~kind nt infant prodigy; w~lich adj odd, peculiar; w~n vr to be surprised ♦ vt to surprise; sich w~n über +akk to be surprised at; w~schön adj beautiful; w~voll adj wonderful

Wundstarrkrampf ['vʊntʃtarkrampf] m tetanus, lockjaw

Wunsch [vʊnʃ] (-(e)s, ⁺e) m wish

wünschen ['vynʃən] vt to wish; sich dat etw ~ to want sth, to wish for sth; ~swert adj desirable

wurde etc ['vʊrdə] vb siehe werden

Würde ['vʏrdə] f dignity; (Stellung) honour; w~voll adj dignified

würdig ['vʏrdɪç] adj worthy (würdevoll) dignified; ~en vt to appreciate

Wurf [vʊrf] (-s, ⁺e) m throw; (Junge) litter

Würfel ['vʏrfəl] (-s, -) m dice; (MATH) cube; ~becher m (dice) cup; w~n vi to play dice ♦ vt to dice; ~zucker m lump sugar

würgen ['vʏrgən] vt, vi to choke

Wurm [vʊrm] (-(e)s, ⁺er) m worm; w~stichig adj worm-ridden

Wurst [vʊrst] (-, ⁺e) f sausage; das ist mir ~ (umg) I don't care, I don't give a damn

Würstchen ['vʏrstçən] nt sausage

Würze ['vʏrtsə] f seasoning, spice

Wurzel ['vʊrtsəl] (-, -n) f root

würzen ['vʏrtsən] vt to season, to spice

würzig adj spicy

wusch etc [vʊʃ] vb siehe waschen

wusste ▲ etc ['vʊstə] vb siehe wissen

wüst [vyːst] adj untidy, messy; (ausschweifend) wild; (öde) waste; (umg: heftig) terrible; W~e f desert

Wut [vuːt] (-) f rage, fury; ~anfall m fit of rage

wüten ['vyːtən] vi to rage; ~d adj furious, mad

X, x

X-Beine ['ɪksbaɪnə] pl knock-knees

x-beliebig [ɪksbə'liːbɪç] adj any (whatever)

xerokopieren [kseroko'piːrən] vt to xerox, to photocopy

x-mal ['ɪksmaːl] adv any number of times, n times

Xylofon ▲, Xylophon [ksylo'foːn] (-s, -e) nt xylophone

Y, y

Yacht (-, -en) f siehe Jacht

Ypsilon ['ʏpsilɔn] (-(s), -s) nt the letter Y

Z, z

Zacke ['tsakə] f point; (Bergzacke) jagged peak; (Gabelzacke) prong; (Kammzacke) tooth

zackig ['tsakɪç] adj jagged; (umg) smart; (Tempo) brisk

zaghaft ['tsaːkhaft] adj timid

zäh [tsɛː] adj tough; (Mensch) tenacious;

(Flüssigkeit) thick; *(schleppend)* sluggish; **Z~igkeit** f toughness; tenacity

Zahl [tsa:l] **(-, -en)** f number; **z~bar** adj payable; **z~en** vt, vi to pay; **z~en bitte!** the bill please!

zählen ['tsɛ:lən] vt, vi to count; ~ **auf** +akk to count on; ~ **zu** to be numbered among

Zahlenschloss ▲ nt combination lock

Zähler ['tsɛ:lər] **(-s, -)** m *(TECH)* meter; *(MATH)* numerator

Zahl- zW: **z~los** adj countless; **z~reich** adj numerous; ~**tag** m payday; ~**ung** f payment; ~**ungsanweisung** f giro transfer order; **z~ungsfähig** adj solvent; ~**wort** nt numeral

zahm [tsa:m] adj tame

zähmen ['tsɛ:mən] vt to tame; *(fig)* to curb

Zahn [tsa:n] **(-(e)s, ⁀e)** m tooth; ~**arzt** m dentist; ~**ärztin** f *(female)* dentist; ~**bürste** f toothbrush; ~**fleisch** nt gums pl; ~**pasta** f toothpaste; ~**rad** nt cog(wheel); ~**schmerzen** pl toothache sg; ~**stein** m tartar; ~**stocher** **(-s, -)** m toothpick

Zange ['tsaŋə] f pliers pl; *(Zuckerzange etc)* tongs pl; *(Beißzange, ZOOL)* pincers pl; *(MED)* forceps pl

zanken ['tsaŋkən] vi, vr to quarrel

zänkisch ['tsɛŋkɪʃ] adj quarrelsome

Zäpfchen ['tsɛpfçən] nt *(ANAT)* uvula; *(MED)* suppository

Zapfen ['tsapfən] **(-s, -)** m plug; *(BOT)* cone; *(Eiszapfen)* icicle

zappeln ['tsapəln] vi to wriggle; to fidget

zart [tsa:rt] adj *(weich, leise)* soft; *(Fleisch)* tender; *(fein, schwächlich)* delicate; **Z~heit** f softness; tenderness; delicacy

zärtlich ['tsɛːrtlɪç] adj tender, affectionate

Zauber ['tsaubər] **(-s, -)** m magic; *(~bann)* spell; ~**ei** f magic; ~**er** **(-s, -)** m magician; conjuror; **z~haft** adj magical, enchanting; ~**künstler** m conjuror; ~**kunststück** nt conjuring trick; **z~n** vi to conjure, to practise magic

zaudern ['tsaudərn] vi to hesitate

Zaum [tsaum] **(-(e)s, Zäume)** m bridle; **etw im ~ halten** to keep sth in check

Zaun [tsaun] **(-(e)s, Zäune)** m fence

z. B. abk *(= zum Beispiel)* e.g.

Zebra ['tse:bra] nt zebra; ~**streifen** m zebra crossing

Zeche ['tsɛçə] f *(Rechnung)* bill; *(Bergbau)* mine

Zeh [tse:] **(-s, -en)** m toe

Zehe [tse:ə] f toe; *(Knoblauchzehe)* clove

zehn [tse:n] num ten; ~**te(r, s)** adj tenth; **Z~tel** **(-s, -)** nt tenth (part)

Zeich- [tsaiç] zW: ~**en** **(-s, -)** nt sign; **z~nen** vt to draw; *(kennzeichnen)* to mark; *(unterzeichnen)* to sign ♦ vi to draw; to sign; ~**ner** **(-s, -)** m artist; **technischer ~ner** draughtsman; ~**nung** f drawing; *(Markierung)* markings pl

Zeige- ['tsaigə] zW: ~**finger** m index finger; **z~n** vt to show ♦ vi to point ♦ vr to show o.s.; **z~n auf** +akk to point to; to point at; **es wird sich z~n** time will tell; **es zeigte sich, dass ...** it turned out that ...; ~**r** **(-s, -)** m pointer; *(Uhrzeiger)* hand

Zeile ['tsailə] f line; *(Häuserzeile)* row

Zeit [tsait] **(-, -en)** f time; *(GRAM)* tense; **sich** dat ~ **lassen** to take one's time; **von ~ zu ~** from time to time; **siehe zurzeit;** ~**alter** nt age; ~**ansage** f *(TEL)* speaking clock; ~**arbeit** f *(COMM)* temporary job; **z~gemäß** adj in keeping with the times; ~**genosse** m contemporary; **z~ig** adj early; **z~lich** adj temporal; ~**lupe** f slow motion; **z~raubend** adj time-consuming; ~**raum** m period; ~**rechnung** f time, era; **nach/vor unserer ~rechnung** A.D./B.C.; ~**schrift** f periodical; ~**ung** f newspaper; ~**vertreib** m pastime, diversion; **z~weilig** adj temporary; **z~weise** adv for a time; ~**wort** nt verb

Zelle ['tsɛlə] f cell; *(Telefonzelle)* callbox

Zellstoff m cellulose

Zelt [tsɛlt] **(-(e)s, -e)** nt tent; **z~en** vi to camp; ~**platz** m camp site

Zement [tse'mɛnt] **(-(e)s, -e)** m cement; **z~ieren** vt to cement

zensieren [tsɛn'zi:rən] vt to censor; *(SCH)* to mark

Zensur [tsɛn'zu:r] f censorship; *(SCH)* mark

Zentimeter [tsɛnti'me:tər] *m od nt* centimetre

Zentner ['tsɛntnər] (**-s, -**) *m* hundredweight

zentral [tsɛn'tra:l] *adj* central; **Z~e** *f* central office; (*TEL*) exchange; **Z~heizung** *f* central heating

Zentrum ['tsɛntrʊm] (**-s, Zentren**) *nt* centre

zerbrechen [tsɛr'brɛçən] (*unreg*) *vt, vi* to break

zerbrechlich *adj* fragile

zer'drücken *vt* to squash, to crush; (*Kartoffeln*) to mash

Zeremonie [tseremo'ni:] *f* ceremony

Zerfall [tsɛr'fal] *m* decay; **z~en** (*unreg*) *vi* to disintegrate, to decay; (*sich gliedern*): **z~en (in** +*akk*) to fall (into)

zer'gehen (*unreg*) *vi* to melt, to dissolve

zerkleinern [tsɛr'klaɪnərn] *vt* to reduce to small pieces

zerlegbar [tsɛr'le:kba:r] *adj* able to be dismantled

zerlegen [tsɛr'le:gən] *vt* to take to pieces; (*Fleisch*) to carve; (*Satz*) to analyse

zermürben [tsɛr'myrbən] *vt* to wear down

zerquetschen [tsɛr'kvɛtʃən] *vt* to squash

zer'reißen (*unreg*) *vt* to tear to pieces ♦ *vi* to tear, to rip

zerren ['tsɛrən] *vt* to drag ♦ *vi*: **~ (an** +*dat*) to tug (at)

zer'rinnen (*unreg*) *vi* to melt away

zerrissen [tsɛr'rɪsən] *adj* torn, tattered; **Z~heit** *f* tattered state; (*POL*) disunion, discord; (*innere Z~heit*) disintegration

Zerrung *f* (*MED*): **eine ~** pulled muscle

zerrütten [tsɛr'rʏtən] *vt* to wreck, to destroy

zer'schlagen (*unreg*) *vt* to shatter, to smash ♦ *vr* to fall through

zer'schneiden (*unreg*) *vt* to cut up

zer'setzen *vt, vr* to decompose, to dissolve

zer'springen (*unreg*) *vi* to shatter, to burst

Zerstäuber [tsɛr'ʃtɔybər] (**-s, -**) *m* atomizer

zerstören [tsɛr'ʃtø:rən] *vt* to destroy

Zerstörung *f* destruction

zerstreu- [tsɛr'ʃtrɔy] *zW*: **~en** *vt* to disperse, to scatter; (*unterhalten*) to divert; (*Zweifel etc*) to dispel ♦ *vr* to disperse, to scatter; to be dispelled; **~t** *adj* scattered; (*Mensch*)

absent-minded; **Z~theit** *f* absent-mindedness; **Z~ung** *f* dispersion; (*Ablenkung*) diversion

zerstückeln [tsɛr'ʃtʏkəln] *vt* to cut into pieces

zer'teilen *vt* to divide into parts

Zertifikat [tsɛrtifi'ka:t] (**-(e)s, -e**) *nt* certificate

zer'treten (*unreg*) *vt* to crush underfoot

zertrümmern [tsɛr'trʏmərn] *vt* to shatter; (*Gebäude etc*) to demolish

Zettel ['tsɛtəl] (**-s, -**) *m* piece of paper, slip; (*Notizzettel*) note; (*Formular*) form

Zeug [tsɔyk] (**-(e)s, -e**) (*umg*) *nt* stuff; (*Ausrüstung*) gear; **dummes ~** (stupid) nonsense; **das ~ haben zu** to have the makings of; **sich ins ~ legen** to put one's shoulder to the wheel

Zeuge ['tsɔygə] (**-n, -n**) *m* witness; **z~n** *vi* to bear witness, to testify ♦ *vt* (*Kind*) to father; **es zeugt von ...** it testifies to ...; **~naussage** *f* evidence; **Zeugin** ['tsɔygɪn] *f* witness

Zeugnis ['tsɔygnɪs] (**-ses, -se**) *nt* certificate; (*SCH*) report; (*Referenz*) reference; (*Aussage*) evidence, testimony; **~ geben von** to be evidence of, to testify to

z. H(d). *abk* (= *zu Händen*) attn.

Zickzack ['tsɪktsak] (**-(e)s, -e**) *m* zigzag

Ziege ['tsi:gə] *f* goat

Ziegel ['tsi:gəl] (**-s, -**) *m* brick; (*Dachziegel*) tile

ziehen ['tsi:ən] (*unreg*) *vt* to draw; (*zerren*) to pull; (*SCHACH etc*) to move; (*züchten*) to rear ♦ *vi* to draw; (*umziehen, wandern*) to move; (*Rauch, Wolke etc*) to drift; (*reißen*) to pull ♦ *vb unpers*: **es zieht** there is a draught, it's draughty ♦ *vr* (*Gummi*) to stretch; (*Grenze etc*) to run; (*Gespräche*) to be drawn out; **etw nach sich ~** to lead to sth, to entail sth

Ziehung ['tsi:ʊŋ] *f* (*Losziehung*) drawing

Ziel [tsi:l] (**-(e)s, -e**) *nt* (*einer Reise*) destination; (*SPORT*) finish; (*MIL*) target; (*Absicht*) goal; **z~bewusst** ▲ *adj* decisive; **z~en** *vi*: **z~en (auf** +*akk*) to aim (at); **z~los** *adj* aimless; **~scheibe** *f* target; **z~strebig**

adj purposeful

ziemlich ['tsi:mlıç] *adj* quite a; fair ♦ *adv* rather; quite a bit

zieren ['tsi:rən] *vr* to act coy

zierlich ['tsi:rlıç] *adj* dainty

Ziffer ['tsıfər] (-, -n) *f* figure, digit; **~blatt** *nt* dial, clock-face

zig [tsık] (*umg*) *adj* umpteen

Zigarette [tsiga'rɛtə] *f* cigarette

Zigaretten- *zW*: **~automat** *m* cigarette machine; **~schachtel** *f* cigarette packet; **~spitze** *f* cigarette holder

Zigarre [tsi'garə] *f* cigar

Zigeuner(in) [tsi'gɔynər(ın)] (-s, -) *m(f)* gipsy

Zimmer ['tsımər] (-s, -) *nt* room; **~lautstärke** *f* reasonable volume; **~mädchen** *nt* chambermaid; **~mann** *m* carpenter; **z~n** *vt* to make (from wood); **~nachweis** *m* accommodation office; **~pflanze** *f* indoor plant; **~service** *m* room service

zimperlich ['tsımpərlıç] *adj* squeamish; (*pingelig*) fussy, finicky

Zimt [tsımt] (-(e)s, -e) *m* cinnamon

Zink [tsıŋk] (-(e)s) *nt* zinc

Zinn [tsın] (-(e)s) *nt* (*Element*) tin; (*in ~waren*) pewter; **~soldat** *m* tin soldier

Zins [tsıns] (-es, -en) *m* interest; **~eszins** *m* compound interest; **~fuß** *m* rate of interest; **z~los** *adj* interest-free; **~satz** *m* rate of interest

Zipfel ['tsıpfəl] (-s, -) *m* corner; (*spitz*) tip; (*Hemdzipfel*) tail; (*Wurstzipfel*) end

zirka ['tsırka] *adv* (round) about

Zirkel ['tsırkəl] (-s, -) *m* circle; (*MATH*) pair of compasses

Zirkus ['tsırkus] (-, -se) *m* circus

zischen ['tsıʃən] *vi* to hiss

Zitat [tsi'ta:t] (-(e)s, -e) *nt* quotation, quote

zitieren [tsi'ti:rən] *vt* to quote

Zitrone [tsi'tro:nə] *f* lemon; **~nlimonade** *f* lemonade; **~nsaft** *m* lemon juice

zittern ['tsıtərn] *vi* to tremble

zivil [tsi'vi:l] *adj* civil; (*Preis*) moderate; **Z~(s)** *nt* plain clothes *pl*; (*MIL*) civilian clothing; **Z~courage** *f* courage of one's convictions;

Z~dienst *m* community service;

Z~isation [tsivilizatsi'o:n] *f* civilization;

Z~isationskrankheit *f* disease peculiar to civilization; **~i'sieren** *vt* to civilize

---
Zivildienst
---

i A young German has to complete his 13 months' **Zivildienst** or service to the community if he has opted out of military service as a conscientious objector. This is usually done in a hospital or old people's home. About 18% of young Germans choose to do this as an alternative to the **Wehrdienst**.

Zivilist [tsivi'lıst] *m* civilian

zögern ['tsø:gərn] *vi* to hesitate

Zoll [tsɔl] (-(e)s, ¨e) *m* customs *pl*; (*Abgabe*) duty; **~abfertigung** *f* customs clearance; **~amt** *nt* customs office; **~beamte(r)** *m* customs official; **~erklärung** *f* customs declaration; **z~frei** *adj* duty-free; **~kontrolle** *f* customs check; **z~pflichtig** *adj* liable to duty, dutiable

Zone ['tso:nə] *f* zone

Zoo [tso:] (-s, -s) *m* zoo; **~loge** [tsoo'lo:gə] (-n, -n) *m* zoologist; **~lo'gie** *f* zoology; **z~'logisch** *adj* zoological

Zopf [tsɔpf] (-(e)s, ¨e) *m* plait; pigtail; **alter ~** antiquated custom

Zorn [tsɔrn] (-(e)s) *m* anger; **z~ig** *adj* angry

zottig ['tsɔtıç] *adj* shaggy

z. T. *abk* = **zum Teil**

SCHLÜSSELWORT
---

zu [tsu:] *präp +dat* **1** (*örtlich*) to; **zum Bahnhof/Arzt gehen** to go to the station/ doctor; **zur Schule/Kirche gehen** to go to school/church; **sollen wir zu euch gehen?** shall we go to your place?; **sie sah zu ihm hin** she looked towards him; **zum Fenster herein** through the window; **zu meiner Linken** to *od* on my left

2 (*zeitlich*) at; **zu Ostern** at Easter; **bis zum 1. Mai** until May 1st; (*nicht später als*) by May 1st; **zu meiner Zeit** in my time

3 (*Zusatz*) with; **Wein zum Essen trinken**

to drink wine with one's meal; **sich zu jdm setzen** to sit down beside sb; **setz dich doch zu uns** (come and) sit with us; **Anmerkungen zu etw** notes on sth **4** (*Zweck*) for; **Wasser zum Waschen** water for washing; **Papier zum Schreiben** paper to write on; **etw zum Geburtstag bekommen** to get sth for one's birthday **5** (*Veränderung*) into; **zu etw werden** to turn into sth; **jdn zu etw machen** to make sb (into) sth; **zu Asche verbrennen** to burn to ashes

6 (*mit Zahlen*): **3 zu 2** (*SPORT*) 3-2; **das Stück zu 2 Mark** at 2 marks each; **zum ersten Mal** for the first time

7: **zu meiner Freude** *etc* to my joy *etc*; **zum Glück** luckily; **zu Fuß** on foot; **es ist zum Weinen** it's enough to make you cry

♦ *konj* to; **etw zu essen** sth to eat; **um besser sehen zu können** in order to see better; **ohne es zu wissen** without knowing it; **noch zu bezahlende Rechnungen** bills that are still to be paid

♦ *adv* **1** (*allzu*) too; **zu sehr** too much; **zu viel** too much; **zu wenig** too little

2 (*örtlich*) toward(s); **er kam auf mich zu** he came up to me

3 (*geschlossen*) shut, closed; **die Geschäfte haben zu** the shops are closed; „**auf/zu**" (*Wasserhahn etc*) "on/off"

4 (*umg: los*): **nur zu!** just keep on!; **mach zu!** hurry up!

zualler- [tsuˈʔalər] *zW*: **~erst** [-ˈʔeːrst] *adv* first of all; **~letzt** [-ˈlɛtst] *adv* last of all

Zubehör [ˈtsuːbəhøːr] (**-(e)s, -e**) *nt* accessories *pl*

zubereiten [ˈtsuːbəraɪtən] *vt* to prepare

zubilligen [ˈtsuːbɪlɪɡən] *vt* to grant

zubinden [ˈtsuːbɪndən] (*unreg*) *vt* to tie up

zubringen [ˈtsuːbrɪŋən] (*unreg*) *vt* (*Zeit*) to spend

Zubringer (**-s, -**) *m* (*Straße*) approach *od* slip road

Zucchini [tsʊˈkiːniː] *pl* (*BOT, KOCH*) courgette (*BRIT*), zucchini (*US*)

Zucht [tsʊxt] (**-, -en**) *f* (*von Tieren*) breeding;

(*von Pflanzen*) cultivation; (*Rasse*) breed; (*Erziehung*) raising; (*Disziplin*) discipline

züchten [ˈtsʏçtən] *vt* (*Tiere*) to breed; (*Pflanzen*) to cultivate, to grow; **Züchter** (**-s, -**) *m* breeder; grower

Zuchthaus *nt* prison, penitentiary (*US*)

züchtigen [ˈtsʏçtɪɡən] *vt* to chastise

Züchtung *f* (*Zuchtart, Sorte: von Tier*) breed; (: *von Pflanze*) variety

zucken [ˈtsʊkən] *vi* to jerk, to twitch; (*Strahl etc*) to flicker ♦ *vt* (*Schultern*) to shrug

Zucker [ˈtsʊkər] (**-s, -**) *m* sugar; (*MED*) diabetes; **~guss** ▲ *m* icing; **z~krank** *adj* diabetic; **~krankheit** *f* (*MED*) diabetes; **z~n** *vt* to sugar; **~rohr** *nt* sugar cane; **~rübe** *f* sugar beet

Zuckung [ˈtsʊkʊŋ] *f* convulsion, spasm; (*leicht*) twitch

zudecken [ˈtsuːdɛkən] *vt* to cover (up)

zudem [tsuˈdeːm] *adv* in addition (to this)

zudringlich [ˈtsuːdrɪŋlɪç] *adj* forward, pushing, obtrusive

zudrücken [ˈtsuːdrʏkən] *vt* to close; **ein Auge ~** to turn a blind eye

zueinander [tsuʔaɪˈnandər] *adv* to one other; (*in Verbindung*) together

zuerkennen [ˈtsuːʔɛrkɛnən] (*unreg*) *vt* to award; **jdm etw ~** to award sth to sb, to award sb sth

zuerst [tsuˈʔeːrst] *adv* first; (*zu Anfang*) at first; **~ einmal** first of all

Zufahrt [ˈtsuːfaːrt] *f* approach; **~sstraße** *f* approach road; (*von Autobahn etc*) slip road

Zufall [ˈtsuːfal] *m* chance; (*Ereignis*) coincidence; **durch ~** by accident; **so ein ~** what a coincidence; **z~en** (*unreg*) *vi* to close, to shut; (*Anteil, Aufgabe*) to fall

zufällig [ˈtsuːfɛlɪç] *adj* chance ♦ *adv* by chance; (*in Frage*) by any chance

Zuflucht [ˈtsuːflʊxt] *f* recourse; (*Ort*) refuge

zufolge [tsuˈfɔlɡə] *präp* (+*dat od gen*) judging by; (*laut*) according to

zufrieden [tsuˈfriːdən] *adj* content(ed), satisfied; **~ geben** to be content *od* satisfied (with); **~ stellen** to satisfy

zufrieren [ˈtsuːfriːrən] (*unreg*) *vi* to freeze up *od* over

Spelling Reform: ▲ *new spelling* △ *old spelling (to be phased out)*

zufügen ['tsuːfyːgən] *vt* to add; (*Leid etc*): (**jdm**) **etw ~** to cause (sb) sth

Zufuhr ['tsuːfuːr] *f* (-, -en) (*Herbeibringen*) supplying; (*MET*) influx

Zug [tsuːk] *m* (-(e)s, ᵘe) (*EISENB*) train; (*Luftzug*) draught; (*Ziehen*) pull(ing); (*Gesichtszug*) feature; (*SCHACH etc*) move; (*Schriftzug*) stroke; (*Atemzug*) breath; (*Charakterzug*) trait; (*an Zigarette*) puff, pull, drag; (*Schluck*) gulp; (*Menschengruppe*) procession; (*von Vögeln*) flight; (*MIL*) platoon; **etw in vollen Zügen genießen** to enjoy sth to the full

Zu- ['tsuː] *zW:* **~gabe** *f* extra; (*in Konzert etc*) encore; **~gang** *m* access, approach; **z~gänglich** *adj* accessible; (*Mensch*) approachable

zugeben ['tsuːgeːbən] (*unreg*) *vt* (*beifügen*) to add, to throw in; (*zugestehen*) to admit; (*erlauben*) to permit

zugehen ['tsuːgeːən] (*unreg*) *vi* (*schließen*) to shut; **es geht dort seltsam zu** there are strange goings-on there; **auf jdn/etw ~** to walk towards sb/sth; **dem Ende ~** to be finishing

Zugehörigkeit ['tsuːgəhøːrɪçkaɪt] *f:* **~ (zu)** membership (of), belonging (to)

Zügel ['tsyːgəl] *m* (-s, -) rein(s); (*fig*) curb; **z~n** *vt* to curb; (*Pferd*) to rein in

zuge- ['tsuːgə] *zW:* **Z~ständnis** (-ses, -se) *nt* concession; **~stehen** (*unreg*) *vt* to admit; (*Rechte*) to concede

Zugführer *m* (*EISENB*) guard

zugig ['tsuːgɪç] *adj* draughty

zügig ['tsyːgɪç] *adj* speedy, swift

zugreifen ['tsuːgraɪfən] (*unreg*) *vi* to seize *od* grab at; (*helfen*) to help; (*beim Essen*) to help o.s.

Zugrestaurant *nt* dining car

zugrunde, zu Grunde [tsuːˈgrʊndə] *adv:* **~ gehen** to collapse; (*Mensch*) to perish; **einer Sache** *dat* **etw ~ legen** to base sth on sth; **einer Sache** *dat* **~ liegen** to be based on sth; **~ richten** to ruin, to destroy

zugunsten, zu Gunsten [tsuːˈgʊnstən] *präp* (+gen *od* dat) in favour of

zugute [tsuːˈguːtə] *adv:* **jdm etw ~ halten** to concede sth to sb; **jdm ~ kommen** to be of assistance to sb

Zugvogel *m* migratory bird

zuhalten ['tsuːhaltən] (*unreg*) *vt* to keep closed ♦ *vi:* **auf jdn/etw ~** to make a beeline for sb/sth

Zuhälter ['tsuːhɛltər] *m* (-s, -) pimp

Zuhause [tsuːˈhauzə] *nt* (-) home

zuhause [tsuːˈhauzə] *adv* (*österreichisch, schweizerisch*) at home

zuhören ['tsuːhøːrən] *vi* to listen

Zuhörer (-s, -) *m* listener

zukleben ['tsuːkleːbən] *vt* to paste up

zukommen ['tsuːkɔmən] (*unreg*) *vi* to come up; **auf jdn ~** to come up to sb; **jdm etw ~ lassen** to give sb sth; **etw auf sich ~ lassen** to wait and see; **jdm ~** (*sich gehören*) to be fitting for sb

Zukunft ['tsuːkʊnft] *f* (-, Zukünfte) future; **zukünftig** ['tsuːkʏnftɪç] *adj* future ♦ *adv* in future; **mein zukünftiger Mann** my husband to be

Zulage ['tsuːlaːgə] *f* bonus

zulassen ['tsuːlasən] (*unreg*) *vt* (*hereinlassen*) to admit; (*erlauben*) to permit; (*Auto*) to license; (*umg: nicht öffnen*) to (keep) shut

zulässig ['tsuːlɛsɪç] *adj* permissible, permitted

Zulassung *f* (*amtlich*) authorization; (*von Kfz*) licensing

zulaufen ['tsuːlaufən] (*unreg*) *vi* (*subj: Mensch*): **~ auf jdn/etw** to run up to sb/ sth; (: *Straße*): **~ auf** to lead towards

zuleide, zu Leide [tsuːˈlaɪdə] *adv:* **jdm etw ~ tun** to hurt *od* harm sb

zuletzt [tsuːˈlɛtst] *adv* finally, at last

zuliebe [tsuːˈliːbə] *adv:* **jdm ~** to please sb

zum [tsʊm] = **zu dem**; **~ dritten Mal** for the third time; **~ Scherz** as a joke; **~ Trinken** for drinking

zumachen ['tsuːmaxən] *vt* to shut; (*Kleidung*) to do up, to fasten ♦ *vi* to shut; (*umg*) to hurry up

zu- *zW:* **~mal** [tsuːˈmaːl] *konj* especially (as); **~meist** [tsuːˈmaɪst] *adv* mostly; **~mindest** [tsuːˈmɪndəst] *adv* at least

zumutbar ['tsu:mu:tbaːr] *adj* reasonable

zumute, zu Mute [tsu'muːtə] *adv*: **wie ist ihm ~?** how does he feel?

zumuten ['tsu:muːtən] *vt*: **(jdm) etw ~** to expect *od* ask sth (of sb)

Zumutung ['tsu:muːtʊŋ] *f* unreasonable expectation *od* demand, impertinence

zunächst [tsu'nɛːçst] *adv* first of all; **~ einmal** to start with

Zunahme ['tsu:naːmə] *f* increase

Zuname ['tsu:naːmə] *m* surname

Zünd- [tsynd] *ZW*: **z~en** *vi* (*Feuer*) to light, to ignite; (*Motor*) to fire; (*begeistern*): **bei jdm z~en** to fire sb (with enthusiasm); **z~end** *adj* fiery; **~er** (**-s, -**) *m* fuse; (*MIL*) detonator; **~holz** ['tsynt-] *nt* match; **~kerze** *f* (*AUT*) spark(ing) plug; **~schloss** ▲ *nt* ignition lock; **~schlüssel** *m* ignition key; **~schnur** *f* fuse wire; **~stoff** *m* (*fig*) inflammatory stuff; **~ung** *f* ignition

zunehmen ['tsu:neːmən] (*unreg*) *vi* to increase, to grow; (*Mensch*) to put on weight

Zuneigung ['tsu:naigʊŋ] *f* affection

Zunft [tsunft] (**-, ²e**) *f* guild

zünftig ['tsynftiç] *adj* proper, real; (*Handwerk*) decent

Zunge ['tsuŋə] *f* tongue

zunichte [tsu'niçtə] *adv*: **~ machen** to ruin, to destroy; **~ werden** to come to nothing

zunutze, zu Nutze [tsu'nʊtsə] *adv*: **sich** *dat* **etw ~ machen** to make use of sth

zuoberst [tsu'joːbərst] *adv* at the top

zupfen ['tsʊpfən] *vt* to pull, to pick, to pluck; (*Gitarre*) to pluck

zur [tsuːr] = **zu der**

zurate, zu Rate [tsu'raːtə] *adv*: **jdn ~ ziehen** to consult sb

zurechnungsfähig ['tsu:rɛçnʊŋsfɛːiç] *adj* responsible, accountable

zurecht- [tsu'rɛçt] *ZW*: **~finden** (*unreg*) *vr* to find one's way (about); **~kommen** (*unreg*) *vi* to (be able to) cope, to manage; **~legen** *vt* to get ready; (*Ausrede etc*) to have ready; **~machen** *vt* to prepare ♦ *vr* to get ready; **~weisen** (*unreg*) *vt* to reprimand

zureden ['tsu:reːdən] *vi*: **jdm ~** to persuade *od* urge sb

zurück [tsu'rʏk] *adv* back; **~behalten** (*unreg*) *vt* to keep back; **~bekommen** (*unreg*) *vt* to get back; **~bleiben** (*unreg*) *vi* (*Mensch*) to remain behind; (*nicht nachkommen*) to fall behind, to lag; (*Schaden*) to remain; **~bringen** (*unreg*) *vt* to bring back; **~fahren** (*unreg*) *vi* to travel back; (*vor Schreck*) to recoil, to start ♦ *vt* to drive back; **~finden** (*unreg*) *vi* to find one's way back; **~fordern** *vt* to demand back; **~führen** *vt* to lead back; **etw auf etw** *akk* **~führen** to trace sth back to sth; **~geben** (*unreg*) *vt* to give back; (*antworten*) to retort with; **~geblieben** *adj* retarded; **~gehen** (*unreg*) *vi* to go back; (*fallen*) to go down, to fall; (*zeitlich*): **~gehen (auf** +*akk*) to date back (to); **~gezogen** *adj* retired, withdrawn; **~halten** (*unreg*) *vt* to hold back; (*Mensch*) to restrain; (*hindern*) to prevent ♦ *vr* (*reserviert sein*) to be reserved; (*im Essen*) to hold back; **~haltend** *adj* reserved; **Z~haltung** *f* reserve; **~kehren** *vi* to return; **~kommen** (*unreg*) *vi* to come back; **auf etw** *akk* **~kommen** to return to sth; **~lassen** (*unreg*) *vt* to leave behind; **~legen** *vt* to put back; (*Geld*) to put by; (*reservieren*) to keep back; (*Strecke*) to cover; **~nehmen** (*unreg*) *vt* to take back; **~stellen** *vt* to put back, to replace; (*aufschieben*) to put off, to postpone; (*Interessen*) to defer; (*Ware*) to keep; **~treten** (*unreg*) *vi* to step back; (*vom Amt*) to retire; **gegenüber etw** *od* **hinter etw** *dat* **~treten** to diminish in importance in view of sth; **~weisen** (*unreg*) *vt* to turn down; (*Mensch*) to reject; **~zahlen** *vt* to repay, to pay back; (*verauslagt*) **~ziehen** (*unreg*) *vt* to pull back; (*Angebot*) to withdraw ♦ *vr* to retire

Zuruf ['tsu:ruːf] *m* shout, cry

zurzeit [tsʊr'tsait] *adv* at the moment

Zusage ['tsu:za:gə] *f* promise; (*Annahme*) consent; **z~n** *vt* to promise ♦ *vi* to accept; **jdm z~n** (*gefallen*) to agree with *od* please sb

zusammen [tsu'zamən] *adv* together;

Z~arbeit f cooperation; **~arbeiten** vi to cooperate; **~beißen** (unreg) vt (Zähne) to clench; **~brechen** (unreg) vi to collapse; (Mensch auch) to break down; **~bringen** (unreg) vt to bring od get together; (Geld) to get; (Sätze) to put together; **Z~bruch** m collapse; **~fassen** vt to summarize; (vereinigen) to unite; **Z~fassung** f summary, résumé; **~fügen** vt to join (together), to unite; **~halten** (unreg) vi to stick together; **Z~hang** m connection; **im/aus dem Z~hang** in/out of context; **~hängen** (unreg) vi to be connected od linked; **~kommen** (unreg) vi to meet, to assemble; (sich ereignen) to occur at once od together; **~legen** vt to put together; (stapeln) to pile up; (falten) to fold; (verbinden) to combine, to unite; (Termine, Fest) to amalgamate; (Geld) to collect; **~nehmen** (unreg) vt to summon up ♦ vr to pull o.s. together; **alles ~genommen** all in all; **~passen** vi to go well together, to match; **~schließen** (unreg) vt, vr to join (together); **Z~schluss** ▲ m amalgamation; **~schreiben** (unreg) vt to write as one word; (Bericht) to put together; **Z~sein** (-s) nt get-together; **~setzen** vt to put together ♦ vr (Stoff) to be composed of; (Menschen) to get together; **Z~setzung** f composition; **~stellen** vt to put together; to compile; **Z~stoß** m collision; **~stoßen** (unreg) vi to collide; **~treffen** (unreg) vi to coincide; (Menschen) to meet; **Z~treffen** nt coincidence; meeting; **~zählen** vt to add up; **~ziehen** (unreg) vt (verengern) to draw together; (vereinigen) to bring together; (addieren) to add up ♦ vr to shrink; (sich bilden) to form, to develop

zusätzlich ['tsu:zɛtslɪç] adj additional ♦ adv in addition

zuschauen ['tsu:ʃauən] vi to watch, to look on; **Zuschauer(in)** (-s, -) m(f) spectator ♦ pl (THEAT) audience sg

zuschicken ['tsu:ʃɪkən] vt: **(jdm etw) ~** to send od to forward (sth to sb)

Zuschlag ['tsu:ʃla:k] m extra charge, surcharge; **z~en** (unreg) vt (Tür) to slam; (Ball) to hit; (bei Auktion) to knock down; (Steine etc) to knock into shape ♦ vi (Fenster, Tür) to shut; (Mensch) to hit, to punch; **~karte** f (EISENB) surcharge ticket; **z~pflichtig** adj subject to surcharge

zuschneiden ['tsu:ʃnaɪdən] (unreg) vt to cut out; to cut to size

zuschrauben ['tsu:ʃraubən] vt to screw down od up

zuschreiben ['tsu:ʃraɪbən] (unreg) vt (fig) to ascribe, to attribute; (COMM) to credit

Zuschrift ['tsu:ʃrɪft] f letter, reply

zuschulden, zu Schulden [tsu'ʃuldən] adv: **sich** dat **etw ~ kommen lassen** to make o.s. guilty of sth

Zuschuss ▲ ['tsu:ʃʊs] m subsidy, allowance

zusehen ['tsu:ze:ən] (unreg) vi to watch; (dafür sorgen) to take care; **jdm/etw ~** to watch sb/sth; **~ds** adv visibly

zusenden ['tsu:zɛndən] (unreg) vt to forward, to send on

zusichern ['tsu:zɪçərn] vt: **jdm etw ~** to assure sb of sth

zuspielen ['tsu:ʃpi:lən] vt, vi to pass

zuspitzen ['tsu:ʃpɪtsən] vt to sharpen ♦ vr (Lage) to become critical

zusprechen ['tsu:ʃprɛçən] (unreg) vt (zuerkennen) to award ♦ vi to speak; **jdm etw ~** to award sb sth od sth to sb; **jdm Trost ~** to comfort sb; **dem Essen/ Alkohol ~** to eat/drink a lot

Zustand ['tsu:ʃtant] m state, condition

zustande, zu Stande [tsu'ʃtandə] adv: **~ bringen** to bring about; **~ kommen** to come about

zuständig ['tsu:ʃtɛndɪç] adj responsible; **Z~keit** f competence, responsibility

zustehen ['tsu:ʃte:ən] (unreg) vi: **jdm ~** to be sb's right

zustellen ['tsu:ʃtɛlən] vt (verstellen) to block; (Post etc) to send

Zustellung f delivery

zustimmen ['tsu:ʃtɪmən] vi to agree

Zustimmung f agreement, consent

zustoßen ['tsu:ʃto:sən] (unreg) vi (fig) to happen

Rechtschreibreform: ▲ *neue Schreibung* △ *alte Schreibung (auslaufend)*

zutage, zu Tage [tsu'ta:gə] *adv*: ~ **bringen** to bring to light; ~ **treten** to come to light

Zutaten ['tsu:ta:tən] *pl* ingredients

zuteilen ['tsu:taɪlən] *vt* (*Arbeit, Rolle*) to designate, assign; (*Aktien, Wohnung*) to allocate

zutiefst [tsu'ti:fst] *adv* deeply

zutragen ['tsu:tra:gən] (*unreg*) *vt* to bring; (*Klatsch*) to tell ♦ *vr* to happen

zutrau- ['tsu:trau] *zW*: **Z~en (-s)** *nt*: **Z~en (zu)** trust (in); **~en** *vt*: **jdm etw ~en** to credit sb with sth; **~lich** *adj* trusting, friendly

zutreffen ['tsu:trɛfən] (*unreg*) *vi* to be correct; to apply; **~d** *adj* (*richtig*) accurate; **Z~des bitte unterstreichen** please underline where applicable

Zutritt ['tsu:trɪt] *m* access, admittance

Zutun ['tsu:tu:n] (-s) *nt* assistance

zuverlässig ['tsu:fɛrlɛsɪç] *adj* reliable; **Z~keit** *f* reliability

zuversichtlich ['tsu:fɛrzɪçtlɪç] *adj* confident

zuvor [tsu'fo:r] *adv* before, previously; **~kommen** (*unreg*) *vi* +*dat* to anticipate; **jdm ~kommen** to beat sb to it; **~kommend** *adj* obliging, courteous

Zuwachs ['tsu:vaks] (-es) *m* increase, growth; (*umg*) addition; **Z~en** (*unreg*) *vi* to become overgrown; (*Wunde*) to heal (up)

zuwege, zu Wege [tsu've:gə] *adv*: **etw ~ bringen** to accomplish sth

zuweilen [tsu'vaɪlən] *adv* at times, now and then

zuweisen ['tsu:vaɪzən] (*unreg*) *vt* to assign, to allocate

zuwenden ['tsu:vɛndən] (*unreg*) *vt* (+*dat*) to turn (towards) ♦ *vr*: **sich jdm/etw ~** to devote o.s. to sb/sth; to turn to sb/sth

zuwider [tsu'vi:dər] *adv*: **etw ist jdm ~** sb loathes sth, sb finds sth repugnant; **~handeln** *vi*: **einer Sache** *dat* **~handeln** to act contrary to sth; **einem Gesetz ~handeln** to contravene a law

zuziehen ['tsu:tsi:ən] (*unreg*) *vt* (*schließen*: *Vorhang*) to draw, to close; (*herberufen*: *Experten*) to call in ♦ *vi* to move in, to

come; **sich** *dat* **etw ~** (*Krankheit*) to catch sth; (*Zorn*) to incur sth

zuzüglich ['tsu:tsy:klɪç] *präp* +*gen* plus, with the addition of

Zwang [tsvaŋ] **(-(e)s, ⁝e)** *m* compulsion, coercion

zwängen ['tsvɛŋən] *vt, vr* to squeeze

zwanglos *adj* informal

Zwangs- *zW*: **~arbeit** *f* forced labour; (*Strafe*) hard labour; **~lage** *f* predicament, tight corner; **z~läufig** *adj* necessary, inevitable

zwanzig ['tsvantsɪç] *num* twenty

zwar [tsva:r] *adv* to be sure, indeed; **das ist ~ ..., aber ...** that may be ... but ...; **und ~ am Sonntag** on Sunday to be precise; **und ~ so schnell, dass ...** in fact so quickly that ...

Zweck [tsvɛk] **(-(e)s, -e)** *m* purpose, aim; **es hat keinen ~** there's no point; **z~dienlich** *adj* practical; expedient

Zwecke *f* hobnail; (*Heftzwecke*) drawing pin, thumbtack (*US*)

Zweck- *zW*: **z~los** *adj* pointless; **z~mäßig** *adj* suitable, appropriate; **z~s** *präp* +*gen* for the purpose of

zwei [tsvaɪ] *num* two; **Z~bettzimmer** *nt* twin room; **z~deutig** *adj* ambiguous; (*unanständig*) suggestive; **~erlei** *adj*: **~erlei Stoff** two different kinds of material; **~erlei Meinung** of differing opinions; **~fach** *adj* double

Zweifel ['tsvaɪfəl] **(-s, -)** *m* doubt; **z~haft** *adj* doubtful, dubious; **z~los** *adj* doubtless; **z~n** *vi*: **(an etw** *dat*) **z~n** to doubt (sth)

Zweig [tsvaɪk] **(-(e)s, -e)** *m* branch; **~stelle** *f* branch (office)

zwei- *zW*: **~hundert** *num* two hundred; **~mal** *adv* twice; **~sprachig** *adj* bilingual; **~spurig** *adj* (*AUT*) two-lane; **~stimmig** *adj* for two voices

zweit [tsvaɪt] *adv*: **zu ~** together; (*bei mehreren Paaren*) in twos

zweitbeste(r, s) *adj* second best

zweite(r, s) *adj* second

zweiteilig ['tsvaɪtaɪlɪç] *adj* (*Gruppe*) two-piece; (*Fernsehfilm*) two-part; (*Kleidung*)

Spelling Reform: ▲ *new spelling* △ *old spelling (to be phased out)*

two-piece

zweit- *zW*: **~ens** *adv* secondly; **~größte(r, s)** *adj* second largest; **~klassig** *adj* second-class; **~letzte(r, s)** *adj* last but one, penultimate; **~rangig** *adj* second-rate

Zwerchfell ['tsverçfel] *nt* diaphragm

Zwerg [tsverk] **(-(e)s, -e)** *m* dwarf

Zwetsch(g)e ['tsvetʃ(g)ə] *f* plum

Zwieback ['tsvi:bak] **(-(e)s, -e)** *m* rusk

Zwiebel ['tsvi:bəl] **(-, -n)** *f* onion; (*Blumenzwiebel*) bulb

Zwie- ['tsvi:] *zW*: **z~lichtig** *adj* shady, dubious; **z~spältig** *adj* (*Gefühle*) conflicting; (*Charakter*) contradictory; **~tracht** *f* discord, dissension

Zwilling ['tsvilɪŋ] **(-s, -e)** *m* twin; **~e** *pl* (*ASTROL*) Gemini

zwingen ['tsvɪŋən] (*unreg*) *vt* to force; **~d** *adj* (*Grund etc*) compelling

zwinkern ['tsvɪŋkərn] *vi* to blink; (*absichtlich*) to wink

Zwirn [tsvɪrn] **(-(e)s, -e)** *m* thread

zwischen ['tsvɪʃən] *präp* (+akk od dat) between; **Z~bemerkung** *f* (incidental) remark; **Z~ding** *nt* cross; **~durch** *adv* in between; (*räumlich*) here and there; **Z~ergebnis** *nt* intermediate result; **Z~fall** *m* incident; **Z~frage** *f* question; **Z~handel** *m* middlemen *pl*; middleman's trade; **Z~landung** *f* (*AVIAT*) stopover; **~menschlich** *adj* interpersonal; **Z~raum** *m* space; **Z~ruf** *m* interjection; **Z~stecker** *m* adaptor (plug); **Z~zeit** *f* interval; **in der Z~zeit** in the interim, meanwhile

zwitschern ['tsvɪtʃərn] *vt, vi* to twitter, to chirp

zwo [tsvo:] *num* two

zwölf [tsvœlf] *num* twelve

Zyklus ['tsy:klus] **(-, Zyklen)** *m* cycle

Zylinder [tsi'lɪndər] **(-s, -)** *m* cylinder; (*Hut*) top hat

Zyniker ['tsy:nikər] **(-s, -)** *m* cynic

zynisch ['tsy:nɪʃ] *adj* cynical

Zypern ['tsy:pərn] *nt* Cyprus

Zyste ['tsystə] *f* cyst

zz., zzt. *abk* = **zurzeit**

VERB TABLES

Introduction

The **Verb Tables** in the following section contain 52 tables of German verbs in alphabetical order. Each table shows you the following forms: **Present, Perfect, Future, Subjunctive, Imperfect, Conditional, Imperative** and the **Present** and **Past Participles**.

In order to help you use the verbs shown in the Verb Tables correctly, there are also a number of example phrases at the bottom of each page to show the verb as it is used in context.

In German there are **regular** verbs or **weak** verbs (their forms follow the normal rules) and **irregular** or **strong** verbs (their forms do not follow the normal rules) and **mixed** verbs (their forms have features of both **weak** and **strong** verbs).

The **Verb Tables** given show one **weak** verb – machen, Verb Table 27 and three **mixed** verbs – bringen, Verb Table 6; denken, Verb Table 7 and kennen Verb Table 20. The rest of the verbs shown are **strong** verbs.

For a further list of German **irregular** verb forms see pages 609–613.

▶ **bieten** (to offer)

PRESENT

ich	biete
du	bietest
er	bietet
wir	bieten
ihr	bietet
sie	bieten

PRESENT SUBJUNCTIVE

ich	biete
du	bietest
er	biete
wir	bieten
ihr	bietet
sie	bieten

PERFECT

ich	habe geboten
du	hast geboten
er	hat geboten
wir	haben geboten
ihr	habt geboten
sie	haben geboten

IMPERFECT

ich	bot
du	bot(e)st
er	bot
wir	boten
ihr	botet
sie	boten

FUTURE

ich	werde bieten
du	wirst bieten
er	wird bieten
wir	werden bieten
ihr	werdet bieten
sie	werden bieten

CONDITIONAL

ich	würde bieten
du	würdest bieten
er	würde bieten
wir	würden bieten
ihr	würdet bieten
sie	würden bieten

IMPERATIVE

biet(e)!/bieten wir!/bietet!
bieten Sie!

PAST PARTICIPLE

geboten

PRESENT PARTICIPLE

bietend

EXAMPLE PHRASES

*Er **bot** ihm die Hand.* He held out his hand to him.
*Für das Bild wurden 2000 Euro **geboten**.* There was a bid of 2000 euros for the painting.
*Diese Stadt hat nichts zu **bieten**.* This town has nothing to offer.

ich = I **du** = you **er** = he **wir** = we/one **ihr** = you **sie** = they

▶ **bitten** (to request)

PRESENT

ich	bitte
du	bittest
er	bittet
wir	bitten
ihr	bittet
sie	bitten

PRESENT SUBJUNCTIVE

ich	bitte
du	bittest
er	bitte
wir	bitten
ihr	bittet
sie	bitten

PERFECT

ich	habe gebeten
du	hast gebeten
er	hat gebeten
wir	haben gebeten
ihr	habt gebeten
sie	haben gebeten

IMPERFECT

ich	bat
du	bat(e)st
er	bat
wir	baten
ihr	batet
sie	baten

FUTURE

ich	werde bitten
du	wirst bitten
er	wird bitten
wir	werden bitten
ihr	werdet bitten
sie	werden bitten

CONDITIONAL

ich	würde bitten
du	würdest bitten
er	würde bitten
wir	würden bitten
ihr	würdet bitten
sie	würden bitten

IMPERATIVE

bitt(e)!/bitten wir!/bittet!
bitten Sie!

PAST PARTICIPLE

gebeten

PRESENT PARTICIPLE

bittend

EXAMPLE PHRASES

*Sie **bat** ihn um Hilfe.* She asked him for help
*Herr Müller lässt **bitten**.* Mr Müller will see you now.
*Man **hat** die Bevölkerung um Mithilfe **geboten**.* The public was asked for assistance.

---

ich = I **du** = you **er** = he **wir** = we/one **ihr** = you **sie** = they

▶ **bleiben** (to remain)

PRESENT

ich	bleibe
du	bleibst
er	bleibt
wir	bleiben
ihr	bleibt
sie	bleiben

PRESENT SUBJUNCTIVE

ich	bleibe
du	bleibest
er	bleibe
wir	bleiben
ihr	bleibet
sie	bleiben

PERFECT

ich	bin geblieben
du	bist geblieben
er	ist geblieben
wir	sind geblieben
ihr	seid geblieben
sie	sind geblieben

IMPERFECT

ich	blieb
du	bliebst
er	blieb
wir	blieben
ihr	bliebt
sie	blieben

FUTURE

ich	werde bleiben
du	wirst bleiben
er	wird bleiben
wir	werden bleiben
ihr	werdet bleiben
sie	werden bleiben

CONDITIONAL

ich	würde bleiben
du	würdest bleiben
er	würde bleiben
wir	würden bleiben
ihr	würdet bleiben
sie	würden bleiben

IMPERATIVE

bleib(e)!/bleiben wir!/bleibt!
bleiben Sie!

PAST PARTICIPLE

geblieben

PRESENT PARTICIPLE

bleibend

EXAMPLE PHRASES

*Hoffentlich **bleibt** das Wetter schön.* I hope the weather will stay fine.
*Vom Kuchen **ist** nur noch ein Stück **geblieben**.* There's only one piece of cake left.
*Dieses Erlebnis **blieb** in meiner Erinnerung.* This experience stayed with me.

ich = I **du** = you **er** = he **wir** = we/one **ihr** = you **sie** = they

▶ **brechen** (to break)

PRESENT

ich	breche
du	brichst
er	bricht
wir	brechen
ihr	brecht
sie	brechen

PRESENT SUBJUNCTIVE

ich	breche
du	brechest
er	breche
wir	brechen
ihr	brechet
sie	brechen

PERFECT

ich	habe gebrochen*
du	hast gebrochen
er	hat gebrochen
wir	haben gebrochen
ihr	habt gebrochen
sie	haben gebrochen

IMPERFECT

ich	brach
du	brachst
er	brach
wir	brachen
ihr	bracht
sie	brachen

FUTURE

ich	werde brechen
du	wirst brechen
er	wird brechen
wir	werden brechen
ihr	werdet brechen
sie	werden brechen

CONDITIONAL

ich	würde brechen
du	würdest brechen
er	würde brechen
wir	würden brechen
ihr	würdet brechen
sie	würden brechen

IMPERATIVE

brich!/brechen wir!/brecht!
brechen Sie!
OR: ich bin/wäre gebrochen
etc (when intransitive).

PAST PARTICIPLE

gebrochen

PRESENT PARTICIPLE

brechend

EXAMPLE PHRASES

*Mir **bricht** das Herz.* It breaks my heart.
*Der Sturz **brach** ihm fast den Arm.* The fall almost broke his arm.
*Sie **hat** ihr Versprechen **gebrochen**.* She broke her promise.

ich = I **du** = you **er** = he **wir** = we/one **ihr** = you **sie** = they

▶ **bringen** (to bring)

PRESENT

ich	bringe
du	bringst
er	bringt
wir	bringen
ihr	bringt
sie	bringen

PRESENT SUBJUNCTIVE

ich	bringe
du	bringest
er	bringe
wir	bringen
ihr	bringet
sie	bringen

PERFECT

ich	habe gebracht
du	hast gebracht
er	hat gebracht
wir	haben gebracht
ihr	habt gebracht
sie	haben gebracht

IMPERFECT

ich	brachte
du	brachtest
er	brachte
wir	brachten
ihr	brachtet
sie	brachten

FUTURE

ich	werde bringen
du	wirst bringen
er	wird bringen
wir	werden bringen
ihr	werdet bringen
sie	werden bringen

CONDITIONAL

ich	würde bringen
du	würdest bringen
er	würde bringen
wir	würden bringen
ihr	würdet bringen
sie	würden bringen

IMPERATIVE

bring(e)!/bringen wir!/bringt!
bringen Sie!

PAST PARTICIPLE

gebracht

PRESENT PARTICIPLE

bringend

EXAMPLE PHRASES

*Kannst du mich zum Flughafen **bringen**?* Can you take me to the airport?
*Max **hat** mir Blumen **gebracht**.* Max brought me flowers.
*Das **brachte** mich auf eine Idee.* It gave me an idea.

---

ich = I **du** = you **er** = he **wir** = we/one **ihr** = you **sie** = they

▶ **denken** (to think)

PRESENT

ich	denke
du	denkst
er	denkt
wir	denken
ihr	denkt
sie	denken

PRESENT SUBJUNCTIVE

ich	denke
du	denkest
er	denke
wir	denken
ihr	denket
sie	denken

PERFECT

ich	habe gedacht
du	hast gedacht
er	hat gedacht
wir	haben gedacht
ihr	habt gedacht
sie	haben gedacht

IMPERFECT

ich	dachte
du	dachtest
er	dachte
wir	dachten
ihr	dachtet
sie	dachten

FUTURE

ich	werde denken
du	wirst denken
er	wird denken
wir	werden denken
ihr	werdet denken
sie	werden denken

CONDITIONAL

ich	würde denken
du	würdest denken
er	würde denken
wir	würden denken
ihr	würdet denken
sie	würden denken

IMPERATIVE

denk(e)!/denken wir!/denkt!
denken Sie!

PAST PARTICIPLE

gedacht

PRESENT PARTICIPLE

denkend

EXAMPLE PHRASES

*Wie **denken** Sie darüber?* What do you think about it?
*Das war für ihn **gedacht**.* It was meant for him.
*Es war das Erste, woran ich **dachte**.* It was the first thing I thought of.

---

ich = I **du** = you **er** = he **wir** = we/one **ihr** = you **sie** = they

▶ dürfen (to be allowed to)

PRESENT

ich	darf
du	darfst
er	darf
wir	dürfen
ihr	dürft
sie	dürfen

PRESENT SUBJUNCTIVE

ich	dürfe
du	dürfest
er	dürfe
wir	dürfen
ihr	dürfet
sie	dürfen

PERFECT

ich	habe gedurft/dürfen
du	hast gedurft/dürfen
er	hat gedurft/dürfen
wir	haben gedurft/dürfen
ihr	habt gedurft/dürfen
sie	haben gedurft/dürfen

IMPERFECT

ich	durfte
du	durftest
er	durfte
wir	durften
ihr	durftet
sie	durften

FUTURE

ich	werde dürfen
du	wirst dürfen
er	wird dürfen
wir	werden dürfen
ihr	werdet dürfen
sie	werden dürfen

CONDITIONAL

ich	würde dürfen
du	würdest dürfen
er	würde dürfen
wir	würden dürfen
ihr	würdet dürfen
sie	würden dürfen

IMPERATIVE

PAST PARTICIPLE

gedurft/dürfen*

PRESENT PARTICIPLE

dürfend

*The second form is used when combined with an infinitive construction.

EXAMPLE PHRASES

Darf ich ins Kino? Can I go to the cinema?
*Das **würde** ich zu Hause nicht dürfen.* I wouldn't be allowed to do that at home.
*Das **dürfen** Sie mir glauben.* You can take my word for it.

ich = I **du** = you **er** = he **wir** = we/one **ihr** = you **sie** = they

▶ empfehlen (to recommend)

PRESENT

ich	empfehle
du	empfiehlst
er	empfiehlt
wir	empfehlen
ihr	empfehlt
sie	empfehlen

PRESENT SUBJUNCTIVE

ich	empfehle
du	empfehlest
er	empfehle
wir	empfehlen
ihr	empfehlet
sie	empfehlen

PERFECT

ich	habe empfohlen
du	hast empfohlen
er	hat empfohlen
wir	haben empfohlen
ihr	habt empfohlen
sie	haben empfohlen

IMPERFECT

ich	empfahl
du	empfahlst
er	empfahl
wir	empfahlen
ihr	empfahlt
sie	empfahlen

FUTURE

ich	werde empfehlen
du	wirst empfehlen
er	wird empfehlen
wir	werden empfehlen
ihr	werdet empfehlen
sie	werden empfehlen

CONDITIONAL

ich	würde empfehlen
du	würdest empfehlen
er	würde empfehlen
wir	würden empfehlen
ihr	würdet empfehlen
sie	würden empfehlen

IMPERATIVE

empfiehl!/empfehlen wir!
empfehlt!/empfehlen Sie!

PAST PARTICIPLE

empfohlen

PRESENT PARTICIPLE

empfehlend

EXAMPLE PHRASES

*Ich **würde** Ihnen **empfehlen**, zu gehen.* I would advise you to go.
*Was **empfiehlst** du mir zu tun?* What would you recommend I do?
*Dieses Restaurant wurde uns **empfohlen**.* This restaurant has been recommended to us.

ich = I **du** = you **er** = he **wir** = we/one **ihr** = you **sie** = they

▶ essen (to eat)

PRESENT

ich	esse
du	isst
er	isst
wir	essen
ihr	esst
sie	essen

PRESENT SUBJUNCTIVE

ich	esse
du	essest
er	esse
wir	essen
ihr	esset
sie	essen

PERFECT

ich	habe gegessen
du	hast gegessen
er	hat gegessen
wir	haben gegessen
ihr	habt gegessen
sie	haben gegessen

IMPERFECT

ich	aß
du	aßest
er	aß
wir	aßen
ihr	aßt
sie	aßen

FUTURE

ich	werde essen
du	wirst essen
er	wird essen
wir	werden essen
ihr	werdet essen
sie	werden essen

CONDITIONAL

ich	würde essen
du	würdest essen
er	würde essen
wir	würden essen
ihr	würdet essen
sie	würden essen

IMPERATIVE

iss!/essen wir!/esst!/essen Sie!

PAST PARTICIPLE

gegessen

PRESENT PARTICIPLE

essend

EXAMPLE PHRASES

*Ich **esse** kein Fleisch.* I don't eat meat.
*Wir **haben** nichts **gegessen.*** We haven't had anything to eat.
*Ich möchte was **essen.*** I'd like something to eat.

---

ich = I **du** = you **er** = he **wir** = we/one **ihr** = you **sie** = they

▶ fahren (to drive/to go)

PRESENT

ich	fahre
du	fährst
er	fährt
wir	fahren
ihr	fahrt
sie	fahren

PRESENT SUBJUNCTIVE

ich	fahre
du	fahrest
er	fahre
wir	fahren
ihr	fahret
sie	fahren

PERFECT

ich	bin gefahren*
du	bist gefahren
er	ist gefahren
wir	sind gefahren
ihr	seid gefahren
sie	sind gefahren

IMPERFECT

ich	fuhr
du	fuhrst
er	fuhr
wir	fuhren
ihr	fuhrt
sie	fuhren

FUTURE

ich	werde fahren
du	wirst fahren
er	wird fahren
wir	werden fahren
ihr	werdet fahren
sie	werden fahren

CONDITIONAL

ich	würde fahren
du	würdest fahren
er	würde fahren
wir	würden fahren
ihr	würdet fahren
sie	würden fahren

IIMPERATIVE

fahr(e)!/fahren wir!/fahrt!
fahren Sie!
OR: ich habe/hätte gefahren
etc (*when transitive*).

PAST PARTICIPLE

gefahren

PRESENT PARTICIPLE

fahrend

EXAMPLE PHRASES

*Sie **fahren** mit dem Bus in die Schule.* They go to school by bus.
*Rechts **fahren**!* Drive on the right!
*Ich **bin** mit der Familie nach Spanien **gefahren**.* I went to Spain with my family.

ich = I **du** = you **er** = he **wir** = we/one **ihr** = you **sie** = they

▶ fallen (to fall)

PRESENT

ich	falle
du	fällst
er	fällt
wir	fallen
ihr	fallt
sie	fallen

PRESENT SUBJUNCTIVE

ich	falle
du	fallest
er	falle
wir	fallen
ihr	fallet
sie	fallen

PERFECT

ich	bin gefallen
du	bist gefallen
er	ist gefallen
wir	sind gefallen
ihr	seid gefallen
sie	sind gefallen

IMPERFECT

ich	fiel
du	fielst
er	fiel
wir	fielen
ihr	fielt
sie	fielen

FUTURE

ich	werde fallen
du	wirst fallen
er	wird fallen
wir	werden fallen
ihr	werdet fallen
sie	werden fallen

CONDITIONAL

ich	würde fallen
du	würdest fallen
er	würde fallen
wir	würden fallen
ihr	würdet fallen
sie	würden fallen

IMPERATIVE

fall(e)!/fallen wir!/fallt!
fallen Sie!

PAST PARTICIPLE

gefallen

PRESENT PARTICIPLE

fallend

EXAMPLE PHRASES

*Er **fiel** vom Fahrrad.* He fell off his bike.
*Ich **bin** durch die Prüfung **gefallen**.* I failed my exam.
*Die Aktien **fielen** im Kurs.* Share prices went down.

---

ich = I **du** = you **er** = he **wir** = we/one **ihr** = you **sie** = they

▶ **finden** (to find)

PRESENT

ich	finde
du	findest
er	findet
wir	finden
ihr	findet
sie	finden

PRESENT SUBJUNCTIVE

ich	finde
du	findest
er	finde
wir	finden
ihr	findet
sie	finden

PERFECT

ich	habe gefunden
du	hast gefunden
er	hat gefunden
wir	haben gefunden
ihr	habt gefunden
sie	haben gefunden

IMPERFECT

ich	fand
du	fand(e)st
er	fand
wir	fanden
ihr	fandet
sie	fanden

FUTURE

ich	werde finden
du	wirst finden
er	wird finden
wir	werden finden
ihr	werdet finden
sie	werden finden

CONDITIONAL

ich	würde finden
du	würdest finden
er	würde finden
wir	würden finden
ihr	würdet finden
sie	würden finden

IMPERATIVE

find(e)!/finden wir!/findet!
finden Sie!

PAST PARTICIPLE

gefunden

PRESENT PARTICIPLE

findend

EXAMPLE PHRASES

*Hast du deine Brieftasche **gefunden**?* Have you found your wallet?
*Er **fand** den Mut, sie zu fragen.* He found the courage to ask her.
*Ich **finde**, sie ist eine gute Lehrerin.* I think she's a good teacher.

---

ich = I **du** = you **er** = he **wir** = we/one **ihr** = you **sie** = they

▶ **fliegen** (to fly)

PRESENT

ich	fliege
du	fliegst
er	fliegt
wir	fliegen
ihr	fliegt
sie	fliegen

PRESENT SUBJUNCTIVE

ich	fliege
du	fliegest
er	fliege
wir	fliegen
ihr	flieget
sie	fliegen

PERFECT

ich	habe geflogen*
du	hast geflogen
er	hat geflogen
wir	haben geflogen
ihr	habt geflogen
sie	haben geflogen

IMPERFECT

ich	flog
du	flogst
er	flog
wir	flogen
ihr	flogt
sie	flogen

FUTURE

ich	werde fliegen
du	wirst fliegen
er	wird fliegen
wir	werden fliegen
ihr	werdet fliegen
sie	werden fliegen

CONDITIONAL

ich	würde fliegen
du	würdest fliegen
er	würde fliegen
wir	würden fliegen
ihr	würdet fliegen
sie	würden fliegen

IMPERATIVE

flieg(e)!/fliegen wir!/fliegt!
fliegen Sie!
OR: ich bin/wäre geflogen
etc (when intransitive).

PAST PARTICIPLE

geflogen

PRESENT PARTICIPLE

fliegend

EXAMPLE PHRASES

Wir **flogen** zusammen nach Spanien. We flew together to Spain.
Die Zeit **fliegt**. Time flies.
Er **ist** von der Schule **geflogen**. He was chucked out of school.

▶ geben (to give)

PRESENT

ich	gebe
du	gibst
er	gibt
wir	geben
ihr	gebt
sie	geben

PRESENT SUBJUNCTIVE

ich	gebe
du	gebest
er	gebe
wir	geben
ihr	gebet
sie	geben

PERFECT

ich	habe gegeben
du	hast gegeben
er	hat gegeben
wir	haben gegeben
ihr	habt gegeben
sie	haben gegeben

IMPERFECT

ich	gab
du	gabst
er	gab
wir	gaben
ihr	gabt
sie	gaben

FUTURE

ich	werde geben
du	wirst geben
er	wird geben
wir	werden geben
ihr	werdet geben
sie	werden geben

CONDITIONAL

ich	würde geben
du	würdest geben
er	würde geben
wir	würden geben
ihr	würdet geben
sie	würden geben

IMPERATIVE

gib!/geben wir!/gebt!
geben Sie!

PAST PARTICIPLE

gegeben

PRESENT PARTICIPLE

gebend

EXAMPLE PHRASES

*Er **gab** mir das Geld für die Bücher.* He gave me the money for the books.
*Was **gibt** es im Kino?* What's on at the cinema?
*Wir **würden** alles darum **geben**, ins Finale zu kommen.* We would give anything
to reach the finals.

ich = I **du** = you **er** = he **wir** = we/one **ihr** = you **sie** = they

▶ gehen (to go)

PRESENT		**PRESENT SUBJUNCTIVE**	
ich	gehe	ich	gehe
du	gehst	du	gehest
er	geht	er	gehe
wir	gehen	wir	gehen
ihr	geht	ihr	gehet
sie	gehen	sie	gehen

PERFECT		**IMPERFECT**	
ich	bin gegangen	ich	ging
du	bist gegangen	du	gingst
er	ist gegangen	er	ging
wir	sind gegangen	wir	gingen
ihr	seid gegangen	ihr	gingt
sie	sind gegangen	sie	gingen

FUTURE		**CONDITIONAL**	
ich	werde gehen	ich	würde gehen
du	wirst gehen	du	würdest gehen
er	wird gehen	er	würde gehen
wir	werden gehen	wir	würden gehen
ihr	werdet gehen	ihr	würdet gehen
sie	werden gehen	sie	würden gehen

IMPERATIVE

geh(e)!/gehen wir!/geht!
gehen Sie!

PAST PARTICIPLE

gegangen

PRESENT PARTICIPLE

gehend

EXAMPLE PHRASES

*Die Kinder **gingen** ins Haus.* The children went into the house.
*Wie **geht** es dir?* How are you?
*Wir **sind** gestern schwimmen **gegangen**.* We went swimming yesterday.

ich = I **du** = you **er** = he **wir** = we/one **ihr** = you **sie** = they

▶ haben (to have)

PRESENT

ich	habe
du	hast
er	hat
wir	haben
ihr	habt
sie	haben

PRESENT SUBJUNCTIVE

ich	habe
du	habest
er	habe
wir	haben
ihr	habet
sie	haben

PERFECT

ich	habe gehabt
du	hast gehabt
er	hat gehabt
wir	haben gehabt
ihr	habt gehabt
sie	haben gehabt

IMPERFECT

ich	hatte
du	hattest
er	hatte
wir	hatten
ihr	hattet
sie	hatten

FUTURE

ich	werde haben
du	wirst haben
er	wird haben
wir	werden haben
ihr	werdet haben
sie	werden haben

CONDITIONAL

ich	würde haben
du	würdest haben
er	würde haben
wir	würden haben
ihr	würdet haben
sie	würden haben

IMPERATIVE

hab(e)!/haben wir!/habt!
haben Sie!

PAST PARTICIPLE

gehabt

PRESENT PARTICIPLE

habend

EXAMPLE PHRASES

Hast du eine Schwester? Have you got a sister?
Er hatte Hunger. He was hungry.
Ich hätte gern ein Eis. I'd like an ice cream.
Sie hat heute Geburtstag. It's her birthday today.

ich = I **du** = you **er** = he **wir** = we/one **ihr** = you **sie** = they

▶ halten (to hold)

PRESENT		PRESENT SUBJUNCTIVE	
ich	halte	ich	halte
du	hältst	du	haltest
er	hält	er	halte
wir	halten	wir	halten
ihr	haltet	ihr	haltet
sie	halten	sie	halten

PERFECT		IMPERFECT	
ich	habe gehalten	ich	hielt
du	hast gehalten	du	hielt(e)st
er	hat gehalten	er	hielt
wir	haben gehalten	wir	hielten
ihr	habt gehalten	ihr	hieltet
sie	haben gehalten	sie	hielten

FUTURE		CONDITIONAL	
ich	werde halten	ich	würde halten
du	wirst halten	du	würdest halten
er	wird halten	er	würde halten
wir	werden halten	wir	würden halten
ihr	werdet halten	ihr	würdet halten
sie	werden halten	sie	würden halten

IMPERATIVE

halt(e)!/halten wir!/haltet!
halten Sie!

PAST PARTICIPLE

gehalten

PRESENT PARTICIPLE

haltend

EXAMPLE PHRASES

*Kannst du das mal **halten**?* Can you hold that for a moment?
*Der Bus **hielt** vor dem Rathaus.* The bus stopped in front of the town hall.
*Ich **habe** sie für deine Mutter **gehalten**.* I took her for your mother.

ich = I **du** = you **er** = he **wir** = we/one **ihr** = you **sie** = they

▶ helfen (to help)

PRESENT

ich	helfe
du	hilfst
er	hilft
wir	helfen
ihr	helft
sie	helfen

PRESENT SUBJUNCTIVE

ich	helfe
du	helfest
er	helfe
wir	helfen
ihr	helfet
sie	helfen

PERFECT

ich	habe geholfen
du	hast geholfen
er	hat geholfen
wir	haben geholfen
ihr	habt geholfen
sie	haben geholfen

IMPERFECT

ich	half
du	halfst
er	half
wir	halfen
ihr	halft
sie	halfen

FUTURE

ich	werde helfen
du	wirst helfen
er	wird helfen
wir	werden helfen
ihr	werdet helfen
sie	werden helfen

CONDITIONAL

ich	würde helfen
du	würdest helfen
er	würde helfen
wir	würden helfen
ihr	würdet helfen
sie	würden helfen

IMPERATIVE

hilf!/helfen wir!/helft!
helfen Sie!

PAST PARTICIPLE

geholfen

PRESENT PARTICIPLE

helfend

EXAMPLE PHRASES

Er **hat** mir dabei **geholfen**. He helped me with it.
Diese Arznei **hilft** gegen Kopfschmerzen. This medicine is good for headaches.
Sein Vorschlag **half** mir wenig. His suggestion was not much help to me.

ich = I **du** = you **er** = he **wir** = we/one **ihr** = you **sie** = they

▶ kennen (to know) *(be acquainted with)*

PRESENT		PRESENT SUBJUNCTIVE	
ich	kenne	ich	kenne
du	kennst	du	kennest
er	kennt	er	kenne
wir	kennen	wir	kennen
ihr	kennt	ihr	kennet
sie	kennen	sie	kennen

PERFECT		IMPERFECT	
ich	habe gekannt	ich	kannte
du	hast gekannt	du	kanntest
er	hat gekannt	er	kannte
wir	haben gekannt	wir	kannten
ihr	habt gekannt	ihr	kanntet
sie	haben gekannt	sie	kannten

FUTURE		CONDITIONAL	
ich	werde kennen	ich	würde kennen
du	wirst kennen	du	würdest kennen
er	wird kennen	er	würde kennen
wir	werden kennen	wir	würden kennen
ihr	werdet kennen	ihr	würdet kennen
sie	werden kennen	sie	würden kennen

IMPERATIVE

kenn(e)!/kennen wir!/kennt!
kennen Sie!

PAST PARTICIPLE

gekannt

PRESENT PARTICIPLE

kennend

EXAMPLE PHRASES

Ich kenne ihn nicht. I don't know him.
Er kannte kein Erbarmen. He knew no mercy.
Kennst du mich noch? Do you remember me?

ich = I **du** = you **er** = he **wir** = we/one **ihr** = you **sie** = they

▶ **kommen** (to come)

PRESENT

ich	komme
du	kommst
er	kommt
wir	kommen
ihr	kommt
sie	kommen

PRESENT SUBJUNCTIVE

ich	komme
du	kommest
er	komme
wir	kommen
ihr	kommet
sie	kommen

PERFECT

ich	bin gekommen
du	bist gekommen
er	ist gekommen
wir	sind gekommen
ihr	seid gekommen
sie	sind gekommen

IMPERFECT

ich	kam
du	kamst
er	kam
wir	kamen
ihr	kamt
sie	kamen

FUTURE

ich	werde kommen
du	wirst kommen
er	wird kommen
wir	werden kommen
ihr	werdet kommen
sie	werden kommen

CONDITIONAL

ich	würde kommen
du	würdest kommen
er	würde kommen
wir	würden kommen
ihr	würdet kommen
sie	würden kommen

IMPERATIVE

komm(e)!/kommen wir!
kommt!/kommen Sie!

PAST PARTICIPLE

gekommen

PRESENT PARTICIPLE

kommend

EXAMPLE PHRASES

*Er **kam** die Straße entlang.* He was coming along the street.
*Ich **komme** zu deiner Party.* I'm coming to your party.
*Woher **kommst** du?* Where do you come from?

---

ich = I **du** = you **er** = he **wir** = we/one **ihr** = you **sie** = they

▶ können (to be able to)

PRESENT		PRESENT SUBJUNCTIVE	
ich	kann	ich	könne
du	kannst	du	könnest
er	kann	er	könne
wir	können	wir	können
ihr	könnt	ihr	könnet
sie	können	sie	können

PERFECT		IMPERFECT	
ich	habe gekonnt/können	ich	konnte
du	hast gekonnt/können	du	konntest
er	hat gekonnt/können	er	konnte
wir	haben gekonnt/können	wir	konnten
ihr	habt gekonnt/können	ihr	konntet
sie	haben gekonnt/können	sie	konnten

FUTURE		CONDITIONAL	
ich	werde können	ich	würde können
du	wirst können	du	würdest können
er	wird können	er	würde können
wir	werden können	wir	würden können
ihr	werdet können	ihr	würdet können
sie	werden können	sie	würden können

IMPERATIVE

PAST PARTICIPLE

gekonnt/können*

PRESENT PARTICIPLE

könnend

The second form is used when combined with an infinitive construction.

EXAMPLE PHRASES

Er **kann** gut schwimmen. He can swim well.
Sie **konnte** kein Wort Deutsch. She couldn't speak a word of German.
Kann ich gehen? Can I go?

ich = I **du** = you **er** = he **wir** = we/one **ihr** = you **sie** = they

▶ lassen (to leave; to allow)

PRESENT

ich	lasse
du	lässt
er	lässt
wir	lassen
ihr	lasst
sie	lassen

PRESENT SUBJUNCTIVE

ich	lasse
du	lassest
er	lasse
wir	lassen
ihr	lasset
sie	lassen

PERFECT

ich	habe gelassen
du	hast gelassen
er	hat gelassen
wir	haben gelassen
ihr	habt gelassen
sie	haben gelassen

IMPERFECT

ich	ließ
du	ließest
er	ließ
wir	ließen
ihr	ließt
sie	ließen

FUTURE

ich	werde lassen
du	wirst lassen
er	wird lassen
wir	werden lassen
ihr	werdet lassen
sie	werden lassen

CONDITIONAL

ich	würde lassen
du	würdest lassen
er	würde lassen
wir	würden lassen
ihr	würdet lassen
sie	würden lassen

IMPERATIVE

lass!/lassen wir!/lasst!
lassen Sie!

PAST PARTICIPLE

gelassen/lassen*

PRESENT PARTICIPLE

lassend

*The second form is used when combined with an infinitive construction.

EXAMPLE PHRASES

Sie ließ uns warten. She kept us waiting.
Ich lasse den Hund nicht auf das Sofa. I won't let the dog get up on the sofa.
Sie haben ihn allein im Auto gelassen. They left him alone in the car.

ich = I **du** = you **er** = he **wir** = we/one **ihr** = you **sie** = they

▶ laufen (to run)

PRESENT

ich	laufe
du	läufst
er	läuft
wir	laufen
ihr	lauft
sie	laufen

PRESENT SUBJUNCTIVE

ich	laufe
du	laufest
er	laufe
wir	laufen
ihr	laufet
sie	laufen

PERFECT

ich	bin gelaufen
du	bist gelaufen
er	ist gelaufen
wir	sind gelaufen
ihr	seid gelaufen
sie	sind gelaufen

IMPERFECT

ich	lief
du	liefst
er	lief
wir	liefen
ihr	lieft
sie	liefen

FUTURE

ich	werde laufen
du	wirst laufen
er	wird laufen
wir	werden laufen
ihr	werdet laufen
sie	werden laufen

CONDITIONAL

ich	würde laufen
du	würdest laufen
er	würde laufen
wir	würden laufen
ihr	würdet laufen
sie	würden laufen

IIMPERATIVE

lauf(e)!/laufen wir!/lauft!
laufen Sie!

PAST PARTICIPLE

gelaufen

PRESENT PARTICIPLE

laufend

EXAMPLE PHRASES

*Er **lief** so schnell er konnte.* He ran as fast as he could.
*Sie **läuft** ständig zur Polizei.* She's always going to the police.
*Das Schiff **ist** auf Grund **gelaufen**.* The ship ran aground.

ich = I **du** = you **er** = he **wir** = we/one **ihr** = you **sie** = they

► **lesen** (to read)

PRESENT

ich	lese
du	liest
er	liest
wir	lesen
ihr	lest
sie	lesen

PRESENT SUBJUNCTIVE

ich	lese
du	lesest
er	lese
wir	lesen
ihr	leset
sie	lesen

PERFECT

ich	habe gelesen
du	hast gelesen
er	hat gelesen
wir	haben gelesen
ihr	habt gelesen
sie	haben gelesen

IMPERFECT

ich	las
du	lasest
er	las
wir	lasen
ihr	last
sie	lasen

FUTURE

ich	werde lesen
du	wirst lesen
er	wird lesen
wir	werden lesen
ihr	werdet lesen
sie	werden lesen

CONDITIONAL

ich	würde lesen
du	würdest lesen
er	würde lesen
wir	würden lesen
ihr	würdet lesen
sie	würden lesen

IMPERATIVE

lies!/lesen wir!/lest!/lesen Sie!

PAST PARTICIPLE

gelesen

PRESENT PARTICIPLE

lesend

EXAMPLE PHRASES

Das **habe** *ich in der Zeitung* **gelesen**. I read it in the newspaper.
Es war in ihrem Gesicht zu lesen. It was written all over her face.
Dieses Buch **liest** *sich gut.* This book is a good read.

ich = I **du** = you **er** = he **wir** = we/one **ihr** = you **sie** = they

▶ liegen (to lie)

PRESENT

ich	liege
du	liegst
er	liegt
wir	liegen
ihr	liegt
sie	liegen

PRESENT SUBJUNCTIVE

ich	liege
du	liegest
er	liege
wir	liegen
ihr	lieget
sie	liegen

PERFECT

ich	habe gelegen
du	hast gelegen
er	hat gelegen
wir	haben gelegen
ihr	habt gelegen
sie	haben gelegen

IMPERFECT

ich	lag
du	lagst
er	lag
wir	lagen
ihr	lagt
sie	lagen

FUTURE

ich	werde liegen
du	wirst liegen
er	wird liegen
wir	werden liegen
ihr	werdet liegen
sie	werden liegen

CONDITIONAL

ich	würde liegen
du	würdest liegen
er	würde liegen
wir	würden liegen
ihr	würdet liegen
sie	würden liegen

IMPERATIVE

lieg(e)!/liegen wir!/liegt!
liegen Sie!

PAST PARTICIPLE

gelegen

PRESENT PARTICIPLE

liegend

EXAMPLE PHRASES

*Wir **lagen** den ganzen Tag am Strand.* We lay on the beach all day.
*Köln **liegt** am Rhein.* Cologne is on the Rhine.
*Es **hat** daran **gelegen**, dass ich krank war.* It was because I was ill.

ich = I **du** = you **er** = he **wir** = we/one **ihr** = you **sie** = they

▶ **machen** (to do *or* to make)

PRESENT

ich	mache
du	machst
er	macht
wir	machen
ihr	macht
sie	machen

PRESENT SUBJUNCTIVE

ich	mache
du	machest
er	mache
wir	machen
ihr	machet
sie	machen

PERFECT

ich	habe gemacht
du	hast gemacht
er	hat gemacht
wir	haben gemacht
ihr	habt gemacht
sie	haben gemacht

IMPERFECT

ich	machte
du	machtest
er	machte
wir	machten
ihr	machtet
sie	machten

FUTURE

ich	werde machen
du	wirst machen
er	wird machen
wir	werden machen
ihr	werdet machen
sie	werden machen

CONDITIONAL

ich	würde machen
du	würdest machen
er	würde machen
wir	würden machen
ihr	würdet machen
sie	würden machen

IMPERATIVE

mach!/macht!/machen Sie!

PAST PARTICIPLE

gemacht

PRESENT PARTICIPLE

machend

EXAMPLE PHRASES

*Was **machst** du?* What are you doing?
*Ich **habe** die Betten **gemacht**.* I made the beds.
*Ich **werde** es morgen **machen**.* I'll do it tomorrow.

---

ich = I **du** = you **er** = he **wir** = we/one **ihr** = you **sie** = they

▶ **mögen** (to like)

PRESENT

ich	mag
du	magst
er	mag
wir	mögen
ihr	mögt
sie	mögen

PRESENT SUBJUNCTIVE

ich	möge
du	mögest
er	möge
wir	mögen
ihr	möget
sie	mögen

PERFECT

ich	habe gemocht/mögen
du	hast gemocht/mögen
er	hat gemocht/mögen
wir	haben gemocht/mögen
ihr	habt gemocht/mögen
sie	haben gemocht/mögen

IMPERFECT

ich	mochte
du	mochtest
er	mochte
wir	mochten
ihr	mochtet
sie	mochten

FUTURE

ich	werde mögen
du	wirst mögen
er	wird mögen
wir	werden mögen
ihr	werdet mögen
sie	werden mögen

CONDITIONAL

ich	würde mögen
du	würdest mögen
er	würde mögen
wir	würden mögen
ihr	würdet mögen
sie	würden mögen

IMPERATIVE

PAST PARTICIPLE

gemocht/mögen

PRESENT PARTICIPLE

mögend

The second form is used when combined with an infinitive construction.

EXAMPLE PHRASES

*Ich **mag** gern Vanilleeis.* I like vanilla ice cream.
*Er **mochte** sie nicht danach fragen.* He didn't want to ask her about it.
*Ich **habe** ihn noch nie **gemocht**.* I never liked him.

ich = I **du** = you **er** = he **wir** = we/one **ihr** = you **sie** = they

▶ müssen (to have to)

PRESENT

ich	muss
du	musst
er	muss
wir	müssen
ihr	müsst
sie	müssen

PRESENT SUBJUNCTIVE

ich	müsse
du	müssest
er	müsse
wir	müssen
ihr	müsset
sie	müssen

PERFECT

ich	habe gemusst/müssen
du	hast gemusst/müssen
er	hat gemusst/müssen
wir	haben gemusst/müssen
ihr	habt gemusst/müssen
sie	haben gemusst/müssen

IMPERFECT

ich	musste
du	musstest
er	musste
wir	mussten
ihr	musstet
sie	mussten

FUTURE

ich	werde müssen
du	wirst müssen
er	wird müssen
wir	werden müssen
ihr	werdet müssen
sie	werden müssen

CONDITIONAL

ich	würde müssen
du	würdest müssen
er	würde müssen
wir	würden müssen
ihr	würdet müssen
sie	würden müssen

IMPERATIVE

PAST PARTICIPLE

gemusst/müssen*

PRESENT PARTICIPLE

müssend

The second form is used when combined with an infinitive construction.

EXAMPLE PHRASES

Ich muss aufs Klo. I must go to the loo.
Wir müssen jeden Abend unsere Hausaufgaben machen. We have to do our homework every night.
Sie hat abwaschen müssen. She had to wash up.

---

ich = I **du** = you **er** = he **wir** = we/one **ihr** = you **sie** = they

▶ nehmen (to take)

PRESENT

ich	nehme
du	nimmst
er	nimmt
wir	nehmen
ihr	nehmt
sie	nehmen

PRESENT SUBJUNCTIVE

ich	nehme
du	nehmest
er	nehme
wir	nehmen
ihr	nehmet
sie	nehmen

PERFECT

ich	habe genommen
du	hast genommen
er	hat genommen
wir	haben genommen
ihr	habt genommen
sie	haben genommen

IMPERFECT

ich	nahm
du	nahmst
er	nahm
wir	nahmen
ihr	nahmt
sie	nahmen

FUTURE

ich	werde nehmen
du	wirst nehmen
er	wird nehmen
wir	werden nehmen
ihr	werdet nehmen
sie	werden nehmen

CONDITIONAL

ich	würde nehmen
du	würdest nehmen
er	würde nehmen
wir	würden nehmen
ihr	würdet nehmen
sie	würden nehmen

IMPERATIVE

nimm!/nehmen wir!/nehmt!
nehmen Sie!

PAST PARTICIPLE

genommen

PRESENT PARTICIPLE

nehmend

EXAMPLE PHRASES

Hast du den Bus in die Stadt **genommen**? Did you take the bus into town?
Wie viel **nimmst** du dafür? How much will you take for it?
Er **nahm** sich vom Brot. He helped himself to bread.

ich = I du = you er = he wir = we/one ihr = you sie = they

▶ schlafen (to sleep)

PRESENT

ich	schlafe
du	schläfst
er	schläft
wir	schlafen
ihr	schlaft
sie	schlafen

PRESENT SUBJUNCTIVE

ich	schlafe
du	schlafest
er	schlafe
wir	schlafen
ihr	schlafet
sie	schlafen

PERFECT

ich	habe geschlafen
du	hast geschlafen
er	hat geschlafen
wir	haben geschlafen
ihr	habt geschlafen
sie	haben geschlafen

IMPERFECT

ich	schlief
du	schliefst
er	schlief
wir	schliefen
ihr	schlieft
sie	schliefen

FUTURE

ich	werde schlafen
du	wirst schlafen
er	wird schlafen
wir	werden schlafen
ihr	werdet schlafen
sie	werden schlafen

CONDITIONAL

ich	würde schlafen
du	würdest schlafen
er	würde schlafen
wir	würden schlafen
ihr	würdet schlafen
sie	würden schlafen

IMPERATIVE

schlaf(e)!/schlafen wir!/schlaft!
schlafen Sie!

PAST PARTICIPLE

geschlafen

PRESENT PARTICIPLE

schlafend

EXAMPLE PHRASES

Sie **schläft** immer noch. She's still asleep.
Heute Nacht **wirst** du bestimmt gut **schlafen**. I'm sure you'll sleep well tonight.
Er **schlief** während des Unterrichts. He slept during lessons.

ich = I **du** = you **er** = he **wir** = we/one **ihr** = you **sie** = they

▶ schneiden (to cut)

PRESENT

ich	schneide
du	schneidest
er	schneidet
wir	schneiden
ihr	schneidet
sie	schneiden

PRESENT SUBJUNCTIVE

ich	schneide
du	schneidest
er	schneide
wir	schneiden
ihr	schneidet
sie	schneiden

PERFECT

ich	habe geschnitten
du	hast geschnitten
er	hat geschnitten
wir	haben geschnitten
ihr	habt geschnitten
sie	haben geschnitten

IMPERFECT

ich	schnitt
du	schnittst
er	schnitt
wir	schnitten
ihr	schnittet
sie	schnitten

FUTURE

ich	werde schneiden
du	wirst schneiden
er	wird schneiden
wir	werden schneiden
ihr	werdet schneiden
sie	werden schneiden

CONDITIONAL

ich	würde schneiden
du	würdest schneiden
er	würde schneiden
wir	würden schneiden
ihr	würdet schneiden
sie	würden schneiden

IMPERATIVE

schneid(e)!/schneiden wir!
schneidet!/schneiden Sie!

PAST PARTICIPLE

geschnitten

PRESENT PARTICIPLE

schneidend

EXAMPLE PHRASES

*Sie **schneidet** ihm die Haare.* She cuts his hair.
*Ich **habe** mir in den Finger **geschnitten**.* I've cut my finger.
*Sie **schnitt** die Tomaten in Scheiben.* She sliced the tomatoes.

---

ich = I **du** = you **er** = he **wir** = we/one **ihr** = you **sie** = they

▶ schreiben (to write)

PRESENT

ich	schreibe
du	schreibst
er	schreibt
wir	schreiben
ihr	schreibt
sie	schreiben

PRESENT SUBJUNCTIVE

ich	schreibe
du	schreibest
er	schreibe
wir	schreiben
ihr	schreibet
sie	schreiben

PERFECT

ich	habe geschrieben
du	hast geschrieben
er	hat geschrieben
wir	haben geschrieben
ihr	habt geschrieben
sie	haben geschrieben

IMPERFECT

ich	schrieb
du	schriebst
er	schrieb
wir	schrieben
ihr	schriebt
sie	schrieben

FUTURE

ich	werde schreiben
du	wirst schreiben
er	wird schreiben
wir	werden schreiben
ihr	werdet schreiben
sie	werden schreiben

CONDITIONAL

ich	würde schreiben
du	würdest schreiben
er	würde schreiben
wir	würden schreiben
ihr	würdet schreiben
sie	würden schreiben

IMPERATIVE

schreib(e)!/schreiben wir!
schreibt!/schreiben Sie!

PAST PARTICIPLE

geschrieben

PRESENT PARTICIPLE

schreibend

EXAMPLE PHRASES

Er schrieb das Wort an die Tafel. He wrote the word on the blackboard.
Wie schreibst du deinen Namen? How do you spell your name?
Sie hat mir einen Brief geschrieben. She wrote me a letter.

ich = I **du** = you **er** = he **wir** = we/one **ihr** = you **sie** = they

▶ sehen (to see)

PRESENT		PRESENT SUBJUNCTIVE	
ich	sehe	ich	sehe
du	siehst	du	sehest
er	sieht	er	sehe
wir	sehen	wir	sehen
ihr	seht	ihr	sehet
sie	sehen	sie	sehen

PERFECT		IMPERFECT	
ich	habe gesehen	ich	sah
du	hast gesehen	du	sahst
er	hat gesehen	er	sah
wir	haben gesehen	wir	sahen
ihr	habt gesehen	ihr	saht
sie	haben gesehen	sie	sahen

FUTURE		CONDITIONAL	
ich	werde sehen	ich	würde sehen
du	wirst sehen	du	würdest sehen
er	wird sehen	er	würde sehen
wir	werden sehen	wir	würden sehen
ihr	werdet sehen	ihr	würdet sehen
sie	werden sehen	sie	würden sehen

IMPERATIVE

sieh(e)!/sehen wir!/seht!
sehen Sie!

PAST PARTICIPLE

gesehen

PRESENT PARTICIPLE

sehend

EXAMPLE PHRASES

*Mein Vater **sieht** schlecht.* My father has bad eyesight.
*Ich **habe** diesen Film noch nicht **gesehen**.* I haven't seen this film yet.
*Er **sah** auf die Uhr.* He looked at his watch.

ich = I **du** = you **er** = he **wir** = we/one **ihr** = you **sie** = they

▶ **sein** (to be)

PRESENT

ich	bin
du	bist
er	ist
wir	sind
ihr	seid
sie	sind

PRESENT SUBJUNCTIVE

ich	sei
du	sei(e)st
er	sei
wir	seien
ihr	seiet
sie	seien

PERFECT

ich	bin gewesen
du	bist gewesen
er	ist gewesen
wir	sind gewesen
ihr	seid gewesen
sie	sind gewesen

IMPERFECT

ich	war
du	warst
er	war
wir	waren
ihr	wart
sie	waren

FUTURE

ich	werde sein
du	wirst sein
er	wird sein
wir	werden sein
ihr	werdet sein
sie	werden sein

CONDITIONAL

ich	würde sein
du	würdest sein
er	würde sein
wir	würden sein
ihr	würdet sein
sie	würden sein

IMPERATIVE

sei!/seien wir!/seid!/seien Sie!

PAST PARTICIPLE

gewesen

PRESENT PARTICIPLE

seiend

EXAMPLE PHRASES

*Er **ist** zehn Jahre alt.* He is ten years old.
*Mir **ist** kalt.* I'm cold.
*Wir **waren** gestern im Theater.* We were at the theatre yesterday.
***Seid** ruhig!* Be quiet!

---

ich = I **du** = you **er** = he **wir** = we/one **ihr** = you **sie** = they

▶ singen (to sing)

PRESENT

ich	singe
du	singst
er	singt
wir	singen
ihr	singt
sie	singen

PRESENT SUBJUNCTIVE

ich	singe
du	singest
er	singe
wir	singen
ihr	singet
sie	singen

PERFECT

ich	habe gesungen
du	hast gesungen
er	hat gesungen
wir	haben gesungen
ihr	habt gesungen
sie	haben gesungen

IMPERFECT

ich	sang
du	sangst
er	sang
wir	sangen
ihr	sangt
sie	sangen

FUTURE

ich	werde singen
du	wirst singen
er	wird singen
wir	werden singen
ihr	werdet singen
sie	werden singen

CONDITIONAL

ich	würde singen
du	würdest singen
er	würde singen
wir	würden singen
ihr	würdet singen
sie	würden singen

IMPERATIVE

sing(e)!/singen wir!/singt!
singen Sie!

PAST PARTICIPLE

gesungen

PRESENT PARTICIPLE

singend

EXAMPLE PHRASES

*Sie **sang** das Kind in den Schlaf.* She sang the child to sleep.
*Er **singt** nicht gut.* He's a bad singer.
*Ich **habe** dieses Lied früher oft **gesungen**.* I used to sing this song a lot.

ich = I **du** = you **er** = he **wir** = we/one **ihr** = you **sie** = they

▶ sitzen (to sit)

PRESENT

ich	sitze
du	sitzt
er	sitzt
wir	sitzen
ihr	sitzt
sie	sitzen

PRESENT SUBJUNCTIVE

ich	sitze
du	sitzest
er	sitze
wir	sitzen
ihr	sitzet
sie	sitzen

PERFECT

ich	habe gesessen
du	hast gesessen
er	hat gesessen
wir	haben gesessen
ihr	habt gesessen
sie	haben gesessen

IMPERFECT

ich	saß
du	saßest
er	saß
wir	saßen
ihr	saßt
sie	saßen

FUTURE

ich	werde sitzen
du	wirst sitzen
er	wird sitzen
wir	werden sitzen
ihr	werdet sitzen
sie	werden sitzen

CONDITIONAL

ich	würde sitzen
du	würdest sitzen
er	würde sitzen
wir	würden sitzen
ihr	würdet sitzen
sie	würden sitzen

IMPERATIVE

sitz(e)!/sitzen wir!/sitzt!
sitzen Sie!

PAST PARTICIPLE

gesessen

PRESENT PARTICIPLE

sitzend

EXAMPLE PHRASES

Er saß auf meinem Stuhl. He was sitting on my chair.
Deine Krawatte sitzt nicht richtig. Your tie isn't straight.
Ich habe zwei Jahre über dieser Arbeit gesessen. I've spent two years on this piece of work.

ich = I **du** = you **er** = he **wir** = we/one **ihr** = you **sie** = they

▶ sprechen (to speak)

PRESENT

ich	spreche
du	sprichst
er	spricht
wir	sprechen
ihr	sprecht
sie	sprechen

PRESENT SUBJUNCTIVE

ich	spreche
du	sprechest
er	spreche
wir	sprechen
ihr	sprechet
sie	sprechen

PERFECT

ich	habe gesprochen
du	hast gesprochen
er	hat gesprochen
wir	haben gesprochen
ihr	habt gesprochen
sie	haben gesprochen

IMPERFECT

ich	sprach
du	sprachst
er	sprach
wir	sprachen
ihr	spracht
sie	sprachen

FUTURE

ich	werde sprechen
du	wirst sprechen
er	wird sprechen
wir	werden sprechen
ihr	werdet sprechen
sie	werden sprechen

CONDITIONAL

ich	würde sprechen
du	würdest sprechen
er	würde sprechen
wir	würden sprechen
ihr	würdet sprechen
sie	würden sprechen

IMPERATIVE

sprich!/sprechen wir!/sprecht!
sprechen Sie!

PAST PARTICIPLE

gesprochen

PRESENT PARTICIPLE

sprechend

EXAMPLE PHRASES

Er **spricht** kein Italienisch. He doesn't speak Italian.
Ich **würde** dich gern privat **sprechen**. I would like to speak to you privately.
Hast du mit ihr **gesprochen**? Have you spoken to her?

ich = I **du** = you **er** = he **wir** = we/one **ihr** = you **sie** = they

▶ stehen (to stand)

PRESENT

ich	stehe
du	stehst
er	steht
wir	stehen
ihr	steht
sie	stehen

PRESENT SUBJUNCTIVE

ich	stehe
du	stehest
er	stehe
wir	stehen
ihr	stehet
sie	stehen

PERFECT

ich	habe gestanden
du	hast gestanden
er	hat gestanden
wir	haben gestanden
ihr	habt gestanden
sie	haben gestanden

IMPERFECT

ich	stand
du	stand(e)st
er	stand
wir	standen
ihr	standet
sie	standen

FUTURE

ich	werde stehen
du	wirst stehen
er	wird stehen
wir	werden stehen
ihr	werdet stehen
sie	werden stehen

CONDITIONAL

ich	würde stehen
du	würdest stehen
er	würde stehen
wir	würden stehen
ihr	würdet stehen
sie	würden stehen

IMPERATIVE

steh(e)!/stehen wir!/steht!
stehen Sie!

PAST PARTICIPLE

gestanden

PRESENT PARTICIPLE

stehend

EXAMPLE PHRASES

Wir **standen** an der Bushaltestelle. We stood at the bus stop.
Es **hat** in der Zeitung **gestanden**. It was in the newspaper.
Dieses Kleid **würde** dir gut **stehen**. This dress would suit you.

ich = I **du** = you **er** = he **wir** = we/one **ihr** = you **sie** = they

▶ sterben (to die)

PRESENT

ich	sterbe
du	stirbst
er	stirbt
wir	sterben
ihr	sterbt
sie	sterben

PRESENT SUBJUNCTIVE

ich	sterbe
du	sterbest
er	sterbe
wir	sterben
ihr	sterbet
sie	sterben

PERFECT

ich	bin gestorben
du	bist gestorben
er	ist gestorben
wir	sind gestorben
ihr	seid gestorben
sie	sind gestorben

IMPERFECT

ich	starb
du	starbst
er	starb
wir	starben
ihr	starbt
sie	starben

FUTURE

ich	werde sterben
du	wirst sterben
er	wird sterben
wir	werden sterben
ihr	werdet sterben
sie	werden sterben

CONDITIONAL

ich	würde sterben
du	würdest sterben
er	würde sterben
wir	würden sterben
ihr	würdet sterben
sie	würden sterben

IMPERATIVE

stirb!/sterben wir!/sterbt!
sterben Sie!

PAST PARTICIPLE

gestorben

PRESENT PARTICIPLE

sterbend

EXAMPLE PHRASES

*Er **starb** eines natürlichen Todes.* He died a natural death.
*Shakespeare **ist** 1616 **gestorben**.* Shakespeare died in 1616.
*Daran **wirst** du nicht **sterben**!* It won't kill you!

ich = I **du** = you **er** = he **wir** = we/one **ihr** = you **sie** = they

▶ tragen (to wear, to carry)

PRESENT

ich	trage
du	trägst
er	trägt
wir	tragen
ihr	tragt
sie	tragen

PRESENT SUBJUNCTIVE

ich	trage
du	tragest
er	trage
wir	tragen
ihr	traget
sie	tragen

PERFECT

ich	habe getragen
du	hast getragen
er	hat getragen
wir	haben getragen
ihr	habt getragen
sie	haben getragen

IMPERFECT

ich	trug
du	trugst
er	trug
wir	trugen
ihr	trugt
sie	trugen

FUTURE

ich	werde tragen
du	wirst tragen
er	wird tragen
wir	werden tragen
ihr	werdet tragen
sie	werden tragen

CONDITIONAL

ich	würde tragen
du	würdest tragen
er	würde tragen
wir	würden tragen
ihr	würdet tragen
sie	würden tragen

IMPERATIVE

trag(e)!/tragen wir!/tragt!
tragen Sie!

PAST PARTICIPLE

getragen

PRESENT PARTICIPLE

tragend

EXAMPLE PHRASES

*Ich **trug** ihren Koffer zum Bahnhof.* I carried her case to the station.
*Du **trägst** die ganze Verantwortung dafür.* You bear the full responsibility for it.
*Ich **würde** meine Haare gern länger **tragen**.* I'd like to wear my hair longer.

---

ich = I **du** = you **er** = he **wir** = we/one **ihr** = you **sie** = they

▶ **treffen** (to meet)

PRESENT

ich	treffe
du	triffst
er	trifft
wir	treffen
ihr	trefft
sie	treffen

PRESENT SUBJUNCTIVE

ich	treffe
du	treffest
er	treffe
wir	treffen
ihr	treffet
sie	treffen

PERFECT

ich	habe getroffen
du	hast getroffen
er	hat getroffen
wir	haben getroffen
ihr	habt getroffen
sie	haben getroffen

IMPERFECT

ich	traf
du	trafst
er	traf
wir	trafen
ihr	traft
sie	trafen

FUTURE

ich	werde treffen
du	wirst treffen
er	wird treffen
wir	werden treffen
ihr	werdet treffen
sie	werden treffen

CONDITIONAL

ich	würde treffen
du	würdest treffen
er	würde treffen
wir	würden treffen
ihr	würdet treffen
sie	würden treffen

IMPERATIVE

triff!/treffen wir!/trefft!
treffen Sie!

PAST PARTICIPLE

getroffen

PRESENT PARTICIPLE

treffend

EXAMPLE PHRASES

*Sie **trifft** sich zweimal pro Woche mit ihm.* She meets with him twice a week.
*Der Schuss **traf** ihn am Kopf.* The shot hit him in the head.
*Du **hast** das Ziel gut **getroffen**.* You hit the target well.

---

ich = I   **du** = you   **er** = he   **wir** = we/one   **ihr** = you   **sie** = they

▶ **trinken** (to drink)

PRESENT

ich	trinke
du	trinkst
er	trinkt
wir	trinken
ihr	trinkt
sie	trinken

PRESENT SUBJUNCTIVE

ich	trinke
du	trinkest
er	trinke
wir	trinken
ihr	trinket
sie	trinken

PERFECT

ich	habe getrunken
du	hast getrunken
er	hat getrunken
wir	haben getrunken
ihr	habt getrunken
sie	haben getrunken

IMPERFECT

ich	trank
du	trankst
er	trank
wir	tranken
ihr	trankt
sie	tranken

FUTURE

ich	werde trinken
du	wirst trinken
er	wird trinken
wir	werden trinken
ihr	werdet trinken
sie	werden trinken

CONDITIONAL

ich	würde trinken
du	würdest trinken
er	würde trinken
wir	würden trinken
ihr	würdet trinken
sie	würden trinken

IMPERATIVE

trink(e)!/trinken wir!/trinkt!
trinken Sie!

PAST PARTICIPLE

getrunken

PRESENT PARTICIPLE

trinkend

EXAMPLE PHRASES

*Er **trank** die ganze Flasche leer.* He drank the whole bottle.
*Ich **habe** zu viel **getrunken**.* I've had too much to drink.
*Wollen wir etwas **trinken** gehen?* Shall we go for a drink?

ich = I **du** = you **er** = he **wir** = we/one **ihr** = you **sie** = they

▶ tun (to do)

PRESENT

ich	tue
du	tust
er	tut
wir	tun
ihr	tut
sie	tun

PRESENT SUBJUNCTIVE

ich	tue
du	tuest
er	tue
wir	tuen
ihr	tuet
sie	tuen

PERFECT

ich	habe getan
du	hast getan
er	hat getan
wir	haben getan
ihr	habt getan
sie	haben getan

IMPERFECT

ich	tat
du	tat(e)st
er	tat
wir	taten
ihr	tatet
sie	taten

FUTURE

ich	werde tun
du	wirst tun
er	wird tun
wir	werden tun
ihr	werdet tun
sie	werden tun

CONDITIONAL

ich	würde tun
du	würdest tun
er	würde tun
wir	würden tun
ihr	würdet tun
sie	würden tun

IMPERATIVE

tu(e)!/tun wir!/tut!/tun Sie!

PAST PARTICIPLE

getan

PRESENT PARTICIPLE

tuend

EXAMPLE PHRASES

*Ich **werde** das auf keinen Fall **tun**.* There is no way I'll do that.
*So etwas **tut** man nicht!* That is just not done!
*Sie **tat**, als ob sie schliefe.* She pretended to be sleeping.

---

ich = I **du** = you **er** = he **wir** = we/one **ihr** = you **sie** = they

▶ vergessen (to forget)

PRESENT

ich	vergesse
du	vergisst
er	vergisst
wir	vergessen
ihr	vergesst
sie	vergessen

PRESENT SUBJUNCTIVE

ich	vergesse
du	vergessest
er	vergesse
wir	vergessen
ihr	vergesset
sie	vergessen

PERFECT

ich	habe vergessen
du	hast vergessen
er	hat vergessen
wir	haben vergessen
ihr	habt vergessen
sie	haben vergessen

IMPERFECT

ich	vergaß
du	vergaßest
er	vergaß
wir	vergaßen
ihr	vergaßt
sie	vergaßen

FUTURE

ich	werde vergessen
du	wirst vergessen
er	wird vergessen
wir	werden vergessen
ihr	werdet vergessen
sie	werden vergessen

CONDITIONAL

ich	würde vergessen
du	würdest vergessen
er	würde vergessen
wir	würden vergessen
ihr	würdet vergessen
sie	würden vergessen

IMPERATIVE

vergiss!/vergessen wir!
vergesst!/vergessen Sie!

PAST PARTICIPLE

vergessen

PRESENT PARTICIPLE

vergessend

EXAMPLE PHRASES

*Ich **habe** seinen Namen vergessen.* I've forgotten his name.
*Sie **vergaß**, die Blumen zu gießen.* She forgot to water the flowers.
*Sie **vergisst** ständig ihre Bücher.* She always forgets to bring her books.

ich = I **du** = you **er** = he **wir** = we/one **ihr** = you **sie** = they

▶ **verlieren** (to lose)

PRESENT

ich	verliere
du	verlierst
er	verliert
wir	verlieren
ihr	verliert
sie	verlieren

PRESENT SUBJUNCTIVE

ich	verliere
du	verlierest
er	verliere
wir	verlieren
ihr	verlieret
sie	verlieren

PERFECT

ich	habe verloren
du	hast verloren
er	hat verloren
wir	haben verloren
ihr	habt verloren
sie	haben verloren

IMPERFECT

ich	verlor
du	verlorst
er	verlor
wir	verloren
ihr	verlort
sie	verloren

FUTURE

ich	werde verlieren
du	wirst verlieren
er	wird verlieren
wir	werden verlieren
ihr	werdet verlieren
sie	werden verlieren

CONDITIONAL

ich	würde verlieren
du	würdest verlieren
er	würde verlieren
wir	würden verlieren
ihr	würdet verlieren
sie	würden verlieren

IMPERATIVE

verlier(e)!/verlieren wir!
verliert!/verlieren Sie!

PAST PARTICIPLE

verloren

PRESENT PARTICIPLE

verlierend

EXAMPLE PHRASES

*Wenn du **verlierst**, musst du 10 Euro Strafe zahlen.* If you lose, you'll have to pay a 10 euro penalty.
*Wir **haben** drei Spiele hintereinander **verloren**.* We lost three matches in a row.
*Er **verlor** kein Wort darüber.* He didn't say a word about it.

---

ich = I **du** = you **er** = he **wir** = we/one **ihr** = you **sie** = they

▶ wachsen* (to grow)

PRESENT

ich	wachse
du	wächst
er	wächst
wir	wachsen
ihr	wachst
sie	wachsen

PRESENT SUBJUNCTIVE

ich	wachse
du	wachsest
er	wachse
wir	wachsen
ihr	wachset
sie	wachsen

PERFECT

ich	bin gewachsen
du	bist gewachsen
er	ist gewachsen
wir	sind gewachsen
ihr	seid gewachsen
sie	sind gewachsen

IMPERFECT

ich	wuchs
du	wuchsest
er	wuchs
wir	wuchsen
ihr	wuchst
sie	wuchsen

FUTURE

ich	werde wachsen
du	wirst wachsen
er	wird wachsen
wir	werden wachsen
ihr	werdet wachsen
sie	werden wachsen

CONDITIONAL

ich	würde wachsen
du	würdest wachsen
er	würde wachsen
wir	würden wachsen
ihr	würdet wachsen
sie	würden wachsen

IMPERATIVE

wachs(e)!/wachsen wir!
wachst!/wachsen Sie!

*Conjugated as a weak verb when
the meaning is "to wax".

PAST PARTICIPLE

gewachsen

PRESENT PARTICIPLE

wachsend

EXAMPLE PHRASES

*Der Baum **wächst** nicht mehr.* The tree has stopped growing.
*Er ließ sich einen Bart **wachsen**.* He grew a beard.
*Sie **ist** gut **gewachsen**.* She has a good figure.

ich = I **du** = you **er** = he **wir** = we/one **ihr** = you **sie** = they

▶ **waschen** (to wash)

PRESENT

ich	wasche
du	wäschst
er	wäscht
wir	waschen
ihr	wascht
sie	waschen

PRESENT SUBJUNCTIVE

ich	wasche
du	waschest
er	wasche
wir	waschen
ihr	waschet
sie	waschen

PERFECT

ich	habe gewaschen
du	hast gewaschen
er	hat gewaschen
wir	haben gewaschen
ihr	habt gewaschen
sie	haben gewaschen

IMPERFECT

ich	wusch
du	wuschest
er	wusch
wir	wuschen
ihr	wuscht
sie	wuschen

FUTURE

ich	werde waschen
du	wirst waschen
er	wird waschen
wir	werden waschen
ihr	werdet waschen
sie	werden waschen

CONDITIONAL

ich	würde waschen
du	würdest waschen
er	würde waschen
wir	würden waschen
ihr	würdet waschen
sie	würden waschen

IMPERATIVE

wasch(e)!/waschen wir!
wascht!/waschen Sie!

PAST PARTICIPLE

gewaschen

PRESENT PARTICIPLE

waschend

EXAMPLE PHRASES

*Ich **habe** mir die Hände **gewaschen**.* I washed my hands.
*Er **wäscht** sich jeden Tag.* He washes every day.
*Die Katze **wusch** sich in der Sonne.* The cat was washing itself in the sunshine.

---

ich = I **du** = you **er** = he **wir** = we/one **ihr** = you **sie** = they

▶ **werden** (to become)

PRESENT

ich	werde
du	wirst
er	wird
wir	werden
ihr	werdet
sie	werden

PRESENT SUBJUNCTIVE

ich	werde
du	werdest
er	werde
wir	werden
ihr	werdet
sie	werden

PERFECT

ich	bin geworden/worden
du	bist geworden/worden
er	ist geworden/worden
wir	sind geworden/worden
ihr	seid geworden/worden
sie	sind geworden/worden

IMPERFECT

ich	wurde
du	wurdest
er	wurde
wir	wurden
ihr	wurdet
sie	wurden

FUTURE

ich	werde werden
du	wirst werden
er	wird werden
wir	werden werden
ihr	werdet werden
sie	werden werden

CONDITIONAL

ich	würde werden
du	würdest werden
er	würde werden
wir	würden werden
ihr	würdet werden
sie	würden werden

IMPERATIVE

werde!/werden wir!/werdet!
werden Sie!

PAST PARTICIPLE

geworden/worden*

PRESENT PARTICIPLE

werdend

The second form is used when combined with an infinitive construction.

EXAMPLE PHRASES

*Mir **wird** schlecht.* I feel ill.
*Ich will Lehrerin **werden**.* I want to be a teacher.
*Der Kuchen **ist** gut **geworden**.* The cake turned out well.

ich = I **du** = you **er** = he **wir** = we/one **ihr** = you **sie** = they

▶ wissen (to know)

PRESENT

ich	weiß
du	weißt
er	weiß
wir	wissen
ihr	wisst
sie	wissen

PRESENT SUBJUNCTIVE

ich	wisse
du	wissest
er	wisse
wir	wissen
ihr	wisset
sie	wissen

PERFECT

ich	habe gewusst
du	hast gewusst
er	hat gewusst
wir	haben gewusst
ihr	habt gewusst
sie	haben gewusst

IMPERFECT

ich	wusste
du	wusstest
er	wusste
wir	wussten
ihr	wusstet
sie	wussten

FUTURE

ich	werde wissen
du	wirst wissen
er	wird wissen
wir	werden wissen
ihr	werdet wissen
sie	werden wissen

CONDITIONAL

ich	würde wissen
du	würdest wissen
er	würde wissen
wir	würden wissen
ihr	würdet wissen
sie	würden wissen

IMPERATIVE

wisse!/wissen wir!/wisset!
wissen Sie!

PAST PARTICIPLE

gewusst

PRESENT PARTICIPLE

wissend

EXAMPLE PHRASES

*Ich **weiß** nicht.* I don't know.
*Er **hat** nichts davon **gewusst**.* He didn't know anything about it.
*Sie **wussten**, wo das Kino war.* They knew where the cinema was.

---

ich = I **du** = you **er** = he **wir** = we/one **ihr** = you **sie** = they

▶ wollen (to want)

PRESENT

ich	will
du	willst
er	will
wir	wollen
ihr	wollt
sie	wollen

PRESENT SUBJUNCTIVE

ich	wolle
du	wollest
er	wolle
wir	wollen
ihr	wollet
sie	wollen

PERFECT

ich	habe gewollt/wollen
du	hast gewollt/wollen
er	hat gewollt/wollen
wir	haben gewollt/wollen
ihr	habt gewollt/wollen
sie	haben gewollt/wollen

IMPERFECT

ich	wollte
du	wolltest
er	wollte
wir	wollten
ihr	wolltet
sie	wollten

FUTURE

ich	werde wollen
du	wirst wollen
er	wird wollen
wir	werden wollen
ihr	werdet wollen
sie	werden wollen

CONDITIONAL

ich	würde wollen
du	würdest wollen
er	würde wollen
wir	würden wollen
ihr	würdet wollen
sie	würden wollen

IMPERATIVE

wolle!/wollen wir!/wollt!
wollen Sie!

PAST PARTICIPLE

gewollt/wollen*

PRESENT PARTICIPLE

wollend

The second form is used when combined with an infinitive construction.

EXAMPLE PHRASES

*Er **will** nach London gehen.* He wants to go to London.
*Das **habe** ich nicht **gewollt**.* I didn't want this to happen.
*Sie **wollten** nur mehr Geld.* All they wanted was more money.

ich = I **du** = you **er** = he **wir** = we/one **ihr** = you **sie** = they

▶ ziehen (to go/to pull)

PRESENT

ich	ziehe
du	ziehst
er	zieht
wir	ziehen
ihr	zieht
sie	ziehen

PRESENT SUBJUNCTIVE

ich	ziehe
du	ziehest
er	ziehe
wir	ziehen
ihr	ziehet
sie	ziehen

PERFECT

ich	bin/habe gezogen
du	bist/hast gezogen
er	ist/hat gezogen
wir	sind/haben gezogen
ihr	seid/habt gezogen
sie	sind/haben gezogen

IMPERFECT

ich	zog
du	zogst
er	zog
wir	zogen
ihr	zogt
sie	zogen

FUTURE

ich	werde ziehen
du	wirst ziehen
er	wird ziehen
wir	werden ziehen
ihr	werdet ziehen
sie	werden ziehen

CONDITIONAL

ich	würde ziehen
du	würdest ziehen
er	würde ziehen
wir	würden ziehen
ihr	würdet ziehen
sie	würden ziehen

IMPERATIVE

zieh(e)!/ziehen wir!/zieht!
ziehen Sie!

PAST PARTICIPLE

gezogen

PRESENT PARTICIPLE

ziehend

EXAMPLE PHRASES

*Sie **zog** mich am Ärmel.* She pulled at my sleeve.
*Seine Familie **ist** nach München **gezogen**.* His family has moved to Munich.
*In diesem Zimmer **zieht** es.* There's a draught in this room.

---

ich = I **du** = you **er** = he **wir** = we/one **ihr** = you **sie** = they

ENGLISH – GERMAN
ENGLISCH – DEUTSCH

A, a

A [eɪ] n (MUS) A nt; **~ road**
Hauptverkehrsstraße f

a [eɪ, ə] (before vowel or silent h: **an**) indef art **1**
ein; eine; **a woman** eine Frau; **a book** ein
Buch; **an eagle** ein Adler; **she's a doctor**
sie ist Ärztin
2 (instead of the number "one") ein, eine; **a
year ago** vor einem Jahr; **a hundred/
thousand** etc **pounds** (ein) hundert/(ein)
tausend etc Pfund
3 (in expressing ratios, prices etc) pro; **3 a
day/week** 3 pro Tag/Woche, 3 am Tag/in
der Woche; **10 km an hour** 10 km pro
Stunde/in der Stunde

A.A. n abbr = **Alcoholics Anonymous**;
(BRIT) = **Automobile Association**

A.A.A. (US) n abbr = **American Automobile
Association**

aback [ə'bæk] adv: **to be taken ~** verblüfft
sein

abandon [ə'bændən] vt (give up) aufgeben;
(desert) verlassen ♦ n Hingabe f

abate [ə'beɪt] vi nachlassen, sich legen

abattoir ['æbətwɑːr] (BRIT) n Schlachthaus nt

abbey ['æbɪ] n Abtei f

abbot ['æbət] n Abt m

abbreviate [ə'briːvɪeɪt] vt abkürzen;
abbreviation [əbriːvɪ'eɪʃən] n Abkürzung f

abdicate ['æbdɪkeɪt] vt aufgeben ♦ vi
abdanken

abdomen ['æbdəmen] n Unterleib m

abduct [æb'dʌkt] vt entführen

aberration [æbə'reɪʃən] n (geistige)
Verwirrung f

abet [ə'bet] vt see **aid**

abeyance [ə'beɪəns] n: **in ~** in der Schwebe;
(disuse) außer Kraft

abide [ə'baɪd] vt vertragen; leiden; **~ by** vt
sich halten an +acc

ability [ə'bɪlɪtɪ] n (power) Fähigkeit f; (skill)
Geschicklichkeit f

abject ['æbdʒekt] adj (liar) übel; (poverty)
größte(r, s); (apology) zerknirscht

ablaze [ə'bleɪz] adj in Flammen

able ['eɪbl] adj geschickt, fähig; **to be ~ to
do sth** etw tun können; **~-bodied**
['eɪbl'bɒdɪd] adj kräftig; (seaman) Voll-; **ably**
['eɪblɪ] adv geschickt

abnormal [æb'nɔːməl] adj regelwidrig,
abnorm

aboard [ə'bɔːd] adv, prep an Bord +gen

abode [ə'bəud] n: **of no fixed ~** ohne festen
Wohnsitz

abolish [ə'bɒlɪʃ] vt abschaffen; **abolition**
[æbə'lɪʃən] n Abschaffung f

abominable [ə'bɒmɪnəbl] adj scheußlich

aborigine [æbə'rɪdʒɪnɪ] n Ureinwohner m

abort [ə'bɔːt] vt abtreiben; fehlgebären; **~ion**
[ə'bɔːʃən] n Abtreibung f; (miscarriage)
Fehlgeburt f; **~ive** adj misslungen

abound [ə'baund] vi im Überfluss vorhanden
sein; **to ~ in** Überfluss haben an +dat

about [ə'baut] adv **1** (approximately) etwa,
ungefähr; **about a hundred/thousand** etc
etwa hundert/tausend etc; **at about 2
o'clock** etwa um 2 Uhr; **I've just about
finished** ich bin gerade fertig
2 (referring to place) herum, umher; **to
leave things lying about** Sachen
herumliegen lassen; **to run/walk** etc **about**
herumrennen/gehen etc
3: **to be about to do sth** im Begriff sein,
etw zu tun; **he was about to go to bed** er
wollte gerade ins Bett gehen
♦ prep **1** (relating to) über +acc; **a book**

about London ein Buch über London; **what is it about?** worum geht es?; (*book etc*) wovon handelt es?; **we talked about it** wir haben darüber geredet; **what** *or* **how about doing this?** wollen wir das machen? 2 (*referring to place*) um (... herum); **to walk about the town** in der Stadt herumgehen; **her clothes were scattered about the room** ihre Kleider waren über das ganze Zimmer verstreut

about-turn [ə'baut'tə:n] *n* Kehrtwendung *f*

above [ə'bʌv] *adv* oben ♦ *prep* über; **~ all** vor allem; **~ board** *adj* offen, ehrlich

abrasive [ə'breɪzɪv] *adj* Abschleif-; (*personality*) zermürbend, aufreibend

abreast [ə'brest] *adv* nebeneinander; **to keep ~ of** Schritt halten mit

abroad [ə'brɔ:d] *adv* (*be*) im Ausland; (*go*) ins Ausland

abrupt [ə'brʌpt] *adj* (*sudden*) abrupt, jäh; (*curt*) schroff; **~ly** *adv* abrupt

abscess ['æbsɪs] *n* Geschwür *nt*

abscond [əb'skɔnd] *vi* flüchten, sich davonmachen

abseil ['æbseɪl] *vi* (*also:* **~ down**) sich abseilen

absence ['æbsəns] *n* Abwesenheit *f*

absent ['æbsənt] *adj* abwesend, nicht da; (*lost in thought*) geistesabwesend; **~-minded** *adj* zerstreut

absolute ['æbsəlu:t] *adj* absolut; (*power*) unumschränkt; (*rubbish*) vollkommen, rein; **~ly** [æbsə'lu:tlɪ] *adv* absolut, vollkommen; **~ly!** ganz bestimmt!

absolve [əb'zɔlv] *vt* entbinden; freisprechen

absorb [əb'zɔ:b] *vt* aufsaugen, absorbieren; (*fig*) ganz in Anspruch nehmen, fesseln; **to be ~ed in a book** in ein Buch vertieft sein; **~ent cotton** (*US*) *n* Verbandwatte *f*; **~ing** *adj* aufsaugend; (*fig*) packend; **absorption** [əb'zɔ:pʃən] *n* Aufsaugung *f*, Absorption *f*; (*fig*) Versunkenheit *f*

abstain [əb'steɪn] *vi* (*in vote*) sich enthalten; **to ~ from** (*keep from*) sich enthalten +*gen*

abstemious [əb'sti:mɪəs] *adj* enthaltsam

abstinence ['æbstɪnəns] *n* Enthaltsamkeit *f*

abstract ['æbstrækt] *adj* abstrakt

absurd [əb'sɔ:d] *adj* absurd

abundance [ə'bʌndəns] *n*: **~ (of)** Überfluss *m* (an +*dat*); **abundant** [ə'bʌndənt] *adj* reichlich

abuse [*n* ə'bju:s, *vb* ə'bju:z] *n* (*rude language*) Beschimpfung *f*; (*ill usage*) Missbrauch *m*; (*bad practice*) (Amts)missbrauch *m* ♦ *vt* (*misuse*) missbrauchen; **abusive** [ə'bju:sɪv] *adj* beleidigend, Schimpf-

abysmal [ə'bɪzməl] *adj* scheußlich; (*ignorance*) bodenlos

abyss [ə'bɪs] *n* Abgrund *m*

AC *abbr* (= *alternating current*) Wechselstrom *m*

academic [ækə'demɪk] *adj* akademisch; (*theoretical*) theoretisch ♦ *n* Akademiker(in) *m(f)*

academy [ə'kædəmɪ] *n* (*school*) Hochschule *f*; (*society*) Akademie *f*

accelerate [æk'seləreɪt] *vi* schneller werden; (*AUT*) Gas geben ♦ *vt* beschleunigen; **acceleration** [æksələ'reɪʃən] *n* Beschleunigung *f*; **accelerator** [æk'seləreɪtə] *n* Gas(pedal) *nt*

accent ['æksənt] *n* Akzent *m*, Tonfall *m*; (*mark*) Akzent *m*; (*stress*) Betonung *f*

accept [ək'sept] *vt* (*take*) annehmen; (*agree to*) akzeptieren; **~able** *adj* annehmbar; **~ance** *n* Annahme *f*

access ['ækses] *n* Zugang *m*; **~ible** [æk'sesəbl] *adj* (*easy to approach*) zugänglich; (*within reach*) (leicht) erreichbar

accessory [æk'sesərɪ] *n* Zubehörteil *nt*; **toilet accessories** Toilettenartikel *pl*

accident ['æksɪdənt] *n* Unfall *m*; (*coincidence*) Zufall *m*; **by ~** zufällig; **~al** [æksɪ'dentl] *adj* unbeabsichtigt; **~ally** [æksɪ'dentəlɪ] *adv* zufällig; **~ insurance** *n* Unfallversicherung *f*; **~-prone** *adj*: **to be ~-prone** zu Unfällen neigen

acclaim [ə'kleɪm] *vt* zujubeln +*dat* ♦ *n* Beifall *m*

acclimatize [ə'klaɪmətaɪz] *vt*: **to become ~d (to)** sich gewöhnen (an +*acc*), sich akklimatisieren (in +*dat*)

accommodate [ə'kɔmədeɪt] *vt*

unterbringen; (*hold*) Platz haben für; (*oblige*) (aus)helfen +*dat*

accommodating [ə'kɒmədeɪtɪŋ] *adj* entgegenkommend

accommodation [əkɒmə'deɪʃən] (*US* **accommodations**) *n* Unterkunft *f*

accompany [ə'kʌmpəni] *vt* begleiten

accomplice [ə'kʌmplɪs] *n* Helfershelfer *m*, Komplize *m*

accomplish [ə'kʌmplɪʃ] *vt* (*fulfil*) durchführen; (*finish*) vollenden; (*aim*) erreichen; ~ed *adj* vollendet, ausgezeichnet; ~ment *n* (*skill*) Fähigkeit *f*; (*completion*) Vollendung *f*; (*feat*) Leistung *f*

accord [ə'kɔːd] *n* Übereinstimmung *f* ♦ *vt* gewähren; **of one's own** ~ freiwillig; ~ing **to** nach, laut +*gen*; ~ance *n*: **in** ~ance **with** in Übereinstimmung mit; ~ingly *adv* danach, dementsprechend

accordion [ə'kɔːdiən] *n* Akkordeon *nt*

accost [ə'kɒst] *vt* ansprechen

account [ə'kaunt] *n* (*bill*) Rechnung *f*; (*narrative*) Bericht *m*; (*report*) Rechenschaftsbericht *m*; (*in bank*) Konto *nt*; (*importance*) Geltung *f*; ~s *npl* (*FIN*) Bücher *pl*; **on** ~ auf Rechnung; **of no** ~ ohne Bedeutung; **on no** ~ keinesfalls; **on** ~ **of** wegen; **to take into** ~ berücksichtigen; ~ **for** *vt fus* (*expenditure*) Rechenschaft ablegen für; **how do you** ~ **for that?** wie erklären Sie (sich) das?; ~able *adj* verantwortlich; ~ancy [ə'kauntənsi] *n* Buchhaltung *f*; ~ant [ə'kauntənt] *n* Wirtschaftsprüfer(in) *m(f)*; ~ **number** *n* Kontonummer *f*

accumulate [ə'kjuːmjuleɪt] *vt* ansammeln ♦ *vi* sich ansammeln

accuracy ['ækjurəsi] *n* Genauigkeit *f*

accurate ['ækjurɪt] *adj* genau; ~ly *adv* genau, richtig

accusation [ækju'zeɪʃən] *n* Anklage *f*, Beschuldigung *f*

accuse [ə'kjuːz] *vt* anklagen, beschuldigen; ~d *n* Angeklagte(r) *f(m)*

accustom [ə'kʌstəm] *vt*: **to** ~ **sb (to sth)** jdn (an etw *acc*) gewöhnen; ~ed *adj* gewohnt

ace [eɪs] *n* Ass *nt*; (*inf*) Ass *nt*, Kanone *f*

ache [eɪk] *n* Schmerz *m* ♦ *vi* (*be sore*) schmerzen, wehtun

achieve [ə'tʃiːv] *vt* zustande *or* zu Stande bringen; (*aim*) erreichen; ~ment *n* Leistung *f*; (*act*) Erreichen *nt*

acid ['æsɪd] *n* Säure *f* ♦ *adj* sauer, scharf; ~ **rain** *n* saure(r) Regen *m*

acknowledge [ək'nɒlɪdʒ] *vt* (*receipt*) bestätigen; (*admit*) zugeben; ~ment *n* Anerkennung *f*; (*letter*) Empfangsbestätigung *f*

acne ['ækni] *n* Akne *f*

acorn ['eɪkɔːn] *n* Eichel *f*

acoustic [ə'kuːstɪk] *adj* akustisch; ~s *npl* Akustik *f*

acquaint [ə'kweɪnt] *vt* vertraut machen; **to be** ~ed **with sb** mit jdm bekannt sein; ~ance *n* (*person*) Bekannte(r) *f(m)*; (*knowledge*) Kenntnis *f*

acquire [ə'kwaɪə*] *vt* erwerben; **acquisition** [ækwɪ'zɪʃən] *n* Errungenschaft *f*; (*act*) Erwerb *m*

acquit [ə'kwɪt] *vt* (*free*) freisprechen; **to** ~ **o.s. well** sich bewähren; ~tal *n* Freispruch *m*

acre ['eɪkə*] *n* Morgen *m*

acrid ['ækrɪd] *adj* (*smell, taste*) bitter; (*smoke*) beißend

acrobat ['ækrəbæt] *n* Akrobat *m*

across [ə'krɒs] *prep* über +*acc* ♦ *adv* hinüber, herüber; **he lives** ~ **the river** er wohnt auf der anderen Seite des Flusses; **ten metres** ~ zehn Meter breit; **he lives** ~ **from us** er wohnt uns gegenüber; **to run/swim** ~ hinüberlaufen/schwimmen

acrylic [ə'krɪlɪk] *adj* Acryl-

act [ækt] *n* (*deed*) Tat *f*; (*JUR*) Gesetz *nt*; (*THEAT*) Akt *m*; (: *turn*) Nummer *f* ♦ *vi* (*take ~ion*) handeln; (*behave*) sich verhalten; (*pretend*) vorgeben; (*THEAT*) spielen ♦ *vt* (*in play*) spielen; **to** ~ **as** fungieren als; ~ing *adj* stellvertretend ♦ *n* Schauspielkunst *f*; (*performance*) Aufführung *f*

action ['ækʃən] *n* (*deed*) Tat *f*; Handlung *f*; (*motion*) Bewegung *f*; (*way of working*) Funktionieren *nt*; (*battle*) Einsatz *m*, Gefecht *nt*; (*lawsuit*) Klage *f*, Prozess *m*; **out of** ~

(person) nicht einsatzfähig; *(thing)* außer Betrieb; **to take ~** etwas unternehmen; **~ replay** *n (TV)* Wiederholung *f*

activate ['æktɪveɪt] *vt (mechanism)* betätigen; *(CHEM, PHYS)* aktivieren

active ['æktɪv] *adj (brisk)* rege, tatkräftig; *(working)* aktiv; *(GRAM)* aktiv, Tätigkeits-; **~ly** *adv* aktiv; *(dislike)* offen

activity [æk'tɪvɪtɪ] *n* Aktivität *f*; *(doings)* Unternehmungen *pl*; *(occupation)* Tätigkeit *f*; **~ holiday** *n* Aktivurlaub *m*

actor ['æktər] *n* Schauspieler *m*

actress ['æktrɪs] *n* Schauspielerin *f*

actual ['æktjuəl] *adj* wirklich; **~ly** *adv* tatsächlich; **~ly no** eigentlich nicht

acumen ['ækjumən] *n* Scharfsinn *m*

acute [ə'kjuːt] *adj (severe)* heftig, akut; *(keen)* scharfsinnig

ad [æd] *n abbr = advertisement

A.D. *adv abbr (= Anno Domini)* n. Chr.

adamant ['ædəmənt] *adj* eisern; hartnäckig

adapt [ə'dæpt] *vt* anpassen ♦ *vi:* **to ~ (to)** sich anpassen (an *+acc*); **~able** *adj* anpassungsfähig; **~ation** [ædæp'teɪʃən] *n (THEAT etc)* Bearbeitung *f*; *(adjustment)* Anpassung *f*; **~er**, **~or** *n (ELEC)* Zwischenstecker *m*

add [æd] *vt (join)* hinzufügen; *(numbers: also:* **~ up)** addieren; **~ up** *vi (make sense)* stimmen; **~ up to** *vt fus* ausmachen

adder ['ædər] *n* Kreuzotter *f*, Natter *f*

addict ['ædɪkt] *n* Süchtige(r) *f(m)*; **~ed** [ə'dɪktɪd] *adj:* **~ed to** -süchtig; **~ion** [ə'dɪkʃən] *n* Sucht *f*; **~ive** [ə'dɪktɪv] *adj:* **to be ~ive** süchtig machen

addition [ə'dɪʃən] *n* Anhang *m*, Addition *f*; *(MATH)* Addition *f*, Zusammenzählen *nt*; **in ~** zusätzlich, außerdem; **~al** *adj* zusätzlich, weiter

additive ['ædɪtɪv] *n* Zusatz *m*

address [ə'dres] *n* Adresse *f*; *(speech)* Ansprache *f* ♦ *vt (letter)* adressieren; *(speak to)* ansprechen; *(make speech to)* eine Ansprache halten an *+acc*

adept ['ædept] *adj* geschickt; **to be ~ at** gut sein in *+dat*

adequate ['ædɪkwɪt] *adj* angemessen

adhere [əd'hɪər] *vi:* **to ~ to** haften an *+dat*; *(fig)* festhalten an *+dat*

adhesive [əd'hiːzɪv] *adj* klebend; Kleb(e)- ♦ *n* Klebstoff *m*; **~ tape** *n (BRIT)* Klebestreifen *m*; *(US)* Heftpflaster *nt*

ad hoc [æd'hɔk] *adj (decision, committee)* Ad-hoc- ♦ *adv* ad hoc

adjacent [ə'dʒeɪsənt] *adj* benachbart; **~ to** angrenzend an *+acc*

adjective ['ædʒɛktɪv] *n* Adjektiv *nt*, Eigenschaftswort *nt*

adjoining [ə'dʒɔɪnɪŋ] *adj* benachbart, Neben-

adjourn [ə'dʒə:n] *vt* vertagen ♦ *vi* abbrechen

adjudicate [ə'dʒu:dɪkeɪt] *vi* entscheiden, ein Urteil fällen

adjust [ə'dʒʌst] *vt (alter)* anpassen; *(put right)* regulieren, richtig stellen ♦ *vi:* sich anpassen; **~able** *adj* verstellbar

ad-lib [æd'lɪb] *vt, vi* improvisieren ♦ *adv:* **ad lib** aus dem Stegreif

administer [əd'mɪnɪstər] *vt (manage)* verwalten; *(dispense)* ausüben; *(justice)* sprechen; *(medicine)* geben; **administration** [ədmɪnɪs'treɪʃən] *n* Verwaltung *f*; *(POL)* Regierung *f*; **administrative** [əd'mɪnɪstrətɪv] *adj* Verwaltungs-; **administrator** [əd'mɪnɪstreɪtər] *n* Verwaltungsbeamte(r) *f(m)*

Admiralty ['ædmərəltɪ] *(BRIT) n* Admiralität *f*

admiration [ædmə'reɪʃən] *n* Bewunderung *f*

admire [əd'maɪər] *vt (respect)* bewundern; *(love)* verehren; **~r** *n* Bewunderer *m*

admission [əd'mɪʃən] *n (entrance)* Einlass *m*; *(fee)* Eintritt(spreis *m) m*; *(confession)* Geständnis *nt*; **~ charge** *n* Eintritt(spreis *m*

admit [əd'mɪt] *vt (let in)* einlassen; *(confess)* gestehen; *(accept)* anerkennen; **~tance** *n* Zulassung *f*; **~tedly** *adv* zugegebenermaßen

admonish [əd'mɒnɪʃ] *vt* ermahnen

ad nauseam [æd'nɔ:sɪæm] *adv (repeat, talk)* endlos

ado [ə'du:] *n:* **without more ~** ohne weitere Umstände

adolescence [ædəu'lesns] n Jugendalter nt;
adolescent [ædəu'lesnt] adj jugendlich ♦ n
Jugendliche(r) f(m)

adopt [ə'dɔpt] vt (child) adoptieren; (idea)
übernehmen; **~ion** [ə'dɔpʃən] n Adoption f;
Übernahme f

adore [ə'dɔː] vt anbeten; verehren

adorn [ə'dɔːn] vt schmücken

Adriatic [eɪdrɪ'ætɪk] n: **the ~ (Sea)** die Adria

adrift [ə'drɪft] adv Wind und Wellen
preisgegeben

adult ['ædʌlt] n Erwachsene(r) f(m)

adultery [ə'dʌltərɪ] n Ehebruch m

advance [ədvɑːns] n (progress) Vorrücken
nt; (money) Vorschuss m ♦ vt (move forward)
vorrücken; (money) vorschießen; (argument)
vorbringen ♦ vi vorwärts gehen; **in ~** im
Voraus; **~ booking** n Vorverkauf m; **~d** adj
(ahead) vorgerückt; (modern)
fortgeschritten; (study) für Fortgeschrittene

advantage [əd'vɑːntɪdʒ] n Vorteil m; **to
have an ~ over sb** jdm gegenüber im
Vorteil sein; **to take ~ of** (misuse)
ausnutzen; (profit from) Nutzen ziehen aus;
~ous [ædvən'teɪdʒəs] adj vorteilhaft

advent ['ædvənt] n Ankunft f; **A~** Advent m

adventure [əd'ventʃə] n Abenteuer nt;
adventurous adj abenteuerlich, waghalsig

adverb ['ædvɜːb] n Adverb nt,
Umstandswort nt

adversary ['ædvəsərɪ] n Gegner m

adverse ['ædvɜːs] adj widrig; **adversity**
[ədvɜːsɪtɪ] n Widrigkeit f, Missgeschick nt

advert ['ædvɜːt] n Anzeige f; **~ise** ['ædvətaɪz]
vt werben für ♦ vi annoncieren; **to ~ise for
sth** etw (per Anzeige) suchen; **~isement**
[ədvɜːtɪsmənt] n Anzeige f, Inserat nt; **~iser**
n (in newspaper etc) Inserent m; **~ising** n
Werbung f

advice [əd'vaɪs] n Rat(schlag) m

advisable [ədvaɪzəbl] adj ratsam

advise [ədvaɪz] vt: **to ~ (sb)** (jdm) raten;
~dly [ədvaɪzɪdlɪ] adv (deliberately) bewusst;
~r n Berater m; **advisory** [ədvaɪzərɪ] adj
beratend, Beratungs-

advocate [vb 'ædvəkeɪt, n 'ædvəkət] vt
vertreten ♦ n Befürworter(in) m(f)

Aegean [iː'dʒiːən] n: **the ~ (Sea)** die Ägäis

aerial ['eərɪəl] n Antenne f ♦ adj Luft-

aerobics [eə'rəubɪks] n Aerobic nt

aerodynamic ['eərəudaɪ'næmɪk] adj
aerodynamisch

aeroplane ['eərəpleɪn] n Flugzeug nt

aerosol ['eərəsɔl] n Aerosol nt; Sprühdose f

aesthetic [iːs'θetɪk] adj ästhetisch

afar [ə'fɑː] adv: **from ~** aus der Ferne

affable ['æfəbl] adj umgänglich

affair [ə'feə] n (concern) Angelegenheit f;
(event) Ereignis nt; (love ~) Verhältnis nt; **~s**
npl (business) Geschäfte pl

affect [ə'fekt] vt (influence) (ein)wirken auf
+acc; (move deeply) bewegen; **this change
doesn't ~ us** diese Änderung betrifft uns
nicht; **~ed** adj affektiert, gekünstelt

affection [ə'fekʃən] n Zuneigung f; **~ate** adj
liebevoll

affiliated [ə'fɪlɪeɪtɪd] adj angeschlossen

affinity [ə'fɪnɪtɪ] n (attraction) gegenseitige
Anziehung f; (relationship) Verwandtschaft f

affirmative [ə'fɜːmətɪv] adj bestätigend

afflict [ə'flɪkt] vt quälen, heimsuchen

affluence ['æfluəns] n (wealth) Wohlstand
m; **affluent** adj wohlhabend, Wohlstands-

afford [ə'fɔːd] vt sich dat leisten; (yield)
bieten, einbringen

afield [ə'fiːld] adv: **far ~** weit fort

afloat [ə'fləut] adj: **to be ~** schwimmen

afoot [ə'fut] adv **im** Gang

afraid [ə'freɪd] adj ängstlich; **to be ~ of**
Angst haben vor +dat; **to be ~ to do sth**
sich scheuen, etw zu tun; **I am ~ I have ...**
ich habe leider ...; **I'm ~ so/not** leider/
leider nicht; **I am ~ that ...** ich fürchte(,
dass) ...

afresh [ə'freʃ] adv von neuem

Africa ['æfrɪkə] n Afrika nt; **~n** adj afrikanisch
♦ n Afrikaner(in) m(f)

after ['ɑːftə] prep nach; (following, seeking)
hinter ... dat ... her; (in imitation) nach, im
Stil von ♦ adv: **soon ~** bald danach ♦ conj
nachdem; **what are you ~?** was wollen
Sie?; **~ he left** nachdem er gegangen war;
~ you! nach Ihnen!; **~ all** letzten Endes; **~
having shaved** als er sich rasiert hatte;

~effects npl Nachwirkungen pl; ~math n Auswirkungen pl; ~noon n Nachmittag m; ~s (inf) n (dessert) Nachtisch m; ~-sales service (BRIT) n Kundendienst m; ~shave (lotion) n Rasierwasser nt; ~sun n Aftersunlotion f; ~thought n nachträgliche(r) Einfall m; ~wards adv danach, nachher

again [ə'gɛn] adv wieder, noch einmal; (besides) außerdem, ferner; ~ and ~ immer wieder

against [ə'gɛnst] prep gegen

age [eɪdʒ] n (of person) Alter nt; (in history) Zeitalter nt ♦ vi altern, alt werden ♦ vt älter machen; **to come of** ~ mündig werden; **20 years of** ~ 20 Jahre alt; **it's been** ~s **since** ... es ist ewig her, seit ...

aged¹ [eɪdʒd] adj ... Jahre alt, -jährig

aged² [eɪdʒɪd] adj (elderly) betagt ♦ npl: **the** ~ die Alten pl

age group n Altersgruppe f

age limit n Altersgrenze f

agency [eɪdʒənsɪ] n Agentur f; Vermittlung f; (CHEM) Wirkung f; **through** or **by the** ~ **of** ... mithilfe or mit Hilfe von ...

agenda [ə'dʒɛndə] n Tagesordnung f

agent [eɪdʒənt] n (COMM) Vertreter m; (spy) Agent m

aggravate ['ægrəveɪt] vt (make worse) verschlimmern; (irritate) reizen

aggregate ['ægrɪgɪt] n Summe f

aggression [ə'grɛʃən] n Aggression f; **aggressive** [ə'grɛsɪv] adj aggressiv

aghast [ə'gɑːst] adj entsetzt

agile ['ædʒaɪl] adj flink, agil; (mind) rege

agitate ['ædʒɪteɪt] vt rütteln; **to** ~ **for** sich stark machen für

AGM n abbr (= annual general meeting) JHV f

ago [ə'gəu] adv: **two days** ~ vor zwei Tagen; **not long** ~ vor kurzem; **it's so long** ~ es ist schon so lange her

agog [ə'gɒg] adj gespannt

agonizing ['ægənaɪzɪŋ] adj quälend

agony ['ægənɪ] n Qual f; **to be in** ~ Qualen leiden

agree [ə'griː] vt (date) vereinbaren ♦ vi (have same opinion, correspond) übereinstimmen; (consent) zustimmen; (be in harmony) sich vertragen; **to** ~ **to sth** einer Sache dat zustimmen; **to** ~ **that** ... (admit) zugeben, dass ...; **to** ~ **to do sth** sich bereit erklären, etw zu tun; **garlic doesn't** ~ **with me** Knoblauch vertrage ich nicht; **I** ~ einverstanden, ich stimme zu; **to** ~ **on sth** sich auf etw acc einigen; ~**able** adj (pleasing) liebenswürdig; (willing to consent) einverstanden; ~**d** adj vereinbart; ~**ment** n (~ing) Übereinstimmung f; (contract) Vereinbarung f, Vertrag m; **to be in** ~**ment** übereinstimmen

agricultural [ægrɪ'kʌltʃərəl] adj landwirtschaftlich, Landwirtschafts-

agriculture ['ægrɪkʌltʃər] n Landwirtschaft f

aground [ə'graund] adv: **to run** ~ auf Grund laufen

ahead [ə'hɛd] adv vorwärts; **to be** ~ voraus sein; ~ **of time** der Zeit voraus; **go right** or **straight** ~ gehen Sie geradeaus; fahren Sie geradeaus

aid [eɪd] n (assistance) Hilfe f, Unterstützung f; (person) Hilfe f; (thing) Hilfsmittel nt ♦ vt unterstützen, helfen +dat; **in** ~ **of** zugunsten or zu Gunsten +gen; **to** ~ **and abet sb** jdm Beihilfe leisten

aide [eɪd] n (person) Gehilfe m; (MIL) Adjutant m

AIDS [eɪdz] n abbr (= acquired immune deficiency syndrome) Aids nt; **AIDS-related** aidsbedingt

ailing ['eɪlɪŋ] adj kränkelnd

ailment ['eɪlmənt] n Leiden nt

aim [eɪm] vt (gun, camera) richten ♦ vi (with gun: also: **take** ~) zielen; (intend) beabsichtigen ♦ n (intention) Absicht f, Ziel nt; (pointing) Zielen nt, Richten nt; **to** ~ **at sth** auf etw dat richten; (fig) etw anstreben; **to** ~ **to do sth** vorhaben, etw zu tun; ~**less** adj ziellos; ~**lessly** adv ziellos

ain't [eɪnt] (inf) = **am not**; **are not**; **is not**; **has not**; **have not**

air [eər] n Luft f; (manner) Miene f, Anschein m; (MUS) Melodie f ♦ vt lüften; (fig) an die Öffentlichkeit bringen ♦ cpd Luft-; **by** ~ (travel) auf dem Luftweg; **to be on the** ~

(RADIO, TV: programme) gesendet werden; **~bed** (BRIT) adj mit Klimaanlage; **~-conditioned** adj mit Klimaanlage; **~-conditioning** n Klimaanlage f; **~craft** n Flugzeug nt, Maschine f; **~craft carrier** n Flugzeugträger m; **~field** n Flugplatz m; **~ force** n Luftwaffe f; **~ freshener** n Raumspray nt; **~gun** n Luftgewehr nt; **~ hostess** (BRIT) n Stewardess f; **~ letter** (BRIT) n Luftpostbrief m; **~lift** n Luftbrücke f; **~line** n Luftverkehrsgesellschaft f; **~liner** n Verkehrsflugzeug nt; **~lock** n Luftblase f; **~mail** n: **by ~mail** mit Luftpost; **~ miles** npl ≈ Flugkilometer m; **~plane** (US) n Flugzeug nt, Maschine f; **~port** n Flughafen m, Flugplatz m; **~ raid** n Luftangriff m; **~sick** adj luftkrank; **~space** n Luftraum m; **~strip** n Landestreifen m; **~ terminal** n Terminal m; **~tight** adj luftdicht; **~ traffic controller** n Fluglotse m; **~y** adj luftig; (manner) leichtfertig

aisle [aɪl] n Gang m; **~ seat** n Sitz m am Gang

ajar [ə'dʒɑːʳ] adv angelehnt; einen Spalt offen

alarm [ə'lɑːm] n (warning) Alarm m; (bell etc) Alarmanlage f; (anxiety) Sorge f ♦ vt erschrecken; **~ call** n (in hotel etc) Weckruf m; **~ clock** n Wecker m

Albania [æl'beɪnɪə] n Albanien nt

albeit [ɔːl'biːɪt] conj obgleich

album ['ælbəm] n Album nt

alcohol ['ælkəhɔl] n Alkohol m; **~-free** adj alkoholfrei; **~ic** [ælkə'hɔlɪk] adj (drink) alkoholisch ♦ n Alkoholiker(in) m(f); **~ism** n Alkoholismus m

alert [ə'lɜːt] adj wachsam ♦ n Alarm m ♦ vt alarmieren; **to be on the ~** wachsam sein

Algeria [æl'dʒɪərɪə] n Algerien nt

alias ['eɪlɪəs] adv alias ♦ n Deckname m

alibi ['ælɪbaɪ] n Alibi nt

alien ['eɪlɪən] n Ausländer m ♦ adj (foreign) ausländisch; (strange) fremd; **~ to** fremd +dat; **~ate** vt entfremden

alight [ə'laɪt] adj brennend; (of building) in Flammen ♦ vi (descend) aussteigen; (bird) sich setzen

align [ə'laɪn] vt ausrichten

alike [ə'laɪk] adj gleich, ähnlich ♦ adv gleich, ebenso; **to look ~** sich dat ähnlich sehen

alimony ['ælɪmənɪ] n Unterhalt m, Alimente pl

alive [ə'laɪv] adj (living) lebend; (lively) lebendig, aufgeweckt; **~ (with)** (full of) voll (von), wimmelnd (von)

KEYWORD

---

all [ɔːl] adj alle(r, s); **all day/night** den ganzen Tag/die ganze Nacht; **all men are equal** alle Menschen sind gleich; **all five came** alle fünf kamen; **all the books/food** die ganzen Bücher/das ganze Essen; **all the time** die ganze Zeit (über); **all his life** sein ganzes Leben (lang)
♦ pron 1 alles; **I ate it all, I ate all of it** ich habe alles gegessen; **all of us/the boys went** wir gingen alle/alle Jungen gingen; **we all sat down** wir setzten uns alle
2 (in phrases): **above all** vor allem; **after all** schließlich; **at all: not at all** (in answer to question) überhaupt nicht; (in answer to thanks) gern geschehen; **I'm not at all tired** ich bin überhaupt nicht müde; **anything at all will do** es ist egal, welche(r, s); **all in all** alles in allem
♦ adv ganz; **all alone** ganz allein; **it's not as hard as all that** so schwer ist es nun auch wieder nicht; **all the more/the better** umso mehr/besser; **all but** fast; **the score is 2 all** es steht 2 zu 2

---

allay [ə'leɪ] vt (fears) beschwichtigen

all clear n Entwarnung f

allegation [ælɪ'geɪʃən] n Behauptung f

allege [ə'ledʒ] vt (declare) behaupten; (falsely) vorgeben; **~dly** adv angeblich

allegiance [ə'liːdʒəns] n Treue f

allergic [ə'lɜːdʒɪk] adj: **~ (to)** allergisch (gegen)

allergy ['ælədʒɪ] n Allergie f

alleviate [ə'liːvɪeɪt] vt lindern

alley ['ælɪ] n Gasse f, Durchgang m

alliance [ə'laɪəns] n Bund m, Allianz f

allied ['ælaɪd] adj vereinigt; (powers) alliiert; **~ (to)** verwandt (mit)

all: ~-in (BRIT) adj, adv (charge) alles inbegriffen, Gesamt-; ~-in **wrestling** n Freistilringen nt; ~-**night** adj (café, cinema) die ganze Nacht geöffnet, Nacht-

allocate ['æləkeɪt] vt zuteilen

allot [ə'lɒt] vt zuteilen; ~**ment** n (share) Anteil m; (plot) Schrebergarten m

all-out ['ɔ:laut] adj total; **all out** adv mit voller Kraft

allow [ə'lau] vt (permit) erlauben, gestatten; (grant) bewilligen; (deduct) abziehen; (concede): **to ~ that ...** annehmen, dass ...; **to ~ sb sth** jdm etw erlauben, jdm etw gestatten; **to ~ sb to do sth** jdm erlauben or gestatten, etw zu tun; ~ **for** vt fus berücksichtigen, einplanen; ~**ance** n Beihilfe f; **to make ~ances for** berücksichtigen

alloy ['ælɔɪ] n Metalllegierung f

all: ~ **right** adv (well) gut; (correct) richtig; (as answer) okay; ~-**round** adj (sportsman) allseitig, Allround-; (view) Rundum-; ~-**time** adj (record, high) ... aller Zeiten, Höchst-

allude [ə'lu:d] vi: **to ~ to** hinweisen auf +acc, anspielen auf +acc

alluring [ə'ljuərɪŋ] adj verlockend

ally [n 'ælaɪ, vb ə'laɪ] n Verbündete(r) f(m); (POL) Alliierte(r) f(m) ♦ vr: **to ~ o.s. with** sich verbünden mit

almighty [ɔ:l'maɪtɪ] adj allmächtig

almond ['ɑ:mənd] n Mandel f

almost ['ɔ:lməust] adv fast, beinahe

alms [ɑ:mz] npl Almosen nt

alone [ə'ləun] adj, adv allein; **to leave sth ~** etw sein lassen; **let ~ ...** geschweige denn ...

along [ə'lɒŋ] prep entlang, längs ♦ adv (onward) vorwärts, weiter; ~ **with** zusammen mit; **he was limping ~** er humpelte einher; **all ~** (all the time) die ganze Zeit; ~**side** adv (walk) nebenher; (come) nebendran; (be) daneben ♦ prep (walk, compared with) neben +dat; (come) neben +acc; (be) entlang, neben +dat; (of ship) längsseits +gen

aloof [ə'lu:f] adj zurückhaltend ♦ adv fern; **to stand ~** abseits stehen

aloud [ə'laud] adv laut

alphabet ['ælfəbet] n Alphabet nt; ~**ical** [ælfə'betɪkl] adj alphabetisch

alpine ['ælpaɪn] adj alpin, Alpen-

Alps [ælps] npl: **the ~** die Alpen pl

already [ɔ:l'redɪ] adv schon, bereits

alright ['ɔ:l'raɪt] (BRIT) adv = **all right**

Alsatian [æl'seɪʃən] n (dog) Schäferhund m

also ['ɔ:lsəu] adv auch, außerdem

altar ['ɔltə'] n Altar m

alter ['ɔltə'] vt ändern; (dress) umändern; ~**ation** [ɔltə'reɪʃən] n Änderung f; Umänderung f; (to building) Umbau m

alternate [adj ɒl'tə:nɪt, vb 'ɒltə:neɪt] adj abwechselnd ♦ vi abwechseln; **on ~ days** jeden zweiten Tag

alternating ['ɔltə:neɪtɪŋ] adj: ~ **current** Wechselstrom m; **alternative** [ɒl'tə:nətɪv] adj andere(r, s) ♦ n Alternative f; **alternative medicine** Alternativmedizin f; **alternatively** adv im anderen Falle; **alternatively one could ...** oder man könnte ...; **alternator** ['ɔltə:neɪtə'] n (AUT) Lichtmaschine f

although [ɔ:l'ðəu] conj obwohl

altitude ['æltɪtju:d] n Höhe f

alto ['æltəu] n Alt m

altogether [ɔ:ltə'geðə'] adv (on the whole) im Ganzen genommen; (entirely) ganz und gar

aluminium [ælju'mɪnɪəm] (BRIT) n Aluminium nt

aluminum [ə'lu:mɪnəm] (US) n Aluminium nt

always ['ɔ:lweɪz] adv immer

Alzheimer's (disease) ['æltshaɪməz-] n (MED) Alzheimerkrankheit f

AM n abbr (= Assembly Member) Mitglied nt der walisischen Versammlung

am [æm] see **be**

a.m. adv abbr (= ante meridiem) vormittags

amalgamate [ə'mælgəmeɪt] vi (combine) sich vereinigen ♦ vt (mix) amalgamieren

amass [ə'mæs] vt anhäufen

amateur ['æmətə'] n Amateur m; (pej) Amateur m, Stümper m; ~**ish** (pej) adj dilettantisch, stümperhaft

amaze [ə'meɪz] vt erstaunen; **to be ~d (at)** erstaunt sein (über); ~**ment** n höchste(s)

Erstaunen nt; **amazing** adj höchst
erstaunlich

Amazon ['æmazan] n (GEOG) Amazonas m

ambassador [æm'bæsədəʳ] n Botschafter m

amber ['æmbəʳ] n Bernstein m; **at ~** (BRIT:
AUT) auf Gelb, gelb

ambiguous [æm'bɪgjuəs] adj zweideutig;
(not clear) unklar

ambition [æm'bɪʃən] n Ehrgeiz m;
ambitious adj ehrgeizig

amble ['æmbl] vi (usu: ~ along) schlendern

ambulance ['æmbjuləns] n Krankenwagen
m; ~ **man** (irreg) n Sanitäter m

ambush ['æmbuʃ] n Hinterhalt m ♦ vt (aus
dem Hinterhalt) überfallen

amenable [ə'mi:nəbl] adj gefügig; ~ **(to)**
(reason) zugänglich (+dat); (flattery)
empfänglich (für)

amend [ə'mɛnd] vt (law etc) abändern,
ergänzen; **to make ~s** etw wieder
gutmachen; ~**ment** n Abänderung f

amenities [ə'mi:nɪtɪz] npl Einrichtungen pl

America [ə'mɛrɪkə] n Amerika nt; ~**n** adj
amerikanisch ♦ n Amerikaner(in) m(f)

amiable ['eɪmɪəbl] adj liebenswürdig

amicable ['æmɪkəbl] adj freundschaftlich;
(settlement) gütlich

amid(st) [ə'mɪd(st)] prep mitten in or unter
+dat

amiss [ə'mɪs] adv: **to take sth ~** etw übel
nehmen; **there's something ~** da stimmt
irgendetwas nicht

ammonia [ə'məunɪə] n Ammoniak nt

ammunition [æmju'nɪʃən] n Munition f

amnesia [æm'ni:zɪə] n Gedächtnisverlust m

amnesty ['æmnɪstɪ] n Amnestie f

amok [ə'mɔk] adv: **to run ~** Amok laufen

among(st) [ə'mʌŋ(st)] prep unter

amoral [æ'mɔrəl] adj unmoralisch

amorous ['æmərəs] adj verliebt

amount [ə'maunt] n (of money) Betrag m; (of
water, sand) Menge f ♦ vi: **to ~ to** (total)
sich belaufen auf +acc; **a great ~ of time/
energy** ein großer Aufwand an Zeit/
Energie (dat); **this ~s to treachery** das
kommt Verrat gleich; **he won't ~ to much**
aus ihm wird nie was

amp(ere) [æmp(ɛəʳ)] n Ampere nt

amphibian [æm'fɪbɪən] n Amphibie f

ample ['æmpl] adj (portion) reichlich; (dress)
weit, groß; ~ **time** genügend Zeit

amplifier ['æmplɪfaɪəʳ] n Verstärker m

amuse [ə'mju:z] vt (entertain) unterhalten;
(make smile) belustigen; ~**ment** n (feeling)
Unterhaltung f; (recreation) Zeitvertreib m;
~**ment arcade** n Spielhalle f; ~**ment
park** n Vergnügungspark m

an [æn, ən] see **a**

anaemia [ə'ni:mɪə] n Anämie f; **anaemic**
adj blutarm

anaesthetic [ænɪs'θɛtɪk] n
Betäubungsmittel nt; **under ~** unter
Narkose; **anaesthetist** [æ'ni:sθɪtɪst] n
Anästhesist(in) m(f)

analgesic [ænæl'dʒi:sɪk] n
schmerzlindernde(s) Mittel nt

analog(ue) ['ænələg] adj Analog-

analogy [ə'nælədʒɪ] n Analogie f

analyse ['ænəlaɪz] (BRIT) vt analysieren

analyses [ə'næləsi:z] (BRIT) npl of **analysis**

analysis [ə'næləsɪs] (pl **analyses**) n Analyse f

analyst ['ænəlɪst] n Analytiker(in) m(f)

analytic(al) [ænə'lɪtɪk(l)] adj analytisch

analyze ['ænəlaɪz] (US) vt = **analyse**

anarchy ['ænəkɪ] n Anarchie f

anatomy [ə'nætəmɪ] n (structure) anato-
mische(r) Aufbau m; (study) Anatomie f

ancestor ['ænsɪstəʳ] n Vorfahr m

anchor ['æŋkəʳ] n Anker m ♦ vi (also: **to
drop ~**) ankern, vor Anker gehen ♦ vt
verankern; **to weigh ~** den Anker lichten

anchovy ['æntʃəvɪ] n Sardelle f

ancient ['eɪnʃənt] adj alt; (car etc) uralt

ancillary [æn'sɪlərɪ] adj Hilfs-

and [ænd] conj und; ~ **so on** und so weiter;
try ~ come versuche zu kommen; **better ~
better** immer besser

Andes ['ændi:z] npl: **the ~** die Anden pl

anemia etc [ə'ni:mɪə] (US) n = **anaemia** etc

anesthetic etc [ænɪs'θɛtɪk] (US) n =
anaesthetic etc

anew [ə'nju:] adv von neuem

angel ['eɪndʒəl] n Engel m

anger ['æŋgəʳ] n Zorn m ♦ vt ärgern

angina [æn'dʒaɪnə] n Angina f

angle ['æŋgl] n Winkel m; (point of view) Standpunkt m

angler ['æŋglə'] n Angler m

Anglican ['æŋglɪkən] adj anglikanisch ♦ n Anglikaner(in) m(f)

angling ['æŋglɪŋ] n Angeln nt

angrily ['æŋgrɪlɪ] adv ärgerlich, böse

angry ['æŋgrɪ] adj ärgerlich, ungehalten, böse; (wound) entzündet; **to be ~ with sb** auf jdn böse sein; **to be ~ at sth** über etw acc verärgert sein

anguish ['æŋgwɪʃ] n Qual f

angular ['æŋgjulə'] adj eckig, winkelförmig; (face) kantig

animal ['ænɪməl] n Tier nt; (living creature) Lebewesen nt ♦ adj tierisch

animate [vb 'ænɪmeɪt, adj 'ænɪmɪt] vt beleben ♦ adj lebhaft; ~**d** adj lebendig; (film) Zeichentrick-

animosity [ænɪ'mɔsɪtɪ] n Feindseligkeit f, Abneigung f

aniseed ['ænɪsiːd] n Anis m

ankle ['æŋkl] n (Fuß)knöchel m; ~ **sock** n Söckchen nt

annex [n 'æneks, vb ə'neks] n (BRIT: also: ~**e**) Anbau m ♦ vt anfügen; (POL) annektieren, angliedern

annihilate [ə'naɪəleɪt] vt vernichten

anniversary [ænɪ'vɜːsərɪ] n Jahrestag m

announce [ə'nauns] vt ankündigen, anzeigen; ~**ment** n Ankündigung f; (official) Bekanntmachung f; ~**r** n Ansager(in) m(f)

annoy [ə'nɔɪ] vt ärgern; **don't get ~ed!** reg dich nicht auf!; ~**ance** n Ärgernis nt, Störung f; ~**ing** adj ärgerlich; (person) lästig

annual ['ænjuəl] adj jährlich; (salary) Jahres- ♦ n (plant) einjährige Pflanze f; (book) Jahrbuch nt; ~**ly** adv jährlich

annul [ə'nʌl] vt aufheben, annullieren

annum ['ænəm] n see **per**

anonymous [ə'nɔnɪməs] adj anonym

anorak ['ænəræk] n Anorak m, Windjacke f

anorexia [ænə'reksɪə] n (MED) Magersucht f

another [ə'nʌðə'] adj, pron (different) ein(e) andere(r, s); (additional) noch eine(r, s); see

also **one**

answer ['ɑːnsə'] n Antwort f ♦ vi antworten; (on phone) sich melden ♦ vt (person) antworten +dat; (letter, question) beantworten; (telephone) gehen an +acc, abnehmen; (door) öffnen; **in ~ to your letter** in Beantwortung Ihres Schreibens; **to ~ the phone** ans Telefon gehen; **to ~ the bell** or **the door** aufmachen; ~ **back** vi frech sein; ~ **for** vt fus: **to ~ for sth** für etw verantwortlich sein; ~**able** adj: **to be ~able to sb for sth** jdm gegenüber für etw verantwortlich sein; ~**ing machine** n Anrufbeantworter m

ant [ænt] n Ameise f

antagonism [æn'tægənɪzəm] n Antagonismus m

antagonize [æn'tægənaɪz] vt reizen

Antarctic [ænt'ɑːktɪk] adj antarktisch ♦ n: **the ~** die Antarktis

antelope ['æntɪləup] n Antilope f

antenatal ['æntɪ'neɪtl] adj vor der Geburt; ~ **clinic** n Sprechstunde f für werdende Mütter

antenna [æn'tenə] n (BIOL) Fühler m; (RAD) Antenne f

antennae [æn'teniː] npl of **antenna**

anthem ['ænθəm] n Hymne f; **national ~** Nationalhymne f

anthology [æn'θɔlədʒɪ] n Gedichtsammlung f, Anthologie f

anti- ['æntɪ] prefix Gegen-, Anti-

anti-aircraft ['æntɪ'eəkrɑːft] adj Flugabwehr-

antibiotic ['æntɪbaɪ'ɔtɪk] n Antibiotikum nt

antibody ['æntɪbɔdɪ] n Antikörper m

anticipate [æn'tɪsɪpeɪt] vt (expect: trouble, question) erwarten, rechnen mit; (look forward to) sich freuen auf +acc; (do first) vorwegnehmen; (foresee) ahnen, vorhersehen; **anticipation** [æntɪsɪ'peɪʃən] n Erwartung f; (foreshadowing) Vorwegnahme f

anticlimax ['æntɪ'klaɪmæks] n Ernüchterung f

anticlockwise ['æntɪ'klɔkwaɪz] adv entgegen dem Uhrzeigersinn

antics ['æntɪks] npl Possen pl

anti: ~cyclone n Hoch nt, Hochdruckgebiet nt; ~depressant n Antidepressivum nt; ~dote n Gegenmittel nt; ~freeze n Frostschutzmittel nt; ~histamine n Antihistamin nt

antiquated ['æntɪkweɪtɪd] adj antiquiert

antique [æn'tiːk] n Antiquität f ♦ adj antik; (old-fashioned) altmodisch; ~ shop n Antiquitätenladen m; antiquity [æn'tɪkwɪtɪ] n Altertum nt

antiseptic [æntɪ'septɪk] n Antiseptikum nt ♦ adj antiseptisch

antisocial ['æntɪ'səʊʃəl] adj (person) ungesellig; (law) unsozial

antlers ['æntləz] npl Geweih nt

anus ['eɪnəs] n After m

anvil ['ænvɪl] n Amboss m

anxiety [æŋ'zaɪətɪ] n Angst f; (worry) Sorge f; anxious ['æŋkʃəs] adj ängstlich; (worried) besorgt; to be anxious to do sth etw unbedingt tun wollen

---

KEYWORD

any ['enɪ] adj 1 (in questions etc): have you any butter? haben Sie (etwas) Butter?; have you any children? haben Sie Kinder?; if there are any tickets left falls noch Karten da sind

2 (with negative): I haven't any money/books ich habe kein Geld/keine Bücher

3 (no matter which) jede(r, s) (beliebige); any colour (at all) jede beliebige Farbe; choose any book you like nehmen Sie ein beliebiges Buch

4 (in phrases): in any case in jedem Fall; any day now jeden Tag; at any moment jeden Moment; at any rate auf jeden Fall

♦ pron 1 (in questions etc): have you got any? haben Sie welche?; can any of you sing? kann (irgend)einer von euch singen?

2 (with negative): I haven't any (of them) ich habe keinen/keines (davon)

3 (no matter which one(s)): take any of those books (you like) nehmen Sie irgendeines dieser Bücher

♦ adv 1 (in questions etc): do you want any more soup/sandwiches? möchten Sie noch Suppe/Brote?; are you feeling any better? fühlen Sie sich etwas besser?

2 (with negative): I can't hear him any more ich kann ihn nicht mehr hören

---

anybody ['enɪbɔdɪ] pron (no matter who) jede(r); (in questions etc) (irgend)jemand, (irgend)eine(r); (with negative): I can't see ~ ich kann niemanden sehen

anyhow ['enɪhaʊ] adv (at any rate): I shall go ~ ich gehe sowieso; (haphazardly): do it ~ machen Sie es, wie Sie wollen

anyone ['enɪwʌn] pron = anybody

KEYWORD

anything ['enɪθɪŋ] pron 1 (in questions etc) (irgend)etwas; can you see anything? können Sie etwas sehen?

2 (with negative): I can't see anything ich kann nichts sehen

3 (no matter what): you can say anything you like Sie können sagen, was Sie wollen; anything will do irgendetwas (wird genügen), irgendeine(r, s) (wird genügen); he'll eat anything er isst alles

---

anyway ['enɪweɪ] adv (at any rate) auf jeden Fall; (besides): ~, I couldn't come even if I wanted to jedenfalls könnte ich nicht kommen, selbst wenn ich wollte; why are you phoning, ~? warum rufst du überhaupt an?

anywhere ['enɪweəʳ] adv (in questions etc) irgendwo; (: with direction) irgendwohin; (no matter where) überall; (: with direction) überallhin; (with negative): I can't see him ~ ich kann ihn nirgendwo or nirgends sehen; can you see him ~? siehst du ihn irgendwo?; put the books down ~ leg die Bücher irgendwohin

apart [ə'pɑːt] adv (parted) auseinander; (away) beiseite, abseits; 10 miles ~ 10 Meilen auseinander; to take ~ auseinander nehmen; ~ from prep außer

apartheid [ə'pɑːteɪt] n Apartheid f

apartment [ə'pɑːtmənt] (US) n Wohnung f; ~ building (US) n Wohnhaus nt

apathy ['æpəθɪ] n Teilnahmslosigkeit f,

Apathie f

ape [eɪp] n (Menschen)affe m ♦ vt nachahmen

aperitif [əˈperɪtiːf] n Aperitif m

aperture [ˈæpətʃjuəʳ] n Öffnung f; (PHOT) Blende f

APEX [ˈeɪpeks] n abbr (AVIAT: = advance purchase excursion) APEX (im Voraus reservierte(r) Fahrkarte/Flugschein zu reduzierten Preisen)

apex [ˈeɪpeks] n Spitze f

apiece [əˈpiːs] adv pro Stück; (per person) pro Kopf

apologetic [əpɔləˈdʒetɪk] adj entschuldigend; **to be ~** sich sehr entschuldigen

apologize [əˈpɔlədʒaɪz] vi: **to ~ (for sth to sb)** sich (für etw bei jdm) entschuldigen; **apology** n Entschuldigung f

apostle [əˈpɔsl] n Apostel m

apostrophe [əˈpɔstrəfɪ] n Apostroph m

appal [əˈpɔːl] vt erschrecken; **~ling** adj schrecklich

apparatus [æpəˈreɪtəs] n Gerät nt

apparel [əˈpærəl] (US) n Kleidung f

apparent [əˈpærənt] adj offenbar; **~ly** adv anscheinend

apparition [æpəˈrɪʃən] n (ghost) Erscheinung f, Geist m

appeal [əˈpiːl] vi dringend ersuchen; (JUR) Berufung einlegen ♦ n Aufruf m; (JUR) Berufung f; **to ~ for** dringend bitten um; **to ~ to** sich wenden an +acc; (to public) appellieren an +acc; **it doesn't ~ to me** es gefällt mir nicht; **~ing** adj ansprechend

appear [əˈpɪəʳ] vi (come into sight) erscheinen; (be seen) auftauchen; (seem) scheinen; **it would ~ that ...** anscheinend ...; **~ance** n (coming into sight) Erscheinen nt; (outward show) Äußere(s) nt

appease [əˈpiːz] vt beschwichtigen

appendices [əˈpendɪsiːz] npl of **appendix**

appendicitis [əpendɪˈsaɪtɪs] n Blinddarmentzündung f

appendix [əˈpendɪks] (pl **appendices**) n (in book) Anhang m; (MED) Blinddarm m

appetite [ˈæpɪtaɪt] n Appetit m; (fig) Lust f

appetizer [ˈæpɪtaɪzəʳ] n Appetitanreger m; **appetizing** [ˈæpɪtaɪzɪŋ] adj appetitanregend

applaud [əˈplɔːd] vi Beifall klatschen, applaudieren ♦ vt Beifall klatschen +dat; **applause** [əˈplɔːz] n Beifall m, Applaus m

apple [ˈæpl] n Apfel m; **~ tree** n Apfelbaum m

appliance [əˈplaɪəns] n Gerät nt

applicable [əˈplɪkəbl] adj anwendbar; (in forms) zutreffend

applicant [ˈæplɪkənt] n Bewerber(in) m(f)

application [æplɪˈkeɪʃən] n (request) Antrag m; (for job) Bewerbung f; (putting into practice) Anwendung f; (hard work) Fleiß m; **~ form** n Bewerbungsformular nt

applied [əˈplaɪd] adj angewandt

apply [əˈplaɪ] vi (be suitable) zutreffen; (ask): **to ~ (to)** sich wenden (an +acc); (request): **to ~ for** sich melden für +acc ♦ vt (place on) auflegen; (cream) auftragen; (put into practice) anwenden; **to ~ for sth** sich um etw bewerben; **to ~ o.s. to sth** sich bei etw anstrengen

appoint [əˈpɔɪnt] vt (to office) ernennen, berufen; (settle) festsetzen; **~ment** n (meeting) Verabredung f; (at hairdresser etc) Bestellung f; (in business) Termin m; (choice for a position) Ernennung f; (UNIV) Berufung f

appraisal [əˈpreɪzl] n Beurteilung f

appreciable [əˈpriːʃəbl] adj (perceptible) merklich; (able to be estimated) abschätzbar

appreciate [əˈpriːʃɪeɪt] vt (value) zu schätzen wissen; (understand) einsehen ♦ vi (increase in value) im Wert steigen; **appreciation** [əpriːʃɪˈeɪʃən] n Wertschätzung f; (COMM) Wertzuwachs m; **appreciative** [əˈpriːʃɪətɪv] adj (showing thanks) dankbar; (showing liking) anerkennend

apprehend [æprɪˈhend] vt (arrest) festnehmen; (understand) erfassen

apprehension [æprɪˈhenʃən] n Angst f

apprehensive [æprɪˈhensɪv] adj furchtsam

apprentice [əˈprentɪs] n Lehrling m; **~ship** n Lehrzeit f

approach [əˈprəʊtʃ] vi sich nähern ♦ vt herantreten an +acc; (problem) herangehen an +*acc* ♦ *n* Annäherung *f*; (*to problem*) Ansatz *m*; (*path*) Zugang *m*, Zufahrt *f*; ~**able** *adj* zugänglich

appropriate [*adj* əˈprəuprɪɪt, *vb* əˈprəuprɪeɪt] *adj* angemessen; (*remark*) angebracht ♦ *vt* (*take for o.s.*) sich aneignen; (*set apart*) bereitstellen

approval [əˈpruːvəl] *n* (*show of satisfaction*) Beifall *m*; (*permission*) Billigung *f*; **on ~** (*COMM*) bei Gefallen

approve [əˈpruːv] *vt*, *vi* billigen; **I don't ~ of it/him** ich halte nichts davon/von ihm; ~**d school** (*BRIT*) *n* Erziehungsheim *nt*

approximate [*adj* əˈprɒksɪmɪt, *vb* əˈprɒksɪmeɪt] *adj* annähernd, ungefähr ♦ *vt* nahe kommen +*dat*; ~**ly** *adv* rund, ungefähr

apricot [ˈeɪprɪkɒt] *n* Aprikose *f*

April [ˈeɪprəl] *n* April *m*; ~ **Fools' Day** *n* der erste April

apron [ˈeɪprən] *n* Schürze *f*

apt [æpt] *adj* (*suitable*) passend; (*able*) begabt; (*likely*): **to be ~ to do sth** dazu neigen, etw zu tun

aptitude [ˈæptɪtjuːd] *n* Begabung *f*

aqualung [ˈækwəlʌŋ] *n* Unterwasseratmungsgerät *nt*

aquarium [əˈkwɛərɪəm] *n* Aquarium *nt*

Aquarius [əˈkwɛərɪəs] *n* Wassermann *m*

aquatic [əˈkwætɪk] *adj* Wasser-

Arab [ˈærəb] *n* Araber(in) *m(f)*

Arabia [əˈreɪbɪə] *n* Arabien *nt*; ~**n** *adj* arabisch

Arabic [ˈærəbɪk] *adj* arabisch ♦ *n* Arabisch *nt*

arable [ˈærəbl] *adj* bebaubar, Kultur-

arbitrary [ˈɑːbɪtrərɪ] *adj* willkürlich

arbitration [ɑːbɪˈtreɪʃən] *n* Schlichtung *f*

arc [ɑːk] *n* Bogen *m*

arcade [ɑːˈkeɪd] *n* Säulengang *m*; (*with video games*) Spielhalle *f*

arch [ɑːtʃ] *n* Bogen *m* ♦ *vt* überwölben; (*back*) krumm machen

archaeologist [ɑːkɪˈɒlədʒɪst] *n* Archäologe *m*

archaeology [ɑːkɪˈɒlədʒɪ] *n* Archäologie *f*

archaic [ɑːˈkeɪɪk] *adj* altertümlich

archbishop [ɑːtʃˈbɪʃəp] *n* Erzbischof *m*

archenemy [ˈɑːtʃˈenəmɪ] *n* Erzfeind *m*

archeology *etc* [ɑːkɪˈɒlədʒɪ] (*US*) = **archaeology** *etc*

archery [ˈɑːtʃərɪ] *n* Bogenschießen *nt*

architect [ˈɑːkɪtekt] *n* Architekt(in) *m(f)*; ~**ural** [ɑːkɪˈtektʃərəl] *adj* architektonisch; ~**ure** *n* Architektur *f*

archives [ˈɑːkaɪvz] *npl* Archiv *nt*

archway [ˈɑːtʃweɪ] *n* Bogen *m*

Arctic [ˈɑːktɪk] *adj* arktisch ♦ *n*: **the ~** die Arktis

ardent [ˈɑːdənt] *adj* glühend

arduous [ˈɑːdjuəs] *adj* mühsam

are [ɑːr] *see* **be**

area [ˈɛərɪə] *n* Fläche *f*; (*of land*) Gebiet *nt*; (*part of sth*) Teil *m*, Abschnitt *m*

arena [əˈriːnə] *n* Arena *f*

aren't [ɑːnt] = **are not**

Argentina [ɑːdʒənˈtiːnə] *n* Argentinien *nt*; **Argentinian** [ɑːdʒənˈtɪnɪən] *adj* argentinisch ♦ *n* Argentinier(in) *m(f)*

arguably [ˈɑːgjuəblɪ] *adv* wohl

argue [ˈɑːgjuː] *vi* diskutieren; (*angrily*) streiten; **argument** *n* (*theory*) Argument *nt*; (*reasoning*) Argumentation *f*; (*row*) Auseinandersetzung *f*, Streit *m*; **to have an argument** sich streiten; **argumentative** [ɑːgjuˈmentətɪv] *adj* streitlustig

aria [ˈɑːrɪə] *n* Arie *f*

Aries [ˈɛərɪz] *n* Widder *m*

arise [əˈraɪz] (*pt* **arose**, *pp* **arisen**) *vi* aufsteigen; (*get up*) aufstehen; (*difficulties etc*) entstehen; (*case*) vorkommen; **to ~ from sth** herrühren von etw; ~**n** [əˈrɪzn] *pp* of **arise**

aristocracy [ærɪsˈtɒkrəsɪ] *n* Adel *m*, Aristokratie *f*; **aristocrat** [ˈærɪstəkræt] *n* Adlige(r) *f(m)*, Aristokrat(in) *m(f)*

arithmetic [əˈrɪθmətɪk] *n* Rechnen *nt*, Arithmetik *f*

arm [ɑːm] *n* Arm *m*; (*branch of military service*) Zweig *m* ♦ *vt* bewaffnen; ~**s** *npl* (*weapons*) Waffen *pl*

armaments [ˈɑːməmənts] *npl* Ausrüstung *f*

armchair [ˈɑːmtʃɛər] *n* Lehnstuhl *m*

armed [ɑːmd] *adj* (*forces*) Streit-, bewaffnet; ~ **robbery** *n* bewaffnete(r) Raubüberfall *m*

armistice ['ɑːmɪstɪs] n Waffenstillstand m

armour ['ɑːmə*] (US **armor**) n (knight's) Rüstung f; (MIL) Panzerplatte f; **~ed car** n Panzerwagen m

armpit ['ɑːmpɪt] n Achselhöhle f

armrest ['ɑːmrest] n Armlehne f

army ['ɑːmɪ] n Armee f, Heer nt; (host) Heer nt

aroma [ə'rəumə] n Duft m, Aroma nt; **~therapy** [ərəumə'θerəpɪ] n Aromatherapie f; **~tic** [ærə'mætɪk] adj aromatisch, würzig

arose [ə'rəuz] pt of **arise**

around [ə'raund] adv ringsherum; (almost) ungefähr ♦ prep um ... herum; **is he ~?** ist er hier?

arrange [ə'reɪndʒ] vt (time, meeting) festsetzen; (holidays) festlegen; (flowers, hair, objects) anordnen; **I ~d to meet him** ich habe mit ihm ausgemacht, ihn zu treffen; **it's all ~d** es ist alles arrangiert; **~ment** n (order) Reihenfolge f; (agreement) Vereinbarung f; **~ments** npl (plans) Pläne pl

array [ə'reɪ] n (collection) Ansammlung f

arrears [ə'rɪəz] npl (of debts) Rückstand m; (of work) Unerledigte(s) nt; **in ~** im Rückstand

arrest [ə'rest] vt (person) verhaften; (stop) aufhalten ♦ n Verhaftung f; **under ~** in Haft

arrival [ə'raɪvl] n Ankunft f

arrive [ə'raɪv] vi ankommen; **to ~ at** ankommen in +dat, ankommen bei

arrogance ['ærəgəns] n Überheblichkeit f, Arroganz f; **arrogant** ['ærəgənt] adj überheblich, arrogant

arrow ['ærəu] n Pfeil m

arse [ɑːs] (infl) n Arsch m (!)

arsenal ['ɑːsɪnl] n Waffenlager nt, Zeughaus nt

arsenic ['ɑːsnɪk] n Arsen nt

arson ['ɑːsn] n Brandstiftung f

art [ɑːt] n Kunst f; **A~s** npl (UNIV) Geisteswissenschaften pl

artery ['ɑːtərɪ] n Schlagader f, Arterie f

art gallery n Kunstgalerie f

arthritis [ɑː'θraɪtɪs] n Arthritis f

artichoke ['ɑːtɪtʃəuk] n Artischocke f;

Jerusalem ~ Erdartischocke f

article ['ɑːtɪkl] n (PRESS, GRAM) Artikel m; (thing) Gegenstand m, Artikel m; (clause) Abschnitt m, Paragraf m; **~ of clothing** Kleidungsstück nt

articulate [adj ɑː'tɪkjulɪt, vb ɑː'tɪkjuleɪt] adj (able to express o.s.) redegewandt; (speaking clearly) deutlich, verständlich ♦ vt (connect) zusammenfügen, gliedern; **to be ~** sich gut ausdrücken können; **~d vehicle** n Sattelschlepper m

artificial [ɑːtɪ'fɪʃəl] adj künstlich, Kunst-; **~ respiration** n künstliche Atmung f

artisan ['ɑːtɪzæn] n gelernte(r) Handwerker m

artist ['ɑːtɪst] n Künstler(in) m(f); **~ic** [ɑː'tɪstɪk] adj künstlerisch; **~ry** n künstlerische(s) Können nt

art school n Kunsthochschule f

KEYWORD

as [æz] conj 1 (referring to time) als; **as the years went by** mit den Jahren; **he came in as I was leaving** als er hereinkam, ging ich gerade; **as from tomorrow** ab morgen

2 (in comparisons): **as big as** so groß wie; **twice as big as** zweimal so groß wie; **as much/many as** so viel/so viele wie; **as soon as** sobald

3 (since, because) da; **he left early as he had to be home by 10** er ging früher, da er um 10 zu Hause sein musste

4 (referring to manner, way) wie; **do as you wish** mach was du willst; **as she said** wie sie sagte

5 (concerning): **as for or to that** was das betrifft or angeht

6: **as if or though** als ob

♦ prep als; see also **long**; **he works as a driver** er arbeitet als Fahrer; see also **such**; **he gave it to me as a present** er hat es mir als Geschenk gegeben; see also **well**

a.s.a.p. abbr = **as soon as possible**

asbestos [æz'bestəs] n Asbest m

ascend [ə'send] vi aufsteigen ♦ vt besteigen; **ascent** n Aufstieg m; Besteigung f

ascertain [æsə'teɪn] *vt* feststellen

ascribe [ə'skraɪb] *vt*: **to ~ sth to sth / sth to sb** etw einer Sache/jdm etw zuschreiben

ash [æʃ] *n* Asche *f*; (*tree*) Esche *f*

ashamed [ə'ʃeɪmd] *adj* beschämt; **to be ~ of sth** sich für etw schämen

ashen ['æʃən] *adj* (*pale*) aschfahl

ashore [ə'ʃɔːr] *adv* an Land

ashtray ['æʃtreɪ] *n* Aschenbecher *m*

Ash Wednesday *n* Aschermittwoch *m*

Asia ['eɪʃə] *n* Asien *nt*; **~n** *adj* asiatisch ♦ *n* Asiat(in) *m(f)*

aside [ə'saɪd] *adv* beiseite

ask [ɑːsk] *vt* fragen; (*permission*) bitten um; **~ him his name** frage ihn nach seinem Namen; **he ~ed to see you** er wollte dich sehen; **to ~ sb to do sth** jdn bitten, etw zu tun; **to ~ sb about sth** jdn nach etw fragen; **to ~ (sb) a question** (jdn) etwas fragen; **to ~ sb out to dinner** jdn zum Essen einladen; **~ after** *vt fus* fragen nach; **~ for** *vt fus* bitten um

askance [ə'skɑːns] *adv*: **to look ~ at sb** jdn schief ansehen

asking price ['ɑːskɪŋ-] *n* Verkaufspreis *m*

asleep [ə'sliːp] *adj*: **to be ~** schlafen; **to fall ~** einschlafen

asparagus [əs'pærəgəs] *n* Spargel *m*

aspect ['æspekt] *n* Aspekt *m*

aspersions [əs'pɜːʃənz] *npl*: **to cast ~ on sb/sth** sich abfällig über jdn/etw äußern

asphyxiation [æsfɪksɪ'eɪʃən] *n* Erstickung *f*

aspirations [æspə'reɪʃənz] *npl*: **to have ~ towards sth** etw anstreben

aspire [əs'paɪər] *vi*: **to ~** to streben nach

aspirin ['æsprɪn] *n* Aspirin *nt*

ass [æs] *n* (*also fig*) Esel *m*; (*US: inf!*) Arsch *m* (!)

assailant [ə'seɪlənt] *n* Angreifer *m*

assassin [ə'sæsɪn] *n* Attentäter(in) *m(f)*; **~ate** *vt* ermorden; **~ation** [əsæsɪ'neɪʃən] *n* (geglückte(s)) Attentat *nt*

assault [ə'sɔːlt] *n* Angriff *m* ♦ *vt* überfallen; (*woman*) herfallen über +*acc*

assemble [ə'sɛmbl] *vt* versammeln; (*parts*) zusammensetzen ♦ *vi* sich versammeln; **assembly** *n* (*meeting*) Versammlung *f*; (*construction*) Zusammensetzung *f*, Montage *f*; **assembly line** *n* Fließband *nt*

assent [ə'sɛnt] *n* Zustimmung *f*

assert [ə'sɜːt] *vt* erklären; **~ion** *n* Behauptung *f*

assess [ə'sɛs] *vt* schätzen; **~ment** *n* Bewertung *f*, Einschätzung *f*; **~or** *n* Steuerberater *m*

asset ['æsɛt] *n* Vorteil *m*, Wert *m*; **~s** *npl* (*FIN*) Vermögen *nt*; (*estate*) Nachlass *m*

assign [ə'saɪn] *vt* zuweisen; **~ment** *n* Aufgabe *f*, Auftrag *m*

assimilate [ə'sɪmɪleɪt] *vt* sich aneignen, aufnehmen

assist [ə'sɪst] *vt* beistehen +*dat*; **~ance** *n* Unterstützung *f*, Hilfe *f*; **~ant** *n* Assistent(in) *m(f)*, Mitarbeiter(in) *m(f)*; (*BRIT: also:* **shop ~ant**) Verkäufer(in) *m(f)*

associate [*n* ə'səʊʃɪɪt, *vb* ə'səʊʃɪeɪt] *n* (*partner*) Kollege *m*, Teilhaber *m*; (*member*) außerordentliche(s) Mitglied *nt* ♦ *vt* verbinden ♦ *vi* (*keep company*) verkehren; **association** [əsəʊsɪ'eɪʃən] *n* Verband *m*, Verein *m*; (*PSYCH*) Assoziation *f*; (*link*) Verbindung *f*

assorted [ə'sɔːtɪd] *adj* gemischt

assortment [ə'sɔːtmənt] *n* Sammlung *f*; (*COMM*): **~ (of)** Sortiment *nt* (von), Auswahl *f* (an +*dat*)

assume [ə'sjuːm] *vt* (*take for granted*) annehmen; (*put on*) annehmen, sich geben; **~d name** *n* Deckname *m*

assumption [ə'sʌmpʃən] *n* Annahme *f*

assurance [ə'ʃʊərəns] *n* (*firm statement*) Versicherung *f*; (*confidence*) Selbstsicherheit *f*; (*insurance*) (Lebens)versicherung *f*

assure [ə'ʃʊər] *vt* (*make sure*) sicherstellen; (*convince*) versichern +*dat*; (*life*) versichern

asterisk ['æstərɪsk] *n* Sternchen *nt*

asthma ['æsmə] *n* Asthma *nt*

astonish [ə'stɒnɪʃ] *vt* erstaunen; **~ment** *n* Erstaunen *nt*

astound [ə'staʊnd] *vt* verblüffen

astray [ə'streɪ] *adv* in die Irre; auf Abwege; **to go ~** (*go wrong*) sich vertun; **to lead ~** irreführen

astride [ə'straɪd] *adv* rittlings ♦ *prep* rittlings

auf

astrologer [əs'trɔlədʒər] *n* Astrologe *m*, Astrologin *f*; **astrology** *n* Astrologie *f*

astronaut ['æstrənɔ:t] *n* Astronaut(in) *m(f)*

astronomer [əs'trɔnəmər] *n* Astronom *m*

astronomical [æstrə'nɔmɪkl] *adj* astronomisch; *(success)* riesig

astronomy [əs'trɔnəmi] *n* Astronomie *f*

astute [əs'tju:t] *adj* scharfsinnig; schlau, gerissen

asylum [ə'saɪləm] *n (home)* Heim *nt*; *(refuge)* Asyl *nt*

KEYWORD

at [æt] *prep* **1** *(referring to position, direction)* an +*dat*, bei +*dat*; *(with place)* in +*dat*; **at the top** an der Spitze; **at home/school** zu Hause/in der Schule; **at the baker's** beim Bäcker; **to look at sth** auf etw *acc* blicken; **to throw sth at sb** etw nach jdm werfen

2 *(referring to time)*: **at 4 o'clock** um 4 Uhr; **at night** bei Nacht; **at Christmas** zu Weihnachten; **at times** manchmal

3 *(referring to rates, speed etc)*: **at £1 a kilo** zu £1 pro Kilo; **two at a time** zwei auf einmal; **at 50 km/h** mit 50 km/h

4 *(referring to manner)*: **at a stroke** mit einem Schlag; **at peace** in Frieden

5 *(referring to activity)*: **to be at work** bei der Arbeit sein; **to play at cowboys** Cowboy spielen; **to be good at sth** gut in etw *dat* sein

6 *(referring to cause)*: **shocked/surprised/annoyed at sth** schockiert/überrascht/verärgert über etw *acc*; **I went at his suggestion** ich ging auf seinen Vorschlag hin

---

ate [eɪt] *pt of* **eat**

atheist ['eɪθɪɪst] *n* Atheist(in) *m(f)*

Athens ['æθɪnz] *n* Athen *nt*

athlete ['æθli:t] *n* Athlet *m*, Sportler *m*

athletic [æθ'letɪk] *adj* sportlich, athletisch; **~s** *n* Leichtathletik *f*

Atlantic [ət'læntɪk] *adj* atlantisch ♦ *n*: **the ~ (Ocean)** der Atlantik

atlas ['ætləs] *n* Atlas *m*

ATM *abbr (= automated teller machine)* Geldautomat *m*

atmosphere ['ætməsfɪər] *n* Atmosphäre *f*

atom ['ætəm] *n* Atom *nt*; *(fig)* bisschen *nt*; **~ic** [ə'tɔmɪk] *adj* atomar, Atom-; **~(ic) bomb** *n* Atombombe *f*

atomizer ['ætəmaɪzər] *n* Zerstäuber *m*

atone [ə'təun] *vi* sühnen; **to ~ for sth** etw sühnen

atrocious [ə'trəuʃəs] *adj* grässlich

atrocity [ə'trɔsɪtɪ] *n* Scheußlichkeit *f*; *(deed)* Gräueltat *f*

attach [ə'tætʃ] *vt (fasten)* befestigen; **to be ~ed to sb/sth** an jdm/etw hängen; **to ~ importance etc to sth** Wichtigkeit *etc* auf etw *acc* legen, einer Sache *dat* Wichtigkeit *etc* beimessen

attaché case [ə'tæʃeɪ] *n* Aktenkoffer *m*

attachment [ə'tætʃmənt] *n (tool)* Zubehörteil *nt*; *(love)*: **~ (to sb)** Zuneigung *f* (zu jdm)

attack [ə'tæk] *vt* angreifen ♦ *n* Angriff *m*; *(MED)* Anfall *m*; **~er** *n* Angreifer(in) *m(f)*

attain [ə'teɪn] *vt* erreichen; **~ments** *npl* Kenntnisse *pl*

attempt [ə'tempt] *n* Versuch *m* ♦ *vt* versuchen; **~ed murder** Mordversuch *m*

attend [ə'tend] *vt (go to)* teilnehmen (an +*dat*); *(lectures)* besuchen; **to ~ to** *(needs)* nachkommen +*dat*; *(person)* sich kümmern um; **~ance** *n (presence)* Anwesenheit *f*; *(people present)* Besucherzahl *f*; **good ~ance** gute Teilnahme; **~ant** *n (companion)* Begleiter(in) *m(f)*; Gesellschafter(in) *m(f)*; *(in car park etc)* Wächter(in) *m(f)*; *(servant)* Bedienstete(r) *mf* ♦ *adj* begleitend; *(fig)* damit verbunden

attention [ə'tenʃən] *n* Aufmerksamkeit *f*; *(care)* Fürsorge *f*; *(for machine etc)* Pflege *f* ♦ *excl (MIL)* Achtung!; **for the ~ of ...** zu Händen (von) ...

attentive [ə'tentɪv] *adj* aufmerksam

attic ['ætɪk] *n* Dachstube *f*, Mansarde *f*

attitude ['ætɪtju:d] *n (mental)* Einstellung *f*

attorney [ə'tə:nɪ] *n (solicitor)* Rechtsanwalt *m*; **A~ General** *n* Justizminister *m*

attract [ə'trækt] *vt* anziehen; *(attention)*

erregen; ~ion n Anziehungskraft f; (thing)
Attraktion f; ~ive adj attraktiv

attribute [n 'ætrɪbjuːt, vb ə'trɪbjuːt] n
Eigenschaft f, Attribut nt ♦ vt zuschreiben

attrition [ə'trɪʃən] n: war of ~
Zermürbungskrieg m

aubergine ['əubəʒiːn] n Aubergine f

auburn ['ɔːbən] adj kastanienbraun

auction ['ɔːkʃən] n (also: sale by ~)
Versteigerung f, Auktion f ♦ vt versteigern;
~eer [ɔːkʃə'nɪə] n Versteigerer m

audacity [ɔː'dæsɪtɪ] n (boldness) Wagemut m;
(impudence) Unverfrorenheit f

audible ['ɔːdɪbl] adj hörbar

audience ['ɔːdɪəns] n Zuhörer pl, Zuschauer
pl; (with queen) Audienz f

audiotypist ['ɔːdɪəʊtaɪpɪst] n Phonotypistin
f, Fonotypistin f

audiovisual ['ɔːdɪəʊ'vɪzjʊəl] adj audiovisuell

audit ['ɔːdɪt] vt prüfen

audition [ɔː'dɪʃən] n Probe f

auditor ['ɔːdɪtə] n (accountant)
Rechnungsprüfer(in) m(f), Buchprüfer m

auditorium [ɔːdɪ'tɔːrɪəm] n Zuschauerraum
m

augment [ɔːg'mɛnt] vt vermehren

augur ['ɔːgə] vi bedeuten, voraussagen; this
~s well das ist ein gutes Omen

August ['ɔːgəst] n August m

aunt [ɑːnt] n Tante f; ~ie n Tantchen nt; ~y
n = auntie

au pair ['əu'pɛə] n (also: ~ girl)
Aupairmädchen nt, Au-pair-Mädchen nt

aura ['ɔːrə] n Nimbus m

auspicious [ɔːs'pɪʃəs] adj günstig;
verheißungsvoll

austere [ɔs'tɪə] adj streng; (room) nüchtern;
austerity [ɔs'tɛrɪtɪ] n Strenge f; (POL)
wirtschaftliche Einschränkung f

Australia [ɔs'treɪlɪə] n Australien nt; ~n adj
australisch ♦ n Australier(in) m(f)

Austria ['ɔstrɪə] n Österreich nt; ~n adj
österreichisch ♦ n Österreicher(in) m(f)

authentic [ɔː'θɛntɪk] adj echt, authentisch

author ['ɔːθə] n Autor m, Schriftsteller m;
(beginner) Urheber m, Schöpfer m

authoritarian [ɔːθɔrɪ'tɛərɪən] adj autoritär

authoritative [ɔː'θɔrɪtətɪv] adj (account)
maßgeblich; (manner) herrisch

authority [ɔː'θɔrɪtɪ] n (power) Autorität f;
(expert) Autorität f, Fachmann m; the
authorities npl (ruling body) die Behörden
pl

authorize ['ɔːθəraɪz] vt bevollmächtigen;
(permit) genehmigen

auto ['ɔːtəu] (US) n Auto nt, Wagen m

autobiography [ɔːtəbaɪ'ɔgrəfɪ] n
Autobiografie f

autograph ['ɔːtəgrɑːf] n (of celebrity)
Autogramm nt ♦ vt mit Autogramm
versehen

automatic [ɔːtə'mætɪk] adj automatisch ♦ n
(gun) Selbstladepistole f; (car) Automatik m;
~ally adv automatisch

automation [ɔːtə'meɪʃən] n Automatisierung
f

automobile ['ɔːtəməbiːl] (US) n Auto(mobil)
nt

autonomous [ɔː'tɔnəməs] adj autonom;
autonomy n Autonomie f

autumn ['ɔːtəm] n Herbst m

auxiliary [ɔːg'zɪlɪərɪ] adj Hilfs-

Av. abbr = avenue

avail [ə'veɪl] vt: to ~ o.s. of sth sich einer
Sache gen bedienen ♦ n: to no ~ nutzlos

availability [əveɪlə'bɪlɪtɪ] n Erhältlichkeit f,
Vorhandensein nt

available [ə'veɪləbl] adj erhältlich; zur
Verfügung stehend; (person) erreichbar,
abkömmlich

avalanche ['ævəlɑːnʃ] n Lawine f

Ave. abbr = avenue

avenge [ə'vɛndʒ] vt rächen, sühnen

avenue ['ævənjuː] n Allee f

average ['ævərɪdʒ] n Durchschnitt m ♦ adj
durchschnittlich, Durchschnitts- ♦ vt
(figures) den Durchschnitt nehmen von;
(perform) durchschnittlich leisten; (in car etc)
im Schnitt fahren; on ~ durchschnittlich,
im Durchschnitt; ~ out vi: to ~ out at im
Durchschnitt betragen

averse [ə'vɜːs] adj: to be ~ to doing sth
eine Abneigung dagegen haben, etw zu
tun

avert [ə'vɜːt] vt (*turn away*) abkehren; (*prevent*) abwehren

aviary ['eɪvɪərɪ] n Vogelhaus nt

aviation [eɪvɪ'eɪʃən] n Luftfahrt f, Flugwesen nt

avid ['ævɪd] adj: ~ **(for)** gierig (auf +acc)

avocado [ævə'kɑːdəʊ] n (*BRIT: also:* ~ **pear**) Avocado(birne) f

avoid [ə'vɔɪd] vt vermeiden

await [ə'weɪt] vt erwarten, entgegensehen +dat

awake [ə'weɪk] (*pt* **awoke**, *pp* **awoken** *or* **awaked**) adj wach ♦ vt (auf)wecken ♦ vi aufwachen; **to be** ~ wach sein; ~**ning** n Erwachen nt

award [ə'wɔːd] n (*prize*) Preis m ♦ vt: **to** ~ **(sb sth)** (jdm etw) zuerkennen

aware [ə'weə] adj bewusst; **to be** ~ sich bewusst sein; ~**ness** n Bewusstsein nt

awash [ə'wɒʃ] adj überflutet

away [ə'weɪ] adv weg, fort; **two hours** ~ **by car** zwei Autostunden entfernt; **the holiday was two weeks** ~ es war noch zwei Wochen bis zum Urlaub; **two kilometres** ~ zwei Kilometer entfernt; ~ **match** n (*SPORT*) Auswärtsspiel nt

awe [ɔː] n Ehrfurcht f; ~**-inspiring** adj Ehrfurcht gebietend; ~**some** adj Ehrfurcht gebietend

awful ['ɔːfəl] adj (*very bad*) furchtbar; ~**ly** adv furchtbar, sehr

awhile [ə'waɪl] adv eine Weile

awkward ['ɔːkwəd] adj (*clumsy*) ungeschickt, linkisch; (*embarrassing*) peinlich

awning ['ɔːnɪŋ] n Markise f

awoke [ə'wəuk] pt of **awake**; ~**n** pp of **awake**

awry [ə'raɪ] adv schief; (*plans*) schief gehen

axe [æks] (*US* **ax**) n Axt f, Beil nt ♦ vt (*end suddenly*) streichen

axes[1] ['æksɪz] npl of **axe**

axes[2] ['æksiːz] npl of **axis**

axis ['æksɪs] (*pl* **axes**) n Achse f

axle ['æksl] n Achse f

ay(e) [aɪ] excl (*yes*) ja

azalea [ə'zeɪlɪə] n Azalee f

B, b

B [biː] n (*MUS*) H nt; ~ **road** (*BRIT*) Landstraße f

B.A. n abbr = **Bachelor of Arts**

babble ['bæbl] vi schwätzen

baby ['beɪbɪ] n Baby nt; ~ **carriage** (*US*) n Kinderwagen m; ~ **food** n Babynahrung f; ~**-sit** vi Kinder hüten, babysitten; ~**-sitter** n Babysitter m; ~**sitting** n Babysitten nt, Babysitting nt; ~ **wipe** n Ölpflegetuch nt

bachelor ['bætʃələr] n Junggeselle m; **B~ of Arts** Bakkalaureus m der philosophischen Fakultät; **B~ of Science** Bakkalaureus m der Naturwissenschaften

back [bæk] n (*of person, horse*) Rücken m; (*of house*) Rückseite f; (*of train*) Ende nt; (*FOOTBALL*) Verteidiger m ♦ vt (*support*) unterstützen; (*wager*) wetten auf +acc; (*car*) rückwärts fahren ♦ vi (*go ~wards*) rückwärts gehen *or* fahren ♦ adj hintere(r, s) ♦ adv zurück; (*to the rear*) nach hinten; ~ **down** vi zurückstecken; ~ **out** vi sich zurückziehen; (*inf*) kneifen; ~ **up** vt (*support*) unterstützen; (*car*) zurücksetzen; (*COMPUT*) eine Sicherungskopie machen von; ~**ache** n Rückenschmerzen pl; ~**bencher** (*BRIT*) n Parlamentarier(in) m(f); ~**bone** n Rückgrat nt; (*support*) Rückhalt m; ~**cloth** n Hintergrund m; ~**date** vt rückdatieren; ~**drop** n (*THEAT*) = **backcloth**; (*~ground*) Hintergrund m; ~**fire** vi (*plan*) fehlschlagen; (*TECH*) fehlzünden; ~**ground** n Hintergrund m; (*person's education*) Vorbildung f; **family ~ground** Familienverhältnisse pl; ~**hand** n (*TENNIS: also:* ~**hand stroke**) Rückhand f; ~**hander** (*BRIT*) n (*bribe*) Schmiergeld nt; ~**ing** n (*support*) Unterstützung f; ~**lash** n (*fig*) Gegenschlag m; ~**log** n (*of work*) Rückstand m; ~ **number** n (*PRESS*) alte Nummer f; ~**pack** n Rucksack m; ~**packer** n Rucksacktourist(in) m(f); ~ **pain** n Rückenschmerzen pl; ~ **pay** n (Gehalts- or Lohn)nachzahlung f; ~ **payments** npl

Zahlungsrückstände pl; ~ **seat** n (AUT)
Rücksitz m; **~side** (inf) n Hintern m;
~stage adv hinter den Kulissen; **~stroke** n
Rückenschwimmen nt; **~up** adj (COMPUT)
Sicherungs- ♦ n (COMPUT) Sicherungskopie
f; **~ward** adj (less developed)
zurückgeblieben; (primitive) rückständig;
~wards adv rückwärts; **~water** n (fig) Kaff
nt; **~yard** n Hinterhof m

bacon ['beɪkən] n Schinkenspeck m
bacteria [bæk'tɪərɪə] npl Bakterien pl
bad [bæd] adj schlecht, schlimm; **to go ~**
schlecht werden
bade [bæd] pt of **bid**
badge [bædʒ] n Abzeichen nt
badger ['bædʒə*] n Dachs m
badly ['bædlɪ] adv schlecht, schlimm; **~**
wounded schwer verwundet; **he needs it**
~ off (for
money) dringend Geld nötig haben
badminton ['bædmɪntən] n Federball m,
Badminton nt
bad-tempered ['bæd'tempəd] adj schlecht
gelaunt
baffle ['bæfl] vt (puzzle) verblüffen
bag [bæg] n (sack) Beutel m; (paper) Tüte f;
(handbag) Tasche f; (suitcase) Koffer m; (inf:
old woman) alte Schachtel f ♦ vt (put in sack)
in einen Sack stecken; (hunting) erlegen; **~s**
of (inf: lots of) eine Menge +acc; **~gage**
['bægɪdʒ] n Gepäck nt; **~ allowance** n
Freigepäck nt; **~ reclaim** n
Gepäckausgabe f; **~gy** ['bægɪ] adj bauschig,
sackartig
bagpipes ['bægpaɪps] npl Dudelsack m
bail [beɪl] n (money) Kaution f ♦ vt (prisoner:
usu: grant ~ to) gegen Kaution freilassen;
(boat: also: ~ **out**) ausschöpfen; **on ~**
(prisoner) gegen Kaution freigelassen; **to ~**
sb out die Kaution für jdn stellen; see also
bale
bailiff ['beɪlɪf] n Gerichtsvollzieher(in) m(f)
bait [beɪt] n Köder m ♦ vt mit einem Köder
versehen; (fig) ködern
bake [beɪk] vt, vi backen; **~d beans**
gebackene Bohnen pl; **~d potatoes** npl in
der Schale gebackene Kartoffeln pl; **~r** n

Bäcker m; **~ry** n Bäckerei f; **baking** n
Backen nt; **baking powder** n Backpulver
nt
balance ['bæləns] n (scales) Waage f;
(equilibrium) Gleichgewicht nt; (FIN: state of
account) Saldo m; (difference) Bilanz f;
(amount remaining) Restbetrag m ♦ vt
(weigh) wägen; (make equal) ausgleichen; **~**
of trade/payments Handels-/
Zahlungsbilanz f; **~d** adj ausgeglichen; **~**
sheet n Bilanz f, Rechnungsabschluss m
balcony ['bælkənɪ] n Balkon m
bald [bɔːld] adj kahl; (statement) knapp
bale [beɪl] n Ballen m; **bale out** vi (from a
plane) abspringen
ball [bɔːl] n Ball m; **~ bearing** n Kugellager
nt
ballet ['bæleɪ] n Ballett nt; **~ dancer** n
Balletttänzer(in) m(f); **~ shoe** n
Ballettschuh m
balloon [bə'luːn] n (Luft)ballon m
ballot ['bælət] n (geheime) Abstimmung f
ballpoint (pen) ['bɔːlpɔɪnt-] n
Kugelschreiber m
ballroom ['bɔːlrum] n Tanzsaal m
Baltic ['bɔːltɪk] n: **the ~ (Sea)** die Ostsee
bamboo [bæm'buː] n Bambus m
ban [bæn] n Verbot nt ♦ vt verbieten
banana [bə'nɑːnə] n Banane f
band [bænd] n Band nt; (group) Gruppe f; (of
criminals) Bande f; (MUS) Kapelle f, Band f;
~ together vi sich zusammentun
bandage ['bændɪdʒ] n Verband m; (elastic)
Bandage f ♦ vt (cut) verbinden; (broken
limb) bandagieren
Bandaid ['bændeɪd] (® US) n Heftpflaster nt
bandit ['bændɪt] n Bandit m, Räuber m
bandwagon ['bændwægən] n: **to jump on**
the ~ (fig) auf den fahrenden Zug
aufspringen
bandy ['bændɪ] vt wechseln; **~-legged** adj
o-beinig, O-beinig
bang [bæŋ] n (explosion) Knall m; (blow) Hieb
m ♦ vt, vi knallen
Bangladesh [bæŋglə'deʃ] n Bangladesch nt
bangle ['bæŋgl] n Armspange f
bangs [bæŋz] (US) npl (fringe) Pony m

banish [ˈbænɪʃ] vt verbannen

banister(s) [ˈbænɪstə(z)] n(pl) (Treppen)geländer nt

bank [bæŋk] n (raised ground) Erdwall m; (of lake etc) Ufer nt; (FIN) Bank f ♦ vt (tilt: AVIAT) in die Kurve bringen; (money) einzahlen; **on** vt fus: **to ~ on sth** mit etw rechnen; **~ account** n Bankkonto nt; **~ card** n Scheckkarte f; **~er** n Bankier m; **~er's card** (BRIT) n = bank card; **B~ holiday** (BRIT) n gesetzliche(r) Feiertag m; **~ing** n Bankwesen nt; **~note** n Banknote f; **~ rate** n Banksatz m

---
bank holiday
---

i Als **bank holiday** wird in Großbritannien ein gesetzlicher Feiertag bezeichnet, an dem die Banken geschlossen sind. Die meisten dieser Feiertage, abgesehen von Weihnachten und Ostern, fallen auf Montage im Mai und August. An diesen langen Wochenenden (bank holiday weekends) fahren viele Briten in Urlaub, so dass dann auf den Straßen, Flughäfen und bei der Bahn sehr viel Betrieb ist.

---

bankrupt [ˈbæŋkrʌpt] adj: **to be ~** bankrott sein; **to go ~** Bankrott machen; **~cy** n Bankrott m

bank statement n Kontoauszug m

banned [bænd] adj: **he was ~ from driving** (BRIT) ihm wurde Fahrverbot erteilt

banner [ˈbænə] n Banner nt

banns [bænz] npl Aufgebot nt

baptism [ˈbæptɪzəm] n Taufe f

baptize [bæpˈtaɪz] vt taufen

bar [bɑː] n (rod) Stange f; (obstacle) Hindernis nt; (of chocolate) Tafel f; (of soap) Stück nt; (for food, drink) Buffet nt, Bar f; (pub) Wirtschaft f; (MUS) Takt(strich) m ♦ vt (fasten) verriegeln; (hinder) versperren; (exclude) ausschließen; **behind ~s** hinter Gittern; **the B~:** **to be called to the B~** als Anwalt zugelassen werden; **~ none** ohne Ausnahme

barbaric [bɑːˈbærɪk] adj primitiv, unkultiviert

barbecue [ˈbɑːbɪkjuː] n Barbecue nt

barbed wire [ˈbɑːbd-] n Stacheldraht m

barber [ˈbɑːbə] n Herrenfriseur m

bar code n (COMM) Registrierkode f

bare [bɛə] adj nackt; (trees, country) kahl; (mere) bloß ♦ vt entblößen; **~back** adv ungesattelt; **~faced** adj unverfroren; **~foot** adj, adv barfuß; **~ly** adv kaum, knapp

bargain [ˈbɑːgɪn] n (sth cheap) günstiger Kauf; (agreement: written) Kaufvertrag m; (: oral) Geschäft nt; **into the ~** obendrein; **~ for** vt: **he got more than he ~ed for** er erlebte sein blaues Wunder

barge [bɑːdʒ] n Lastkahn m; **~ in** vi hereinplatzen; **~ into** vt rennen gegen

bark [bɑːk] n (of tree) Rinde f; (of dog) Bellen nt ♦ vi (dog) bellen

barley [ˈbɑːlɪ] n Gerste f; **~ sugar** n Malzbonbon m

bar: **~maid** n Bardame f; **~man** (irreg) n Barkellner m; **~ meal** n einfaches Essen in einem Pub

barn [bɑːn] n Scheune f

barometer [bəˈrɒmɪtə] n Barometer nt

baron [ˈbærən] n Baron m; **~ess** n Baronin f

barracks [ˈbærəks] npl Kaserne f

barrage [ˈbærɑːʒ] n (gunfire) Sperrfeuer nt; (dam) Staudamm m; Talsperre f

barrel [ˈbærəl] n Fass nt; (of gun) Lauf m

barren [ˈbærən] adj unfruchtbar

barricade [bærɪˈkeɪd] n Barrikade f ♦ vt verbarrikadieren

barrier [ˈbærɪə] n (obstruction) Hindernis nt; (fence) Schranke f

barring [ˈbɑːrɪŋ] prep außer im Falle +gen

barrister [ˈbærɪstə] (BRIT) n Rechtsanwalt m

barrow [ˈbærəʊ] n (cart) Schubkarren m

bartender [ˈbɑːtendə] (US) n Barmann or -kellner m

barter [ˈbɑːtə] vt handeln

base [beɪs] n (bottom) Boden m, Basis f; (MIL) Stützpunkt m ♦ vt gründen; (opinion, theory): **to be ~d on** basieren auf +dat ♦ adj (low) gemein; **I'm ~d in London** ich wohne in London; **~ball** [ˈbeɪsbɔːl] n Baseball m; **~ment** [ˈbeɪsmənt] n Kellergeschoss nt

bases[1] [ˈbeɪsɪz] npl of **base**

bases[2] [ˈbeɪsiːz] npl of **basis**

bash [bæʃ] (*inf*) *vt* (heftig) schlagen

bashful ['bæʃful] *adj* schüchtern

basic ['beɪsɪk] *adj* grundlegend; **~s** *npl*: **the ~s** das Wesentliche *sg*; **~ally** *adv* im Grunde

basil ['bæzl] *n* Basilikum *nt*

basin ['beɪsn] *n* (*dish*) Schüssel *f*; (*for washing, also valley*) Becken *nt*; (*dock*) (Trocken)becken *nt*

basis ['beɪsɪs] (*pl* **bases**) *n* Basis *f*, Grundlage *f*

bask [bɑːsk] *vi*: **to ~ in the sun** sich sonnen

basket ['bɑːskɪt] *n* Korb *m*; **~ball** *n* Basketball *m*

bass [beɪs] *n* (*MUS, also instrument*) Bass *m*; (*voice*) Bassstimme *f*; **~ drum** *n* große Trommel

bassoon [bə'suːn] *n* Fagott *nt*

bastard ['bɑːstəd] *n* Bastard *m*; (*inf!*) Arschloch *nt* (*!*)

bat [bæt] *n* (*SPORT*) Schlagholz *nt*; Schläger *m*; (*ZOOL*) Fledermaus *f* ♦ *vt*: **he didn't ~ an eyelid** er hat nicht mit der Wimper gezuckt

batch [bætʃ] *n* (*of letters*) Stoß *m*; (*of samples*) Satz *m*

bated ['beɪtɪd] *adj*: **with ~ breath** mit angehaltenem Atem

bath [bɑːθ] *n* Bad *nt*; (~ *tub*) Badewanne *f* ♦ *vt* baden; **to have a ~** baden; *see also* **baths**

bathe [beɪð] *vt*, *vi* baden; **~r** *n* Badende(r) *f(m)*

bathing ['beɪðɪŋ] *n* Baden *nt*; **~ cap** *n* Badekappe *f*; **~ costume** *n* Badeanzug *m*; **~ suit** (*US*) *n* Badeanzug *m*; **~ trunks** (*BRIT*) *npl* Badehose *f*

bath: **~robe** *n* Bademantel *m*; **~room** *n* Bad(ezimmer *nt*) *nt*; **~s** *npl* (Schwimm)bad *nt*; **~ towel** *n* Badetuch *nt*

baton ['bætən] *n* (*of police*) Gummiknüppel *m*; (*MUS*) Taktstock *m*

batter ['bætər] *vt* verprügeln ♦ *n* Schlagteig *m*; (*for cake*) Biskuitteig *m*; **~ed** *adj* (*hat, pan*) verbeult

battery ['bætərɪ] *n* (*ELEC*) Batterie *f*; (*MIL*) Geschützbatterie *f*

battery farming *n* (Hühner- *etc*)

batterien *pl*

battle ['bætl] *n* Schlacht *f*; (*small*) Gefecht *nt* ♦ *vi* kämpfen; **~field** *n* Schlachtfeld *nt*; **~ship** *n* Schlachtschiff *nt*

Bavaria [bə'veərɪə] *n* Bayern *nt*; **~n** *adj* bay(e)risch ♦ *n* (*person*) Bayer(in) *m(f)*

bawdy ['bɔːdɪ] *adj* unflätig

bawl [bɔːl] *vi* brüllen

bay [beɪ] *n* (*of sea*) Bucht *f* ♦ *vi* bellen; **to keep at ~** unter Kontrolle halten; **~ window** *n* Erkerfenster *nt*

bazaar [bə'zɑːr] *n* Basar *m*

B. & B. *abbr* = **bed and breakfast**

BBC *n abbr* (= *British Broadcasting Corporation*) BBC *f or m*

B.C. *adv abbr* (= *before Christ*) v. Chr.

KEYWORD

be [biː] (*pt* **was**, **were**, *pp* **been**) *aux vb*
1 (*with present participle: forming continuous tenses*): **what are you doing?** was machst du (gerade)?; **it is raining** es regnet; **I've been waiting for you for hours** ich warte schon seit Stunden auf dich

2 (*with pp: forming passives*): **to be killed** getötet werden; **the thief was nowhere to be seen** der Dieb war nirgendwo zu sehen

3 (*in tag questions*): **it was fun, wasn't it?** es hat Spaß gemacht, nicht wahr?

4 (+*to* +*infin*): **the house is to be sold** das Haus soll verkauft werden; **he's not to open it** er darf es nicht öffnen

♦ *vb* +*complement* **1** (*usu*) sein; **I'm tired** ich bin müde; **I'm hot/cold** mir ist heiß/kalt; **he's a doctor** er ist Arzt; **2 and 2 are 4** 2 und 2 ist *or* sind 4; **she's tall/pretty** sie ist groß/hübsch; **be careful/quiet** sei vorsichtig/ruhig

2 (*of health*): **how are you?** wie geht es dir?; **he's very ill** er ist sehr krank; **I'm fine now** jetzt geht es mir gut

3 (*of age*): **how old are you?** wie alt bist du?; **I'm sixteen (years old)** ich bin sechzehn (Jahre alt)

4 (*cost*): **how much was the meal?** was *or* wie viel hat das Essen gekostet?; **that'll be £5.75, please** das macht £5.75, bitte

♦ vi 1 (exist, occur etc) sein; **is there a God?** gibt es einen Gott?; **be that as it may** wie dem auch sei; **so be it** also gut 2 (referring to place) sein; **I won't be here tomorrow** iche werde morgen nicht hier sein

3 (referring to movement): **where have you been?** wo bist du gewesen?; **I've been in the garden** ich war im Garten

♦ impers vb 1 (referring to time, distance, weather) sein; **it's 5 o'clock** es ist 5 Uhr; **it's 10 km to the village** es sind 10 km bis zum Dorf; **it's too hot/cold** es ist zu heiß/kalt

2 (emphatic): **it's me** ich bins; **it's the postman** es ist der Briefträger

beach [biːtʃ] n Strand m ♦ vt (ship) auf den Strand setzen

beacon ['biːkən] n (signal) Leuchtfeuer nt; (traffic ~) Bake f

bead [biːd] n Perle f; (drop) Tropfen m

beak [biːk] n Schnabel m

beaker ['biːkər] n Becher m

beam [biːm] n (of wood) Balken m; (of light) Strahl m; (smile) strahlende(s) Lächeln nt ♦ vi strahlen

bean [biːn] n Bohne f; (also: **baked ~s**) gebackene Bohnen pl; **~ sprouts** npl Sojasprossen pl

bear [bɛər] (pt **bore**, pp **borne**) n Bär m ♦ vt (weight, crops) tragen; (tolerate) ertragen; (young) gebären ♦ vi: **to ~ right/left** sich rechts/links halten; **~ out** vt (suspicions etc) bestätigen; **~ up** vi sich halten

beard [bɪəd] n Bart m; **~ed** adj bärtig

bearer ['bɛərər] n Träger m

bearing ['bɛərɪŋ] n (posture) Haltung f; (relevance) Relevanz f; (relation) Bedeutung f; (TECH) Kugellager nt; **~s** npl (direction) Orientierung f; (also: **ball ~s**) (Kugel)lager nt

beast [biːst] n Tier nt, Vieh nt; (person) Biest nt

beat [biːt] (pt **beat**, pp **beaten**) n (stroke) Schlag m; (pulsation) (Herz)schlag m; (police round) Runde f; Revier nt; (MUS) Takt m;

Beat m ♦ vt, vi schlagen; **to ~ it** abhauen; **off the ~en track** abgelegen; **~ off** vt abschlagen; **~ up** vt zusammenschlagen; **~en** pp of **beat**; **~ing** n Prügel pl

beautiful ['bjuːtɪful] adj schön; **~ly** adv ausgezeichnet

beauty ['bjuːtɪ] n Schönheit f; **~ salon** n Schönheitssalon m; **~ spot** n Schönheitsfleck m; (BRIT: TOURISM) (besonders) schöne(r) Ort m

beaver ['biːvər] n Biber m

became [bɪ'keɪm] pt of **become**

because [bɪ'kɔz] conj weil ♦ prep: **~ of** wegen +gen, wegen +dat (inf)

beck [bek] n: **to be at the ~ and call of sb** nach jds Pfeife tanzen

beckon ['bekən] vt, vi: **to ~ to sb** jdm ein Zeichen geben

become [bɪ'kʌm] (irreg: like **come**) vi werden ♦ vt werden; (clothes) stehen +dat

becoming [bɪ'kʌmɪŋ] adj (suitable) schicklich; (clothes) kleidsam

bed [bed] n Bett nt; (of river) Flussbett nt; (foundation) Schicht f; (in garden) Beet nt; **to go to ~** zu Bett gehen; **~ and breakfast** n Übernachtung f mit Frühstück; **~clothes** npl Bettwäsche f; **~ding** n Bettzeug nt

---

Bed and Breakfast

ⓘ **Bed and Breakfast** bedeutet "Übernachtung mit Frühstück", wobei sich dies in Großbritannien nicht auf Hotels, sondern auf kleinere Pensionen, Privathäuser und Bauernhöfe bezieht, wo man wesentlich preisgünstiger übernachten kann als in Hotels. Oft wird für Bed and Breakfast, auch B & B genannt, durch ein entsprechendes Schild im Garten oder an der Einfahrt geworben.

---

bedlam ['bedləm] n (uproar) tolle(s) Durcheinander nt

bed linen n Bettwäsche f

bedraggled [bɪ'dræɡld] adj ramponiert

bed: ~ridden adj bettlägerig; **~room** n Schlafzimmer nt; **~side** n: **at the ~side** am Bett; **~sit(ter)** (BRIT) n Einzimmerwohnung

f, möblierte(s) Zimmer nt; **~spread** n
Tagesdecke f; **~time** n Schlafenszeit f

)ee [bi:] n Biene f

)eech [bi:tʃ] n Buche f

)eef [bi:f] n Rindfleisch nt; **roast ~** Roastbeef
nt; **~burger** n Hamburger m

)eehive ['bi:haɪv] n Bienenstock m

)eeline ['bi:laɪn] n: **to make a ~ for**
schnurstracks zugehen auf +acc

)een [bi:n] pp of **be**

)eer [bɪəʳ] n Bier nt

)eet [bi:t] n (vegetable) Rübe f; (US: also: **red
~**) Rote Bete f or Rübe f

)eetle ['bi:tl] n Käfer m

)eetroot ['bi:tru:t] (BRIT) n Rote Bete f

)efore [bɪ'fɔ:ʳ] prep vor ♦ conj bevor ♦ adv (of
time) zuvor; früher; **the week ~** die Woche
zuvor or vorher; **I've done it ~** das hab ich
schon mal getan; **~ going** bevor er/sie etc
geht/ging; **~ she goes** bevor sie geht;
~hand adv im Voraus

)eg [beg] vt, vi (implore) dringend bitten;
(alms) betteln

)egan [bɪ'gæn] pt of **begin**

)eggar ['begəʳ] n Bettler(in) m(f)

)egin [bɪ'gɪn] (pt **began**, pp **begun**) vt, vi
anfangen, beginnen; (found) gründen; **to ~
doing** or **to do sth** anfangen or beginnen,
etw zu tun; **to ~ with** zunächst (einmal);
~ner n Anfänger m; **~ning** n Anfang m

)egun [bɪ'gʌn] pp of **begin**

)ehalf [bɪ'hɑ:f] n: **on ~ of** im Namen +gen;
on my ~ für mich

)ehave [bɪ'heɪv] vi sich benehmen;
behaviour [bɪ'heɪvjəʳ] (US **behavior**) n
Benehmen nt

)eheld [bɪ'held] pt, pp of **behold**

)ehind [bɪ'haɪnd] prep hinter ♦ adv (late) im
Rückstand; (in the rear) hinten ♦ n (inf)
Hinterteil nt; **~ the scenes** (fig) hinter den
Kulissen

)ehold [bɪ'həʊld] (irreg: like **hold**) vt
erblicken

)eige [beɪʒ] adj beige

)eijing [beɪ'dʒɪŋ] n Peking nt

)eing ['bi:ɪŋ] n (existence) (Da)sein nt;
(person) Wesen nt; **to come into ~**

entstehen

Belarus [belə'rus] n Weißrussland nt

belated [bɪ'leɪtɪd] adj verspätet

belch [beltʃ] vi rülpsen ♦ vt (smoke)
ausspeien

belfry ['belfrɪ] n Glockenturm m

Belgian ['beldʒən] adj belgisch ♦ n
Belgier(in) m(f)

Belgium ['beldʒəm] n Belgien nt

belie [bɪ'laɪ] vt Lügen strafen +acc

belief [bɪ'li:f] n Glaube m; (conviction)
Überzeugung f; **~ in sb/sth** Glaube an
jdn/etw

believe [bɪ'li:v] vt glauben +dat; (think)
glauben, meinen, denken ♦ vi (have faith)
glauben; **to ~ in sth** an etw acc glauben;
~r n Gläubige(r) f(m)

belittle [bɪ'lɪtl] vt herabsetzen

bell [bel] n Glocke f

belligerent [bɪ'lɪdʒərənt] adj (person)
streitsüchtig; (country) Krieg führend

bellow ['beləʊ] vt, vi brüllen

bellows ['beləʊz] npl (TECH) Gebläse nt; (for
fire) Blasebalg m

belly ['belɪ] n Bauch m

belong [bɪ'lɒŋ] vi gehören; **to ~ to sb** jdm
gehören; **to ~ to a club** etc einem Klub etc
angehören; **~ings** npl Habe f

beloved [bɪ'lʌvɪd] adj innig geliebt ♦ n
Geliebte(r) f(m)

below [bɪ'ləʊ] prep unter ♦ adv unten

belt [belt] n (band) Riemen m; (round waist)
Gürtel m ♦ vt (fasten) mit Riemen
befestigen; (inf: beat) schlagen; **~way** (US)
n (AUT: ring road) Umgehungsstraße f

bemused [bɪ'mju:zd] adj verwirrt

bench [bentʃ] n (seat) Bank f; (workshop)
Werkbank f; (judge's seat) Richterbank f;
(judges) Richter pl

bend [bend] (pt, pp **bent**) vt (curve) biegen;
(stoop) beugen ♦ vi sich biegen; sich
beugen ♦ n Biegung f; (BRIT: in road) Kurve
f; **~ down** or **over** vi sich bücken

beneath [bɪ'ni:θ] prep unter ♦ adv darunter

benefactor ['benɪfæktəʳ] n Wohltäter(in)
m(f)

beneficial [benɪ'fɪʃəl] adj vorteilhaft; (to

health) heilsam

benefit ['benɪfɪt] *n (advantage)* Nutzen *m* ♦ *vt* fördern ♦ *vi*: **to ~ (from)** Nutzen ziehen (aus)

Benelux ['benɪlʌks] *n* Beneluxstaaten *pl*

benevolent [bɪ'nevələnt] *adj* wohlwollend

benign [bɪ'naɪn] *adj (person)* gütig; *(climate)* mild

bent [bent] *pt, pp of* **bend** ♦ *n (inclination)* Neigung *f* ♦ *adj (inf: dishonest)* unehrlich; **to be ~ on** versessen sein auf +*acc*

bequest [bɪ'kwest] *n* Vermächtnis *nt*

bereaved [bɪ'riːvd] *npl*: **the ~** die Hinterbliebenen *pl*

beret ['bereɪ] *n* Baskenmütze *f*

Berlin [bɜː'lɪn] *n* Berlin *nt*

berm [bɜːm] *(US) n (AUT)* Seitenstreifen *m*

berry ['berɪ] *n* Beere *f*

berserk [bə'sɜːk] *adj*: **to go ~** wild werden

berth [bɜːθ] *n (for ship)* Ankerplatz *m*; *(in ship)* Koje *f*; *(in train)* Bett *nt* ♦ *vt* am Kai festmachen ♦ *vi* anlegen

beseech [bɪ'siːtʃ] *(pt, pp* **besought**) *vt* anflehen

beset [bɪ'set] *(pt, pp* **beset**) *vt* bedrängen

beside [bɪ'saɪd] *prep* neben, bei; *(except)* außer; **to be ~ o.s. (with)** außer sich sein (vor +*dat*); **that's ~ the point** das tut nichts zur Sache

besides [bɪ'saɪdz] *prep* außer, neben ♦ *adv* außerdem

besiege [bɪ'siːdʒ] *vt (MIL)* belagern; *(surround)* umlagern, bedrängen

besought [bɪ'sɔːt] *pt, pp of* **beseech**

best [best] *adj* beste(r, s) ♦ *adv* am besten; **the ~ part of** *(quantity)* das meiste +*gen*; **at ~** höchstens; **to make the ~ of it** das Beste daraus machen; **to do one's ~** sein Bestes tun; **to the ~ of my knowledge** meines Wissens; **to the ~ of my ability** so gut ich kann; **for the ~** zum Besten; **~-before date** *n* Mindesthaltbarkeitsdatum *nt*; **~ man** *n* Trauzeuge *m*

bestow [bɪ'stəʊ] *vt* verleihen

bet [bet] *(pt, pp* **bet** *or* **betted**) *n* Wette *f* ♦ *vt, vi* wetten

betray [bɪ'treɪ] *vt* verraten

better ['betər] *adj, adv* besser ♦ *vt* verbessern ♦ *n*: **to get the ~ of sb** jdn überwinden; **he thought ~ of it** er hat sich eines Besseren besonnen; **you had ~ leave** Sie gehen jetzt wohl besser; **to get ~** *(MED)* gesund werden; **~ off** *adj (richer)* wohlhabender

betting ['betɪŋ] *n* Wetten *nt*; **~ shop** *(BRIT) n* Wettbüro *nt*

between [bɪ'twiːn] *prep* zwischen; *(among)* unter ♦ *adv* dazwischen

beverage ['bevərɪdʒ] *n* Getränk *nt*

bevy ['bevɪ] *n* Schar *f*

beware [bɪ'weər] *vt, vi* sich hüten vor +*dat*; **"~ of the dog"** „Vorsicht, bissiger Hund!"

bewildered [bɪ'wɪldəd] *adj* verwirrt

beyond [bɪ'jɒnd] *prep (place)* jenseits +*gen*; *(time)* über ... hinaus; *(out of reach)* außerhalb +*gen* ♦ *adv* darüber hinaus; **~ doubt** ohne Zweifel; **~ repair** nicht mehr zu reparieren

bias ['baɪəs] *n (slant)* Neigung *f*; *(prejudice)* Vorurteil *nt*; **~(s)ed** *adj* voreingenommen

bib [bɪb] *n* Latz *m*

Bible ['baɪbl] *n* Bibel *f*

bicarbonate of soda [baɪ'kɑːbənɪt-] *n* Natron *nt*

bicker ['bɪkər] *vi* zanken

bicycle ['baɪsɪkl] *n* Fahrrad *nt*

bid [bɪd] *(pt* **bade** *or* **bid**, *pp* **bid(den)**) *n (offer)* Gebot *nt*; *(attempt)* Versuch *m* ♦ *vt, vi (offer)* bieten; **to ~ farewell** Lebewohl sagen; **~der** *n (person)* Steigerer *m*; **the highest ~der** der Meistbietende; **~ding** *n (command)* Geheiß *nt*

bide [baɪd] *vt*: **to ~ one's time** abwarten

bifocals [baɪ'fəʊklz] *npl* Bifokalbrille *f*

big [bɪg] *adj* groß; **~ dipper** [-'dɪpər] *n* Achterbahn *f*; **~headed** ['bɪg'hedɪd] *adj* eingebildet

bigot ['bɪgət] *n* Frömmler *m*; **~ed** *adj* bigott; **~ry** *n* Bigotterie *f*

big top *n* Zirkuszelt *nt*

bike [baɪk] *n* Rad *nt*

bikini [bɪ'kiːnɪ] *n* Bikini *m*

bile [baɪl] *n (BIOL)* Galle *f*

bilingual [baɪ'lɪŋgwəl] *adj* zweisprachig

bill [bɪl] *n (account)* Rechnung *f*; *(POL)*

Gesetzentwurf *m*; (*US: FIN*) Geldschein *m*; **to fit** *or* **fill the ~** (*fig*) der/die/das Richtige sein; **"post no ~s"** „Plakate ankleben verboten"; **~board** ['bɪlbɔːd] *n* Reklameschild *nt*

billet ['bɪlɪt] *n* Quartier *nt*

billfold ['bɪlfəʊld] (*US*) *n* Geldscheintasche *f*

billiards ['bɪljədz] *n* Billard *nt*

billion ['bɪljən] *n* (*BRIT*) Billion *f*; (*US*) Milliarde *f*

bimbo ['bɪmbəʊ] (*inf: pej*) *n* Puppe *f*, Häschen *nt*

bin [bɪn] *n* Kasten *m*; (*dustbin*) (Abfall)eimer *m*

bind [baɪnd] (*pt, pp* **bound**) *vt* (*tie*) binden; (*tie together*) zusammenbinden; (*oblige*) verpflichten; **~ing** *n* (Buch)einband *m* ♦ *adj* verbindlich

binge [bɪndʒ] (*inf*) *n* Sauferei *f*

bingo ['bɪŋgəʊ] *n* Bingo *nt*

binoculars [bɪ'nɔkjʊləz] *npl* Fernglas *nt*

bio... [baɪəʊ] *prefix*: **~chemistry** *n* Biochemie *f*; **~degradable** *adj* biologisch abbaubar; **~graphy** *n* Biografie *f*; **~logical** [baɪə'lɔdʒɪkl] *adj* biologisch; **~logy** [baɪ'ɔlədʒɪ] *n* Biologie *f*

birch [bɜːtʃ] *n* Birke *f*

bird [bɜːd] *n* Vogel *m*; (*BRIT: inf: girl*) Mädchen *nt*; **~'s-eye view** *n* Vogelschau *f*; **~ watcher** *n* Vogelbeobachter(in) *m(f)*; **~ watching** *n* Vogelbeobachten *nt*

Biro ['baɪərəʊ] ® *n* Kugelschreiber *m*

birth [bɜːθ] *n* Geburt *f*; **to give ~ to** zur Welt bringen; **~ certificate** *n* Geburtsurkunde *f*; **~ control** *n* Geburtenkontrolle *f*; **~day** *n* Geburtstag *m*; **~day card** *n* Geburtstagskarte *f*; **~place** *n* Geburtsort *m*; **~ rate** *n* Geburtenrate *f*

biscuit ['bɪskɪt] *n* Keks *m*

bisect [baɪ'sɛkt] *vt* halbieren

bishop ['bɪʃəp] *n* Bischof *m*

bit [bɪt] *pt of* **bite** ♦ *n* bisschen, Stückchen *nt*; (*horse's*) Gebiss *nt*; (*COMPUT*) Bit *nt*; **a ~ tired** etwas müde

bitch [bɪtʃ] *n* (*dog*) Hündin *f*; (*unpleasant woman*) Weibsstück *nt*

bite [baɪt] (*pt* **bit**, *pp* **bitten**) *vt, vi* beißen ♦ *n*

Biss *m*; (*mouthful*) Bissen *m*; **to ~ one's nails** Nägel kauen; **let's have a ~ to eat** lass uns etwas essen

bitten ['bɪtn] *pp of* **bite**

bitter ['bɪtər] *adj* bitter; (*memory etc*) schmerzlich; (*person*) verbittert ♦ *n* (*BRIT: beer*) dunkle(s) Bier *nt*; **~ness** *n* Bitterkeit *f*

blab [blæb] *vi* klatschen ♦ *vt* (*also: ~ out*) ausplaudern

black [blæk] *adj* schwarz; (*night*) finster ♦ *vt* schwärzen; (*shoes*) wichsen; (*eye*) blau schlagen; (*BRIT: INDUSTRY*) boykottieren; **to give sb a ~ eye** jdm ein blaues Auge schlagen; **in the ~** (*bank account*) in den schwarzen Zahlen; **~ and blue** *adj* grün und blau; **~berry** *n* Brombeere *f*; **~bird** *n* Amsel *f*; **~board** *n* (Wand)tafel *f*; **~ coffee** *n* schwarze(r) Kaffee *m*; **~currant** *n* schwarze Johannisbeere *f*; **~en** *vt* schwärzen; (*fig*) verunglimpfen; **B~ Forest** *n* Schwarzwald *m*; **~ ice** *n* Glatteis *nt*; **~leg** (*BRIT*) *n* Streikbrecher(in) *m(f)*; **~list** *n* schwarze Liste *f*; **~mail** *n* Erpressung *f* ♦ *vt* erpressen; **~ market** *n* Schwarzmarkt *m*; **~out** *n* Verdunklung *f*; (*MED*): **to have a ~out** bewusstlos werden; **~ pudding** *n* ≈ Blutwurst *f*; **B~ Sea** *n*: **the B~ Sea** das Schwarze Meer; **~ sheep** *n* schwarze(s) Schaf *nt*; **~smith** *n* Schmied *m*; **~ spot** *n* (*AUT*) Gefahrenstelle *f*; (*for unemployment etc*) schwer betroffene(s) Gebiet *nt*

bladder ['blædər] *n* Blase *f*

blade [bleɪd] *n* (*of weapon*) Klinge *f*; (*of grass*) Halm *m*; (*of oar*) Ruderblatt *nt*

blame [bleɪm] *n* Tadel *m*, Schuld *f* ♦ *vt* Vorwürfe machen +*dat*; **to ~ sb for sth** jdm die Schuld an etw *dat* geben; **he is to ~** er ist daran schuld

bland [blænd] *adj* mild

blank [blæŋk] *adj* leer, unbeschrieben; (*look*) verdutzt; (*verse*) Blank- ♦ *n* (*space*) Lücke *f*; Zwischenraum *m*; (*cartridge*) Platzpatrone *f*; **~ cheque** *n* Blankoscheck *m*; (*fig*) Freibrief *m*

blanket ['blæŋkɪt] *n* (Woll)decke *f*

blare [bleər] *vi* (*radio*) plärren; (*horn*) tuten; (*MUS*) schmettern

blasé [ˈblɑːzeɪ] *adj* blasiert

blast [blɑːst] *n* Explosion *f*; (*of wind*) Windstoß *m* ♦ *vt* (*blow up*) sprengen; ~! (*inf*) verflixt!; ~**off** *n* (*SPACE*) (Raketen)abschuss *m*

blatant [ˈbleɪtənt] *adj* offenkundig

blaze [bleɪz] *n* (*fire*) lodernde(s) Feuer *nt* ♦ *vi* lodern ♦ *vt*: **to ~ a trail** Bahn brechen

blazer [ˈbleɪzər] *n* Blazer *m*

bleach [bliːtʃ] *n* (*also:* **household ~**) Bleichmittel *nt* ♦ *vt* bleichen; ~**ed** *adj* gebleicht

bleachers [ˈbliːtʃəz] (*US*) *npl* (*SPORT*) unüberdachte Tribüne *f*

bleak [bliːk] *adj* kahl, rau; (*future*) trostlos

bleary-eyed [ˈblɪərɪˈaɪd] *adj* triefäugig; (*on waking up*) mit verschlafenen Augen

bleat [bliːt] *vi* blöken; (*fig: complain*) meckern

bled [bled] *pt, pp* of **bleed**

bleed [bliːd] (*pt, pp* **bled**) *vi* bluten ♦ *vt* (*draw blood*) zur Ader lassen; **to ~ to death** verbluten

bleeper [ˈbliːpər] *n* (*of doctor etc*) Funkrufempfänger *m*

blemish [ˈblemɪʃ] *n* Makel *m* ♦ *vt* verunstalten

blend [blend] *n* Mischung *f* ♦ *vt* mischen ♦ *vi* sich mischen; ~**er** *n* Mixer *m*, Mixgerät *nt*

bless [bles] (*pt, pp* **blessed**) *vt* segnen; (*give thanks*) preisen; (*make happy*) glücklich machen; ~ **you!** Gesundheit!; ~**ing** *n* Segen *m*; (*at table*) Tischgebet *nt*; (*happiness*) Wohltat *f*; Segen *m*; (*good wish*) Glück *nt*

blew [bluː] *pt* of **blow**

blimey [ˈblaɪmɪ] (*BRIT: inf*) *excl* verflucht

blind [blaɪnd] *adj* blind; (*corner*) unübersichtlich ♦ *n* (*for window*) Rouleau *nt* ♦ *vt* blenden; ~ **alley** *n* Sackgasse *f*; ~**fold** *n* Augenbinde *f* ♦ *adj, adv* mit verbundenen Augen ♦ *vt*: **to ~fold sb** jdm die Augen verbinden; ~**ly** *adv* blind; (*fig*) blindlings; ~**ness** *n* Blindheit *f*; ~ **spot** *n* (*AUT*) tote(r) Winkel *m*; (*fig*) schwache(r) Punkt *m*

blink [blɪŋk] *vi* blinzeln; ~**ers** *npl* Scheuklappen *pl*

bliss [blɪs] *n* (Glück)seligkeit *f*

blister [ˈblɪstər] *n* Blase *f* ♦ *vi* Blasen werfen

blitz [blɪts] *n* Luftkrieg *m*

blizzard [ˈblɪzəd] *n* Schneesturm *m*

bloated [ˈbləʊtɪd] *adj* aufgedunsen; (*inf: full*) nudelsatt

blob [blɒb] *n* Klümpchen *nt*

bloc [blɒk] *n* (*POL*) Block *m*

block [blɒk] *n* (*of wood*) Block *m*, Klotz *m*; (*of houses*) Häuserblock *m* ♦ *vt* hemmen; ~**ade** [blɒˈkeɪd] *n* Blockade *f* ♦ *vt* blockieren; ~**age** *n* Verstopfung *f*; ~**buster** *n* Knüller *m*; ~ **letters** *npl* Blockbuchstaben *pl*; ~ **of flats** (*BRIT*) *n* Häuserblock *m*

bloke [bləʊk] (*BRIT: inf*) *n* Kerl *m*, Typ *m*

blond(e) [blɒnd] *adj* blond ♦ *n* Blondine *f*

blood [blʌd] *n* Blut *nt*; ~ **donor** *n* Blutspender *m*; ~ **group** *n* Blutgruppe *f*; ~ **poisoning** *n* Blutvergiftung *f*; ~ **pressure** *n* Blutdruck *m*; ~**shed** *n* Blutvergießen *nt*; ~**shot** *adj* blutunterlaufen; ~ **sports** *npl* Jagdsport, Hahnenkampf *etc*; ~**stained** *adj* blutbefleckt; ~**stream** *n* Blut *nt*, Blutkreislauf *m*; ~ **test** *n* Blutprobe *f*; ~**thirsty** *adj* blutrünstig; ~ **vessel** *n* Blutgefäß *nt*; ~**y** *adj* blutig; (*BRIT: inf*) verdammt; ~**y-minded** (*BRIT: inf*) *adj* stur

bloom [bluːm] *n* Blüte *f*; (*freshness*) Glanz *m* ♦ *vi* blühen

blossom [ˈblɒsəm] *n* Blüte *f* ♦ *vi* blühen

blot [blɒt] *n* Klecks *m* ♦ *vt* beklecksen; (*ink*) (ab)löschen; ~ **out** *vt* auslöschen

blotchy [ˈblɒtʃɪ] *adj* fleckig

blotting paper [ˈblɒtɪŋ-] *n* Löschpapier *nt*

blouse [blauz] *n* Bluse *f*

blow [bləʊ] (*pt* **blew**, *pp* **blown**) *n* Schlag *m* ♦ *vt* blasen ♦ *vi* (*wind*) wehen; **to ~ one's nose** sich *dat* die Nase putzen; ~ **away** *vt* wegblasen; ~ **down** *vt* umwehen; ~ **off** *vt* wegwehen ♦ *vi* wegfliegen; ~ **out** *vi* ausgehen; ~ **over** *vi* vorübergehen; ~ **up** *vi* explodieren ♦ *vt* sprengen; ~**dry** *n*: **to have a ~dry** sich föhnen lassen ♦ *vt* föhnen; ~**lamp** (*BRIT*) *n* Lötlampe *f*; ~**n** *pp* of **blow**; ~**out** *n* (*AUT*) geplatzte(r) Reifen *m*; ~**torch** *n* = **blowlamp**

blue [bluː] *adj* blau; (*inf: unhappy*) niedergeschlagen; (*obscene*) pornografisch;

(joke) anzüglich ♦ n: **out of the ~** (fig) aus heiterem Himmel; **to have the ~s** traurig sein; **~bell** n Glockenblume f; **~bottle** n Schmeißfliege f; **~ film** n Pornofilm m; **~print** n (fig) Entwurf m

bluff [blʌf] vi bluffen, täuschen ♦ n (deception) Bluff m; **to call sb's ~** es darauf ankommen lassen

blunder [ˈblʌndəʳ] n grobe(r) Fehler m, Schnitzer m ♦ vi einen groben Fehler machen

blunt [blʌnt] adj (knife) stumpf; (talk) unverblümt ♦ vt abstumpfen

blur [bləːʳ] n Fleck m ♦ vt verschwommen machen

blurb [bləːb] n Waschzettel m

blush [blʌʃ] vi erröten

blustery [ˈblʌstərɪ] adj stürmisch

boar [bɔːʳ] n Keiler m, Eber m

board [bɔːd] n (of wood) Brett nt; (of card) Pappe f; (committee) Ausschuss m; (of firm) Aufsichtsrat m; (SCH) Direktorium nt ♦ vt (train) einsteigen in +acc; (ship) an Bord gehen +gen; **on ~** (AVIAT, NAUT) an Bord; **~ and lodging** Unterkunft f und Verpflegung; **full/half ~** (BRIT) Voll-/Halbpension f; **to go by the ~** flachfallen, über Bord gehen; **~ up** vt mit Brettern vernageln; **~er** n Kostgänger m; (SCH) Internatsschüler(in) m(f); **~ game** n Brettspiel nt; **~ing card** n (AVIAT, NAUT) Bordkarte f; **~ing house** n Pension f; **~ing school** n Internat nt; **~room** n Sitzungszimmer nt

boast [bəust] vi prahlen ♦ vt sich rühmen +gen ♦ n Großtuerei f; Prahlerei f; **to ~ about** or **of sth** mit etw prahlen

boat [bəut] n Boot nt; (ship) Schiff nt; **~er** n (hat) Kreissäge f; **~swain** n = **bosun**; **~ train** n Zug m mit Fährenanschluss

bob [bɔb] vi sich auf und nieder bewegen; **~ up** vi auftauchen

bobbin [ˈbɔbɪn] n Spule f

bobby [ˈbɔbɪ] (BRIT: inf) n Bobby m

bobsleigh [ˈbɔbsleɪ] n Bob m

bode [bəud] vi: **to ~ well/ill** ein gutes/ schlechtes Zeichen sein

bodily [ˈbɔdɪlɪ] adj, adv körperlich

body [ˈbɔdɪ] n Körper m; (dead) Leiche f; (group) Mannschaft f; (AUT) Karosserie f; (trunk) Rumpf m; **~ building** nt Bodybuilding nt; **~guard** n Leibwache f; **~work** n Karosserie f

bog [bɔg] n Sumpf m ♦ vt: **to get ~ged down** sich festfahren

boggle [ˈbɔgl] vi stutzen; **the mind ~s** es ist kaum auszumalen

bog-standard adj stinknormal (inf)

bogus [ˈbəugəs] adj unecht, Schein-

boil [bɔɪl] vt, vi kochen ♦ n (MED) Geschwür nt; **to come to the** (BRIT) or a (US) **~** zu kochen anfangen; **to ~ down to** (fig) hinauslaufen auf +acc; **~ over** vi überkochen; **~ed egg** n (weich) gekochte(s) Ei nt; **~ed potatoes** npl Salzkartoffeln pl; **~er** n Boiler m; **~er suit** (BRIT) n Arbeitsanzug m; **~ing point** n Siedepunkt m

boisterous [ˈbɔɪstərəs] adj ungestüm

bold [bəuld] adj (fearless) unerschrocken; (handwriting) fest und klar

bollard [ˈbɔləd] n (NAUT) Poller m; (BRIT: AUT) Pfosten m

bolt [bəult] n Bolzen m; (lock) Riegel m ♦ adv: **~ upright** kerzengerade ♦ vt verriegeln; (swallow) verschlingen ♦ vi (horse) durchgehen

bomb [bɔm] n Bombe f ♦ vt bombardieren; **~ard** [bɔmˈbɑːd] vt bombardieren; **~ardment** [bɔmˈbɑːdmənt] n Beschießung f; **~ disposal** n: **~ disposal unit** Bombenräumkommando nt; **~er** n Bomber m; (terrorist) Bombenattentäter(in) m(f); **~ing** n Bomben nt; **~shell** n (fig) Bombe f

bona fide [ˈbəunəˈfaɪdɪ] adj echt

bond [bɔnd] n (link) Band nt; (FIN) Schuldverschreibung f

bondage [ˈbɔndɪdʒ] n Sklaverei f

bone [bəun] n Knochen m; (of fish) Gräte f; (piece of ~) Knochensplitter m ♦ vt die Knochen herausnehmen +dat; (fish) entgräten; **~ dry** adj (inf) knochentrocken; **~ idle** adj stinkfaul; **~ marrow** n (ANAT) Knochenmark nt

bonfire [ˈbɔnfaɪəʳ] n Feuer nt im Freien

bonnet ['bɒnɪt] *n* Haube *f*; (*for baby*) Häubchen *nt*; (*BRIT: AUT*) Motorhaube *f*

bonus ['bəunəs] *n* Bonus *m*; (*annual ~*) Prämie *f*

bony ['bəunɪ] *adj* knochig, knochendürr

boo [bu:] *vt* auspfeifen

booby trap ['bu:bɪ-] *n* Falle *f*

book [buk] *n* Buch *nt* ♦ *vt* (*ticket etc*) vorbestellen; (*person*) verwarnen; **~s** *npl* (*COMM*) Bücher *pl*; **~case** *n* Bücherregal *nt*, Bücherschrank *m*; **~ing office** (*BRIT*) *n* (*RAIL*) Fahrkartenschalter *m*; (*THEAT*) Vorverkaufsstelle *f*; **~-keeping** *n* Buchhaltung *f*; **~let** *n* Broschüre *f*; **~maker** *n* Buchmacher *m*; **~seller** *n* Buchhändler *m*; **~shelf** *n* Bücherbord *nt*; **~shop** ['bukʃɒp], **~store** *n* Buchhandlung *f*

boom [bu:m] *n* (*noise*) Dröhnen *nt*; (*busy period*) Hochkonjunktur *f* ♦ *vi* dröhnen

boon [bu:n] *n* Wohltat *f*, Segen *m*

boost [bu:st] *n* Auftrieb *m*; (*fig*) Reklame *f* ♦ *vt* Auftrieb geben; **~er** *n* (*MED*) Wiederholungsimpfung *f*

boot [bu:t] *n* Stiefel *m*; (*BRIT: AUT*) Kofferraum *m* ♦ *vt* (*kick*) einen Fußtritt geben; (*COMPUT*) laden; **to ~** (*in addition*) obendrein

booth [bu:ð] *n* (*at fair*) Bude *f*; (*telephone ~*) Zelle *f*; (*voting ~*) Kabine *f*

booze [bu:z] (*inf*) *n* Alkohol *m*, Schnaps *m* ♦ *vi* saufen

border ['bɔ:dər] *n* Grenze *f*; (*edge*) Kante *f*; (*in garden*) (Blumen)rabatte *f* ♦ *adj* Grenz-; **the B~s** *Grenzregion zwischen England und Schottland*; **~ on** *vt* grenzen an *+acc*; **~line** *n* Grenze *f*; **~line case** *n* Grenzfall *m*

bore [bɔ:r] *pt of* **bear** ♦ *vt* bohren; (*weary*) langweilen ♦ *n* (*person*) Langweiler *m*; (*thing*) langweilige Sache *f*; (*of gun*) Kaliber *nt*; **I am ~d** ich langweile mich; **~dom** *n* Langeweile *f*

boring ['bɔ:rɪŋ] *adj* langweilig

born [bɔ:n] *adj*: **to be ~** geboren werden

borne [bɔ:n] *pp of* **bear**

borough ['bʌrə] *n* Stadt(gemeinde) *f*, Stadtbezirk *m*

borrow ['bɒrəu] *vt* borgen

Bosnia (and) Herzegovina ['bɔznɪə (ənd) ha:tsəgəu'vi:nə] *n* Bosnien und Herzegovina *nt*; **~n** *n* Bosnier(in) *m(f)* ♦ *adj* bosnisch

bosom ['buzəm] *n* Busen *m*

boss [bɒs] *n* Chef *m*, Boss *m* ♦ *vt*: **to ~ around** *or* **about** herumkommandieren; **~y** *adj* herrisch

bosun ['bəusn] *n* Bootsmann *m*

botany ['bɒtənɪ] *n* Botanik *f*

botch [bɒtʃ] *vt* (*also: ~ up*) verpfuschen

both [bəuθ] *adj* beide(s) ♦ *pron* beide(s) ♦ *adv*: **~ X and Y** sowohl X wie *or* als auch Y; **~ (of) the books** sie beide Bücher; **~ of us went, we ~ went** wir gingen beide

bother ['bɒðər] *vt* (*pester*) quälen ♦ *vi* (*fuss*) sich aufregen ♦ *n* Mühe *f*, Umstand *m*; **to ~ doing sth** sich *dat* die Mühe machen, etw zu tun; **what a ~!** wie ärgerlich!

bottle ['bɒtl] *n* Flasche *f* ♦ *vt* (*in Flaschen*) abfüllen; **~ up** *vt* aufstauen; **~ bank** *n* Altglascontainer *m*; **~d beer** *n* Flaschenbier *nt*; **~d water** *n* in Flaschen abgefülltes Wasser; **~neck** *n* (*also fig*) Engpass *m*; **~ opener** *n* Flaschenöffner *m*

bottom ['bɒtəm] *n* Boden *m*; (*of person*) Hintern *m*; (*riverbed*) Flussbett *nt* ♦ *adj* unterste(r, s)

bough [bau] *n* Zweig *m*, Ast *m*

bought [bɔ:t] *pt, pp of* **buy**

boulder ['bəuldər] *n* Felsbrocken *m*

bounce [bauns] *vi* (*person*) herumhüpfen; (*ball*) hochspringen; (*cheque*) platzen ♦ *vt* (auf)springen lassen ♦ *n* (*rebound*) Aufprall *m*; **~r** *n* Rausschmeißer *m*

bound [baund] *pt, pp of* **bind** ♦ *n* Grenze *f*; (*leap*) Sprung *m* ♦ *vi* (*spring, leap*) (auf)springen ♦ *adj* (*obliged*) gebunden, verpflichtet; **out of ~s** Zutritt verboten; **to be ~ to do sth** verpflichtet sein, etw zu tun; **it's ~ to happen** es muss so kommen; **to be ~ for ...** nach ... fahren

boundary ['baundrɪ] *n* Grenze *f*

bouquet ['bukeɪ] *n* Strauß *m*; (*of wine*) Blume *f*

bourgeois ['buəʒwɑ:] *adj* kleinbürgerlich, bourgeois ♦ *n* Spießbürger(in) *m(f)*

bout [baut] *n* (*of illness*) Anfall *m*; (*of contest*)

Kampf m

bow[1] [bəu] n (ribbon) Schleife f; (weapon, MUS) Bogen m

bow[2] [bau] n (with head, body) Verbeugung f; (of ship) Bug m ♦ vi sich verbeugen; (submit): **to ~ to** sich beugen +dat

bowels ['bauəlz] npl (ANAT) Darm m

bowl [bəul] n (basin) Schüssel f; (of pipe) (Pfeifen)kopf m; (wooden ball) (Holz)kugel f ♦ vt, vi (die Kugel) rollen

bow-legged ['bəu'legıd] adj o-beinig, O-beinig

bowler ['bəulə'] n Werfer m; (BRIT: also: ~ **hat**) Melone f

bowling ['bəulıŋ] n Kegeln nt; ~ **alley** n Kegelbahn f; ~ **green** n Rasen m zum Bowlingspiel

bowls n (game) Bowlsspiel nt

bow tie [bəu-] n Fliege f

box [bɒks] n (also: **cardboard** ~) Schachtel f; (bigger than box) Kasten m; (THEAT) Loge f ♦ vt einpacken ♦ vi boxen; ~**er** n Boxer m; ~**er shorts** (BRIT) npl Boxershorts pl; ~**ing** n (SPORT) Boxen nt; B~**ing Day** (BRIT) n zweite(r) Weihnachtsfeiertag m; ~**ing gloves** npl Boxhandschuhe pl; ~**ing ring** n Boxring m; ~ **office** n (Theater)kasse f; ~**room** n Rumpelkammer f

---

Boxing Day

Boxing Day (26.12.) ist ein Feiertag in Großbritannien. Wenn Weihnachten auf ein Wochenende fällt, wird der Feiertag am nächsten darauf folgenden Wochentag nachgeholt. Der Name geht auf einen alten Brauch zurück; früher erhielten Händler und Lieferanten an diesem Tag ein Geschenk, die so genannte *Christmas Box*.

---

boy [bɔɪ] n Junge m

boycott ['bɔɪkɒt] n Boykott m ♦ vt boykottieren

boyfriend ['bɔɪfrend] n Freund m

boyish ['bɔɪʃ] adj jungenhaft

B.R. n abbr = **British Rail**

bra [brɑː] n BH m

brace [breɪs] n (TECH) Stütze f; (MED)

Klammer f ♦ vt stützen; ~**s** npl (BRIT) Hosenträger pl; **to ~ o.s. for sth** (fig) sich auf etw acc gefasst machen

bracelet ['breɪslɪt] n Armband nt

bracing ['breɪsɪŋ] adj kräftigend

bracken ['brækən] n Farnkraut nt

bracket ['brækɪt] n Halter m, Klammer f; (in punctuation) Klammer f; (group) Gruppe f ♦ vt einklammern; (fig) in dieselbe Gruppe einordnen

brag [bræg] vi sich rühmen

braid [breɪd] n (hair) Flechte f; (trim) Borte f

Braille [breɪl] n Blindenschrift f

brain [breɪn] n (ANAT) Gehirn nt; (intellect) Intelligenz f, Verstand m; (person) kluge(r) Kopf m; ~**s** npl (intelligence) Verstand m; ~**child** n Erfindung f; ~**wash** vt eine Gehirnwäsche vornehmen bei; ~**wave** n Geistesblitz m; ~**y** adj gescheit

braise [breɪz] vt schmoren

brake [breɪk] n Bremse f ♦ vt, vi bremsen; ~ **fluid** n Bremsflüssigkeit f; ~ **light** n Bremslicht nt

bramble ['bræmbl] n Brombeere f

bran [bræn] n Kleie f; (food) Frühstücksflocken pl

branch [brɑːntʃ] n Ast m; (division) Zweig m ♦ vi (also: ~ **out**: road) sich verzweigen

brand [brænd] n (COMM) Marke f, Sorte f; (on cattle) Brandmal nt ♦ vt brandmarken; (COMM) ein Warenzeichen geben +dat

brandish ['brændɪʃ] vt (drohend) schwingen

brand-new ['brænd'njuː] adj funkelnagelneu

brandy ['brændı] n Weinbrand m, Kognak m

brash [bræʃ] adj unverschämt

brass [brɑːs] n Messing nt; **the ~** (MUS) das Blech; ~ **band** n Blaskapelle f

brassière ['bræsɪə'] n Büstenhalter m

brat [bræt] n Gör nt

bravado [brə'vɑːdəu] n Tollkühnheit f

brave [breɪv] adj tapfer ♦ vt die Stirn bieten +dat; ~**ry** n Tapferkeit f

brawl [brɔːl] n Rauferei f

brawn [brɔːn] n (ANAT) Muskeln pl; (strength) Muskelkraft f

bray [breɪ] vi schreien

brazen ['breɪzn] adj (shameless) unverschämt

♦ *vt*: **to ~ it out** sich mit Lügen und Betrügen durchsetzen

brazier ['breɪzɪəʳ] *n* (*of workmen*) offene(r) Kohlenofen *m*

Brazil [brə'zɪl] *n* Brasilien *nt*; **~ian** *adj* brasilianisch ♦ *n* Brasilianer(in) *m(f)*

breach [briːtʃ] *n* (*gap*) Lücke *f*; (*MIL*) Durchbruch *m*; (*of discipline*) Verstoß *m* (gegen die Disziplin); (*of faith*) Vertrauensbruch *m* ♦ *vt* durchbrechen; **~ of contract** Vertragsbruch *m*; **~ of the peace** öffentliche Ruhestörung *f*

bread [bred] *n* Brot *nt*; **~ and butter** Butterbrot *nt*; **~bin** *n* Brotkasten *m*; **~ box** (*US*) *n* Brotkasten *m*; **~crumbs** *npl* Brotkrumen *pl*; (*COOK*) Paniermehl *nt*; **~line** *n*: **to be on the ~line** sich gerade so durchschlagen

breadth [bretθ] *n* Breite *f*

breadwinner ['bredwɪnəʳ] *n* Ernährer *m*

break [breɪk] (*pt* **broke**, *pp* **broken**) *vt* (*destroy*) (ab- or zer)brechen; (*promise*) brechen, nicht einhalten ♦ *vi* (*fall apart*) auseinander brechen; (*collapse*) zusammenbrechen; (*dawn*) anbrechen ♦ *n* (*gap*) Lücke *f*; (*chance*) Chance *f*, Gelegenheit *f*; (*fracture*) Bruch *m*; (*rest*) Pause *f*; **~ down** *vt* (*figures, data*) aufschlüsseln; (*undermine*) überwinden ♦ *vi* (*car*) eine Panne haben; (*person*) zusammenbrechen; **~ even** *vi* die Kosten decken; **~ free** *vi* sich losreißen; **~ in** *vt* (*horse*) zureiten ♦ *vi* (*burglar*) einbrechen; **~ into** *vt fus* (*house*) einbrechen in +*acc*; **~ loose** *vi* sich losreißen; **~ off** *vi* abbrechen; **~ open** *vt* (*door etc*) aufbrechen; **~ out** *vi* ausbrechen; **to ~ out in spots** Pickel bekommen; **~ up** *vi* zerbrechen; (*fig*) sich zerstreuen; (*BRIT: SCH*) in die Ferien gehen ♦ *vt* brechen; **~age** *n* Bruch *m*, Beschädigung *f*; **~down** *n* (*TECH*) Panne *f*; (*MED: also*: **nervous ~down**) Zusammenbruch *m*; **~down van** (*BRIT*) *n* Abschleppwagen *m*; **~er** *n* Brecher *m*

breakfast ['brekfəst] *n* Frühstück *nt*

break: **~-in** *n* Einbruch *m*; **~ing** *n*: **~ing and entering** (*JUR*) Einbruch *m*; **~through** *n* Durchbruch *m*; **~water** *n* Wellenbrecher *m*

breast [brest] *n* Brust *f*; **~-feed** (*irreg: like* **feed**) *vt*, *vi* stillen; **~-stroke** *n* Brustschwimmen *nt*

breath [breθ] *n* Atem *m*; **out of ~** außer Atem; **under one's ~** flüsternd

Breathalyzer ['breθəlaɪzəʳ] ® *n* Röhrchen *nt*

breathe [briːð] *vt*, *vi* atmen; **~ in** *vt*, *vi* einatmen; **~ out** *vt*, *vi* ausatmen; **~r** *n* Verschnaufpause *f*; **breathing** *n* Atmung *f*

breathless ['breθlɪs] *adj* atemlos

breathtaking ['breθteɪkɪŋ] *adj* atemberaubend

bred [bred] *pt*, *pp of* **breed**

breed [briːd] (*pt*, *pp* **bred**) *vi* sich vermehren ♦ *vt* züchten ♦ *n* (*race*) Rasse *f*, Zucht *f*; **~ing** *n* Züchtung *f*; (*upbringing*) Erziehung *f*

breeze [briːz] *n* Brise *f*; **breezy** *adj* windig; (*manner*) munter

brevity ['brevɪtɪ] *n* Kürze *f*

brew [bruː] *vt* (*beer*) brauen ♦ *vi* (*storm*) sich zusammenziehen; **~ery** *n* Brauerei *f*

bribe [braɪb] *n* Bestechungsgeld *nt*, Bestechungsgeschenk *nt* ♦ *vt* bestechen; **~ry** ['braɪbərɪ] *n* Bestechung *f*

bric-a-brac ['brɪkəbræk] *n* Nippes *pl*

brick [brɪk] *n* Backstein *m*; **~layer** *n* Maurer *m*; **~works** *n* Ziegelei *f*

bridal ['braɪdl] *adj* Braut-

bride [braɪd] *n* Braut *f*; **~groom** *n* Bräutigam *m*; **~smaid** *n* Brautjungfer *f*

bridge [brɪdʒ] *n* Brücke *f*; (*NAUT*) Kommandobrücke *f*; (*CARDS*) Bridge *nt*; (*ANAT*) Nasenrücken *m* ♦ *vt* eine Brücke schlagen über +*acc*; (*fig*) überbrücken

bridle ['braɪdl] *n* Zaum *m* ♦ *vt* (*fig*) zügeln; (*horse*) aufzäumen; **~ path** *n* Reitweg *m*

brief [briːf] *adj* kurz ♦ *n* (*JUR*) Akten *pl* ♦ *vt* instruieren; **~s** *npl* (*underwear*) Schlüpfer *m*, Slip *m*; **~case** *n* Aktentasche *f*; **~ing** *n* (*genaue*) Anweisung *f*; **~ly** *adv* kurz

brigadier [brɪgə'dɪəʳ] *n* Brigadegeneral *m*

bright [braɪt] *adj* hell; (*cheerful*) heiter; (*idea*) klug; **~en (up)** ['braɪtn-] *vt* aufhellen; (*person*) aufheitern ♦ *vi* sich aufhellen

brilliance ['brɪljəns] *n* Glanz *m*; (*of person*)

Scharfsinn m

brilliant ['brɪljənt] *adj* glänzend

brim [brɪm] *n* Rand *m*

brine [braɪn] *n* Salzwasser *nt*

bring [brɪŋ] (*pt, pp* **brought**) *vt* bringen; ~ **about** *vt* zustande *or* zu Stande bringen; ~ **back** *vt* zurückbringen; ~ **down** *vt* (*price*) senken; ~ **forward** *vt* (*meeting*) vorverlegen; (*COMM*) übertragen; ~ **in** *vt* hereinbringen; (*harvest*) einbringen; ~ **off** *vt* davontragen; (*success*) erzielen; ~ **out** *vt* (*object*) herausbringen; ~ **round** *or* to *vt* wieder zu sich bringen; ~ **up** *vt* aufziehen; (*question*) zur Sprache bringen

brink [brɪŋk] *n* Rand *m*

brisk [brɪsk] *adj* lebhaft

bristle ['brɪsl] *n* Borste *f* ♦ *vi* sich sträuben; **bristling with** strotzend vor +*dat*

Britain ['brɪtən] *n* (*also:* **Great ~**) Großbritannien *nt*

British ['brɪtɪʃ] *adj* britisch ♦ *npl:* **the ~** die Briten *pl;* ~ **Isles** *npl:* **the ~ Isles** die Britischen Inseln *pl;* ~ **Rail** *n* die Britischen Eisenbahnen

Briton ['brɪtən] *n* Brite *m*, Britin *f*

Brittany ['brɪtənɪ] *n* die Bretagne

brittle ['brɪtl] *adj* spröde

broach [brəʊtʃ] *vt* (*subject*) anschneiden

broad [brɔːd] *adj* breit; (*hint*) deutlich; (*general*) allgemein; (*accent*) stark; **in ~ daylight** am helllichten Tag; ~**band** *n* Breitband *nt;* ~**cast** (*pt, pp* **broadcast**) *n* Rundfunkübertragung *f* ♦ *vt, vi* übertragen, senden; ~**en** *vt* erweitern ♦ *vi* sich erweitern; ~**ly** *adv* allgemein gesagt; ~~**minded** *adj* tolerant

broccoli ['brɔkəlɪ] *n* Brokkoli *pl*

brochure ['brəʊʃjʊə'] *n* Broschüre *f*

broil [brɔɪl] *vt* (*grill*) grillen

broke [brəʊk] *pt of* **break** ♦ *adj* (*inf*) pleite

broken ['brəʊkn] *pp of* **break** ♦ *adj:* ~ **leg** gebrochenes Bein; **in ~ English** in gebrochenem Englisch; ~~**hearted** *adj* untröstlich

broker ['brəʊkə'] *n* Makler *m*

brolly ['brɔlɪ] (*BRIT: inf*) *n* Schirm *m*

bronchitis [brɔŋ'kaɪtɪs] *n* Bronchitis *f*

bronze [brɔnz] *n* Bronze *f*

brooch [brəʊtʃ] *n* Brosche *f*

brood [bruːd] *n* Brut *f* ♦ *vi* brüten

brook [brʊk] *n* Bach *m*

broom [brum] *n* Besen *m*

Bros. *abbr* = **Brothers**

broth [brɔθ] *n* Suppe *f*, Fleischbrühe *f*

brothel ['brɔθl] *n* Bordell *nt*

brother ['brʌðə'] *n* Bruder *m;* ~~**in-law** *n* Schwager *m*

brought [brɔːt] *pt, pp of* **bring**

brow [braʊ] *n* (*eyebrow*) (Augen)braue *f;* (*forehead*) Stirn *f;* (*of hill*) Bergkuppe *f*

brown [braʊn] *adj* braun ♦ *n* Braun *nt* ♦ *vt* bräunen; ~ **bread** *n* Mischbrot *nt;* **B~ie** *n* Wichtel *m;* ~ **paper** *n* Packpapier *nt*

browse [braʊz] *vi* (*in books*) blättern; (*in shop*) schmökern, herumschauen; ~**r** *n* (*COMPUT*) Browser *m*

bruise [bruːz] *n* Bluterguss *m*, blaue(r) Fleck *m* ♦ *vt* einen blauen Fleck geben ♦ *vi* einen blauen Fleck bekommen

brunt [brʌnt] *n* volle Wucht *f*

brush [brʌʃ] *n* Bürste *f;* (*for sweeping*) Handbesen *m;* (*for painting*) Pinsel *m;* (*fight*) kurze(r) Kampf *m;* (*MIL*) Scharmützel *nt;* (*fig*) Auseinandersetzung *f* ♦ *vt* (*clean*) bürsten; (*sweep*) fegen; (*usu:* ~ *past,* ~ *against*) streifen; ~ **aside** *vt* abtun; ~ **up** *vt* (*knowledge*) auffrischen; ~**wood** *n* Gestrüpp *nt*

brusque [bruːsk] *adj* schroff

Brussels ['brʌslz] *n* Brüssel *nt;* ~ **sprout** *n* Rosenkohl *m*

brutal ['bruːtl] *adj* brutal

brute [bruːt] *n* (*person*) Scheusal *nt* ♦ *adj:* **by ~ force** mit roher Kraft

B.Sc. *n abbr* = **Bachelor of Science**

BSE *n abbr* (= *bovine spongiform encephalopathy*) BSE *f*

bubble ['bʌbl] *n* (Luft)blase *f* ♦ *vi* sprudeln; (*with joy*) übersprudeln; ~ **bath** *n* Schaumbad *nt;* ~ **gum** *n* Kaugummi *m or nt*

buck [bʌk] *n* Bock *m;* (*US: inf*) Dollar *m* ♦ *vi* bocken; **to pass the ~ (to sb)** die Verantwortung (auf jdn) abschieben; ~ **up** (*inf*) *vi* sich zusammenreißen

bucket ['bʌkɪt] n Eimer m

Buckingham Palace

ⓘ **Buckingham Palace** ist die offizielle
Londoner Residenz der britischen
Monarchen und liegt am St James Park. Der
Palast wurde 1703 für den Herzog von
Buckingham erbaut, 1762 von George III.
gekauft, zwischen 1821 und 1836 von John
Nash umgebaut, und Anfang des 20.
Jahrhunderts teilweise neu gestaltet. Teile
des Buckingham Palace sind heute der
Öffentlichkeit zugänglich.

buckle ['bʌkl] n Schnalle f ♦ vt (an- or
zusammen)schnallen ♦ vi (bend) sich
verziehen

bud [bʌd] n Knospe f ♦ vi knospen, keimen

Buddhism ['budɪzəm] n Buddhismus m;
Buddhist adj buddhistisch ♦ n
Buddhist(in) m(f)

budding ['bʌdɪŋ] adj angehend

buddy ['bʌdɪ] (inf) n Kumpel m

budge [bʌdʒ] vt, vi (sich) von der Stelle
rühren

budgerigar ['bʌdʒərɪgɑːr] n Wellensittich m

budget ['bʌdʒɪt] n Budget nt; (POL) Haushalt
m ♦ vi: **to ~ for sth** etw einplanen

budgie ['bʌdʒɪ] n = **budgerigar**

buff [bʌf] adj (colour) lederfarben ♦ n
(enthusiast) Fan m

buffalo ['bʌfələu] (pl ~ or ~es) n (BRIT) Büffel
m; (US: bison) Bison m

buffer ['bʌfər] n Puffer m; (COMPUT)
Pufferspeicher m; ~ zone n Pufferzone f

buffet¹ ['bʌfɪt] n (blow) Schlag m ♦ vt
(herum)stossen

buffet² ['bufeɪ] (BRIT) n (bar) Imbissraum m,
Erfrischungsraum m; (food) (kaltes) Büfett
nt; ~ car (BRIT) n Speisewagen m

bug [bʌg] n (also fig) Wanze f ♦ vt
verwanzen; **the room is bugged** das
Zimmer ist verwanzt

bugle ['bjuːgl] n Jagdhorn nt; (MIL: MUS)
Bügelhorn nt

build [bɪld] n (pt, pp **built**) vt bauen ♦ n
Körperbau m; ~ up vt aufbauen; ~er n

Bauunternehmer m; ~ing n Gebäude nt;
~ing society (BRIT) n Bausparkasse f

built [bɪlt] pt, pp of **build**; ~-in adj (cupboard)
eingebaut; ~-up area n Wohngebiet nt

bulb [bʌlb] n (BOT) (Blumen)zwiebel f; (ELEC)
Glühlampe f, Birne f

Bulgaria [bʌl'geərɪə] n Bulgarien nt; ~n adj
bulgarisch ♦ n Bulgare m, Bulgarin f; (LING)
Bulgarisch nt

bulge [bʌldʒ] n Wölbung f ♦ vi sich wölben

bulk [bʌlk] n Größe f, Masse f; (greater part)
Großteil m; **in ~** (COMM) en gros; **the ~ of**
der größte Teil +gen; ~head n Schott nt;
~y adj (sehr) umfangreich; (goods) sperrig

bull [bul] n Bulle m; (cattle) Stier m; ~dog n
Bulldogge f

bulldozer ['buldəuzər] n Planierraupe f

bullet ['bulɪt] n Kugel f

bulletin ['bulɪtɪn] n Bulletin nt,
Bekanntmachung f

bulletproof ['bulɪtpruːf] adj kugelsicher

bullfight ['bulfaɪt] n Stierkampf m; ~er n
Stierkämpfer m; ~ing n Stierkampf m

bullion ['buljən] n Barren m

bullock ['bulək] n Ochse m

bullring ['bulrɪŋ] n Stierkampfarena f

bull's-eye ['bulzaɪ] n Zentrum nt

bully ['bulɪ] n Raufbold m ♦ vt einschüchtern

bum [bʌm] n (inf: backside) Hintern m;
(tramp) Landstreicher m

bumblebee ['bʌmblbiː] n Hummel f

bump [bʌmp] n (blow) Stoß m; (swelling)
Beule f ♦ vt, vi stoßen, prallen; ~ **into** vt
fus stoßen gegen ♦ vt (person) treffen; ~er
n (AUT) Stoßstange f ♦ adj (edition) dick;
(harvest) Rekord-

bumpy ['bʌmpɪ] adj holprig

bun [bʌn] n Korinthenbrötchen nt

bunch [bʌntʃ] n (of flowers) Strauß m; (of
keys) Bund m; (of people) Haufen m; ~es npl
(in hair) Zöpfe pl

bundle ['bʌndl] n Bündel nt ♦ vt (also: ~ up)
bündeln

bungalow ['bʌŋgələu] n einstöckige(s) Haus
nt, Bungalow m

bungle ['bʌŋgl] vt verpfuschen

bunion ['bʌnjən] n entzündete(r) Fußballen *m*

bunk [bʌŋk] *n* Schlafkoje *f;* ~ **beds** *npl* Etagenbett *nt*

bunker ['bʌŋkəʳ] *n (coal store)* Kohlenbunker *m; (GOLF)* Sandloch *nt*

bunny ['bʌnɪ] *n (also:* ~ **rabbit)** Häschen *nt*

bunting ['bʌntɪŋ] *n* Fahnentuch *nt*

buoy [bɔɪ] *n* Boje *f; (lifebuoy)* Rettungsboje *f;* ~**ant** *adj (floating)* schwimmend; *(fig)* heiter

burden ['bɜːdn] *n (weight)* Ladung *f*, Last *f; (fig)* Bürde *f ♦ vt* belasten

bureau ['bjʊərəʊ] *(pl* ~**x)** *n (BRIT: writing desk)* Sekretär *m; (US: chest of drawers)* Kommode *f; (for information etc)* Büro *nt*

bureaucracy [bjʊəˈrɔkrəsɪ] *n* Bürokratie *f*

bureaucrat ['bjʊərəkræt] *n* Bürokrat(in) *m(f)*

bureaux ['bjʊərəʊz] *npl of* **bureau**

burglar ['bɜːgləʳ] *n* Einbrecher *m;* ~ **alarm** *n* Einbruchssicherung *f;* ~**y** *n* Einbruch *m*

burial ['berɪəl] *n* Beerdigung *f*

burly ['bɜːlɪ] *adj* stämmig

Burma ['bɜːmə] *n* Birma *nt*

burn [bɜːn] *(pt, pp* **burned** *or* **burnt)** *vt* verbrennen *♦ vi* brennen *♦ n* Brandwunde *f;* ~ **down** *vt, vi* abbrennen; ~**er** *n* Brenner *m;* ~**ing** *adj* brennend; ~**t** [bɜːnt] *pt, pp of* **burn**

burrow ['bʌrəʊ] *n (of fox)* Bau *m; (of rabbit)* Höhle *f ♦ vt* eingraben

bursar ['bɜːsəʳ] *n* Kassenverwalter *m*, Quästor *m;* ~**y** *(BRIT)* Stipendium *nt*

burst [bɜːst] *(pt, pp* **burst)** *vt* zerbrechen *♦ vi* platzen *♦ n (outburst)* Explosion *f; (outbreak)* Ausbruch *m; (in pipe)* Bruch(stelle *f) m;* **to** ~ **into flames** in Flammen aufgehen; **to** ~ **into tears** in Tränen ausbrechen; **to** ~ **out laughing** in Gelächter ausbrechen; ~ **into** *vt fus (room etc)* platzen in *+acc;* ~ **open** *vi* aufbrechen

bury ['berɪ] *vt* vergraben; *(in grave)* beerdigen

bus [bʌs] *n* (Auto)bus *m*, Omnibus *m*

bush [bʊʃ] *n* Busch *m;* **to beat about the** ~ wie die Katze um den heißen Brei herumgehen; ~**y** ['bʊʃɪ] *adj* buschig

busily ['bɪzɪlɪ] *adv* geschäftig

business ['bɪznɪs] *n* Geschäft *nt; (concern)*

Angelegenheit *f;* **it's none of your** ~ es geht dich nichts an; **to mean** ~ es ernst meinen; **to be away on** ~ geschäftlich verreist sein; **it's my** ~ **to ...** es ist meine Sache, zu ...; ~**like** *adj* geschäftsmäßig; ~**man** *(irreg) n* Geschäftsmann *m;* ~ **trip** *n* Geschäftsreise *f;* ~**woman** *(irreg) n* Geschäftsfrau *f*

busker ['bʌskəʳ] *(BRIT) n* Straßenmusikant *m*

bus: ~ **shelter** *n* Wartehäuschen *nt;* ~ **station** *n* Busbahnhof *m;* ~ **stop** *n* Bushaltestelle *f*

bust [bʌst] *n* Büste *f ♦ adj (broken)* kaputt(gegangen); *(business)* pleite; **to go** ~ Pleite machen

bustle ['bʌsl] *n* Getriebe *nt ♦ vi* hasten

bustling ['bʌslɪŋ] *adj* geschäftig

busy ['bɪzɪ] *adj* beschäftigt; *(road)* belebt *♦ vt:* **to** ~ **o.s.** sich beschäftigen; ~**body** *n* Übereifrige(r) *mf;* ~ **signal** *(US) n (TEL)* Besetztzeichen *nt*

KEYWORD

but [bʌt] *conj* 1 *(yet)* aber; **not X but Y** nicht X sondern Y

2 *(however):* **I'd love to come, but I'm busy** ich würde gern kommen, bin aber beschäftigt

3 *(showing disagreement, surprise etc):* **but that's fantastic!** (aber) das ist ja fantastisch!

♦ prep (apart from, except): **nothing but trouble** nichts als Ärger; **no-one but him can do it** niemand außer ihn kann es machen; **but for you/your help** ohne dich/deine Hilfe; **anything but that** alles, nur das nicht

♦ adv (just, only): **she's but a child** sie ist noch ein Kind; **had I but known** wenn ich es nur gewusst hätte; **I can but try** ich kann es immerhin versuchen; **all but finished** so gut wie fertig

---

butcher ['bʊtʃəʳ] *n* Metzger *m; (murderer)* Schlächter *m ♦ vt* schlachten; *(kill)* abschlachten; ~**'s (shop)** *n* Metzgerei *f*

butler ['bʌtləʳ] *n* Butler *m*

butt [bʌt] *n* (*cask*) große(s) Fass *nt*; (*BRIT: fig: target*) Zielscheibe *f*; (*of gun*) Kolben *m*; (*of cigarette*) Stummel *m* ♦ *vt* (mit dem Kopf) stoßen; ~ **in** *vi* sich einmischen

butter ['bʌtə'] *n* Butter *f* ♦ *vt* buttern; ~**bean** *n* Wachsbohne *f*; ~**cup** *n* Butterblume *f*

butterfly ['bʌtəflaɪ] *n* Schmetterling *m*; (*SWIMMING: also:* ~ **stroke**) Butterflystil *m*

buttocks ['bʌtəks] *npl* Gesäß *nt*

button ['bʌtn] *n* Knopf *m* ♦ *vt, vi* (*also:* ~ **up**) zuknöpfen

buttress ['bʌtrɪs] *n* Strebepfeiler *m*; Stützbogen *m*

buxom ['bʌksəm] *adj* drall

buy [baɪ] (*pt, pp* **bought**) *vt* kaufen ♦ *n* Kauf *m*; **to ~ sb a drink** jdm einen Drink spendieren; ~**er** *n* Käufer(in) *m(f)*

buzz [bʌz] *n* Summen *nt* ♦ *vi* summen; ~**er** ['bʌzə'] *n* Summer *m*; ~ **word** *n* Modewort *nt*

KEYWORD

by [baɪ] *prep* **1** (*referring to cause, agent*) of, durch; **killed by lightning** vom Blitz getötet; **a painting by Picasso** ein Gemälde von Picasso

2 (*referring to method, manner*): **by bus/car/train** mit dem Bus/Auto/Zug; **to pay by cheque** per Scheck bezahlen; **by moonlight** bei Mondschein; **by saving hard, he ...** indem er eisern sparte, ... er ...

3 (*via, through*) über +*acc*; **he came in by the back door** er kam durch die Hintertür herein

4 (*close to, past*) bei, an +*dat*; **a holiday by the sea** ein Urlaub am Meer; **she rushed by me** sie eilte an mir vorbei

5 (*not later than*): **by 4 o'clock** bis 4 Uhr; **by this time tomorrow** morgen um diese Zeit; **by the time I got here it was too late** als ich hier ankam, war es zu spät

6 (*during*): **by day** bei Tag

7 (*amount*): **by the kilo/metre** kiloweise/meterweise; **paid by the hour** stundenweise bezahlt

8 (*MATH, measure*): **to divide by 3** durch 3

teilen; **to multiply by 3** mit 3 malnehmen; **a room 3 metres by 4** ein Zimmer 3 mal 4 Meter; **it's broader by a metre** es ist (um) einem Meter breiter

9 (*according to*) nach; **it's all right by me** von mir aus gern

10: **(all) by oneself** *etc* ganz allein

11: **by the way** übrigens

♦ *adv* **1** *see* **go**; **pass** *etc*

2: **by and by** irgendwann; (*with past tenses*) nach einiger Zeit; **by and large** (*on the whole*) im Großen und Ganzen

---

bye(-bye) ['baɪ('baɪ)] *excl* (auf) Wiedersehen

by(e)-law ['baɪlɔ:] *n* Verordnung *f*

by-election ['baɪɪlekʃən] (*BRIT*) *n* Nachwahl *f*

bygone ['baɪgɔn] *adj* vergangen ♦ *n*: **let ~s be ~s** lass(t) das Vergangene vergangen sein

bypass ['baɪpɑːs] *n* Umgehungsstraße *f* ♦ *vt* umgehen

by-product ['baɪprɔdʌkt] *n* Nebenprodukt *nt*

bystander ['baɪstændə'] *n* Zuschauer *m*

byte [baɪt] *n* (*COMPUT*) Byte *nt*

byword ['baɪwə:d] *n* Inbegriff *m*

C, c

C [si:] *n* (*MUS*) C *nt*

C. *abbr* (= *centigrade*) C

C.A. *abbr* = **chartered accountant**

cab [kæb] *n* Taxi *nt*; (*of train*) Führerstand *m*; (*of truck*) Führersitz *m*

cabaret ['kæbəreɪ] *n* Kabarett *nt*

cabbage ['kæbɪdʒ] *n* Kohl(kopf) *m*

cabin ['kæbɪn] *n* Hütte *f*; (*NAUT*) Kajüte *f*; (*AVIAT*) Kabine *f*; ~ **crew** *n* (*AVIAT*) Flugbegleitpersonal *nt*; ~ **cruiser** *n* Motorjacht *f*

cabinet ['kæbɪnɪt] *n* Schrank *m*; (*for china*) Vitrine *f*; (*POL*) Kabinett *nt*; ~-**maker** *n* Kunsttischler *m*

cable ['keɪbl] *n* Drahtseil *nt*, Tau *nt*; (*TEL*) (Leitungs)kabel *nt*; (*telegram*) Kabel *nt* ♦ *vt* kabeln, telegrafieren; ~ **car** *n* Seilbahn *f*; ~ **television** *n* Kabelfernsehen *nt* cache [kæʃ] n geheime(s) (Waffen)lager nt; geheime(s) (Proviant)lager nt

cackle ['kækl] vi gackern

cacti ['kæktaɪ] npl of **cactus**

cactus ['kæktəs] (pl cacti) n Kaktus m, Kaktee f

caddie ['kædɪ] n (GOLF) Golfjunge m; caddy ['kædɪ] n = **caddie**

cadet [kə'det] n Kadett m

cadge [kædʒ] vt schmarotzen

Caesarean [sɪ'zɛərɪən] adj: ~ **(section)** Kaiserschnitt m

café ['kæfeɪ] n Café nt, Restaurant nt

cafeteria [kæfɪ'tɪərɪə] n Selbstbedienungsrestaurant nt

caffein(e) ['kæfi:n] n Koffein nt

cage [keɪdʒ] n Käfig m ♦ vt einsperren

cagey ['keɪdʒɪ] adj geheimnistuerisch, zurückhaltend

cagoule [kə'gu:l] n Windhemd nt

Cairo ['kaɪərəʊ] n Kairo nt

cajole [kə'dʒəʊl] vt überreden

cake [keɪk] n Kuchen m; (of soap) Stück nt; ~d adj verkrustet

calamity [kə'læmɪtɪ] n Unglück nt, (Schicksals)schlag m

calcium ['kælsɪəm] n Kalzium nt

calculate ['kælkjʊleɪt] vt berechnen, kalkulieren; calculating adj berechnend; calculation [kælkjʊ'leɪʃən] n Berechnung f; calculator n Rechner m

calendar ['kæləndər] n Kalender m; ~ month n Kalendermonat m

calf [kɑ:f] (pl calves) n Kalb nt; (also: ~skin) Kalbsleder nt; (ANAT) Wade f

calibre ['kælɪbər] (US caliber) n Kaliber nt

call [kɔ:l] vt rufen; (name) nennen; (meeting) einberufen; (awaken) wecken; (TEL) anrufen ♦ vi (shout) rufen; (visit: also: ~ in, ~ round) vorbeikommen ♦ n (shout) Ruf m; (TEL) Anruf m; to be ~ed heißen; on ~ in Bereitschaft; ~ back vi (return) wiederkommen; (TEL) zurückrufen; ~ for fus (demand) erfordern, verlangen; (fetch) abholen; ~ off vt (cancel) absagen; ~ on vt fus (visit) besuchen; (turn to) bitten; ~ out vi rufen; ~ up vt (MIL) einberufen;

~box (BRIT) n Telefonzelle f; ~ centre n Telefoncenter nt, Callcenter nt; ~er n Besucher(in) m(f); (TEL) Anrufer m; ~ girl n Callgirl nt; ~-in (US) n (phone-in) Phone-in nt; ~ing n (vocation) Berufung f; ~ing card (US) n Visitenkarte f

callous ['kæləs] adj herzlos

calm [kɑ:m] n Ruhe f; (NAUT) Flaute f ♦ vt beruhigen ♦ adj ruhig; (person) gelassen; ~ down vi sich beruhigen ♦ vt beruhigen

Calor gas ['kælər-] ® n Propangas nt

calorie ['kælərɪ] n Kalorie f

calves [kɑ:vz] npl of **calf**

Cambodia [kæm'bəʊdɪə] n Kambodscha nt

camcorder ['kæmkɔːdər] n Camcorder m

came [keɪm] pt of **come**

cameo ['kæmɪəʊ] n Kamee f

camera ['kæmərə] n Fotoapparat m; (CINE, TV) Kamera f; in ~ unter Ausschluss der Öffentlichkeit; ~man (irreg) n Kameramann m; ~phone n Fotohandy nt

camouflage ['kæməflɑːʒ] n Tarnung f ♦ vt tarnen

camp [kæmp] n Lager nt ♦ vi zelten, campen ♦ adj affektiert

campaign [kæm'peɪn] n Kampagne f; (MIL) Feldzug m ♦ vi (MIL) Krieg führen; (fig) werben, Propaganda machen; (POL) den Wahlkampf führen

camp: ~ bed ['kæmp'bed] (BRIT) n Campingbett nt; ~er ['kæmpər] n Camper(in) m(f); (vehicle) Campingwagen m; ~ing ['kæmpɪŋ] n: to go ~ing zelten, Camping machen; ~ing gas (US) n Campinggas nt; ~site ['kæmpsaɪt] n Campingplatz m

campus ['kæmpəs] n Universitätsgelände nt, Campus m

can¹ [kæn] n Büchse f, Dose f; (for water) Kanne f ♦ vt konservieren, in Büchsen einmachen

┌─── KEYWORD ───┐

can² [kæn] (negative cannot, can't, conditional could) aux vb 1 (be able to, know how to) können; **I can see you tomorrow, if you like** ich könnte Sie morgen sehen, wenn Sie wollen; **I can swim** ich kann schwimmen; **can you speak German?** sprechen Sie Deutsch? 2 (*may*) können, dürfen; **could I have a word with you?** könnte ich Sie kurz sprechen?

Canada [ˈkænədə] n Kanada nt; **Canadian** [kəˈneɪdɪən] adj kanadisch ♦ n Kanadier(in) m(f)

canal [kəˈnæl] n Kanal m

canapé [ˈkænəpeɪ] n Cocktail- or Appetithappen m

canary [kəˈneərɪ] n Kanarienvogel m

cancel [ˈkænsəl] vt absagen; (*delete*) durchstreichen; (*train*) streichen; ~**lation** [kænsəˈleɪʃən] n Absage f; Streichung f

cancer [ˈkænsər] n (ASTROL: C~) Krebs m

candid [ˈkændɪd] adj offen, ehrlich

candidate [ˈkændɪdeɪt] n Kandidat(in) m(f)

candle [ˈkændl] n Kerze f; ~**light** n Kerzenlicht nt; ~**stick** n (also: ~ **holder**) Kerzenhalter m

candour [ˈkændər] (US **candor**) n Offenheit f

candy [ˈkændɪ] n Kandis(zucker) m; (US) Bonbons pl; ~**floss** (BRIT) n Zuckerwatte f

cane [keɪn] n (BOT) Rohr nt; (*stick*) Stock m ♦ (BRIT: *beat*) schlagen

canine [ˈkeɪnaɪn] adj Hunde-

canister [ˈkænɪstər] n Blechdose f

cannabis [ˈkænəbɪs] n Hanf m, Haschisch nt

canned [kænd] adj Büchsen-, eingemacht

cannon [ˈkænən] (pl ~ or ~**s**) n Kanone f

cannot [ˈkænɔt] = **can not**

canny [ˈkænɪ] adj schlau

canoe [kəˈnuː] n Kanu nt; ~**ing** n Kanusport m, Kanufahren nt

canon [ˈkænən] n (*clergyman*) Domherr m; (*standard*) Grundsatz m

can-opener [ˈkænəupnər] n Büchsenöffner m

canopy [ˈkænəpɪ] n Baldachin m

can't [kænt] = **can not**

cantankerous [kænˈtæŋkərəs] adj zänkisch, mürrisch

canteen [kænˈtiːn] n Kantine f; (BRIT: of cutlery) Besteckkasten m

canter [ˈkæntər] n Kanter m ♦ vi in kurzem Galopp reiten

canvas [ˈkænvəs] n Segeltuch nt; (*sail*) Segel nt; (*for painting*) Leinwand f; **under ~** (*camping*) in Zelten

canvass [ˈkænvəs] vt um Stimmen werben; ~**ing** n Wahlwerbung f

canyon [ˈkænjən] n Felsenschlucht f

cap [kæp] n Mütze f; (*of pen*) Kappe f; (*of bottle*) Deckel m ♦ vt (*surpass*) übertreffen; (SPORT) aufstellen; (*put limit on*) einen Höchstsatz festlegen für

capability [keɪpəˈbɪlɪtɪ] n Fähigkeit f

capable [ˈkeɪpəbl] adj fähig

capacity [kəˈpæsɪtɪ] n Fassungsvermögen nt; (*ability*) Fähigkeit f; (*position*) Eigenschaft f

cape [keɪp] n (*garment*) Cape nt, Umhang m; (GEOG) Kap nt

caper [ˈkeɪpər] n (COOK: usu: ~**s**) Kaper f; (*prank*) Kapriole f

capital [ˈkæpɪtl] n (~ *city*) Hauptstadt f; (FIN) Kapital nt; (~ *letter*) Großbuchstabe m; ~ **gains tax** n Kapitalertragssteuer f; ~**ism** n Kapitalismus m; ~**ist** adj kapitalistisch ♦ n Kapitalist(in) m(f); ~**ize** vi: **to ~ize on** Kapital schlagen aus; ~ **punishment** n Todesstrafe f

Capitol

ℹ **Capitol** ist das Gebäude in Washington auf dem Capitol Hill, in dem der Kongress der USA zusammentritt. Die Bezeichnung wird in vielen amerikanischen Bundesstaaten auch für das Parlamentsgebäude des jeweiligen Staates verwendet.

Capricorn [ˈkæprɪkɔːn] n Steinbock m

capsize [kæpˈsaɪz] vt, vi kentern

capsule [ˈkæpsjuːl] n Kapsel f

captain [ˈkæptɪn] n Kapitän m; (MIL) Hauptmann m ♦ vt anführen

caption [ˈkæpʃən] n (*heading*) Überschrift f; (*to picture*) Unterschrift f

captivate [ˈkæptɪveɪt] vt fesseln

captive [ˈkæptɪv] n Gefangene(r) f(m) ♦ adj gefangen (gehalten); **captivity** [kæpˈtɪvɪtɪ] *n* Gefangenschaft *f*

capture ['kæptʃə'] *vt* gefangen nehmen; (*place*) erobern; (*attention*) erregen ♦ *n* Gefangennahme *f*; (*data ~*) Erfassung *f*

car [kɑː'] *n* Auto *nt*, Wagen *m*; (*RAIL*) Wagen *m*

caramel ['kærəməl] *n* Karamelle *f*, Karamellbonbon *m or nt*; (*burnt sugar*) Karamell *m*

carat ['kærət] *n* Karat *nt*

caravan ['kærəvæn] *n* (*BRIT*) Wohnwagen *m*; (*in desert*) Karawane *f*; **~ning** *n* Caravaning *nt*, Urlaub *m* im Wohnwagen; **~ site** (*BRIT*) *n* Campingplatz *m* für Wohnwagen

carbohydrate [kɑːbəu'haɪdreɪt] *n* Kohlenhydrat *nt*

carbon ['kɑːbən] *n* Kohlenstoff *m*; **~ copy** *n* Durchschlag *m*; **~ dioxide** *n* Kohlendioxyd *nt*; **~ monoxide** *n* Kohlenmonoxyd *nt*; **~ paper** *n* Kohlepapier *nt*

car boot sale *n* auf einem Parkplatz stattfindender Flohmarkt mit dem Kofferraum als Auslage

carburettor [kɑːbju'retə'] (*US* **carburetor**) *n* Vergaser *m*

carcass ['kɑːkəs] *n* Kadaver *m*

card [kɑːd] *n* Karte *f*; **~board** *n* Pappe *f*; **~ game** *n* Kartenspiel *nt*

cardiac ['kɑːdɪæk] *adj* Herz-

cardigan ['kɑːdɪgən] *n* Strickjacke *f*

cardinal ['kɑːdɪnl] *adj*: **~ number** Kardinalzahl *f* ♦ *n* (*REL*) Kardinal *m*

card index *n* Kartei *f*; (*in library*) Katalog *m*

cardphone *n* Kartentelefon *nt*

care [keə'] *n* (*of teeth, car etc*) Pflege *f*; (*of children*) Fürsorge *f*; (*~fulness*) Sorgfalt *f*; (*worry*) Sorge *f* ♦ *vi*: **to ~ about** sich kümmern um; **~ of** bei; **in sb's ~** in jds Obhut; **I don't ~** das ist mir egal; **I couldn't ~ less** es ist mir doch völlig egal; **to take ~** aufpassen; **to take ~ of** sorgen für; **to take ~ to do sth** sich bemühen, etw zu tun; **~ for** *vt* sorgen für; (*like*) mögen

career [kə'rɪə'] *n* Karriere *f*, Laufbahn *f* ♦ *vi* (*also*: **~ along**) rasen; **~ woman** (*irreg*) *n* Karrierefrau *f*

care: **~free** *adj* sorgenfrei; **~ful** *adj*

sorgfältig; **(be) ~ful!** pass auf!; **~fully** *adv* vorsichtig; (*methodically*) sorgfältig; **~less** *adj* nachlässig; **~lessness** *n* Nachlässigkeit *f*; **~r** *n* (*MED*) Betreuer(in) *m(f)*

caress [kə'rɛs] *n* Liebkosung *f* ♦ *vt* liebkosen

caretaker ['keəteɪkə'] *n* Hausmeister *m*

car ferry *n* Autofähre *f*

cargo ['kɑːgəu] (*pl* **~es**) *n* Schiffsladung *f*

car hire *n* Autovermietung *f*

Caribbean [kærɪ'biːən] *n*: **the ~ (Sea)** die Karibik

caricature ['kærɪkətjuə'] *n* Karikatur *f*

caring ['keərɪŋ] *adj* (*society, organization*) sozial eingestellt; (*person*) liebevoll

carnage ['kɑːnɪdʒ] *n* Blutbad *nt*

carnation [kɑː'neɪʃən] *n* Nelke *f*

carnival ['kɑːnɪvl] *n* Karneval *m*, Fasching *m*; (*US: fun fair*) Kirmes *f*

carnivorous [kɑː'nɪvərəs] *adj* Fleisch fressend

carol ['kærəl] *n*: **(Christmas) ~** (Weihnachts)lied *nt*

carp [kɑːp] *n* (*fish*) Karpfen *m*

car park (*BRIT*) *n* Parkplatz *m*; (*covered*) Parkhaus *nt*

carpenter ['kɑːpɪntə'] *n* Zimmermann *m*; **carpentry** ['kɑːpɪntrɪ] *n* Zimmerei *f*

carpet ['kɑːpɪt] *n* Teppich *m* ♦ *vt* mit einem Teppich auslegen; **~ bombing** *n* Flächenbombardierung *f*; **~ slippers** *npl* Pantoffeln *pl*; **~ sweeper** ['kɑːpɪtswiːpə'] *n* Teppichkehrer *m*

car phone *n* (*TEL*) Autotelefon *nt*

car rental (*US*) *n* Autovermietung *f*

carriage ['kærɪdʒ] *n* Kutsche *f*; (*RAIL, of typewriter*) Wagen *m*; (*of goods*) Beförderung *f*; (*bearing*) Haltung *f*; **~ return** *n* (*on typewriter*) Rücklauftaste *f*; **~way** (*BRIT*) *n* (*part of road*) Fahrbahn *f*

carrier ['kærɪə'] *n* Träger(in) *m(f)*; (*COMM*) Spediteur *m*; **~ bag** (*BRIT*) *n* Tragetasche *m*

carrot ['kærət] *n* Möhre *f*, Karotte *f*

carry ['kærɪ] *vt, vi* tragen; **to get carried away** (*fig*) sich nicht mehr bremsen können; **~ on** *vi* (*continue*) weitermachen; (*inf: complain*) Theater machen; **~ out** *vt* (*orders*) ausführen; (*investigation*) durchführen;~**cot** (BRIT) n Babytragetasche f;~**on** (inf) n (fuss) Theater nt

cart [kɑːt] n Wagen m, Karren m ♦ vt schleppen

cartilage [ˈkɑːtɪlɪdʒ] n Knorpel m

carton [ˈkɑːtən] n Karton m; (of milk) Tüte f

cartoon [kɑːˈtuːn] n (PRESS) Karikatur f; (comic strip) Comics pl; (CINE) (Zeichen)trickfilm m

cartridge [ˈkɑːtrɪdʒ] n Patrone f

carve [kɑːv] vt (wood) schnitzen; (stone) meißeln; (meat) (vor)schneiden;~ **up** vt aufschneiden;**carving** [ˈkɑːvɪŋ] n Schnitzerei f;**carving knife** n Tran(s)chiermesser nt

car wash n Autowäsche f

cascade [kæsˈkeɪd] n Wasserfall m ♦ vi kaskadenartig herabfallen

case [keɪs] n (box) Kasten m; (BRIT: also: **suitcase**) Koffer m; (JUR, matter) Fall m; **in** ~ falls, im Falle; **in any** ~ jedenfalls, auf jeden Fall

cash [kæʃ] n (Bar)geld nt ♦ vt einlösen; ~ **on delivery** per Nachnahme;~ **book** n Kassenbuch nt;~ **card** n Scheckkarte f;~ **desk** (BRIT) n Kasse f;~ **dispenser** n Geldautomat m

cashew [kæˈʃuː] n (also: ~ **nut**) Cashewnuss f

cash flow n Cashflow m

cashier [kæˈʃɪər] n Kassierer(in) m(f)

cashmere [ˈkæʃmɪər] n Kaschmirwolle f

cash register n Registrierkasse f

casing [ˈkeɪsɪŋ] n Gehäuse nt

casino [kəˈsiːnəu] n Kasino nt

casket [ˈkɑːskɪt] n Kästchen nt; (US: coffin) Sarg m

casserole [ˈkæsərəul] n Kasserolle f; (food) Auflauf m

cassette [kæˈset] n Kassette f; ~ **player** n Kassettengerät nt

cast [kɑːst] (pt, pp **cast**) vt werfen; (horns) verlieren; (metal) gießen; (THEAT) besetzen; (vote) abgeben ♦ n (THEAT) Besetzung f; (also: **plaster** ~) Gipsverband m; ~ **off** vi (NAUT) losmachen

castaway [ˈkɑːstəweɪ] n Schiffbrüchige(r) f(m)

caste [kɑːst] n Kaste f

caster sugar [ˈkɑːstə-] (BRIT) n Raffinade f

casting vote [ˈkɑːstɪŋ-] (BRIT) n entscheidende Stimme f

cast iron n Gusseisen nt

castle [ˈkɑːsl] n Burg f; Schloss nt; (CHESS) Turm m

castor [ˈkɑːstər] n (wheel) Laufrolle f

castor oil n Rizinusöl nt

castrate [kæsˈtreɪt] vt kastrieren

casual [ˈkæʒjul] adj (attitude) nachlässig; (dress) leger; (meeting) zufällig; (work) Gelegenheits-;~**ly** adv (dress) zwanglos, leger; (remark) beiläufig

casualty [ˈkæʒjultɪ] n Verletzte(r) f(m); (dead) Tote(r) f(m); (also: ~ **department**) Unfallstation f

cat [kæt] n Katze f

catalogue [ˈkætəlɔg] (US **catalog**) n Katalog m ♦ vt katalogisieren

catalyst [ˈkætəlɪst] n Katalysator m

catalytic converter [kætəˈlɪtɪk kənˈvɜːtər] n Katalysator m

catapult [ˈkætəpʌlt] n Schleuder f

cataract [ˈkætərækt] n (MED) graue(r) Star m

catarrh [kəˈtɑːr] n Katarr(h) m

catastrophe [kəˈtæstrəfi] n Katastrophe f

catch [kætʃ] (pt, pp **caught**) vt fangen; (arrest) fassen; (train) erreichen; (person: by surprise) ertappen; (also: ~ **up**) einholen ♦ vi (fire) in Gang kommen; (in branches etc) hängen bleiben ♦ n (fish etc) Fang m; (trick) Haken m; (of lock) Sperrhaken m; **to** ~ **an illness** sich dat eine Krankheit holen; **to** ~ **fire** Feuer fangen; ~ **on** vi (understand) begreifen; (grow popular) ankommen; ~ **up** vi (fig) aufholen; ~**ing** [ˈkætʃɪŋ] adj ansteckend; ~**ment area** [ˈkætʃmənt-] (BRIT) n Einzugsgebiet nt; ~ **phrase** n Slogan m; ~**y** [ˈkætʃi] adj (tune) eingängig

categoric(al) [kætɪˈgɔrɪk(l)] adj kategorisch

category [ˈkætɪgəri] n Kategorie f

cater [ˈkeɪtər] vi versorgen; ~ **for** (BRIT) vt fus (party) ausrichten; (needs) eingestellt sein auf +acc; ~**er** n Lieferant(in) m(f) von Speisen und Getränken; ~**ing** n

Gastronomie f

caterpillar ['kætəpɪlər] n Raupe f; ~ **track** ® n Gleiskette f

cathedral [kə'θi:drəl] n Kathedrale f, Dom m

Catholic ['kæθəlɪk] adj (REL) katholisch ♦ n Katholik(in) m(f); c~ adj (tastes etc) vielseitig

CAT scan [kæt-] n Computertomografie f

Catseye ['kæts'aɪ] (BRIT: ®) n (AUT) Katzenauge nt

cattle ['kætl] npl Vieh nt

catty ['kætɪ] adj gehässig

caucus ['kɔ:kəs] n (POL) Gremium nt; (US: meeting) Sitzung f

caught [kɔ:t] pt, pp of **catch**

cauliflower ['kɒlɪflaʊər] n Blumenkohl m

cause [kɔ:z] n Ursache f; (purpose) Sache f ♦ vt verursachen

causeway ['kɔ:zweɪ] n Damm m

caustic ['kɔ:stɪk] adj ätzend; (fig) bissig

caution ['kɔ:ʃən] n Vorsicht f; (warning) Verwarnung f ♦ vt verwarnen; **cautious** ['kɔ:ʃəs] adj vorsichtig

cavalry ['kævəlrɪ] n Kavallerie f

cave [keɪv] n Höhle f; ~ **in** vi einstürzen; ~**man** (irreg) n Höhlenmensch m

cavern ['kævən] n Höhle f

caviar(e) ['kævɪɑ:ʳ] n Kaviar m

cavity ['kævɪtɪ] n Loch nt

cavort [kə'vɔ:t] vi umherspringen

C.B. n abbr (= Citizens' Band (Radio)) CB

C.B.I. n abbr (= Confederation of British Industry) ≈ BDI m

cc n abbr = **carbon copy; cubic centimetres**

CCTV n abbr (= closed-circuit television) Videoüberwachung f

CD n abbr (= compact disc) CD f

CDI n abbr (= Compact Disk Interactive) CD-I f

CD player n CD-Spieler m

CD-ROM n abbr (= compact disc read-only memory) CD-Rom f

cease [si:s] vi aufhören ♦ vt beenden; ~**fire** n Feuereinstellung f; ~**less** adj unaufhörlich

cedar ['si:dər] n Zeder f

ceiling ['si:lɪŋ] n Decke f; (fig) Höchstgrenze f

celebrate ['selɪbreɪt] vt, vi feiern; ~**d** adj gefeiert; **celebration** [selɪ'breɪʃən] n Feier f

celebrity [sɪ'lebrɪtɪ] n gefeierte Persönlichkeit f

celery ['selərɪ] n Sellerie m or f

celibacy ['selɪbəsɪ] n Zölibat nt or m

cell [sel] n Zelle f; (ELEC) Element nt

cellar ['selər] n Keller m

cello ['tʃeləʊ] n Cello nt

Cellophane ['seləfeɪn] ® n Cellophan nt ®

cellphone ['selfəʊn] n Funktelefon nt

cellular ['seljʊlər] adj zellular

cellulose ['seljʊləʊs] n Zellulose f

Celt [kelt, selt] n Kelte m, Keltin f; ~**ic** ['keltɪk, 'seltɪk] adj keltisch

cement [sə'ment] n Zement m ♦ vt zementieren; ~ **mixer** n Betonmischmaschine f

cemetery ['semɪtrɪ] n Friedhof m

censor ['sensər] n Zensor m ♦ vt zensieren; ~**ship** n Zensur f

censure ['senʃər] vt rügen

census ['sensəs] n Volkszählung f

cent [sent] n (coin) Cent m; see also **per cent**

centenary [sen'ti:nərɪ] n Jahrhundertfeier f

center ['sentər] (US) n = **centre**

centigrade ['sentɪgreɪd] adj Celsius

centimetre ['sentɪmi:tər] (US **centimeter**) n Zentimeter nt

centipede ['sentɪpi:d] n Tausendfüßler m

central ['sentrəl] adj zentral; C~ **America** n Mittelamerika nt; ~ **heating** n Zentralheizung f; ~**ize** vt zentralisieren; ~ **reservation** (BRIT) n (AUT) Mittelstreifen m

centre ['sentər] (US **center**) n Zentrum nt ♦ vt zentrieren; ~-**forward** n (SPORT) Mittelstürmer m; ~-**half** n (SPORT) Stopper m

century ['sentjʊrɪ] n Jahrhundert nt

ceramic [sɪ'ræmɪk] adj keramisch; ~**s** npl Keramiken pl

cereal ['sɪərɪəl] n (grain) Getreide nt; (at breakfast) Getreideflocken pl

cerebral ['serɪbrəl] adj zerebral; (intellectual) geistig

ceremony ['serɪmənɪ] n Zeremonie f; **to**

stand on ~ förmlich sein

certain ['sɜːtən] *adj* sicher; (*particular*) gewiss; **for ~** ganz bestimmt; **~ly** *adv* sicher, bestimmt; **~ty** *n* Gewissheit *f*

certificate [sə'tɪfɪkɪt] *n* Bescheinigung *f*; (*SCH etc*) Zeugnis *nt*

certified mail ['sɜːtɪfaɪd-] (*US*) *n* Einschreiben *nt*

certified public accountant ['sɜːtɪfaɪd-] (*US*) *n* geprüfte(r) Buchhalter *m*

certify ['sɜːtɪfaɪ] *vt* bescheinigen

cervical ['sɜːvɪkl] *adj* (*smear, cancer*) Gebärmutterhals-

cervix ['sɜːvɪks] *n* Gebärmutterhals *m*

cf. *abbr* (= *compare*) vgl.

CFC *n abbr* (= *chlorofluorocarbon*) FCKW *m*

ch. *abbr* (= *chapter*) Kap.

chafe [tʃeɪf] *vt* scheuern

chaffinch ['tʃæfɪntʃ] *n* Buchfink *m*

chain [tʃeɪn] *n* Kette *f* ♦ *vt* (*also:* ~ **up**) anketten; **~ reaction** *n* Kettenreaktion *f*; **~-smoke** *vi* kettenrauchen; **~ store** *n* Kettenladen *m*

chair [tʃeə*r*] *n* Stuhl *m*; (*armchair*) Sessel *m*; (*UNIV*) Lehrstuhl *m* ♦ *vt* (*meeting*) den Vorsitz führen bei; **~lift** *n* Sessellift *m*; **~man** (*irreg*) *n* Vorsitzende(r) *m*

chalet ['ʃæleɪ] *n* Chalet *nt*

chalk [tʃɔːk] *n* Kreide *f*

challenge ['tʃælɪndʒ] *n* Herausforderung *f* ♦ *vt* herausfordern; (*contest*) bestreiten; **challenging** *adj* (*tone*) herausfordernd; (*work*) anspruchsvoll

chamber ['tʃeɪmbə*r*] *n* Kammer *f*; ~ **of commerce** Handelskammer *f*; **~maid** *n* Zimmermädchen *nt*; ~ **music** *n* Kammermusik *f*

chamois ['ʃæmwɑː] *n* Gämse *f*

champagne [ʃæm'peɪn] *n* Champagner *m*, Sekt *m*

champion ['tʃæmpɪən] *n* (*SPORT*) Meister(in) *m(f)*; (*of cause*) Verfechter(in) *m(f)*; **~ship** *n* Meisterschaft *f*

chance [tʃɑːns] *n* (*luck*) Zufall *m*; (*possibility*) Möglichkeit *f*; (*opportunity*) Gelegenheit *f*, Chance *f*; (*risk*) Risiko *nt* ♦ *adj* zufällig ♦ *vt*: **to ~ it** es darauf ankommen lassen; **by ~**

zufällig; **to take a ~** ein Risiko eingehen

chancellor ['tʃɑːnsələ*r*] *n* Kanzler *m*; **C~ of the Exchequer** (*BRIT*) *n* Schatzkanzler *m*

chandelier [ʃændə'lɪə*r*] *n* Kronleuchter *m*

change [tʃeɪndʒ] *vt* ändern; (*replace, COMM: money*) wechseln; (*exchange*) umtauschen; (*transform*) verwandeln ♦ *vi* sich ändern; (~ *trains*) umsteigen; (~ *clothes*) sich umziehen ♦ *n* Veränderung *f*; (*money returned*) Wechselgeld *nt*; (*coins*) Kleingeld *nt*; **to ~ one's mind** es sich *dat* anders überlegen; **to ~ into sth** (*be transformed*) sich in etw *acc* verwandeln; **for a ~** zur Abwechslung; **~able** *adj* (*weather*) wechselhaft; **~ machine** *n* Geldwechselautomat *m*; **~over** *n* Umstellung *f*

changing ['tʃeɪndʒɪŋ] *adj* veränderlich; **~ room** (*BRIT*) *n* Umkleideraum *m*

channel ['tʃænl] *n* (*stream*) Bachbett *nt*; (*NAUT*) Straße *f*; (*TV*) Kanal *m*; (*fig*) Weg *m* ♦ *vt* (*efforts*) lenken; **the (English) C~** der Ärmelkanal; **~-hopping** *n* (*TV*) ständiges Umschalten; **C~ Islands** *npl*: **the C~ Islands** die Kanalinseln *pl*; **C~ Tunnel** *n*: **the C~ Tunnel** der Kanaltunnel

chant [tʃɑːnt] *n* Gesang *m*; (*of fans*) Sprechchor *m* ♦ *vt* intonieren

chaos ['keɪɔs] *n* Chaos *nt*

chap [tʃæp] (*inf*) *n* Kerl *m*

chapel ['tʃæpl] *n* Kapelle *f*

chaperon ['ʃæpərəʊn] *n* Anstandsdame *f*

chaplain ['tʃæplɪn] *n* Kaplan *m*

chapped [tʃæpt] *adj* (*skin, lips*) spröde

chapter ['tʃæptə*r*] *n* Kapitel *nt*

char [tʃɑː*r*] *vt* (*burn*) verkohlen

character ['kærɪktə*r*] *n* Charakter *m*, Wesen *nt*; (*in novel, film*) Figur *f*; **~istic** [kærɪktə'rɪstɪk] *adj*: **~istic (of sb/sth)** (für jdn/etw) charakteristisch ♦ *n* Kennzeichen *nt*; **~ize** *vt* charakterisieren, kennzeichnen

charade [ʃə'rɑːd] *n* Scharade *f*

charcoal ['tʃɑːkəʊl] *n* Holzkohle *f*

charge [tʃɑːdʒ] *n* (*cost*) Preis *m*; (*JUR*) Anklage *f*; (*explosive*) Ladung *f*; (*attack*) Angriff *m* ♦ *vt* (*gun, battery*) laden; (*price*) verlangen; (*JUR*) anklagen; (*MIL*) angreifen ♦ *vi* (*rush*) (an)stürmen; **bank ~s**

Bankgebühren pl; **free of ~** kostenlos; **to reverse the ~s** (TEL) ein R-Gespräch führen; **to be in ~ of** verantwortlich sein für; **to take ~** (die Verantwortung) übernehmen; **to ~ sth (up) to sb's account** jdm etw in Rechnung stellen; **~ card** n Kundenkarte f

charitable ['tʃærɪtəbl] adj wohltätig; (lenient) nachsichtig

charity ['tʃærɪtɪ] n (institution) Hilfswerk nt; (attitude) Nächstenliebe f

charm [tʃɑːm] n Charme m; (spell) Bann m; (object) Talisman m ♦ vt bezaubern; **~ing** adj reizend

chart [tʃɑːt] n Tabelle f; (NAUT) Seekarte f ♦ vt (course) abstecken

charter ['tʃɑːtəʳ] vt chartern ♦ n Schutzbrief m; **~ed accountant** n Wirtschaftsprüfer(in) m(f); **~ flight** n Charterflug m

chase [tʃeɪs] vt jagen, verfolgen ♦ n Jagd f

chasm ['kæzəm] n Kluft f

chassis ['ʃæsɪ] n Fahrgestell nt

chat [tʃæt] vi (also: **have a ~**) plaudern ♦ n Plauderei f; **~ show** (BRIT) n Talkshow f

chatter ['tʃætəʳ] vi schwatzen; (teeth) klappern ♦ n Geschwätz nt; **~box** n Quasselstrippe f

chatty ['tʃætɪ] adj geschwätzig

chauffeur ['ʃəʊfəʳ] n Chauffeur m

chauvinist ['ʃəʊvɪnɪst] n (male ~) Chauvi m (inf)

cheap [tʃiːp] adj, adv billig; **~ day return** n Tagesrückfahrkarte f (zu einem günstigeren Tarif); **~ly** adv billig

cheat [tʃiːt] vt, vi betrügen; (SCH) mogeln ♦ n Betrüger(in) m(f)

check [tʃek] vt (examine) prüfen; (make sure) nachsehen; (control) kontrollieren; (restrain) zügeln; (stop) anhalten ♦ n (examination, restraint) Kontrolle f; (bill) Rechnung f; (pattern) Karo(muster) nt; (US) = **cheque** ♦ adj (pattern, cloth) kariert; **~ in** vi (in hotel, airport) einchecken ♦ vt (luggage) abfertigen lassen; **~ out** vi (of hotel) abreisen; **~ up** vi nachschauen; **~ up on** vt kontrollieren; **~ered** (US) adj =

chequered; **~ers** (US) n (draughts) Damespiel nt; **~-in (desk)** n Abfertigung f; **~ing account** (US) n (current account) Girokonto nt; **~mate** n Schachmatt nt; **~out** n Kasse f; **~point** n Kontrollpunkt m; **~ room** (US) n (left-luggage office) Gepäckaufbewahrung f; **~up** n (Nach)prüfung f; (MED) (ärztliche) Untersuchung f

cheek [tʃiːk] n Backe f; (fig) Frechheit f; **~bone** n Backenknochen m; **~y** adj frech

cheep [tʃiːp] vi piepsen

cheer [tʃɪəʳ] n (usu pl) Hurra- or Beifallsruf m ♦ vt zujubeln; (encourage) aufmuntern ♦ vi jauchzen; **~s!** Prost!; **~ up** vi bessere Laune bekommen ♦ vt aufmuntern; **~ up!** nun lach doch mal!; **~ful** adj fröhlich

cheerio [tʃɪərɪ'əʊ] (BRIT) excl tschüss!

cheese [tʃiːz] n Käse m; **~board** n (gemischte) Käseplatte f

cheetah ['tʃiːtə] n Gepard m

chef [ʃef] n Küchenchef m

chemical ['kemɪkl] adj chemisch ♦ n Chemikalie f

chemist ['kemɪst] n (BRIT: pharmacist) Apotheker m, Drogist m; (scientist) Chemiker m; **~ry** n Chemie f; **~'s (shop)** (BRIT) n Apotheke f, Drogerie f

cheque [tʃek] (BRIT) n Scheck m; **~book** n Scheckbuch nt; **~ card** n Scheckkarte f

chequered ['tʃekəd] adj (fig) bewegt

cherish ['tʃerɪʃ] vt (person) lieben; (hope) hegen

cherry ['tʃerɪ] n Kirsche f

chess [tʃes] n Schach nt; **~board** n Schachbrett nt; **~man** (irreg) n Schachfigur f

chest [tʃest] n (ANAT) Brust f; (box) Kiste f; **~ of drawers** Kommode f

chestnut ['tʃesnʌt] n Kastanie f

chew [tʃuː] vt, vi kauen; **~ing gum** n Kaugummi m

chic [ʃiːk] adj schick, elegant

chick [tʃɪk] n Küken nt; (US: inf: girl) Biene f

chicken ['tʃɪkɪn] n Huhn nt; (food) Hähnchen nt; **~ out** (inf) vi kneifen

chickenpox ['tʃɪkɪnpɒks] n Windpocken pl

chicory ['tʃɪkərɪ] n (in coffee) Zichorie f; (plant) Chicorée f, Schikoree f

chief [tʃiːf] n (of tribe) Häuptling m; (COMM) Chef m ♦ adj Haupt-; ~ **executive** n Geschäftsführer(in) m(f); ~**ly** adv hauptsächlich

chilblain ['tʃɪlbleɪn] n Frostbeule f

child [tʃaɪld] (pl ~**ren**) n Kind nt; ~**birth** n Entbindung f; ~**hood** n Kindheit f; ~**ish** adj kindisch; ~**like** adj kindlich; ~ **minder** (BRIT) n Tagesmutter f; ~**ren** ['tʃɪldrən] npl of **child**; ~ **seat** n Kindersitz m

Chile ['tʃɪlɪ] n Chile nt; ~**an** adj chilenisch

chill [tʃɪl] n Kühle f; (MED) Erkältung f ♦ vt (CULIN) kühlen

chilli ['tʃɪlɪ] n Peperoni pl; (meal, spice) Chili m

chilly ['tʃɪlɪ] adj kühl, frostig

chime [tʃaɪm] n Geläut nt ♦ vi ertönen

chimney ['tʃɪmnɪ] n Schornstein m; ~ **sweep** n Schornsteinfeger(in) m(f)

chimpanzee [tʃɪmpæn'ziː] n Schimpanse m

chin [tʃɪn] n Kinn nt

China ['tʃaɪnə] n China nt

china ['tʃaɪnə] n Porzellan nt

Chinese [tʃaɪ'niːz] adj chinesisch ♦ n (inv) Chinese m, Chinesin f; (LING) Chinesisch nt

chink [tʃɪŋk] n (opening) Ritze f; (noise) Klirren nt

chip [tʃɪp] n (of wood etc) Splitter m; (in poker etc; US: crisp) Chip m ♦ vt absplittern; ~**s** npl (BRIT: COOK) Pommes frites pl; ~ **in** vi Zwischenbemerkungen machen

---

Chip shop

i Chip shop, auch fish-and-chip shop, ist die traditionelle britische Imbissbude, in der vor allem fritierte Fischfilets und Pommes frites, aber auch andere einfache Mahlzeiten angeboten werden. Früher wurde das Essen zum Mitnehmen in Zeitungspapier verpackt. Manche chip shops haben auch einen Essraum.

---

chiropodist [kɪ'rɔpədɪst] (BRIT) n Fußpfleger(in) m(f)

chirp [tʃəːp] vi zwitschern

chisel ['tʃɪzl] n Meißel m

chit [tʃɪt] n Notiz f

chivalrous ['ʃɪvəlrəs] adj ritterlich; **chival** ['ʃɪvlrɪ] n Ritterlichkeit f

chives [tʃaɪvz] npl Schnittlauch m

chlorine ['klɔːriːn] n Chlor nt

chock-a-block ['tʃɔkə'blɔk] adj voll gepfropft

chock-full [tʃɔk'ful] adj voll gepfropft

chocolate ['tʃɔklɪt] n Schokolade f

choice [tʃɔɪs] n Wahl f; (of goods) Auswahl ♦ adj Qualitäts-

choir ['kwaɪə*] n Chor m; ~**boy** n Chorkna m

choke [tʃəuk] vi ersticken ♦ vt erdrosseln; (block) (ab)drosseln ♦ n (AUT) Starterklapp f

cholera ['kɔlərə] n Cholera f

cholesterol [kə'lestərɔl] n Cholesterin nt

choose [tʃuːz] (pt **chose**, pp **chosen**) vt wählen; **choosy** ['tʃuːzɪ] adj wählerisch

chop [tʃɔp] vt (wood) spalten; (COOK: also: ~ **up**) (zer)hacken ♦ n Hieb m; (COOK) Kotelett nt; ~**s** npl (jaws) Lefzen pl

chopper ['tʃɔpə*] n (helicopter) Hubschraub m

choppy ['tʃɔpɪ] adj (sea) bewegt

chopsticks ['tʃɔpstɪks] npl (Ess)stäbchen p

choral ['kɔːrəl] adj Chor-

chord [kɔːd] n Akkord m

chore [tʃɔː*] n Pflicht f; ~**s** npl (housework) Hausarbeit f

choreographer [kɔrɪ'ɔgrəfə*] n Choreograf(in) m(f)

chorister ['kɔrɪstə*] n Chorsänger(in) m(f)

chortle ['tʃɔːtl] vi glucksen

chorus ['kɔːrəs] n Chor m; (in song) Refrain m

chose [tʃəuz] pt of **choose**

chosen ['tʃəuzn] pp of **choose**

chowder ['tʃaudə*] (US) n sämige Fischsupp f

Christ [kraɪst] n Christus m

christen ['krɪsn] vt taufen; ~**ing** n Taufe f

Christian ['krɪstɪən] adj christlich ♦ n Christ(in) m(f); ~**ity** [krɪstɪ'ænɪtɪ] n Christentum nt; ~ **name** n Vorname m

hristmas ['krɪsməs] n Weihnachten pl; **Happy** or **Merry ~!** frohe or fröhliche Weihnachten!; **~ card** n Weihnachtskarte f; **~ Day** n der erste Weihnachtstag; **~ Eve** n Heiligabend m; **~ tree** n Weihnachtsbaum m

hrome [krəʊm] n Verchromung f

hromium ['krəʊmɪəm] n Chrom nt

hronic ['krɒnɪk] adj chronisch

hronicle ['krɒnɪkl] n Chronik f

hronological [krɒnə'lɒdʒɪkl] adj chronologisch

hubby ['tʃʌbɪ] adj rundlich

huck [tʃʌk] vt werfen; (BRIT: also: **~ up**); **~ in** hinwerfen; **~ out** vt (person) rauswerfen; (old clothes etc) wegwerfen

huckle ['tʃʌkl] vi in sich hineinlachen

hug [tʃʌg] vi tuckern

hunk [tʃʌŋk] n Klumpen m; (of food) Brocken m

hurch [tʃɜːtʃ] n Kirche f; **~yard** n Kirchhof m

hurn [tʃɜːn] n (for butter) Butterfass nt; (for milk) Milchkanne f; **~ out** (inf) vt produzieren

hute [ʃuːt] n Rutsche f; (rubbish ~) Müllschlucker m

hutney ['tʃʌtnɪ] n Chutney nt

IA (US) n abbr (= Central Intelligence Agency) CIA m

ID (BRIT) n abbr (= Criminal Investigation Department) ≈ Kripo f

der ['saɪdər] n Apfelwein m

gar [sɪ'gɑː'] n Zigarre f

garette [sɪgə'rɛt] n Zigarette f; **~ case** n Zigarettenetui nt; **~ end** n Zigarettenstummel m

inderella [sɪndə'rɛlə] n Aschenbrödel nt

nders ['sɪndəz] npl Asche f

ne camera ['sɪnɪ-] (BRIT) n Filmkamera f

ne film (BRIT) n Schmalfilm m

nema ['sɪnəmə] n Kino nt

nnamon ['sɪnəmən] n Zimt m

rcle ['sɜːkl] n Kreis m; (in cinema etc) Rang m ♦ vi kreisen ♦ vt (surround) umgeben; (move round) kreisen um

rcuit ['sɜːkɪt] n (track) Rennbahn f; (lap) Runde f; (ELEC) Stromkreis m

circular ['sɜːkjʊlə'] adj rund ♦ n Rundschreiben nt

circulate ['sɜːkjʊleɪt] vi zirkulieren ♦ vt in Umlauf setzen; **circulation** [sɜːkju'leɪʃən] n (of blood) Kreislauf m; (of newspaper) Auflage f; (of money) Umlauf m

circumcise ['sɜːkəmsaɪz] vt beschneiden

circumference [sə'kʌmfərəns] n (Kreis)umfang m

circumspect ['sɜːkəmspɛkt] adj umsichtig

circumstances ['sɜːkəmstənsɪz] npl Umstände pl; (financial) Verhältnisse pl

circumvent [sɜːkəm'vɛnt] vt umgehen

circus ['sɜːkəs] n Zirkus m

CIS n abbr (= Commonwealth of Independent States) GUS f

cistern ['sɪstən] n Zisterne f; (of W.C.) Spülkasten m

cite [saɪt] vt zitieren, anführen

citizen ['sɪtɪzn] n Bürger(in) m(f); **~ship** n Staatsbürgerschaft f

citrus fruit ['sɪtrəs-] n Zitrusfrucht f

city ['sɪtɪ] n Großstadt f; **the C~** die City, das Finanzzentrum Londons

city technology college n ≈ Technische Fachschule f

civic ['sɪvɪk] adj (of town) städtisch; (of citizen) Bürger-; **~ centre** (BRIT) n Stadtverwaltung f

civil ['sɪvɪl] adj bürgerlich; (not military) zivil; (polite) höflich; **~ engineer** n Bauingenieur m; **~ian** [sɪ'vɪlɪən] n Zivilperson f ♦ adj zivil, Zivil-

civilization [sɪvɪlaɪ'zeɪʃən] n Zivilisation f

civilized ['sɪvɪlaɪzd] adj zivilisiert

civil: **~ law** n Zivilrecht nt; **~ servant** n Staatsbeamte(r) m; **C~ Service** n Staatsdienst m; **~ war** n Bürgerkrieg m

clad [klæd] adj: **~ in** gehüllt in +acc

claim [kleɪm] vt beanspruchen; (have opinion) behaupten ♦ vi (for insurance) Ansprüche geltend machen ♦ n (demand) Forderung f; (right) Anspruch m; (pretension) Behauptung f; **~ant** n Antragsteller(in) m(f)

clairvoyant [klɛə'vɔɪənt] n Hellseher(in) m(f)

clam [klæm] n Venusmuschel f

clamber ['klæmbə'] vi kraxeln

clammy ['klæmɪ] adj klamm

clamour ['klæmə'] vi: to ~ for sth nach etw verlangen

clamp [klæmp] n Schraubzwinge f ♦ vt einspannen; (AUT: wheel) krallen; ~ down on vt fus Maßnahmen ergreifen gegen

clan [klæn] n Clan m

clandestine [klæn'dɛstɪn] adj geheim

clang [klæŋ] vi scheppern

clap [klæp] vi klatschen ♦ vt Beifall klatschen +dat ♦ n (of hands) Klatschen nt; (of thunder) Donnerschlag m; ~ping n Klatschen nt

claret ['klærət] n rote(r) Bordeaux(wein) m

clarify ['klærɪfaɪ] vt klären, erklären

clarinet [klærɪ'nɛt] n Klarinette f

clarity ['klærɪtɪ] n Klarheit f

clash [klæʃ] n (fig) Konflikt m ♦ vi zusammenprallen; (colours) sich beißen; (argue) sich streiten

clasp [klɑːsp] n Griff m; (on jewels, bag) Verschluss m ♦ vt umklammern

class [klɑːs] n Klasse f ♦ vt einordnen; ~-conscious adj klassenbewusst

classic ['klæsɪk] n Klassiker m ♦ adj klassisch; ~al adj klassisch

classified ['klæsɪfaɪd] adj (information) Geheim-; ~ advertisement n Kleinanzeige f

classify ['klæsɪfaɪ] vt klassifizieren

classmate ['klɑːsmeɪt] n Klassenkamerad(in) m(f)

classroom ['klɑːsrum] n Klassenzimmer nt

clatter ['klætə'] vi klappern; (feet) trappeln

clause [klɔːz] n (JUR) Klausel f; (GRAM) Satz m

claustrophobia [klɔːstrə'fəubɪə] n Platzangst f

claw [klɔː] n Kralle f ♦ vt (zer)kratzen

clay [kleɪ] n Lehm m; (for pots) Ton m

clean [kliːn] adj sauber ♦ vt putzen; (clothes) reinigen; ~ out vt gründlich putzen; ~ up vt aufräumen; ~-cut adj (person) adrett; (clear) klar; ~er n (person) Putzfrau f; ~er's n (also: dry ~er's) Reinigung f; ~ing n Putzen nt; (clothes) Reinigung f; ~liness ['klɛnlɪnɪs] n Reinlichkeit f

cleanse [klɛnz] vt reinigen; ~r n (for face) Reinigungsmilch f

clean-shaven ['kliːn'ʃeɪvn] adj glatt rasie

cleansing department ['klɛnzɪŋ-] (BRIT) Stadtreinigung f

clear [klɪə'] adj klar; (road) frei ♦ vt (road e freimachen; (obstacle) beseitigen; (JUR: suspect) freisprechen ♦ vi klar werden; (fo sich lichten ♦ adv: ~ of von ... entfernt; t ~ the table den Tisch abräumen; ~ up aufräumen; (solve) aufklären; ~ance ['klɪərəns] n (removal) Räumung f; (free space) Lichtung f; (permission) Freigabe f; ~-cut adj (case) eindeutig; ~ing n Lichtu f; ~ing bank (BRIT) n Clearingbank f; ~ly adv klar; (obviously) eindeutig; ~way (BRI n (Straße f mit) Halteverbot nt

cleaver ['kliːvə'] n Hackbeil f

cleft [klɛft] n (in rock) Spalte f

clementine ['klɛməntaɪn] n (fruit) Klementine f

clench [klɛntʃ] vt (teeth) zusammenbeißen (fist) ballen

clergy ['klɜːdʒɪ] n Geistliche(n) pl; ~man (irreg) n Geistliche(r) m

clerical ['klɛrɪkl] adj (office) Schreib-, Büro (REL) geistlich

clerk [klɑːk, (US) klɜːrk] n (in office) Büroangestellte(r) mf; (US: sales person) Verkäufer(in) m(f)

clever ['klɛvə'] adj klug; (crafty) schlau

cliché ['kliːʃeɪ] n Klischee nt

click [klɪk] vt (tongue) schnalzen mit; (heels zusammenklappen; ~ on vt (COMPUT) anklicken

client ['klaɪənt] n Klient(in) m(f); ~ele [kliːɑːn'tɛl] n Kundschaft f

cliff [klɪf] n Klippe f

climate ['klaɪmɪt] n Klima nt

climax ['klaɪmæks] n Höhepunkt m

climb [klaɪm] vt besteigen ♦ vi steigen, klettern ♦ n Aufstieg m; ~-down n Abstie m; ~er n Bergsteiger(in) m(f); ~ing n Bergsteigen nt

clinch [klɪntʃ] vt (decide) entscheiden; (dea festmachen

cling [klɪŋ] (pt, pp clung) vi (clothes) eng anliegen; to ~ to sich festklammern an +

clinic ['klɪnɪk] n Klinik f; ~al adj klinisch

ink [klɪŋk] vi klimpern

ip [klɪp] n Spange f; (also: **paper ~**) Klammer f ♦ vt (papers) heften; (hair, hedge) stutzen; **~pers** npl (for hedge) Heckenschere f; (for hair) Haarschneidemaschine f; **~ping** n Ausschnitt m

oak [kləuk] n Umhang m ♦ vt hüllen; **~room** n (for coats) Garderobe f; (BRIT: W.C.) Toilette f

ock [klɔk] n Uhr f; **~ in** or **on** vi stempeln; **~ off** or **out** vi stempeln; **~wise** adv im Uhrzeigersinn; **~work** n Uhrwerk nt ♦ adj zum Aufziehen

og [klɔg] n Holzschuh m ♦ vt verstopfen

oister ['klɔɪstər] n Kreuzgang m

one[1] [kləun] n Klon m ♦ vt klonen

ose[1] [kləus] adj (near) in der Nähe; (friend, connection, print) eng; (relative) nahe; (result) knapp; (examination) eingehend; (weather) schwül; (room) stickig ♦ adv nahe, dicht; **~by** in der Nähe; **~ at hand** in der Nähe; **to have a ~ shave** (fig) mit knapper Not davonkommen

ose[2] [kləuz] vt (shut) schließen; (end) beenden ♦ vi (shop etc) schließen; (door etc) sich schließen ♦ n Ende nt; **~ down** vi schließen; **~d** adj (shop etc) geschlossen; **~d shop** n Gewerkschaftszwang m

ose-knit ['kləus'nɪt] adj eng zusammengewachsen

osely ['kləuslɪ] adv (watch) eng; (carefully) genau

oset ['klɔzɪt] n Schrank m

ose-up ['kləusʌp] n Nahaufnahme f

osure ['kləuʒər] n Schließung f

ot [klɔt] n (of blood) Blutgerinnsel nt; (fool) Blödmann m ♦ vi gerinnen

oth [klɔθ] n (material) Tuch nt; (rag) Lappen m

othe [kləuð] vt kleiden

othes [kləuðz] npl Kleider pl; **~ brush** n Kleiderbürste f; **~ line** n Wäscheleine f; **~ peg, ~ pin** (US) n Wäscheklammer f

othing ['kləuðɪŋ] n Kleidung f

otted cream ['klɔtɪd-] (BRIT) n Sahne aus erhitzter Milch

oud [klaud] n Wolke f; **~burst** n

Wolkenbruch m; **~y** adj bewölkt; (liquid) trüb

clout [klaut] vt hauen

clove [kləuv] n Gewürznelke f; **~ of garlic** Knoblauchzehe f

clover ['kləuvər] n Klee m

clown [klaun] n Clown m ♦ vi (also: **~ about, ~ around**) kaspern

cloying ['klɔɪɪŋ] adj (taste, smell) übersüß

club [klʌb] n (weapon) Knüppel m; (society) Klub m; (also: **golf ~**) Golfschläger m ♦ vt prügeln ♦ vi: **to ~ together** zusammenlegen; **~s** npl (CARDS) Kreuz nt; **~ car** (US) n (RAIL) Speisewagen m; **~ class** n (AVIAT) Club-Klasse f; **~house** n Klubhaus nt

cluck [klʌk] vi glucken

clue [klu:] n Anhaltspunkt m; (in crosswords) Frage f; **I haven't a ~** (ich hab) keine Ahnung

clump [klʌmp] n Gruppe f

clumsy ['klʌmzɪ] adj (person) unbeholfen; (shape) unförmig

clung [klʌŋ] pt, pp of **cling**

cluster ['klʌstər] n (of trees etc) Gruppe f ♦ vi sich drängen, sich scharen

clutch [klʌtʃ] n Griff m; (AUT) Kupplung f ♦ vt sich festklammern an +dat

clutter ['klʌtər] vt voll pfropfen; (desk) übersäen

CND n abbr = **Campaign for Nuclear Disarmament**

Co. abbr = **county; company**

c/o abbr (= care of) c/o

coach [kəutʃ] n (bus) Reisebus m; (horse-drawn) Kutsche f; (RAIL) (Personen)wagen m; (trainer) Trainer m ♦ vt (SCH) Nachhilfeunterricht geben +dat; (SPORT) trainieren; **~ trip** n Busfahrt f

coal [kəul] n Kohle f; **~ face** n Streb m

coalition [kəuə'lɪʃən] n Koalition f

coalman ['kəulmən] (irreg) n Kohlenhändler m

coal mine n Kohlenbergwerk nt

coarse [kɔ:s] adj grob; (fig) ordinär

coast [kəust] n Küste f ♦ vi dahinrollen; (AUT) im Leerlauf fahren; **~al** adj Küsten-;

~guard n Küstenwache f; **~line** n Küste(nlinie) f

coat [kəut] n Mantel m; (on animals) Fell nt; (of paint) Schicht f ♦ vt überstreichen; **~hanger** n Kleiderbügel m; **~ing** n Überzug m; (of paint) Schicht f; **~ of arms** n Wappen nt

coax [kəuks] vt beschwatzen

cob [kɔb] n see **corn**

cobbler ['kɔblə^r] n Schuster m

cobbles ['kɔblz] npl Pflastersteine pl

cobweb ['kɔbweb] n Spinnennetz nt

cocaine [kə'keɪn] n Kokain nt

cock [kɔk] n Hahn m ♦ vt (gun) entsichern; **~erel** ['kɔkərl] n junge(r) Hahn m; **~eyed** adj (fig) verrückt

cockle ['kɔkl] n Herzmuschel f

cockney ['kɔknɪ] n echte(r) Londoner m

cockpit ['kɔkpɪt] n (AVIAT) Pilotenkanzel f

cockroach ['kɔkrəutʃ] n Küchenschabe f

cocktail ['kɔkteɪl] n Cocktail m; **~ cabinet** n Hausbar f; **~ party** n Cocktailparty f

cocoa ['kəukəu] n Kakao m

coconut ['kəukənʌt] n Kokosnuss f

cocoon [kə'ku:n] n Kokon m

cod [kɔd] n Kabeljau m

C.O.D. abbr = **cash on delivery**

code [kəud] n Kode m; (JUR) Kodex m

cod-liver oil ['kɔdlɪvə-] n Lebertran m

coercion [kəu'ə:ʃən] n Zwang m

coffee ['kɔfɪ] n Kaffee m; **~ bar** (BRIT) n Café nt; **~ bean** n Kaffeebohne f; **~ break** n Kaffeepause f; **~pot** n Kaffeekanne f; **~ table** n Couchtisch m

coffin ['kɔfɪn] n Sarg m

cog [kɔg] n (Rad)zahn m

cognac ['kɔnjæk] n Kognak m

coherent [kəu'hɪərənt] adj zusammenhängend; (person) verständlich

coil [kɔɪl] n Rolle f; (ELEC) Spule f; (contraceptive) Spirale f ♦ vt aufwickeln

coin [kɔɪn] n Münze f ♦ vt prägen; **~age** ['kɔɪnɪdʒ] n (word) Prägung f; **~ box** (BRIT) n Münzfernsprecher m

coincide [kəuɪn'saɪd] vi (happen together) zusammenfallen; (agree) übereinstimmen; **~nce** [kəu'ɪnsɪdəns] n Zufall m

coinphone ['kɔɪnfəun] n Münzfernsprech m

Coke [kəuk] ® n (drink) Coca-Cola ® f

coke [kəuk] n Koks m

colander ['kɔləndə^r] n Durchschlag m

cold [kəuld] adj kalt ♦ n Kälte f; (MED) Erkältung f; **I'm ~** mir ist kalt; **to catch ~** sich erkälten; **in ~ blood** kaltblütig; **to give sb the ~ shoulder** jdm die kalte Schulter zeigen; **~ly** adv kalt; **~-shoulder** vt die kalte Schulter zeigen +dat; **~ sore** n Erkältungsbläschen nt

coleslaw ['kəulslɔ:] n Krautsalat m

colic ['kɔlɪk] n Kolik f

collaborate [kə'læbəreɪt] vi zusammenarbeiten

collapse [kə'læps] vi (people) zusammenbrechen; (things) einstürzen ♦ n Zusammenbruch m; Einsturz m; **collapsible** adj zusammenklappbar, Klapp-

collar ['kɔlə^r] n Kragen m; **~bone** n Schlüsselbein nt

collateral [kə'lætərl] n (zusätzliche) Sicherheit f

colleague ['kɔli:g] n Kollege m, Kollegin f

collect [kə'lekt] vt sammeln; (BRIT: call and pick up) abholen ♦ vi sich sammeln ♦ adv: **to call ~** (US: TEL) ein R-Gespräch führen; **~ion** [kə'lekʃən] n Sammlung f; (REL) Kollekte f; (of post) Leerung f; **~ive** [kə'lektɪv] adj gemeinsam; (POL) kollektiv; **~or** [kə'lektə^r] n Sammler m; (tax ~or) (Steuer)einnehmer m

college ['kɔlɪdʒ] n (UNIV) College nt; (TECH) Fach-, Berufsschule f

collide [kə'laɪd] vi zusammenstoßen

collie ['kɔlɪ] n Collie m

colliery ['kɔlɪərɪ] (BRIT) n Zeche f

collision [kə'lɪʒən] n Zusammenstoß m

colloquial [kə'ləukwɪəl] adj umgangssprachlich

colon ['kəulən] n Doppelpunkt m; (MED) Dickdarm m

colonel ['kə:nl] n Oberst m

colonial [kə'ləunɪəl] adj Kolonial-

colonize ['kɔlənaɪz] vt kolonisieren

olony ['kɒlənɪ] n Kolonie f

olour ['kʌlə'] (US **color**) n Farbe f ♦ vt (also fig) färben ♦ vi sich verfärben; **~s** npl (of club) Fahne f; **~ bar** n Rassenschranke f; **~-blind** adj farbenblind; **~ed** adj farbig; **~ film** n Farbfilm m; **~ful** adj bunt; (personality) schillernd; **~ing** n (complexion) Gesichtsfarbe f; (substance) Farbstoff m; **~ scheme** n Farbgebung f; **~ television** n Farbfernsehen nt

olt [kəult] n Fohlen nt

olumn ['kɒləm] n Säule f; (MIL) Kolonne f; (of print) Spalte f; **~ist** ['kɒləmnɪst] n Kolumnist m

oma ['kəumə] n Koma nt

omb [kəum] n Kamm m ♦ vt kämmen; (search) durchkämmen

ombat ['kɒmbæt] n Kampf m ♦ vt bekämpfen

ombination [kɒmbɪ'neɪʃən] n Kombination f

ombine [vb kəm'baɪn, n 'kɒmbaɪn] vt verbinden ♦ vi sich vereinigen ♦ n (COMM) Konzern m; **~ (harvester)** n Mähdrescher m

ombustion [kəm'bʌstʃən] n Verbrennung f

ome [kʌm] (pt **came**, pp **come**) vi kommen; **to ~ undone** aufgehen; **~ about** vi geschehen; **~ across** vt fus (find) stoßen auf +acc; **~ away** vi (person) weggehen; (handle etc) abgehen; **~ back** vi zurückkommen; **~ by** vt fus (find): **to ~ by sth** zu etw kommen; **~ down** vi (price) fallen; **~ forward** vi (volunteer) sich melden; **~ from** vt fus (result) kommen von; **where do you ~ from?** wo kommen Sie her?; **I ~ from London** ich komme aus London; **~ in** vi hereinkommen; (train) einfahren; **~ in for** vt fus abkriegen; **~ into** vt fus (inherit) erben; **~ off** vi (handle) abgehen; (succeed) klappen; **~ on** vi (progress) vorankommen; **~ on!** komm!; (hurry) beeil dich!; **~ out** vi herauskommen; **~ round** vi (MED) wieder zu sich kommen; **~ to** vi (MED) wieder zu sich kommen ♦ vt fus (bill) sich belaufen auf +acc; **~ up** vi hochkommen; (sun)

aufgehen; (problem) auftauchen; **~ up against** vt fus (resistance, difficulties) stoßen auf +acc; **~ upon** vt fus stoßen auf +acc; **~ up with** vt fus sich einfallen lassen

comedian [kə'miːdɪən] n Komiker m; **comedienne** [kəmiːdɪ'ɛn] n Komikerin f

comedown ['kʌmdaun] n Abstieg m

comedy ['kɒmɪdɪ] n Komödie f

comet ['kɒmɪt] n Komet m

comeuppance [kʌm'ʌpəns] n: **to get one's ~** seine Quittung bekommen

comfort ['kʌmfət] n Komfort m; (consolation) Trost m ♦ vt trösten; **~able** adj bequem; **~ably** adv (sit etc) bequem; (live) angenehm; **~ station** (US) n öffentliche Toilette f

comic ['kɒmɪk] n Comic(heft) nt; (comedian) Komiker m ♦ adj (also: **~al**) komisch; **~ strip** n Comicstrip m

coming ['kʌmɪŋ] n Kommen nt; **~(s) and going(s)** n(pl) Kommen und Gehen nt

comma ['kɒmə] n Komma nt

command [kə'mɑːnd] n Befehl m; (control) Führung f; (MIL) Kommando nt; (mastery) Beherrschung f ♦ vt befehlen +dat; (MIL) kommandieren; (be able to get) verfügen über +acc; **~eer** [kɒmən'dɪə'] vt requirieren; **~er** n Kommandant m; **~ment** n (REL) Gebot nt

commando [kə'mɑːndəu] n Kommandotruppe nt; (person) Mitglied nt einer Kommandotruppe

commemorate [kə'mɛməreɪt] vt gedenken +gen

commence [kə'mɛns] vt, vi beginnen

commend [kə'mɛnd] vt (recommend) empfehlen; (praise) loben

commensurate [kə'mɛnʃərɪt] adj: **~ with sth** einer Sache dat entsprechend

comment ['kɒmɛnt] n Bemerkung f ♦ vi: **to ~ (on)** sich äußern (zu); **~ary** n Kommentar m; **~ator** n Kommentator m; (TV) Reporter(in) m(f)

commerce ['kɒmə:s] n Handel m

commercial [kə'mə:ʃəl] adj kommerziell, geschäftlich; (training) kaufmännisch ♦ n (TV) Fernsehwerbung f; **~ break** n

Werbespot *m*; ~ize *vt* kommerzialisieren
commiserate [kə'mɪzəreɪt] *vi*: **to ~ with** Mitleid haben mit
commission [kə'mɪʃən] *n* (*act*) Auftrag *m*; (*fee*) Provision *f*; (*body*) Kommission *f* ♦ *vt* beauftragen; (*MIL*) zum Offizier ernennen; (*work of art*) in Auftrag geben; **out of ~** außer Betrieb; **~er** *n* (*POLICE*) Polizeipräsident *m*
commit [kə'mɪt] *vt* (*crime*) begehen; (*entrust*) anvertrauen; **to ~ o.s.** sich festlegen; **~ment** *n* Verpflichtung *f*
committee [kə'mɪtɪ] *n* Ausschuss *m*
commodity [kə'mɔdɪtɪ] *n* Ware *f*
common ['kɔmən] *adj* (*cause*) gemeinsam; (*pej*) gewöhnlich; (*widespread*) üblich, häufig ♦ *n* Gemeindeland *nt*; **C~s** *npl* (*BRIT*): **the C~s** das Unterhaus; **~er** *n* Bürgerliche(r) *mf*; **~ law** *n* Gewohnheitsrecht *nt*; **~ly** *adv* gewöhnlich; **C~ Market** *n* Gemeinsame(r) Markt *m*; **~place** *adj* alltäglich; **~ room** *n* Gemeinschaftsraum *m*; **~ sense** *n* gesunde(r) Menschenverstand *m*; **C~wealth** *n*: **the C~wealth** das Commonwealth
commotion [kə'məuʃən] *n* Aufsehen *nt*
communal ['kɔmjuːnl] *adj* Gemeinde-; Gemeinschafts-
commune [*n* 'kɔmjuːn, *vb* kə'mjuːn] *n* Kommune *f* ♦ *vi*: **to ~ with** sich mitteilen +*dat*
communicate [kə'mjuːnɪkeɪt] *vt* (*transmit*) übertragen ♦ *vi* (*be in touch*) in Verbindung stehen; (*make self understood*) sich verständigen; **communication** [kəmjuːnɪ'keɪʃən] *n* (*message*) Mitteilung *f*; (*making understood*) Kommunikation *f*; **communication cord** (*BRIT*) *n* Notbremse *f*
communion [kə'mjuːnɪən] *n* (*also:* **Holy C~**) Abendmahl *nt*, Kommunion *f*
communism ['kɔmjunɪzəm] *n* Kommunismus *m*; **communist** ['kɔmjunɪst] *n* Kommunist(in) *m(f)* ♦ *adj* kommunistisch
community [kə'mjuːnɪtɪ] *n* Gemeinschaft *f*; **~ centre** *n* Gemeinschaftszentrum *nt*; **~**

chest (*US*) *n* Wohltätigkeitsfonds *m*; **~ home** (*BRIT*) *n* Erziehungsheim *nt*
commutation ticket [kɔmju'teɪʃən-] (*US*) Zeitkarte *f*
commute [kə'mjuːt] *vi* pendeln ♦ *vt* umwandeln; **~r** *n* Pendler *m*
compact [*adj* kəm'pækt, *n* 'kɔmpækt] *adj* kompakt ♦ *n* (*for make-up*) Puderdose *f*; **~ disc** *n* Compactdisc *f*, Compact Disc *f*; **~ disc player** *n* CD-Spieler *m*
companion [kəm'pænjən] *n* Begleiter(in) *m(f)*; **~ship** *n* Gesellschaft *f*
company ['kʌmpənɪ] *n* Gesellschaft *f*; (*COMM*) Firma *f*, Gesellschaft *f*; **to keep sb ~** jdm Gesellschaft leisten; **~ secretary** (*BRIT*) *n* ≈ Prokurist(in) *m(f)*
comparable ['kɔmpərəbl] *adj* vergleichbar
comparative [kəm'pærətɪv] *adj* (*relative*) relativ; **~ly** *adv* verhältnismäßig
compare [kəm'peər] *vt* vergleichen ♦ *vi* sich vergleichen lassen; **comparison** [kəm'pærɪsn] *n* Vergleich *m*; **in comparison (with)** im Vergleich (mit *or* zu)
compartment [kəm'pɑːtmənt] *n* (*RAIL*) Abteil *nt*; (*in drawer*) Fach *nt*
compass ['kʌmpəs] *n* Kompass *m*; **~es** *npl* (*MATH etc: also:* **pair of ~es**) Zirkel *m*
compassion [kəm'pæʃən] *n* Mitleid *nt*; **~ate** *adj* mitfühlend
compatible [kəm'pætɪbl] *adj* vereinbar; (*COMPUT*) kompatibel
compel [kəm'pel] *vt* zwingen
compensate ['kɔmpənseɪt] *vt* entschädigen ♦ *vi*: **to ~ for** Ersatz leisten für; **compensation** [kɔmpən'seɪʃən] *n* Entschädigung *f*
compère ['kɔmpeər] *n* Conférencier *m*
compete [kəm'piːt] *vi* (*take part*) teilnehmen; (*vie with*) konkurrieren
competent ['kɔmpɪtənt] *adj* kompetent
competition [kɔmpɪ'tɪʃən] *n* (*contest*) Wettbewerb *m*; (*COMM, rivalry*) Konkurrenz *f*; **competitive** [kəm'petɪtɪv] *adj* Konkurrenz-; (*COMM*) konkurrenzfähig; **competitor** [kəm'petɪtər] *n* (*COMM*) Konkurrent(in) *m(f)*; (*participant*) Teilnehmer(in) *m(f)*

compile [kəm'paɪl] *vt* zusammenstellen

complacency [kəm'pleɪsnsɪ] *n* Selbstzufriedenheit *f*

complacent [kəm'pleɪsnt] *adj* selbstzufrieden

complain [kəm'pleɪn] *vi* sich beklagen; *(formally)* sich beschweren; ~t *n* Klage *f*; *(formal ~t)* Beschwerde *f*; *(MED)* Leiden *nt*

complement [*n* 'komplɪmənt, *vb* 'komplɪment] *n* Ergänzung *f*; *(ship's crew etc)* Bemannung *f* ♦ *vt* ergänzen; ~ary [komplɪ'mentərɪ] *adj* (sich) ergänzend

complete [kəm'pliːt] *adj* *(full)* vollkommen, ganz; *(finished)* fertig ♦ *vt* vervollständigen; *(finish)* beenden; *(fill in: form)* ausfüllen; ~ly *adv* ganz; **completion** [kəm'pliːʃən] *n* Fertigstellung *f*; *(of contract etc)* Abschluss *m*

complex ['kompleks] *adj* kompliziert

complexion [kəm'plekʃən] *n* Gesichtsfarbe *f*; *(fig)* Aspekt *m*

complexity [kəm'pleksɪtɪ] *n* Kompliziertheit *f*

compliance [kəm'plaɪəns] *n* Fügsamkeit *f*, Einwilligung *f*; **in ~ with sth** einer Sache *dat* gemäß

complicate ['komplɪkeɪt] *vt* komplizieren; ~d *adj* kompliziert; **complication** [komplɪ'keɪʃən] *n* Komplikation *f*

compliment [*n* 'komplɪmənt, *vb* 'komplɪment] *n* Kompliment *nt* ♦ *vt* ein Kompliment machen +*dat*; ~s *npl* *(greetings)* Grüße *pl*; **to pay sb a ~** jdm ein Kompliment machen; ~ary [komplɪ'mentərɪ] *adj* schmeichelhaft; *(free)* Frei-, Gratis-

comply [kəm'plaɪ] *vi*: **to ~ with** erfüllen +*acc*; entsprechen +*dat*

component [kəm'pəunənt] *adj* Teil- ♦ *n* Bestandteil *m*

compose [kəm'pəuz] *vt* *(music)* komponieren; *(poetry)* verfassen; **to ~ o.s.** sich sammeln; ~d *adj* gefasst; ~r *n* Komponist(in) *m(f)*; **composition** ['kompə'zɪʃən] *n* *(MUS)* Komposition *f*; *(SCH)* Aufsatz *m*; *(structure)* Zusammensetzung *f*, Aufbau *m*

composure [kəm'pəuʒə*ʳ*] *n* Fassung *f*

compound ['kompaund] *n* *(CHEM)* Verbindung *f*; *(enclosure)* Lager *nt*; *(LING)* Kompositum *nt* ♦ *adj* zusammengesetzt; *(fracture)* kompliziert; ~ **interest** *n* Zinseszins *m*

comprehend [komprɪ'hend] *vt* begreifen; **comprehension** *n* Verständnis *nt*

comprehensive [komprɪ'hensɪv] *adj* umfassend ♦ *n* = **comprehensive school**; ~ **insurance** *n* Vollkasko *nt*; ~ **school** *(BRIT)* *n* Gesamtschule *f*

compress [*vb* kəm'pres, *n* 'kompres] *vt* komprimieren ♦ *n* *(MED)* Kompresse *f*

comprise [kəm'praɪz] *vt* *(also:* **be ~d of)** umfassen, bestehen aus

compromise ['komprəmaɪz] *n* Kompromiss *m* ♦ *vt* kompromittieren ♦ *vi* einen Kompromiss schließen

compulsion [kəm'pʌlʃən] *n* Zwang *m*; **compulsive** [kəm'pʌlsɪv] *adj* zwanghaft; **compulsory** [kəm'pʌlsərɪ] *adj* obligatorisch

computer [kəm'pjuːtə*ʳ*] *n* Computer *m*, Rechner *m*; ~ **game** *n* Computerspiel *nt*; ~-**generated** *adj* computergeneriert; ~**ize** *vt* *(information)* computerisieren; *(company, accounts)* auf Computer umstellen; ~ **programmer** *n* Programmierer(in) *m(f)*; ~ **programming** *n* Programmieren *nt*; ~ **science** *n* Informatik *f*; **computing** [kəm'pjuːtɪŋ] *n* *(science)* Informatik *f*; *(work)* Computerei *f*

comrade ['komrɪd] *n* Kamerad *m*; *(POL)* Genosse *m*

con [kon] *vt* hereinlegen ♦ *n* Schwindel *nt*

concave ['konkeɪv] *adj* konkav

conceal [kən'siːl] *vt* *(secret)* verschweigen; *(hide)* verbergen

concede [kən'siːd] *vt* *(grant)* gewähren; *(point)* zugeben ♦ *vi* *(admit defeat)* nachgeben

conceit [kən'siːt] *n* Einbildung *f*; ~ed *adj* eingebildet

conceivable [kən'siːvəbl] *adj* vorstellbar

conceive [kən'siːv] *vt* *(idea)* ausdenken; *(imagine)* sich vorstellen; *(baby)* empfangen ♦ *vi* empfangen

concentrate ['konsəntreɪt] *vi* sich konzentrieren ♦ *vt* konzentrieren; **to ~ on sth** sich auf etw *acc* konzentrieren;

concentration [kɔnsən'treɪʃən] n
Konzentration f; **concentration camp** n
Konzentrationslager nt, KZ nt

concept ['kɔnsɛpt] n Begriff m

conception [kən'sɛpʃən] n (idea) Vorstellung
f; (BIOL) Empfängnis f

concern [kən'sə:n] n (affair) Angelegenheit
f; (COMM) Unternehmen nt; (worry) Sorge f
♦ vt (interest) angehen; (be about) handeln
von; (have connection with) betreffen; **to be
~ed (about)** sich Sorgen machen (um);
~ing prep hinsichtlich +gen

concert ['kɔnsət] n Konzert nt

concerted [kən'sə:tɪd] adj gemeinsam

concert hall n Konzerthalle f

concertina [kɔnsə'ti:nə] n Handharmonika f

concerto [kən'tʃɜːtəu] n Konzert nt

concession [kən'sɛʃən] n (yielding)
Zugeständnis nt; **tax ~** Steuerkonzession f

conciliation [kənsɪlɪ'eɪʃən] n Versöhnung f;
(official) Schlichtung f

concise [kən'saɪs] adj präzis

conclude [kən'klu:d] vt (end) beenden;
(treaty) (ab)schließen; (decide) schließen,
folgern; **conclusion** [kən'klu:ʒən] n
(Ab)schluss m; (deduction) Schluss m;
conclusive [kən'klu:sɪv] adj schlüssig

concoct [kən'kɔkt] vt zusammenbrauen;
~ion [kən'kɔkʃən] n Gebräu nt

concourse ['kɔŋkɔːs] n (Bahnhofs)halle f,
Vorplatz m

concrete ['kɔŋkriːt] n Beton m ♦ adj konkret

concur [kən'kɜːr] vi übereinstimmen

concurrently [kən'kʌrntlɪ] adv gleichzeitig

concussion [kən'kʌʃən] n
(Gehirn)erschütterung f

condemn [kən'dɛm] vt (JUR) verurteilen;
(building) abbruchreif erklären

condensation [kɔndən'seɪʃən] n
Kondensation f

condense [kən'dɛns] vi (CHEM)
kondensieren ♦ vt (fig) zusammendrängen;
~d milk n Kondensmilch f

condescending [kɔndɪ'sɛndɪŋ] adj
herablassend

condition [kən'dɪʃən] n (state) Zustand m;
(presupposition) Bedingung f ♦ vt (hair etc)

behandeln; (accustom) gewöhnen; **~s** npl
(circumstances) Verhältnisse pl; **on ~ that ...**
unter der Bedingung, dass ...; **~al** adj
bedingt; **~er** n (for hair) Spülung f; (for
fabrics) Weichspüler m

condolences [kən'dəulənsɪz] npl Beileid nt

condom ['kɔndəm] n Kondom nt or m

condominium [kɔndə'mɪnɪəm] (US) n
Eigentumswohnung f; (block)
Eigentumsblock m

condone [kən'dəun] vt gutheißen

conducive [kən'djuːsɪv] adj: **~ to** dienlich
+dat

conduct [n 'kɔndʌkt, vb kən'dʌkt] n
(behaviour) Verhalten nt; (management)
Führung f ♦ vt führen; (MUS) dirigieren;
~ed tour n Führung f; **~or** [kən'dʌktər] n
(of orchestra) Dirigent m; (in bus, US: on
train) Schaffner m; (ELEC) Leiter m; **~ress**
[kən'dʌktrɪs] n (in bus) Schaffnerin f

cone [kəun] n (MATH) Kegel m; (for ice cream)
(Waffel)tüte f; (BOT) Tannenzapfen m

confectioner's (shop) [kən'fɛkʃənəz-] n
Konditorei f; **~y** [kən'fɛkʃənrɪ] n Süßigkeiten
pl

confederation [kənfɛdə'reɪʃən] n Bund m

confer [kən'fɜːr] vt (degree) verleihen ♦ vi
(discuss) konferieren, verhandeln; **~ence**
['kɔnfərəns] n Konferenz f

confess [kən'fɛs] vt, vi gestehen; (ECCL)
beichten; **~ion** [kən'fɛʃən] n Geständnis nt;
(ECCL) Beichte f; **~ional** n Beichtstuhl m

confide [kən'faɪd] vi: **to ~ in** (sich)
anvertrauen +dat

confidence ['kɔnfɪdns] n Vertrauen nt;
(assurance) Selbstvertrauen nt; (secret)
Geheimnis nt; **in ~** (speak, write) vertraulich;
~ trick n Schwindel m

confident ['kɔnfɪdənt] adj (sure) überzeugt;
(self-assured) selbstsicher

confidential [kɔnfɪ'dɛnʃəl] adj vertraulich

confine [kən'faɪn] vt (limit) beschränken;
(lock up) einsperren; **~d** adj (space) eng;
~ment n (in prison) Haft f; (MED)
Wochenbett nt; **~s** ['kɔnfaɪnz] npl Grenzen
pl

confirm [kən'fɜːm] vt bestätigen; **~ation**

[kɔnfəˈmeɪʃən] n Bestätigung f; (REL)
Konfirmation f; ~ed adj unverbesserlich;
(bachelor) eingefleischt

confiscate [ˈkɔnfɪskeɪt] vt beschlagnahmen

conflict [n ˈkɔnflɪkt, vb kənˈflɪkt] n Konflikt m
♦ vi im Widerspruch stehen; ~ing
[kənˈflɪktɪŋ] adj widersprüchlich

conform [kənˈfɔːm] vi: to ~ (to) (things)
entsprechen +dat; (people) sich anpassen
+dat; (to rules) sich richten (nach)

confound [kənˈfaʊnd] vt verblüffen;
(confuse) durcheinander bringen

confront [kənˈfrʌnt] vt (enemy)
entgegentreten +dat; (problems) sich stellen
+dat; to ~ sb with sth jdn mit etw
konfrontieren; ~ation [kɔnfrənˈteɪʃən] n
Konfrontation f

confuse [kənˈfjuːz] vt verwirren; (sth with
sth) verwechseln; ~d adj verwirrt;
confusing adj verwirrend; confusion
[kənˈfjuːʒən] n (perplexity) Verwirrung f;
(mixing up) Verwechslung f; (tumult) Aufruhr
m

congeal [kənˈdʒiːl] vi (freeze) gefrieren; (clot)
gerinnen

congested [kənˈdʒestɪd] adj überfüllt

congestion [kənˈdʒestʃən] n Stau m

conglomerate [kənˈglɔmərɪt] n (COMM,
GEOL) Konglomerat nt

conglomeration [kənglɔməˈreɪʃən] n
Anhäufung f

congratulate [kənˈgrætjuleɪt] vt: to ~ sb
(on sth) jdn (zu etw) beglückwünschen;
congratulations [kəngrætjuˈleɪʃənz] npl
Glückwünsche pl; congratulations!
gratuliere!, herzlichen Glückwunsch!

congregate [ˈkɔngrɪgeɪt] vi sich
versammeln; congregation [kɔngrɪˈgeɪʃən]
n Gemeinde f

congress [ˈkɔngres] n Kongress m; C~man
(irreg: US) n Mitglied nt des amerikanischen
Repräsentantenhauses

conifer [ˈkɔnɪfəʳ] n Nadelbaum m

conjunction [kənˈdʒʌŋkʃən] n Verbindung f;
(GRAM) Konjunktion f

conjunctivitis [kəndʒʌŋktɪˈvaɪtɪs] n
Bindehautentzündung f

conjure [ˈkʌndʒəʳ] vi zaubern; ~ up vt
heraufbeschwören; ~r n Zauberkünstler(in)
m(f)

conk out [kɔŋk-] (inf) vi den Geist aufgeben

con man (irreg) n Schwindler m

connect [kəˈnekt] vt verbinden; (ELEC)
anschließen; to be ~ed with eine
Beziehung haben zu; (be related to)
verwandt sein mit; ~ion [kəˈnekʃən] n
Verbindung f; (relation) Zusammenhang m;
(ELEC, TEL, RAIL) Anschluss m

connive [kəˈnaɪv] vi: to ~ at stillschweigend
dulden

connoisseur [kɔnɪˈsəːʳ] n Kenner m

conquer [ˈkɔŋkəʳ] vt (feelings) überwinden;
(enemy) besiegen; (country) erobern; ~or n
Eroberer m

conquest [ˈkɔŋkwest] n Eroberung f

cons [kɔnz] npl see convenience; pro

conscience [ˈkɔnʃəns] n Gewissen nt

conscientious [kɔnʃɪˈenʃəs] adj
gewissenhaft

conscious [ˈkɔnʃəs] adj bewusst; (MED) bei
Bewusstsein; ~ness n Bewusstsein nt

conscript [ˈkɔnskrɪpt] n Wehrpflichtige(r) m;
~ion [kənˈskrɪpʃən] n Wehrpflicht f

consecutive [kənˈsekjutɪv] adj aufeinander
folgend

consensus [kənˈsensəs] n allgemeine
Übereinstimmung f

consent [kənˈsent] n Zustimmung f ♦ vi
zustimmen

consequence [ˈkɔnsɪkwəns] n (importance)
Bedeutung f; (effect) Folge f

consequently [ˈkɔnsɪkwəntlɪ] adv folglich

conservation [kɔnsəˈveɪʃən] n Erhaltung f;
(nature ~) Umweltschutz m

conservative [kənˈsəːvətɪv] adj konservativ;
C~ (BRIT) adj konservativ ♦ n
Konservative(r) mf

conservatory [kənˈsəːvətrɪ] n (room)
Wintergarten m

conserve [kənˈsəːv] vt erhalten

consider [kənˈsɪdəʳ] vt überlegen; (take into
account) in Betracht ziehen; (regard as)
halten für; to ~ doing sth daran denken,
etw zu tun; ~able [kənˈsɪdərəbl] adj

beträchtlich; **~ably** *adv* beträchtlich; **~ate**
adj rücksichtsvoll; **~ation** [kənsıdə'reıʃən] *n*
Rücksicht(nahme) *f*; (*thought*) Erwägung *f*;
~ing *prep* in Anbetracht +*gen*

consign [kən'saın] *vt* übergeben; **~ment** *n*
Sendung *f*

consist [kən'sıst] *vi*: **to ~ of** bestehen aus

consistency [kən'sıstənsı] *n* (*of material*)
Konsistenz *f*; (*of argument, person*)
Konsequenz *f*

consistent [kən'sıstənt] *adj* (*person*)
konsequent; (*argument*) folgerichtig

consolation [kɒnsə'leıʃən] *n* Trost *m*

console[1] [kən'səul] *vt* trösten

console[2] ['kɒnsəul] *n* Kontroll(pult) *nt*

consolidate [kən'sɒlıdeıt] *vt* festigen

consommé [kən'sɒmeı] *n* Fleischbrühe *f*

consonant ['kɒnsənənt] *n* Konsonant *m*,
Mitlaut *m*

conspicuous [kən'spıkjuəs] *adj* (*prominent*)
auffällig; (*visible*) deutlich sichtbar

conspiracy [kən'spırəsı] *n* Verschwörung *f*

conspire [kən'spaıə[r]] *vi* sich verschwören

constable ['kʌnstəbl] (*BRIT*) *n* Polizist(in)
m(f); **chief ~** Polizeipräsident *m*;
constabulary [kən'stæbjulərı] *n* Polizei *f*

constant ['kɒnstənt] *adj* (*continuous*) ständig;
(*unchanging*) konstant; **~ly** *adv* ständig

constellation [kɒnstə'leıʃən] *n* Sternbild *nt*

consternation [kɒnstə'neıʃən] *n* Bestürzung
f

constipated ['kɒnstıpeıtıd] *adj* verstopft;
constipation [kɒnstı'peıʃən] *n* Verstopfung
f

constituency [kən'stıtjuənsı] *n* Wahlkreis *m*

constituent [kən'stıtjuənt] *n* (*person*) Wähler
m; (*part*) Bestandteil *m*

constitute ['kɒnstıtju:t] *vt* (*make up*) bilden;
(*amount to*) darstellen

constitution [kɒnstı'tju:ʃən] *n* Verfassung *f*;
~al *adj* Verfassungs-

constraint [kən'streınt] *n* Zwang *m*;
(*shyness*) Befangenheit *f*

construct [kən'strʌkt] *vt* bauen; **~ion**
[kən'strʌkʃən] *n* Konstruktion *f*; (*building*)
Bau *m*; **~ive** *adj* konstruktiv

construe [kən'stru:] *vt* deuten

consul ['kɒnsl] *n* Konsul *m*; **~ate** *n* Konsulat
nt

consult [kən'sʌlt] *vt* um Rat fragen; (*doctor*)
konsultieren; (*book*) nachschlagen in +*dat*;
~ant *n* (*MED*) Facharzt *m*; (*other specialist*)
Gutachter *m*; **~ation** [kɒnsəl'teıʃən] *n*
Beratung *f*; (*MED*) Konsultation *f*; **~ing
room** *n* Sprechzimmer *nt*

consume [kən'sju:m] *vt* verbrauchen; (*food*)
konsumieren; **~r** *n* Verbraucher *m*; **~r
goods** *npl* Konsumgüter *pl*; **~rism** *n*
Konsum *m*; **~r society** *n*
Konsumgesellschaft *f*

consummate ['kɒnsʌmeıt] *vt* (*marriage*)
vollziehen

consumption [kən'sʌmpʃən] *n* Verbrauch
m; (*of food*) Konsum *m*

cont. *abbr* (= *continued*) Forts.

contact ['kɒntækt] *n* (*touch*) Berührung *f*;
(*connection*) Verbindung *f*; (*person*) Kontakt
m ♦ *vt* sich in Verbindung setzen mit; **~
lenses** *npl* Kontaktlinsen *pl*

contagious [kən'teıdʒəs] *adj* ansteckend

contain [kən'teın] *vt* enthalten; **to ~ o.s.**
sich zügeln; **~er** *n* Behälter *m*; (*transport*)
Container *m*

contaminate [kən'tæmıneıt] *vt*
verunreinigen

cont'd *abbr* (= *continued*) Forts.

contemplate ['kɒntəmpleıt] *vt* (*look at*)
(nachdenklich) betrachten; (*think about*)
überdenken; (*plan*) vorhaben

contemporary [kən'tempərərı] *adj*
zeitgenössisch ♦ *n* Zeitgenosse *m*

contempt [kən'tempt] *n* Verachtung *f*; **~ of
court** (*JUR*) Missachtung *f* des Gerichts;
~ible *adj* verachtenswert; **~uous** *adj*
verächtlich

contend [kən'tend] *vt* (*argue*) behaupten
♦ *vi* kämpfen; **~er** *n* (*for post*) Bewerber(in)
m(f); (*SPORT*) Wettkämpfer(in) *m(f)*

content [*adj, vb* kən'tent, *n* 'kɒntent] *adj*
zufrieden ♦ *vt* befriedigen ♦ *n* (*also:* **~s**)
Inhalt *m*; **~ed** *adj* zufrieden

contention [kən'tenʃən] *n* (*dispute*) Streit *m*;
(*argument*) Behauptung *f*

contentment [kən'tentmənt] *n* Zufriedenheit f

contest [n 'kɒntest, vb kən'test] n
(Wett)kampf m ♦ vt (dispute) bestreiten;
(JUR) anfechten; (POL) kandidieren in +dat;
~ant [kən'testənt] n Bewerber(in) m(f)

context ['kɒntekst] n Zusammenhang m

continent ['kɒntɪnənt] n Kontinent m; **the
C~** (BRIT) das europäische Festland; ~al
[kɒntɪ'nentl] adj kontinental; ~al **breakfast**
n kleines Frühstück nt; ~al **quilt** (BRIT) n
Federbett nt

contingency [kən'tɪndʒənsɪ] n Möglichkeit f

contingent [kən'tɪndʒənt] n Kontingent nt

continual [kən'tɪnjuəl] adj (endless)
fortwährend; (repeated) immer
wiederkehrend; ~**ly** adv immer wieder

continuation [kəntɪnju'eɪʃən] n Fortsetzung
f

continue [kən'tɪnju:] vi (person)
weitermachen; (thing) weitergehen ♦ vt
fortsetzen

continuity [kɒntɪ'nju:ɪtɪ] n Kontinuität f

continuous [kən'tɪnjuəs] adj
ununterbrochen; ~ **stationery** n
Endlospapier nt

contort [kən'tɔ:t] vt verdrehen; ~**ion**
[kən'tɔ:ʃən] n Verzerrung f

contour ['kɒntuə'] n Umriss m; (also: ~ **line**)
Höhenlinie f

contraband ['kɒntrəbænd] n
Schmuggelware f

contraception [kɒntrə'sepʃən] n
Empfängnisverhütung f

contraceptive [kɒntrə'septɪv] n
empfängnisverhütende(s) Mittel nt ♦ adj
empfängnisverhütend

contract [n 'kɒntrækt, vb kən'trækt] n Vertrag
m ♦ vi (muscle, metal) sich zusammenziehen
♦ vt zusammenziehen; **to ~ to do sth**
(COMM) sich vertraglich verpflichten, etw zu
tun; ~**ion** [kən'trækʃən] n (shortening)
Verkürzung f; ~**or** [kən'træktə'] n
Unternehmer m

contradict [kɒntrə'dɪkt] vt widersprechen
+dat; ~**ion** [kɒntrə'dɪkʃən] n Widerspruch m

contraflow ['kɒntrəfləʊ] n (AUT)
Gegenverkehr m

contraption [kən'træpʃən] (inf) n Apparat m

contrary[1] ['kɒntrərɪ] adj (opposite)
entgegengesetzt ♦ n Gegenteil nt; **on the ~**
im Gegenteil

contrary[2] [kən'treərɪ] adj (obstinate)
widerspenstig

contrast [n 'kɒntrɑ:st, vb kən'trɑ:st] n
Kontrast m ♦ vt entgegensetzen; ~**ing**
[kən'trɑ:stɪŋ] adj Kontrast-

contravene [kɒntrə'vi:n] vt verstoßen
gegen

contribute [kən'trɪbju:t] vt, vi: **to ~ to**
beitragen zu; **contribution** [kɒntrɪ'bju:ʃən]
n Beitrag m; **contributor** [kən'trɪbjutə'] n
Beitragende(r) f(m)

contrive [kən'traɪv] vt ersinnen ♦ vi: **to ~ to
do sth** es schaffen, etw zu tun

control [kən'trəʊl] vt (direct, test)
kontrollieren ♦ n Kontrolle f; ~**s** npl (of
vehicle) Steuerung f; (of engine) Schalttafel f;
to be in ~ of (business, office) leiten; (group
of children) beaufsichtigen; **out of ~** außer
Kontrolle; **under ~** unter Kontrolle; ~**led
substance** n verschreibungspflichtiges
Medikament; ~ **panel** n Schalttafel f; ~
room n Kontrollraum m; ~ **tower** (AVIAT) n
Kontrollturm m

controversial [kɒntrə'və:ʃl] adj umstritten;
controversy ['kɒntrəvə:sɪ] n Kontroverse f

conurbation [kɒnə'beɪʃən] n Ballungsgebiet
nt

convalesce [kɒnvə'les] vi genesen;
convalescence [kɒnvə'lesns] n Genesung f

convector [kən'vektə'] n Heizlüfter m

convene [kən'vi:n] vt zusammenrufen ♦ vi
sich versammeln

convenience [kən'vi:nɪəns] n
Annehmlichkeit f; **all modern ~s** or (BRIT)
mod cons mit allem Komfort; **at your ~**
wann es Ihnen passt

convenient [kən'vi:nɪənt] adj günstig

convent ['kɒnvənt] n Kloster nt

convention [kən'venʃən] n Versammlung f;
(custom) Konvention f; ~**al** adj
konventionell

convent school n Klosterschule f

converge [kən'və:dʒ] vi zusammenlaufen

conversant [kən'vɜːsnt] *adj*: **to be ~ with** bewandert sein in +*dat*

conversation [kɔnvə'seɪʃən] *n* Gespräch *nt*; **~al** *adj* Unterhaltungs-

converse [*n* 'kɔnvɜːs, *vb* kən'vɜːs] *n* Gegenteil *nt* ♦ *vi* sich unterhalten

conversion [kən'vɜːʃən] *n* Umwandlung *f*; (*REL*) Bekehrung *f*

convert [*vb* kən'vɜːt, *n* 'kɔnvɜːt] *vt* (*change*) umwandeln; (*REL*) bekehren ♦ *n* Bekehrte(r) *mf*; Konvertit(in) *m(f)*; **~ible** *n* (*AUT*) Kabriolett *nt* ♦ *adj* umwandelbar; (*FIN*) konvertierbar

convex ['kɔnveks] *adj* konvex

convey [kən'veɪ] *vt* (*carry*) befördern; (*feelings*) vermitteln; **~or belt** *n* Fließband *nt*

convict [*vb* kən'vɪkt, *n* 'kɔnvɪkt] *vt* verurteilen ♦ *n* Häftling *m*; **~ion** [kən'vɪkʃən] *n* (*verdict*) Verurteilung *f*; (*belief*) Überzeugung *f*

convince [kən'vɪns] *vt* überzeugen; **~d** *adj*: **~d that** überzeugt davon, dass; **convincing** *adj* überzeugend

convoluted ['kɔnvəluːtɪd] *adj* verwickelt; (*style*) gewunden

convoy ['kɔnvɔɪ] *n* (*of vehicles*) Kolonne *f*; (*protected*) Konvoi *m*

convulse [kən'vʌls] *vt* zusammenzucken lassen; **to be ~d with laughter** sich vor Lachen krümmen; **convulsion** *n* (*esp MED*) Zuckung *f*, Krampf *m*

coo [kuː] *vi* gurren

cook [kuk] *vt, vi* kochen ♦ *n* Koch *m*, Köchin *f*; **~ book** *n* Kochbuch *nt*; **~er** *n* Herd *m*; **~ery** *n* Kochkunst *f*; **~ery book** (*BRIT*) *n* = **cook book**; **~ie** (*US*) *n* Plätzchen *nt*; **~ing** *n* Kochen *nt*

cool [kuːl] *adj* kühl ♦ *vt, vi* (ab)kühlen; **~ down** *vt, vi* (*fig*) (sich) beruhigen; **~ness** *n* Kühle *f*; (*of temperament*) kühle(r) Kopf *m*

coop [kuːp] *n* Hühnerstall *m* ♦ *vt*: **~ up** (*fig*) einpferchen

cooperate [kəu'ɔpəreɪt] *vi* zusammenarbeiten; **cooperation** [kəuɔpə'reɪʃən] *n* Zusammenarbeit *f*

cooperative [kəu'ɔpərətɪv] *adj* hilfsbereit; (*COMM*) genossenschaftlich ♦ *n* (*of farmers*) Genossenschaft *f*; (*~ store*) Konsumladen *m*

coordinate [*vb* kəu'ɔːdɪneɪt, *n* kəu'ɔːdɪnət] *vt* koordinieren ♦ *n* (*MATH*) Koordinate *f*; **~s** *npl* (*clothes*) Kombinationen *pl*

coordination [kəuɔːdɪ'neɪʃən] *n* Koordination *f*

cop [kɔp] (*inf*) *n* Polyp *m*, Bulle *m*

cope [kəup] *vi*: **to ~ with** fertig werden mit

copious ['kəupɪəs] *adj* reichhaltig

copper ['kɔpə'] *n* (*metal*) Kupfer *nt*; (*inf: policeman*) Polyp *m*, Bulle *m*; **~s** *npl* (*money*) Kleingeld *nt*

copse [kɔps] *n* Unterholz *nt*

copy ['kɔpɪ] *n* (*imitation*) Kopie *f*; (*of book etc*) Exemplar *nt*; (*of newspaper*) Nummer *f* ♦ *vt* kopieren, abschreiben; **~right** *n* Copyright *nt*

coral ['kɔrəl] *n* Koralle *f*; **~ reef** *n* Korallenriff *nt*

cord [kɔːd] *n* Schnur *f*; (*ELEC*) Kabel *nt*

cordial ['kɔːdɪəl] *adj* herzlich ♦ *n* Fruchtsaft *m*

cordon ['kɔːdn] *n* Absperrkette *f*; **~ off** *vt* abriegeln

corduroy ['kɔːdərɔɪ] *n* Kord(samt) *m*

core [kɔː'] *n* Kern *m* ♦ *vt* entkernen

cork [kɔːk] *n* (*bark*) Korkrinde *f*; (*stopper*) Korken *m*; **~screw** *n* Korkenzieher *m*

corn [kɔːn] *n* (*BRIT: wheat*) Getreide *nt*, Korn *nt*; (*US: maize*) Mais *m*; (*on foot*) Hühnerauge *nt*; **~ on the cob** Maiskolben *m*

corned beef ['kɔːnd-] *n* Cornedbeef *nt*, Corned Beef *nt*

corner ['kɔːnə'] *n* Ecke *f*; (*on road*) Kurve *f* ♦ *vt* in die Enge treiben; (*market*) monopolisieren ♦ *vi* (*AUT*) in die Kurve gehen; **~stone** *n* Eckstein *m*

cornet ['kɔːnɪt] *n* (*MUS*) Kornett *nt*; (*BRIT: of ice cream*) Eistüte *f*

corn: ~flakes ['kɔːnfleɪks] *npl* Cornflakes *pl* ®; **~flour** ['kɔːnflauə'] (*BRIT*) *n* Maizena *nt* ®; **~starch** ['kɔːnstɑːtʃ] (*US*) *n* Maizena *nt* ®

corny ['kɔːnɪ] *adj* (*joke*) blöd(e)

coronary ['kɔrənərɪ] *n* (*also: ~ thrombosis*) Herzinfarkt *m* coronation [kɒrə'neɪʃən] n Krönung f

coroner ['kɒrənəʳ] n Untersuchungsrichter m

corporal ['kɔ:pərl] n Obergefreite(r) m ♦ adj:
~ punishment Prügelstrafe f

corporate ['kɔ:pərɪt] adj gemeinschaftlich,
korporativ

corporation [kɔ:pə'reɪʃən] n (of town)
Gemeinde f; (COMM) Körperschaft f,
Aktiengesellschaft f

corps [kɔ:ʳ] (pl ~) n (Armee)korps nt

corpse [kɔ:ps] n Leiche f

corral [kə'rɑ:l] n Pferch m, Korral m

correct [kə'rekt] adj (accurate) richtig;
(proper) korrekt ♦ vt korrigieren; ~ion
[kə'rekʃən] n Berichtigung f

correlation [kɒrɪ'leɪʃən] n
Wechselbeziehung f

correspond [kɒrɪs'pɒnd] vi (agree)
übereinstimmen; (exchange letters)
korrespondieren; ~ence n (similarity)
Entsprechung f; (letters) Briefwechsel m,
Korrespondenz f; ~ence course n
Fernkurs m; ~ent n (PRESS) Berichterstatter
m

corridor ['kɒrɪdɔ:ʳ] n Gang m

corroborate [kə'rɒbəreɪt] vt bestätigen

corrode [kə'rəud] vt zerfressen ♦ vi rosten

corrosion [kə'rəuʒən] n Korrosion f

corrugated ['kɒrəgeɪtɪd] adj gewellt; ~ iron
n Wellblech nt

corrupt [kə'rʌpt] adj korrupt ♦ vt verderben;
(bribe) bestechen; ~ion [kə'rʌpʃən] n
Verdorbenheit f; (bribery) Bestechung f

corset ['kɔ:sɪt] n Korsett nt

Corsica ['kɔ:sɪkə] n Korsika nt

cosmetics [kɒz'metɪks] npl Kosmetika pl

cosmic ['kɒzmɪk] adj kosmisch

cosmonaut ['kɒzmənɔ:t] n Kosmonaut(in)
m(f)

cosmopolitan [kɒzmə'pɒlɪtn] adj
international; (city) Welt-

cosmos ['kɒzmɒs] n Kosmos m

cost [kɒst] (pt, pp cost) n Kosten pl, Preis m
♦ vt, vi kosten; ~s npl (JUR) Kosten pl; how
much does it ~? wie viel kostet das?; at all
~s um jeden Preis

co-star ['kəustɑ:ʳ] n zweite(r) or weitere(r)
Hauptdarsteller(in) m(f)

cost: ~-effective adj rentabel; ~ly ['kɒstlɪ]
adj kostspielig; ~-of-living ['kɒstəv'lɪvɪŋ]
adj (index) Lebenshaltungskosten-; ~ price
(BRIT) n Selbstkostenpreis m

costume ['kɒstju:m] n Kostüm nt; (fancy
dress) Maskenkostüm nt; (BRIT: also:
swimming ~) Badeanzug m; ~ jewellery
n Modeschmuck m

cosy ['kəuzɪ] (BRIT) adj behaglich;
(atmosphere) gemütlich

cot [kɒt] n (BRIT: child's) Kinderbett(chen) nt;
(US: camp bed) Feldbett nt

cottage ['kɒtɪdʒ] n kleine(s) Haus nt; ~
cheese n Hüttenkäse m; ~ industry n
Heimindustrie f; ~ pie n Auflauf mit
Hackfleisch und Kartoffelbrei

cotton ['kɒtn] n Baumwolle f; (thread) Garn
nt; ~ on to (inf) vt kapieren; ~ candy (US)
n Zuckerwatte f; ~ wool (BRIT) n Watte f

couch [kautʃ] n Couch f

couchette [ku:'ʃet] n (on train, boat)
Liegewagenplatz m

cough [kɒf] vi husten ♦ n Husten m; ~ drop
n Hustenbonbon nt

could [kud] pt of can²

couldn't ['kudnt] = could not

council ['kaunsl] n (of town) Stadtrat m; ~
estate (BRIT) n Siedlung f des sozialen
Wohnungsbaus; ~ house (BRIT) n Haus nt
des sozialen Wohnungsbaus; ~lor
['kaunslə'] n Stadtrat m/-rätin f

counsel ['kaunsl] n (barrister) Anwalt m;
(advice) Rat(schlag) m ♦ vt beraten; ~lor
['kaunslə'] n Berater m

count [kaunt] vt, vi zählen ♦ n (reckoning)
Abrechnung f; (nobleman) Graf m; ~ on vt
zählen auf +acc

countenance ['kauntɪnəns] n (old) Antlitz nt
♦ vt (tolerate) gutheißen

counter ['kauntə'] n (in shop) Ladentisch m;
(in café) Theke f; (in bank, post office)
Schalter m ♦ vt entgegnen

counteract [kauntər'ækt] vt
entgegenwirken +dat

counterfeit ['kauntəfɪt] n Fälschung f ♦ vt
fälschen ♦ adj gefälscht

counterfoil ['kauntəfɔɪl] n (Kontroll)abschnitt m

counterpart ['kauntəpɑːt] n (object) Gegenstück nt; (person) Gegenüber nt

counterproductive ['kauntəprə'dʌktɪv] adj destruktiv

countersign ['kauntəsaɪn] vt gegenzeichnen

countess ['kauntɪs] n Gräfin f

countless ['kauntlɪs] adj zahllos, unzählig

country ['kʌntrɪ] n Land nt;~ **dancing** (BRIT) n Volkstanz m;~ **house** n Landhaus nt;~**man** (irreg) n (national) Landsmann m; (rural) Bauer m;~**side** n Landschaft f

county ['kauntɪ] n Landkreis m; (BRIT) Grafschaft f

coup [kuː] (pl ~s) n Coup m; (also: ~ **d'état**) Staatsstreich m, Putsch m

couple ['kʌpl] n Paar nt ♦ vt koppeln; **a ~ of** ein paar

coupon ['kuːpɒn] n Gutschein m

coups [kuː] npl of **coup**

courage ['kʌrɪdʒ] n Mut m;~**ous** [kə'reɪdʒəs] adj mutig

courgette [kuə'ʒet] (BRIT) n Zucchini f or pl

courier ['kurɪəʳ] n (for holiday) Reiseleiter m; (messenger) Kurier m

course [kɔːs] n (race) Bahn f; (of stream) Lauf m; (golf ~) Platz m; (NAUT, SCH) Kurs m; (in meal) Gang m; **of ~** natürlich

court [kɔːt] n (royal) Hof m; (JUR) Gericht nt ♦ vt (woman) gehen mit; (danger) herausfordern; **to take to ~** vor Gericht bringen

courteous ['kə:tɪəs] adj höflich

courtesy ['kə:təsɪ] n Höflichkeit f

courtesy bus, courtesy coach n gebührenfreier Bus m

court: ~ **house** (US) n Gerichtsgebäude nt; ~**ier** ['kɔːtɪəʳ] n Höfling m;~ **martial** ['kɔːt'mɑːʃəl] (pl ~**s martial**) n Kriegsgericht nt ♦ vt vor ein Kriegsgericht stellen;~**room** n Gerichtssaal m;~**s martial** npl of **court martial**;~**yard** ['kɔːtjɑːd] n Hof m

cousin ['kʌzn] n Cousin m, Vetter m; Kusine f

cove [kəuv] n kleine Bucht f

covenant ['kʌvənənt] n (ECCL) Bund m; (JUR) Verpflichtung f

cover ['kʌvəʳ] vt (spread over) bedecken; (shield) abschirmen; (include) sich erstrecken über +acc; (protect) decken; (distance) zurücklegen; (report on) berichten über +acc ♦ n (lid) Deckel m; (for bed) Decke f; (MIL) Bedeckung f; (of book) Einband m; (of magazine) Umschlag m; (insurance) Versicherung f; **to take ~** (from rain) sich unterstellen; (MIL) in Deckung gehen; **under ~** (indoors) drinnen; **under ~ of** im Schutze +gen; **under separate ~** (COMM) mit getrennter Post; **to ~ up for sb** jdn decken;~**age** n (PRESS: reports) Berichterstattung f; (distribution) Verbreitung f;~ **charge** n Bedienungsgeld nt;~**ing** n Bedeckung f;~**ing letter** (US ~ **letter**) n Begleitbrief m;~ **note** n (INSURANCE) vorläufige(r) Versicherungsschein m

covert ['kʌvət] adj geheim

cover-up ['kʌvərʌp] n Vertuschung f

cow [kau] n Kuh f ♦ vt einschüchtern

coward ['kauəd] n Feigling m;~**ice** ['kauədɪs] n Feigheit f;~**ly** adj feige

cower ['kauəʳ] vi kauern

coy [kɔɪ] adj schüchtern

coyote [kɔɪ'əutɪ] n Präriewolf m

cozy ['kauzɪ] (US) adj = **cosy**

CPA (US) n abbr = **certified public accountant**

crab [kræb] n Krebs m

crab apple n Holzapfel m

crack [kræk] n Riss m, Sprung m; (noise) Knall m; (drug) Crack nt ♦ vt (break) springen lassen; (joke) reißen; (nut, safe) knacken; (whip) knallen lassen ♦ vi springen ♦ adj erstklassig; (troops) Elite-;~ **down** vi: **to ~ down (on)** hart durchgreifen (bei);~ **up** vi (fig) zusammenbrechen

cracked [krækt] adj (glass, plate, ice) gesprungen; (rib, bone) gebrochen, angeknackst (umg); (broken) gebrochen; (surface, walls) rissig; (inf: mad) übergeschnappt

cracker ['krækəʳ] n (firework) Knallkörper m, Kracher m; (biscuit) Keks m; (Christmas ~)

Knallbonbon nt
crackle ['krækl] vi knistern; (fire) prasseln
cradle ['kreɪdl] n Wiege f
craft [krɑːft] n (skill) (Hand- or
Kunst)fertigkeit f; (trade) Handwerk nt;
(NAUT) Schiff nt; ~sman (irreg) n
Handwerker m; ~smanship n (quality)
handwerkliche Ausführung f; (ability)
handwerkliche(s) Können nt
crafty ['krɑːftɪ] adj schlau
crag [kræg] n Klippe f
cram [kræm] vt voll stopfen ♦ vi (learn)
pauken; **to ~ sth into sth** etw in etw acc
stopfen
cramp [kræmp] n Krampf m ♦ vt (limit)
einengen; (hinder) hemmen; ~ed adj
(position) verkrampft; (space) eng
crampon ['kræmpən] n Steigeisen nt
cranberry ['krænbərɪ] n Preiselbeere f
crane [kreɪn] n (machine) Kran m; (bird)
Kranich m
crank [kræŋk] n (lever) Kurbel f; (person)
Spinner m; ~shaft n Kurbelwelle f
cranny ['krænɪ] n see **nook**
crash [kræʃ] n (noise) Krachen nt; (with cars)
Zusammenstoß m; (with plane) Absturz m;
(COMM) Zusammenbruch m ♦ vt (plane)
abstürzen mit ♦ vi (cars) zusammenstoßen;
(plane) abstürzen; (economy)
zusammenbrechen; (noise) knallen; ~
course n Schnellkurs m; ~ **helmet** n
Sturzhelm m; ~ **landing** n Bruchlandung f
crass [kræs] adj krass
crate [kreɪt] n (also fig) Kiste f
crater ['kreɪtər] n Krater m
cravat(e) [krə'væt] n Halstuch nt
crave [kreɪv] vt verlangen nach
crawl [krɔːl] vi kriechen; (baby) krabbeln ♦ n
Kriechen nt; (swim) Kraul nt
crayfish ['kreɪfɪʃ] n inv (freshwater) Krebs m;
(saltwater) Languste f
crayon ['kreɪən] n Buntstift m
craze [kreɪz] n Fimmel m
crazy ['kreɪzɪ] adj verrückt
creak [kriːk] vi knarren
cream [kriːm] n (from milk) Rahm m, Sahne
f; (polish, cosmetic) Creme f; (fig: people)

Elite f ♦ adj cremefarbig; ~ **cake** n
Sahnetorte f; ~ **cheese** n Rahmquark m;
~y adj sahnig
crease [kriːs] n Falte f ♦ vt falten; (wrinkle)
zerknittern ♦ vi (wrinkle up) knittern; ~d adj
zerknittert, faltig
create [kriː'eɪt] vt erschaffen; (cause)
verursachen; **creation** [kriː'eɪʃən] n
Schöpfung f; **creative** adj kreativ; **creator**
n Schöpfer m
creature ['kriːtʃər] n Geschöpf nt
crèche [kreʃ] n Krippe f
credence ['kriːdns] n: **to lend** or **give ~ to**
sth etw dat Glauben schenken
credentials [krɪ'denʃlz] npl
Beglaubigungsschreiben nt
credibility [kredɪ'bɪlɪtɪ] n Glaubwürdigkeit f
credible ['kredɪbl] adj (person) glaubwürdig;
(story) glaubhaft
credit ['kredɪt] n (also COMM) Kredit m ♦ vt
Glauben schenken +dat; (COMM)
gutschreiben; ~**s** npl (of film) Mitwirkenden
pl; ~**able** adj rühmlich; ~ **card** n
Kreditkarte f; ~**or** n Gläubiger m
creed [kriːd] n Glaubensbekenntnis nt
creek [kriːk] n (inlet) kleine Bucht f; (US:
river) kleine(r) Wasserlauf m
creep [kriːp] (pt, pp **crept**) vi kriechen; ~**er**
n Kletterpflanze f; ~**y** adj (frightening)
gruselig
cremate [krɪ'meɪt] vt einäschern;
cremation [krɪ'meɪʃən] n Einäscherung f;
crematorium [kremə'tɔːrɪəm] n
Krematorium nt
crêpe [kreɪp] n Krepp m; ~ **bandage** (BRIT)
n Elastikbinde f
crept [krept] pt, pp of **creep**
crescent ['kresnt] n (of moon) Halbmond m
cress [kres] n Kresse f
crest [krest] n (of cock) Kamm m; (of wave)
Wellenkamm m; (coat of arms) Wappen nt
crestfallen ['krestfɔːlən] adj
niedergeschlagen
Crete [kriːt] n Kreta nt
crevice ['krevɪs] n Riss m
crew [kruː] n Besatzung f, Mannschaft f; ~~
cut n Bürstenschnitt m; ~ **neck** n runde(r)

Ausschnitt *m*

crib [krɪb] *n* (bed) Krippe *f* ♦ *vt* (inf) spicken

crick [krɪk] *n* Muskelkrampf *m*

cricket ['krɪkɪt] *n* (insect) Grille *f*; (game) Kricket *nt*

crime [kraɪm] *n* Verbrechen *nt*

criminal ['krɪmɪnl] *n* Verbrecher *m* ♦ *adj* kriminell; (act) strafbar

crimson ['krɪmzn] *adj* leuchtend rot

cringe [krɪndʒ] *vi* sich ducken

crinkle ['krɪŋkl] *vt* zerknittern

cripple ['krɪpl] *n* Krüppel *m* ♦ *vt* lahm legen; (MED) verkrüppeln

crisis ['kraɪsɪs] (*pl* **crises**) *n* Krise *f*

crisp [krɪsp] *adj* knusprig; ~**s** (BRIT) *npl* Chips *pl*

crisscross ['krɪskrɔs] *adj* gekreuzt, Kreuz-

criteria [kraɪ'tɪərɪə] *npl of* **criterion**

criterion [kraɪ'tɪərɪən] (*pl* **criteria**) *n* Kriterium *nt*

critic ['krɪtɪk] *n* Kritiker(in) *m(f)*; ~**al** *adj* kritisch; ~**ally** *adv* kritisch; (ill) gefährlich; ~**ism** ['krɪtɪsɪzəm] *n* Kritik *f*; ~**ize** ['krɪtɪsaɪz] *vt* kritisieren

croak [krəuk] *vi* krächzen; (frog) quaken

Croatia [krəu'eɪʃə] *n* Kroatien *nt*

crochet ['krəuʃeɪ] *n* Häkelei *f*

crockery ['krɔkərɪ] *n* Geschirr *nt*

crocodile ['krɔkədaɪl] *n* Krokodil *nt*

crocus ['krəukəs] *n* Krokus *m*

croft [krɔft] (BRIT) *n* kleine(s) Pachtgut *nt*

crony ['krəunɪ] (inf) *n* Kumpel *m*

crook [kruk] *n* (criminal) Gauner *m*; (stick) Hirtenstab *m*

crooked ['krukɪd] *adj* krumm

crop [krɔp] *n* (harvest) Ernte *f*; (riding ~) Reitpeitsche *f* ♦ *vt* ernten; ~ **up** *vi* passieren

croquet ['krəukeɪ] *n* Krocket *nt*

croquette [krə'ket] *n* Krokette *f*

cross [krɔs] *n* Kreuz *nt* ♦ *vt* (road) überqueren; (legs) übereinander legen; kreuzen ♦ *adj* (annoyed) böse; ~ **out** *vt* streichen; ~ **over** *vi* hinübergehen; ~**bar** *n* Querstange *f*; ~~**country** (race) *n* Geländelauf *m*; ~~**examine** *vt* ins Kreuzverhör nehmen; ~~**eyed** *adj*: **to be**

~~**eyed** schielen; ~**fire** *n* Kreuzfeuer *nt*; ~**ing** *n* (~roads) (Straßen)kreuzung *f*; (of ship) Überfahrt *f*; (for pedestrians) Fußgängerüberweg *m*; ~**ing guard** (US) *n* Schülerlotse *m*; ~ **purposes** *npl*: **to be at** ~ **purposes** aneinander vorbeireden; ~~**reference** *n* Querverweis *m*; ~**roads** *n* Straßenkreuzung *f*; (fig) Scheideweg *m*; ~ **section** *n* Querschnitt *m*; ~**walk** (US) *n* Fußgängerüberweg *m*; ~**wind** *n* Seitenwind *m*; ~**word** (puzzle) *n* Kreuzworträtsel *nt*

crotch [krɔtʃ] *n* Zwickel *m*; (ANAT) Unterleib *nt*

crouch [krautʃ] *vi* hocken

crow [krəu] *n* (bird) Krähe *f*; (of cock) Krähen *nt* ♦ *vi* krähen

crowbar ['krəubɑː*r*] *n* Stemmeisen *nt*

crowd [kraud] *n* Menge *f* ♦ *vt* (fill) überfüllen ♦ *vi* drängen; ~**ed** *adj* überfüllt

crown [kraun] *n* Krone *f*; (of head, hat) Kopf *m* ♦ *vt* krönen; ~ **jewels** *npl* Kronjuwelen *pl*; ~ **prince** *n* Kronprinz *m*

crow's-feet ['krəuzfiːt] *npl* Krähenfüße *pl*

crucial ['kruːʃl] *adj* entscheidend

crucifix ['kruːsɪfɪks] *n* Kruzifix *nt*; ~**ion** [kruːsɪ'fɪkʃən] *n* Kreuzigung *f*

crude [kruːd] *adj* (raw) roh; (humour, behaviour) grob; (basic) primitiv; ~ (**oil**) *n* Rohöl *nt*

cruel ['kruəl] *adj* grausam; ~**ty** *n* Grausamkeit *f*

cruise [kruːz] *n* Kreuzfahrt *f* ♦ *vi* kreuzen; ~**r** *n* (MIL) Kreuzer *m*

crumb [krʌm] *n* Krume *f*

crumble ['krʌmbl] *vt*, *vi* zerbröckeln; **crumbly** *adj* krümelig

crumpet ['krʌmpɪt] *n* Tee(pfann)kuchen *m*

crumple ['krʌmpl] *vt* zerknittern

crunch [krʌntʃ] *n*: **the** ~ (fig) der Knackpunkt ♦ *vt* knirschen; ~**y** *adj* knusprig

crusade [kruː'seɪd] *n* Kreuzzug *m*

crush [krʌʃ] *n* Gedränge *nt* ♦ *vt* zerdrücken; (rebellion) unterdrücken

crust [krʌst] *n* Kruste *f*

crutch [krʌtʃ] *n* Krücke *f*

crux [krʌks] *n* springende(r) Punkt *m*

cry [kraɪ] vi (shout) schreien; (weep) weinen
♦ n (call) Schrei m; ~ off vi (plötzlich) absagen

crypt [krɪpt] n Krypta f

cryptic ['krɪptɪk] adj hintergründig

crystal ['krɪstl] n Kristall m; (glass) Kristallglas nt; (mineral) Bergkristall m; ~-clear adj kristallklar

crystallize ['krɪstəlaɪz] vt, vi kristallisieren; (fig) klären

CSA n abbr (= Child Support Agency) Amt zur Regelung von Unterhaltszahlungen für Kinder

CTC (BRIT) n abbr = city technology college

cub [kʌb] n Junge(s) nt; (also: C~ scout) Wölfling m

Cuba ['kjuːbə] n Kuba nt; ~n adj kubanisch ♦ n Kubaner(in) m(f)

cubbyhole ['kʌbɪhəʊl] n Eckchen nt

cube [kjuːb] n Würfel m ♦ vt (MATH) hoch drei nehmen

cubic ['kjuːbɪk] adj würfelförmig; (centimetre etc) Kubik-; ~ capacity n Fassungsvermögen nt

cubicle ['kjuːbɪkl] n Kabine f

cuckoo ['kʊkuː] n Kuckuck m; ~ clock n Kuckucksuhr f

cucumber ['kjuːkʌmbə*] n Gurke f

cuddle ['kʌdl] vt, vi herzen, drücken (inf)

cue [kjuː] n (THEAT) Stichwort nt; (snooker ~) Billardstock m

cuff [kʌf] n (BRIT: of shirt, coat etc) Manschette f; Aufschlag m; (US) = turn-up; off the ~ aus dem Handgelenk; ~link n Manschettenknopf m

cuisine [kwɪˈziːn] n Kochkunst f, Küche f

cul-de-sac ['kʌldəsæk] n Sackgasse f

culinary ['kʌlɪnərɪ] adj Koch-

cull [kʌl] vt (select) auswählen

culminate ['kʌlmɪneɪt] vi gipfeln; culmination [kʌlmɪˈneɪʃən] n Höhepunkt m

culottes [kjuːˈlɒts] npl Hosenrock m

culpable ['kʌlpəbl] adj schuldig

culprit ['kʌlprɪt] n Täter m

cult [kʌlt] n Kult m

cultivate ['kʌltɪveɪt] vt (AGR) bebauen; (mind) bilden; cultivation [kʌltɪˈveɪʃən] n

(AGR) Bebauung f; (of person) Bildung f

cultural ['kʌltʃərəl] adj kulturell, Kultur-

culture ['kʌltʃə*] n Kultur f; ~d adj gebildet

cumbersome ['kʌmbəsəm] adj (object) sperrig

cumulative ['kjuːmjʊlətɪv] adj gehäuft

cunning ['kʌnɪŋ] n Verschlagenheit f ♦ adj schlau

cup [kʌp] n Tasse f; (prize) Pokal m

cupboard ['kʌbəd] n Schrank m

cup tie (BRIT) n Pokalspiel nt

curate ['kjʊərɪt] n (Catholic) Kurat m; (Protestant) Vikar m

curator [kjʊəˈreɪtə*] n Kustos m

curb [kɜːb] vt zügeln ♦ n (on spending etc) Einschränkung f; (US) Bordstein m

curdle ['kɜːdl] vi gerinnen

cure [kjʊə*] n Heilmittel nt; (process) Heilverfahren nt ♦ vt heilen

curfew ['kɜːfjuː] n Ausgangssperre f; Sperrstunde f

curio ['kjʊərɪəʊ] n Kuriosität f

curiosity [kjʊərɪˈɒsɪtɪ] n Neugier f

curious ['kjʊərɪəs] adj neugierig; (strange) seltsam

curl [kɜːl] n Locke f ♦ vt locken ♦ vi sich locken; ~ up vi sich zusammenrollen; (person) sich ankuscheln; ~er n Lockenwickler m; ~y ['kɜːlɪ] adj lockig

currant ['kʌrnt] n Korinthe f

currency ['kʌrnsɪ] n Währung f; to gain ~ an Popularität gewinnen

current ['kʌrnt] n Strömung f ♦ adj (expression) gängig, üblich; (issue) neueste; ~ account (BRIT) n Girokonto nt; ~ affairs npl Zeitgeschehen nt; ~ly adv zurzeit

curricula [kəˈrɪkjʊlə] npl of curriculum

curriculum [kəˈrɪkjʊləm] (pl ~s or curricula) n Lehrplan m; ~ vitae [-ˈviːtaɪ] n Lebenslauf m

curry ['kʌrɪ] n Currygericht nt ♦ vt: to ~ favour with sich einschmeicheln bei; ~ powder n Curry(pulver) m

curse [kɜːs] vi (swear): to ~ (at) fluchen (auf or über +acc) ♦ vt (insult) verwünschen ♦ n Fluch m

cursor ['kɜːsə*] n (COMPUT) Cursor m

cursory ['kə:sərɪ] *adj* flüchtig

curt [kə:t] *adj* schroff

curtail [kə:'teɪl] *vt* abkürzen; *(rights)* einschränken

curtain ['kə:tn] *n* Vorhang *m*

curts(e)y ['kə:tsɪ] *n* Knicks *m* ♦ *vi* knicksen

curve [kə:v] *n* Kurve *f*; *(of body, vase etc)* Rundung *f* ♦ *vi* sich biegen; *(hips, breasts)* sich runden; *(road)* einen Bogen machen

cushion ['kuʃən] *n* Kissen *nt* ♦ *vt* dämpfen

custard ['kʌstəd] *n* Vanillesoße *f*

custodian [kʌs'təʊdɪən] *n* Kustos *m*, Verwalter(in) *m(f)*

custody ['kʌstədɪ] *n* Aufsicht *f*; *(police ~)* Haft *f*; **to take into ~** verhaften

custom ['kʌstəm] *n* *(tradition)* Brauch *m*; *(COMM)* Kundschaft *f*; **~ary** *adj* üblich

customer ['kʌstəmə*r*] *n* Kunde *m*, Kundin *f*

customized ['kʌstəmaɪzd] *adj* *(car etc)* mit Spezialausrüstung

custom-made ['kʌstəm'meɪd] *adj* speziell angefertigt

customs ['kʌstəmz] *npl* Zoll *m*; **~ duty** *n* Zollabgabe *f*; **~ officer** *n* Zollbeamte(r) *m*, Zollbeamtin *f*

cut [kʌt] *(pt, pp* **cut***) vt* schneiden; *(wages)* kürzen; *(prices)* heruntersetzen ♦ *vi* schneiden; *(intersect)* sich schneiden ♦ *n* Schnitt *m*; *(wound)* Schnittwunde *f*; *(in income etc)* Kürzung *f*; *(share)* Anteil *m*; **to ~ a tooth** zahnen; **~ down** *vt (tree)* fällen; *(reduce)* einschränken; **~ off** *vt (also fig)* abschneiden; *(allowance)* sperren; **~ out** *vt (shape)* ausschneiden; *(delete)* streichen; **~ up** *vt (meat)* aufschneiden; **~back** *n* Kürzung *f*

cute [kju:t] *adj* niedlich

cuticle ['kju:tɪkl] *n* Nagelhaut *f*

cutlery ['kʌtlərɪ] *n* Besteck *nt*

cutlet ['kʌtlɪt] *n (pork)* Kotelett *nt*; *(veal)* Schnitzel *nt*

cut: ~out *n (cardboard ~out)* Ausschneidemodell *nt*; **~-price, ~-rate** *(US) adj* verbilligt; **~throat** *n* Verbrechertyp *m* ♦ *adj* mörderisch

cutting ['kʌtɪŋ] *adj* schneidend ♦ *n (BRIT: PRESS)* Ausschnitt *m*; *(: RAIL)* Durchstich *m*

CV *n abbr* = **curriculum vitae**

cwt *abbr* = **hundredweight(s)**

cyanide ['saɪənaɪd] *n* Zyankali *nt*

cybercafé ['saɪbəkæfeɪ] *n* Internet-Café *nt*

cyberspace ['saɪbəspeɪs] *n* Cyberspace *m*

cycle ['saɪkl] *n* Fahrrad *nt*; *(series)* Reihe *f* ♦ *vi* Rad fahren; **~ hire** *n* Fahrradverleih *m*; **~ lane, ~ path** *n* (Fahr)radweg *m*; **cycling** *n* Radfahren *nt*; **cyclist** *n* Radfahrer(in) *m(f)*

cyclone ['saɪkləʊn] *n* Zyklon *m*

cygnet ['sɪgnɪt] *n* junge(r) Schwan *m*

cylinder ['sɪlɪndə*r*] *n* Zylinder *m*; *(TECH)* Walze *f*

cymbals ['sɪmblz] *npl* Becken *nt*

cynic ['sɪnɪk] *n* Zyniker(in) *m(f)*; **~al** *adj* zynisch; **~ism** ['sɪnɪsɪzəm] *n* Zynismus *m*

cypress ['saɪprɪs] *n* Zypresse *f*

Cyprus ['saɪprəs] *n* Zypern *nt*

cyst [sɪst] *n* Zyste *f*

cystitis [sɪs'taɪtɪs] *n* Blasenentzündung *f*

czar [za:*r*] *n* Zar *m*

Czech [tʃek] *adj* tschechisch ♦ *n* Tscheche *m*, Tschechin *f*

Czechoslovakia [tʃekəslə'vækɪə] *(HIST) n* die Tschechoslowakei; **~n** *adj* tschechoslowakisch ♦ *n* Tschechoslowake *m*, Tchechoslowakin *f*

D, d

D [di:] *n (MUS)* D *nt*

dab [dæb] *vt (wound, paint)* betupfen ♦ *n (little bit)* bisschen *nt*; *(of paint)* Tupfer *m*

dabble ['dæbl] *vi*: **to ~ in sth** in etw *dat* machen

dad [dæd] *n* Papa *m*, Vati *m*; **~dy** ['dædɪ] *n* Papa *m*, Vati *m*; **~dy-long-legs** *n* Weberknecht *m*

daffodil ['dæfədɪl] *n* Osterglocke *f*

daft [dɑ:ft] *(inf) adj* blöd(e), doof

dagger ['dægə*r*] *n* Dolch *m*

daily ['deɪlɪ] *adj* täglich ♦ *n (PRESS)* Tageszeitung *f*; *(BRIT: cleaner)* Haushaltshilfe *f* ♦ *adv* täglich

dainty ['deɪntɪ] *adj* zierlich

dairy ['dɛərɪ] *n (shop)* Milchgeschäft *nt*; *(on*

farm) Molkerei f ♦ *adj* Milch-; **~ farm***n* Hof
m mit Milchwirtschaft; **~ produce***n*
Molkereiprodukte *pl*; **~ products***npl*
Milchprodukte *pl*, Molkereiprodukte *pl*; **~
store** (*US*) *n* Milchgeschäft *nt*

dais ['deɪɪs] *n* Podium *nt*

daisy ['deɪzɪ] *n* Gänseblümchen *nt*

dale [deɪl] *n* Tal *nt*

dam [dæm] *n* (Stau)damm m ♦ *vt* stauen

damage ['dæmɪdʒ] *n* Schaden *m* ♦ *vt*
beschädigen; **~s** *npl* (*JUR*) Schaden(s)ersatz
m

damn [dæm] *vt* verdammen ♦ *n* (*inf*): **I don't
give a ~** das ist mir total egal ♦ *adj* (*inf*:
also: **~ed**) verdammt; **~ it!** verflucht!; **~ing**
adj vernichtend

damp [dæmp] *adj* feucht ♦ *n* Feuchtigkeit *f*
♦ *vt* (*also:* **~en**) befeuchten; (*discourage*)
dämpfen

damson ['dæmzən] *n* Damaszenerpflaume *f*

dance [dɑːns] *n* Tanz *m* ♦ *vi* tanzen; **~ hall**
n Tanzlokal *nt*; **~r** *n* Tänzer(in) *m(f)*;
dancing *n* Tanzen *nt*

dandelion ['dændɪlaɪən] *n* Löwenzahn *m*

dandruff ['dændrəf] *n* (Kopf)schuppen *pl*

Dane [deɪn] *n* Däne *m*, Dänin *f*

danger ['deɪndʒə*r*] *n* Gefahr *f*; **~!** (*sign*)
Achtung!; **to be in ~ of doing sth** Gefahr
laufen, etw zu tun; **~ous** *adj* gefährlich

dangle ['dæŋgl] *vi* baumeln ♦ *vt*
herabhängen lassen

Danish ['deɪnɪʃ] *adj* dänisch ♦ *n* Dänisch *nt*

dare [dɛə*r*] *vt* herausfordern ♦ *vi*: **to ~ (to)
do sth** es wagen, etw zu tun; **I ~ say** ich
würde sagen; **daring** ['dɛərɪŋ] *adj*
(*audacious*) verwegen; (*bold*) wagemutig;
(*dress*) gewagt ♦ *n* Mut *m*

dark [dɑːk] *adj* dunkel; (*fig*) düster, trübe;
(*deep colour*) dunkel- ♦ *n* Dunkelheit *f*; **to be
left in the ~ about** im Dunkeln sein über
+*acc*; **after ~** nach Anbruch der Dunkelheit;
~en *vt, vi* verdunkeln; **~ glasses** *npl*
Sonnenbrille *f*; **~ness** *n* Finsternis *nt*;
~room *n* Dunkelkammer *f*

darling ['dɑːlɪŋ] *n* Liebling *m* ♦ *adj* lieb

darn [dɑːn] *vt* stopfen

dart [dɑːt] *n* (*weapon*) Pfeil *m*; (*in sewing*)

Abnäher *m* ♦ *vi* sausen; **~s** *n* (*game*)
Pfeilwerfen *nt*; **~board***n* Zielscheibe *f*

dash [dæʃ] *n* Sprung *m*; (*mark*)
(Gedanken)strich *m*; (*small amount*)
bisschen *nt* ♦ *vt* (*hopes*) zunichte machen
♦ *vi* stürzen; **~ away** *vi* davonstürzen; **~
off** *vi* davonstürzen

dashboard ['dæʃbɔːd] *n* Armaturenbrett *nt*

dashing ['dæʃɪŋ] *adj* schneidig

data ['deɪtə] *n* Einzelheiten *pl*, Daten *pl*;
~base*n* Datenbank *f*; **~ processing***n*
Datenverarbeitung *f*

date [deɪt] *n* Datum *nt*; (*for meeting etc*)
Termin *m*; (*with person*) Verabredung *f*;
(*fruit*) Dattel *f* ♦ *vt* (*letter etc*) datieren; (*person*) gehen mit; **~ of birth**
Geburtsdatum *nt*; **to ~** bis heute; **out of ~**
überholt; **up to ~** (*clothes*) modisch; (*report*)
up-to-date; (*with news*) auf dem Laufenden;
~d *adj* altmodisch; **~ rape***n*
Vergewaltigung *f* nach einem Rendezvous

daub [dɔːb] *vt* beschmieren; (*paint*)
schmieren

daughter ['dɔːtə*r*] *n* Tochter *f*; **~-in-law***n*
Schwiegertochter *f*

daunting ['dɔːntɪŋ] *adj* entmutigend

dawdle ['dɔːdl] *vi* trödeln

dawn [dɔːn] *n* Morgendämmerung *f* ♦ *vi*
dämmern; (*fig*): **it ~ed on him that ...**
dämmerte ihm, dass ...

day [deɪ] *n* Tag *m*; **the ~ before/after** am
Tag zuvor/danach; **the ~ after tomorrow**
übermorgen; **the ~ before yesterday**
vorgestern; **by ~** am Tage; **~break***n*
Tagesanbruch *m*; **~dream** *vi* mit offenen
Augen träumen; **~light** *n* Tageslicht *nt*; **~
return** (*BRIT*) *n* Tagesrückfahrkarte *f*; **~time**
n Tageszeit *f*; **~-to-~** *adj* alltäglich

daze [deɪz] *vt* betäuben ♦ *n* Betäubung *f*; **in
a ~** benommen

dazzle ['dæzl] *vt* blenden

DC *abbr* (= *direct current*) Gleichstrom *m*

D-day ['diːdeɪ] *n* (*HIST*) *Tag der Invasion
durch die Alliierten* (6.6.44); (*fig*) der Tag X

deacon ['diːkən] *n* Diakon *m*

dead [dɛd] *adj* tot; (*without feeling*) gefühllos
♦ *adv* ganz; (*exactly*) genau ♦ *npl*: **the ~** die

Toten *pl*; **to shoot sb ~** jdn erschießen; **~ tired** todmüde; **to stop ~** abrupt stehen bleiben; **~en** *vt* (*pain*) abtöten; (*sound*) ersticken; **~ end** *n* Sackgasse *f*; **~ heat** *n* tote(s) Rennen *nt*; **~line** *n* Stichtag *m*; **~lock** *n* Stillstand *m*; **~ loss** (*inf*) *n*: **to be a ~ loss** ein hoffnungsloser Fall sein; **~ly** *adj* tödlich; **~pan** *adj* undurchdringlich; **D~ Sea** *n*: **the D~ Sea** das Tote Meer

deaf [def] *adj* taub; **~en** *vt* taub machen; **~ening** *adj* (*noise*) ohrenbetäubend; (*noise*) lautstark; **~-mute** *n* Taubstumme(r) *mf*; **~ness** *n* Taubheit *f*

deal [di:l] (*pt, pp* **dealt**) *n* Geschäft *nt* ♦ *vt* austeilen; (*CARDS*) geben; **a great ~ of** sehr viel; **~ in** *vt fus* handeln mit; **~ with** *vt fus* (*person*) behandeln; (*subject*) sich befassen mit; (*problem*) in Angriff nehmen; **~er** *n* (*COMM*) Händler *m*; (*CARDS*) Kartengeber *m*; **~ings** *npl* (*FIN*) Geschäfte *pl*; (*relations*) Beziehungen *pl*; **~t** [delt] *pt, pp of* **deal**

dean [di:n] *n* (*Protestant*) Superintendent *m*; (*Catholic*) Dechant *m*; (*UNIV*) Dekan *m*

dear [dɪə^r] *adj* lieb; (*expensive*) teuer ♦ *n* Liebling *m* ♦ *excl*: **~ me!** du liebe Zeit!; **D~ Sir** Sehr geehrter Herr!; **D~ John** Lieber John!; **~ly** *adv* (*love*) herzlich; (*pay*) teuer

death [deθ] *n* Tod *m*; (*statistic*) Todesfall *m*; **~ certificate** *n* Totenschein *m*; **~ly** *adj* totenähnlich, Toten-; **~ penalty** *n* Todesstrafe *f*; **~ rate** *n* Sterblichkeitsziffer *f*

debar [dɪ'bɑ:^r] *vt* ausschließen

debase [dɪ'beɪs] *vt* entwerten

debatable [dɪ'beɪtəbl] *adj* anfechtbar

debate [dɪ'beɪt] *n* Debatte *f* ♦ *vt* debattieren, diskutieren; (*consider*) überlegen

debilitating [dɪ'bɪlɪteɪtɪŋ] *adj* schwächend

debit ['debɪt] *n* Schuldposten *m* ♦ *vt* belasten

debris ['debri:] *n* Trümmer *pl*

debt [det] *n* Schuld *f*; **to be in ~** verschuldet sein; **~or** *n* Schuldner *m*

debunk [di:'bʌŋk] *vt* entlarven

decade ['dekeɪd] *n* Jahrzehnt *nt*

decadence ['dekədəns] *n* Dekadenz *f*

decaff ['di:kæf] (*inf*) *n* koffeinfreier Kaffee

decaffeinated [dɪ'kæfɪneɪtɪd] *adj* koffeinfrei

decanter [dɪ'kæntə^r] *n* Karaffe *f*

decay [dɪ'keɪ] *n* Verfall *m*; (*tooth ~*) Karies *m* ♦ *vi* verfallen; (*teeth, meat etc*) faulen; (*leaves etc*) verrotten

deceased [dɪ'si:st] *adj* verstorben

deceit [dɪ'si:t] *n* Betrug *m*; **~ful** *adj* falsch

deceive [dɪ'si:v] *vt* täuschen

December [dɪ'sembə^r] *n* Dezember *m*

decency ['di:sənsɪ] *n* Anstand *m*

decent ['di:sənt] *adj* (*respectable*) anständig; (*pleasant*) annehmbar

deception [dɪ'sepʃən] *n* Betrug *m*

deceptive [dɪ'septɪv] *adj* irreführend

decibel ['desɪbel] *n* Dezibel *nt*

decide [dɪ'saɪd] *vt* entscheiden ♦ *vi* sich entscheiden; **to ~ on sth** etw beschließen; **~d** *adj* entschieden; **~dly** [dɪ'saɪdɪdlɪ] *adv* entschieden

deciduous [dɪ'sɪdjuəs] *adj* Laub-

decimal ['desɪməl] *adj* dezimal ♦ *n* Dezimalzahl *f*; **~ point** *n* Komma *nt*

decipher [dɪ'saɪfə^r] *vt* entziffern

decision [dɪ'sɪʒən] *n* Entscheidung *f*, Entschluss *m*

decisive [dɪ'saɪsɪv] *adj* entscheidend; (*person*) entschlossen

deck [dek] *n* (*NAUT*) Deck *nt*; (*of cards*) Pack *m*; **~chair** *n* Liegestuhl *m*

declaration [deklə'reɪʃən] *n* Erklärung *f*

declare [dɪ'kleə^r] *vt* erklären; (*CUSTOMS*) verzollen

decline [dɪ'klaɪn] *n* (*decay*) Verfall *m*; (*lessening*) Rückgang *m* ♦ *vt* (*invitation*) ablehnen ♦ *vi* (*say no*) ablehnen; (*of strength*) nachlassen

decode ['di:'kəud] *vt* entschlüsseln; **~r** *n* (*TV*) Decoder *m*

decompose [di:kəm'pəuz] *vi* (sich) zersetzen

décor ['deɪkɔ:^r] *n* Ausstattung *f*

decorate ['dekəreɪt] *vt* (*room: paper*) tapezieren; (*: paint*) streichen; (*adorn*) (aus)schmücken; (*cake*) verzieren; (*honour*) auszeichnen; **decoration** [dekə'reɪʃən] *n* (*of house*) (Wand)dekoration *f*; (*medal*) Orden *m*; **decorator** ['dekəreɪtə^r] *n* Maler *m*, Anstreicher *m*

decorum [dɪ'kɔ:rəm] *n* Anstand *m*

decoy ['di:kɔɪ] n Lockvogel m

decrease [n 'di:kri:s, vb di:'kri:s] n Abnahme f ♦ vt vermindern ♦ vi abnehmen

decree [dɪ'kri:] n Erlass m; **~ nisi** n vorläufige(s) Scheidungsurteil nt

decrepit [dɪ'krepɪt] adj hinfällig

dedicate ['dedɪkeɪt] vt widmen; **~d** adj hingebungsvoll, engagiert; (COMPUT) dediziert; **dedication** [dedɪ'keɪʃən] n (devotion) Ergebenheit f; (in book) Widmung f

deduce [dɪ'dju:s] vt: **to ~ sth (from sth)** etw (aus etw) ableiten, etw (aus etw) schließen

deduct [dɪ'dʌkt] vt abziehen; **~ion** [dɪ'dʌkʃən] n (of money) Abzug m; (conclusion) (Schluss)folgerung f

deed [di:d] n Tat f; (document) Urkunde f

deem [di:m] vt: **to ~ sb/sth (to be) sth** jdn/etw für etw halten

deep [di:p] adj tief ♦ adv: **the spectators stood 20 ~** die Zuschauer standen in 20 Reihen hintereinander; **to be 4m ~** 4 Meter tief sein; **~en** vt vertiefen ♦ vi (darkness) tiefer werden; **~ end** n: **the ~ end** (of swimming pool) das Tiefe; **~-freeze** n Tiefkühlung f; **~-fry** vt fritttieren; **~ly** adv tief; **~-sea diving** n Tiefseetauchen nt; **~-seated** adj tief sitzend

deer [dɪə¹] n Reh nt; **~skin** n Hirsch-/Rehleder nt

deface [dɪ'feɪs] vt entstellen

defamation [defə'meɪʃən] n Verleumdung f

default [dɪ'fɔ:lt] n Versäumnis nt; (COMPUT) Standardwert m ♦ vi versäumen; **by ~** durch Nichterscheinen

defeat [dɪ'fi:t] n Niederlage f ♦ vt schlagen; **~ist** adj defätistisch ♦ n Defätist m

defect [n 'di:fekt, vb dɪ'fekt] n Fehler m ♦ vi überlaufen; **~ive** [dɪ'fektɪv] adj fehlerhaft

defence [dɪ'fens] n Verteidigung f; **~less** adj wehrlos

defend [dɪ'fend] vt verteidigen; **~ant** n Angeklagte(r) m; **~er** n Verteidiger m

defense [dɪ'fens] (US) n = **defence**

defensive [dɪ'fensɪv] adj defensiv ♦ n: **on the ~** in der Defensive

defer [dɪ'fə:¹] vt verschieben

deference ['defərəns] n Rücksichtnahme f

defiance [dɪ'faɪəns] n Trotz m, Unnachgiebigkeit f; **in ~ of sth** einer Sache dat zum Trotz

defiant [dɪ'faɪənt] adj trotzig, unnachgiebig

deficiency [dɪ'fɪʃənsɪ] n (lack) Mangel m; (weakness) Schwäche f

deficient [dɪ'fɪʃənt] adj mangelhaft

deficit ['defɪsɪt] n Defizit nt

defile [vb dɪ'faɪl, n 'di:faɪl] vt beschmutzen ♦ n Hohlweg m

define [dɪ'faɪn] vt bestimmen; (explain) definieren

definite ['defɪnɪt] adj (fixed) definitiv; (clear) eindeutig; **~ly** adv bestimmt

definition [defɪ'nɪʃən] n Definition f

deflate [di:'fleɪt] vt die Luft ablassen aus

deflect [dɪ'flekt] vt ablenken

deformity [dɪ'fɔ:mɪtɪ] n Missbildung f

defraud [dɪ'frɔ:d] vt betrügen

defrost [di:'frɒst] vt (fridge) abtauen; (food) auftauen; **~er** (US) n (demister) Gebläse nt

deft [deft] adj geschickt

defunct [dɪ'fʌŋkt] adj verstorben

defuse [di:'fju:z] vt entschärfen

defy [dɪ'faɪ] vt (disobey) sich widersetzen +dat; (orders, death) trotzen +dat; (challenge) herausfordern

degenerate [v dɪ'dʒenəreɪt, adj dɪ'dʒenərɪt] vi degenerieren ♦ adj degeneriert

degrading [dɪ'greɪdɪŋ] adj erniedrigend

degree [dɪ'gri:] n Grad m; (UNIV) Universitätsabschluss m; **by ~s** allmählich; **to some ~** zu einem gewissen Grad

dehydrated [di:haɪ'dreɪtɪd] adj (person) ausgetrocknet

de-ice ['di:'aɪs] vt enteisen

deign [deɪn] vi sich herablassen

deity ['di:ɪtɪ] n Gottheit f

dejected [dɪ'dʒektɪd] adj niedergeschlagen

delay [dɪ'leɪ] vt (hold back) aufschieben ♦ vi (linger) sich aufhalten ♦ n Aufschub m, Verzögerung f; (of train etc) Verspätung f; **to be ~ed** (train) Verspätung haben; **without ~** unverzüglich

delectable [dɪ'lektəbl] adj köstlich; (fig) reizend

delegate [n 'dɛlɪgɪt, vb 'dɛlɪgeɪt] n Delegierte(r) mf ♦ vt delegieren

delete [dɪ'liːt] vt (aus)streichen

deliberate [adj dɪ'lɪbərɪt, vb dɪ'lɪbəreɪt] adj (intentional) absichtlich; (slow) bedächtig ♦ vi (consider) überlegen; (debate) sich beraten; ~ly adv absichtlich

delicacy ['dɛlɪkəsɪ] n Zartheit f; (weakness) Anfälligkeit f; (food) Delikatesse f

delicate ['dɛlɪkɪt] adj (fine) fein; (fragile) zart; (situation) heikel; (MED) empfindlich

delicatessen [dɛlɪkə'tɛsn] n Feinkostgeschäft nt

delicious [dɪ'lɪʃəs] adj lecker

delight [dɪ'laɪt] n Wonne f ♦ vt entzücken; **to take ~ in sth** Freude an etw dat haben; ~ed adj: **~ed (at** or **with sth)** entzückt (über +acc etw); **~ed to do sth** etw sehr gern tun; ~ful adj entzückend, herrlich

delinquency [dɪ'lɪŋkwənsɪ] n Kriminalität f

delinquent [dɪ'lɪŋkwənt] n Straffällige(r) mf ♦ adj straffällig

delirious [dɪ'lɪrɪəs] adj im Fieberwahn

deliver [dɪ'lɪvə^r] vt (goods) (ab)liefern; (letter) zustellen; (speech) halten; ~y n (Ab)lieferung f; (of letter) Zustellung f; (of speech) Vortragsweise f; (MED) Entbindung f; **to take ~y of** in Empfang nehmen

delude [dɪ'luːd] vt täuschen

deluge ['dɛljuːdʒ] n Überschwemmung f; (fig) Flut f ♦ vt (fig) überfluten

delusion [dɪ'luːʒən] n (Selbst)täuschung f

de luxe [də'lʌks] adj Luxus-

delve [dɛlv] vi: **to ~ into** sich vertiefen in +acc

demand [dɪ'mɑːnd] vt verlangen ♦ n (request) Verlangen nt; (COMM) Nachfrage f; **in ~** gefragt; **on ~** auf Verlangen; ~ing adj anspruchsvoll

demean [dɪ'miːn] vt: **to ~ o.s.** sich erniedrigen

demeanour [dɪ'miːnə^r] (US **demeanor**) n Benehmen nt

demented [dɪ'mɛntɪd] adj wahnsinnig

demister [diː'mɪstə^r] n (AUT) Gebläse nt

demo ['dɛməʊ] (inf) n abbr (= demonstration) Demo f

democracy [dɪ'mɒkrəsɪ] n Demokratie f

democrat ['dɛməkræt] n Demokrat m; **democratic** [dɛmə'krætɪk] adj demokratisch

demolish [dɪ'mɒlɪʃ] vt abreißen; (fig) vernichten

demolition [dɛmə'lɪʃən] n Abbruch m

demon ['diːmən] n Dämon m

demonstrate ['dɛmənstreɪt] vt, vi demonstrieren; **demonstration** [dɛmən'streɪʃən] n Demonstration f; **demonstrator** [dɛmən'streɪtə^r] n (POL) Demonstrant(in) m(f)

demote [dɪ'məʊt] vt degradieren

demure [dɪ'mjʊə^r] adj ernst

den [dɛn] n (of animal) Höhle f; (study) Bude f

denatured alcohol [diː'neɪtʃəd-] (US) n ungenießbar gemachte(r) Alkohol m

denial [dɪ'naɪəl] n Leugnung f; **official ~** Dementi nt

denim ['dɛnɪm] adj Denim-; ~s npl Denimjeans pl

Denmark ['dɛnmɑːk] n Dänemark nt

denomination [dɪnɒmɪ'neɪʃən] n (ECCL) Bekenntnis nt; (type) Klasse f; (FIN) Wert m

denote [dɪ'nəʊt] vt bedeuten

denounce [dɪ'naʊns] vt brandmarken

dense [dɛns] adj dicht; (stupid) schwer von Begriff; ~ly adv dicht; **density** ['dɛnsɪtɪ] n Dichte f; **single/double density disk** Diskette f mit einfacher/doppelter Dichte

dent [dɛnt] n Delle f ♦ vt (also: **make a ~ in**) einbeulen

dental ['dɛntl] adj Zahn-; **~ surgeon** n = **dentist**

dentist ['dɛntɪst] n Zahnarzt(ärztin) m(f)

dentures ['dɛntʃəz] npl Gebiss nt

deny [dɪ'naɪ] vt leugnen; (officially) dementieren; (help) abschlagen

deodorant [diː'əʊdərənt] n Deodorant nt

depart [dɪ'pɑːt] vi abfahren; **to ~ from** (fig: differ from) abweichen von

department [dɪ'pɑːtmənt] n (COMM) Abteilung f; (UNIV) Seminar nt; (POL) Ministerium nt; **~ store** n Warenhaus nt

departure [dɪ'pɑːtʃə^r] n (of person) Abreise f; (of train) Abfahrt f; (of plane) Abflug m; **new**

~ Neuerung *f*;~ **lounge** *n* (*at airport*) Abflughalle *f*

depend [dɪ'pend] *vi*: **to ~ on** abhängen von; (*rely on*) angewiesen sein auf +*acc*; **it ~s** es kommt darauf an; **~ing on the result ...** abhängend vom Resultat ...;~**able** *adj* zuverlässig;~**ant** *n* Angehörige(r) *f(m)*; ~**ence** *n* Abhängigkeit *f*;~**ent** *adj* abhängig ♦ *n* = **dependant**; ~**ent on** abhängig von

depict [dɪ'pɪkt] *vt* schildern

depleted [dɪ'pli:tɪd] *adj* aufgebraucht

deplorable [dɪ'plɔ:rəbl] *adj* bedauerlich

deploy [dɪ'plɔɪ] *vt* einsetzen

depopulation ['di:pɔpju'leɪʃən] *n* Entvölkerung *f*

deport [dɪ'pɔ:t] *vt* deportieren;~**ation** [di:pɔ:'teɪʃən] *n* Abschiebung *f*

deportment [dɪ'pɔ:tmənt] *n* Betragen *nt*

deposit [dɪ'pɔzɪt] *n* (*in bank*) Guthaben *nt*; (*down payment*) Anzahlung *f*; (*security*) Kaution *f*; (*CHEM*) Niederschlag *m* ♦ *vt* (*in bank*) deponieren; (*put down*) niederlegen; ~ **account** *n* Sparkonto *nt*

depot ['depəu] *n* Depot *nt*

depraved [dɪ'preɪvd] *adj* verkommen

depreciate [dɪ'pri:ʃɪet] *vi* im Wert sinken; **depreciation** [dɪprɪ:ʃɪ'eɪʃən] *n* Wertminderung *f*

depress [dɪ'pres] *vt* (*press down*) niederdrücken; (*in mood*) deprimieren;~**ed** *adj* deprimiert;~**ion** [dɪ'preʃən] *n* (*mood*) Depression *f*; (*in trade*) Wirtschaftskrise *f*; (*hollow*) Vertiefung *f*, (*MET*) Tief(druckgebiet) *nt*

deprivation [deprɪ'veɪʃən] *n* Not *f*

deprive [dɪ'praɪv] *vt*: **to ~ sb of sth** jdn einer Sache *gen* berauben;~**d** *adj* (*child*) sozial benachteiligt; (*area*) unterentwickelt

depth [depθ] *n* Tiefe *f*; **in the ~s of despair** in tiefster Verzweiflung

deputation [depju'teɪʃən] *n* Abordnung *f*

deputize ['depjutaɪz] *vi*: **to ~ (for sb)** (jdn) vertreten

deputy ['depjutɪ] *adj* stellvertretend ♦ *n* (Stell)vertreter *m*;~ **head** (*BRIT: SCOL*) *n* Konrektor(in) *m(f)*

derail [dɪ'reɪl] *vt*: **to be ~ed** entgleisen; ~**ment** *n* Entgleisung *f*

deranged [dɪ'reɪndʒd] *adj* verrückt

derby ['də:rbɪ] (*US*) *n* Melone *f*

derelict ['derɪlɪkt] *adj* verlassen

deride [dɪ'raɪd] *vt* auslachen

derisory [dɪ'raɪsərɪ] *adj* spöttisch

derivative [dɪ'rɪvətɪv] *n* Derivat *nt* ♦ *adj* abgeleitet

derive [dɪ'raɪv] *vt* (*get*) gewinnen; (*deduce*) ableiten ♦ *vi* (*come from*) abstammen

dermatitis [də:mə'taɪtɪs] *n* Hautentzündung *f*

derogatory [dɪ'rɔgətərɪ] *adj* geringschätzig

derrick ['derɪk] *n* Drehkran *m*

descend [dɪ'send] *vt, vi* hinuntersteigen; **to ~ from** abstammen von;~**ant** *n* Nachkomme *m*;**descent** [dɪ'sent] *n* (*coming down*) Abstieg *m*; (*origin*) Abstammung *f*

describe [dɪs'kraɪb] *vt* beschreiben

description [dɪs'krɪpʃən] *n* Beschreibung *f*; (*sort*) Art *f*

descriptive [dɪs'krɪptɪv] *adj* beschreibend; (*word*) anschaulich

desecrate ['desɪkreɪt] *vt* schänden

desert [*n* 'dezət, *vb* dɪ'zə:t] *n* Wüste *f* ♦ *vt* verlassen; (*temporarily*) im Stich lassen ♦ *vi* (*MIL*) desertieren; **~s** *npl* (*what one deserves*): **to get one's just ~s** seinen gerechten Lohn bekommen;~**er** *n* Deserteur *m*;~**ion** [dɪ'zə:ʃən] *n* (*of wife*) Verlassen *nt*; (*MIL*) Fahnenflucht *f*;~ **island** *n* einsame Insel *f*

deserve [dɪ'zə:v] *vt* verdienen;**deserving** *adj* verdienstvoll

design [dɪ'zaɪn] *n* (*plan*) Entwurf *m*; (*planning*) Design *nt* ♦ *vt* entwerfen

designate [*vb* 'dezɪgneɪt, *adj* 'dezɪgnɪt] *vt* bestimmen ♦ *adj* designiert

designer [dɪ'zaɪnər] *n* Designer(in) *m(f)*; (*TECH*) Konstrukteur(in) *m(f)*; (*fashion ~*) Modeschöpfer(in) *m(f)*

desirable [dɪ'zaɪərəbl] *adj* wünschenswert

desire [dɪ'zaɪər] *n* Wunsch *m*, Verlangen *nt* ♦ *vt* (*lust*) begehren; (*ask for*) wollen

desk [desk] *n* Schreibtisch *m*; (*BRIT: in shop, restaurant*) Kasse *f*;~**top publishing** *n*

Desktop-Publishing *nt*

desolate ['dɛsəlɪt] *adj* öde; *(sad)* trostlos; **desolation** [dɛsə'leɪʃən] *n* Trostlosigkeit *f*

despair [dɪs'pɛəʳ] *n* Verzweiflung *f* ♦ *vi:* **to ~ (of)** verzweifeln (an +*dat*)

despatch [dɪs'pætʃ] *n, vt* = **dispatch**

desperate ['dɛspərɪt] *adj* verzweifelt; **~ly** *adv* verzweifelt; **desperation** [dɛspə'reɪʃən] *n* Verzweiflung *f*

despicable [dɪs'pɪkəbl] *adj* abscheulich

despise [dɪs'paɪz] *vt* verachten

despite [dɪs'paɪt] *prep* trotz +*gen*

despondent [dɪs'pɔndənt] *adj* mutlos

dessert [dɪ'zɜːt] *n* Nachtisch *m*; **~spoon** *n* Dessertlöffel *m*

destination [dɛstɪ'neɪʃən] *n* (of person) (Reise)ziel *nt*; (of goods) Bestimmungsort *m*

destiny ['dɛstɪnɪ] *n* Schicksal *nt*

destitute ['dɛstɪtjuːt] *adj* Not leidend

destroy [dɪs'trɔɪ] *vt* zerstören; **~er** *n* (NAUT) Zerstörer *m*

destruction [dɪs'trʌkʃən] *n* Zerstörung *f*

destructive [dɪs'trʌktɪv] *adj* zerstörend

detach [dɪ'tætʃ] *vt* loslösen; **~able** *adj* abtrennbar; **~ed** *adj* (attitude) distanziert; (house) Einzel-; **~ment** *n* (fig) Abstand *m*; (MIL) Sonderkommando *nt*

detail ['diːteɪl] *n* Einzelheit *f*, Detail *nt* ♦ *vt* (relate) ausführlich berichten; (appoint) abkommandieren; **in ~** im Detail; **~ed** *adj* detailliert

detain [dɪ'teɪn] *vt* aufhalten; (imprison) in Haft halten

detect [dɪ'tɛkt] *vt* entdecken; **~ion** *n* [dɪ'tɛkʃən] *n* Aufdeckung *f*; **~ive** *n* Detektiv *m*; **~ive story** *n* Kriminalgeschichte *f*, Krimi *m*

détente [deɪ'tɑːnt] *n* Entspannung *f*

detention [dɪ'tɛnʃən] *n* Haft *f*; (SCH) Nachsitzen *nt*

deter [dɪ'tɜːʳ] *vt* abschrecken

detergent [dɪ'tɜːdʒənt] *n* Waschmittel *nt*

deteriorate [dɪ'tɪərɪəreɪt] *vi* sich verschlechtern; **deterioration** [dɪtɪərɪə'reɪʃən] *n* Verschlechterung *f*

determination [dɪtɜːmɪ'neɪʃən] *n* Entschlossenheit *f*

determine [dɪ'tɜːmɪn] *vt* bestimmen; **~d** *adj* entschlossen

deterrent [dɪ'tɛrənt] *n* Abschreckungsmittel *nt*

detest [dɪ'tɛst] *vt* verabscheuen

detonate ['dɛtəneɪt] *vt* explodieren lassen ♦ *vi* detonieren

detour ['diːtuəʳ] *n* Umweg *m*; (US: AUT: diversion) Umleitung *f* ♦ *vt* (US: AUT: traffic) umleiten

detract [dɪ'trækt] *vi:* **to ~ from** schmälern

detriment ['dɛtrɪmənt] *n:* **to the ~ of** zum Schaden +*gen*; **~al** [dɛtrɪ'mɛntl] *adj* schädlich

devaluation [diːvæljʊ'eɪʃən] *n* Abwertung *f*

devastate ['dɛvəsteɪt] *vt* verwüsten; (fig: shock): **to be ~d by** niedergeschmettert sein von; **devastating** *adj* verheerend

develop [dɪ'vɛləp] *vt* entwickeln; (resources) erschließen ♦ *vi* sich entwickeln; **~ing country** *n* Entwicklungsland *nt*; **~ment** *n* Entwicklung *f*

deviate ['diːvɪeɪt] *vi* abweichen

device [dɪ'vaɪs] *n* Gerät *nt*

devil ['dɛvl] *n* Teufel *m*

devious ['diːvɪəs] *adj* (means) krumm; (person) verschlagen

devise [dɪ'vaɪz] *vt* entwickeln

devoid [dɪ'vɔɪd] *adj:* **~ of** ohne

devolution [diːvə'luːʃən] *n* (POL) Dezentralisierung *f*

devote [dɪ'vəut] *vt:* **to ~ sth (to sth)** etw (einer Sache *dat*) widmen; **~d** *adj* ergeben; **~e** [dɛvəu'tiː] *n* Anhänger(in) *m(f)*, Verehrer(in) *m(f)*; **devotion** [dɪ'vəuʃən] *n* (piety) Andacht *f*; (loyalty) Ergebenheit *f*, Hingabe *f*

devour [dɪ'vauəʳ] *vt* verschlingen

devout [dɪ'vaut] *adj* andächtig

dew [djuː] *n* Tau *m*

dexterity [dɛks'tɛrɪtɪ] *n* Geschicklichkeit *f*

DHSS (BRIT) *n abbr* = **Department of Health and Social Security**

diabetes [daɪə'biːtiːz] *n* Zuckerkrankheit *f*

diabetic [daɪə'bɛtɪk] *adj* zuckerkrank; (food) Diabetiker- ♦ *n* Diabetiker *m*

diabolical [daɪə'bɔlɪkl] (inf) *adj* (weather, behaviour) saumäßig

diagnose [daɪəg'nəuz] *vt* diagnostizieren

diagnoses [daɪəg'nəusi:z] *npl of* **diagnosis**

diagnosis [daɪəg'nəusɪs] *n* Diagnose *f*

diagonal [daɪ'ægənl] *adj* diagonal ♦ *n* Diagonale *f*

diagram ['daɪəgræm] *n* Diagramm *nt*, Schaubild *nt*

dial ['daɪəl] *n* (TEL) Wählscheibe *f*; (of clock) Zifferblatt *nt* ♦ *vt* wählen

dialect ['daɪəlekt] *n* Dialekt *m*

dialling code ['daɪəlɪŋ-] *n* Vorwahl *f*

dialling tone *n* Amtszeichen *nt*

dialogue ['daɪəlɔg] *n* Dialog *m*

dial tone (US) *n* = **dialling tone**

diameter [daɪ'æmɪtə*r*] *n* Durchmesser *m*

diamond ['daɪəmənd] *n* Diamant *m*; **~s** *npl* (CARDS) Karo *nt*

diaper ['daɪəpə*r*] (US) *n* Windel *f*

diaphragm ['daɪəfræm] *n* Zwerchfell *nt*

diarrhoea [daɪə'ri:ə] (US **diarrhea**) *n* Durchfall *m*

diary ['daɪərɪ] *n* Taschenkalender *m*; (account) Tagebuch *nt*

dice [daɪs] *n* Würfel *pl* ♦ *vt* in Würfel schneiden

dictate [dɪk'teɪt] *vt* diktieren; **~s** ['dɪkteɪts] *npl* Gebote *pl*; **dictation** [dɪk'teɪʃən] *n* Diktat *nt*

dictator [dɪk'teɪtə*r*] *n* Diktator *m*; **~ship** [dɪk'teɪtəʃɪp] *n* Diktatur *f*

dictionary ['dɪkʃənrɪ] *n* Wörterbuch *nt*

did [dɪd] *pt of* **do**

didn't ['dɪdnt] = **did not**

die [daɪ] *vi* sterben; **to be dying for sth** etw unbedingt haben wollen; **to be dying to do sth** darauf brennen, etw zu tun; **~ away** *vi* nachlassen; **~ down** *vi* nachlassen; **~ out** *vi* aussterben

diesel ['di:zl] *n* (car) Diesel *m*; **~ engine** *n* Dieselmotor *m*; **~ oil** *n* Dieselkraftstoff *m*

diet ['daɪət] *n* Nahrung *f*; (special food) Diät *f*; (slimming) Abmagerungskur *f* ♦ *vi* (also: **be on a ~**) eine Abmagerungskur machen

differ ['dɪfə*r*] *vi* sich unterscheiden; (disagree) anderer Meinung sein; **~ence** *n* Unterschied *m*; **~ent** *adj* anders; (two things) verschieden; **~entiate** [dɪfə'renʃɪeɪt]

vt, *vi* unterscheiden; **~ently** *adv* anders; (from one another) unterschiedlich

difficult ['dɪfɪkəlt] *adj* schwierig; **~y** *n* Schwierigkeit *f*

diffident ['dɪfɪdənt] *adj* schüchtern

diffuse [*adj* dɪ'fju:s, *vb* dɪ'fju:z] *adj* langatmig ♦ *vt* verbreiten

dig [dɪg] (*pt*, *pp* **dug**) *vt* graben ♦ *n* (prod) Stoß *m*; (remark) Spitze *f*; (archaeological) Ausgrabung *f*; **~ in** *vi* (MIL) sich eingraben; **~ into** *vt fus* (savings) angreifen; **~ up** *vt* ausgraben; (fig) aufgabeln

digest [*vb* daɪ'dʒest, *n* 'daɪdʒest] *vt* verdauen ♦ *n* Auslese *f*; **~ion** [dɪ'dʒestʃən] *n* Verdauung *f*

digit ['dɪdʒɪt] *n* Ziffer *f*; (ANAT) Finger *m*; **~al** *adj* digital, Digital-; **~al camera** *n* Digitalkamera *f*; **~al TV** *n* Digitalfernsehen *nt*

dignified ['dɪgnɪfaɪd] *adj* würdevoll

dignity ['dɪgnɪtɪ] *n* Würde *f*

digress [daɪ'gres] *vi* abschweifen

digs [dɪgz] (BRIT: inf) *npl* Bude *f*

dilapidated [dɪ'læpɪdeɪtɪd] *adj* baufällig

dilate [daɪ'leɪt] *vt* weiten ♦ *vi* sich weiten

dilemma [daɪ'lemə] *n* Dilemma *nt*

diligent ['dɪlɪdʒənt] *adj* fleißig

dilute [daɪ'lu:t] *vt* verdünnen

dim [dɪm] *adj* trübe; (stupid) schwer von Begriff ♦ *vt* verdunkeln; **to ~ one's headlights** (esp US) abblenden

dime [daɪm] (US) *n* Zehncentstück *nt*

dimension [daɪ'menʃən] *n* Dimension *f*

diminish [dɪ'mɪnɪʃ] *vt*, *vi* verringern

diminutive [dɪ'mɪnjutɪv] *adj* winzig ♦ *n* Verkleinerungsform *f*

dimmer ['dɪmə*r*] (US) *n* (AUT) Abblendschalter *m*; **~s** *npl* Abblendlicht *nt*; (sidelights) Begrenzungsleuchten *pl*

dimple ['dɪmpl] *n* Grübchen *nt*

din [dɪn] *n* Getöse *nt*

dine [daɪn] *vi* speisen; **~r** *n* Tischgast *m*; (RAIL) Speisewagen *m*

dinghy ['dɪŋgɪ] *n* Dingi *nt*; **rubber ~** Schlauchboot *nt*

dingy ['dɪndʒɪ] *adj* armselig

dining car (BRIT) *n* Speisewagen *m*

dining room ['daɪnɪŋ-] *n* Esszimmer *nt*; (in

hotel) Speisezimmer nt

dinner ['dɪnəʳ] n (*lunch*) Mittagessen nt; (*evening*) Abendessen nt; (*public*) Festessen nt; ~ **jacket** n Smoking m; ~ **party** n Tischgesellschaft f; ~ **time** n Tischzeit f

dinosaur ['daɪnəsɔːʳ] n Dinosaurier m

dint [dɪnt] n: **by ~ of** durch

diocese ['daɪəsɪs] n Diözese f

dip [dɪp] n (*hollow*) Senkung f; (*bathe*) kurze(s) Baden nt ♦ vt eintauchen; (*BRIT: AUT*) abblenden ♦ vi (*slope*) sich senken, abfallen

diploma [dɪ'pləumə] n Diplom nt

diplomacy [dɪ'pləuməsɪ] n Diplomatie f

diplomat ['dɪpləmæt] n Diplomat(in) m(f); ~**ic** [dɪplə'mætɪk] adj diplomatisch

dip stick n Ölmessstab m

dipswitch ['dɪpswɪtʃ] (*BRIT*) n (*AUT*) Abblendschalter m

dire [daɪəʳ] adj schrecklich

direct [daɪ'rekt] adj direkt ♦ vt leiten; (*film*) die Regie führen +gen; (*aim*) richten; (*order*) anweisen; **can you ~ me to ...?** können Sie mir sagen, wo ich zu ... komme?; ~ **debit** n (*BRIT*) Einzugsauftrag m; (*transaction*) automatische Abbuchung f

direction [dɪ'rekʃən] n Richtung f; (*CINE*) Regie f; Leitung f; ~**s** npl (*for use*) Gebrauchsanleitung f; (*orders*) Anweisungen pl; **sense of ~** Orientierungssinn m

directly [dɪ'rektlɪ] adv direkt; (*at once*) sofort

director [dɪ'rektəʳ] n Direktor m; (*of film*) Regisseur m

directory [dɪ'rektərɪ] n (*TEL*) Telefonbuch nt; ~ **enquiries**, ~ **assistance** (*US*) n (Fernsprech)auskunft f

dirt [dɜːt] n Schmutz m, Dreck m; ~-**cheap** adj spottbillig; ~**y** adj schmutzig ♦ vt beschmutzen; ~**y trick** n gemeine(r) Trick m

disability [dɪsə'bɪlɪtɪ] n Körperbehinderung f

disabled [dɪs'eɪbld] adj körperbehindert

disadvantage [dɪsəd'vɑːntɪdʒ] n Nachteil m

disagree [dɪsə'griː] vi nicht übereinstimmen; (*quarrel*) (sich) streiten; (*food*): **to ~ with sb** jdm nicht bekommen; ~**able** adj

unangenehm; ~**ment** n (*between persons*) Streit m; (*between things*) Widerspruch m

disallow ['dɪsə'lau] vt nicht zulassen

disappear [dɪsə'pɪəʳ] vi verschwinden; ~**ance** n Verschwinden nt

disappoint [dɪsə'pɔɪnt] vt enttäuschen; ~**ed** adj enttäuscht; ~**ment** n Enttäuschung f

disapproval [dɪsə'pruːvəl] n Missbilligung f

disapprove [dɪsə'pruːv] vi: **to ~ of** missbilligen

disarm [dɪs'ɑːm] vt entwaffnen; (*POL*) abrüsten; ~**ament** n Abrüstung f

disarray [dɪsə'reɪ] n: **to be in ~** (*army*) in Auflösung (begriffen) sein; (*clothes*) in unordentlichen Zustand sein

disaster [dɪ'zɑːstəʳ] n Katastrophe f; **disastrous** [dɪ'zɑːstrəs] adj verhängnisvoll

disband [dɪs'bænd] vt auflösen ♦ vi auseinander gehen

disbelief ['dɪsbə'liːf] n Ungläubigkeit f

disc [dɪsk] n Scheibe f; (*record*) (Schall)platte f; (*COMPUT*) = **disk**

discard [dɪs'kɑːd] vt ablegen

discern [dɪ'sɜːn] vt erkennen; ~**ing** adj scharfsinnig

discharge [vb dɪs'tʃɑːdʒ, n 'dɪstʃɑːdʒ] vt (*ship*) entladen; (*duties*) nachkommen +dat; (*dismiss*) entlassen; (*gun*) abschießen; (*JUR*) freisprechen ♦ n (*of ship, ELEC*) Entladung f; (*dismissal*) Entlassung f; (*MED*) Ausfluss m

disciple [dɪ'saɪpl] n Jünger m

discipline ['dɪsɪplɪn] n Disziplin f ♦ vt (*train*) schulen; (*punish*) bestrafen

disc jockey n Diskjockey m

disclaim [dɪs'kleɪm] vt nicht anerkennen

disclose [dɪs'kləuz] vt enthüllen; **disclosure** [dɪs'kləuʒəʳ] n Enthüllung f

disco ['dɪskəu] n abbr = **discotheque**

discoloured [dɪs'kʌləd] (*US* **discolored**) adj verfärbt

discomfort [dɪs'kʌmfət] n Unbehagen nt

disconcert [dɪskən'sɜːt] vt aus der Fassung bringen

disconnect [dɪskə'nekt] vt abtrennen

discontent [dɪskən'tent] n Unzufriedenheit f; ~**ed** adj unzufrieden

discontinue [dɪskən'tɪnjuː] vt einstellen

discord ['dɪskɔːd] n Zwietracht f; (noise) Dissonanz f

discotheque ['dɪskəutek] n Diskothek f

discount [n 'dɪskaunt, vb dɪs'kaunt] n Rabatt m ♦ vt außer Acht lassen

discourage [dɪs'kʌrɪdʒ] vt entmutigen; (prevent) abraten

discourteous [dɪs'kəːtɪəs] adj unhöflich

discover [dɪs'kʌvəʳ] vt entdecken;~y n Entdeckung f

discredit [dɪs'krɛdɪt] vt in Verruf bringen

discreet [dɪs'kriːt] adj diskret

discrepancy [dɪs'krɛpənsɪ] n Diskrepanz f

discriminate [dɪs'krɪmɪneɪt] vi unterscheiden; **to ~ against** diskriminieren; **discriminating** adj anspruchsvoll; **discrimination** [dɪskrɪmɪ'neɪʃən] n Urteilsvermögen nt; (pej) Diskriminierung f

discuss [dɪs'kʌs] vt diskutieren, besprechen; ~**ion** [dɪs'kʌʃən] n Diskussion f, Besprechung f

disdain [dɪs'deɪn] n Verachtung f

disease [dɪ'ziːz] n Krankheit f

disembark [dɪsɪm'baːk] vi von Bord gehen

disenchanted ['dɪsɪn'tʃaːntɪd] adj desillusioniert

disengage [dɪsɪn'geɪdʒ] vt (AUT) auskuppeln

disentangle [dɪsɪn'tæŋgl] vt entwirren

disfigure [dɪs'fɪgəʳ] vt entstellen

disgrace [dɪs'greɪs] n Schande f ♦ vt Schande bringen über +acc;~**ful** adj unerhört

disgruntled [dɪs'grʌntld] adj verärgert

disguise [dɪs'gaɪz] vt verkleiden; (feelings) verhehlen ♦ n Verkleidung f; **in ~** verkleidet, maskiert

disgust [dɪs'gʌst] n Abscheu f ♦ vt anwidern; ~**ed** adj angeekelt; (at sb's behaviour) empört;~**ing** adj widerlich

dish [dɪʃ] n Schüssel f; (food) Gericht nt; **to do** or **wash the ~es** abwaschen;~ **up** vt auftischen;~ **cloth** n Spüllappen m

dishearten [dɪs'haːtn] vt entmutigen

dishevelled [dɪ'ʃɛvəld] adj (hair) zerzaust; (clothing) ungepflegt

dishonest [dɪs'ɔnɪst] adj unehrlich

dishonour [dɪs'ɔnəʳ] (US **dishonor**) n

Unehre f;~**able** adj unehrenhaft

dishtowel ['dɪʃtauəl] n Geschirrtuch nt

dishwasher ['dɪʃwɔʃəʳ] n Geschirrspülmaschine f

disillusion [dɪsɪ'luːʒən] vt enttäuschen, desillusionieren

disincentive [dɪsɪn'sɛntɪv] n Entmutigung f

disinfect [dɪsɪn'fɛkt] vt desinfizieren;~**ant** n Desinfektionsmittel nt

disintegrate [dɪs'ɪntɪgreɪt] vi sich auflösen

disinterested [dɪs'ɪntrəstɪd] adj uneigennützig; (inf) uninteressiert

disjointed [dɪs'dʒɔɪntɪd] adj unzusammenhängend

disk [dɪsk] n (COMPUT) Diskette f; **single/ double sided ~** einseitige/beidseitige Diskette;~ **drive** n Diskettenlaufwerk nt; ~**ette** [dɪs'kɛt] (US) n = **disk**

dislike [dɪs'laɪk] n Abneigung f ♦ vt nicht leiden können

dislocate ['dɪsləkeɪt] vt auskugeln

dislodge [dɪs'lɔdʒ] vt verschieben; (MIL) aus der Stellung werfen

disloyal [dɪs'lɔɪəl] adj treulos

dismal ['dɪzml] adj trostlos, trübe

dismantle [dɪs'mæntl] vt demontieren

dismay [dɪs'meɪ] n Bestürzung f ♦ vt bestürzen

dismiss [dɪs'mɪs] vt (employee) entlassen; (idea) von sich weisen; (send away) wegschicken; (JUR) abweisen;~**al** n Entlassung f

dismount [dɪs'maunt] vi absteigen

disobedience [dɪsə'biːdɪəns] n Ungehorsam m;**disobedient** adj ungehorsam

disobey [dɪsə'beɪ] vt nicht gehorchen +dat

disorder [dɪs'ɔːdəʳ] n (confusion) Verwirrung f; (commotion) Aufruhr m; (MED) Erkrankung f

disorderly [dɪs'ɔːdəlɪ] adj (untidy) unordentlich; (unruly) ordnungswidrig

disorganized [dɪs'ɔːgənaɪzd] adj unordentlich

disorientated [dɪs'ɔːrɪənteɪtɪd] adj (person: after journey) verwirrt

disown [dɪs'əun] vt (child) verstoßen

disparaging [dɪs'pærɪdʒɪŋ] adj

geringschätzig

dispassionate [dɪsˈpæʃənət] *adj* objektiv

dispatch [dɪsˈpætʃ] *vt* (*goods*) abschicken, abfertigen ♦ *n* Absendung *f*; (*esp MIL*) Meldung *f*

dispel [dɪsˈpel] *vt* zerstreuen

dispensary [dɪsˈpensərɪ] *n* Apotheke *f*

dispense [dɪsˈpens] *vt* verteilen, austeilen; ~ **with** *vt fus* verzichten auf +*acc*; ~**r** *n* (*container*) Spender *m*; **dispensing** *adj*: **dispensing chemist** (*BRIT*) Apotheker *m*

dispersal [dɪsˈpəːsl] *n* Zerstreuung *f*

disperse [dɪsˈpəːs] *vt* zerstreuen ♦ *vi* sich verteilen

dispirited [dɪsˈpɪrɪtɪd] *adj* niedergeschlagen

displace [dɪsˈpleɪs] *vt* verschieben; ~**d person** *n* Verschleppte(r) *mf*

display [dɪsˈpleɪ] *n* (*of goods*) Auslage *f*; (*of feeling*) Zurschaustellung *f* ♦ *vt* zeigen; (*ostentatiously*) vorführen; (*goods*) ausstellen

displease [dɪsˈpliːz] *vt* missfallen +*dat*

displeasure [dɪsˈpleʒə*] *n* Missfallen *nt*

disposable [dɪsˈpəuzəbl] *adj* Wegwerf-; ~ **nappy** *n* Papierwindel *f*

disposal [dɪsˈpəuzl] *n* (*of property*) Verkauf *m*; (*throwing away*) Beseitigung *f*; **to be at one's ~** einem zur Verfügung stehen

dispose [dɪsˈpəuz] *vi*: **to ~ of** loswerden; ~**d** *adj* geneigt

disposition [dɪspəˈzɪʃən] *n* Wesen *nt*

disproportionate [dɪsprəˈpɔːʃənət] *adj* unverhältnismäßig

disprove [dɪsˈpruːv] *vt* widerlegen

dispute [dɪsˈpjuːt] *n* Streit *m*; (*also:* **industrial ~**) Arbeitskampf *m* ♦ *vt* bestreiten

disqualify [dɪsˈkwɔlɪfaɪ] *vt* disqualifizieren

disquiet [dɪsˈkwaɪət] *n* Unruhe *f*

disregard [dɪsrɪˈgɑːd] *vt* nicht (be)achten

disrepair [ˈdɪsrɪˈpeə*] *n*: **to fall into ~** verfallen

disreputable [dɪsˈrepjutəbl] *adj* verrufen

disrespectful [dɪsrɪˈspektful] *adj* respektlos

disrupt [dɪsˈrʌpt] *vt* stören; (*service*) unterbrechen; ~**ion** [dɪsˈrʌpʃən] *n* Störung *f*; Unterbrechung *f*

dissatisfaction [dɪssætɪsˈfækʃən] *n* Unzufriedenheit *f*; **dissatisfied** [dɪsˈsætɪsfaɪd] *adj* unzufrieden

dissect [dɪˈsekt] *vt* zerlegen, sezieren

dissent [dɪˈsent] *n* abweichende Meinung *f*

dissertation [dɪsəˈteɪʃən] *n* wissenschaftliche Arbeit *f*; (*Ph.D.*) Doktorarbeit *f*

disservice [dɪsˈsəːvɪs] *n*: **to do sb a ~** jdm einen schlechten Dienst erweisen

dissident [ˈdɪsɪdnt] *adj* anders denkend ♦ *n* Dissident *m*

dissimilar [dɪˈsɪmɪlə*] *adj*: ~ **(to sb/sth)** (jdm/etw) unähnlich

dissipate [ˈdɪsɪpeɪt] *vt* (*waste*) verschwenden; (*scatter*) zerstreuen

dissociate [dɪˈsəuʃɪeɪt] *vt* trennen

dissolve [dɪˈzɔlv] *vt* auflösen ♦ *vi* sich auflösen

dissuade [dɪˈsweɪd] *vt*: **to ~ sb from doing sth** jdn davon abbringen, etw zu tun

distance [ˈdɪstns] *n* Entfernung *f*; **in the ~** in der Ferne; **distant** *adj* entfernt, fern; (*with time*) fern

distaste [dɪsˈteɪst] *n* Abneigung *f*; ~**ful** *adj* widerlich

distended [dɪsˈtendɪd] *adj* (*stomach*) aufgebläht

distil [dɪsˈtɪl] *vt* destillieren; ~**lery** *n* Brennerei *f*

distinct [dɪsˈtɪŋkt] *adj* (*separate*) getrennt; (*clear*) klar, deutlich; **as ~ from** im Unterschied zu; ~**ion** [dɪsˈtɪŋkʃən] *n* Unterscheidung *f*; (*eminence*) Auszeichnung *f*; ~**ive** *adj* bezeichnend

distinguish [dɪsˈtɪŋgwɪʃ] *vt* unterscheiden; ~**ed** *adj* (*eminent*) berühmt; ~**ing** *adj* bezeichnend

distort [dɪsˈtɔːt] *vt* verdrehen; (*misrepresent*) entstellen; ~**ion** [dɪsˈtɔːʃən] *n* Verzerrung *f*

distract [dɪsˈtrækt] *vt* ablenken; ~**ing** *adj* verwirrend; ~**ion** [dɪsˈtrækʃən] *n* (*distress*) Raserei *f*; (*diversion*) Zerstreuung *f*

distraught [dɪsˈtrɔːt] *adj* bestürzt

distress [dɪsˈtres] *n* Not *f*; (*suffering*) Qual *f* ♦ *vt* quälen; ~**ing** *adj* erschütternd; ~ **signal** *n* Notsignal *nt*

distribute [dɪsˈtrɪbjuːt] *vt* verteilen; **distribution** [dɪstrɪˈbjuːʃən] *n* Verteilung *f*;

distributor n Verteiler m

district ['dɪstrɪkt] n (of country) Kreis m; (of town) Bezirk m; ~ **attorney** (US) n Oberstaatsanwalt m; ~ **nurse** n Kreiskrankenschwester f

distrust [dɪs'trʌst] n Misstrauen nt ♦ vt misstrauen +dat

disturb [dɪs'tɜːb] vt stören; (agitate) erregen; ~**ance** n Störung f; ~**ed** adj beunruhigt; **emotionally** ~**ed** emotional gestört; ~**ing** adj beunruhigend

disuse [dɪs'juːs] n: **to fall into** ~ außer Gebrauch kommen; ~**d** [dɪs'juːzd] adj außer Gebrauch; (mine, railway line) stillgelegt

ditch [dɪtʃ] n Graben m ♦ vt (person) loswerden; (plan) fallen lassen

dither ['dɪðə*] vi verdattert sein

ditto ['dɪtəʊ] adv dito, ebenfalls

divan [dɪ'væn] n Liegesofa nt

dive [daɪv] n (into water) Kopfsprung m; (AVIAT) Sturzflug m ♦ vi tauchen; ~**r** n Taucher m

diverge [daɪ'vɜːdʒ] vi auseinander gehen

diverse [daɪ'vɜːs] adj verschieden

diversion [daɪ'vɜːʃən] n Ablenkung f; (BRIT: AUT) Umleitung f

diversity [daɪ'vɜːsɪtɪ] n Vielfalt f

divert [daɪ'vɜːt] vt ablenken; (traffic) umleiten

divide [dɪ'vaɪd] vt teilen ♦ vi sich teilen; ~**d highway** (US) n Schnellstraße f

divine [dɪ'vaɪn] adj göttlich

diving ['daɪvɪŋ] n (SPORT) Turmspringen nt; (underwater ~) Tauchen nt; ~ **board** n Sprungbrett nt

divinity [dɪ'vɪnɪtɪ] n Gottheit f; (subject) Religion f

division [dɪ'vɪʒən] n Teilung f; (MIL) Division f; (part) Abteilung f; (in opinion) Uneinigkeit f; (BRIT: POL) (Abstimmung f durch) Hammelsprung f

divorce [dɪ'vɔːs] n (Ehe)scheidung f ♦ vt scheiden; ~**d** adj geschieden; ~**e** [dɪvɔː'siː] n Geschiedene(r) f(m)

divulge [daɪ'vʌldʒ] vt preisgeben

DIY (BRIT) n abbr = **do-it-yourself**

dizzy ['dɪzɪ] adj schwindlig

DJ n abbr = **disc jockey**

DNA fingerprinting n genetische Fingerabdrücke pl

KEYWORD

---

do [duː] (pt **did**, pp **done**) n (inf: party etc) Fete f
♦ aux vb **1** (in negative constructions and questions): **I don't understand** ich verstehe nicht; **didn't you know?** wusstest du das nicht?; **what do you think?** was meinen Sie?
2 (for emphasis, in polite phrases): **she does seem rather tired** sie scheint wirklich sehr müde zu sein; **do sit down/help yourself** setzen Sie sich doch hin/greifen Sie doch zu
3 (used to avoid repeating vb): **she swims better than I do** sie schwimmt besser als ich; **she lives in Glasgow - so do I** sie wohnt in Glasgow - ich auch
4 (in tag questions): **you like him, don't you?** du magst ihn doch, oder?
♦ vt **1** (carry out, perform etc) tun, machen; **what are you doing tonight?** was machst du heute Abend?; **I've got nothing to do** ich habe nichts zu tun; **to do one's hair/nails** sich die Haare/Nägel machen
2 (AUT etc) fahren
♦ vi **1** (act, behave): **do as I do** mach wie ich
2 (get on, fare): **he's doing well/badly at school** er ist gut/schlecht in der Schule; **how do you do?** guten Tag
3 (be suitable) gehen; (be sufficient) reichen; **to make do (with)** auskommen mit

do away with vt (kill) umbringen; (abolish: law etc) abschaffen

do up vt (laces, dress, buttons) zumachen; (room, house) renovieren

do with vt (need) brauchen; (be connected) zu tun haben mit

do without vt, vi auskommen ohne

---

docile ['dəʊsaɪl] adj gefügig

dock [dɒk] n Dock nt; (JUR) Anklagebank f
♦ vi ins Dock gehen; ~**er** n Hafenarbeiter m; ~**yard** n Werft f

doctor ['dɔktər] n Arzt m, Ärztin f; (UNIV) Doktor m ♦ vt (fig) fälschen; (drink etc) etw beimischen +dat; **D~ of Philosophy** n Doktor m der Philosophie

document ['dɔkjumənt] n Dokument nt; **~ary** [dɔkju'mɛntəri] n Dokumentarbericht m; (film) Dokumentarfilm m ♦ adj dokumentarisch; **~ation** [dɔkjumən'teɪʃən] n dokumentarische(r) Nachweis m

dodge [dɔdʒ] n Kniff m ♦ vt ausweichen +dat

dodgems ['dɔdʒəmz] (BRIT) npl Autoskooter m

doe [dəu] n (roe deer) Ricke f; (red deer) Hirschkuh f; (rabbit) Weibchen nt

does [dʌz] vb see **do; ~n't** = **does not**

dog [dɔg] n Hund m; **~ collar** n Hundehalsband nt; (ECCL) Kragen m des Geistlichen; **~-eared** adj mit Eselsohren

dogged ['dɔgɪd] adj hartnäckig

dogsbody ['dɔgzbɔdɪ] n Mädchen nt für alles

doings ['duɪŋz] npl (activities) Treiben nt

do-it-yourself ['du:ɪtjɔː'sɛlf] n Do-it-yourself nt

doldrums ['dɔldrəmz] npl: **to be in the ~** (business) Flaute haben; (person) deprimiert sein

dole [dəul] (BRIT) n Stempelgeld nt; **to be on the ~** stempeln gehen; **~ out** vt ausgeben, austeilen

doleful ['dəulful] adj traurig

doll [dɔl] n Puppe f ♦ vt: **to ~ o.s. up** sich aufdonnern

dollar ['dɔlər] n Dollar m

dolphin ['dɔlfin] n Delfin m, Delphin m

dome [dəum] n Kuppel f

domestic [də'mɛstɪk] adj häuslich; (within country) Innen-, Binnen-; (animal) Haus-; **~ated** adj (person) häuslich; (animal) zahm

dominant ['dɔmɪnənt] adj vorherrschend

dominate ['dɔmɪneɪt] vt beherrschen

domineering [dɔmɪ'nɪərɪŋ] adj herrisch

dominion [də'mɪnɪən] n (rule) Regierungsgewalt f; (land) Staatsgebiet nt mit Selbstverwaltung

domino ['dɔmɪnəu] (pl **~es**) n Dominostein m; **~es** n (game) Domino(spiel) nt

don [dɔn] (BRIT) n akademische(r) Lehrer m

donate [də'neɪt] vt (blood, money) spenden; (lot of money) stiften; **donation** [də'neɪʃən] n Spende f

done [dʌn] pp of **do**

donkey ['dɔŋkɪ] n Esel m

donor ['dəunər] n Spender m; **~ card** n Organspenderausweis m

don't [dəunt] = **do not**

doodle ['du:dl] vi kritzeln

doom [du:m] n böse(s) Geschick nt; (downfall) Verderben nt ♦ vt: **to be ~ed** zum Untergang verurteilt sein; **~sday** n der Jüngste Tag

door [dɔːr] n Tür f; **~bell** n Türklingel f; **~ handle** n Türklinke f; **~man** (irreg) n Türsteher m; **~mat** n Fußmatte f; **~step** n Türstufe f; **~way** n Türöffnung f

dope [dəup] n (drug) Aufputschmittel nt ♦ vt (horse) dopen

dopey ['dəupɪ] (inf) adj bekloppt

dormant ['dɔːmənt] adj latent

dormitory ['dɔːmɪtrɪ] n Schlafsaal m

dormouse ['dɔːmaus] (pl **-mice**) n Haselmaus f

DOS [dɔs] n abbr (= disk operating system) DOS nt

dosage ['dəusɪdʒ] n Dosierung f

dose [dəus] n Dosis f

dosh [dɔʃ] (inf) n (money) Moos nt, Knete f

doss house ['dɔs-] (BRIT) n Bleibe f

dot [dɔt] n Punkt m; **~ted with** übersät mit; **on the ~** pünktlich

dote [dəut]: **to ~ on** vt fus vernarrt sein in +acc

dotted line ['dɔtɪd-] n punktierte Linie f

double ['dʌbl] adj, adv doppelt ♦ n Doppelgänger m ♦ vt verdoppeln ♦ vi sich verdoppeln; **~s** npl (TENNIS) Doppel nt; **on** or **at the ~** im Laufschritt; **~ bass** n Kontrabass m; **~ bed** n Doppelbett nt; **~ bend** (BRIT) n S-Kurve f; **~-breasted** adj zweireihig; **~-cross** vt hintergehen; **~-decker** n Doppeldecker m; **~ glazing** (BRIT) n Doppelverglasung f; **~ room** n Doppelzimmer nt

doubly ['dʌblɪ] adv doppelt

doubt [daut] n Zweifel m ♦ vt bezweifeln; **~ful** adj zweifelhaft; **~less** adv ohne Zweifel

dough [dəu] n Teig m; **~nut** n Berliner m

douse [dauz] vt (drench) mit Wasser begießen, durchtränken; (extinguish) ausmachen

dove [dʌv] n Taube f

dovetail ['dʌvteɪl] vi (plans) übereinstimmen

dowdy ['daudɪ] adj unmodern

down [daun] n (fluff) Flaum m; (hill) Hügel m ♦ adv unten; (motion) herunter; hinunter ♦ prep: **to go ~ the street** die Straße hinuntergehen; **~ with X!** nieder mit X!; **~-and-out** n Tramp m; **~-at-heel** adj schäbig; **~cast** adj niedergeschlagen; **~fall** n Sturz m; **~hearted** adj niedergeschlagen; **~hill** adv bergab; **~ payment** n Anzahlung f; **~pour** n Platzregen m; **~right** adj ausgesprochen; **~size** vi (ECON: company) sich verkleinern

---

Downing Street

i **Downing Street** ist die Straße in London, die von Whitehall zum St James Park führt und in der sich der offizielle Wohnsitz des Premierministers (Nr. 10) und des Finanzministers (Nr. 11) befindet. Im weiteren Sinne bezieht sich der Begriff Downing Street auf die britische Regierung.

Down's syndrome [daunz-] n (MED) Down-Syndrom nt

down: **~stairs** adv unten; (motion) nach unten; **~stream** adv flussabwärts; **~-to-earth** adj praktisch; **~town** adv in der Innenstadt; (motion) in die Innenstadt; **~under** (BRIT: inf) adv in/nach Australien/ Neuseeland; **~ward** adj Abwärts-, nach unten ♦ adv abwärts, nach unten; **~wards** adv abwärts, nach unten

dowry ['dauri] n Mitgift f

doz. abbr (= dozen) Dtzd.

doze [dəuz] vi dösen; **~ off** vi einnicken

dozen ['dʌzn] n Dutzend nt; **a ~ books** ein Dutzend Bücher; **~s of** dutzende or Dutzende von

Dr. abbr = **doctor**; **drive**

drab [dræb] adj düster, eintönig

draft [drɑːft] n Entwurf m; (FIN) Wechsel m; (US: MIL) Einberufung f ♦ vt skizzieren; see also **draught**

draftsman ['drɑːftsmən] (US: irreg) n = **draughtsman**

drag [dræg] vt schleppen; (river) mit einem Schleppnetz absuchen ♦ vi sich (dahin)schleppen ♦ n (bore) etwas Blödes; **in ~** als Tunte; **a man in ~** eine Tunte; **~ on** vi sich in die Länge ziehen; **~ and drop** vt (COMPUT) Drag & Drop nt

dragon ['drægn] n Drache m; **~fly** ['drægənflaɪ] n Libelle f

drain [dreɪn] n Abfluss m; (fig: burden) Belastung f ♦ vt ableiten; (exhaust) erschöpfen ♦ vi (of water) abfließen; **~age** n Kanalisation f; **~ing board** (US~board) n Ablaufbrett nt; **~pipe** n Abflussrohr nt

dram [dræm] n Schluck m

drama ['drɑːmə] n Drama nt; **~tic** [drə'mætɪk] adj dramatisch; **~tist** ['dræmətɪst] n Dramatiker m; **~tize** ['dræmətaɪz] vt (events) dramatisieren; (for TV etc) bearbeiten

drank [dræŋk] pt of **drink**

drape [dreɪp] vt drapieren; **~s** (US) npl Vorhänge pl

drastic ['dræstɪk] adj drastisch

draught [drɑːft] (US **draft**) n Zug m; (NAUT) Tiefgang m; **~s** n Damespiel nt; **on ~** (beer) vom Fass; **~ beer** n Bier nt vom Fass; **~board** (BRIT) n Zeichenbrett nt

draughtsman ['drɑːftsmən] (irreg) n technische(r) Zeichner m

draw [drɔː] (pt drew, pp drew) vt ziehen; (crowd) anlocken; (picture) zeichnen; (money) abheben; (water) schöpfen ♦ vi (SPORT) unentschieden spielen ♦ n (SPORT) Unentschieden nt; (lottery) Ziehung f; **~near** vi näher rücken; **~ out** vi (train) ausfahren; (lengthen) sich hinziehen; **~ up** vi (stop) halten ♦ vt (document) aufsetzen

drawback ['drɔːbæk] n Nachteil m

drawbridge ['drɔːbrɪdʒ] n Zugbrücke f

drawer [drɔːʳ] n Schublade f

drawing [ˈdrɔːɪŋ] n Zeichnung f; Zeichnen nt; ~ **board** n Reißbrett nt; ~ **pin** (BRIT) n Reißzwecke f; ~ **room** n Salon m

drawl [drɔːl] n schleppende Sprechweise f

drawn [drɔːn] pp of **draw**

dread [dred] n Furcht f ♦ vt fürchten; ~**ful** adj furchtbar

dream [driːm] (pt, pp **dreamed** or **dreamt**) n Traum m ♦ vt träumen ♦ vi: **to** ~ **(about)** träumen (von); ~**er** n Träumer m; ~**t** [dremt] pt, pp of **dream**; ~**y** adj verträumt

dreary [ˈdrɪərɪ] adj trostlos, öde

dredge [dredʒ] vt ausbaggern

dregs [dregz] npl Bodensatz m; (fig) Abschaum m

drench [drentʃ] vt durchnässen

dress [dres] n Kleidung f; (garment) Kleid nt ♦ vt anziehen; (MED) verbinden; **to get ~ed** sich anziehen; ~ **up** vi sich fein machen; ~ **circle** (BRIT) n erste(r) Rang m; ~**er** n (furniture) Anrichte f; ~**ing** n (MED) Verband m; (COOK) Soße f; ~**ing gown** (BRIT) n Morgenrock m; ~**ing room** n (THEAT) Garderobe f; (SPORT) Umkleideraum m; ~**ing table** n Toilettentisch m; ~**maker** n Schneiderin f; ~ **rehearsal** n Generalprobe f

drew [druː] pt of **draw**

dribble [ˈdrɪbl] vi sabbern ♦ vt (ball) dribbeln

dried [draɪd] adj getrocknet; (fruit) Dörr-, gedörrt(e, r, s); ~ **milk** n Milchpulver nt

drier [ˈdraɪəʳ] n = **dryer**

drift [drɪft] n Strömung f; (snowdrift) Schneewehe f; (fig) Richtung f ♦ vi sich treiben lassen; ~**wood** n Treibholz nt

drill [drɪl] n Bohrer m; (MIL) Drill m ♦ vt bohren; (MIL) ausbilden ♦ vi: **to** ~ **(for)** bohren (nach)

drink [drɪŋk] (pt **drank**, pp **drunk**) n Getränk nt; (spirits) Drink m ♦ vt, vi trinken; **to have a** ~ etwas trinken; ~**er** n Trinker m; ~**ing water** n Trinkwasser nt

drip [drɪp] n Tropfen m ♦ vi tropfen; ~-**dry** adj bügelfrei; ~**ping** n Bratenfett nt

drive [draɪv] (pt **drove**, pp **driven**) n Fahrt f; (road) Einfahrt f; (campaign) Aktion f; (energy) Schwung m; (SPORT) Schlag m; (also: **disk** ~) Diskettenlaufwerk nt ♦ vt (car) fahren; (animals, people, objects) treiben; (power) antreiben ♦ vi fahren; **left-/right-hand** ~ Links-/Rechtssteuerung f; **to** ~ **sb mad** jdn verrückt machen; ~-**by shooting** n Schusswaffenangriff aus einem vorbeifahrenden Wagen

drivel [ˈdrɪvl] n Faselei f

driven [ˈdrɪvn] pp of **drive**

driver [ˈdraɪvəʳ] n Fahrer m; ~**'s license** (US) n Führerschein m

driveway [ˈdraɪvweɪ] n Auffahrt f; (longer) Zufahrtsstraße f

driving [ˈdraɪvɪŋ] adj (rain) stürmisch; ~ **instructor** n Fahrlehrer m; ~ **lesson** n Fahrstunde f; ~ **licence** (BRIT) n Führerschein m; ~ **school** n Fahrschule f; ~ **test** n Fahrprüfung f

drizzle [ˈdrɪzl] n Nieselregen m ♦ vi nieseln

droll [drəul] adj drollig

drone [drəun] n (sound) Brummen nt; (bee) Drohne f

drool [druːl] vi sabbern

droop [druːp] vi (schlaff) herabhängen

drop [drɔp] n (of liquid) Tropfen m; (fall) Fall m ♦ vt fallen lassen; (lower) senken; (abandon) fallen lassen ♦ vi (fall) herunterfallen; ~**s** npl (MED) Tropfen pl; ~ **off** vi (sleep) einschlafen ♦ vt (passenger) absetzen; ~ **out** vi (withdraw) ausscheiden; ~-**out** n Aussteiger m; ~**per** n Pipette f; ~**pings** npl Kot m

drought [draut] n Dürre f

drove [drəuv] pt of **drive**

drown [draun] vt ertränken; (sound) übertönen ♦ vi ertrinken

drowsy [ˈdrauzɪ] adj schläfrig

drudgery [ˈdrʌdʒərɪ] n Plackerei f

drug [drʌg] n (MED) Arznei f; (narcotic) Rauschgift nt ♦ vt betäuben; ~ **addict** n Rauschgiftsüchtige(r) f(m); ~**gist** (US) n Drogist(in) m(f); ~**store** (US) n Drogerie f

drum [drʌm] n Trommel f ♦ vi trommeln; ~**s** npl (MUS) Schlagzeug nt; ~**mer** n Trommler m

drunk [drʌŋk] pp of **drink** ♦ adj betrunken ♦ n (also: ~**ard**) Trinker(in) m(f); ~**en** adj betrunken

dry [draɪ] adj trocken ♦ vt (ab)trocknen ♦ vi trocknen; ~ **up** vi austrocknen ♦ vt (dishes) abtrocknen; ~ **cleaner's** n chemische Reinigung f; ~ **cleaning** n chemische Reinigung f; ~**er** n Trockner m; (US: spin-dryer) (Wäsche)schleuder f; ~ **goods store** (US) n Kurzwarengeschäft nt; ~**ness** n Trockenheit f; ~ **rot** n Hausschwamm m

DSS (BRIT) n abbr (= Department of Social Security) ≈ Sozialministerium nt

DTP n abbr (= desktop publishing) DTP nt

dual ['djuəl] adj doppelt; ~ **carriageway** (BRIT) n zweispurige Fahrbahn f; ~ **nationality** n doppelte Staatsangehörigkeit f; ~~**purpose** adj Mehrzweck-

dubbed [dʌbd] adj (film) synchronisiert

dubious ['dju:bɪəs] adj zweifelhaft

duchess ['dʌtʃɪs] n Herzogin f

duck [dʌk] n Ente f ♦ vi sich ducken; ~**ling** n Entchen nt

duct [dʌkt] n Röhre f

dud [dʌd] n Niete f ♦ adj (cheque) ungedeckt

due [dju:] adj fällig; (fitting) angemessen ♦ n Gebühr f; (right) Recht nt ♦ adv (south etc) genau; ~**s** npl (for club) Beitrag m; (NAUT) Gebühren pl; ~ **to** wegen +gen

duel ['djuəl] n Duell nt

duet [dju:'et] n Duett nt

duffel ['dʌfl] adj: ~ **bag** Matchbeutel m, Matchsack m

dug [dʌg] pt, pp of **dig**

duke [dju:k] n Herzog m

dull [dʌl] adj (colour, weather) trübe; (stupid) schwer von Begriff; (boring) langweilig ♦ vt abstumpfen

duly ['dju:lɪ] adv ordnungsgemäß

dumb [dʌm] adj stumm; (inf: stupid) doof, blöde; ~**founded** [dʌm'faundɪd] adj verblüfft

dummy ['dʌmɪ] n Schneiderpuppe f; (substitute) Attrappe f; (BRIT: for baby) Schnuller m ♦ adj Schein-

dump [dʌmp] n Abfallhaufen m; (MIL) Stapelplatz m; (inf: place) Nest nt ♦ vt abladen, auskippen; ~**ing** n (COMM) Schleuderexport m; (of rubbish)

Schuttabladen nt

dumpling ['dʌmplɪŋ] n Kloß m, Knödel m

dumpy ['dʌmpɪ] adj pummelig

dunce [dʌns] n Dummkopf m

dune [dju:n] n Düne f

dung [dʌŋ] n Dünger m

dungarees [dʌŋgə'ri:z] npl Latzhose f

dungeon ['dʌndʒən] n Kerker m

dupe [dju:p] n Gefoppte(r) m ♦ vt hintergehen, anführen

duplex ['dju:plɛks] (US) n zweistöckige Wohnung f

duplicate [n 'dju:plɪkət, vb 'dju:plɪkeɪt] n Duplikat nt ♦ vt verdoppeln; (make copies) kopieren; **in** ~ in doppelter Ausführung

duplicity [dju:'plɪsɪtɪ] n Doppelspiel nt

durable ['djuərəbl] adj haltbar

duration [djuə'reɪʃən] n Dauer f

duress [djuə'rɛs] n: **under** ~ unter Zwang

during ['djuərɪŋ] prep während +gen

dusk [dʌsk] n Abenddämmerung f

dust [dʌst] n Staub m ♦ vt abstauben; (sprinkle) bestäuben; ~**bin** (BRIT) n Mülleimer m; ~**er** n Staubtuch nt; ~ **jacket** n Schutzumschlag m; ~**man** (BRIT: irreg) n Müllmann m; ~**y** adj staubig

Dutch [dʌtʃ] adj holländisch, niederländisch ♦ n (LING) Holländisch nt, Niederländisch nt; **the** ~ npl (people) die Holländer pl, die Niederländer pl; **to go** ~ getrennte Kasse machen; ~**man/woman** (irreg) n Holländer(in) m(f), Niederländer(in) m(f)

dutiful ['dju:tɪful] adj pflichtbewusst

duty ['dju:tɪ] n Pflicht f; (job) Aufgabe f; (tax) Einfuhrzoll m; **on** ~ im Dienst; ~ **chemist's** n Apotheke f im Bereitschaftsdienst; ~~**free** adj zollfrei

duvet ['du:veɪ] (BRIT) n Daunendecke nt

DVD n abbr (= digital video disc) DVD f

dwarf [dwɔ:f] (pl **dwarves**) n Zwerg m ♦ vt überragen

dwell [dwɛl] (pt, pp **dwelt**) vi wohnen; ~ **on** vt fus verweilen bei; ~**ing** n Wohnung f

dwelt [dwɛlt] pt, pp of **dwell**

dwindle ['dwɪndl] vi schwinden

dye [daɪ] n Farbstoff m ♦ vt färben

dying ['daɪɪŋ] adj (person) sterbend;

(moments) letzt

dyke [daik] *(BRIT) n (channel)* Kanal *m;*
(barrier) Deich *m,* Damm *m*

dynamic [dai'næmik] *adj* dynamisch

dynamite ['dainəmait] *n* Dynamit *nt*

dyslexia [dis'leksiə] *n* Legasthenie *f*

E, e

E [i:] *n (MUS)* E *nt*

each [i:tʃ] *adj* jeder/jede/jedes ♦ *pron* (ein)
jeder/(eine) jede/(ein) jedes; **~ other**
einander, sich; **they have two books ~** sie
haben je zwei Bücher

eager ['i:gə'] *adj* eifrig

eagle ['i:gl] *n* Adler *m*

ear [iə'] *n* Ohr *nt; (of corn)* Ähre *f;* **~ache** *n*
Ohrenschmerzen *pl;* **~drum** *n* Trommelfell
nt

earl [ə:l] *n* Graf *m*

earlier ['ə:liə'] *adj, adv* früher; **I can't come**
any ~ ich kann nicht früher *or* eher
kommen

early ['ə:li] *adj, adv* früh; **~ retirement** *n*
vorzeitige Pensionierung

earmark ['iəma:k] *vt* vorsehen

earn [ə:n] *vt* verdienen

earnest ['ə:nist] *adj* ernst; **in ~** im Ernst

earnings ['ə:niŋz] *npl* Verdienst *m*

ear: ~phones ['iəfəunz] *npl* Kopfhörer *pl;*
~ring ['iəriŋ] *n* Ohrring *m;* **~shot** ['iəʃɔt] *n*
Hörweite *f*

earth [ə:θ] *n* Erde *f;* (*BRIT: ELEC)* Erdung *f* ♦ *vt*
erden; **~enware** *n* Steingut *nt;* **~quake** *n*
Erdbeben *nt;* **~y** *adj* roh

earwig ['iəwig] *n* Ohrwurm *m*

ease [i:z] *n (simplicity)* Leichtigkeit *f; (social)*
Ungezwungenheit *f* ♦ *vt (pain)* lindern;
(burden) erleichtern; **at ~** ungezwungen;
(MIL) rührt euch!; **~ off** *or* **up** *vi*
nachlassen

easel ['i:zl] *n* Staffelei *f*

easily ['i:zili] *adv* leicht

east [i:st] *n* Osten *m* ♦ *adj* östlich ♦ *adv* nach
Osten

Easter ['i:stə'] *n* Ostern *nt;* **~ egg** *n* Osterei

nt

east: ~erly *adj* östlich, Ost-; **~ern** *adj*
östlich; **~ward(s)** *adv* ostwärts

easy ['i:zi] *adj (task)* einfach; *(life)* bequem;
(manner) ungezwungen, natürlich ♦ *adv*
leicht; **~ chair** *n* Sessel *m;* **~-going** *adj*
gelassen, *(lax)* lässig

eat [i:t] *(pt* **ate***, pp* **eaten***) vt* essen; *(animals)*
fressen; *(destroy)* (zer)fressen ♦ *vi* essen;
fressen; **~ away** *vt* zerfressen; **~ into** *vt*
fus zerfressen; **~en** *pp of* **eat**

eau de Cologne ['əudəkə'ləun] *n*
Kölnischwasser *nt*

eaves [i:vz] *npl* Dachrand *m*

eavesdrop ['i:vzdrɔp] *vi* lauschen; **to ~ on**
sb jdn belauschen

ebb [eb] *n* Ebbe *f* ♦ *vi (fig: also:* **~ away***)*
(ab)ebben

ebony ['ebəni] *n* Ebenholz *nt*

EC *n abbr (= European Community)* EG *f*

ECB *n abbr (= European Central Bank)* EZB *f*

eccentric [ik'sentrik] *adj* exzentrisch ♦ *n*
Exzentriker(in) *m(f)*

ecclesiastical [ikli:zi'æstikl] *adj* kirchlich

echo ['ekəu] *(pl* **~es***) n* Echo *nt* ♦ *vt*
zurückwerfen; *(fig)* nachbeten ♦ *vi*
widerhallen

eclipse [i'klips] *n* Finsternis *f* ♦ *vt* verfinstern

ecology [i'kɔlədʒi] *n* Ökologie *f*

e-commerce ['i:kɔmə:s] *n* Onlinehandel *m*

economic [i:kə'nɔmik] *adj* wirtschaftlich;
~al *adj* wirtschaftlich; *(person)* sparsam; **~**
refugee *n* Wirtschaftsflüchtling *m;* **~s** *n*
Volkswirtschaft *f*

economist [i'kɔnəmist] *n*
Volkswirt(schaftler) *m*

economize [i'kɔnəmaiz] *vi* sparen

economy [i'kɔnəmi] *n (thrift)* Sparsamkeit *f;*
(of country) Wirtschaft *f;* **~ class** *n*
Touristenklasse *f*

ecstasy ['ekstəsi] *n* Ekstase *f; (drug)* Ecstasy
nt; **ecstatic** [eks'tætik] *adj* hingerissen

ECU ['eikju:] *n abbr (= European Currency*
Unit) ECU *m*

eczema ['eksimə] *n* Ekzem *nt*

edge [edʒ] *n* Rand *m; (of knife)* Schneide *f*
♦ *vt (SEWING)* einfassen; **on ~** *(fig)* = **edgy;**

to ~ **away from** langsam abrücken von; **~ways** adv: **he couldn't get a word in ~ways** er kam überhaupt nicht zu Wort

edgy ['edʒɪ] adj nervös

edible ['edɪbl] adj essbar

edict ['iːdɪkt] n Erlass m

edit ['edɪt] vt redigieren; **~ion** [ɪ'dɪʃən] n Ausgabe f; **~or** n (of newspaper) Redakteur m; (of book) Lektor m; **~orial** [edɪ'tɔːrɪəl] adj Redaktions- ♦ n Leitartikel m

educate ['edjukeɪt] vt erziehen, (aus)bilden; **~d** adj gebildet; **education** [edju'keɪʃən] n (teaching) Unterricht m; (system) Schulwesen nt; (schooling) Erziehung f; Bildung f; **educational** adj pädagogisch

eel [iːl] n Aal m

eerie ['ɪərɪ] adj unheimlich

effect [ɪ'fekt] n Wirkung f ♦ vt bewirken; **~s** npl (sound, visual) Effekte pl; **in ~** in der Tat; **to take ~** (law) in Kraft treten; (drug) wirken; **~ive** adj wirksam, effektiv; **~ively** adv wirksam, effektiv

effeminate [ɪ'femɪnɪt] adj weibisch

effervescent [efə'vesnt] adj (also fig) sprudelnd

efficiency [ɪ'fɪʃənsɪ] n Leistungsfähigkeit f

efficient [ɪ'fɪʃənt] adj tüchtig; (TECH) leistungsfähig; (method) wirksam

effigy ['efɪdʒɪ] n Abbild nt

effort ['efət] n Anstrengung f; **~less** adj mühelos

effusive [ɪ'fjuːsɪv] adj überschwänglich

e.g. adv abbr (= exempli gratia) z. B.

egalitarian [ɪgælɪ'teərɪən] adj Gleichheits-, egalitär

egg [eg] n Ei nt; **~ on** vt anstacheln; **~cup** n Eierbecher m; **~plant** (esp US) n Aubergine f; **~shell** n Eierschale f

ego ['iːgəu] n Ich nt, Selbst nt; **~tism** ['egəutɪzəm] n Ichbezogenheit f; **~tist** ['egəutɪst] n Egozentriker m

Egypt ['iːdʒɪpt] n Ägypten nt; **~ian** [ɪ'dʒɪpʃən] adj ägyptisch ♦ n Ägypter(in) m(f)

eiderdown ['aɪdədaun] n Daunendecke f

eight [eɪt] num acht; **~een** num achtzehn; **~h** [eɪtθ] adj achte(r, s) ♦ n Achtel nt; **~y** num achtzig

Eire ['ɛərə] n Irland nt

either ['aɪðə] conj: **~ ... or** entweder ... oder ♦ pron: **~ of the two** eine(r, s) von beiden ♦ adj: **on ~ side** auf beiden Seiten ♦ adv: **I don't ~** ich auch nicht; **I don't want ~** ich will keins von beiden

eject [ɪ'dʒekt] vt ausstoßen, vertreiben

eke [iːk] vt: **to ~ out** strecken

elaborate [adj ɪ'læbərɪt, vb ɪ'læbəreɪt] adj sorgfältig ausgearbeitet, ausführlich ♦ vt sorgfältig ausarbeiten ♦ vi ausführlich darstellen

elapse [ɪ'læps] vi vergehen

elastic [ɪ'læstɪk] n Gummiband nt ♦ adj elastisch; **~ band** (BRIT) n Gummiband nt

elated [ɪ'leɪtɪd] adj froh

elation [ɪ'leɪʃən] n gehobene Stimmung f

elbow ['elbəu] n Ellbogen m

elder ['eldə] adj älter ♦ n Ältere(r) f(m); **~ly** adj ältere(r, s) ♦ npl: **the ~ly** die Älteren pl; **eldest** ['eldɪst] adj älteste(r, s) ♦ n Älteste(r) f(m)

elect [ɪ'lekt] vt wählen ♦ adj zukünftig; **~ion** [ɪ'lekʃən] n Wahl f; **~ioneering** [ɪlekʃə'nɪərɪŋ] n Wahlpropaganda f; **~or** n Wähler m; **~oral** adj Wahl-; **~orate** n Wähler pl, Wählerschaft f

electric [ɪ'lektrɪk] adj elektrisch, Elektro-; **~al** adj elektrisch; **~ blanket** n Heizdecke f; **~ chair** n elektrische(r) Stuhl m; **~ fire** n elektrische(r) Heizofen m

electrician [ɪlek'trɪʃən] n Elektriker m

electricity [ɪlek'trɪsɪtɪ] n Elektrizität f

electrify [ɪ'lektrɪfaɪ] vt elektrifizieren; (fig) elektrisieren

electrocute [ɪ'lektrəkjuːt] vt durch elektrischen Strom töten

electronic [ɪlek'trɔnɪk] adj elektronisch, Elektronen-; **~ mail** n E-Mail f; **~s** n Elektronik f

elegance ['elɪgəns] n Eleganz f; **elegant** ['elɪgənt] adj elegant

element ['elɪmənt] n Element nt; **~ary** [elɪ'mentərɪ] adj einfach; (primary) Grund-

elephant ['elɪfənt] n Elefant m

elevate ['elɪveɪt] vt emporheben; **elevation** [elɪ'veɪʃən] n (height) Erhebung f; (ARCHIT)

(Quer)schnitt m; elevator (US) n Fahrstuhl m, Aufzug m

eleven [ɪ'lɛvn] num elf; ~ses (BRIT) npl ≈ zweite(s) Frühstück nt; ~th adj elfte(r, s)

elicit [ɪ'lɪsɪt] vt herausbekommen

eligible ['ɛlɪdʒəbl] adj wählbar; to be ~ for a pension pensionsberechtigt sein

eliminate [ɪ'lɪmɪneɪt] vt ausschalten

elite [eɪ'liːt] n Elite f

elm [ɛlm] n Ulme f

elocution [ɛlə'kjuːʃən] n Sprecherziehung f

elongated ['iːlɔŋɡeɪtɪd] adj verlängert

elope [ɪ'ləup] vi entlaufen

eloquence ['ɛləkwəns] n Beredsamkeit f; eloquent adj redegewandt

else [ɛls] adv sonst; who ~? wer sonst?; somebody ~ jemand anders; or ~ sonst; ~where adv anderswo, woanders

elude [ɪ'luːd] vt entgehen +dat

elusive [ɪ'luːsɪv] adj schwer fassbar

emaciated [ɪ'meɪsɪeɪtɪd] adj abgezehrt

e-mail ['iːmeɪl] n abbr (= electronic mail) E-Mail f ♦ vti mailen

emancipation [ɪmænsɪ'peɪʃən] n Emanzipation f; Freilassung f

embankment [ɪm'bæŋkmənt] n (of river) Uferböschung f; (of road) Straßendamm m

embargo [ɪm'bɑːɡəu] (pl ~es) n Embargo nt

embark [ɪm'bɑːk] vi sich einschiffen; ~ on vt fus unternehmen; ~ation [emba:'keɪʃən] n Einschiffung f

embarrass [ɪm'bærəs] vt in Verlegenheit bringen; ~ed adj verlegen; ~ing adj peinlich; ~ment n Verlegenheit f

embassy ['embəsɪ] n Botschaft f

embed [ɪm'bɛd] vt einbetten

embellish [ɪm'bɛlɪʃ] vt verschönern

embers ['embəz] npl Glut(asche) f

embezzle [ɪm'bɛzl] vt unterschlagen; ~ment n Unterschlagung f

embitter [ɪm'bɪtər] vt verbittern

embody [ɪm'bɔdɪ] vt (ideas) verkörpern; (new features) (in sich) vereinigen

embossed [ɪm'bɔst] adj geprägt

embrace [ɪm'breɪs] vt umarmen; (include) einschließen ♦ vi sich umarmen ♦ n Umarmung f

embroider [ɪm'brɔɪdər] vt (be)sticken; (story) ausschmücken; ~y n Stickerei f

emerald ['emərəld] n Smaragd m

emerge [ɪ'mɜːdʒ] vi auftauchen; (truth) herauskommen; ~nce n Erscheinen nt

emergency [ɪ'mɜːdʒənsɪ] n Notfall m; ~ cord (US) n Notbremse f; ~ exit n Notausgang m; ~ landing n Notlandung f; ~ services npl Notdienste pl

emery board ['emərɪ-] n Papiernagelfeile f

emigrant ['emɪɡrənt] n Auswanderer m

emigrate ['emɪɡreɪt] vi auswandern; emigration [emɪ'ɡreɪʃən] n Auswanderung f

eminence ['emɪnəns] n hohe(r) Rang m

eminent ['emɪnənt] adj bedeutend

emission [ɪ'mɪʃən] n Ausströmen nt; ~s npl Emissionen fpl

emit [ɪ'mɪt] vt von sich dat geben

emotion [ɪ'məuʃən] n Emotion f, Gefühl nt; ~al adj (person) emotional; (scene) ergreifend

emotive [ɪ'məutɪv] adj gefühlsbetont

emperor ['empərər] n Kaiser m

emphases ['emfəsiːz] npl of emphasis

emphasis ['emfəsɪs] n (LING) Betonung f; (fig) Nachdruck m; emphasize ['emfəsaɪz] vt betonen

emphatic [em'fætɪk] adj nachdrücklich; ~ally adv nachdrücklich

empire ['empaɪər] n Reich nt

empirical [em'pɪrɪkl] adj empirisch

employ [ɪm'plɔɪ] vt (hire) anstellen; (use) verwenden; ~ee [ɪmplɔɪ'iː] n Angestellte(r) f(m); ~er n Arbeitgeber(in) m(f); ~ment n Beschäftigung f; ~ment agency n Stellenvermittlung f

empower [ɪm'pauər] vt: to ~ sb to do sth jdn ermächtigen, etw zu tun

empress ['emprɪs] n Kaiserin f

emptiness ['emptɪnɪs] n Leere f

empty ['emptɪ] adj leer ♦ n (bottle) Leergut nt ♦ vt (contents) leeren; (container) ausleeren ♦ vi (water) abfließen; (river) münden; (house) sich leeren; ~-handed adj mit leeren Händen

EMU ['iːmjuː] n abbr (= economic and monetary union) EWU f

emulate ['emjuleɪt] vt nacheifern +dat

emulsion [ɪ'mʌlʃən] n Emulsion f

enable [ɪ'neɪbl] vt: to ~ sb to do sth es jdm ermöglichen, etw zu tun

enact [ɪ'nækt] vt (law) erlassen; (play) aufführen; (role) spielen

enamel [ɪ'næməl] n Email nt; (of teeth) (Zahn)schmelz m

encased [ɪn'keɪst] adj: ~ in (enclosed) eingeschlossen in +dat; (covered) verkleidet mit

enchant [ɪn'tʃɑːnt] vt bezaubern; ~ing adj entzückend

encircle [ɪn'sɜːkl] vt umringen

encl. abbr (= enclosed) Anl.

enclose [ɪn'kləuz] vt einschließen; to ~ sth (in or with a letter) (einem Brief) beilegen; ~d (in letter) beiliegend, anbei; enclosure [ɪn'kləuʒər] n Einfriedung f; (in letter) Anlage f

encompass [ɪn'kʌmpəs] vt (include) umfassen

encore [ɒŋ'kɔːr] n Zugabe f

encounter [ɪn'kauntər] n Begegnung f; (MIL) Zusammenstoß m ♦ vt treffen; (resistance) stoßen auf +acc

encourage [ɪn'kʌrɪdʒ] vt ermutigen; ~ment n Ermutigung f, Förderung f; encouraging adj ermutigend, viel versprechend

encroach [ɪn'krəutʃ] vi: to ~ (up)on eindringen in +acc; (time) in Anspruch nehmen

encrusted [ɪn'krʌstɪd] adj: ~ with besetzt mit

encyclop(a)edia [ensaɪkləu'piːdɪə] n Konversationslexikon nt

end [end] n Ende nt, Schluss m; (purpose) Zweck m ♦ vt (also: bring to an ~, put an ~ to) beenden ♦ vi zu Ende gehen; in the ~ zum Schluss; on ~ (object) hochkant; to stand on ~ (hair) zu Berge stehen; for hours on ~ stundenlang; ~ up vi landen

endanger [ɪn'deɪndʒər] vt gefährden; ~ed species n eine vom Aussterben bedrohte Art

endearing [ɪn'dɪərɪŋ] adj gewinnend

endeavour [ɪn'devər] (US endeavor) n Bestrebung f ♦ vi sich bemühen

ending ['endɪŋ] n Ende nt

endless ['endlɪs] adj endlos

endorse [ɪn'dɔːs] vt unterzeichnen; (approve) unterstützen; ~ment n (AUT) Eintrag m

endow [ɪn'dau] vt: to ~ sb with sth jdm etw verleihen; (with money) jdm etw stiften

endurance [ɪn'djuərəns] n Ausdauer f

endure [ɪn'djuər] vt ertragen ♦ vi (last) (fort)dauern

enemy ['enəmɪ] n Feind m ♦ adj feindlich

energetic [enə'dʒetɪk] adj tatkräftig

energy ['enədʒɪ] n Energie f

enforce [ɪn'fɔːs] vt durchsetzen

engage [ɪn'geɪdʒ] vt (employ) einstellen; (in conversation) verwickeln; (TECH) einschalten ♦ vi (TECH) ineinander greifen; (clutch) fassen; to ~ in sich beteiligen an +dat; ~d adj verlobt; (BRIT: TEL, toilet) besetzt; (: busy) beschäftigt; to get ~d sich verloben; ~d tone (BRIT) n (TEL) Besetztzeichen nt; ~ment n (appointment) Verabredung f; (to marry) Verlobung f; (MIL) Gefecht nt; ~ment ring n Verlobungsring m; engaging adj gewinnend

engender [ɪn'dʒendər] vt hervorrufen

engine ['endʒɪn] n (AUT) Motor m; (RAIL) Lokomotive f; ~ driver n Lok(omotiv)führer(in) m(f)

engineer [endʒɪ'nɪər] n Ingenieur m; (US: RAIL) Lok(omotiv)führer(in) m(f); ~ing [endʒɪ'nɪərɪŋ] n Technik f

England ['ɪŋglənd] n England nt

English ['ɪŋglɪʃ] adj englisch ♦ n (LING) Englisch nt; the ~ npl (people) die Engländer pl; ~ Channel n: the ~ Channel der Ärmelkanal m; ~man/ woman (irreg) n Engländer(in) m(f)

engraving [ɪn'greɪvɪŋ] n Stich m

engrossed [ɪn'grəust] adj vertieft

engulf [ɪn'gʌlf] vt verschlingen

enhance [ɪn'hɑːns] vt steigern, heben

enigma [ɪ'nɪgmə] n Rätsel nt; ~tic [enɪg'mætɪk] adj rätselhaft

enjoy [ɪn'dʒɔɪ] vt genießen; (privilege) besitzen; to ~ o.s. sich amüsieren; ~able *adj* erfreulich; **~ment** *n* Genuss *m*, Freude *f*

enlarge [ɪn'lɑːdʒ] *vt* erweitern; (PHOT) vergrößern ♦ *vi*: **to ~ on sth** etw weiter ausführen; **~ment** *n* Vergrößerung *f*

enlighten [ɪn'laɪtn] *vt* aufklären; **~ment** *n*: **the E~ment** (HIST) die Aufklärung

enlist [ɪn'lɪst] *vt* gewinnen ♦ *vi* (MIL) sich melden

enmity ['enmɪtɪ] *n* Feindschaft *f*

enormity [ɪ'nɔːmɪtɪ] *n* Ungeheuerlichkeit *f*

enormous [ɪ'nɔːməs] *adj* ungeheuer

enough [ɪ'nʌf] *adj, adv* genug; **funnily ~** komischerweise

enquire [ɪn'kwaɪə'] *vt, vi* = **inquire**

enrage [ɪn'reɪdʒ] *vt* wütend machen

enrich [ɪn'rɪtʃ] *vt* bereichern

enrol [ɪn'rəul] *vt* einschreiben ♦ *vi* (register) sich anmelden; **~ment** *n* (for course) Anmeldung *f*

en route [ɔn'ruːt] *adv* unterwegs

ensign ['ensaɪn, 'ensən] *n* (NAUT) Flagge *f*; (MIL) Fähnrich *m*

enslave [ɪn'sleɪv] *vt* versklaven

ensue [ɪn'sjuː] *vi* folgen, sich ergeben

en suite [ɔnswiːt] *adj*: **room with ~ bathroom** Zimmer *nt* mit eigenem Bad

ensure [ɪn'ʃuə'] *vt* garantieren

entail [ɪn'teɪl] *vt* mit sich bringen

entangle [ɪn'tæŋgl] *vt* verwirren, verstricken; **~d** *adj*: **to become ~d (in)** (in net, rope etc) sich verfangen (in +dat)

enter ['entə'] *vt* eintreten in +dat, betreten; (club) beitreten +dat; (in book) eintragen ♦ *vi* hereinkommen, hineingehen; **~ for** *vt fus* sich beteiligen an +dat; **~ into** *vt fus* (agreement) eingehen; (plans) eine Rolle spielen bei; **~ (up)on** *vt fus* beginnen

enterprise ['entəpraɪz] *n* (in person) Initiative *f*; (COMM) Unternehmen *nt*; **enterprising** ['entəpraɪzɪŋ] *adj* unternehmungslustig

entertain [entə'teɪn] *vt* (guest) bewirten; (amuse) unterhalten; **~er** *n* Unterhaltungskünstler(in) *m(f)*; **~ing** *adj* unterhaltsam; **~ment** *n* Unterhaltung *f*

enthralled [ɪn'θrɔːld] *adj* gefesselt

enthusiasm [ɪn'θuːzɪæzəm] *n* Begeisterung *f*

enthusiast [ɪn'θuːzɪæst] *n* Enthusiast *m*; **~ic** [ɪnθuːzɪ'æstɪk] *adj* begeistert

entice [ɪn'taɪs] *vt* verleiten, locken

entire [ɪn'taɪə'] *adj* ganz; **~ly** *adv* ganz, völlig; **~ty** [ɪn'taɪərətɪ] *n*: **in its ~ty** in seiner Gesamtheit

entitle [ɪn'taɪtl] *vt* (allow) berechtigen; (name) betiteln; **~d** *adj* (book) mit dem Titel; **to be ~d to sth** das Recht auf etw *acc* haben; **to be ~d to do sth** das Recht haben, etw zu tun

entity ['entɪtɪ] *n* Ding *nt*, Wesen *nt*

entourage [ɔntu'rɑːʒ] *n* Gefolge *nt*

entrails ['entreɪlz] *npl* Eingeweide *pl*

entrance [*n* 'entrns, *vb* ɪn'trɑːns] *n* Eingang *m*; (entering) Eintritt *m* ♦ *vt* hinreißen; **~ examination** *n* Aufnahmeprüfung *f*; **~ fee** *n* Eintrittsgeld *nt*; **~ ramp** (US) *n* (AUT) Einfahrt *f*

entrant ['entrnt] *n* (for exam) Kandidat *m*; (in race) Teilnehmer *m*

entreat [en'triːt] *vt* anflehen

entrenched [en'trentʃt] *adj* (fig) verwurzelt

entrepreneur ['ɔntrəprə'nəː'] *n* Unternehmer(in) *m(f)*

entrust [ɪn'trʌst] *vt*: **to ~ sb with sth** or **sth to sb** jdm etw anvertrauen

entry ['entrɪ] *n* Eingang *m*; (THEAT) Auftritt *m*; (in account) Eintragung *f*; (in dictionary) Eintrag *m*; **"no ~"** "Eintritt verboten"; (for cars) "Einfahrt verboten"; **~ form** *n* Anmeldeformular *nt*; **~ phone** *n* Sprechanlage *f*

enumerate [ɪ'njuːməreɪt] *vt* aufzählen

enunciate [ɪ'nʌnsɪeɪt] *vt* aussprechen

envelop [ɪn'veləp] *vt* einhüllen

envelope ['envələup] *n* Umschlag *m*

enviable ['envɪəbl] *adj* beneidenswert

envious ['envɪəs] *adj* neidisch

environment [ɪn'vaɪərnmənt] *n* Umgebung *f*; (ECOLOGY) Umwelt *f*; **~al** [ɪnvaɪərn'mentl] *adj* Umwelt-; **~-friendly** *adj* umweltfreundlich

envisage [ɪn'vɪzɪdʒ] *vt* sich *dat* vorstellen

envoy ['envɔɪ] *n* Gesandte(r) *mf*

envy ['envɪ] *n* Neid *m* ♦ *vt*: **to ~ sb sth** jdn um etw beneiden

enzyme ['enzaɪm] *n* Enzym *nt*

epic ['ɛpɪk] n Epos nt ♦ adj episch
epidemic [ɛpɪ'dɛmɪk] n Epidemie f
epilepsy ['ɛpɪlɛpsɪ] n Epilepsie f; epileptic [ɛpɪ'lɛptɪk] adj epileptisch ♦ n Epileptiker(in) m(f)
episode ['ɛpɪsəud] n (incident) Vorfall m; (story) Episode f
epitaph ['ɛpɪtɑːf] n Grabschrift f
epitomize [ɪ'pɪtəmaɪz] vt verkörpern
equable ['ɛkwəbl] adj ausgeglichen
equal ['iːkwl] adj gleich ♦ n Gleichgestellte(r) mf ♦ vt gleichkommen +dat; ~ to the task der Aufgabe gewachsen; equality [iː'kwɔlɪtɪ] n Gleichheit f; (equal rights) Gleichberechtigung f; ~ize vt gleichmachen ♦ vi (SPORT) ausgleichen; ~izer n (SPORT) Ausgleich(streffer) m; ~ly adv gleich
equanimity [ɛkwə'nɪmɪtɪ] n Gleichmut m
equate [ɪ'kweɪt] vt gleichsetzen
equation [ɪ'kweɪʃən] n Gleichung f
equator [ɪ'kweɪtə*] n Äquator m
equestrian [ɪ'kwɛstrɪən] adj Reit-
equilibrium [iːkwɪ'lɪbrɪəm] n Gleichgewicht nt
equinox ['iːkwɪnɔks] n Tagundnachtgleiche f
equip [ɪ'kwɪp] vt ausrüsten; to be well ~ped gut ausgerüstet sein; ~ment n Ausrüstung f; (TECH) Gerät nt
equitable ['ɛkwɪtəbl] adj gerecht, billig
equities ['ɛkwɪtɪz] (BRIT) npl (FIN) Stammaktien pl
equivalent [ɪ'kwɪvələnt] adj gleichwertig, entsprechend ♦ n Äquivalent nt; (in money) Gegenwert m; ~ to gleichwertig +dat, entsprechend +dat
equivocal [ɪ'kwɪvəkl] adj zweideutig
era ['ɪərə] n Epoche f, Ära f
eradicate [ɪ'rædɪkeɪt] vt ausrotten
erase [ɪ'reɪz] vt ausradieren; (tape) löschen; ~r n Radiergummi m
erect [ɪ'rɛkt] adj aufrecht ♦ vt errichten; ~ion [ɪ'rɛkʃən] n Errichtung f; (ANAT) Erektion f
ERM n abbr (= Exchange Rate Mechanism) Wechselkursmechanismus m
erode [ɪ'rəud] vt zerfressen; (land)

auswaschen
erotic [ɪ'rɔtɪk] adj erotisch
err [əː] vi sich irren
errand ['ɛrənd] n Besorgung f
erratic [ɪ'rætɪk] adj unberechenbar
erroneous [ɪ'rəunɪəs] adj irrig
error ['ɛrə*] n Fehler m
erupt [ɪ'rʌpt] vi ausbrechen; ~ion [ɪ'rʌpʃən] n Ausbruch m
escalate ['ɛskəleɪt] vi sich steigern
escalator ['ɛskəleɪtə*] n Rolltreppe f
escape [ɪs'keɪp] n Flucht f; (of gas) Entweichen nt ♦ vi entkommen; (prisoners) fliehen; (leak) entweichen ♦ vt entkommen +dat; escapism n Flucht f (vor der Wirklichkeit)
escort [n 'ɛskɔːt, vb ɪs'kɔːt] n (person accompanying) Begleiter m; (guard) Eskorte f ♦ vt (lady) begleiten; (MIL) eskortieren
Eskimo ['ɛskɪməu] n Eskimo(frau) m(f)
especially [ɪs'pɛʃlɪ] adv besonders
espionage ['ɛspɪənɑːʒ] n Spionage f
esplanade [ɛsplə'neɪd] n Promenade f
Esquire [ɪs'kwaɪə*] n: J. Brown ~ Herrn J. Brown
essay ['ɛseɪ] n Aufsatz m; (LITER) Essay m
essence ['ɛsns] n (quality) Wesen nt; (extract) Essenz f
essential [ɪ'sɛnʃl] adj (necessary) unentbehrlich; (basic) wesentlich ♦ n Allernötigste(s) nt; ~ly adv eigentlich
establish [ɪs'tæblɪʃ] vt (set up) gründen; (prove) nachweisen; ~ed adj anerkannt; (belief, laws etc) herrschend; ~ment n (setting up) Einrichtung f
estate [ɪs'teɪt] n Gut nt; (BRIT: housing ~) Siedlung f; (will) Nachlass m; ~ agent (BRIT) n Grundstücksmakler m; ~ car (BRIT) n Kombiwagen m
esteem [ɪs'tiːm] n Wertschätzung f
esthetic [ɪs'θɛtɪk] (US) adj = aesthetic
estimate [n 'ɛstɪmət, vb 'ɛstɪmeɪt] n Schätzung f; (of price) (Kosten)voranschlag m ♦ vt schätzen; estimation [ɛstɪ'meɪʃən] n Einschätzung f; (esteem) Achtung f
estranged [ɪs'treɪndʒd] adj entfremdet
estuary ['ɛstjuərɪ] n Mündung f

etc *abbr* (= *et cetera*) usw.

etching ['etʃɪŋ] *n* Kupferstich *m*

eternal [ɪ'tɜːnl] *adj* ewig

eternity [ɪ'tɜːnɪtɪ] *n* Ewigkeit *f*

ether ['iːθə*r*] *n* Äther *m*

ethical ['eθɪkl] *adj* ethisch

ethics ['eθɪks] *n* Ethik *f* ♦ *npl* Moral *f*

Ethiopia [iːθɪ'əʊpɪə] *n* Äthiopien *nt*

ethnic ['eθnɪk] *adj* Volks-, ethnisch; ~ **minority** *n* ethnische Minderheit *f*

ethos ['iːθɒs] *n* Gesinnung *f*

e-ticket ['iːtɪkɪt] *n* E-Ticket *nt*

etiquette ['etɪket] *n* Etikette *f*

EU *abbr* (= *European Union*) EU *f*

euphemism ['juːfəmɪzəm] *n* Euphemismus *m*

euro ['jʊərəʊ] *n* (*FIN*) Euro *m*

Eurocheque ['jʊərəʊtʃek] *n* Euroscheck *m*

Euroland ['jʊərəʊlænd] *n* Eurozone *f*, Euroland *nt*

Europe ['jʊərəp] *n* Europa *nt*; ~**an** [jʊərə'piːən] *adj* europäisch ♦ *n* Europäer(in) *m(f)*; ~**an Community** *n*: **the ~an Community** die Europäische Gemeinschaft

Euro-sceptic ['jʊərəʊskeptɪk] *n* Kritiker der Europäischen Gemeinschaft

evacuate [ɪ'vækjʊeɪt] *vt* (*place*) räumen; (*people*) evakuieren; **evacuation** [ɪvækjʊ'eɪʃən] *n* Räumung *f*; Evakuierung *f*

evade [ɪ'veɪd] *vt* (*escape*) entkommen +*dat*; (*avoid*) meiden; (*duty*) sich entziehen +*dat*

evaluate [ɪ'væljʊeɪt] *vt* bewerten; (*information*) auswerten

evaporate [ɪ'væpəreɪt] *vi* verdampfen ♦ *vt* verdampfen lassen; ~**d milk** *n* Kondensmilch *f*

evasion [ɪ'veɪʒən] *n* Umgehung *f*

evasive [ɪ'veɪsɪv] *adj* ausweichend

eve [iːv] *n*: **on the ~ of** am Vorabend +*gen*

even ['iːvn] *adj* eben; gleichmäßig; (*score etc*) unentschieden; (*number*) gerade ♦ *adv*: ~ **you** sogar du; **to get ~ with sb** jdm heimzahlen; ~ **if** selbst wenn; ~ **so** dennoch; ~ **though** obwohl; ~ **more** sogar noch mehr; ~ **out** *vt* sich ausgleichen

evening ['iːvnɪŋ] *n* Abend *m*; **in the ~** abends, am Abend; ~ **class** *n* Abendschule *f*; ~ **dress** *n* (*man's*) Gesellschaftsanzug *m*; (*woman's*) Abendkleid *nt*

event [ɪ'vent] *n* (*happening*) Ereignis *nt*; (*SPORT*) Disziplin *f*; **in the ~ of** im Falle +*gen*; ~**ful** *adj* ereignisreich

eventual [ɪ'ventʃʊəl] *adj* (*final*) schließlich; ~**ity** [ɪventʃu'ælɪtɪ] *n* Möglichkeit *f*; ~**ly** *adv* am Ende; (*given time*) schließlich

ever ['evə*r*] *adv* (*always*) immer; (*at any time*) je(mals) ♦ *conj* seit; ~ **since** seitdem; **have you ~ seen it?** haben Sie es je gesehen?; ~**green** *n* Immergrün *nt*; ~**lasting** *adj* immer während

every ['evrɪ] *adj* jede(r, s); ~ **other/third day** jeden zweiten/dritten Tag; ~ **one of them** alle; **I have ~ confidence in him** ich habe uneingeschränktes Vertrauen in ihn; **we wish you ~ success** wir wünschen Ihnen viel Erfolg; **he's ~ bit as clever as his brother** er ist genauso klug wie sein Bruder; ~ **now and then** ab und zu; ~**body** *pron* = **everyone**; ~**day** *adj* (*daily*) täglich; (*commonplace*) alltäglich, Alltags-; ~**one** *pron* jeder, alle *pl*; ~**thing** *pron* alles; ~**where** *adv* überall(hin); (*wherever*) wohin; ~**where you go** wohin du auch gehst

evict [ɪ'vɪkt] *vt* ausweisen; ~**ion** [ɪ'vɪkʃən] *n* Ausweisung *f*

evidence ['evɪdns] *n* (*sign*) Spur *f*; (*proof*) Beweis *m*; (*testimony*) Aussage *f*

evident ['evɪdnt] *adj* augenscheinlich; ~**ly** *adv* offensichtlich

evil ['iːvl] *adj* böse ♦ *n* Böse *nt*

evocative [ɪ'vɒkətɪv] *adj*: **to be ~ of sth** an etw *acc* erinnern

evoke [ɪ'vəʊk] *vt* hervorrufen

evolution [iːvə'luːʃən] *n* Entwicklung *f*; (*of life*) Evolution *f*

evolve [ɪ'vɒlv] *vt* entwickeln ♦ *vi* sich entwickeln

ewe [juː] *n* Mutterschaf *nt*

ex- [eks] *prefix* Ex-, Alt-, ehemalig

exacerbate [eks'æsəbeɪt] *vt* verschlimmern

exact [ɪg'zækt] *adj* genau ♦ *vt* (*demand*) verlangen; ~**ing** *adj* anspruchsvoll; ~**ly** *adv* genau

exaggerate [ɪg'zædʒəreɪt] *vt, vi* übertreiben; **exaggeration** [ɪgzædʒə'reɪʃən] *n*

Übertreibung f

exalted [ɪg'zɔːltɪd] adj (position, style) hoch; (person) exaltiert

exam [ɪg'zæm] n abbr (SCH) = **examination**

examination [ɪgzæmɪ'neɪʃən] n Untersuchung f; (SCH) Prüfung f, Examen nt; (customs) Kontrolle f

examine [ɪg'zæmɪn] vt untersuchen; (SCH) prüfen; (consider) erwägen; ~r n Prüfer m

example [ɪg'zɑːmpl] n Beispiel nt; **for ~** zum Beispiel

exasperate [ɪg'zɑːspəreɪt] vt zur Verzweiflung bringen; **exasperating** adj ärgerlich, zum Verzweifeln bringend; **exasperation** [ɪgzɑːspə'reɪʃən] n Verzweiflung f

excavate ['ɛkskəveɪt] vt ausgraben; **excavation** [ɛkskə'veɪʃən] n Ausgrabung f

exceed [ɪk'siːd] vt überschreiten; (hopes) übertreffen; **~ingly** adv äußerst

excel [ɪk'sɛl] vi sich auszeichnen; **~lence** ['ɛksələns] n Vortrefflichkeit f; **E~lency** ['ɛksələns] n: **His E~lency** Seine Exzellenz f; **~lent** ['ɛksələnt] adj ausgezeichnet

except [ɪk'sɛpt] prep (also: **~ for**, **~ing**) außer +dat ♦ vt ausnehmen; **~ion** [ɪk'sɛpʃən] n Ausnahme f; **to take ~ion to** Anstoß nehmen an +dat; **~ional** [ɪk'sɛpʃənl] adj außergewöhnlich

excerpt ['ɛksəːpt] n Auszug m

excess [ɪk'sɛs] n Übermaß nt; **an ~ of** ein Übermaß an +dat; **~ baggage** n Mehrgepäck nt; **~ fare** n Nachlösegebühr f; **~ive** adj übermäßig

exchange [ɪks'tʃeɪndʒ] n Austausch m; (also: **telephone ~**) Zentrale f ♦ vt (goods) tauschen; (greetings) austauschen; (money, blows) wechseln; **~ rate** n Wechselkurs m

Exchequer [ɪks'tʃekə[r]] (BRIT) n: **the ~** das Schatzamt

excise ['ɛksaɪz] n Verbrauchssteuer f

excite [ɪk'saɪt] vt erregen; **to get ~d** sich aufregen; **~ment** n Aufregung f; **exciting** adj spannend

exclaim [ɪks'kleɪm] vi ausrufen

exclamation [ɛksklə'meɪʃən] n Ausruf m; **~ mark** n Ausrufezeichen nt

exclude [ɪks'kluːd] vt ausschließen

exclusion [ɪks'kluːʒən] n Ausschluss m; **~ zone** n Sperrzone f

exclusive [ɪks'kluːsɪv] adj (select) exklusiv; (sole) ausschließlich, Allein-; **~ of** exklusive +gen; **~ly** adv nur, ausschließlich

excrement ['ɛkskrəmənt] n Kot m

excruciating [ɪks'kruːʃɪeɪtɪŋ] adj qualvoll

excursion [ɪks'kəːʃən] n Ausflug m

excusable [ɪks'kjuːzəbl] adj entschuldbar

excuse [n ɪks'kjuːs, vb ɪks'kjuːz] n Entschuldigung f ♦ vt entschuldigen; **~ me!** entschuldigen Sie!

ex-directory ['ɛksdɪ'rɛktərɪ] (BRIT) adj: **to be ~** nicht im Telefonbuch stehen

execute ['ɛksɪkjuːt] vt (carry out) ausführen; (kill) hinrichten; **execution** [ɛksɪ'kjuːʃən] n Ausführung f; (killing) Hinrichtung f; **executioner** [ɛksɪ'kjuːʃnə[r]] n Scharfrichter m

executive [ɪg'zɛkjutɪv] n (COMM) Geschäftsführer m; (POL) Exekutive f ♦ adj Exekutiv-, ausführend

executor [ɪg'zɛkjutə[r]] n Testamentsvollstrecker m

exemplary [ɪg'zɛmplərɪ] adj musterhaft

exemplify [ɪg'zɛmplɪfaɪ] vt veranschaulichen

exempt [ɪg'zɛmpt] adj befreit ♦ vt befreien; **~ion** [ɪg'zɛmpʃən] n Befreiung f

exercise ['ɛksəsaɪz] n Übung f ♦ vt (power) ausüben; (muscle, patience) üben; (dog) ausführen ♦ vi Sport treiben; **~ bike** n Heimtrainer m; **~ book** n (Schul)heft nt

exert [ɪg'zəːt] vt (influence) ausüben; **to ~ o.s.** sich anstrengen; **~ion** [ɪg'zəːʃən] n Anstrengung f

exhale [ɛks'heɪl] vt, vi ausatmen

exhaust [ɪg'zɔːst] n (fumes) Abgase pl; (pipe) Auspuffrohr nt ♦ vt erschöpfen; **~ed** adj erschöpft; **~ion** [ɪg'zɔːstʃən] n Erschöpfung f; **~ive** adj erschöpfend

exhibit [ɪg'zɪbɪt] n (JUR) Beweisstück nt; (ART) Ausstellungsstück nt ♦ vt ausstellen; **~ion** [ɛksɪ'bɪʃən] n (ART) Ausstellung f; (of temper etc) Zurschaustellung f; **~ionist** [ɛksɪ'bɪʃənɪst] n Exhibitionist m

exhilarating [ɪg'zɪləreɪtɪŋ] adj erhebend

ex-husband n Ehemann m

exile ['eksaıl] n Exil nt; (*person*) Verbannte(r) f(m) ♦ vt verbannen

exist [ıg'zıst] vi existieren; **~ence** n Existenz f; **~ing** adj bestehend

exit ['eksıt] n Ausgang m; (*THEAT*) Abgang m ♦ vi (*THEAT*) abtreten; (*COMPUT*) aus einem Programm herausgehen; **~ poll** n bei Wahlen unmittelbar nach Verlassen der Wahllokale durchgeführte Umfrage; **~ramp** (*US*) n (*AUT*) Ausfahrt f

exodus ['eksədəs] n Auszug m

exonerate [ıg'zɔnəreıt] vt entlasten

exorbitant [ıg'zɔːbıtnt] adj übermäßig; (*price*) Fantasie-

exotic [ıg'zɔtık] adj exotisch

expand [ıks'pænd] vt ausdehnen ♦ vi sich ausdehnen

expanse [ıks'pæns] n Fläche f

expansion [ıks'pænʃən] n Erweiterung f

expatriate [eks'pætrıət] n Ausländer(in) m(f)

expect [ıks'pekt] vt erwarten; (*suppose*) annehmen ♦ vi: **to be ~ing** ein Kind erwarten; **~ancy** n Erwartung f; **~ant mother** n werdende Mutter f; **~ation** [ekspek'teıʃən] n Hoffnung f

expedient [ıks'piːdıənt] adj zweckdienlich ♦ n (Hilfs)mittel nt

expedition [ekspə'dıʃən] n Expedition f

expel [ıks'pel] vt ausweisen; (*student*) (ver)weisen

expend [ıks'pend] vt (*effort*) aufwenden; **~iture** n Ausgaben pl

expense [ıks'pens] n Kosten pl; **~s** npl (*COMM*) Spesen pl; **at the ~ of** auf Kosten von; **~ account** n Spesenkonto nt; **expensive** [ıks'pensıv] adj teuer

experience [ıks'pıərıəns] n (*incident*) Erlebnis nt; (*practice*) Erfahrung f ♦ vt erleben; **~d** adj erfahren

experiment [ıks'perımənt] n Versuch m, Experiment nt ♦ vi experimentieren; **~al** [ıksperı'mentl] adj experimentell

expert ['ekspəːt] n Fachmann m; (*official*) Sachverständige(r) m ♦ adj erfahren; **~ise** [ekspəː'tiːz] n Sachkenntnis f

expire [ıks'paıər] vi (*end*) ablaufen; (*ticket*) verfallen; (*die*) sterben; **expiry** n Ablauf m

explain [ıks'pleın] vt erklären

explanation [eksplə'neıʃən] n Erklärung f; **explanatory** [ıks'plænətrı] adj erklärend

explicit [ıks'plısıt] adj ausdrücklich

explode [ıks'pləud] vi explodieren ♦ vt (*bomb*) sprengen

exploit [n 'eksplɔıt, vb ıks'plɔıt] n (Helden)tat f ♦ vt ausbeuten; **~ation** [eksplɔı'teıʃən] n Ausbeutung f

exploration [eksplə'reıʃən] n Erforschung f

exploratory [ıks'plɔrətrı] adj Probe-

explore [ıks'plɔː] vt (*travel*) erforschen; (*search*) untersuchen; **~r** n Erforscher(in) m(f)

explosion [ıks'pləuʒən] n Explosion f; (*fig*) Ausbruch m

explosive [ıks'pləusıv] adj explosiv, Spreng- ♦ n Sprengstoff m

export [vb eks'pɔːt, n 'ekspɔːt] vt exportieren ♦ n Export m ♦ cpd (*trade*) Export-; **~er** [eks'pɔːtər] n Exporteur m

expose [ıks'pəuz] vt (*to danger etc*) aussetzen; (*impostor*) entlarven; **to ~ sb to sth** jdn einer Sache dat aussetzen; **~d** adj (*position*) exponiert; **exposure** [ıks'pəuʒər] n (*MED*) Unterkühlung f; (*PHOT*) Belichtung f; **exposure meter** n Belichtungsmesser m

express [ıks'pres] adj ausdrücklich; (*speedy*) Express-, Eil- ♦ n (*RAIL*) Schnellzug m ♦ adv (*send*) per Express ♦ vt ausdrücken; **to ~ o.s.** sich ausdrücken; **~ion** [ıks'preʃən] n Ausdruck m; **~ive** adj ausdrucksvoll; **~ly** adv ausdrücklich; **~way** (*US*) n (*urban motorway*) Schnellstraße f

expulsion [ıks'pʌlʃən] n Ausweisung f

exquisite [eks'kwızıt] adj erlesen

extend [ıks'tend] vt (*visit etc*) verlängern; (*building*) ausbauen; (*hand*) ausstrecken; (*welcome*) bieten ♦ vi (*land*) sich erstrecken

extension [ıks'tenʃən] n Erweiterung f; (*of building*) Anbau m; (*TEL*) Apparat m

extensive [ıks'tensıv] adj (*knowledge*) umfassend; (*use*) weitgehend, weit gehend

extent [ıks'tent] n Ausdehnung f; (*fig*) Ausmaß nt; **to a certain ~** bis zu einem

gewissen Grade; **to such an ~ that ...**
dermaßen, dass ...; **to what ~?** inwieweit?
extenuating [ɪks'tɛnjuetɪŋ] *adj* mildernd
exterior [ɛks'tɪərɪəʳ] *adj* äußere(r, s), Außen-
♦ *n* Äußere(s) *nt*
exterminate [ɪks'tə:mɪneɪt] *vt* ausrotten
external [ɛks'tə:nl] *adj* äußere(r, s), Außen-
extinct [ɪks'tɪŋkt] *adj* ausgestorben; **~ion**
[ɪks'tɪŋkʃən] *n* Aussterben *nt*
extinguish [ɪks'tɪŋgwɪʃ] *vt* (aus)löschen
extort [ɪks'tɔ:t] *vt* erpressen; **~ion** [ɪks'tɔ:ʃən]
n Erpressung *f*; **~ionate** [ɪks'tɔ:ʃnɪt] *adj*
überhöht, erpresserisch

extra ['ɛkstrə] *adj* zusätzlich ♦ *adv* besonders
♦ *n* (for car etc) Extra *nt*; (charge) Zuschlag
m; (THEAT) Statist *m* ♦ *prefix* außer...

extract [*v* ɪks'trækt, *n* 'ɛkstrækt] *vt*
(heraus)ziehen ♦ *n* (from book etc) Auszug
m; (COOK) Extrakt *m*
extracurricular ['ɛkstrəkə'rɪkjʊləʳ] *adj*
außerhalb des Stundenplans
extradite ['ɛkstrədaɪt] *vt* ausliefern
extramarital ['ɛkstrə'mærɪtl] *adj*
außerehelich
extramural ['ɛkstrə'mjʊərl] *adj* (course)
Volkshochschul-
extraordinary [ɪks'trɔ:dnrɪ] *adj*
außerordentlich; (amazing) erstaunlich
extravagance [ɪks'trævəgəns] *n*
Verschwendung *f*; (lack of restraint)
Zügellosigkeit *f*; (an ~) Extravaganz *f*
extravagant [ɪks'trævəgənt] *adj* extravagant
extreme [ɪks'tri:m] *adj* (edge) äußerste(r, s),
hinterste(r, s); (cold) äußerste(r, s);
(behaviour) außergewöhnlich, übertrieben
♦ *n* Extrem *nt*; **~ly** *adv* äußerst, höchst;
extremist *n* Extremist(in) *m(f)*
extremity [ɪks'trɛmɪtɪ] *n* (end) Spitze *f*,
äußerste(s) Ende *nt*; (hardship) bitterste Not
f; (ANAT) Hand *f*; Fuß *m*
extricate ['ɛkstrɪkeɪt] *vt* losmachen, befreien
extrovert ['ɛkstrəvə:t] *n* extrovertierte(r)
Mensch *m*
exuberant [ɪg'zju:bərnt] *adj* ausgelassen
exude [ɪg'zju:d] *vt* absondern
eye [aɪ] *n* Auge *nt*; (of needle) Öhr *nt* ♦ *vt*
betrachten; (up and down) mustern; **to**

keep an ~ on aufpassen auf +*acc*; **~ball** *n*
Augapfel *m*; **~bath** *n* Augenbad *nt*; **~brow**
n Augenbraue *f*; **~brow pencil** *n*
Augenbrauenstift *m*; **~drops** *npl*
Augentropfen *pl*; **~lash** *n* Augenwimper *f*;
~lid *n* Augenlid *nt*; **~liner** *n* Eyeliner *nt*; **~-
opener** *n*: **that was an ~-opener** das hat
mir/ihm etc die Augen geöffnet; **~shadow**
n Lidschatten *m*; **~sight** *n* Sehkraft *f*;
~sore *n* Schandfleck *m*; **~ witness** *n*
Augenzeuge *m*

F, f

F [ɛf] *n* (MUS) F *nt*
F. *abbr* (= Fahrenheit) F
fable ['feɪbl] *n* Fabel *f*
fabric ['fæbrɪk] *n* Stoff *m*; (fig) Gefüge *nt*
fabrication [fæbrɪ'keɪʃən] *n* Erfindung *f*
fabulous ['fæbjʊləs] *adj* sagenhaft
face [feɪs] *n* Gesicht *nt*; (surface) Oberfläche
f; (of clock) Zifferblatt *nt* ♦ *vt* (point towards)
liegen zu; (situation, difficulty) sich stellen
+*dat*; **~ down** (person) mit dem Gesicht
nach unten; (card) mit der Vorderseite nach
unten; **to make** *or* **pull a ~** das Gesicht
verziehen; **in the ~ of** angesichts +*gen*; **on
the ~ of it** so, wie es aussieht; **~ to ~** Auge
in Auge; **to ~ up to sth** einer Sache *dat* ins
Auge sehen; **~ cloth** (BRIT) *n* Waschlappen
m; **~ cream** *n* Gesichtscreme *f*; **~ lift** *n*
Facelifting *nt*; **~ powder** *n* (Gesichts)puder
m
facet ['fæsɪt] *n* Aspekt *m*; (of gem) Facette *f*,
Fassette *f*
facetious [fə'si:ʃəs] *adj* witzig
face value *n* Nennwert *m*; **to take sth at
(its) ~** (fig) etw für bare Münze nehmen
facial ['feɪʃl] *adj* Gesichts-
facile ['fæsaɪl] *adj* (easy) leicht
facilitate [fə'sɪlɪteɪt] *vt* erleichtern
facilities [fə'sɪlɪtɪz] *npl* Einrichtungen *pl*;
credit ~ Kreditmöglichkeiten *pl*
facing ['feɪsɪŋ] *adj* zugekehrt ♦ *prep*
gegenüber
facsimile [fæk'sɪmɪlɪ] *n* Faksimile *nt*;

(*machine*) Telekopierer *m*

fact [fækt] *n* Tatsache *f*; **in ~** in der Tat

faction ['fækʃən] *n* Splittergruppe *f*

factor ['fæktə'] *n* Faktor *m*

factory ['fæktərɪ] *n* Fabrik *f*

factual ['fæktjʊəl] *adj* sachlich

faculty ['fækəltɪ] *n* Fähigkeit *f*; (UNIV) Fakultät *f*; (US: *teaching staff*) Lehrpersonal *nt*

fad [fæd] *n* Tick *m*; (*fashion*) Masche *f*

fade [feɪd] *vi* (*lose colour*) verblassen; (*dim*) nachlassen; (*sound, memory*) schwächer werden; (*wilt*) verwelken

fag [fæg] (*inf*) *n* (*cigarette*) Kippe *f*

fail [feɪl] *vt* (*exam*) nicht bestehen; (*student*) durchfallen lassen; (*courage*) verlassen; (*memory*) im Stich lassen ♦ *vi* (*supplies*) zu Ende gehen; (*student*) durchfallen; (*eyesight*) nachlassen; (*light*) schwächer werden; (*crop*) fehlschlagen; (*remedy*) nicht wirken; **to ~ to do sth** (*neglect*) es unterlassen, etw zu tun; (*be unable*) es nicht schaffen, etw zu tun; **without ~** unbedingt; **~ing** *n* Schwäche *f* ♦ *prep* mangels +*gen*; **~ure** ['feɪljə'] *n* (*person*) Versager *m*; (*act*) Versagen *nt*; (TECH) Defekt *m*

faint [feɪnt] *adj* schwach ♦ *n* Ohnmacht *f* ♦ *vi* ohnmächtig werden

fair [fɛə'] *adj* (*just*) gerecht, fair; (*hair*) blond; (*skin*) hell; (*weather*) schön; (*not very good*) mittelmäßig; (*sizeable*) ansehnlich ♦ *adv* (*play*) fair ♦ *n* (COMM) Messe *f*; (BRIT: *funfair*) Jahrmarkt *m*; **~ly** *adv* (*honestly*) gerecht, fair; (*rather*) ziemlich; **~ness** *n* Fairness *f*

fairy ['fɛərɪ] *n* Fee *f*; **~ tale** *n* Märchen *nt*

faith [feɪθ] *n* Glaube *m*; (*trust*) Vertrauen *nt*; (*sect*) Bekenntnis *nt*; **~ful** *adj* treu; **~fully** *adv* treu; **yours ~fully** (BRIT) hochachtungsvoll

fake [feɪk] *n* (*thing*) Fälschung *f*; (*person*) Schwindler *m* ♦ *adj* vorgetäuscht ♦ *vt* fälschen

falcon ['fɔːlkən] *n* Falke *m*

fall [fɔːl] (*pt* **fell**, *pp* **fallen**) *n* Fall *m*, Sturz *m*; (*decrease*) Fallen *nt*; (*of snow*) (Schnee)fall *m*; (US: *autumn*) Herbst *m* ♦ *vi* (*also fig*) fallen; (*night*) hereinbrechen; **~s** *npl* (*waterfall*) Fälle *pl*; **to ~ flat** platt hinfallen;

(*joke*) nicht ankommen; **~ back** *vi* zurückweichen; **~ back on** *vt fus* zurückgreifen auf +*acc*; **~ behind** *vi* zurückbleiben; **~ down** *vi* (*person*) hinfallen; (*building*) einstürzen; **~ for** *vt fus* (*trick*) hereinfallen auf +*acc*; (*person*) sich verknallen in +*acc*; **~ in** *vi* (*roof*) einstürzen; **~ off** *vi* herunterfallen; (*diminish*) sich vermindern; **~ out** *vi* sich streiten; (MIL) wegtreten; **~ through** *vi* (*plan*) ins Wasser fallen

fallacy ['fæləsɪ] *n* Trugschluss *m*

fallen ['fɔːlən] *pp* of **fall**

fallible ['fæləbl] *adj* fehlbar

fallout ['fɔːlaut] *n* radioaktive(r) Niederschlag *m*; **~ shelter** *n* Atombunker *m*

fallow ['fæləu] *adj* brach(liegend)

false [fɔːls] *adj* falsch; (*artificial*) künstlich; **under ~ pretences** unter Vorspiegelung falscher Tatsachen; **~ alarm** *n* Fehlalarm *m*; **~ teeth** (BRIT) *npl* Gebiss *nt*

falter ['fɔːltə'] *vi* schwanken; (*in speech*) stocken

fame [feɪm] *n* Ruhm *m*

familiar [fə'mɪlɪə'] *adj* bekannt; (*intimate*) familiär; **to be ~ with** vertraut sein mit; **~ize** *vt* vertraut machen

family ['fæmɪlɪ] *n* Familie *f*; (*relations*) Verwandtschaft *f*; **~ business** *n* Familienunternehmen *nt*; **~ doctor** *n* Hausarzt *m*

famine ['fæmɪn] *n* Hungersnot *f*

famished ['fæmɪʃt] *adj* ausgehungert

famous ['feɪməs] *adj* berühmt

fan [fæn] *n* (*folding*) Fächer *m*; (ELEC) Ventilator *m*; (*admirer*) Fan *m* ♦ *vt* fächeln; **~ out** *vi* sich (fächerförmig) ausbreiten

fanatic [fə'nætɪk] *n* Fanatiker(in) *m(f)*

fan belt *n* Keilriemen *m*

fanciful ['fænsɪful] *adj* (*odd*) seltsam; (*imaginative*) fantasievoll

fancy ['fænsɪ] *n* (*liking*) Neigung *f*; (*imagination*) Einbildung *f* ♦ *adj* schick ♦ *vt* (*like*) gern haben; wollen; (*imagine*) sich einbilden; **he fancies her** er mag sie; **~ dress** *n* Maskenkostüm *nt*; **~-dress ball** *n* Maskenball *m*

fang [fæŋ] *n* Fangzahn *m*; (*of snake*) Giftzahn *m*

fantastic [fæn'tæstɪk] *adj* fantastisch

fantasy ['fæntəsɪ] *n* Fantasie *f*

far [fɑːʳ] *adj* weit ♦ *adv* weit entfernt; (*very much*) weitaus; **by ~** bei weitem; **so ~** so weit; bis jetzt; **go as ~ as the station** gehen Sie bis zum Bahnhof; **as ~ as I know** soweit *or* soviel ich weiß; **~away** *adj* weit entfernt

farce [fɑːs] *n* Farce *f*; **farcical** ['fɑːsɪkl] *adj* lächerlich

fare [fɛəʳ] *n* Fahrpreis *m*; Fahrgeld *nt*; (*food*) Kost *f*; **half/full ~** halber/voller Fahrpreis *m*

Far East *n*: **the ~** der Ferne Osten

farewell [fɛə'wɛl] *n* Abschied(sgruß) *m* ♦ *excl* lebe wohl!

farm [fɑːm] *n* Bauernhof *m*, Farm *f* ♦ *vt* bewirtschaften; **~er** *n* Bauer *m*, Landwirt *m*; **~hand** *n* Landarbeiter *m*; **~house** *n* Bauernhaus *nt*; **~ing** *n* Landwirtschaft *f*; **~land** *n* Ackerland *nt*; **~yard** *n* Hof *m*

far-reaching ['fɑː'riːtʃɪŋ] *adj* (*reform, effect*) weitreichend, weit reichend

fart [fɑːt] (*infl*) *n* Furz *m* ♦ *vi* furzen

farther ['fɑːðəʳ] *adv* weiter; **farthest** ['fɑːðɪst] *adj* fernste(r, s) ♦ *adv* am weitesten

fascinate ['fæsɪneɪt] *vt* faszinieren; **fascinating** *adj* faszinierend; **fascination** [fæsɪ'neɪʃən] *n* Faszination *f*

fascism ['fæʃɪzəm] *n* Faschismus *m*

fashion ['fæʃən] *n* (*of clothes*) Mode *f*; (*manner*) Art *f* (und Weise *f*) ♦ *vt* machen; **in ~** in Mode; **out of ~** unmodisch; **~able** *adj* (*clothes*) modisch; (*place*) elegant; **~ show** *n* Mode(n)schau *f*

fast [fɑːst] *adj* schnell; (*firm*) fest ♦ *adv* schnell; fest ♦ *n* Fasten *nt* ♦ *vi* fasten; **to be ~** (*clock*) vorgehen

fasten ['fɑːsn] *vt* (*attach*) befestigen; (*with rope*) zuschnüren; (*seat belt*) festmachen; (*coat*) zumachen ♦ *vi* sich schließen lassen; **~er** *n* Verschluss *m*; **~ing** *n* Verschluss *m*

fast food *n* Fastfood *nt*, Fast Food *nt*

fastidious [fæs'tɪdɪəs] *adj* wählerisch

fat [fæt] *adj* dick ♦ *n* Fett *nt*

fatal ['feɪtl] *adj* tödlich; (*disastrous*)

verhängnisvoll; **~ity** [fə'tælɪtɪ] *n* (*road death etc*) Todesopfer *nt*; **~ly** *adv* tödlich

fate [feɪt] *n* Schicksal *nt*; **~ful** *adj* (*prophetic*) schicksalsschwer; (*important*) schicksalhaft

father ['fɑːðəʳ] *n* Vater *m*; (*REL*) Pater *m*; **~-in-law** *n* Schwiegervater *m*; **~ly** *adj* väterlich

fathom ['fæðəm] *n* Klafter *m* ♦ *vt* ausloten; (*fig*) ergründen

fatigue [fə'tiːg] *n* Ermüdung *f*

fatten ['fætn] *vt* dick machen; (*animals*) mästen ♦ *vi* dick werden

fatty ['fætɪ] *adj* fettig ♦ *n* (*inf*) Dickerchen *nt*

fatuous ['fætjuəs] *adj* albern, affig

faucet ['fɔːsɪt] (*US*) *n* Wasserhahn *m*

fault [fɔːlt] *n* (*defect*) Defekt *m*; (*ELEC*) Störung *f*; (*blame*) Schuld *f*; (*GEOG*) Verwerfung *f*; **it's your ~** du bist daran schuld; **to find ~ with (sth/sb)** etwas auszusetzen haben an (etw/jdm); **at ~** im Unrecht; **~less** *adj* tadellos; **~y** *adj* fehlerhaft, defekt

fauna ['fɔːnə] *n* Fauna *f*

favour ['feɪvəʳ] (*US* **favor**) *n* (*approval*) Wohlwollen *nt*; (*kindness*) Gefallen *m* ♦ *vt* (*prefer*) vorziehen; **in ~ of** für; zugunsten *or* zu Gunsten +*gen*; **to find ~ with sb** bei jdm Anklang finden; **~able** ['feɪvrəbl] *adj* günstig; **~ite** ['feɪvrɪt] *adj* Lieblings- ♦ *n* (*child*) Liebling *m*; (*SPORT*) Favorit *m*

fawn [fɔːn] *adj* rehbraun ♦ *n* (*animal*) (Reh)kitz *nt* ♦ *vi*: **to ~ (up)on** (*fig*) katzbuckeln vor +*dat*

fax [fæks] *n* (*document*) Fax *nt*; (*machine*) Telefax *nt* ♦ *vt*: **to ~ sth to sb** jdm etw faxen

FBI (*US*) *n abbr* (= *Federal Bureau of Investigation*) FBI *nt*

fear [fɪəʳ] *n* Furcht *f* ♦ *vt* fürchten; **~ful** *adj* (*timid*) furchtsam; (*terrible*) fürchterlich; **~less** *adj* furchtlos

feasible ['fiːzəbl] *adj* durchführbar

feast [fiːst] *n* Festmahl *nt*; (*REL: also*: ~ **day**) Feiertag *m* ♦ *vi*: **to ~ (on)** sich gütlich tun (an +*dat*)

feat [fiːt] *n* Leistung *f*

feather ['fɛðəʳ] *n* Feder *f*

feature ['fiːtʃəʳ] *n* (Gesichts)zug *m*;

(*important part*) Grundzug m; (*CINE, PRESS*) Feature nt ♦ vt darstellen; (*advertising etc*) groß herausbringen ♦ vi vorkommen; **featuring X** mit X; ~ **film** n Spielfilm m

February ['februəri] n Februar m

fed [fed] pt, pp of **feed**

federal ['fedərəl] adj Bundes-

federation [fedə'reɪʃən] n (*society*) Verband m; (*of states*) Staatenbund m

fed up adj: **to be ~ with sth** etw satt haben; **I'm ~** ich habe die Nase voll

fee [fiː] n Gebühr f

feeble ['fiːbl] adj (*person*) schwach; (*excuse*) lahm

feed [fiːd] (pt, pp **fed**) n (*for animals*) Futter nt ♦ vt füttern; (*support*) ernähren; (*data*) eingeben; **to ~ on** fressen; **~back** n (*information*) Feed-back nt, Feedback nt; **~ing bottle** (*BRIT*) n Flasche f

feel [fiːl] (pt, pp **felt**) n: **it has a soft ~** es fühlt sich weich an ♦ vt (*sense*) fühlen; (*touch*) anfassen; (*think*) meinen ♦ vi (*person*) sich fühlen; (*thing*) sich anfühlen; **to get the ~ of sth** sich an etw acc gewöhnen; **I ~ cold** mir ist kalt; **I ~ like a cup of tea** ich habe Lust auf eine Tasse Tee; **~ about** or **around** vi herumsuchen; **~er** n Fühler m; **~ing** n Gefühl nt; (*opinion*) Meinung f

feet [fiːt] npl of **foot**

feign [feɪn] vt vortäuschen

feline ['fiːlaɪn] adj katzenartig

fell [fel] pt of **fall** ♦ vt (*tree*) fällen

fellow ['feləu] n (*man*) Kerl m; ~ **citizen** n Mitbürger(in) m(f); ~ **countryman** (*irreg*) n Landsmann m; ~ **men** npl Mitmenschen pl; **~ship** n (*group*) Körperschaft f; (*friendliness*) Kameradschaft f; (*scholarship*) Forschungsstipendium nt; ~ **student** n Kommilitone m, Kommilitonin f

felony ['feləni] n schwere(s) Verbrechen nt

felt [felt] pt, pp of **feel** ♦ n Filz m; **~-tip pen** n Filzstift m

female ['fiːmeɪl] n (*of animals*) Weibchen nt ♦ adj weiblich

feminine ['femɪnɪn] adj (*LING*) weiblich; (*qualities*) fraulich

feminist ['femɪnɪst] n Feminist(in) m(f)

fence [fens] n Zaun m ♦ vt (*also*: ~ **in**) einzäunen ♦ vi fechten; **fencing** ['fensɪŋ] n Zaun m; (*SPORT*) Fechten nt

fend [fend] vi: **to ~ for o.s.** sich (allein) durchschlagen; ~ **off** vt abwehren

fender ['fendə'] n Kaminvorsetzer m; (*US: AUT*) Kotflügel m

ferment [vb fə'ment, n 'fɜːment] vi (*CHEM*) gären ♦ n (*unrest*) Unruhe f

fern [fɜːn] n Farn m

ferocious [fə'rəuʃəs] adj wild, grausam

ferret ['ferɪt] n Frettchen nt ♦ vt: **to ~ out** aufspüren

ferry ['feri] n Fähre f ♦ vt übersetzen

fertile ['fɜːtaɪl] adj fruchtbar

fertilize ['fɜːtɪlaɪz] vt (*AGR*) düngen; (*BIOL*) befruchten; **~r** n (*Kunst*)dünger m

fervent ['fɜːvənt] adj (*admirer*) glühend; (*hope*) innig

fervour ['fɜːvə'] (*US* **fervor**) n Leidenschaft f

fester ['festə'] vi eitern

festival ['festɪvəl] n (*REL etc*) Fest nt; (*ART, MUS*) Festspiele pl

festive ['festɪv] adj festlich; **the ~ season** (*Christmas*) die Festzeit; **festivities** [fes'tɪvɪtɪz] npl Feierlichkeiten pl

festoon [fes'tuːn] vt: **to ~ with** schmücken mit

fetch [fetʃ] vt holen; (*in sale*) einbringen

fetching ['fetʃɪŋ] adj reizend

fête [feɪt] n Fest nt

fetus ['fiːtəs] (*esp US*) n = **foetus**

feud [fjuːd] n Fehde f

feudal ['fjuːdl] adj Feudal-

fever ['fiːvə'] n Fieber nt; **~ish** adj (*MED*) fiebrig; (*fig*) fieberhaft

few [fjuː] adj wenig; **a ~** einige; **~er** adj weniger; **~est** adj wenigste(r,s)

fiancé [fɪ'ɑːnseɪ] n Verlobte(r) m; ~ **e** n Verlobte f

fib [fɪb] n Flunkerei f ♦ vi flunkern

fibre ['faɪbə'] (*US* **fiber**) n Faser f; **~glass** n Glaswolle f

fickle ['fɪkl] adj unbeständig

fiction ['fɪkʃən] n (*novels*) Romanliteratur f; (*story*) Erdichtung f; **~al** adj erfunden

fictitious [fɪkˈtɪʃəs] adj erfunden, fingiert

fiddle [ˈfɪdl] n Geige f; (trick) Schwindelei f
♦ vt (BRIT: accounts) frisieren; ~ **with** vt fus herumfummeln an +dat

fidelity [fɪˈdelɪtɪ] n Treue f

fidget [ˈfɪdʒɪt] vi zappeln

field [fiːld] n Feld nt; (range) Gebiet nt; ~ **marshal** n Feldmarschall m; ~**work** n Feldforschung f

fiend [fiːnd] n Teufel m

fierce [fɪəs] adj wild

fiery [ˈfaɪərɪ] adj (person) hitzig

fifteen [fɪfˈtiːn] num fünfzehn

fifth [fɪfθ] adj fünfte(r, s) ♦ n Fünftel nt

fifty [ˈfɪftɪ] num fünfzig; ~-**fifty** adj, adv halbe-halbe, fifty-fifty (inf)

fig [fɪg] n Feige f

fight [faɪt] (pt, pp fought) n Kampf m; (brawl) Schlägerei f; (argument) Streit m ♦ vt kämpfen gegen; sich schlagen mit; (fig) bekämpfen ♦ vi kämpfen; sich schlagen; streiten; ~**er** n Kämpfer(in) m(f); (plane) Jagdflugzeug nt; ~**ing** n Kämpfen nt; (war) Kampfhandlungen pl

figment [ˈfɪgmənt] n: ~ **of the imagination** reine Einbildung f

figurative [ˈfɪgjurətɪv] adj bildlich

figure [ˈfɪgər] n (of person) Figur f; (person) Gestalt f; (number) Ziffer f ♦ vt (US: imagine) glauben ♦ vi (appear) erscheinen; ~ **out** vt herausbekommen; ~**head** n (NAUT, fig) Galionsfigur f; ~ **of speech** n Redensart f

file [faɪl] n (tool) Feile f; (dossier) Akte f; (folder) Aktenordner m; (COMPUT) Datei f; (row) Reihe f ♦ vt (metal, nails) feilen; (papers) abheften; (claim) einreichen ♦ vi: **to** ~ **in/out** hintereinander hereinkommen/ hinausgehen; **to** ~ **past** vorbeimarschieren; **filing** [ˈfaɪlɪŋ] n Ablage f; **filing cabinet** n Aktenschrank m

fill [fɪl] vt füllen; (occupy) ausfüllen; (satisfy) sättigen ♦ n: **to eat one's** ~ sich richtig satt essen; ~ **in** vt (hole) (auf)füllen; (form) ausfüllen; ~ **up** vt (container) auffüllen; (form) ausfüllen ♦ vt (AUT) tanken

fillet [ˈfɪlɪt] n Filet nt; ~ **steak** n Filetsteak nt

filling [ˈfɪlɪŋ] n (COOK) Füllung f; (for tooth) (Zahn)plombe f; ~ **station** n Tankstelle f

film [fɪlm] n Film m ♦ vt (scene) filmen; ~ **star** n Filmstar m

filter [ˈfɪltər] n Filter m ♦ vt filtern; ~ **lane** n (BRIT) Abbiegespur f; ~-**tipped** adj Filter-

filth [fɪlθ] n Dreck m; ~**y** adj dreckig; (weather) scheußlich

fin [fɪn] n Flosse f

final [ˈfaɪnl] adj letzte(r, s); End-; (conclusive) endgültig ♦ n (FOOTBALL etc) Endspiel nt; ~**s** npl (UNIV) Abschlussexamen nt; (SPORT) Schlussrunde f

finale [fɪˈnɑːlɪ] n (MUS) Finale nt

final: ~**ist** n Schlussrundenteilnehmer m; ~**ize** vt endgültige Form geben +dat; abschließen; ~**ly** adv (lastly) zuletzt; (eventually) endlich; (irrevocably) endgültig

finance [faɪˈnæns] n Finanzwesen nt ♦ vt finanzieren; ~**s** npl (funds) Finanzen pl; **financial** [faɪˈnænʃəl] adj Finanz-; finanziell

find [faɪnd] (pt, pp found) vt finden ♦ n Fund m; **to** ~ **sb guilty** jdn für schuldig erklären; ~ **out** vt herausfinden; ~**ings** npl (JUR) Ermittlungsergebnis nt; (of report) Befund m

fine [faɪn] adj fein; (good) gut; (weather) schön ♦ adv (well) gut; (small) klein ♦ n (JUR) Geldstrafe f ♦ vt (JUR) mit einer Geldstrafe belegen; ~ **arts** npl schöne(n) Künste pl

finger [ˈfɪŋgər] n Finger m ♦ vt befühlen; ~**nail** n Fingernagel m; ~**print** n Fingerabdruck m; ~**tip** n Fingerspitze f

finicky [ˈfɪnɪkɪ] adj pingelig

finish [ˈfɪnɪʃ] n Ende nt; (SPORT) Ziel nt; (of object) Verarbeitung f; (of paint) Oberflächenwirkung f ♦ vt beenden; (book) zu Ende lesen ♦ vi aufhören; (SPORT) ans Ziel kommen; **to be** ~**ed with sth** fertig sein mit etw; **to** ~ **doing sth** mit etw fertig werden; ~ **off** vt (complete) fertig machen; (kill) den Gnadenstoß geben +dat; (knock out) erledigen (umg); ~ **up** vt (food) aufessen; (drink) austrinken ♦ vi (end up) enden; ~**ing line** n Ziellinie f; ~**ing school** n Mädchenpensionat nt

finite [ˈfaɪnaɪt] adj endlich, begrenzt

Finland [ˈfɪnlənd] n Finnland nt

Finn [fɪn] n Finne m, Finnin f; **~ish** adj finnisch ♦ n (LING) Finnisch nt

fir [fɜːʳ] n Tanne f

fire ['faɪəʳ] n Feuer nt; (in house etc) Brand m ♦ vt (gun) abfeuern; (imagination) entzünden; (dismiss) hinauswerfen ♦ vi (AUT) zünden; **to be on ~** brennen; **~ alarm** n Feueralarm m; **~arm** n Schusswaffe f; **~ brigade** (BRIT) n Feuerwehr f; **~ department** (US) n Feuerwehr f; **~ engine** n Feuerwehrauto nt; **~ escape** n Feuerleiter f; **~ extinguisher** n Löschgerät nt; **~man** (irreg) n Feuerwehrmann m; **~place** n Kamin m; **~side** n Kamin m; **~ station** n Feuerwehrwache f; **~wood** n Brennholz nt; **~works** npl Feuerwerk nt; **~ squad** n Exekutionskommando nt

firm [fɜːm] adj fest ♦ n Firma f; **~ly** ['fɜːmlɪ] adv (grasp, speak) fest; (push, tug) energisch; (decide) endgültig

first [fɜːst] adj erste(r, s) ♦ adv zuerst; (arrive) als Erste(r); (happen) zum ersten Mal ♦ n (person: in race) Erste(r) mf; (UNIV) Eins f; (AUT) erste(r) Gang m; **at ~** zuerst; **~ of all** zuallererst; **~ aid** n erste Hilfe f; **~-aid kit** n Verbandskasten m; **~-class** adj erstklassig; (travel) erster Klasse; **~-hand** adj aus erster Hand; **~ lady** (US) n First Lady f; **~ly** adv erstens; **~ name** n Vorname m; **~-rate** adj erstklassig

fiscal ['fɪskl] adj Finanz-

fish [fɪʃ] n inv Fisch m ♦ vi fischen; angeln; **to go ~ing** angeln gehen; (in sea) fischen gehen; **~erman** (irreg) n Fischer m; **~ farm** n Fischzucht f; **~ fingers** (BRIT) npl Fischstäbchen pl; **~ing boat** n Fischerboot nt; **~ing line** n Angelschnur f; **~ing rod** n Angel(rute) f; **~ing tackle** n (for sport) Angelgeräte pl; **~monger's (shop)** n Fischhändler m; **~ slice** n Fischvorlegemesser nt; **~ sticks** (US) npl = **fish fingers**

fishy ['fɪʃɪ] (inf) adj (suspicious) faul

fission ['fɪʃən] n Spaltung f

fissure ['fɪʃəʳ] n Riss m

fist [fɪst] n Faust f

fit [fɪt] adj (MED) gesund; (SPORT) in Form, fit; (suitable) geeignet ♦ vt passen +dat; (insert, attach) einsetzen ♦ vi passen; (in space, gap) hineinpassen ♦ n (of clothes) Sitz m; (MED, of anger) Anfall m; (of laughter) Krampf m; **by ~s and starts** (move) ruckweise; (work) unregelmäßig; **~ in** vi hineinpassen; (fig: person) passen; **~ out** vt (also: **~ up**) ausstatten; **~ful** adj (sleep) unruhig; **~ment** n Einrichtungsgegenstand m; **~ness** n (suitability) Eignung f; (MED) Gesundheit f; (SPORT) Fitness f; **~ted carpet** n Teppichboden m; **~ted kitchen** n Einbauküche f; **~ter** n (TECH) Monteur m; **~ting** adj passend ♦ n (of dress) Anprobe f; (piece of equipment) (Ersatz)teil nt; **~tings** npl (equipment) Zubehör nt; **~ting room** n Anproberaum m

five [faɪv] num fünf; **~r** (inf) n (BRIT) Fünfpfundnote f; (US) Fünfdollarnote f

fix [fɪks] vt befestigen; (settle) festsetzen; (repair) reparieren ♦ n: **in a ~** in der Klemme; **~ up** vt (meeting) arrangieren; **to ~ sb up with sth** jdm etw acc verschaffen; **~ation** [fɪk'seɪʃən] n Fixierung f; **~ed** [fɪkst] adj fest; **~ture** ['fɪkstʃəʳ] n Installationsteil nt; (SPORT) Spiel nt

fizzy ['fɪzɪ] adj Sprudel-, sprudelnd

flabbergasted ['flæbəɡɑːstɪd] (inf) adj platt

flabby ['flæbɪ] adj wabbelig

flag [flæɡ] n Fahne f ♦ vi (strength) nachlassen; (spirit) erlahmen; **~ down** vt anhalten; **~pole** ['flæɡpəʊl] n Fahnenstange f

flair [flɛəʳ] n Talent nt

flak [flæk] n Flakfeuer nt

flake [fleɪk] n (of snow) Flocke f; (of rust) Schuppe f ♦ vi (also: **~ off**) abblättern

flamboyant [flæm'bɔɪənt] adj extravagant

flame [fleɪm] n Flamme f

flamingo [flə'mɪŋɡəʊ] n Flamingo m

flammable ['flæməbl] adj brennbar

flan [flæn] (BRIT) n Obsttorte f

flank [flæŋk] n Flanke f ♦ vt flankieren

flannel ['flænl] n Flanell m; (BRIT: also: **face ~**) Waschlappen m; (: inf) Geschwafel nt; **~s** npl (trousers) Flanellhose f

flap [flæp] n Klappe f; (inf: crisis) (helle) Aufregung f ♦ vt (wings) schlagen mit ♦ vi flattern

flare [flɛəʳ] n (signal) Leuchtsignal nt; (in skirt etc) Weite f; ~ **up** vi aufflammen; (fig) aufbrausen; (revolt) (plötzlich) ausbrechen

flash [flæʃ] n Blitz m; (also: news ~) Kurzmeldung f; (PHOT) Blitzlicht nt ♦ vt aufleuchten lassen ♦ vi aufleuchten; **in a ~** im Nu; ~ **by** or **past** vi vorbeirasen; ~**back** n Rückblende f; ~**bulb** n Blitzlichtbirne f; ~ **cube** n Blitzwürfel m; ~**light** n Blitzlicht nt

flashy ['flæʃɪ] (pej) adj knallig

flask [flɑːsk] n (CHEM) Kolben m; (also: **vacuum ~**) Thermosflasche f ®

flat [flæt] adj flach; (dull) matt; (MUS) erniedrigt; (beer) schal; (tyre) platt ♦ n (BRIT: rooms) Wohnung f; (MUS) b nt; (AUT) Platte(r) m; **to work ~ out** auf Hochtouren arbeiten; ~**ly** adv glatt; ~**-screen** adj (TV, COMPUT) mit flachem Bildschirm; ~**ten** vt (also: ~**ten out**) ebnen

flatter ['flætəʳ] vt schmeicheln +dat; ~**ing** adj schmeichelhaft; ~**y** n Schmeichelei f

flatulence ['flætjuləns] n Blähungen pl

flaunt [flɔːnt] vt prunken mit

flavour ['fleɪvəʳ] (US **flavor**) n Geschmack m ♦ vt würzen; ~**ed** adj: **strawberry-~ed** mit Erdbeergeschmack; ~**ing** n Würze f

flaw [flɔː] n Fehler m; ~**less** adj einwandfrei

flax [flæks] n Flachs m; ~**en** adj flachsfarben

flea [fliː] n Floh m

fleck [flɛk] n (mark) Fleck m; (pattern) Tupfen m

fled [flɛd] pt, pp of **flee**

flee [fliː] (pt, pp **fled**) vi fliehen ♦ vt fliehen vor +dat; (country) fliehen aus

fleece [fliːs] n Vlies nt ♦ vt (inf) schröpfen

fleet [fliːt] n Flotte f

fleeting ['fliːtɪŋ] adj flüchtig

Flemish ['flɛmɪʃ] adj flämisch

flesh [flɛʃ] n Fleisch nt; ~ **wound** n Fleischwunde f

flew [fluː] pt of **fly**

flex [flɛks] n Kabel nt ♦ vt beugen; ~**ibility** [flɛksɪ'bɪlɪtɪ] n Biegsamkeit f; (fig) Flexibilität f; ~**ible** adj biegsam; (plans) flexibel

flick [flɪk] n leichte(r) Schlag m ♦ vt leicht schlagen; ~ **through** vt fus durchblättern

flicker ['flɪkəʳ] n Flackern nt ♦ vi flackern

flier ['flaɪəʳ] n Flieger m

flight [flaɪt] n Flug m; (fleeing) Flucht f; (also: ~ **of steps**) Treppe f; **to take** ~ die Flucht ergreifen; ~ **attendant** (US) n Steward(ess) m(f); ~ **deck** n Flugdeck nt

flimsy ['flɪmzɪ] adj (thin) hauchdünn; (excuse) fadenscheinig

flinch [flɪntʃ] vi: **to** ~ (**away from**) zurückschrecken (vor +dat)

fling [flɪŋ] (pt, pp **flung**) vt schleudern

flint [flɪnt] n Feuerstein m

flip [flɪp] vt werfen

flippant ['flɪpənt] adj schnippisch

flipper ['flɪpəʳ] n Flosse f

flirt [flɜːt] vi flirten ♦ n: **he/she is a** ~ er/sie flirtet gern

flit [flɪt] vi flitzen

float [fləut] n (FISHING) Schwimmer m; (esp in procession) Plattformwagen m ♦ vi schwimmen; (in air) schweben ♦ vt (COMM) gründen; (currency) floaten

flock [flɒk] n (of sheep, REL) Herde f; (of birds) Schwarm m

flog [flɒg] vt prügeln; (inf: sell) verkaufen

flood [flʌd] n Überschwemmung f; (fig) Flut f ♦ vt überschwemmen; ~**ing** n Überschwemmung f; ~**light** n Flutlicht nt

floor [flɔːʳ] n (Fuß)boden m; (storey) Stock m ♦ vt (person) zu Boden schlagen; **ground** ~ (BRIT) Erdgeschoss nt; **first** ~ (BRIT) erste(r) Stock m; (US) Erdgeschoss nt; ~**board** n Diele f; ~ **show** n Kabarettvorstellung f

flop [flɒp] n Plumps m; (failure) Reinfall m ♦ vi (fail) durchfallen

floppy ['flɒpɪ] adj hängend; ~ (**disk**) n (COMPUT) Diskette f

flora ['flɔːrə] n Flora f; ~**l** adj Blumen-

florist ['flɒrɪst] n Blumenhändler(in) m(f); ~**'s** (**shop**) n Blumengeschäft nt

flotation [fləu'teɪʃən] n (FIN) Auflegung f

flounce [flauns] n Volant m

flounder ['flaundəʳ] vi (fig) ins Schleudern kommen ♦ n (ZOOL) Flunder f

flour ['flauǝ^r] n Mehl nt
flourish ['flʌrɪʃ] vi blühen; gedeihen ♦ n *(waving)* Schwingen nt; *(of trumpets)* Tusch m, Fanfare f
flout [flaut] vt missachten
flow [flǝu] n Fließen nt; *(of sea)* Flut f ♦ vi fließen; ~ **chart** n Flussdiagramm nt
flower ['flauǝ^r] n Blume f ♦ vi blühen; ~ **bed** n Blumenbeet nt; ~**pot** n Blumentopf m; ~**y** adj *(style)* blumenreich
flown [flǝun] pp of **fly**
flu [flu:] n Grippe f
fluctuate ['flʌktjueɪt] vi schwanken; **fluctuation** [flʌktju'eɪʃǝn] n Schwankung f
fluency ['flu:ǝnsɪ] n Flüssigkeit f
fluent ['flu:ǝnt] adj fließend; ~**ly** adv fließend
fluff [flʌf] n Fussel f; ~**y** adj flaumig
fluid ['flu:ɪd] n Flüssigkeit f ♦ adj flüssig; *(fig: plans)* veränderbar
fluke [flu:k] *(inf)* n Dusel m
flung [flʌŋ] pt, pp of **fling**
fluoride ['fluǝraɪd] n Fluorid nt; ~**toothpaste** n Fluorzahnpasta f
flurry ['flʌrɪ] n *(of snow)* Gestöber nt; *(of activity)* Aufregung f
flush [flʌʃ] n Erröten nt; *(excited)* Glühen nt ♦ vt (aus)spülen ♦ vi erröten ♦ adj glatt; ~ **out** vt aufstöbern; ~**ed** adj rot
flustered ['flʌstǝd] adj verwirrt
flute [flu:t] n Querflöte f
flutter ['flʌtǝ^r] n Flattern nt ♦ vi flattern
flux [flʌks] n: **in a state of ~** im Fluss
fly [flaɪ] *(pt* **flew**, *pp* **flown**) n *(insect)* Fliege f; *(on trousers: also:* **flies**) (Hosen)schlitz m ♦ vt fliegen ♦ vi fliegen; *(flee)* fliehen; *(flag)* wehen; ~ **away** or **off** vi *(bird, insect)* wegfliegen; ~-**drive** n: ~-**drive holiday** Fly & Drive-Urlaub m; ~**ing** n Fliegen nt ♦ adj: **with ~ing colours** mit fliegenden Fahnen; ~**ing start** gute(r) Start m; ~**ing visit** Stippvisite f; ~**ing saucer** n fliegende Untertasse f; ~**over** *(BRIT)* n Überführung f; ~**sheet** n *(for tent)* Regendach nt
foal [fǝul] n Fohlen nt
foam [fǝum] n Schaum m ♦ vi schäumen; ~ **rubber** n Schaumgummi m
fob [fɔb] vt: **to ~ sb off with sth** jdm etw

andrehen; *(with promise)* jdn mit etw abspeisen
focal ['fǝukl] adj Brenn-; ~ **point** n *(of room, activity)* Mittelpunkt m
focus ['fǝukǝs] *(pl* ~**es**) n Brennpunkt m ♦ vt *(attention)* konzentrieren; *(camera)* scharf einstellen ♦ vi: **to ~ (on)** sich konzentrieren (auf +acc); **in ~** scharf eingestellt; **out of ~** unscharf
fodder ['fɔdǝ^r] n Futter nt
foe [fǝu] n Feind m
foetus ['fi:tǝs] *(US* **fetus**) n Fötus m
fog [fɔg] n Nebel m; ~**gy** adj neblig; ~ **lamp** *(BRIT)*, ~ **light** *(US)* n *(AUT)* Nebelscheinwerfer m
foil [fɔɪl] vt vereiteln ♦ n *(metal, also fig)* Folie f; *(FENCING)* Florett nt
fold [fǝuld] n *(bend, crease)* Falte f; *(AGR)* Pferch m ♦ vt falten; ~ **up** vt *(map etc)* zusammenfalten ♦ vi *(business)* eingehen; ~**er** n Schnellhefter m; ~**ing** adj *(chair etc)* Klapp-
foliage ['fǝulɪdʒ] n Laubwerk nt
folk [fǝuk] npl Leute pl ♦ adj Volks-; ~**s** npl *(family)* Leute pl; ~**lore** ['fǝuklɔ:^r] n *(study)* Volkskunde f; *(tradition)* Folklore f; ~ **song** n Volkslied nt; *(modern)* Folksong m
follow ['fɔlǝu] vt folgen +dat; *(fashion)* mitmachen ♦ vi folgen; ~ **up** vt verfolgen; ~**er** n Anhänger(in) m(f); ~**ing** adj folgend ♦ n *(people)* Gefolgschaft f; ~-**on call** n weiteres Gespräch in einer Telefonzelle um Guthaben zu verbrauchen
folly ['fɔlɪ] n Torheit f
fond [fɔnd] adj: **to be ~ of** gern haben
fondle ['fɔndl] vt streicheln
font [fɔnt] n Taufbecken nt
food [fu:d] n Essen nt; *(fodder)* Futter nt; ~ **mixer** n Küchenmixer m; ~ **poisoning** n Lebensmittelvergiftung f; ~ **processor** n Küchenmaschine f; ~**stuffs** npl Lebensmittel pl
fool [fu:l] n Narr m, Närrin f ♦ vt *(deceive)* hereinlegen ♦ vi *(also:* ~ **around**) (herum)albern; ~**hardy** adj tollkühn; ~**ish** adj albern; ~**proof** adj idiotensicher
foot [fut] *(pl* **feet**) n Fuß m ♦ vt *(bill)*

bezahlen; **on ~** zu Fuß
footage ['futɪdʒ] *n* (CINE) Filmmaterial *nt*
football ['futbɔːl] *n* Fußball *m*; (*game:* BRIT)
Fußball *m*; (: US) Football *m*; ~ **player** *n*
(BRIT: *also:* **~er**) Fußballspieler *m*, Fußballer
m; (US) Footballer *m*

Football Pools

i Football Pools, *umgangssprachlich*
auch the pools *genannt, ist das in*
Großbritannien sehr beliebte Fußballtoto,
bei dem auf die Ergebnisse der
samstäglichen Fußballspiele gewettet wird.
Teilnehmer schicken ihren ausgefüllten
Totoschein vor den Spielen an die
Totogesellschaft und vergleichen nach den
Spielen die Ergebnisse mit ihrem Schein. Die
Gewinne können sehr hoch sein und
gelegentlich Millionen von Pfund betragen.

---

foot: **~brake** *n* Fußbremse *f*; **~bridge** *n*
Fußgängerbrücke *f*; **~hills** *npl* Ausläufer *pl*;
~hold *n* Halt *m*; **~ing** *n* Halt *m*; (*fig*)
Verhältnis *nt*; **~lights** *npl* Rampenlicht *nt*;
~man (*irreg*) *n* Bedienstete(r) *m*; **~note** *n*
Fußnote *f*; **~path** *n* Fußweg *m*; **~print** *n*
Fußabdruck *m*; **~sore** *adj* fußkrank; **~step**
n Schritt *m*; **~wear** *n* Schuhzeug *nt*

KEYWORD

for [fɔːʳ] *prep* **1** für; **is this for me?** ist das für
mich?; **the train for London** der Zug nach
London; **he went for the paper** er ging die
Zeitung holen; **give it to me – what for?**
gib es mir – warum?

2 (*because of*) wegen; **for this reason** aus
diesem Grunde

3 (*referring to distance*): **there are**
roadworks for 5 km die Baustelle ist 5 km
lang; **we walked for miles** wir sind
meilenweit gegangen

4 (*referring to time*) seit; (: *with future sense*)
für; **he was away for 2 years** er war zwei
Jahre lang weg

5 (*+infin clauses*): **it is not for me to decide**
das kann ich nicht entscheiden; **for this to**
be possible ... damit dies möglich wird/

wurde ...

6 (*in spite of*) trotz *+gen or (inf) dat* ; **for all**
his complaints obwohl er sich ständig
beschwert

♦ *conj* denn

---

forage ['fɒrɪdʒ] *n* (Vieh)futter *nt*
foray ['fɒreɪ] *n* Raubzug *m*
forbad(e) [fə'bæd] *pt of* **forbid**
forbid [fə'bɪd] (*pt* **forbad(e)**, *pp* **forbidden**)
vt verbieten; **~ding** *adj* einschüchternd
force [fɔːs] *n* Kraft *f*; (*compulsion*) Zwang *m*
♦ *vt* zwingen; (*lock*) aufbrechen; **the F~s**
npl (BRIT) die Streitkräfte; **in ~** (*rule*) gültig;
(*group*) in großer Stärke; **~d** *adj* (*smile*)
gezwungen; (*landing*) Not-; **~~feed** *vt*
zwangsernähren; **~ful** *adj* (*speech*) kraftvoll;
(*personality*) resolut
forceps ['fɔːseps] *npl* Zange *f*
forcibly ['fɔːsəblɪ] *adv* zwangsweise
ford [fɔːd] *n* Furt *f* ♦ *vt* durchwaten
fore [fɔːʳ] *n*: **to the ~** in den Vordergrund;
~arm ['fɔːrɑːm] *n* Unterarm *m*; **~boding**
[fɔː'bəudɪŋ] *n* Vorahnung *f*; **~cast** ['fɔːkɑːst]
(*irreg: like* **cast**) *n* Vorhersage *f* ♦ *vt*
voraussagen; **~court** ['fɔːkɔːt] *n* (*of garage*)
Vorplatz *m*; **~fathers** ['fɔːfɑːðəz] *npl*
Vorfahren *pl*; **~finger** ['fɔːfɪŋgəʳ] *n*
Zeigefinger *m*; **~front** ['fɔːfrʌnt] *n* Spitze *f*
forego [fɔː'gəu] (*irreg: like* **go**) *vt* verzichten
auf *+acc*
fore: **~gone** ['fɔːgɒn] *adj*: **it's a ~gone**
conclusion es steht von vornherein fest;
~ground ['fɔːgraund] *n* Vordergrund *m*;
~head ['fɒrɪd] *n* Stirn *f*
foreign ['fɒrɪn] *adj* Auslands-; (*accent*)
ausländisch; (*trade*) Außen-; (*body*) Fremd-;
~er *n* Ausländer(in) *m(f)*; **~ exchange** *n*
Devisen *pl*; **F~ Office** (BRIT) *n*
Außenministerium *nt*; **F~ Secretary** (BRIT)
n Außenminister *m*
fore: **~leg** *n* Vorderbein *nt*; **~man**
(*irreg*) *n* Vorarbeiter *m*; **~most** *adj* erste(r,
s) ♦ *adv*: **first and ~most** vor allem
forensic [fə'rensɪk] *adj* gerichtsmedizinisch
fore: **~runner** *n* Vorläufer *m*; **~see**
[fɔː'siː] (*irreg: like* **see**) *vt* vorhersehen;

~**seeable** adj absehbar; ~**shadow**
[fɔː'ʃædəu] vt andeuten; ~**sight** ['fɔːsaɪt] n
Voraussicht f

forest ['fɒrɪst] n Wald m

forestall [fɔː'stɔːl] vt zuvorkommen +dat

forestry ['fɒrɪstrɪ] n Forstwirtschaft f

foretaste ['fɔːteɪst] n Vorgeschmack m

foretell [fɔː'tɛl] (irreg: like tell) vt
vorhersagen

forever [fə'rɛvəʳ] adv für immer

foreword ['fɔːwɜːd] n Vorwort nt

forfeit ['fɔːfɪt] n Einbuße f ♦ vt verwirken

forgave [fə'geɪv] pt of **forgive**

forge [fɔːdʒ] n Schmiede f ♦ vt fälschen;
(iron) schmieden; ~ **ahead** vi Fortschritte
machen; ~**d** adj gefälscht; ~**d banknotes**
Blüten (inf) pl; ~**r** n Fälscher m; ~**ry** n
Fälschung f

forget [fə'gɛt] (pt **forgot**, pp **forgotten**) vt, vi
vergessen; ~**ful** adj vergesslich; ~-**me-not**
n Vergissmeinnicht nt

forgive [fə'gɪv] (pt **forgave**, pp **forgiven**) vt
verzeihen; **to ~ sb (for sth)** jdm (etw)
verzeihen; ~**ness** n Verzeihung f

forgot [fə'gɒt] pt of **forget**; ~**ten** pp of **forget**

fork [fɔːk] n Gabel f; (in road) Gabelung f ♦ vi
(road) sich gabeln; ~ **out** (inf) vt (pay)
blechen; ~-**lift truck** n Gabelstapler m

forlorn [fə'lɔːn] adj (person) verlassen; (hope)
vergeblich

form [fɔːm] n Form f; (type) Art f; (figure)
Gestalt f; (SCH) Klasse f; (bench) (Schul)bank
f; (document) Formular nt ♦ vt formen; (be
part of) bilden

formal ['fɔːməl] adj formell; (occasion)
offiziell; ~**ly** adv (ceremoniously) formell;
(officially) offiziell

format ['fɔːmæt] n Format nt ♦ vt (COMPUT)
formatieren

formation [fɔː'meɪʃən] n Bildung f; (AVIAT)
Formation f

formative ['fɔːmətɪv] adj (years) formend

former ['fɔːməʳ] adj früher; (opposite of latter)
erstere(r, s); ~**ly** adv früher

formidable ['fɔːmɪdəbl] adj furchtbar

formula ['fɔːmjulə] (pl ~**e** or ~**s**) n Formel f;
~**e** ['fɔːmjuliː] npl of **formula**; ~**te**

['fɔːmjuleɪt] vt formulieren

fort [fɔːt] n Feste f, Fort nt

forte ['fɔːtɪ] n Stärke f, starke Seite f

forth [fɔːθ] adv: **and so ~** und so weiter;
~**coming** adj kommend; (character)
entgegenkommend; ~**right** adj offen;
~**with** adv umgehend

fortify ['fɔːtɪfaɪ] vt (ver)stärken; (protect)
befestigen

fortitude ['fɔːtɪtjuːd] n Seelenstärke f

fortnight ['fɔːtnaɪt] (BRIT) n vierzehn Tage pl;
~**ly** (BRIT) adj zweiwöchentlich ♦ adv alle
vierzehn Tage

fortress ['fɔːtrɪs] n Festung f

fortunate ['fɔːtʃənɪt] adj glücklich; ~**ly** adv
glücklicherweise, zum Glück

fortune ['fɔːtʃən] n Glück nt; (money)
Vermögen nt; ~-**teller** n Wahrsager(in)
m(f)

forty ['fɔːtɪ] num vierzig

forum ['fɔːrəm] n Forum nt

forward ['fɔːwəd] adj vordere(r, s);
(movement) Vorwärts-; (person) vorlaut;
(planning) Voraus- ♦ adv vorwärts ♦ n
(SPORT) Stürmer m ♦ vt (send) schicken;
(help) fördern; ~**s** adv vorwärts

fossil ['fɒsl] n Fossil nt, Versteinerung f

foster ['fɒstəʳ] vt (talent) fördern; ~ **child** n
Pflegekind nt; ~ **mother** n Pflegemutter f

fought [fɔːt] pt, pp of **fight**

foul [faul] adj schmutzig; (language) gemein;
(weather) schlecht ♦ n (SPORT) Foul nt ♦ vt
(mechanism) blockieren; (SPORT) foulen; ~
play n (SPORT) Foulspiel nt; (LAW)
Verbrechen nt

found [faund] pt, pp of **find** ♦ vt gründen;
~**ation** [faun'deɪʃən] n (act) Gründung f;
(fig) Fundament nt; (also: ~**ation cream**)
Grundierungscreme f; ~**ations** npl (of
house) Fundament nt; ~**er** n Gründer(in)
m(f) ♦ vi sinken

foundry ['faundrɪ] n Gießerei f

fountain ['fauntɪn] n (Spring)brunnen m; ~
pen n Füllfederhalter m

four [fɔːʳ] num vier; **on all ~s** auf allen
vieren; ~-**poster** n Himmelbett nt; ~**some**
n Quartett nt; ~**teen** num vierzehn;

~teenth *adj* vierzehnte(r, s); ~th *adj* vierte(r, s)

fowl [faul] *n* Huhn *nt*; (*food*) Geflügel *nt*

fox [fɔks] *n* Fuchs *m* ♦ *vt* täuschen

foyer ['fɔɪeɪ] *n* Foyer *nt*, Vorhalle *f*

fraction ['frækʃən] *n* (MATH) Bruch *m*; (*part*) Bruchteil *m*

fracture ['fræktʃə⁸] *n* (MED) Bruch *m* ♦ *vt* brechen

fragile ['frædʒaɪl] *adj* zerbrechlich

fragment ['frægmənt] *n* Bruchstück *nt*; (*small part*) Splitter *m*

fragrance ['freɪgrəns] *n* Duft *m*; fragrant ['freɪgrənt] *adj* duftend

frail [freɪl] *adj* schwach, gebrechlich

frame [freɪm] *n* Rahmen *m*; (*of spectacles: also:* ~s) Gestell *nt*; (*body*) Gestalt *f* ♦ *vt* einrahmen; to ~ sb (*inf: incriminate*) jdm etwas anhängen; ~ of mind Verfassung *f*; ~work *n* Rahmen *m*; (*of society*) Gefüge *nt*

France [frɑːns] *n* Frankreich *nt*

franchise ['fræntʃaɪz] *n* (POL) (aktives) Wahlrecht *nt*; (COMM) Lizenz *f*

frank [fræŋk] *adj* offen ♦ *vt* (*letter*) frankieren; ~ly *adv* offen gesagt

frantic ['fræntɪk] *adj* verzweifelt

fraternal [frə'tɜːnl] *adj* brüderlich

fraternity [frə'tɜːnɪtɪ] *n* (*club*) Vereinigung *f*; (*spirit*) Brüderlichkeit *f*; (US: SCH) Studentenverbindung *f*

fraternize ['frætənaɪz] *vi* fraternisieren

fraud [frɔːd] *n* (*trickery*) Betrug *m*; (*person*) Schwindler(in) *m(f)*; ~ulent ['frɔːdjulənt] *adj* betrügerisch

fraught [frɔːt] *adj*: ~ with voller +*gen*

fray [freɪ] *vt, vi* ausfransen; tempers were ~ed die Gemüter waren erhitzt

freak [friːk] *n* Monstrosität *f* ♦ *cpd* (*storm etc*) anormal

freckle ['frekl] *n* Sommersprosse *f*

free [friː] *adj* frei; (*loose*) lose; (*liberal*) freigebig ♦ *vt* (*set* ~) befreien; (*unblock*) freimachen; ~ (of charge) gratis, umsonst; for ~ gratis, umsonst; ~dom ['friːdəm] *n* Freiheit *f*; F~fone ® *n*: call F~fone 0800 ... rufen Sie gebührenfrei 0800 ... an; ~-for-all *n* (*fight*) allgemeine(s)

Handgemenge *nt*; ~ gift *n* Geschenk *nt*; ~ kick *n* Freistoß *m*; ~lance *adj* frei; (*artist*) freischaffend; ~ly *adv* frei; (*admit*) offen; F~post ® *n* ≈ Gebühr zahlt Empfänger; ~-range *adj* (*hen*) Farmhof-; (*eggs*) Land-; ~ trade *n* Freihandel *m*; ~way (US) *n* Autobahn *f*; ~wheel *vi* im Freilauf fahren; ~ will *n*: of one's own ~ will aus freien Stücken

freeze [friːz] (*pt* froze, *pp* frozen) *vi* gefrieren; (*feel cold*) frieren ♦ *vt* (*also fig*) einfrieren ♦ *n* (*fig, FIN*) Stopp *m*; ~r *n* Tiefkühltruhe *f*; (*in fridge*) Gefrierfach *nt*; freezing *adj* eisig; (*freezing cold*) eiskalt; freezing point *n* Gefrierpunkt *m*

freight [freɪt] *n* Fracht *f*; ~ train *n* Güterzug *m*

French [frentʃ] *adj* französisch ♦ *n* (LING) Französisch *nt*; the ~ *npl* (*people*) die Franzosen *pl*; ~ bean *n* grüne Bohne *f*; ~ fried potatoes (BRIT) *npl* Pommes frites *pl*; ~ fries (US) *npl* Pommes frites *pl*; ~ horn *n* (MUS) (Wald)horn *nt*; ~ kiss *n* Zungenkuss *m*; ~ loaf *n* Baguette *f*; ~man/woman (*irreg*) *n* Franzose *m*/Französin *f*; ~ window *n* Verandatür *f*

frenzy ['frenzɪ] *n* Raserei *f*

frequency ['friːkwənsɪ] *n* Häufigkeit *f*; (PHYS) Frequenz *f*

frequent [*adj* 'friːkwənt, *vb* frɪ'kwent] *adj* häufig ♦ *vt* (*regelmäßig*) besuchen; ~ly *adv* (*often*) häufig, oft

fresh [freʃ] *adj* frisch; ~en *vi* (*also:* ~en up) (sich) auffrischen; (*person*) sich frisch machen; ~er (*inf: BRIT*) *n* (UNIV) Erstsemester *nt*; ~ly *adv* gerade; ~man (*irreg*) (US) *n* = fresher; ~ness *n* Frische *f*; ~water *adj* (*fish*) Süßwasser-

fret [fret] *vi* sich *dat* Sorgen machen

friar ['fraɪə⁸] *n* Klosterbruder *m*

friction ['frɪkʃən] *n* (*also fig*) Reibung *f*

Friday ['fraɪdɪ] *n* Freitag *m*

fridge [frɪdʒ] (BRIT) *n* Kühlschrank *m*

fried [fraɪd] *adj* gebraten

friend [frend] *n* Freund(in) *m(f)*; ~ly *adj* freundlich; (*relations*) freundschaftlich; ~ly fire *n* Beschuss *m* durch die eigene Seite;

~ship n Freundschaft f

frieze [fri:z] n Fries m

frigate ['frɪgɪt] n Fregatte f

fright [fraɪt] n Schrecken m; **to take ~** es mit der Angst zu tun bekommen; **~en** vt erschrecken; **to be ~ened** Angst haben; **~ening** adj schrecklich; **~ful** (inf) adj furchtbar

frigid ['frɪdʒɪd] adj frigide

frill [frɪl] n Rüsche f

fringe [frɪndʒ] n Besatz m; (BRIT: of hair) Pony m; (fig) Peripherie f; **~ benefits** npl zusätzliche Leistungen pl

Frisbee ['frɪzbɪ] ® n Frisbee ® nt

frisk [frɪsk] vt durchsuchen

frisky ['frɪskɪ] adj lebendig, ausgelassen

fritter ['frɪtəʳ] vt: **~ away** vergeuden

frivolous ['frɪvələs] adj frivol

frizzy ['frɪzɪ] adj kraus

fro [frəʊ] adv see **to**

frock [frɒk] n Kleid nt

frog [frɒg] n Frosch m; **~man** (irreg) n Froschmann m

frolic ['frɒlɪk] vi ausgelassen sein

KEYWORD

---

from [frɒm] prep 1 (indicating starting place) of; (indicating origin etc) aus +dat; **a letter / telephone call from my sister** ein Brief / Anruf von meiner Schwester; **where do you come from?** woher kommen Sie?; **to drink from the bottle** aus der Flasche trinken

2 (indicating time) von ... an; (: past) seit; **from one o'clock to** or **until** or **till two** von ein Uhr bis zwei; **from January (on)** ab Januar

3 (indicating distance) von ... (entfernt)

4 (indicating price, number etc) ab +dat; **from £10** ab £10; **there were from 20 to 30 people there** es waren zwischen 20 und 30 Leute da

5 (indicating difference): **he can't tell red from green** er kann nicht zwischen Rot und Grün unterscheiden; **to be different from sb / sth** anders sein als jd / etw

6 (because of, based on): **from what he**

says aus dem, was er sagt; **weak from hunger** schwach vor Hunger

front [frʌnt] n Vorderseite f; (of house) Fassade f; (promenade: also: **sea ~**) Strandpromenade f; (MIL, POL, MET) Front f; (fig: appearances) Fassade f ♦ adj (forward) vordere(r, s), Vorder-; (first) vorderste(r, s); **in ~** vorne; **in ~ of** vor; **~age** ['frʌntɪdʒ] n Vorderfront f; **~ door** n Haustür f; **~ier** ['frʌntɪəʳ] n Grenze f; **~ page** n Titelseite f; **~ room** (BRIT) n Wohnzimmer nt; **~-wheel drive** n Vorderradantrieb m

frost [frɒst] n Frost m; **~bite** n Erfrierung f; **~ed** adj (glass) Milch-; **~y** adj frostig

froth [frɒθ] n Schaum m

frown [fraʊn] n Stirnrunzeln nt ♦ vi die Stirn runzeln

froze [frəʊz] pt of **freeze**

frozen ['frəʊzn] pp of **freeze**

frugal ['fru:gl] adj sparsam, bescheiden

fruit [fru:t] n inv (as collective) Obst nt; (particular) Frucht f; **~ful** adj fruchtbar; **~ion** [fru:'ɪʃən] n: **to come to ~ion** in Erfüllung gehen; **~ juice** n Fruchtsaft m; **~ machine** n (BRIT) Spielautomat m; **~ salad** n Obstsalat m

frustrate [frʌs'treɪt] vt vereiteln; **~d** adj gehemmt; (PSYCH) frustriert

fry [fraɪ] (pt, pp **fried**) vt braten ♦ npl: **small ~** kleine Fische pl; **~ing pan** n Bratpfanne f

ft. abbr = **foot; feet**

fuddy-duddy ['fʌdɪdʌdɪ] n altmodische(r) Kauz m

fudge [fʌdʒ] n Fondant m

fuel ['fjʊəl] n Treibstoff m; (for heating) Brennstoff m; (for lighter) Benzin nt; **~ oil** n (diesel fuel) Heizöl nt; **~ tank** n Tank m

fugitive ['fju:dʒɪtɪv] n Flüchtling m

fulfil [ful'fɪl] vt (duty) erfüllen; (promise) einhalten; **~ment** n Erfüllung f

full [ful] adj (box, bottle, price) voll; (person: satisfied) satt; (member, power, employment) Voll-; (complete) vollständig, Voll-; (speed) höchste(r, s); (skirt) weit ♦ adv: **~ well** sehr wohl; **in ~** vollständig; **a ~ two hours** volle zwei Stunden; **~-length** *adj* (*lifesize*) lebensgroß; **a ~-length photograph** eine Ganzaufnahme; **~ moon** *n* Vollmond *m*; **~-scale** *adj* (*attack*) General-; (*drawing*) in Originalgröße; **~ stop** *n* Punkt *m*; **~-time** *adj* (*job*) Ganztags- ♦ *adv* (*work*) ganztags ♦ *n* (*SPORT*) Spielschluss *nt*; **~-y** *adv* völlig; **~y fledged** *adj* (*also fig*) flügge; **~y licensed** *adj* (*hotel, restaurant*) mit voller Schankkonzession *or* -erlaubnis

fumble ['fʌmbl] *vi*: **to ~ (with)** herumfummeln (an +*dat*)

fume [fju:m] *vi* qualmen; (*fig*) kochen (*inf*); **~s** *npl* (*of fuel, car*) Abgase *pl*

fumigate ['fju:mɪgeɪt] *vt* ausräuchern

fun [fʌn] *n* Spaß *m*; **to make ~ of** sich lustig machen über +*acc*

function ['fʌŋkʃən] *n* Funktion *f*; (*occasion*) Veranstaltung *f* ♦ *vi* funktionieren; **~al** *adj* funktionell

fund [fʌnd] *n* (*money*) Geldmittel *pl*, Fonds *m*; (*store*) Vorrat *m*; **~s** *npl* (*resources*) Mittel *pl*

fundamental [fʌndə'mentl] *adj* fundamental, grundlegend

funeral ['fju:nərəl] *n* Beerdigung *f*; **~ parlour** *n* Leichenhalle *f*; **~ service** *n* Trauergottesdienst *m*

funfair ['fʌnfeəʳ] (*BRIT*) *n* Jahrmarkt *m*

fungi ['fʌŋgaɪ] *npl* of **fungus**

fungus ['fʌŋgəs] *n* Pilz *m*

funnel ['fʌnl] *n* Trichter *m*; (*NAUT*) Schornstein *m*

funny ['fʌnɪ] *adj* komisch

fur [fɜːʳ] *n* Pelz *m*; **~ coat** *n* Pelzmantel *m*

furious ['fjuərɪəs] *adj* wütend; (*attempt*) heftig

furlong ['fɜːlɒŋ] *n* = 201.17 m

furnace ['fɜːnɪs] *n* (Brenn)ofen *m*

furnish ['fɜːnɪʃ] *vt* einrichten; (*supply*) versehen; **~ings** *npl* Einrichtung *f*

furniture ['fɜːnɪtʃəʳ] *n* Möbel *pl*; **piece of ~** Möbelstück *nt*

furrow ['fʌrəu] *n* Furche *f*

furry ['fɜːrɪ] *adj* (*tongue*) pelzig; (*animal*) Pelz-

further ['fɜːðəʳ] *adj* weitere(r, s) ♦ *adv* weiter ♦ *vt* fördern; **~ education** *n* Weiterbildung

f; Erwachsenenbildung *f*; **~more** *adv* ferner

furthest ['fɜːðɪst] *superl* of **far**

furtive ['fɜːtɪv] *adj* verstohlen

fury ['fjuərɪ] *n* Wut *f*, Zorn *m*

fuse [fju:z] (*US* **fuze**) *n* (*ELEC*) Sicherung *f*; (*of bomb*) Zünder *m* ♦ *vt* verschmelzen ♦ *vi* (*BRIT*: *ELEC*) durchbrennen; **~ box** *n* Sicherungskasten *m*

fuselage ['fju:zəlɑ:ʒ] *n* Flugzeugrumpf *m*

fusion ['fju:ʒən] *n* Verschmelzung *f*

fuss [fʌs] *n* Theater *nt*; **~y** *adj* kleinlich

futile ['fju:taɪl] *adj* zwecklos, sinnlos; **futility** [fju:'tɪlɪtɪ] *n* Zwecklosigkeit *f*

future ['fju:tʃəʳ] *adj* zukünftig ♦ *n* Zukunft *f*; **in (the) ~** in Zukunft

fuze [fju:z] (*US*) = **fuse**

fuzzy ['fʌzɪ] *adj* (*indistinct*) verschwommen; (*hair*) kraus

G, g

G [dʒi:] *n* (*MUS*) G *nt*

G7 *n abbr* (= Group of Seven) G7 *f*

gabble ['gæbl] *vi* plappern

gable ['geɪbl] *n* Giebel *m*

gadget ['gædʒɪt] *n* Vorrichtung *f*

Gaelic ['geɪlɪk] *adj* gälisch ♦ *n* (*LING*) Gälisch *nt*

gaffe [gæf] *n* Fauxpas *m*

gag [gæg] *n* Knebel *m*; (*THEAT*) Gag *m* ♦ *vt* knebeln

gaiety ['geɪɪtɪ] *n* Fröhlichkeit *f*

gain [geɪn] *vt* (*obtain*) erhalten; (*win*) gewinnen ♦ *vi* (*clock*) vorgehen ♦ *n* Gewinn *m*; **to ~ in sth** an etw *dat* gewinnen; **~ on** *vt fus* einholen

gait [geɪt] *n* Gang *m*

gal. *abbr* = **gallon**

gala ['gɑ:lə] *n* Fest *nt*

galaxy ['gæləksɪ] *n* Sternsystem *nt*

gale [geɪl] *n* Sturm *m*

gallant ['gælənt] *adj* tapfer; (*polite*) galant

gallbladder [gɔ:l-] *n* Gallenblase *f*

gallery ['gælərɪ] *n* (*also*: **art ~**) Galerie *f*

galley ['gælɪ] *n* (*ship's kitchen*) Kombüse *f*; (*ship*) Galeere *f*

gallon ['gælən] n Gallone f

gallop ['gæləp] n Galopp m ♦ vi galoppieren

gallows ['gæləuz] n Galgen m

gallstone ['gɔːlstəun] n Gallenstein m

galore [gə'lɔːʳ] adv in Hülle und Fülle

galvanize ['gælvənaız] vt (metal) galvanisieren; (fig) elektrisieren

gambit ['gæmbıt] n (fig): **opening ~** (einleitende(r)) Schachzug m

gamble ['gæmbl] vi (um Geld) spielen ♦ vt (risk) aufs Spiel setzen ♦ n Risiko nt; **~r** n Spieler(in) m(f); **gambling** n Glücksspiel nt

game [geım] n Spiel nt; (hunting) Wild nt ♦ adj: **~ (for)** bereit (zu); **~keeper** n Wildhüter m; **~s console** n (COMPUT) Gameboy m ®, Konsole f

gammon ['gæmən] n geräucherte(r) Schinken m

gamut ['gæmət] n Tonskala f

gang [gæŋ] n (of criminals, youths) Bande f; (of workmen) Kolonne f ♦ vi: **to ~ up on sb** sich gegen jdn verschwören

gangrene ['gæŋgriːn] n Brand m

gangster ['gæŋstəʳ] n Gangster m

gangway ['gæŋweı] n (NAUT) Laufplanke f; (aisle) Gang m

gaol [dʒeıl] (BRIT) n, vt = **jail**

gap [gæp] n Lücke f

gape [geıp] vi glotzen; **gaping** ['geıpıŋ] adj (wound) klaffend; (hole) gähnend

garage ['gæraːʒ] n Garage f; (for repair) (Auto)reparaturwerkstatt f; (for petrol) Tankstelle f

garbage ['gaːbıdʒ] n Abfall m; **~ can** (US) n Mülltonne f

garbled ['gaːbld] adj (story) verdreht

garden ['gaːdn] n Garten m; **~s** npl (public park) Park m; (private) Gartenanlagen pl; **~er** n Gärtner(in) m(f); **~ing** n Gärtnern nt

gargle ['gaːgl] vi gurgeln

gargoyle ['gaːgɔıl] n Wasserspeier m

garish ['gɛərıʃ] adj grell

garland ['gaːlənd] n Girlande f

garlic ['gaːlık] n Knoblauch m

garment ['gaːmənt] n Kleidungsstück nt

garnish ['gaːnıʃ] vt (food) garnieren

garrison ['gærısn] n Garnison f

garter ['gaːtəʳ] n Strumpfband nt; (US) Strumpfhalter m

gas [gæs] n Gas nt; (esp US: petrol) Benzin nt ♦ vt vergasen; **~ cooker** (BRIT) n Gasherd m; **~ cylinder** n Gasflasche f; **~ fire** n Gasofen m

gash [gæʃ] n klaffende Wunde f ♦ vt tief verwunden

gasket ['gæskıt] n Dichtungsring m

gas mask n Gasmaske f

gas meter n Gaszähler m

gasoline ['gæsəliːn] (US) n Benzin nt

gasp [gaːsp] vi keuchen; (in surprise) tief Luft holen ♦ n Keuchen nt

gas: ~ ring n Gasring m; **~ station** (US) n Tankstelle f; **~ tap** n Gashahn m

gastric ['gæstrık] adj Magen-

gate [geıt] n Tor nt; (barrier) Schranke f

gateau ['gætəu] (pl **~x**) n Torte f

gatecrash ['geıtkræʃ] (BRIT) vt (party) platzen in +acc

gateway ['geıtweı] n Toreingang m

gather ['gæðəʳ] vt (people) versammeln; (things) sammeln; (understand) annehmen ♦ vi (assemble) sich versammeln; **to ~ speed** schneller werden; **to ~ (from)** schließen (aus); **~ing** n Versammlung f

gauche [gəuʃ] adj linkisch

gaudy ['gɔːdı] adj schreiend

gauge [geıdʒ] n (instrument) Messgerät nt; (RAIL) Spurweite f; (dial) Anzeiger m; (measure) Maß nt ♦ vt (ab)messen; (fig) abschätzen

gaunt [gɔːnt] adj hager

gauze [gɔːz] n Gaze f

gave [geıv] pt of **give**

gay [geı] adj (homosexual) schwul; (lively) lustig

gaze [geız] n Blick m ♦ vi starren; **to ~ at sth** etw dat anstarren

gazelle [gə'zɛl] n Gazelle f

gazumping [gə'zʌmpıŋ] (BRIT) n Hausverkauf an Höherbietenden trotz Zusage an anderen

GB n abbr = **Great Britain**

GCE (BRIT) n abbr = **General Certificate of Education**

GCSE (BRIT) n abbr = **General Certificate of Secondary Education**

gear [gɪəʳ] n Getriebe nt; (equipment) Ausrüstung f; (AUT) Gang m ♦ vt (fig: adapt): **to be ~ed to** ausgerichtet sein auf +acc; **top ~** höchste(r) Gang m; **high ~** (US) höchste(r) Gang m; **low ~** niedrige(r) Gang m; **in ~** eingekuppelt; **~ box** n Getriebe(gehäuse) nt; **~ lever** n Schalthebel m; **~ shift** (US) n Schalthebel m

geese [giːs] npl of **goose**

gel [dʒɛl] n Gel nt

gelatin(e) ['dʒɛlətiːn] n Gelatine f

gem [dʒɛm] n Edelstein m; (fig) Juwel nt

Gemini ['dʒɛmɪnaɪ] n Zwillinge pl

gender ['dʒɛndəʳ] n (GRAM) Geschlecht nt

gene [dʒiːn] n Gen nt

general ['dʒɛnərəl] n General m ♦ adj allgemein; **~ delivery** (US) n Ausgabe(schalter m) f postlagernder Sendungen; **~ election** n allgemeine Wahlen pl; **~ize** vi verallgemeinern; **~ knowledge** n Allgemeinwissen nt; **~ly** adv allgemein, im Allgemeinen; **~ practitioner** n praktische(r) Arzt m, praktische Ärztin f

generate ['dʒɛnəreɪt] vt erzeugen

generation [dʒɛnə'reɪʃən] n Generation f; (act) Erzeugung f

generator ['dʒɛnəreɪtəʳ] n Generator m

generosity [dʒɛnə'rɒsɪtɪ] n Großzügigkeit f

generous ['dʒɛnərəs] adj großzügig

genetic [dʒɪ'nɛtɪk] adj genetisch; **~ally** adv genetisch; **~ally modified** genmanipuliert; **~ engineering** n Gentechnik f; **~ fingerprinting** [-'fɪŋɡəprɪntɪŋ] n genetische Fingerabdrücke pl

genetics [dʒɪ'nɛtɪks] n Genetik f

Geneva [dʒɪ'niːvə] n Genf nt

genial ['dʒiːnɪəl] adj freundlich, jovial

genitals ['dʒɛnɪtlz] npl Genitalien pl

genius ['dʒiːnɪəs] n Genie nt

genocide ['dʒɛnəusaɪd] n Völkermord m

gent [dʒɛnt] n abbr = **gentleman**

genteel [dʒɛn'tiːl] adj (polite) wohlanständig; (affected) affektiert

gentle ['dʒɛntl] adj sanft, zart

gentleman ['dʒɛntlmən] (irreg) n Herr m; (polite) Gentleman m

gentleness ['dʒɛntlnɪs] n Zartheit f, Milde f

gently ['dʒɛntlɪ] adv zart, sanft

gentry ['dʒɛntrɪ] n Landadel m

gents [dʒɛnts] n: **G~** (lavatory) Herren pl

genuine ['dʒɛnjuɪn] adj echt

geographic(al) [dʒɪə'ɡræfɪk(l)] adj geografisch

geography [dʒɪ'ɒɡrəfɪ] n Geografie f

geological [dʒɪə'lɒdʒɪkl] adj geologisch

geology [dʒɪ'ɒlədʒɪ] n Geologie f

geometric(al) [dʒɪə'mɛtrɪk(l)] adj geometrisch

geometry [dʒɪ'ɒmətrɪ] n Geometrie f

geranium [dʒɪ'reɪnɪəm] n Geranie f

geriatric [dʒɛrɪ'ætrɪk] adj Alten- ♦ n Greis(in) m(f)

germ [dʒəːm] n Keim m; (MED) Bazillus m

German ['dʒəːmən] adj deutsch ♦ n Deutsche(r) f(m); (LING) Deutsch nt; **~ measles** n Röteln pl; **~y** n Deutschland nt

germination [dʒəːmɪ'neɪʃən] n Keimen nt

gesticulate [dʒɛs'tɪkjulert] vi gestikulieren

gesture ['dʒɛstjəʳ] n Geste f

KEYWORD

get [gɛt] (pt, pp **got**, pp **gotten** (US)) vi 1 (become, be) werden; **to get old/tired** alt/müde werden; **to get married** heiraten
2 (go) (an)kommen, gehen
3 (begin): **to get to know sb** jdn kennen lernen; **let's get going** or **started!** fangen wir an!
4 (modal aux vb): **you've got to do it** du musst es tun
♦ vt 1: **to get sth done** (do) etw machen; (have done) etw machen lassen; **to get sth going** or **to go** etw in Gang bringen or bekommen; **to get sb to do sth** jdn dazu bringen, etw zu tun
2 (obtain: money, permission, results) erhalten; (find: job, flat) finden; (fetch: person, object) holen; **to get sth for sb** jdm etw besorgen; **get me Mr Jones, please** (TEL) verbinden Sie mich bitte mit Mr Jones
3 (receive: present, letter) bekommen, kriegen; (acquire: reputation etc) erwerben

4(*catch*) bekommen, kriegen; (*hit: target etc*) treffen, erwischen; **get him!** (*to dog*) fass!

5(*take, move*) bringen; **to get sth to sb** jdm etw bringen

6(*understand*) verstehen; (*hear*) mitbekommen; **I've got it!** ich habs!

7(*have, possess*): **to have got sth** etw haben

get about *vi* herumkommen; (*news*) sich verbreiten

get along *vi* (*people*) (gut) zurechtkommen; (*depart*) sich *acc* auf den Weg machen

get at *vt* (*facts*) herausbekommen; **to get at sb** (*nag*) an jdm herumnörgeln

get away *vi* (*leave*) sich *acc* davonmachen; (*escape*): **to get away from sth** von etw *dat* entkommen; **to get away with sth** mit etw davonkommen

get back *vi* (*return*) zurückkommen ♦ *vt* zurückbekommen

get by *vi* (*pass*) vorbeikommen; (*manage*) zurechtkommen

get down *vi* (her)untergehen ♦ *vt* (*depress*) fertig machen; **to get down to** in Angriff nehmen; (*find time to do*) kommen zu

get in *vi* (*train*) ankommen; (*arrive home*) heimkommen

get into *vt* (*enter*) hinein-/hereinkommen in +*acc*; (: *car, train etc*) einsteigen in +*acc*; (*clothes*) anziehen

get off *vi* (*from train etc*) aussteigen; (*from horse*) absteigen ♦ *vt* aussteigen aus; absteigen von

get on *vi* (*progress*) vorankommen; (*be friends*) auskommen; (*age*) alt werden; (*onto train etc*) einsteigen; (*onto horse*) aufsteigen ♦ *vt* einsteigen in +*acc*; auf etw *acc* aufsteigen

get out *vi* (*of house*) herauskommen; (*of vehicle*) aussteigen ♦ *vt* (*take out*) herausholen

get out of *vt* (*duty etc*) herumkommen um

get over *vt* (*illness*) sich *acc* erholen von;

(*surprise*) verkraften; (*news*) fassen; (*loss*) sich abfinden mit

get round *vt* herumkommen; (*fig: person*) herumkriegen

get through to *vt* (*TEL*) durchkommen zu

get together *vi* zusammenkommen

get up *vi* aufstehen ♦ *vt* hinaufbringen; (*go up*) hinaufgehen; (*organize*) auf die Beine stellen

get up to *vt* (*reach*) erreichen; (*prank etc*) anstellen

getaway ['gɛtəweɪ] *n* Flucht *f*

get-up ['gɛtʌp] (*inf*) *n* Aufzug *m*

geyser ['giːzə^r] *n* Geiser *m*; (*heater*) Durchlauferhitzer *m*

ghastly ['gɑːstlɪ] *adj* grässlich

gherkin ['gɜːkɪn] *n* Gewürzgurke *f*

ghetto ['gɛtəu] *n* G(h)etto *nt*; ~ **blaster** *n* (große(r)) Radiorekorder *m*

ghost [gəust] *n* Gespenst *nt*

giant ['dʒaɪənt] *n* Riese *m* ♦ *adj* riesig, Riesen-

gibberish ['dʒɪbərɪʃ] *n* dumme(s) Geschwätz *nt*

gibe [dʒaɪb] *n* spöttische Bemerkung *f*

giblets ['dʒɪblɪts] *npl* Geflügelinnereien *pl*

giddiness ['gɪdɪnɪs] *n* Schwindelgefühl *nt*

giddy ['gɪdɪ] *adj* schwindlig

gift [gɪft] *n* Geschenk *nt*; (*ability*) Begabung *f*; ~**ed** *adj* begabt; ~ **shop** *n* Geschenkladen *m*; ~ **token**, ~ **voucher** *n* Geschenkgutschein *m*

gigantic [dʒaɪˈgæntɪk] *adj* riesenhaft

giggle ['gɪgl] *vi* kichern ♦ *n* Gekicher *nt*

gild [gɪld] *vt* vergolden

gill [dʒɪl] *n* (1/4 *pint*) Viertelpinte *f*

gills [gɪlz] *npl* (*of fish*) Kiemen *pl*

gilt [gɪlt] *n* Vergoldung *f* ♦ *adj* vergoldet; ~-**edged** *adj* mündelsicher

gimmick ['gɪmɪk] *n* Gag *m*

gin [dʒɪn] *n* Gin *m*

ginger ['dʒɪndʒə^r] *n* Ingwer *m*; ~ **ale** *n* Ingwerbier *nt*; ~ **beer** *n* Ingwerbier *nt*; ~**bread** *n* Pfefferkuchen *m*; ~-**haired** *adj* rothaarig

gingerly ['dʒɪndʒəlɪ] *adv* behutsam

gipsy ['dʒɪpsɪ] n Zigeuner(in) m(f)

giraffe [dʒɪ'rɑːf] n Giraffe f

girder ['gəːdə^r] n Eisenträger m

girdle ['gəːdl] n Hüftgürtel m

girl [gəːl] n Mädchen nt; **an English ~** eine (junge) Engländerin; **~friend** n Freundin f; **~ish** adj mädchenhaft

giro ['dʒaɪrəʊ] n (bank ~) Giro nt; (post office ~) Postscheckverkehr m

girth [gəːθ] n (measure) Umfang m; (strap) Sattelgurt m

gist [dʒɪst] n Wesentliche(s) nt

give [gɪv] (pt **gave**, pp **given**) vt geben ♦ vi (break) nachgeben; **~ away** vt verschenken; (betray) verraten; **~ back** vt zurückgeben; **~ in** vi nachgeben ♦ vt (hand in) abgeben; **~ off** vt abgeben; **~ out** vt verteilen; (announce) bekannt geben; **~ up** vt, vi aufgeben; **to ~ o.s. up** sich stellen; (after siege) sich ergeben; **~ way** vi (BRIT: traffic) Vorfahrt lassen; (to feelings): **to ~ way to** nachgeben +dat

glacier ['glæsɪə^r] n Gletscher m

glad [glæd] adj froh; **~ly** ['glædlɪ] adv gern(e)

glamorous ['glæmərəs] adj reizvoll

glamour ['glæmə^r] n Glanz m

glance [glɑːns] n Blick m ♦ vi: **to ~ (at)** (hin)blicken (auf +acc); **~ off** vt fus (fly off) abprallen von; **glancing** ['glɑːnsɪŋ] adj (blow) Streif-

gland [glænd] n Drüse f

glare [glɛə^r] n (light) grelle(s) Licht nt; (stare) wilde(r) Blick m ♦ vi grell scheinen; (angrily): **to ~ at** böse ansehen; **glaring** ['glɛərɪŋ] adj (injustice) schreiend; (mistake) krass

glass [glɑːs] n Glas nt; (mirror: also: **looking ~**) Spiegel m; **~es** npl (spectacles) Brille f; **~house** n Gewächshaus nt; **~ware** n Glaswaren pl; **~y** adj glasig

glaze [gleɪz] vt verglasen; (finish with a ~) glasieren ♦ n Glasur f; **~d** adj (eye) glasig; (pot) glasiert; **glazier** ['gleɪzɪə^r] n Glaser m

gleam [gliːm] n Schimmer m ♦ vi schimmern

glean [gliːn] vt (fig) ausfindig machen

glen [glɛn] n Bergtal nt

glib [glɪb] adj oberflächlich

glide [glaɪd] vi gleiten; **~r** n (AVIAT) Segelflugzeug nt; **gliding** ['glaɪdɪŋ] n Segelfliegen nt

glimmer ['glɪmə^r] n Schimmer m

glimpse [glɪmps] n flüchtige(r) Blick m ♦ vt flüchtig erblicken

glint [glɪnt] n Glitzern nt ♦ vi glitzern

glisten ['glɪsn] vi glänzen

glitter ['glɪtə^r] vi funkeln ♦ n Funkeln nt

gloat [gləʊt] vi: **to ~ over** sich weiden an +dat

global ['gləʊbl] adj: **~ warming** globale(r) Temperaturanstieg m

globe [gləʊb] n Erdball m; (sphere) Globus m

gloom [gluːm] n (darkness) Dunkel nt; (depression) düstere Stimmung f; **~y** adj düster

glorify ['glɔːrɪfaɪ] vt verherrlichen

glorious ['glɔːrɪəs] adj glorreich

glory ['glɔːrɪ] n Ruhm m

gloss [glɒs] n (shine) Glanz m; **~ over** vt fus übertünchen

glossary ['glɒsərɪ] n Glossar nt

glossy ['glɒsɪ] adj (surface) glänzend

glove [glʌv] n Handschuh m; **~ compartment** n (AUT) Handschuhfach nt

glow [gləʊ] vi glühen ♦ n Glühen nt

glower ['glaʊə^r] vi: **to ~ at** finster anblicken

glucose ['gluːkəʊs] n Traubenzucker m

glue [gluː] n Klebstoff m ♦ vt kleben

glum [glʌm] adj bedrückt

glut [glʌt] n Überfluss m

glutton ['glʌtn] n Vielfraß m; **a ~ for work** ein Arbeitstier nt

glycerin(e) ['glɪsəriːn] n Glyzerin nt

GM abbr = **genetically modified**

gnarled [nɑːld] adj knorrig

gnat [næt] n Stechmücke f

gnaw [nɔː] vt nagen an +dat

gnome [nəʊm] n Gnom m

go [gəʊ] (pt **went**, pp **gone**, pl **~es**) vi gehen; (travel) reisen, fahren; (depart: train) (ab)fahren; (be sold) verkauft werden; (work) gehen, funktionieren; (fit, suit) passen; (become) werden; (break etc) nachgeben ♦ n (energy) Schwung m;

(attempt) Versuch m; **he's ~ing to do it** er wird es tun; **to ~ for a walk** spazieren gehen; **to ~ dancing** tanzen gehen; **how did it ~?** wie was?; **to ~ with** *(be suitable)* passen zu; **to have a ~ at sth** etw versuchen; **to be on the ~** auf Trab sein; **whose ~ is it?** wer ist dran?; **~ about** *vi (rumour)* umgehen ♦ *vt fus:* **how do I ~ about this?** wie packe ich das an?; **~ after** *vt fus (pursue: person)* nachgehen +*dat;* **~ ahead** *vi (proceed)* weitergehen; **~ along** *vi* dahingehen, dahinfahren ♦ *vt* entlanggehen, entlangfahren; **to ~ along with** *(support)* zustimmen +*dat;* **~ away** *vi (depart)* weggehen; **~ back** *vi (return)* zurückgehen; **~ back on** *vt fus (promise)* nicht halten; **~ by** *(years, time)* vergehen ♦ *vt fus* sich richten nach; **~ down** *vi (sun)* untergehen ♦ *vt fus* hinuntergehen, hinunterfahren; **~ for** *vt fus (fetch)* holen *(gehen); (like)* mögen; *(attack)* sich stürzen auf +*acc;* **~ in** *vi* hineingehen; **~ in for** *vt fus (competition)* teilnehmen an; **~ into** *vt fus (enter)* hineingehen in +*acc; (study)* sich befassen mit; **~ off** *vi (depart)* weggehen; *(lights)* ausgehen; *(milk etc)* sauer werden; *(explode)* losgehen ♦ *vt fus (dislike)* nicht mehr mögen; **~ on** *vi (continue)* weitergehen; *(inf: complain)* meckern; *(lights)* angehen; **to ~ on with sth** mit etw weitermachen; **~ out** *vi (fire, light)* ausgehen; *(of house)* hinausgehen; **~ over** *vi (ship)* kentern ♦ *vt fus (examine, check)* durchgehen; **~ past** *vi:* **to ~ past sth** an etw *dat* vorbeigehen; **~ round** *vi (visit):* **to ~ round (to sb's)** (bei jdm) vorbeigehen; **~ through** *vt fus (town etc)* durchgehen, durchfahren; **~ up** *vi (price)* steigen; **~ with** *vt fus (suit)* zu etw passen; **~ without** *vt fus* sich behelfen ohne; *(food)* entbehren

goad [gəud] *vt* anstacheln

go-ahead ['gəuəhed] *adj* zielstrebig; *(progressive)* fortschrittlich ♦ *n* grüne(s) Licht *nt*

goal [gəul] *n* Ziel *nt;* (SPORT) Tor *nt;* **~keeper** *n* Torwart *m;* **~ post** *n*

Torpfosten *m*

goat [gəut] *n* Ziege *f*

gobble ['gɔbl] *vt (also:* **~ down, ~ up)** hinunterschlingen

go-between ['gəubɪtwiːn] *n* Mittelsmann *m*

god [gɔd] *n* Gott *m;* **G~** *n* Gott *m;* **~child** *n* Patenkind *nt;* **~daughter** *n* Patentochter *f;* **~dess** *n* Göttin *f;* **~father** *n* Pate *m;* **~forsaken** *adj* gottverlassen; **~mother** *n* Patin *f;* **~send** *n* Geschenk *nt* des Himmels; **~son** *n* Patensohn *m*

goggles ['gɔglz] *npl* Schutzbrille *f*

going ['gəuɪŋ] *n* (HORSE-RACING) Bahn *f* ♦ *adj (rate)* gängig; *(concern)* gut gehend; **it's hard ~** es ist schwierig

gold [gəuld] *n* Gold *nt* ♦ *adj* golden; **~en** *adj* golden, Gold-; **~fish** *n* Goldfisch *m;* **~mine** *n* Goldgrube *f;* **~-plated** *adj* vergoldet; **~smith** *n* Goldschmied(in) *m(f)*

golf [gɔlf] *n* Golf *nt;* **~ ball** *n* Golfball *m;* *(on typewriter)* Kugelkopf *m;* **~ club** *n (society)* Golfklub *m; (stick)* Golfschläger *m;* **~ course** *n* Golfplatz *m;* **~er** *n* Golfspieler(in) *m(f)*

gondola ['gɔndələ] *n* Gondel *f*

gone [gɔn] *pp of* **go**

gong [gɔŋ] *n* Gong *m*

good [gud] *n (benefit)* Wohl *nt; (moral excellence)* Güte *f* ♦ *adj* gut; **~s** *npl (merchandise etc)* Waren *pl,* Güter *pl;* **a ~ deal (of)** ziemlich viel; **a ~ many** ziemlich viele; **~ morning!** guten Morgen!; **~ afternoon!** guten Tag!; **~ evening!** guten Abend!; **~ night!** gute Nacht!; **would you be ~ enough to …?** könnten Sie bitte …?

goodbye [gud'bai] *excl* auf Wiedersehen!

good: **G~ Friday** *n* Karfreitag *m;* **~-looking** *adj* gut aussehend; **~-natured** *adj* gutmütig; *(joke)* harmlos; **~ness** *n* Güte *f;* *(virtue)* Tugend *f;* **~s train** *n* (BRIT) *n* Güterzug *m;* **~will** *n (favour)* Wohlwollen *nt;* (COMM) Firmenansehen *nt*

goose [guːs] *n (pl* **geese)** Gans *f*

gooseberry ['guzbərɪ] *n* Stachelbeere *f*

gooseflesh ['guːsfleʃ] *n* Gänsehaut *f*

goose pimples *npl* Gänsehaut *f*

gore [gɔːr] *vt* aufspießen ♦ *n* Blut *nt*

gorge [gɔ:dʒ] n Schlucht f ♦ vt: **to ~ o.s.** (sich voll) fressen

gorgeous ['gɔ:dʒəs] adj prächtig

gorilla [gə'rɪlə] n Gorilla m

gorse [gɔ:s] n Stechginster m

gory ['gɔ:rɪ] adj blutig

go-slow ['gəu'sləu] (BRIT) n Bummelstreik m

gospel ['gɔspl] n Evangelium nt

gossip ['gɔsɪp] n Klatsch m; (person) Klatschbase f ♦ vi klatschen

got [gɔt] pt, pp of **get**

gotten ['gɔtn] (US) pp of **get**

gout [gaut] n Gicht f

govern ['gʌvən] vt regieren; verwalten

governess ['gʌvənɪs] n Gouvernante f

government ['gʌvnmənt] n Regierung f

governor ['gʌvənə] n Gouverneur m

gown [gaun] n Gewand nt; (UNIV) Robe f

G.P. n abbr = **general practitioner**

grab [græb] vt packen

grace [greɪs] n Anmut f; (blessing) Gnade f; (prayer) Tischgebet nt ♦ vt (adorn) zieren; (honour) auszeichnen; **5 days'** ~ 5 Tage Aufschub; **~ful** adj anmutig

gracious ['greɪʃəs] adj gnädig; (kind) freundlich

grade [greɪd] n Grad m; (slope) Gefälle nt ♦ vt (classify) einstufen; ~ **crossing** (US) n Bahnübergang m; ~ **school** (US) n Grundschule f

gradient ['greɪdɪənt] n Steigung f; Gefälle nt

gradual ['grædjuəl] adj allmählich; **~ly** adv allmählich

graduate [n 'grædjuɪt, vb 'grædjueɪt] n: **to be a** ~ das Staatsexamen haben ♦ vi das Staatsexamen machen; **graduation** [grædju'eɪʃən] n Abschlussfeier f

graffiti [grə'fi:tɪ] npl Graffiti pl

graft [grɑ:ft] n (hard work) Schufterei f; (MED) Verpflanzung f ♦ vt pfropfen; (fig) aufpfropfen; (MED) verpflanzen

grain [greɪn] n Korn nt; (in wood) Maserung f

gram [græm] n Gramm nt

grammar ['græmə] n Grammatik f; ~ **school** (BRIT) n Gymnasium nt; **grammatical** [grə'mætɪkl] adj grammat(ikal)isch

gramme [græm] n = **gram**

granary ['grænərɪ] n Kornspeicher m

grand [grænd] adj großartig; **~child** (pl **~children**) n Enkelkind nt, Enkel(in) m(f); **~dad** n Opa m; **~daughter** n Enkelin f; **~eur** ['grændʒə] n Erhabenheit f; **~father** n Großvater m; **~iose** ['grændɪəus] adj (imposing) großartig; (pompous) schwülstig; **~ma** n Oma f; **~mother** n Großmutter f; **~pa** n = **granddad**; **~parents** npl Großeltern pl; ~ **piano** n Flügel m; **~son** n Enkel m; **~stand** n Haupttribüne f

granite ['grænɪt] n Granit m

granny ['grænɪ] n Oma f

grant [grɑ:nt] vt gewähren ♦ n Unterstützung f; (UNIV) Stipendium nt; **to take sth for ~ed** etw als selbstverständlich (an)nehmen

granulated sugar ['grænjuleɪtɪd-] n Zuckerraffinade f

granule ['grænju:l] n Körnchen nt

grape [greɪp] n (Wein)traube f

grapefruit ['greɪpfru:t] n Pampelmuse f, Grapefruit f

graph [grɑ:f] n Schaubild nt; **~ic** ['græfɪk] adj (descriptive) anschaulich; (drawing) grafisch; **~ics** npl Grafik f

grapple ['græpl] vi: **to ~ with** kämpfen mit

grasp [grɑ:sp] vt ergreifen; (understand) begreifen ♦ n Griff m; (of subject) Beherrschung f; **~ing** adj habgierig

grass [grɑ:s] n Gras nt; **~hopper** n Heuschrecke f; **~land** n Weideland nt; **~-roots** adj an der Basis; ~ **snake** n Ringelnatter f

grate [greɪt] n Kamin m ♦ vi (sound) knirschen ♦ vt (cheese etc) reiben; **to ~ on the nerves** auf die Nerven gehen

grateful ['greɪtful] adj dankbar

grater ['greɪtə] n Reibe f

gratify ['grætɪfaɪ] vt befriedigen; **~ing** adj erfreulich

grating ['greɪtɪŋ] n (iron bars) Gitter nt ♦ adj (noise) knirschend

gratitude ['grætɪtju:d] n Dankbarkeit f

gratuity [grə'tju:ɪtɪ] n Gratifikation f

grave [greɪv] n Grab nt ♦ adj (serious) ernst

gravel ['grævl] n Kies m

gravestone ['greɪvstəun] n Grabstein m

graveyard ['greɪvjɑːd] n Friedhof m

gravity ['grævɪtɪ] n Schwerkraft f; (seriousness) Schwere f

gravy ['greɪvɪ] n (Braten)soße f

gray [greɪ] adj = **grey**

graze [greɪz] vi grasen ♦ vt (touch) streifen; (MED) abschürfen ♦ n Abschürfung f

grease [griːs] n (fat) Fett nt; (lubricant) Schmiere f ♦ vt (ab)schmieren; ~proof (BRIT) adj (paper) Butterbrot-; **greasy** ['griːsɪ] adj fettig

great [greɪt] adj groß; (inf: good) prima; **G~ Britain** n Großbritannien nt; ~~ **grandfather** n Urgroßvater m; ~~ **grandmother** n Urgroßmutter f; ~**ly** adv sehr

Greece [griːs] n Griechenland nt

greed [griːd] n (also: ~**iness**) Gier f; (meanness) Geiz m; ~(**iness**) **for** Gier nach; ~**y** adj gierig

Greek [griːk] adj griechisch ♦ n Grieche m, Griechin f; (LING) Griechisch nt

green [griːn] adj grün ♦ n (village ~) Dorfwiese f; ~ **belt** n Grüngürtel m; ~ **card** n (AUT) grüne Versicherungskarte f; ~**ery** n Grün nt; grüne(s) Laub nt; ~**gage** n Reneklode f, Reineclaude f; ~**grocer** (BRIT) n Obst- und Gemüsehändler m; ~**house** n Gewächshaus nt; ~**house effect** n Treibhauseffekt m; ~**house gas** n Treibhausgas nt

Greenland ['griːnlənd] n Grönland nt

greet [griːt] vt grüßen; ~**ing** n Gruß m; ~**ing(s) card** n Glückwunschkarte f

gregarious [grə'gɛərɪəs] adj gesellig

grenade [grə'neɪd] n Granate f

grew [gruː] pt of **grow**

grey [greɪ] adj grau; ~**-haired** adj grauhaarig; ~**hound** n Windhund m

grid [grɪd] n Gitter nt; (ELEC) Leitungsnetz nt; (on map) Gitternetz nt

gridlock ['grɪdlɒk] n (AUT: traffic jam) totale(r) Stau m; ~**ed** adj: **to be ~ed** (roads) total verstopft sein; (talks etc) festgefahren sein

grief [griːf] n Gram m, Kummer m

grievance ['griːvəns] n Beschwerde f

grieve [griːv] vi sich grämen ♦ vt betrüben

grievous ['griːvəs] adj: ~ **bodily harm** (JUR) schwere Körperverletzung f

grill [grɪl] n Grill m ♦ vt (BRIT) grillen; (question) in die Mangel nehmen

grille [grɪl] n (AUT) (Kühler)gitter nt

grim [grɪm] adj grimmig; (situation) düster

grimace [grɪ'meɪs] n Grimasse f ♦ vi Grimassen schneiden

grime [graɪm] n Schmutz m; **grimy** ['graɪmɪ] adj schmutzig

grin [grɪn] n Grinsen nt ♦ vi grinsen

grind [graɪnd] (pt, pp **ground**) vt mahlen; (US: meat) durch den Fleischwolf drehen; (sharpen) schleifen; (teeth) knirschen mit ♦ n (bore) Plackerei f

grip [grɪp] n Griff m; (suitcase) Handkoffer m ♦ vt packen; ~**ping** adj (exciting) spannend

grisly ['grɪzlɪ] adj grässlich

gristle ['grɪsl] n Knorpel m

grit [grɪt] n Splitt m; (courage) Mut m ♦ vt (teeth) zusammenbeißen; (road) (mit Splitt be)streuen

groan [grəun] n Stöhnen nt ♦ vi stöhnen

grocer ['grəusəʳ] n Lebensmittelhändler m; ~**ies** npl Lebensmittel pl; ~'**s (shop)** n Lebensmittelgeschäft nt

groggy ['grɒgɪ] adj benommen

groin [grɔɪn] n Leistengegend f

groom [gruːm] n (also: **bridegroom**) Bräutigam m; (for horses) Pferdeknecht m ♦ vt (horse) striegeln; (**well-**)~**ed** gepflegt

groove [gruːv] n Rille f, Furche f

grope [grəup] vi tasten; ~ **for** vt fus suchen nach

gross [grəus] adj (coarse) dick, plump; (bad) grob, schwer; (COMM) brutto; ~**ly** adv höchst

grotesque [grə'tɛsk] adj grotesk

grotto ['grɒtəu] n Grotte f

ground [graund] pt, pp of **grind** ♦ n Boden m; (land) Grundbesitz m; (reason) Grund m; (US: also: ~ **wire**) Endleitung f ♦ vi (run ashore) stranden, auflaufen; ~**s** npl (dregs) Bodensatz m; (around house)

(Garten)anlagen *pl*; **on the ~** am Boden; **to the ~** zu Boden; **to gain/lose ~** Boden gewinnen/verlieren; **~ cloth** (*US*) *n* = **groundsheet**; **~ing** *n* (*instruction*) Anfangsunterricht *m*; **~less** *adj* grundlos; **~sheet** (*BRIT*) *n* Zeltboden *m*; **~ staff** *n* Bodenpersonal *nt*; **~ work** *n* Grundlage *f*

roup [gruːp] *n* Gruppe *f* ♦ *vt* (*also*: **~ together**) gruppieren ♦ *vi* sich gruppieren

rouse [graus] *n inv* (*bird*) schottische(s) Moorhuhn *nt*

rove [grəuv] *n* Gehölz *nt*, Hain *m*

rovel ['grɔvl] *vi* (*fig*) kriechen

row [grəu] (*pt* **grew**, *pp* **grown**) *vi* wachsen; (*become*) werden ♦ *vt* (*raise*) anbauen; **~ up** *vi* aufwachsen; **~er** *n* Züchter *m*; **~ing** *adj* zunehmend

rowl [graul] *vi* knurren

rown [grəun] *pp of* **grow**; **~-up** *n* Erwachsene(r) *mf*

rowth [grəuθ] *n* Wachstum *nt*; (*increase*) Zunahme *f*; (*of beard etc*) Wuchs *m*

rub [grʌb] *n* Made *f*, Larve *f*; (*inf*: *food*) Futter *nt*; **~by** ['grʌbɪ] *adj* schmutzig

rudge [grʌdʒ] *n* Groll *m* ♦ *vt*: **to ~ sb sth** jdm etw missgönnen; **to bear sb a ~** einen Groll gegen jdn hegen

ruelling ['gruəlɪŋ] *adj* (*climb*, *race*) mörderisch

ruesome ['gruːsəm] *adj* grauenhaft

ruff [grʌf] *adj* barsch

rumble ['grʌmbl] *vi* murren

rumpy ['grʌmpɪ] *adj* verdrießlich

runt [grʌnt] *vi* grunzen ♦ *n* Grunzen *nt*

-string ['dʒiːstrɪŋ] *n* Minislip *m*

uarantee [gærən'tiː] *n* Garantie *f* ♦ *vt* garantieren

uard [gɑːd] *n* (*sentry*) Wache *f*; (*BRIT*: *RAIL*) Zugbegleiter *m* ♦ *vt* bewachen

uarded ['gɑːdɪd] *adj* vorsichtig

uardian ['gɑːdɪən] *n* Vormund *m*; (*keeper*) Hüter *m*

uard's van ['gɑːdz] (*BRIT*) *n* (*RAIL*) Dienstwagen *m*

uerrilla [gə'rɪlə] *n* Guerilla(kämpfer) *m*; **~ warfare** *n* Guerillakrieg *m*

guess [gɛs] *vt*, *vi* (er)raten, schätzen ♦ *n* Vermutung *f*; **~work** *n* Raterei *f*

guest [gɛst] *n* Gast *m*; **~ house** *n* Pension *f*; **~ room** *n* Gastzimmer *nt*

guffaw [gʌ'fɔː] *vi* schallend lachen

guidance ['gaɪdəns] *n* (*control*) Leitung *f*; (*advice*) Beratung *f*

guide [gaɪd] *n* Führer *m*; (*also*: **girl ~**) Pfadfinderin *f* ♦ *vt* führen; **~book** *n* Reiseführer *m*; **~ dog** *n* Blindenhund *m*; **~lines** *npl* Richtlinien *pl*

guild [gɪld] *n* (*HIST*) Gilde *f*

guillotine ['gɪləti:n] *n* Guillotine *f*

guilt [gɪlt] *n* Schuld *f*; **~y** *adj* schuldig

guinea pig ['gɪnɪ-] *n* Meerschweinchen *nt*; (*fig*) Versuchskaninchen *nt*

guise [gaɪz] *n*: **in the ~ of** in der Form +*gen*

guitar [gɪ'tɑː] *n* Gitarre *f*

gulf [gʌlf] *n* Golf *m*; (*fig*) Abgrund *m*

gull [gʌl] *n* Möwe *f*

gullet ['gʌlɪt] *n* Schlund *m*

gullible ['gʌlɪbl] *adj* leichtgläubig

gully ['gʌlɪ] *n* (*Wasser*)rinne *f*

gulp [gʌlp] *vt* (*also*: **~ down**) hinunterschlucken ♦ *vi* (*gasp*) schlucken

gum [gʌm] *n* (*around teeth*) Zahnfleisch *nt*; (*glue*) Klebstoff *m*; (*also*: **chewing ~**) Kaugummi *m* ♦ *vt* gummieren; **~boots** (*BRIT*) *npl* Gummistiefel *pl*

gun [gʌn] *n* Schusswaffe *f*; **~boat** *n* Kanonenboot *nt*; **~fire** *n* Geschützfeuer *nt*; **~man** (*irreg*) *n* bewaffnete(r) Verbrecher *m*; **~point** *n*: **at ~point** mit Waffengewalt; **~powder** *n* Schießpulver *nt*; **~shot** *n* Schuss *m*

gurgle ['gəːgl] *vi* gluckern

gush [gʌʃ] *vi* (*rush out*) hervorströmen; (*fig*) schwärmen

gust [gʌst] *n* Windstoß *m*, Bö *f*

gusto ['gʌstəu] *n* Genuss *m*, Lust *f*

gut [gʌt] *n* (*ANAT*) Gedärme *pl*; (*string*) Darm *m*; **~s** *npl* (*fig*) Schneid *m*

gutter ['gʌtər] *n* Dachrinne *f*; (*in street*) Gosse *f*

guttural ['gʌtərl] *adj* guttural, Kehl-

guy [gaɪ] *n* (*also*: **~rope**) Halteseil *nt*; (*man*) Typ *m*, Kerl *m*

Guy Fawkes' Night

i **Guy Fawkes' Night**, *auch bonfire night genannt, erinnert an den Gunpowder Plot, einen Attentatsversuch auf James I. und sein Parlament am 5. November 1605. Einer der Verschwörer, Guy Fawkes, wurde auf frischer Tat ertappt, als er das Parlamentsgebäude in die Luft sprengen wollte. Vor der Guy Fawkes' Night basteln Kinder in Großbritannien eine Puppe des Guy Fawkes, mit der sie Geld für Feuerwerkskörper von Passanten erbetteln, und die dann am 5. November auf einem Lagerfeuer mit Feuerwerk verbrannt wird.*

---

guzzle ['gʌzl] *vt, vi (drink)* saufen; *(eat)* fressen
gym [dʒɪm] *n (also: ~nasium)* Turnhalle *f; (also: ~nastics)* Turnen *nt*
gymnast ['dʒɪmnæst] *n* Turner(in) *m(f)*
gymnastics [dʒɪm'næstɪks] *n* Turnen *nt*, Gymnastik *f*
gym shoes *npl* Turnschuhe *pl*
gynaecologist [gaɪnɪ'kɒlədʒɪst] *(US* **gynecologist**) *n* Frauenarzt(-ärztin) *m(f)*
gypsy ['dʒɪpsɪ] *n* = **gipsy**
gyrate [dʒaɪ'reɪt] *vi* kreisen

H, h

haberdashery [hæbə'dæʃərɪ] *(BRIT) n* Kurzwaren *pl*
habit ['hæbɪt] *n* (An)gewohnheit *f; (monk's)* Habit *nt or m*
habitable ['hæbɪtəbl] *adj* bewohnbar
habitat ['hæbɪtæt] *n* Lebensraum *m*
habitual [hə'bɪtjuəl] *adj* gewohnheitsmäßig; **~ly** *adv* gewöhnlich
hack [hæk] *vt* hacken ♦ *n* Hieb *m; (writer)* Schreiberling *m*
hacker ['hækər] *n (COMPUT)* Hacker *m*
hackneyed ['hæknɪd] *adj* abgedroschen
had [hæd] *pt, pp of* **have**
haddock ['hædək] *(pl ~ or ~s) n* Schellfisch *m*

hadn't ['hædnt] = **had not**
haemorrhage ['hemərɪdʒ] *(US* **hemorrhage**) *n* Blutung *f*
haemorrhoids ['hemərɔɪdz] *(US* **hemorrhoids**) *npl* Hämorr(ho)iden *pl*
haggard ['hægəd] *adj* abgekämpft
haggle ['hægl] *vi* feilschen
Hague [heɪg] *n (GEOG)* **The ~** Den Haag *nt*
hail [heɪl] *n* Hagel *m* ♦ *vt* umjubeln ♦ *vi* hageln; **~stone** *n* Hagelkorn *nt*
hair [hɛər] *n* Haar *nt*, Haare *pl; (one ~)* Haar *nt;* **~brush** *n* Haarbürste *f;* **~cut** *n* Haarschnitt *m;* **to get a ~cut** sich *dat* die Haare schneiden lassen; **~do** *n* Frisur *f;* **~dresser** *n* Friseur *m*, Friseuse *f;* **~dresser's** *n* Friseursalon *m;* **~ dryer** *n* Trockenhaube *f; (hand-held)* Föhn *m*, Fön ®; **~ gel** *n* Haargel *nt;* **~grip** *n* Klemme *f;* **~net** *n* Haarnetz *nt;* **~pin** *n* Haarnadel *f;* **~pin bend** *(US* **~pin curve**) *n* Haarnadelkurve *f;* **~raising** *adj* haarsträubend; **~ removing cream** *n* Enthaarungscreme *nt;* **~ spray** *n* Haarspr *nt;* **~style** *n* Frisur *f*
hairy ['hɛərɪ] *adj* haarig
hake [heɪk] *n* Seehecht *m*
half [hɑːf] *(pl* **halves**) *n* Hälfte *f* ♦ *adj* halb ♦ *adv* halb, zur Hälfte; **~ an hour** eine halbe Stunde; **two and a ~** zweieinhalb; **t cut sth in ~** etw halbieren; **~ a dozen** ein halbes Dutzend, sechs; **~ board** *n* Halbpension *f;* **~caste** *n* Mischling *m;* **~ fare** *n* halbe(r) Fahrpreis *m;* **~hearted** *a* lustlos; **~hour** *n* halbe Stunde *f;* **~price** *n:* **(at) ~price** zum halben Preis; **~ term** *(BRIT) n (SCH)* Ferien *pl* in der Mitte des Trimesters; **~time** *n* Halbzeit *f; ~way* *ad* halbwegs, auf halbem Wege
halibut ['hælɪbət] *n inv* Heilbutt *m*
hall [hɔːl] *n* Saal *m; (entrance ~)* Hausflur *m (building)* Halle *f;* **~ of residence** *(BRIT) n* Studentenwohnheim *nt*
hallmark ['hɔːlmɑːk] *n* Stempel *m*
hallo [hə'ləʊ] *excl* = **hello**
Hallowe'en ['hæləʊ'iːn] *n* Tag *m* vor Allerheiligen

Hallowe'en

Hallowe'en *ist der 31. Oktober, der Vorabend von Allerheiligen und nach ltem Glauben der Abend, an dem man Geister und Hexen sehen kann. In Großbritannien und vor allem in den USA eiern die Kinder Hallowe'en, indem sie sich erkleiden und mit selbst gemachten aternen aus Kürbissen von Tür zu Tür iehen.*

allucination [həluːsɪˈneɪʃən] *n* Halluzination *f*

allway [ˈhɔːlweɪ] *n* Korridor *m*

alo [ˈheɪləu] *n* Heiligenschein *m*

alt [hɔːlt] *n* Halt *m* ♦ *vt, vi* anhalten

alve [hɑːv] *vt* halbieren

alves [hɑːvz] *pl of* **half**

am [hæm] *n* Schinken *m*

amburger [ˈhæmbɜːgəˀ] *n* Hamburger *m*

amlet [ˈhæmlɪt] *n* Weiler *m*

ammer [ˈhæməˀ] *n* Hammer *m* ♦ *vt, vi* hämmern

ammock [ˈhæmək] *n* Hängematte *f*

amper [ˈhæmpəˀ] *vt* (be)hindern ♦ *n* Picknickkorb *m*

amster [ˈhæmstəˀ] *n* Hamster *m*

and [hænd] *n* Hand *f*; (*of clock*) (Uhr)zeiger *m*; (*worker*) Arbeiter *m* ♦ *vt* (*pass*) geben; **to give sb a ~** jdm helfen; **at ~** nahe; **to ~** zur Hand; **in ~** (*under control*) unter Kontrolle; (*being done*) im Gange; (*extra*) übrig; **on ~** zur Verfügung; **on the one ~ ..., on the other ~ ...** einerseits ..., andererseits ...; **~ in** *vt* abgeben; (*forms*) einreichen; **~ out** *vt* austeilen; **~ over** *vt* (*deliver*) übergeben; (*surrender*) abgeben; (: *prisoner*) ausliefern; **~bag** *n* Handtasche *f*; **~book** *n* Handbuch *nt*; **~brake** *n* Handbremse *f*; **~cuffs** *npl* Handschellen *pl*; **~ful** *n* Hand *f* voll; (*inf: person*) Plage *f*

andicap [ˈhændɪkæp] *n* Handikap *nt* ♦ *vt* benachteiligen; **mentally/physically ~ped** geistig/körperlich behindert

andicraft [ˈhændɪkrɑːft] *n* Kunsthandwerk *nt*

handiwork [ˈhændɪwɜːk] *n* Arbeit *f*; (*fig*) Werk *nt*

handkerchief [ˈhæŋkətʃɪf] *n* Taschentuch *nt*

handle [ˈhændl] *n* (*of door etc*) Klinke *f*; (*of cup etc*) Henkel *m*; (*for winding*) Kurbel *f* ♦ *vt* (*touch*) anfassen; (*deal with: things*) sich befassen mit; (: *people*) umgehen mit; **~bar(s)** *n(pl)* Lenkstange *f*

hand: ~ luggage *n* Handgepäck *nt*; **~made** *adj* handgefertigt; **~out** *n* (*distribution*) Verteilung *f*; (*charity*) Geldzuwendung *f*; (*leaflet*) Flugblatt *nt*; **~rail** *n* Geländer *nt*; (*on ship*) Reling *f*; **~set** *n* (*TEL*) Hörer *m*; **please replace the ~set** bitte legen Sie auf; **~shake** *n* Händedruck *f*

handsome [ˈhænsəm] *adj* gut aussehend

handwriting [ˈhændraɪtɪŋ] *n* Handschrift *f*

handy [ˈhændɪ] *adj* praktisch; (*shops*) leicht erreichbar; **~man** [ˈhændɪmæn] (*irreg*) *n* Bastler *m*

hang [hæŋ] (*pt, pp* **hung**) *vt* aufhängen; (*pt, pp* **hanged**: *criminal*) hängen ♦ *vi* hängen ♦ *n*: **to get the ~ of sth** (*inf*) bei etw herauskriegen; **~ about, ~ around** *vi* sich herumtreiben; **~ on** *vi* (*wait*) warten; **~ up** *vi* (*TEL*) auflegen

hangar [ˈhæŋəˀ] *n* Hangar *m*

hanger [ˈhæŋəˀ] *n* Kleiderbügel *m*

hanger-on [ˈhæŋərɒn] *n* Anhänger(in) *m(f)*

hang [ˈhæŋ-]: **~-gliding** *n* Drachenfliegen *nt*; **~over** *n* Kater *m*; **~-up** *n* Komplex *m*

hanker [ˈhæŋkəˀ] *vi*: **to ~ for** *or* **after** sich sehnen nach

hankie [ˈhæŋkɪ] *n abbr* = **handkerchief**

hanky [ˈhæŋkɪ] *n abbr* = **handkerchief**

haphazard [hæpˈhæzəd] *adj* zufällig

happen [ˈhæpən] *vi* sich ereignen, passieren; **as it ~s I'm going there today** zufällig(erweise) gehe ich heute (dort)hin; **~ing** *n* Ereignis *nt*

happily [ˈhæpɪlɪ] *adv* glücklich; (*fortunately*) glücklicherweise

happiness [ˈhæpɪnɪs] *n* Glück *nt*

happy [ˈhæpɪ] *adj* glücklich; **~ birthday!** alles Gute zum Geburtstag!; **~-go-lucky** *adj* sorglos; **~ hour** *n* Happy Hour *f*

harass ['hærəs] vt plagen; **~ment** n
Belästigung f
harbour ['hɑːbəʳ] (US **harbor**) n Hafen m
♦ vt (hope etc) hegen; (criminal etc)
Unterschlupf gewähren
hard [hɑːd] adj (firm) hart; (difficult) schwer;
(harsh) hart(herzig) ♦ adv (work) hart; (try)
sehr; (push, hit) fest; **no ~ feelings!** ich
nehme es dir nicht übel; **~ of hearing**
schwerhörig; **to be ~ done by** übel dran
sein; **~back** n kartonierte Ausgabe f; **~
cash** n Bargeld nt; **~ disk** n (COMPUT)
Festplatte f; **~en** vt erhärten; (fig) verhärten
♦ vi hart werden; (fig) sich verhärten; **~-
headed** adj nüchtern; **~ labour** n
Zwangsarbeit f
hardly ['hɑːdlɪ] adv kaum
hard: ~ship n Not f; **~ shoulder** (BRIT) n
(AUT) Seitenstreifen m; **~ up** adj knapp bei
Kasse; **~ware** n Eisenwaren pl; (COMPUT)
Hardware f; **~ware shop** n
Eisenwarenhandlung f; **~-wearing** adj
strapazierfähig; **~-working** adj fleißig
hardy ['hɑːdɪ] adj widerstandsfähig
hare [hɛəʳ] n Hase m; **~-brained** adj
schwachsinnig
harm [hɑːm] n Schaden m ♦ vt schaden
+dat; **out of ~'s way** in Sicherheit; **~ful** adj
schädlich; **~less** adj harmlos
harmonica [hɑːˈmɒnɪkə] n Mundharmonika
f
harmonious [hɑːˈməʊnɪəs] adj harmonisch
harmonize ['hɑːmənaɪz] vt abstimmen ♦ vi
harmonieren
harmony ['hɑːmənɪ] n Harmonie f
harness ['hɑːnɪs] n Geschirr nt ♦ vt (horse)
anschirren; (fig) nutzbar machen
harp [hɑːp] n Harfe f ♦ vi: **to ~ on about sth**
auf etw dat herumreiten
harpoon [hɑːˈpuːn] n Harpune f
harrowing ['hærəʊɪŋ] adj nervenaufreibend
harsh [hɑːʃ] adj (rough) rau; (severe) streng;
~ness n Härte f
harvest ['hɑːvɪst] n Ernte f ♦ vt, vi ernten
has [hæz] vb see **have**
hash [hæʃ] vt klein hacken ♦ n (mess)
Kuddelmuddel m

hashish ['hæʃɪʃ] n Haschisch nt
hasn't ['hæznt] = **has not**
hassle ['hæsl] (inf) n Theater nt
haste [heɪst] n Eile f; **~n** ['heɪsn] vt
beschleunigen ♦ vi eilen; **hasty** adj hastig
(rash) vorschnell
hat [hæt] n Hut m
hatch [hætʃ] n (NAUT: also: **~way**) Luke f; (
house) Durchreiche f ♦ vi (young)
ausschlüpfen ♦ vt (brood) ausbrüten; (plo
aushecken; **~back** n (AUT) (Aut
nt mit) Heckklappe f
hatchet ['hætʃɪt] n Beil nt
hate [heɪt] vt hassen ♦ n Hass m; **~ful** adj
verhasst
hatred ['heɪtrɪd] n Hass m
haughty ['hɔːtɪ] adj hochnäsig, überheblic
haul [hɔːl] vt ziehen ♦ n (catch) Fang m;
~age n Spedition f; **~ier** (US **hauler**) n
Spediteur m
haunch [hɔːntʃ] n Lende f
haunt [hɔːnt] vt (ghost) spuken in +dat;
(memory) verfolgen; (pub) häufig besuche
♦ n Lieblingsplatz m; **the castle is ~ed** in
dem Schloss spukt es

KEYWORD

have [hæv] (pt, pp **had**) aux vb **1** haben; (
with vbs of motion) sein; **to have arrived/
slept** angekommen sein/geschlafen habe
to have been gewesen sein; **having eate**
or **when he had eaten, he left** nachdem
er gegessen hatte, ging er
2 (in tag questions): **you've done it,
haven't you?** du hast es doch gemacht,
oder nicht?
3 (in short answers and questions): **you've
made a mistake – so I have/no I haven**
du hast einen Fehler gemacht – ja,
stimmt/nein; **we haven't paid – yes we
have!** wir haben nicht bezahlt – doch; **I'v
been there before, have you?** ich war
schon einmal da, du auch?
♦ modal aux vb (be obliged): **to have (got)**
to do sth etw tun müssen; **you haven't t
tell her** du darfst es ihr nicht erzählen
♦ vt **1** (possess) haben; **he has (got) blue**

eyes er hat blaue Augen; **I have (got) an idea** ich habe eine Idee
2 (*referring to meals etc*): **to have breakfast/a cigarette** frühstücken/eine Zigarette rauchen
3 (*receive, obtain etc*) haben; **may I have your address?** kann ich Ihre Adresse haben?; **to have a baby** ein Kind bekommen
4 (*maintain, allow*): **he will have it that he is right** er besteht darauf, dass er Recht hat; **I won't have it** das lasse ich mir nicht bieten
5: to have sth done etw machen lassen; **to have sb do sth** jdn etw machen lassen; **he soon had them all laughing** er brachte sie alle zum Lachen
6 (*experience, suffer*): **she had her bag stolen** man hat ihr die Tasche gestohlen; **he had his arm broken** er hat sich den Arm gebrochen
7 (*+noun: take, hold etc*): **to have a walk/ rest** spazieren gehen/sich ausruhen; **to have a meeting/party** eine Besprechung/ Party haben
have out *vt*: **to have it out with sb** (*settle problem*) etw mit jdm bereden

aven ['heivn] *n* Zufluchtsort *m*
aven't ['hævnt] = **have not**
avoc ['hævək] *n* Verwüstung *f*
awk [hɔːk] *n* Habicht *m*
ay [hei] *n* Heu *nt*; ~ **fever** *n* Heuschnupfen *m*; ~**stack** *n* Heuschober *m*
aywire ['heiwaiəʳ] (*inf*) *adj* durcheinander
azard ['hæzəd] *n* Risiko *nt* ♦ *vt* aufs Spiel setzen; ~**ous** *adj* gefährlich; ~ **(warning) lights** *npl* (*AUT*) Warnblinklicht *nt*
aze [heiz] *n* Dunst *m*
azelnut ['heizlnʌt] *n* Haselnuss *f*
azy ['heizi] *adj* (*misty*) dunstig; (*vague*) verschwommen
e [hiː] *pron* er
ead [hed] *n* Kopf *m*; (*leader*) Leiter *m* ♦ *vt* (an)führen, leiten; (*ball*) köpfen; ~**s (or tails)** Kopf (oder Zahl); ~ **first** mit dem Kopf nach unten; ~ **over heels** kopfüber;

~ **for** *vt fus* zugehen auf +*acc*; ~**ache** *n* Kopfschmerzen *pl*; ~**dress** *n* Kopfschmuck *m*; ~**ing** *n* Überschrift *f*; ~**lamp** (*BRIT*) *n* Scheinwerfer *m*; ~**land** *n* Landspitze *f*; ~**light** *n* Scheinwerfer *m*; ~**line** *n* Schlagzeile *f*; ~**long** *adv* kopfüber; ~**master** *n* (*of primary school*) Rektor *m*; (*of secondary school*) Direktor *m*; ~**mistress** *n* Rektorin *f*; Direktorin *f*; ~**office** *n* Zentrale *f*; ~**-on** *adj* Frontal-; ~**phones** *npl* Kopfhörer *pl*; ~**quarters** *npl* Zentrale *f*; (*MIL*) Hauptquartier *nt*; ~**rest** *n* Kopfstütze *f*; ~**room** *n* (*of bridges etc*) lichte Höhe *f*; ~**scarf** *n* Kopftuch *nt*; ~**strong** *adj* eigenwillig; ~**teacher** (*BRIT*) *n* Schulleiter(in) *m(f)*; (*of secondary school also*) Direktor(in) *m*; ~ **waiter** *n* Oberkellner *m*; ~**way** *n* Fortschritte *pl*; ~**wind** *n* Gegenwind *m*; ~**y** *adj* berauschend
heal [hiːl] *vt* heilen ♦ *vi* verheilen
health [helθ] *n* Gesundheit *f*; ~ **food** *n* Reformkost *f*; **H~ Service** (*BRIT*) *n*: **the H~ Service** das Gesundheitswesen; ~**y** *adj* gesund
heap [hiːp] *n* Haufen *m* ♦ *vt* häufen
hear [hiəʳ] (*pt, pp* **heard**) *vt* hören; (*listen to*) anhören ♦ *vi* hören; ~**d** [həːd] *pt, pp of* **hear**; ~**ing** *n* Gehör *nt*; (*JUR*) Verhandlung *f*; ~**ing aid** *n* Hörapparat *m*; ~**say** *n* Hörensagen *nt*
hearse [həːs] *n* Leichenwagen *m*
heart [haːt] *n* Herz *nt*; ~**s** *npl* (*CARDS*) Herz *nt*; **by ~** auswendig; ~ **attack** *n* Herzanfall *m*; ~**beat** *n* Herzschlag *m*; ~**breaking** *adj* herzzerbrechend; ~**broken** *adj* untröstlich; ~**burn** *n* Sodbrennen *nt*; ~ **failure** *n* Herzschlag *m*; ~**felt** *adj* aufrichtig
hearth [haːθ] *n* Herd *m*
heartily ['haːtili] *adv* herzlich; (*eat*) herzhaft
heartless ['haːtlis] *adj* herzlos
hearty ['haːti] *adj* kräftig; (*friendly*) freundlich
heat [hiːt] *n* Hitze *f*; (*of food, water etc*) Wärme *f*; (*SPORT: also*: **qualifying ~**) Ausscheidungsrunde *f* ♦ *vt* (*house*) heizen; (*substance*) heiß machen, erhitzen; ~ **up** *vi* warm werden ♦ *vt* aufwärmen; ~**ed** *adj* erhitzt; (*fig*) hitzig; ~**er** *n* (Heiz)ofen *m*

heath [hi:θ] (*BRIT*) *n* Heide *f*
heathen ['hi:ðən] *n* Heide *m*/Heidin *f* ♦ *adj* heidnisch, Heiden-
heather ['heðə'] *n* Heidekraut *nt*
heat: ~**ing** *n* Heizung *f*; ~~**seeking** *adj* Wärme suchend; ~**stroke** *n* Hitzschlag *m*; ~ **wave** *n* Hitzewelle *f*
heave [hi:v] *vt* hochheben; (*sigh*) ausstoßen ♦ *vi* wogen; (*breast*) sich heben ♦ *n* Heben *nt*
heaven ['hevn] *n* Himmel *m*; ~**ly** *adj* himmlisch
heavily ['hevili] *adv* schwer
heavy ['hevi] *adj* schwer; ~ **goods vehicle** *n* Lastkraftwagen *m*; ~**weight** *n* (*SPORT*) Schwergewicht *nt*
Hebrew ['hi:bru:] *adj* hebräisch ♦ *n* (*LING*) Hebräisch *nt*
Hebrides ['hebridi:z] *npl* Hebriden *pl*
heckle ['hekl] *vt* unterbrechen
hectic ['hektik] *adj* hektisch
he'd [hi:d] = **he had; he would**
hedge [hedʒ] *n* Hecke *f* ♦ *vt* einzäunen ♦ *vi* (*fig*) ausweichen; **to ~ one's bets** sich absichern
hedgehog ['hedʒhɔg] *n* Igel *m*
heed [hi:d] *vt* (*also:* **take ~ of**) beachten ♦ *n* Beachtung *f*; ~**less** *adj* achtlos
heel [hi:l] *n* Ferse *f*; (*of shoe*) Absatz *m* ♦ *vt* mit Absätzen versehen
hefty ['hefti] *adj* (*person*) stämmig; (*portion*) reichlich
heifer ['hefə'] *n* Färse *f*
height [hait] *n* (*of person*) Größe *f*; (*of object*) Höhe *f*; ~**en** *vt* erhöhen
heir [eə'] *n* Erbe *m*; ~**ess** ['ɛəres] *n* Erbin *f*; ~**loom** *n* Erbstück *nt*
held [held] *pt*, *pp of* **hold**
helicopter ['helikɔptə'] *n* Hubschrauber *m*
heliport ['helipɔ:t] *n* Hubschrauber-landeplatz *m*
hell [hel] *n* Hölle *f* ♦ *excl* verdammt!
he'll [hi:l] = **he will; he shall**
hellish ['heliʃ] *adj* höllisch, verteufelt
hello [hə'ləu] *excl* hallo
helm [helm] *n* Ruder *nt*, Steuer *nt*
helmet ['helmit] *n* Helm *m*

help [help] *n* Hilfe *f* ♦ *vt* helfen +*dat*; **I can't ~ it** ich kann nichts dafür; ~ **yourself** bedienen Sie sich; ~**er** *n* Helfer *m*; ~**ful** *adj* hilfreich; ~**ing** *n* Portion *f*; ~**less** *adj* hilflos
hem [hem] *n* Saum *m* ♦ *vt* säumen; ~ **in** *vt* einengen
hemorrhage ['heməridʒ] (*US*) *n* = **haemorrhage**
hemorrhoids ['hemərɔidz] (*US*) *npl* = **haemorrhoids**
hen [hen] *n* Henne *f*
hence [hens] *adv* von jetzt an; (*therefore*) daher; ~**forth** *adv* von nun an; (*from then on*) von da an
henchman ['hentʃmən] (*irreg*) *n* Gefolgsmann *m*
her [hə:'] *pron* (*acc*) sie; (*dat*) ihr ♦ *adj* ihr; *see also* **me; my**
herald ['herəld] *n* (Vor)bote *m* ♦ *vt* verkünden
heraldry ['herəldri] *n* Wappenkunde *f*
herb [hə:b] *n* Kraut *nt*
herd [hə:d] *n* Herde *f*
here [hiə'] *adv* hier; (*to this place*) hierher; ~**after** [hiər'ɑ:ftə'] *adv* hernach, künftig ♦ *n* Jenseits *nt*; ~**by** [hiə'bai] *adv* hiermit
hereditary [hi'reditri] *adj* erblich
heredity [hi'rediti] *n* Vererbung *f*
heritage ['heritidʒ] *n* Erbe *nt*
hermit ['hə:mit] *n* Einsiedler *m*
hernia ['hə:niə] *n* Bruch *m*
hero ['hiərəu] (*pl* ~**es**) *n* Held *m*; ~**ic** [hi'rəuik] *adj* heroisch
heroin ['herəuin] *n* Heroin *nt*
heroine ['herəuin] *n* Heldin *f*
heroism ['herəuizəm] *n* Heldentum *nt*
heron ['herən] *n* Reiher *m*
herring ['heriŋ] *n* Hering *m*
hers [hə:z] *pron* ihre(r, s); *see also* **mine**[2]
herself [hə:'self] *pron* sich (selbst); (*emphat*) selbst; *see also* **oneself**
he's [hi:z] = **he is; he has**
hesitant ['hezitənt] *adj* zögernd
hesitate ['heziteit] *vi* zögern; **hesitation** [hezi'teiʃən] *n* Zögern *nt*
heterosexual ['hetərəu'seksjuəl] *adj* heterosexuell ♦ *n* Heterosexuelle(r) *mf*

ew [hju:] (*pt* **hewed**, *pp* **hewn**) *vt* hauen, hacken

exagonal [hɛkˈsægənl] *adj* sechseckig

eyday [ˈheɪdeɪ] *n* Blüte *f*, Höhepunkt *m*

GV *n abbr* = **heavy goods vehicle**

i [haɪ] *excl* he, hallo

ibernate [ˈhaɪbəneɪt] *vi* Winterschlaf *m* halten; **hibernation** [haɪbəˈneɪʃən] *n* Winterschlaf *m*

iccough [ˈhɪkʌp] *vi* den Schluckauf haben; **~s** *npl* Schluckauf *m*

iccup [ˈhɪkʌp] = **hiccough**

id [hɪd] *pt of* **hide**; **~den** [ˈhɪdn] *pp of* **hide**

ide [haɪd] (*pt* **hid**, *pp* **hidden**) *n* (*skin*) Haut *f*, Fell *nt* ♦ *vt* verstecken ♦ *vi* sich verstecken; **~-and-seek** *n* Versteckspiel *nt*; **~away** *n* Versteck *nt*

ideous [ˈhɪdɪəs] *adj* abscheulich

iding [ˈhaɪdɪŋ] *n* (*beating*) Tracht *f* Prügel; **to be in ~** (*concealed*) sich versteckt halten; **~ place** *n* Versteck *nt*

i-fi [ˈhaɪfaɪ] *n* Hi-Fi *nt* ♦ *adj* Hi-Fi-

igh [haɪ] *adj* hoch; (*wind*) stark ♦ *adv* hoch; **it is 20m ~** es ist 20 Meter hoch; **~brow** *adj* (*betont*) intellektuell; **~chair** *n* Hochstuhl *m*; **~er education** *n* Hochschulbildung *f*; **~-handed** *adj* eigenmächtig; **~-heeled** *adj* hochhackig; **~ jump** *n* (*SPORT*) Hochsprung *m*; **H~lands** *npl*: **the H~lands** das schottische Hochland; **~light** *n* (*fig*) Höhepunkt *m* ♦ *vt* hervorheben; **~ly** *adv* höchst; **~ly strung** *adj* überempfindlich; **~ness** *n* Höhe *f*; **Her H~ness** Ihre Hoheit *f*; **~-pitched** *adj* hoch; **~-rise block** *n* Hochhaus *nt*; **~ school** (*US*) *n* Oberschule *f*; **~ season** (*BRIT*) *n* Hochsaison *f*; **~ street** (*BRIT*) *n* Hauptstraße *f*

ighway [ˈhaɪweɪ] *n* Landstraße *f*; **H~ Code** (*BRIT*) *n* Straßenverkehrsordnung *f*

ijack [ˈhaɪdʒæk] *vt* entführen; **~er** *n* Entführer(in) *m(f)*

ike [haɪk] *vi* wandern ♦ *n* Wanderung *f*; **~r** *n* Wanderer *m*; **hiking** *n* Wandern *nt*

ilarious [hɪˈlɛərɪəs] *adj* lustig

ill [hɪl] *n* Berg *m*; **~side** *n* (Berg)hang *m*; **~ walking** *n* Bergwandern *nt*; **~y** *adj* hügelig

hilt [hɪlt] *n* Heft *nt*; **(up) to the ~** ganz und gar

him [hɪm] *pron* (*acc*) ihn; (*dat*) ihm; *see also* **me**; **~self** *pron* sich (selbst); (*emphatic*) selbst; *see also* **oneself**

hind [haɪnd] *adj* hinter, Hinter-

hinder [ˈhɪndər] *vt* (*stop*) hindern; (*delay*) behindern; **hindrance** *n* (*delay*) Behinderung *f*; (*obstacle*) Hindernis *nt*

hindsight [ˈhaɪndsaɪt] *n*: **with ~** im nachhinein

Hindu [ˈhɪnduː] *n* Hindu *m*

hinge [hɪndʒ] *n* Scharnier *nt*; (*on door*) Türangel *f* ♦ *vi* (*fig*): **to ~ on** abhängen von

hint [hɪnt] *n* Tipp *m*; (*trace*) Anflug *m* ♦ *vt*: **to ~ that** andeuten, dass ♦ *vi*: **to ~ at** andeuten

hip [hɪp] *n* Hüfte *f*

hippie [ˈhɪpɪ] *n* Hippie *m*

hippo [ˈhɪpəu] (*inf*) *n* Nilpferd *nt*

hippopotami [hɪpəˈpɔtəmaɪ] *npl of* **hippopotamus**

hippopotamus [hɪpəˈpɔtəməs] (*pl* **~es** *or* **hippopotami**) *n* Nilpferd *nt*

hire [ˈhaɪər] *vt* (*worker*) anstellen; (*BRIT: car*) mieten ♦ *n* Miete *f*; **for ~** (*taxi*) frei; **~(d) car** (*BRIT*) *n* Mietwagen *m*, Leihwagen *m*; **~ purchase** (*BRIT*) *n* Teilzahlungskauf *m*

his [hɪz] *adj* sein ♦ *pron* seine(r, s); *see also* **my**; **mine²**

hiss [hɪs] *vi* zischen ♦ *n* Zischen *nt*

historian [hɪˈstɔːrɪən] *n* Historiker *m*

historic [hɪˈstɔrɪk] *adj* historisch; **~al** *adj* historisch, geschichtlich

history [ˈhɪstərɪ] *n* Geschichte *f*

hit [hɪt] (*pt*, *pp* **hit**) *vt* schlagen; (*injure*) treffen ♦ *n* (*blow*) Schlag *m*; (*success*) Erfolg *m*; (*MUS*) Hit *m*; **to ~ it off with sb** prima mit jdm auskommen; **~-and-run driver** *n* jemand, der Fahrerflucht begeht

hitch [hɪtʃ] *vt* festbinden; (*also: ~ up*) hochziehen ♦ *n* (*difficulty*) Haken *m*; **to ~ a lift** trampen; **~hike** *vi* trampen; **~hiker** *n* Tramper *m*; **~hiking** *n* Trampen *nt*

hi-tech [ˈhaɪtɛk] *adj* Hightech- ♦ *n* Spitzentechnologie *f*

hitherto [hɪðəˈtuː] *adv* bislang

hit man (inf) (irreg) n Killer m

HIV n abbr: **HIV-negative/-positive** HIV-negativ/-positiv

hive [haɪv] n Bienenkorb m

HMS abbr = **His/Her Majesty's Ship**

hoard [hɔːd] n Schatz m ♦ vt horten, hamstern

hoarding ['hɔːdɪŋ] n Bretterzaun m; (BRIT: for posters) Reklamewand f

hoarse [hɔːs] adj heiser, rau

hoax [həʊks] n Streich m

hob [hɒb] n Kochmulde f

hobble ['hɒbl] vi humpeln

hobby ['hɒbɪ] n Hobby nt

hobby-horse ['hɒbɪhɔːs] n (fig) Steckenpferd nt

hobo ['həʊbəʊ] (US) n Tippelbruder m

hockey ['hɒkɪ] n Hockey nt

hoe [həʊ] n Hacke f ♦ vt hacken

hog [hɒg] n Schlachtschwein m ♦ vt mit Beschlag belegen; **to go the whole ~** aufs Ganze gehen

hoist [hɔɪst] n Winde f ♦ vt hochziehen

hold [həʊld] (pt, pp **held**) vt halten; (contain) enthalten; (be able to contain) fassen; (breath) anhalten; (meeting) abhalten ♦ vi (withstand pressure) aushalten ♦ n (grasp) Halt m; (NAUT) Schiffsraum m; **~ the line!** (TEL) bleiben Sie am Apparat!; **to ~ one's own** sich behaupten; **~ back** vt zurückhalten; **~ down** vt niederhalten; (job) behalten; **~ off** vt (enemy) abwehren; **~ on** vi sich festhalten; (resist) durchhalten; (wait) warten; **~ on to** vt fus festhalten an +dat; (keep) behalten; **~ out** vt hinhalten ♦ vi aushalten; **~ up** vt (delay) aufhalten; (rob) überfallen; **~all** (BRIT) n Reisetasche f; **~er** n Behälter m; **~ing** n (share) (Aktien)anteil m; **~up** n (BRIT: in traffic) Stockung f; (robbery) Überfall m; (delay) Verzögerung f

hole [həʊl] n Loch nt; **~ in the wall** (inf) n (cash dispenser) Geldautomat m

holiday ['hɒlɪdeɪ] n (day) Feiertag m; freie(r) Tag m; (vacation) Urlaub m; (SCH) Ferien pl; **~-maker** (BRIT) n Urlauber(in) m(f); **~ resort** n Ferienort m

Holland ['hɒlənd] n Holland nt

hollow ['hɒləʊ] adj hohl; (fig) leer ♦ n Vertiefung f; **~ out** vt aushöhlen

holly ['hɒlɪ] n Stechpalme f

holocaust ['hɒləkɔːst] n Inferno nt

holster ['həʊlstər] n Pistolenhalfter m

holy ['həʊlɪ] adj heilig; **H~ Ghost** or **Spirit** n: **the H~ Ghost** or **Spirit** der Heilige Geist

homage ['hɒmɪdʒ] n Huldigung f; **to pay to** huldigen +dat

home [həʊm] n Zuhause nt; (institution) Heim nt, Anstalt f ♦ adj einheimisch; (POL) inner ♦ adv heim, nach Hause; **at ~** zu Hause; **~ address** n Heimatadresse f; **~coming** n Heimkehr f; **~land** n Heimat(land nt) f; **~less** adj obdachlos; **~ly** adj häuslich; (US: ugly) unscheinbar; **~ made** adj selbst gemacht; **~ match** adj Heimspiel nt; **H~ Office** (BRIT) n Innenministerium nt; **~ page** n (COMPUT) Homepage f; **~ rule** n Selbstverwaltung f; **H~ Secretary** (BRIT) n Innenminister(in) m(f); **~sick** adj: **to be ~sick** Heimweh haben; **~ town** n Heimatstadt f; **~ward** adj (journey) Heim-; **~work** n Hausaufgaben pl

homicide ['hɒmɪsaɪd] (US) n Totschlag m

homoeopathic [həʊmɪə'pæθɪk] (US **homeopathic**) adj homöopathisch; **homoeopathy** [həʊmɪ'ɒpəθɪ] (US **homeopathy**) n Homöopathie f

homogeneous [hɒməʊ'dʒiːnɪəs] adj homogen

homosexual [hɒməʊ'seksjʊəl] adj homosexuell ♦ n Homosexuelle(r) mf

honest ['ɒnɪst] adj ehrlich; **~ly** adv ehrlich; **~y** n Ehrlichkeit f

honey ['hʌnɪ] n Honig m; **~comb** n Honigwabe f; **~moon** n Flitterwochen pl, Hochzeitsreise f; **~suckle** ['hʌnɪsʌkl] n Geißblatt nt

honk [hɒŋk] vi hupen

honor etc ['ɒnər] (US) vt, n = **honour** etc

honorary ['ɒnərərɪ] adj Ehren-

honour ['ɒnər] (US **honor**) vt ehren; (cheque) einlösen ♦ n Ehre f; **~able** adj ehrenwert; (intention) ehrenhaft; **~s degree** n (UNIV) akademischer Grad mit Prüfung im

Spezialfach

hood [hud] *n* Kapuze *f*; (*BRIT: AUT*) Verdeck *nt*; (*US: AUT*) Kühlerhaube *f*

hoof [hu:f] (*pl* **hooves**) *n* Huf *m*

hook [huk] *n* Haken *m* ♦ *vt* einhaken

hooligan ['hu:lɪgən] *n* Rowdy *m*

hoop [hu:p] *n* Reifen *m*

hooray [hu:'reɪ] *excl* = **hurrah**

hoot [hu:t] *vi* (*AUT*) hupen; **~er** *n* (*NAUT*) Dampfpfeife *f*; (*BRIT: AUT*) (Auto)hupe *f*

Hoover ['hu:vər] (®; *BRIT*) *n* Staubsauger *m* ♦ *vt*: **to h~** staubsaugen, Staub saugen

hooves [hu:vz] *npl pl of* **hoof**

hop [hɔp] *vi* hüpfen, hopsen ♦ *n* (*jump*) Hopser *m*

hope [həup] *vt, vi* hoffen ♦ *n* Hoffnung *f*; **I ~ so/not** hoffentlich/hoffentlich nicht; **~ful** *adj* hoffnungsvoll; (*promising*) viel versprechend; **~fully** *adv* hoffentlich; **~less** *adj* hoffnungslos

hops [hɔps] *npl* Hopfen *m*

horizon [hə'raɪzn] *n* Horizont *m*; **~tal** [hɔrɪ'zɔntl] *adj* horizontal

hormone ['hɔ:məun] *n* Hormon *nt*

horn [hɔ:n] *n* Horn *nt*; (*AUT*) Hupe *f*

hornet ['hɔ:nɪt] *n* Hornisse *f*

horny ['hɔ:nɪ] *adj* schwielig; (*US: inf*) scharf

horoscope ['hɔrəskəup] *n* Horoskop *nt*

horrendous [hə'rendəs] *adj* (*crime*) abscheulich; (*error*) schrecklich

horrible ['hɔrɪbl] *adj* fürchterlich

horrid ['hɔrɪd] *adj* scheußlich

horrify ['hɔrɪfaɪ] *vt* entsetzen

horror ['hɔrər] *n* Schrecken *m*; **~ film** *n* Horrorfilm *m*

hors d'oeuvre [ɔ:'də:vrə] *n* Vorspeise *f*

horse [hɔ:s] *n* Pferd *nt*; **~back** *n*: **on ~back** beritten; **~ chestnut** *n* Rosskastanie *f*; **~man/woman** (*irreg*) *n* Reiter(in) *m(f)*; **~power** *n* Pferdestärke *f*; **~-racing** *n* Pferderennen *nt*; **~radish** *n* Meerrettich *m*; **~shoe** *n* Hufeisen *nt*

horticulture ['hɔ:tɪkʌltʃər] *n* Gartenbau *m*

hose [həuz] *n* (*also:* **~pipe**) Schlauch *m*

hosiery ['həuzɪərɪ] *n* Strumpfwaren *pl*

hospitable ['hɔspɪtəbl] *adj* gastfreundlich

hospital ['hɔspɪtl] *n* Krankenhaus *nt*

hospitality [hɔspɪ'tælɪtɪ] *n* Gastfreundschaft *f*

host [həust] *n* Gastgeber *m*; (*innkeeper*) (Gast)wirt *m*; (*large number*) Heerschar *f*; (*ECCL*) Hostie *f*

hostage ['hɔstɪdʒ] *n* Geisel *f*

hostel ['hɔstl] *n* Herberge *f*; (*also:* **youth ~**) Jugendherberge *f*

hostess ['həustɪs] *n* Gastgeberin *f*

hostile ['hɔstaɪl] *adj* feindlich; **hostility** [hɔ'stɪlɪtɪ] *n* Feindschaft *f*; **hostilities** *npl* (*fighting*) Feindseligkeiten *pl*

hot [hɔt] *adj* heiß; (*food, water*) warm; (*spiced*) scharf; **I'm ~** mir ist heiß; **~bed** (*fig*) Nährboden *m*; **~ dog** *n* heiße(s) Würstchen *nt*

hotel [həu'tel] *n* Hotel *nt*; **~ier** [həu'telɪər] *n* Hotelier *m*

hot: ~house *n* Treibhaus *nt*; **~ line** *n* (*POL*) heiße(r) Draht *m*; **~ly** *adv* (*argue*) hitzig; **~plate** *n* Kochplatte *f*; **~pot** ['hɔtpɔt] *n* (*BRIT*) *n* Fleischeintopf *m*; **~-water bottle** *n* Wärmflasche *f*

hound [haund] *n* Jagdhund *m* ♦ *vt* hetzen

hour ['auər] *n* Stunde *f*; (*time of day*) (Tages)zeit *f*; **~ly** *adj, adv* stündlich

house [*n* haus, *vb* hauz] *n* Haus *nt* ♦ *vt* unterbringen; **on the ~** auf Kosten des Hauses; **~ arrest** *n* (*POL, MIL*) Hausarrest *m*; **~boat** *n* Hausboot *nt*; **~breaking** *n* Einbruch *m*; **~coat** *n* Morgenmantel *m*; **~hold** *n* Haushalt *m*; **~keeper** *n* Haushälterin *f*; **~keeping** *n* Haushaltung *f*; **~-warming party** *n* Einweihungsparty *f*; **~wife** (*irreg*) *n* Hausfrau *f*; **~work** *n* Hausarbeit *f*

housing ['hauzɪŋ] *n* (*act*) Unterbringung *f*; (*houses*) Wohnungen *pl*; (*POL*) Wohnungsbau *m*; (*covering*) Gehäuse *nt*; **~ estate** (*US* **~ development**) *n* (Wohn)siedlung *f*

hovel ['hɔvl] *n* elende Hütte *f*

hover ['hɔvər] *vi* (*bird*) schweben; (*person*) herumstehen; **~craft** *n* Luftkissenfahrzeug *nt*

how [hau] *adv* wie; **~ are you?** wie geht es Ihnen?; **~ much milk?** wie viel Milch?; **~**

many people? wie viele Leute?

however [hau'ɛvə'] *adv (but)* (je)doch, aber; **~ you phrase it** wie Sie es auch ausdrücken

howl [haul] *n* Heulen *nt ♦ vi* heulen

H.P. *abbr* = **hire purchase**

h.p. *abbr* = **horsepower**

H.Q. *abbr* = **headquarters**

HTML *abbr (= hypertext markup language)* HTML

hub [hʌb] *n* Radnabe *f*

hubbub ['hʌbʌb] *n* Tumult *m*

hubcap ['hʌbkæp] *n* Radkappe *f*

huddle ['hʌdl] *vi:* **to ~ together** sich zusammendrängen

hue [hju:] *n* Färbung *f*; **~ and cry** *n* Zetergeschrei *nt*

huff [hʌf] *n:* **to go into a ~** einschnappen

hug [hʌg] *vt* umarmen *♦ n* Umarmung *f*

huge [hju:dʒ] *adj* groß, riesig

hulk [hʌlk] *n (ship)* abgetakelte(s) Schiff *nt; (person)* Koloss *m*

hull [hʌl] *n* Schiffsrumpf *m*

hullo [hə'ləu] *excl* = **hello**

hum [hʌm] *vt, vi* summen

human ['hju:mən] *adj* menschlich *♦ n (also: ~ being)* Mensch *m*

humane [hju:'meɪn] *adj* human

humanitarian [hju:mænɪ'tɛərɪən] *adj* humanitär

humanity [hju:'mænɪtɪ] *n* Menschheit *f; (kindliness)* Menschlichkeit *f*

humble ['hʌmbl] *adj* demütig; *(modest)* bescheiden *♦ vt* demütigen

humbug ['hʌmbʌg] *n* Humbug *m; (BRIT: sweet)* Pfefferminzbonbon *nt*

humdrum ['hʌmdrʌm] *adj* stumpfsinnig

humid ['hju:mɪd] *adj* feucht; **~ity** [hju:'mɪdɪtɪ] *n* Feuchtigkeit *f*

humiliate [hju:'mɪlɪeɪt] *vt* demütigen; **humiliation** [hju:mɪlɪ'eɪʃən] *n* Demütigung *f*

humility [hju:'mɪlɪtɪ] *n* Demut *f*

humor ['hju:mə'] *(US) n, vt* = **humour**

humorous ['hju:mərəs] *adj* humorvoll

humour ['hju:mə'] *(US* **humor**) *n (fun)* Humor *m; (mood)* Stimmung *f ♦ vt* bei Stimmung halten

hump [hʌmp] *n* Buckel *m*

hunch [hʌntʃ] *n* Buckel *m; (premonition)* (Vor)ahnung *f*; **~back** *n* Bucklige(r) *mf*; **~ed** *adj* gekrümmt

hundred ['hʌndrəd] *num* hundert; **~weight** *n* Zentner *m (BRIT = 50.8 kg; US = 45.3 kg)*

hung [hʌŋ] *pt, pp of* **hang**

Hungarian [hʌŋ'gɛərɪən] *adj* ungarisch *♦ n* Ungar(in) *m(f); (LING)* Ungarisch *nt*

Hungary ['hʌŋgərɪ] *n* Ungarn *nt*

hunger ['hʌŋgə'] *n* Hunger *m ♦ vi* hungern

hungry ['hʌŋgrɪ] *adj* hungrig; **to be ~** Hunger haben

hunk [hʌŋk] *n (of bread)* Stück *nt*

hunt [hʌnt] *vt, vi* jagen *♦ n* Jagd *f*; **to ~ for** suchen; **~er** *n* Jäger *m*; **~ing** *n* Jagd *f*

hurdle ['hə:dl] *n (also fig)* Hürde *f*

hurl [hə:l] *vt* schleudern

hurrah [hu'rɑ:] *n* Hurra *nt*

hurray [hu'reɪ] *n* Hurra *nt*

hurricane ['hʌrɪkən] *n* Orkan *m*

hurried ['hʌrɪd] *adj* eilig; *(hasty)* übereilt; **~ly** *adv* übereilt, hastig

hurry ['hʌrɪ] *n* Eile *f ♦ vi* sich beeilen *♦ vt* (an)treiben; *(job)* übereilen; **to be in a ~** es eilig haben; **~ up** *vi* sich beeilen *♦ vt (person)* zur Eile antreiben; *(work)* vorantreiben

hurt [hə:t] *(pt, pp* **hurt**) *vt* wehtun +*dat; (injure, fig)* verletzen *♦ vi* wehtun; **~ful** *adj* schädlich; *(remark)* verletzend

hurtle ['hə:tl] *vi* sausen

husband ['hʌzbənd] *n* (Ehe)mann *m*

hush [hʌʃ] *n* Stille *f ♦ vt* zur Ruhe bringen *♦ excl* pst, still

husky ['hʌskɪ] *adj (voice)* rau *♦ n* Eskimohund *m*

hustle ['hʌsl] *vt (push)* stoßen; *(hurry)* antreiben *♦ n:* **~ and bustle** Geschäftigkeit *f*

hut [hʌt] *n* Hütte *f*

hutch [hʌtʃ] *n* (Kaninchen)stall *m*

hyacinth ['haɪəsɪnθ] *n* Hyazinthe *f*

hydrant ['haɪdrənt] *n (also:* **fire ~**) Hydrant *m*

hydraulic [haɪ'drɔ:lɪk] *adj* hydraulisch

hydroelectric ['haɪdrəu'lektrɪk] *adj (energy)* durch Wasserkraft erzeugt; **~ power station** *n* Wasserkraftwerk *nt*

hydrofoil ['haɪdrəfɔɪl] *n* Tragflügelboot *nt*

hydrogen ['haɪdrədʒən] *n* Wasserstoff *m*

hyena [haɪ'iːnə] *n* Hyäne *f*

hygiene ['haɪdʒiːn] *n* Hygiene *f*; **hygienic** [haɪ'dʒiːnɪk] *adj* hygienisch

hymn [hɪm] *n* Kirchenlied *nt*

hype [haɪp] (*inf*) *n* Publicity *f*

hypermarket ['haɪpəmɑːkɪt] (*BRIT*) *n* Hypermarket *m*

hypertext ['haɪpətekst] *n* (*COMPUT*) Hypertext *m*

hyphen ['haɪfn] *n* Bindestrich *m*

hypnosis [hɪp'nəʊsɪs] *n* Hypnose *f*

hypnotize ['hɪpnətaɪz] *vt* hypnotisieren

hypocrisy [hɪ'pɒkrɪsɪ] *n* Heuchelei *f*

hypocrite ['hɪpəkrɪt] *n* Heuchler *m*; **hypocritical** [hɪpə'krɪtɪkl] *adj* scheinheilig, heuchlerisch

hypothermia [haɪpə'θɜːmɪə] *n* Unterkühlung *f*

hypotheses [haɪ'pɒθɪsiːz] *npl of* **hypothesis**

hypothesis [haɪ'pɒθɪsɪs] (*pl* **hypotheses**) *n* Hypothese *f*

hypothetic(al) [haɪpəʊ'θetɪk(l)] *adj* hypothetisch

hysterical [hɪ'sterɪkl] *adj* hysterisch

hysterics [hɪ'sterɪks] *npl* hysterische(r) Anfall *m*

I, i

I [aɪ] *pron* ich

ice [aɪs] *n* Eis *nt* ♦ *vt* (*COOK*) mit Zuckerguss überziehen ♦ *vi* (*also:* ~ **up**) vereisen; ~ **axe** *n* Eispickel *m*; ~**berg** *n* Eisberg *m*; ~**box** (*US*) *n* Kühlschrank *m*; ~ **cream** *n* Eis *nt*; ~ **cube** *n* Eiswürfel *m*; ~**d** [aɪst] *adj* (*cake*) mit Zuckerguss überzogen, glasiert; (*tea, coffee*) Eis-; ~ **hockey** *n* Eishockey *nt*

Iceland ['aɪslənd] *n* Island *nt*

ice: ~ **lolly** (*BRIT*) *n* Eis *nt* am Stiel; ~ **rink** *n* (Kunst)eisbahn *f*; ~ **skating** *n* Schlittschuhlaufen *nt*

icicle ['aɪsɪkl] *n* Eiszapfen *m*

icing ['aɪsɪŋ] *n* (*on cake*) Zuckerguss *m*; (*on window*) Vereisung *f*; ~ **sugar** (*BRIT*) *n* Puderzucker *m*

icon ['aɪkɒn] *n* Ikone *f*; (*COMPUT*) Icon *nt*

icy ['aɪsɪ] *adj* (*slippery*) vereist; (*cold*) eisig

I'd [aɪd] = **I would**; **I had**

idea [aɪ'dɪə] *n* Idee *f*

ideal [aɪ'dɪəl] *n* Ideal *nt* ♦ *adj* ideal

identical [aɪ'dentɪkl] *adj* identisch; (*twins*) eineiig

identification [aɪdentɪfɪ'keɪʃən] *n* Identifizierung *f*; **means of** ~ Ausweispapiere *pl*

identify [aɪ'dentɪfaɪ] *vt* identifizieren; (*regard as the same*) gleichsetzen

Identikit [aɪ'dentɪkɪt] ® *n*: ~ **picture** *n* Phantombild *nt*

identity [aɪ'dentɪtɪ] *n* Identität *f*; ~ **card** *n* Personalausweis *m*

ideology [aɪdɪ'ɒlədʒɪ] *n* Ideologie *f*

idiom ['ɪdɪəm] *n* (*expression*) Redewendung *f*; (*dialect*) Idiom *nt*; ~**atic** [ɪdɪə'mætɪk] *adj* idiomatisch

idiosyncrasy [ɪdɪəʊ'sɪŋkrəsɪ] *n* Eigenart *f*

idiot ['ɪdɪət] *n* Idiot(in) *m(f)*; ~**ic** [ɪdɪ'ɒtɪk] *adj* idiotisch

idle ['aɪdl] *adj* (*doing nothing*) untätig; (*lazy*) faul; (*useless*) nutzlos; (*machine*) still(stehend); (*threat, talk*) leer ♦ *vi* (*machine*) leer laufen ♦ *vt*: **to ~ away the time** die Zeit vertrödeln; ~**ness** *n* Müßiggang *m*; Faulheit *f*

idol ['aɪdl] *n* Idol *nt*; ~**ize** *vt* vergöttern

i.e. *abbr* (= *id est*) d. h.

---KEYWORD---

if [ɪf] *conj* **1** wenn; (*in case also*) falls; **if I were you** wenn ich Sie wäre
2 (*although*): **(even) if** (selbst *or* auch) wenn
3 (*whether*) ob
4: **if so/not** wenn ja/nicht; **if only ...** wenn ... doch nur ...; **if only I could** wenn ich doch nur könnte; *see also* **as**

---

ignite [ɪg'naɪt] *vt* (an)zünden ♦ *vi* sich entzünden; **ignition** [ɪg'nɪʃən] *n* Zündung *f*; **to switch on/off the ignition** den Motor anlassen/abstellen; **ignition key** *n* (*AUT*) Zündschlüssel *m*

ignorance ['ɪgnərəns] *n* Unwissenheit *f*

ignorant ['ɪgnərənt] *adj* unwissend; **to be ~ of** nicht wissen

ignore [ɪg'nɔːʳ] *vt* ignorieren

I'll [aɪl] = **I will**; **I shall**

ill [ɪl] *adj* krank ♦ *n* Übel *nt* ♦ *adv* schlecht; **~-advised** *adj* unklug; **~-at-ease** *adj* unbehaglich

illegal [ɪ'liːgl] *adj* illegal

illegible [ɪ'ledʒɪbl] *adj* unleserlich

illegitimate [ɪlɪ'dʒɪtɪmət] *adj* unehelich

ill-fated [ɪl'feɪtɪd] *adj* unselig

ill feeling *n* Verstimmung *f*

illicit [ɪ'lɪsɪt] *adj* verboten

illiterate [ɪ'lɪtərət] *adj* ungebildet

ill-mannered [ɪl'mænəd] *adj* ungehobelt

illness ['ɪlnɪs] *n* Krankheit *f*

illogical [ɪ'lɒdʒɪkl] *adj* unlogisch

ill-treat [ɪl'triːt] *vt* misshandeln

illuminate [ɪ'luːmɪneɪt] *vt* beleuchten; **illumination** [ɪluːmɪ'neɪʃən] *n* Beleuchtung *f*; **illuminations** *pl* (*decorative lights*) festliche Beleuchtung *f*

illusion [ɪ'luːʒən] *n* Illusion *f*; **to be under the ~ that ...** sich *dat* einbilden, dass ...

illustrate ['ɪləstreɪt] *vt* (*book*) illustrieren; (*explain*) veranschaulichen; **illustration** [ɪlə'streɪʃən] *n* Illustration *f*; (*explanation*) Veranschaulichung *f*

illustrious [ɪ'lʌstrɪəs] *adj* berühmt

I'm [aɪm] = **I am**

image ['ɪmɪdʒ] *n* Bild *nt*; (*public ~*) Image *nt*; **~ry** *n* Symbolik *f*

imaginary [ɪ'mædʒɪnərɪ] *adj* eingebildet; (*world*) Fantasie-

imagination [ɪmædʒɪ'neɪʃən] *n* Einbildung *f*; (*creative*) Fantasie *f*

imaginative [ɪ'mædʒɪnətɪv] *adj* fantasiereich, einfallsreich

imagine [ɪ'mædʒɪn] *vt* sich vorstellen; (*wrongly*) sich einbilden

imbalance [ɪm'bæləns] *n* Unausgeglichenheit *f*

imbecile ['ɪmbəsiːl] *n* Schwachsinnige(r) *mf*

imitate ['ɪmɪteɪt] *vt* imitieren; **imitation** [ɪmɪ'teɪʃən] *n* Imitation *f*

immaculate [ɪ'mækjulət] *adj* makellos; (*dress*) tadellos; (*ECCL*) unbefleckt

immaterial [ɪmə'tɪərɪəl] *adj* unwesentlich; **it is ~ whether ...** es ist unwichtig, ob ...

immature [ɪmə'tjuəʳ] *adj* unreif

immediate [ɪ'miːdɪət] *adj* (*instant*) sofortig; (*near*) unmittelbar; (*relatives*) nächste(r, s); (*needs*) dringlich; **~ly** *adv* sofort; **~ly next to** direkt neben

immense [ɪ'mɛns] *adj* unermesslich

immerse [ɪ'məːs] *vt* eintauchen; **to be ~d in** (*fig*) vertieft sein in +*acc*

immersion heater [ɪ'məːʃən-] (*BRIT*) *n* Boiler *m*

immigrant ['ɪmɪgrənt] *n* Einwanderer *m*

immigrate ['ɪmɪgreɪt] *vi* einwandern; **immigration** [ɪmɪ'greɪʃən] *n* Einwanderung *f*

imminent ['ɪmɪnənt] *adj* bevorstehend

immobile [ɪ'məubaɪl] *adj* unbeweglich; **immobilize** [ɪ'məubɪlaɪz] *vt* lähmen

immoral [ɪ'mɔrl] *adj* unmoralisch; **~ity** [ɪmɔ'rælɪtɪ] *n* Unsittlichkeit *f*

immortal [ɪ'mɔːtl] *adj* unsterblich

immune [ɪ'mjuːn] *adj* (*secure*) sicher; (*MED*) immun; **~ from** sicher vor +*dat*; **immunity** *n* (*MED, JUR*) Immunität *f*; (*fig*) Freiheit *f*; **immunize** ['ɪmjunaɪz] *vt* immunisieren

impact ['ɪmpækt] *n* Aufprall *m*; (*fig*) Wirkung *f*

impair [ɪm'pɛəʳ] *vt* beeinträchtigen

impart [ɪm'pɑːt] *vt* mitteilen; (*knowledge*) vermitteln; (*exude*) abgeben

impartial [ɪm'pɑːʃl] *adj* unparteiisch

impassable [ɪm'pɑːsəbl] *adj* unpassierbar

impassive [ɪm'pæsɪv] *adj* gelassen

impatience [ɪm'peɪʃəns] *n* Ungeduld *f*; **impatient** *adj* ungeduldig; **impatiently** *adv* ungeduldig

impeccable [ɪm'pɛkəbl] *adj* tadellos

impede [ɪm'piːd] *vt* (be)hindern; **impediment** [ɪm'pɛdɪmənt] *n* Hindernis *nt*; **speech impediment** Sprachfehler *m*

impending [ɪm'pɛndɪŋ] *adj* bevorstehend

impenetrable [ɪm'pɛnɪtrəbl] *adj* (*also fig*) undurchdringlich

imperative [ɪm'pɛrətɪv] *adj* (*necessary*) unbedingt erforderlich

imperceptible [ɪmpəˈsɛptɪbl] *adj* nicht wahrnehmbar

imperfect [ɪmˈpəːfɪkt] *adj (faulty)* fehlerhaft; **~ion** [ɪmpəˈfɛkʃən] *n* Unvollkommenheit *f*; *(fault)* Fehler *m*

imperial [ɪmˈpɪərɪəl] *adj* kaiserlich

impersonal [ɪmˈpəːsənl] *adj* unpersönlich

impersonate [ɪmˈpəːsəneɪt] *vt* sich ausgeben als; *(for fun)* imitieren

impertinent [ɪmˈpəːtɪnənt] *adj* unverschämt, frech

impervious [ɪmˈpəːvɪəs] *adj (fig)*: **~ (to)** unempfänglich (für)

impetuous [ɪmˈpɛtjuəs] *adj* ungestüm

impetus [ˈɪmpətəs] *n* Triebkraft *f*; *(fig)* Auftrieb *m*

impinge [ɪmˈpɪndʒ]: **~ on** *vt* beeinträchtigen

implacable [ɪmˈplækəbl] *adj* unerbittlich

implement [*n* ˈɪmplɪmənt, *vb* ˈɪmplɪmɛnt] *n* Werkzeug *nt* ♦ *vt* ausführen

implicate [ˈɪmplɪkeɪt] *vt* verwickeln; **implication** [ɪmplɪˈkeɪʃən] *n (effect)* Auswirkung *f*; *(in crime)* Verwicklung *f*

implicit [ɪmˈplɪsɪt] *adj (suggested)* unausgesprochen; *(utter)* vorbehaltlos

implore [ɪmˈplɔːr] *vt* anflehen

imply [ɪmˈplaɪ] *vt (hint)* andeuten; *(be evidence for)* schließen lassen auf +acc

impolite [ɪmpəˈlaɪt] *adj* unhöflich

import [*vb* ɪmˈpɔːt, *n* ˈɪmpɔːt] *vt* einführen ♦ *n* Einfuhr *f*; *(meaning)* Bedeutung *f*

importance [ɪmˈpɔːtns] *n* Bedeutung *f*

important [ɪmˈpɔːtənt] *adj* wichtig; **it's not ~** es ist unwichtig

importer [ɪmˈpɔːtər] *n* Importeur *m*

impose [ɪmˈpəuz] *vt, vi*: **to ~ (on)** auferlegen (+dat); *(penalty, sanctions)* verhängen (gegen); **to ~ (o.s.) on sb** sich jdm aufdrängen

imposing [ɪmˈpəuzɪŋ] *adj* eindrucksvoll

imposition [ɪmpəˈzɪʃən] *n (of burden, fine)* Auferlegung *f*; **to be an ~** *(on person)* eine Zumutung sein

impossible [ɪmˈpɒsɪbl] *adj* unmöglich

impostor [ɪmˈpɒstər] *n* Hochstapler *m*

impotent [ˈɪmpətnt] *adj* machtlos; *(sexually)* impotent

impound [ɪmˈpaund] *vt* beschlagnahmen

impoverished [ɪmˈpɒvərɪʃt] *adj* verarmt

impracticable [ɪmˈpræktɪkəbl] *adj* undurchführbar

impractical [ɪmˈpræktɪkl] *adj* unpraktisch

imprecise [ɪmprɪˈsaɪs] *adj* ungenau

impregnable [ɪmˈprɛgnəbl] *adj (castle)* uneinnehmbar

impregnate [ˈɪmprɛgneɪt] *vt (saturate)* sättigen; *(fertilize)* befruchten

impress [ɪmˈprɛs] *vt (influence)* beeindrucken; *(imprint)* (auf)drücken; **to ~ sth on sb** jdm etw einschärfen; **~ed** *adj* beeindruckt; **~ion** [ɪmˈprɛʃən] *n* Eindruck *m*; *(on wax, footprint)* Abdruck *m*; *(of book)* Auflage *f*; *(take-off)* Nachahmung *f*; **I was under the ~ion** ich hatte den Eindruck; **~ionable** *adj* leicht zu beeindrucken; **~ive** *adj* eindrucksvoll

imprint [ˈɪmprɪnt] *n* Abdruck *m*

imprison [ɪmˈprɪzn] *vt* ins Gefängnis schicken; **~ment** *n* Inhaftierung *f*

improbable [ɪmˈprɒbəbl] *adj* unwahrscheinlich

impromptu [ɪmˈprɒmptjuː] *adj, adv* aus dem Stegreif, improvisiert

improper [ɪmˈprɒpər] *adj (indecent)* unanständig; *(unsuitable)* unpassend

improve [ɪmˈpruːv] *vt* verbessern ♦ *vi* besser werden; **~ment** *n* (Ver)besserung *f*

improvise [ˈɪmprəvaɪz] *vt, vi* improvisieren

imprudent [ɪmˈpruːdnt] *adj* unklug

impudent [ˈɪmpjudnt] *adj* unverschämt

impulse [ˈɪmpʌls] *n* Impuls *m*; **to act on ~** spontan handeln; **impulsive** [ɪmˈpʌlsɪv] *adj* impulsiv

impure [ɪmˈpjuər] *adj (dirty)* verunreinigt; *(bad)* unsauber; **impurity** [ɪmˈpjuərɪtɪ] *n* Unreinheit *f*; *(TECH)* Verunreinigung *f*

KEYWORD

in [ɪn] *prep* **1** *(indicating place, position)* in +dat; *(with motion)* in +acc; **in here/there** hier/dort; **in London** in London; **in the United States** in den Vereinigten Staaten **2** *(indicating time: during)* in +dat; **in summer** im Sommer; **in 1988** (im Jahre)

1988; **in the afternoon** nachmittags, am Nachmittag
3 (*indicating time: in the space of*) innerhalb von; **I'll see you in 2 weeks** *or* **in 2 weeks' time** ich sehe Sie in zwei Wochen
4 (*indicating manner, circumstances, state etc*) in +*dat*; **in the sun/rain** in der Sonne/im Regen; **in English/French** auf Englisch/Französisch; **in a loud/soft voice** mit lauter/leiser Stimme
5 (*with ratios, numbers*): **1 in 10** jeder Zehnte; **20 pence in the pound** 20 Pence pro Pfund; **they lined up in twos** sie stellten sich in Zweierreihe auf
6 (*referring to people, works*): **the disease is common in children** die Krankheit ist bei Kindern häufig; **in Dickens** bei Dickens; **we have a loyal friend in him** er ist uns ein treuer Freund
7 (*indicating profession etc*): **to be in teaching/the army** Lehrer(in)/beim Militär sein; **to be in publishing** im Verlagswesen arbeiten
8 (*with present participle*): **in saying this, I ...** wenn ich das sage, ... ich; **in accepting this view, he ...** weil er diese Meinung akzeptierte, ... er
♦ *adv*: **to be in** (*person: at home, work*) da sein; (*train, ship, plane*) angekommen sein; (*in fashion*) in sein; **to ask sb in** jdn hereinbitten; **to run/limp etc in** hereingerannt/gehumpelt etc kommen
♦ *n*: **the ins and outs** (*of proposal, situation etc*) die Feinheiten

in. *abbr* = **inch**
inability [ɪnəˈbɪlɪtɪ] *n* Unfähigkeit *f*
inaccessible [ɪnəkˈsesɪbl] *adj* unzugänglich
inaccurate [ɪnˈækjʊrət] *adj* ungenau; (*wrong*) unrichtig
inactivity [ɪnækˈtɪvɪtɪ] *n* Untätigkeit *f*
inadequate [ɪnˈædɪkwət] *adj* unzulänglich
inadvertently [ɪnədˈvɜːtntlɪ] *adv* unabsichtlich
inadvisable [ɪnədˈvaɪzəbl] *adj* nicht ratsam
inane [ɪˈneɪn] *adj* dumm, albern
inanimate [ɪnˈænɪmət] *adj* leblos

inappropriate [ɪnəˈprəʊprɪət] *adj* (*clothing*) ungeeignet; (*remark*) unangebracht
inarticulate [ɪnɑːˈtɪkjʊlət] *adj* unklar
inasmuch as [ɪnəzˈmʌtʃ-] *adv* da; (*in so far as*) so weit
inaudible [ɪnˈɔːdɪbl] *adj* unhörbar
inauguration [ɪnɔːgjʊˈreɪʃən] *n* Eröffnung *f*; (*feierliche*) Amtseinführung *f*
inborn [ɪnˈbɔːn] *adj* angeboren
inbred [ɪnˈbred] *adj* angeboren
Inc. *abbr* = **incorporated**
incalculable [ɪnˈkælkjʊləbl] *adj* (*consequences*) unabsehbar
incapable [ɪnˈkeɪpəbl] *adj*: ~ **(of doing sth)** unfähig(, etw zu tun)
incapacitate [ɪnkəˈpæsɪteɪt] *vt* untauglich machen
incapacity [ɪnkəˈpæsɪtɪ] *n* Unfähigkeit *f*
incarcerate [ɪnˈkɑːsəreɪt] *vt* einkerkern
incarnation [ɪnkɑːˈneɪʃən] *n* (*ECCL*) Menschwerdung *f*; (*fig*) Inbegriff *m*
incendiary [ɪnˈsendɪərɪ] *adj* Brand-
incense [*n* ˈɪnsens, *vb* ɪnˈsens] *n* Weihrauch *m* ♦ *vt* erzürnen
incentive [ɪnˈsentɪv] *n* Anreiz *m*
incessant [ɪnˈsesnt] *adj* unaufhörlich
incest [ˈɪnsest] *n* Inzest *m*
inch [ɪntʃ] *n* Zoll *m* ♦ *vi*: **to ~ forward** sich Stückchen für Stückchen vorwärts bewegen; **to be within an ~ of** kurz davor sein; **he didn't give an ~** er gab keinen Zentimeter nach
incidence [ˈɪnsɪdns] *n* Auftreten *nt*; (*of crime*) Quote *f*
incident [ˈɪnsɪdnt] *n* Vorfall *m*; (*disturbance*) Zwischenfall *m*
incidental [ɪnsɪˈdentl] *adj* (*music*) Begleit-; (*unimportant*) nebensächlich; (*remark*) beiläufig; **~ly** *adv* übrigens
incinerator [ɪnˈsɪnəreɪtə*] *n* Verbrennungsofen *m*
incision [ɪnˈsɪʒən] *n* Einschnitt *m*
incisive [ɪnˈsaɪsɪv] *adj* (*style*) treffend; (*person*) scharfsinnig
incite [ɪnˈsaɪt] *vt* anstacheln
inclination [ɪnklɪˈneɪʃən] *n* Neigung *f*
incline [*n* ˈɪnklaɪn, *vb* ɪnˈklaɪn] *n* Abhang *m*

♦ vt neigen; (fig) veranlassen ♦ vi sich neigen; **to be ~d to do sth** dazu neigen, etw zu tun

include [ɪnˈkluːd] vt einschließen; (on list, in group) aufnehmen; **including** prep: **including X** X inbegriffen; **inclusion** [ɪnˈkluːʒən] n Aufnahme f; **inclusive** [ɪnˈkluːsɪv] adj einschließlich; (COMM) inklusive; **inclusive of** einschließlich +gen

incoherent [ɪnkəʊˈhɪərənt] adj zusammenhanglos

income [ˈɪnkʌm] n Einkommen nt; (from business) Einkünfte pl; **~ tax** n Lohnsteuer f; (of self-employed) Einkommensteuer f

incoming [ˈɪnkʌmɪŋ] adj: **~ flight** eintreffende Maschine f

incomparable [ɪnˈkɒmpərəbl] adj unvergleichlich

incompatible [ɪnkəmˈpætɪbl] adj unvereinbar; (people) unverträglich

incompetence [ɪnˈkɒmpɪtns] n Unfähigkeit f; **incompetent** adj unfähig

incomplete [ɪnkəmˈpliːt] adj unvollständig

incomprehensible [ɪnkɒmprɪˈhensɪbl] adj unverständlich

inconceivable [ɪnkənˈsiːvəbl] adj unvorstellbar

incongruous [ɪnˈkɒŋgruəs] adj seltsam; (remark) unangebracht

inconsiderate [ɪnkənˈsɪdərət] adj rücksichtslos

inconsistency [ɪnkənˈsɪstənsɪ] n Widersprüchlichkeit f; (state) Unbeständigkeit f

inconsistent [ɪnkənˈsɪstnt] adj (action, speech) widersprüchlich; (person, work) unbeständig; **~ with** nicht übereinstimmend mit

inconspicuous [ɪnkənˈspɪkjuəs] adj unauffällig

incontinent [ɪnˈkɒntɪnənt] adj (MED) nicht fähig, Stuhl und Harn zurückzuhalten

inconvenience [ɪnkənˈviːnjəns] n Unbequemlichkeit f; (trouble to others) Unannehmlichkeiten pl

inconvenient [ɪnkənˈviːnjənt] adj ungelegen; (journey) unbequem

incorporate [ɪnˈkɔːpəreɪt] vt (include) aufnehmen; (contain) enthalten; **~d** adj: **~d company** (US) eingetragene Aktiengesellschaft f

incorrect [ɪnkəˈrekt] adj unrichtig

incorrigible [ɪnˈkɒrɪdʒɪbl] adj unverbesserlich

incorruptible [ɪnkəˈrʌptɪbl] adj unzerstörbar; (person) unbestechlich

increase [n ˈɪnkriːs, vb ɪnˈkriːs] n Zunahme f; (pay ~) Gehaltserhöhung f; (in size) Vergrößerung f ♦ vt erhöhen; (wealth, rage) vermehren; (business) erweitern ♦ vi zunehmen; (prices) steigen; (in size) größer werden; (in number) sich vermehren; **increasing** adj (number) steigend; **increasingly** [ɪnˈkriːsɪŋlɪ] adv zunehmend

incredible [ɪnˈkredɪbl] adj unglaublich

incredulous [ɪnˈkredjuləs] adj ungläubig

increment [ˈɪnkrɪmənt] n Zulage f

incriminate [ɪnˈkrɪmɪneɪt] vt belasten

incubation [ɪnkjuˈbeɪʃən] n Ausbrüten nt

incubator [ˈɪnkjubeɪtə*] n Brutkasten m

incumbent [ɪnˈkʌmbənt] n ♦ adj: **it is ~ on him to ...** es obliegt ihm, ...

incur [ɪnˈkəː*] vt sich zuziehen; (debts) machen

incurable [ɪnˈkjuərəbl] adj unheilbar

indebted [ɪnˈdetɪd] adj (obliged): **~ (to sb)** (jdm) verpflichtet

indecent [ɪnˈdiːsnt] adj unanständig; **~ assault** (BRIT) n Notzucht f; **~ exposure** n Exhibitionismus m

indecisive [ɪndɪˈsaɪsɪv] adj (battle) nicht entscheidend; (person) unentschlossen

indeed [ɪnˈdiːd] adv tatsächlich, in der Tat; **yes ~!** allerdings!

indefinite [ɪnˈdefɪnɪt] adj unbestimmt; **~ly** adv auf unbestimmte Zeit; (wait) unbegrenzt lange

indelible [ɪnˈdelɪbl] adj unauslöschlich

indemnity [ɪnˈdemnɪtɪ] n (insurance) Versicherung f; (compensation) Entschädigung f

independence [ɪndɪˈpendns] n Unabhängigkeit f; **independent** adj unabhängig

---

Independence Day

i **Independence Day** *(der 4. Juli)* ist in den USA ein gesetzlicher Feiertag zum Gedenken an die Unabhängigkeitserklärung am 4. Juli 1776, mit der die 13 amerikanischen Kolonien ihre Freiheit und Unabhängigkeit von Großbritannien erklärten.

---

indestructible [ɪndɪs'trʌktəbl] *adj* unzerstörbar

indeterminate [ɪndɪ'tə:mɪnɪt] *adj* unbestimmt

index ['ɪndeks] *(pl* **~es** *or* **indices)** *n* Index *m;* **~ card** *n* Karteikarte *f;* **~ finger** *n* Zeigefinger *m;* **~-linked** *(US* **~ed)** *adj (salaries)* der Inflationsrate *dat* angeglichen; *(pensions)* dynamisch

India ['ɪndɪə] *n* Indien *nt;* **~n** *adj* indisch ♦ *n* Inder(in) *m(f);* **American ~n** Indianer(in) *m(f);* **~n Ocean** *n:* **the ~n Ocean** der Indische Ozean

indicate ['ɪndɪkeɪt] *vt* anzeigen; *(hint)* andeuten; **indication** [ɪndɪ'keɪʃən] *n* Anzeichen *nt;* *(information)* Angabe *f;* **indicative** [ɪn'dɪkətɪv] *adj:* **indicative of** bezeichnend für; **indicator** *n* (An)zeichen *nt;* *(AUT)* Richtungsanzeiger *m*

indict [ɪn'daɪt] *vt* anklagen; **~ment** *n* Anklage *f*

indifference [ɪn'dɪfrəns] *n* Gleichgültigkeit *f;* Unwichtigkeit *f;* **indifferent** *adj* gleichgültig; *(mediocre)* mäßig

indigenous [ɪn'dɪdʒɪnəs] *adj* einheimisch

indigestion [ɪndɪ'dʒestʃən] *n* Verdauungsstörung *f*

indignant [ɪn'dɪgnənt] *adj:* **to be ~ about sth** über etw *acc* empört sein

indignation [ɪndɪg'neɪʃən] *n* Entrüstung *f*

indignity [ɪn'dɪgnɪtɪ] *n* Demütigung *f*

indirect [ɪndɪ'rekt] *adj* indirekt

indiscreet [ɪndɪs'kri:t] *adj (insensitive)* taktlos; *(telling secrets)* indiskret; **indiscretion** [ɪndɪs'kreʃən] *n* Taktlosigkeit *f;* Indiskretion *f*

indiscriminate [ɪndɪs'krɪmɪnət] *adj* wahllos;

kritiklos

indispensable [ɪndɪs'pensəbl] *adj* unentbehrlich

indisposed [ɪndɪs'pəuzd] *adj* unpässlich

indisputable [ɪndɪs'pju:təbl] *adj* unbestreitbar; *(evidence)* unanfechtbar

indistinct [ɪndɪs'tɪŋkt] *adj* undeutlich

individual [ɪndɪ'vɪdjuəl] *n* Individuum *nt* ♦ *adj* individuell; *(case)* Einzel-; *(of, for one person)* eigen, individuell; *(characteristic)* eigentümlich; **~ly** *adv* einzeln, individuell

indivisible [ɪndɪ'vɪzɪbl] *adj* unteilbar

indoctrinate [ɪn'dɒktrɪneɪt] *vt* indoktrinieren

Indonesia [ɪndə'ni:zɪə] *n* Indonesien *nt*

indoor ['ɪndɔ:ʳ] *adj* Haus-; Zimmer-; Innen-; *(SPORT)* Hallen-; **~s** [ɪn'dɔ:z] *adv* drinnen, im Haus

induce [ɪn'dju:s] *vt* dazu bewegen; *(reaction)* herbeiführen

induction course [ɪn'dʌkʃən-] *(BRIT)* *n* Einführungskurs *m*

indulge [ɪn'dʌldʒ] *vt (give way)* nachgeben +*dat; (gratify)* frönen +*dat* ♦ *vi:* **to ~ (in)** frönen (+*dat);* **~nce** *n* Nachsicht *f;* *(enjoyment)* Genuss *m;* **~nt** *adj* nachsichtig; *(pej)* nachgiebig

industrial [ɪn'dʌstrɪəl] *adj* Industrie-, industriell; *(dispute, injury)* Arbeits-; **~ action** *n* Arbeitskampfmaßnahmen *pl;* **~ estate** *(BRIT)* *n* Industriegebiet *nt;* **~ist** *n* Industrielle(r) *mf;* **~ize** *vt* industrialisieren; **~ park** *(US)* *n* Industriegebiet *nt*

industrious [ɪn'dʌstrɪəs] *adj* fleißig

industry ['ɪndəstrɪ] *n* Industrie *f;* *(diligence)* Fleiß *m*

inebriated [ɪ'ni:brɪeɪtɪd] *adj* betrunken

inedible [ɪn'edɪbl] *adj* ungenießbar

ineffective [ɪnɪ'fektɪv] *adj* unwirksam; *(person)* untauglich

ineffectual [ɪnɪ'fektjuəl] *adj* = **ineffective**

inefficiency [ɪnɪ'fɪʃənsɪ] *n* Ineffizienz *f*

inefficient [ɪnɪ'fɪʃənt] *adj* ineffizient; *(ineffective)* unwirksam

inept [ɪ'nept] *adj (remark)* unpassend; *(person)* ungeeignet

inequality [ɪnɪ'kwɒlɪtɪ] *n* Ungleichheit *f*

inert [ɪ'nə:t] *adj* träge; *(CHEM)* inaktiv;

(*motionless*) unbeweglich

inescapable [ɪnɪˈskeɪpəbl] *adj* unvermeidbar

inevitable [ɪnˈɛvɪtəbl] *adj* unvermeidlich; **inevitably** *adv* zwangsläufig

inexcusable [ɪnɪksˈkjuːzəbl] *adj* unverzeihlich

inexhaustible [ɪnɪɡˈzɔːstɪbl] *adj* unerschöpflich

inexpensive [ɪnɪkˈspɛnsɪv] *adj* preiswert

inexperience [ɪnɪkˈspɪərɪəns] *n* Unerfahrenheit *f*; **~d** *adj* unerfahren

inexplicable [ɪnɪkˈsplɪkəbl] *adj* unerklärlich

inextricably [ɪnɪkˈstrɪkəblɪ] *adv* untrennbar

infallible [ɪnˈfælɪbl] *adj* unfehlbar

infamous [ˈɪnfəməs] *adj* (*deed*) schändlich; (*person*) niederträchtig

infancy [ˈɪnfənsɪ] *n* frühe Kindheit *f*; (*fig*) Anfangsstadium *nt*

infant [ˈɪnfənt] *n* kleine(s) Kind *nt*, Säugling *m*; **~ile** [-aɪl] *adj* kindisch, infantil; **~ school** (*BRIT*) *n* Vorschule *f*

infatuated [ɪnˈfætjʊeɪtɪd] *adj* vernarrt; **to become ~ with** sich vernarren in +*acc*; **infatuation** [ɪnfætjuˈeɪʃən] *n*: **infatuation (with)** Vernarrtheit *f* (in +*acc*)

infect [ɪnˈfɛkt] *vt* anstecken (*also fig*); **~ed with** (*illness*) infiziert mit; **~ion** [ɪnˈfɛkʃən] *n* Infektion *f*; **~ious** [ɪnˈfɛkʃəs] *adj* ansteckend

infer [ɪnˈfɜː] *vt* schließen

inferior [ɪnˈfɪərɪə] *adj* (*rank*) untergeordnet; (*quality*) minderwertig ♦ *n* Untergebene(r) *m*; **~ity** [ɪnfɪərɪˈɒrɪtɪ] *n* Minderwertigkeit *f*; (*in rank*) untergeordnete Stellung *f*; **~ity complex** *n* Minderwertigkeitskomplex *m*

infernal [ɪnˈfɜːnl] *adj* höllisch

infertile [ɪnˈfɜːtaɪl] *adj* unfruchtbar; **infertility** [ɪnfəˈtɪlɪtɪ] *n* Unfruchtbarkeit *f*

infested [ɪnˈfɛstɪd] *adj*: **to be ~ with** wimmeln von

infidelity [ɪnfɪˈdɛlɪtɪ] *n* Untreue *f*

infighting [ˈɪnfaɪtɪŋ] *n* Nahkampf *m*

infiltrate [ˈɪnfɪltreɪt] *vt* infiltrieren; (*spies*) einschleusen ♦ *vi* (*MIL, liquid*) einsickern; (*POL*) **to ~ (into)** unterwandern (+*acc*)

infinite [ˈɪnfɪnɪt] *adj* unendlich

infinitive [ɪnˈfɪnɪtɪv] *n* Infinitiv *m*

infinity [ɪnˈfɪnɪtɪ] *n* Unendlichkeit *f*

infirm [ɪnˈfɜːm] *adj* gebrechlich; **~ary** *n* Krankenhaus *nt*

inflamed [ɪnˈfleɪmd] *adj* entzündet

inflammable [ɪnˈflæməbl] (*BRIT*) *adj* feuergefährlich

inflammation [ɪnfləˈmeɪʃən] *n* Entzündung *f*

inflatable [ɪnˈfleɪtəbl] *adj* aufblasbar

inflate [ɪnˈfleɪt] *vt* aufblasen; (*tyre*) aufpumpen; (*prices*) hoch treiben; **inflation** [ɪnˈfleɪʃən] *n* Inflation *f*; **inflationary** [ɪnˈfleɪʃənərɪ] *adj* (*increase*) inflationistisch; (*situation*) inflationär

inflexible [ɪnˈflɛksɪbl] *adj* (*person*) nicht flexibel; (*opinion*) starr; (*thing*) unbiegsam

inflict [ɪnˈflɪkt] *vt*: **to ~ sth on sb** jdm etw zufügen; (*wound*) jdm etw beibringen

influence [ˈɪnflʊəns] *n* Einfluss *m* ♦ *vt* beeinflussen

influential [ɪnflʊˈɛnʃl] *adj* einflussreich

influenza [ɪnflʊˈɛnzə] *n* Grippe *f*

influx [ˈɪnflʌks] *n* (*of people*) Zustrom *m*; (*of ideas*) Eindringen *nt*

infomercial [ˈɪnfəʊməːʃl] *n* Werbeinformationssendung *f*

inform [ɪnˈfɔːm] *vt* informieren ♦ *vi*: **to ~ on sb** jdn denunzieren; **to keep sb ~ed** jdn auf dem Laufenden halten

informal [ɪnˈfɔːml] *adj* zwanglos; **~ity** [ɪnfɔːˈmælɪtɪ] *n* Ungezwungenheit *f*

informant [ɪnˈfɔːmənt] *n* Informant(in) *m(f)*

information [ɪnfəˈmeɪʃən] *n* Auskunft *f*, Information *f*; **a piece of ~** eine Auskunft, eine Information; **~ desk** *n* Auskunftsschalter *m*; **~ office** *n* Informationsbüro *nt*

informative [ɪnˈfɔːmətɪv] *adj* informativ; (*person*) mitteilsam

informer [ɪnˈfɔːmə] *n* Denunziant(in) *m(f)*

infra-red [ˌɪnfrəˈrɛd] *adj* infrarot

infrequent [ɪnˈfriːkwənt] *adj* selten

infringe [ɪnˈfrɪndʒ] *vt* (*law*) verstoßen gegen; **~ upon** *vt* verletzen; **~ment** *n* Verstoß *m*, Verletzung *f*

infuriating [ɪnˈfjʊərɪeɪtɪŋ] *adj* ärgerlich

ingenuity [ɪndʒɪˈnjuːɪtɪ] *n* Genialität *f*

ingenuous [ɪnˈdʒɛnjʊəs] *adj* aufrichtig; (*naive*) naiv

ingot ['ɪŋgət] n Barren m

ingrained [ɪn'greɪnd] adj tief sitzend

ingratiate [ɪn'greɪʃɪeɪt] vt: **to ~ o.s. with sb** sich bei jdm einschmeicheln

ingratitude [ɪn'grætɪtjuːd] n Undankbarkeit f

ingredient [ɪn'griːdɪənt] n Bestandteil m; (COOK) Zutat f

inhabit [ɪn'hæbɪt] vt bewohnen; **~ant** n Bewohner(in) m(f); (of island, town) Einwohner(in) m(f)

inhale [ɪn'heɪl] vt einatmen; (MED, cigarettes) inhalieren

inherent [ɪn'hɪərənt] adj: **~ (in)** innewohnend (+dat)

inherit [ɪn'herɪt] vt erben; **~ance** n Erbe nt, Erbschaft f

inhibit [ɪn'hɪbɪt] vt hemmen; **to ~ sb from doing sth** jdn daran hindern, etw zu tun; **~ion** [ɪnhɪ'bɪʃən] n Hemmung f

inhospitable [ɪnhɔs'pɪtəbl] adj (person) ungastlich; (country) unwirtlich

inhuman [ɪn'hjuːmən] adj unmenschlich

initial [ɪ'nɪʃl] adj anfänglich, Anfangs- ♦ n Initiale f ♦ vt abzeichnen; (POL) paraphieren; **~ly** adv anfangs

initiate [ɪ'nɪʃɪeɪt] vt einführen; (negotiations) einleiten; **to ~ proceedings against sb** (JUR) gerichtliche Schritte gegen jdn einleiten; **initiation** [ɪnɪʃɪ'eɪʃən] n Einführung f; Einleitung f

initiative [ɪ'nɪʃɪətɪv] n Initiative f

inject [ɪn'dʒekt] vt einspritzen; (fig) einflößen; **~ion** [ɪn'dʒekʃən] n Spritze f

injunction [ɪn'dʒʌŋkʃən] n Verfügung f

injure ['ɪndʒər] vt verletzen; **~d** adj (person, arm) verletzt; **injury** ['ɪndʒərɪ] n Verletzung f; **to play injury time** (SPORT) nachspielen

injustice [ɪn'dʒʌstɪs] n Ungerechtigkeit f

ink [ɪŋk] n Tinte f

inkling ['ɪŋklɪŋ] n (dunkle) Ahnung f

inlaid ['ɪnleɪd] adj eingelegt, Einlege-

inland [adj 'ɪnlənd, adv ɪn'lænd] adj Binnen-; (domestic) Inlands-; ♦ adv landeinwärts; **~ revenue** (BRIT) n Fiskus m

in-laws ['ɪnlɔːz] npl (parents-in-law) Schwiegereltern pl; (others) angeheiratete Verwandte pl

inlet ['ɪnlet] n Einlass m; (bay) kleine Bucht f

inmate ['ɪnmeɪt] n Insasse m

inn [ɪn] n Gasthaus nt, Wirtshaus nt

innate [ɪ'neɪt] adj angeboren

inner ['ɪnər] adj inner, Innen-; (fig) verborgen; **~ city** n Innenstadt f; **~ tube** n (of tyre) Schlauch m

innings ['ɪnɪŋz] n (CRICKET) Innenrunde f

innocence ['ɪnəsns] n Unschuld f; (ignorance) Unkenntnis f

innocent ['ɪnəsnt] adj unschuldig

innocuous [ɪ'nɔkjuəs] adj harmlos

innovation [ɪnəu'veɪʃən] n Neuerung f

innuendo [ɪnju'endəu] n (versteckte) Anspielung f

innumerable [ɪ'njuːmrəbl] adj unzählig

inoculation [ɪnɔkju'leɪʃən] n Impfung f

inopportune [ɪn'ɔpətjuːn] adj (remark) unangebracht; (visit) ungelegen

inordinately [ɪ'nɔːdɪnətlɪ] adv unmäßig

inpatient ['ɪnpeɪʃənt] n stationäre(r) Patient m/stationäre Patientin f

input ['ɪnput] n (COMPUT) Eingabe f; (power ~) Energiezufuhr f; (of energy, work) Aufwand m

inquest ['ɪnkwest] n gerichtliche Untersuchung f

inquire [ɪn'kwaɪər] vi sich erkundigen ♦ vt (price) sich erkundigen nach; **~ into** vt untersuchen; **inquiry** [ɪn'kwaɪərɪ] n (question) Erkundigung f; (investigation) Untersuchung f; **inquiries** Auskunft f; **inquiry office** (BRIT) n Auskunft(sbüro nt) f

inquisitive [ɪn'kwɪzɪtɪv] adj neugierig

ins. abbr = **inches**

insane [ɪn'seɪn] adj wahnsinnig; (MED) geisteskrank; **insanity** [ɪn'sænɪtɪ] n Wahnsinn m

insatiable [ɪn'seɪʃəbl] adj unersättlich

inscribe [ɪn'skraɪb] vt eingravieren; **inscription** [ɪn'skrɪpʃən] n (on stone) Inschrift f; (in book) Widmung f

insect ['ɪnsekt] n Insekt nt; **~icide** [ɪn'sektɪsaɪd] n Insektenvertilgungsmittel nt; **~ repellent** n Insektenbekämpfungsmittel nt

insecure [ɪnsɪ'kjuər] adj (person) unsicher;

(thing) nicht fest *or* sicher; **insecurity** [ɪnsɪˈkjʊərɪtɪ] *n* Unsicherheit *f*

insemination [ɪnsemɪˈneɪʃən] *n*: **artificial ~** künstliche Befruchtung *f*

insensible [ɪnˈsensɪbl] *adj* (*unconscious*) bewusstlos

insensitive [ɪnˈsensɪtɪv] *adj* (*to pain*) unempfindlich; (*unfeeling*) gefühllos

inseparable [ɪnˈseprəbl] *adj* (*people*) unzertrennlich; (*word*) untrennbar

insert [*vb* ɪnˈsɜːt, *n* ˈɪnsɜːt] *vt* einfügen; (*coin*) einwerfen; (*stick into*) hineinstecken; (*advertisement*) aufgeben ♦ *n* (*in book*) Einlage *f*; (*in magazine*) Beilage *f*; **~ion** [ɪnˈsɜːʃən] *n* Einfügung *f*; (*PRESS*) Inserat *nt*

in-service [ˈɪnˈsɜːvɪs] *adj* (*training*) berufsbegleitend

inshore [ˈɪnˈʃɔːr] *adj* Küsten- ♦ *adv* an der Küste

inside [ˈɪnˈsaɪd] *n* Innenseite *f*, Innere(s) *nt* ♦ *adj* innere(r, s), Innen- ♦ *adv* (*place*) innen; (*direction*) nach innen, hinein ♦ *prep* (*place*) in +*dat*; (*direction*) in +*acc* ... hinein; (*time*) innerhalb +*gen*; **~s** *npl* (*inf*) Eingeweide *nt*; **~ 10 minutes** unter 10 Minuten; **~ information** *n* interne Informationen *pl*; **~ lane** *n* (*AUT*: *in Britain*) linke Spur; **~ out** *adv* linksherum; (*know*) in- und auswendig

insider dealing, insider trading [ɪnˈsaɪdər-] *n* (*STOCK EXCHANGE*) Insiderhandel *m*

insidious [ɪnˈsɪdɪəs] *adj* heimtückisch

insight [ˈɪnsaɪt] *n* Einsicht *f*; **~ into** Einblick *m* in +*acc*

insignificant [ɪnsɪɡˈnɪfɪknt] *adj* unbedeutend

insincere [ɪnsɪnˈsɪər] *adj* unaufrichtig

insinuate [ɪnˈsɪnjʊeɪt] *vt* (*hint*) andeuten

insipid [ɪnˈsɪpɪd] *adj* fad(e)

insist [ɪnˈsɪst] *vi*: **to ~ (on)** bestehen (auf +*acc*); **~ence** *n* Bestehen *nt*; **~ent** *adj* hartnäckig; (*urgent*) dringend

insole [ˈɪnsəʊl] *n* Einlegesohle *f*

insolence [ˈɪnsələns] *n* Frechheit *f*

insolent [ˈɪnsələnt] *adj* frech

insoluble [ɪnˈsɒljʊbl] *adj* unlösbar; (*CHEM*) unlöslich

insolvent [ɪnˈsɒlvənt] *adj* zahlungsunfähig

insomnia [ɪnˈsɒmnɪə] *n* Schlaflosigkeit *f*

inspect [ɪnˈspekt] *vt* prüfen; (*officially*) inspizieren; **~ion** [ɪnˈspekʃən] *n* Inspektion *f*; **~or** *n* (*official*) Inspektor *m*; (*police*) Polizeikommissar *m*; (*BRIT*: *on buses, trains*) Kontrolleur *m*

inspiration [ɪnspəˈreɪʃən] *n* Inspiration *f*

inspire [ɪnˈspaɪər] *vt* (*person*) inspirieren; **to ~ sth in sb** (*respect*) jdm etw einflößen; (*hope*) etw in jdm wecken

instability [ɪnstəˈbɪlɪtɪ] *n* Unbeständigkeit *f*, Labilität *f*

install [ɪnˈstɔːl] *vt* (*put in*) installieren; (*telephone*) anschließen; (*establish*) einsetzen; **~ation** [ɪnstəˈleɪʃən] *n* (*of person*) (Amts)einsetzung *f*; (*of machinery*) Installierung *f*; (*machines etc*) Anlage *f*

instalment [ɪnˈstɔːlmənt] (*US* **installment**) *n* Rate *f*; (*of story*) Fortsetzung *f*; **to pay in ~s** in Raten zahlen

instance [ˈɪnstəns] *n* Fall *m*; (*example*) Beispiel *nt*; **for ~** zum Beispiel; **in the first ~** zunächst

instant [ˈɪnstənt] *n* Augenblick *m* ♦ *adj* augenblicklich, sofortig; **~aneous** [ɪnstənˈteɪnɪəs] *adj* unmittelbar; **~ coffee** *n* Pulverkaffee *m*; **~ly** *adv* sofort

instead [ɪnˈsted] *adv* stattdessen; **~ of** *prep* anstatt +*gen*

instep [ˈɪnstep] *n* Spann *m*; (*of shoe*) Blatt *nt*

instil [ɪnˈstɪl] *vt* (*fig*): **to ~ sth in sb** jdm etw beibringen

instinct [ˈɪnstɪŋkt] *n* Instinkt *m*; **~ive** [ɪnˈstɪŋktɪv] *adj* instinktiv

institute [ˈɪnstɪtjuːt] *n* Institut *nt* ♦ *vt* einführen; (*search*) einleiten

institution [ɪnstɪˈtjuːʃən] *n* Institution *f*; (*home*) Anstalt *f*

instruct [ɪnˈstrʌkt] *vt* anweisen; (*officially*) instruieren; **~ion** [ɪnˈstrʌkʃən] *n* Unterricht *m*; **~ions** *npl* (*orders*) Anweisungen *pl*; (*for use*) Gebrauchsanweisung *f*; **~or** *n* Lehrer *m*

instrument [ˈɪnstrumənt] *n* Instrument *nt*; **~al** [ɪnstruˈmentl] *adj* (*MUS*) Instrumental-;

(*helpful*): **~al (in)** behilflich (bei); **~ panel** *n* Armaturenbrett *nt*

insubordinate [ɪnsəˈbɔːdənɪt] *adj* aufsässig, widersetzlich

insufferable [ɪnˈsʌfrəbl] *adj* unerträglich

insufficient [ɪnsəˈfɪʃənt] *adj* ungenügend

insular [ˈɪnsjulər] *adj* (*fig*) engstirnig

insulate [ˈɪnsjuleɪt] *vt* (*ELEC*) isolieren; (*fig*): **to ~ (from)** abschirmen (vor +*dat*); **insulating tape** *n* Isolierband *nt*; **insulation** [ɪnsjuˈleɪʃən] *n* Isolierung *f*

insulin [ˈɪnsjulɪn] *n* Insulin *nt*

insult [*n* ˈɪnsʌlt, *vb* ɪnˈsʌlt] *n* Beleidigung *f* ♦ *vt* beleidigen

insurance [ɪnˈʃuərəns] *n* Versicherung *f*; **fire/life ~** Feuer-/Lebensversicherung; **~ agent** *n* Versicherungsvertreter *m*; **~ policy** *n* Versicherungspolice *f*

insure [ɪnˈʃuər] *vt* versichern

intact [ɪnˈtækt] *adj* unversehrt

intake [ˈɪnteɪk] *n* (*place*) Einlassöffnung *f*; (*act*) Aufnahme *f*; (*BRIT*: *SCH*): **an ~ of 200 a year** ein Neuzugang von 200 im Jahr

intangible [ɪnˈtændʒɪbl] *adj* nicht greifbar

integral [ˈɪntɪɡrəl] *adj* (*essential*) wesentlich; (*complete*) vollständig; (*MATH*) Integral-

integrate [ˈɪntɪɡreɪt] *vt* integrieren ♦ *vi* sich integrieren

integrity [ɪnˈtɛɡrɪtɪ] *n* (*honesty*) Redlichkeit *f*, Integrität *f*

intellect [ˈɪntəlɛkt] *n* Intellekt *m*; **~ual** [ɪntəˈlɛktjuəl] *adj* geistig, intellektuell ♦ *n* Intellektuelle(r) *mf*

intelligence [ɪnˈtɛlɪdʒəns] *n* (*understanding*) Intelligenz *f*; (*news*) Information *f*; (*MIL*) Geheimdienst *m*; **~ service** *n* Nachrichtendienst *m*, Geheimdienst *m*

intelligent [ɪnˈtɛlɪdʒənt] *adj* intelligent; **~ly** *adv* klug; (*write*, *speak*) verständlich

intelligentsia [ɪntɛlɪˈdʒɛntsɪə] *n* Intelligenz *f*

intelligible [ɪnˈtɛlɪdʒɪbl] *adj* verständlich

intend [ɪnˈtɛnd] *vt* beabsichtigen; **that was ~ed for you** das war für dich gedacht

intense [ɪnˈtɛns] *adj* stark, intensiv; (*person*) ernsthaft; **~ly** *adv* äußerst; (*study*) intensiv

intensify [ɪnˈtɛnsɪfaɪ] *vt* verstärken, intensivieren

intensity [ɪnˈtɛnsɪtɪ] *n* Intensität *f*

intensive [ɪnˈtɛnsɪv] *adj* intensiv; **~ care unit** *n* Intensivstation *f*

intent [ɪnˈtɛnt] *n* Absicht *f* ♦ *adj*: **to be ~ on doing sth** fest entschlossen sein, etw zu tun; **to all ~s and purposes** praktisch

intention [ɪnˈtɛnʃən] *n* Absicht *f*; **~al** *adj* absichtlich

intently [ɪnˈtɛntlɪ] *adv* konzentriert

interact [ɪntərˈækt] *vi* aufeinander einwirken; **~ion** [ɪntərˈækʃən] *n* Wechselwirkung *f*; **~ive** *adj* (*COMPUT*) interaktiv

intercept [ɪntəˈsɛpt] *vt* abfangen

interchange [*n* ˈɪntətʃeɪndʒ, *vb* ɪntəˈtʃeɪndʒ] *n* (*exchange*) Austausch *m*; (*on roads*) Verkehrskreuz *nt* ♦ *vt* austauschen; **~able** [ɪntəˈtʃeɪndʒəbl] *adj* austauschbar

intercom [ˈɪntəkɔm] *n* (Gegen)sprechanlage *f*

intercourse [ˈɪntəkɔːs] *n* (*exchange*) Beziehungen *pl*; (*sexual*) Geschlechtsverkehr *m*

interest [ˈɪntrɪst] *n* Interesse *nt*; (*FIN*) Zinsen *pl*; (*COMM*: *share*) Anteil *m*; (*group*) Interessengruppe *f* ♦ *vt* interessieren; **~ed** *adj* (*having claims*) beteiligt; (*attentive*) interessiert; **to be ~ed in** sich interessieren für; **~ing** *adj* interessant; **~ rate** *n* Zinssatz *m*

interface [ˈɪntəfeɪs] *n* (*COMPUT*) Schnittstelle *f*, Interface *nt*

interfere [ɪntəˈfɪər] *vi*: **to ~ (with)** (*meddle*) sich einmischen (in +*acc*); (*disrupt*) stören +*acc*; **~nce** [ɪntəˈfɪərəns] *n* Einmischung *f*; (*TV*) Störung *f*

interim [ˈɪntərɪm] *n*: **in the ~** inzwischen

interior [ɪnˈtɪərɪər] *n* Innere(s) *nt* ♦ *adj* innere(r, s), Innen-; **~ designer** *n* Innenarchitekt(in) *m(f)*

interjection [ɪntəˈdʒɛkʃən] *n* Ausruf *m*

interlock [ɪntəˈlɔk] *vi* ineinander greifen

interlude [ˈɪntəluːd] *n* Pause *f*

intermediary [ɪntəˈmiːdɪərɪ] *n* Vermittler *m*

intermediate [ɪntəˈmiːdɪət] *adj* Zwischen-, Mittel-

interminable [ɪnˈtəːmɪnəbl] *adj* endlos

intermission [ɪntəˈmɪʃən] *n* Pause *f*

intermittent [ɪntə'mɪtnt] *adj* periodisch, stoßweise

intern [*vb* ɪn'tə:n, *n* 'ɪntə:n] *vt* internieren ♦ *n* (*US*) Assistenzarzt *m*/-ärztin *f*

internal [ɪn'tə:nl] *adj* (*inside*) innere(r, s); (*domestic*) Inlands-; **~ly** *adv* innen; (*MED*) innerlich; **"not to be taken ~ly"** „nur zur äußerlichen Anwendung"; **Internal Revenue Service** (*US*) *n* Finanzamt *nt*

international [ɪntə'næʃənl] *adj* international ♦ *n* (*SPORT*) Nationalspieler(in) *m(f)*; (: *match*) internationale(s) Spiel *nt*

Internet ['ɪntənet] *n*: **the ~** das Internet; **~ café** *n* Internet-Café *nt*

interplay ['ɪntəpleɪ] *n* Wechselspiel *nt*

interpret [ɪn'tə:prɪt] *vt* (*explain*) auslegen, interpretieren; (*translate*) dolmetschen; **~er** *n* Dolmetscher(in) *m(f)*

interrelated [ɪntərɪ'leɪtɪd] *adj* untereinander zusammenhängend

interrogate [ɪn'terəugeɪt] *vt* verhören; **interrogation** [ɪnterəu'geɪʃən] *n* Verhör *nt*

interrupt [ɪntə'rʌpt] *vt* unterbrechen; **~ion** [ɪntə'rʌpʃən] *n* Unterbrechung *f*

intersect [ɪntə'sekt] *vt* (durch)schneiden ♦ *vi* sich schneiden; **~ion** [ɪntə'sekʃən] *n* (*of roads*) Kreuzung *f*; (*of lines*) Schnittpunkt *m*

intersperse [ɪntə'spə:s] *vt*: **to ~ sth with sth** etw mit etw durchsetzen

intertwine [ɪntə'twaɪn] *vt* verflechten ♦ *vi* sich verflechten

interval ['ɪntəvl] *n* Abstand *m*; (*BRIT: THEAT, SPORT*) Pause *f*; **at ~s** in Abständen

intervene [ɪntə'vi:n] *vi* dazwischenliegen; (*act*): **to ~ (in)** einschreiten (gegen); **intervention** [ɪntə'venʃən] *n* Eingreifen *nt*, Intervention *f*

interview ['ɪntəvju:] *n* (*PRESS etc*) Interview *nt*; (*for job*) Vorstellungsgespräch *nt* ♦ *vt* interviewen; **~er** *n* Interviewer *m*

intestine [ɪn'testɪn] *n*: **large/small ~** Dick-/Dünndarm *m*

intimacy ['ɪntɪməsɪ] *n* Intimität *f*

intimate [*adj* 'ɪntɪmət, *vb* 'ɪntɪmeɪt] *adj* (*inmost*) innerste(r, s); (*knowledge*) eingehend; (*familiar*) vertraut; (*friends*) eng ♦ *vt* andeuten

intimidate [ɪn'tɪmɪdeɪt] *vt* einschüchtern

into ['ɪntu] *prep* (*motion*) in +*acc* ... hinein; **5 ~ 25** 25 durch 5

intolerable [ɪn'tɔlərəbl] *adj* unerträglich

intolerant [ɪn'tɔlərnt] *adj*: **~ of** unduldsam gegen(über)

intoxicate [ɪn'tɔksɪkeɪt] *vt* berauschen; **~d** *adj* betrunken; **intoxication** [ɪntɔksɪ'keɪʃən] *n* Rausch *m*

intractable [ɪn'træktəbl] *adj* schwer zu handhaben; (*problem*) schwer lösbar

intranet ['ɪntrənet] *n* Intranet *nt*

intransitive [ɪn'trænsɪtɪv] *adj* intransitiv

intravenous [ɪntrə'vi:nəs] *adj* intravenös

in-tray ['ɪntreɪ] *n* Eingangskorb *m*

intrepid [ɪn'trepɪd] *adj* unerschrocken

intricate ['ɪntrɪkət] *adj* kompliziert

intrigue [ɪn'tri:g] *n* Intrige *f* ♦ *vt* faszinieren ♦ *vi* intrigieren

intrinsic [ɪn'trɪnsɪk] *adj* innere(r, s); (*difference*) wesentlich

introduce [ɪntrə'dju:s] *vt* (*person*) vorstellen; (*sth new*) einführen; (*subject*) anschneiden; **to ~ sb to sb** jdm jdn vorstellen; **to ~ sb to sth** jdn in etw *acc* einführen; **introduction** [ɪntrə'dʌkʃən] *n* Einführung *f*; (*to book*) Einleitung *f*; **introductory** [ɪntrə'dʌktərɪ] *adj* Einführungs-, Vor-

introspective [ɪntrəu'spektɪv] *adj* nach innen gekehrt

introvert ['ɪntrəuvə:t] *n* Introvertierte(r) *mf* ♦ *adj* introvertiert

intrude [ɪn'tru:d] *vi*: **to ~ (on sb/sth)** (jdn/etw) stören; **~r** *n* Eindringling *m*

intrusion [ɪn'tru:ʒən] *n* Störung *f*

intrusive [ɪn'tru:sɪv] *adj* aufdringlich

intuition [ɪntju:'ɪʃən] *n* Intuition *f*

inundate ['ɪnʌndeɪt] *vt* überschwemmen

invade [ɪn'veɪd] *vt* einfallen in +*acc*; **~r** *n* Eindringling *m*

invalid[1] ['ɪnvəlɪd] *n* (*disabled*) Invalide *m* ♦ *adj* (*ill*) krank; (*disabled*) invalide

invalid[2] [ɪn'vælɪd] *adj* (*not valid*) ungültig

invaluable [ɪn'væljuəbl] *adj* unschätzbar

invariable [ɪn'veərɪəbl] *adj* unveränderlich; **invariably** *adv* ausnahmslos

invent [ɪn'vent] *vt* erfinden; **~ion** [ɪn'venʃən]

n Erfindung *f;* **~ive** *adj* erfinderisch; **~or** *n* Erfinder *m*

inventory ['ɪnvəntrɪ] *n* Inventar *nt*

inverse [ɪn'vɜːs] *n* Umkehrung *f* ♦ *adj* umgekehrt

invert [ɪn'vɜːt] *vt* umdrehen; **~ed commas** (*BRIT*) *npl* Anführungsstriche *pl*

invest [ɪn'vest] *vt* investieren

investigate [ɪn'vestɪgeɪt] *vt* untersuchen; **investigation** [ɪnvestɪ'geɪʃən] *n* Untersuchung *f;* **investigator** [ɪn'vestɪgeɪtə'] *n* Untersuchungsbeamte(r) *m*

investiture [ɪn'vestɪtʃə'] *n* Amtseinsetzung *f*

investment [ɪn'vestmənt] *n* Investition *f*

investor [ɪn'vestə'] *n* (Geld)anleger *m*

invigilate [ɪn'vɪdʒɪleɪt] *vi* (*in exam*) Aufsicht führen ♦ *vt* Aufsicht führen bei

invigorating [ɪn'vɪgəreɪtɪŋ] *adj* stärkend

invincible [ɪn'vɪnsɪbl] *adj* unbesiegbar

invisible [ɪn'vɪzɪbl] *adj* unsichtbar

invitation [ɪnvɪ'teɪʃən] *n* Einladung *f*

invite [ɪn'vaɪt] *vt* einladen

invoice ['ɪnvɔɪs] *n* Rechnung *f* ♦ *vt* (*goods*): **to ~ sb for sth** jdm etw *acc* in Rechnung stellen

invoke [ɪn'vəuk] *vt* anrufen

involuntary [ɪn'vɔləntrɪ] *adj* unabsichtlich

involve [ɪn'vɔlv] *vt* (*entangle*) verwickeln; (*entail*) mit sich bringen; **~d** *adj* verwickelt; **~ment** *n* Verwicklung *f*

inward ['ɪnwəd] *adj* innere(r, s); (*curve*) Innen- ♦ *adv* nach innen; **~ly** *adv* im Innern; **~s** *adv* nach innen

I/O *abbr* (*COMPUT*) (= input/output) I/O

iodine ['aɪəudiːn] *n* Jod *nt*

ioniser ['aɪənaɪzə'] *n* Ionisator *m*

iota [aɪ'əutə] *n* (*fig*) bisschen *nt*

IOU *n abbr* (= I owe you) Schuldschein *m*

IQ *n abbr* (= intelligence quotient) IQ *m*

IRA *n abbr* (= Irish Republican Army) IRA *f*

Iran [ɪ'rɑːn] *n* Iran *m;* **~ian** [ɪ'reɪnɪən] *adj* iranisch ♦ *n* Iraner(in) *m(f);* (*LING*) Iranisch *nt*

Iraq [ɪ'rɑːk] *n* Irak *m;* **~i** *adj* irakisch ♦ *n* Iraker(in) *m(f)*

irate [aɪ'reɪt] *adj* zornig

Ireland ['aɪələnd] *n* Irland *nt*

iris ['aɪrɪs] (*pl* **~es**) *n* Iris *f*

Irish ['aɪrɪʃ] *adj* irisch ♦ *npl:* **the ~** die Iren *pl,* die Irländer *pl;* **~man** (*irreg*) *n* Ire *m,* Irländer *m;* **~ Sea** *n:* **the ~ Sea** die Irische See *f;* **~woman** (*irreg*) *n* Irin *f,* Irländerin *f*

irksome ['ɜːksəm] *adj* lästig

iron ['aɪən] *n* Eisen *nt;* (*for ~ing*) Bügeleisen *nt* ♦ *adj* eisern ♦ *vt* bügeln; **~ out** *vt* (*also fig*) ausbügeln; **Iron Curtain** *n* (*HIST*) Eiserne(r) Vorhang *m*

ironic(al) [aɪ'rɔnɪk(l)] *adj* ironisch; (*coincidence etc*) witzig

iron: ~ing *n* Bügeln *nt;* (*laundry*) Bügelwäsche *f;* **~ing board** *n* Bügelbrett *nt;* **~monger's (shop)** *n* Eisen- und Haushaltswarenhandlung *f*

irony ['aɪrənɪ] *n* Ironie *f*

irrational [ɪ'ræʃənl] *adj* irrational

irreconcilable [ɪrekən'saɪləbl] *adj* unvereinbar

irrefutable [ɪrɪ'fjuːtəbl] *adj* unwiderlegbar

irregular [ɪ'regjulə'] *adj* unregelmäßig; (*shape*) ungleich(mäßig); (*fig*) unüblich; (*: behaviour*) ungehörig

irrelevant [ɪ'reləvənt] *adj* belanglos, irrelevant

irreparable [ɪ'repərəbl] *adj* nicht wieder gutzumachen

irreplaceable [ɪrɪ'pleɪsəbl] *adj* unersetzlich

irresistible [ɪrɪ'zɪstɪbl] *adj* unwiderstehlich

irrespective [ɪrɪ'spektɪv] *adj:* **~ of** *prep* ungeachtet +*gen*

irresponsible [ɪrɪ'spɔnsɪbl] *adj* verantwortungslos

irreverent [ɪ'revərnt] *adj* respektlos

irrevocable [ɪ'revəkəbl] *adj* unwiderrufbar

irrigate ['ɪrɪgeɪt] *vt* bewässern

irritable ['ɪrɪtəbl] *adj* reizbar

irritate ['ɪrɪteɪt] *vt* irritieren, reizen (*also MED*); **irritating** *adj* ärgerlich, irritierend; **he is irritating** er kann einem auf die Nerven gehen; **irritation** [ɪrɪ'teɪʃən] *n* (*anger*) Ärger *m;* (*MED*) Reizung *f*

IRS *n abbr* = **Internal Revenue Service**

is [ɪz] *vb see* **be**

Islam ['ɪzlɑːm] *n* Islam *m;* **~ic** [ɪz'læmɪk] *adj* islamisch

island ['aɪlənd] *n* Insel *f*; **~er** *n* Inselbewohner(in) *m(f)*

isle [aɪl] *n* (kleine) Insel *f*

isn't ['ɪznt] = **is not**

isolate ['aɪsəleɪt] *vt* isolieren; **~d** *adj* isoliert; *(case)* Einzel-; **isolation** [aɪsə'leɪʃən] *n* Isolierung *f*

ISP *n abbr* (= *Internet Service Provider*) Internet-Anbieter *m*

Israel ['ɪzreɪl] *n* Israel *nt*; **~i** [ɪz'reɪlɪ] *adj* israelisch ♦ *n* Israeli *mf*

issue ['ɪʃjuː] *n* (*matter*) Frage *f*; (*outcome*) Ausgang *m*; (*of newspaper, shares*) Ausgabe *f*; (*offspring*) Nachkommenschaft *f* ♦ *vt* ausgeben; (*warrant*) erlassen; (*documents*) ausstellen; (*orders*) erteilen; (*books*) herausgeben; (*verdict*) aussprechen; **to be at ~** zur Debatte stehen; **to take ~ with sb over sth** jdm in etw *dat* widersprechen

KEYWORD

it [ɪt] *pron* **1** (*specific: subject*) er/sie/es; (: *direct object*) ihn/sie/es; (: *indirect object*) ihm/ihr/ihm; **about/from/in/of it** darüber/davon/darin/davon

2 (*impers*) es; **it's raining** es regnet; **it's Friday tomorrow** morgen ist Freitag; **who is it? – it's me** wer ist da? – ich (bin)s

Italian [ɪ'tæljən] *adj* italienisch ♦ *n* Italiener(in) *m(f)*; (*LING*) Italienisch *nt*

italic [ɪ'tælɪk] *adj* kursiv; **~s** *npl* Kursivschrift *f*

Italy ['ɪtəlɪ] *n* Italien *nt*

itch [ɪtʃ] *n* Juckreiz *m*; (*fig*) Lust *f* ♦ *vi* jucken; **to be ~ing to do sth** darauf brennen, etw zu tun; **~y** *adj* juckend

it'd ['ɪtd] = **it would; it had**

item ['aɪtəm] *n* Gegenstand *m*; (*on list*) Posten *m*; (*in programme*) Nummer *f*; (*in agenda*) (Programm)punkt *m*; (*in newspaper*) (Zeitungs)notiz *f*; **~ize** *vt* verzeichnen

itinerant [ɪ'tɪnərənt] *adj* umherreisend

itinerary [aɪ'tɪnərərɪ] *n* Reiseroute *f*

it'll ['ɪtl] = **it will; it shall**

its [ɪts] *adj* (*masculine, neuter*) sein; (*feminine*) ihr

it's [ɪts] = **it is; it has**

itself [ɪt'self] *pron* sich (selbst); (*emphatic*) selbst

ITV (*BRIT*) *n abbr* = **Independent Television**

I.U.D. *n abbr* (= *intra-uterine device*) Pessar *nt*

I've [aɪv] = **I have**

ivory ['aɪvərɪ] *n* Elfenbein *nt*

ivy ['aɪvɪ] *n* Efeu *nt*

J, j

jab [dʒæb] *vt* (hinein)stechen ♦ *n* Stich *m*, Stoß *m*; (*inf*) Spritze *f*

jack [dʒæk] *n* (*AUT*) (Wagen)heber *m*; (*CARDS*) Bube *m*; **~ up** *vt* aufbocken

jackal ['dʒækl] *n* (*ZOOL*) Schakal *m*

jackdaw ['dʒækdɔː] *n* Dohle *f*

jacket ['dʒækɪt] *n* Jacke *f*; (*of book*) Schutzumschlag *m*; (*TECH*) Ummantelung *f*; **~ potatoes** *npl* in der Schale gebackene Kartoffeln *pl*

jackknife ['dʒæknaɪf] *vi* (*truck*) sich zusammenschieben

jack plug *n* (*ELEC*) Buchsenstecker *m*

jackpot ['dʒækpɒt] *n* Haupttreffer *m*

jaded ['dʒeɪdɪd] *adj* ermattet

jagged ['dʒægɪd] *adj* zackig

jail [dʒeɪl] *n* Gefängnis *nt* ♦ *vt* einsperren; **~er** *n* Gefängniswärter *m*

jam [dʒæm] *n* Marmelade *f*; (*also:* **traffic ~**) (Verkehrs)stau *m*; (*inf: trouble*) Klemme *f* ♦ *vt* (*wedge*) einklemmen; (*cram*) hineinzwängen; (*obstruct*) blockieren ♦ *vi* sich verklemmen; **to ~ sth into sth** etw in etw *acc* hineinstopfen

Jamaica [dʒə'meɪkə] *n* Jamaika *nt*

jam jar *n* Marmeladenglas *nt*

jammed [dʒæmd] *adj*: **it's ~** es klemmt

jam-packed [dʒæm'pækt] *adj* überfüllt, proppenvoll

jangle ['dʒæŋgl] *vt, vi* klimpern

janitor ['dʒænɪtə'] *n* Hausmeister *m*

January ['dʒænjuərɪ] *n* Januar *m*

Japan [dʒə'pæn] *n* Japan *nt*; **~ese** [dʒæpə'niːz] *adj* japanisch ♦ *n inv* Japaner(in) *m(f)*; (*LING*) Japanisch *nt*

jar [dʒɑː'] *n* Glas *nt* ♦ *vi* kreischen; (*colours*

etc) nicht harmonieren

jargon ['dʒɑːgən] *n* Fachsprache *f*, Jargon *m*

jaundice ['dʒɔːndɪs] *n* Gelbsucht *f*; **~d** *adj* (*fig*) missgünstig

jaunt [dʒɔːnt] *n* Spritztour *f*

javelin ['dʒævlɪn] *n* Speer *m*

jaw [dʒɔː] *n* Kiefer *m*

jay [dʒeɪ] *n* (ZOOL) Eichelhäher *m*

jaywalker ['dʒeɪwɔːkəʳ] *n* unvorsichtige(r) Fußgänger *m*

jazz [dʒæz] *n* Jazz *m*; **~ up** *vt* (MUS) verjazzen; (*enliven*) aufpolieren

jealous ['dʒɛləs] *adj* (*envious*) missgünstig; (*husband*) eifersüchtig; **~y** *n* Missgunst *f*; Eifersucht *f*

jeans [dʒiːnz] *npl* Jeans *pl*

Jeep [dʒiːp] ® *n* Jeep *m* ®

jeer [dʒɪəʳ] *vi*: **to ~ (at sb)** (über jdn) höhnisch lachen, (jdn) verspotten

Jehovah's Witness [dʒɪˈhəʊvəz-] *n* Zeuge *m*/Zeugin *f* Jehovas

jelly ['dʒɛlɪ] *n* Gelee *nt*; (*dessert*) Grütze *f*; **~fish** *n* Qualle *f*

jeopardize ['dʒɛpədaɪz] *vt* gefährden

jeopardy ['dʒɛpədɪ] *n*: **to be in jeopardy** in Gefahr sein

jerk [dʒɜːk] *n* Ruck *m*; (*inf: idiot*) Trottel *m* ♦ *vt* ruckartig bewegen ♦ *vi* sich ruckartig bewegen

jerky ['dʒɜːkɪ] *adj* (*movement*) ruckartig; (*ride*) rüttelnd

jersey ['dʒɜːzɪ] *n* Pullover *m*

jest [dʒɛst] *n* Scherz *m* ♦ *vi* spaßen; **in ~** im Spaß

Jesus ['dʒiːzəs] *n* Jesus *m*

jet [dʒɛt] *n* (*stream: of water etc*) Strahl *m*; (*spout*) Düse *f*; (AVIAT) Düsenflugzeug *nt*; **~-black** *adj* rabenschwarz; **~ engine** *n* Düsenmotor *m*; **~ lag** *n* Jetlag *m*

jettison ['dʒɛtɪsn] *vt* über Bord werfen

jetty ['dʒɛtɪ] *n* Landesteg *m*, Mole *f*

Jew [dʒuː] *n* Jude *m*

jewel ['dʒuːəl] *n* (*also fig*) Juwel *nt*; **~ler** (US **jeweler**) *n* Juwelier *m*; **~ler's (shop)** *n* Juwelier *m*; **~lery** (US **jewelry**) *n* Schmuck *m*

Jewess ['dʒuːɪs] *n* Jüdin *f*

Jewish ['dʒuːɪʃ] *adj* jüdisch

jibe [dʒaɪb] *n* spöttische Bemerkung *f*

jiffy ['dʒɪfɪ] (*inf*) *n*: **in a ~** sofort

jigsaw ['dʒɪgsɔː] *n* (*also:* **~ puzzle**) Puzzle(spiel) *nt*

jilt [dʒɪlt] *vt* den Laufpass geben +*dat*

jingle ['dʒɪŋgl] *n* (*advertisement*) Werbesong *m* ♦ *vi* klimpern; (*bells*) bimmeln ♦ *vt* klimpern mit; bimmeln lassen

jinx [dʒɪŋks] *n*: **there's a ~ on it** es ist verhext

jitters ['dʒɪtəz] (*inf*) *npl*: **to get the ~** einen Bammel kriegen

job [dʒɔb] *n* (*piece of work*) Arbeit *f*; (*position*) Stellung *f*; (*duty*) Aufgabe *f*; (*difficulty*) Mühe *f*; **it's a good ~ he ...** es ist ein Glück, dass er ...; **just the ~** genau das Richtige; **J~centre** (BRIT) *n* Arbeitsamt *nt*; **~less** *adj* arbeitslos

jockey ['dʒɔkɪ] *n* Jockei *m*, Jockey *m* ♦ *vi*: **to ~ for position** sich in eine gute Position drängeln

jocular ['dʒɔkjʊləʳ] *adj* scherzhaft

jog [dʒɔg] *vt* (an)stoßen ♦ *vi* (*run*) joggen; **to ~ along** vor sich *acc* hinwursteln; (*work*) seinen Gang gehen; **~ging** *n* Jogging *nt*

join [dʒɔɪn] *vt* (*club*) beitreten +*dat*; (*person*) sich anschließen +*dat*; (*fasten*): **to ~ (sth to sth)** (etw mit etw) verbinden ♦ *vi* (*unite*) sich vereinigen ♦ *n* Verbindungsstelle *f*, Naht *f*; **~ in** *vt, vi*: **to ~ in (sth)** (bei etw) mitmachen; **~ up** *vi* (MIL) zur Armee gehen

joiner ['dʒɔɪnəʳ] *n* Schreiner *m*; **~y** *n* Schreinerei *f*

joint [dʒɔɪnt] *n* (TECH) Fuge *f*; (*of bones*) Gelenk *nt*; (*of meat*) Braten *m*; (*inf: place*) Lokal *nt* ♦ *adj* gemeinsam; **~ account** *n* (*with bank etc*) gemeinsame(s) Konto *nt*; **~ly** *adv* gemeinsam

joke [dʒəʊk] *n* Witz *m* ♦ *vi* Witze machen; **to play a ~ on sb** jdm einen Streich spielen

joker ['dʒəʊkəʳ] *n* Witzbold *m*; (CARDS) Joker *m*

jolly ['dʒɔlɪ] *adj* lustig ♦ *adv* (*inf*) ganz schön

jolt [dʒəʊlt] *n* (*shock*) Schock *m*; (*jerk*) Stoß *m*

♦ vt (push) stoßen; (shake) durchschütteln; (fig) aufrütteln ♦ vi holpern

Jordan ['dʒɔːdən] n Jordanien nt

jostle ['dʒɔsl] vt anrempeln

jot [dʒɔt] n: **not one ~** kein Jota nt; **~ down** vt notieren; **~ter** (BRIT) n Notizblock m

journal ['dʒəːnl] n (diary) Tagebuch nt; (magazine) Zeitschrift f; **~ism** n Journalismus m; **~ist** n Journalist(in) m(f)

journey ['dʒəːnɪ] n Reise f

jovial ['dʒəuvɪəl] adj jovial

joy [dʒɔɪ] n Freude f; **~ful** adj freudig; **~ous** adj freudig; **~ ride** n Schwarzfahrt f; **~rider** n Autodieb, der den Wagen nur für eine Spritztour stiehlt; **~stick** n Steuerknüppel m; (COMPUT) Joystick m

J.P. n abbr = **Justice of the Peace**

Jr abbr = **junior**

jubilant ['dʒuːbɪlnt] adj triumphierend

jubilee ['dʒuːbɪliː] n Jubiläum nt

judge [dʒʌdʒ] n Richter m; (fig) Kenner m ♦ vt (JUR: person) die Verhandlung führen über +acc; (case) verhandeln; (assess) beurteilen; (estimate) einschätzen; **~ment** n (JUR) Urteil nt; (ECCL) Gericht nt; (ability) Urteilsvermögen nt

judicial [dʒuː'dɪʃl] adj gerichtlich, Justiz-

judiciary [dʒuː'dɪʃɪərɪ] n Gerichtsbehörden pl; (judges) Richterstand m

judicious [dʒuː'dɪʃəs] adj weise

judo ['dʒuːdəu] n Judo nt

jug [dʒʌg] n Krug m

juggernaut ['dʒʌgənɔːt] (BRIT) n (huge truck) Schwertransporter m

juggle ['dʒʌgl] vt, vi jonglieren; **~r** n Jongleur m

Jugoslav etc ['juːgəu'slɑːv] = **Yugoslav** etc

juice [dʒuːs] n Saft m; **juicy** ['dʒuːsɪ] adj (also fig) saftig

jukebox ['dʒuːkbɔks] n Musikautomat m

July [dʒuː'laɪ] n Juli m

jumble ['dʒʌmbl] n Durcheinander nt ♦ vt (also: **~ up**) durcheinander werfen; (facts) durcheinander bringen

jumble sale (BRIT) n Basar m, Flohmarkt m

Jumble sale

ⓘ **Jumble sale** ist ein Wohltätigkeitsbasar, meist in einer Aula oder einem Gemeindehaus abgehalten, bei dem alle möglichen Gebrauchtwaren (vor allem Kleidung, Spielzeug, Bücher, Geschirr und Möbel) verkauft werden. Der Erlös fließt entweder einer Wohltätigkeitsorganisation zu oder wird für örtliche Zwecke verwendet, z.B. die Pfadfinder, die Grundschule, Reparatur der Kirche usw.

---

jumbo (jet) ['dʒʌmbəu-] n Jumbo(jet) m

jump [dʒʌmp] vi springen; (nervously) zusammenzucken ♦ vt überspringen ♦ n Sprung m; **to ~ the queue** (BRIT) sich vordrängeln

jumper ['dʒʌmpər] n (BRIT: pullover) Pullover m; (US: dress) Trägerkleid nt

jump leads BRIT, **jumper cables** US npl Überbrückungskabel nt

jumpy ['dʒʌmpɪ] adj nervös

Jun. abbr = **junior**

junction ['dʒʌŋkʃən] n (BRIT: of roads) (Straßen)kreuzung f; (RAIL) Knotenpunkt m

juncture ['dʒʌŋktʃər] n: **at this ~** in diesem Augenblick

June [dʒuːn] n Juni m

jungle ['dʒʌŋgl] n Dschungel m

junior ['dʒuːnɪər] adj (younger) jünger; (after name) junior; (SPORT) Junioren-; (lower position) untergeordnet; (for young people) Junioren- ♦ n Jüngere(r) mf; **~ school** (BRIT) n Grundschule f

junk [dʒʌŋk] n (rubbish) Plunder m; (ship) Dschunke f; **~ bond** n (COMM) niedrig eingestuftes Wertpapier mit hohen Ertragschancen bei erhöhtem Risiko; **~ food** n Junk food nt; **~ mail** n Reklame, die unangefordert in den Briefkasten gesteckt wird; **~ shop** n Ramschladen m

Junr abbr = **junior**

jurisdiction [dʒuərɪs'dɪkʃən] n Gerichtsbarkeit f; (range of authority) Zuständigkeit(sbereich m) f

juror ['dʒʊərər] n Geschworene(r) mf; (*in competition*) Preisrichter m

jury ['dʒʊərɪ] n (*court*) Geschworene pl; (*panel*) Jury f

just [dʒʌst] adj gerecht ♦ adv (*recently, now*) gerade, eben; (*barely*) gerade noch; (*exactly*) genau, gerade; (*only*) nur, bloß; (*a small distance*) gleich; (*absolutely*) einfach; ~ **as I arrived** gerade als ich ankam; ~ **as nice** genauso nett; ~ **as well** umso besser; ~ **now** soeben, gerade; ~ **try** versuch es mal; **she's ~ left** sie ist gerade or (so)eben gegangen; **he's ~ done it** er hat es gerade or (so)eben getan; ~ **before** gerade or kurz bevor; ~ **enough** gerade genug; **he ~ missed** er hat fast or beinahe getroffen

justice ['dʒʌstɪs] n (*fairness*) Gerechtigkeit f; **J~ of the Peace** n Friedensrichter m

justifiable [dʒʌstɪ'faɪəbl] adj berechtigt

justification [dʒʌstɪfɪ'keɪʃən] n Rechtfertigung f

justify ['dʒʌstɪfaɪ] vt rechtfertigen; (*text*) justieren

justly ['dʒʌstlɪ] adv (*say*) mit Recht; (*condemn*) gerecht

jut [dʒʌt] vi (*also*: ~ **out**) herausragen, vorstehen

juvenile ['dʒuːvənaɪl] adj (*young*) jugendlich; (*for the young*) Jugend- ♦ n Jugendliche(r) mf

juxtapose ['dʒʌkstəpəʊz] vt nebeneinander stellen

K, k

K [keɪ] abbr (= one thousand) Tsd.; (= kilobyte) K

kangaroo [kæŋgə'ruː] n Känguru nt

karate [kə'rɑːtɪ] n Karate nt

kebab [kə'bæb] n Kebab m

keel [kiːl] n Kiel m; **on an even ~** (fig) im Lot

keen [kiːn] adj begeistert; (*wind, blade, intelligence*) scharf; (*sight, hearing*) gut; **to be ~ to do** or **on doing sth** etw unbedingt tun wollen; **to be ~ on sth/sb** scharf auf etw/jdn sein

keep [kiːp] (pt, pp **kept**) vt (*retain*) behalten; (*have*) haben; (*animals, one's word*) halten; (*support*) versorgen; (*maintain in state*) halten; (*preserve*) aufbewahren; (*restrain*) abhalten ♦ vi (*continue in direction*) sich halten; (*food*) sich halten; (*remain: quiet etc*) bleiben ♦ n Unterhalt m; (*tower*) Burgfried m; (*inf*): **for ~s** für immer; **to ~ sth to o.s.** etw für sich behalten; **it ~s happening** es passiert immer wieder; ~ **back** vt fern halten; (*information*) verschweigen; ~ **on** vi: ~ **on doing sth** etw immer weiter tun; ~ **out** vt nicht hereinlassen; "~ **out**" „Eintritt verboten!"; ~ **up** vi Schritt halten ♦ vt aufrechterhalten; (*continue*) weitermachen; **to ~ up with** Schritt halten mit; ~**er** n Wärter(in) m(f); (*goalkeeper*) Torhüter(in) m(f); ~**-fit** n Keep-fit nt; ~**ing** n (*care*) Obhut f; **in ~ing with** in Übereinstimmung mit; ~**sake** n Andenken nt

keg [keg] n Fass nt

kennel ['kɛnl] n Hundehütte f; ~**s** npl: **to put a dog in ~s** (*for boarding*) einen Hund in Pflege geben

Kenya ['kɛnjə] n Kenia nt; ~**n** adj kenianisch ♦ n Kenianer(in) m(f)

kept [kɛpt] pt, pp of **keep**

kerb [kɜːb] n (BRIT) Bordstein m

kernel ['kɜːnl] n Kern m

kerosene ['kɛrəsiːn] n Kerosin nt

kettle ['kɛtl] n Kessel m; ~**drum** n Pauke f

key [kiː] n Schlüssel m; (*of piano, typewriter*) Taste f; (MUS) Tonart f ♦ vt (*also*: ~ **in**) eingeben; ~**board** n Tastatur f; ~**ed up** adj (*person*) überdreht; ~**hole** n Schlüsselloch nt; ~**hole surgery** n minimal invasive Chirurgie f, Schlüssellochchirurgie f; ~**note** n Grundton m; ~ **ring** n Schlüsselring m

khaki ['kɑːkɪ] n K(h)aki nt ♦ adj k(h)aki(farben)

kick [kɪk] vt einen Fußtritt geben +dat, treten ♦ vi treten; (*baby*) strampeln; (*horse*) ausschlagen ♦ n (Fuß)tritt m; (*thrill*) Spaß m; **he does it for ~s** er macht das aus Jux;

~ **off** vi (SPORT) anstoßen; **~-off** n (SPORT) Anstoß m

kid [kɪd] n (inf: child) Kind nt; (goat) Zicklein nt; (leather) Glacéleder nt, Glaceeleder nt ♦ vi (inf) Witze machen

kidnap ['kɪdnæp] vt entführen; **~per** n Entführer m; **~ping** n Entführung f

kidney ['kɪdnɪ] n Niere f

kill [kɪl] vt töten, umbringen ♦ vi töten ♦ n (hunting) (Jagd)beute f; **~er** n Mörder(in) m(f); **~ing** n Mord m; **~joy** n Spaßverderber(in) m(f)

kiln [kɪln] n Brennofen m

kilo ['kiːləu] n Kilo nt; **~byte** n (COMPUT) Kilobyte nt; **~gram(me)** n Kilogramm nt; **~metre** ['kɪləmiːtər] (US **kilometer**) n Kilometer m; **~watt** n Kilowatt nt

kilt [kɪlt] n Schottenrock m

kind [kaɪnd] adj freundlich ♦ n Art f; **a ~ of** eine Art von; **(two) of a ~** (zwei) von der gleichen Art; **in ~** auf dieselbe Art; (in goods) in Naturalien

kindergarten ['kɪndəgɑːtn] n Kindergarten m

kind-hearted [kaɪnd'hɑːtɪd] adj gutherzig

kindle ['kɪndl] vt (set on fire) anzünden; (rouse) reizen, (er)wecken

kindly ['kaɪndlɪ] adj freundlich ♦ adv liebenswürdig(erweise); **would you ~ ...?** wären Sie so freundlich und ...?

kindness ['kaɪndnɪs] n Freundlichkeit f

kindred ['kɪndrɪd] adj: **~ spirit** Gleichgesinnte(r) mf

king [kɪŋ] n König m; **~dom** n Königreich nt

kingfisher ['kɪŋfɪʃər] n Eisvogel m

king-size(d) ['kɪŋsaɪz(d)] adj (cigarette) Kingsize

kinky ['kɪŋkɪ] (inf) adj (person, ideas) verrückt; (sexual) abartig

kiosk ['kiːɔsk] (BRIT) n (TEL) Telefonhäuschen nt

kipper ['kɪpər] n Räucherhering m

kiss [kɪs] n Kuss m ♦ vt küssen ♦ vi: **they ~ed** sie küssten sich; **~ of life** (BRIT) n: **the ~ of life** Mund-zu-Mund-Beatmung f

kit [kɪt] n Ausrüstung f; (tools) Werkzeug nt

kitchen ['kɪtʃɪn] n Küche f; **~ sink** n

Spülbecken nt

kite [kaɪt] n Drachen m

kitten ['kɪtn] n Kätzchen nt

kitty ['kɪtɪ] n (money) Kasse f

km abbr (= kilometre) km

knack [næk] n Dreh m, Trick m

knapsack ['næpsæk] n Rucksack m; (MIL) Tornister m

knead [niːd] vt kneten

knee [niː] n Knie nt; **~cap** n Kniescheibe f

kneel [niːl] (pt, pp **knelt**) vi (also: ~ **down**) knien

knelt [nɛlt] pt, pp of **kneel**

knew [njuː] pt of **know**

knickers ['nɪkəz] (BRIT) npl Schlüpfer m

knife [naɪf] (pl **knives**) n Messer nt ♦ vt erstechen

knight [naɪt] n Ritter m; (chess) Springer m; **~hood** n (title): **to get a ~hood** zum Ritter geschlagen werden

knit [nɪt] vt stricken ♦ vi stricken; (bones) zusammenwachsen; **~ting** n (occupation) Stricken nt; (work) Strickzeug nt; **~ting needle** n Stricknadel f; **~wear** n Strickwaren pl

knives [naɪvz] pl of **knife**

knob [nɔb] n Knauf m; (on instrument) Knopf m; (BRIT: of butter etc) kleine(s) Stück nt

knock [nɔk] vt schlagen; (criticize) heruntermachen ♦ vi: **to ~ at** or **on the door** an die Tür klopfen ♦ n Schlag m; (on door) Klopfen nt; **~ down** vt umwerfen; (with car) anfahren; **~ off** vt (do quickly) hinhauen; (inf: steal) klauen ♦ vi (finish) Feierabend machen; **~ out** vt ausschlagen; (BOXING) k. o. schlagen; **~ over** vt (person, object) umwerfen; (with car) anfahren; **~er** n (on door) Türklopfer m; **~out** n K.-o.-Schlag m; (fig) Sensation f

knot [nɔt] n Knoten m ♦ vt (ver)knoten

knotty ['nɔtɪ] adj (fig) kompliziert

know [nəu] (pt **knew**, pp **known**) vt, vi wissen; (be able to) können; (be acquainted with) kennen; (recognize) erkennen; **to ~ how to do sth** wissen, wie man etw macht, etw tun können; **to ~ about** or **of sth/sb** etw/jdn kennen; **~-all** n Alleswisser

m; **~-how** n Kenntnis f, Know-how nt;
~ing adj (look, smile) wissend; (intentionally) **~ingly** adv
wissend; (intentionally) wissentlich
knowledge ['nɔlɪdʒ] n Wissen nt, Kenntnis
f; **~able** adj informiert
known [nəun] pp of **know**
knuckle ['nʌkl] n Fingerknöchel m
K.O. n abbr = **knockout**
Koran [kɔ'rɑːn] n Koran m
Korea [kə'rɪə] n Korea nt
kosher ['kəuʃəʳ] adj koscher

L, l

L [εl] abbr (BRIT: AUT) (= learner) am Auto
angebrachtes Kennzeichen für Fahrschüler; =
lake; (= large) gr.; (= left) l.
l. abbr = **litre**
lab [læb] (inf) n Labor nt
label ['leɪbl] n Etikett nt ♦ vt etikettieren
labor etc ['leɪbəʳ] (US) = **labour** etc
laboratory [lə'bɔrətərɪ] n Laboratorium nt
laborious [lə'bɔːrɪəs] adj mühsam
labour ['leɪbəʳ] (US **labor**) n Arbeit f;
(workmen) Arbeitskräfte pl; (MED) Wehen pl
♦ vi: **to ~ (at)** sich abmühen (mit) ♦ vt
breittreten (inf); **in ~** (MED) in den Wehen;
L~ (BRIT: also: **the L~ party**) die Labour
Party; **~ed** adj (movement) gequält; (style)
schwerfällig; **~er** n Arbeiter m; **farm ~er**
(Land)arbeiter m
lace [leɪs] n (fabric) Spitze f; (of shoe)
Schnürsenkel m; (braid) Litze f ♦ vt (also: ~
up) (zu)schnüren
lack [læk] n Mangel m ♦ vt nicht haben; **sb
~s sth** jdm fehlt etw nom; **to be ~ing**
fehlen; **sb is ~ing in sth** es fehlt jdm an
etw dat; **for** or **through ~ of** aus Mangel an
+dat
lacquer ['lækəʳ] n Lack m
lad [læd] n Junge m
ladder ['lædəʳ] n Leiter f; (BRIT: in tights)
Laufmasche f ♦ vt (BRIT: tights) Laufmaschen
bekommen in +dat
laden ['leɪdn] adj beladen, voll
ladle ['leɪdl] n Schöpfkelle f

lady ['leɪdɪ] n Dame f; (title) Lady f; **young ~**
junge Dame; **the ladies' (room)** die
Damentoilette; **~bird** (US **~bug**) n
Marienkäfer m; **~like** adj damenhaft,
vornehm; **~ship** n: **your L~ship** Ihre
Ladyschaft
lag [læg] vi (also: ~ **behind**) zurückbleiben
♦ vt (pipes) verkleiden
lager ['lɑːgəʳ] n helle(s) Bier nt
lagging ['lægɪŋ] n Isolierung f
lagoon [lə'guːn] n Lagune f
laid [leɪd] pt, pp of **lay**; **~ back** (inf) adj cool
lain [leɪn] pp of **lie**
lair [lεəʳ] n Lager nt
lake [leɪk] n See m
lamb [læm] n Lamm nt; (meat) Lammfleisch
nt; **~ chop** n Lammkotelett nt; **~swool** n
Lammwolle f
lame [leɪm] adj lahm; (excuse) faul
lament [lə'ment] n Klage f ♦ vt beklagen
laminated ['læmɪneɪtɪd] adj beschichtet
lamp [læmp] n Lampe f; (in street)
Straßenlaterne f; **~post** n Laternenpfahl m;
~shade n Lampenschirm m
lance [lɑːns] n Lanze f; **~ corporal** (BRIT) n
Obergefreite(r) m
land [lænd] n Land nt ♦ vi (from ship) an
Land gehen; (AVIAT, end up) landen ♦ vt
(obtain) kriegen; (passengers) absetzen;
(goods) abladen; (troops, space probe)
landen; **~fill site** n ['lændfɪl-] n Mülldeponie
f; **~ing** n Landung f; (on stairs)
(Treppen)absatz m; **~ing gear** n
Fahrgestell nt; **~ing stage** (BRIT) n
Landesteg m; **~ing strip** n Landebahn f;
~lady n (Haus)wirtin f; **~locked** adj
landumschlossen, Binnen-; **~lord** n (of
house) Hauswirt m, Besitzer m; (of pub)
Gastwirt m; (of area) Grundbesitzer m;
~mark n Wahrzeichen nt; (fig) Meilenstein
m; **~owner** n Grundbesitzer m; **~scape** n
Landschaft f; **~ gardener** n
Landschaftsgärtner(in) m(f); **~slide** n
(GEOG) Erdrutsch m; (POL)
überwältigende(r) Sieg m
lane [leɪn] n (in town) Gasse f; (in country)
Weg m; (of motorway) Fahrbahn f, Spur f;

(SPORT) Bahn f; **"get in ~"** „bitte einordnen"

language ['læŋgwɪdʒ] n Sprache f; **bad ~** unanständige Ausdrücke pl; **~ laboratory** n Sprachlabor nt

languish ['læŋgwɪʃ] vi schmachten

lank [læŋk] adj dürr

lanky ['læŋkɪ] adj schlaksig

lantern ['læntən] n Laterne f

lap [læp] n Schoß m; (SPORT) Runde f ♦ vt (also: **~ up**) auflecken ♦ vi (water) plätschern

lapel [lə'pɛl] n Revers nt or m

Lapland ['læplænd] n Lappland nt

lapse [læps] n (moral) Fehltritt m ♦ vi (decline) nachlassen; (expire) ablaufen; (claims) erlöschen; **to ~ into bad habits** sich schlechte Gewohnheiten angewöhnen

laptop (computer) ['læptɒp-] n Laptop(-Computer) m

lard [lɑːd] n Schweineschmalz nt

larder ['lɑːdə'] n Speisekammer f

large [lɑːdʒ] adj groß; **at ~** auf freiem Fuß; **~ly** adv zum größten Teil; **~-scale** adj groß angelegt, Groß-

lark [lɑːk] n (bird) Lerche f; (joke) Jux m; **~ about** (inf) vi herumalbern

laryngitis [lærɪn'dʒaɪtɪs] n Kehlkopfentzündung f

laser ['leɪzə'] n Laser m; **~ printer** n Laserdrucker m

lash [læʃ] n Peitschenhieb m; (eyelash) Wimper f ♦ vt (rain) schlagen gegen; (whip) peitschen; (bind) festbinden; **~ out** vi (with fists) um sich schlagen

lass [læs] n Mädchen nt

lasso [læ'suː] n Lasso nt

last [lɑːst] adj letzte(r, s) ♦ adv zuletzt; (~ time) das letzte Mal ♦ vi (continue) dauern; (remain good) sich halten; (money) ausreichen; **at ~** endlich; **~ night** gestern Abend; **~ week** letzte Woche; **~ but one** vorletzte(r, s); **~-ditch** adj (attempt) in letzter Minute; **~ing** adj dauerhaft; (shame etc) andauernd; **~ly** adv schließlich; **~-minute** adj in letzter Minute

latch [lætʃ] n Riegel m

late [leɪt] adj spät; (dead) verstorben ♦ adv spät; (after proper time) zu spät; **to be ~** zu spät kommen; **of ~** in letzter Zeit; **in ~ May** Ende Mai; **~comer** n Nachzügler(in) m(f); **~ly** adv in letzter Zeit; **later** ['leɪtə'] adj (date) später; (version) neuer ♦ adv später

lateral ['lætərəl] adj seitlich

latest ['leɪtɪst] adj (fashion) neueste(r, s) ♦ n (news) Neu(e)ste(s) nt; **at the ~** spätestens

lathe [leɪð] n Drehbank f

lather ['lɑːðə'] n (Seifen)schaum m ♦ vt einschäumen ♦ vi schäumen

Latin ['lætɪn] n Latein nt ♦ adj lateinisch; (Roman) römisch; **~ America** n Lateinamerika nt; **~ American** adj lateinamerikanisch

latitude ['lætɪtjuːd] n (GEOG) Breite f; (freedom) Spielraum m

latter ['lætə'] adj (second of two) letztere; (coming at end) letzte(r, s), später ♦ n: **the ~** der/die/das letztere, die letzteren; **~ly** adv in letzter Zeit

lattice ['lætɪs] n Gitter nt

laudable ['lɔːdəbl] adj löblich

laugh [lɑːf] n Lachen nt ♦ vi lachen; **~ at** vt lachen über +acc; **~ off** vt lachend abtun; **~able** adj lachhaft; **~ing stock** n Zielscheibe f des Spottes; **~ter** n Gelächter nt

launch [lɔːntʃ] n (of ship) Stapellauf m; (of rocket) Abschuss m; (boat) Barkasse f; (of product) Einführung f ♦ vt (set afloat) vom Stapel lassen; (rocket) (ab)schießen; (product) auf den Markt bringen; **~(ing) pad** n Abschussrampe f

launder ['lɔːndə'] vt waschen

Launderette [lɔːn'drɛt] (® BRIT) n Waschsalon m

Laundromat ['lɔːndrəmæt] (® US) n Waschsalon m

laundry ['lɔːndrɪ] n (place) Wäscherei f; (clothes) Wäsche f; **to do the ~** waschen

laureate ['lɔːrɪət] adj see **poet**

laurel ['lɒrl] n Lorbeer m

lava ['lɑːvə] n Lava f

lavatory ['lævətərɪ] n Toilette f

lavender ['lævəndəʳ] n Lavendel m

lavish ['lævɪʃ] adj (extravagant) verschwenderisch; (generous) großzügig ♦ vt (money): **to ~ sth on sth** etw auf etw acc verschwenden; (attention, gifts): **to ~ sth on sb** jdn mit etw überschütten

law [lɔ:] n Gesetz nt; (system) Recht nt; (as studies) Jura no art; **~-abiding** adj gesetzestreu; **~ and order** n Recht nt und Ordnung f; **~ court** n Gerichtshof m; **~ful** adj gesetzlich; **~less** adj gesetzlos

lawn [lɔ:n] n Rasen m; **~mower** n Rasenmäher m; **~ tennis** n Rasentennis m

law: **~ school** n Rechtsakademie f; **~suit** n Prozess m; **~yer** n Rechtsanwalt m, Rechtsanwältin f

lax [læks] adj (behaviour) nachlässig; (standards) lax

laxative ['læksətɪv] n Abführmittel nt

lay [leɪ] (pt, pp **laid**) pt of **lie** ♦ adj Laien- ♦ vt (place) legen; (table) decken; (egg) legen; (trap) stellen; (money) wetten; **~ aside** vt zurücklegen; **~ by** vt (set aside) beiseite legen; **~ down** vt hinlegen; (rules) vorschreiben; (arms) strecken; **to ~ down the law** Vorschriften machen; **~ off** vt (workers) (vorübergehend) entlassen; **~ on** vt (water, gas) anschließen; (concert etc) veranstalten; **~ out** vt (her)auslegen; (money) ausgeben; (corpse) aufbahren; **~ up** vt (subj: illness) ans Bett fesseln; **~about** n Faulenzer m; **~-by** n (BRIT) Parkbucht f; (bigger) Rastplatz m

layer ['leɪəʳ] n Schicht f

layman ['leɪmən] (irreg) n Laie m

layout ['leɪaʊt] n Anlage f; (ART) Lay-out nt, Layout nt

laze [leɪz] vi faulenzen

laziness ['leɪzɪnɪs] n Faulheit f

lazy ['leɪzɪ] adj faul; (slow-moving) träge

lb. abbr = **pound** (weight)

lead¹ [lɛd] n (chemical) Blei nt; (of pencil) (Bleistift)mine f ♦ adj bleiern, Blei-

lead² [li:d] (pt, pp **led**) n (front position) Führung f; (distance, time ahead) Vorsprung f; (example) Vorbild nt; (clue) Tipp m; (of police) Spur f; (THEAT) Hauptrolle f; (dog's) Leine f ♦ vt (guide) führen; (group etc) leiten ♦ vi (be first) führen; **in the ~** (SPORT, fig) in Führung; **~ astray** vt irreführen; **~ away** vt wegführen; (prisoner) abführen; **~ back** vi zurückführen; **~ on** vt anführen; **~ on to** vt (induce) dazu bringen; **~ to** vt (street) (hin)führen nach; (result in) führen zu; **~ up to** vt (drive) führen zu; (speaker etc) hinführen auf +acc

leaded petrol ['lɛdɪd-] n verbleites Benzin nt

leaden ['lɛdn] adj (sky, sea) bleiern; (heavy: footsteps) bleischwer

leader ['li:dəʳ] n Führer m, Leiter m; (of party) Vorsitzende(r) m; (PRESS) Leitartikel m; **~ship** n (office) Leitung f; (quality) Führerschaft f

lead-free ['lɛdfri:] adj (petrol) bleifrei

leading ['li:dɪŋ] adj führend; **~ lady** n (THEAT) Hauptdarstellerin f; **~ light** n (person) führende(r) Geist m

lead singer [li:d-] n Leadsänger(in) m(f)

leaf [li:f] (pl **leaves**) n Blatt nt ♦ vi: **to ~ through** durchblättern; **to turn over a new ~** einen neuen Anfang machen

leaflet ['li:flɪt] n (advertisement) Prospekt m; (pamphlet) Flugblatt nt; (for information) Merkblatt nt

league [li:g] n (union) Bund m; (SPORT) Liga f; **to be in ~ with** unter einer Decke stecken mit

leak [li:k] n undichte Stelle f; (in ship) Leck nt ♦ vt (liquid etc) durchlassen ♦ vi (pipe etc) undicht sein; (liquid etc) auslaufen; **the information was ~ed to the enemy** die Information wurde dem Feind zugespielt; **~ out** vi (liquid etc) auslaufen; (information) durchsickern; **~y** ['li:kɪ] adj undicht

lean [li:n] (pt, pp **leaned** or **leant**) adj mager ♦ vi sich neigen ♦ vt (to ~): **to ~ against sth** an etw dat angelehnt sein; sich an etw acc anlehnen; **~ back** vi sich zurücklehnen; **~ forward** vi sich vorbeugen; **~ on** vt fus sich stützen auf +acc; **~ out** vi sich hinauslehnen; **~ over** vi sich hinüberbeugen; **~ing** n Neigung f ♦ adj schief; **~t** [lɛnt] pt, pp of **lean**; **~-to** n

Anbau *m*

leap [liːp] (*pt, pp* **leaped** *or* **leapt**) *n* Sprung *m* ♦ *vi* springen; **~frog** *n* Bockspringen *nt*; **~t** [lɛpt] *pt, pp of* **leap**; **~ year** *n* Schaltjahr *nt*

learn [ləːn] (*pt, pp* **learned** *or* **learnt**) *vt, vi* lernen; (*find out*) erfahren; **to ~ how to do sth** etw (er)lernen; **~ed** [ˈləːnɪd] *adj* gelehrt; **~er** *n* Anfänger(in) *m(f)*; (*AUT: BRIT: also:* **~er driver**) Fahrschüler(in) *m(f)*; **~ing** *n* Gelehrsamkeit *f*; **~t** [ləːnt] *pt, pp of* **learn**

lease [liːs] *n* (*of property*) Mietvertrag *m* ♦ *vt* pachten

leash [liːʃ] *n* Leine *f*

least [liːst] *adj* geringste(r, s) ♦ *adv* am wenigsten ♦ *n* Mindeste(s) *nt*; **the ~ possible effort** möglichst geringer Aufwand; **at ~** zumindest; **not in the ~!** durchaus nicht!

leather [ˈlɛðər] *n* Leder *nt*

leave [liːv] (*pt, pp* **left**) *vt* verlassen; (*~ behind*) zurücklassen; (*forget*) vergessen; (*allow to remain*) lassen; (*after death*) hinterlassen; (*entrust*): **to ~ sth to sb** jdm etw überlassen ♦ *vi* weggehen, wegfahren; (*for journey*) abreisen; (*bus, train*) abfahren ♦ *n* Erlaubnis *f*; (*MIL*) Urlaub *m*; **to be left** (*remain*) übrig bleiben; **there's some milk left over** es ist noch etwas Milch übrig; **on ~** auf Urlaub; **~ behind** *vt* (*person, object*) dalassen; (*forget*) liegen lassen, stehen lassen; **~ out** *vt* auslassen; **~ of absence** *n* Urlaub *m*

leaves [liːvz] *pl of* **leaf**

Lebanon [ˈlɛbənən] *n* Libanon *m*

lecherous [ˈlɛtʃərəs] *adj* lüstern

lecture [ˈlɛktʃər] *n* Vortrag *m*; (*UNIV*) Vorlesung *f* ♦ *vi* einen Vortrag halten; (*UNIV*) lesen ♦ *vt* (*scold*) abkanzeln; **to give a ~ on** sth einen Vortrag über etw halten; **~r** [ˈlɛktʃərər] *n* Vortragende(r) *mf*; (*BRIT: UNIV*) Dozent(in) *m(f)*

led [lɛd] *pt, pp of* **lead²**

ledge [lɛdʒ] *n* Leiste *f*; (*window ~*) Sims *m or nt*; (*of mountain*) (Fels)vorsprung *m*

ledger [ˈlɛdʒər] *n* Hauptbuch *nt*

leech [liːtʃ] *n* Blutegel *m*

leek [liːk] *n* Lauch *m*

leer [lɪər] *vi*: **to ~ (at sb)** (nach jdm) schielen

leeway [ˈliːweɪ] *n* (*fig*): **to have some ~** etwas Spielraum haben

left [lɛft] *pt, pp of* **leave** ♦ *adj* linke(r, s) ♦ *n* (*side*) linke Seite *f* ♦ *adv* links; **on the ~** links; **to the ~** nach links; **the L~** (*POL*) die Linke *f*; **~-hand** *adj*: **~-hand drive** mit Linkssteuerung; **~-handed** *adj* linkshändig; **~-hand side** *n* linke Seite *f*; **~-luggage locker** *n* Gepäckschließfach *nt*; **~-luggage (office)** (*BRIT*) *n* Gepäckaufbewahrung *f*; **~-overs** *npl* Reste *pl*; **~-wing** *adj* linke(r, s)

leg [lɛg] *n* Bein *nt*; (*of meat*) Keule *f*; (*stage*) Etappe *f*; **1st/2nd ~** (*SPORT*) 1./2. Etappe

legacy [ˈlɛgəsɪ] *n* Erbe *nt*, Erbschaft *f*

legal [ˈliːgl] *adj* gesetzlich; (*allowed*) legal; **~ holiday** (*US*) *n* gesetzliche(r) Feiertag *m*; **~ize** *vt* legalisieren; **~ly** *adv* gesetzlich; legal; **~ tender** *n* gesetzliche(s) Zahlungsmittel *nt*

legend [ˈlɛdʒənd] *n* Legende *f*; **~ary** *adj* legendär

leggings [ˈlɛgɪŋz] *npl* Leggings *pl*

legible [ˈlɛdʒəbl] *adj* leserlich

legislation [lɛdʒɪsˈleɪʃən] *n* Gesetzgebung *f*; **legislative** [ˈlɛdʒɪslətɪv] *adj* gesetzgebend; **legislature** [ˈlɛdʒɪslətʃər] *n* Legislative *f*

legitimate [lɪˈdʒɪtɪmət] *adj* rechtmäßig, legitim; (*child*) ehelich

legroom [ˈlɛgruːm] *n* Platz *m* für die Beine

leisure [ˈlɛʒər] *n* Freizeit *f*; **to be at ~** Zeit haben; **~ centre** *n* Freizeitzentrum *nt*; **~ly** *adj* gemächlich

lemon [ˈlɛmən] *n* Zitrone *f*; (*colour*) Zitronengelb *nt*; **~ade** [lɛməˈneɪd] *n* Limonade *f*; **~ tea** *n* Zitronentee *m*

lend [lɛnd] (*pt, pp* **lent**) *vt* leihen; **to ~ sb sth** jdm etw leihen; **~ing library** *n* Leihbibliothek *f*

length [lɛŋθ] *n* Länge *f*; (*of road, pipe etc*) Strecke *f*; (*of material*) Stück *nt*; **at ~** (*lengthily*) ausführlich; (*at last*) schließlich; **~en** *vt* verlängern ♦ *vi* länger werden; **~ways** *adv* längs; **~y** *adj* sehr lang, langatmig

lenient [ˈliːnɪənt] *adj* nachsichtig

lens [lɛnz] *n* Linse *f*; (PHOT) Objektiv *nt*

Lent [lɛnt] *n* Fastenzeit *f*

lent [lɛnt] *pt, pp of* **lend**

lentil ['lɛntɪl] *n* Linse *f*

Leo ['liːəu] *n* Löwe *m*

leotard ['liːətɑːd] *n* Trikot *nt*, Gymnastikanzug *m*

leper ['lɛpə*] *n* Leprakranke(r) *f(m)*

leprosy ['lɛprəsɪ] *n* Lepra *f*

lesbian ['lɛzbɪən] *adj* lesbisch ♦ *n* Lesbierin *f*

less [lɛs] *adj, adv* weniger ♦ *n* weniger ♦ *pron* weniger; **~ than half** weniger als die Hälfte; **~ than ever** weniger denn je; **~ and ~** immer weniger; **the ~ he works** je weniger er arbeitet; **~en** ['lɛsn] *vi* abnehmen ♦ *vt* verringern, verkleinern; **~er** ['lɛsə*] *adj* kleiner, geringer; **to a ~er extent** in geringerem Maße

lesson ['lɛsn] *n* (SCH) Stunde *f*; (unit of study) Lektion *f*; (fig) Lehre *f*; (ECCL) Lesung *f*; **a maths ~** eine Mathestunde

lest [lɛst] *conj*: **~ it happen** damit es nicht passiert

let [lɛt] (*pt, pp* **let**) *vt* lassen; (BRIT: lease) vermieten; **to ~ sb do sth** jdn etw tun lassen; **to ~ sb know sth** jdn etw wissen lassen; **~'s go!** gehen wir!; **~ him come** soll er doch kommen; **~ down** *vt* hinunterlassen; (disappoint) enttäuschen; **~ go** *vi* loslassen ♦ *vt* (things) loslassen; (person) gehen lassen; **~ in** *vt* hereinlassen; (water) durchlassen; **~ off** *vt* (gun) abfeuern; (steam) ablassen; (forgive) laufen lassen; **~ on** *vi* durchblicken lassen; (pretend) vorgeben; **~ out** *vt* herauslassen; (scream) fahren lassen; **~ up** *vi* nachlassen; (stop) aufhören

lethal ['liːθl] *adj* tödlich

lethargic [lɛ'θɑːdʒɪk] *adj* lethargisch

letter ['lɛtə*] *n* Brief *m*; (of alphabet) Buchstabe *m*; **~ bomb** *n* Briefbombe *f*; **~box** (BRIT) *n* Briefkasten *m*; **~ing** *n* Beschriftung *f*; **~ of credit** *n* Akkreditiv *m*

lettuce ['lɛtɪs] *n* (Kopf)salat *m*

let-up ['lɛtʌp] (inf) *n* Nachlassen *nt*

leukaemia [luːˈkiːmɪə] (US **leukemia**) *n* Leukämie *f*

level ['lɛvl] *adj* (ground) eben; (at same height) auf gleicher Höhe; (equal) gleich gut; (head) kühl ♦ *adv* auf gleicher Höhe ♦ *n* (instrument) Wasserwaage *f*; (altitude) Höhe *f*; (flat place) ebene Fläche *f*; (position on scale) Niveau *nt*; (amount, degree) Grad *m* ♦ *vt* (ground) einebnen; **to draw ~ with** gleichziehen mit; **to be ~ with** auf einer Höhe sein mit; **A ~s** (BRIT) ≈ Abitur *nt*; **O ~s** (BRIT) ≈ mittlere Reife *f*; **on the ~** (fig: honest) ehrlich; **to ~ sth at sb** (blow) etw versetzen; (remark) etw gegen jdn richten; **~ off** *or* **out** *vi* flach *or* eben werden; (fig) sich ausgleichen; (plane) horizontal fliegen ♦ *vt* (ground) planieren; (differences) ausgleichen; **~ crossing** (BRIT) *n* Bahnübergang *m*; **~-headed** *adj* vernünftig

lever ['liːvə*] *n* Hebel *m*; (fig) Druckmittel *nt* ♦ *vt* (hoch)stemmen; **~age** *n* Hebelkraft *f*; (fig) Einfluss *m*

levy ['lɛvɪ] *n* (of taxes) Erhebung *f*; (tax) Abgaben *pl*; (MIL) Aushebung *f* ♦ *vt* erheben; (MIL) ausheben

lewd [luːd] *adj* unzüchtig, unanständig

liability [laɪə'bɪlətɪ] *n* (burden) Belastung *f*; (duty) Pflicht *f*; (debt) Verpflichtung *f*; (responsibility) Haftung *f*; (proneness) Anfälligkeit *f*

liable ['laɪəbl] *adj* (responsible) haftbar; (prone) anfällig; **to be ~ for sth** etw *dat* unterliegen; **it's ~ to happen** es kann leicht vorkommen

liaise [liː'eɪz] *vi*: **to ~ (with sb)** (mit jdm) zusammenarbeiten; **liaison** *n* Verbindung *f*

liar ['laɪə*] *n* Lügner *m*

libel ['laɪbl] *n* Verleumdung *f* ♦ *vt* verleumden

liberal ['lɪbərl] *adj* (generous) großzügig; (open-minded) aufgeschlossen; (POL) liberal

liberate ['lɪbəreɪt] *vt* befreien; **liberation** [lɪbə'reɪʃən] *n* Befreiung *f*

liberty ['lɪbətɪ] *n* Freiheit *f*; (permission) Erlaubnis *f*; **to be at ~ to do sth** etw tun dürfen; **to take the ~ of doing sth** sich *dat* erlauben, etw zu tun

Libra ['liːbrə] *n* Waage *f*

librarian [laɪˈbrɛərɪən] n Bibliothekar(in) m(f)
library [ˈlaɪbrərɪ] n Bibliothek f; (lending ~)
Bücherei f
Libya [ˈlɪbɪə] n Libyen nt; ~**n** adj libysch ♦ n
Libyer(in) m(f)
lice [laɪs] npl of **louse**
licence [ˈlaɪsns] (US **license**) n (permit)
Erlaubnis f; (also: **driving ~**, (US) **driver's ~**)
Führerschein m
license [ˈlaɪsns] (US) = **licence** ♦ vt
genehmigen, konzessionieren; ~**d** adj (for
alcohol) konzessioniert (für den
Alkoholausschank); ~ **plate** (US) n (AUT)
Nummernschild nt
lichen [ˈlaɪkən] n Flechte f
lick [lɪk] vt lecken ♦ n Lecken nt; **a ~ of paint**
ein bisschen Farbe
licorice [ˈlɪkərɪs] (US) n = **liquorice**
lid [lɪd] n Deckel m; (eyelid) Lid nt
lie [laɪ] (pt **lay**, pp **lain**) vi (rest, be situated)
liegen; (put o.s. in position) sich legen; (pt,
pp lied: tell lies) lügen ♦ n Lüge f; **to ~ low**
(fig) untertauchen; ~ **about** vi (things)
herumliegen; (people) faulenzen; ~**-down**
(BRIT) n: **to have a ~-down** ein Nickerchen
machen; ~**-in** (BRIT) n: **to have a ~-in** sich
ausschlafen
lieu [luː] n: **in ~ of** anstatt +gen
lieutenant [lefˈtɛnənt, (US) luːˈtɛnənt] n
Leutnant m
life [laɪf] (pl **lives**) n Leben nt; ~ **assurance**
(BRIT) n = **life insurance**; ~**belt** (BRIT) n
Rettungsring m; ~**boat** n Rettungsboot nt;
~**guard** n Rettungsschwimmer m; ~
insurance n Lebensversicherung f; ~
jacket n Schwimmweste f; ~**less** adj
(dead) leblos; (dull) langweilig; ~**like** adj
lebenswahr, naturgetreu; ~**line** n
Rettungsleine f; (fig) Rettungsanker m;
~**long** adj lebenslang; ~ **preserver** (US) n
= **lifebelt**; ~**-saver** n Lebensretter(in) m(f);
~**-saving** adj lebensrettend, Rettungs-; ~
sentence n lebenslängliche Freiheitsstrafe
f; ~ **span** n Lebensspanne f; ~**style** n
Lebensstil m; ~ **support system** n (MED)
Lebenserhaltungssystem nt; ~**time** n: **in
his ~time** während er lebte; **once in a**

~**time** einmal im Leben
lift [lɪft] vt hochheben ♦ vi sich heben ♦ n
(BRIT: elevator) Aufzug m, Lift m; **to give sb
a ~** jdn mitnehmen; ~**-off** n Abheben nt
(vom Boden)
ligament [ˈlɪgəmənt] n Band nt
light [laɪt] (pt, pp **lighted** or **lit**) n Licht nt;
(for cigarette etc): **have you got a ~?** haben
Sie Feuer? ♦ vt beleuchten; (fire, cigarette)
anmachen; (lamp) anzünden ♦ adj
(bright) hell; (pale) hell-; (not heavy, easy)
leicht; (punishment) milde; (touch) leicht; ~**s**
npl (AUT) Beleuchtung f; ~ **up** vi (lamp)
angehen; (face) aufleuchten ♦ vt (illuminate)
beleuchten; (~s) anmachen; ~ **bulb** n
Glühbirne f; ~**en** vi (brighten) hell werden;
(~ning) blitzen ♦ vt (give ~ to) erhellen;
(hair) aufhellen; (gloom) aufheitern; (make
less heavy) leichter machen; (fig) erleichtern;
~**er** n Feuerzeug nt; ~**-headed** adj
(thoughtless) leichtsinnig; (giddy) schwindlig;
~**-hearted** adj leichtherzig, fröhlich;
~**house** n Leuchtturm m; ~**ing** n
Beleuchtung f; ~**ly** adv leicht; (irresponsibly)
leichtfertig; **to get off ~ly** mit einem blauen
Auge davonkommen; ~**ness** n (of weight)
Leichtigkeit f; (of colour) Helle f
lightning [ˈlaɪtnɪŋ] n Blitz m; ~ **conductor**
(US ~ **rod**) n Blitzableiter m
light: ~ **pen** n Lichtstift m; ~**weight** adj
(suit) leicht; ~**weight** n (BOXING)
Leichtgewichtler m; ~ **year** n Lichtjahr nt
like [laɪk] vt mögen, gern haben ♦ prep wie
♦ adj (similar) ähnlich; (equal) gleich ♦ n:
the ~ dergleichen; **I would** or **I'd ~** ich
möchte gern; **would you ~ a coffee?**
möchten Sie einen Kaffee?; **to be** or **look ~
sb/sth** jdm/etw ähneln; **that's just ~ him**
das ist typisch für ihn; **do it ~ this** mach es
so; **it is nothing ~ ...** es ist nicht zu
vergleichen mit ...; **what does it look ~?**
wie sieht es aus?; **what does it sound ~?**
wie hört es sich an?; **what does it taste ~?**
wie schmeckt es?; **his ~s and dislikes** was
er mag und was er nicht mag; ~**able** adj
sympathisch
likelihood [ˈlaɪklɪhud] n Wahrscheinlichkeit f

likely ['laɪklɪ] *adj* wahrscheinlich; **he's ~ to leave** er geht möglicherweise; **not ~!** wohl kaum!

likeness ['laɪknɪs] *n* Ähnlichkeit *f*; (*portrait*) Bild *nt*

likewise ['laɪkwaɪz] *adv* ebenso

liking ['laɪkɪŋ] *n* Zuneigung *f*; (*taste*) Vorliebe *f*

lilac ['laɪlək] *n* Flieder *m* ♦ *adj* (*colour*) fliederfarben

lily ['lɪlɪ] *n* Lilie *f*; **~ of the valley** *n* Maiglöckchen *nt*

limb [lɪm] *n* Glied *nt*

limber up ['lɪmbər-] *vi* sich auflockern; (*fig*) sich vorbereiten

limbo ['lɪmbəʊ] *n*: **to be in ~** (*fig*) in der Schwebe sein

lime [laɪm] *n* (*tree*) Linde *f*; (*fruit*) Limone *f*; (*substance*) Kalk *m*

limelight ['laɪmlaɪt] *n*: **to be in the ~** (*fig*) im Rampenlicht stehen

limestone ['laɪmstəʊn] *n* Kalkstein *m*

limit ['lɪmɪt] *n* Grenze *f*; (*inf*) Höhe *f* ♦ *vt* begrenzen, einschränken; **~ation** [lɪmɪ'teɪʃən] *n* Einschränkung *f*; **~ed** *adj* beschränkt; **to be ~ed to** sich beschränken auf +*acc*; **~ed (liability) company** (*BRIT*) *n* Gesellschaft *f* mit beschränkter Haftung

limousine ['lɪməziːn] *n* Limousine *f*

limp [lɪmp] *n* Hinken *nt* ♦ *vi* hinken ♦ *adj* schlaff

limpet ['lɪmpɪt] *n* (*fig*) Klette *f*

line [laɪn] *n* Linie *f*; (*rope*) Leine *f*; (*on face*) Falte *f*; (*row*) Reihe *f*; (*of hills*) Kette *f*; (*US: queue*) Schlange *f*; (*company*) Linie *f*, Gesellschaft *f*; (*RAIL*) Strecke *f*; (*TEL*) Leitung *f*; (*written*) Zeile *f*; (*direction*) Richtung *f*; (*fig: business*) Branche *f*; (*range of items*) Kollektion *f* ♦ *vt* (*coat*) füttern; (*border*) säumen; **~s** *npl* (*RAIL*) Gleise *pl*; **in ~ with** in Übereinstimmung mit; **~ up** *vi* sich aufstellen ♦ *vt* aufstellen; (*prepare*) sorgen für; (*support*) mobilisieren; (*surprise*) planen; **~ar** ['lɪnɪə] *adj* gerade; (*measure*) Längen-; **~d** *adj* (*face*) faltig; (*paper*) liniert

linen ['lɪnɪn] *n* Leinen *nt*; (*sheets etc*) Wäsche *f*

liner ['laɪnər] *n* Überseedampfer *m*

linesman ['laɪnzmən] (*irreg*) *n* (*SPORT*) Linienrichter *m*

line-up ['laɪnʌp] *n* Aufstellung *f*

linger ['lɪŋgər] *vi* (*remain long*) verweilen; (*taste*) (zurück)bleiben; (*delay*) zögern, verharren

lingerie ['lænʒəriː] *n* Damenunterwäsche *f*

lingering ['lɪŋgərɪŋ] *adj* (*doubt*) zurückbleibend; (*disease*) langwierig; (*taste*) nachhaltend; (*look*) lang

lingo ['lɪŋgəʊ] (*pl* **~es**) (*inf*) *n* Sprache *f*

linguist ['lɪŋgwɪst] *n* Sprachkundige(r) *mf*; (*UNIV*) Sprachwissenschaftler(in) *m(f)*; **~ic** [lɪŋ'gwɪstɪk] *adj* sprachlich; sprachwissenschaftlich; **~ics** *n* Sprachwissenschaft *f*, Linguistik *f*

lining ['laɪnɪŋ] *n* Futter *nt*

link [lɪŋk] *n* Glied *nt*; (*connection*) Verbindung *f* ♦ *vt* verbinden; **~s** *npl* (*GOLF*) Golfplatz *m*; **~ up** *vt* verbinden ♦ *vi* zusammenkommen; (*companies*) sich zusammenschließen; **~-up** *n* (*TEL*) Verbindung *f*; (*of spaceships*) Kopplung *f*

lino ['laɪnəʊ] *n* = **linoleum**

linoleum [lɪ'nəʊlɪəm] *n* Linoleum *nt*

linseed oil ['lɪnsiːd-] *n* Leinöl *nt*

lion ['laɪən] *n* Löwe *m*; **~ess** *n* Löwin *f*

lip [lɪp] *n* Lippe *f*; (*of jug*) Schnabel *m*; **to pay ~ service (to)** ein Lippenbekenntnis ablegen (zu)

liposuction ['lɪpəʊsʌkʃən] *n* Fettabsaugen *nt*

lip: **~read** (*irreg*) *vi* von den Lippen ablesen; **~ salve** *n* Lippenbalsam *m*; **~stick** *n* Lippenstift *m*

liqueur [lɪ'kjʊər] *n* Likör *m*

liquid ['lɪkwɪd] *n* Flüssigkeit *f* ♦ *adj* flüssig

liquidate ['lɪkwɪdeɪt] *vt* liquidieren

liquidize ['lɪkwɪdaɪz] *vt* (*COOK*) (im Mixer) pürieren; **~r** ['lɪkwɪdaɪzə'] *n* Mixgerät *nt*

liquor ['lɪkər] *n* Alkohol *m*

liquorice ['lɪkərɪs] (*BRIT*) *n* Lakritze *f*

liquor store (*US*) *n* Spirituosengeschäft *nt*

Lisbon ['lɪzbən] *n* Lissabon *nt*

lisp [lɪsp] *n* Lispeln *nt* ♦ *vt, vi* lispeln

list [lɪst] *n* Liste *f*, Verzeichnis *nt*; (*of ship*) Schlagseite *f* ♦ *vt* (*write down*) eine Liste machen von; (*verbally*) aufzählen ♦ *vi* (*ship*) Schlagseite haben

listen ['lɪsn] *vi* hören; **~ to** *vt* zuhören +*dat*; **~er** *n* (Zu)hörer(in) *m(f)*

listless ['lɪstlɪs] *adj* lustlos

lit [lɪt] *pt*, *pp* of **light**

liter ['liːtəʳ] (*US*) *n* = **litre**

literacy ['lɪtərəsɪ] *n* Fähigkeit *f* zu lesen und zu schreiben

literal ['lɪtərəl] *adj* buchstäblich; (*translation*) wortwörtlich; **~ly** *adv* wörtlich; buchstäblich

literary ['lɪtərərɪ] *adj* literarisch

literate ['lɪtərət] *adj* des Lesens und Schreibens kundig

literature ['lɪtrɪtʃəʳ] *n* Literatur *f*

litigation [lɪtɪ'geɪʃən] *n* Prozess *m*

litre ['liːtəʳ] (*US* **liter**) *n* Liter *m*

litter ['lɪtəʳ] *n* (*rubbish*) Abfall *m*; (*of animals*) Wurf *m* ♦ *vt* in Unordnung bringen; **to be ~ed with** übersät sein mit; **~ bin** (*BRIT*) *n* Abfalleimer *m*

little ['lɪtl] *adj* klein ♦ *adv*, *n* wenig; **a ~** ein bisschen; **~ by ~** nach und nach

live¹ [laɪv] *adj* lebendig; (*MIL*) scharf; (*ELEC*) geladen; (*broadcast*) live

live² [lɪv] *vi* leben; (*dwell*) wohnen ♦ *vt* (*life*) führen; **~ down** *vt*: **I'll never ~ it down** das wird man mir nie vergessen; **~ on** *vi* weiterleben ♦ *vt fus*: **to ~ on sth** von etw leben; **~ together** *vi* zusammenleben; (*share a flat*) zusammenwohnen; **~ up to** *vt* (*standards*) gerecht werden +*dat*; (*principles*) anstreben; (*hopes*) entsprechen +*dat*

livelihood ['laɪvlɪhud] *n* Lebensunterhalt *m*

lively ['laɪvlɪ] *adj* lebhaft, lebendig

liven up ['laɪvn-] *vt* beleben

liver ['lɪvəʳ] *n* (*ANAT*) Leber *f*

lives [laɪvz] *pl* of **life**

livestock ['laɪvstɔk] *n* Vieh *nt*

livid ['lɪvɪd] *adj* bläulich; (*furious*) fuchsteufelswild

living ['lɪvɪŋ] *n* (Lebens)unterhalt *m* ♦ *adj* lebendig; (*language etc*) lebend; **to earn** or **make a ~** sich *dat* seinen Lebensunterhalt verdienen; **~ conditions** *npl*

Wohnverhältnisse *pl*; **~ room** *n* Wohnzimmer *nt*; **~ standards** *npl* Lebensstandard *m*; **~ wage** *n* ausreichender Lohn *m*

lizard ['lɪzəd] *n* Eidechse *f*

load [ləud] *n* (*burden*) Last *f*; (*amount*) Ladung *f* ♦ *vt* (*also*: **~ up**) (be)laden; (*COMPUT*) laden; (*camera*) Film einlegen in +*acc*; (*gun*) laden; **a ~ of**, **~s of** (*fig*) jede Menge; **~ed** *adj* beladen; (*dice*) präpariert; (*question*) Fang-; (*inf*: *rich*) steinreich; **~ing bay** *n* Ladeplatz *m*

loaf [ləuf] (*pl* **loaves**) *n* Brot *nt* ♦ *vi* (*also*: **~ about**, **~ around**) herumlungern, faulenzen

loan [ləun] *n* Leihgabe *f*; (*FIN*) Darlehen *nt* ♦ *vt* leihen; **on ~** geliehen

loath [ləuθ] *adj*: **to be ~ to do sth** etw ungern tun

loathe [ləuð] *vt* verabscheuen

loaves [ləuvz] *pl* of **loaf**

lobby ['lɔbɪ] *n* Vorhalle *f*; (*POL*) Lobby *f* ♦ *vt* politisch beeinflussen (wollen)

lobster ['lɔbstəʳ] *n* Hummer *m*

local ['ləukl] *adj* ortsansässig, Orts- ♦ *n* (*pub*) Stammwirtschaft *f*; **the ~s** *npl* (*people*) die Ortsansässigen *pl*; **~ anaesthetic** *n* (*MED*) örtliche Betäubung *f*; **~ authority** *n* städtische Behörden *pl*; **~ call** *n* (*TEL*) Ortsgespräch *nt*; **~ government** *n* Gemeinde-/Kreisverwaltung *f*; **~ity** [ləu'kælɪtɪ] *n* Ort *m*; **~ly** *adv* örtlich, am Ort

locate [ləu'keɪt] *vt* ausfindig machen; (*establish*) errichten; **location** [ləu'keɪʃən] *n* Platz *m*, Lage *f*; **on location** (*CINE*) auf Außenaufnahme

loch [lɔx] (*SCOTTISH*) *n* See *m*

lock [lɔk] *n* Schloss *nt*; (*NAUT*) Schleuse *f*; (*of hair*) Locke *f* ♦ *vt* (*fasten*) (ver)schließen ♦ *vi* (*door etc*) sich schließen (lassen); (*wheels*) blockieren; **~ up** *vt* (*criminal, mental patient*) einsperren; (*house*) abschließen

locker ['lɔkəʳ] *n* Spind *m*

locket ['lɔkɪt] *n* Medaillon *nt*

lock ['lɔk-]: **~out** *n* Aussperrung *f*; **~smith** *n* Schlosser(in) *m(f)*; **~up** *n* (*jail*) Gefängnis *nt*; (*garage*) Garage *f*

locum ['ləukəm] *n* (*MED*) Vertreter(in) *m(f)*

lodge [lɒdʒ] *n* (*gatehouse*) Pförtnerhaus *nt*; (*freemasons'*) Loge *f* ♦ *vi* (*get stuck*) stecken (bleiben); (*in Untermiete*): **to ~ (with)** wohnen (bei) ♦ *vt* (*protest*) einreichen; **~r** *n* (Unter)mieter *m*; **lodgings** *n* (Miet)wohnung *f*

loft [lɒft] *n* (Dach)boden *m*

lofty ['lɒftɪ] *adj* hoch(ragend); (*proud*) hochmütig

log [lɒg] *n* Klotz *m*; (*book*) = **logbook**

logbook ['lɒgbuk] *n* Bordbuch *nt*; (*for lorry*) Fahrtenschreiber *m*; (*AUT*) Kraftfahrzeugbrief *m*

loggerheads ['lɒgəhedz] *npl*: **to be at ~** sich in den Haaren liegen

logic ['lɒdʒɪk] *n* Logik *f*; **~al** *adj* logisch

log in *or* **on** *vi* (*COMPUT*) einloggen

log off *or* **out** *vi* (*COMPUT*) ausloggen

logistics [lɒ'dʒɪstɪks] *npl* Logistik *f*

logo ['ləugəu] *n* Firmenzeichen *nt*

loin [lɔɪn] *n* Lende *f*

loiter ['lɔɪtə*] *vi* herumstehen

loll [lɒl] *vi* (*also*: **~ about**) sich rekeln *or* räkeln

lollipop ['lɒlɪpɒp] *n* (Dauer)lutscher *m*; **~ man/lady** (*irreg*; *BRIT*) ≈ Schülerlotse *m*

Lollipop man/lady

ⓘ **Lollipop man/lady** *heißen in Großbritannien die Männer bzw. Frauen, die mit Hilfe eines runden Stoppschildes den Verkehr anhalten, damit Schulkinder die Straße überqueren können. Der Name bezieht sich auf die Form des Schildes, die an einen Lutscher erinnert.*

lolly ['lɒlɪ] (*inf*) *n* (*sweet*) Lutscher *m*

London ['lʌndən] *n* London *nt*; **~er** *n* Londoner(in) *m(f)*

lone [ləun] *adj* einsam

loneliness ['ləunlɪnɪs] *n* Einsamkeit *f*

lonely ['ləunlɪ] *adj* einsam

loner ['ləunə*] *n* Einzelgänger(in) *m(f)*

long [lɒŋ] *adj*; (*distance*) weit ♦ *adv* lange ♦ *vi*: **to ~ for** sich sehnen nach; **before ~** bald; **as ~ as** solange; **in the ~ run** auf die Dauer; **don't be ~!** beeil dich!;

how ~ is the street? wie lang ist die Straße?; **how ~ is the lesson?** wie lange dauert die Stunde?; **6 metres ~** 6 Meter lang; **6 months ~** 6 Monate lang; **all night ~** die ganze Nacht; **he no ~er comes** er kommt nicht mehr; **~ ago** vor langer Zeit; **~ before** lange vorher; **at ~ last** endlich; **~-distance** *adj* Fern-

longevity [lɒn'dʒevɪtɪ] *n* Langlebigkeit *f*

long: **~-haired** *adj* langhaarig; **~hand** *n* Langschrift *f*; **~ing** *n* Sehnsucht *f* ♦ *adj* sehnsüchtig

longitude ['lɒŋgɪtjuːd] *n* Längengrad *m*

long: **~ jump** *n* Weitsprung *m*; **~-life** *adj* (*batteries etc*) mit langer Lebensdauer; **~-lost** *adj* längst verloren geglaubt; **~-playing record** *n* Langspielplatte *f*; **~-range** *adj* Langstrecken-, Fern-; **~-sighted** *adj* weitsichtig; **~-standing** *adj* alt, seit langer Zeit bestehend; **~-suffering** *adj* schwer geprüft; **~-term** *adj* langfristig; **~ wave** *n* Langwelle *f*; **~-winded** *adj* langatmig

loo [luː] (*BRIT*: *inf*) *n* Klo *nt*

look [luk] *vi* schauen; (*seem*) aussehen; (*building etc*): **to ~ on to the sea** aufs Meer gehen ♦ *n* Blick *m*; **~s** *npl* (*appearance*) Aussehen *nt*; **~ after** *vt* (*care for*) sorgen für; (*watch*) aufpassen auf +*acc*; **~ at** *vt* ansehen; (*consider*) sich überlegen; **~ back** *vi* sich umsehen; (*fig*) zurückblicken; **~ down on** *vt* (*fig*) herabsehen auf +*acc*; **~ for** *vt* (*seek*) suchen; **~ forward to** *vt* sich freuen auf +*acc*; (*in letters*): **we ~ forward to hearing from you** wir hoffen, bald von Ihnen zu hören; **~ into** *vt* untersuchen; **~ on** *vi* zusehen; **~ out** *vi* hinaussehen; (*take care*) aufpassen; **~ out for** *vt* Ausschau halten nach; (*be careful*) Acht geben auf +*acc*; **~ round** *vi* sich umsehen; **~ to** *vt* (*take care of*) Acht geben auf +*acc*; (*rely on*) sich verlassen auf +*acc*; **~ up** *vi* aufblicken; (*improve*) sich bessern ♦ *vt* (*word*) nachschlagen; (*person*) besuchen; **~ up to** *vt* aufsehen zu; **~out** *n* (*watch*) Ausschau *f*; (*person*) Wachposten *m*; (*place*) Ausguck *m*; (*prospect*) Aussichten *pl*; **to be on the ~ out**

for sth nach etw Ausschau halten
loom [luːm] n Webstuhl m ♦ vi sich abzeichnen
loony [ˈluːnɪ] (inf) n Verrückte(r) mf
loop [luːp] n Schlaufe f; **~hole** n (fig) Hintertürchen nt
loose [luːs] adj lose, locker; (free) frei; (inexact) unpräzise ♦ vt lösen, losbinden; **~ change** n Kleingeld nt; **~ chippings** npl (on road) Rollsplit m; **~ end** n: **to be at a ~ end** (BRIT) or **at ~ ends** (US) nicht wissen, was man tun soll; **~ly** adv locker, lose; **~n** vt lockern, losmachen
loot [luːt] n Beute f ♦ vt plündern
lop off [lɔp-] vt abhacken
lopsided [ˈlɔpˈsaɪdɪd] adj schief
lord [lɔːd] n (ruler) Herr m; (BRIT: title) Lord m; **the L~** (God) der Herr; **the (House of) L~s** das Oberhaus; **~ship** n: **Your L~ship** Eure Lordschaft
lorry [ˈlɔrɪ] (BRIT) n Lastwagen m; **~ driver** (BRIT) n Lastwagenfahrer(in) m(f)
lose [luːz] (pt, pp **lost**) vt verlieren; (chance) verpassen ♦ vi verlieren; **to ~ (time)** (clock) nachgehen; **~r** n Verlierer m
loss [lɔs] n Verlust m; **at a ~** (COMM) mit Verlust; (unable) außerstande, außer Stande
lost [lɔst] pt, pp of **lose** ♦ adj verloren; **~ property** (US **~ and found**) n Fundsachen pl
lot [lɔt] n (quantity) Menge f; (fate, at auction) Los nt; (inf: people, things) Haufen m; **the ~** alles; (people) alle; **a ~ of** (with sg) viel; (with pl) viele; **~s of** massenhaft, viel(e); **I read a ~** ich lese viel; **to draw ~s for sth** etw verlosen
lotion [ˈləʊʃən] n Lotion f
lottery [ˈlɔtərɪ] n Lotterie f
loud [laʊd] adj laut; (showy) schreiend ♦ adv laut; **~ly** adv laut; **~speaker** n Lautsprecher m
lounge [laʊndʒ] n (in hotel) Gesellschaftsraum m; (in house) Wohnzimmer nt ♦ vi sich herumlümmeln
louse [laʊs] (pl **lice**) n Laus f
lousy [ˈlaʊzɪ] adj (fig) miserabel
lout [laʊt] n Lümmel m

louvre [ˈluːvər] (US **louver**) adj (door, window) Jalousie-
lovable [ˈlʌvəbl] adj liebenswert
love [lʌv] n Liebe f; (person) Liebling m; (SPORT) null ♦ vt (person) lieben; (activity) gerne mögen; **to be in ~ with sb** in jdn verliebt sein; **to make ~** sich lieben; **for the ~ of** aus Liebe zu; **"15 ~"** (TENNIS) „15 null"; **to ~ to do sth** etw (sehr) gerne tun; **~ affair** n (Liebes)verhältnis nt; **~ letter** n Liebesbrief m; **~ life** n Liebesleben nt
lovely [ˈlʌvlɪ] adj schön
lover [ˈlʌvər] n Liebhaber(in) m(f)
loving [ˈlʌvɪŋ] adj liebend, liebevoll
low [ləʊ] adj niedrig; (rank) niedere(r, s); (level, note, neckline) tief; (intelligence, density) gering; (vulgar) ordinär; (not loud) leise; (depressed) gedrückt ♦ adv (not high) niedrig; (not loudly) leise ♦ n (~ point) Tiefstand m; (MET) Tief nt; **to feel ~** sich mies fühlen; **to turn (down) ~** leiser stellen; **~ alcohol** adj alkoholarm; **~-calorie** adj kalorienarm; **~-cut** adj (dress) tief ausgeschnitten; **~er** vt herunterlassen; (eyes, gun) senken; (reduce) herabsetzen, senken ♦ vr: **to ~er o.s.** (fig) sich herablassen zu; **~er sixth** (BRIT) n (SCOL) ≈ zwölfte Klasse; **~-fat** adj fettarm, Mager-; **~lands** npl (GEOG) Flachland nt; **~ly** adj bescheiden; **~-lying** adj tief gelegen
loyal [ˈlɔɪəl] adj treu; **~ty** n Treue f; **~ty card** n Kundenkarte f
lozenge [ˈlɔzɪndʒ] n Pastille f
L-plates [ˈelpleɪts] (BRIT) npl L-Schild nt

L-Plates

ⓘ Als **L-Plates** werden in Großbritannien die weißen Schilder mit einem roten „L" bezeichnet, die an jedem von einem Fahrschüler geführten Fahrzeug befestigt werden müssen. Fahrschüler bekommen einen vorläufigen Führerschein und dürfen damit unter Aufsicht eines erfahrenen Autofahrers auf allen Straßen außer Autobahnen fahren.

Ltd abbr (= limited company) GmbH
lubricant [ˈluːbrɪkənt] n Schmiermittel nt

lubricate [ˈluːbrɪkeɪt] vt schmieren

lucid [ˈluːsɪd] adj klar; (sane) bei klarem Verstand; (moment) licht

luck [lʌk] n Glück nt; **bad** or **hard** or **tough** ~! (so ein) Pech!; **good** ~! viel Glück!; ~**ily** adv glücklicherweise, zum Glück; ~**y** adj Glücks-; **to be** ~**y** Glück haben

lucrative [ˈluːkrətɪv] adj einträglich

ludicrous [ˈluːdɪkrəs] adj grotesk

lug [lʌg] vt schleppen

luggage [ˈlʌgɪdʒ] n Gepäck nt; ~ **rack** n Gepäcknetz nt

lukewarm [ˈluːkwɔːm] adj lauwarm; (indifferent) lau

lull [lʌl] n Flaute f ♦ vt einlullen; (calm) beruhigen

lullaby [ˈlʌləbaɪ] n Schlaflied nt

lumbago [lʌmˈbeɪgəu] n Hexenschuss m

lumber [ˈlʌmbəʳ] n Plunder m; (wood) Holz nt; ~**jack** n Holzfäller m

luminous [ˈluːmɪnəs] adj Leucht-

lump [lʌmp] n Klumpen m; (MED) Schwellung f; (in breast) Knoten m; (of sugar) Stück nt ♦ vt (also: ~ **together**) zusammentun; (judge together) in einen Topf werfen; ~ **sum** n Pauschalsumme f; ~**y** adj klumpig

lunacy [ˈluːnəsɪ] n Irrsinn m

lunar [ˈluːnəʳ] adj Mond-

lunatic [ˈluːnətɪk] n Wahnsinnige(r) mf ♦ adj wahnsinnig, irr

lunch [lʌntʃ] n Mittagessen nt; ~**eon** [ˈlʌntʃən] n Mittagessen nt; ~**eon meat** n Frühstücksfleisch nt; ~**eon voucher** (BRIT) n Essenmarke f; ~**time** n Mittagszeit f

lung [lʌŋ] n Lunge f

lunge [lʌndʒ] vi (also: ~ **forward**) (los)stürzen; **to** ~ **at** sich stürzen auf +acc

lurch [lɜːtʃ] vi taumeln; (NAUT) schlingern ♦ n Ruck m; (NAUT) Schlingern nt; **to leave sb in the** ~ jdn im Stich lassen

lure [luəʳ] n Köder m; (fig) Lockung f ♦ vt (ver)locken

lurid [ˈluərɪd] adj (shocking) grausig, widerlich; (colour) grell

lurk [lɜːk] vi lauern

luscious [ˈlʌʃəs] adj köstlich

lush [lʌʃ] adj satt; (vegetation) üppig

lust [lʌst] n Wollust f; (greed) Gier f ♦ vi: **to** ~ **after** gieren nach

lustre [ˈlʌstəʳ] (US **luster**) n Glanz m

Luxembourg [ˈlʌksəmbɜːg] n Luxemburg nt

luxuriant [lʌgˈzjuərɪənt] adj üppig

luxurious [lʌgˈzjuərɪəs] adj luxuriös, Luxus-

luxury [ˈlʌkʃərɪ] n Luxus m ♦ cpd Luxus-

lying [ˈlaɪɪŋ] n Lügen nt ♦ adj verlogen

lynx [lɪŋks] n Luchs m

lyric [ˈlɪrɪk] n Lyrik f ♦ adj lyrisch; ~**s** pl (words for song) (Lied)text m; ~**al** adj lyrisch, gefühlvoll

M, m

m abbr = **metre**; **mile**; **million**

M.A. n abbr = **Master of Arts**

mac [mæk] (BRIT: inf) n Regenmantel m

macaroni [mækəˈrəunɪ] n Makkaroni pl

machine [məˈʃiːn] n Maschine f ♦ vt (dress etc) mit der Maschine nähen; ~ **gun** n Maschinengewehr nt; ~ **language** n (COMPUT) Maschinensprache f; ~**ry** n Maschinerie f

macho [ˈmætʃəu] adj macho

mackerel [ˈmækrl] n Makrele f

mackintosh [ˈmækɪntɔʃ] (BRIT) n Regenmantel m

mad [mæd] adj verrückt; (dog) tollwütig; (angry) wütend; ~ **about** (fond of) verrückt nach, versessen auf +acc

madam [ˈmædəm] n gnädige Frau f

madden [ˈmædn] vt verrückt machen; (make angry) ärgern

made [meɪd] pt, pp of **make**

made-to-measure [ˈmeɪdtəˈmeʒəʳ] (BRIT) adj Maß-

mad [ˈmæd-]: ~**ly** adv wahnsinnig; ~**man** (irreg) n Verrückte(r) m, Irre(r) m; ~**ness** n Wahnsinn m

magazine [mægəˈziːn] n Zeitschrift f; (in gun) Magazin m

maggot [ˈmægət] n Made f

magic [ˈmædʒɪk] n Zauberei f, Magie f; (fig) Zauber m ♦ adj magisch, Zauber-; ~**al** adj magisch; **~ian** [mə'dʒɪʃən] n Zauberer m

magistrate ['mædʒɪstreɪt] n (Friedens)richter m

magnanimous [mæg'nænɪməs] adj großmütig

magnet ['mægnɪt] n Magnet m; **~ic** [mæg'nɛtɪk] adj magnetisch; **~ic tape** n Magnetband nt; **~ism** n Magnetismus m; (fig) Ausstrahlungskraft f

magnificent [mæg'nɪfɪsnt] adj großartig

magnify ['mægnɪfaɪ] vt vergrößern; **~ing glass** n Lupe f

magnitude ['mægnɪtjuːd] n (size) Größe f; (importance) Ausmaß nt

magpie ['mægpaɪ] n Elster f

mahogany [mə'hɔgənɪ] n Mahagoni nt ♦ cpd Mahagoni-

maid [meɪd] n Dienstmädchen nt; **old ~** alte Jungfer f

maiden ['meɪdn] n Maid f ♦ adj (flight, speech) Jungfern-; **~ name** n Mädchenname m

mail [meɪl] n Post f ♦ vt aufgeben; **~ box** (US) n Briefkasten m; **~ing list** n Anschreibeliste f; **~ order** n Bestellung f durch die Post; **~ order firm** n Versandhaus nt

maim [meɪm] vt verstümmeln

main [meɪn] adj hauptsächlich, Haupt- ♦ n (pipe) Hauptleitung f; **the ~s** npl (ELEC) das Stromnetz; **in the ~** im Großen und Ganzen; **~frame** n (COMPUT) Großrechner m; **~land** n Festland nt; **~ly** adv hauptsächlich; **~ road** n Hauptstraße f; **~stay** n (fig) Hauptstütze f; **~stream** n Hauptrichtung f

maintain [meɪn'teɪn] vt (machine, roads) instand or in Stand halten; (support) unterhalten; (keep up) aufrechterhalten; (claim) behaupten; (innocence) beteuern

maintenance ['meɪntənəns] n (TECH) Wartung f; (of family) Unterhalt m

maize [meɪz] n Mais m

majestic [mə'dʒɛstɪk] adj majestätisch

majesty ['mædʒɪstɪ] n Majestät f

major ['meɪdʒər] n Major m ♦ adj (MUS) Dur; (more important) Haupt-; (bigger) größer

Majorca [mə'jɔːkə] n Mallorca nt

majority [mə'dʒɔrɪtɪ] n Mehrheit f; (JUR) Volljährigkeit f

make [meɪk] (pt, pp **made**) vt machen; (appoint) ernennen (zu); (cause to do sth) veranlassen; (reach) erreichen; (in time) schaffen; (earn) verdienen ♦ n Marke f; **to ~ sth happen** etw geschehen lassen; **to ~ it** es schaffen; **what time do you ~ it?** wie spät hast du es?; **to ~ do with** auskommen mit; **~ for** vi gehen/fahren nach; **~ out** vt (write out) ausstellen; (understand) verstehen; **~ up** vt machen; (face) schminken; (quarrel) beilegen; (story etc) erfinden ♦ vi sich versöhnen; **~ up for** vt wieder gutmachen; (COMM) vergüten; **~-believe** n Fantasie f; **~r** n (COMM) Hersteller m; **~shift** adj behelfsmäßig, Not-; **~up** n Schminke f, Make-up nt; **~-up remover** n Make-up-Entferner m; **making** n: **in the making** im Entstehen; **to have the makings of** das Zeug haben zu

malaria [mə'lɛərɪə] n Malaria f

Malaysia [mə'leɪzɪə] n Malaysia nt

male [meɪl] n Mann m; (animal) Männchen nt ♦ adj männlich

malevolent [mə'levələnt] adj übel wollend

malfunction [mæl'fʌŋkʃən] n (MED) Funktionsstörung f; (of machine) Defekt m

malice ['mælɪs] n Bosheit f; **malicious** [mə'lɪʃəs] adj böswillig, gehässig

malign [mə'laɪn] vt verleumden ♦ adj böse

malignant [mə'lɪgnənt] adj bösartig

mall [mɔːl] n (also: **shopping ~**) Einkaufszentrum nt

malleable ['mælɪəbl] adj formbar

mallet ['mælɪt] n Holzhammer m

malnutrition [mælnjuː'trɪʃən] n Unterernährung f

malpractice [mæl'præktɪs] n Amtsvergehen nt

malt [mɔːlt] n Malz nt

Malta ['mɔːltə] n Malta nt; **Maltese** [mɔːl'tiːz] adj inv maltesisch ♦ n inv Malteser(in) m(f)

maltreat [mæl'triːt] vt misshandeln

mammal ['mæml] n Säugetier nt

mammoth ['mæməθ] n Mammut nt ♦ adj Mammut-

man [mæn] (pl **men**) n Mann m; (human race) der Mensch, die Menschen pl ♦ vt bemannen; **an old ~** ein alter Mann, ein Greis m; **~ and wife** Mann und Frau

manage ['mænɪdʒ] vi zurechtkommen ♦ vt (control) führen, leiten; (cope with) fertig werden mit; **~able** adj (person, animal) fügsam; (object) handlich; **~ment** n (control) Führung f, Leitung f; (directors) Management nt; **~r** n Geschäftsführer m; **~ress** [mænɪdʒə'res] n Geschäftsführerin f; **~rial** [mænɪ'dʒɪərɪəl] adj (post) leitend; (problem etc) Management-; **managing** ['mænɪdʒɪŋ] adj: **managing director** Betriebsleiter m

mandarin ['mændərɪn] n (fruit) Mandarine f

mandatory ['mændətərɪ] adj obligatorisch

mane [meɪn] n Mähne f

maneuver [mə'nu:vər] (US) = **manoeuvre**

manfully ['mænfəlɪ] adv mannhaft

mangle ['mæŋgl] vt verstümmeln ♦ n Mangel f

mango ['mæŋgəʊ] (pl **~es**) n Mango(pflaume) f

mangy ['meɪndʒɪ] adj (dog) räudig

man [mæn-]: **~handle** vt grob behandeln; **~hole** n (Straßen)schacht m; **~hood** n Mannesalter nt; (~liness) Männlichkeit f; **~-hour** n Arbeitsstunde f; **~hunt** n Fahndung f

mania ['meɪnɪə] n Manie f; **~c** ['meɪnɪæk] n Wahnsinnige(r) mf

manic ['mænɪk] adj (behaviour, activity) hektisch

manicure ['mænɪkjʊər] n Maniküre f; **~ set** n Necessaire nt, Nessessär f

manifest ['mænɪfest] vt offenbaren ♦ adj offenkundig; **~ation** [mænɪfes'teɪʃən] n (sign) Anzeichen nt

manifesto [mænɪ'festəʊ] n Manifest nt

manipulate [mə'nɪpjʊleɪt] vt handhaben; (fig) manipulieren

man [mæn-]: **~kind** n Menschheit f; **~ly** ['mænlɪ] adj männlich; mannhaft; **~-made** adj (fibre) künstlich

manner ['mænər] n Art f, Weise f; **~s** npl (behaviour) Manieren pl; **in a ~ of speaking** sozusagen; **~ism** n (of person) Angewohnheit f; (of style) Manieriertheit f

manoeuvre [mə'nu:vər] (US **maneuver**) vt, vi manövrieren ♦ n (MIL) Feldzug m; (general) Manöver m, Schachzug m

manor ['mænər] n Landgut nt

manpower ['mænpaʊər] n Arbeitskräfte pl

mansion ['mænʃən] n Villa f

manslaughter ['mænslɔ:tər] n Totschlag m

mantelpiece ['mæntlpi:s] n Kaminsims m

manual ['mænjʊəl] adj manuell, Hand- ♦ n Handbuch nt

manufacture [mænjʊ'fæktʃər] vt herstellen ♦ n Herstellung f; **~r** n Hersteller m

manure [mə'njʊər] n Dünger m

manuscript ['mænjʊskrɪpt] n Manuskript nt

Manx [mæŋks] adj der Insel Man

many ['menɪ] adj, pron viele; **a great ~** sehr viele; **~ a time** ein

map [mæp] n (Land)karte f; (of town) Stadtplan m ♦ vt eine Karte machen von; **~ out** vt (fig) ausarbeiten

maple ['meɪpl] n Ahorn m

mar [mɑ:r] vt verderben

marathon ['mærəθən] n (SPORT) Marathonlauf m; (fig) Marathon m

marble ['mɑ:bl] n Marmor m; (for game) Murmel f

March [mɑ:tʃ] n März m

march [mɑ:tʃ] vi marschieren ♦ n Marsch m

mare [mɛər] n Stute f

margarine [mɑ:dʒə'ri:n] n Margarine f

margin ['mɑ:dʒɪn] n Rand m; (extra amount) Spielraum m; (COMM) Spanne f; **~al** adj (note) Rand-; (difference etc) geringfügig; **~al (seat)** n (POL) Wahlkreis, der nur mit knapper Mehrheit gehalten wird

marigold ['mærɪgəʊld] n Ringelblume f

marijuana [mærɪ'wɑ:nə] n Marihuana f

marina [mə'ri:nə] n Jachthafen m

marinate ['mærɪneɪt] vt marinieren

marine [mə'ri:n] adj Meeres-, See- ♦ n (MIL) Marineinfanterist m

marital ['mærɪtl] adj ehelich, Ehe-; **~ status** n Familienstand m maritime ['mærɪtaɪm] adj See-

mark [maːk] n (HIST: coin) Mark f; (spot) Fleck m; (scar) Kratzer m; (sign) Zeichen nt; (target) Ziel nt; (SCH) Note f ♦ vt (make ~ on) Flecken/Kratzer machen auf +acc; (indicate) markieren; (exam) korrigieren; to ~ time (also fig) auf der Stelle treten; ~ out vt bestimmen; (area) abstecken; ~ed adj deutlich; ~er n (in book) (Lese)zeichen nt; (on road) Schild nt

market ['maːkɪt] n Markt m; (stock ~) Börse f ♦ vt (COMM: new product) auf den Markt bringen; ~ garden (BRIT) n Handelsgärtnerei f; ~ing n Marketing nt; ~ research n Marktforschung f; ~ value n Marktwert m

marksman ['maːksmən] (irreg) n Scharfschütze m

marmalade ['maːməleɪd] n Orangenmarmelade f

maroon [mə'ruːn] vt aussetzen ♦ adj (colour) kastanienbraun

marquee [maː'kiː] n große(s) Zelt nt

marriage ['mærɪdʒ] n Ehe f; (wedding) Heirat f; ~ bureau n Heiratsinstitut nt; ~ certificate n Heiratsurkunde f

married ['mærɪd] adj (person) verheiratet; (couple, life) Ehe-

marrow ['mærəu] n (Knochen)mark nt; (BOT) Kürbis m

marry ['mærɪ] vt (join) trauen; (take as husband, wife) heiraten ♦ vi (also: get married) heiraten

marsh [maːʃ] n Sumpf m

marshal ['maːʃl] n (US) Bezirkspolizeichef m ♦ vt (an)ordnen, arrangieren

marshy ['maːʃɪ] adj sumpfig

martial law ['maːʃl] n Kriegsrecht nt

martyr ['maːtə*] n (also fig) Märtyrer(in) m(f) ♦ vt zum Märtyrer machen; ~dom n Martyrium nt

marvel ['maːvl] n Wunder nt ♦ vi: to ~ (at) sich wundern (über +acc); ~lous (US marvelous) adj wunderbar

Marxist ['maːksɪst] n Marxist(in) m(f)

marzipan ['maːzɪpæn] n Marzipan nt

mascara [mæs'kaːrə] n Wimperntusche f

mascot ['mæskət] n Maskottchen nt

masculine ['mæskjulɪn] adj männlich

mash [mæʃ] n Brei m; ~ed potatoes npl Kartoffelbrei m or -püree nt

mask [maːsk] n (also fig) Maske f ♦ vt maskieren, verdecken

mason ['meɪsn] n (stonemason) Steinmetz m; (freemason) Freimaurer m; ~ry n Mauerwerk nt

masquerade [mæskə'reɪd] n Maskerade f ♦ vi: to ~ as sich ausgeben als

mass [mæs] n Masse f; (greater part) Mehrheit f; (REL) Messe f ♦ vi sich sammeln; the ~es npl (people) die Masse(n) f(pl)

massacre ['mæsəkə*] n Blutbad nt ♦ vt niedermetzeln, massakrieren

massage ['mæsaːʒ] n Massage f ♦ vt massieren

massive ['mæsɪv] adj gewaltig, massiv

mass media npl Massenmedien pl

mass production n Massenproduktion f

mast [maːst] n Mast m

master ['maːstə*] n Herr m; (NAUT) Kapitän m; (teacher) Lehrer m; (artist) Meister m ♦ vt meistern; (language etc) beherrschen; ~ly adj meisterhaft; ~mind n Kapazität f ♦ vt geschickt lenken; M~ of Arts n Magister m der philosophischen Fakultät; M~ of Science n Magister m der naturwissenschaftlichen Fakultät; ~piece n Meisterwerk nt; ~ plan n kluge(r) Plan m; ~y n Können nt

masturbate ['mæstəbeɪt] vi masturbieren, onanieren

mat [mæt] n Matte f; (for table) Untersetzer m ♦ adj = matt

match [mætʃ] n Streichholz nt; (sth corresponding) Pendant nt; (SPORT) Wettkampf m; (ball games) Spiel nt ♦ vt (be like, suit) passen zu; (equal) gleichkommen +dat ♦ vi zusammenpassen; it's a good ~ (for) es passt gut (zu); ~box n Streichholzschachtel f; ~ing adj passend

mate [meɪt] n (companion) Kamerad m; (spouse) Lebensgefährte m; (of animal) Weibchen nt/Männchen nt; (NAUT) Schiffsoffizier m ♦ vi (animals) sich paaren

♦ *vt (animals)* paaren

material [mə'tɪərɪəl] *n* Material *nt*; *(for book, cloth)* Stoff *m* ♦ *adj (important)* wesentlich; *(damage)* Sach-; *(comforts etc)* materiell; **~s** *npl (for building etc)* Materialien *pl*; **~istic** [mətɪərɪə'lɪstɪk] *adj* materialistisch; **~ize** *vi* sich verwirklichen, zustande *or* zu Stande kommen

maternal [mə'tə:nl] *adj* mütterlich, Mutter-

maternity [mə'tə:nɪtɪ] *adj (dress)* Umstands-; *(benefit)* Wochen-; **~ hospital** *n* Entbindungsheim *nt*

math [mæθ] *(US) n* = **maths**

mathematical [mæθə'mætɪkl] *adj* mathematisch; **mathematics** *n* Mathematik *f*; **maths** *(US* **math)** *n* Mathe *f*

matinée ['mætɪneɪ] *n* Matinee *f*

matrices ['meɪtrɪsi:z] *npl of* **matrix**

matriculation [mətrɪkju'leɪʃən] *n* Immatrikulation *f*

matrimonial [mætrɪ'məʊnɪəl] *adj* ehelich, Ehe-

matrimony ['mætrɪmənɪ] *n* Ehestand *m*

matrix ['meɪtrɪks] *(pl* **matrices)** *n* Matrize *f*; *(GEOL etc)* Matrix *f*

matron ['meɪtrən] *n (MED)* Oberin *f*; *(SCH)* Hausmutter *f*

matt [mæt] *adj (paint)* matt

matted ['mætɪd] *adj* verfilzt

matter ['mætə*] *n (substance)* Materie *f*; *(affair)* Angelegenheit *f* ♦ *vi* darauf ankommen; **no – how/what** egal wie/was; **what is the ~?** was ist los?; **as a ~ of course** selbstverständlich; **as a ~ of fact** eigentlich; **it doesn't ~** es macht nichts; **~-of-fact** *adj* sachlich, nüchtern

mattress ['mætrɪs] *n* Matratze *f*

mature [mə'tjuə*] *adj* reif ♦ *vi* reif werden; **maturity** [mə'tjuərɪtɪ] *n* Reife *f*

maul [mɔ:l] *vt* übel zurichten

maxima ['mæksɪmə] *npl of* **maximum**

maximum ['mæksɪməm] *(pl* **maxima)** *adj* Höchst-, Maximal- ♦ *n* Maximum *nt*

May [meɪ] *n* Mai *m*

may [meɪ] *(conditional* **might)** *vi (be possible)* können; *(have permission)* dürfen; **he ~ come** er kommt vielleicht; **~be** ['meɪbi:]

adv vielleicht

May Day *n* der 1. Mai

mayhem ['meɪhem] *n* Chaos *nt*; *(US)* Körperverletzung *f*

mayonnaise [meɪə'neɪz] *n* Majonäse *f*, Mayonnaise *f*

mayor [meə*] *n* Bürgermeister *m*; **~ess** *n* Bürgermeisterin *f*; *(wife)* (die) Frau *f* Bürgermeister

maypole ['meɪpəʊl] *n* Maibaum *m*

maze [meɪz] *n* Irrgarten *m*; *(fig)* Wirrwarr *nt*

M.D. *abbr* = **Doctor of Medicine**

KEYWORD
---

me [mi:] *pron* **1** *(direct)* mich; **it's me** ich bins

2 *(indirect)* mir; **give them to me** gib sie mir

3 *(after prep: +acc)* mich; *(: +dat)* mir; **with/without me** mit mir/ohne mich

---

meadow ['medəʊ] *n* Wiese *f*

meagre ['mi:gə*] *(US* **meager)** *adj* dürftig, spärlich

meal [mi:l] *n* Essen *nt*, Mahlzeit *f*; *(grain)* Schrotmehl *nt*; **to have a ~** essen (gehen); **~time** *n* Essenszeit *f*

mean [mi:n] *(pt, pp* **meant)** *adj (stingy)* geizig; *(spiteful)* gemein; *(average)* durchschnittlich, Durchschnitts- ♦ *vt (signify)* bedeuten; *(intend)* vorhaben, beabsichtigen ♦ *n (average)* Durchschnitt *m*; **~s** *npl (wherewithal)* Mittel *pl*; *(wealth)* Vermögen *nt*; **do you ~ me?** meinst du mich?; **do you ~ it?** meinst du das ernst?; **what do you ~?** was willst du damit sagen?; **to be ~t for sb/sth** für jdn/etw bestimmt sein; **by ~s of** durch; **by all ~s** selbstverständlich; **by no ~s** keineswegs

meander [mɪ'ændə*] *vi* sich schlängeln

meaning ['mi:nɪŋ] *n* Bedeutung *f*; *(of life)* Sinn *m*; **~ful** *adj* bedeutungsvoll; *(life)* sinnvoll; **~less** *adj* sinnlos

meanness ['mi:nnɪs] *n (stinginess)* Geiz *m*; *(spitefulness)* Gemeinheit *f*

meant [ment] *pt, pp of* **mean**

meantime ['mi:ntaɪm] *adv* inzwischen

meanwhile ['mi:nwaɪl] *adv* inzwischen

measles ['mi:zlz] *n* Masern *pl*

measly ['mi:zlɪ] (*inf*) *adj* poplig

measure ['mɛʒəʳ] *vt, vi* messen ♦ *n* Maß *nt*; (*step*) Maßnahme *f*; **~ments** *npl* Maße *pl*

meat [mi:t] *n* Fleisch *nt*; **cold ~** Aufschnitt *m*; **~ ball** *n* Fleischkloß *m*; **~ pie** *n* Fleischpastete *f*; **~y** *adj* fleischig; (*fig*) gehaltvoll

Mecca ['mɛkə] *n* Mekka *nt* (*also fig*)

mechanic [mɪ'kænɪk] *n* Mechaniker *m*; **~al** *adj* mechanisch; **~s** *n* Mechanik *f* ♦ *npl* Technik *f*

mechanism ['mɛkənɪzəm] *n* Mechanismus *m*

mechanize ['mɛkənaɪz] *vt* mechanisieren

medal ['mɛdl] *n* Medaille *f*; (*decoration*) Orden *m*; **~list** (*US* **medalist**) *n* Medaillengewinner(in) *m(f)*

meddle ['mɛdl] *vi*: **to ~ (in)** sich einmischen (in +*acc*); **to ~ with sth** sich an etw *dat* zu schaffen machen

media ['mi:dɪə] *npl* Medien *pl*

mediaeval [mɛdɪ'i:vl] *adj* = **medieval**

median ['mi:dɪən] (*US*) *n* (*also:* **~ strip**) Mittelstreifen *m*

mediate ['mi:dɪeɪt] *vi* vermitteln; **mediator** *n* Vermittler *m*

Medicaid ['mɛdɪkeɪd] (®) *US*) *n* medizinisches Versorgungsprogramm für sozial Schwache

medical ['mɛdɪkl] *adj* medizinisch; Medizin-; ärztlich ♦ *n* (ärztliche) Untersuchung *f*

Medicare ['mɛdɪkɛəʳ] (*US*) *n* staatliche Krankenversicherung besonders für Ältere

medicated ['mɛdɪkeɪtɪd] *adj* medizinisch

medication [mɛdɪ'keɪʃən] *n* (*drugs etc*) Medikamente *pl*

medicinal [mɛ'dɪsɪnl] *adj* medizinisch, Heil-

medicine ['mɛdsɪn] *n* Medizin *f*; (*drugs*) Arznei *f*

medieval [mɛdɪ'i:vl] *adj* mittelalterlich

mediocre [mi:dɪ'əukəʳ] *adj* mittelmäßig

meditate ['mɛdɪteɪt] *vi* meditieren; **to ~ (on sth)** (über etw *acc*) nachdenken; **meditation** [mɛdɪ'teɪʃən] *n* Nachsinnen *nt*; Meditation *f*

Mediterranean [mɛdɪtə'reɪnɪən] *adj*

Mittelmeer-; (*person*) südländisch; **the ~ (Sea)** das Mittelmeer

medium ['mi:dɪəm] *adj* mittlere(r, s), Mittel-, mittel- ♦ *n* Mitte *f*; (*means*) Mittel *nt*; (*person*) Medium *nt*; **happy ~** goldener Mittelweg; **~-sized** *adj* mittelgroß; **~ wave** *n* Mittelwelle *f*

medley ['mɛdlɪ] *n* Gemisch *nt*

meek [mi:k] *adj* sanft(mütig)

meet [mi:t] (*pt, pp* **met**) *vt* (*encounter*) treffen, begegnen +*dat*; (*by arrangement*) sich treffen mit; (*difficulties*) stoßen auf +*acc*; (*get to know*) kennen lernen; (*fetch*) abholen; (*join*) zusammentreffen mit; (*satisfy*) entsprechen +*dat* ♦ *vi* sich treffen; (*become acquainted*) sich kennen lernen; **~ with** *vt* (*problems*) stoßen auf +*acc*; (*US: people*) zusammentreffen mit; **~ing** *n* Treffen *nt*; (*business ~ing*) Besprechung *f*; (*of committee*) Sitzung *f*; (*assembly*) Versammlung *f*

mega- ['mɛgə-] (*inf*) *prefix* Mega-; **~byte** *n* (*COMPUT*) Megabyte *nt*; **~phone** *n* Megafon *nt*, Megaphon *nt*

melancholy ['mɛlənkəlɪ] *adj* (*person*) melancholisch; (*sight, event*) traurig

mellow ['mɛləu] *adj* mild, weich; (*fruit*) reif; (*fig*) gesetzt ♦ *vi* reif werden

melodious [mɪ'ləudɪəs] *adj* wohlklingend

melody ['mɛlədɪ] *n* Melodie *f*

melon ['mɛlən] *n* Melone *f*

melt [mɛlt] *vi* schmelzen; (*anger*) verfliegen ♦ *vt* schmelzen; **~ away** *vi* dahinschmelzen; **~ down** *vt* einschmelzen; **~down** *n* (*in nuclear reactor*) Kernschmelze *f*; **~ing point** *n* Schmelzpunkt *m*; **~ing pot** *n* (*fig*) Schmelztiegel *m*

member ['mɛmbəʳ] *n* Mitglied *nt*; (*of tribe, species*) Angehörige(r) *f(m)*; (*ANAT*) Glied *nt*; **M~ of Parliament** (*BRIT*) Parlamentsmitglied *nt*; **M~ of the European Parliament** (*BRIT*) *n* Mitglied *nt* des Europäischen Parlaments; **M~ of the Scottish Parliament** *n* Mitglied *nt* des schottischen Parlaments; **~ship** *n* Mitgliedschaft *f*; **to seek ~ship of** einen Antrag auf Mitgliedschaft stellen; **~ship**

card n Mitgliedskarte f

memento [mə'mɛntəu] n Andenken nt

memo ['mɛməu] n Mitteilung f

memoirs ['mɛmwɑːz] npl Memoiren pl

memorable ['mɛmərəbl] adj denkwürdig

memoranda [mɛmə'rændə] npl of **memorandum**

memorandum [mɛmə'rændəm] (pl **memoranda**) n Mitteilung f

memorial [mɪ'mɔːrɪəl] n Denkmal nt ♦ adj Gedenk-

memorize ['mɛməraɪz] vt sich einprägen

memory ['mɛmərɪ] n Gedächtnis nt; (of computer) Speicher m; (sth recalled) Erinnerung f

men [mɛn] pl of **man** ♦ n (human race) die Menschen pl

menace ['mɛnɪs] n Drohung f; Gefahr f ♦ vt bedrohen; **menacing** adj drohend

menagerie [mɪ'nædʒərɪ] n Tierschau f

mend [mɛnd] vt reparieren, flicken ♦ vi (ver)heilen ♦ n ausgebesserte Stelle f; **on the ~** auf dem Wege der Besserung; **~ing** n (articles) Flickarbeit f

menial ['miːnɪəl] adj niedrig

meningitis [mɛnɪn'dʒaɪtɪs] n Hirnhautentzündung f, Meningitis f

menopause ['mɛnəupɔːz] n Wechseljahre pl, Menopause f

menstruation [mɛnstru'eɪʃən] n Menstruation f

mental ['mɛntl] adj geistig, Geistes-; (arithmetic) Kopf-; (hospital) Nerven-; (cruelty) seelisch; (inf: abnormal) verrückt; **~ity** [mɛn'tælɪtɪ] n Mentalität f

menthol ['mɛnθɒl] n Menthol nt

mention ['mɛnʃən] n Erwähnung f ♦ vt erwähnen; **don't ~ it!** bitte (sehr), gern geschehen

mentor ['mɛntɔːr] n Mentor m

menu ['mɛnjuː] n Speisekarte f

MEP n abbr = **Member of the European Parliament**

mercenary ['mɜːsɪnərɪ] adj (person) geldgierig ♦ n Söldner m

merchandise ['mɜːtʃəndaɪz] n (Handels)ware f

merchant ['mɜːtʃənt] n Kaufmann m; **~ bank** (BRIT) n Handelsbank f; **~ navy** (US **~ marine**) n Handelsmarine f

merciful ['mɜːsɪful] adj gnädig

merciless ['mɜːsɪlɪs] adj erbarmungslos

mercury ['mɜːkjurɪ] n Quecksilber nt

mercy ['mɜːsɪ] n Erbarmen nt; Gnade f; **at the ~ of** ausgeliefert +dat

mere [mɪər] adj bloß; **~ly** adv bloß

merge [mɜːdʒ] vt verbinden; (COMM) fusionieren ♦ vi verschmelzen; (roads) zusammenlaufen; (COMM) fusionieren; **~r** n (COMM) Fusion f

meringue [mə'ræŋ] n Baiser nt

merit ['mɛrɪt] n Verdienst nt; (advantage) Vorzug m ♦ vt verdienen

mermaid ['mɜːmeɪd] n Wassernixe f

merry ['mɛrɪ] adj fröhlich; **~-go-round** n Karussell nt

mesh [mɛʃ] n Masche f

mesmerize ['mɛzməraɪz] vt hypnotisieren; (fig) faszinieren

mess [mɛs] n Unordnung f; (dirt) Schmutz m; (trouble) Schwierigkeiten pl; (MIL) Messe f; **~ about** or **around** vi (play the fool) herumalbern; (do nothing in particular) herumgammeln; **~ about** or **around with** vt fus (tinker with) herummurksen an +dat; **~ up** vt verpfuschen; (make untidy) in Unordnung bringen

message ['mɛsɪdʒ] n Mitteilung f; **to get the ~** kapieren

messenger ['mɛsɪndʒər] n Bote m

Messrs ['mɛsəz] abbr (on letters) die Herren

messy ['mɛsɪ] adj schmutzig; (untidy) unordentlich

met [mɛt] pt, pp of **meet**

metabolism [mɛ'tæbəlɪzəm] n Stoffwechsel m

metal ['mɛtl] n Metall nt; **~lic** adj metallisch; (made of ~) aus Metall

metaphor ['mɛtəfər] n Metapher f

meteorology [miːtɪə'rɒlədʒɪ] n Meteorologie f

meter ['miːtər] n Zähler m; (US) = **metre**

method ['mɛθəd] n Methode f; **~ical** [mɪ'θɒdɪkl] adj methodisch; **M~ist**

['mɛθədɪst] *adj* methodistisch ♦ *n* Methodist(in) *m(f)*; **~ology** [mɛθə'dɔlədʒɪ] *n* Methodik *f*

meths [mɛθs] (*BRIT*) *n(pl)* = **methylated spirit(s)**

methylated spirit(s) ['mɛθɪleɪtɪd-] (*BRIT*) *n* (Brenn)spiritus *m*

meticulous [mɪ'tɪkjuləs] *adj* (über)genau

metre ['miːtəʳ] (*US* **meter**) *n* Meter *m* or *nt*

metric ['mɛtrɪk] *adj* (*also:* **~al**) metrisch

metropolitan [mɛtrə'pɔlɪtn] *adj* der Großstadt; **M~ Police** (*BRIT*) *n*: **the M~ Police** die Londoner Polizei

mettle ['mɛtl] *n* Mut *m*

mew [mjuː] *vi* (*cat*) miauen

mews [mjuːz] *n*: **~ cottage** ehemaliges Kutscherhäuschen

Mexican ['mɛksɪkən] *adj* mexikanisch ♦ *n* Mexikaner(in) *m(f)*

Mexico ['mɛksɪkəu] *n* Mexiko *nt*

miaow [miː'au] *vi* miauen

mice [maɪs] *pl of* **mouse**

micro ['maɪkrəu] *n* (*also:* **~computer**) Mikrocomputer *m*; **~chip** *n* Mikrochip *m*; **~cosm** ['maɪkrəukɔzəm] *n* Mikrokosmos *m*; **~phone** *n* Mikrofon *nt*, Mikrophon *nt*; **~scope** *n* Mikroskop *nt*; **~wave** *n* (*also:* **~wave oven**) Mikrowelle(nherd *m*) *f*

mid [mɪd] *adj*: **in ~ afternoon** am Nachmittag; **in ~ air** in der Luft; **in ~ May** Mitte Mai

midday [mɪd'deɪ] *n* Mittag *m*

middle ['mɪdl] *n* Mitte *f*; (*waist*) Taille *f* ♦ *adj* mittlere(r, s), Mittel-; **in the ~ of** mitten in +*dat*; **~-aged** *adj* mittleren Alters; **M~ Ages** *npl*: **the M~ Ages** das Mittelalter; **~-class** *adj* Mittelstands-; **M~ East** *n*: **the M~ East** der Nahe Osten; **~man** (*irreg*) *n* (*COMM*) Zwischenhändler *m*; **~ name** *n* zweiter Vorname *m*; **~ weight** *n* (*BOXING*) Mittelgewicht *nt*

middling ['mɪdlɪŋ] *adj* mittelmäßig

midge [mɪdʒ] *n* Mücke *f*

midget ['mɪdʒɪt] *n* Liliputaner(in) *m(f)*

midnight ['mɪdnaɪt] *n* Mitternacht *f*

midriff ['mɪdrɪf] *n* Taille *f*

midst [mɪdst] *n*: **in the ~ of** (*persons*) mitten

unter +*dat*; (*things*) mitten in +*dat*

mid [mɪd] **-]: ~summer** *n* Hochsommer *m*; **~way** *adv* auf halbem Wege ♦ *adj* Mittel-; **~week** *adv* in der Mitte der Woche

midwife ['mɪdwaɪf] (*irreg*) *n* Hebamme *f*; **~ry** ['mɪdwɪfərɪ] *n* Geburtshilfe *f*

midwinter [mɪd'wɪntəʳ] *n* tiefste(r) Winter *m*

might [maɪt] *vi see* **may** ♦ *n* Macht *f*, Kraft *f*; **I ~ come** ich komme vielleicht; **~y** *adj, adv* mächtig

migraine ['miːgreɪn] *n* Migräne *f*

migrant ['maɪgrənt] *adj* Wander-; (*bird*) Zug-

migrate [maɪ'greɪt] *vi* (ab)wandern; (*birds*) (fort)ziehen; **migration** [maɪ'greɪʃən] *n* Wanderung *f*, Zug *m*

mike [maɪk] *n* = **microphone**

Milan [mɪ'læn] *n* Mailand *nt*

mild [maɪld] *adj* mild; (*medicine, interest*) leicht; (*person*) sanft ♦ *n* (*beer*) leichtes dunkles Bier

mildew ['mɪldjuː] *n* (*on plants*) Mehltau *m*; (*on food*) Schimmel *m*

mildly ['maɪldlɪ] *adv* leicht; **to put it ~** gelinde gesagt

mile [maɪl] *n* Meile *f*; **~age** *n* Meilenzahl *f*; **~ometer** *n* = **milometer**; **~stone** *n* (*also fig*) Meilenstein *m*

militant ['mɪlɪtnt] *adj* militant ♦ *n* Militante(r) *mf*

military ['mɪlɪtərɪ] *adj* militärisch, Militär-, Wehr-

militate ['mɪlɪteɪt] *vi*: **to ~ against** entgegenwirken +*dat*

militia [mɪ'lɪʃə] *n* Miliz *f*

milk [mɪlk] *n* Milch *f* ♦ *vt* (*also fig*) melken; **~ chocolate** *n* Milchschokolade *f*; **~man** (*irreg*) *n* Milchmann *m*; **~ shake** *n* Milchmixgetränk *nt*; **~y** *adj* milchig; **M~y Way** *n* Milchstraße *f*

mill [mɪl] *n* Mühle *f*; (*factory*) Fabrik *f* ♦ *vt* mahlen ♦ *vi* umherlaufen

millennia [mɪ'lenɪə] *npl of* **millennium**

millennium [mɪ'lenɪəm] (*pl* **~s** *or* **millennia**) *n* Jahrtausend *nt*; **~ bug** *n* (*COMPUT*) Jahrtausendfehler *m*

miller ['mɪləʳ] *n* Müller *m*

milligram(me) ['mɪlɪgræm] *n* Milligramm *nt*

millimetre ['mɪlɪmiːtər] (*US* **millimeter**) *n* Millimeter *m*

million ['mɪljən] *n* Million *f*; **a ~ times** tausendmal; **~aire** [mɪljəˈnɛər] *n* Millionär(in) *m(f)*

millstone ['mɪlstəʊn] *n* Mühlstein *m*

milometer [maɪˈlɒmɪtər] *n* ≈ Kilometerzähler *m*

mime [maɪm] *n* Pantomime *f* ♦ *vt, vi* mimen

mimic ['mɪmɪk] *n* Mimiker *m* ♦ *vt* nachahmen; **~ry** *n* Nachahmung *f*; (*BIOL*) Mimikry *f*

min. *abbr* = **minutes; minimum**

mince [mɪns] *vt* (zer)hacken ♦ *n* (*meat*) Hackfleisch *nt*; **~meat** *n* süße Pastetenfüllung *f*; **~ pie** *n* gefüllte (süße) Pastete *f*; **~r** *n* Fleischwolf *m*

mind [maɪnd] *n* Verstand *m*, Geist *m*; (*opinion*) Meinung *f* ♦ *vt* aufpassen auf +*acc*; (*object to*) etwas haben gegen; **on my ~** auf dem Herzen; **to my ~** meiner Meinung nach; **to be out of one's ~** wahnsinnig sein; **to bear** *or* **keep in ~** bedenken; **to change one's ~** es sich *dat* anders überlegen; **to make up one's ~** sich entschließen; **I don't ~** das macht mir nichts aus; **~ you, ...** allerdings ...; **never ~!** macht nichts!; **"~ the step"** „Vorsicht Stufe"; **~ your own business** kümmern Sie sich um Ihre eigenen Angelegenheiten; **~er** *n* Aufpasser(in) *m(f)*; **~ful** *adj*: **~ful of** achtsam auf +*acc*; **~less** *adj* sinnlos

mine¹ [maɪn] *n* (*coalmine*) Bergwerk *nt*; (*MIL*) Mine *f* ♦ *vt* abbauen; (*MIL*) verminen

mine² [maɪn] *pron* meine(r, s); **that book is ~** das Buch gehört mir; **a friend of ~** ein Freund von mir

minefield ['maɪnfiːld] *n* Minenfeld *nt*

miner ['maɪnər] *n* Bergarbeiter *m*

mineral ['mɪnərəl] *adj* mineralisch, Mineral- ♦ *n* Mineral *nt*; **~s** *npl* (*BRIT*: *soft drinks*) alkoholfreie Getränke *pl*; **~ water** *n* Mineralwasser *nt*

minesweeper ['maɪnswiːpər] *n* Minensuchboot *nt*

mingle ['mɪŋgl] *vi*: **to ~ (with)** sich mischen (unter +*acc*)

miniature ['mɪnətʃər] *adj* Miniatur- ♦ *n* Miniatur *f*

minibus ['mɪnɪbʌs] *n* Kleinbus *m*

Minidisc ['mɪnɪdɪsk] *n* Minidisc ® *f*

minimal ['mɪnɪml] *adj* minimal

minimize ['mɪnɪmaɪz] *vt* auf das Mindestmaß beschränken

minimum ['mɪnɪməm] (*pl* **minima**) *n* Minimum *nt* ♦ *adj* Mindest-

mining ['maɪnɪŋ] *n* Bergbau *m* ♦ *adj* Bergbau-, Berg-

miniskirt ['mɪnɪskəːt] *n* Minirock *m*

minister ['mɪnɪstər] *n* (*BRIT*: *POL*) Minister *m*; (*ECCL*) Pfarrer *m* ♦ *vi*: **to ~ to sb/sb's needs** sich um jdn kümmern; **~ial** [mɪnɪsˈtɪərɪəl] *adj* ministeriell, Minister-

ministry ['mɪnɪstrɪ] *n* (*BRIT*: *POL*) Ministerium *nt*; (*ECCL*: *office*) geistliche(s) Amt *nt*

mink [mɪŋk] *n* Nerz *m*

minnow ['mɪnəʊ] *n* Elritze *f*

minor ['maɪnər] *adj* kleiner; (*operation*) leicht; (*problem, poet*) unbedeutend; (*MUS*) Moll ♦ *n* (*BRIT*: *under 18*) Minderjährige(r) *mf*

minority [maɪˈnɒrɪtɪ] *n* Minderheit *f*

mint [mɪnt] *n* Minze *f*; (*sweet*) Pfefferminzbonbon *nt* ♦ *vt* (*coins*) prägen; **the (Royal** (*BRIT*) *or* **US** (*US*)) **M~** die Münzanstalt; **in ~ condition** in tadellosem Zustand

minus ['maɪnəs] *n* Minuszeichen *nt*; (*amount*) Minusbetrag *m* ♦ *prep* minus, weniger

minuscule ['mɪnəskjuːl] *adj* winzig

minute¹ [maɪˈnjuːt] *adj* winzig; (*detailed*) minutiös, minuziös

minute² ['mɪnɪt] *n* Minute *f*; (*moment*) Augenblick *m*; **~s** *npl* (*of meeting etc*) Protokoll *nt*

miracle ['mɪrəkl] *n* Wunder *nt*

miraculous [mɪˈrækjʊləs] *adj* wunderbar

mirage ['mɪrɑːʒ] *n* Fata Morgana *f*

mire ['maɪər] *n* Morast *m*

mirror ['mɪrər] *n* Spiegel *m* ♦ *vt* (wider)spiegeln

mirth [məːθ] *n* Heiterkeit *f*

misadventure [mɪsədˈventʃər] *n* Missgeschick *nt*, Unfall *m*

misanthropist [mɪˈzænθrəpɪst] *n*

Menschenfeind *m*

misapprehension ['mɪsæprɪ'henʃən] *n*
Missverständnis *nt*

misbehave [mɪsbɪ'heɪv] *vi* sich schlecht
benehmen

miscalculate [mɪs'kælkjuleɪt] *vt* falsch
berechnen

miscarriage ['mɪskærɪdʒ] *n* (*MED*)
Fehlgeburt *f*; ~ **of justice** Fehlurteil *nt*

miscellaneous [mɪsɪ'leɪnɪəs] *adj*
verschieden

mischief ['mɪstʃɪf] *n* Unfug *m*;

mischievous ['mɪstʃɪvəs] *adj* (*person*)
durchtrieben; (*glance*) verschmitzt; (*rumour*)
bösartig

misconception ['mɪskən'sepʃən] *n*
fälschliche Annahme *f*

misconduct [mɪs'kɔndʌkt] *n* Vergehen *nt*;
professional ~ Berufsvergehen *nt*

misconstrue [mɪskən'struː] *vt*
missverstehen

misdemeanour [mɪsdɪ'miːnəʳ] (*US*
misdemeanor) *n* Vergehen *nt*

miser ['maɪzəʳ] *n* Geizhals *m*

miserable ['mɪzərəbl] *adj* (*unhappy*)
unglücklich; (*headache, weather*)
fürchterlich; (*poor*) elend; (*contemptible*)
erbärmlich

miserly ['maɪzəlɪ] *adj* geizig

misery ['mɪzərɪ] *n* Elend *nt*, Qual *f*

misfire [mɪs'faɪəʳ] *vi* (*gun*) versagen; (*engine*)
fehlzünden; (*plan*) fehlgehen

misfit ['mɪsfɪt] *n* Außenseiter *m*

misfortune [mɪs'fɔːtʃən] *n* Unglück *nt*

misgiving(s) [mɪs'gɪvɪŋ(z)] *n(pl)* Bedenken
pl

misguided [mɪs'gaɪdɪd] *adj* fehlgeleitet;
(*opinions*) irrig

mishandle [mɪs'hændl] *vt* falsch handhaben

mishap ['mɪshæp] *n* Missgeschick *nt*

misinform [mɪsɪn'fɔːm] *vt* falsch
unterrichten

misinterpret [mɪsɪn'təːprɪt] *vt* falsch
auffassen

misjudge [mɪs'dʒʌdʒ] *vt* falsch beurteilen

mislay [mɪs'leɪ] (*irreg: like* **lay**) *vt* verlegen

mislead [mɪs'liːd] (*irreg: like* **lead**2) *vt*

(*deceive*) irreführen; ~**ing** *adj* irreführend

mismanage [mɪs'mænɪdʒ] *vt* schlecht
verwalten

misnomer [mɪs'nəuməʳ] *n* falsche
Bezeichnung *f*

misplace [mɪs'pleɪs] *vt* verlegen

misprint ['mɪsprɪnt] *n* Druckfehler *m*

Miss [mɪs] *n* Fräulein *nt*

miss [mɪs] *vt* (*fail to hit, catch*) verfehlen; (*not
notice*) verpassen; (*be too late*) versäumen,
verpassen; (*omit*) auslassen; (*regret the
absence of*) vermissen ♦ *vi* fehlen ♦ *n* (*shot*)
Fehlschuss *m*; (*failure*) Fehlschlag *m*; **I ~ you**
du fehlst mir; ~ **out** *vt* auslassen

misshapen [mɪs'ʃeɪpən] *adj* missgestaltet

missile ['mɪsaɪl] *n* Rakete *f*

missing [mɪsɪŋ] *adj* (*person*) vermisst;
(*thing*) fehlend; **to be ~** fehlen

mission ['mɪʃən] *n* (*work*) Auftrag *m*;
(*people*) Delegation *f*; (*REL*) Mission *f*; ~**ary**
n Missionar(in) *m(f)*; ~ **statement** *n*
Kurzdarstellung *f* der Firmenphilosophie

misspell ['mɪs'spel] (*irreg: like* **spell**) *vt*
falsch schreiben

misspent ['mɪs'spent] *adj* (*youth*) vergeudet

mist [mɪst] *n* Dunst *m*, Nebel *m* ♦ *vi* (*also: ~
over, ~ up*) sich trüben; (*BRIT: windows*) sich
beschlagen

mistake [mɪs'teɪk] (*irreg: like* **take**) *n* Fehler
m ♦ *vt* (*misunderstand*) missverstehen; (*mix
up*): **to ~** (**sth for sth**) (etw mit etw)
verwechseln; **to make a ~** einen Fehler
machen; **by ~** aus Versehen; **to ~ A for B** A
mit B verwechseln; ~**n** *pp of* **mistake** ♦ *adj*
(*idea*) falsch; **to be ~n** sich irren

mister ['mɪstəʳ] *n* (*inf*) Herr *m; see* **Mr**

mistletoe ['mɪsltəu] *n* Mistel *f*

mistook [mɪs'tuk] *pt of* **mistake**

mistress ['mɪstrɪs] *n* (*teacher*) Lehrerin *f*; (*in
house*) Herrin *f*; (*lover*) Geliebte *f; see* **Mrs**

mistrust [mɪs'trʌst] *vt* misstrauen +*dat*

misty ['mɪstɪ] *adj* neblig

misunderstand [mɪsʌndə'stænd] (*irreg: like*
understand) *vt, vi* missverstehen, falsch
verstehen; ~**ing** *n* Missverständnis *nt*;
(*disagreement*) Meinungsverschiedenheit *f*

misuse [*n* mɪs'juːs, *vb* mɪs'juːz] *n* falsche(r)

Gebrauch *m* ♦ *vt* falsch gebrauchen

mitigate ['mɪtɪgeɪt] *vt* mildern

mitt(en) ['mɪt(n)] *n* Fausthandschuh *m*

mix [mɪks] *vt* (*blend*) (ver)mischen ♦ *vi* (*liquids*) sich (ver)mischen lassen; (*people: get on*) sich vertragen; (: *associate*) Kontakt haben ♦ *n* (*~ture*) Mischung *f*; **~ up** *vt* zusammenmischen; (*confuse*) verwechseln; **~ed** *adj* gemischt; **~ed-up** *adj* durcheinander; **~er** *n* (*for food*) Mixer *m*; **~ture** *n* Mischung *f*; **~-up** *n* Durcheinander *nt*

mm *abbr* (= *millimetre(s)*) mm

moan [məun] *n* Stöhnen *nt*; (*complaint*) Klage *f* ♦ *vi* stöhnen; (*complain*) maulen

moat [məut] *n* (Burg)graben *m*

mob [mɔb] *n* Mob *m*; (*the masses*) Pöbel *m* ♦ *vt* herfallen über +*acc*

mobile ['məubaɪl] *adj* beweglich; (*library etc*) fahrbar ♦ *n* (*decoration*) Mobile *nt*; **~ home** *n* Wohnwagen *m*; **~ phone** *n* (TEL) Mobiltelefon *nt*; **mobility** [məu'bɪlɪtɪ] *n* Beweglichkeit *f*; **mobilize** ['məubɪlaɪz] *vt* mobilisieren

mock [mɔk] *vt* verspotten; (*defy*) trotzen +*dat* ♦ *adj* Schein-; **~ery** *n* Spott *m*; (*person*) Gespött *nt*

mod [mɔd] *adj see* **convenience**

mode [məud] *n* (Art *f* und) Weise *f*

model ['mɔdl] *n* Modell *nt*; (*example*) Vorbild *nt*; (*in fashion*) Mannequin *nt* ♦ *adj* (*railway*) Modell-; (*perfect*) Muster-; vorbildlich ♦ *vt* (*make*) bilden; (*clothes*) vorführen ♦ *vi* als Mannequin arbeiten

modem ['məudem] *n* (COMPUT) Modem *nt*

moderate [*adj, n* 'mɔdərət, *vb* 'mɔdəreɪt] *adj* gemäßigt ♦ *n* (POL) Gemäßigte(r) *mf* ♦ *vi* sich mäßigen ♦ *vt* mäßigen; **moderation** [mɔdə'reɪʃən] *n* Mäßigung *f*; **in moderation** mit Maßen

modern ['mɔdən] *adj* modern; (*history, languages*) neuere(r, s); **~ize** *vt* modernisieren

modest ['mɔdɪst] *adj* bescheiden; **~y** *n* Bescheidenheit *f*

modicum ['mɔdɪkəm] *n* bisschen *nt*

modification [mɔdɪfɪ'keɪʃən] *n*

(Ab)änderung *f*

modify ['mɔdɪfaɪ] *vt* abändern

module ['mɔdjuːl] *n* (*component*) (Bau)element *nt*; (SPACE) (Raum)kapsel *f*

mogul ['məugl] *n* (*fig*) Mogul *m*

mohair ['məuhɛə] *n* Mohär *m*, Mohair *m*

moist [mɔɪst] *adj* feucht; **~en** ['mɔɪsn] *vt* befeuchten; **~ure** ['mɔɪstʃə] *n* Feuchtigkeit *f*; **~urizer** ['mɔɪstʃəraɪzə] *n* Feuchtigkeitscreme *f*

molar ['məulə] *n* Backenzahn *m*

molasses [mə'læsɪz] *n* Melasse *f*

mold [məuld] (US) = **mould**

mole [məul] *n* (*spot*) Leberfleck *m*; (*animal*) Maulwurf *m*; (*pier*) Mole *f*

molest [mə'lest] *vt* belästigen

mollycoddle ['mɔlɪkɔdl] *vt* verhätscheln

molt [məult] (US) *vi* = **moult**

molten ['məultən] *adj* geschmolzen

mom [mɔm] (US) *n* = **mum**

moment ['məumənt] *n* Moment *m*, Augenblick *m*; (*importance*) Tragweite *f*; **at the ~** im Augenblick; **~ary** *adj* kurz; **~ous** [məu'mentəs] *adj* folgenschwer

momentum [məu'mentəm] *n* Schwung *m*; **to gather ~** in Fahrt kommen

mommy ['mɔmɪ] (US) *n* = **mummy**

Monaco ['mɔnəkəu] *n* Monaco *nt*

monarch ['mɔnək] *n* Herrscher(in) *m(f)*; **~y** *n* Monarchie *f*

monastery ['mɔnəstərɪ] *n* Kloster *nt*

monastic [mə'næstɪk] *adj* klösterlich, Kloster-

Monday ['mʌndɪ] *n* Montag *m*

monetary ['mʌnɪtərɪ] *adj* Geld-; (*of currency*) Währungs-

money ['mʌnɪ] *n* Geld *nt*; **to make ~** Geld verdienen; **~ belt** *n* Geldgürtel *m*; **~lender** *n* Geldverleiher *m*; **~ order** *n* Postanweisung *f*; **~-spinner** (*inf*) *n* Verkaufsschlager *m*

mongol ['mɔngəl] *n* (MED) mongoloide(s) Kind *nt* ♦ *adj* mongolisch; (MED) mongoloid

mongrel ['mʌngrəl] *n* Promenadenmischung *f*

monitor ['mɔnɪtə] *n* (SCH) Klassenordner *m*; (*television ~*) Monitor *m* ♦ *vt* (*broadcasts*) abhören; *(control)* überwachen

monk [mʌŋk] *n* Mönch *m*

monkey ['mʌŋkɪ] *n* Affe *m*; **~ nut** *n (BRIT)* Erdnuss *f*; **~ wrench** *n (TECH)* Engländer *m*, Franzose *m*

monochrome ['mɒnəkrəʊm] *adj* schwarzweiß, schwarzweiß

monopolize [mə'nɒpəlaɪz] *vt* beherrschen

monopoly [mə'nɒpəlɪ] *n* Monopol *nt*

monosyllable ['mɒnəsɪləbl] *n* einsilbige(s) Wort *nt*

monotone ['mɒnətəʊn] *n* gleich bleibende(r) Ton(fall) *m*; **to speak in a ~** monoton sprechen; **monotonous** [mə'nɒtənəs] *adj* eintönig; **monotony** [mə'nɒtənɪ] *n* Eintönigkeit *f*, Monotonie *f*

monsoon [mɒn'suːn] *n* Monsun *m*

monster ['mɒnstəʳ] *n* Ungeheuer *nt*; *(person)* Scheusal *nt*

monstrosity [mɒn'strɒsɪtɪ] *n* Ungeheuerlichkeit *f*; *(thing)* Monstrosität *f*

monstrous ['mɒnstrəs] *adj (shocking)* grässlich, ungeheuerlich; *(huge)* riesig

month [mʌnθ] *n* Monat *m*; **~ly** *adj* monatlich, Monats- ♦ *adv* einmal im Monat ♦ *n (magazine)* Monatsschrift *f*

monument ['mɒnjumənt] *n* Denkmal *nt*; **~al** [mɒnju'mentl] *adj (huge)* gewaltig; *(ignorance)* ungeheuer

moo [muː] *vi* muhen

mood [muːd] *n* Stimmung *f*, Laune *f*; **to be in a good/bad ~** gute/schlechte Laune haben; **~y** *adj* launisch

moon [muːn] *n* Mond *m*; **~light** *n* Mondlicht *nt*; **~lighting** *n* Schwarzarbeit *f*; **~lit** *adj* mondhell

moor [mʊəʳ] *n* Heide *f*, Hochmoor *nt* ♦ *vt (ship)* festmachen, verankern ♦ *vi* anlegen; **~ings** *npl* Liegeplatz *m*; **~land** ['mʊələnd] *n* Heidemoor *nt*

moose [muːs] *n* Elch *m*

mop [mɒp] *n* Mopp *m* ♦ *vt* (auf)wischen; **~ up** *vt* aufwischen

mope [məʊp] *vi* Trübsal blasen

moped ['məʊpɛd] *n* Moped *nt*

moral ['mɒrl] *adj* moralisch; *(values)* sittlich; *(virtuous)* tugendhaft ♦ *n* Moral *f*; **~s** *npl*

(ethics) Moral *f*

morale [mɒ'rɑːl] *n* Moral *f*

morality [mə'rælɪtɪ] *n* Sittlichkeit *f*

morass [mə'ræs] *n* Sumpf *m*

morbid ['mɔːbɪd] *adj* krankhaft; *(jokes)* makaber

KEYWORD

more [mɔːʳ] *adj (greater in number etc)* mehr; *(additional)* noch mehr; **do you want (some) more tea?** möchten Sie noch etwas Tee?; **I have no** *or* **I don't have any more money** ich habe kein Geld mehr ♦ *pron (greater amount)* mehr; *(further or additional amount)* noch mehr; **is there any more?** gibt es noch mehr?; *(left over)* ist noch etwas da?; **there's no more** es ist nichts mehr da

♦ *adv* mehr; **more dangerous/easily** *etc* **(than)** gefährlicher/einfacher *etc* (als); **more and more** immer mehr; **more and more excited** immer aufgeregter; **more or less** mehr oder weniger; **more than ever** mehr denn je; **more beautiful than ever** schöner denn je

---

moreover [mɔː'rəʊvəʳ] *adv* überdies

morgue [mɔːg] *n* Leichenschauhaus *nt*

Mormon ['mɔːmən] *n* Mormone *m*, Mormonin *f*

morning ['mɔːnɪŋ] *n* Morgen *m*; **in the ~** am Morgen; **7 o'clock in the ~** 7 Uhr morgens; **~ sickness** *n* (Schwangerschafts)übelkeit *f*

Morocco [mə'rɒkəʊ] *n* Marokko *nt*

moron ['mɔːrɒn] *n* Schwachsinnige(r) *mf*

morose [mə'rəʊs] *adj* mürrisch

morphine ['mɔːfiːn] *n* Morphium *nt*

Morse [mɔːs] *n (also: ~ code)* Morsealphabet *nt*

morsel ['mɔːsl] *n* Bissen *m*

mortal ['mɔːtl] *adj* sterblich; *(deadly)* tödlich; *(very great)* Todes- ♦ *n (human being)* Sterbliche(r) *mf*; **~ity** [mɔː'tælɪtɪ] *n* Sterblichkeit *f*; *(death rate)* Sterblichkeitsziffer *f*

mortar ['mɔːtəʳ] *n (for building)* Mörtel *m*;

(MIL) Granatwerfer *m*

mortgage ['mɔːgɪdʒ] *n* Hypothek *f ♦ vt* hypothekarisch belasten; **~ company** *(US)* *n* ≈ Bausparkasse *f*

mortify ['mɔːtɪfaɪ] *vt* beschämen

mortuary ['mɔːtjuərɪ] *n* Leichenhalle *f*

mosaic [məʊ'zeɪɪk] *n* Mosaik *nt*

Moscow ['mɒskəʊ] *n* Moskau *nt*

Moslem ['mɒzləm] = **Muslim**

mosque [mɒsk] *n* Moschee *f*

mosquito [mɒs'kiːtəʊ] *(pl ~es) n* Moskito *m*

moss [mɒs] *n* Moos *nt*

most [məʊst] *adj* meiste(r, s) *♦ adv* am meisten; *(very)* höchst *♦ n* das meiste, der größte Teil; *(people)* die meisten; **~ men** die meisten Männer; **at the (very) ~** allerhöchstens; **to make the ~ of** das Beste machen aus; **a ~ interesting book** ein höchstinteressantes Buch; **~ly** *adv* größtenteils

MOT *(BRIT) n abbr* (= *Ministry of Transport*): **the MOT (test)** ≈ der TÜV

motel [məʊ'tel] *n* Motel *nt*

moth [mɒθ] *n* Nachtfalter *m*; *(wool-eating)* Motte *f*; **~ball** *n* Mottenkugel *f*

mother ['mʌðə*] *n* Mutter *f ♦ vt* bemuttern; **~hood** *n* Mutterschaft *f*; **~-in-law** *n* Schwiegermutter *f*; **~ly** *adj* mütterlich; **~-of-pearl** *n* Perlmut *nt*; **M~'s Day** *(BRIT) n* Muttertag *m*; **~-to-be** *n* werdende Mutter *f*; **~ tongue** *n* Muttersprache *f*

motion ['məʊʃən] *n* Bewegung *f*; *(in meeting)* Antrag *m ♦ vt, vi*: **to ~ (to) sb** jdm winken, jdm zu verstehen geben; **~less** *adj* regungslos; **~ picture** *n* Film *m*

motivated ['məʊtɪveɪtɪd] *adj* motiviert

motivation [məʊtɪ'veɪʃən] *n* Motivierung *f*

motive ['məʊtɪv] *n* Motiv *nt*, Beweggrund *m ♦ adj* treibend

motley ['mɒtlɪ] *adj* bunt

motor ['məʊtə*] *n* Motor *m*; *(BRIT: inf: vehicle)* Auto *nt ♦ adj* Motor-; **~bike** *n* Motorrad *nt*; **~boat** *n* Motorboot *nt*; **~car** *(BRIT) n* Auto *nt*; **~cycle** *n* Motorrad *nt*; **~cyclist** *n* Motorradfahrer(in) *m(f)*; **~ing** *(BRIT) n* Autofahren *nt ♦ adj* Auto-; **~ist** *n* Autofahrer(in) *m(f)*; **~ mechanic** *n*

Kraftfahrzeugmechaniker(in) *m(f)*, Kfz-Mechaniker(in) *m(f)*; **~ racing** *(BRIT) n* Autorennen *nt*; **~ vehicle** *n* Kraftfahrzeug *nt*; **~way** *(BRIT) n* Autobahn *f*

mottled ['mɒtld] *adj* gesprenkelt

mould [məʊld] *(US* **mold***) n* Form *f*; *(mildew)* Schimmel *m ♦ vt (also fig)* formen; **~y** *adj* schimmelig

moult [məʊlt] *(US* **molt***) vi* sich mausern

mound [maʊnd] *n* (Erd)hügel *m*

mount [maʊnt] *n (liter: hill)* Berg *m*; *(horse)* Pferd *nt*; *(for jewel etc)* Fassung *f ♦ vt (horse)* steigen auf +*acc*; *(put in setting)* fassen; *(exhibition)* veranstalten; *(attack)* unternehmen *♦ vi (also: ~ up)* sich häufen; *(on horse)* aufsitzen

mountain ['maʊntɪn] *n* Berg *m ♦ cpd* Berg-; **~ bike** *n* Mountainbike *nt*; **~eer** *n* Bergsteiger(in) *m(f)*; **~eering** [maʊntɪ'nɪərɪŋ] *n* Bergsteigen *nt*; **~ous** *adj* bergig; **~ rescue team** *n* Bergwacht *f*; **~side** *n* Berg(ab)hang *m*

mourn [mɔːn] *vt* betrauen, beklagen *♦ vi*: **to ~ (for sb)** (um jdn) trauern; **~er** *n* Trauernde(r) *mf*; **~ful** *adj* traurig; **~ing** *n (grief)* Trauer *f ♦ cpd (dress)* Trauer-; **in ~ing** *(period etc)* in Trauer; *(dress)* in Trauerkleidung *f*

mouse [maʊs] *(pl* **mice***) n* Maus *f*; **~trap** *n* Mausefalle *f*; **~ mat, ~ pad** *(COMPUT)* Mousepad *nt*

mousse [muːs] *n (COOK)* Creme *f*; *(cosmetic)* Schaumfestiger *m*

moustache [məs'tɑːʃ] *n* Schnurrbart *m*

mousy ['maʊsɪ] *adj (colour)* mausgrau; *(person)* schüchtern

mouth [maʊθ] *n* Mund *m*; *(opening)* Öffnung *f*; *(of river)* Mündung *f*; **~ful** *n* Mund *m* voll; **~ organ** *n* Mundharmonika *f*; **~piece** *n* Mundstück *nt*; *(fig)* Sprachrohr *nt*; **~wash** *n* Mundwasser *nt*; **~watering** *adj* lecker, appetitlich

movable ['muːvəbl] *adj* beweglich

move [muːv] *n (~ment)* Bewegung *f*; *(in game)* Zug *m*; *(step)* Schritt *m*; *(of house)* Umzug *m ♦ vt* bewegen; *(people)* transportieren; *(in job)* versetzen;

(*emotionally*) bewegen ♦ *vi* sich bewegen; (*vehicle, ship*) fahren; (~ *house*) umziehen; **to get a ~ on** sich beeilen; **to ~ sb to do sth** jdn veranlassen, etw zu tun; ~ **about** *or* **around** *vi* sich hin und her bewegen; (*travel*) unterwegs sein; ~ **along** *vi* weitergehen; (*cars*) weiterfahren; ~ **away** *vi* weggehen; ~ **back** *vi* zurückgehen; (*to the rear*) zurückweichen; ~ **forward** *vi* vorwärts gehen, sich vorwärts bewegen ♦ *vt* vorschieben; (*time*) vorverlegen; ~ **in** *vi* (*to house*) einziehen; (*troops*) einrücken; ~ **on** *vi* weitergehen ♦ *vt* weitergehen lassen; ~ **out** *vi* (*of house*) ausziehen; (*troops*) abziehen; ~ **over** *vi* zur Seite rücken; ~ **up** *vi* aufsteigen; (*in job*) befördert werden ♦ *vt* nach oben bewegen; (*in job*) befördern; ~**ment** ['muːvmənt] *n* Bewegung *f*

movie ['muːvɪ] *n* Film *m*; **to go to the ~s** ins Kino gehen; ~ **camera** *n* Filmkamera *f*

moving ['muːvɪŋ] *adj* beweglich; (*touching*) ergreifend

mow [məu] (*pt* **mowed**, *pp* **mowed** *or* **mown**) *vt* mähen; ~ **down** *vt* (*fig*) niedermähen; ~**er** *n* (*lawnmower*) Rasenmäher *m*; ~**n** *pp of* **mow**

MP *n abbr* = **Member of Parliament**

MP3 player *n* MP3-Spieler *m*

m.p.h. *abbr* = **miles per hour**

Mr ['mɪstər] (*US* **Mr.**) *n* Herr *m*

Mrs ['mɪsɪz] (*US* **Mrs.**) *n* Frau *f*

Ms [mɪz] (*US* **Ms.**) *n* (= *Miss or Mrs*) Frau *f*

M.Sc. *n abbr* = **Master of Science**

MSP *n abbr* (= *Member of the Scottish Parliament*) Mitglied *nt* des schottischen Parlaments

much [mʌtʃ] *adj* viel ♦ *adv* sehr; viel ♦ *n* viel, eine Menge; **how ~ is it?** wie viel kostet das?; **too ~** zu viel; **it's not ~** es ist nicht viel; **as ~ as** so sehr, so viel; **however ~ he tries** sosehr er es auch versucht

muck [mʌk] *n* Mist *m*; (*fig*) Schmutz *m*; ~ **about** *or* **around** (*inf*) *vi*: **to ~ about** *or* **around (with sth)** (an etw *dat*) herumalbern; ~ **up** *vt* (*inf: ruin*) vermasseln; (*dirty*) dreckig machen; ~**y** *adj* (*dirty*) dreckig

mud [mʌd] *n* Schlamm *m*

muddle ['mʌdl] *n* Durcheinander *nt* ♦ *vt* (*also:* ~ **up**) durcheinander bringen; ~ **through** *vi* sich durchwursteln

mud ['mʌd]-: ~**dy** *adj* schlammig; ~**guard** *n* Schutzblech *nt*; ~**-slinging** (*inf*) *n* Verleumdung *f*

muesli ['mjuːzlɪ] *n* Müsli *nt*

muffin ['mʌfɪn] *n* süße(s) Teilchen *nt*

muffle ['mʌfl] *vt* (*sound*) dämpfen; (*wrap up*) einhüllen; ~**d** *adj* gedämpft; ~**r** (*US*) *n* (*AUT*) Schalldämpfer *m*

mug [mʌg] *n* (*cup*) Becher *m*; (*inf: face*) Visage *f*; (: *fool*) Trottel *m* ♦ *vt* überfallen und ausrauben; ~**ger** *n* Straßenräuber *m*; ~**ging** *n* Überfall *m*

muggy ['mʌgɪ] *adj* (*weather*) schwül

mule [mjuːl] *n* Maulesel *m*

mull [mʌl]: ~ **over** *vt* nachdenken über +*acc*

multicoloured ['mʌltɪkʌləd] (*US* **multicolored**) *adj* mehrfarbig

multi-level ['mʌltɪlevl] (*US*) *adj* = **multistorey**

multiple ['mʌltɪpl] *n* Vielfache(s) *nt* ♦ *adj* mehrfach; (*many*) mehrere; ~ **sclerosis** *n* multiple Sklerose *f*

multiplex cinema ['mʌltɪpleks-] *n* Kinocenter *nt*

multiplication [mʌltɪplɪ'keɪʃən] *n* Multiplikation *f*; (*increase*) Vervielfachung *f*

multiply ['mʌltɪplaɪ] *vt*: **to ~ (by)** multiplizieren (mit) ♦ *vi* (*BIOL*) sich vermehren

multistorey ['mʌltɪ'stɔːrɪ] (*BRIT*) *adj* (*building, car park*) mehrstöckig

multitude ['mʌltɪtjuːd] *n* Menge *f*

mum [mʌm] (*BRIT: inf*) Mutti *f* ♦ *adj*: **to keep ~ (about)** den Mund halten (über +*acc*)

mumble ['mʌmbl] *vt, vi* murmeln ♦ *n* Gemurmel *nt*

mummy ['mʌmɪ] *n* (*dead body*) Mumie *f*; (*BRIT: inf*) Mami *f*

mumps [mʌmps] *n* Mumps *m*

munch [mʌntʃ] *vt, vi* mampfen

mundane [mʌn'deɪn] *adj* banal

municipal [mjuː'nɪsɪpl] *adj* städtisch, Stadt-

mural ['mjuərl] *n* Wandgemälde *nt*

murder ['mɜːdər] *n* Mord *m* ♦ *vt* ermorden; ~**er** *n* Mörder *m*; ~**ous** *adj* Mord-; (*fig*) mörderisch

murky ['mɜːkɪ] *adj* finster

murmur ['mɜːmər] *n* Murmeln *nt*; *(of water, wind)* Rauschen *nt* ♦ *vt, vi* murmeln

muscle ['mʌsl] *n* Muskel *m*; ~ **in** *vi* mitmischen; **muscular** ['mʌskjulər] *adj* Muskel-; *(strong)* muskulös

museum [mjuːˈzɪəm] *n* Museum *nt*

mushroom ['mʌʃrum] *n* Champignon *m*; Pilz *m* ♦ *vi* (*fig*) emporschießen

music ['mjuːzɪk] *n* Musik *f*; *(printed)* Noten *pl*; ~**al** *adj* (*sound*) melodisch; *(person)* musikalisch ♦ *n* (*show*) Musical *nt*; ~**al instrument** *n* Musikinstrument *nt*; ~ **centre** *n* Stereoanlage *f*; ~ **hall** (*BRIT*) *n* Varietee *nt*, Varieté *nt*; ~**ian** [mjuːˈzɪʃən] *n* Musiker(in) *m(f)*

Muslim ['mʌzlɪm] *adj* moslemisch ♦ *n* Moslem *m*

muslin ['mʌzlɪn] *n* Musselin *m*

mussel ['mʌsl] *n* Miesmuschel *f*

must [mʌst] *vb aux* müssen; *(in negation)* dürfen ♦ *n* Muss *nt*; **the film is a** ~ den Film muss man einfach gesehen haben

mustard ['mʌstəd] *n* Senf *m*

muster ['mʌstər] *vt* (*MIL*) antreten lassen; *(courage)* zusammennehmen

mustn't ['mʌsnt] = **must not**

musty ['mʌstɪ] *adj* muffig

mute [mjuːt] *adj* stumm ♦ *n* (*person*) Stumme(r) *mf*; (*MUS*) Dämpfer *m*; ~**d** *adj* gedämpft

mutilate ['mjuːtɪleɪt] *vt* verstümmeln

mutiny ['mjuːtɪnɪ] *n* Meuterei *f* ♦ *vi* meutern

mutter ['mʌtər] *vt, vi* murmeln

mutton ['mʌtn] *n* Hammelfleisch *nt*

mutual ['mjuːtʃuəl] *adj* gegenseitig; beiderseitig; ~**ly** *adv* gegenseitig; für beide Seiten

muzzle ['mʌzl] *n* (*of animal*) Schnauze *f*; (*for animal*) Maulkorb *m*; (*of gun*) Mündung *f* ♦ *vt* einen Maulkorb anlegen +*dat*

my [maɪ] *adj* mein; **this is** ~ **car** das ist mein Auto; **I've washed** ~ **hair** ich habe mir die Haare gewaschen

myself [maɪˈself] *pron* mich *acc*; mir *dat*; *(emphatic)* selbst; *see also* **oneself**

mysterious [mɪsˈtɪərɪəs] *adj* geheimnisvoll

mystery ['mɪstərɪ] *n* (*secret*) Geheimnis *nt*; *(sth difficult)* Rätsel *nt*

mystify ['mɪstɪfaɪ] *vt* ein Rätsel *nt* sein +*dat*; verblüffen

mystique [mɪsˈtiːk] *n* geheimnisvolle Natur *f*

myth [mɪθ] *n* Mythos *m*; (*fig*) Erfindung *f*; ~**ology** [mɪˈθɒlədʒɪ] *n* Mythologie *f*

N, n

n/a *abbr* (= *not applicable*) nicht zutreffend

nab [næb] (*inf*) *vt* schnappen

naff [næf] (*BRIT: inf*) *adj* blöd

nag [næg] *n* (*horse*) Gaul *m*; (*person*) Nörgler(in) *m(f)* ♦ *vt, vi*: **to** ~ (**at**) **sb** an jdm herumnörgeln; ~**ging** *adj* (*doubt*) nagend ♦ *n* Nörgelei *f*

nail [neɪl] *n* Nagel *m* ♦ *vt* nageln; **to** ~ **sb down to doing sth** jdn darauf festnageln, etw zu tun; ~**brush** *n* Nagelbürste *f*; ~**file** *n* Nagelfeile *f*; ~ **polish** *n* Nagellack *m*; ~ **polish remover** *n* Nagellackentferner *m*; ~ **scissors** *npl* Nagelschere *f*; ~ **varnish** (*BRIT*) *n* = **nail polish**

naïve [naɪˈiːv] *adj* naiv

naked ['neɪkɪd] *adj* nackt

name [neɪm] *n* Name *m*; (*reputation*) Ruf *m* ♦ *vt* nennen; (*sth new*) benennen; (*appoint*) ernennen; **by** ~ mit Namen; **I know him only by** ~ ich kenne ihn nur dem Namen nach; **what's your** ~? wie heißen Sie?; **in the** ~ **of** im Namen +*gen*; (*for the sake of*) um +*gen* ... willen; ~**less** *adj* namenlos; ~**ly** *adv* nämlich; ~**sake** *n* Namensvetter *m*

nanny ['nænɪ] *n* Kindermädchen *nt*

nap [næp] *n* (*sleep*) Nickerchen *nt*; (*on cloth*) Strich *m* ♦ *vi*: **to be caught** ~**ping** (*fig*) überrumpelt werden

nape [neɪp] *n* Nacken *m*

napkin ['næpkɪn] *n* (*at table*) Serviette *f*; (*BRIT: for baby*) Windel *f*

nappy ['næpɪ] (*BRIT*) *n* (*for baby*) Windel *f*; ~ **rash** *n* wunde Stellen *pl*

narcotic [naːˈkɒtɪk] *adj* betäubend ♦ *n* Betäubungsmittel *nt*

narrative ['nærətɪv] n Erzählung f ♦ adj erzählend

narrator [nə'reɪtəʳ] n Erzähler(in) m(f)

narrow ['nærəʊ] adj eng, schmal; (limited) beschränkt ♦ vi sich verengen; **to have a ~ escape** mit knapper Not davonkommen; **to ~ sth down to sth** etw auf etw acc einschränken; **~ly** adv (miss) knapp; (escape) mit knapper Not; **~-minded** adj engstirnig

nasty ['nɑːstɪ] adj ekelhaft, fies; (business, wound) schlimm

nation ['neɪʃən] n Nation f, Volk nt; **~al** ['næʃənl] adj national, National-, Landes- ♦ n Staatsangehörige(r) mf; **~al anthem** (BRIT) n Nationalhymne f; **~al dress** n Tracht f; **N~al Health Service** (BRIT) n staatliche(r) Gesundheitsdienst m; **N~al Insurance** (BRIT) n Sozialversicherung f; **~alism** ['næʃnəlɪzəm] n Nationalismus m; **~alist** ['næʃnəlɪst] n Nationalist(in) m(f) ♦ adj nationalistisch; **~ality** [næʃə'nælɪtɪ] n Staatsangehörigkeit f; **~alize** ['næʃnəlaɪz] vt verstaatlichen; **~ally** ['næʃnəlɪ] adv national, auf Staatsebene; **~al park** (BRIT) n Nationalpark m; **~wide** ['neɪʃənwaɪd] adj, adv allgemein, landesweit

---

National Trust

ⓘ Der **National Trust** ist ein 1895 gegründeter Natur- und Denkmalschutzverband in Großbritannien, der Gebäude und Gelände von besonderem historischen oder ästhetischen Interesse erhält und der Öffentlichkeit zugänglich macht. Viele Gebäude im Besitz des National Trust sind (z.T. gegen ein Eintrittsgeld) zu besichtigen.

---

native ['neɪtɪv] n (born in) Einheimische(r) mf; (original inhabitant) Eingeborene(r) mf ♦ adj einheimisch; Eingeborenen-; (belonging to birth) heimatlich, Heimat-; (inborn) angeboren, natürlich; **a ~ of Germany** ein gebürtiger Deutscher; **a ~ speaker of French** ein französischer Muttersprachler; **N~ American** n Indianer(in) m(f), Ureinwohner(in) m(f) Amerikas; **~ language** n Muttersprache f

Nativity [nə'tɪvɪtɪ] n: **the ~** Christi Geburt no art

NATO ['neɪtəʊ] n abbr (= North Atlantic Treaty Organization) NATO f

natural ['nætʃrəl] adj natürlich; Natur-; (inborn) (an)geboren; **~ gas** n Erdgas nt; **~ist** n Naturkundler(in) m(f); **~ly** adv natürlich

nature ['neɪtʃəʳ] n Natur f; **by ~** von Natur (aus)

naught [nɔːt] n = **nought**

naughty ['nɔːtɪ] adj (child) unartig, ungezogen; (action) ungehörig

nausea ['nɔːsɪə] n (sickness) Übelkeit f; (disgust) Ekel m; **~te** ['nɔːsɪeɪt] vt anekeln

nautical ['nɔːtɪkl] adj nautisch; See-; (expression) seemännisch

naval ['neɪvl] adj Marine-, Flotten-; **~ officer** n Marineoffizier m

nave [neɪv] n Kirchen(haupt)schiff nt

navel ['neɪvl] n Nabel m

navigate ['nævɪgeɪt] vi navigieren; **navigation** [nævɪ'geɪʃən] n Navigation f; **navigator** ['nævɪgeɪtəʳ] n Steuermann m; (AVIAT) Navigator m; (AUT) Beifahrer(in) m(f)

navvy ['nævɪ] (BRIT) n Straßenarbeiter m

navy ['neɪvɪ] n (Kriegs)marine f ♦ adj (also: ~ blue) marineblau

Nazi ['nɑːtsɪ] n Nazi m

NB abbr (= nota bene) NB

near [nɪəʳ] adj nah ♦ adv in der Nähe ♦ prep (also: ~ to: space) in der Nähe +gen; (: time) um +acc ... herum ♦ vt sich nähern +dat; **a ~ miss** knapp daneben; **~by** adj nahe (gelegen) ♦ adv in der Nähe; **~ly** adv fast; **I ~ly fell** ich wäre fast gefallen; **~side** n (AUT) Beifahrerseite f ♦ adj auf der Beifahrerseite; **~-sighted** adj kurzsichtig

neat [niːt] adj (tidy) ordentlich; (solution) sauber; (pure) pur; **~ly** adv (tidily) ordentlich

necessarily ['nesɪsrɪlɪ] adv unbedingt

necessary ['nesɪsrɪ] adj notwendig, nötig; **he did all that was ~** er erledigte alles, was nötig war; **it is ~ to/that ...** man nötig war; **it is ~ to/that ...** man muss ...

necessitate [nɪ'sesɪteɪt] vt erforderlich machen

necessity [nɪ'sesɪtɪ] n (need) Not f; (compulsion) Notwendigkeit f; **necessities** npl (things needed) das Notwendigste

neck [nɛk] n Hals m ♦ vi (inf) knutschen; ~ **and** ~ Kopf an Kopf; **~lace** ['nɛklɪs] n Halskette f; **~line** ['nɛklaɪn] n Ausschnitt m; **~tie** ['nɛktaɪ] (US) n Krawatte f

née [neɪ] adj geborene

need [niːd] n Bedürfnis nt; (lack) Mangel m; (necessity) Notwendigkeit f; (poverty) Not f ♦ vt brauchen; **I ~ to do it** ich muss es tun; **you don't ~ to go** du brauchst nicht zu gehen

needle ['niːdl] n Nadel f ♦ vt (fig: inf) ärgern

needless ['niːdlɪs] adj unnötig; ~ **to say** natürlich

needlework ['niːdlwɜːk] n Handarbeit f

needn't ['niːdnt] = need not

needy ['niːdɪ] adj bedürftig

negative ['nɛgətɪv] n (PHOT) Negativ nt ♦ adj negativ; (answer) abschlägig; ~ **equity** n Differenz zwischen gefallenem Wert und hypothekarischer Belastung eines Wohneigentums

neglect [nɪ'glɛkt] vt vernachlässigen ♦ n Vernachlässigung f; **~ed** adj vernachlässigt

negligee ['nɛglɪʒeɪ] n Negligee nt, Negligé nt

negligence ['nɛglɪdʒəns] n Nachlässigkeit f

negligible ['nɛglɪdʒɪbl] adj unbedeutend, geringfügig

negotiable [nɪ'gəʊʃɪəbl] adj (cheque) übertragbar, einlösbar

negotiate [nɪ'gəʊʃɪeɪt] vi verhandeln ♦ vt (treaty) abschließen; (difficulty) überwinden; (corner) nehmen; **negotiation** [nɪgəʊʃɪ'eɪʃən] n Verhandlung f; **negotiator** n Unterhändler m

neigh [neɪ] vi wiehern

neighbour ['neɪbər] (US **neighbor**) n Nachbar(in) m(f); **~hood** n Nachbarschaft f; Umgebung f; **~ing** adj benachbart, angrenzend; **~ly** adj (person, attitude) nachbarlich

neither ['naɪðər] adj, pron keine(r, s) (von

beiden) ♦ conj: **he can't do it, and ~ can I** er kann es nicht und ich auch nicht ♦ adv: ~ **good nor bad** weder gut noch schlecht; ~ **story is true** keine der beiden Geschichten stimmt

neon ['niːɔn] n Neon nt; ~ **light** n Neonlampe f

nephew ['nevjuː] n Neffe m

nerve [nɜːv] n Nerv m; (courage) Mut m; (impudence) Frechheit f; **to have a fit of ~s** in Panik geraten; **~-racking** adj nervenaufreibend

nervous ['nɜːvəs] adj (of the nerves) Nerven-; (timid) nervös, ängstlich; ~ **breakdown** n Nervenzusammenbruch m; **~ness** n Nervosität f

nest [nɛst] n Nest nt ♦ vi nisten; ~ **egg** n (fig) Notgroschen m

nestle ['nɛsl] vi sich kuscheln

Net [nɛt] n: **the ~** das Internet

net [nɛt] n Netz nt ♦ adj netto, Netto- ♦ vt netto einnehmen; **~ball** n Netzball m

Netherlands ['nɛðələndz] npl: **the ~** die Niederlande pl

nett [nɛt] adj = net

netting ['nɛtɪŋ] n Netz(werk) nt

nettle ['nɛtl] n Nessel f

network ['nɛtwɜːk] n Netz nt

neurotic [njuə'rɔtɪk] adj neurotisch

neuter ['njuːtər] adj (BIOL) geschlechtslos; (GRAM) sächlich ♦ vt kastrieren

neutral ['njuːtrəl] adj neutral ♦ n (AUT) Leerlauf m; **~ity** [njuː'trælɪtɪ] n Neutralität f; **~ize** vt (fig) ausgleichen

never ['nevər] adv nie(mals); **I ~ went** ich bin gar nicht gegangen; ~ **in my life** nie im Leben; **~-ending** adj endlos; **~theless** [nevəðə'les] adv trotzdem, dennoch

new [njuː] adj neu; **N~ Age** adj Newage-, New-Age-; **~comer** ['njuːkʌmər] n Neuankömmling m; **~-fangled** (pej) adj neumodisch; **~-found** adj neu entdeckt; **~ly** adv frisch, neu; **~lyweds** npl Frischvermählte pl; ~ **moon** n Neumond m

news [njuːz] n Nachricht f; (RAD, TV) Nachrichten pl; **a piece of ~** eine

Nachricht; **~ agency** n Nachrichtenagentur f; **~agent** (BRIT) n Zeitungshändler m; **~caster** n Nachrichtensprecher(in) m(f); **~ flash** n Kurzmeldung f; **~letter** n Rundschreiben nt; **~paper** n Zeitung f; **~print** n Zeitungspapier nt; **~reader** n = **newscaster**; **~reel** n Wochenschau f; **~ stand** n Zeitungsstand m

newt [njuːt] n Wassermolch m

New Year n Neujahr nt; **~'s Day** n Neujahrstag m; **~'s Eve** n Silvester(abend m) nt

New Zealand [-ˈziːlənd] n Neuseeland nt; **~er** n Neuseeländer(in) m(f)

next [nɛkst] adj nächste(r, s) ♦ adv (after) dann, darauf; (~ time) das nächste Mal; **the ~ day** am nächsten or folgenden Tag; **~ time** das nächste Mal; **~ year** nächstes Jahr; **~ door** adv nebenan ♦ adj (neighbour, flat) von nebenan; **~ of kin** n nächste(r) Verwandte(r) mf; **~ to** prep neben; **~ to nothing** so gut wie nichts

NHS n abbr = **National Health Service**

nib [nɪb] n Spitze f

nibble [ˈnɪbl] vt knabbern an +dat

nice [naɪs] adj (person) nett; (thing) schön; (subtle) fein; **~-looking** adj gut aussehend; **~ly** adv gut, nett; **~ties** [ˈnaɪsɪtɪz] npl Feinheiten pl

nick [nɪk] n Einkerbung f ♦ vt (inf: steal) klauen; **in the ~ of time** gerade rechtzeitig

nickel [ˈnɪkl] n Nickel nt; (US) Nickel m (5 cents)

nickname [ˈnɪkneɪm] n Spitzname m ♦ vt taufen

nicotine patch [ˈnɪkətiːn-] n Nikotinpflaster nt

niece [niːs] n Nichte f

Nigeria [naɪˈdʒɪərɪə] n Nigeria nt

niggling [ˈnɪglɪŋ] adj pedantisch; (doubt, worry) quälend

night [naɪt] n Nacht f; (evening) Abend m; **the ~ before last** vorletzte Nacht; **at** or **by ~** (before midnight) abends; (after midnight) nachts; **~cap** n (drink) Schlummertrunk m; **~club** n Nachtlokal nt; **~dress** n

Nachthemd nt; **~fall** n Einbruch m der Nacht; **~ gown** n = **nightdress**; **~ie** (inf) n Nachthemd nt

nightingale [ˈnaɪtɪŋgeɪl] n Nachtigall f

night: ~life [ˈnaɪtlaɪf] n Nachtleben nt; **~ly** [ˈnaɪtlɪ] adj, adv jeden Abend; jede Nacht; **~mare** [ˈnaɪtmɛəʳ] n Albtraum m; **~ porter** n Nachtportier m; **~ school** n Abendschule f; **~ shift** n Nachtschicht f; **~time** n Nacht f

nil [nɪl] n Null f

Nile [naɪl] n: **the ~** der Nil

nimble [ˈnɪmbl] adj beweglich

nine [naɪn] num neun; **~teen** num neunzehn; **~ty** num neunzig

ninth [naɪnθ] adj neunte(r, s)

nip [nɪp] vt kneifen ♦ n Kneifen nt

nipple [ˈnɪpl] n Brustwarze f

nippy [ˈnɪpɪ] (inf) adj (person) flink; (BRIT: car) flott; (: cold) frisch

nitrogen [ˈnaɪtrədʒən] n Stickstoff m

KEYWORD
---

no [nəu] (pl **noes**) adv (opposite of yes) nein; **to answer no** (to question) mit Nein antworten; (to request) Nein or nein sagen; **no thank you** nein, danke
♦ adj (not any) kein(e); **I have no money/time** ich habe kein Geld/keine Zeit; **"no smoking"** „Rauchen verboten"
♦ n Nein nt; (no vote) Neinstimme f

---

nobility [nəuˈbɪlɪtɪ] n Adel m

noble [ˈnəubl] adj (rank) adlig; (splendid) nobel, edel

nobody [ˈnəubədɪ] pron niemand, keiner

nocturnal [nɔkˈtəːnl] adj (tour, visit) nächtlich; (animal) Nacht-

nod [nɔd] vi nicken ♦ vt nicken mit ♦ n Nicken nt; **~ off** vi einnicken

noise [nɔɪz] n (sound) Geräusch nt; (unpleasant, loud) Lärm m; **noisy** [ˈnɔɪzɪ] adj laut; (crowd) lärmend

nominal [ˈnɔmɪnl] adj nominell

nominate [ˈnɔmɪneɪt] vt (suggest) vorschlagen; (in election) aufstellen; (appoint) ernennen; **nomination**

[nɔmɪ'neɪʃən] n (election) Nominierung f; (appointment) Ernennung f; **nominee** [nɔmɪ'niː] n Kandidat(in) m(f)

non... [nɔn] prefix Nicht-, un-; **~-alcoholic** adj alkoholfrei

nonchalant ['nɔnʃələnt] adj lässig

non-committal [nɔnkə'mɪtl] adj (reserved) zurückhaltend; (uncommitted) unverbindlich

nondescript ['nɔndɪskrɪpt] adj mittelmäßig

none [nʌn] adj, pron kein(e, er, es) ♦ adv: **he's ~ the worse for it** es hat ihm nicht geschadet; **~ of you** keiner von euch; **I've ~ left** ich habe keinen mehr

nonentity [nɔ'nentɪtɪ] n Null f (inf)

nonetheless ['nʌnðə'les] adv nichtsdestoweniger

non-existent [nɔnɪg'zɪstənt] adj nicht vorhanden

non-fiction [nɔn'fɪkʃən] n Sachbücher pl

nonplussed [nɔn'plʌst] adj verdutzt

nonsense ['nɔnsəns] n Unsinn m

non: **~-smoker** n Nichtraucher(in) m(f); **~-smoking** adj Nichtraucher-; **~-stick** adj (pan, surface) Teflon- ®; **~-stop** adj Nonstop-, Non-Stop-

noodles ['nuːdlz] npl Nudeln pl

nook [nuk] n Winkel m; **~s and crannies** Ecken und Winkel

noon [nuːn] n (12 Uhr) Mittag m

no one ['nəuwʌn] pron = **nobody**

noose [nuːs] n Schlinge f

nor [nɔː] conj = **neither** ♦ adv see **neither**

norm [nɔːm] n (convention) Norm f; (rule, requirement) Vorschrift f

normal ['nɔːməl] adj normal; **~ly** adv normal; (usually) normalerweise

Normandy ['nɔːməndɪ] n Normandie f

north [nɔːθ] n Norden m ♦ adj nördlich, Nord- ♦ adv nördlich, nach or im Norden; **N~ Africa** n Nordafrika nt; **N~ America** n Nordamerika nt; **~-east** n Nordosten m; **~erly** ['nɔːðəlɪ] adj nördlich; **~ern** ['nɔːðən] adj nördlich, Nord-; **N~ern Ireland** n Nordirland nt; **N~ Pole** n Nordpol m; **N~ Sea** n Nordsee f; **~ward(s)** ['nɔːθwəd(z)] adv nach Norden; **~-west** n Nordwesten m

Norway ['nɔːweɪ] n Norwegen nt

Norwegian [nɔː'wiːdʒən] adj norwegisch ♦ n Norweger(in) m(f); (LING) Norwegisch nt

nose [nəuz] n Nase f ♦ vi: **to ~ about** herumschnüffeln; **~bleed** n Nasenbluten nt; **~ dive** n Sturzflug m; **~y** adj = **nosy**

nostalgia [nɔs'tældʒɪə] n Nostalgie f; **nostalgic** adj nostalgisch

nostril ['nɔstrɪl] n Nasenloch nt

nosy ['nəuzɪ] (inf) adj neugierig

not [nɔt] adv nicht; **he is ~** or **isn't here** er ist nicht hier; **it's too late, isn't it?** es ist zu spät, oder or nicht wahr?; **~ yet/now** noch nicht/nicht jetzt; see also **all**; **only**

notably ['nəutəblɪ] adv (especially) besonders; (noticeably) bemerkenswert

notary ['nəutərɪ] n Notar(in) m(f)

notch [nɔtʃ] n Kerbe f, Einschnitt m

note [nəut] n (MUS) Note f, Ton m; (short letter) Nachricht f; (POL) Note f; (comment, attention) Notiz f; (of lecture etc) Aufzeichnung f; (banknote) Schein m; (fame) Ruf m ♦ vt (observe) bemerken; (also: **~ down**) notieren; **~book** n Notizbuch nt; **~d** adj bekannt; **~pad** n Notizblock m; **~paper** n Briefpapier nt

nothing ['nʌθɪŋ] n nichts; **~ new/much** nichts Neues/nicht viel; **for ~** umsonst

notice ['nəutɪs] n (announcement) Bekanntmachung f; (warning) Ankündigung f; (dismissal) Kündigung f ♦ vt bemerken; **to take ~ of** beachten; **at short ~** kurzfristig; **until further ~** bis auf weiteres; **to hand in one's ~** kündigen; **~able** adj merklich; **~ board** n Anschlagtafel f

notify ['nəutɪfaɪ] vt benachrichtigen

notion ['nəuʃən] n Idee f

notorious [nəu'tɔːrɪəs] adj berüchtigt

notwithstanding [nɔtwɪθ'stændɪŋ] adv trotzdem; **~ this** ungeachtet dessen

nought [nɔːt] n Null f

noun [naun] n Substantiv nt

nourish ['nʌrɪʃ] vt nähren; **~ing** adj nahrhaft; **~ment** n Nahrung f

novel ['nɔvl] n Roman m ♦ adj neu(artig); **~ist** n Schriftsteller(in) m(f); **~ty** n Neuheit f

November [nəu'vɛmbər] n November m
novice ['nɔvɪs] n Neuling m
now [nau] adv jetzt; **right ~** jetzt, gerade;
by ~ inzwischen; **just ~** gerade; **~ and
then, ~ and again** ab und zu, manchmal;
from ~ on von jetzt an; **~adays** adv
heutzutage
nowhere ['nəuwɛər] adv nirgends
nozzle ['nɔzl] n Düse f
nuclear ['nju:klɪər] adj (energy etc) Atom-,
Kern-
nuclei ['nju:klɪaɪ] npl of **nucleus**
nucleus ['nju:klɪəs] n Kern m
nude [nju:d] adj nackt ♦ n (ART) Akt m; **in
the ~** nackt
nudge [nʌdʒ] vt leicht anstoßen
nudist ['nju:dɪst] n Nudist(in) m(f)
nudity ['nju:dɪtɪ] n Nacktheit f
nuisance ['nju:sns] n Ärgernis nt; **what a ~!**
wie ärgerlich!
nuke [nju:k] (inf) n Kernkraftwerk nt ♦ vt
atomar vernichten
null [nʌl] adj: **~ and void** null und nichtig
numb [nʌm] adj taub, gefühllos ♦ vt
betäuben
number ['nʌmbər] n Nummer f; (numeral
also) Zahl f; (quantity) (An)zahl f ♦ vt
nummerieren; (amount to) sein; **to be ~ed
among** gezählt werden zu; **a ~ of** (several)
einige; **they were ten in ~** sie waren zehn
an der Zahl; **~ plate** (BRIT) n (AUT)
Nummernschild nt
numeral ['nju:mərəl] n Ziffer f
numerate ['nju:mərɪt] adj rechenkundig
numerical [nju:'mɛrɪkl] adj (order)
zahlenmäßig
numerous ['nju:mərəs] adj zahlreich
nun [nʌn] n Nonne f
nurse [nə:s] n Krankenschwester f; (for
children) Kindermädchen nt ♦ vt (patient)
pflegen; (doubt etc) hegen
nursery ['nə:sərɪ] n (for children)
Kinderzimmer nt; (for plants) Gärtnerei f;
(for trees) Baumschule f; **~ rhyme** n
Kinderreim m; **~ school** n Kindergarten m;
~ slope (BRIT) n (SKI) Idiotenhügel m (inf),
Anfängerhügel m

nursing ['nə:sɪŋ] n (profession) Krankenpflege
f; **~ home** n Privatklinik f
nurture ['nə:tʃər] vt aufziehen
nut [nʌt] n Nuss f; (TECH) Schraubenmutter f;
(inf) Verrückte(r) mf; **he's ~s** er ist verrückt;
~crackers ['nʌtkrækəz] npl Nussknacker m
nutmeg ['nʌtmɛg] n Muskat(nuss f) m
nutrient ['nju:trɪənt] n Nährstoff m
nutrition [nju:'trɪʃən] n Nahrung f;
nutritious [nju:'trɪʃəs] adj nahrhaft
nutshell ['nʌtʃɛl] n Nussschale f; **in a ~** (fig)
kurz gesagt
nutter ['nʌtər] (BRIT: inf) n Spinner(in) m(f)
nylon ['naɪlɔn] n Nylon nt ♦ adj Nylon-

O, o

oak [əuk] n Eiche f ♦ adj Eichen(holz)-
O.A.P. abbr = **old-age pensioner**
oar [ɔ:r] n Ruder nt
oases [əu'eɪsi:z] npl of **oasis**
oasis [əu'eɪsɪs] n Oase f
oath [əuθ] n (statement) Eid m, Schwur m;
(swearword) Fluch m
oatmeal ['əutmi:l] n Haferschrot m
oats [əuts] npl Hafer m
obedience [ə'bi:dɪəns] n Gehorsam m
obedient [ə'bi:dɪənt] adj gehorsam
obesity [əu'bi:sɪtɪ] n Fettleibigkeit f
obey [ə'beɪ] vt, vi: **to ~ (sb)** (jdm) gehorchen
obituary [ə'bɪtjuərɪ] n Nachruf m
object [n 'ɔbdʒɪkt, vb əb'dʒɛkt] n (thing)
Gegenstand m, Objekt nt; (purpose) Ziel nt
♦ vi dagegen sein; **expense is no ~**
Ausgaben spielen keine Rolle; **I ~!** ich
protestiere!; **to ~ to sth** Einwände gegen
etw haben; (morally) Anstoß an etw acc
nehmen; **to ~ that** einwenden, dass; **~ion**
[əb'dʒɛkʃən] n (reason against) Einwand m,
Einspruch m; (dislike) Abneigung f; **I have
no ~ion to ...** ich habe nichts gegen ...
einzuwenden; **~ionable** [əb'dʒɛkʃənəbl] adj
nicht einwandfrei; (language) anstößig
objective [əb'dʒɛktɪv] n Ziel nt ♦ adj objektiv
obligation [ɔblɪ'geɪʃən] n Verpflichtung f;
without ~ unverbindlich; **obligatory**

[əˈblɪɡətərɪ] *adj* obligatorisch

oblige [əˈblaɪdʒ] *vt* (*compel*) zwingen; (*do a favour*) einen Gefallen tun +*dat*; **to be ~d to sb for sth** jdm für etw verbunden sein

obliging [əˈblaɪdʒɪŋ] *adj* entgegenkommend

oblique [əˈbliːk] *adj* schräg, schief ♦ *n* Schrägstrich *m*

obliterate [əˈblɪtəreɪt] *vt* auslöschen

oblivion [əˈblɪvɪən] *n* Vergessenheit *f*

oblivious [əˈblɪvɪəs] *adj* nicht bewusst

oblong [ˈɒblɒŋ] *n* Rechteck *nt* ♦ *adj* länglich

obnoxious [əbˈnɒkʃəs] *adj* widerlich

oboe [ˈəʊbəʊ] *n* Oboe *f*

obscene [əbˈsiːn] *adj* obszön; **obscenity** [əbˈsɛnɪtɪ] *n* Obszönität *f*; **obscenities** *npl* (*oaths*) Zoten *pl*

obscure [əbˈskjʊəʳ] *adj* unklar; (*indistinct*) undeutlich; (*unknown*) unbekannt, obskur; (*dark*) düster ♦ *vt* verdunkeln; (*view*) verbergen; (*confuse*) verwirren; **obscurity** [əbˈskjʊərɪtɪ] *n* Unklarheit *f*; (*darkness*) Dunkelheit *f*

observance [əbˈzɜːvəns] *n* Befolgung *f*

observant [əbˈzɜːvənt] *adj* aufmerksam

observation [ɒbzəˈveɪʃən] *n* (*noticing*) Beobachtung *f*; (*surveillance*) Überwachung *f*; (*remark*) Bemerkung *f*

observatory [əbˈzɜːvətrɪ] *n* Sternwarte *f*, Observatorium *nt*

observe [əbˈzɜːv] *vt* (*notice*) bemerken; (*watch*) beobachten; (*customs*) einhalten; **~r** *n* Beobachter(in) *m(f)*

obsess [əbˈsɛs] *vt* verfolgen, quälen; **~ion** [əbˈsɛʃən] *n* Besessenheit *f*, Wahn *m*; **~ive** *adj* krankhaft

obsolete [ˈɒbsəliːt] *adj* überholt, veraltet

obstacle [ˈɒbstəkl] *n* Hindernis *nt*; **~ race** *n* Hindernisrennen *nt*

obstetrics [ɒbˈstɛtrɪks] *n* Geburtshilfe *f*

obstinate [ˈɒbstɪnɪt] *adj* hartnäckig, stur

obstruct [əbˈstrʌkt] *vt* versperren; (*pipe*) verstopfen; (*hinder*) hemmen; **~ion** [əbˈstrʌkʃən] *n* Versperrung *f*; Verstopfung *f*; (*obstacle*) Hindernis *nt*

obtain [əbˈteɪn] *vt* erhalten, bekommen; (*result*) erzielen

obtrusive [əbˈtruːsɪv] *adj* aufdringlich

obvious [ˈɒbvɪəs] *adj* offenbar, offensichtlich; **~ly** *adv* offensichtlich

occasion [əˈkeɪʒən] *n* Gelegenheit *f*; (*special event*) Ereignis *nt*; (*reason*) Anlass *m* ♦ *vt* veranlassen; **~al** *adj* gelegentlich; **~ally** *adv* gelegentlich

occupant [ˈɒkjʊpənt] *n* Inhaber(in) *m(f)*; (*of house*) Bewohner(in) *m(f)*

occupation [ɒkjuˈpeɪʃən] *n* (*employment*) Tätigkeit *f*, Beruf *m*; (*pastime*) Beschäftigung *f*; (*of country*) Besetzung *f*, Okkupation *f*; **~al hazard** *n* Berufsrisiko *nt*

occupier [ˈɒkjʊpaɪəʳ] *n* Bewohner(in) *m(f)*

occupy [ˈɒkjʊpaɪ] *vt* (*take possession of*) besetzen; (*seat*) belegen; (*live in*) bewohnen; (*position, office*) bekleiden; (*position in sb's life*) einnehmen; (*time*) beanspruchen; **to ~ o.s. with sth** sich mit etw beschäftigen; **to ~ o.s. by doing sth** sich damit beschäftigen, etw zu tun

occur [əˈkɜːʳ] *vi* vorkommen; **to ~ to sb** jdm einfallen; **~rence** *n* (*event*) Ereignis *nt*; (*appearing*) Auftreten *nt*

ocean [ˈəʊʃən] *n* Ozean *m*, Meer *nt*; **~-going** *adj* Hochsee-

o'clock [əˈklɒk] *adv*: **it is 5 ~** es ist 5 Uhr

OCR *n abbr* = **optical character reader**

octagonal [ɒkˈtæɡənl] *adj* achteckig

October [ɒkˈtəʊbəʳ] *n* Oktober *m*

octopus [ˈɒktəpəs] *n* Krake *f*; (*small*) Tintenfisch *m*

odd [ɒd] *adj* (*strange*) sonderbar; (*not even*) ungerade; (*sock etc*) einzeln; (*surplus*) übrig; **60-~** so um die 60; **at ~ times** ab und zu; **to be the ~ one out** (*person*) das fünfte Rad am Wagen sein; (*thing*) nicht dazugehören; **~ity** *n* (*strangeness*) Merkwürdigkeit *f*; (*queer person*) seltsame(r) Kauz *m*; (*thing*) Kuriosität *f*; **~-job man** (*irreg*) *n* Mädchen *nt* für alles; **~ jobs** *npl* gelegentlich anfallende Arbeiten; **~ly** *adv* seltsam; **~ments** *npl* Reste *pl*; **~s** *npl* Chancen *pl*; (*betting*) Gewinnchancen *pl*; **it makes no ~s** es spielt keine Rolle; **at ~s** uneinig; **~s and ends** *npl* Krimskrams *m*

odometer [ɔˈdɒmɪtəʳ] (*esp US*) *n* Tacho(meter) *m*

odour ['əʊdəʳ] (*US* **odor**) *n* Geruch *m*

KEYWORD

of [ɒv, əv] *prep* **1** von +*dat*; *use of gen*; **the history of Germany** die Geschichte Deutschlands; **a friend of ours** ein Freund von uns; **a boy of 10** ein 10-jähriger Junge; **that was kind of you** das war sehr freundlich von Ihnen

2 (*expressing quantity, amount, dates etc*): **a kilo of flour** ein Kilo Mehl; **how much of this do you need?** wie viel brauchen Sie (davon)?; **there were 3 of them** (*people*) sie waren zu dritt; (*objects*) es gab 3 (davon); **a cup of tea/vase of flowers** eine Tasse Tee/Vase mit Blumen; **the 5th of July** der 5. Juli

3 (*from, out of*) aus; **a bridge made of wood** eine Holzbrücke, eine Brücke aus Holz

off [ɒf] *adj, adv* (*absent*) weg, fort; (*switch*) aus(geschaltet), ab(geschaltet); (*BRIT: food: bad*) schlecht; (*cancelled*) abgesagt ♦ *prep* von +*dat*; **to be ~** (*to leave*) gehen; **to be ~ sick** krank sein; **a day ~** ein freier Tag; **to have an ~ day** einen schlechten Tag haben; **he had his coat ~** er hatte seinen Mantel aus; **10% ~** (*COMM*) 10% Rabatt; **5 km ~ (the road)** 5 km (von der Straße) entfernt; **~ the coast** vor der Küste; **I'm ~ meat** (*no longer eat it*) ich esse kein Fleisch mehr; (*no longer like it*) ich mag kein Fleisch mehr; **on the ~ chance** auf gut Glück

offal ['ɒfl] *n* Innereien *pl*

off-colour ['ɒf'kʌləʳ] *adj* nicht wohl

offence [ə'fɛns] (*US* **offense**) *n* (*crime*) Vergehen *nt*, Straftat *f*; (*insult*) Beleidigung *f*; **to take ~ at** gekränkt sein wegen

offend [ə'fɛnd] *vt* beleidigen; **~er** *n* Gesetzesübertreter *m*

offense [ə'fɛns] (*US*) *n* = **offence**

offensive [ə'fɛnsɪv] *adj* (*unpleasant*) übel, abstoßend; (*weapon*) Kampf-; (*remark*) verletzend ♦ *n* Angriff *m*

offer ['ɒfəʳ] *n* Angebot *f* ♦ *vt* anbieten; (*opinion*) äußern; (*resistance*) leisten; **on ~**

zum Verkauf angeboten; **~ing** *n* Gabe *f*

offhand [ɒf'hænd] *adj* lässig ♦ *adv* ohne weiteres

office ['ɒfɪs] *n* Büro *nt*; (*position*) Amt *nt*; **doctor's ~** (*US*) Praxis *f*; **to take ~** sein Amt antreten; (*POL*) die Regierung übernehmen; **~ automation** *n* Büroautomatisierung *f*; **~ block** (*US* **~ building**) *n* Büro(hoch)haus *nt*; **~ hours** *npl* Dienstzeit *f*; (*US: MED*) Sprechstunde *f*

officer ['ɒfɪsəʳ] *n* (*MIL*) Offizier *m*; (*public ~*) Beamte(r) *m*

official [ə'fɪʃl] *adj* offiziell, amtlich ♦ *n* Beamte(r) *m*; **~dom** *n* Beamtentum *nt*

officiate [ə'fɪʃɪeɪt] *vi* amtieren

officious [ə'fɪʃəs] *adj* aufdringlich

offing ['ɒfɪŋ] *n*: **in the ~** in (Aus)sicht

Off-licence

🛈 **Off-licence** *ist ein Geschäft (oder eine Theke in einer Gaststätte), wo man alkoholische Getränke kaufen kann, die aber anderswo konsumiert werden müssen. In solchen Geschäften, die oft von landesweiten Ketten betrieben werden, kann man auch andere Getränke, Süßigkeiten, Zigaretten und Knabbereien kaufen.*

off: **~licence** (*BRIT*) *n* (*shop*) Wein- und Spirituosenhandlung *f*; **~line** *adj* (*COMPUT*) Offline- ♦ *adv* (*COMPUT*) offline; **~peak** *adj* (*charges*) verbilligt; **~putting** (*BRIT*) *adj* (*person, remark etc*) abstoßend; **~road vehicle** *n* Geländefahrzeug *nt*; **~season** *adj* außer Saison; **~set** (*irreg: like* **set**) *vt* ausgleichen ♦ *n* (*also:* **~set printing**) Offset(druck) *m*; **~shoot** *n* (*fig: of organization*) Zweig *m*; (: *of discussion etc*) Randergebnis *nt*; **~shore** *adv* in einiger Entfernung von der Küste ♦ *adj* küstennah, Küsten-; **~side** *adj* (*SPORT*) im Abseits ♦ *adv* abseits ♦ *n* (*AUT*) Fahrerseite *f*; **~spring** *n* Nachkommenschaft *f*; (*one*) Sprössling *m*; **~stage** *adv* hinter den Kulissen; **~the-cuff** *adj* unvorbereitet, aus dem Stegreif; **~the-peg** (*US* **~the-rack**) *adv* von der Stange; **~white** *adj* naturweiß

Oftel ['ɔftel] n Überwachungsgremium zum Verbraucherschutz nach Privatisierung der Telekommunikationsindustrie

often ['ɔfn] adv oft

Ofwat ['ɔfwɔt] n Überwachungsgremium zum Verbraucherschutz nach Privatisierung der Wasserindustrie

ogle ['əugl] vt liebäugeln mit

oil [ɔil] n Öl nt ♦ vt ölen; **~can** n Ölkännchen nt; **~field** n Ölfeld nt; **~ filter** n (AUT) Ölfilter m; **~-fired** adj Öl-; **~ painting** n Ölgemälde nt; **~ rig** n Ölplattform f; **~skins** npl Ölzeug nt; **~ slick** n Ölteppich m; **~ tanker** n (Öl)tanker m; **~ well** n Ölquelle f; **~y** adj ölig; (dirty) ölbeschmiert

ointment ['ɔintmənt] n Salbe f

O.K. ['əu'kei] excl in Ordnung, O. K., o. k. ♦ adj in Ordnung ♦ vt genehmigen

okay ['əu'kei] = **O.K.**

old [əuld] adj alt; **how ~ are you?** wie alt bist du?; **he's 10 years ~** er ist 10 Jahre alt; **~er brother** ältere(r) Bruder m; **~ age** n Alter nt; **~-age pensioner** (BRIT) n Rentner(in) m(f); **~-fashioned** adj altmodisch

olive ['ɔliv] n (fruit) Olive f; (colour) Olive nt ♦ adj Oliven-; (coloured) olivenfarbig; **~ oil** n Olivenöl nt

Olympic [əu'limpik] adj olympisch; **the ~ Games, the ~s** die Olympischen Spiele

omelet(te) ['ɔmlit] n Omelett nt

omen ['əumən] n Omen nt

ominous ['ɔminəs] adj bedrohlich

omission [əu'miʃən] n Auslassung f; (neglect) Versäumnis nt

omit [əu'mit] vt auslassen; (fail to do) versäumen

KEYWORD

on [ɔn] prep **1** (indicating position) auf +dat; (with vb of motion) auf +acc; (on vertical surface, part of body) an +dat/acc; **it's on the table** es ist auf dem Tisch; **she put the book on the table** sie legte das Buch auf den Tisch; **on the left** links

2 (indicating means, method, condition etc): **on foot** (go, be) zu Fuß; **on the train/**

plane (go) mit dem Zug/Flugzeug; (be) im Zug/Flugzeug; **on the telephone/ television** am Telefon/im Fernsehen; **to be on drugs** Drogen nehmen; **to be on holiday/business** im Urlaub/auf Geschäftsreise sein

3 (referring to time): **on Friday** (am) Freitag; **on Fridays** freitags; **on June 20th** am 20. Juni; **a week on Friday** Freitag in einer Woche; **on arrival he ...** als er ankam, ... er ...

4 (about, concerning) über +acc

♦ adv **1** (referring to dress) an; **she put her boots/hat on** sie zog ihre Stiefel an/setzte ihren Hut auf

2 (further, continuously) weiter; **to walk on** weitergehen

♦ adj **1** (functioning, in operation: machine, TV, light) an; (: tap) aufgedreht; (: brakes) angezogen; **is the meeting still on?** findet die Versammlung noch statt?; **there's a good film on** es läuft ein guter Film

2: that's not on! (inf: of behaviour) das liegt nicht drin!

once [wʌns] adv einmal ♦ conj wenn ... einmal; **~ he had left/it was done** nachdem er gegangen war/es fertig war; **at ~** (at the same time) gleichzeitig; (immediately) sofort; **~ a week** einmal in der Woche; **~ more** noch einmal; **~ and for all** ein für alle Mal; **~ upon a time** es war einmal

oncoming ['ɔnkʌmiŋ] adj (traffic) Gegen-, entgegenkommend

KEYWORD

one [wʌn] num eins; (with noun, referring back to noun) ein/eine/ein; **it is one** (o'clock) es ist eins, es ist ein Uhr; **one hundred and fifty** einhundertfünfzig

♦ adj **1** (sole) einzige(r, s); **the one book which** das einzige Buch, welches

2 (same) derselbe/dieselbe/dasselbe; **they came in the one car** sie kamen alle in dem einen Auto

3 (indef): **one day I discovered ...** eines Tages bemerkte ich ...

◆ *pron* 1 eine(r, s); **do you have a red one?** haben Sie einen roten/eine rote/ein rotes?; **this one** diese(r, s); **that one** der/die/das; **which one?** welche(r, s)?; **one by one** einzeln

2: **one another** einander; **do you two ever see one another?** seht ihr beide euch manchmal?

3 (*impers*) man; **one never knows** man kann nie wissen; **to cut one's finger** sich in den Finger schneiden

one: **~-armed bandit** *n* einarmiger Bandit *m*; **~-day excursion** (*US*) *n* (*day return*) Tagesrückfahrkarte *f*; **~-man** *adj* Einmann-; **~-man band** *n* Einmannkapelle *f*; (*fig*) Einmannbetrieb *m*; **~-off** (*BRIT: inf*) *n* Einzelfall *m*

oneself [wʌn'sɛlf] *pron* (*reflexive: after prep*) sich; (*~ personally*) sich selbst *or* selber; (*emphatic*) (sich) selbst; **to hurt ~** sich verletzen

one: **~-sided** *adj* (*argument*) einseitig; **~-to-~** *adj* (*relationship*) eins-zu-eins; **~-upmanship** *n* die Kunst, anderen um eine Nasenlänge voraus zu sein; **~-way** *adj* (*street*) Einbahn-

ongoing [ˈɒŋɡəʊɪŋ] *adj* momentan; (*progressing*) sich entwickelnd

onion [ˈʌnjən] *n* Zwiebel *f*

on-line [ˈɒnlaɪn] *adj* (*COMPUT*) Online-

onlooker [ˈɒnlʊkəʳ] *n* Zuschauer(in) *m(f)*

only [ˈəʊnlɪ] *adv* nur, bloß ◆ *adj* einzige(r, s) ◆ *conj* nur, bloß; **an ~ child** ein Einzelkind; **not ~ ... but also ...** nicht nur ..., sondern auch ...

onset [ˈɒnsɛt] *n* (*start*) Beginn *m*

onshore [ˈɒnʃɔːʳ] *adj* (*wind*) See-

onslaught [ˈɒnslɔːt] *n* Angriff *m*

onto [ˈɒntʊ] *prep* = **on to**

onus [ˈəʊnəs] *n* Last *f*, Pflicht *f*

onward(s) [ˈɒnwəd(z)] *adv* (*place*) voran, vorwärts; **from that day ~** von dem Tag an; **from today ~** ab heute

ooze [uːz] *vi* sickern

opaque [əʊˈpeɪk] *adj* undurchsichtig

OPEC [ˈəʊpɛk] *n abbr* (= Organization of Petroleum-Exporting Countries) OPEC *f*

open [ˈəʊpn] *adj* offen; (*public*) öffentlich; (*mind*) aufgeschlossen ◆ *vt* öffnen, aufmachen; (*trial, motorway, account*) eröffnen ◆ *vi* (*begin*) anfangen; (*shop*) aufmachen; (*door, flower*) aufgehen; (*play*) Premiere haben; **in the ~ (-air)** im Freien; **~ on to** *vt fus* sich öffnen auf *+acc*; **~ up** *vt* (*route*) erschließen; (*shop, prospects*) eröffnen ◆ *vi* aufgehen; **~ing** *n* (*hole*) Öffnung *f*; (*beginning*) Anfang *m*; (*good chance*) Gelegenheit *f*; **~ing hours** *npl* Öffnungszeiten *pl*; **~ learning centre** *n* Weiterbildungseinrichtung auf Teilzeitbasis; **~ly** *adv* offen; (*publicly*) öffentlich; **~-minded** *adj* aufgeschlossen; **~-necked** *adj* offen; **~-plan** *adj* (*office*) Großraum-; (*flat etc*) offen angelegt

---

Open University

ⓘ **Open University** *ist eine 1969 in Großbritannien gegründete Fernuniversität für Spätstudierende. Der Unterricht findet durch Fernseh- und Radiosendungen statt, schriftliche Arbeiten werden mit der Post verschickt, und der Besuch von Sommerkursen ist Pflicht. Die Studenten müssen eine bestimmte Anzahl von Unterrichtseinheiten in einem bestimmten Zeitraum absolvieren und für die Verleihung eines akademischen Grades eine Mindestzahl von Scheinen machen.*

---

opera [ˈɒpərə] *n* Oper *f*; **~ house** *n* Opernhaus *nt*

operate [ˈɒpəreɪt] *vt* (*machine*) bedienen; (*brakes, light*) betätigen ◆ *vi* (*machine*) laufen, in Betrieb sein; (*person*) arbeiten; (*MED*): **to ~ on** operieren

operatic [ɒpəˈrætɪk] *adj* Opern-

operating [ˈɒpəreɪtɪŋ] *adj*: **~ table/theatre** Operationstisch *m*/-saal *m*

operation [ɒpəˈreɪʃən] *n* (*working*) Betrieb *m*; (*MED*) Operation *f*; (*undertaking*) Unternehmen *nt*; (*MIL*) Einsatz *m*; **to be in ~** (*JUR*) in Kraft sein; (*machine*) in Betrieb sein; **to have an ~** (*MED*) operiert werden;

~al adj einsatzbereit

operative ['ɔpərətɪv] adj wirksam

operator ['ɔpəreɪtə'] n (of machine) Arbeiter m; (TEL) Telefonist(in) m(f)

opinion [ə'pɪnjən] n Meinung f; **in my ~** meiner Meinung nach; **~ated** adj starrsinnig; **~ poll** n Meinungsumfrage f

opponent [ə'pəunənt] n Gegner m

opportunity [ɔpə'tju:nɪtɪ] n Gelegenheit f, Möglichkeit f; **to take the ~ of doing sth** die Gelegenheit ergreifen, etw zu tun

oppose [ə'pəuz] vt entgegentreten +dat; (argument, idea) ablehnen; (plan) bekämpfen; **to be ~d to sth** gegen etw sein; **as ~d to** im Gegensatz zu; **opposing** adj gegnerisch; (points of view) entgegengesetzt

opposite ['ɔpəzɪt] adj (house) gegenüberliegend; (direction) entgegengesetzt ♦ adv gegenüber ♦ prep gegenüber ♦ n Gegenteil nt

opposition [ɔpə'zɪʃən] n (resistance) Widerstand m; (POL) Opposition f; (contrast) Gegensatz m

oppress [ə'prɛs] vt unterdrücken; (heat etc) bedrücken; **~ion** [ə'prɛʃən] n Unterdrückung f; **~ive** adj (authority, law) repressiv; (burden, thought) bedrückend; (heat) drückend

opt [ɔpt] vi: **to ~ for** sich entscheiden für; **to ~ to do sth** sich entscheiden, etw zu tun; **to ~ out of sth** sich drücken vor +dat

optical ['ɔptɪkl] adj (illusion) optisch; **~ character reader** n optische(s) Lesegerät nt

optician [ɔp'tɪʃən] n Optiker m

optimist ['ɔptɪmɪst] n Optimist m; **~ic** [ɔptɪ'mɪstɪk] adj optimistisch

optimum ['ɔptɪməm] adj optimal

option ['ɔpʃən] n Wahl f; (COMM) Option f; **to keep one's ~s open** sich alle Möglichkeiten offen halten; **~al** adj freiwillig; (subject) wahlfrei; **~al extras** npl Extras auf Wunsch

or [ɔ:'] conj oder; **he could not read ~ write** er konnte weder lesen noch schreiben; **~ else** sonst

oral ['ɔ:rəl] adj mündlich ♦ n (exam) mündliche Prüfung f

orange ['ɔrɪndʒ] n (fruit) Apfelsine f, Orange f; (colour) Orange nt ♦ adj orange

orator ['ɔrətə'] n Redner(in) m(f)

orbit ['ɔ:bɪt] n Umlaufbahn f

orbital (motorway) ['ɔ:bɪtəl-] n Ringautobahn f

orchard ['ɔ:tʃəd] n Obstgarten m

orchestra ['ɔ:kɪstrə] n Orchester nt; (US: seating) Parkett nt; **~l** [ɔ:'kɛstrəl] adj Orchester-, orchestral

orchid ['ɔ:kɪd] n Orchidee f

ordain [ɔ:'deɪn] vt (ECCL) weihen

ordeal [ɔ:'di:l] n Qual f

order ['ɔ:də'] n (sequence) Reihenfolge f; (good arrangement) Ordnung f; (command) Befehl m; (JUR) Anordnung f; (peace) Ordnung f; (condition) Zustand m; (rank) Klasse f; (COMM) Bestellung f; (ECCL, honour) Orden m ♦ vt (also: **put in ~**) ordnen; (command) befehlen; (COMM) bestellen; **in ~** in der Reihenfolge; **in ~ to do sth** um etw zu tun; **on ~** (COMM) auf Bestellung; **to ~ sb to do sth** jdm befehlen, etw zu tun; **to ~ sth** (command) etw acc befehlen; **~ form** n Bestellschein m; **~ly** n (MIL) Sanitäter m; (MED) Pfleger m ♦ adj (tidy) ordentlich; (well-behaved) ruhig

ordinary ['ɔ:dnrɪ] adj gewöhnlich ♦ n: **out of the ~** außergewöhnlich

Ordnance Survey ['ɔ:dnəns-] (BRIT) n amtliche(r) Kartografiedienst m

ore [ɔ:'] n Erz nt

organ ['ɔ:gən] n (MUS) Orgel f; (BIOL, fig) Organ nt

organic [ɔ:'gænɪk] adj (food, farming etc) biodynamisch

organization [ɔ:gənaɪ'zeɪʃən] n Organisation f; (make-up) Struktur f

organize ['ɔ:gənaɪz] vt organisieren; **~r** n Organisator m, Veranstalter m

orgasm ['ɔ:gæzəm] n Orgasmus m

orgy ['ɔ:dʒɪ] n Orgie f

Orient ['ɔ:rɪənt] n Orient m; **o~al** [ɔ:rɪ'ɛntl] adj orientalisch

origin ['ɔrɪdʒɪn] n Ursprung m; (of the world)

Anfang m, Entstehung f; **~al** [ə'rɪdʒɪnl] adj
(first) ursprünglich; (painting) original; (idea)
originell ♦ n Original nt; **~ally** adv
ursprünglich; originell; **~ate** [ə'rɪdʒɪneɪt] vi
entstehen ♦ vt ins Leben rufen; **to ~ate
from** stammen aus

Orkney ['ɔːknɪ] npl (also: **the ~ Islands**) die
Orkneyinseln pl

ornament ['ɔːnəmənt] n Schmuck m; (on
mantelpiece) Nippesfigur f; **~al** [ɔːnə'mentl]
adj Zier-

ornate [ɔː'neɪt] adj reich verziert

orphan ['ɔːfn] n Waise f, Waisenkind nt ♦ vt:
to be ~ed Waise werden; **~age** n
Waisenhaus nt

orthodox ['ɔːθədɔks] adj orthodox; **~y** n
Orthodoxie f; (fig) Konventionalität f

orthopaedic [ɔːθə'piːdɪk] (US **orthopedic**)
adj orthopädisch

ostentatious [ɔsten'teɪʃəs] adj großtuerisch,
protzig

ostracize ['ɔstrəsaɪz] vt ausstoßen

ostrich ['ɔstrɪtʃ] n Strauß m

other ['ʌðə'] adj andere(r, s) ♦ pron andere(r,
s) ♦ adv: **~ than** anders als; **the ~ (one)**
der/die/das andere; **the ~ day** neulich; **~s**
(~ people) andere; **~wise** adv (in a different
way) anders; (or else) sonst

otter ['ɔtə'] n Otter m

ouch [autʃ] excl aua

ought [ɔːt] vb aux sollen; **I ~ to do it** ich
sollte es tun; **this ~ to have been
corrected** das hätte korrigiert werden
sollen

ounce [auns] n Unze f

our ['auə'] adj unser; see also **my**; **~s** pron
unsere(r, s); see also **mine²**; **~selves** pron
uns (selbst); (emphatic) (wir) selbst; see also
oneself

oust [aust] vt verdrängen

out [aut] adv hinaus/heraus; (not indoors)
draußen; (not alight) aus; (unconscious)
bewusstlos; (results) bekannt gegeben; **to
eat/go ~** auswärts essen/ausgehen; **~
there** da draußen; **he is ~** (absent) er ist
nicht da; **he was ~ in his calculations**
seine Berechnungen waren nicht richtig; **~**

loud laut; **~ of** aus; (away from) außerhalb
+gen; **to be ~ of milk** etc keine Milch etc
mehr haben; **~ of order** außer Betrieb; **~-
and-~** adj (liar, thief etc) ausgemacht;
~back n Hinterland nt; **~board (motor)** n
Außenbordmotor m; **~break** n Ausbruch
m; **~burst** n Ausbruch m; **~cast** n
Ausgestoßene(r) mf; **~come** n Ergebnis nt;
~crop n (of rock) Felsnase f; **~cry** n Protest
m; **~dated** adj überholt; **~do** (irreg: like
do) vt übertrumpfen; **~door** adj Außen-;
(SPORT) im Freien; **~doors** adv im Freien

outer ['autə'] adj äußere(r, s); **~ space** n
Weltraum m

outfit ['autfɪt] n Kleidung f

out: ~going adj (character) aufgeschlossen;
~goings (BRIT) npl Ausgaben pl; **~grow**
(irreg: like grow) vt (clothes) herauswachsen
aus; (habit) ablegen; **~house** n
Nebengebäude nt

outing ['autɪŋ] n Ausflug m

outlandish [aut'lændɪʃ] adj eigenartig

out: ~law n Geächtete(r) f(m) ♦ vt ächten;
(thing) verbieten; **~lay** n Auslage f; **~let** n
Auslass m, Abfluss m; (also: **retail ~let**)
Absatzmarkt m; (US: ELEC) Steckdose f; (for
emotions) Ventil nt

outline ['autlaɪn] n Umriss m

out: ~live vt überleben; **~look** n (also fig)
Aussicht f; (attitude) Einstellung f; **~lying**
adj entlegen; (district) Außen-; **~moded** adj
veraltet; **~number** vt zahlenmäßig
überlegen sein +dat; **~-of-date** adj
(passport) abgelaufen; (clothes etc)
altmodisch; (ideas etc) überholt; **~-of-the-
way** adj abgelegen; **~patient** n
ambulante(r) Patient m/ambulante
Patientin f; **~post** n (MIL, fig) Vorposten m;
~put n Leistung f, Produktion f; (COMPUT)
Ausgabe f

outrage ['autreɪdʒ] n (cruel deed)
Ausschreitung f; (indecency) Skandal m ♦ vt
(morals) verstoßen gegen; (person)
empören; **~ous** [aut'reɪdʒəs] adj unerhört

outreach worker [aut'riːtʃ-] n
Streetworker(in) m(f)

outright [adv aut'raɪt, adj 'autraɪt] adv (at

once) sofort; *(openly)* ohne Umschweife ♦ *adj (denial)* völlig; *(sale)* Total-; *(winner)* unbestritten

outset ['autset] *n* Beginn *m*

outside [aut'saɪd] *n* Außenseite *f* ♦ *adj* äußere(r, s), Außen-; *(chance)* gering ♦ *adv* außen ♦ *prep* außerhalb +*gen*; **at the ~** *(fig)* maximal; *(time)* spätestens; **to go ~** nach draußen gehen; **~ lane** *n (AUT)* äußere Spur *f*; **~ line** *n (TEL)* Amtsanschluss *m*; **~r** *n* Außenseiter(in) *m(f)*

out: **~size** *adj* übergroß; **~skirts** *npl* Stadtrand *m*; **~spoken** *adj* freimütig; **~standing** *adj* hervorragend; *(debts etc)* ausstehend; **~stay** *vt:* **to ~stay one's welcome** länger bleiben als erwünscht; **~stretched** *adj* ausgestreckt; **~strip** *vt* übertreffen; **~ tray** *n* Ausgangskorb *m*

outward ['autwəd] *adj* äußere(r, s); *(journey)* Hin-; *(freight)* ausgehend ♦ *adv* nach außen; **~ly** *adv* äußerlich

outweigh [aut'weɪ] *vt (fig)* überwiegen

outwit [aut'wɪt] *vt* überlisten

oval ['əuvl] *adj* oval ♦ *n* Oval *nt*

> **Oval Office**
>
> *i* Oval Office, ein großer ovaler Raum im Weißen Haus, ist das private Büro des amerikanischen Präsidenten. Im weiteren Sinne bezieht sich dieser Begriff oft auf die Präsidentschaft selbst.

ovary ['əuvərɪ] *n* Eierstock *m*

ovation [əu'veɪʃən] *n* Beifallssturm *m*

oven ['ʌvn] *n* Backofen *m*; **~proof** *adj* feuerfest

over ['əuvə*] *adv (across)* hinüber/herüber; *(finished)* vorbei; *(left)* übrig; *(again)* wieder, noch einmal ♦ *prep* über ♦ *prefix (excessively)* übermäßig; **~ here** hier(hin); **~ there** dort(hin); **all ~** *(everywhere)* überall; *(finished)* vorbei; **~ and ~** immer wieder; **~ and above** darüber hinaus; **to ask sb ~** jdn einladen; **to bend ~** sich bücken

overall [*adj, n* 'əuvərɔːl, *adv* əuvər'ɔːl] *adj (situation)* allgemein; *(length)* Gesamt- ♦ *n (BRIT)* Kittel *m* ♦ *adv* insgesamt; **~s** *npl (for man)* Overall *m*

over: **~awe** *vt (frighten)* einschüchtern; *(make impression)* überwältigen; **~balance** *vi* Übergewicht bekommen; **~bearing** *adj* aufdringlich; **~board** *adv* über Bord; **~book** *vi* überbuchen

overcast ['əuvəkɑːst] *adj* bedeckt

overcharge [əuvə'tʃɑːdʒ] *vt:* **to ~ sb** von jdm zu viel verlangen

overcoat ['əuvəkəut] *n* Mantel *m*

overcome [əuvə'kʌm] *(irreg: like* **come***) vt* überwinden

over: **~crowded** *adj* überfüllt; **~crowding** *n* Überfüllung *f*; **~do** *(irreg: like* **do***) vt (cook too much)* verkochen; *(exaggerate)* übertreiben; **~done** *adj* übertrieben; *(COOK)* verbraten, verkocht; **~dose** *n* Überdosis *f*; **~draft** *n* (Konto)überziehung *f*; **~drawn** *adj (account)* überzogen; **~due** *adj* überfällig; **~estimate** *vt* überschätzen; **~excited** *adj* überreizt; *(children)* aufgeregt

overflow [əuvə'fləu] *vi* überfließen ♦ *n (excess)* Überschuss *m*; *(also:* **~ pipe***)* Überlaufrohr *nt*

overgrown [əuvə'grəun] *adj (garden)* verwildert

overhaul [*vb* əuvə'hɔːl, *n* 'əuvəhɔːl] *vt (car)* überholen; *(plans)* überprüfen ♦ *n* Überholung *f*

overhead [*adv* əuvə'hed, *adj, n* 'əuvəhed] *adv* oben ♦ *adj* Hoch-; *(wire)* oberirdisch; *(lighting)* Decken- ♦ *n (US)* = **overheads**; **~s** *npl (costs)* allgemeine Unkosten *pl*; **~ projector** *n* Overheadprojektor *m*

over: **~hear** *(irreg: like* **hear***) vt* (mit an)hören; **~heat** *vi (engine)* heiß laufen; **~joyed** *adj* überglücklich; **~kill** *n (fig)* Rundumschlag *m*

overland ['əuvəlænd] *adj* Überland- ♦ *adv (travel)* über Land

overlap [*vb* əuvə'læp, *n* 'əuvəlæp] *vi* sich überschneiden; *(objects)* sich teilweise decken ♦ *n* Überschneidung *f*

over: **~leaf** *adv* umseitig; **~load** *vt* überladen; **~look** *vt (view from above)* überblicken; *(not notice)* übersehen; *(pardon)* hinwegsehen über +*acc*

vernight [adv əuvə'naɪt, adj 'əuvənaɪt] adv über Nacht ♦ adj (journey) Nacht-; **~ stay** Übernachtung f; **to stay ~** übernachten

verpass ['əuvəpɑːs] n Überführung f

verpower [əuvə'pauə^r] vt überwältigen

ver: ~rate vt überschätzen; **~ride** (irreg: like **ride**) vt (order, decision) aufheben; (objection) übergehen; **~riding** adj vorherrschend; **~rule** vt verwerfen; **~run** (irreg: like **run**) vt (country) einfallen in; (time limit) überziehen

verseas [əuvə'siːz] adv nach/in Übersee ♦ adj überseeisch, Übersee-

verseer ['əuvəsiə^r] n Aufseher m

vershadow [əuvə'ʃædəu] vt überschatten

vershoot [əuvə'ʃuːt] (irreg: like **shoot**) vt (runway) hinausschießen über +acc

versight ['əuvəsaɪt] n (mistake) Versehen nt

ver: ~sleep (irreg: like **sleep**) vi verschlafen; **~spill** n (Bevölkerungs)überschuss m; **~state** vt übertreiben; **~step** vt: **to ~step the mark** zu weit gehen

vert [əu'vɜːt] adj offen(kundig)

vertake [əuvə'teɪk] (irreg: like **take**) vt, vi überholen

ver: ~throw (irreg: like **throw**) vt (POL) stürzen; **~time** n Überstunden pl; **~tone** n (fig) Note f

verture ['əuvətʃuə^r] n Ouvertüre f

ver: ~turn vt, vi umkippen; **~weight** adj zu dick; **~whelm** [əuvə'welm] vt überwältigen; **~work** n Überarbeitung f ♦ vt überlasten ♦ vi sich überarbeiten; **~wrought** adj überreizt

we [əu] vt schulden; **to ~ sth to sb** (money) jdm etw schulden; (favour etc) jdm etw verdanken; **owing to** prep wegen +gen

wl [aul] n Eule f

wn [əun] vt besitzen ♦ adj eigen; **a room of my ~** mein eigenes Zimmer; **to get one's ~ back** sich rächen; **on one's ~** allein; **~ up** vi: **to ~ up (to sth)** (etw) zugeben; **~er** n Besitzer(in) m(f); **~ership** n Besitz m

x [ɔks] (pl **~en**) n Ochse m

xtail ['ɔksteɪl] n: **~ soup** Ochsenschwanzsuppe f

xygen ['ɔksɪdʒən] n Sauerstoff m; **~ mask**

n Sauerstoffmaske f; **~ tent** n Sauerstoffzelt nt

oyster ['ɔɪstə^r] n Auster f

oz. abbr = **ounce(s)**

ozone ['əuzəun] n Ozon nt; **~-friendly** adj (aerosol) ohne Treibgas; (fridge) FCKW-frei; **~ hole** n Ozonloch nt; **~ layer** n Ozonschicht f

P, p

p abbr = **penny; pence**

pa [pɑː] (inf) n Papa m

P.A. n abbr = **personal assistant; public address system**

p.a. abbr = **per annum**

pace [peɪs] n Schritt m; (speed) Tempo nt ♦ vi schreiten; **to keep ~ with** Schritt halten mit; **~maker** n Schrittmacher m

pacific [pə'sɪfɪk] adj pazifisch ♦ n: **the P~ (Ocean)** der Pazifik

pacifist ['pæsɪfɪst] n Pazifist m

pacify ['pæsɪfaɪ] vt befrieden; (calm) beruhigen

pack [pæk] n (of goods) Packung f; (of hounds) Meute f; (of cards) Spiel nt; (gang) Bande f ♦ vt (case) packen; (clothes) einpacken ♦ vi packen; **to ~ sb off to ...** jdn nach ... schicken; **~ it in!** lass es gut sein!

package ['pækɪdʒ] n Paket nt; **~ tour** n Pauschalreise f

packed [pækt] adj abgepackt; **~ lunch** n Lunchpaket nt

packet ['pækɪt] n Päckchen nt

packing ['pækɪŋ] n (action) Packen nt; (material) Verpackung f; **~ case** n (Pack)kiste f

pact [pækt] n Pakt m, Vertrag m

pad [pæd] n (of paper) (Schreib)block m; (stuffing) Polster nt ♦ vt polstern; **~ding** n Polsterung f

paddle ['pædl] n Paddel nt; (US: SPORT) Schläger m ♦ vt (boat) paddeln ♦ vi (in sea) plan(t)schen; **~ steamer** n Raddampfer m

paddling pool ['pædlɪŋ-] (BRIT) n

Plan(t)schbecken nt

paddock ['pædək] n Koppel f

paddy field ['pædɪ-] n Reisfeld nt

padlock ['pædlɔk] n Vorhängeschloss nt ♦ vt verschließen

paediatrics [piːdɪ'ætrɪks] (US **pediatrics**) n Kinderheilkunde f

pagan ['peɪgən] adj heidnisch ♦ n Heide m, Heidin f

page [peɪdʒ] n Seite f; (person) Page m ♦ vt (in hotel) ausrufen lassen

pageant ['pædʒənt] n Festzug m; **~ry** n Gepränge nt

pager ['peɪdʒər] n (TEL) Funkrufempfänger m, Piepser m (inf)

paging device ['peɪdʒɪŋ-] n (TEL) = **pager**

paid [peɪd] pt, pp of **pay** ♦ adj bezahlt; **to put ~ to** (BRIT) zunichte machen

pail [peɪl] n Eimer m

pain [peɪn] n Schmerz m; **to be in ~** Schmerzen haben; **on ~ of death** bei Todesstrafe; **to take ~s to do sth** sich dat Mühe geben, etw zu tun; **~ed** adj (expression) gequält; **~ful** adj (physically) schmerzhaft; (embarrassing) peinlich; (difficult) mühsam; **~fully** adv (fig: very) schrecklich; **~killer** n Schmerzmittel nt; **~less** adj schmerzlos; **~staking** ['zteɪkɪŋ] adj gewissenhaft

paint [peɪnt] n Farbe f ♦ vt anstreichen; (picture) malen; **to ~ the door blue** die Tür blau streichen; **~brush** n Pinsel m; **~er** n Maler m; **~ing** n Malerei f; (picture) Gemälde nt; **~work** n Anstrich m; (of car) Lack m

pair [peər] n Paar nt; **~ of scissors** Schere f; **~ of trousers** Hose f

pajamas [pə'dʒɑːməz] (US) npl Schlafanzug m

Pakistan [pɑːkɪ'stɑːn] n Pakistan nt; **~i** adj pakistanisch ♦ n Pakistani mf

pal [pæl] (inf) n Kumpel m

palace ['pæləs] n Palast m, Schloss nt

palatable ['pælɪtəbl] adj schmackhaft

palate ['pælɪt] n Gaumen m

palatial [pə'leɪʃəl] adj palastartig

pale [peɪl] adj blass, bleich ♦ n: **to be**

beyond the ~ die Grenzen überschreiten

Palestine ['pælɪstaɪn] n Palästina nt; **Palestinian** [pælɪs'tɪnɪən] adj palästinensisch ♦ n Palästinenser(in) m(f)

palette ['pælɪt] n Palette f

paling ['peɪlɪŋ] n (stake) Zaunpfahl m; (fence) Lattenzaun m

pall [pɔːl] vi jeden Reiz verlieren, verblassen

pallet ['pælɪt] n (for goods) Palette f

pallid ['pælɪd] adj blass, bleich

pallor ['pælər] n Blässe f

palm [pɑːm] n (of hand) Handfläche f; (also: **~ tree**) Palme f ♦ vt: **to ~ sth off on sb** jdm etw andrehen; **P~ Sunday** n Palmsonntag m

palpable ['pælpəbl] adj (also fig) greifbar

palpitation [pælpɪ'teɪʃən] n Herzklopfen nt

paltry ['pɔːltrɪ] adj armselig

pamper ['pæmpər] vt verhätscheln

pamphlet ['pæmflət] n Broschüre f

pan [pæn] n Pfanne f ♦ vi (CINE) schwenken

panache [pə'næʃ] n Schwung m

pancake ['pænkeɪk] n Pfannkuchen m

pancreas ['pæŋkrɪəs] n Bauchspeicheldrüse f

panda ['pændə] n Panda m; **~ car** (BRIT) n (Funk)streifenwagen m

pandemonium [pændɪ'məʊnɪəm] n Hölle f, (noise) Höllenlärm m

pander ['pændər] vi: **to ~ to** sich richten nach

pane [peɪn] n (Fenster)scheibe f

panel ['pænl] n (of wood) Tafel f; (TV) Diskussionsrunde f; **~ling** (US **paneling**) n Täfelung f

pang [pæŋ] n: **~s of hunger** quälende(r) Hunger m; **~s of conscience** Gewissensbisse pl

panic ['pænɪk] n Panik f ♦ vi in Panik geraten; **don't ~** (nur) keine Panik; **~ky** adj (person) überängstlich; **~-stricken** adj von panischem Schrecken erfasst; (look) panisch

pansy ['pænzɪ] n Stiefmütterchen nt; (inf) Schwule(r) m

pant [pænt] vi keuchen; (dog) hecheln

panther ['pænθər] n Pant(h)er m

~anties ['pæntɪz] npl (Damen)slip m

~antihose ['pæntɪhəʊz] (US) n Strumpfhose f

~antomime ['pæntəmaɪm] (BRIT) n Märchenkomödie f um Weihnachten

---

Pantomime

ⓘ **Pantomime** oder umgangssprachlich **panto** ist in Großbritannien ein zur Weihnachtszeit aufgeführtes Märchenspiel mit possenhaften Elementen, Musik, Standardrollen (ein als Frau verkleideter Mann, ein Junge, ein Bösewicht) und aktuellen Witzen. Publikumsbeteiligung wird gern gesehen (z.B. warnen die Kinder den Helden mit dem Ruf "He's behind you" vor einer drohenden Gefahr), und viele der Witze sprechen vor allem Erwachsene an, so dass pantomimes Unterhaltung für die ganze Familie bieten.

~antry ['pæntrɪ] n Vorratskammer f

~ants [pænts] npl (BRIT: woman's) Schlüpfer m; (: man's) Unterhose f; (US: trousers) Hose f

~apal ['peɪpəl] adj päpstlich

~aper ['peɪpə*] n Papier nt; (newspaper) Zeitung f; (essay) Referat nt ♦ adj Papier-, aus Papier ♦ vt (wall) tapezieren; **~s** npl (identity ~s) Ausweis(papiere pl) m; **~back** n Taschenbuch nt; **~ bag** n Tüte f; **~ clip** n Büroklammer f; **~ hankie** n Tempotaschentuch nt ®; **~weight** n Briefbeschwerer m; **~work** n Schreibarbeit f

~ar [pɑː*] n (COMM) Nennwert m; (GOLF) Par nt; **on a ~ with** ebenbürtig +dat

~arable ['pærəbl] n (REL) Gleichnis nt

~arachute ['pærəʃuːt] n Fallschirm m ♦ vi (mit dem Fallschirm) abspringen

~arade [pə'reɪd] n Parade f ♦ vt aufmarschieren lassen; (fig) zur Schau stellen ♦ vi paradieren, vorbeimarschieren

~aradise ['pærədaɪs] n Paradies nt

~aradox ['pærədɒks] n Paradox nt; **~ically** [pærə'dɒksɪklɪ] adv paradoxerweise

~araffin ['pærəfɪn] (BRIT) n Paraffin nt

paragraph ['pærəgrɑːf] n Absatz m

parallel ['pærəlɛl] adj parallel ♦ n Parallele f

paralyse ['pærəlaɪz] (US **paralyze**) vt (MED) lähmen, paralysieren; (fig: organization, production etc) lahm legen; **~d** adj gelähmt; **paralysis** [pə'rælɪsɪs] n Lähmung f

paralyze ['pærəlaɪz] (US) = **paralyse** vt

parameter [pə'ræmɪtə*] n Parameter m; **~s** npl (framework, limits) Rahmen m

paramount ['pærəmaʊnt] adj höchste(r, s), oberste(r, s)

paranoid ['pærənɔɪd] adj (person) an Verfolgungswahn leidend, paranoid; (feeling) krankhaft

parapet ['pærəpɪt] n Brüstung f

paraphernalia [pærəfə'neɪlɪə] n Zubehör nt, Utensilien pl

paraphrase ['pærəfreɪz] vt umschreiben

paraplegic [pærə'pliːdʒɪk] n Querschnittsgelähmte(r) f(m)

parasite ['pærəsaɪt] n (also fig) Schmarotzer m, Parasit m

parasol ['pærəsɒl] n Sonnenschirm m

paratrooper ['pærətruːpə*] n Fallschirmjäger m

parcel ['pɑːsl] n Paket nt ♦ vt (also: ~ **up**) einpacken

parch [pɑːtʃ] vt (aus)dörren; **~ed** adj ausgetrocknet; (person) am Verdursten

parchment ['pɑːtʃmənt] n Pergament nt

pardon ['pɑːdn] n Verzeihung f ♦ vt (JUR) begnadigen; **~ me!, I beg your ~!** verzeihen Sie bitte!; **~ me?** (US) wie bitte?; **(I beg your) ~?** wie bitte?

parent ['pɛərənt] n Elternteil m; **~s** npl (mother and father) Eltern pl; **~al** [pə'rɛntl] adj elterlich, Eltern-

parentheses [pə'rɛnθɪsiːz] npl of **parenthesis**

parenthesis [pə'rɛnθɪsɪs] n Klammer f; (sentence) Parenthese f

Paris ['pærɪs] n Paris nt

parish ['pærɪʃ] n Gemeinde f

park [pɑːk] n Park m ♦ vt, vi parken

parking ['pɑːkɪŋ] n Parken nt; **"no ~"** „Parken verboten"; **~ lot** (US) n Parkplatz m; **~ meter** n Parkuhr f; **~ ticket** n

Strafzettel *m*

parlance ['pɑːləns] *n* Sprachgebrauch *m*

parliament ['pɑːləmənt] *n* Parlament *nt*;
~ary [pɑːlə'mentərɪ] *adj* parlamentarisch,
Parlaments-

parlour ['pɑːlər] (*US* **parlor**) *n* Salon *m*

parochial [pə'rəʊkɪəl] *adj* (*narrow-minded*)
eng(stirnig)

parole [pə'rəʊl] *n*: **on ~** (*prisoner*) auf
Bewährung

parrot ['pærət] *n* Papagei *m*

parry ['pærɪ] *vt* parieren, abwehren

parsley ['pɑːslɪ] *n* Petersilie *f*

parsnip ['pɑːsnɪp] *n* Pastinake *f*

parson ['pɑːsn] *n* Pfarrer *m*

part [pɑːt] *n* (*piece*) Teil *m*; (*THEAT*) Rolle *f*; (*of
machine*) Teil *m* ♦ *adv* = **partly**; ♦ *vt*
trennen; (*hair*) scheiteln ♦ *vi* (*people*) sich
trennen; **to take ~ in** teilnehmen an +*dat*;
to take sth in good ~ etw nicht übel
nehmen; **to take sb's ~** sich auf jds Seite
acc stellen; **for my ~** ich für meinen Teil;
for the most ~ meistens, größtenteils; **in ~
exchange** (*BRIT*) in Zahlung; **~ with** *vt fus*
hergeben; (*renounce*) aufgeben; **~ial** ['pɑːʃl]
adj (*incomplete*) teilweise; (*biased*) parteiisch;
to be ~ial to eine (besondere) Vorliebe
haben für

participant [pɑː'tɪsɪpənt] *n* Teilnehmer(in)
m(f)

participate [pɑː'tɪsɪpeɪt] *vi*: **to ~ (in)**
teilnehmen an +*dat*); **participation**
[pɑːtɪsɪ'peɪʃən] *n* Teilnahme *f*; (*sharing*)
Beteiligung *f*

participle ['pɑːtɪsɪpl] *n* Partizip *nt*

particle ['pɑːtɪkl] *n* Teilchen *nt*

particular [pə'tɪkjulər] *adj* bestimmt; (*exact*)
genau; (*fussy*) eigen; **in ~** besonders; **~ly**
adv besonders

particulars *npl* (*details*) Einzelheiten *pl*; (*of
person*) Personalien *pl*

parting ['pɑːtɪŋ] *n* (*separation*) Abschied *m*;
(*BRIT: of hair*) Scheitel *m* ♦ *adj* Abschieds-

partition [pɑː'tɪʃən] *n* (*wall*) Trennwand *f*;
(*division*) Teilung *f* ♦ *vt* aufteilen

partly ['pɑːtlɪ] *adv* zum Teil, teilweise

partner ['pɑːtnər] *n* Partner *m* ♦ *vt* der

Partner sein von; **~ship** *n* Partnerschaft *f*;
(*COMM*) Teilhaberschaft *f*

partridge ['pɑːtrɪdʒ] *n* Rebhuhn *nt*

part-time ['pɑːt'taɪm] *adj* Teilzeit- ♦ *adv*
stundenweise

party ['pɑːtɪ] *n* (*POL, JUR*) Partei *f*; (*group*)
Gesellschaft *f*; (*celebration*) Party *f* ♦ *adj*
(*dress*) Party-; (*politics*) Partei-; **~ line** (*TE*
Gemeinschaftsanschluss *m*

pass [pɑːs] *vt* (*on foot*) vorbeigehen an +*dat*
(*driving*) vorbeifahren an +*dat*; (*surpass*)
übersteigen; (*hand on*) weitergeben;
(*approve*) genehmigen; (*time*) verbringen;
(*exam*) bestehen ♦ *vi* (*go by*) vorbeigehen;
vorbeifahren; (*years*) vergehen; (*be
successful*) bestehen ♦ *n* (*in mountains,
SPORT*) Pass *m*; (*permission*) Passierschein *m*
(*in exam*): **to get a ~** bestehen; **to ~ sth
through sth** etw durch etw führen; **to
make a ~ at sb** (*inf*) bei jdm
Annäherungsversuche machen; **~ away**
(*euph*) verscheiden; **~ by** *vi* vorbeigehen;
vorbeifahren; (*years*) vergehen; **~ on** *vt*
weitergeben; **~ out** *vi* (*faint*) ohnmächtig
werden; **~ up** *vt* vorbeigehen lassen;
~able *adj* (*road*) passierbar; (*fairly good*)
passabel

passage ['pæsɪdʒ] *n* (*corridor*) Gang *m*; (*in
book*) (Text)stelle *f*; (*voyage*) Überfahrt *f*;
~way *n* Durchgang *m*

passbook ['pɑːsbʊk] *n* Sparbuch *nt*

passenger ['pæsɪndʒər] *n* Passagier *m*; (*on
bus*) Fahrgast *m*

passer-by [pɑːsə'baɪ] *n* Passant(in) *m(f)*

passing ['pɑːsɪŋ] *adj* (*car*) vorbeifahrend;
(*thought, affair*) momentan ♦ *n*: **in ~**
beiläufig; **~ place** (*AUT*) Ausweichstelle *f*

passion ['pæʃən] *n* Leidenschaft *f*; **~ate** *ad*
leidenschaftlich

passive ['pæsɪv] *adj* passiv; (*LING*) passivisc
~ smoking *n* Passivrauchen *nt*

Passover ['pɑːsəʊvər] *n* Passahfest *nt*

passport ['pɑːspɔːt] *n* (Reise)pass *m*; **~
control** *n* Passkontrolle *f*; **~ office** *n*
Passamt *nt*

password ['pɑːswɜːd] *n* Parole *f*, Kennwort
nt, Losung *f*

ast [pɑːst] *prep (motion)* an +*dat* ... vorbei; *(position)* hinter +*dat*; *(later than)* nach ♦ *adj (years)* vergangen; *(president etc)* ehemalig ♦ *n* Vergangenheit *f*; **he's ~ forty** er ist über vierzig; **for the ~ few/3 days** in den letzten paar/3 Tagen; **to run ~** vorbeilaufen; **ten/quarter ~ eight** zehn/ Viertel nach acht

asta ['pæstə] *n* Teigwaren *pl*

aste [peɪst] *n (fish ~ etc)* Paste *f*; *(glue)* Kleister *m* ♦ *vt* kleben

asteurized ['pæstʃəraɪzd] *adj* pasteurisiert

astime ['pɑːstaɪm] *n* Zeitvertreib *m*

astor ['pɑːstəʳ] *n* Pfarrer *m*

astry ['peɪstrɪ] *n* Blätterteig *m*; **pastries** *npl (tarts etc)* Stückchen *pl*

asture ['pɑːstʃəʳ] *n* Weide *f*

asty [*n* 'pæstɪ, *adj* 'peɪstɪ] *n* (Fleisch)pastete *f* ♦ *adj* blässlich, käsig

at [pæt] *n* leichte(r) Schlag *m*, Klaps *m* ♦ *vt* tätscheln

atch [pætʃ] *n* Fleck *m* ♦ *vt* flicken; **(to go through) a bad ~** eine Pechsträhne (haben); **~ up** *vt* flicken; *(quarrel)* beilegen; **~ed** *adj* geflickt; **~y** *adj (irregular)* ungleichmäßig

âté ['pæteɪ] *n* Pastete *f*

atent ['peɪtnt] *n* Patent *nt* ♦ *vt* patentieren lassen; *(by authorities)* patentieren ♦ *adj* offenkundig; **~ leather** *n* Lackleder *nt*

aternal [pə'tɜːnl] *adj* väterlich

aternity [pə'tɜːnɪtɪ] *n* Vaterschaft *f*

ath [pɑːθ] *n* Pfad *m*; Weg *m*

athetic [pə'θetɪk] *adj (very bad)* kläglich

athological [pæθə'lɒdʒɪkl] *adj* pathologisch

athology [pə'θɒlədʒɪ] *n* Pathologie *f*

athos ['peɪθɒs] *n* Rührseligkeit *f*

athway ['pɑːθweɪ] *n* Weg *m*

atience ['peɪʃns] *n* Geduld *f*; *(BRIT: CARDS)* Patience *f*

atient ['peɪʃnt] *n* Patient(in) *m(f)*, Kranke(r) *mf* ♦ *adj* geduldig

atio ['pætɪəʊ] *n* Terrasse *f*

atriotic [pætrɪ'ɒtɪk] *adj* patriotisch

atrol [pə'trəʊl] *n* Patrouille *f*; *(police)* Streife *f* ♦ *vt* patrouillieren in +*dat* ♦ *vi (police)* die

Runde machen; *(MIL)* patrouillieren; **~ car** *n* Streifenwagen *m*; **~man** *(US) (irreg)* *n* (Streifen)polizist *m*

patron ['peɪtrən] *n (in shop)* (Stamm)kunde *m*; *(in hotel)* (Stamm)gast *m*; *(supporter)* Förderer *m*; **~ of the arts** Mäzen *m*; **~age** ['pætrənɪdʒ] *n* Schirmherrschaft *f*; **~ize** ['pætrənaɪz] *vt (support)* unterstützen; *(shop)* besuchen; *(treat condescendingly)* von oben herab behandeln; **~ saint** *n* Schutzpatron(in) *m(f)*

patter ['pætəʳ] *n (sound: of feet)* Trappeln *nt*; *(: of rain)* Prasseln *nt*; *(sales talk)* Gerede *nt* ♦ *vi (feet)* trappeln; *(rain)* prasseln

pattern ['pætən] *n* Muster *nt*; *(SEWING)* Schnittmuster *nt*; *(KNITTING)* Strickanleitung *f*

pauper ['pɔːpəʳ] *n* Arme(r) *mf*

pause [pɔːz] *n* Pause *f* ♦ *vi* innehalten

pave [peɪv] *vt* pflastern; **to ~ the way for** den Weg bahnen für

pavement ['peɪvmənt] *(BRIT)* *n* Bürgersteig *m*

pavilion [pə'vɪlɪən] *n* Pavillon *m*; *(SPORT)* Klubhaus *nt*

paving ['peɪvɪŋ] *n* Straßenpflaster *nt*; **~ stone** *n* Pflasterstein *m*

paw [pɔː] *n* Pfote *f*; *(of big cats)* Tatze *f*, Pranke *f* ♦ *vt (scrape)* scharren; *(handle)* betatschen

pawn [pɔːn] *n* Pfand *nt*; *(chess)* Bauer *m* ♦ *vt* verpfänden; **~broker** *n* Pfandleiher *m*; **~shop** *n* Pfandhaus *nt*

pay [peɪ] *(pt, pp* paid*) n* Bezahlung *f*, Lohn *m* ♦ *vt* bezahlen ♦ *vi (be profitable)* sich bezahlt machen; **to ~ attention (to)** Acht geben (auf +*acc*); **to ~ sb a visit** jdn besuchen; **~ back** *vt* zurückzahlen; **~ for** *vt fus* bezahlen; **~ in** *vt* einzahlen; **~ off** *vt* abzahlen ♦ *vi (scheme, decision)* sich bezahlt machen; **~ up** *vi* bezahlen; **~able** *adj* zahlbar, fällig; **~ee** *n* Zahlungsempfänger *m*; **~ envelope** *(US)* *n* Lohntüte *f*; **~ment** *n* Bezahlung *f*; **advance ~ment** Vorauszahlung *f*; **monthly ~ment** monatliche Rate *f*; **~ packet** *(BRIT)* *n* Lohntüte *f*; **~phone** *n* Münzfernsprecher

m; **~roll** *n* Lohnliste *f;* **~ slip** *n* Lohn-/
Gehaltsstreifen *m;* **~ television** *n*
Abonnenten-Fernsehen *nt*
PC *n abbr* = **personal computer**
p.c. *abbr* = **per cent**
pea [piː] *n* Erbse *f*
peace [piːs] *n* Friede(n) *m;* **~able** *adj*
friedlich; **~ful** *adj* friedlich, ruhig;
~keeping *adj* Friedens-
peach [piːtʃ] *n* Pfirsich *m*
peacock ['piːkɔk] *n* Pfau *m*
peak [piːk] *n* Spitze *f;* (*of mountain*) Gipfel *m;*
(*fig*) Höhepunkt *m;* **~ hours** *npl* (*traffic*)
Hauptverkehrszeit *f;* (*telephone, electricity*)
Hauptbelastungszeit *f;* **~ period** *n* Stoßzeit
f, Hauptzeit *f*
peal [piːl] *n* (Glocken)läuten *nt;* **~s of
laughter** schallende(s) Gelächter *nt*
peanut ['piːnʌt] *n* Erdnuss *f;* **~ butter** *n*
Erdnussbutter *f*
pear [pɛəʳ] *n* Birne *f*
pearl [pɜːl] *n* Perle *f*
peasant ['peznt] *n* Bauer *m*
peat [piːt] *n* Torf *m*
pebble ['pebl] *n* Kiesel *m*
peck [pek] *vt, vi* picken ♦ *n* (*with beak*)
Schnabelhieb *m;* (*kiss*) flüchtige(r) Kuss *m;*
~ing order *n* Hackordnung *f;* **~ish** (*BRIT:
inf*) *adj* ein bisschen hungrig
peculiar [pɪ'kjuːlɪəʳ] *adj* (*odd*) seltsam; **~ to**
charakteristisch für; **~ity** [pɪkjuːlɪ'ærɪtɪ] *n*
(*singular quality*) Besonderheit *f;*
(*strangeness*) Eigenartigkeit *f*
pedal ['pedl] *n* Pedal *nt* ♦ *vt, vi* (*cycle*) fahren,
Rad fahren
pedantic [pɪ'dæntɪk] *adj* pedantisch
peddler ['pedləʳ] *n* Hausierer(in) *m(f);* (*of
drugs*) Drogenhändler(in) *m(f)*
pedestal ['pedəstl] *n* Sockel *m*
pedestrian [pɪ'destrɪən] *n* Fußgänger *m*
♦ *adj* Fußgänger-; (*humdrum*) langweilig; **~
crossing** (*BRIT*) *n* Fußgängerübergang *m;*
~ized *n* in eine Fußgängerzone
umgewandelt; **~ precinct** (*BRIT*), **~ zone**
(*US*) *n* Fußgängerzone *f*
pediatrics [piːdɪ'ætrɪks] (*US*) *n* = **paediatrics**
pedigree ['pedɪgriː] *n* Stammbaum *m* ♦ *cpd*

(*animal*) reinrassig, Zucht-
pee [piː] (*inf*) *vi* pissen, pinkeln
peek [piːk] *vi* gucken
peel [piːl] *n* Schale *f* ♦ *vt* schälen ♦ *vi* (*paint
etc*) abblättern; (*skin*) sich schälen
peep [piːp] *n* (*BRIT: look*) kurze(r) Blick *m;*
(*sound*) Piepsen *nt* ♦ *vi* (*BRIT: look*) gucken;
~ out *vi* herausgucken; **~hole** *n* Gucklock
nt
peer [pɪəʳ] *vi* starren; (*peep*) gucken ♦ *n*
(*nobleman*) Peer *m;* (*equal*) Ebenbürtige(r)
m; **~age** *n* Peerswürde *f*
peeved [piːvd] *adj* (*person*) sauer
peg [peg] *n* (*stake*) Pflock *m;* (*BRIT: also:*
clothes ~) Wäscheklammer *f*
Pekinese [piːkɪ'niːz] *n* (*dog*) Pekinese *m*
pelican ['pelɪkən] *n* Pelikan *m;* **~ crossing**
(*BRIT*) *n* (*AUT*) Ampelüberweg *m*
pellet ['pelɪt] *n* Kügelchen *nt*
pelmet ['pelmɪt] *n* Blende *f*
pelt [pelt] *vt* bewerfen ♦ *vi* (*rain*) schütten
♦ *n* Pelz *m,* Fell *nt*
pelvis ['pelvɪs] *n* Becken *nt*
pen [pen] *n* (*fountain ~*) Federhalter *m;* (*ballpoint ~*) Kuli *m;* (*for sheep*) Pferch *m*
penal ['piːnl] *adj* Straf-; **~ize** *vt* (*punish*)
bestrafen; (*disadvantage*) benachteiligen
penalty ['penltɪ] *n* Strafe *f;* (*FOOTBALL*)
Elfmeter *m;* **~ (kick)** *n* Elfmeter *m*
penance ['penəns] *n* Buße *f*
pence [pens] (*BRIT*) *npl of* **penny**
pencil ['pensl] *n* Bleistift *m;* **~ case** *n*
Federmäppchen *nt;* **~ sharpener** *n*
Bleistiftspitzer *m*
pendant ['pendnt] *n* Anhänger *m*
pending ['pendɪŋ] *prep* bis (zu) ♦ *adj*
unentschieden, noch offen
pendulum ['pendjuləm] *n* Pendel *nt*
penetrate ['penɪtreɪt] *vt* durchdringen;
(*enter into*) eindringen in +*acc;*
penetration [penɪ'treɪʃən] *n* Durchdringen
nt; Eindringen *nt*
penfriend ['penfrend] (*BRIT*) *n* Brieffreund(in
m(f)
penguin ['pengwɪn] *n* Pinguin *m*
penicillin [penɪ'sɪlɪn] *n* Penizillin *nt*
peninsula [pə'nɪnsjulə] *n* Halbinsel *f*

enis ['pi:nɪs] n Penis m

enitentiary [penɪ'tenʃərɪ] (US) n Zuchthaus nt

enknife ['pennaɪf] n Federmesser nt

en name n Pseudonym nt

enniless ['penɪlɪs] adj mittellos

enny ['penɪ] (pl **pennies** or (BRIT) **pence**) n Penny m; (US) Centstück nt

enpal ['penpæl] n Brieffreund(in) m(f)

ension ['penʃən] n Rente f; ~er (BRIT) n Rentner(in) m(f); ~ fund n Rentenfonds m; ~ plan n Rentenversicherung f

ensive ['pensɪv] adj nachdenklich

Pentagon

Pentagon *heißt das fünfeckige Gebäude in Arlington, Virginia, in dem das amerikanische Verteidigungsministerium untergebracht ist. Im weiteren Sinne bezieht sich dieses Wort auf die amerikanische Militärführung.*

entathlon [pen'tæθlən] n Fünfkampf m

entecost ['pentɪkɔst] n Pfingsten pl or nt

enthouse ['penthaʊs] n Dach-terrassenwohnung f

ent-up ['pentʌp] adj (feelings) angestaut

enultimate [pe'nʌltɪmət] adj vorletzte(r, s)

eople ['pi:pl] n (nation) Volk nt ♦ npl (persons) Leute pl; (inhabitants) Bevölkerung f ♦ vt besiedeln; **several ~ came** mehrere Leute kamen; **~ say that ...** man sagt, dass ...

epper ['pepər] n Pfeffer m; (vegetable) Paprika m ♦ vt (pelt) bombardieren; ~ mill n Pfeffermühle f; ~mint n (plant) Pfefferminze f; (sweet) Pfefferminz nt

ep talk [pep-] (inf) n Anstachelung f

er [pə:ʳ] prep pro; ~ day/person pro Tag/Person; ~ annum adv pro Jahr; ~ capita adj (income) Pro-Kopf- ♦ adv pro Kopf

erceive [pə'si:v] vt (realize) wahrnehmen; (understand) verstehen

er cent n Prozent nt; **percentage** [pə'sentɪdʒ] n Prozentsatz m

erception [pə'sepʃən] n Wahrnehmung f; (insight) Einsicht f

perceptive [pə'septɪv] adj (person) aufmerksam; (analysis) tief gehend

perch [pə:tʃ] n Stange f; (fish) Flussbarsch m ♦ vi sitzen, hocken

percolator ['pə:kəleɪtəʳ] n Kaffeemaschine f

percussion [pə'kʌʃən] n (MUS) Schlagzeug nt

perennial [pə'renɪəl] adj wiederkehrend; (everlasting) unvergänglich

perfect [adj, n 'pə:fɪkt, vb pə'fekt] adj vollkommen; (crime, solution) perfekt ♦ n (GRAM) Perfekt nt ♦ vt vervollkommnen; ~ion n Vollkommenheit f; ~ly adv vollkommen, perfekt; (quite) ganz, einfach

perforate ['pə:fəreɪt] vt durchlöchern; **perforation** [pə:fə'reɪʃən] n Perforieren nt; (line of holes) Perforation f

perform [pə'fɔ:m] vt (carry out) durch- or ausführen; (task) verrichten; (THEAT) spielen, geben ♦ vi (THEAT) auftreten; ~ance n Durchführung f; (efficiency) Leistung f; (show) Vorstellung f; ~er n Künstler(in) m(f)

perfume ['pə:fju:m] n Duft m; (lady's) Parfüm nt

perhaps [pə'hæps] adv vielleicht

peril ['perɪl] n Gefahr f

perimeter [pə'rɪmɪtəʳ] n Peripherie f; (of circle etc) Umfang m

period ['pɪərɪəd] n Periode f; (GRAM) Punkt m; (MED) Periode f ♦ adj (costume) historisch; ~ic [pɪərɪ'ɔdɪk] adj periodisch; ~ical [pɪərɪ'ɔdɪkl] n Zeitschrift f; ~ically [pɪərɪ'ɔdɪklɪ] adv periodisch

peripheral [pə'rɪfərəl] adj Rand-, peripher ♦ n (COMPUT) Peripheriegerät nt

perish ['perɪʃ] vi umkommen; (fruit) verderben; ~able adj leicht verderblich

perjury ['pə:dʒərɪ] n Meineid m

perk [pə:k] (inf) n (fringe benefit) Vergünstigung f; ~ up vi munter werden; ~y adj keck

perm [pə:m] n Dauerwelle f

permanent ['pə:mənənt] adj dauernd, ständig

permeate ['pə:mɪeɪt] vt, vi durchdringen

permissible [pə'mɪsɪbl] adj zulässig

permission [pə'mɪʃən] n Erlaubnis f

permissive [pəˈmɪsɪv] *adj* nachgiebig; **the ~ society** die permissive Gesellschaft

permit [*n* ˈpəːmɪt, *vb* pəˈmɪt] *n* Zulassung *f* ♦ *vt* erlauben, zulassen

perpendicular [pəːpənˈdɪkjuləʳ] *adj* senkrecht

perpetrate [ˈpəːpɪtreɪt] *vt* begehen

perpetual [pəˈpetjuəl] *adj* dauernd, ständig

perpetuate [pəˈpetjueɪt] *vt* verewigen, bewahren

perplex [pəˈpleks] *vt* verblüffen

persecute [ˈpəːsɪkjuːt] *vt* verfolgen; **persecution** [pəːsɪˈkjuːʃən] *n* Verfolgung *f*

perseverance [pəːsɪˈvɪərns] *n* Ausdauer *f*

persevere [pəːsɪˈvɪəʳ] *vi* durchhalten

Persian [ˈpəːʃən] *adj* persisch ♦ *n* Perser(in) *m(f)*; **the (Persian) Gulf** der Persische Golf

persist [pəˈsɪst] *vi* (*in belief etc*) bleiben; (*rain, smell*) andauern; (*continue*) nicht aufhören; **to ~ in** bleiben bei; **~ence** *n* Beharrlichkeit *f*; **~ent** *adj* beharrlich; (*unending*) ständig

person [ˈpəːsn] *n* Person *f*; **in ~** persönlich; **~able** *adj* gut aussehend; **~al** *adj* persönlich; (*private*) privat; (*of body*) körperlich, Körper-; **~al assistant** *n* Assistent(in) *m(f)*; **~al column** *n* private Kleinanzeigen *pl*; **~al computer** *n* Personalcomputer *m*; **~ality** [pəːsəˈnælɪtɪ] *n* Persönlichkeit *f*; **~ally** *adv* persönlich; **~al organizer** *n* Terminplaner *m*, Zeitplaner *m*; (*electronic*) elektronisches Notizbuch *nt*; **~al stereo** *n* Walkman *m* ®; **~ify** [pəːˈsɔnɪfaɪ] *vt* verkörpern

personnel [pəːsəˈnel] *n* Personal *nt*

perspective [pəˈspektɪv] *n* Perspektive *f*

Perspex [ˈpəːspeks] ® *n* Acrylglas *nt*, Akrylglas *nt*

perspiration [pəːspɪˈreɪʃən] *n* Transpiration *f*

perspire [pəˈspaɪəʳ] *vi* transpirieren

persuade [pəˈsweɪd] *vt* überreden; (*convince*) überzeugen

persuasion [pəˈsweɪʒən] *n* Überredung *f*; Überzeugung *f*

persuasive [pəˈsweɪsɪv] *adj* überzeugend

pert [pəːt] *adj* keck

pertaining [pəːˈteɪnɪŋ]: **~ to** *prep* betreffend +*acc*

pertinent [ˈpəːtɪnənt] *adj* relevant

perturb [pəˈtəːb] *vt* beunruhigen

pervade [pəˈveɪd] *vt* erfüllen

perverse [pəˈvəːs] *adj* pervers; (*obstinate*) eigensinnig

pervert [pəˈvəːt, *vb* pəˈvəːt] *n* perverse(r) Mensch *m* ♦ *vt* verdrehen; (*morally*) verderben

pessimist [ˈpesɪmɪst] *n* Pessimist *m*; **~ic** *adj* pessimistisch

pest [pest] *n* (*insect*) Schädling *m*; (*fig: person*) Nervensäge *f*; (*: thing*) Plage *f*; **~er** [ˈpestəʳ] *vt* plagen; **~icide** [ˈpestɪsaɪd] *n* Insektenvertilgungsmittel *nt*

pet [pet] *n* (*animal*) Haustiere *nt* ♦ *vt* liebkosen, streicheln

petal [ˈpetl] *n* Blütenblatt *nt*

peter out [ˈpiːtə-] *vi* allmählich zu Ende gehen

petite [pəˈtiːt] *adj* zierlich

petition [pəˈtɪʃən] *n* Bittschrift *f*

petrified [ˈpetrɪfaɪd] *adj* versteinert; (*person*) starr (vor Schreck)

petrify [ˈpetrɪfaɪ] *vt* versteinern; (*person*) erstarren lassen

petrol [ˈpetrəl] (*BRIT*) *n* Benzin *nt*, Kraftstoff *m*; **two-/four-star ~** ≈ Normal-/ Superbenzin *nt*; **~ can** *n* Benzinkanister *m*

petroleum [pəˈtrəuliəm] *n* Petroleum *nt*

petrol: ~ pump (*BRIT*) *n* (*in car*) Benzinpumpe *f*; (*at garage*) Zapfsäule *f*; **~ station** (*BRIT*) *n* Tankstelle *f*; **~ tank** (*BRIT*) *n* Benzintank *m*

petticoat [ˈpetɪkəut] *n* Unterrock *m*

petty [ˈpetɪ] *adj* (*unimportant*) unbedeutend; (*mean*) kleinlich; **~ cash** *n* Portokasse *f*; **~ officer** *n* Maat *m*

pew [pjuː] *n* Kirchenbank *f*

pewter [ˈpjuːtəʳ] *n* Zinn *nt*

phantom [ˈfæntəm] *n* Phantom *nt*

pharmacist [ˈfɑːməsɪst] *n* Pharmazeut *m*; (*druggist*) Apotheker *m*

pharmacy [ˈfɑːməsɪ] *n* Pharmazie *f*; (*shop*) Apotheke *f*

phase [feɪz] *n* Phase *f* ♦ *vt*: **to ~ sth in** etw allmählich einführen; **to ~ sth out** etw auslaufen lassen

Ph.D. *n abbr* = **Doctor of Philosophy**

pheasant ['feznt] *n* Fasan *m*

phenomena [fə'nɔmɪnə] *npl of* **phenomenon**

phenomenon [fə'nɔmɪnən] *n* Phänomen *nt*

philanthropist [fɪ'lænθrəpɪst] *n* Philanthrop *m*, Menschenfreund *m*

Philippines ['fɪlɪpiːnz] *npl*: **the ~** die Philippinen *pl*

philosopher [fɪ'lɔsəfəˈ] *n* Philosoph *m*; **philosophical** [fɪlə'sɔfɪkl] *adj* philosophisch; **philosophy** [fɪ'lɔsəfɪ] *n* Philosophie *f*

phlegm [flɛm] *n* (MED) Schleim *m*

phobia ['fəubjə] *n* (*irrational fear: of insects, flying, water etc*) Phobie *f*

phone [fəun] *n* Telefon *nt* ♦ *vt, vi* telefonieren, anrufen; **to be on the ~** telefonieren; **~ back** *vt, vi* zurückrufen; **~ up** *vt, vi* anrufen; **~ bill** *n* Telefonrechnung *f*; **~ book** *n* Telefonbuch *nt*; **~ booth** *n* Telefonzelle *f*; **~ box** *n* Telefonzelle *f*; **~ call** *n* Telefonanruf *m*; **~card** *n* (TEL) Telefonkarte *f*; **~-in** *n* (RAD, TV) Phone-in *nt*; **~ number** *n* Telefonnummer *f*

phonetics [fə'nɛtɪks] *n* Phonetik *f*

phoney ['fəunɪ] (*inf*) *adj* unecht ♦ *n* (*person*) Schwindler *m*; (*thing*) Fälschung *f*; (*banknote*) Blüte *f*

phony ['fəunɪ] *adj, n* = **phoney**

photo ['fəutəu] *n* Foto *nt*; **~copier** ['fəutəukɔpɪəˈ] *n* Kopiergerät *nt*; **~copy** ['fəutəukɔpɪ] *n* Fotokopie *f* ♦ *vt* fotokopieren; **~genic** [fəutəu'dʒɛnɪk] *adj* fotogen; **~graph** *n* Fotografie *f*, Aufnahme *f* ♦ *vt* fotografieren; **~grapher** ['fəutəgræf] *n* Fotograf *m*; **~graphic** [fəutə'græfɪk] *adj* fotografisch; **~graphy** [fə'tɔgrafɪ] *n* Fotografie *f*

phrase [freɪz] *n* Satz *m*; (*expression*) Ausdruck *m* ♦ *vt* ausdrücken, formulieren; **~book** *n* Sprachführer *m*

physical ['fɪzɪkl] *adj* physikalisch; (*bodily*) körperlich, physisch; **~ education** *n* Turnen *nt*; **~ly** *adv* physikalisch

physician [fɪ'zɪʃən] *n* Arzt *m*

physicist ['fɪzɪsɪst] *n* Physiker(in) *m(f)*

physics ['fɪzɪks] *n* Physik *f*

physiotherapist [fɪzɪəu'θerəpɪst] *n* Physiotherapeut(in) *m(f)*

physiotherapy [fɪzɪəu'θerəpɪ] *n* Heilgymnastik *f*, Physiotherapie *f*

physique [fɪ'ziːk] *n* Körperbau *m*

pianist ['piːənɪst] *n* Pianist(in) *m(f)*

piano [pɪ'ænəu] *n* Klavier *nt*

pick [pɪk] *n* (*tool*) Pickel *m*; (*choice*) Auswahl *f* ♦ *vt* (*fruit*) pflücken; (*choose*) auswählen; **take your ~** such dir etwas aus; **to ~ sb's pocket** jdn bestehlen; **~ on** *vt fus* (*person*) herumhacken auf +*dat*; **~ out** *vt* auswählen; **~ up** *vi* (*improve*) sich erholen ♦ *vt* (*lift up*) aufheben; (*learn*) (schnell) mitbekommen; (*collect*) abholen; (*girl*) (sich *dat*) anlachen; (AUT: *passenger*) mitnehmen; (*speed*) gewinnen an +*dat*; **to ~ o.s. up** aufstehen

picket ['pɪkɪt] *n* (*striker*) Streikposten *m* ♦ *vt* (*factory*) (Streik)posten aufstellen vor +*dat* ♦ *vi* (Streik)posten stehen

pickle ['pɪkl] *n* (*salty mixture*) Pökel *m*; (*inf*) Klemme *f* ♦ *vt* (*in Essig*) einlegen; einpökeln

pickpocket ['pɪkpɔkɪt] *n* Taschendieb *m*

pick-up ['pɪkʌp] *n* (BRIT: *on record player*) Tonabnehmer *m*; (*small truck*) Lieferwagen *m*

picnic ['pɪknɪk] *n* Picknick *nt* ♦ *vi* picknicken; **~ area** *n* Rastplatz *m*

pictorial [pɪk'tɔːrɪəl] *adj* in Bildern

picture ['pɪktʃəˈ] *n* Bild *nt* ♦ *vt* (*visualize*) sich *dat* vorstellen; **the ~s** *npl* (BRIT) das Kino; **~ book** *n* Bilderbuch *nt*; **~ message** *n* Bildnachricht *f*

picturesque [pɪktʃə'rɛsk] *adj* malerisch

pie [paɪ] *n* (*meat*) Pastete *f*; (*fruit*) Torte *f*

piece [piːs] *n* Stück *nt* ♦ *vt*: **to ~ together** zusammenstückeln; (*fig*) sich *dat* zusammenreimen; **to take to ~s** in Einzelteile zerlegen; **~meal** *adv* stückweise, Stück für Stück; **~work** *n* Akkordarbeit *f*

pie chart *n* Kreisdiagramm *nt*

pier [pɪəˈ] *n* Pier *m*, Mole *f*

pierce [pɪəs] *vt* durchstechen, durchbohren (*also look*); **~d** *adj* durchgestochen; **piercing** ['pɪəsɪŋ] *adj* (*cry*) durchdringend

pig [pɪg] *n* Schwein *nt*

pigeon ['pɪdʒən] n Taube f; **~hole** n (compartment) Ablegefach nt

piggy bank ['pɪgɪ-] n Sparschwein nt

pig: ~headed ['pɪg'hɛdɪd] adj dickköpfig; **~let** ['pɪglɪt] n Ferkel nt; **~skin** ['pɪgskɪn] n Schweinsleder nt; **~sty** ['pɪgstaɪ] n Schweinestall m; **~tail** ['pɪgteɪl] n Zopf m

pike [paɪk] n Pike f; (fish) Hecht m

pilchard ['pɪltʃəd] n Sardine f

pile [paɪl] n Haufen m; (of books, wood) Stapel m; (in ground) Pfahl m; (on carpet) Flausch m ♦ vt (also: ~ up) anhäufen ♦ vi (also: ~ up) sich anhäufen

piles [paɪlz] npl Hämorr(ho)iden pl

pile-up ['paɪlʌp] n (AUT) Massenzusammenstoß m

pilfering ['pɪlfərɪŋ] n Diebstahl m

pilgrim ['pɪlgrɪm] n Pilger(in) m(f); **~age** n Wallfahrt f

pill [pɪl] n Tablette f, Pille f; **the ~** die (Antibaby)pille

pillage ['pɪlɪdʒ] vt plündern

pillar ['pɪlə'] n Pfeiler m, Säule f (also fig); **~ box** (BRIT) n Briefkasten m

pillion ['pɪljən] n Soziussitz m

pillow ['pɪləʊ] n Kissen nt; **~case** n Kissenbezug m

pilot ['paɪlət] n Pilot m; (NAUT) Lotse m ♦ adj (scheme etc) Versuchs- ♦ vt führen; (ship) lotsen; **~ light** n Zündflamme f

pimp [pɪmp] n Zuhälter m

pimple ['pɪmpl] n Pickel m

PIN n abbr (= personal identification number) PIN f

pin [pɪn] n Nadel f; (for sewing) Stecknadel f; (TECH) Stift m, Bolzen m ♦ vt stecken; (keep in one position) pressen, drücken; **to ~ sth to sth** etw an etw acc heften; **to ~ sth on sb** (fig) jdm etw anhängen; **~s and needles** Kribbeln nt; **~ down** vt (fig: person): **to ~ sb down** (to sth) jdn (auf etw acc) festnageln

pinafore ['pɪnəfɔ:'] n Schürze f; **~ dress** n Kleiderrock m

pinball ['pɪnbɔ:l] n Flipper m

pincers ['pɪnsəz] npl Kneif- or Beißzange f; (MED) Pinzette f

pinch [pɪntʃ] n Zwicken nt, Kneifen nt; (of salt) Prise f ♦ vt zwicken, kneifen; (inf: steal) klauen ♦ vi (shoe) drücken; **at a ~** notfalls, zur Not

pincushion ['pɪnkuʃən] n Nadelkissen nt

pine [paɪn] n (also: ~ tree) Kiefer f ♦ vi: **to ~ for** sich sehnen nach; **~ away** vi sich zu Tode sehnen

pineapple ['paɪnæpl] n Ananas f

ping [pɪŋ] n Klingeln nt; **~-pong** ® n Pingpong nt

pink [pɪŋk] adj rosa inv ♦ n Rosa nt; (BOT) Nelke f

pinnacle ['pɪnəkl] n Spitze f

PIN (number) n Geheimnummer f

pinpoint ['pɪnpɔɪnt] vt festlegen

pinstripe ['pɪnstraɪp] n Nadelstreifen m

pint [paɪnt] n Pint nt; (BRIT: inf: of beer) große(s) Bier nt

pioneer [paɪə'nɪə'] n Pionier m; (fig also) Bahnbrecher m

pious ['paɪəs] adj fromm

pip [pɪp] n Kern m; **the ~s** npl (BRIT: RAD) das Zeitzeichen

pipe [paɪp] n (smoking) Pfeife f; (tube) Rohr nt; (in house) (Rohr)leitung f ♦ vt (durch Rohre) leiten; (MUS) blasen; **~s** npl (also: bagpipes) Dudelsack m; **~ down** vi (be quiet) die Luft anhalten; **~ cleaner** n Pfeifenreiniger m; **~ dream** n Luftschloss nt; **~line** n (for oil) Pipeline f; **~r** n Pfeifer m; (bagpipes) Dudelsackbläser m

piping ['paɪpɪŋ] adv: **~ hot** siedend heiß

pique [pi:k] n gekränkte(r) Stolz m

pirate ['paɪərət] n Pirat m, Seeräuber m; **~d** adj: **~d version** Raubkopie f; **~ radio** (BRIT) n Piratensender m

Pisces ['paɪsi:z] n Fische pl

piss [pɪs] (inf) vi pissen; **~ed** (inf) adj (drunk) voll

pistol ['pɪstl] n Pistole f

piston ['pɪstən] n Kolben m

pit [pɪt] n Grube f; (THEAT) Parterre nt; (orchestra ~) Orchestergraben m ♦ vt (mark with scars) zerfressen; (compare): **to ~ sb against sb** jdn an jdm messen; **the ~s** npl (MOTOR RACING) die Boxen pl

pitch [pɪtʃ] n Wurf m; (of trader) Stand m; (SPORT) (Spiel)feld nt; (MUS) Tonlage f; (substance) Pech nt ♦ vt werfen; (set up) aufschlagen ♦ vi (NAUT) rollen; **to ~ a tent** ein Zelt aufbauen; **~-black** adj pechschwarz; **~ed battle** n offene Schlacht f

piteous ['pɪtɪəs] adj kläglich, erbärmlich

pitfall ['pɪtfɔːl] n (fig) Falle f

pith [pɪθ] n Mark nt

pithy ['pɪθɪ] adj prägnant

pitiful ['pɪtɪful] adj (deserving pity) bedauernswert; (contemptible) jämmerlich

pitiless ['pɪtɪlɪs] adj erbarmungslos

pittance ['pɪtns] n Hungerlohn m

pity ['pɪtɪ] n (sympathy) Mitleid nt ♦ vt Mitleid haben mit; **what a ~!** wie schade!

pivot ['pɪvət] n Drehpunkt m ♦ vi: **to ~ (on)** sich drehen (um)

pizza ['piːtsə] n Pizza f

placard ['plækɑːd] n Plakat nt, Anschlag m

placate [plə'keɪt] vt beschwichtigen

place [pleɪs] n Platz m; (spot) Stelle f; (town etc) Ort m ♦ vt setzen, stellen, legen; (order) aufgeben; (SPORT) platzieren; (identify) unterbringen; **to take ~** stattfinden; **out of ~** nicht am rechten Platz; (fig: remark) unangebracht; **in the first ~** erstens; **to change ~s with sb** mit jdm den Platz tauschen; **to be ~d third** (in race, exam) auf dem dritten Platz liegen

placid ['plæsɪd] adj gelassen, ruhig

plagiarism ['pleɪdʒərɪzəm] n Plagiat nt

plague [pleɪg] n Pest f; (fig) Plage f ♦ vt plagen

plaice [pleɪs] n Scholle f

plaid [plæd] n Plaid nt

plain [pleɪn] adj (clear) klar, deutlich; (simple) einfach, schlicht; (not beautiful) alltäglich ♦ n Ebene f; **in ~ clothes** (police) in Zivil(kleidung); **~ chocolate** n Bitterschokolade f

plaintiff ['pleɪntɪf] n Kläger m

plaintive ['pleɪntɪv] adj wehleidig

plait [plæt] n Zopf m ♦ vt flechten

plan [plæn] n Plan m ♦ vt, vi planen; **according to ~** planmäßig; **to ~ to do sth**

vorhaben, etw zu tun

plane [pleɪn] n Ebene f; (AVIAT) Flugzeug nt; (tool) Hobel m; (tree) Platane f

planet ['plænɪt] n Planet m

plank [plæŋk] n Brett nt

planning ['plænɪŋ] n Planung f; **family ~** Familienplanung f; **~ permission** n Baugenehmigung f

plant [plɑːnt] n Pflanze f; (TECH) (Maschinen)anlage f; (factory) Fabrik f, Werk nt ♦ vt pflanzen; (set firmly) stellen; **~ation** [plæn'teɪʃən] n Plantage f

plaque [plæk] n Gedenktafel f; (on teeth) (Zahn)belag m

plaster ['plɑːstəʳ] n Gips m; (in house) Verputz m; (BRIT: also: **sticking ~**) Pflaster nt; (for fracture: ~ of Paris) Gipsverband m ♦ vt gipsen; (hole) zugipsen; (ceiling) verputzen; (fig: with pictures etc) bekleben, verkleben; **~ed** (inf) adj besoffen; **~er** n Gipser m

plastic ['plæstɪk] n Plastik nt or f ♦ adj (made of ~) Plastik-; (ART) plastisch, bildend; **~ bag** n Plastiktüte f

plasticine ['plæstɪsiːn] ® n Plastilin nt

plastic surgery n plastische Chirurgie f

plate [pleɪt] n Teller m; (gold/silver ~) vergoldete(s)/versilberte(s) Tafelgeschirr nt; (in book) (Bild)tafel f

plateau ['plætəʊ] (pl **~s** or **~x**) n (GEOG) Plateau nt, Hochebene f

plateaux ['plætəʊz] npl of **plateau**

plate glass n Tafelglas nt

platform ['plætfɔːm] n (at meeting) Plattform f, Podium nt; (RAIL) Bahnsteig m; (POL) Parteiprogramm nt; **~ ticket** n Bahnsteigkarte f

platinum ['plætɪnəm] n Platin nt

platoon [plə'tuːn] n (MIL) Zug m

platter ['plætəʳ] n Platte f

plausible ['plɔːzɪbl] adj (theory, excuse, statement) plausibel; (person) überzeugend

play [pleɪ] n (also TECH) Spiel nt; (THEAT) (Theater)stück nt ♦ vt spielen; (another team) spielen gegen ♦ vi spielen; **to ~ safe** auf Nummer sicher or Sicher gehen; **~ down** vt herunterspielen; **~ up** vi (cause

trouble) frech werden; (*bad leg etc*) wehtun
♦ vt (*person*) plagen; **to ~ up to sb** jdm
flattieren; **~-acting** n Schauspielerei f; **~er**
n Spieler(in) m(f); **~ful** adj spielerisch;
~ground n Spielplatz m; **~group** n
Kindergarten m; **~ing card** n Spielkarte f;
~ing field n Sportplatz m; **~mate** n
Spielkamerad m; **~-off** n (*SPORT*)
Entscheidungsspiel nt; **~pen** n Laufstall m;
~school n = **playgroup**; **~thing** n
Spielzeug nt; **~time** n (kleine) Pause f;
~wright ['pleɪraɪt] n Theaterschriftsteller m

plc abbr (= *public limited company*) AG

plea [pliː] n Bitte f; (*general appeal*) Appell m;
(*JUR*) Plädoyer nt; **~ bargaining** n (*LAW*)
*Aushandeln der Strafe zwischen
Staatsanwaltschaft und Verteidigung*

plead [pliːd] vt (*poverty*) zur Entschuldigung
anführen; (*JUR: sb's case*) vertreten ♦ vi (*beg*)
dringend bitten; (*JUR*) plädieren; **to ~ with
sb** jdn dringend bitten

pleasant ['plɛznt] adj angenehm; **~ries** npl
(*polite remarks*) Nettigkeiten pl

please [pliːz] vt, vi (*be agreeable to*) gefallen
+dat; **~!** bitte!; **~ yourself!** wie du willst!;
~d adj zufrieden; (*glad*): **~d (about sth)**
erfreut (über etw acc); **~d to meet you**
angenehm; **pleasing** ['pliːzɪŋ] adj erfreulich

pleasure ['plɛʒər] n Freude f ♦ cpd
Vergnügungs-; **"it's a ~"** „gern
geschehen"

pleat [pliːt] n Falte f

plectrum ['plɛktrəm] n Plektron nt

pledge [plɛdʒ] n Pfand nt; (*promise*)
Versprechen nt ♦ vt verpfänden; (*promise*)
geloben, versprechen

plentiful ['plɛntɪful] adj reichlich

plenty ['plɛntɪ] n Fülle f, Überfluss m; **~ of**
eine Menge, viel

pleurisy ['pluərɪsɪ] n Rippenfellentzündung f

pliable ['plaɪəbl] adj biegsam; (*person*)
beeinflussbar

pliers ['plaɪəz] npl (Kneif)zange f

plight [plaɪt] n (Not)lage f

plimsolls ['plɪmsəlz] (*BRIT*) npl Turnschuhe pl

plinth [plɪnθ] n Sockel m

P.L.O. n abbr (= *Palestine Liberation*

Organization) PLO f

plod [plɒd] vi (*work*) sich abplagen; (*walk*)
trotten

plonk [plɒŋk] n (*BRIT: inf: wine*) billige(r)
Wein m ♦ vt: **to ~ sth down** etw hinknallen

plot [plɒt] n Komplott nt; (*story*) Handlung f;
(*of land*) Grundstück nt ♦ vt markieren;
(*curve*) zeichnen; (*movements*) nachzeichnen
♦ vi (*plan secretly*) sich verschwören

plough [plaʊ] (*US* **plow**) n Pflug m ♦ vt
pflügen; **~ back** vt (*COMM*) wieder in das
Geschäft stecken; **~ through** vt fus (*water*)
durchpflügen; (*book*) sich kämpfen durch

plow [plaʊ] (*US*) = **plough**

ploy [plɔɪ] n Masche f

pluck [plʌk] vt (*fruit*) pflücken; (*guitar*)
zupfen; (*goose etc*) rupfen ♦ n Mut m; **to ~
up courage** all seinen Mut
zusammennehmen

plug [plʌg] n Stöpsel m; (*ELEC*) Stecker m;
(*inf: publicity*) Schleichwerbung f; (*AUT*)
Zündkerze f ♦ vt (zu)stopfen; (*inf: advertise*)
Reklame machen für; **~ in** vt (*ELEC*)
anschließen

plum [plʌm] n Pflaume f, Zwetsch(g)e f

plumage ['pluːmɪdʒ] n Gefieder nt

plumber ['plʌmər] n Klempner m,
Installateur m; **plumbing** ['plʌmɪŋ] n (*craft*)
Installieren nt; (*fittings*) Leitungen pl

plummet ['plʌmɪt] vi (ab)stürzen

plump [plʌmp] adj rundlich, füllig ♦ vt
plumpsen lassen; **to ~ for** (*inf: choose*) sich
entscheiden für

plunder ['plʌndər] n Plünderung f; (*loot*)
Beute f ♦ vt plündern

plunge [plʌndʒ] n Sturz m ♦ vt stoßen ♦ vi
(sich) stürzen; **to take the ~** den Sprung
wagen; **plunging** ['plʌndʒɪŋ] adj (*neckline*)
offenherzig

plural ['pluərəl] n Plural m, Mehrzahl f

plus [plʌs] n (*also:* **~ sign**) Plus(zeichen) nt
♦ prep plus, und; **ten/twenty ~** mehr als
zehn/zwanzig

plush [plʌʃ] adj (*also:* **~y:** inf) feudal

ply [plaɪ] vt (*trade*) (be)treiben; (*with
questions*) zusetzen +dat; (*ship, taxi*)
befahren ♦ vi (*ship, taxi*) verkehren ♦ n:

three-~ (*wool*) Dreifach-; **to ~ sb with drink** jdn zum Trinken animieren; **~wood** n Sperrholz nt

P.M. n abbr = **prime minister**

p.m. adv abbr (= *post meridiem*) nachmittags

pneumatic drill n Presslufthammer m

pneumonia [nju:'məuniə] n Lungenentzündung f

poach [pəutʃ] vt (*COOK*) pochieren; (*game*) stehlen ♦ vi (*steal*) wildern; **~ed** adj (*egg*) verloren; **~er** n Wilddieb m

P.O. Box n abbr = **Post Office Box**

pocket ['pɔkɪt] n Tasche f; (*of resistance*) (Widerstands)nest nt ♦ vt einstecken; **to be out of ~** (*BRIT*) draufzahlen; **~book** n Taschenbuch nt; **~ calculator** n Taschenrechner m; **~ knife** n Taschenmesser m; **~ money** n Taschengeld nt

pod [pɔd] n Hülse f; (*of peas also*) Schote f

podgy ['pɔdʒɪ] adj pummelig

podiatrist [pɔ'di:ətrɪst] (*US*) n Fußpfleger(in) m(f)

poem ['pəuɪm] n Gedicht nt

poet ['pəuɪt] n Dichter m, Poet m; **~ic** [pəu'etɪk] adj poetisch, dichterisch; **~ laureate** n Hofdichter m; **~ry** n Poesie f; (*poems*) Gedichte pl

poignant ['pɔɪnjənt] adj (*touching*) ergreifend

point [pɔɪnt] n (*also in discussion, scoring*) Punkt m; (*spot*) Punkt m, Stelle f; (*sharpened tip*) Spitze f; (*moment*) (Zeit)punkt m; (*purpose*) Zweck m; (*idea*) Argument nt; (*decimal*) Dezimalstelle f; (*personal characteristic*) Seite f ♦ vt zeigen mit; (*gun*) richten ♦ vi zeigen; **~s** npl (*RAIL*) Weichen pl; **to be on the ~ of doing sth** drauf und dran sein, etw zu tun; **to make a ~ of** Wert darauf legen; **to get the ~** verstehen, worum es geht; **to come to the ~** zur Sache kommen; **there's no ~ (in doing sth)** es hat keinen Sinn(, etw zu tun); **~ out** vt hinweisen auf +acc; **~ to** vt fus zeigen auf +acc; **~-blank** adv (*at close range*) aus nächster Entfernung; (*bluntly*) unverblümt; **~ed** adj (*also fig*) spitz, scharf;

~edly adv (*fig*) spitz; **~er** n Zeigestock m; (*on dial*) Zeiger m; **~less** adj sinnlos; **~ of view** n Stand- or Gesichtspunkt m

poise [pɔɪz] n Haltung f; (*fig*) Gelassenheit f

poison ['pɔɪzn] n (*also fig*) Gift nt ♦ vt vergiften; **~ing** n Vergiftung f; **~ous** adj giftig, Gift-

poke [pəuk] vt stoßen; (*put*) stecken; (*fire*) schüren; (*hole*) bohren; **~ about** vi herumstochern; (*nose around*) herumwühlen

poker ['pəukə'] n Schürhaken m; (*CARDS*) Poker nt

poky ['pəukɪ] adj eng

Poland ['pəulənd] n Polen nt

polar ['pəulə'] adj Polar-, polar; **~ bear** n Eisbär m

Pole [pəul] n Pole m, Polin f

pole [pəul] n Stange f, Pfosten m; (*flagpole, telegraph ~*) Stange f, Mast m; (*ELEC, GEOG*) Pol m; (*SPORT: vaulting ~*) Stab m; (*ski ~*) Stock m; **~ bean** n (*US*) (*runner bean*) Stangenbohne f; **~ vault** n Stabhochsprung m

police [pə'li:s] n Polizei f ♦ vt kontrollieren; **~ car** n Polizeiwagen m; **~man** (*irreg*) n Polizist m; **~ state** n Polizeistaat m; **~ station** n (Polizei)revier nt, Wache f; **~woman** (*irreg*) n Polizistin f

policy ['pɔlɪsɪ] n Politik f; (*insurance*) (Versicherungs)police f

polio ['pəulɪəu] n (spinale) Kinderlähmung f, Polio f

Polish ['pəulɪʃ] adj polnisch ♦ n (*LING*) Polnisch nt

polish ['pɔlɪʃ] n Politur f; (*for floor*) Wachs nt; (*for shoes*) Creme f; (*for nails*) Lack m; (*shine*) Glanz m; (*of furniture*) Politur f; (*fig*) Schliff m ♦ vt polieren; (*shoes*) putzen; (*fig*) den letzten Schliff geben +dat; **~ off** vt (*inf: food*) wegputzen; (: *drink*) hinunterschütten; **~ed** adj glänzend; (*manners*) verfeinert

polite [pə'laɪt] adj höflich; **~ly** adv höflich; **~ness** n Höflichkeit f

politic-: ~al [pə'lɪtɪkl] adj politisch; **~ally** [pə'lɪtɪklɪ] adv politisch; **~ally correct**

politisch korrekt; **~ian** [pɔliˈtiʃən] n Politiker m; **~s** npl Politik f

polka dot [ˈpɔlkə-] n Tupfen m

poll [pəul] n Abstimmung f; (in election) Wahl f; (votes cast) Wahlbeteiligung f; (opinion ~) Umfrage f ♦ vt (votes) erhalten

pollen [ˈpɔlən] n (BOT) Blütenstaub m, Pollen m

polling [ˈpəulɪŋ-]: **~ booth** (BRIT) n Wahlkabine f; **~ day** (BRIT) n Wahltag m; **~ station** (BRIT) n Wahllokal nt

pollute [pəˈluːt] vt verschmutzen, verunreinigen; **~d** adj verschmutzt; **pollution** [pəˈluːʃən] n Verschmutzung f

polo [ˈpəuləu] n Polo nt; **~ neck** n (also: **~-necked sweater**) Rollkragen m; Rollkragenpullover m; **~ shirt** n Polohemd nt

polystyrene [pɔliˈstaɪriːn] n Styropor nt

polytechnic [pɔliˈtɛknɪk] n technische Hochschule f

polythene [ˈpɔliθiːn] n Plastik nt; **~ bag** n Plastiktüte f

pomegranate [ˈpɔmɪɡrænɪt] n Granatapfel m

pompom [ˈpɔmpɔm] n Troddel f, Pompon m

pompous [ˈpɔmpəs] adj aufgeblasen; (language) geschwollen

pond [pɔnd] n Teich m, Weiher m

ponder [ˈpɔndə*] vt nachdenken über +acc; **~ous** adj schwerfällig

pong [pɔŋ] (BRIT: inf) n Mief m

pontiff [ˈpɔntɪf] n Pontifex m

pontoon [pɔnˈtuːn] n Ponton m; (CARDS) 17-und-4 nt

pony [ˈpəunɪ] n Pony nt; **~tail** n Pferdeschwanz m; **~ trekking** (BRIT) n Ponyreiten nt

poodle [ˈpuːdl] n Pudel m

pool [puːl] n (swimming ~) Schwimmbad nt; (: private) Swimmingpool m; (of liquid, blood) Lache f; (fund) (gemeinsame) Kasse f; (billiards) Poolspiel nt ♦ vt (money etc) zusammenlegen; (football) **~s** Toto nt

poor [puə*] adj arm; (not good) schlecht ♦ npl: **the ~** die Armen pl; **~ in** (resources)

arm an +dat; **~ly** adv schlecht; (dressed) ärmlich ♦ adj schlecht

pop [pɔp] n Knall m; (music) Popmusik f; (drink) Limo(nade) f; (US: inf) Pa m ♦ vt (put) stecken; (balloon) platzen lassen ♦ vi knallen; **~ in** vi kurz vorbeigehen or vorbeikommen; **~ out** vi (person) kurz rausgehen; (thing) herausspringen; **~ up** vi auftauchen; **~corn** n Puffmais m

pope [pəup] n Papst m

poplar [ˈpɔplə*] n Pappel f

poppy [ˈpɔpɪ] n Mohn m

Popsicle [ˈpɔpsɪkl] (® US) n (ice lolly) Eis am Stiel

populace [ˈpɔpjuləs] n Volk nt

popular [ˈpɔpjulə*] adj beliebt, populär; (of the people) volkstümlich; (widespread) allgemein; **~ity** [pɔpjuˈlærɪtɪ] n Beliebtheit f, Popularität f; **~ly** adv allgemein, überall

population [pɔpjuˈleɪʃən] n Bevölkerung f; (of town) Einwohner pl

populous [ˈpɔpjuləs] adj dicht besiedelt

porcelain [ˈpɔːslɪn] n Porzellan nt

porch [pɔːtʃ] n Vorbau m, Veranda f

porcupine [ˈpɔːkjupaɪn] n Stachelschwein n

pore [pɔː*] n Pore f ♦ vi: **to ~ over** brüten über +dat

pork [pɔːk] n Schweinefleisch nt

porn [pɔːn] n Porno m; **~ographic** [pɔːnəˈɡræfɪk] adj pornografisch; **~ography** [pɔːˈnɔɡrəfɪ] n Pornografie f

porous [ˈpɔːrəs] adj porös; (skin) porig

porpoise [ˈpɔːpəs] n Tümmler m

porridge [ˈpɔrɪdʒ] n Haferbrei m

port [pɔːt] n Hafen m; (town) Hafenstadt f; (NAUT: left side) Backbord nt; (wine) Portwein m; **~ of call** Anlaufhafen m

portable [ˈpɔːtəbl] adj tragbar

porter [ˈpɔːtə*] n Pförtner(in) m(f); (for luggage) (Gepäck)träger m

portfolio [pɔːtˈfəuliəu] n (case) Mappe f; (POL) Geschäftsbereich m; (FIN) Portefeuille nt; (of artist) Kollektion f

porthole [ˈpɔːthəul] n Bullauge nt

portion [ˈpɔːʃən] n Teil m, Stück nt; (of food) Portion f

portrait [ˈpɔːtreɪt] n Porträt nt

portray [pɔː'treɪ] vt darstellen; **~al** n Darstellung f

Portugal ['pɔːtjugl] n Portugal nt

Portuguese [pɔːtju'giːz] adj portugiesisch ♦ n inv Portugiese m, Portugiesin f; (LING) Portugiesisch nt

pose [pəʊz] n Stellung f, Pose f; (affectation) Pose f ♦ vi posieren ♦ vt stellen

posh [pɔʃ] (inf) adj (piek)fein

position [pə'zɪʃən] n Stellung f; (place) Lage f; (job) Stelle f; (attitude) Standpunkt m ♦ vt aufstellen

positive ['pɔzɪtɪv] adj positiv; (convinced) sicher; (definite) eindeutig

posse ['pɔsɪ] (US) n Aufgebot nt

possess [pə'zes] vt besitzen; **~ion** [pə'zeʃən] n Besitz m; **~ive** adj besitzergreifend, eigensüchtig

possibility [pɔsɪ'bɪlɪtɪ] n Möglichkeit f

possible ['pɔsɪbl] adj möglich; **as big as ~** so groß wie möglich, möglichst groß; **possibly** adv möglicherweise, vielleicht; **I cannot possibly come** ich kann unmöglich kommen

post [pəʊst] n (BRIT: letters, delivery) Post f; (pole) Pfosten m, Pfahl m; (place of duty) Posten m; (job) Stelle f ♦ vt (notice) anschlagen; (BRIT: letters) aufgeben; (: appoint) versetzen; (soldiers) aufstellen; **~age** n Postgebühr f, Porto nt; **~al** adj Post-; **~al order** n Postanweisung f; **~box** (BRIT) n Briefkasten m; **~card** n Postkarte f; **~code** (BRIT) n Postleitzahl f

postdate ['pəʊst'deɪt] vt (cheque) nachdatieren

poster ['pəʊstə'] n Plakat nt, Poster nt

poste restante [pəʊst'restɑːnt] n Aufbewahrungsstelle f für postlagernde Sendungen

posterior [pɔs'tɪərɪə'] (inf) n Hintern m

posterity [pɔs'terɪtɪ] n Nachwelt f

postgraduate ['pəʊst'grædjuət] n Weiterstudierende(r) mf

posthumous ['pɔstjuməs] adj post(h)um

postman ['pəʊstmən] (irreg) n Briefträger m

postmark ['pəʊstmɑːk] n Poststempel m

post-mortem [pəʊst'mɔːtəm] n Autopsie f

post office n Postamt nt, Post f; (organization) Post f; **Post Office Box** n Postfach n

postpone [pəʊs'pəʊn] vt verschieben

postscript ['pəʊstskrɪpt] n Postskript nt; (to affair) Nachspiel nt

posture ['pɔstʃə'] n Haltung f ♦ vi posieren

postwar [pəʊst'wɔː'] adj Nachkriegs-

postwoman ['pəʊstwʊmən] (irreg) n Briefträgerin f

posy ['pəʊzɪ] n Blumenstrauß m

pot [pɔt] n Topf m; (teapot) Kanne f; (inf: marijuana) Hasch m ♦ vt (plant) eintopfen; **to go to ~** (inf: work) auf den Hund kommen

potato [pə'teɪtəʊ] (pl **~es**) n Kartoffel f; **~ peeler** n Kartoffelschäler m

potent ['pəʊtnt] adj stark; (argument) zwingend

potential [pə'tenʃl] adj potenziell, potentiell ♦ n Potenzial nt, Potential nt; **~ly** adv potenziell, potentiell

pothole ['pɔthəʊl] n (in road) Schlagloch nt; (BRIT: underground) Höhle f; **potholing** (BRIT) n: **to go potholing** Höhlen erforschen

potion ['pəʊʃən] n Trank m

potluck [pɔt'lʌk] n: **to take ~ with sth** etw auf gut Glück nehmen

pot plant n Topfpflanze f

potter ['pɔtə'] n Töpfer m ♦ vi herumhantieren; **~y** n Töpferwaren pl; (place) Töpferei f

potty ['pɔtɪ] adj (inf: mad) verrückt ♦ n Töpfchen nt

pouch [paʊtʃ] n Beutel m

pouf(fe) [puːf] n Sitzkissen nt

poultry ['pəʊltrɪ] n Geflügel nt

pounce [paʊns] vi sich stürzen ♦ n Sprung m, Satz m; **to ~ on** sich stürzen auf +acc

pound [paʊnd] n (FIN, weight) Pfund nt; (for cars, animals) Auslösestelle f ♦ vt (zer)stampfen ♦ vi klopfen, hämmern; **~ sterling** n Pfund Sterling nt

pour [pɔː'] vt gießen, schütten ♦ vi gießen; (crowds etc) strömen; **~ away** vt abgießen; **~ in** vi (people) hereinströmen; **~ off** vt abgießen; **~ out** vi (people) herausströmen

♦ vt (drink) einschenken; ~ing adj: ~ing
rain strömende(r) Regen m

pout [paut] vi schmollen

poverty ['pɔvətɪ] n Armut f; ~-stricken adj
verarmt, sehr arm

powder ['paudəʳ] n Pulver nt; (cosmetic)
Puder m ♦ vt pulverisieren; to ~ one's
nose sich dat die Nase pudern; ~
compact n Puderdose f; ~ed milk n
Milchpulver nt; ~ room n Damentoilette f;
~y adj pulverig

power ['pauəʳ] n (also POL) Macht f; (ability)
Fähigkeit f; (strength) Stärke f; (MATH)
Potenz f; (ELEC) Strom m ♦ vt betreiben,
antreiben; to be in ~ (POL etc) an der
Macht sein; ~ cut n Stromausfall m; ~ed
adj: ~ed by betrieben mit; ~ failure (US) n
Stromausfall m; ~ful adj (person) mächtig;
(engine, government) stark; ~less adj
machtlos; ~ point (BRIT) n elektrische(r)
Anschluss m; ~ station n Elektrizitätswerk
nt; ~ struggle n Machtkampf m

p.p. abbr (= per procurationem): p.p. J. Smith
i. A. J. Smith

PR n abbr = public relations

practicable ['præktɪkəbl] adj durchführbar

practical ['præktɪkl] adj praktisch; ~ity
[præktɪ'kælɪtɪ] n (of person) praktische
Veranlagung f; (of situation etc)
Durchführbarkeit f; ~ joke n Streich m; ~ly
adv praktisch

practice ['præktɪs] n Übung f; (reality, also of
doctor, lawyer) Praxis f; (custom) Brauch m;
(in business) Usus m ♦ vt, vi (US) = practise;
in ~ (in reality) in der Praxis; out of ~
außer Übung; practicing (US) adj =
practising

practise ['præktɪs] (US practice) vt üben;
(profession) ausüben ♦ vi (sich) üben;
(doctor, lawyer) praktizieren; practising (US
practicing) adj praktizierend; (Christian etc)
aktiv

practitioner [præk'tɪʃənəʳ] n praktische(r)
Arzt m, praktische Ärztin f

pragmatic [præg'mætɪk] adj pragmatisch

prairie ['preərɪ] n Prärie f, Steppe f

praise [preɪz] n Lob m ♦ vt loben; ~worthy

adj lobenswert

pram [præm] (BRIT) n Kinderwagen m

prance [prɑːns] vi (horse) tänzeln; (person)
stolzieren

prank [præŋk] n Streich m

prawn [prɔːn] n Garnele f; Krabbe f; ~
cocktail n Krabbencocktail m

pray [preɪ] vi beten; ~er [preəʳ] n Gebet nt

preach [priːtʃ] vi predigen; ~er n Prediger
m

preamble [prɪ'æmbl] n Einleitung f

precarious [prɪ'keərɪəs] adj prekär, unsicher

precaution [prɪ'kɔːʃən] n
(Vorsichts)maßnahme f

precede [prɪ'siːd] vi vorausgehen ♦ vt
vorausgehen +dat; ~nce ['presɪdəns] n
Vorrang m; ~nt ['presɪdənt] n Präzedenzfall
m; preceding [prɪ'siːdɪŋ] adj vorhergehend

precinct ['priːsɪŋkt] n (US: district) Bezirk m;
~s npl (round building) Gelände nt; (area,
environs) Umgebung f; pedestrian ~
Fußgängerzone f; shopping ~
Geschäftsviertel nt

precious ['preʃəs] adj kostbar, wertvoll;
(affected) pretiös, preziös, geziert

precipice ['presɪpɪs] n Abgrund m

precipitate [adj prɪ'sɪpɪtɪt, vb prɪ'sɪpɪteɪt] adj
überstürzt, übereilt ♦ vt hinunterstürzen;
(events) heraufbeschwören

precise [prɪ'saɪs] adj genau, präzis; ~ly adv
genau, präzis

precision [prɪ'sɪʒən] n Präzision f

preclude [prɪ'kluːd] vt ausschließen

precocious [prɪ'kəuʃəs] adj frühreif

preconceived [priːkən'siːvd] adj (idea)
vorgefasst

precondition ['priːkən'dɪʃən] n
Vorbedingung f, Voraussetzung f

precursor [priː'kɜːsəʳ] n Vorläufer m

predator ['predətəʳ] n Raubtier nt

predecessor ['priːdɪsesəʳ] n Vorgänger m

predicament [prɪ'dɪkəmənt] n missliche
Lage f

predict [prɪ'dɪkt] vt voraussagen; ~able adj
vorhersagbar; ~ion [prɪ'dɪkʃən] n
Voraussage f

predominantly [prɪ'dɔmɪnəntlɪ] adv

überwiegend, hauptsächlich
predominate [prɪ'dɔmɪneɪt] *vi*
vorherrschen; (*fig*) vorherrschen,
überwiegen
pre-eminent [pri:'emɪnənt] *adj*
hervorragend, herausragend
pre-empt [pri:'emt] *vt* (*action, decision*)
vorwegnehmen
preen [pri:n] *vt* putzen; **to ~ o.s.** (*person*)
sich brüsten
prefab ['pri:fæb] *n* Fertighaus *nt*
preface ['prefəs] *n* Vorwort *nt*
prefect ['pri:fekt] *n* Präfekt *m*; (*SCH*)
Aufsichtsschüler(in) *m(f)*
prefer [prɪ'fɜ:ʳ] *vt* vorziehen, lieber mögen;
to ~ to do sth etw lieber tun; **~ably**
['prefrəblɪ] *adv* vorzugsweise, am liebsten;
~ence ['prefrəns] *n* Präferenz *f*, Vorzug *m*;
~ential [prefə'renʃəl] *adj* bevorzugt,
Vorzugs-
prefix ['pri:fɪks] *n* Vorsilbe *f*, Präfix *nt*
pregnancy ['pregnənsɪ] *n* Schwangerschaft *f*
pregnant ['pregnənt] *adj* schwanger
prehistoric ['pri:hɪs'tɔrɪk] *adj* prähistorisch,
vorgeschichtlich
prejudice ['predʒudɪs] *n* (*bias*)
Voreingenommenheit *f*; (*opinion*) Vorurteil
nt; (*harm*) Schaden *m* ♦ *vt* beeinträchtigen;
~d *adj* (*person*) voreingenommen
preliminary [prɪ'lɪmɪnərɪ] *adj* einleitend,
Vor-
prelude ['prelju:d] *n* Vorspiel *nt*; (*fig*) Auftakt
m
premarital ['pri:'mærɪtl] *adj* vorehelich
premature ['premətʃuəʳ] *adj* vorzeitig,
verfrüht; (*birth*) Früh-
premeditated [pri:'medɪteɪtɪd] *adj* geplant;
(*murder*) vorsätzlich
premenstrual syndrome [pri:'menstruəl-]
n prämenstruelles Syndrom *nt*
premier ['premɪəʳ] *adj* erste(r, s) ♦ *n* Premier
m
première ['premɪeəʳ] *n* Premiere *f*;
Uraufführung *f*
Premier League [-li:g] *n* ≈ 1. Bundesliga
(*höchste Spielklasse im Fußball*)
premise ['premɪs] *n* Voraussetzung *f*,

Prämisse *f*; **~s** *npl* (*shop*) Räumlichkeiten *pl*;
(*grounds*) Gelände *nt*; **on the ~s** im Hause
premium ['pri:mɪəm] *n* Prämie *f*; **to be at a
~** über pari stehen; **~ bond** (*BRIT*) *n*
Prämienanleihe *f*
premonition [premə'nɪʃən] *n* Vorahnung *f*
preoccupation [pri:ɔkju'peɪʃən] *n* Sorge *f*
preoccupied [pri:'ɔkjupaɪd] *adj* (*look*)
geistesabwesend
prep [prep] *n* (*SCH*) Hausaufgabe *f*
prepaid [pri:'peɪd] *adj* vorausbezahlt; (*letter*)
frankiert
preparation [prepə'reɪʃən] *n* Vorbereitung *f*
preparatory [prɪ'pærətərɪ] *adj*
Vor(bereitungs)-; **~ school** *n* (*BRIT*) *private
Vorbereitungsschule für die Public School*;
(*US*) *private Vorbereitungsschule für die
Hochschule*
prepare [prɪ'peəʳ] *vt* vorbereiten ♦ *vi* sich
vorbereiten; **to ~ for/prepare sth for**
sich/etw vorbereiten auf *+acc*; **to be ~d to
...** bereit sein zu ...
preponderance [prɪ'pɔndərns] *n*
Übergewicht *nt*
preposition [prepə'zɪʃən] *n* Präposition *f*,
Verhältniswort *nt*
preposterous [prɪ'pɔstərəs] *adj* absurd
prep school *n* = **preparatory school**
prerequisite [pri:'rekwɪzɪt] *n* (*unerlässliche*)
Voraussetzung *f*
prerogative [prɪ'rɔgətɪv] *n* Vorrecht *nt*
Presbyterian [prezbɪ'tɪərɪən] *adj*
presbyterianisch ♦ *n* Presbyterier(in) *m(f)*
preschool ['pri:sku:l] *adj* Vorschul-
prescribe [prɪ'skraɪb] *vt* vorschreiben; (*MED*)
verschreiben
prescription [prɪ'skrɪpʃən] *n* (*MED*) Rezept *nt*
presence ['prezns] *n* Gegenwart *f*; **~ of
mind** Geistesgegenwart *f*
present [*adj, n* 'preznt, *vb* prɪ'zent] *adj* (*here*)
anwesend; (*current*) gegenwärtig ♦ *n*
Gegenwart *f*; (*gift*) Geschenk *nt* ♦ *vt*
vorlegen; (*introduce*) vorstellen; (*show*)
zeigen; (*give*): **to ~ sb with sth** jdm etw
überreichen; **at ~** im Augenblick; **to give
sb a ~** jdm ein Geschenk machen; **~able**
[prɪ'zentəbl] *adj* präsentabel; **~ation**

[prezn'teɪʃən] n Überreichung f; **~-day** adj heutig; **~er** [prɪ'zentəʳ] n (RAD, TV) Moderator(in) m(f); **~ly** adv bald; (at ~) im Augenblick

preservation [prezə'veɪʃən] n Erhaltung f

preservative [prɪ'zɜːvətɪv] n Konservierungsmittel nt

preserve [prɪ'zɜːv] vt erhalten; (food) einmachen ♦ n (jam) Eingemachte(s) nt; (reserve) Schutzgebiet nt

preside [prɪ'zaɪd] vi den Vorsitz haben

president ['prezɪdənt] n Präsident m; **~ial** [prezɪ'denʃl] adj Präsidenten-; (election) Präsidentschafts-; (system) Präsidial-

press [pres] n Presse f; (printing house) Druckerei f ♦ vt drücken; (iron) bügeln; (urge) (be)drängen ♦ vi drücken; to be **~ed for time** unter Zeitdruck stehen; to **~ for sth** drängen auf etw acc; **~ on** vi vorwärts drängen; **~ agency** n Presseagentur f; **~ conference** n Pressekonferenz f; **~ed** adj (clothes) gebügelt; **~ing** adj dringend; **~ stud** (BRIT) n Druckknopf m; **~-up** (BRIT) n Liegestütz m

pressure ['preʃəʳ] n Druck m; **~ cooker** n Schnellkochtopf m; **~ gauge** n Druckmesser m

pressurized ['preʃəraɪzd] adj Druck-

prestige [pres'tiːʒ] n Prestige nt; **prestigious** [pres'tɪdʒəs] adj Prestige-

presumably [prɪ'zjuːməblɪ] adv vermutlich

presume [prɪ'zjuːm] vt, vi annehmen; to **~ to do sth** sich erlauben, etw zu tun; **presumption** [prɪ'zʌmpʃən] n Annahme f; **presumptuous** [prɪ'zʌmpʃəs] adj anmaßend

pretence [prɪ'tens] (US **pretense**) n Vorgabe f, Vortäuschung f; (false claim) Vorwand m

pretend [prɪ'tend] vt vorgeben, so tun als ob ... ♦ vi so tun; to **~ to sth** Anspruch erheben auf etw acc

pretense [prɪ'tens] (US) n = **pretence**

pretension [prɪ'tenʃən] n Anspruch m; (impudent claim) Anmaßung f

pretentious [prɪ'tenʃəs] adj angeberisch

pretext ['priːtekst] n Vorwand m

pretty ['prɪtɪ] adj hübsch ♦ adv (inf) ganz schön

prevail [prɪ'veɪl] vi siegen; (custom) vorherrschen; to **~ against** or **over** siegen über +acc; to **~ (up)on sb to do sth** jdn dazu bewegen, etw zu tun; **~ing** adj vorherrschend

prevalent ['prevələnt] adj vorherrschend

prevent [prɪ'vent] vt (stop) verhindern, verhüten; to **~ sb from doing sth** jdn (daran) hindern, etw zu tun; **~ative** n Vorbeugungsmittel nt; **~ion** [prɪ'venʃən] n Verhütung f; **~ive** adj vorbeugend, Schutz-

preview ['priːvjuː] n private Voraufführung f; (trailer) Vorschau f

previous ['priːvɪəs] adj früher, vorherig; **~ly** adv früher

prewar [priː'wɔːʳ] adj Vorkriegs-

prey [preɪ] n Beute f; **~ on** vt fus Jagd machen auf +acc; **it was ~ing on his mind** es quälte sein Gewissen

price [praɪs] n Preis m; (value) Wert m ♦ vt (label) auszeichnen; **~less** adj (also fig) unbezahlbar; **~ list** n Preisliste f

prick [prɪk] n Stich m ♦ vt, vi stechen; to **~ up one's ears** die Ohren spitzen

prickle ['prɪkl] n Stachel m, Dorn m

prickly ['prɪklɪ] adj stachelig; (fig: person) reizbar; **~ heat** n Hitzebläschen pl

pride [praɪd] n Stolz m; (arrogance) Hochmut m ♦ vt: to **~ o.s. on sth** auf etw acc stolz sein

priest [priːst] n Priester m; **~hood** n Priesteramt nt

prim [prɪm] adj prüde

primarily ['praɪmərɪlɪ] adv vorwiegend

primary ['praɪmərɪ] adj (main) Haupt-; (SCH) Grund-; **~ school** (BRIT) n Grundschule f

prime [praɪm] adj erste(r, s); (excellent) erstklassig ♦ vt vorbereiten; (gun) laden; **in the ~ of life** in der Blüte der Jahre; **~ minister** n Premierminister m, Ministerpräsident m; **~r** ['praɪməʳ] n Fibel f

primeval [praɪ'miːvl] adj vorzeitlich; (forests) Ur-

primitive ['prɪmɪtɪv] adj primitiv

primrose ['prɪmrəʊz] n (gelbe) Primel f

primus (stove) ['praɪməs-] (® BRIT) n

Primuskocher *m*

prince [prɪns] *n* Prinz *m*; (*ruler*) Fürst *m*; **princess** [prɪn'sɛs] *n* Prinzessin *f*; Fürstin *f*

principal ['prɪnsɪpl] *adj* Haupt- ♦ *n* (*SCH*) (Schul)direktor *m*, Rektor *m*; (*money*) (Grund)kapital *nt*

principle ['prɪnsɪpl] *n* Grundsatz *m*, Prinzip *nt*; **in ~** im Prinzip; **on ~** aus Prinzip, prinzipiell

print [prɪnt] *n* Druck *m*; (*made by feet, fingers*) Abdruck *m*; (*PHOT*) Abzug *m* ♦ *vt* drucken; (*name*) in Druckbuchstaben schreiben; (*PHOT*) abziehen; **out of ~** vergriffen; **~ed matter** *n* Drucksache *f*; **~er** *n* Drucker *m*; **~ing** *n* Drucken *nt*; (*of photos*) Abziehen *nt*; **~out** *n* (*COMPUT*) Ausdruck *m*

prior ['praɪə*r*] *adj* früher ♦ *n* Prior *m*; **~ to sth** vor etw *dat*; **~ to going abroad, she had ...** bevor sie ins Ausland ging, hatte sie ...

priority [praɪ'ɔrɪtɪ] *n* Vorrang *m*; Priorität *f*

prise [praɪz] *vt*: **to ~ open** aufbrechen

prison ['prɪzn] *n* Gefängnis *nt* ♦ *adj* Gefängnis-; (*system etc*) Strafvollzugs-; **~er** *n* Gefangene(r) *mf*

pristine ['prɪstiːn] *adj* makellos

privacy ['prɪvəsɪ] *n* Ungestörtheit *f*, Ruhe *f*; Privatleben *nt*

private ['praɪvɪt] *adj* privat, Privat-; (*secret*) vertraulich, geheim ♦ *n* einfache(r) Soldat *m*; **"~"** (*on envelope*) „persönlich"; (*on door*) „Privat"; **in ~** privat, unter vier Augen; **~ enterprise** *n* Privatunternehmen *nt*; **~ eye** *n* Privatdetektiv *m*; **~ property** *n* Privatbesitz *m*; **~ school** *n* Privatschule *f*; **privatize** *vt* privatisieren

privet ['prɪvɪt] *n* Liguster *m*

privilege ['prɪvɪlɪdʒ] *n* Privileg *nt*; **~d** *adj* bevorzugt, privilegiert

privy ['prɪvɪ] *adj* geheim, privat; **P~ Council** *n* Geheime(r) Staatsrat *m*

prize [praɪz] *n* Preis *m* ♦ *adj* (*example*) erstklassig; (*idiot*) Voll- ♦ *vt* (hoch) schätzen; **~-giving** *n* Preisverteilung *f*; **~winner** *n* Preisträger(in) *m(f)*

pro [prəʊ] *n* (*professional*) Profi *m*; **the ~s and cons** das Für und Wider

probability [prɔbə'bɪlɪtɪ] *n*

Wahrscheinlichkeit *f*

probable ['prɔbəbl] *adj* wahrscheinlich; **probably** *adv* wahrscheinlich

probation [prə'beɪʃən] *n* Probe(zeit) *f*; (*JUR*) Bewährung *f*; **on ~** auf Probe; auf Bewährung

probe [prəʊb] *n* Sonde *f*; (*enquiry*) Untersuchung *f* ♦ *vt, vi* erforschen

problem ['prɔbləm] *n* Problem *nt*; **~atic** [prɔblə'mætɪk] *adj* problematisch

procedure [prə'siːdʒə*r*] *n* Verfahren *nt*

proceed [prə'siːd] *vi* (*advance*) vorrücken; (*start*) anfangen; (*carry on*) fortfahren; (*set about*) vorgehen; **~ings** *npl* Verfahren *nt*

proceeds ['prəʊsiːdz] *npl* Erlös *m*

process ['prəʊsɛs] *n* Prozess *m*; (*method*) Verfahren *nt* ♦ *vt* bearbeiten; (*food*) verarbeiten; (*film*) entwickeln; **~ing** *n* (*PHOT*) Entwickeln *nt*

procession [prə'sɛʃən] *n* Prozession *f*, Umzug *m*; **funeral ~** Trauerprozession *f*

pro-choice [prəʊ'tʃɔɪs] *adj* (*movement*) Pro-Abtreibungs-; **~ campaigner** Abtreibungsbefürworter(in) *m(f)*

proclaim [prə'kleɪm] *vt* verkünden

procrastinate [prəʊ'kræstɪneɪt] *vi* zaudern

procure [prə'kjuə*r*] *vt* beschaffen

prod [prɔd] *vt* stoßen ♦ *n* Stoß *m*

prodigal ['prɔdɪgl] *adj*: **~ (with *or* of)** verschwenderisch (mit)

prodigy ['prɔdɪdʒɪ] *n* Wunder *nt*

produce [*n* 'prɔdjuːs, *vb* prə'djuːs] *n* (*AGR*) (Boden)produkte *pl*, (Natur)erzeugnis *nt* ♦ *vt* herstellen, produzieren; (*cause*) hervorrufen; (*farmer*) erzeugen; (*yield*) liefern, bringen; (*play*) inszenieren; **~r** *n* Hersteller *m*, Produzent *m* (*also CINE*); Erzeuger *m*

product ['prɔdʌkt] *n* Produkt *nt*, Erzeugnis *nt*; **~ion** [prə'dʌkʃən] *n* Produktion *f*, Herstellung *f*; (*thing*) Erzeugnis *nt*, Produkt *nt*; (*THEAT*) Inszenierung *f*; **~ion line** *n* Fließband *nt*; **~ive** [prə'dʌktɪv] *adj* produktiv; (*fertile*) ertragreich, fruchtbar

productivity [prɔdʌk'tɪvɪtɪ] *n* Produktivität *f*

profane [prə'feɪn] *adj* weltlich, profan; (*language etc*) gotteslästerlich

profess [prə'fɛs] vt bekennen; (*show*) zeigen; (*claim to be*) vorgeben

profession [prə'fɛʃən] n Beruf m; (*declaration*) Bekenntnis nt; ~**al** n Fachmann m; (*expert*) fachlich; (SPORT) Berufsspieler(in) m(f) ♦ adj Berufs-; (*expert*) fachlich; (*player*) professionell; ~**ally** adv beruflich, fachmännisch

professor [prə'fɛsə^r] n Professor m

proficiency [prə'fɪʃənsɪ] n Können nt

proficient [prə'fɪʃənt] adj fähig

profile ['prəʊfaɪl] n Profil nt; (*fig: report*) Kurzbiografie f

profit ['prɒfɪt] n Gewinn m ♦ vi: **to ~ (by or from)** profitieren (von); ~**ability** [prɒfɪtə'bɪlɪtɪ] n Rentabilität f; ~**able** adj einträglich, rentabel; ~**eering** [prɒfɪ'tɪərɪŋ] n Profitmacherei f

profound [prə'faʊnd] adj tief

profuse [prə'fjuːs] adj überreich; ~**ly** [prə'fjuːslɪ] adv überschwänglich; (*sweat*) reichlich; **profusion** [prə'fjuːʒən] n: **profusion (of)** Überfülle f (von), Überfluss m (an +dat)

program ['prəʊɡræm] n (COMPUT) Programm nt ♦ vt (*machine*) programmieren, ~**me** (US **program**) n Programm nt ♦ vt planen; (*computer*) programmieren; ~**mer** (US **programer**) n Programmierer(in) m(f)

progress [n 'prəʊɡrɛs, vb prə'ɡrɛs] n Fortschritt m ♦ vi fortschreiten, weitergehen; **in ~** im Gang; ~**ion** [prə'ɡrɛʃən] n Folge f; ~**ive** [prə'ɡrɛsɪv] adj fortschrittlich, progressiv

prohibit [prə'hɪbɪt] vt verbieten; **to ~ sb from doing sth** jdm untersagen, etw zu tun; ~**ion** [prəʊɪ'bɪʃən] n Verbot nt; (US) Alkoholverbot nt, Prohibition f; ~**ive** adj unerschwinglich

project [n 'prɒdʒɛkt, vb prə'dʒɛkt] n Projekt nt ♦ vt vorausplanen; (*film etc*) projizieren; (*personality, voice*) zum Tragen bringen ♦ vi (*stick out*) hervorragen, (her)vorstehen

projectile [prə'dʒɛktaɪl] n Geschoss nt

projection [prə'dʒɛkʃən] n Projektion f; (*sth prominent*) Vorsprung m

projector [prə'dʒɛktə^r] n Projektor m

proletariat [prəʊlɪ'tɛərɪət] n Proletariat nt

pro-life [prəʊ'laɪf] adj (*movement*) Anti-Abtreibungs-; **~ campaigner** Abtreibungsgegner(in) m(f)

prolific [prə'lɪfɪk] adj fruchtbar; (*author etc*) produktiv

prologue ['prəʊlɒɡ] n Prolog m; (*event*) Vorspiel nt

prolong [prə'lɒŋ] vt verlängern

prom [prɒm] n abbr = **promenade**; **promenade concert**

Prom

ⓘ **Prom** (promenade concert) ist in Großbritannien ein Konzert, bei dem ein Teil der Zuhörer steht (ursprünglich spazieren ging). Die seit 1895 alljährlich stattfindenden Proms (seit 1941 immer in der Londoner Royal Albert Hall) zählen zu den bedeutendsten Musikereignissen in England. Der letzte Abend der Proms steht ganz im Zeichen des Patriotismus und gipfelt im Singen des Lieds „Land of Hope and Glory". In den USA und Kanada steht das Wort für promenade, ein Ball an einer High School oder einem College.

---

promenade [prɒmə'nɑːd] n Promenade f; **~ concert** n Promenadenkonzert nt

prominence ['prɒmɪnəns] n (große) Bedeutung f

prominent ['prɒmɪnənt] adj bedeutend; (*politician*) prominent; (*easily seen*) herausragend, auffallend

promiscuous [prə'mɪskjʊəs] adj lose

promise ['prɒmɪs] n Versprechen nt; (*hope: ~ of sth*) Aussicht f auf etw acc ♦ vt, vi versprechen; **promising** adj viel versprechend

promontory ['prɒməntrɪ] n Vorsprung m

promote [prə'məʊt] vt befördern; (*help on*) fördern, unterstützen; ~**r** n (*in entertainment, sport*) Veranstalter m; (*for charity etc*) Organisator m; **promotion** [prə'məʊʃən] n (*in rank*) Beförderung f; (*furtherance*) Förderung f; (COMM): **promotion (of)** Werbung f (für)

prompt [prɒmpt] *adj* prompt, schnell ♦ *adv* (*punctually*) genau ♦ *n* (COMPUT) Meldung *f* ♦ *vt* veranlassen; (THEAT) soufflieren +*dat*; **to ~ sb to do sth** jdn dazu veranlassen, etw zu tun; **~ly** *adv* sofort

prone [prəun] *adj* hingestreckt; **to be ~ to sth** zu etw neigen

prong [prɒŋ] *n* Zinke *f*

pronoun ['prəunaun] *n* Fürwort *nt*

pronounce [prə'nauns] *vt* aussprechen; (JUR) verkünden ♦ *vi*: **to ~ (on)** sich äußern (zu)

pronunciation [prənʌnsı'eıʃən] *n* Aussprache *f*

proof [pruːf] *n* Beweis *m*; (PRINT) Korrekturfahne *f*; (*of alcohol*) Alkoholgehalt *m* ♦ *adj* sicher

prop [prɒp] *n* (*also fig*) Stütze *f*; (THEAT) Requisit *nt* ♦ *vt* (*also:* ~ **up**) (ab)stützen

propaganda [prɒpə'gændə] *n* Propaganda *f*

propel [prə'pel] *vt* (an)treiben; **~ler** *n* Propeller *m*; **~ling pencil** (BRIT) *n* Drehbleistift *m*

propensity [prə'pensıtı] *n* Tendenz *f*

proper ['prɒpə'] *adj* richtig; (*seemly*) schicklich; **~ly** *adv* richtig; **~ noun** *n* Eigenname *m*

property ['prɒpətı] *n* Eigentum *nt*; (*quality*) Eigenschaft *f*; (*land*) Grundbesitz *m*; **~ owner** *n* Grundbesitzer *m*

prophecy ['prɒfısı] *n* Prophezeiung *f*

prophesy ['prɒfısaı] *vt* prophezeien

prophet ['prɒfıt] *n* Prophet *m*

proportion [prə'pɔːʃən] *n* Verhältnis *nt*; (*share*) Teil *m* ♦ *vt*: **to ~ (to)** abstimmen (auf +*acc*); **~al** *adj* proportional; **~ate** *adj* verhältnismäßig

proposal [prə'pəuzl] *n* Vorschlag *m*; (*of marriage*) Heiratsantrag *m*

propose [prə'pəuz] *vt* vorschlagen; (*toast*) ausbringen ♦ *vi* (*offer marriage*) einen Heiratsantrag machen; **to ~ to do sth** beabsichtigen, etw zu tun

proposition [prɒpə'zıʃən] *n* Angebot *nt*; (*statement*) Satz *m*

proprietor [prə'praıətə'] *n* Besitzer *m*, Eigentümer *m*

propriety [prə'praıətı] *n* Anstand *m*

pro rata [prəu'rɑːtə] *adv* anteilmäßig

prose [prəuz] *n* Prosa *f*

prosecute ['prɒsıkjuːt] *vt* (strafrechtlich) verfolgen; **prosecution** [prɒsı'kjuːʃən] *n* (JUR) strafrechtliche Verfolgung *f*; (*party*) Anklage *f*; **prosecutor** *n* Vertreter *m* der Anklage; **Public Prosecutor** Staatsanwalt *m*

prospect [*n* 'prɒspekt, *vb* prə'spekt] *n* Aussicht *f* ♦ *vt* auf Bodenschätze hin untersuchen ♦ *vi*: **to ~ (for)** suchen (nach); **~ing** ['prɒspektıŋ] *n* (*for minerals*) Suche *f*; **~ive** [prə'spektıv] *adj* (*son-in-law etc*) zukünftig; (*customer, candidate*) voraussichtlich

prospectus [prə'spektəs] *n* (Werbe)prospekt *m*

prosper ['prɒspə'] *vi* blühen, gedeihen; (*person*) erfolgreich sein; **~ity** [prɒ'sperıtı] *n* Wohlstand *m*; **~ous** *adj* wohlhabend, reich

prostitute ['prɒstıtjuːt] *n* Prostituierte *f*

prostrate ['prɒstreıt] *adj* ausgestreckt (liegend)

protagonist [prə'tægənıst] *n* Hauptperson *f*, Held *m*

protect [prə'tekt] *vt* (be)schützen; **~ed species** *n* geschützte Art; **~ion** [prə'tekʃən] *n* Schutz *m*; **~ive** *adj* Schutz-, (be)schützend

protégé ['prəuteʒeı] *n* Schützling *m*

protein ['prəutiːn] *n* Protein *nt*, Eiweiß *nt*

protest [*n* 'prəutest, *vb* prə'test] *n* Protest *m* ♦ *vi* protestieren ♦ *vt* (*affirm*) beteuern

Protestant ['prɒtıstənt] *adj* protestantisch ♦ *n* Protestant(in) *m(f)*

protester [prə'testə'] *n* (*demonstrator*) Demonstrant(in) *m(f)*

protracted [prə'træktıd] *adj* sich hinziehend

protrude [prə'truːd] *vi* (her)vorstehen

proud [praud] *adj*: **~ (of)** stolz (auf +*acc*)

prove [pruːv] *vt* beweisen ♦ *vi*: **to ~ (to be) correct** sich als richtig erweisen; **to ~ o.s.** sich bewähren

proverb ['prɒvəːb] *n* Sprichwort *nt*; **~ial** [prə'vəːbıəl] *adj* sprichwörtlich

provide [prə'vaıd] *vt* versehen; (*supply*) besorgen; **to ~ sb with sth** jdn mit etw versorgen; **~ for** *vt fus* sorgen für; *(emergency)* Vorkehrungen treffen für; **~d (that)** *conj* vorausgesetzt(, dass)

providing [prə'vaɪdɪŋ] *conj* vorausgesetzt(, dass)

province ['prɒvɪns] *n* Provinz *f*; *(division of work)* Bereich *m*; **provincial** [prə'vɪnʃəl] *adj* provinziell, Provinz-

provision [prə'vɪʒən] *n* Vorkehrung *f*; *(condition)* Bestimmung *f*; **~s** *npl (food)* Vorräte *pl*, Proviant *m*; **~al** *adj* provisorisch

proviso [prə'vaɪzəʊ] *n* Bedingung *f*

provocative [prə'vɒkətɪv] *adj* provozierend

provoke [prə'vəʊk] *vt* provozieren; *(cause)* hervorrufen

prowess ['praʊɪs] *n* überragende(s) Können *nt*

prowl [praʊl] *vi* herumstreichen; *(animal)* schleichen ♦ *n*: **on the ~** umherstreifend; **~er** *n* Herumtreiber(in) *m(f)*

proximity [prɒk'sɪmɪtɪ] *n* Nähe *f*

proxy ['prɒksɪ] *n* (Stell)vertreter *m*; *(authority, document)* Vollmacht *f*; **by ~** durch einen Stellvertreter

prudent ['pru:dnt] *adj* klug, umsichtig

prudish ['pru:dɪʃ] *adj* prüde

prune [pru:n] *n* Backpflaume *f* ♦ *vt* ausputzen; *(fig)* zurechtstutzen

pry [praɪ] *vi*: **to ~ (into)** seine Nase stecken (in +*acc*)

PS *n abbr* (= *postscript*) PS

pseudonym ['sju:dənɪm] *n* Pseudonym *nt*, Deckname *m*

psychiatric [saɪkɪ'ætrɪk] *adj* psychiatrisch

psychiatrist [saɪ'kaɪətrɪst] *n* Psychiater *m*

psychic ['saɪkɪk] *adj (also:* **~al)** übersinnlich; *(person)* paranormal begabt

psychoanalyse [saɪkəʊ'ænəlaɪz] *(US* **psychoanalyze)** *vt* psychoanalytisch behandeln; **psychoanalyst** [saɪkəʊ'ænəlɪst] *n* Psychoanalytiker(in) *m(f)*

psychological [saɪkə'lɒdʒɪkl] *adj* psychologisch; **psychologist** [saɪ'kɒlədʒɪst] *n* Psychologe *m*, Psychologin *f*; **psychology** [saɪ'kɒlədʒɪ] *n* Psychologie *f*

PTO *abbr* = **please turn over**

pub [pʌb] *n abbr* (= *public house*) Kneipe *f*

---

pubic ['pju:bɪk] *adj* Scham-

public ['pʌblɪk] *adj* öffentlich ♦ *n (also:* **general ~)** Öffentlichkeit *f*; **in ~** in der Öffentlichkeit; **~ address system** *n* Lautsprecheranlage *f*

publican ['pʌblɪkən] *n* Wirt *m*

publication [pʌblɪ'keɪʃən] *n* Veröffentlichung *f*

public: **~ company** *n* Aktiengesellschaft *f*; **~ convenience** *(BRIT)* *n* öffentliche Toiletten *pl*; **~ holiday** *n* gesetzliche(r) Feiertag *m*; **~ house** *(BRIT)* *n* Lokal *nt*, Kneipe *f*

publicity [pʌb'lɪsɪtɪ] *n* Publicity *f*, Werbung *f*

publicize ['pʌblɪsaɪz] *vt* bekannt machen; *(advertise)* Publicity machen für

publicly ['pʌblɪklɪ] *adv* öffentlich

public: **~ opinion** *n* öffentliche Meinung *f*; **~ relations** *npl* Publicrelations *pl*, Public Relations *pl*; **~ school** *n (BRIT)* Privatschule *f*; *(US)* staatliche Schule *f*; **~-spirited** *adj* mit Gemeinschaftssinn; **~ transport** *n* öffentliche Verkehrsmittel *pl*

publish ['pʌblɪʃ] *vt* veröffentlichen; *(event)* bekannt geben; **~er** *n* Verleger *m*; **~ing** *n (business)* Verlagswesen *nt*

pub lunch *n* in Pubs servierter Imbiss

pucker ['pʌkər] *vt (face)* verziehen; *(lips)* kräuseln

pudding ['pʊdɪŋ] *n (BRIT: course)* Nachtisch *m*; Pudding *m*; **black ~** ≈ Blutwurst *f*

puddle ['pʌdl] *n* Pfütze *f*

puff [pʌf] *n (of wind etc)* Stoß *m*; *(cosmetic)*

Puderquaste f ♦ vt blasen, pusten; (*pipe*)
paffen ♦ vi keuchen, schnaufen; (*smoke*)
paffen; **to ~ out smoke** Rauch ausstoßen;
~ pastry (*US* **~ paste**) n Blätterteig m; **~y**
adj aufgedunsen

pull [pul] n Ruck m; (*influence*) Beziehung f
♦ vt ziehen; (*trigger*) abdrücken ♦ vi ziehen;
to ~ sb's leg jdn auf den Arm nehmen; **to
~ to pieces** in Stücke reißen; (*fig*)
verreißen; **to ~ one's punches** sich
zurückhalten; **to ~ one's weight** sich in die
Riemen legen; **to ~ o.s. together** sich
zusammenreißen; **~ apart** vt (*break*)
zerreißen; (*dismantle*) auseinander nehmen;
(*separate*) trennen; **~ down** vt (*house*)
abreißen; **~ in** vi hineinfahren; (*stop*)
anhalten; (*RAIL*) einfahren; **~ off** vt (*deal
etc*) abschließen; **~ out** vi (*car*)
herausfahren; (*fig: partner*) aussteigen ♦ vt
herausziehen; **~ over** vi (*AUT*) an die Seite
fahren; **~ through** vi durchkommen; **~
up** vi anhalten ♦ vt (*uproot*) herausreißen;
(*stop*) anhalten

pulley [ˈpulɪ] n Rolle f, Flaschenzug m
pullover [ˈpuləʊvəʳ] n Pullover m
pulp [pʌlp] n Brei m; (*of fruit*) Fruchtfleisch nt
pulpit [ˈpulpɪt] n Kanzel f
pulsate [pʌlˈseɪt] vi pulsieren
pulse [pʌls] n Puls m; **~s** npl (*BOT*)
Hülsenfrüchte pl
pummel [ˈpʌml] vt mit den Fäusten
bearbeiten
pump [pʌmp] n Pumpe f; (*shoe*) leichter
(Tanz)schuh m ♦ vt pumpen; **~ up** vt (*tyre*)
aufpumpen
pumpkin [ˈpʌmpkɪn] n Kürbis m
pun [pʌn] n Wortspiel nt
punch [pʌntʃ] n (*tool*) Locher m; (*blow*)
(Faust)schlag m; (*drink*) Punsch m, Bowle f
♦ vt lochen; (*strike*) schlagen, boxen; **~ line**
n Pointe f; **~-up** (*BRIT: inf*) n Keilerei f
punctual [ˈpʌŋktjʊəl] adj pünktlich
punctuate [ˈpʌŋktjuet] vt mit Satzzeichen
versehen; (*fig*) unterbrechen; **punctuation**
[pʌŋktjuˈeɪʃən] n Zeichensetzung f,
Interpunktion f
puncture [ˈpʌŋktʃəʳ] n Loch nt; (*AUT*)

Reifenpanne f ♦ vt durchbohren
pundit [ˈpʌndɪt] n Gelehrte(r) m
pungent [ˈpʌndʒənt] adj scharf
punish [ˈpʌnɪʃ] vt bestrafen; (*in boxing etc*)
übel zurichten; **~ment** n Strafe f; (*action*)
Bestrafung f
punk [pʌŋk] n (*also:* **~ rocker**) Punker(in)
m(f); (*also:* **~ rock**) Punk m; (*US: inf:
hoodlum*) Ganove m
punt [pʌnt] n Stechkahn m
punter [ˈpʌntəʳ] (*BRIT*) n (*better*) Wetter m
puny [ˈpjuːnɪ] adj kümmerlich
pup [pʌp] n = **puppy**
pupil [ˈpjuːpl] n Schüler(in) m(f); (*in eye*)
Pupille f
puppet [ˈpʌpɪt] n Puppe f; Marionette f
puppy [ˈpʌpɪ] n junge(r) Hund m
purchase [ˈpɜːtʃɪs] n Kauf m; (*grip*) Halt m
♦ vt kaufen, erwerben; **~r** n Käufer(in) m(f)
pure [pjuəʳ] adj (*also fig*) rein; **~ly** [ˈpjuəlɪ]
adv rein
purgatory [ˈpɜːgətərɪ] n Fegefeuer nt
purge [pɜːdʒ] n (*also POL*) Säuberung f ♦ vt
reinigen; (*body*) entschlacken
purify [ˈpjuərɪfaɪ] vt reinigen
purity [ˈpjuərɪtɪ] n Reinheit f
purple [ˈpɜːpl] adj violett; (*face*) dunkelrot
purport [pɜːˈpɔːt] vt vorgeben
purpose [ˈpɜːpəs] n Zweck m, Ziel nt; (*of
person*) Absicht f; **on ~** absichtlich; **~ful** adj
zielbewusst, entschlossen
purr [pɜːʳ] n Schnurren nt ♦ vi schnurren
purse [pɜːs] n Portemonnaie nt, Portmonee
nt, Geldbeutel m ♦ vt (*lips*)
zusammenpressen, schürzen
purser [ˈpɜːsəʳ] n Zahlmeister m
pursue [pəˈsjuː] vt verfolgen; (*study*)
nachgehen +dat; **~r** n Verfolger m; **pursuit**
[pəˈsjuːt] n Verfolgung f; (*occupation*)
Beschäftigung f
pus [pʌs] n Eiter m
push [puʃ] n Stoß m, Schub m; (*MIL*) Vorstoß
m ♦ vt stoßen, schieben; (*button*) drücken;
(*idea*) durchsetzen ♦ vi stoßen, schieben; **~
aside** vt beiseite schieben; **~ off** (*inf*) vi
abschieben; **~ on** vi weitermachen; **~
through** vt durchdrücken; (*policy*)

durchsetzen; **~ up** vt (*total*) erhöhen; (*prices*) hoch treiben; **~chair** (*BRIT*) n (Kinder)sportwagen m; **~er** n (*drug dealer*) Pusher m; **~over** (*inf*) n Kinderspiel nt; **~ up** (*US*) n (*press-up*) Liegestütz m; **~y** (*inf*) adj aufdringlich

puss [pʊs] n Mieze(katze) f; **~y(cat)** n Mieze(katze) f

put [pʊt] (*pt, pp* put) vt setzen, stellen, legen; (*express*) ausdrücken, sagen; (*write*) schreiben; **~ about** vi (*turn back*) wenden ♦ vt (*spread*) verbreiten; **~ across** vt (*explain*) erklären; **~ away** vt (*store*) beiseite legen; **~ back** vt zurückstellen *or* -legen; **~ by** vt zurücklegen, sparen; **~ down** vt hinstellen *or* -legen; (*rebellion*) niederschlagen; (*animal*) einschläfern; (*in writing*) niederschreiben; **~ forward** vt (*idea*) vorbringen; (*clock*) vorstellen; **~ in** vt (*application, complaint*) einreichen; **~ off** vt verschieben; (*discourage*): **to ~ sb off sth** jdn von etw abbringen; **~ on** vt (*clothes etc*) anziehen; (*light etc*) anschalten, anmachen; (*play etc*) aufführen; (*brake*) anziehen; **~ out** vt (*hand etc*) (her)ausstrecken; (*news, rumour*) verbreiten; (*light etc*) ausschalten, ausmachen; **~ through** vt (*TEL: person*) verbinden; (: *call*) durchstellen; **~ up** vt (*tent*) aufstellen; (*building*) errichten; (*price*) erhöhen; (*person*) unterbringen; **~ up with** vt fus sich abfinden mit

putrid [ˈpjuːtrɪd] adj faul

putt [pʌt] vt (*golf*) putten ♦ n (*golf*) Putten nt; **~ing green** n kleine(r) Golfplatz m nur zum Putten

putty [ˈpʌtɪ] n Kitt m; (*fig*) Wachs nt

put-up [ˈpʊtʌp] adj: **~ job** abgekartete(s) Spiel nt

puzzle [ˈpʌzl] n Rätsel nt; (*toy*) Geduldspiel nt ♦ vt verwirren ♦ vi sich den Kopf zerbrechen; **~d** adj verdutzt, verblüfft; **puzzling** adj rätselhaft, verwirrend

pyjamas [pəˈdʒɑːməz] (*BRIT*) npl Schlafanzug m, Pyjama m

pylon [ˈpaɪlən] n Mast m

pyramid [ˈpɪrəmɪd] n Pyramide f

Q, q

quack [kwæk] n Quaken nt; (*doctor*) Quacksalber m ♦ vi quaken

quad [kwɒd] n abbr = **quadrangle**; **quadruplet**

quadrangle [ˈkwɒdræŋgl] n (*court*) Hof m; (*MATH*) Viereck nt

quadruple [kwɒˈdruːpl] adj ♦ vi sich vervierfachen ♦ vt vervierfachen

quadruplets [kwɒˈdruːplɪts] npl Vierlinge pl

quagmire [ˈkwæɡmaɪəʳ] n Morast m

quail [kweɪl] n (*bird*) Wachtel f ♦ vi (vor Angst) zittern

quaint [kweɪnt] adj kurios; malerisch

quake [kweɪk] vi beben, zittern ♦ n abbr = **earthquake**

qualification [kwɒlɪfɪˈkeɪʃən] n Qualifikation f; (*sth which limits*) Einschränkung f

qualified [ˈkwɒlɪfaɪd] adj (*competent*) qualifiziert; (*limited*) bedingt

qualify [ˈkwɒlɪfaɪ] vt (*prepare*) befähigen; (*limit*) einschränken ♦ vi sich qualifizieren; **to ~ as a doctor/lawyer** sein medizinisches/juristisches Staatsexamen machen

quality [ˈkwɒlɪtɪ] n Qualität f; (*characteristic*) Eigenschaft f

> **Quality press**

> ⓘ **Quality press** *bezeichnet die seriösen Tages- und Wochenzeitungen, im Gegensatz zu den Massenblättern. Diese Zeitungen sind fast alle großformatig und wenden sich an den anspruchsvolleren Leser, der voll informiert sein möchte und bereit ist, für die Zeitungslektüre viel Zeit aufzuwenden. Siehe auch* **tabloid press**.

quality time n intensiv genutzte Zeit

qualm [kwɑːm] n Bedenken nt

quandary [ˈkwɒndrɪ] n: **to be in a ~** in Verlegenheit sein

quantity [ˈkwɒntɪtɪ] n Menge f; **~ surveyor**

n Baukostenkalkulator m

quarantine ['kwɒrəntiːn] n Quarantäne f

quarrel ['kwɒrl] n Streit m ♦ vi sich streiten; **~some** adj streitsüchtig

quarry ['kwɒrɪ] n Steinbruch m; (animal) Wild nt; (fig) Opfer nt

quarter ['kwɔːtər] n Viertel nt; (of year) Quartal nt ♦ vt (divide) vierteln; (MIL) einquartieren; **~s** npl (esp MIL) Quartier nt; **~ of an hour** Viertelstunde f; **~ final** n Viertelfinale nt; **~ly** adj vierteljährlich

quartet(te) [kwɔː'tet] n Quartett nt

quartz [kwɔːts] n Quarz m

quash [kwɒʃ] vt (verdict) aufheben

quaver ['kweɪvər] vi (tremble) zittern

quay [kiː] n Kai m

queasy ['kwiːzɪ] adj übel

queen [kwiːn] n Königin f; **~ mother** n Königinmutter f

queer [kwɪər] adj seltsam ♦ n (inf: homosexual) Schwule(r) m

quell [kwel] vt unterdrücken

quench [kwentʃ] vt (thirst) löschen

querulous ['kwerʊləs] adj nörglerisch

query ['kwɪərɪ] n (question) (An)frage f; (question mark) Fragezeichen nt ♦ vt in Zweifel ziehen, infrage or in Frage stellen

quest [kwest] n Suche f

question ['kwestʃən] n Frage f ♦ vt (ask) (be)fragen; (suspect) verhören; (doubt) infrage or in Frage stellen, bezweifeln; **beyond ~** ohne Frage; **out of the ~** ausgeschlossen; **~able** adj zweifelhaft; **~ mark** n Fragezeichen nt

questionnaire [kwestʃə'neər] n Fragebogen m

queue [kjuː] (BRIT) n Schlange f ♦ vi (also: ~ up) Schlange stehen

quibble ['kwɪbl] vi kleinlich sein

quick [kwɪk] adj schnell ♦ n (of nail) Nagelhaut f; **be ~!** mach schnell!; **cut to the ~** (fig) tief getroffen; **~en** vt (hasten) beschleunigen ♦ vi sich beschleunigen; **~ly** adv schnell; **~sand** n Treibsand m; **~-witted** adj schlagfertig

quid [kwɪd] (BRIT: inf) n Pfund nt

quiet ['kwaɪət] adj (without noise) leise;

(peaceful, calm) still, ruhig ♦ n Stille f, Ruhe f ♦ vt, vi (US) = **quieten**; **keep ~!** sei still!; **~en** vi (also: **~en down**) ruhig werden ♦ vt beruhigen; **~ly** adv leise, ruhig; **~ness** n Ruhe f, Stille f

quilt [kwɪlt] n (continental ~) Steppdecke f

quin [kwɪn] n abbr = **quintuplet**

quintuplets [kwɪn'tjuːplɪts] npl Fünflinge pl

quip [kwɪp] n witzige Bemerkung f

quirk [kwəːk] n (oddity) Eigenart f

quit [kwɪt] (pt, pp **quit** or **quitted**) vt verlassen ♦ vi aufhören

quite [kwaɪt] adv (completely) ganz, völlig; (fairly) ziemlich; **~ a few of them** ziemlich viele von ihnen; **~ (so)!** richtig!

quits [kwɪts] adj quitt; **let's call it ~** lassen wirs gut sein

quiver ['kwɪvər] vi zittern ♦ n (for arrows) Köcher m

quiz [kwɪz] n (competition) Quiz nt ♦ vt prüfen; **~zical** adj fragend

quota ['kwəʊtə] n Anteil m; (COMM) Quote f

quotation [kwəʊ'teɪʃən] n Zitat nt; (price) Kostenvoranschlag m; **~ marks** npl Anführungszeichen pl

quote [kwəʊt] n = **quotation** ♦ vi (from book) zitieren ♦ vt zitieren; (price) angeben

R, r

rabbi ['ræbaɪ] n Rabbiner m; (title) Rabbi m

rabbit ['ræbɪt] n Kaninchen nt; **~ hole** n Kaninchenbau m; **~ hutch** n Kaninchenstall m

rabble ['ræbl] n Pöbel m

rabies ['reɪbiːz] n Tollwut f

RAC (BRIT) n abbr = **Royal Automobile Club**

raccoon [rə'kuːn] n Waschbär m

race [reɪs] n (species) Rasse f; (competition) Rennen nt; (on foot) Rennen nt, Wettlauf m; (rush) Hetze f ♦ vt um die Wette laufen mit; (horses) laufen lassen ♦ vi (run) rennen; (in contest) am Rennen teilnehmen; **~ car** (US) n = **racing car**; **~ car driver** (US) n = **racing driver**; **~course** n (for horses) Rennbahn f; **~horse** n Rennpferd nt; **~r** n (*person*) Rennfahrer(in) *m(f)*; (*car*) Rennwagen *m*; ~**track** *n* (*for cars etc*) Rennstrecke *f*

racial ['reɪʃl] *adj* Rassen-

racing ['reɪsɪŋ] *n* Rennen *nt*; ~ **car** (*BRIT*) *n* Rennwagen *m*; ~ **driver** (*BRIT*) *n* Rennfahrer *m*

racism ['reɪsɪzəm] *n* Rassismus *m*; **racist** ['reɪsɪst] *n* Rassist *m* ♦ *adj* rassistisch

rack [ræk] *n* Ständer *m*, Gestell *nt* ♦ *vt* plagen; **to go to ~ and ruin** verfallen; **to ~ one's brains** sich *dat* den Kopf zerbrechen

racket ['rækɪt] *n* (*din*) Krach *m*; (*scheme*) (Schwindel)geschäft *nt*; (*TENNIS*) (Tennis)schläger *m*

racquet ['rækɪt] *n* (Tennis)schläger *m*

racy ['reɪsɪ] *adj* gewagt; (*style*) spritzig

radar ['reɪdɑːʳ] *n* Radar *nt or m*

radial ['reɪdɪəl] *adj* (*also: US:* **~-ply**) radial

radiant ['reɪdɪənt] *adj* strahlend; (*giving out rays*) Strahlungs-

radiate ['reɪdɪeɪt] *vi* ausstrahlen; (*roads, lines*) strahlenförmig wegführen ♦ *vt* ausstrahlen; **radiation** [reɪdɪ'eɪʃən] *n* (Aus)strahlung *f*

radiator ['reɪdɪeɪtəʳ] *n* (*for heating*) Heizkörper *m*; (*AUT*) Kühler *m*

radical ['rædɪkl] *adj* radikal

radii ['reɪdɪaɪ] *npl of* **radius**

radio ['reɪdɪəu] *n* Rundfunk *m*, Radio *nt*; (*set*) Radio *nt*, Radioapparat *m*; **on the ~** im Radio; ~**active** ['reɪdɪəu'æktɪv] *adj* radioaktiv; ~ **cassette** *n* Radiorekorder *m*; ~**-controlled** *adj* ferngesteuert; ~**logy** [reɪdɪ'ɔlədʒɪ] *n* Strahlenkunde *f*; ~ **station** *n* Rundfunkstation *f*; ~**therapy** ['reɪdɪəu'θerəpɪ] *n* Röntgentherapie *f*

radish ['rædɪʃ] *n* (*big*) Rettich *m*; (*small*) Radieschen *nt*

radius ['reɪdɪəs] (*pl* **radii**) *n* Radius *m*; (*area*) Umkreis *m*

RAF *n abbr* = **Royal Air Force**

raffle ['ræfl] *n* Verlosung *f*, Tombola *f* ♦ *vt* verlosen

raft [rɑːft] *n* Floß *nt*

rafter ['rɑːftəʳ] *n* Dachsparren *m*

rag [ræg] *n* (*cloth*) Lumpen *m*, Lappen *m*; (*inf: newspaper*) Käseblatt *nt*; (*UNIV: for*

charity) studentische Sammelaktion *f* ♦ *vt* (*BRIT*) auf den Arm nehmen; ~**s** *npl* (*cloth*) Lumpen *pl*; ~ **doll** *n* Flickenpuppe *f*

rage [reɪdʒ] *n* Wut *f*; (*fashion*) große Mode *f* ♦ *vi* wüten, toben

ragged ['rægɪd] *adj* (*edge*) gezackt; (*clothes*) zerlumpt

raid [reɪd] *n* Überfall *m*; (*MIL*) Angriff *m*; (*by police*) Razzia *f* ♦ *vt* überfallen

rail [reɪl] *n* (*also RAIL*) Schiene *f*; (*on stair*) Geländer *nt*; (*of ship*) Reling *f*; ~**s** *npl* (*RAIL*) Geleise *pl*; **by ~** per Bahn; ~**ing(s)** *n(pl)* Geländer *nt*; ~**road** (*US*) *n* Eisenbahn *f*; ~**way** (*BRIT*) *n* Eisenbahn *f*; ~**way line** (*BRIT*) *n* (Eisen)bahnlinie *f*; (*track*) Gleis *nt*; ~**wayman** (*irreg; BRIT*) *n* Eisenbahner *m*; ~**way station** (*BRIT*) *n* Bahnhof *m*

rain [reɪn] *n* Regen *m* ♦ *vt, vi* regnen; **in the ~** im Regen; **it's ~ing** es regnet; ~**bow** *n* Regenbogen *m*; ~**coat** *n* Regenmantel *m*; ~**drop** *n* Regentropfen *m*; ~**fall** *n* Niederschlag *m*; ~**forest** *n* Regenwald *m*; ~**y** *adj* (*region, season*) Regen-; (*day*) regnerisch, verregnet

raise [reɪz] *n* (*esp US: increase*) (Gehalts)erhöhung *f* ♦ *vt* (*lift*) (hoch)heben; (*increase*) erhöhen; (*question*) aufwerfen; (*doubts*) äußern; (*funds*) beschaffen; (*family*) großziehen; (*livestock*) züchten; **to ~ one's voice** die Stimme erheben

raisin ['reɪzn] *n* Rosine *f*

rake [reɪk] *n* Rechen *m*, Harke *f*; Wüstling *m* ♦ *vt* rechen, harken; (*search*) (durch)suchen

rally ['rælɪ] *n* (*POL etc*) Kundgebung *f*; (*AUT*) Rallye *f* ♦ *vt* (*MIL*) sammeln ♦ *vi* Kräfte sammeln; ~ **round** *vt fus* (sich) scharen um; (*help*) zu Hilfe kommen +*dat* ♦ *vi* zu Hilfe kommen

RAM [ræm] *n abbr* (= **random access memory**) RAM *m*

Ramadan ['ræmədɑːn] *n* Ramadan *m*

ram [ræm] *n* Widder *m* ♦ *vt* (*hit*) rammen; (*stuff*) (hinein)stopfen

ramble ['ræmbl] *n* Wanderung *f* ♦ *vi* (*talk*) schwafeln; ~**r** *n* Wanderer *m*; **rambling** *adj* (*speech*) weitschweifig; (*town*) ausgedehnt

ramp [ræmp] *n* Rampe *f*; **on/off ~** (*US: AUT*)

Ein-/Ausfahrt f

rampage [ræm'peɪdʒ] n: **to be on the ~** randalieren ♦ vi randalieren

rampant ['ræmpənt] adj wild wuchernd

rampart ['ræmpɑːt] n (Schutz)wall m

ram raid n Raubüberfall, bei dem eine Geschäftsfront mit einem Fahrzeug gerammt wird

ramshackle ['ræmʃækl] adj baufällig

ran [ræn] pt of **run**

ranch [rɑːntʃ] n Ranch f

rancid ['rænsɪd] adj ranzig

rancour ['ræŋkəʳ] (US **rancor**) n Verbitterung f, Groll m

random ['rændəm] adj ziellos, wahllos ♦ n: **at ~** aufs Geratewohl; **~ access** n (COMPUT) wahlfreie(r) Zugriff m

randy ['rændɪ] (BRIT: inf) adj geil, scharf

rang [ræŋ] pt of **ring**

range [reɪndʒ] n Reihe f; (of mountains) Kette f; (COMM) Sortiment nt; (reach) (Reich)weite f; (of gun) Schussweite f; (for shooting practice) Schießplatz m; (stove) (großer) Herd m ♦ vt (set in row) anordnen, aufstellen; (roam) durchstreifen ♦ vi: **to ~ over** (wander) umherstreifen in +dat; (extend) sich erstrecken auf +acc; **a ~ of** (selection) eine (große) Auswahl an +dat; **prices ranging from £5 to £10** Preise, die sich zwischen £5 und £10 bewegen; **~r** ['reɪndʒəʳ] n Förster m

rank [ræŋk] n (row) Reihe f; (BRIT: also: **taxi ~**) (Taxi)stand m; (MIL) Rang m; (social position) Stand m ♦ vi (have ~): **to ~ among** gehören zu ♦ adj (strong-smelling) stinkend; (extreme) kraß; **the ~ and file** (fig) die breite Masse

rankle ['ræŋkl] vi nagen

ransack ['rænsæk] vt (plunder) plündern; (search) durchwühlen

ransom ['rænsəm] n Lösegeld nt; **to hold sb to ~** jdn gegen Lösegeld festhalten

rant [rænt] vi hochtrabend reden

rap [ræp] n Schlag m; (music) Rap m ♦ vt klopfen

rape [reɪp] n Vergewaltigung f; (BOT) Raps m ♦ vt vergewaltigen; **~(seed) oil** n Rapsöl nt

rapid ['ræpɪd] adj rasch, schnell; **~ity** [rə'pɪdɪtɪ] n Schnelligkeit f; **~s** npl Stromschnellen pl

rapist ['reɪpɪst] n Vergewaltiger m

rapport [ræ'pɔːʳ] n gute(s) Verhältnis nt

rapture ['ræptʃəʳ] n Entzücken nt; **rapturous** ['ræptʃərəs] adj (applause) stürmisch; (expression) verzückt

rare [rɛəʳ] adj selten, rar; (underdone) nicht durchgebraten; **~ly** ['rɛəlɪ] adv selten

raring ['rɛərɪŋ] adj: **to be ~ to go** (inf) es kaum erwarten können, bis es losgeht

rarity ['rɛərɪtɪ] n Seltenheit f

rascal ['rɑːskl] n Schuft m

rash [ræʃ] adj übereilt; (reckless) unbesonnen ♦ n (Haut)ausschlag m

rasher ['ræʃəʳ] n Speckscheibe f

raspberry ['rɑːzbərɪ] n Himbeere f

rasping ['rɑːspɪŋ] adj (noise) kratzend; (voice) krächzend

rat [ræt] n (animal) Ratte f; (person) Halunke m

rate [reɪt] n (proportion) Rate f; (price) Tarif m; (speed) Tempo nt ♦ vt (ein)schätzen; **~s** npl (BRIT: tax) Grundsteuer f; **to ~ as** für etw halten; **~able value** (BRIT) n Einheitswert m (als Bemessungsgrundlage); **~payer** (BRIT) n Steuerzahler(in) m(f)

rather ['rɑːðəʳ] adv (in preference) lieber, eher; (to some extent) ziemlich; **I would** or **I'd ~ go** ich würde lieber gehen; **it's ~ expensive** (quite) es ist ziemlich teuer; (too) es ist etwas zu teuer; **there's ~ a lot** es ist ziemlich viel

ratify ['rætɪfaɪ] vt (POL) ratifizieren

rating ['reɪtɪŋ] n Klasse f

ratio ['reɪʃɪəʊ] n Verhältnis nt; **in the ~ of 100 to 1** im Verhältnis 100 zu 1

ration ['ræʃən] n (usu pl) Ration f ♦ vt rationieren

rational ['ræʃənl] adj rational

rationale [ræʃə'nɑːl] n Grundprinzip nt

rationalize ['ræʃnəlaɪz] vt rationalisieren

rat race n Konkurrenzkampf m

rattle ['rætl] n (sound) Rasseln nt; (toy) Rassel f ♦ vi ratteln, klappern ♦ vt rasseln mit; **~snake** n Klapperschlange f

raucous ['rɔːkəs] *adj* heiser, rau

rave [reɪv] *vi* (*talk wildly*) fantasieren; (*rage*) toben ♦ *n* (BRIT: *inf*: *party*) Rave *m*, Fete *f*

raven ['reɪvən] *n* Rabe *m*

ravenous ['rævənəs] *adj* heißhungrig

ravine [rə'viːn] *n* Schlucht *f*

raving ['reɪvɪŋ] *adj*: **~ lunatic** völlig Wahnsinnige(r) *mf*

ravishing ['rævɪʃɪŋ] *adj* atemberaubend

raw [rɔː] *adj* roh; (*tender*) wund (gerieben); (*inexperienced*) unerfahren; **to get a ~ deal** (*inf*) schlecht wegkommen; **~ material** *n* Rohmaterial *nt*

ray [reɪ] *n* (*of light*) Strahl *m*; **~ of hope** Hoffnungsschimmer *m*

raze [reɪz] *vt* (*also*: **~ to the ground**) dem Erdboden gleichmachen

razor ['reɪzər] *n* Rasierapparat *m*; **~ blade** *n* Rasierklinge *f*

Rd *abbr* = **road**

RE (BRIT: SCH) *abbr* (= *religious education*) Religionsunterricht *m*

re [riː] *prep* (COMM) betreffs +*gen*

reach [riːtʃ] *n* Reichweite *f*; (*of river*) Strecke *f* ♦ *vt* (*arrive at*) erreichen; (*give*) reichen ♦ *vi* (*stretch*) sich erstrecken; **within ~** (*shops etc*) in erreichbarer Weite *or* Entfernung; **out of ~** außer Reichweite; **to ~ for** (*try to get*) langen nach; **~ out** *vi* die Hand ausstrecken; **to ~ out for sth** nach etw greifen

react [riː'ækt] *vi* reagieren; **~ion** [riː'ækʃən] *n* Reaktion *f*; **~or** [riː'æktər] *n* Reaktor *m*

read¹ [red] *pt, pp of* **read²**

read² [riːd] (*pt, pp* **read**) *vt, vi* lesen; (*aloud*) vorlesen; **~ out** *vt* vorlesen; **~able** *adj* leserlich; (*worth ~ing*) lesenswert; **~er** *n* (*person*) Leser(in) *m(f)*; **~ership** *n* Leserschaft *f*

readily ['redɪlɪ] *adv* (*willingly*) bereitwillig; (*easily*) prompt

readiness ['redɪnɪs] *n* (*willingness*) Bereitwilligkeit *f*; (*being ready*) Bereitschaft *f*; **in ~** (*prepared*) bereit

reading ['riːdɪŋ] *n* Lesen *nt*

readjust [riːə'dʒʌst] *vt* neu einstellen ♦ *vi* (*person*): **to ~ to** sich wieder anpassen an

ready ['redɪ] *adj* (*prepared, willing*) bereit ♦ *adv*: **~-cooked** vorgekocht ♦ *n*: **at the ~** bereit; **~-made** *adj* gebrauchsfertig, Fertig-; (*clothes*) Konfektions-; **~ money** *n* Bargeld *nt*; **~ reckoner** *n* Rechentabelle *f*; **~-to-wear** *adj* Konfektions-

real [rɪəl] *adj* wirklich; (*actual*) eigentlich; (*not fake*) echt; **in ~ terms** effektiv; **~ estate** *n* Grundbesitz *m*; **~istic** [rɪə'lɪstɪk] *adj* realistisch

reality [riː'ælɪtɪ] *n* Wirklichkeit *f*, Realität *f*; **in ~** in Wirklichkeit

realization [rɪəlaɪ'zeɪʃən] *n* (*understanding*) Erkenntnis *f*; (*fulfilment*) Verwirklichung *f*

realize ['rɪəlaɪz] *vt* (*understand*) begreifen; (*make real*) verwirklichen; **I didn't ~ ...** ich wusste nicht, ...

really ['rɪəlɪ] *adv* wirklich; **~?** (*indicating interest*) tatsächlich?; (*expressing surprise*) wirklich?

realm [relm] *n* Reich *nt*

realtor ['rɪəltɔːr] (US) *n* Grundstücks-makler(in) *m(f)*

reap [riːp] *vt* ernten

reappear [riːə'pɪər] *vi* wieder erscheinen

rear [rɪər] *adj* hintere(r, s), Rück- ♦ *n* Rückseite *f*; (*last part*) Schluss *m* ♦ *vt* (*bring up*) aufziehen ♦ *vi* (*horse*) sich aufbäumen; **~guard** *n* Nachhut *f*

rearmament [riː'ɑːməmənt] *n* Wiederaufrüstung *f*

rearrange [riːə'reɪndʒ] *vt* umordnen

rear-view mirror ['rɪəvjuː-] *n* Rückspiegel *m*

reason ['riːzn] *n* (*cause*) Grund *m*; (*ability to think*) Verstand *m*; (*sensible thoughts*) Vernunft *f* ♦ *vi* (*think*) denken; (*use arguments*) argumentieren; **it stands to ~ that** es ist logisch, dass; **to ~ with sb** mit jdm diskutieren; **~able** *adj* vernünftig; **~ably** *adv* vernünftig; (*fairly*) ziemlich; **~ed** *adj* (*argument*) durchdacht; **~ing** *n* Urteilen *nt*; (*argumentation*) Beweisführung *f*

reassurance [riːə'ʃuərəns] *n* Beruhigung *f*; (*confirmation*) Bestätigung *f*; **reassure** [riːə'ʃuər] *vt* beruhigen; **to reassure sb of**

sth jdm etw versichern
rebate ['riːbeɪt] n Rückzahlung f
rebel [n 'rebl, vb rɪ'bel] n Rebell m ♦ vi
rebellieren; **~lion** [rɪ'beljən] n Rebellion f,
Aufstand m; **~lious** [rɪ'beljəs] adj rebellisch
rebirth [riː'bɜːθ] n Wiedergeburt f
rebound [vb rɪ'baund, n 'riːbaund] vi
zurückprallen ♦ n Rückprall m
rebuff [rɪ'bʌf] n Abfuhr f ♦ vt abblitzen
lassen
rebuild [riː'bɪld] (irreg) vt wieder aufbauen;
(fig) wieder herstellen
rebuke [rɪ'bjuːk] n Tadel m ♦ vt tadeln,
rügen
rebut [rɪ'bʌt] vt widerlegen
recall [vb rɪ'kɔːl, n 'riːkɔl] vt (call back)
zurückrufen; (remember) sich erinnern an
+acc ♦ n Rückruf m
recap ['riːkæp] vt, vi wiederholen
rec'd abbr (= received) Eing.
recede [rɪ'siːd] vi zurückweichen; **receding**
adj: **receding hairline** Stirnglatze f
receipt [rɪ'siːt] n (document) Quittung f;
(receiving) Empfang m; **~s** npl (ECON)
Einnahmen pl
receive [rɪ'siːv] vt erhalten; (visitors etc)
empfangen; **~r** n (TEL) Hörer m
recent ['riːsnt] adj vor kurzem (geschehen),
neulich; (modern) neu; **~ly** adv kürzlich,
neulich
receptacle [rɪ'septɪkl] n Behälter m
reception [rɪ'sepʃən] n Empfang m; **~ desk**
n Empfang m; (in hotel) Rezeption f; **~ist** n
(in hotel) Empfangschef m, Empfangsdame
f; (MED) Sprechstundenhilfe f
receptive [rɪ'septɪv] adj aufnahmebereit
recess [rɪ'ses] n (break) Ferien pl; (hollow)
Nische f
recession [rɪ'seʃən] n Rezession f
recharge [riː'tʃɑːdʒ] vt (battery) aufladen
recipe ['resɪpɪ] n Rezept nt
recipient [rɪ'sɪpɪənt] n Empfänger m
reciprocal [rɪ'sɪprəkl] adj gegenseitig;
(mutual) wechselseitig
recital [rɪ'saɪtl] n Vortrag m
recite [rɪ'saɪt] vt vortragen, aufsagen
reckless ['rekləs] adj leichtsinnig; (driving)

fahrlässig
reckon ['rekən] vt (count) rechnen,
berechnen, errechnen; (estimate) schätzen;
(think): **I ~ that ...** ich nehme an, dass ...; **~**
on vt fus rechnen mit; **~ing** n (calculation)
Rechnen nt
reclaim [rɪ'kleɪm] vt (expenses)
zurückverlangen; (land): **to ~ (from sth)**
(etw dat) gewinnen; **reclamation**
[reklə'meɪʃən] n (of land) Gewinnung f
recline [rɪ'klaɪn] vi sich zurücklehnen;
reclining adj Liege-
recluse [rɪ'kluːs] n Einsiedler m
recognition [rekəg'nɪʃən] n (recognizing)
Erkennen nt; (acknowledgement)
Anerkennung f; **transformed beyond ~**
völlig verändert
recognizable ['rekəgnaɪzəbl] adj erkennbar
recognize ['rekəgnaɪz] vt erkennen; (POL,
approve) anerkennen; **to ~ as** anerkennen
als; **to ~ by** erkennen an +dat
recoil [rɪ'kɔɪl] vi (in horror) zurückschrecken;
(rebound) zurückprallen; (person): **to ~ from**
doing sth davor zurückschrecken, etw zu
tun
recollect [rekə'lekt] vt sich erinnern an +acc;
~ion [rekə'lekʃən] n Erinnerung f
recommend [rekə'mend] vt empfehlen;
~ation [rekəmen'deɪʃən] n Empfehlung f
recompense ['rekəmpens] n (compensation)
Entschädigung f; (reward) Belohnung f ♦ vt
entschädigen; belohnen
reconcile ['rekənsaɪl] vt (facts) vereinbaren;
(people) versöhnen; **to ~ o.s. to sth** sich
mit etw abfinden; **reconciliation**
[rekənsɪlɪ'eɪʃən] n Versöhnung f
recondition [riːkən'dɪʃən] vt (machine)
generalüberholen
reconnoitre [rekə'nɔɪtə*] (US **reconnoiter**) vt
erkunden ♦ vi aufklären
reconsider [riːkən'sɪdə*] vt von neuem
erwägen, noch einmal überdenken ♦ vi es
noch einmal überdenken
reconstruct [riːkən'strʌkt] vt wieder
aufbauen; (crime) rekonstruieren
record [n 'rekɔːd, vb rɪ'kɔːd] n Aufzeichnung
f; (MUS) Schallplatte f; (best performance)

Rekord m ♦ vt aufzeichnen; (*music etc*) aufnehmen; **off the ~** vertraulichi, im Vertrauen; **in ~ time** in Rekordzeit; **~ card** n (*in file*) Karteikarte f; **~ed delivery** (*BRIT*) n (*POST*) Einschreiben nt; **~er** n (*TECH*) Registriergerät nt; (*MUS*) Blockflöte f; **~ holder** n (*SPORT*) Rekordinhaber m; **~ing** n (*MUS*) Aufnahme f; **~ player** n Plattenspieler m

recount [rɪˈkaunt] vt (*tell*) berichten

re-count [ˈriːkaunt] n Nachzählung f

recoup [rɪˈkuːp] vt: **to ~ one's losses** seinen Verlust wieder gutmachen

recourse [rɪˈkɔːs] n: **to have ~ to** Zuflucht nehmen zu *or* bei

recover [rɪˈkʌvəʳ] vt (*get back*) zurückerhalten ♦ vi sich erholen

re-cover [riːˈkʌvəʳ] vt (*quilt etc*) neu überziehen

recovery [rɪˈkʌvərɪ] n Wiedererlangung f; (*of health*) Erholung f

recreate [riːkrɪˈeɪt] vt wieder herstellen

recreation [rekrɪˈeɪʃən] n Erholung f; **~al** adj Erholungs-; **~al drug** n Freizeitdroge f

recrimination [rɪkrɪmɪˈneɪʃən] n Gegenbeschuldigung f

recruit [rɪˈkruːt] n Rekrut m ♦ vt rekrutieren; **~ment** n Rekrutierung f

rectangle [ˈrektæŋgl] n Rechteck nt; **rectangular** [rekˈtæŋgjuləʳ] adj rechteckig, rechtwinklig

rectify [ˈrektɪfaɪ] vt berichtigen

rector [ˈrektəʳ] n (*REL*) Pfarrer m; (*SCH*) Direktor(in) m(f); **~y** [ˈrektərɪ] n Pfarrhaus nt

recuperate [rɪˈkjuːpəreɪt] vi sich erholen

recur [rɪˈkəːʳ] vi sich wiederholen; **~rence** n Wiederholung f; **~rent** adj wiederkehrend

recycle [riːˈsaɪkl] vt wieder verwerten, wieder aufbereiten; **recycling** n Recycling nt

red [red] n Rot nt; (*POL*) Rote(r) m ♦ adj rot; **in the ~** in den roten Zahlen; **~ carpet treatment** n Sonderbehandlung f, große(r) Bahnhof m; **R~ Cross** n Rote(s) Kreuz nt; **~currant** n rote Johannisbeere f; **~den** vi sich röten; (*blush*) erröten ♦ vt röten; **~dish** adj rötlich

redecorate [riːˈdekəreɪt] vt neu tapezieren, neu streichen

redeem [rɪˈdiːm] vt (*COMM*) einlösen; (*save*) retten; **~ing** adj: **~ing feature** versöhnende(s) Moment nt

redeploy [riːdɪˈplɔɪ] vt (*resources*) umverteilen

red: ~-haired [redˈheəd] adj rothaarig; **~-handed** [redˈhændɪd] adv: **to be caught ~-handed** auf frischer Tat ertappt werden; **~head** [ˈredhed] n Rothaarige(r) mf; **~ herring** n Ablenkungsmanöver nt; **~-hot** [redˈhɔt] adj rot glühend

redirect [riːdaɪˈrekt] vt umleiten

red light n: **to go through a ~** (*AUT*) bei Rot über die Ampel fahren; **red-light district** n Strichviertel nt

redo [riːˈduː] (*irreg: like* do) vt nochmals machen

redolent [ˈredələnt] adj: **~ of** (*fig*) erinnernd an +acc

redouble [riːˈdʌbl] vt: **to ~ one's efforts** seine Anstrengungen verdoppeln

redress [rɪˈdres] vt wieder gutmachen

red: R~ Sea n: **the R~ Sea** das Rote Meer; **~skin** [ˈredskɪn] n Rothaut f; **~ tape** n Bürokratismus m

reduce [rɪˈdjuːs] vt (*speed, temperature*) vermindern; (*photo*) verkleinern; **"~ speed now"** (*AUT*) ≃ „langsam"; **to ~ the price (to)** den Preis herabsetzen (auf +acc); **at a ~d price** zum ermäßigten Preis

reduction [rɪˈdʌkʃən] n Verminderung f; Verkleinerung f; Herabsetzung f; (*amount of money*) Nachlass m

redundancy [rɪˈdʌndənsɪ] n Überflüssigkeit f; (*of workers*) Entlassung f

redundant [rɪˈdʌndnt] adj überflüssig; (*workers*) ohne Arbeitsplatz; **to be made ~** arbeitslos werden

reed [riːd] n Schilf nt; (*MUS*) Rohrblatt nt

reef [riːf] n Riff nt

reek [riːk] vi: **to ~ (of)** stinken (nach)

reel [riːl] n Spule f, Rolle f ♦ vt (*also: ~ in*) wickeln, spulen ♦ vi (*stagger*) taumeln

ref [ref] (*inf*) n abbr (= referee) Schiri m

refectory [rɪˈfektərɪ] n (*UNIV*) Mensa f; (*SCH*)

Speisesaal m; (ECCL) Refektorium nt

refer [rɪ'fəːʳ] vt: **to ~ sb to sb/sth** jdn an jdn/etw verweisen ♦ vi: **to ~ to** (to book) nachschlagen in +dat; (mention) sich beziehen auf +acc

referee [rɛfə'riː] n Schiedsrichter m; (BRIT: for job) Referenz f ♦ vt schiedsrichtern

reference ['rɛfrəns] n (for job) Referenz f; (in book) Verweis m; (number, code) Aktenzeichen nt; (allusion): **~ (to)** Anspielung (auf +acc); **with ~ to** in Bezug auf +acc; **~ book** n Nachschlagewerk nt; **~ number** n Aktenzeichen nt

referenda [rɛfə'rɛndə] npl of **referendum**

referendum [rɛfə'rɛndəm] (pl **-da**) n Volksabstimmung f

refill [vb riː'fɪl, n 'riːfɪl] vt nachfüllen ♦ n (for pen) Ersatzmine f

refine [rɪ'faɪn] vt (purify) raffinieren; **~d** adj kultiviert; **~ment** n Kultiviertheit f; **~ry** n Raffinerie f

reflect [rɪ'flɛkt] vt (light) reflektieren; (fig) (wider)spiegeln ♦ vi (meditate): **to ~ (on)** nachdenken (über +acc); **it ~s badly/well on him** das stellt ihn in ein schlechtes/ gutes Licht; **~ion** [rɪ'flɛkʃən] n Reflexion f; (image) Spiegelbild nt; (thought) Überlegung f; **on ~ion** wenn man sich dat das recht überlegt

reflex ['riːflɛks] adj Reflex- ♦ n Reflex m; **~ive** [rɪ'flɛksɪv] adj reflexiv

reform [rɪ'fɔːm] n Reform f ♦ vt (person) bessern; **~atory** (US) n Besserungsanstalt f

refrain [rɪ'freɪn] vi: **to ~ from** unterlassen ♦ n Refrain m

refresh [rɪ'frɛʃ] vt erfrischen; **~er course** (BRIT) n Wiederholungskurs m; **~ing** adj erfrischend; **~ments** npl Erfrischungen pl

refrigeration [rɪfrɪdʒə'reɪʃən] n Kühlung f

refrigerator [rɪ'frɪdʒəreɪtəʳ] n Kühlschrank m

refuel [riː'fjuəl] vt, vi auftanken

refuge ['rɛfjuːdʒ] n Zuflucht f; **to take ~ in** sich flüchten in +acc; **~e** [rɛfjuː'dʒiː] n Flüchtling m

refund [n 'riːfʌnd, vb rɪ'fʌnd] n Rückvergütung f ♦ vt zurückerstatten

refurbish [riː'fəːbɪʃ] vt aufpolieren

refusal [rɪ'fjuːzəl] n (Ver)weigerung f; **first ~** Vorkaufsrecht nt

refuse[1] [rɪ'fjuːz] vt abschlagen ♦ vi sich weigern

refuse[2] ['rɛfjuːs] n Abfall m, Müll m; **~ collection** n Müllabfuhr f

refute [rɪ'fjuːt] vt widerlegen

regain [rɪ'geɪn] vt wiedergewinnen; (consciousness) wiedererlangen

regal ['riːgl] adj königlich

regalia [rɪ'geɪlɪə] npl Insignien pl

regard [rɪ'gɑːd] n Achtung f ♦ vt ansehen; **to send one's ~s to sb** jdn grüßen lassen; **"with kindest ~s"** "mit freundlichen Grüßen"; **~ing** or **as ~s** or **with ~ to** bezüglich +gen, in Bezug auf +acc; **~less** adj: **~less of** ohne Rücksicht auf +acc ♦ adv trotzdem

regenerate [rɪ'dʒɛnəreɪt] vt erneuern

régime [reɪ'ʒiːm] n Regime nt

regiment [n 'rɛdʒɪmənt, vb 'rɛdʒɪmɛnt] n Regiment nt ♦ vt (fig) reglementieren; **~al** [rɛdʒɪ'mɛntl] adj Regiments-

region ['riːdʒən] n Region f; **in the ~ of** (fig) so um; **~al** adj örtlich, regional

register ['rɛdʒɪstəʳ] n Register nt ♦ vt (list) registrieren; (emotion) zeigen; (write down) eintragen ♦ vi (at hotel) sich eintragen; (with police) sich melden; (make impression) wirken, ankommen; **~ed** (BRIT) adj (letter) Einschreibe-, eingeschrieben; **~ed trademark** n eingetragene(s) Warenzeichen n

registrar ['rɛdʒɪstrɑːʳ] n Standesbeamte(r) m

registration [rɛdʒɪs'treɪʃən] n (act) Registrierung f; (AUT: also: **~ number**) polizeiliche(s) Kennzeichen nt

registry ['rɛdʒɪstrɪ] n Sekretariat nt; **~ office** (BRIT) n Standesamt nt; **to get married in a ~ office** standesamtlich heiraten

regret [rɪ'grɛt] n Bedauern nt ♦ vt bedauern; **~fully** adv mit Bedauern, ungern; **~table** adj bedauerlich

regroup [riː'gruːp] vt umgruppieren ♦ vi sich umgruppieren

regular ['rɛgjuləʳ] adj regelmäßig; (usual) üblich; (inf) regelrecht ♦ n (client etc)

Stammkunde m; ~ity [regju'lærɪtɪ] n
Regelmäßigkeit f; ~ly adv regelmäßig

regulate ['regjuleɪt] vt regeln, regulieren;
regulation [regju'leɪʃən] n (rule) Vorschrift f;
(control) Regulierung f

rehabilitation ['riːəbɪlɪ'teɪʃən] n (of criminal)
Resozialisierung f

rehearsal [rɪ'həːsəl] n Probe f

rehearse [rɪ'həːs] vt proben

reign [reɪn] n Herrschaft f ♦ vi herrschen

reimburse [riːɪm'bəːs] vt: **to ~ sb for sth**
jdn für etw entschädigen, jdm etw
zurückzahlen

rein [reɪn] n Zügel m

reincarnation [riːɪnkɑː'neɪʃən] n
Wiedergeburt f

reindeer ['reɪndɪəʳ] n Ren nt

reinforce [riːɪn'fɔːs] vt verstärken; ~d
concrete n Stahlbeton m; ~ment n
Verstärkung f; ~ments npl (MIL)
Verstärkungstruppen pl

reinstate [riːɪn'steɪt] vt wieder einsetzen

reissue [riː'ɪʃuː] vt neu herausgeben

reiterate [riː'ɪtəreɪt] vt wiederholen

reject [n 'riːdʒekt, vb rɪ'dʒekt] n (COMM)
Ausschuss(artikel) m ♦ vt ablehnen; ~ion
[rɪ'dʒekʃən] n Zurückweisung f

rejoice [rɪ'dʒɔɪs] vi: **to ~ at or over** sich
freuen über +acc

rejuvenate [rɪ'dʒuːvəneɪt] vt verjüngen

rekindle [riː'kɪndl] vt wieder anfachen

relapse [rɪ'læps] n Rückfall m

relate [rɪ'leɪt] vt (tell) erzählen; (connect)
verbinden ♦ vi: **to ~** zusammenhängen
mit; (form relationship) eine Beziehung
aufbauen zu; ~d adj: ~d (to) verwandt
(mit); **relating** prep: **relating to** bezüglich
+gen; **relation** [rɪ'leɪʃən] n Verwandte(r) mf;
(connection) Beziehung f; **relationship** n
Verhältnis n, Beziehung f

relative ['relətɪv] n Verwandte(r) mf ♦ adj
relativ; ~ly adv verhältnismäßig

relax [rɪ'læks] vi (slacken) sich lockern;
(muscles, person) sich entspannen ♦ vt (ease)
lockern, entspannen; ~ation [riːlæk'seɪʃən] n
Entspannung f; ~ed adj entspannt, locker;
~ing adj entspannend

relay [n 'riːleɪ, vb rɪ'leɪ] n (SPORT) Staffel f ♦ vt
(message) weiterleiten; (RAD, TV) übertragen

release [rɪ'liːs] n (freedom) Entlassung f;
(TECH) Auslöser m ♦ vt befreien; (prisoner)
entlassen; (report, news) verlautbaren,
bekannt geben

relegate ['relɪgeɪt] vt (SPORT): **to be ~d**
absteigen

relent [rɪ'lent] vi nachgeben; ~less adj
unnachgiebig

relevant ['relɪvənt] adj wichtig, relevant; ~
to relevant für

reliability [rɪlaɪə'bɪlɪtɪ] n Zuverlässigkeit f

reliable [rɪ'laɪəbl] adj zuverlässig; **reliably**
adv zuverlässig; **to be reliably informed**
that ... aus zuverlässiger Quelle wissen,
dass ...

reliance [rɪ'laɪəns] n: ~ **(on)** Abhängigkeit f
(von)

relic ['relɪk] n (from past) Überbleibsel nt;
(REL) Reliquie f

relief [rɪ'liːf] n Erleichterung f; (help) Hilfe f;
(person) Ablösung f

relieve [rɪ'liːv] vt (ease) erleichtern; (help)
entlasten; (person) ablösen; **to ~ sb of sth**
jdm etw abnehmen; **to ~ o.s.** (euph) sich
erleichtern (euph); ~d adj erleichtert

religion [rɪ'lɪdʒən] n Religion f; **religious**
[rɪ'lɪdʒəs] adj religiös

relinquish [rɪ'lɪŋkwɪʃ] vt aufgeben

relish ['relɪʃ] n Würze f ♦ vt genießen; **to ~**
doing gern tun

relocate [riːləu'keɪt] vt verlegen ♦ vi
umziehen

reluctance [rɪ'lʌktəns] n Widerstreben nt,
Abneigung f

reluctant [rɪ'lʌktənt] adj widerwillig; ~ly adv
ungern

rely [rɪ'laɪ] vt fus: **to ~ on** sich verlassen auf
+acc

remain [rɪ'meɪn] vi (be left) übrig bleiben;
(stay) bleiben; ~der n Rest m; ~ing adj
übrig (geblieben); ~s npl Überreste pl

remake ['riːmeɪk] n (CINE) Neuverfilmung f

remand [rɪ'mɑːnd] n: **on ~** in
Untersuchungshaft ♦ vt: **to ~ in custody** in
Untersuchungshaft schicken; ~ **home**

(*BRIT*) n Untersuchungsgefängnis nt für Jugendliche

remark [rɪ'mɑːk] n Bemerkung f ♦ vt bemerken; **~able** adj bemerkenswert; **remarkably** adv außergewöhnlich

remarry [riː'mærɪ] vi sich wieder verheiraten

remedial [rɪ'miːdɪəl] adj Heil-; (*teaching*) Hilfsschul-

remedy ['remədɪ] n Mittel nt ♦ vt (*pain*) abhelfen +dat; (*trouble*) in Ordnung bringen

remember [rɪ'membər] vt sich erinnern an +acc; **remembrance** [rɪ'membrəns] n Erinnerung f; (*official*) Gedenken nt; **R~ Day** n ≃ Volkstrauertag m

---
Remembrance Day

ⓘ **Remembrance Day** *oder* **Remembrance Sunday** *ist der britische Gedenktag für die Gefallenen der beiden Weltkriege und anderer Konflikte. Er fällt auf einen Sonntag vor oder nach dem 11. November (am 11. November 1918 endete der erste Weltkrieg) und wird mit einer Schweigeminute, Kranzniederlegungen an Kriegerdenkmälern und dem Tragen von Ansteckbadeln in Form einer Mohnblume begangen.*

---

remind [rɪ'maɪnd] vt: **to ~ sb to do sth** jdn daran erinnern, etw zu tun; **to ~ sb of sth** jdn an etw acc erinnern; **she ~s me of her mother** sie erinnert mich an ihre Mutter; **~er** n Mahnung f

reminisce [remɪ'nɪs] vi in Erinnerungen schwelgen; **~nt** [remɪ'nɪsnt] adj: **to be ~nt of sth** an etw acc erinnern

remiss [rɪ'mɪs] adj nachlässig

remission [rɪ'mɪʃən] n Nachlass m; (*of debt, sentence*) Erlass m

remit [rɪ'mɪt] vt (*money*): **to ~ (to)** überweisen (an +acc); **~tance** n Geldanweisung f

remnant ['remnənt] n Rest m; **~s** npl (*COMM*) Einzelstücke pl

remorse [rɪ'mɔːs] n Gewissensbisse pl; **~ful** adj reumütig; **~less** adj unbarmherzig

remote [rɪ'məut] adj abgelegen; (*slight*)

gering; **~ control** n Fernsteuerung f; **~ly** adv entfernt

remould ['riːməuld] (*BRIT*) n runderneuerte(r) Reifen m

removable [rɪ'muːvəbl] adj entfernbar

removal [rɪ'muːvəl] n Beseitigung f; (*of furniture*) Umzug m; (*from office*) Entlassung f; **~ van** (*BRIT*) n Möbelwagen m

remove [rɪ'muːv] vt beseitigen, entfernen; **~rs** npl Möbelspedition f

remuneration [rɪmjuːnə'reɪʃən] n Vergütung f, Honorar nt

render ['rendər] vt machen; (*translate*) übersetzen; **~ing** (*MUS*) Wiedergabe f

rendezvous ['rɔndɪvuː] n (*meeting*) Rendezvous nt; (*place*) Treffpunkt m ♦ vi sich treffen

renew [rɪ'njuː] vt erneuern; (*contract, licence*) verlängern; (*replace*) ersetzen; **~able** adj regenerierbar; **~al** n Erneuerung f; Verlängerung f

renounce [rɪ'nauns] vt (*give up*) verzichten auf +acc; (*disown*) verstoßen

renovate ['renəveɪt] vt renovieren; (*building*) restaurieren

renown [rɪ'naun] n Ruf m; **~ed** adj namhaft

rent [rent] n Miete f; (*for land*) Pacht f ♦ vt (*hold as tenant*) mieten; pachten; (*let*) vermieten; verpachten; (*car etc*) mieten; (*firm*) vermieten; **~al** n Miete f

renunciation [rɪnʌnsɪ'eɪʃən] n: **~ (of)** Verzicht m (auf +acc)

reorganize [riː'ɔːgənaɪz] vt umgestalten, reorganisieren

rep [rep] n abbr (*COMM*) = **representative**; (*THEAT*) = **repertory**

repair [rɪ'peər] n Reparatur f ♦ vt reparieren; (*damage*) wieder gutmachen; **in good / bad ~** in gutem/schlechtem Zustand; **~ kit** n Werkzeugkasten m

repartee [repɑː'tiː] n Witzeleien pl

repatriate [riː'pætrieɪt] vt in die Heimat zurückschicken

repay [riː'peɪ] vt (*irreg*) zurückzahlen; (*reward*) vergelten; **~ment** n Rückzahlung f; (*fig*) Vergeltung f

repeal [rɪ'piːl] vt aufheben

repeat [rɪ'piːt] n (RAD, TV) Wiederholung(ssendung) f ♦ vt wiederholen; **~edly** adv wiederholt

repel [rɪ'pel] vt (drive back) zurückschlagen; (disgust) abstoßen; **~lent** adj abstoßend ♦ n: **insect ~lent** Insektenmittel nt

repent [rɪ'pent] vt, vi: **to ~ (of)** bereuen; **~ance** n Reue f

repercussion [riːpə'kʌʃən] n Auswirkung f; **to have ~s** ein Nachspiel haben

repertory ['repətərɪ] n Repertoire nt

repetition [repɪ'tɪʃən] n Wiederholung f

repetitive [rɪ'petɪtɪv] adj sich wiederholend

replace [rɪ'pleɪs] vt ersetzen; (put back) zurückstellen; **~ment** n Ersatz m

replay ['riːpleɪ] n (of match) Wiederholungsspiel nt; (of tape, film) Wiederholung f

replenish [rɪ'plenɪʃ] vt ergänzen

replica ['replɪkə] n Kopie f

reply [rɪ'plaɪ] n Antwort f ♦ vi antworten; **~ coupon** n Antwortschein m

report [rɪ'pɔːt] n Bericht m; (BRIT: SCH) Zeugnis nt ♦ vt (tell) berichten; (give information against) melden; (to police) anzeigen ♦ vi (make ~) Bericht erstatten; (present o.s.): **to ~ (to sb)** sich (bei jdm) melden; **~ card** n (US, SCOTTISH) n Zeugnis nt; **~edly** adv wie verlautet; **~er** n Reporter m

reprehensible [reprɪ'hensɪbl] adj tadelnswert

represent [reprɪ'zent] vt darstellen; (speak for) vertreten; **~ation** [reprɪzen'teɪʃən] n Darstellung f; (being ~ed) Vertretung f; **~ations** npl (protest) Vorhaltungen pl; **~ative** n (person) Vertreter m; (US: POL) Abgeordnete(r) mf ♦ adj repräsentativ

repress [rɪ'pres] vt unterdrücken; **~ion** [rɪ'preʃən] n Unterdrückung f

reprieve [rɪ'priːv] n (JUR) Begnadigung f; (fig) Gnadenfrist f ♦ vt (JUR) begnadigen

reprimand ['reprɪmaːnd] n Verweis m ♦ vt einen Verweis erteilen +dat

reprint [n 'riːprɪnt, vb riː'prɪnt] n Neudruck m ♦ vt wieder abdrucken

reprisal [rɪ'praɪzl] n Vergeltung f

reproach [rɪ'prəʊtʃ] n Vorwurf m ♦ vt Vorwürfe machen +dat; **to ~ sb with sth** jdm etw vorwerfen; **~ful** adj vorwurfsvoll

reproduce [riːprə'djuːs] vt reproduzieren ♦ vi (have offspring) sich vermehren; **reproduction** [riːprə'dʌkʃən] n (ART, PHOT) Reproduktion f; (breeding) Fortpflanzung f; **reproductive** [riːprə'dʌktɪv] adj reproduktiv; (breeding) Fortpflanzungs-

reprove [rɪ'pruːv] vt tadeln

reptile ['reptaɪl] n Reptil nt

republic [rɪ'pʌblɪk] n Republik f

repudiate [rɪ'pjuːdɪeɪt] vt zurückweisen

repugnant [rɪ'pʌgnənt] adj widerlich

repulse [rɪ'pʌls] vt (drive back) zurückschlagen; (reject) abweisen

repulsive [rɪ'pʌlsɪv] adj abstoßend

reputable ['repjutəbl] adj angesehen

reputation [repju'teɪʃən] n Ruf m

reputed [rɪ'pjuːtɪd] adj angeblich; **~ly** [rɪ'pjuːtɪdlɪ] adv angeblich

request [rɪ'kwest] n Bitte f ♦ vt (thing) erbitten; **to ~ sth of** or **from sb** jdn um etw bitten; (formally) jdn um etw ersuchen; **~ stop** n (BRIT) Bedarfshaltestelle f

require [rɪ'kwaɪər] vt (need) brauchen; (demand) erfordern; **~ment** n (condition) Anforderung f; (need) Bedarf m

requisite ['rekwɪzɪt] adj erforderlich

requisition [rekwɪ'zɪʃən] n Anforderung f ♦ vt beschlagnahmen

rescue ['reskjuː] n Rettung f ♦ vt retten; **~ party** n Rettungsmannschaft f; **~r** n Retter m

research [rɪ'səːtʃ] n Forschung f ♦ vi forschen ♦ vt erforschen; **~er** n Forscher m

resemblance [rɪ'zembləns] n Ähnlichkeit f

resemble [rɪ'zembl] vt ähneln +dat

resent [rɪ'zent] vt übel nehmen; **~ful** adj nachtragend, empfindlich; **~ment** n Verstimmung f, Unwille m

reservation [rezə'veɪʃən] n (booking) Reservierung f; (THEAT) Vorbestellung f; (doubt) Vorbehalt m; (land) Reservat nt

reserve [rɪ'zəːv] n (store) Vorrat m, Reserve f; (manner) Zurückhaltung f; (game ~) Naturschutzgebiet nt; (SPORT)

Ersatzspieler(in) *m(f)* ♦ *vt* reservieren; (*judgement*) sich *dat* vorbehalten; **~s** *npl* (*MIL*) Reserve *f*; **in ~** in Reserve; **~d** *adj* reserviert

reshuffle [riː'ʃʌfl] *n* (*POL*): **cabinet ~** Kabinettsumbildung *f* ♦ *vt* (*POL*) umbilden

reside [rɪ'zaɪd] *vi* wohnen, ansässig sein

residence ['rezɪdəns] *n* (*house*) Wohnsitz *m*; (*living*) Aufenthalt *m*; **~ permit** (*BRIT*) *n* Aufenthaltserlaubnis *f*

resident ['rezɪdənt] *n* (*in house*) Bewohner *m*; (*in area*) Einwohner *m* ♦ *adj* wohnhaft, ansässig; **~ial** [rezɪ'denʃəl] *adj* Wohn-

residue ['rezɪdjuː] *n* Rest *m*; (*CHEM*) Rückstand *m*; (*fig*) Bodensatz *m*

resign [rɪ'zaɪn] *vt* (*office*) aufgeben, zurücktreten von ♦ *vi* (*from office*) zurücktreten; (*employee*) kündigen; **to be ~ed to sth, to ~ o.s. to sth** sich mit etw abfinden; **~ation** [rezɪg'neɪʃən] *n* (*from job*) Kündigung *f*; (*POL*) Rücktritt *m*; (*submission*) Resignation *f*; **~ed** *adj* resigniert

resilience [rɪ'zɪliəns] *n* Spannkraft *f*; (*of person*) Unverwüstlichkeit *f*; **resilient** [rɪ'zɪliənt] *adj* unverwüstlich

resin ['rezɪn] *n* Harz *nt*

resist [rɪ'zɪst] *vt* widerstehen +*dat*; **~ance** *n* Widerstand *m*

resit [*vb* riː'sɪt, *n* 'riːsɪt] *vt* (*exam*) wiederholen ♦ *n* Wiederholung(sprüfung) *f*

resolute ['rezəluːt] *adj* entschlossen, resolut; **resolution** [rezə'luːʃən] *n* (*firmness*) Entschlossenheit *f*; (*intention*) Vorsatz *m*; (*decision*) Beschluss *m*

resolve [rɪ'zɒlv] *n* Entschlossenheit *f* ♦ *vt* (*decide*) beschließen ♦ *vi* sich lösen; **~d** *adj* (*fest*) entschlossen

resonant ['rezənənt] *adj* voll

resort [rɪ'zɔːt] *n* (*holiday place*) Erholungsort *m*; (*help*) Zuflucht *f* ♦ *vi*: **to ~ to** Zuflucht nehmen zu; **as a last ~** als letzter Ausweg

resound [rɪ'zaund] *vi*: **to ~ (with)** widerhallen (von); **~ing** *adj* nachhallend; (*success*) groß

resource [rɪ'sɔːs] *n* Findigkeit *f*; **~s** *npl* (*financial*) Geldmittel *pl*; (*natural*) Bodenschätze *pl*; **~ful** *adj* findig

respect [rɪs'pekt] *n* Respekt *m* ♦ *vt* achten, respektieren; **~s** *npl* (*regards*) Grüße *pl*; **with ~ to** in Bezug auf +*acc*, hinsichtlich +*gen*; **in this ~** in dieser Hinsicht; **~able** *adj* anständig; (*not bad*) leidlich; **~ful** *adj* höflich

respective [rɪs'pektɪv] *adj* jeweilig; **~ly** *adv* beziehungsweise

respiration [respɪ'reɪʃən] *n* Atmung *f*

respite ['respaɪt] *n* Ruhepause *f*

resplendent [rɪs'plendənt] *adj* strahlend

respond [rɪs'pɒnd] *vi* antworten; (*react*): **to ~ (to)** reagieren (auf +*acc*); **response** [rɪs'pɒns] *n* Antwort *f*; Reaktion *f*; (*to advert*) Resonanz *f*

responsibility [rɪspɒnsɪ'bɪlɪtɪ] *n* Verantwortung *f*

responsible [rɪs'pɒnsɪbl] *adj* verantwortlich; (*reliable*) verantwortungsvoll

responsive [rɪs'pɒnsɪv] *adj* empfänglich

rest [rest] *n* Ruhe *f*; (*break*) Pause *f*; (*remainder*) Rest *m* ♦ *vi* sich ausruhen; (*be supported*) (auf)liegen ♦ *vt* (*lean*): **to ~ sth on/against sth** etw gegen etw *acc* lehnen; **the ~ of them** die Übrigen; **it ~s with him to ...** es liegt bei ihm, zu ...

restaurant ['restərɒŋ] *n* Restaurant *nt*; **~ car** (*BRIT*) *n* Speisewagen *m*

restful ['restful] *adj* erholsam, ruhig

rest home *n* Erholungsheim *nt*

restive ['restɪv] *adj* unruhig

restless ['restlɪs] *adj* unruhig

restoration [restə'reɪʃən] *n* Rückgabe *f*; (*of building etc*) Rückerstattung *f*

restore [rɪ'stɔː] *vt* (*order*) wieder herstellen; (*customs*) wieder einführen; (*person to position*) wieder einsetzen; (*give back*) zurückgeben; (*renovate*) restaurieren

restrain [rɪs'treɪn] *vt* zurückhalten; (*curiosity etc*) beherrschen; (*person*): **to ~ sb from doing sth** jdn davon abhalten, etw zu tun; **~ed** *adj* (*style etc*) gedämpft, verhalten; **~t** *n* (*self-control*) Zurückhaltung *f*

restrict [rɪs'trɪkt] *vt* einschränken; **~ion** [rɪs'trɪkʃən] *n* Einschränkung *f*; **~ive** *adj* einschränkend

rest room (*US*) *n* Toilette *f*

restructure [riː'strʌktʃəʳ] vt umstrukturieren

result [rɪ'zʌlt] n Resultat nt, Folge f; (of exam, game) Ergebnis nt ♦ vi: **to ~ in sth** etw zur Folge haben; **as a ~ of** als Folge +gen

resume [rɪ'zjuːm] vt fortsetzen; (occupy again) wieder einnehmen ♦ vi (work etc) wieder beginnen

résumé ['reɪzjuːmeɪ] n Zusammenfassung f

resumption [rɪ'zʌmpʃən] n Wiederaufnahme f

resurgence [rɪ'səːdʒəns] n Wiedererwachen nt

resurrection [rezə'rekʃən] n Auferstehung f

resuscitate [rɪ'sʌsɪteɪt] vt wieder beleben; **resuscitation** [rɪsʌsɪ'teɪʃən] n Wiederbelebung f

retail [n, adj 'riːteɪl, vb 'riː'teɪl] n Einzelhandel m ♦ adj Einzelhandels- ♦ vt im Kleinen verkaufen ♦ vi im Einzelhandel kosten; **~er** ['riːteɪləʳ] n Einzelhändler m, Kleinhändler m; **~ price** n Ladenpreis m

retain [rɪ'teɪn] vt (keep) (zurück)behalten; **~er** n (fee) (Honorar)vorschuss m

retaliate [rɪ'tælieɪt] vi zum Vergeltungsschlag ausholen; **retaliation** [rɪtælɪ'eɪʃən] n Vergeltung f

retarded [rɪ'tɑːdɪd] adj zurückgeblieben

retch [retʃ] vi würgen

retentive [rɪ'tentɪv] adj (memory) gut

reticent ['retɪsnt] adj schweigsam

retina ['retɪnə] n Netzhaut f

retire [rɪ'taɪəʳ] vi (from work) in den Ruhestand treten; (withdraw) sich zurückziehen; (go to bed) schlafen gehen; **~d** adj (person) pensioniert, im Ruhestand; **~ment** n Ruhestand m

retiring [rɪ'taɪərɪŋ] adj zurückhaltend

retort [rɪ'tɔːt] n (reply) Erwiderung f ♦ vi (scharf) erwidern

retrace [riː'treɪs] vt zurückverfolgen; **to ~ one's steps** denselben Weg zurückgehen

retract [rɪ'trækt] vt (statement) zurücknehmen; (claws) einziehen ♦ vi einen Rückzieher machen; **~able** adj (aerial) ausziehbar

retrain [riː'treɪn] vt umschulen

retread ['riːtred] n (tyre) Reifen m mit erneuerter Lauffläche

retreat [rɪ'triːt] n Rückzug m; (place) Zufluchtsort m ♦ vi sich zurückziehen

retribution [retrɪ'bjuːʃən] n Strafe f

retrieval [rɪ'triːvəl] n Wiedergewinnung f

retrieve [rɪ'triːv] vt wiederbekommen; (rescue) retten; **~r** n Apportierhund m

retrograde ['retrəgreɪd] adj (step) Rück-; (policy) rückschrittlich

retrospect ['retrəspekt] n: **in ~** im Rückblick, rückblickend; **~ive** [retrə'spektɪv] adj (action) rückwirkend; (look) rückblickend

return [rɪ'təːn] n Rückkehr f; (profits) Ertrag m; (BRIT: rail ticket etc) Rückfahrkarte f; (: plane ticket) Rückflugkarte f ♦ adj (journey, match) Rück- ♦ vi zurückkehren, zurückkommen ♦ vt zurückgeben, zurückschicken; (pay back) zurückzahlen; (elect) wählen; (verdict) aussprechen; **~s** npl (COMM) Gewinn m; (receipts) Einkünfte pl; **in ~** dafür; **by ~ of post** postwendend; **many happy ~s!** herzlichen Glückwunsch zum Geburtstag!

reunion [riː'juːnɪən] n Wiedervereinigung f; (SCH etc) Treffen nt

reunite [riːjuː'naɪt] vt wieder vereinigen

reuse [riː'juːz] vt wieder verwenden, wieder verwerten

rev [rev] n abbr (AUT: = revolution) Drehzahl f

revamp [riː'væmp] vt aufpolieren

reveal [rɪ'viːl] vt enthüllen; **~ing** adj aufschlussreich

revel ['revl] vi: **to ~ in sth/in doing sth** seine Freude an etw dat haben/daran haben, etw zu tun

revelation [revə'leɪʃən] n Offenbarung f

revelry ['revlrɪ] n Rummel m

revenge [rɪ'vendʒ] n Rache f; **to take ~ on** sich rächen an +dat

revenue ['revənjuː] n Einnahmen pl

reverberate [rɪ'vəːbəreɪt] vi widerhallen

revere [rɪ'vɪəʳ] vt (ver)ehren; **~nce** ['revərəns] n Ehrfurcht f

Reverend ['revərənd] adj: **the ~ Robert Martin** ≃ Pfarrer Robert Martin

reversal [rɪ'vəːsl] n Umkehrung f

reverse [rɪ'vəːs] n Rückseite f; (AUT: gear)

Rückwärtsgang *m* ♦ *adj* (*order, direction*)
entgegengesetzt ♦ *vt* umkehren ♦ *vi* (*BRIT:*
AUT) rückwärts fahren; **~-charge call** (*BRIT*)
n R-Gespräch *nt*; **reversing lights** *npl*
(*AUT*) Rückfahrscheinwerfer *pl*

revert [rɪ'vəːt] *vi*: **to ~ to** zurückkehren zu;
(*to bad state*) zurückfallen in +*acc*

review [rɪ'vjuː] *n* (*of book*) Rezension *f*;
(*magazine*) Zeitschrift *f* ♦ *vt* Rückschau
halten auf +*acc*; (*MIL*) mustern; (*book*)
rezensieren; (*reexamine*) von neuem
untersuchen; **~er** *n* (*critic*) Rezensent *m*

revise [rɪ'vaɪz] *vt* (*book*) überarbeiten;
(*reconsider*) ändern, revidieren; **revision**
[rɪ'vɪʒən] *n* Prüfung *f*; (*COMM*) Revision *f*;
(*SCH*) Wiederholung *f*

revitalize [riː'vaɪtəlaɪz] *vt* neu beleben

revival [rɪ'vaɪvəl] *n* Wiederbelebung *f*; (*REL*)
Erweckung *f*; (*THEAT*) Wiederaufnahme *f*

revive [rɪ'vaɪv] *vt* wieder beleben; (*fig*)
wieder auffrischen ♦ *vi* wieder erwachen;
(*fig*) wieder aufleben

revoke [rɪ'vəuk] *vt* aufheben

revolt [rɪ'vəult] *n* Aufstand *m*, Revolte *f* ♦ *vi*
sich auflehnen ♦ *vt* entsetzen; **~ing** *adj*
widerlich

revolution [revə'luːʃən] *n* (*turn*) Umdrehung
f; (*POL*) Revolution *f*; **~ary** *adj* revolutionär
♦ *n* Revolutionär *m*; **~ize** *vt* revolutionieren

revolve [rɪ'vɔlv] *vi* kreisen; (*on own axis*) sich
drehen

revolver [rɪ'vɔlvər] *n* Revolver *m*

revolving door [rɪ'vɔlvɪŋ-] *n* Drehtür *f*

revulsion [rɪ'vʌlʃən] *n* Ekel *m*

reward [rɪ'wɔːd] *n* Belohnung *f* ♦ *vt*
belohnen; **~ing** *adj* lohnend

rewind [riː'waɪnd] (*irreg: like* **wind**) *vt* (*tape*
etc) zurückspulen

rewire [riː'waɪər] *vt* (*house*) neu verkabeln

reword [riː'wəːd] *vt* anders formulieren

rewrite [riː'raɪt] (*irreg: like* **write**) *vt*
umarbeiten, neu schreiben

rheumatism ['ruːmətɪzəm] *n* Rheumatismus
m, Rheuma *nt*

Rhine [raɪn] *n*: **the ~** der Rhein

rhinoceros [raɪ'nɔsərəs] *n* Nashorn *nt*

Rhone [rəun] *n*: **the ~** die Rhone

rhubarb ['ruːbɑːb] *n* Rhabarber *m*

rhyme [raɪm] *n* Reim *m*

rhythm ['rɪðm] *n* Rhythmus *m*

rib [rɪb] *n* Rippe *f* ♦ *vt* (*mock*) hänseln,
aufziehen

ribbon ['rɪbən] *n* Band *nt*; **in ~s** (*torn*) in
Fetzen

rice [raɪs] *n* Reis *m*; **~ pudding** *n* Milchreis
m

rich [rɪtʃ] *adj* reich; (*food*) reichhaltig ♦ *npl*:
the ~ die Reichen *pl*; **~es** *npl* Reichtum *m*;
~ly *adv* reich; (*deserve*) völlig

rickets ['rɪkɪts] *n* Rachitis *f*

rickety ['rɪkɪtɪ] *adj* wack(e)lig

rickshaw ['rɪkʃɔː] *n* Rikscha *f*

ricochet ['rɪkəʃeɪ] *n* Abprallen *nt*; (*shot*)
Querschläger *m* ♦ *vi* abprallen

rid [rɪd] (*pt, pp* **rid**) *vt* befreien; **to get ~ of**
loswerden

riddle ['rɪdl] *n* Rätsel *nt* ♦ *vt*: **to be ~d with**
völlig durchlöchert sein von

ride [raɪd] (*pt* **rode**, *pp* **ridden**) *n* (*in vehicle*)
Fahrt *f*; (*on horse*) Ritt *m* ♦ *vt* (*horse*) reiten;
(*bicycle*) fahren ♦ *vi* fahren, reiten; **to take**
sb for a ~ mit jdm eine Fahrt *etc* machen;
(*fig*) jdn aufs Glatteis führen; **~r** *n* Reiter *m*

ridge [rɪdʒ] *n* Kamm *m*; (*of roof*) First *m*

ridicule ['rɪdɪkjuːl] *n* Spott *m* ♦ *vt* lächerlich
machen

ridiculous [rɪ'dɪkjuləs] *adj* lächerlich

riding ['raɪdɪŋ] *n* Reiten *nt*; **~ school** *n*
Reitschule *f*

rife [raɪf] *adj* weit verbreitet; **to be ~**
grassieren; **to be ~ with** voll sein von

riffraff ['rɪfræf] *n* Pöbel *m*

rifle ['raɪfl] *n* Gewehr *nt* ♦ *vt* berauben; **~**
range *n* Schießstand *m*

rift [rɪft] *n* Spalte *f*; (*fig*) Bruch *m*

rig [rɪg] *n* (*oil ~*) Bohrinsel *f* ♦ *vt* (*election etc*)
manipulieren; **~ out** (*BRIT*) *vt* ausstatten; **~**
up *vt* zusammenbasteln; **~ging** *n* Takelage
f

right [raɪt] *adj* (*correct, just*) richtig, recht; (*~*
side) rechte(r, s) ♦ *n* Recht *nt*; (*not left, POL*)
Rechte *f* ♦ *adv* (*on the ~*) rechts; (*to the ~*)
nach rechts; (*look, work*) richtig, recht;
(*directly*) gerade; (*exactly*) genau ♦ *vt* in

Ordnung bringen, korrigieren ♦ excl gut; **on the ~** rechts; **to be in the ~** im Recht sein; **by ~s** von Rechts wegen; **to be ~** Recht haben; **~ away** sofort; **~ now** in diesem Augenblick, eben; **~ in the middle** genau in der Mitte; **~ angle** n rechte(r) Winkel m; **~eous** ['raɪtʃəs] adj rechtschaffen; **~ful** adj rechtmäßig; **~-hand** adj: **~-hand drive** mit Rechtssteuerung; **~-handed** adj rechtshändig; **~-hand man** (irreg) n rechte Hand f; **~-hand side** n rechte Seite f; **~ly** adv mit Recht; **~ of way** n Vorfahrt f; **~-wing** adj rechtsorientiert

rigid ['rɪdʒɪd] adj (stiff) starr, steif; (strict) streng; **~ity** [rɪ'dʒɪdɪtɪ] n Starrheit f; Strenge f

rigmarole ['rɪgmərəul] n Gewäsch nt

rigor ['rɪgə*] (US) n = **rigour**

rigorous ['rɪgərəs] adj streng

rigour ['rɪgə*] (US **rigor**) n Strenge f, Härte f

rile [raɪl] vt ärgern

rim [rɪm] n (edge) Rand m; (of wheel) Felge f

rind [raɪnd] n Rinde f

ring [rɪŋ] (pt **rang**, pp **rung**) n Ring m; (of people) Kreis m; (arena) Manege f; (of telephone) Klingeln nt ♦ vt, vi (bell) läuten; (BRIT) anrufen; **~ back** (BRIT) vt, vi zurückrufen; **~ off** (BRIT) vi aufhängen; **~ up** (BRIT) vt anrufen; **~ binder** n Ringbuch nt; **~ing** n Klingeln nt; (of large bell) Läuten nt; (in ears) Klingen nt; **~ing tone** n (TEL) Rufzeichen nt

ringleader ['rɪŋliːdə*] n Anführer m, Rädelsführer m

ringlets ['rɪŋlɪts] npl Ringellocken pl

ring road n Umgehungsstraße f

ringtone ['rɪŋtəun] n Klingelton m

rink [rɪŋk] n (ice ~) Eisbahn f

rinse [rɪns] n Spülen nt ♦ vt spülen

riot ['raɪət] n Aufruhr m ♦ vi randalieren; **to run ~** (people) randalieren; (vegetation) wuchern; **~er** n Aufrührer m; **~ous** adj aufrührerisch; (noisy) lärmend

rip [rɪp] n Schlitz m, Riss m ♦ vt, vi (zer)reißen; **~cord** n Reißleine f

ripe [raɪp] adj reif; **~n** vi reifen ♦ vt reifen lassen

rip-off ['rɪpɔf] (inf) n: **it's a ~~!** das ist Wucher!

ripple ['rɪpl] n kleine Welle f ♦ vt kräuseln ♦ vi sich kräuseln

rise [raɪz] (pt **rose**, pp **risen**) n (slope) Steigung f; (esp in wages: BRIT) Erhöhung f; (growth) Aufstieg m ♦ vi (sun) aufgehen; (smoke) aufsteigen; (mountain) sich erheben; (ground) ansteigen; (prices) steigen; (in revolt) sich erheben; **to give ~ to** Anlass geben zu; **to ~ to the occasion** sich der Lage gewachsen zeigen; **~n** [rɪzn] pp of **rise**; **~r** ['raɪzə*] n: **to be an early ~r** ein(e) Frühaufsteher(in) m(f) sein; **rising** ['raɪzɪŋ] adj (tide, prices) steigend; (sun, moon) aufgehend ♦ n (uprising) Aufstand m

risk [rɪsk] n Gefahr f, Risiko nt ♦ vt (venture) wagen; (chance loss of) riskieren, aufs Spiel setzen; **to take** or **run the ~ of doing sth** das Risiko eingehen, etw zu tun; **at ~** in Gefahr; **at one's own ~** auf eigene Gefahr; **~y** adj riskant

risqué ['riːskeɪ] adj gewagt

rissole ['rɪsəul] n Fleischklößchen nt

rite [raɪt] n Ritus m; **last ~s** Letzte Ölung f

ritual ['rɪtjuəl] n Ritual nt ♦ adj ritual, Ritual-; (fig) rituell

rival ['raɪvl] n Rivale m, Konkurrent m ♦ adj rivalisierend ♦ vt rivalisieren mit; (COMM) konkurrieren mit; **~ry** n Rivalität f; Konkurrenz f

river ['rɪvə*] n Fluss m, Strom m ♦ cpd (port, traffic) Fluss-; **up/down ~** flussaufwärts/ -abwärts; **~bank** n Flussufer nt; **~bed** n Flussbett nt

rivet ['rɪvɪt] n Niete f ♦ vt (fasten) (ver)nieten

Riviera [rɪvɪ'ɛərə] n: **the ~** die Riviera

road [rəud] n Straße f ♦ cpd Straßen-; **major/minor ~** Haupt-/Nebenstraße f; **~ accident** n Verkehrsunfall m; **~block** n Straßensperre f; **~hog** n Verkehrsrowdy m; **~ map** n Straßenkarte f; **~ rage** n Aggressivität f im Straßenverkehr; **~ safety** n Verkehrssicherheit f; **~side** n Straßenrand m ♦ adj an der Landstraße (gelegen); **~ sign** n Straßenschild nt; **~ user** n Verkehrsteilnehmer m; **~way** n Fahrbahn f;

~ works npl Straßenbauarbeiten pl; **~worthy** adj verkehrssicher

roam [rəum] vi (umher)streifen ♦ vt durchstreifen

roar [rɔːʳ] n Brüllen nt, Gebrüll nt ♦ vi brüllen; **to ~ with laughter** vor Lachen brüllen; **to do a ~ing trade** ein Riesengeschäft machen

roast [rəust] n Braten m ♦ vt braten, schmoren; **~ beef** n Roastbeef nt

rob [rɔb] vt bestehlen, berauben; (bank) ausrauben; **to ~ sb of sth** jdm etw rauben; **~ber** n Räuber m; **~bery** n Raub m

robe [rəub] n (dress) Gewand nt; (US) Hauskleid nt; (judge's) Robe f

robin ['rɔbɪn] n Rotkehlchen nt

robot ['rəubɔt] n Roboter m

robust [rəu'bʌst] adj (person) robust; (appetite, economy) gesund

rock [rɔk] n Felsen m; (BRIT: sweet) Zuckerstange f ♦ vt wiegen, schaukeln; **on the ~s** (drink) mit Eis(würfeln); (marriage) gescheitert; (ship) aufgelaufen; **~ and roll** n Rock und Roll m; **~-bottom** n (fig) Tiefpunkt m; **~ery** n Steingarten m

rocket ['rɔkɪt] n Rakete f

rocking chair ['rɔkɪŋ-] n Schaukelstuhl m

rocking horse n Schaukelpferd nt

rocky ['rɔkɪ] adj felsig

rod [rɔd] n (bar) Stange f; (stick) Rute f

rode [rəud] pt of **ride**

rodent ['rəudnt] n Nagetier nt

roe [rəu] n (also: **~ deer**) Reh nt; (of fish: also: **hard ~**) Rogen m; **soft ~** Milch f

rogue [rəug] n Schurke m

role [rəul] n Rolle f; **~ play** n Rollenspiel nt

roll [rəul] n Rolle f; (bread) Brötchen nt; (list) (Namens)liste f; (of drum) Wirbel m ♦ vt (turn) rollen, (herum)wälzen; (grass etc) walzen ♦ vi (swing) schlingern; (sound) rollen, grollen; **~ about** or **around** vi herumkugeln; (ship) schlingern; (dog etc) sich wälzen; **~ by** vi (time) verfließen; **~ over** vi sich (herum)drehen; **~ up** vi (arrive) kommen, auftauchen ♦ vt (carpet) aufrollen; **~ call** n Namensaufruf m; **~er** n Rolle f, Walze f; (road ~er) Straßenwalze f;

R~erblade ® n Rollerblade m; **~er coaster** n Achterbahn f; **~er skates** npl Rollschuhe pl; **~-skating** n Rollschuhlaufen nt

rolling ['rəulɪŋ] adj (landscape) wellig; **~ pin** n Nudel- or Wellholz nt; **~ stock** n Wagenmaterial nt

ROM [rɔm] n abbr (= read only memory) ROM m

Roman ['rəumən] adj römisch ♦ n Römer(in) m(f); **~ Catholic** adj römisch-katholisch ♦ n Katholik(in) m(f)

romance [rə'mæns] n Romanze f; (story) (Liebes)roman m

Romania [rəu'meɪnɪə] n = **Rumania**; **~n** n = **Rumanian**

Roman numeral n römische Ziffer

romantic [rə'mæntɪk] adj romantisch; **~ism** [rə'mæntɪsɪzəm] n Romantik f

Rome [rəum] n Rom nt

romp [rɔmp] n Tollen nt ♦ vi (also: **~ about**) herumtollen

rompers ['rɔmpəz] npl Spielanzug m

roof [ruːf] (pl **~s**) n Dach nt; (of mouth) Gaumen m ♦ vt überdachen, überdecken; **~ing** n Deckmaterial nt; **~ rack** n (AUT) Dachgepäckträger m

rook [ruk] n (bird) Saatkrähe f; (chess) Turm m

room [ruːm] n Zimmer nt, Raum m; (space) Platz m; (fig) Spielraum m; **~s** npl (accommodation) Wohnung f; **"~s to let** (BRIT) or **for rent** (US)" „Zimmer zu vermieten"; **single/double ~** Einzel-/ Doppelzimmer nt; **~ing house** n (US) Mietshaus nt (mit möblierten Wohnungen); **~mate** n Mitbewohner(in) m(f); **~ service** n Zimmerbedienung f; **~y** adj geräumig

roost [ruːst] n Hühnerstange f ♦ vi auf der Stange hocken

rooster ['ruːstəʳ] n Hahn m

root [ruːt] n (also fig) Wurzel f ♦ vi wurzeln; **~ about** vi (fig) herumwühlen; **~ for** vt fus Stimmung machen für; **~ out** vt ausjäten; (fig) ausrotten

rope [rəup] n Seil nt ♦ vt (tie) festschnüren; **to know the ~s** sich auskennen; **to ~ sb in** jdn gewinnen; **~ off** vt absperren;

~ ladder *n* Strickleiter *f*

rosary ['rəʊzərɪ] *n* Rosenkranz *m*

rose [rəʊz] *pt of* **rise** ♦ *n* Rose *f* ♦ *adj* Rosen-, rosenrot

rosé ['rəʊzeɪ] *n* Rosé *m*

rosebud ['rəʊzbʌd] *n* Rosenknospe *f*

rosebush ['rəʊzbʊʃ] *n* Rosenstock *m*

rosemary ['rəʊzmərɪ] *n* Rosmarin *m*

rosette [rəʊ'zet] *n* Rosette *f*

roster ['rɒstə*] *n* Dienstplan *m*

rostrum ['rɒstrəm] *n* Rednerbühne *f*

rosy ['rəʊzɪ] *adj* rosig

rot [rɒt] *n* Fäulnis *f*; (*nonsense*) Quatsch *m* ♦ *vi* verfaulen ♦ *vt* verfaulen lassen

rota ['rəʊtə] *n* Dienstliste *f*

rotary ['rəʊtərɪ] *adj* rotierend

rotate [rəʊ'teɪt] *vt* rotieren lassen; (*take turns*) turnusmäßig wechseln ♦ *vi* rotieren; **rotating** *adj* rotierend; **rotation** [rəʊ'teɪʃən] *n* Umdrehung *f*

rote [rəʊt] *n*: **by ~** auswendig

rotten ['rɒtn] *adj* faul; (*fig*) schlecht, gemein; **to feel ~** (*ill*) sich elend fühlen

rotund [rəʊ'tʌnd] *adj* rundlich

rouble ['ruːbl] (*US* **ruble**) *n* Rubel *m*

rough [rʌf] *adj* (*not smooth*) rau; (*path*) uneben; (*violent*) roh, grob; (*crossing*) stürmisch; (*without comforts*) hart, unbequem; (*unfinished, makeshift*) grob; (*approximate*) ungefähr ♦ *n* (*BRIT: person*) Rowdy *m*, Rohling *m*; (*GOLF*): **in the ~** im Rau ♦ *vt*: **to ~ it** primitiv leben; **to sleep ~** im Freien schlafen; **~age** *n* Ballaststoffe *pl*; **~-and-ready** *adj* provisorisch; (*work*) zusammengehauen; **~ copy** *n* Entwurf *m*; **~ draft** *n* Entwurf *m*; **~ly** *adv* grob; (*about*) ungefähr; **~ness** *f* Rauheit *f*; (*of manner*) Ungeschliffenheit *f*

roulette [ruː'let] *n* Roulett(e) *nt*

Roumania [ruː'meɪnɪə] *n* = **Rumania**

round [raʊnd] *adj* rund; (*figures*) aufgerundet ♦ *adv* (*in a circle*) rundherum ♦ *prep* um ... herum ♦ *n* Runde *f*; (*of ammunition*) Magazin *nt* ♦ *vt* (*corner*) biegen um; **all ~** überall; **the long way ~** der Umweg; **all the year ~** das ganze Jahr über; **it's just ~ the corner** (*fig*) es ist gerade um die Ecke;

~ the clock rund um die Uhr; **to go ~ to sb's (house)** jdn besuchen; **to go ~ the back** hintenherum gehen; **enough to go ~** genug für alle; **to go the ~s** (*story*) die Runde machen; **a ~ of applause** ein Beifall *m*; **a ~ of drinks** eine Runde Drinks; **a ~ of sandwiches** ein Sandwich *nt* or *m*, ein belegtes Brot; **~ off** *vt* abrunden; **~ up** *vt* (*end*) abschließen; (*figures*) aufrunden; (*criminals*) hochnehmen; **~about** *n* (*BRIT: traffic*) Kreisverkehr *m*; (: *merry-go-~*) Karussell *nt* ♦ *adj* auf Umwegen; **~ers** *npl* (*game*) ≈ Schlagball *m*; **~ly** *adv* (*fig*) gründlich; **~-shouldered** *adj* mit abfallenden Schultern; **~ trip** *n* Rundreise *f*; **~up** *n* Zusammentreiben *nt*, Sammeln *nt*

rouse [raʊz] *vt* (*waken*) (auf)wecken; (*stir up*) erregen; **rousing** *adj* (*welcome*) stürmisch; (*speech*) zündend

route [ruːt] *n* Weg *m*, Route *f*; **~ map** (*BRIT*) *n* (*for journey*) Streckenkarte *f*

routine [ruː'tiːn] *n* Routine *f* ♦ *adj* Routine-

row¹ [raʊ] *n* (*noise*) Lärm *m*; (*dispute*) Streit *m* ♦ *vi* sich streiten

row² [rəʊ] *n* (*line*) Reihe *f* ♦ *vt, vi* (*boat*) rudern; **in a ~** (*fig*) hintereinander; **~boat** ['rəʊbəʊt] (*US*) *n* Ruderboot *nt*

rowdy ['raʊdɪ] *adj* rüpelhaft ♦ *n* (*person*) Rowdy *m*

rowing ['rəʊɪŋ] *n* Rudern *nt*; (*SPORT*) Rudersport *m*; **~ boat** (*BRIT*) *n* Ruderboot *nt*

royal ['rɔɪəl] *adj* königlich, Königs-; **R~ Air Force** *n* Königliche Luftwaffe *f*; **~ty** ['rɔɪəltɪ] *n* (*family*) königliche Familie *f*; (*for novel etc*) Tantieme *f*

rpm *abbr* (= *revs per minute*) U/min

R.S.V.P. *abbr* (= *répondez s'il vous plaît*) u. A. w. g.

Rt. Hon. (*BRIT*) *abbr* (= *Right Honourable*) Abgeordnete(r) *mf*

rub [rʌb] *n* (*with cloth*) Polieren *nt*; (*on person*) Reiben *nt* ♦ *vt* reiben; **to ~ sb up** (*BRIT*) or **to ~ sb** (*US*) **the wrong way** jdn aufreizen; **~ off** *vi* (*also fig*): **to ~ off (on)** abfärben (auf +*acc*); **~ out** *vt* herausreiben; (*with eraser*) ausradieren

rubber ['rʌbə*] *n* Gummi *m*; (*BRIT*)

Radiergummi m; ~ **band** n Gummiband
nt; ~ **plant** n Gummibaum m
rubbish ['rʌbɪʃ] n (waste) Abfall m;
(nonsense) Blödsinn m, Quatsch m; ~ **bin**
(BRIT) n Mülleimer m; ~ **dump** n
Müllabladeplatz m
rubble ['rʌbl] n (Stein)schutt m
ruby ['ruːbɪ] n Rubin m ♦ adj rubinrot
rucksack ['rʌksæk] n Rucksack m
rudder ['rʌdər] n Steuerruder nt
ruddy ['rʌdɪ] adj (colour) rötlich; (inf: bloody)
verdammt
rude [ruːd] adj unverschämt; (shock) hart;
(awakening) unsanft; (unrefined, rough) grob;
~**ness** n Unverschämtheit f; Grobheit f
rudiment ['ruːdɪmənt] n Grundlage f
rueful ['ruːful] adj reuevoll
ruffian ['rʌfɪən] n Rohling m
ruffle ['rʌfl] vt kräuseln
rug [rʌg] n Brücke f; (in bedroom)
Bettvorleger m; (BRIT: for knees) (Reise)decke
f
rugby ['rʌgbɪ] n (also: ~ **football**) Rugby nt
rugged ['rʌgɪd] adj (coastline) zerklüftet;
(features) markig
rugger ['rʌgər] (BRIT: inf) n = rugby
ruin ['ruːɪn] n Ruine f; (downfall) Ruin m ♦ vt
ruinieren; ~**s** npl (fig) Trümmer pl; ~**ous**
adj ruinierend
rule [ruːl] n Regel f; (government) Regierung
f; (for measuring) Lineal nt ♦ vt (govern)
herrschen über +acc, regieren; (decide)
anordnen, entscheiden; (make lines on)
linieren ♦ vi herrschen, regieren;
entscheiden; **as a** ~ in der Regel; ~ **out** vt
ausschließen; ~**d** adj (paper) liniert; ~**r** n
Lineal nt; Herrscher m; ruling ['ruːlɪŋ] adj
(party) Regierungs-; (class) herrschend ♦ n
(JUR) Entscheid m
rum [rʌm] n Rum m
Rumania [ruːˈmeɪnɪə] n Rumänien nt; ~**n** adj
rumänisch ♦ n Rumäne m, Rumänin f;
(LING) Rumänisch nt
rumble ['rʌmbl] n Rumpeln nt; (of thunder)
Grollen nt ♦ vi rumpeln; grollen
rummage ['rʌmɪdʒ] vi durchstöbern
rumour ['ruːmər] (US **rumor**) n Gerücht nt

♦ vt: **it is ~ed that** man sagt or man
munkelt, dass
rump [rʌmp] n Hinterteil nt; ~ **steak** n
Rumpsteak nt
rumpus ['rʌmpəs] n Spektakel m
run [rʌn] (pt **ran**, pp **run**) n Lauf m; (in car)
(Spazier)fahrt f; (series) Serie f, Reihe f; (ski
~) (Ski)abfahrt f; (in stocking) Laufmasche f
♦ vt (cause to ~) laufen lassen; (car, train,
bus) fahren; (race, distance) laufen, rennen;
(manage) leiten; (COMPUT) laufen lassen;
(pass: hand, eye) gleiten lassen ♦ vi laufen;
(move quickly) laufen, rennen; (bus, train)
fahren; (flow) fließen, laufen; (colours)
(ab)färben; **there was a ~ on** (meat, tickets)
es gab einen Ansturm auf +acc; **on the ~**
auf der Flucht; **in the long ~** auf die Dauer;
I'll ~ you to the station ich fahre dich zum
Bahnhof; **to ~ a risk** ein Risiko eingehen; ~
about or **around** vi (children)
umherspringen; ~ **across** vt fus (find)
stoßen auf +acc; ~ **away** vi weglaufen; ~
down vi (clock) ablaufen ♦ vt (production,
factory) allmählich auflösen; (with car)
überfahren; (talk against) heruntermachen;
to be ~ down erschöpft or abgespannt
sein; ~ **in** (BRIT) vt (car) einfahren; ~ **into**
vt fus (meet: person) zufällig treffen; (trouble)
bekommen; (collide with) rennen gegen;
fahren gegen; ~ **off** vi fortlaufen; ~ **out** vi
(person) hinausrennen; (liquid) auslaufen;
(lease) ablaufen; (money) ausgeben; **he ran
out of money/petrol!** ihm ging das Geld/
Benzin aus; ~ **over** vt (in accident)
überfahren; ~ **through** vt (instructions)
durchgehen; ~ **up** vt (debt, bill) machen; ~
up against vt fus (difficulties) stoßen auf
+acc; ~**away** adj (horse) ausgebrochen;
(person) flüchtig
rung [rʌŋ] pp of **ring** ♦ n Sprosse f
runner ['rʌnər] n Läufer(in) m(f); (for sleigh)
Kufe f; ~ **bean** (BRIT) n Stangenbohne f;
~-**up** n Zweite(r) mf
running ['rʌnɪŋ] n (of business) Leitung f; (of
machine) Betrieb m ♦ adj (water) fließend;
(commentary) laufend; **to be in/out of the
~ for sth** im/aus dem Rennen für etw sein;

3 days ~ 3 Tage lang *or* hintereinander; **~ costs** *npl* (*of car, machine*) Unterhaltungskosten *pl*

runny ['rʌnɪ] *adj* dünn; (*nose*) laufend

run-of-the-mill ['rʌnəvðə'mɪl] *adj* gewöhnlich, alltäglich

runt [rʌnt] *n* (*animal*) Kümmerer *m*

run-up ['rʌnʌp] *n*: **the ~~~ to** (*election etc*) die Endphase vor +*dat*

runway ['rʌnweɪ] *n* Startbahn *f*

rupture ['rʌptʃə⁽ʳ⁾] *n* (*MED*) Bruch *m*

rural ['ruərl] *adj* ländlich, Land-

ruse [ruːz] *n* Kniff *m*, List *f*

rush [rʌʃ] *n* Eile *f*, Hetze *f*; (*FIN*) starke Nachfrage *f* ♦ *vt* (*carry along*) auf dem schnellsten Wege schaffen *or* transportieren; (*attack*) losstürmen auf +*acc* ♦ *vi* (*hurry*) eilen, stürzen; **don't ~ me** dräng mich nicht; **~ hour** *n* Hauptverkehrszeit *f*

rusk [rʌsk] *n* Zwieback *m*

Russia ['rʌʃə] *n* Russland *nt*; **~n** *adj* russisch ♦ *n* Russe *m*, Russin *f*; (*LING*) Russisch *nt*

rust [rʌst] *n* Rost *m* ♦ *vi* rosten

rustic ['rʌstɪk] *adj* bäuerlich, ländlich

rustle ['rʌsl] *vi* rauschen, rascheln ♦ *vt* rascheln lassen

rustproof ['rʌstpruːf] *adj* rostfrei

rusty ['rʌstɪ] *adj* rostig

rut [rʌt] *n* (*in track*) Radspur *f*; **to be in a ~** im Trott stecken

ruthless ['ruːθlɪs] *adj* rücksichtslos

rye [raɪ] *n* Roggen *m*; **~ bread** *n* Roggenbrot *nt*

S, s

sabbath ['sæbəθ] *n* Sabbat *m*

sabotage ['sæbətɑːʒ] *n* Sabotage *f* ♦ *vt* sabotieren

saccharin ['sækərɪn] *n* Sa(c)charin *nt*

sachet ['sæʃeɪ] *n* (*of shampoo etc*) Briefchen *nt*, Kissen *nt*

sack [sæk] *n* Sack *m* ♦ *vt* (*inf*) hinauswerfen; (*pillage*) plündern; **to get the ~** rausfliegen; **~ing** *n* (*material*) Sackleinen *nt*; (*inf*)

Rausschmiss *m*

sacrament ['sækrəmənt] *n* Sakrament *nt*

sacred ['seɪkrɪd] *adj* heilig

sacrifice ['sækrɪfaɪs] *n* Opfer *nt* ♦ *vt* (*also fig*) opfern

sacrilege ['sækrɪlɪdʒ] *n* Schändung *f*

sad [sæd] *adj* traurig; **~den** *vt* traurig machen, betrüben

saddle ['sædl] *n* Sattel *m* ♦ *vt* (*burden*): **to ~ sb with sth** jdm etw aufhalsen; **~bag** *n* Satteltasche *f*

sadistic [sə'dɪstɪk] *adj* sadistisch

sadly ['sædlɪ] *adv* traurig; (*unfortunately*) leider

sadness ['sædnɪs] *n* Traurigkeit *f*

s.a.e. *abbr* (= *stamped addressed envelope*) adressierte(r) Rückumschlag *m*

safe [seɪf] *adj* (*careful*) vorsichtig ♦ *n* Safe *m*; **~ and sound** gesund und wohl; **(just) to be on the ~ side** um ganz sicherzugehen; **~ from** (*attack*) sicher vor +*dat*; **~-conduct** *n* freie(s) Geleit *nt*; **~-deposit** *n* (*vault*) Tresorraum *m*; (*box*) Banksafe *m*; **~guard** *n* Sicherung *f* ♦ *vt* sichern, schützen; **~keeping** *n* sichere Verwahrung *f*; **~ly** *adv* sicher; (*arrive*) wohlbehalten; **~ sex** *n* geschützter Sex *m*

safety ['seɪftɪ] *n* Sicherheit *f*; **~ belt** *n* Sicherheitsgurt *m*; **~ pin** *n* Sicherheitsnadel *f*; **~ valve** *n* Sicherheitsventil *nt*

sag [sæg] *vi* (durch)sacken

sage [seɪdʒ] *n* (*herb*) Salbei *m*; (*person*) Weise(r) *mf*

Sagittarius [sædʒɪ'teərɪəs] *n* Schütze *m*

Sahara [sə'hɑːrə] *n*: **the ~ (Desert)** die (Wüste) Sahara

said [sed] *pt, pp of* **say**

sail [seɪl] *n* Segel *nt*; (*trip*) Fahrt *f* ♦ *vt* segeln ♦ *vi* segeln; (*begin voyage: person*) abfahren; (: *ship*) auslaufen; (*fig: cloud etc*) dahinsegeln; **to go for a ~** segeln gehen; **they ~ed into Copenhagen** sie liefen in Kopenhagen ein; **~ through** *vt fus, vi* (*fig*) (es) spielend schaffen; **~boat** (*US*) *n* Segelboot *nt*; **~ing** *n* Segeln *nt*; **~ing ship** *n* Segelschiff *nt*; **~or** *n* Matrose *m*, Seemann *m*

saint [seɪnt] n Heilige(r) mf; **~ly** adj heilig, fromm

sake [seɪk] n: **for the ~ of** um +gen willen

salad ['sæləd] n Salat m; **~ bowl** n Salatschüssel f; **~ cream** (BRIT) n Salatmayonnaise f, Salatmajonäse f; **~ dressing** n Salatsoße f

salary ['sælərɪ] n Gehalt nt

sale [seɪl] n Verkauf m; (reduced prices) Schlussverkauf m; **"for ~"** „zu verkaufen"; **on ~** zu verkaufen; **~room** n Verkaufsraum m; **~s assistant** n Verkäufer(in) m(f); **~s clerk** (US) n Verkäufer(in) m(f); **~sman** (irreg) n Verkäufer m; (representative) Vertreter m; **~s rep** n (COMM) Vertreter(in) m(f); **~swoman** (irreg) n Verkäuferin f

salient ['seɪlɪənt] adj bemerkenswert

saliva [sə'laɪvə] n Speichel m

sallow ['sæləʊ] adj fahl; (face) bleich

salmon ['sæmən] n Lachs m

salon ['sælɔn] n Salon m

saloon [sə'luːn] n (BRIT: AUT) Limousine f; (ship's lounge) Salon m; **~ car** (BRIT) n Limousine f

salt [sɔːlt] n Salz nt ♦ vt (cure) einsalzen; (flavour) salzen; **~cellar** n Salzfass nt; **~water** adj Salzwasser-; **~y** adj salzig

salute [sə'luːt] n (MIL) Gruß m; (with guns) Salutschüsse pl ♦ vt (MIL) salutieren

salvage ['sælvɪdʒ] n (from ship) Bergung f; (property) Rettung f ♦ vt bergen; retten

salvation [sæl'veɪʃən] n Rettung f; **S~ Army** n Heilsarmee f

same [seɪm] adj, pron (similar) gleiche(r, s); (identical) derselbe/dieselbe/dasselbe; **the ~ book as** das gleiche Buch wie; **at the ~ time** zur gleichen Zeit, gleichzeitig; (however) zugleich, andererseits; **all** or **just the ~** trotzdem; **the ~ to you!** gleichfalls!; **to do the ~ (as sb)** das Gleiche tun (wie jd)

sample ['sɑːmpl] n Probe f ♦ vt probieren

sanctify ['sæŋktɪfaɪ] vt weihen

sanctimonious [sæŋktɪ'məʊnɪəs] adj scheinheilig

sanction ['sæŋkʃən] n Sanktion f

sanctity ['sæŋktɪtɪ] n Heiligkeit f; (fig)

Unverletzlichkeit f

sanctuary ['sæŋktjʊərɪ] n (for fugitive) Asyl nt; (refuge) Zufluchtsort m; (for animals) Schutzgebiet nt

sand [sænd] n Sand m ♦ vt (furniture) schmirgeln

sandal ['sændl] n Sandale f

sand: **~box** (US) n = **sandpit**; **~castle** n Sandburg f; **~ dune** n (Sand)düne f; **~paper** n Sandpapier nt; **~pit** n Sandkasten m; **~stone** n Sandstein m

sandwich ['sændwɪtʃ] n Sandwich m or nt ♦ vt (also: **~ in**) einklemmen; **cheese / ham ~** Käse-/Schinkenbrot; **~ed between** eingeklemmt zwischen; **~ board** n Reklametafel f; **~ course** (BRIT) n Theorie und Praxis abwechselnde(r) Ausbildungsgang m

sandy ['sændɪ] adj sandig; (hair) rotblond

sane [seɪn] adj geistig gesund or normal; (sensible) vernünftig, gescheit

sang [sæŋ] pt of **sing**

sanitary ['sænɪtərɪ] adj hygienisch; **~ towel** n (Monats)binde f

sanitation [sænɪ'teɪʃən] n sanitäre Einrichtungen pl; **~ department** (US) n Stadtreinigung f

sanity ['sænɪtɪ] n geistige Gesundheit f; (sense) Vernunft f

sank [sæŋk] pt of **sink**

Santa Claus [sæntə'klɔːz] n Nikolaus m, Weihnachtsmann m

sap [sæp] n (of plants) Saft m ♦ vt (strength) schwächen

sapling ['sæplɪŋ] n junge(r) Baum m

sapphire ['sæfaɪə] n Saphir m

sarcasm ['sɑːkæzm] n Sarkasmus m

sarcastic [sɑː'kæstɪk] adj sarkastisch

sardine [sɑː'diːn] n Sardine f

Sardinia [sɑː'dɪnɪə] n Sardinien nt

sardonic [sɑː'dɒnɪk] adj zynisch

sash [sæʃ] n Schärpe f

sat [sæt] pt, pp of **sit**

Satan ['seɪtn] n Satan m

satchel ['sætʃl] n (for school) Schulmappe f

satellite ['sætəlaɪt] n Satellit m; **~ dish** n (TECH) Parabolantenne f, Satellitenantenne *f;* ~ **television** *n* Satellitenfernsehen *nt*

satisfaction [sætɪsˈfækʃən] *n* Befriedigung *f*, Genugtuung *f;* **satisfactory** [sætɪsˈfæktərɪ] *adj* zufrieden stellend, befriedigend; **satisfied** *adj* befriedigt

satisfy [ˈsætɪsfaɪ] *vt* befriedigen, zufrieden stellen; (*convince*) überzeugen; (*conditions*) erfüllen; **~ing** *adj* befriedigend; (*meal*) sättigend

saturate [ˈsætʃəreɪt] *vt* (durch)tränken

Saturday [ˈsætədɪ] *n* Samstag *m*, Sonnabend *m*

sauce [sɔːs] *n* Soße *f*, Sauce *f;* **~pan** *n* Kasserolle *f*

saucer [ˈsɔːsər] *n* Untertasse *f*

saucy [ˈsɔːsɪ] *adj* frech, keck

Saudi [ˈsaudɪ]: ~ **Arabia** *n* Saudi-Arabien *nt;* ~ (**Arabian**) *adj* saudi-arabisch ♦ *n* Saudi-Araber(in) *m(f)*

sauna [ˈsɔːnə] *n* Sauna *f*

saunter [ˈsɔːntər] *vi* schlendern

sausage [ˈsɒsɪdʒ] *n* Wurst *f;* ~ **roll** *n* Wurst *f* im Schlafrock, Wurstpastete *f*

sauté [ˈsəuteɪ] *adj* Röst-

savage [ˈsævɪdʒ] *adj* wild ♦ *n* Wilde(r) *mf* ♦ *vt* (*animals*) zerfleischen

save [seɪv] *vt* retten; (*money, electricity etc*) sparen; (*strength etc*) aufsparen; (*COMPUT*) speichern ♦ *vi* (*also:* ~ **up**) sparen ♦ *n* (*SPORT*) (Ball)abwehr *f* ♦ *prep, conj* außer, ausgenommen

saving [ˈseɪvɪŋ] *adj:* **the** ~ **grace of** das Versöhnende an +*dat* ♦ *n* Ersparnis *f;* ~**s** *npl* (*money*) Ersparnisse *pl;* ~**s account** *n* Sparkonto *nt;* ~**s bank** *n* Sparkasse *f*

saviour [ˈseɪvjər] (*US* **savior**) *n* (*REL*) Erlöser *m*

savour [ˈseɪvər] (*US* **savor**) *vt* (*taste*) schmecken; (*fig*) genießen; ~**y** *adj* pikant, würzig

saw [sɔː] (*pt* **sawed**, *pp* **sawed** *or* **sawn**) *pt of* **see** ♦ *n* (*tool*) Säge *f* ♦ *vt, vi* sägen; ~**dust** *n* Sägemehl *nt;* ~**mill** *n* Sägewerk *nt;* ~**n-off shotgun** *n* Gewehr *nt* mit abgesägtem Lauf

sax [sæks] (*inf*) *n* Saxofon *nt*, Saxophon *nt*

saxophone [ˈsæksəfəun] *n* Saxofon *nt*, Saxophon *nt*

say [seɪ] (*pt, pp* **said**) *n:* **to have a/no** ~ **in sth** Mitspracherecht/kein Mitspracherecht bei etw haben ♦ *vt, vi* sagen; **let him have his** ~ lass ihn doch reden; **to** ~ **yes/no** Ja/Nein *or* ja/nein sagen; **that goes without** ~**ing** das versteht sich von selbst; **that is to** ~ das heißt; ~**ing** *n* Sprichwort *nt*

scab [skæb] *n* Schorf *m;* (*pej*) Streikbrecher *m*

scaffold [ˈskæfəld] *n* (*for execution*) Schafott *nt;* ~**ing** *n* (Bau)gerüst *nt*

scald [skɔːld] *n* Verbrühung *f* ♦ *vt* (*burn*) verbrühen

scale [skeɪl] *n* (*of fish*) Schuppe *f;* (*MUS*) Tonleiter *f;* (*on map, size*) Maßstab *m;* (*gradation*) Skala *f* ♦ *vt* (*climb*) erklimmen; ~**s** *npl* (*balance*) Waage *f;* **on a large** ~ (*fig*) im Großen, in großem Umfang; ~ **of charges** Gebührenordnung *f;* ~ **down** *vt* verkleinern; ~ **model** *n* maßstabgetreue(s) Modell *nt*

scallop [ˈskɒləp] *n* Kammmuschel *f*

scalp [skælp] *n* Kopfhaut *f*

scamper [ˈskæmpər] *vi:* **to** ~ **away** *or* **off** sich davonmachen

scampi [ˈskæmpɪ] *npl* Scampi *pl*

scan [skæn] *vt* (*examine*) genau prüfen; (*quickly*) überfliegen; (*horizon*) absuchen

scandal [ˈskændl] *n* Skandal *m;* (*piece of gossip*) Skandalgeschichte *f*

Scandinavia [skændɪˈneɪvɪə] *n* Skandinavien *nt;* ~**n** *adj* skandinavisch ♦ *n* Skandinavier(in) *m(f)*

scant [skænt] *adj* knapp; ~**ily** *adv* knapp, dürftig; ~**y** *adj* knapp, unzureichend

scapegoat [ˈskeɪpgəut] *n* Sündenbock *m*

scar [skɑːr] *n* Narbe *f* ♦ *vt* durch Narben entstellen

scarce [skɛəs] *adj* selten, rar; (*goods*) knapp; ~**ly** *adv* kaum; **scarcity** *n* Mangel *m*

scare [skɛər] *n* Schrecken *m* ♦ *vt* erschrecken; **bomb** ~ Bombendrohung *f;* **to** ~ **sb stiff** jdn zu Tode erschrecken; **to be** ~**d** Angst haben; ~ **away** *vt* (*animal*) verscheuchen; ~ **off** *vt* = **scare away;**

~**crow** n Vogelscheuche f
scarf [skɑ:f] (pl **scarves**) n Schal m; (headscarf) Kopftuch nt
scarlet ['skɑ:lɪt] adj scharlachrot ♦ n Scharlachrot nt; ~ **fever** n Scharlach m
scarves [skɑ:vz] npl of **scarf**
scary ['skɛərɪ] (inf) adj schaurig
scathing ['skeɪðɪŋ] adj scharf, vernichtend
scatter ['skætər] vt (sprinkle) (ver)streuen; (disperse) zerstreuen ♦ vi sich zerstreuen; ~**brained** adj flatterhaft, schusselig
scavenger ['skævəndʒər] n (animal) Aasfresser m
scenario [sɪ'nɑ:rɪəu] n (THEAT, CINE) Szenarium nt; (fig) Szenario nt
scene [si:n] n (of happening) Ort m; (of play, incident) Szene f; (view) Anblick m; (argument) Szene f, Auftritt m; ~**ry** ['si:nərɪ] n (THEAT) Bühnenbild nt; (landscape) Landschaft f
scenic ['si:nɪk] adj landschaftlich
scent [sɛnt] n Parfüm nt; (smell) Duft m ♦ vt parfümieren
sceptical ['skɛptɪkl] (US **skeptical**) adj skeptisch
schedule ['ʃɛdju:l, (US) 'skɛdju:l] n (list) Liste f; (plan) Programm nt; (of work) Zeitplan m ♦ vt planen; **on** ~ pünktlich; **to be ahead of/behind** ~ dem Zeitplan voraus/im Rückstand sein; ~**d flight** n (not charter) Linienflug m
scheme [ski:m] n Schema nt; (dishonest) Intrige f; (plan of action) Plan m ♦ vi intrigieren ♦ vt planen; **scheming** ['ski:mɪŋ] adj intrigierend
scholar ['skɒlər] n Gelehrte(r) m; (holding ~ship) Stipendiat m; ~**ly** adj gelehrt; ~**ship** n Gelehrsamkeit f; (grant) Stipendium nt
school [sku:l] n Schule f; (UNIV) Fakultät f ♦ vt schulen; ~ **age** n schulpflichtige(s) Alter nt; ~**book** n Schulbuch nt; ~**boy** n Schüler m; ~**children** npl Schüler pl, Schulkinder pl; ~**days** npl (alte) Schulzeit f; ~**girl** n Schülerin f; ~**ing** n Schulung f, Ausbildung f; ~**master** n Lehrer m; ~**mistress** n Lehrerin f; ~**teacher** n Lehrer(in) m(f)

sciatica [saɪ'ætɪkə] n Ischias m or nt
science ['saɪəns] n Wissenschaft f; (natural ~) Naturwissenschaft f; ~ **fiction** n Sciencefiction f; **scientific** [saɪən'tɪfɪk] adj wissenschaftlich; (natural ~s) naturwissenschaftlich; **scientist** ['saɪəntɪst] n Wissenschaftler(in) m(f)
scintillating ['sɪntɪleɪtɪŋ] adj sprühend
scissors ['sɪzəz] npl Schere f; **a pair of** ~ eine Schere
scoff [skɒf] vt (BRIT: inf: eat) fressen ♦ vi (mock): **to** ~ (**at**) spotten (über +acc)
scold [skəuld] vt schimpfen
scone [skɒn] n weiche(s) Teegebäck nt
scoop [sku:p] n Schaufel f; (news) sensationelle Erstmeldung f; ~ **out** vt herausschaufeln; ~ **up** vt aufschaufeln; (liquid) aufschöpfen
scooter ['sku:tər] n Motorroller m; (child's) Roller m
scope [skəup] n Ausmaß nt; (opportunity) (Spiel)raum m
scorch [skɔ:tʃ] n Brandstelle f ♦ vt versengen; ~**ing** adj brennend
score [skɔ:r] n (in game) Punktzahl f; (final ~) (Spiel)ergebnis nt; (MUS) Partitur f; (line) Kratzer m; (twenty) zwanzig, zwanzig Stück ♦ vt (goal) schießen; (points) machen; (mark) einritzen ♦ vi (keep record) Punkte zählen; **on that** ~ in dieser Hinsicht; **what's the** ~? wie stehts?; **to** ~ **6 out of 10** 6 von 10 Punkten erzielen; ~ **out** vt ausstreichen; ~**board** n Anschreibetafel f; ~**r** n Torschütze m; (recorder) (Auf)schreiber m
scorn [skɔ:n] n Verachtung f ♦ vt verhöhnen; ~**ful** adj verächtlich
Scorpio ['skɔ:pɪəu] n Skorpion m
Scot [skɒt] n Schotte m, Schottin f
Scotch [skɒtʃ] n Scotch m
scotch [skɒtʃ] vt (end) unterbinden
scot-free ['skɒt'fri:] adv: **to get off** ~~ (unpunished) ungeschoren davonkommen
Scotland ['skɒtlənd] n Schottland nt
Scots [skɒts] adj schottisch; ~**man/woman** (irreg) n Schotte m/Schottin f
Scottish ['skɒtɪʃ] adj schottisch

scoundrel ['skaʊndrl] n Schuft m

scour ['skaʊər] vt (search) absuchen; (clean) schrubben

scourge [skə:dʒ] n (whip) Geißel f; (plague) Qual f

scout [skaʊt] n (MIL) Späher m; (also: **boy ~**) Pfadfinder m; **~ around** vi: **to ~ around (for)** sich umsehen (nach)

scowl [skaʊl] n finstere(r) Blick m ♦ vi finster blicken

scrabble ['skræbl] vi (also: **~ around**: search) (herum)tasten; (claw): **to ~ (at)** kratzen (an +dat) ♦ n: **S~** ® Scrabble nt ®

scraggy ['skrægɪ] adj dürr, hager

scram [skræm] (inf) vi abhauen

scramble ['skræmbl] n (climb) Kletterei f; (struggle) Kampf m ♦ vi klettern; (fight) sich schlagen; **to ~ out/through** krabbeln aus/durch; **to ~ for sth** sich um etw raufen; **~d eggs** npl Rührei nt

scrap [skræp] n (bit) Stückchen nt; (fight) Keilerei f; (also: **~ iron**) Schrott m ♦ vt verwerfen ♦ vi (fight) streiten, sich prügeln; **~s** npl (leftovers) Reste pl; (waste) Abfall m; **~book** n Einklebealbum nt; **~ dealer** n Schrotthändler(in) m(f)

scrape [skreɪp] n Kratzen nt; (trouble) Klemme f ♦ vt kratzen; (car) zerkratzen; (clean) abkratzen ♦ vi (make harsh noise) kratzen; **to ~ through** gerade noch durchkommen; **~r** n Kratzer m

scrap: ~ heap n Schrotthaufen m; **on the ~ heap** (fig) beim alten Eisen; **~ iron** n Schrott m; **~ merchant** (BRIT) n Altwarenhändler(in) m(f); **~ paper** n Schmierpapier nt

scrappy ['skræpɪ] adj zusammengestoppelt

scratch [skrætʃ] n (wound) Kratzer m, Schramme f ♦ adj: **~ team** zusammengewürfelte Mannschaft ♦ vt kratzen; (car) zerkratzen ♦ vi (sich) kratzen; **to start from ~** ganz von vorne anfangen; **to be up to ~** den Anforderungen entsprechen

scrawl [skrɔ:l] n Gekritzel nt ♦ vt, vi kritzeln

scrawny ['skrɔ:nɪ] adj (person, neck) dürr

scream [skri:m] n Schrei m ♦ vi schreien

scree [skri:] n Geröll(halde f) nt

screech [skri:tʃ] n Schrei m ♦ vi kreischen

screen [skri:n] n (protective) Schutzschirm m; (CINE) Leinwand f; (TV) Bildschirm m ♦ vt (shelter) (be)schirmen; (film) zeigen, vorführen; **~ing** n (MED) Untersuchung f; **~play** n Drehbuch nt; **~ saver** n (COMPUT) Bildschirmschoner m

screw [skru:] n Schraube f ♦ vt (fasten) schrauben; (vulgar) bumsen; **~ up** vt (paper etc) zerknüllen; (inf: ruin) vermasseln (inf); **~driver** n Schraubenzieher m

scribble ['skrɪbl] n Gekritzel nt ♦ vt kritzeln

script [skrɪpt] n (handwriting) Handschrift f; (for film) Drehbuch nt; (THEAT) Manuskript nt, Text m

Scripture ['skrɪptʃər] n Heilige Schrift f

scroll [skrəʊl] n Schriftrolle f

scrounge [skraʊndʒ] (inf) vt: **to ~ sth off** or **from sb** etw bei jdm abstauben ♦ n: **on the ~** beim Schnorren

scrub [skrʌb] n (clean) Schrubben nt; (in countryside) Gestrüpp nt ♦ vt (clean) schrubben

scruff [skrʌf] n: **by the ~ of the neck** am Genick

scruffy ['skrʌfɪ] adj unordentlich, vergammelt

scrum(mage) ['skrʌm(ɪdʒ)] n Getümmel nt

scruple ['skru:pl] n Skrupel m, Bedenken nt

scrupulous ['skru:pjʊləs] adj peinlich genau, gewissenhaft

scrutinize ['skru:tɪnaɪz] vt genau prüfen; **scrutiny** ['skru:tɪnɪ] n genaue Untersuchung f

scuff [skʌf] vt (shoes) abstoßen

scuffle ['skʌfl] n Handgemenge nt

sculptor ['skʌlptər] n Bildhauer(in) m(f)

sculpture ['skʌlptʃər] n (ART) Bildhauerei f; (statue) Skulptur f

scum [skʌm] n (also fig) Abschaum m

scurry ['skʌrɪ] vi huschen

scuttle ['skʌtl] n (also: **coal ~**) Kohleneimer m ♦ vt (ship) versenken ♦ vi (scamper): **to ~ away** or **off** sich davonmachen

scythe [saɪð] n Sense f

SDP (BRIT) n abbr = **Social Democratic**

Party

sea [si:] n Meer nt, See f; (fig) Meer nt ♦ adj Meeres-, See-; **by ~** (travel) auf dem Seeweg; **on the ~** (boat) auf dem Meer; (town) am Meer; **out to ~** aufs Meer hinaus; **out at ~** aufs Meer; **~board** n Küste f; **~food** n Meeresfrüchte pl; **~ front** n Strandpromenade f; **~going** adj seetüchtig, Hochsee-; **~gull** n Möwe f

seal [si:l] n (animal) Robbe f, Seehund m; (stamp, impression) Siegel nt ♦ vt versiegeln; **~ off** vt (place) abriegeln

sea level n Meeresspiegel m

sea lion n Seelöwe m

seam [si:m] n Saum m; (edges joining) Naht f; (of coal) Flöz nt

seaman ['si:mən] (irreg) n Seemann m

seaplane ['si:pleɪn] n Wasserflugzeug nt

seaport ['si:pɔ:t] n Seehafen m

search [sɜ:tʃ] n (for person, thing) Suche f; (of drawer, pockets, house) Durchsuchung f ♦ vi suchen ♦ vt durchsuchen; **in ~ of** auf der Suche nach; **to ~ for** suchen nach; **~ through** vt durchsuchen; **~ engine** n (COMPUT) Suchmaschine f; **~ing** adj (look) forschend; **~light** n Scheinwerfer m; **~ party** n Suchmannschaft f; **~ warrant** n Durchsuchungsbefehl m

sea: **~shore** ['si:ʃɔ:] n Meeresküste f; **~sick** ['si:sɪk] adj seekrank; **~side** ['si:saɪd] n Küste f; **~side resort** n Badeort m

season ['si:zn] n Jahreszeit f; (Christmas etc) Zeit f, Saison f ♦ vt (flavour) würzen; **~al** adj Saison-; **~ed** adj (fig) erfahren; **~ing** n Gewürz nt, Würze f; **~ ticket** n (RAIL) Zeitkarte f; (THEAT) Abonnement nt

seat [si:t] n Sitz m, Platz m; (in Parliament) Sitz m; (part of body) Gesäß nt; (of trousers) Hosenboden m ♦ vt (place) setzen; (have space for) Sitzplätze bieten für; **to be ~ed** sitzen; **~ belt** n Sicherheitsgurt m

sea: **~ water** n Meerwasser nt; **~weed** ['si:wi:d] n (See)tang m; **~worthy** ['si:wə:ðɪ] adj seetüchtig

sec. abbr (= second(s)) Sek.

secluded [sɪ'klu:dɪd] adj abgelegen

seclusion [sɪ'klu:ʒən] n Zurückgezogenheit f

second ['sekənd] adj zweite(r,s) ♦ adv (in ~ position) an zweiter Stelle ♦ n Sekunde f; (person) Zweite(r) mf; (COMM: imperfect) zweite Wahl f; (SPORT) Sekundant m; (AUT: also: ~ gear) zweite(r) Gang m; (BRIT: UNIV: degree) mittlere Note bei Abschlussprüfungen ♦ vt (support) unterstützen; **~ary** adj zweitrangig; **~ary school** n höhere Schule f, Mittelschule f; **~-class** adj zweiter Klasse; **~hand** adj aus zweiter Hand; (car etc) gebraucht; **~ hand** n (on clock) Sekundenzeiger m; **~ly** adv zweitens

secondment [sɪ'kɔndmənt] (BRIT) n Abordnung f

second-rate ['sekənd'reɪt] adj mittelmäßig

second thoughts npl: **to have ~** es sich dat anders überlegen; **on ~** (BRIT) or **thought** (US) oder lieber (nicht)

secrecy ['si:krəsɪ] n Geheimhaltung f

secret ['si:krɪt] n Geheimnis nt ♦ adj geheim, Geheim-; **in ~** geheim

secretarial [sekrɪ'teərɪəl] adj Sekretärinnen-

secretary ['sekrətərɪ] n Sekretär(in) m(f); **S~ of State** (BRIT) (POL) Minister(in) m(f) (für); **S~ of State (for)**

secretion [sɪ'kri:ʃən] n Absonderung f

secretive ['si:krətɪv] adj geheimtuerisch

secretly ['si:krɪtlɪ] adv geheim

sectarian [sek'teərɪən] adj (riots etc) Konfessions-, zwischen den Konfessionen

section ['sekʃən] n Teil m; (department) Abteilung f; (of document) Abschnitt m

sector ['sektə'] n Sektor m

secular ['sekjulə'] adj weltlich, profan

secure [sɪ'kjuə'] adj (safe) sicher; (firmly fixed) fest ♦ vt (make firm) befestigen, sichern; (obtain) sichern; **security** [sɪ'kjuərɪtɪ] n Sicherheit f; (pledge) Pfand nt; (document) Wertpapier nt; (national security) Staatssicherheit f; **security guard** n Sicherheitsbeamte(r) m, Wächter m, Wache f

sedan [sə'dæn] (US) n (AUT) Limousine f

sedate [sɪ'deɪt] adj gesetzt ♦ vt (MED) ein Beruhigungsmittel geben +dat; **sedation** [sɪ'deɪʃən] n (MED) Einfluss m von Beruhigungsmitteln; **sedative** ['sedɪtɪv] n

Beruhigungsmittel nt ♦ adj beruhigend, einschläfernd

sediment ['sedɪmənt] n (Boden)satz m

seduce [sɪ'djuːs] vt verführen; **seductive** [sɪ'dʌktɪv] adj verführerisch

see [siː] (pt **saw**, pp **seen**) vt sehen; (understand) (ein)sehen, erkennen; (visit) besuchen ♦ vi (be aware) sehen; (find out) nachsehen ♦ n (ECCL: R.C.) Bistum nt; (: Protestant) Kirchenkreis m; **to ~ sb to the door** jdn hinausbegleiten; **to ~ that** (ensure) dafür sorgen, dass; **~ you soon!** bis bald!; **~ about** vt fus sich kümmern um; **~ off** vt: **to ~ sb off** jdn zum Zug etc begleiten; **~ through** vt: **to ~ sth through** etw durchfechten; **to ~ through sb/sth** jdn/ etw durchschauen; **~ to** vt fus: **to ~ to it** dafür sorgen

seed [siːd] n Samen m ♦ vt (TENNIS) platzieren; **to go to ~** (plant) schießen; (fig) herunterkommen; **~ling** n Setzling m; **~y** adj (café) übel; (person) zweifelhaft

seeing ['siːɪŋ] conj: **~ (that)** da

seek [siːk] (pt, pp **sought**) vt suchen

seem [siːm] vi scheinen; **it ~s that ...** es scheint, dass ...; **~ingly** adv anscheinend

seen [siːn] pp of **see**

seep [siːp] vi sickern

seesaw ['siːsɔː] n Wippe f

seethe [siːð] vi: **to ~ with anger** vor Wut kochen

see-through ['siːθruː] adj (dress etc) durchsichtig

segment ['segmənt] n Teil m; (of circle) Ausschnitt m

segregate ['segrɪgeɪt] vt trennen

seize [siːz] vt (grasp) (er)greifen, packen; (power) ergreifen; (take legally) beschlagnahmen; **~ (up)on** vt fus sich stürzen auf +acc; **~ up** vi (TECH) sich festfressen; **seizure** ['siːʒəʳ] n (illness) Anfall m

seldom ['seldəm] adv selten

select [sɪ'lekt] adj ausgewählt ♦ vt auswählen; **~ion** [sɪ'lekʃən] n Auswahl f; **~ive** adj (person) wählerisch

self [self] (pl **selves**) pron selbst ♦ n Selbst

nt, Ich nt; **the ~** das Ich; **~-assured** adj selbstbewusst; **~-catering** (BRIT) adj für Selbstversorger; **~-centred** (US **self-centered**) adj egozentrisch; **~-coloured** (US **self-colored**) adj (of one colour) einfarbig, uni; **~-confidence** n Selbstvertrauen nt, Selbstbewusstsein nt; **~-conscious** adj gehemmt, befangen; **~-contained** adj (complete) (in sich) geschlossen; (person) verschlossen; (BRIT: flat) separat; **~-control** n Selbstbeherrschung f; **~-defence** (US **self-defense**) n Selbstverteidigung f; (JUR) Notwehr f; **~-discipline** n Selbstdisziplin f **~-employed** adj frei(schaffend); **~-evident** adj offensichtlich; **~-governing** adj selbst verwaltet; **~-indulgent** adj zügellos; **~-interest** n Eigennutz m

selfish ['selfɪʃ] adj egoistisch, selbstsüchtig; **~ness** n Egoismus m, Selbstsucht f

self: **~-lessly** adv selbstlos; **~-made** adj: **~-made man** Selfmademan m; **~-pity** n Selbstmitleid nt; **~-portrait** n Selbstbildnis nt; **~-possessed** adj selbstbeherrscht; **~-preservation** n Selbsterhaltung f; **~-reliant** adj unabhängig; **~-respect** n Selbstachtung f; **~-righteous** adj selbstgerecht; **~-sacrifice** n Selbstaufopferung f; **~-satisfied** adj selbstzufrieden; **~-service** adj Selbstbedienungs-; **~-sufficient** adj selbstgenügsam; **~-taught** adj selbst erlernt; **~-taught person** Autodidakt m

sell [sel] (pt, pp **sold**) vt verkaufen ♦ vi verkaufen; (goods) sich verkaufen; **to ~ at o for £10** für £10 verkaufen; **~ off** vt verkaufen; **~ out** vi alles verkaufen; **~-by date** n Verfalldatum nt; **~er** n Verkäufer m; **~ing price** n Verkaufspreis m

Sellotape ['seləuteɪp] (® BRIT) n Tesafilm m ®

sellout ['selaut] n (of tickets): **it was a ~** war ausverkauft

selves [selvz] npl of **self**

semaphore ['seməfɔːʳ] n Winkzeichen pl

semblance ['semblns] n Anschein m

semen ['siːmən] n Sperma nt

semester [sɪ'mestəʳ] (US) n Semester nt

semi ['semɪ] n = **semidetached house**; **~circle** n Halbkreis m; **~colon** n Semikolon nt; **~conductor** n Halbleiter m; **~detached house** (BRIT) n halbe(s) Doppelhaus nt; **~final** n Halbfinale nt

seminary ['semɪnərɪ] n (REL) Priesterseminar nt

semiskilled [semɪ'skɪld] adj angelernt

semi-skimmed [semɪ'skɪmd] adj (milk) teilentrahmt, Halbfett-

senate ['senɪt] n Senat m; **senator** n Senator m

send [send] (pt, pp sent) vt senden, schicken; (inf: inspire) hinreißen; **~ away** vt wegschicken; **~ away for** vt fus anfordern; **~ back** vt zurückschicken; **~ for** vt fus holen lassen; **~ off** vt (goods) abschicken; (BRIT: SPORT: player) vom Feld schicken; **~ out** vt (invitation) aussenden; **~ up** vt hinaufsenden; (BRIT: parody) verulken; **~er** n Absender m; **~-off** n: **to give sb a good ~-off** jdn (ganz) groß verabschieden

senior ['siːnɪəʳ] adj (older) älter; (higher rank) Ober- ♦ n (older person) Ältere(r) mf; (higher ranking) Rangälteste(r) mf; **~ citizen** n ältere(r) Mitbürger(in) m(f); **~ity** [siːnɪ'ɒrɪtɪ] n (of age) höhere(s) Alter nt; (in rank) höhere(r) Dienstgrad m

sensation [sen'seɪʃən] n Gefühl nt; (excitement) Sensation f, Aufsehen nt; **~al** adj (wonderful) wunderbar; (result) sensationell; (headlines etc) reißerisch

sense [sens] n Sinn m; (understanding) Verstand m, Vernunft f; (feeling) Gefühl nt ♦ vt fühlen, spüren; **~ of humour** Humor m; **to make ~** Sinn ergeben; **~less** adj sinnlos; (unconscious) besinnungslos

sensibility [sensɪ'bɪlɪtɪ] n Empfindsamkeit f; (feeling hurt) Empfindlichkeit f; **sensibilities** npl (feelings) Zartgefühl nt

sensible ['sensɪbl] adj vernünftig

sensitive ['sensɪtɪv] adj: **~ (to)** empfindlich (gegen); (artistic) feinfühlig; **sensitivity** [sensɪ'tɪvɪtɪ] n Empfindlichkeit f; (artistic) Feingefühl nt; (tact) Feinfühligkeit f

sensual ['sensjuəl] adj sinnlich

sensuous ['sensjuəs] adj sinnlich

sent [sent] pt, pp of **send**

sentence ['sentns] n Satz m; (JUR) Strafe f; Urteil nt ♦ vt: **to ~ sb to death/to 5 years** jdn zum Tode/zu 5 Jahren verurteilen

sentiment ['sentɪmənt] n Gefühl nt; (thought) Gedanke m; **~al** [sentɪ'mentl] adj sentimental; (of feelings rather than reason) gefühlsmäßig

sentry ['sentrɪ] n (Schild)wache f

separate [adj 'seprɪt, vb 'sepəreɪt] adj getrennt, separat ♦ vt trennen ♦ vi sich trennen; **~ly** adv getrennt; **~s** npl (clothes) Röcke, Pullover etc; **separation** [sepə'reɪʃən] n Trennung f

September [sep'tembəʳ] n September m

septic ['septɪk] adj vereitert, septisch; **~ tank** n Klärbehälter m

sequel ['siːkwl] n Folge f

sequence ['siːkwəns] n (Reihen)folge f

sequin ['siːkwɪn] n Paillette f

Serbia ['sɜːbɪə] n Serbien nt

serene [sɪ'riːn] adj heiter

sergeant ['sɑːdʒənt] n Feldwebel m; (POLICE) (Polizei)wachtmeister m

serial ['sɪərɪəl] n Fortsetzungsroman m; (TV) Fernsehserie f ♦ adj (number) (fort)laufend; **~ize** vt in Fortsetzungen veröffentlichen; in Fortsetzungen senden

series ['sɪərɪz] n inv Serie f, Reihe f

serious ['sɪərɪəs] adj ernst; (injury) schwer; **~ly** adv ernst(haft); (hurt) schwer; **~ness** n Ernst m, Ernsthaftigkeit f

sermon ['sɜːmən] n Predigt f

serrated [sɪ'reɪtɪd] adj gezackt

servant ['sɜːvənt] n Diener(in) m(f)

serve [sɜːv] vt dienen +dat; (guest, customer) bedienen; (food) servieren ♦ vi dienen, nützen; (at table) servieren; (TENNIS) geben, aufschlagen; **it ~s him right** das geschieht ihm recht; **that'll ~ as a table** das geht als Tisch; **to ~ a summons (on sb)** (jdn) vor Gericht laden; **~ out** or **up** vt (food) auftragen, servieren

service ['sɜːvɪs] n (help) Dienst m; (trains etc) Verbindung f; (hotel) Service m, Bedienung f; (set of dishes) Service nt; (REL)

Gottesdienst *m*; (*car*) Inspektion *f*; (*for TVs etc*) Kundendienst *m*; (*TENNIS*) Aufschlag *m* ♦ *vt* (*AUT, TECH*) warten, überholen; **the S~s** *npl* (*armed forces*) die Streitkräfte *pl*; **to be of ~ to sb** jdm einen großen Dienst erweisen; **~ included/not included** Bedienung inbegriffen/nicht inbegriffen; **~able** *adj* brauchbar; **~ area** *n* (*on motorway*) Raststätte *f*; **~ charge** (*BRIT*) *n* Bedienung *f*; **~man** (*irreg*) *n* (*soldier etc*) Soldat *m*; **~ station** *n* (*Groß*)tankstelle *f*

serviette [səː'vɪɛt] *n* Serviette *f*

servile ['səː'vaɪl] *adj* unterwürfig

session ['sɛʃən] *n* Sitzung *f*; (*POL*) Sitzungsperiode *f*; **to be in ~** tagen

set [sɛt] (*pt, pp* **set**) *n* (*collection of things*) Satz *m*, Set *nt*; (*RAD, TV*) Apparat *m*; (*TENNIS*) Satz *m*; (*group of people*) Kreis *m*; (*CINE*) Szene *f*; (*THEAT*) Bühnenbild *nt* ♦ *adj* festgelegt; (*ready*) bereit ♦ *vt* (*place*) setzen, stellen, legen; (*arrange*) (an)ordnen; (*table*) decken; (*time, price*) festsetzen; (*alarm, watch, task*) stellen; (*jewels*) (ein)fassen; (*exam*) ausarbeiten ♦ *vi* (*sun*) untergehen; (*become hard*) fest werden; (*bone*) zusammenwachsen; **to be ~ on doing sth** etw unbedingt tun wollen; **to ~ to music** vertonen; **to ~ on fire** anstecken; **to ~ free** freilassen; **to ~ sth going** etw in Gang bringen; **to ~ sail** losfahren; **~ about** *vt fus* (*task*) anpacken; **~ aside** *vt* beiseite legen; **~ back** *vt*: **to ~ back (by)** zurückwerfen (um); **~ off** *vi* aufbrechen ♦ *vt* (*explode*) sprengen; (*alarm*) losgehen lassen; (*show up well*) hervorheben; **~ out** *vi*: **to ~ out to do sth** vorhaben, etw zu tun ♦ *vt* (*arrange*) anlegen, arrangieren; (*state*) darlegen; **~ up** *vt* (*organization*) aufziehen; (*record*) aufstellen; (*monument*) erstellen; **~back** *n* Rückschlag *m*; **~ meal** *n* Menü *nt*; **~ menu** *n* Tageskarte *f*

settee [sɛ'tiː] *n* Sofa *nt*

setting ['sɛtɪŋ] *n* Hintergrund *m*

settle ['sɛtl] *vt* beruhigen; (*pay*) begleichen, bezahlen; (*agree*) regeln ♦ *vi* sich einleben; (*come to rest*) sich niederlassen; (*sink*) sich setzen; (*calm down*) sich beruhigen; **to ~ for**

sth sich mit etw zufrieden geben; **to ~ on sth** sich für etw entscheiden; **to ~ up with sb** mit jdm abrechnen; **~ down** *vi* (*feel at home*) sich einleben; (*calm down*) sich beruhigen; **~ in** *vi* sich eingewöhnen; **~ment** *n* Regelung *f*; (*payment*) Begleichung *f*; (*colony*) Siedlung *f*; **~r** *n* Siedler *m*

setup ['sɛtʌp] *n* (*situation*) Lage *f*

seven ['sɛvn] *num* sieben; **~teen** *num* siebzehn; **~th** *adj* siebte(r, s) ♦ *n* Siebtel *nt*; **~ty** *num* siebzig

sever ['sɛvəʳ] *vt* abtrennen

several ['sɛvərl] *adj* mehrere, verschiedene ♦ *pron* mehrere; **~ of us** einige von uns

severance ['sɛvərəns] *n*: **~ pay** Abfindung *f*

severe [sɪ'vɪəʳ] *adj* (*strict*) streng; (*serious*) schwer; (*climate*) rau; **severity** [sɪ'vɛrɪtɪ] *n* Strenge *f*; Schwere *f*; Rauheit *f*

sew [səu] (*pt* **sewed**, *pp* **sewn**) *vt, vi* nähen; **~ up** *vt* zunähen

sewage ['suːɪdʒ] *n* Abwässer *pl*

sewer ['suːəʳ] *n* (Abwasser)kanal *m*

sewing ['səuɪŋ] *n* Näharbeit *f*; **~ machine** *n* Nähmaschine *f*

sewn [səun] *pp* of **sew**

sex [sɛks] *n* Sex *m*; (*gender*) Geschlecht *nt*; **to have ~ with sb** mit jdm Geschlechtsverkehr haben; **~ism** *n* Sexismus *m*; **~ist** *adj* sexistisch ♦ *n* Sexist(in) *m(f)*; **~ual** ['sɛksjuəl] *adj* sexuell, geschlechtlich, Geschlechts-; **~uality** [sɛksjuˈælɪtɪ] *n* Sexualität *f*; **~y** *adj* sexy

shabby ['ʃæbɪ] *adj* (*also fig*) schäbig

shack [ʃæk] *n* Hütte *f*

shackles ['ʃæklz] *npl* (*also fig*) Fesseln *pl*, Ketten *pl*

shade [ʃeɪd] *n* Schatten *m*; (*for lamp*) Lampenschirm *m*; (*colour*) Farbton *m* ♦ *vt* abschirmen; **in the ~** im Schatten; **a ~ smaller** ein bisschen kleiner

shadow ['ʃædəu] *n* Schatten *m* ♦ *vt* (*follow*) beschatten ♦ *adj*: **~ cabinet** (*BRIT: POL*) Schattenkabinett *nt*; **~y** *adj* schattig

shady ['ʃeɪdɪ] *adj* schattig; (*fig*) zwielichtig

shaft [ʃɑːft] *n* (*of spear etc*) Schaft *m*; (*in mine*) Schacht *m*; (*TECH*) Welle *f*; (*of light*)

Strahl m

shaggy ['ʃægɪ] adj struppig

shake [ʃeɪk] (pt **shook**, pp **shaken**) vt schütteln, rütteln; (shock) erschüttern ♦ vi (move) schwanken; (tremble) zittern, beben ♦ n (jerk) Schütteln nt, Rütteln nt; **to ~ hands with** die Hand geben +dat; **to ~ one's head** den Kopf schütteln; **~ off** vt abschütteln; **~ up** vt aufschütteln; (fig) aufrütteln; **~n** [ʃeɪkn] pp of **shake**; **shaky** ['ʃeɪkɪ] adj zittrig; (weak) unsicher

shall [ʃæl] vb aux: **I ~ go** ich werde gehen; **~ I open the door?** soll ich die Tür öffnen?; **I'll buy some cake, ~ I?** soll ich Kuchen kaufen?, ich kaufe Kuchen, oder?

shallow ['ʃæləʊ] adj seicht

sham [ʃæm] n Schein m ♦ adj unecht, falsch

shambles ['ʃæmblz] n Durcheinander nt

shame [ʃeɪm] n Scham f; (disgrace, pity) Schande f ♦ vt beschämen; **it is a ~ that** es ist schade, dass; **it is a ~ to do ...** es ist eine Schande, ... zu tun; **what a ~!** wie schade!; **~faced** adj beschämt; **~ful** adj schändlich; **~less** adj schamlos

shampoo [ʃæm'puː] n Shampoo(n) nt ♦ vt (hair) waschen; **~ and set** n Waschen nt und Legen

shamrock ['ʃæmrɒk] n Kleeblatt nt

shandy ['ʃændɪ] n Bier nt mit Limonade

shan't [ʃɑːnt] = **shall not**

shantytown ['ʃæntɪtaʊn] n Bidonville f

shape [ʃeɪp] n Form f ♦ vt formen, gestalten ♦ vi (also: **~ up**) sich entwickeln; **to take ~** Gestalt annehmen; **~d** suffix: **heart-~d** herzförmig; **~less** adj formlos; **~ly** adj wohlproportioniert

share [ʃeəʳ] n (An)teil m; (FIN) Aktie f ♦ vt teilen; **to ~ out (among/between)** verteilen (unter/zwischen); **~holder** n Aktionär(in) m(f)

shark [ʃɑːk] n Hai(fisch) m; (swindler) Gauner m

sharp [ʃɑːp] adj scharf; (pin) spitz; (person) clever; (MUS) erhöht ♦ n Kreuz nt ♦ adv zu hoch; **nine o'clock ~** Punkt neun; **~en** vt schärfen; (pencil) spitzen; **~ener** n (also: **pencil ~ener**) Anspitzer m; **~-eyed** adj

scharfsichtig; **~ly** adv (turn, stop) plötzlich; (stand out, contrast) deutlich; (criticize, retort) scharf

shatter ['ʃætəʳ] vt zerschmettern; (fig) zerstören ♦ vi zerspringen

shave [ʃeɪv] n Rasur f ♦ vi sich rasieren; **to have a ~** sich rasieren (lassen); **~r** n (also: **electric ~r**) Rasierapparat m

shaving ['ʃeɪvɪŋ] n (action) Rasieren nt; **~s** npl (of wood etc) Späne pl; **~ brush** n Rasierpinsel m; **~ cream** n Rasiercreme f; **~ foam** n Rasierschaum m

shawl [ʃɔːl] n Schal m, Umhang m

she [ʃiː] pron sie ♦ adj weiblich

sheaf [ʃiːf] (pl **sheaves**) n Garbe f

shear [ʃɪəʳ] (pt **sheared**, pp **sheared** or **shorn**) vt scheren; **~ off** vi abbrechen; **~s** npl Heckenschere f

sheath [ʃiːθ] n Scheide f; (condom) Kondom m or nt

sheaves [ʃiːvz] npl of **sheaf**

shed [ʃed] (pt, pp **shed**) n Schuppen m; (for animals) Stall m ♦ vt (leaves etc) verlieren; (tears) vergießen

she'd [ʃiːd] = **she had**; **she would**

sheen [ʃiːn] n Glanz m

sheep [ʃiːp] n inv Schaf nt; **~dog** n Schäferhund m; **~ish** adj verlegen; **~skin** n Schaffell nt

sheer [ʃɪəʳ] adj bloß, rein; (steep) steil; (transparent) (hauch)dünn ♦ adv (directly) direkt

sheet [ʃiːt] n Betttuch nt, Bettlaken nt; (of paper) Blatt nt; (of metal etc) Platte f; (of ice) Fläche f

sheikh(h) [ʃeɪk] n Scheich m

shelf [ʃelf] (pl **shelves**) n Bord nt, Regal nt

shell [ʃel] n Schale f; (seashell) Muschel f; (explosive) Granate f ♦ vt (peas) schälen; (fire on) beschießen

she'll [ʃiːl] = **she will**; **she shall**

shellfish ['ʃelfɪʃ] n Schalentier nt; (as food) Meeresfrüchte pl

shell suit n Ballonseidenanzug m

shelter ['ʃeltəʳ] n Schutz m; (air-raid ~) Bunker m ♦ vt schützen, bedecken; (refugees) aufnehmen ♦ vi sich unterstellen;

~ed *adj* (*life*) behütet; (*spot*) geschützt; **~ housing** *n* (*for old people*) Altenwohnungen *pl*; (*for handicapped people*) Behindertenwohnungen *pl*

shelve [ʃɛlv] *vt* aufschieben ♦ *vi* abfallen

shelves [ʃɛlvz] *npl of* **shelf**

shepherd [ˈʃɛpəd] *n* Schäfer *m* ♦ *vt* treiben, führen; **~'s pie** *n Auflauf aus Hackfleisch und Kartoffelbrei*

sheriff [ˈʃɛrɪf] *n* Sheriff *m*; (*SCOTTISH*) Friedensrichter *m*

she's [ʃiːz] = **she is**; **she has**

Shetland [ˈʃɛtlənd] *n* (*also:* **the ~s, the ~ Isles**) die Shetlandinseln *pl*

shield [ʃiːld] *n* Schild *m*; (*fig*) Schirm *m* ♦ *vt* (be)schirmen; (*TECH*) abschirmen

shift [ʃɪft] *n* Verschiebung *f*; (*work*) Schicht *f* ♦ *vt* (ver)rücken, verschieben; (*arm*) wegnehmen ♦ *vi* sich verschieben; **~less** *adj* (*person*) träge; **~ work** *n* Schichtarbeit *f*; **~y** *adj* verschlagen

shilly-shally [ˈʃɪlɪʃælɪ] *vi* zögern

shin [ʃɪn] *n* Schienbein *nt*

shine [ʃaɪn] (*pt, pp* **shone**) *n* Glanz *m*, Schein *m* ♦ *vt* polieren ♦ *vi* scheinen; (*fig*) glänzen; **to ~ a torch on sb** jdn (mit einer Lampe) anleuchten

shingle [ˈʃɪŋɡl] *n* Strandkies *m*; **~s** *npl* (*MED*) Gürtelrose *f*

shiny [ˈʃaɪnɪ] *adj* glänzend

ship [ʃɪp] *n* Schiff *nt* ♦ *vt* verschiffen; **~building** *n* Schiffbau *m*; **~ment** *n* Schiffsladung *f*; **~per** *n* Verschiffer *m*; **~ping** *n* (*act*) Verschiffung *f*; (*~s*) Schifffahrt *f*; **~wreck** *n* Schiffbruch *m*; (*destroyed*) Wrack *nt* ♦ *vt*: **to be ~wrecked** Schiffbruch erleiden; **~yard** *n* Werft *f*

shire [ˈʃaɪə*] (*BRIT*) *n* Grafschaft *f*

shirk [ʃɜːk] *vt* ausweichen +*dat*

shirt [ʃɜːt] *n* (Ober)hemd *nt*; **in ~ sleeves** in Hemdsärmeln

shit [ʃɪt] (*infl*) *excl* Scheiße (!)

shiver [ˈʃɪvə*] *n* Schauer *m* ♦ *vi* frösteln, zittern

shoal [ʃəul] *n* (Fisch)schwarm *m*

shock [ʃɔk] *n* Erschütterung *f*; (*mental*)

Schock *m*; (*ELEC*) Schlag *m* ♦ *vt* erschüttern; (*offend*) schockieren; **~ absorber** *n* Stoßdämpfer *m*; **~ed** *adj* geschockt, schockiert, erschüttert; **~ing** *adj* unerhört

shod [ʃɔd] *pt, pp of* **shoe**

shoddy [ˈʃɔdɪ] *adj* schäbig

shoe [ʃuː] (*pt, pp* **shod**) *n* Schuh *m*; (*of horse*) Hufeisen *nt* ♦ *vt* (*horse*) beschlagen; **~brush** *n* Schuhbürste *f*; **~horn** *n* Schuhlöffel *m*; **~lace** *n* Schnürsenkel *m*; **~ polish** *n* Schuhcreme *f*; **~ shop** *n* Schuhgeschäft *nt*; **~string** *n* (*fig*): **on a ~string** mit sehr wenig Geld

shone [ʃɔn] *pt, pp of* **shine**

shoo [ʃuː] *excl* sch; (*to dog etc*) pfui

shook [ʃuk] *pt of* **shake**

shoot [ʃuːt] (*pt, pp* **shot**) *n* (*branch*) Schössling *m* ♦ *vt* (*gun*) abfeuern; (*goal, arrow*) schießen; (*person*) anschießen; (*kill*) erschießen; (*film*) drehen ♦ *vi* (*move quickly*) schießen; **to ~ (at)** schießen (auf +*acc*); **~ down** *vt* abschießen; **~ in** *vi* hineinschießen; **~ out** *vi* hinausschießen; **~ up** *vi* (*fig*) aus dem Boden schießen; **~ing** *n* Schießerei *f*; **~ing star** *n* Sternschnuppe *f*

shop [ʃɔp] *n* (*esp BRIT*) Geschäft *nt*, Laden *m*; (*workshop*) Werkstatt *f* ♦ *vi* (*also:* **go ~ping**) einkaufen gehen; **~ assistant** (*BRIT*) *n* Verkäufer(in) *m(f)*; **~ floor** (*BRIT*) *n* Werkstatt *f*; **~keeper** *n* Geschäftsinhaber *m*; **~lifting** *n* Ladendiebstahl *m*; **~per** *n* Käufer(in) *m(f)*; **~ping** *n* Einkaufen *nt*, Einkauf *m*; **~ping bag** *n* Einkaufstasche *f*; **~ping centre** (*US* **shopping center**) *n* Einkaufszentrum *nt*; **~-soiled** *adj* angeschmutzt; **~ steward** (*BRIT*) *n* (*INDUSTRY*) Betriebsrat *m*; **~ window** *n* Schaufenster *nt*

shore [ʃɔː*] *n* Ufer *nt*; (*of sea*) Strand *m* ♦ *vt*: **to ~ up** abstützen

shorn [ʃɔːn] *pp of* **shear**

short [ʃɔːt] *adj* kurz; (*person*) klein; (*curt*) kurz angebunden; (*measure*) zu knapp ♦ *n* (*also:* **~ film**) Kurzfilm *m* ♦ *adv* (*suddenly*) plötzlich ♦ *vi* (*ELEC*) einen Kurzschluss haben; **~s** *npl* (*clothes*) Shorts *pl*; **to be ~ of sth** nicht genug von etw haben; **in ~** kurz gesagt; **~ of doing sth** ohne so weit zu gehen, etw zu tun; **everything ~ of ...** alles außer ...; **it is ~ for** das ist die Kurzform von; **to cut ~** abkürzen; **to fall ~ of sth** etw nicht erreichen; **to stop ~** plötzlich anhalten; **to stop ~ of** Halt machen vor; **~age** n Knappheit f, Mangel m; **~bread** n Mürbegebäck nt; **~-change** vt: **to ~-change sb** jdm zu wenig herausgeben; **~-circuit** n Kurzschluss m ♦ vi einen Kurzschluss haben ♦ vt kurzschließen; **~coming** n Mangel m; **~(crust) pastry** (BRIT) n Mürbeteig m; **~-cut** n Abkürzung f; **~en** vt (ab)kürzen; (clothes) kürzer machen; **~fall** n Defizit nt; **~hand** (BRIT) n Stenografie f; **~hand typist** (BRIT) n Stenotypistin f; **~ list** (BRIT) n (for job) engere Wahl f; **~-lived** adj kurzlebig; **~ly** adv bald; **~ notice** n: **at ~ notice** kurzfristig; **~-sighted** (BRIT) adj (also fig) kurzsichtig; **~-staffed** adj: **to be ~-staffed** zu wenig Personal haben; **~-stay** n (car park) Kurzparken nt; **~ story** n Kurzgeschichte f; **~-tempered** adj leicht aufbrausend; **~-term** adj (effect) kurzfristig; **~ wave** n (RAD) Kurzwelle f

shot [ʃɔt] pt, pp of **shoot** ♦ n (from gun) Schuss m; (person) Schütze m; (try) Versuch m; (injection) Spritze f; (PHOT) Aufnahme f; **like a ~** wie der Blitz; **~gun** n Schrotflinte f

should [ʃʊd] vb aux: **I ~ go now** ich sollte jetzt gehen; **he ~ be there now** er sollte eigentlich schon da sein; **I ~ go if I were you** ich würde gehen, wenn ich du wäre; **I ~ like to** ich möchte gerne

shoulder [ˈʃəʊldəʳ] n Schulter f; (BRIT: of road): **hard ~** Seitenstreifen m ♦ vt (rifle) schultern; (fig) auf sich nehmen; **~ bag** n Umhängetasche f; **~ blade** n Schulterblatt nt; **~ strap** n (of dress etc) Träger m

shouldn't [ˈʃʊdnt] = **should not**

shout [ʃaʊt] n Schrei m; (call) Ruf m ♦ vt rufen ♦ vi schreien; **~ down** vt niederbrüllen; **~ing** n Geschrei nt

shove [ʃʌv] n Schubs m, Stoß m ♦ vt

schieben, stoßen, schubsen; (inf: put): **to ~ sth in(to)** sth etw in etw acc hineinschieben; **~ off** vi (NAUT) abstoßen; (fig: inf) abhauen

shovel [ˈʃʌvl] n Schaufel f ♦ vt schaufeln

show [ʃəʊ] (pt **showed**, pp **shown**) n (display) Schau f; (exhibition) Ausstellung f; (CINE, THEAT) Vorstellung f, Show f ♦ vt zeigen; (kindness) erweisen ♦ vi zu sehen sein; **to be on ~** (exhibits etc) ausgestellt sein; **to ~ sb in** jdn hereinführen; **to ~ sb out** jdn hinausbegleiten; **~ off** vi (pej) angeben ♦ vt (display) ausstellen; **~ up** vi (stand out) sich abheben; (arrive) erscheinen ♦ vt aufzeigen; (unmask) bloßstellen; **~ business** n Showbusiness nt; **~down** n Kraftprobe f

shower [ˈʃaʊəʳ] n Schauer m; (of stones) (Stein)hagel m; (~ bath) Dusche f ♦ vi duschen ♦ vt: **to ~ sb with sth** jdn mit etw überschütten; **~proof** adj Wasser abstoßend

showing [ˈʃəʊɪŋ] n Vorführung f

show jumping n Schaureiten nt

shown [ʃəʊn] pp of **show**

show: ~-off [ˈʃəʊɔf] n Angeber(in) m(f); **~piece** [ˈʃəʊpiːs] n Paradestück nt; **~room** [ˈʃəʊrʊm] n Ausstellungsraum m

shrank [ʃræŋk] pt of **shrink**

shred [ʃred] n Fetzen m ♦ vt zerfetzen; (COOK) raspeln; **~der** n (COOK) Gemüseschneider m; (for documents) Reißwolf m

shrewd [ʃruːd] adj clever

shriek [ʃriːk] n Schrei m ♦ vt, vi kreischen, schreien

shrill [ʃrɪl] adj schrill

shrimp [ʃrɪmp] n Krabbe f, Garnele f

shrine [ʃraɪn] n Schrein m; (fig) Gedenkstätte f

shrink [ʃrɪŋk] (pt **shrank**, pp **shrunk**) vi schrumpfen, eingehen ♦ vt einschrumpfen lassen; **to ~ from doing sth** davor zurückschrecken, etw zu tun; **~age** n Schrumpfung f; **~-wrap** vt einschweißen

shrivel [ˈʃrɪvl] vt, vi (also: ~ up) schrumpfen, schrumpeln

shroud [ʃraud] n Leichentuch nt ♦ vt: **~ed in mystery** mit einem Geheimnis umgeben

Shrove Tuesday ['ʃrəuv-] n Fastnachtsdienstag m

shrub [ʃrʌb] n Busch m, Strauch m; **~bery** n Gebüsch nt

shrug [ʃrʌg] n Achselzucken nt ♦ vi, vt: **to ~ (one's shoulders)** die Achseln zucken; **~ off** vt auf die leichte Schulter nehmen

shrunk [ʃrʌŋk] pp of **shrink**

shudder ['ʃʌdər] n Schauder m ♦ vi schaudern

shuffle ['ʃʌfl] vt (cards) mischen; **to ~ (one's feet)** scharren

shun [ʃʌn] vt scheuen, (ver)meiden

shunt [ʃʌnt] vt rangieren

shut [ʃʌt] (pt, pp **shut**) vt schließen, zumachen ♦ vi sich schließen (lassen); **~ down** vt, vi schließen; **~ off** vt (supply) abdrehen; **~ up** vi (keep quiet) den Mund halten ♦ vt (close) zuschließen; **~ter** n Fensterladen m; (PHOT) Verschluss m

shuttle ['ʃʌtl] n (plane, train etc) Pendelflugzeug nt/-zug m etc; (space ~) Raumtransporter m; (also: **~ service**) Pendelverkehr m; **~cock** ['ʃʌtlkɔk] n Federball m; **~ diplomacy** n Pendeldiplomatie f

shy [ʃaɪ] adj schüchtern; **~ness** n Schüchternheit f

Siamese [saɪə'miːz] adj: **~ cat** Siamkatze f

Siberia [saɪ'bɪərɪə] n Sibirien nt

sibling ['sɪblɪŋ] n Geschwister nt

Sicily ['sɪsɪlɪ] n Sizilien nt

sick [sɪk] adj krank; (joke) makaber; **I feel ~** mir ist schlecht; **I was ~** ich habe gebrochen; **to be ~ of sb/sth** jdn/etw satt haben; **~ bay** n (Schiffs)lazarett nt; **~en** vt (disgust) krank machen ♦ vi krank werden; **~ening** adj (annoying) zum Weinen

sickle ['sɪkl] n Sichel f

sick: **~ leave** n: **to be on ~ leave** krankgeschrieben sein; **~ly** adj kränklich, blass; (causing nausea) widerlich; **~ness** n Krankheit f; (vomiting) Übelkeit f, Erbrechen nt; **~ note** n Arbeitsunfähigkeits- bescheinigung f; **~ pay** n Krankengeld

side [saɪd] n Seite f ♦ adj (door, entrance) Seiten-, Neben- ♦ vi: **to ~ with sb** jds Partei ergreifen; **by the ~ of** neben; **~ by ~** nebeneinander; **on all ~s** von allen Seiten; **to take ~s (with)** Partei nehmen (für); **from all ~s** von allen Seiten; **~board** n Sideboard nt; **~boards** (BRIT) npl Koteletten pl; **~burns** npl Koteletten pl; **~car** n Beiwagen m; **~ drum** n (MUS) kleine Trommel; **~ effect** n Nebenwirkung f; **~light** n (AUT) Parkleuchte f; **~line** n (SPORT) Seitenlinie f; (fig: hobby) Nebenbeschäftigung f; **~long** adj Seiten-; **~ order** n Beilage f; **~saddle** adv im Damensattel; **~ show** n Nebenausstellung f; **~step** vt (fig) ausweichen; **~ street** n Seitenstraße f; **~track** vt (fig) ablenken; **~walk** (US) n Bürgersteig m; **~ways** adv seitwärts

siding ['saɪdɪŋ] n Nebengleis nt

sidle ['saɪdl] vi: **to ~ up (to)** sich heranmachen (an +acc)

siege [siːdʒ] n Belagerung f

sieve [sɪv] n Sieb nt ♦ vt sieben

sift [sɪft] vt sieben; (fig) sichten

sigh [saɪ] n Seufzer m ♦ vi seufzen

sight [saɪt] n (power of seeing) Sehvermögen nt; (look) Blick m; (fact of seeing) Anblick m; (of gun) Visier nt ♦ vt sichten; **in ~** in Sicht; **out of ~** außer Sicht; **~seeing** n Besuch m von Sehenswürdigkeiten; **to go ~seeing** Sehenswürdigkeiten besichtigen

sign [saɪn] n Zeichen nt; (notice, road ~ etc) Schild nt ♦ vt unterschreiben; **to ~ sth over to sb** jdm etw überschreiben; **~ on** vi (as unemployed) sich (arbeitslos) melden ♦ vt (employee) anstellen; **~ up** vi (MIL) sich verpflichten ♦ vt verpflichten

signal ['sɪgnl] n Signal nt ♦ vt ein Zeichen geben +dat; **~man** (irreg) n (RAIL) Stellwerkswärter m

signature ['sɪgnətʃər] n Unterschrift f; **~ tune** n Erkennungsmelodie f

signet ring ['sɪgnət-] n Siegelring m

significance [sɪg'nɪfɪkəns] n Bedeutung f

significant [sɪg'nɪfɪkənt] adj (meaning sth)

bedeutsam; (*important*) bedeutend

signify ['sɪgnɪfaɪ] *vt* bedeuten; (*show*) andeuten, zu verstehen geben

sign language *n* Zeichensprache *f*, Fingersprache *f*

signpost ['saɪnpəust] *n* Wegweiser *m*

silence ['saɪləns] *n* Stille *f*; (*of person*) Schweigen *nt* ♦ *vt* zum Schweigen bringen; **~r** *n* (*on gun*) Schalldämpfer *m*; (*BRIT: AUT*) Auspufftopf *m*

silent ['saɪlənt] *adj* still; (*person*) schweigsam; **to remain ~** schweigen; **~ partner** *n* (*COMM*) stille(r) Teilhaber *m*

silicon chip ['sɪlɪkən-] *n* Siliciumchip *m*, Siliziumchip *m*

silk [sɪlk] *n* Seide *f* ♦ *adj* seiden, Seiden-; **~y** *adj* seidig

silly ['sɪlɪ] *adj* dumm, albern

silt [sɪlt] *n* Schlamm *m*, Schlick *m*

silver ['sɪlvər] *n* Silber *nt* ♦ *adj* silbern, Silber-; **~ paper** (*BRIT*) *n* Silberpapier *nt*; **~-plated** *adj* versilbert; **~smith** *n* Silberschmied *m*; **~ware** *n* Silber *nt*; **~y** *adj* silbern

similar ['sɪmɪlər] *adj*: **~ (to)** ähnlich (+*dat*); **~ity** [sɪmɪˈlærɪtɪ] *n* Ähnlichkeit *f*; **~ly** *adv* in ähnlicher Weise

simmer ['sɪmər] *vi* sieden ♦ *vt* sieden lassen

simple ['sɪmpl] *adj* einfach; **~(-minded)** *adj* einfältig

simplicity [sɪmˈplɪsɪtɪ] *n* Einfachheit *f*; (*of person*) Einfältigkeit *f*

simplify ['sɪmplɪfaɪ] *vt* vereinfachen

simply ['sɪmplɪ] *adv* einfach

simulate ['sɪmjuleɪt] *vt* simulieren

simultaneous [sɪməlˈteɪnɪəs] *adj* gleichzeitig

sin [sɪn] *n* Sünde *f* ♦ *vi* sündigen

since [sɪns] *adv* seither ♦ *prep* seit, seitdem ♦ *conj* (*time*) seit; (*because*) da, weil; **~ then** seitdem

sincere [sɪnˈsɪər] *adj* aufrichtig; **~ly** *adv*: **yours ~ly** mit freundlichen Grüßen

sincerity [sɪnˈserɪtɪ] *n* Aufrichtigkeit *f*

sinew ['sɪnjuː] *n* Sehne *f*

sinful ['sɪnful] *adj* sündig, sündhaft

sing [sɪŋ] (*pt* **sang**, *pp* **sung**) *vt*, *vi* singen

Singapore [sɪŋgəˈpɔːr] *n* Singapur *nt*

singe [sɪndʒ] *vt* versengen

singer ['sɪŋər] *n* Sänger(in) *m(f)*

singing ['sɪŋɪŋ] *n* Singen *nt*, Gesang *m*

single ['sɪŋgl] *adj* (*one only*) einzig; (*bed, room*) Einzel-, einzeln; (*unmarried*) ledig; (*BRIT: ticket*) einfach; (*having one part only*) einzeln ♦ *n* (*BRIT: also:* **~ ticket**) einfache Fahrkarte *f*; **in ~ file** hintereinander; **~ out** *vt* aussuchen, auswählen; **~ bed** *n* Einzelbett *nt*; **~-breasted** *adj* einreihig; **~-handed** *adj* allein; **~-minded** *adj* zielstrebig; **~ parent** *n* Alleinerziehende(r) *f(m)*; **~ room** *n* Einzelzimmer *nt*; **~s** *n* (*TENNIS*) Einzel *nt*; **~-track road** *n* einspurige Straße (mit Ausweichstellen); **singly** *adv* einzeln, allein

singular ['sɪŋgjulər] *adj* (*odd*) merkwürdig, seltsam ♦ *n* (*GRAM*) Einzahl *f*, Singular *m*

sinister ['sɪnɪstər] *adj* (*evil*) böse; (*ghostly*) unheimlich

sink [sɪŋk] (*pt* **sank**, *pp* **sunk**) *n* Spülbecken *nt* ♦ *vt* (*ship*) versenken ♦ *vi* sinken; **to ~ sth into** (*teeth, claws*) etw schlagen in +*acc*; **~ in** *vi* (*news etc*) eingehen

sinner ['sɪnər] *n* Sünder(in) *m(f)*

sinus ['saɪnəs] *n* (*ANAT*) Sinus *m*

sip [sɪp] *n* Schlückchen *nt* ♦ *vt* nippen an +*dat*

siphon ['saɪfən] *n* Siphon(flasche *f*) *m*; **~ off** *vt* absaugen; (*fig*) abschöpfen

sir [sər] *n* (*respect*) Herr *m*; (*knight*) Sir *m*; **S~ John Smith** Sir John Smith; **yes ~** ja(wohl, mein Herr)

siren ['saɪərn] *n* Sirene *f*

sirloin ['sɜːlɔɪn] *n* Lendenstück *nt*

sissy ['sɪsɪ] (*inf*) *n* Waschlappen *m*

sister ['sɪstər] *n* Schwester *f*; (*BRIT: nurse*) Oberschwester *f*; (*nun*) Ordensschwester *f*; **~-in-law** *n* Schwägerin *f*

sit [sɪt] (*pt*, *pp* **sat**) *vi* sitzen; (*hold session*) tagen ♦ *vt* (*exam*) machen; **~ down** *vi* sich hinsetzen; **~ in on** *vt fus* dabei sein bei; **~ up** *vi* (*after lying*) sich aufsetzen; (*straight*) sich gerade setzen; (*at night*) aufbleiben

sitcom ['sɪtkɔm] *n abbr* (= *situation comedy*) Situationskomödie *f*

site [saɪt] *n* Platz *m*; (*also:* **building ~**)

Baustelle f ♦ vt legen

sitting ['sɪtɪŋ] n (meeting) Sitzung f; ~ **room** n Wohnzimmer nt

situated ['sɪtjueɪtɪd] adj: **to be ~** liegen

situation [sɪtju'eɪʃən] n Situation f, Lage f; (place) Lage f; (employment) Stelle f; **"~s vacant"** (BRIT) „Stellenangebote" pl

six [sɪks] num sechs; ~**teen** num sechzehn; ~**th** adj sechste(r, s) ♦ n Sechstel f; ~**ty** num sechzig

size [saɪz] n Größe f; (of project) Umfang m; ~ **up** vt (assess) abschätzen, einschätzen; ~**able** adj ziemlich groß, ansehnlich

sizzle ['sɪzl] vi zischen; (COOK) brutzeln

skate [skeɪt] n Schlittschuh m; (fish: pl inv) Rochen m ♦ vi Schlittschuh laufen; ~**board** n Skateboard nt; ~**boarding** n Skateboardfahren nt; ~**r** n Schlittschuhläufer(in) m(f); **skating** ['skeɪtɪŋ] n Eislauf m; **to go skating** Eis laufen gehen; **skating rink** n Eisbahn f

skeleton ['skelɪtn] n Skelett nt; (fig) Gerüst nt; ~ **key** n Dietrich m; ~ **staff** n Notbesetzung f

skeptical ['skeptɪkl] (US) adj = **sceptical**

sketch [sketʃ] n Skizze f; (THEAT) Sketch m ♦ vt skizzieren; ~**book** n Skizzenbuch nt; ~**y** adj skizzenhaft

skewer ['skju:ər] n Fleischspieß m

ski [ski:] n Ski m, Schi m ♦ vi Ski or Schi laufen; ~ **boot** n Skistiefel m

skid [skɪd] n (AUT) Schleudern nt ♦ vi rutschen; (AUT) schleudern

ski: ~**er** ['ski:ər] n Skiläufer(in) m(f); ~**ing** ['ski:ɪŋ] n: **to go ~ing** Ski laufen gehen; ~-**jump** n Sprungschanze f ♦ vi Ski springen

skilful ['skɪlful] adj geschickt

ski-lift n Skilift m

skill [skɪl] n Können nt; ~**ed** adj geschickt; (worker) Fach-, gelernt

skim [skɪm] vt (liquid) abschöpfen; (glide over) gleiten über +acc ♦ vi: ~ **through** (book) überfliegen; ~**med milk** n Magermilch f

skimp [skɪmp] vt (do carelessly) oberflächlich tun; ~**y** adj (dress) knapp

skin [skɪn] n Haut f; (peel) Schale f ♦ vt abhäuten; schälen; ~ **cancer** n Hautkrebs m; ~~-**deep** adj oberflächlich; ~ **diving** n Schwimmtauchen nt; ~~-**head** n Skinhead m; ~**ny** adj dünn; ~**tight** adj (dress etc) hauteng

skip [skɪp] n Sprung m ♦ vi hüpfen; (with rope) Seil springen ♦ vt (pass over) übergehen

ski: ~ **pants** npl Skihosen pl; ~ **pass** n Skipass nt; ~ **pole** n Skistock m

skipper ['skɪpər] n Kapitän m ♦ vt führen

skipping rope ['skɪpɪŋ-] (BRIT) n Hüpfseil nt

skirmish ['skə:mɪʃ] n Scharmützel nt

skirt [skə:t] n Rock m ♦ vt herumgehen um; (fig) umgehen; ~**ing board** (BRIT) n Fußleiste f

ski suit n Skianzug m

skit [skɪt] n Parodie f

ski tow n Schlepplift m

skittle ['skɪtl] n Kegel m; ~**s** n (game) Kegeln nt

skive [skaɪv] (BRIT: inf) vi schwänzen

skulk [skʌlk] vi sich herumdrücken

skull [skʌl] n Schädel m

skunk [skʌŋk] n Stinktier nt

sky [skaɪ] n Himmel m; ~**light** n Oberlicht nt; ~**scraper** n Wolkenkratzer m

slab [slæb] n (of stone) Platte f

slack [slæk] adj (loose) locker; (business) flau; (careless) nachlässig, lasch ♦ vi nachlässig sein ♦ n: **to take up the** ~ straff ziehen; ~**s** npl (trousers) Hose(n pl) f; ~**en** vi (also: ~**en off**) locker werden; (: slow down) stocken, nachlassen ♦ vt (: loosen) lockern

slag [slæg] (BRIT) vt: ~ **off** (criticize) (he)runtermachen

slag heap [slæg-] n Halde f

slain [sleɪn] pp of **slay**

slam [slæm] n Knall m ♦ vt (door) zuschlagen; (throw down) knallen ♦ vi zuschlagen

slander ['slɑ:ndər] n Verleumdung f ♦ vt verleumden

slang [slæŋ] n Slang m; (jargon) Jargon m

slant [slɑ:nt] n Schräge f; (fig) Tendenz f ♦ vt schräg legen ♦ vi schräg liegen; ~**ed** adj schräg; ~**ing** adj schräg

slap [slæp] n Klaps m ♦ vt einen Klaps geben +dat ♦ adv (directly) geradewegs; **~dash** adj salopp; **~stick** n (comedy) Klamauk m; **~-up** (BRIT) adj (meal) erstklassig, prima

slash [slæʃ] n Schnittwunde f ♦ vt (auf)schlitzen

slat [slæt] n Leiste f

slate [sleɪt] n (stone) Schiefer m; (roofing) Dachziegel m ♦ vt (criticize) verreißen

slaughter ['slɔːtər] n (of animals) Schlachten nt; (of people) Gemetzel nt ♦ vt schlachten; (people) niedermetzeln; **~house** n Schlachthof m

Slav [slɑːv] adj slawisch

slave [sleɪv] n Sklave m, Sklavin f ♦ vi schuften, sich schinden; **~ry** n Sklaverei f

slay [sleɪ] (pt **slew**, pp **slain**) vt ermorden

sleazy ['sliːzɪ] adj (place) schmierig

sledge [sledʒ] n Schlitten m

sledgehammer ['sledʒhæmər] n Schmiedehammer m

sledging n Schlittenfahren nt

sleek [sliːk] adj glatt; (shape) rassig

sleep [sliːp] (pt, pp **slept**) n Schlaf m ♦ vi schlafen; **to go to ~** einschlafen; **~ in** vi ausschlafen; (oversleep) verschlafen; **~er** n (person) Schläfer m; (BRIT: RAIL) Schlafwagen m; (: beam) Schwelle f; **~ing bag** n Schlafsack m; **~ing car** n Schlafwagen m; **~ing partner** n = **silent partner**; **~ing pill** n Schlaftablette f; **~less** adj (night) schlaflos; **~walker** n Schlafwandler(in) m(f); **~y** adj schläfrig

sleet [sliːt] n Schneeregen m

sleeve [sliːv] n Ärmel m; (of record) Umschlag m; **~less** adj ärmellos

sleigh [sleɪ] n Pferdeschlitten m

sleight [slaɪt] n: **~ of hand** Fingerfertigkeit f

slender ['slendər] adj schlank; (fig) gering

slept [slept] pt, pp of **sleep**

slew [sluː] vi (veer) (herum)schwenken ♦ pt of **slay**

slice [slaɪs] n Scheibe f ♦ vt in Scheiben schneiden

slick [slɪk] adj (clever) raffiniert, aalglatt ♦ n Ölteppich m

slid [slɪd] pt, pp of **slide**

slide [slaɪd] (pt, pp **slid**) n Rutschbahn f; (PHOT) Dia(positiv) nt; (BRIT: for hair) (Haar)spange f ♦ vt schieben ♦ vi (slip) gleiten, rutschen; **sliding** ['slaɪdɪŋ] adj (door) Schiebe-; **sliding scale** n gleitende Skala f

slight [slaɪt] adj zierlich; (trivial) geringfügig; (small) gering ♦ n Kränkung f ♦ vt (offend) kränken; **not in the ~est** nicht im Geringsten; **~ly** adv etwas, ein bisschen

slim [slɪm] adj schlank; (book) dünn; (chance) gering ♦ vi eine Schlankheitskur machen

slime [slaɪm] n Schleim m

slimming ['slɪmɪŋ] n Schlankheitskur f

slimy ['slaɪmɪ] adj glitschig; (dirty) schlammig; (person) schmierig

sling [slɪŋ] n (MED) Schlinge f; (weapon) Schleuder f ♦ vt schleudern

slip [slɪp] n (mistake) Flüchtigkeitsfehler m; (petticoat) Unterrock m; (of paper) Zettel m ♦ vt (put) stecken, schieben ♦ vi (lose balance) ausrutschen; (move) gleiten, rutschen; (decline) nachlassen; (move smoothly): **to ~ in/out** (person) hinein-/ hinausschlüpfen; **to give sb the ~** jdm entwischen; **~ of the tongue** Versprecher m; **it ~ped my mind** das ist mir entfallen; **to ~ sth on/off** etw über-/abstreifen; **~ away** vi sich wegstehlen; **~ in** vt hineingleiten lassen ♦ vi (errors) sich einschleichen; **~ped disc** n Bandscheibenschaden m

slipper ['slɪpər] n Hausschuh m

slippery ['slɪpərɪ] adj glatt

slip: ~ road (BRIT) n Auffahrt f/Ausfahrt f; **~shod** adj schlampig; **~-up** n Panne f; **~way** n Auslaufbahn f

slit [slɪt] (pt, pp **slit**) n Schlitz m ♦ vt aufschlitzen

slither ['slɪðər] vi schlittern; (snake) sich schlängeln

sliver ['slɪvər] n (of glass, wood) Splitter m; (of cheese) Scheibchen nt

slob [slɒb] (inf) n Klotz m

slog [slɒg] vi (work hard) schuften ♦ n: **it was a ~** es war eine Plackerei

slogan ['sləʊgən] n Schlagwort nt; (COMM)

Werbespruch m

slop [slɔp] vi (also: ~ **over**) überschwappen ♦ vt verschütten

slope [sləup] n Neigung f; (of mountains) (Ab)hang m ♦ vi: **to ~ down** sich senken; **to ~ up** ansteigen; **sloping** ['sləupɪŋ] adj schräg

sloppy ['slɔpɪ] adj schlampig

slot [slɔt] n Schlitz m ♦ vt: **to ~ sth in** etw einlegen

sloth [sləuθ] n (laziness) Faulheit f

slot machine n (BRIT) Automat m; (for gambling) Spielautomat m

slouch [slautʃ] vi: **to ~ about** (laze) herumhängen (inf)

slovenly ['slʌvənlɪ] adj schlampig; (speech) salopp

slow [sləu] adj langsam ♦ adv langsam; **to be ~** (clock) nachgehen; (stupid) begriffsstutzig sein; **"~"** (road sign) „Langsam"; **in ~ motion** in Zeitlupe; **~ down** vi langsamer werden ♦ vt verlangsamen; **~ up** vi sich verlangsamen, sich verzögern ♦ vt aufhalten, langsamer machen; **~ly** adv langsam

sludge [slʌdʒ] n Schlamm m

slug [slʌg] n Nacktschnecke f; (inf: bullet) Kugel f

sluggish ['slʌgɪʃ] adj träge; (COMM) schleppend

sluice [slu:s] n Schleuse f

slum [slʌm] n (house) Elendsquartier nt

slump [slʌmp] n Rückgang m ♦ vi fallen, stürzen

slung [slʌŋ] pt, pp of **sling**

slur [slə:ʳ] n Undeutlichkeit f; (insult) Verleumdung f; **~red** [slə:d] adj (pronunciation) undeutlich

slush [slʌʃ] n (snow) Schneematsch m; **~ fund** n Schmiergeldfonds m

slut [slʌt] n Schlampe f

sly [slaɪ] adj schlau

smack [smæk] n Klaps m ♦ vt einen Klaps geben +dat ♦ vi: **to ~ of** riechen nach; **to ~ one's lips** schmatzen, sich dat die Lippen lecken

small [smɔ:l] adj klein; **in the ~ hours** in den frühen Morgenstunden; **~ ads** (BRIT) npl Kleinanzeigen pl; **~ change** n Kleingeld nt; **~holder** (BRIT) n Kleinbauer m; **~pox** n Pocken pl; **~ talk** n Geplauder nt

smart [smɑ:t] adj (fashionable) elegant, schick; (neat) adrett; (clever) clever; (quick) scharf ♦ vi brennen, schmerzen; **~ card** n Chipkarte f; **~en up** vi sich in Schale werfen ♦ vt herausputzen

smash [smæʃ] n Zusammenstoß m; (TENNIS) Schmetterball m ♦ vt (break) zerschmettern; (destroy) vernichten ♦ vi (break) zersplittern, zerspringen; **~ing** (inf) adj toll

smattering ['smætərɪŋ] n oberflächliche Kenntnis f

smear [smɪəʳ] n Fleck m ♦ vt beschmieren

smell [smel] (pt, pp **smelt** or **smelled**) n Geruch m; (sense) Geruchssinn m ♦ vt riechen ♦ vi: **to ~ (of)** riechen (nach); (fragrantly) duften (nach); **~y** adj übel riechend

smile [smaɪl] n Lächeln nt ♦ vi lächeln

smiling ['smaɪlɪŋ] adj lächelnd

smirk [smə:k] n blöde(s) Grinsen nt

smock [smɔk] n Kittel m

smoke [sməuk] n Rauch m ♦ vt rauchen; (food) räuchern ♦ vi rauchen; **~d** adj (bacon) geräuchert; (glass) Rauch-; **~r** n Raucher(in) m(f); (RAIL) Raucherabteil nt; **~ screen** n Rauchwand f

smoking ['sməukɪŋ] n: **"no ~"** „Rauchen verboten"; **~ compartment** (BRIT), **~ car** (US) n Raucherabteil nt

smoky ['sməukɪ] adj rauchig; (room) verraucht; (taste) geräuchert

smolder ['sməuldəʳ] (US) vi = **smoulder**

smooth [smu:ð] adj glatt ♦ vt (also: ~ **out**) glätten, glatt streichen

smother ['smʌðəʳ] vt ersticken

smoulder ['sməuldəʳ] (US **smolder**) vi schwelen

smudge [smʌdʒ] n Schmutzfleck m ♦ vt beschmieren

smug [smʌg] adj selbstgefällig

smuggle ['smʌgl] vt schmuggeln; **~r** n Schmuggler m

smuggling ['smʌglɪŋ] n Schmuggel m

smutty ['smʌtɪ] adj schmutzig

snack [snæk] n Imbiss m; **~ bar** n Imbissstube f

snag [snæg] n Haken m

snail [sneɪl] n Schnecke f

snake [sneɪk] n Schlange f

snap [snæp] n Schnappen nt; (photograph) Schnappschuss m ♦ adj (decision) schnell ♦ vt (break) zerbrechen; (PHOT) knipsen ♦ vi (break) brechen; (speak) anfauchen; **to ~ shut** zuschnappen; **~ at** vt fus schnappen nach; **~ off** vt (break) abbrechen **~ up** vt aufschnappen; **~shot** n Schnappschuss m

snare [snɛəʳ] n Schlinge f ♦ vt mit einer Schlinge fangen

snarl [snɑːl] n Zähnefletschen nt ♦ vi (dog) knurren

snatch [snætʃ] n (small amount) Bruchteil m ♦ vt schnappen, packen

sneak [sniːk] vi schleichen ♦ n (inf) Petze(r) mf; **~ers** ['sniːkəz] (US) npl Freizeitschuhe pl; **~y** ['sniːkɪ] adj raffiniert

sneer [snɪəʳ] n Hohnlächeln nt ♦ vi spötteln

sneeze [sniːz] n Niesen nt ♦ vi niesen

sniff [snɪf] n Schnüffeln nt ♦ vi schnieben; (smell) schnüffeln ♦ vt schnuppern

snigger ['snɪgəʳ] n Kichern nt ♦ vi hämisch kichern

snip [snɪp] n Schnippel m, Schnipsel m ♦ vt schnippeln

sniper ['snaɪpəʳ] n Heckenschütze m

snippet ['snɪpɪt] n Schnipsel m; (of conversation) Fetzen pl

snivelling ['snɪvlɪŋ] adj weinerlich

snob [snɔb] n Snob m

snooker ['snuːkəʳ] n Snooker nt

snoop [snuːp] vi: **to ~ about** herumschnüffeln

snooze [snuːz] n Nickerchen nt ♦ vi ein Nickerchen machen, dösen

snore [snɔːʳ] vi schnarchen ♦ n Schnarchen nt

snorkel ['snɔːkl] n Schnorchel m

snort [snɔːt] n Schnauben nt ♦ vi schnauben

snout [snaʊt] n Schnauze f

snow [snəʊ] n Schnee m ♦ vi schneien; **~ball** n Schneeball m ♦ vi eskalieren; **~bound** adj eingeschneit; **~drift** n Schneewehe f; **~drop** n Schneeglöckchen nt; **~fall** n Schneefall m; **~flake** n Schneeflocke f; **~man** (irreg) n Schneemann m; **~plough** (US **snowplow**) n Schneepflug m; **~ shoe** n Schneeschuh m; **~storm** n Schneesturm m

snub [snʌb] vt schroff abfertigen ♦ n Verweis m; **~-nosed** adj stupsnasig

snuff [snʌf] n Schnupftabak m

snug [snʌg] adj gemütlich, behaglich

snuggle ['snʌgl] vi: **to ~ up to sb** sich an jdn kuscheln

KEYWORD

so [səʊ] adv **1** (thus) so; (likewise) auch; **so saying he walked away** indem er das sagte, ging er; **if so** wenn ja; **I didn't do it – you did so!** ich hab das nicht gemacht – hast du wohl!; **so do I, so am I** etc ich auch; **so it is!** tatsächlich!; **I hope/think so** hoffentlich/ich glaube schon; **so far** bis jetzt

2 (in comparisons etc: to such a degree) so; **so quickly/big (that)** so schnell/groß, dass; **I'm so glad to see you** ich freue mich so, dich zu sehen

3 : **so many** so viele; **so much work** so viel Arbeit; **I love you so much** ich liebe dich so sehr

4 (phrases): **10 or so** etwa 10; **so long!** (inf: goodbye) tschüss!

♦ conj **1** (expressing purpose): **so as to** um ... zu; **so (that)** damit

2 (expressing result) also; **so I was right after all** ich hatte also doch Recht; **so you see** ... wie du siehst ...

---

soak [səʊk] vt durchnässen; (leave in liquid) einweichen ♦ vi (ein)weichen; **~ in** vi einsickern; **~ up** vt aufsaugen; **~ed** adj völlig durchnässt; **~ing** adj klitschnass, patschnass

so-and-so ['səʊənsəʊ] n (somebody) Soundso m

soap [səʊp] n Seife f; **~flakes** npl Seifenflocken pl; **~ opera** n Familienserie f *(im Fernsehen, Radio)*; **~ powder** n Waschpulver nt; **~y** adj seifig, Seifen-

soar [sɔːʳ] vi aufsteigen; *(prices)* in die Höhe schnellen

sob [sɔb] n Schluchzen nt ♦ vi schluchzen

sober ['səubəʳ] adj *(also fig)* nüchtern; **~ up** vi nüchtern werden

so-called ['səu'kɔːld] adj so genannt

soccer ['sɔkəʳ] n Fußball m

sociable ['səuʃəbl] adj gesellig

social ['səuʃl] adj sozial; *(friendly, living with others)* gesellig ♦ n gesellige(r) Abend m; **~ club** n Verein m *(für Freizeitgestaltung)*; **~ism** n Sozialismus m; **~ist** n Sozialist(in) m(f) ♦ adj sozialistisch; **~ize** vi: **to ~ize (with)** gesellschaftlich verkehren (mit); **~ly** adv gesellschaftlich, privat; **~ security** n Sozialversicherung f; **~ work** n Sozialarbeit f; **~ worker** n Sozialarbeiter(in) m(f)

society [sə'saɪətɪ] n Gesellschaft f; *(fashionable world)* die große Welt

sociology [səusɪ'ɔlədʒɪ] n Soziologie f

sock [sɔk] n Socke f

socket ['sɔkɪt] n *(ELEC)* Steckdose f; *(of eye)* Augenhöhle f

sod [sɔd] n Rasenstück nt; *(inf!)* Saukerl m (!)

soda ['səudə] n Soda f; *(also: ~ water)* Soda(wasser) nt; *(US: also: ~ pop)* Limonade f

sodden ['sɔdn] adj durchweicht

sodium ['səudɪəm] n Natrium nt

sofa ['səufə] n Sofa nt

soft [sɔft] adj weich; *(not loud)* leise; *(weak)* nachgiebig; **~ drink** n alkoholfreie(s) Getränk nt; **~en** ['sɔfn] vt weich machen; *(blow)* abschwächen, mildern ♦ vi weich werden; **~ly** adv sanft; leise; **~ness** n Weichheit f; *(fig)* Sanftheit f

software ['sɔftwɛəʳ] n *(COMPUT)* Software f

soggy ['sɔgɪ] adj *(ground)* sumpfig; *(bread)* aufgeweicht

soil [sɔɪl] n Erde f ♦ vt beschmutzen

solace ['sɔlɪs] n Trost m

solar ['səuləʳ] adj Sonnen-; **~ cell** n Solarzelle f; **~ energy** n Sonnenenergie f; **~ panel** n Sonnenkollektor m; **~ power** n Sonnenenergie f

sold [səuld] pt, pp of **sell**; **~ out** *(COMM)* ausverkauft

solder ['sɔuldəʳ] vt löten

soldier ['səuldʒəʳ] n Soldat m

sole [səul] n Sohle f; *(fish)* Seezunge f ♦ adj alleinig, Allein-; **~ly** adv ausschließlich

solemn ['sɔləm] adj feierlich

sole trader n *(COMM)* Einzelunternehmen nt

solicit [sə'lɪsɪt] vt *(request)* bitten um ♦ vi *(prostitute)* Kunden anwerben

solicitor [sə'lɪsɪtəʳ] n Rechtsanwalt m/-anwältin f

solid ['sɔlɪd] adj *(hard)* fest; *(of same material, not hollow)* massiv; *(without break)* voll, ganz; *(reliable, sensible)* solide ♦ n Festkörper m; **~arity** [sɔlɪ'dærɪtɪ] n Solidarität f; **~ify** [sə'lɪdɪfaɪ] vi fest werden

solitary ['sɔlɪtərɪ] adj einsam, einzeln; **~ confinement** n Einzelhaft f

solitude ['sɔlɪtjuːd] n Einsamkeit f

solo ['səuləu] n Solo nt; **~ist** n Solist(in) m(f)

soluble ['sɔljubl] adj *(substance)* löslich; *(problem)* (auf)lösbar

solution [sə'luːʃən] n *(also fig)* Lösung f; *(of mystery)* Erklärung f

solve [sɔlv] vt (auf)lösen

solvent ['sɔlvənt] adj *(FIN)* zahlungsfähig ♦ n *(CHEM)* Lösungsmittel nt

sombre ['sɔmbəʳ] *(US* **somber)** adj düster

KEYWORD

---

some [sʌm] adj **1** *(a certain amount or number of)* einige; *(a few)* ein paar; *(with singular nouns)* etwas; **some tea/biscuits** etwas Tee/ein paar Plätzchen; **I've got some money, but not much** ich habe ein bisschen Geld, aber nicht viel

2 *(certain: in contrasts)* manche(r, s); **some people say that ...** manche Leute sagen, dass ...

3 *(unspecified)* irgendein(e); **some woman was asking for you** da hat eine Frau nach Ihnen gefragt; **some day** eines Tages; **some day next week** irgendwann nächste Woche

♦ *pron* **1** (*a certain number*) einige; **have you got some?** haben Sie welche?
2 (*a certain amount*) etwas; **I've read some of the book** ich habe das Buch teilweise gelesen
♦ *adv*: **some 10 people** etwa 10 Leute

somebody ['sʌmbədɪ] *pron* = **someone**
somehow ['sʌmhaʊ] *adv* (*in some way, for some reason*) irgendwie
someone ['sʌmwʌn] *pron* jemand; (*direct obj*) jemand(en); (*indirect obj*) jemandem
someplace ['sʌmpleɪs] (*US*) *adv* = **somewhere**
somersault ['sʌməsɔːlt] *n* Salto *m* ♦ *vi* einen Salto machen
something ['sʌmθɪŋ] *pron* etwas
sometime ['sʌmtaɪm] *adv* (*irgend*)einmal
sometimes ['sʌmtaɪmz] *adv* manchmal
somewhat ['sʌmwɔt] *adv* etwas
somewhere ['sʌmweəʳ] *adv* irgendwo; (*to a place*) irgendwohin; **~ else** irgendwo anders
son [sʌn] *n* Sohn *m*
sonar ['səʊnɑːʳ] *n* Echolot *nt*
song [sɒŋ] *n* Lied *nt*
sonic boom ['sɒnɪk-] *n* Überschallknall *m*
son-in-law ['sʌnɪnlɔː] *n* Schwiegersohn *m*
soon [suːn] *adv* bald; **~ afterwards** kurz danach; **~er** *adv* (*time*) früher; (*for preference*) lieber; **~er or later** früher oder später
soot [sʊt] *n* Ruß *m*
soothe [suːð] *vt* (*person*) beruhigen; (*pain*) lindern
sophisticated [sə'fɪstɪkeɪtɪd] *adj* (*person*) kultiviert; (*machinery*) hoch entwickelt
sophomore ['sɒfəmɔːʳ] (*US*) *n* College-student *m* im 2. Jahr
soporific [sɒpə'rɪfɪk] *adj* einschläfernd
sopping ['sɒpɪŋ] *adj* patschnass
soppy ['sɒpɪ] (*inf*) *adj* schmalzig
soprano [sə'prɑːnəʊ] *n* Sopran *m*
sorcerer ['sɔːsərəʳ] *n* Hexenmeister *m*
sordid ['sɔːdɪd] *adj* erbärmlich
sore [sɔːʳ] *adj* schmerzend; (*point*) wund ♦ *n* Wunde *f*; **~ly** *adv* (*tempted*) stark, sehr

sorrow ['sɒrəʊ] *n* Kummer *m*, Leid *nt*; **~ful** *adj* sorgenvoll
sorry ['sɒrɪ] *adj* traurig, erbärmlich; **~!** Entschuldigung!; **to feel ~ for sb** jdn bemitleiden; **I feel ~ for him** er tut mir Leid; **~?** (*pardon*) wie bitte?
sort [sɔːt] *n* Art *f*, Sorte *f* ♦ *vt* (*also:* **~ out**: *papers*) sortieren; (: *problems*) sichten, in Ordnung bringen; **~ing office** *n* Sortierstelle *f*
SOS *n* SOS *nt*
so-so ['səʊsəʊ] *adv* so(so) lala
sought [sɔːt] *pt, pp of* **seek**
soul [səʊl] *n* Seele *f*; (*music*) Soul *m*; **~-destroying** *adj* trostlos; **~ful** *adj* seelenvoll
sound [saʊnd] *adj* (*healthy*) gesund; (*safe*) sicher; (*sensible*) vernünftig; (*theory*) stichhaltig; (*thorough*) tüchtig, gehörig ♦ *adv*: **to be ~ asleep** fest schlafen ♦ *n* (*noise*) Geräusch *nt*, Laut *m*; (*GEOG*) Sund *m* ♦ *vt* erschallen lassen; (*alarm*) (Alarm) schlagen ♦ *vi* (*make a ~*) schallen, tönen; (*seem*) klingen; **to ~ like** sich anhören wie; **~ out** *vt* erforschen; (*person*) auf den Zahn fühlen +*dat*; **~ barrier** *n* Schallmauer *f*; **~ bite** *n* (*RAD, TV*) prägnante(s) Zitat *nt*; **~ effects** *npl* Toneffekte *pl*; **~ly** *adv* (*sleep*) fest; (*beat*) tüchtig; **~proof** *adj* (*room*) schalldicht; **~ track** *n* Tonstreifen *m*; (*music*) Filmmusik *f*
soup [suːp] *n* Suppe *f*; **~ plate** *n* Suppenteller *m*; **~spoon** *n* Suppenlöffel *m*
sour ['saʊəʳ] *adj* (*also fig*) sauer; **it's ~ grapes** (*fig*) die Trauben hängen zu hoch
source [sɔːs] *n* (*also fig*) Quelle *f*
south [saʊθ] *n* Süden *m* ♦ *adj* Süd-, südlich ♦ *adv* nach Süden, südwärts; **S~ Africa** *n* Südafrika *nt*; **S~ African** *adj* südafrikanisch ♦ *n* Südafrikaner(in) *m(f)*; **S~ America** *n* Südamerika *nt*; **S~ American** *adj* südamerikanisch ♦ *n* Südamerikaner(in) *m(f)*; **~-east** *n* Südosten *m*; **~erly** *adj* südlich; **~ern** ['sʌðən] *adj* südlich, Süd-; **S~ Pole** *n* Südpol *m*; **S~ Wales** *n* Südwales *nt*; **~ward(s)** *adv* südwärts, nach Süden; **~-west** *n* Südwesten *m*
souvenir [suːvə'nɪəʳ] *n* Souvenir *nt*

sovereign ['sɔvrɪn] n (*ruler*) Herrscher(in) m(f) ♦ adj (*independent*) souverän

soviet ['səuvɪət] adj sowjetisch; **the S~ Union** die Sowjetunion

sow¹ [sau] n Sau f

sow² [səu] (pt **sowed**, pp **sown**) vt (*also fig*) säen

soya ['sɔɪə] (US **soy**) n: ~ **bean** Sojabohne f; ~ **sauce** Sojasauce f

spa [spɑ:] n (*place*) Kurort m

space [speɪs] n Platz m, Raum m; (*universe*) Weltraum m, All nt; (*length of time*) Abstand m ♦ vt (*also*: ~ **out**) verteilen; ~**craft** n Raumschiff nt; ~**man** (*irreg*) n Raumfahrer m; ~ **ship** n Raumschiff nt

spacing ['speɪsɪŋ] n Abstand m; (*also*: ~ **out**) Verteilung f

spacious ['speɪʃəs] adj geräumig, weit

spade [speɪd] n Spaten m; ~**s** npl (CARDS) Pik nt

Spain [speɪn] n Spanien nt

span [spæn] n Spanne f; (*of bridge etc*) Spannweite f ♦ vt überspannen

Spaniard ['spænjəd] n Spanier(in) m(f)

spaniel ['spænjəl] n Spaniel m

Spanish ['spænɪʃ] adj spanisch ♦ n (LING) Spanisch nt; **the** ~ npl (*people*) die Spanier pl

spank [spæŋk] vt verhauen, versohlen

spanner ['spænər] (BRIT) n Schraubenschlüssel m

spar [spɑ:r] n (NAUT) Sparren m ♦ vi (BOXING) einen Sparring machen

spare [spɛər] adj Ersatz- ♦ n = **spare part** ♦ vt (*lives, feelings*) verschonen; (*trouble*) ersparen; **to** ~ (*surplus*) übrig; ~ **part** n Ersatzteil nt; ~ **time** n Freizeit f; ~ **wheel** n (AUT) Reservereifen m

sparing ['spɛərɪŋ] adj: **to be** ~ **with** geizen mit; ~**ly** adv sparsam; (*eat, spend etc*) in Maßen

spark [spɑ:k] n Funken m; ~**(ing) plug** n Zündkerze f

sparkle ['spɑ:kl] n Funkeln nt; (*gaiety*) Schwung m ♦ vi funkeln; **sparkling** adj funkelnd; (*wine*) Schaum-; (*mineral water*) mit Kohlensäure; (*conversation*) spritzig,

geistreich

sparrow ['spærəu] n Spatz m

sparse [spɑ:s] adj spärlich

spasm ['spæzəm] n (MED) Krampf m; (*fig*) Anfall m; ~**odic** [spæz'mɔdɪk] adj (*fig*) sprunghaft

spastic ['spæstɪk] (*old*) n Spastiker(in) m(f) ♦ adj spastisch

spat [spæt] pt, pp of **spit**

spate [speɪt] n (*fig*) Flut f, Schwall m; **in** ~ (*river*) angeschwollen

spatter ['spætər] vt bespritzen, verspritzen

spatula ['spætjulə] n Spatel m

spawn [spɔ:n] vi laichen ♦ n Laich m

speak [spi:k] (pt **spoke**, pp **spoken**) vt sprechen, reden; (*truth*) sagen; (*language*) sprechen ♦ vi: **to** ~ **(to)** sprechen (mit or zu); **to** ~ **to sb of** or **about sth** mit jdm über etw acc sprechen; ~ **up!** sprich lauter!; ~**er** n Sprecher(in) m(f), Redner(in) m(f); (*loudspeaker*) Lautsprecher m; (POL): **the S~er** der Vorsitzende des Parlaments (BRIT) or des Kongresses (US)

spear [spɪər] n Speer m ♦ vt aufspießen; ~**head** vt (*attack etc*) anführen

spec [spɛk] (*inf*) n: **on** ~ auf gut Glück

special ['spɛʃl] adj besondere(r, s); ~**ist** n (TECH) Fachmann m; (MED) Facharzt m/ Fachärztin f; ~**ity** [spɛʃɪ'ælɪtɪ] n Spezialität f; (*study*) Spezialgebiet nt; ~**ize** vi: **to** ~**ize (in)** sich spezialisieren (auf +acc); ~**ly** adv besonders; (*explicitly*) extra; ~ **needs** adj: ~ **needs children** behinderte Kinder pl; ~**ty** (*esp US*) n = **speciality**

species ['spi:ʃi:z] n Art f

specific [spə'sɪfɪk] adj spezifisch; ~**ally** adv spezifisch

specification [spɛsɪfɪ'keɪʃən] n Angabe f; (*stipulation*) Bedingung f; ~**s** npl (TECH) technische Daten pl

specify ['spɛsɪfaɪ] vt genau angeben

specimen ['spɛsɪmən] n Probe f

speck [spɛk] n Fleckchen nt

speckled ['spɛkld] adj gesprenkelt

specs [spɛks] (*inf*) npl Brille f

spectacle ['spɛktəkl] n Schauspiel nt; ~**s** npl (*glasses*) Brille f

spectacular [spek'tækjulər] *adj* sensationell; (*success etc*) spektakulär

spectator [spek'teɪtər] *n* Zuschauer(in) *m(f)*

spectre ['spektər] (*US* **specter**) *n* Geist *m*, Gespenst *nt*

speculate ['spekjuleɪt] *vi* spekulieren

speech [spiːtʃ] *n* Sprache *f*; (*address*) Rede *f*; (*way one speaks*) Sprechweise *f*; **~less** *adj* sprachlos

speed [spiːd] *n* Geschwindigkeit *f*; (*gear*) Gang *m* ♦ *vi* (*JUR*) (zu) schnell fahren; **at full** *or* **top ~** mit Höchstgeschwindigkeit; **~ up** *vt* beschleunigen ♦ *vi* schneller werden; schneller fahren; **~boat** *n* Schnellboot *nt*; **~ily** *adv* schleunigst; **~ing** *n* Geschwindigkeitsüberschreitung *f*; **~ limit** *n* Geschwindigkeitsbegrenzung *f*; **~ometer** [spɪ'dɒmɪtər] *n* Tachometer *m*; **~way** *n* (*bike racing*) Motorradrennstrecke *f*; **~y** *adj* schnell

spell [spel] (*pt, pp* **spelt** (*BRIT*) *or* **spelled**) *n* (*magic*) Bann *m*; (*period of time*) (eine) Zeit lang ♦ *vt* buchstabieren; (*imply*) bedeuten; **to cast a ~ on sb** jdn verzaubern; **~bound** *adj* (wie) gebannt; **~ing** *n* Rechtschreibung *f*

spelt [spelt] (*BRIT*) *pt, pp of* **spell**

spend [spend] (*pt, pp* **spend**) *vt* (*money*) ausgeben; (*time*) verbringen; **~thrift** *n* Verschwender(in) *m(f)*

spent [spent] *pt, pp of* **spend**

sperm [spəːm] *n* (*BIOL*) Samenflüssigkeit *f*

spew [spjuː] *vt* (er)brechen

sphere [sfɪər] *n* (*globe*) Kugel *f*; (*fig*) Sphäre *f*, Gebiet *nt*; **spherical** ['sferɪkl] *adj* kugelförmig

spice [spaɪs] *n* Gewürz *nt* ♦ *vt* würzen

spick-and-span ['spɪkən'spæn] *adj* blitzblank

spicy ['spaɪsɪ] *adj* (*food*) stark gewürzt; (*fig*) pikant

spider ['spaɪdər] *n* Spinne *f*

spike [spaɪk] *n* Dorn *m*, Spitze *f*

spill [spɪl] (*pt, pp* **spilt** *or* **spilled**) *vt* verschütten ♦ *vi* sich ergießen; **~ over** *vi* überlaufen; (*fig*) sich ausbreiten

spilt [spɪlt] *pt, pp of* **spill**

spin [spɪn] (*pt, pp* **spun**) *n* (*trip in car*) Spazierfahrt *f*; (*AVIAT*) (Ab)trudeln *nt*; (*on ball*) Drall *m* ♦ *vt* (*thread*) spinnen; (*like top*) (herum)wirbeln ♦ *vi* sich drehen; **~ out** *vt* in die Länge ziehen

spinach ['spɪnɪtʃ] *n* Spinat *m*

spinal ['spaɪnl] *adj* Rückgrat-; **~ cord** *n* Rückenmark *nt*

spindly ['spɪndlɪ] *adj* spindeldürr

spin doctor *n* PR-Fachmann *m*, PR-Fachfrau *f*

spin-dryer [spɪn'draɪər] (*BRIT*) *n* Wäscheschleuder *f*

spine [spaɪn] *n* Rückgrat *nt*; (*thorn*) Stachel *m*; **~less** *adj* (*also fig*) rückgratlos

spinning ['spɪnɪŋ] *n* Spinnen *nt*; **~ top** *n* Kreisel *m*; **~ wheel** *n* Spinnrad *nt*

spin-off ['spɪnɒf] *n* Nebenprodukt *nt*

spinster ['spɪnstər] *n* unverheiratete Frau *f*; (*pej*) alte Jungfer *f*

spiral ['spaɪərl] *n* Spirale *f* ♦ *adj* spiralförmig; (*movement etc*) in Spiralen ♦ *vi* sich (hoch)winden); **~ staircase** *n* Wendeltreppe *f*

spire ['spaɪər] *n* Turm *m*

spirit ['spɪrɪt] *n* Geist *m*; (*humour, mood*) Stimmung *f*; (*courage*) Mut *m*; (*verve*) Elan *m*; (*alcohol*) Alkohol *m*; **~s** *npl* (*drink*) Spirituosen *pl*; **in good ~s** gut aufgelegt; **~ed** *adj* beherzt; **~ level** *n* Wasserwaage *f*

spiritual ['spɪrɪtjuəl] *adj* geistig, seelisch; (*REL*) geistlich ♦ *n* Spiritual *nt*

spit [spɪt] (*pt, pp* **spat**) *n* (*for roasting*) (Brat)spieß *m*; (*saliva*) Spucke *f* ♦ *vi* spucken; (*rain*) sprühen; (*make a sound*) zischen; (*cat*) fauchen

spite [spaɪt] *n* Gehässigkeit *f* ♦ *vt* kränken; **in ~ of** trotz; **~ful** *adj* gehässig

spittle ['spɪtl] *n* Speichel *m*, Spucke *f*

splash [splæʃ] *n* Spritzer *m*; (*of colour*) (Farb)fleck *m* ♦ *vt* bespritzen ♦ *vi* spritzen

spleen [spliːn] *n* (*ANAT*) Milz *f*

splendid ['splendɪd] *adj* glänzend

splendour ['splendər] (*US* **splendor**) *n* Pracht *f*

splint [splɪnt] *n* Schiene *f*

splinter ['splɪntər] *n* Splitter *m* ♦ *vi* (zer)splittern

split [splɪt] (*pt, pp* **split**) *n* Spalte *f*; (*fig*) Spaltung *f*; (*division*) Trennung *f* ♦ *vt* spalten *n* ♦ *vi* (*divide*) reißen *n*; ~ **up** *vi* sich trennen

splutter ['splʌtər] *vi* stottern

spoil [spɔɪl] (*pt, pp* **spoilt** *or* **spoiled**) *vt* (*ruin*) verderben; (*child*) verwöhnen; ~**s** *npl* Beute *f*; ~**sport** *n* Spielverderber *m*; ~**t** *pt, pp of* **spoil**

spoke [spəuk] *pt of* **speak** ♦ *n* Speiche *f*; ~**n** *pp of* **speak**

spokesman ['spəuksmən] (*irreg*) *n* Sprecher *m*; **spokeswoman** ['spəukswumən] (*irreg*) *n* Sprecherin *f*

sponge [spʌndʒ] *n* Schwamm *m* ♦ *vt* abwaschen ♦ *vi*: **to ~ on** auf Kosten +*gen* leben; ~ **bag** (*BRIT*) *n* Kulturbeutel *m*; ~ **cake** *n* Rührkuchen *m*

sponsor ['spɔnsər] *n* Sponsor *m* ♦ *vt* fördern; ~**ship** *n* Finanzierung *f*; (*public*) Schirmherrschaft *f*

spontaneous [spɔn'teɪnɪəs] *adj* spontan

spooky ['spuːkɪ] (*inf*) *adj* gespenstisch

spool [spuːl] *n* Spule *f*, Rolle *f*

spoon [spuːn] *n* Löffel *m*; ~**-feed** (*irreg*) *vt* mit dem Löffel füttern; (*fig*) hochpäppeln; ~**ful** *n* Löffel *m* (voll)

sport [spɔːt] *n* Sport *m*; (*person*) feine(r) Kerl *m*; ~**ing** *adj* (*fair*) sportlich, fair; **to give sb a ~ing chance** jdm eine faire Chance geben; ~ **jacket** (*US*) *n* = **sports jacket**; ~**s car** *n* Sportwagen *m*; ~**s jacket** *n* Sportjackett *nt*; ~**sman** (*irreg*) *n* Sportler *m*; ~**smanship** *n* Sportlichkeit *f*; ~**swear** *n* Sportkleidung *f*; ~**swoman** (*irreg*) *n* Sportlerin *f*; ~**y** *adj* sportlich

spot [spɔt] *n* Punkt *m*; (*dirty*) Fleck(en) *m*; (*place*) Stelle *f*; (*MED*) Pickel *m* ♦ *vt* erspähen; (*mistake*) bemerken; **on the ~** an Ort und Stelle; (*at once*) auf der Stelle; ~ **check** *n* Stichprobe *f*; ~**less** *adj* fleckenlos; ~**light** *n* Scheinwerferlicht *nt*; (*lamp*) Scheinwerfer *m*; ~**ted** *adj* gefleckt; ~**ty** *adj* (*face*) pickelig

spouse [spaus] *n* Gatte *m*/Gattin *f*

spout [spaut] *n* (*of pot*) Tülle *f*; (*jet*) Wasserstrahl *m* ♦ *vi* speien

sprain [spreɪn] *n* Verrenkung *f* ♦ *vt* verrenken

sprang [spræŋ] *pt of* **spring**

sprawl [sprɔːl] *vi* sich strecken

spray [spreɪ] *n* Spray *nt*; (*off sea*) Gischt *f*; (*of flowers*) Zweig *m* ♦ *vt* besprühen, sprayen

spread [spred] (*pt, pp* **spread**) *n* (*extent*) Verbreitung *f*; (*inf: meal*) Schmaus *m*; (*for bread*) Aufstrich *m* ♦ *vt* ausbreiten; (*scatter*) verbreiten; (*butter*) streichen ♦ *vi* sich ausbreiten; ~ **out** *vi* (*move apart*) sich verteilen; ~**-eagled** ['spredːɪɡld] *adj*: **to be ~-eagled** alle viere von sich strecken; ~**sheet** *n* Tabellenkalkulation *f*

spree [spriː] *n* (*shopping*) Einkaufsbummel *m*; **to go on a ~** einen draufmachen

sprightly ['spraɪtlɪ] *adj* munter, lebhaft

spring [sprɪŋ] (*pt* **sprang**, *pp* **sprung**) *n* (*leap*) Sprung *m*; (*TECH*) Feder *f*; (*season*) Frühling *m*; (*water*) Quelle *f* ♦ *vi* (*leap*) springen; ~ **up** *vi* (*problem*) auftauchen; ~**board** *n* Sprungbrett *nt*; ~**-clean** *n* (*also:* ~**-cleaning**) Frühjahrsputz *m*; ~**time** *n* Frühling *m*; ~**y** *adj* federnd, elastisch

sprinkle ['sprɪŋkl] *vt* (*salt*) streuen; (*liquid*) sprenkeln; **to ~ water on, to ~ with water** mit Wasser besprengen; ~**r** ['sprɪŋklər] *n* (*for lawn*) Sprenger *m*; (*for fire fighting*) Sprinkler *m*

sprint [sprɪnt] *n* (*race*) Sprint *m* ♦ *vi* (*run fast*) rennen; (*SPORT*) sprinten; ~**er** *n* Sprinter(in) *m(f)*

sprout [spraut] *vi* sprießen

sprouts [sprauts] *npl* (*also:* **Brussels ~**) Rosenkohl *m*

spruce [spruːs] *n* Fichte *f* ♦ *adj* schmuck, adrett

sprung [sprʌŋ] *pp of* **spring**

spry [spraɪ] *adj* flink, rege

spun [spʌn] *pt, pp of* **spin**

spur [spəː] *n* Sporn *m*; (*fig*) Ansporn *m* ♦ *vt* (*also:* ~ **on**: *fig*) anspornen; **on the ~ of the moment** spontan

spurious ['spjuərɪəs] *adj* falsch

spurn [spəːn] *vt* verschmähen

spurt [spəːt] *n* (*jet*) Strahl *m*; (*acceleration*) Spurt *m* ♦ *vi* (*liquid*) schießen

by [spaɪ] n Spion(in) m(f) ♦ vi spionieren ♦ vt erspähen; **~ing** n Spionage f

q. abbr = **square**

quabble ['skwɔbl] n Zank m ♦ vi sich zanken

quad [skwɔd] n (MIL) Abteilung f; (POLICE) Kommando nt

quadron ['skwɔdrn] n (cavalry) Schwadron f; (NAUT) Geschwader nt; (air force) Staffel f

qualid ['skwɔlɪd] adj verkommen

quall [skwɔːl] n Bö(e) f, Windstoß m

qualor ['skwɔlə'] n Verwahrlosung f

quander ['skwɔndə'] vt verschwenden

quare [skweə'] n Quadrat nt; (open space) Platz m; (instrument) Winkel m; (inf: person) Spießer m ♦ adj viereckig; (inf: ideas, tastes) spießig ♦ vt (arrange) ausmachen; (MATH) ins Quadrat erheben ♦ vi (agree) übereinstimmen; **all ~** quitt; **a ~ meal** eine ordentliche Mahlzeit; **2 metres ~** 2 Meter im Quadrat; **1 ~ metre** 1 Quadratmeter; **~ly** adv fest, gerade

quash [skwɔʃ] n (BRIT: drink) Saft m; (game) Squash nt ♦ vt zerquetschen

quat [skwɔt] adj untersetzt ♦ vi hocken; **~ter** n Hausbesetzer m

quawk [skwɔːk] vi kreischen

queak [skwiːk] vi quiek(s)en; (spring, door etc) quietschen

queal [skwiːl] vi schrill schreien

queamish ['skwiːmɪʃ] adj empfindlich

queeze [skwiːz] vt pressen, drücken; (orange) auspressen; **~ out** vt ausquetschen

quelch [skweltʃ] vi platschen

quib [skwɪb] n Knallfrosch m

quid [skwɪd] n Tintenfisch m

quiggle ['skwɪgl] n Schnörkel m

quint [skwɪnt] vi schielen ♦ n: **to have a ~** schielen; **to ~ at sb/sth** nach jdm/etw schielen

quirm [skwɜːm] vi sich winden

quirrel ['skwɪrəl] n Eichhörnchen nt

quirt [skwɜːt] vt, vi spritzen

' abbr (= senior) sen.

t abbr (= saint) hl., St.; (= street) Str.

ab [stæb] n (blow) Stich m; (inf: try) Versuch

m ♦ vt erstechen

stabilize ['steɪbəlaɪz] vt stabilisieren ♦ vi sich stabilisieren

stable ['steɪbl] adj stabil ♦ n Stall m

stack [stæk] n Stapel m ♦ vt stapeln

stadium ['steɪdɪəm] n Stadion nt

staff [stɑːf] n (stick, MIL) Stab m; (personnel) Personal nt; (BRIT: SCH) Lehrkräfte pl ♦ vt besetzen

stag [stæg] n Hirsch m

stage [steɪdʒ] n Bühne f; (of journey) Etappe f; (degree) Stufe f; (point) Stadium nt ♦ vt (put on) aufführen; (simulate) inszenieren; (demonstration) veranstalten; **in ~s** etappenweise; **~coach** n Postkutsche f; **~ door** n Bühneneingang m; **~ manager** n Intendant m

stagger ['stægə'] vi wanken, taumeln ♦ vt (amaze) verblüffen; (hours) staffeln; **~ing** adj unglaublich

stagnant ['stægnənt] adj stagnierend; (water) stehend; **stagnate** [stæg'neɪt] vi stagnieren

stag party n Männerabend m (vom Bräutigam vor der Hochzeit gegeben)

staid [steɪd] adj gesetzt

stain [steɪn] n Fleck m ♦ vt beflecken; **~ed glass window** buntes Glasfenster nt; **~less** adj (steel) rostfrei; **~ remover** n Fleckentferner m

stair [steə'] n (Treppen)stufe f; **~s** npl (flight of steps) Treppe f; **~case** n Treppenhaus nt, Treppe f; **~way** n Treppenaufgang m

stake [steɪk] n (post) Pfahl m; (money) Einsatz m ♦ vt (bet: money) setzen; **to be at ~** auf dem Spiel stehen

stale [steɪl] adj alt; (bread) altbacken

stalemate ['steɪlmeɪt] n (CHESS) Patt nt; (fig) Stillstand m

stalk [stɔːk] n Stängel m, Stiel m ♦ vt (game) jagen; **~ off** vi abstolzieren

stall [stɔːl] n (in stable) Stand m, Box f; (in market) (Verkaufs)stand m ♦ vt (AUT) abwürgen ♦ vi (AUT) stehen bleiben; (fig) Ausflüchte machen; **~s** npl (BRIT: THEAT) Parkett nt

stallion ['stæljən] n Zuchthengst m

stalwart ['stɔːlwət] n treue(r) Anhänger m

stamina ['stæmɪnə] n Durchhaltevermögen nt, Zähigkeit f

stammer ['stæməʳ] n Stottern nt ♦ vt, vi stottern, stammeln

stamp [stæmp] n Briefmarke f; (for document) Stempel m ♦ vi stampfen ♦ vt (mark) stempeln; (mail) frankieren; (foot) stampfen mit; ~ **album** n Briefmarkenalbum nt; ~ **collecting** n Briefmarkensammeln nt

stampede [stæm'piːd] n panische Flucht f

stance [stæns] n Haltung f

stand [stænd] (pt, pp **stood**) n (for objects) Gestell nt; (seats) Tribüne f ♦ vi stehen; (rise) aufstehen; (decision) feststehen ♦ vt setzen, stellen; (endure) aushalten; (person) ausstehen; (nonsense) dulden; **to make a ~** Widerstand leisten; **to ~ for parliament** (BRIT) für das Parlament kandidieren; ~ **by** vi (be ready) bereitstehen ♦ vt fus (opinion) treu bleiben +dat; ~ **down** vi (withdraw) zurücktreten; ~ **for** vt fus (signify) stehen für; (permit, tolerate) hinnehmen; ~ **in for** vt fus einspringen für; ~ **out** vi (be prominent) hervorstechen; ~ **up** vi (rise) aufstehen; ~ **up for** vt fus sich einsetzen für; ~ **up to** vt fus: **to ~ up to sth** einer Sache gut gewachsen sein; **to ~ up to sb** sich jdm gegenüber behaupten

standard ['stændəd] n (measure) Norm f; (flag) Fahne f ♦ adj (size etc) Normal-; ~**s** npl (morals) Maßstäbe pl; ~**ize** vt vereinheitlichen; ~ **lamp** (BRIT) n Stehlampe f; ~ **of living** n Lebensstandard m

stand: ~**-by** n Reserve f; **to be on** ~**-by** in Bereitschaft sein; ~**-by ticket** n (AVIAT) Standbyticket nt; ~**-in** ['stændɪn] n Ersatz m

standing ['stændɪŋ] adj (erect) stehend; (permanent) ständig; (invitation) offen ♦ n (duration) Dauer f; (reputation) Ansehen nt; **of many years'** ~ langjährig; ~ **order** (BRIT) n (at bank) Dauerauftrag m; ~ **room** n Stehplatz m

stand: ~**-offish** [stænd'ɔfɪʃ] adj zurückhaltend, sehr reserviert; ~**point** ['stændpɔɪnt] n Standpunkt m; ~**still**

['stændstɪl] n: **to be at a ~still** stillstehen; t **come to a ~still** zum Stillstand kommen

stank [stæŋk] pt of **stink**

staple ['steɪpl] n (in paper) Heftklammer f; (article) Haupterzeugnis nt ♦ adj Grund-, Haupt- ♦ vt (fest)klammern; ~**r** n Heftmaschine f

star [stɑːʳ] n Stern m; (person) Star m ♦ vi di Hauptrolle spielen ♦ vt: ~**ring ...** in der Hauptrolle/den Hauptrollen ...

starboard ['stɑːbɔːd] n Steuerbord nt

starch [stɑːtʃ] n Stärke f

stardom ['stɑːdəm] n Berühmtheit f

stare [steəʳ] n starre(r) Blick m ♦ vi: **to ~ at** starren auf +acc, anstarren

starfish ['stɑːfɪʃ] n Seestern m

stark [stɑːk] adj öde ♦ adv: ~ **naked** splitternackt

starling ['stɑːlɪŋ] n Star m

starry ['stɑːrɪ] adj Sternen-; ~**-eyed** adj (innocent) blauäugig

start [stɑːt] n Anfang m; (SPORT) Start m; (lead) Vorsprung m ♦ vt in Gang setzen; (car) anlassen ♦ vi anfangen; (car) anspringen; (on journey) aufbrechen; (SPORT) starten; (with fright) zusammenfahren; **to ~ doing** or **to do sth** anfangen, etw zu tun; ~ **off** vi anfangen; (begin moving) losgehen; losfahren; ~ **up** vi anfangen ♦ vt beginnen; (car) anlassen; (engine) starten; ~**er** n (AUT) Anlasser m; (at race) Starter m; (BRIT: COOK) Vorspeise f; ~**ing point** n Ausgangspunkt m

startle ['stɑːtl] vt erschrecken; **startling** ad erschreckend

starvation [stɑː'veɪʃən] n Verhungern nt

starve [stɑːv] vi verhungern ♦ vt verhunger lassen; **I'm starving** ich sterbe vor Hunge

state [steɪt] n (condition) Zustand m; (POL) Staat m ♦ vt erklären; (facts) angeben; **the S~s** (USA) die Staaten; **to be in a ~** durchdrehen; ~**ly** adj würdevoll; ~**ly hon** n herrschaftliches Anwesen nt, Schloss nt; ~**ment** n Aussage f; (POL) Erklärung f; ~**sman** (irreg) n Staatsmann m

static ['stætɪk] n (also: ~ **electricity**) Reibungselektrizität f

tation ['steɪʃən] n (RAIL etc) Bahnhof m; (police etc) Wache f; (in society) Stand m ♦ vt stationieren

tationary ['steɪʃnərɪ] adj stillstehend; (car) parkend

tationer's n (shop) Schreibwarengeschäft nt; ~**y** n Schreibwaren pl

tation master n Bahnhofsvorsteher m

tation wagon n Kombiwagen m

atistics [stə'tɪstɪks] n Statistik f

atue ['stætjuː] n Statue f

ature ['stætʃər] n Größe f

atus ['steɪtəs] n Status m

atute ['stætjuːt] n Gesetz nt; **statutory** ['stætjutrɪ] adj gesetzlich

aunch [stɔːntʃ] adj standhaft

ay [steɪ] n Aufenthalt m ♦ vi bleiben; (reside) wohnen; **to ~ put** an Ort und Stelle bleiben; **to ~ the night** übernachten; **~ behind** vi zurückbleiben; **~ in** vi (at home) zu Hause bleiben; **~ on** vi (continue) länger bleiben; **~ out** vi (of house) wegbleiben; **~ up** vi (at night) aufbleiben; **~ing power** n Durchhaltevermögen nt

ead [sted] n: **in sb's ~** an jds Stelle dat; **to stand sb in good ~** jdm zugute kommen

eadfast ['stedfɑːst] adj standhaft, treu

eadily ['stedɪlɪ] adv stetig, regelmäßig

eady ['stedɪ] adj (firm) fest, stabil; (regular) gleichmäßig; (reliable) beständig; (hand) ruhig; (job, boyfriend) fest ♦ vt festigen; **to ~ o.s. on/against sth** sich stützen auf/ gegen etw acc

eak [steɪk] n Steak nt; (fish) Filet nt

eal [stiːl] (pt **stole**, pp **stolen**) vt stehlen ♦ vi stehlen; (go quietly) sich stehlen

ealth [stelθ] n Heimlichkeit f; ~**y** adj verstohlen, heimlich

eam [stiːm] n Dampf m ♦ vt (COOK) im Dampfbad erhitzen ♦ vi dampfen; ~**engine** n Dampfmaschine f; ~**er** n Dampfer m; ~**roller** n Dampfwalze f; ~**ship** n = **steamer**; ~**y** adj dampfig

eel [stiːl] n Stahl m ♦ adj Stahl-; (fig) stählern; ~**works** n Stahlwerke pl

eep [stiːp] adj steil; (price) gepfeffert ♦ vt einweichen

steeple ['stiːpl] n Kirchturm m; ~**chase** n Hindernisrennen nt

steer [stɪər] vt, vi steuern; (car etc) lenken; ~**ing** n (AUT) Steuerung f; ~**ing wheel** n Steuer- or Lenkrad nt

stem [stem] n Stiel m ♦ vt aufhalten; ~ **from** vt fus abstammen von

stench [stentʃ] n Gestank m

stencil ['stensl] n Schablone f ♦ vt (auf)drucken

stenographer [stɛ'nɔgrəfər] (US) n Stenograf(in) m(f)

step [step] n Schritt m; (stair) Stufe f ♦ vi treten, schreiten; ~ = **stepladder**; **to take ~s** Schritte unternehmen; **in/out of ~ (with)** im/nicht im Gleichklang (mit); ~ **down** vi (fig) abtreten; ~ **off** vt fus aussteigen aus; ~ **up** vt steigern

stepbrother ['stepbrʌðər] n Stiefbruder m

stepdaughter ['stepdɔːtər] n Stieftochter f

stepfather ['stepfɑːðər] n Stiefvater m

stepladder ['steplædər] n Trittleiter f

stepmother ['stepmʌðər] n Stiefmutter f

stepping stone ['stepɪŋ-] n Stein m; (fig) Sprungbrett nt

stepsister ['stepsɪstər] n Stiefschwester f

stepson ['stepsʌn] n Stiefsohn m

stereo ['steriəu] n Stereoanlage f ♦ adj (also: ~**phonic**) stereofonisch, stereophonisch

stereotype ['stɪərɪətaɪp] n (fig) Klischee nt ♦ vt stereotypieren; (fig) stereotyp machen

sterile ['steraɪl] adj steril; (person) unfruchtbar; **sterilize** vt sterilisieren

sterling ['stɜːlɪŋ] adj (FIN) Sterling-; (character) gediegen ♦ n (ECON) das Pfund Sterling; **a pound ~** ein Pfund Sterling

stern [stɜːn] adj streng ♦ n Heck nt, Achterschiff nt

stew [stjuː] n Eintopf m ♦ vt, vi schmoren

steward ['stjuːəd] n Steward m; ~**ess** n Stewardess f

stick [stɪk] (pt, pp **stuck**) n Stock m; (of chalk etc) Stück nt ♦ vt (stab) stechen; (fix) stecken; (put) stellen; (gum) (an)kleben; (inf: tolerate) vertragen ♦ vi (stop) stecken bleiben; (get stuck) klemmen; (hold fast)

kleben, haften; **~ out** *vi (project)*
hervorstehen; **~ up** *vi (project)* in die Höhe
stehen; **~ up for** *vt fus (defend)* eintreten
für; **~er** *n* Aufkleber *m*; **~ing plaster** *n*
Heftpflaster *nt*

stickler ['stɪklə^r] *n*: **~ (for)** Pedant *m (in
+acc)*

stick-up ['stɪkʌp] *(inf) n* (Raub)überfall *m*

sticky ['stɪkɪ] *adj* klebrig; *(atmosphere)* stickig

stiff [stɪf] *adj* steif; *(difficult)* hart; *(paste)* dick;
(drink) stark; **to have a ~ neck** einen steifen
Hals haben; **~en** *vt* versteifen, (ver)stärken
♦ *vi* sich versteifen

stifle ['staɪfl] *vt* unterdrücken; **stifling** *adj*
drückend

stigma ['stɪgmə] *(pl BOT, MED, REL* **~ta**; *fig* **~s)**
n Stigma *nt*

stigmata [stɪg'mɑːtə] *npl of* **stigma**

stile [staɪl] *n* Steige *f*

stiletto [stɪ'letəʊ] *(BRIT) n (also: ~ heel)*
Pfennigabsatz *m*

still [stɪl] *adj* still ♦ *adv* (immer) noch;
(anyhow) immerhin; **~born** *adj* tot
geboren; **~ life** *n* Stilleben *nt*

stilt [stɪlt] *n* Stelze *f*

stilted ['stɪltɪd] *adj* gestelzt

stimulate ['stɪmjʊleɪt] *vt* anregen,
stimulieren

stimuli ['stɪmjʊlaɪ] *npl of* **stimulus**

stimulus ['stɪmjʊləs] *(pl* **-li)** *n* Anregung *f*,
Reiz *m*

sting [stɪŋ] *(pt, pp* **stung)** *n* Stich *m; (organ)*
Stachel *m* ♦ *vi* stechen; *(on skin)* brennen
♦ *vt* stechen

stingy ['stɪndʒɪ] *adj* geizig, knauserig

stink [stɪŋk] *(pt* **stank**, *pp* **stunk)** *n* Gestank
m ♦ *vi* stinken; **~ing** *adj (fig)* widerlich

stint [stɪnt] *n (period)* Betätigung *f;* **to do
one's ~** seine Arbeit tun; *(share)* seinen Teil
beitragen

stipulate ['stɪpjʊleɪt] *vt* festsetzen

stir [stɜː^r] *n* Bewegung *f; (COOK)* Rühren *nt;*
(sensation) Aufsehen *nt* ♦ *vt* (um)rühren ♦ *vi*
sich rühren; **~ up** *vt (mob)* aufhetzen;
(mixture) umrühren; *(dust)* aufwirbeln

stirrup ['stɪrəp] *n* Steigbügel *m*

stitch [stɪtʃ] *n (with needle)* Stich *m; (MED)*

Faden *m; (of knitting)* Masche *f; (pain)* Stic
m ♦ *vt* nähen

stoat [stəʊt] *n* Wiesel *nt*

stock [stɒk] *n* Vorrat *m; (COMM)*
(Waren)lager *nt; (livestock)* Vieh *nt; (COOK)*
Brühe *f; (FIN)* Grundkapital *nt* ♦ *adj* stets
vorrätig; *(standard)* Normal- ♦ *vt (in shop)*
führen; **~s** *npl (FIN)* Aktien *pl;* **in/out of ~**
vorrätig/nicht vorrätig; **to take ~ of**
Inventur machen von; *(fig)* Bilanz ziehen
aus; **~s and shares** Effekten *pl;* **~ up** *vi:*
~ up (with) Reserven anlegen (von);
~broker ['stɒkbrəʊkə^r] *n* Börsenmakler *m;*
cube *n* Brühwürfel *m;* **~ exchange** *n*
Börse *f*

stocking ['stɒkɪŋ] *n* Strumpf *m*

stock: ~ market *n* Börse *f;* **~ phrase** *n*
Standardsatz *m;* **~pile** *n* Vorrat *m* ♦ *vt*
aufstapeln; **~taking** *(BRIT) n (COMM)*
Inventur *f*, Bestandsaufnahme *f*

stocky ['stɒkɪ] *adj* untersetzt

stodgy ['stɒdʒɪ] *adj* pampig

stoke [stəʊk] *vt* schüren

stole [stəʊl] *pt of* **steal** ♦ *n* Stola *f*

stolen ['stəʊln] *pp of* **steal**

stomach ['stʌmək] *n* Bauch *m*, Magen *m*
♦ *vt* vertragen; **~ache** *n* Magen- *or*
Bauchschmerzen *pl*

stone [stəʊn] *n* Stein *m; (BRIT: weight)*
Gewichtseinheit = 6.35 kg ♦ *vt (olive)*
entkernen; *(kill)* steinigen; **~-cold** *adj*
eiskalt; **~-deaf** *adj* stocktaub; **~work** *n*
Mauerwerk *nt;* **stony** ['stəʊnɪ] *adj* steinig

stood [stʊd] *pt, pp of* **stand**

stool [stuːl] *n* Hocker *m*

stoop [stuːp] *vi* sich bücken

stop [stɒp] *n* Halt *m; (bus ~)* Haltestelle *f;*
(punctuation) Punkt *m* ♦ *vt* anhalten; *(brin
to an end)* aufhören (mit), sein lassen ♦ *vi*
aufhören; *(clock)* stehen bleiben; *(remain)*
bleiben; **to ~ doing sth** aufhören, etw zu
tun; **to ~ dead** innehalten; **~ off** *vi* kurz
Halt machen; **~ up** *vt (hole)* zustopfen,
verstopfen; **~gap** *n* Notlösung *f;* **~lights**
npl (AUT) Bremslichter *pl;* **~over** *n (on
journey)* Zwischenaufenthalt *m;* **~page**
['stɒpɪdʒ] *n* (An)halten *nt; (traffic)*

Verkehrsstockung f; (strike)
Arbeitseinstellung f; ~**per** ['stɔpə'] n
Propfen m, Stöpsel m; ~ **press** n letzte
Meldung f; ~**watch** ['stɔpwɔtʃ] n Stoppuhr f

torage ['stɔːrɪdʒ] n Lagerung f; ~ **heater** n
(Nachtstrom)speicherofen m

tore [stɔːʳ] n Vorrat m; (place) Lager nt,
Warenhaus nt; (BRIT: large shop) Kaufhaus
nt; (US) Laden m ♦ vt lagern; ~**s** npl
(supplies) Vorräte pl; ~ **up** vt sich
eindecken mit; ~**room** n Lagerraum m,
Vorratsraum m

torey ['stɔːrɪ] (US **story**) n Stock m

tork [stɔːk] n Storch m

torm [stɔːm] n (also fig) Sturm m ♦ vt, vi
stürmen; ~**y** adj stürmisch

tory ['stɔːrɪ] n Geschichte f; (lie) Märchen
nt; (US) = **storey**; ~**book** n
Geschichtenbuch nt; ~**teller** n
Geschichtenerzähler m

tout [staut] adj (bold) tapfer; (fat) beleibt
♦ n Starkbier nt; (also: **sweet ~**) ≈ Malzbier
nt

tove [stəuv] n (Koch)herd m; (for heating)
Ofen m

tow [stəu] vt verstauen; ~**away** n blinde(r)
Passagier m

traddle ['strædl] vt (horse, fence) rittlings
sitzen auf +dat; (fig) überbrücken

traggle ['strægl] vi (people) nachhinken; ~**r**
n Nachzügler m; **straggly** adj (hair) zottig

traight [streɪt] adj gerade; (honest) offen,
ehrlich; (drink) pur ♦ adv (direct) direkt,
geradewegs; **to put** or **get sth ~** etw in
Ordnung bringen; ~ **away** sofort; ~ **off**
sofort; ~**en** vt (also: ~**en out**) gerade
machen; (fig) klarstellen; ~**-faced** adv ohne
die Miene zu verziehen ♦ adj: **to be ~-
faced** keine Miene verziehen; ~**forward**
adj einfach, unkompliziert

train [streɪn] n Belastung f; (streak, trace)
Zug m; (of music) Fetzen m ♦ vt
überanstrengen; (stretch) anspannen;
(muscle) zerren; (filter) (durch)seihen ♦ vi
sich anstrengen; ~**ed** adj (laugh)
gezwungen; (relations) gespannt; ~**er** n
Sieb nt

strait [streɪt] n Straße f, Meerenge f;
~**jacket** n Zwangsjacke f; ~**-laced** adj
engherzig, streng

strand [strænd] n (of hair) Strähne f; (also fig)
Faden m

stranded ['strændɪd] adj (also fig) gestrandet

strange [streɪndʒ] adj fremd; (unusual)
seltsam; ~**r** n Fremde(r) mf

strangle ['stræŋgl] vt erwürgen; ~**hold** n
(fig) Umklammerung f

strap [stræp] n Riemen m; (on clothes) Träger
m ♦ vt (fasten) festschnallen

strapping ['stræpɪŋ] adj stramm

strata ['strɑːtə] npl of **stratum**

strategic [strə'tiːdʒɪk] adj strategisch

strategy ['strætɪdʒɪ] n (fig) Strategie f

stratum ['strɑːtəm] (pl **-ta**) n Schicht f

straw [strɔː] n Stroh nt; (single stalk, drinking
~) Strohhalm m; **that's the last ~!** das ist
der Gipfel!

strawberry ['strɔːbərɪ] n Erdbeere f

stray [streɪ] adj (animal) verirrt ♦ vi
herumstreunen

streak [striːk] n Streifen m; (in character)
Einschlag m; (in hair) Strähne f ♦ vt streifen
♦ vi zucken; (move quickly) flitzen; ~ **of bad
luck** Pechsträhne f; ~**y** adj gestreift; (bacon)
durchwachsen

stream [striːm] n (brook) Bach m; (fig) Strom
m ♦ vt (SCH) in (Leistungs)gruppen einteilen
♦ vi strömen; **to ~ in/out** (people) hinein-/
hinausströmen

streamer ['striːmə'] n (flag) Wimpel m; (of
paper) Luftschlange f

streamlined ['striːmlaɪnd] adj
stromlinienförmig; (effective) rationell

street [striːt] n Straße f ♦ adj Straßen-; ~**car**
(US) n Straßenbahn f; ~ **lamp** n
Straßenlaterne f; ~ **plan** n Stadtplan m;
~**wise** (inf) adj: **to be ~wise** wissen, wo es
langgeht

strength [streŋθ] n (also fig) Stärke f; Kraft f;
~**en** vt (ver)stärken

strenuous ['strenjuəs] adj anstrengend

stress [stres] n Druck m; (mental) Stress m;
(GRAM) Betonung f ♦ vt betonen

stretch [stretʃ] n Strecke f ♦ vt ausdehnen,

strecken ♦ *vi* sich erstrecken; *(person)* sich strecken; ~ **out** *vi* sich ausstrecken ♦ *vt* ausstrecken

stretcher ['stretʃəʳ] *n* Tragbahre *f*

stretchy ['stretʃɪ] *adj* elastisch, dehnbar

strewn [struːn] *adj*: ~ **with** übersät mit

stricken ['strɪkən] *adj (person)* ergriffen; *(city, country)* heimgesucht; ~ **with** *(disease)* leidend unter +*dat*

strict [strɪkt] *adj (exact)* genau; *(severe)* streng; ~**ly** *adv* streng, genau

stridden ['strɪdn] *pp of* **stride**

stride [straɪd] *(pt* **strode**, *pp* **stridden)** *n* lange(r) Schritt *m* ♦ *vi* schreiten

strident ['straɪdnt] *adj* schneidend, durchdringend

strife [straɪf] *n* Streit *m*

strike [straɪk] *(pt, pp* **struck)** *n* Streik *m*; *(attack)* Schlag *m* ♦ *vt (hit)* schlagen; *(collide)* stoßen gegen; *(come to mind)* einfallen +*dat*; *(find)* finden ♦ *vi (stop work)* streiken; *(attack)* zuschlagen; *(clock)* schlagen; **on** ~ *(workers)* im Streik; **to** ~ **a match** ein Streichholz anzünden; ~ **down** *vt (lay low)* niederschlagen; ~ **out** *vt (cross out)* ausstreichen; ~ **up** *vt (music)* anstimmen; *(friendship)* schließen; ~**r** *n* Streikende(r) *mf*; **striking** ['straɪkɪŋ] *adj* auffallend

string [strɪŋ] *(pt, pp* **strung)** *n* Schnur *f*; *(row)* Reihe *f*; *(MUS)* Saite *f* ♦ *vt*: **to** ~ **together** aneinander reihen ♦ *vi*: **to** ~ **out** *(sich)* verteilen; **the** ~**s** *npl (MUS)* die Streichinstrumente *pl*; **to pull** ~**s** *(fig)* Fäden ziehen; ~ **bean** *n* grüne Bohne *f*; ~**(ed) instrument** *n (MUS)* Saiteninstrument *nt*

stringent ['strɪndʒənt] *adj* streng

strip [strɪp] *n* Streifen *m* ♦ *vt (uncover)* abstreifen, abziehen; *(clothes)* ausziehen; *(TECH)* auseinander nehmen ♦ *vi (undress)* sich ausziehen; ~ **cartoon** *n* Bildserie *f*

stripe [straɪp] *n* Streifen *m*; ~**d** *adj* gestreift

strip lighting *n* Neonlicht *nt*

stripper ['strɪpəʳ] *n* Stripteasetänzerin *f*

strip-search ['strɪpsɜːtʃ] *n* Leibesvisitation *f* *(bei der man sich ausziehen muss)* ♦ *vt*: **to be** ~~~**ed** sich ausziehen müssen und

durchsucht werden

stripy ['straɪpɪ] *adj* gestreift

strive [straɪv] *(pt* **strove**, *pp* **striven)** *vi*: **to** ~ **(for)** streben (nach)

strode [strəʊd] *pt of* **stride**

stroke [strəʊk] *n* Schlag *m*; *(SWIMMING, ROWING)* Stoß *m*; *(MED)* Schlaganfall *m*; *(caress)* Streicheln *nt* ♦ *vt* streicheln; **at a** ~ mit einem Schlag

stroll [strəʊl] *n* Spaziergang *m* ♦ *vi* schlendern; ~**er** *(US) n (pushchair)* Sportwagen *m*

strong [strɒŋ] *adj* stark; *(firm)* fest; **they are 50** ~ sie sind 50 Mann stark; ~**box** *n* Kassette *f*; ~**hold** *n* Hochburg *f*; ~**ly** *adv* stark; ~**room** *n* Tresor *m*

strove [strəʊv] *pt of* **strive**

struck [strʌk] *pt, pp of* **strike**

structure ['strʌktʃəʳ] *n* Struktur *f*, Aufbau *m*; *(building)* Bau *m*

struggle ['strʌgl] *n* Kampf *m* ♦ *vi (fight)* kämpfen

strum [strʌm] *vt (guitar)* klimpern auf +*dat*

strung [strʌŋ] *pt, pp of* **string**

strut [strʌt] *n* Strebe *f*, Stütze *f* ♦ *vi* stolziere

stub [stʌb] *n* Stummel *m*; *(of cigarette)* Kipp *f* ♦ *vt*: **to** ~ **one's toe** sich *dat* den Zeh anstoßen; ~ **out** *vt* ausdrücken

stubble ['stʌbl] *n* Stoppel *f*

stubborn ['stʌbən] *adj* hartnäckig

stuck [stʌk] *pt, pp of* **stick** ♦ *adj (jammed)* klemmend; ~~**up** *adj* hochnäsig

stud [stʌd] *n (button)* Kragenknopf *m*; *(place* Gestüt *nt* ♦ *vt (fig)*: ~**ded with** übersät mit

student ['stjuːdənt] *n* Student(in) *m(f)*; *(US)* Student(in) *m(f)*, Schüler(in) *m(f)* ♦ *adj* Studenten-; ~ **driver** *(US) n* Fahrschüler(in *m(f)*

studio ['stjuːdɪəʊ] *n* Studio *nt*; *(for artist)* Atelier *nt*; ~ **apartment** *(US) n* Appartement *nt*; ~ **flat** *n* Appartement *nt*

studious ['stjuːdɪəs] *adj* lernbegierig

study ['stʌdɪ] *n* Studium *nt*; *(investigation)* Studium *nt*, Untersuchung *f*; *(room)* Arbeitszimmer *nt*; *(essay etc)* Studie *f* ♦ *vt* studieren; *(face)* erforschen; *(evidence)* prüfen ♦ *vi* studieren

tuff [stʌf] n Stoff m; (inf) Zeug nt ♦ vt
stopfen, füllen; (animal) ausstopfen; ~**ing** n
Füllung f; ~**y** adj (room) schwül; (person)
spießig

tumble ['stʌmbl] vi stolpern; **to ~ across**
(fig) zufällig stoßen auf +acc

tumbling block ['stʌmblɪŋ-] n Hindernis
nt

tump [stʌmp] n Stumpf m

tun [stʌn] vt betäuben; (shock)
niederschmettern

tung [stʌŋ] pt, pp of **sting**

tunk [stʌŋk] pp of **stink**

tunned adj benommen, fassungslos

tunning ['stʌnɪŋ] adj betäubend; (news)
überwältigend, umwerfend

tunt [stʌnt] n Kunststück nt, Trick m

tunted ['stʌntɪd] adj verkümmert

tuntman ['stʌntmæn] (irreg) n Stuntman m

tupefy ['stju:pɪfaɪ] vt betäuben; (by news)
bestürzen

tupendous [stju:'pɛndəs] adj erstaunlich,
enorm

tupid ['stju:pɪd] adj dumm; ~**ity** [stju:'pɪdɪtɪ]
n Dummheit f

tupor ['stju:pəʳ] n Betäubung f

turdy ['stɜ:dɪ] adj kräftig, robust

tutter ['stʌtəʳ] n Stottern nt ♦ vi stottern

ty [staɪ] n Schweinestall m

tye [staɪ] n Gerstenkorn nt

tyle [staɪl] n Stil m; (fashion) Mode f;
stylish ['staɪlɪʃ] adj modisch; **stylist**
['staɪlɪst] n (hair stylist) Friseur m, Friseuse f

tylus ['staɪləs] n (Grammofon)nadel f

uave [swɑ:v] adj zuvorkommend

ub... [sʌb] prefix Unter...; ~**conscious** adj
unterbewusst ♦ n: **the ~conscious** das
Unterbewusste; ~**contract** vt (vertraglich)
untervermitteln; ~**divide** vt unterteilen;
~**dued** adj (lighting) gedämpft; (person) still

ubject [n, adj 'sʌbdʒɪkt, vb səb'dʒɛkt] n (of
kingdom) Untertan m; (citizen)
Staatsangehörige(r) mf; (topic) Thema nt;
(SCH) Fach nt; (GRAM) Subjekt nt ♦ adj: **to
be ~ to** unterworfen sein +dat; (exposed)
ausgesetzt sein +dat ♦ vt (subdue)
unterwerfen; (expose) aussetzen; ~**ive**
[səb'dʒɛktɪv] adj subjektiv; ~ **matter** n
Thema nt

sublet [sʌb'lɛt] (irreg: like **let**) vt
untervermieten

sublime [sə'blaɪm] adj erhaben

submachine gun ['sʌbmə'ʃi:n-] n
Maschinenpistole f

submarine ['sʌbmə'ri:n] n Unterseeboot nt,
U-Boot nt

submerge [səb'mɜ:dʒ] vt untertauchen;
(flood) überschwemmen ♦ vi untertauchen

submission [səb'mɪʃən] n (obedience)
Gehorsam m; (claim) Behauptung f; (of
plan) Unterbreitung f; **submissive**
[səb'mɪsɪv] adj demütig, unterwürfig (pej)

submit [səb'mɪt] vt behaupten; (plan)
unterbreiten ♦ vi sich ergeben

subnormal [sʌb'nɔ:ml] adj minderbegabt

subordinate [sə'bɔ:dɪnət] adj untergeordnet
♦ n Untergebene(r) mf

subpoena [sə'pi:nə] n Vorladung f ♦ vt
vorladen

subscribe [səb'skraɪb] vi: **to ~ to** (view etc)
unterstützen; (newspaper) abonnieren; ~**r** n
(to periodical) Abonnent m; (TEL)
Telefonteilnehmer m

subscription [səb'skrɪpʃən] n Abonnement
nt; (money subscribed) (Mitglieds)beitrag m

subsequent ['sʌbsɪkwənt] adj folgend,
später; ~**ly** adv später

subside [səb'saɪd] vi sich senken; ~**nce**
[səb'saɪdns] n Senkung f

subsidiarity [səbsɪdɪ'ærɪtɪ] n (POL)
Subsidiarität f

subsidiary [səb'sɪdɪərɪ] adj Neben- ♦ n
Tochtergesellschaft f

subsidize ['sʌbsɪdaɪz] vt subventionieren

subsidy ['sʌbsɪdɪ] n Subvention f

subsistence [səb'sɪstəns] n Unterhalt m

substance ['sʌbstəns] n Substanz f

substantial [səb'stænʃl] adj (strong) fest,
kräftig; (important) wesentlich; ~**ly** adv
erheblich

substantiate [səb'stænʃɪeɪt] vt begründen,
belegen

substitute ['sʌbstɪtju:t] n Ersatz m ♦ vt
ersetzen; **substitution** [sʌbstɪ'tju:ʃən] n

Ersetzung f

subterfuge ['sʌbtəfjuːdʒ] n Vorwand m; (*trick*) Trick m

subterranean [sʌbtə'reɪnɪən] adj unterirdisch

subtitle ['sʌbtaɪtl] n Untertitel m; ~d adj untertitelt, mit Untertiteln versehen

subtle ['sʌtl] adj fein; ~ty n Feinheit f

subtotal [sʌb'təʊtl] n Zwischensumme f

subtract [səb'trækt] vt abziehen; ~ion [səb'trækʃən] n Abziehen nt, Subtraktion f

suburb ['sʌbɜːb] n Vorort m; **the ~s** die Außenbezirke pl; ~an [sə'bɜːbən] adj Vorort(s)-; ~ia [sə'bɜːbɪə] n Vorstadt f

subversive [səb'vɜːsɪv] adj subversiv

subway ['sʌbweɪ] n (*US*) U-Bahn f; (*BRIT*) Unterführung f

succeed [sək'siːd] vi (*person*) erfolgreich sein, Erfolg haben; (*plan etc also*) gelingen ♦ vt (nach)folgen +dat; **he ~ed in doing it** es gelang ihm, es zu tun; ~ing adj (nach)folgend

success [sək'ses] n Erfolg m; ~ful adj erfolgreich; **to be ~ful (in doing sth)** Erfolg haben (bei etw); ~fully adv erfolgreich

succession [sək'seʃən] n (Aufeinander)folge f; (*to throne*) Nachfolge f

successive [sək'sesɪv] adj aufeinander folgend

successor [sək'sesər] n Nachfolger(in) m(f)

succinct [sək'sɪŋkt] adj knapp

succulent ['sʌkjʊlənt] adj saftig

succumb [sə'kʌm] vi: **to ~ (to)** erliegen (+dat); (*yield*) nachgeben (+dat)

such [sʌtʃ] adj solche(r, s); **~ a book** so ein Buch; **~ books** solche Bücher; **~ courage** so ein Mut; **~ a long trip** so eine lange Reise; **~ a lot of** so viel(e); **~ as** wie; **a noise ~ as to** ein derartiger Lärm, dass; **as ~** an sich; **~-and-~ a time** die und die Zeit

suck [sʌk] vt saugen; (*lollipop etc*) lutschen

sucker ['sʌkər] (*inf*) n Idiot m

suction ['sʌkʃən] n Saugkraft f

sudden ['sʌdn] adj plötzlich; **all of a ~** auf einmal; ~ly adv plötzlich

suds [sʌdz] npl Seifenlauge f; (*lather*) Seifenschaum m

sue [suː] vt verklagen

suede [sweɪd] n Wildleder nt

Suez ['suːɪz] n: **the ~ Canal** der Suezkanal

suffer ['sʌfər] vt (er)leiden ♦ vi leiden; ~er Leidende(r) mf; ~ing n Leiden nt

suffice [sə'faɪs] vi genügen

sufficient [sə'fɪʃənt] adj ausreichend; ~ly adv ausreichend

suffix ['sʌfɪks] n Nachsilbe f

suffocate ['sʌfəkeɪt] vt, vi ersticken

suffrage ['sʌfrɪdʒ] n Wahlrecht nt

sugar ['ʃʊgər] n Zucker m ♦ vt zuckern; **~ beet** n Zuckerrübe f; **~ cane** n Zuckerroh nt; ~y adj süß

suggest [sə'dʒest] vt vorschlagen; (*show*) schließen lassen auf +acc; ~ion [sə'dʒestʃən] n Vorschlag m; ~ive adj anregend; (*indecent*) zweideutig

suicide ['suɪsaɪd] n Selbstmord m; **to commit ~** Selbstmord begehen **~ bomber** n Selbstmordattentäter(in) m(f)

suit [suːt] n Anzug m; (*CARDS*) Farbe f ♦ vt passen +dat; (*clothes*) stehen +dat; **well ~e** (*well matched*) gut zusammenpassend; ~able adj geeignet, passend; ~ably adv passend, angemessen

suitcase ['suːtkeɪs] n (Hand)koffer m

suite [swiːt] n (*of rooms*) Zimmerflucht f; (*of furniture*) Einrichtung f; (*MUS*) Suite f

suitor ['suːtər] n (*JUR*) Kläger(in) m(f)

sulfur ['sʌlfər] (*US*) n = **sulphur**

sulk [sʌlk] vi schmollen; ~y adj schmollend

sullen ['sʌlən] adj mürrisch

sulphur ['sʌlfər] (*US* **sulfur**) n Schwefel m

sultana [sʌl'tɑːnə] n (*fruit*) Sultanine f

sultry ['sʌltrɪ] adj schwül

sum [sʌm] n Summe f; (*money*) Betrag m, Summe f; (*arithmetic*) Rechenaufgabe f; **~ up** vt, vi zusammenfassen

summarize ['sʌmaraɪz] vt kurz zusammenfassen

summary ['sʌmarɪ] n Zusammenfassung f ♦ adj (*justice*) kurzerhand erteilt

summer ['sʌmər] n Sommer m ♦ adj Sommer-; ~house n (*in garden*) Gartenhaus nt; ~time n Sommerzeit f

summit ['sʌmɪt] n Gipfel m; ~

(conference) n Gipfelkonferenz f
summon ['sʌmən] vt herbeirufen; (JUR) vorladen; (gather up) aufbringen; **~s** (JUR) n Vorladung f ♦ vt vorladen
sump [sʌmp] (BRIT) n (AUT) Ölwanne f
sumptuous ['sʌmptjuəs] adj prächtig
sun [sʌn] n Sonne f; **~bathe** vi sich sonnen; **~block** n Sonnenschutzcreme f; **~burn** n Sonnenbrand m; **~burnt** adj sonnenverbrannt, sonnengebräunt; **to be ~burnt** (painfully) einen Sonnenbrand haben
Sunday ['sʌndɪ] n Sonntag m; **~ school** n Sonntagsschule f
sundial ['sʌndaɪəl] n Sonnenuhr f
sundown ['sʌndaun] n Sonnenuntergang m
sundries ['sʌndrɪz] npl (miscellaneous items) Verschiedene(s) nt
sundry ['sʌndrɪ] adj verschieden; **all and ~** alle
sunflower ['sʌnflauər] n Sonnenblume f
sung [sʌŋ] pp of **sing**
sunglasses ['sʌnglɑːsɪz] npl Sonnenbrille f
sunk [sʌŋk] pp of **sink**
sun: ~light ['sʌnlaɪt] n Sonnenlicht nt; **~lit** ['sʌnlɪt] adj sonnenbeschienen; **~ny** ['sʌnɪ] adj sonnig; **~rise** n Sonnenaufgang m; **~ roof** n (AUT) Schiebedach nt; **~screen** ['sʌnskriːn] n Sonnenschutzcreme f; **~set** ['sʌnset] n Sonnenuntergang m; **~shade** ['sʌnʃeɪd] n Sonnenschirm m; **~shine** ['sʌnʃaɪn] n Sonnenschein m; **~stroke** ['sʌnstrəuk] n Hitzschlag m; **~tan** ['sʌntæn] n (Sonnen)bräune f; **~tan oil** n Sonnenöl nt
super ['suːpər] (inf) adj prima, klasse
superannuation [suːpərænjuˈeɪʃən] n Pension f
superb [suːˈpəːb] adj ausgezeichnet, hervorragend
supercilious [suːpəˈsɪlɪəs] adj herablassend
superficial [suːpəˈfɪʃəl] adj oberflächlich
superfluous [suːˈpəːfluəs] adj überflüssig
superhuman [suːpəˈhjuːmən] adj (effort) übermenschlich
superimpose ['suːpərɪm'pəuz] vt übereinander legen
superintendent [suːpərɪn'tendənt] n

Polizeichef m
superior [suːˈpɪərɪər] adj überlegen; (better) besser ♦ n Vorgesetzte(r) mf; **~ity** [supɪərɪˈɔrɪtɪ] n Überlegenheit f
superlative [suːˈpəːlətɪv] adj überragend
super: ~man ['suːpəmæn] (irreg) n Übermensch m; **~market** ['suːpəmɑːkɪt] n Supermarkt m; **~natural** [suːpəˈnætʃərəl] adj übernatürlich; **~power** ['suːpəpauər] n Weltmacht f
supersede [suːpəˈsiːd] vt ersetzen
supersonic ['suːpəˈsɔnɪk] adj Überschall-
superstition [suːpəˈstɪʃən] n Aberglaube m; **superstitious** [suːpəˈstɪʃəs] adj abergläubisch
supervise ['suːpəvaɪz] vt beaufsichtigen, kontrollieren; **supervision** [suːpəˈvɪʒən] n Aufsicht f; **supervisor** ['suːpəvaɪzər] n Aufsichtsperson f; **supervisory** ['suːpəvaɪzərɪ] adj Aufsichts-
supper ['sʌpər] n Abendessen nt
supplant [səˈplɑːnt] vt (person, thing) ersetzen
supple ['sʌpl] adj geschmeidig
supplement [n 'sʌplɪmənt, vb sʌplɪ'ment] n Ergänzung f; (in book) Nachtrag m ♦ vt ergänzen; **~ary** [sʌplɪˈmentərɪ] adj ergänzend; **~ary benefit** (BRIT: old) n ≈ Sozialhilfe f
supplier [səˈplaɪər] n Lieferant m
supplies [səˈplaɪz] npl (food) Vorräte pl; (MIL) Nachschub m
supply [səˈplaɪ] vt liefern ♦ n Vorrat m; (~ing) Lieferung f; see also **supplies**; **~ teacher** (BRIT) n Vertretung f
support [səˈpɔːt] n Unterstützung f; (TECH) Stütze f ♦ vt (hold up) stützen, tragen; (provide for) ernähren; (be in favour of) unterstützen; **~er** n Anhänger(in) m(f)
suppose [səˈpəuz] vt, vi annehmen; **to be ~d to do sth** etw tun sollen; **~dly** [səˈpəuzɪdlɪ] adv angeblich; **supposing** conj angenommen; **supposition** [sʌpəˈzɪʃən] n Voraussetzung f
suppress [səˈpres] vt unterdrücken
supremacy [suˈpreməsɪ] n Vorherrschaft f, Oberhoheit f

supreme [su'pri:m] *adj* oberste(r, s), höchste(r, s)

surcharge ['sə:tʃɑ:dʒ] *n* Zuschlag *m*

sure [ʃuə'] *adj* sicher, gewiss; **~!** (*of course*) klar!; **to make ~ of sth/that** sich einer Sache *gen* vergewissern/vergewissern, dass; **~ enough** (*with past*) tatsächlich; (*with future*) ganz bestimmt; **~-footed** *adj* sicher (auf den Füßen); **~ly** *adv* (*certainly*) sicherlich, gewiss; **~ly it's wrong** das ist doch wohl falsch

surety ['ʃuərəti] *n* Sicherheit *f*

surf [sə:f] *n* Brandung *f*

surface ['sə:fis] *n* Oberfläche *f* ♦ *vt* (*roadway*) teeren ♦ *vi* auftauchen; **~ mail** *n* gewöhnliche Post *f*

surfboard ['sə:fbɔ:d] *n* Surfbrett *nt*

surfeit ['sə:fit] *n* Übermaß *nt*

surfing ['sə:fiŋ] *n* Surfen *nt*

surge [sə:dʒ] *n* Woge *f* ♦ *vi* wogen

surgeon ['sə:dʒən] *n* Chirurg(in) *m(f)*

surgery ['sə:dʒəri] *n* (*BRIT: place*) Praxis *f*; (: *time*) Sprechstunde *f*; (*treatment*) Operation *f*; **to undergo ~** operiert werden; **~ hours** (*BRIT*) *npl* Sprechstunden *pl*

surgical ['sə:dʒikl] *adj* chirurgisch; **~ spirit** (*BRIT*) *n* Wundbenzin *nt*

surly ['sə:li] *adj* verdrießlich, grob

surmount [sə:'maunt] *vt* überwinden

surname ['sə:neim] *n* Zuname *m*

surpass [sə:'pɑ:s] *vt* übertreffen

surplus ['sə:pləs] *n* Überschuss *m* ♦ *adj* überschüssig, Über(schuss)-

surprise [sə'praiz] *n* Überraschung *f* ♦ *vt* überraschen; **~d** *adj* überrascht; **surprising** *adj* überraschend; **surprisingly** *adv* überraschend(erweise)

surrender [sə'rendə'] *n* Kapitulation *f* ♦ *vi* sich ergeben

surreptitious [sʌrəp'tiʃəs] *adj* heimlich; (*look also*) verstohlen

surrogate ['sʌrəgit] *n* Ersatz *m*; **~ mother** *n* Leihmutter *f*

surround [sə'raund] *vt* umgeben; **~ing** *adj* (*countryside*) umliegend; **~ings** *npl* Umgebung *f*; (*environment*) Umwelt *f*

surveillance [sə:'veiləns] *n* Überwachung *f*

survey [*n* 'sə:vei, *vb* sə:'vei] *n* Übersicht *f* ♦ *vt* überblicken; (*land*) vermessen; **~or** [sə'veiə'] *n* Land(ver)messer(in) *m(f)*

survival [sə'vaivl] *n* Überleben *nt*

survive [sə'vaiv] *vt, vi* überleben; **survivor** [sə'vaivə'] *n* Überlebende(r) *mf*

susceptible [sə'septəbl] *adj*: **~ (to)** empfindlich (gegen); (*charms etc*) empfänglich (für)

suspect [*n* 'sʌspekt, *vb* səs'pekt] *n* Verdächtige(r) *mf* ♦ *adj* verdächtig ♦ *vt* verdächtigen; (*think*) vermuten

suspend [səs'pend] *vt* verschieben; (*from work*) suspendieren; (*hang up*) aufhängen; (*SPORT*) sperren; **~ed sentence** *n* (*JUR*) zur Bewährung ausgesetzte Strafe; **~er belt** *n* Strumpf(halter)gürtel *m*; **~ers** *npl* (*BRIT*) Strumpfhalter *m*; (*US*) Hosenträger *m*

suspense [səs'pens] *n* Spannung *f*

suspension [səs'penʃən] *n* (*from work*) Suspendierung *f*; (*SPORT*) Sperrung *f*; (*AUT*) Federung *f*; **~ bridge** *n* Hängebrücke *f*

suspicion [səs'piʃən] *n* Misstrauen *nt*; Verdacht *m*; **suspicious** [səs'piʃəs] *adj* misstrauisch; (*causing ~*) verdächtig

sustain [səs'tein] *vt* (*maintain*) aufrechterhalten; (*confirm*) bestätigen; (*injury*) davontragen; **~able** *adj* (*development, growth etc*) aufrechtzuerhalten; **~ed** *adj* (*effort*) anhaltend

sustenance ['sʌstinəns] *n* Nahrung *f*

swab [swɔb] *n* (*MED*) Tupfer *m*

swagger ['swægə'] *vi* stolzieren

swallow ['swɔləu] *n* (*bird*) Schwalbe *f*; (*of food etc*) Schluck *m* ♦ *vt* (ver)schlucken; **~ up** *vt* verschlingen

swam [swæm] *pt of* swim

swamp [swɔmp] *n* Sumpf *m* ♦ *vt* überschwemmen

swan [swɔn] *n* Schwan *m*

swap [swɔp] *n* Tausch *m* ♦ *vt*: **to ~ sth (for sth)** etw (gegen etw) tauschen *or* eintauschen

swarm [swɔ:m] *n* Schwarm *m* ♦ *vi*: **to ~ be ~ing with** wimmeln von

swarthy ['swɔːðɪ] adj dunkel, braun

swastika ['swɔstɪkə] n Hakenkreuz nt

swat [swɔt] vt totschlagen

sway [sweɪ] vi schwanken; (branches) schaukeln, sich wiegen ♦ vt schwenken; (influence) beeinflussen

swear [sweəʳ] (pt **swore**, pp **sworn**) vi (promise) schwören; (curse) fluchen; **to ~ to sth** schwören auf etw acc;~**word** n Fluch m

sweat [swɛt] n Schweiß m ♦ vi schwitzen

sweater ['swɛtəʳ] n Pullover m

sweatshirt ['swɛtʃəːt] n Sweatshirt nt

sweaty ['swɛtɪ] adj verschwitzt

Swede [swiːd] n Schwede m, Schwedin f

swede [swiːd] (BRIT) n Steckrübe f

Sweden ['swiːdn] n Schweden nt

Swedish ['swiːdɪʃ] adj schwedisch ♦ n (LING) Schwedisch nt

sweep [swiːp] (pt, pp **swept**) n (chimney ~) Schornsteinfeger m ♦ vt fegen, kehren;~ **away** vt wegfegen;~ **past** vi vorbeisausen;~ **up** vt zusammenkehren; ~**ing** adj (gesture) schwungvoll; (statement) verallgemeinernd

sweet [swiːt] n (course) Nachtisch m; (candy) Bonbon nt ♦ adj süß;~**corn** n Zuckermais m;~**en** vt süßen; (fig) versüßen;~**heart** n Liebste(r) mf;~**ness** n Süße f;~ **pea** n Gartenwicke f

swell [swɛl] (pt **swelled**, pp **swollen** or **swelled**) n Seegang m ♦ adj (inf) todschick ♦ vt (numbers) vermehren ♦ vi (also: ~ **up**) (an)schwellen;~**ing** n Schwellung f

sweltering ['swɛltərɪŋ] adj drückend

swept [swɛpt] pt, pp of **sweep**

swerve [swəːv] vt, vi ausscheren

swift [swɪft] n Mauersegler m ♦ adj geschwind, schnell, rasch;~**ly** adv geschwind, schnell, rasch

swig [swɪg] n Zug m

swill [swɪl] n (for pigs) Schweinefutter nt ♦ vt spülen

swim [swɪm] (pt **swam**, pp **swum**) n: **to go for a ~** schwimmen gehen ♦ vi schwimmen ♦ vt (cross) (durch)schwimmen; ~**mer** n Schwimmer(in) m(f);~**ming** n

Schwimmen nt;~**ming cap** n Badehaube f, Badekappe f;~**ming costume** (BRIT) n Badeanzug m;~**ming pool** n Schwimmbecken nt; (private) Swimmingpool m;~**ming trunks** npl Badehose f;~**suit** n Badeanzug m

swindle ['swɪndl] n Schwindel m, Betrug m ♦ vt betrügen

swine [swaɪn] n (also fig) Schwein nt

swing [swɪŋ] (pt, pp **swung**) n (child's) Schaukel f; (movement) Schwung m ♦ vt schwingen ♦ vi schwingen, schaukeln; (turn quickly) schwenken; **in full ~** in vollem Gange;~ **bridge** n Drehbrücke f;~ **door** (BRIT) n Schwingtür f

swingeing ['swɪndʒɪŋ] (BRIT) adj hart; (taxation, cuts) extrem

swinging door ['swɪŋɪŋ-] (US) n Schwingtür f

swipe [swaɪp] n Hieb m ♦ vt (inf: hit) hart schlagen; (: steal) klauen

swirl [swəːl] vi wirbeln

swish [swɪʃ] adj (inf: smart) schick ♦ vi zischen; (grass, skirts) rascheln

Swiss [swɪs] adj Schweizer, schweizerisch ♦ n Schweizer(in) m(f); **the ~** npl (people) die Schweizer pl

switch [swɪtʃ] n (ELEC) Schalter m; (change) Wechsel m ♦ vt (ELEC) schalten; (change) wechseln ♦ vi wechseln;~ **off** vt ab- or ausschalten;~ **on** vt an- or einschalten; ~**board** n Zentrale f; (board) Schaltbrett nt

Switzerland ['swɪtsələnd] n die Schweiz

swivel ['swɪvl] vt (also: ~ **round**) drehen ♦ vi (also: ~ **round**) sich drehen

swollen ['swəʊlən] pp of **swell**

swoon [swuːn] vi (old) in Ohnmacht fallen

swoop [swuːp] n Sturzflug m; (esp by police) Razzia f ♦ vi (also: ~ **down**) stürzen

swop [swɔp] = **swap**

sword [sɔːd] n Schwert nt;~**fish** n Schwertfisch m

swore [swɔːʳ] pt of **swear**

sworn [swɔːn] pp of **swear**

swot [swɔt] vt, vi pauken

swum [swʌm] pp of **swim**

swung [swʌŋ] pt, pp of **swing**

sycamore ['sɪkəmɔːʳ] *n* (*US*) Platane *f*; (*BRIT*) Bergahorn *m*

syllable ['sɪləbl] *n* Silbe *f*

syllabus ['sɪləbəs] *n* Lehrplan *m*

symbol ['sɪmbl] *n* Symbol *nt*; **~ic(al)** [sɪm'bɒlɪk(l)] *adj* symbolisch

symmetry ['sɪmɪtrɪ] *n* Symmetrie *f*

sympathetic [sɪmpə'θetɪk] *adj* mitfühlend

sympathize ['sɪmpəθaɪz] *vi* mitfühlen; **~r** *n* (*POL*) Sympathisant(in) *m(f)*

sympathy ['sɪmpəθɪ] *n* Mitleid *nt*, Mitgefühl *nt*; (*condolence*) Beileid *nt*; **with our deepest ~** mit tief empfundenem Beileid

symphony ['sɪmfənɪ] *n* Sinfonie *f*

symptom ['sɪmptəm] *n* Symptom *nt*; **~atic** [sɪmptə'mætɪk] *adj* (*fig*): **~atic of** bezeichnend für

synagogue ['sɪnəgɔg] *n* Synagoge *f*

synchronize ['sɪŋkrənaɪz] *vt* synchronisieren

syndicate ['sɪndɪkɪt] *n* Konsortium *nt*

synonym ['sɪnənɪm] *n* Synonym *nt*; **~ous** [sɪ'nɒnɪməs] *adj* gleichbedeutend

synopsis [sɪ'nɒpsɪs] *n* Zusammenfassung *f*

synthetic [sɪn'θetɪk] *adj* synthetisch; **~s** *npl* (*man-made fabrics*) Synthetik *f*

syphon ['saɪfən] *n* = **siphon**

Syria ['sɪrɪə] *n* Syrien *nt*

syringe [sɪ'rɪndʒ] *n* Spritze *f*

syrup ['sɪrəp] *n* Sirup *m*; (*of sugar*) Melasse *f*

system ['sɪstəm] *n* System *nt*; **~atic** [sɪstə'mætɪk] *adj* systematisch; **~ disk** *n* (*COMPUT*) Systemdiskette *f*; **~s analyst** *n* Systemanalytiker(in) *m(f)*

T, t

ta [tɑː] (*BRIT: inf*) *excl* danke!

tab [tæb] *n* Aufhänger *m*; (*name ~*) Schild *nt*; **to keep ~s on** (*fig*) genau im Auge behalten

tabby ['tæbɪ] *n* (*also: ~ cat*) getigerte Katze *f*

table ['teɪbl] *n* Tisch *m*; (*list*) Tabelle *f* ♦ *vt* (*PARL: propose*) vorlegen, einbringen; **to lay** *or* **set the ~** den Tisch decken; **~cloth** *n* Tischtuch *nt*; **~ d'hôte** [tɑːbl'dəut] *n* Tagesmenü *nt*; **~ lamp** *n* Tischlampe *f*;

~mat *n* Untersatz *m*; **~ of contents** *n* Inhaltsverzeichnis *nt*; **~spoon** *n* Esslöffel *m*; **~spoonful** *n* Esslöffel *m* (voll)

tablet ['tæblɪt] *n* (*MED*) Tablette *f*

table tennis *n* Tischtennis *nt*

table wine *n* Tafelwein *m*

tabloid ['tæblɔɪd] *n* Zeitung *f* in kleinem Format; (*pej*) Boulevardzeitung *f*

---

tabloid press

🛈 *Der Ausdruck* **tabloid press** *bezieht sich auf kleinformatige Zeitungen (ca 30 x 40cm); sie sind in Großbritannien fast ausschließlich Massenblätter. Im Gegensatz zur* **quality press** *verwenden diese Massenblätter viele Fotos und einen knappen, oft reißerischen Stil. Sie kommen den Lesern entgegen, die mehr Wert auf Unterhaltung legen.*

---

tabulate ['tæbjuleɪt] *vt* tabellarisch ordnen

tacit ['tæsɪt] *adj* stillschweigend

taciturn ['tæsɪtɜːn] *adj* wortkarg

tack [tæk] *n* (*small nail*) Stift *m*; (*US: thumbtack*) Reißzwecke *f*; (*stitch*) Heftstich *m*; (*NAUT*) Lavieren *nt*; (*course*) Kurs *m* ♦ *vt* (*nail*) nageln; (*stitch*) heften ♦ *vi* aufkreuzen

tackle ['tækl] *n* (*for lifting*) Flaschenzug *m*; (*NAUT*) Takelage *f*; (*SPORT*) Tackling *nt* ♦ *vt* (*deal with*) anpacken, in Angriff nehmen; (*person*) festhalten; (*player*) angehen

tacky ['tækɪ] *adj* klebrig

tact [tækt] *n* Takt *m*; **~ful** *adj* taktvoll

tactical ['tæktɪkl] *adj* taktisch

tactics ['tæktɪks] *npl* Taktik *f*

tactless ['tæktlɪs] *adj* taktlos

tadpole ['tædpəul] *n* Kaulquappe *f*

taffy ['tæfɪ] (*US*) *n* Sahnebonbon *nt*

tag [tæg] *n* (*label*) Schild *nt*, Anhänger *m*; (*maker's name*) Etikett *nt*; **~ along** *vi* mitkommen

tail [teɪl] *n* Schwanz *m*; (*of list*) Schluss *m* ♦ *vt* folgen +*dat*; **~ away** *or* **off** *vi* abfallen, schwinden; **~back** (*BRIT*) *n* (*AUT*) (Rück)stau *m*; **~ coat** *n* Frack *m*; **~ end** *n* Schluss *m*, Ende *nt*; **~gate** *n* (*AUT*) Heckklappe *f*

tailor ['teɪləʳ] *n* Schneider *m*; **~ing** *n*

Schneidern nt; **~-made** adj
maßgeschneidert; (fig): **~-made for sb** jdm
wie auf den Leib geschnitten
tailwind ['teɪlwɪnd] n Rückenwind m
tainted ['teɪntɪd] adj verdorben
take [teɪk] (pt **took**, pp **taken**) vt nehmen;
(trip, exam, PHOT) machen; (capture: person)
fassen; (: town; also COMM, FIN) einnehmen;
(carry to a place) bringen; (get for o.s.) sich
dat nehmen; (gain, obtain) bekommen; (put
up with) hinnehmen; (respond to)
aufnehmen; (interpret) auffassen; (assume)
annehmen; (contain) Platz haben für;
(GRAM) stehen mit; **to ~ sth from sb** jdm
etw wegnehmen; **to ~ sth from sth** (MATH:
subtract) etw von etw abziehen; (extract,
quotation) etw einer Sache dat entnehmen;
~ after vt fus ähnlich sein +dat; **~ apart**
vt auseinander nehmen; **~ away** vt
(remove) wegnehmen; (carry off)
wegbringen; **~ back** vt (return)
zurückbringen; (retract) zurücknehmen; **~
down** vt (pull down) abreißen; (write down)
aufschreiben; **~ in** vt (deceive) hereinlegen;
(understand) begreifen; (include)
einschließen; **~ off** vi (plane) starten ♦ vt
(remove) wegnehmen; (clothing) ausziehen;
(imitate) nachmachen; **~ on** vt (undertake)
übernehmen; (engage)
(opponent) antreten gegen; **~ out** vt (girl,
dog) ausführen; (extract) herausnehmen;
(insurance) abschließen; (licence) sich dat
geben lassen; (book) ausleihen; (remove)
entfernen; **to ~ sth out of sth** (drawer,
pocket etc) etw aus etw herausnehmen; **~
over** vt übernehmen ♦ vi **to ~ over from
sb** jdn ablösen; **~ to** vt fus (like) mögen;
(adopt as practice) sich dat angewöhnen; **~
up** vt (raise) aufnehmen; (dress etc) kürzer
machen; (occupy) in Anspruch nehmen;
(engage in) sich befassen mit; **~away** adj
zum Mitnehmen; **~-home pay** n
Nettolohn m; **~n** pp of **take**; **~off** n (AVIAT)
Start m; (imitation) Nachahmung f; **~out**
(US) adj = **takeaway**; **~over** n (COMM)
Übernahme f; **takings** ['teɪkɪŋz] npl (COMM)
Einnahmen pl

talc [tælk] n (also: **~um powder**)
Talkumpuder m
tale [teɪl] n Geschichte f, Erzählung f; **to tell
~s** (fig: lie) Geschichten erfinden
talent ['tælnt] n Talent nt; **~ed** adj begabt
talk [tɔːk] n (conversation) Gespräch nt;
(rumour) Gerede nt; (speech) Vortrag m ♦ vi
sprechen, reden; **~s** npl (POL etc) Gespräche
pl; **to ~ about** sprechen von +dat or über
+acc; **to ~ sb into doing sth** jdn
überreden, etw zu tun; **to ~ sb out of
doing sth** jdm ausreden, etw zu tun; **to ~
shop** fachsimpeln; **~ over** vt besprechen;
~ative adj gesprächig
tall [tɔːl] adj groß; (building) hoch; **to be 1 m
80 ~** 1,80 m groß sein; **~boy** (BRIT) n
Kommode f; **~ story** n übertriebene
Geschichte f
tally ['tælɪ] n Abrechnung f ♦ vi
übereinstimmen
talon ['tælən] n Kralle f
tame [teɪm] adj zahm; (fig) fade
tamper ['tæmpə*] vi: **to ~ with**
herumfuschen an +dat
tampon ['tæmpɒn] n Tampon m
tan [tæn] n (Sonnen)bräune f; (colour)
Gelbbraun nt ♦ adj (colour) (gelb)braun ♦ vt
bräunen ♦ vi braun werden
tang [tæŋ] n Schärfe f
tangent ['tændʒənt] n Tangente f; **to go off
at a ~** (fig) vom Thema abkommen
tangerine [tændʒə'riːn] n Mandarine f
tangible ['tændʒəbl] adj greifbar
tangle ['tæŋgl] n Durcheinander nt; (trouble)
Schwierigkeiten pl; **to get in(to) a ~** sich
verheddern
tank [tæŋk] n (container) Tank m, Behälter m;
(MIL) Panzer m; **~er** ['tæŋkə*] n (ship) Tanker
m; (vehicle) Tankwagen m
tanned [tænd] adj gebräunt
tantalizing ['tæntəlaɪzɪŋ] adj verlockend;
(annoying) quälend
tantamount ['tæntəmaunt] adj: **~ to**
gleichbedeutend mit
tantrum ['tæntrəm] n Wutanfall m
tap [tæp] n Hahn m; (gentle blow) Klopfen nt
♦ vt (strike) klopfen; (supply) anzapfen;

(telephone) abhören; **on ~** *(fig: resources)* zur Hand; **~-dancing** n Steppen nt

tape [teɪp] n Band nt; *(magnetic)* (Ton)band nt; *(adhesive)* Klebstreifen m ♦ vt *(record)* aufnehmen; **~ deck** n Tapedeck nt; **~ measure** n Maßband nt

taper ['teɪpəʳ] vi spitz zulaufen

tape recorder n Tonbandgerät nt

tapestry ['tæpɪstrɪ] n Wandteppich m

tar [tɑː] n Teer m

target ['tɑːgɪt] n Ziel nt; *(board)* Zielscheibe f

tariff ['tærɪf] n *(duty paid)* Zoll m; *(list)* Tarif m

tarmac ['tɑːmæk] n *(AVIAT)* Rollfeld nt

tarnish ['tɑːnɪʃ] vt matt machen; *(fig)* beflecken

tarpaulin [tɑːˈpɔːlɪn] n Plane f

tarragon ['tærəgən] n Estragon m

tart [tɑːt] n (Obst)torte f; *(inf)* Nutte f ♦ adj scharf; **~ up** *(inf)* vt aufmachen; *(person)* auftakeln

tartan ['tɑːtn] n Schottenkaro nt ♦ adj mit Schottenkaro

tartar ['tɑːtəʳ] n Zahnstein m

tartar(e) sauce ['tɑːtə-] n Remoulade f

task [tɑːsk] n Aufgabe f; **to take sb to ~** sich dat jdn vornehmen; **~ force** n Sondertrupp m

tassel ['tæsl] n Quaste f

taste [teɪst] n Geschmack m; *(sense)* Geschmackssinn m; *(small quantity)* Kostprobe f; *(liking)* Vorliebe f ♦ vt schmecken; *(try)* probieren ♦ vi schmecken; **can I have a ~ of this wine?** kann ich diesen Wein probieren?; **to have a ~ for sth** etw mögen; **in good / bad ~** geschmackvoll/geschmacklos; **you can ~ the garlic (in it)** man kann den Knoblauch herausschmecken; **to ~ of sth** nach einer Sache schmecken; **~ful** adj geschmackvoll; **~less** adj *(insipid)* fade; *(in bad ~)* geschmacklos; **tasty** ['teɪstɪ] adj schmackhaft

tattered ['tætəd] adj = **in tatters**

tatters ['tætəz] npl: **in ~** in Fetzen

tattoo [təˈtuː] n *(MIL)* Zapfenstreich m; *(on skin)* Tätowierung f ♦ vt tätowieren

tatty ['tætɪ] *(BRIT: inf)* adj schäbig

taught [tɔːt] pt, pp of **teach**

taunt [tɔːnt] n höhnische Bemerkung f ♦ vt verhöhnen

Taurus ['tɔːrəs] n Stier m

taut [tɔːt] adj straff

tawdry ['tɔːdrɪ] adj (bunt und) billig

tax [tæks] n Steuer f ♦ vt besteuern; *(strain)* strapazieren; *(strength)* angreifen; **~able** adj *(income)* steuerpflichtig; **~ation** [tækˈseɪʃən] n Besteuerung f; *(amount)* Steuerumgehung f; **~ disc** (BRIT) n *(AUT)* Kraftfahrzeugsteuerplakette f; **~ evasion** n Steuerhinterziehung f; **~-free** adj steuerfrei

taxi ['tæksɪ] n Taxi nt ♦ vi *(plane)* rollen; **~ driver** n Taxifahrer m; **~ rank** (BRIT) n Taxistand m; **~ stand** n Taxistand m

tax: ~payer n Steuerzahler m; **~ relief** n Steuerermäßigung f; **~ return** n Steuererklärung f

TB n abbr (= tuberculosis) Tb f, Tbc f

tea [tiː] n Tee m; *(meal)* (frühes) Abendessen nt; **high ~** (BRIT) Abendessen nt; **~ bag** n Teebeutel m; **~ break** (BRIT) n Teepause f

teach [tiːtʃ] (pt, pp **taught**) vt lehren; *(SCH)* lehren, unterrichten; *(show)*: **to ~ sb sth** jdm etw beibringen ♦ vi lehren, unterrichten; **~er** n Lehrer(in) m(f); **~er's pet** n Lehrers Liebling m; **~ing** n *(~er's work)* Unterricht m; *(doctrine)* Lehre f

tea: ~ cloth n Geschirrtuch nt; **~ cosy** n Teewärmer m; **~cup** n Teetasse f; **~ leaves** npl Teeblätter pl

team [tiːm] n *(workers)* Team nt; *(SPORT)* Mannschaft f; *(animals)* Gespann nt; **~work** n Gemeinschaftsarbeit f, Teamarbeit f

teapot ['tiːpɔt] n Teekanne f

tear¹ [tɛəʳ] (pt **tore**, pp **torn**) n Riss m ♦ vt zerreißen; *(muscle)* zerren ♦ vi (zer)reißen; *(rush)* rasen; **~ along** vi *(rush)* entlangrasen; **~ up** vt *(sheet of paper etc)* zerreißen

tear² [tɪəʳ] n Träne f; **~ful** ['tɪəful] adj weinend; *(voice)* weinerlich; **~ gas** ['tɪəgæs] n Tränengas nt

tearoom ['tiːruːm] n Teestube f

tease [tiːz] n Hänsler m ♦ vt necken

tea set n Teeservice nt

teaspoon ['ti:spu:n] n Teelöffel m

teat [ti:t] n (of human) Brustwarze f; (of animal) Zitze f; (of bottle) Sauger m

tea time n (in the afternoon) Teestunde f; (mealtime) Abendessen nt

tea towel n Geschirrtuch nt

technical ['tɛknɪkl] adj technisch; (knowledge, terms) Fach-; **~ity** [tɛknɪ'kælɪtɪ] n technische Einzelheit f; (JUR) Formsache f; **~ly** adv technisch; (speak) spezialisiert; (fig) genau genommen

technician [tɛk'nɪʃən] n Techniker m

technique [tɛk'ni:k] n Technik f

techno ['tɛknəʊ] n Techno m

technological [tɛknə'lɒdʒɪkl] adj technologisch

technology [tɛk'nɒlədʒɪ] n Technologie f

teddy (bear) ['tɛdɪ-] n Teddybär m

tedious ['ti:dɪəs] adj langweilig, ermüdend

tee [ti:] n (GOLF: object) Tee nt

teem [ti:m] vi (swarm): **to ~ (with)** wimmeln (von); **it is ~ing (with rain)** es gießt in Strömen

teenage ['ti:neɪdʒ] adj (fashions etc) Teenager-, jugendlich; **~r** n Teenager m, Jugendliche(r) mf

teens [ti:nz] npl Teenageralter nt

tee-shirt ['ti:ʃə:t] n T-Shirt nt

teeter ['ti:tər] vi schwanken

teeth [ti:θ] npl of **tooth**

teethe [ti:ð] vi zahnen; **teething ring** n Beißring m; **teething troubles** npl (fig) Kinderkrankheiten pl

teetotal ['ti:'təʊtl] adj abstinent

tele: **~communications** npl Fernmeldewesen nt; **~conferencing** n Telefon- or Videokonferenz f; **~gram** n Telegramm nt; **~graph** n Telegraf m; **~graph pole** n Telegrafenmast m

telephone ['tɛlɪfəʊn] n Telefon nt, Fernsprecher m ♦ vt anrufen; (message) telefonisch mitteilen; **to be on the ~** (talking) telefonieren; (possessing phone) Telefon haben; **~ booth** n Telefonzelle f; **~ box** (BRIT) n Telefonzelle f; **~ call** n Telefongespräch nt, Anruf m; **~ directory** n Telefonbuch nt; **~ number** n

Telefonnummer f; **telephonist** [tə'lɛfənɪst] (BRIT) n Telefonist(in) m(f)

telephoto lens ['tɛlɪ'fəʊtəʊ-] n Teleobjektiv nt

telesales ['tɛlɪseɪlz] n Telefonverkauf m

telescope ['tɛlɪskəʊp] n Teleskop nt, Fernrohr nt ♦ vt ineinander schieben

televise ['tɛlɪvaɪz] vt durch das Fernsehen übertragen

television ['tɛlɪvɪʒən] n Fernsehen nt; **on ~** im Fernsehen; **~ (set)** n Fernsehapparat m, Fernseher m

teleworking ['tɛlɪwə:kɪŋ] n Telearbeit f

telex ['tɛlɛks] n Telex nt ♦ vt per Telex schicken

tell [tɛl] (pt, pp **told**) vt (story) erzählen; (secret) ausplaudern; (say, make known) sagen; (distinguish) erkennen; (be sure) wissen ♦ vi (talk) sprechen; (be sure) wissen; (divulge) es verraten; (have effect) sich auswirken; **to ~ sb to do sth** jdm sagen, dass er etw tun soll; **to ~ sb sth** or **sth to sb** jdm etw sagen; **to ~ sb by sth** jdn an etw dat erkennen; **to ~ sth from sth** unterscheiden von; **to ~ of sth** von etw sprechen; **~ off** vt: **to ~ sb off** jdn ausschimpfen

teller ['tɛlər] n Kassenbeamte(r) mf

telling ['tɛlɪŋ] adj verräterisch; (blow) hart

telltale ['tɛlteɪl] adj verräterisch

telly ['tɛlɪ] (BRIT: inf) n abbr (= television) TV nt

temp [tɛmp] n abbr (= temporary) Aushilfssekretärin f

temper ['tɛmpər] n (disposition) Temperament nt; (anger) Zorn m ♦ vt (tone down) mildern; (metal) härten; **to be in a (bad) ~** wütend sein; **to lose one's ~** die Beherrschung verlieren

temperament ['tɛmprəmənt] n Temperament nt; **~al** [tɛmprə'mɛntl] adj (moody) launisch

temperate ['tɛmprət] adj gemäßigt

temperature ['tɛmprətʃər] n Temperatur f; (MED: high ~) Fieber nt; **to have** or **run a ~** Fieber haben

template ['tɛmplɪt] n Schablone f

temple ['tɛmpl] n Tempel m; (ANAT) Schläfe *f*

temporal ['tempərl] *adj (of time)* zeitlich; *(worldly)* irdisch, weltlich

temporarily ['tempərərɪlɪ] *adv* zeitweilig, vorübergehend

temporary ['tempərərɪ] *adj* vorläufig; *(road, building)* provisorisch

tempt [tempt] *vt (persuade)* verleiten; *(attract)* reizen, (ver)locken; **to ~ sb into doing sth** jdn dazu verleiten, etw zu tun; **~ation** [temp'teɪʃən] *n* Versuchung *f*; **~ing** *adj (person)* verführerisch; *(object, situation)* verlockend

ten [ten] *num* zehn

tenable ['tenəbl] *adj* haltbar

tenacious [tə'neɪʃəs] *adj* zäh, hartnäckig

tenacity [tə'næsɪtɪ] *n* Zähigkeit *f*, Hartnäckigkeit *f*

tenancy ['tenənsɪ] *n* Mietverhältnis *nt*

tenant ['tenənt] *n* Mieter *m*; *(of larger property)* Pächter *m*

tend [tend] *vt (look after)* sich kümmern um ♦ *vi:* **to ~ to do sth** etw gewöhnlich tun

tendency ['tendənsɪ] *n* Tendenz *f*; *(of person)* Tendenz *f*, Neigung *f*

tender ['tendər] *adj* zart; *(loving)* zärtlich ♦ *n* *(COMM: offer)* Kostenanschlag *m* ♦ *vt* (an)bieten; *(resignation)* einreichen; **~ness** *n* Zartheit *f*; *(being loving)* Zärtlichkeit *f*

tendon ['tendən] *n* Sehne *f*

tenement ['tenəmənt] *n* Mietshaus *nt*

tennis ['tenɪs] *n* Tennis *nt*; **~ ball** *n* Tennisball *m*; **~ court** *n* Tennisplatz *m*; **~ player** *n* Tennisspieler(in) *m(f)*; **~ racket** *n* Tennisschläger *m*; **~ shoes** *npl* Tennisschuhe *pl*

tenor ['tenər] *n* Tenor *m*

tenpin bowling ['tenpɪn-] *n* Bowling *nt*

tense [tens] *adj* angespannt ♦ *n* Zeitform *f*

tension ['tenʃən] *n* Spannung *f*

tent [tent] *n* Zelt *nt*

tentacle ['tentəkl] *n* Fühler *m*; *(of sea animals)* Fangarm *m*

tentative ['tentətɪv] *adj (movement)* unsicher; *(offer)* Probe-; *(arrangement)* vorläufig; *(suggestion)* unverbindlich; **~ly** *adv* versuchsweise; *(try, move)* vorsichtig

tenterhooks ['tentəhuks] *npl:* **to be on ~** auf die Folter gespannt sein

tenth [tenθ] *adj* zehnte(r, s)

tent peg *n* Hering *m*

tent pole *n* Zeltstange *f*

tenuous ['tenjuəs] *adj* schwach

tenure ['tenjuər] *n (of land)* Besitz *m*; *(of office)* Amtszeit *f*

tepid ['tepɪd] *adj* lauwarm

term [tɜːm] *n (period of time)* Zeit(raum *m*) *f*; *(limit)* Frist *f*; *(SCH)* Quartal *nt*; *(UNIV)* Trimester *nt*; *(expression)* Ausdruck *m* ♦ *vt* (be)nennen; **~s** *npl (conditions)* Bedingungen *pl*; **in the short/long ~** auf kurze/lange Sicht; **to be on good ~s with sb** gut mit jdm auskommen; **to come to ~s with** *(person)* sich einigen mit; *(problem)* sich abfinden mit

terminal ['tɜːmɪnl] *n (BRIT: also:* **coach ~**) Endstation *f*; *(AVIAT)* Terminal *m*; *(COMPUT)* Terminal *nt or m* ♦ *adj* Schluss-; *(MED)* unheilbar; **~ly** *adj (MED):* **~ly ill** unheilbar krank

terminate ['tɜːmɪneɪt] *vt* beenden ♦ *vi* enden, aufhören

termini ['tɜːmɪnaɪ] *npl of* **terminus**

terminus ['tɜːmɪnəs] *(pl* **termini**) *n* Endstation *f*

terrace ['terəs] *n (BRIT: row of houses)* Häuserreihe *f*; *(in garden etc)* Terrasse *f*; **the ~s** *npl (BRIT: SPORT)* die Ränge; **~d** *adj (garden)* terrassenförmig angelegt; *(house)* Reihen-

terrain [te'reɪn] *n* Gelände *nt*

terrible ['terɪbl] *adj* schrecklich, entsetzlich, fürchterlich; **terribly** *adv* fürchterlich

terrier ['terɪər] *n* Terrier *m*

terrific [tə'rɪfɪk] *adj* unwahrscheinlich; **~!** klasse!

terrified *adj:* **to be ~ of sth** vor etw schreckliche Angst haben

terrify ['terɪfaɪ] *vt* erschrecken

territorial [terɪ'tɔːrɪəl] *adj* Gebiets-, territorial

territory ['terɪtərɪ] *n* Gebiet *nt*

terror ['terər] *n* Schrecken *m*

terrorism ['terərɪzəm] *n* Terrorismus *m*; **~ist** *n* Terrorist(in) *m(f)*; **~ize** *vt* terrorisieren

terse [tɜːs] *adj* knapp, kurz, bündig

test [test] *n* Probe *f*; (*examination*) Prüfung *f*; (*PSYCH, TECH*) Test *m* ♦ *vt* prüfen; (*PSYCH*) testen

testicle ['testɪkl] *n* (*ANAT*) Hoden *m*

testify ['testɪfaɪ] *vi* aussagen; **to ~ to sth** etw bezeugen

testimony ['testɪmənɪ] *n* (*JUR*) Zeugenaussage *f*; (*fig*) Zeugnis *nt*

test match *n* (*SPORT*) Länderkampf *m*

test tube *n* Reagenzglas *nt*

tether ['teðəʳ] *vt* anbinden ♦ *n*: **at the end of one's ~** völlig am Ende

text [tekst] *n* Text *m*; (*of document*) Wortlaut *m*; (*text message*) SMS-Nachricht *f*; ♦ *vti* eine SMS schicken; **ich schicke dir eine SMS** I'll send you a text; **~book** *n* Lehrbuch *nt*

textiles ['tekstaɪlz] *npl* Textilien *pl*

texture ['tekstʃəʳ] *n* Beschaffenheit *f*

Thai [taɪ] *adj* thailändisch ♦ *n* Thailänder(in) *m(f)*; **~land** *n* Thailand *nt*

Thames [temz] *n*: **the ~** die Themse

than [ðæn, ðən] *prep* (*in comparisons*) als

thank [θæŋk] *vt* danken +*dat*; **you've him to ~ for your success** Sie haben Ihren Erfolg ihm zu verdanken; **~ you (very much)** danke (vielmals), danke schön; **~ful** *adj* dankbar; **~less** *adj* undankbar; **~s** *npl* Dank *m* ♦ *excl* danke!; **~s to** dank +*gen*; **T~sgiving (Day)** (*US*) *n* Thanksgiving Day *m*

Thanksgiving (Day)

ⓘ **Thanksgiving (Day)** *ist ein Feiertag in den USA, der auf den vierten Donnerstag im November fällt. Er soll daran erinnern, wie die Pilgerväter die gute Ernte im Jahre 1621 feierten. In Kanada gibt es einen ähnlichen Erntedanktag (der aber nichts mit dem Pilgervätern zu tun hat) am zweiten Montag im Oktober.*

KEYWORD

that [ðæt, ðət] *adj* (*demonstrative: pl those*) der/die/das; jene(r, s); **that one** das da

♦ *pron* **1** (*demonstrative: pl those*) das; **who's/what's that?** wer ist da/was ist das?; **is that you?** bist du das?; **that's what he said** genau das hat er gesagt; **what happened after that?** was passierte danach?; **that is** das heißt

2 (*relative: subj*) der/die/das, die; (*: direct obj*) den/die/das, die; (*: indirect obj*) dem/der/dem, denen; **all (that) I have** alles, was ich habe

3 (*relative: of time*): **the day (that)** an dem Tag, als; **the winter (that) he came** in dem Winter, in dem er kam

♦ *conj* dass; **he thought that I was ill** er dachte, dass ich krank sei, er dachte, ich sei krank

♦ *adv* (*demonstrative*) so; **I can't work that much** ich kann nicht so viel arbeiten

thatched [θætʃt] *adj* strohgedeckt; (*cottage*) mit Strohdach

thaw [θɔː] *n* Tauwetter *nt* ♦ *vi* tauen; (*frozen foods, fig: people*) auftauen ♦ *vt* (auf)tauen lassen

KEYWORD

the [ðiː, ðə] *def art* **1** der/die/das; **to play the piano/violin** Klavier/Geige spielen; **I'm going to the butcher's/the cinema** ich gehe zum Fleischer/ins Kino; **Elizabeth the First** Elisabeth die Erste

2 (+*adj to form noun*) das, die; **the rich and the poor** die Reichen und die Armen

3 (*in comparisons*): **the more he works the more he earns** je mehr er arbeitet, desto mehr verdient er

theatre ['θɪətəʳ] (*US* **theater**) *n* Theater *nt*; (*for lectures etc*) Saal *m*; (*MED*) Operationssaal *m*; **~goer** *n* Theaterbesucher(in) *m(f)*; **theatrical** [θɪ'ætrɪkl] *adj* Theater-; (*career*) Schauspieler-; (*showy*) theatralisch

theft [θeft] *n* Diebstahl *m*

their [ðɛəʳ] *adj* ihr; *see also* **my**; **~s** *pron* ihre(r, s); *see also* **mine²**

them [ðem, ðəm] *pron* (*acc*) sie; (*dat*) ihnen; *see also* **me**

theme [θiːm] *n* Thema *nt*; (*MUS*) Motiv *nt*; ~ **park** *n* (thematisch gestalteter) Freizeitpark *m*; ~ **song** *n* Titelmusik *f*

themselves [ðəmˈsɛlvz] *pl pron* (*reflexive*) sich (selbst); (*emphatic*) selbst; *see also* **oneself**

then [ðɛn] *adv* (*at that time*) damals; (*next*) dann ♦ *conj* also, folglich; (*furthermore*) ferner ♦ *adj* damalig; **from ~ on** von da an; **by ~** bis dahin; **the ~ president** der damalige Präsident

theology [θɪˈɔlədʒɪ] *n* Theologie *f*

theoretical [θɪəˈrɛtɪkl] *adj* theoretisch; **~ly** *adv* theoretisch

theory [ˈθɪərɪ] *n* Theorie *f*

therapist [ˈθɛrəpɪst] *n* Therapeut(in) *m(f)*

therapy [ˈθɛrəpɪ] *n* Therapie *f*

KEYWORD

there [ðɛəʳ] *adv* **1**: **there is, there are** es *or* da ist/sind; (*there exists/exist also*) es gibt; **there are 3 of them** (*people, things*) es gibt 3 davon; **there has been an accident** da war ein Unfall

2 (*place*) da, dort; (*direction*) dahin, dorthin; **put it in/on there** leg es dahinein/dorthinauf

3: **there, there** (*esp to child*) na, na

---

there: **~abouts** [ˈðɛərəˈbauts] *adv* (*place*) dort in der Nähe, dort irgendwo; (*amount*): **20 or ~abouts** ungefähr 20; **~after** [ðɛərˈɑːftəʳ] *adv* danach; **~by** [ˈðɛəbaɪ] *adv* dadurch, damit

therefore [ˈðɛəfɔːʳ] *adv* deshalb, daher

there's [ˈðɛəz] = **there is**; **there has**

thermometer [θəˈmɔmɪtəʳ] *n* Thermometer *nt*

Thermos [ˈθəːməs] ® *n* Thermosflasche *f*

thesaurus [θɪˈsɔːrəs] *n* Synonymwörterbuch *nt*

these [ðiːz] *pron, adj* (*pl*) diese

theses [ˈθiːsiːz] *npl of* **thesis**

thesis [ˈθiːsɪs] (*pl* **theses**) *n* (*for discussion*) These *f*; (*UNIV*) Dissertation *f*, Doktorarbeit *f*

they [ðeɪ] *pl pron* sie; (*people in general*) man; **~ say that ...** (*it is said that*) es wird gesagt,

dass ; **~'d** = **they had**; **they would**; **~=** **they shall**; **they will**; **~=** **they are**; **~=** **they have**

thick [θɪk] *adj* dick; (*forest*) dicht; (*liquid*) dickflüssig; (*slow, stupid*) dumm, schwer von Begriff ♦ *n*: **in the ~ of** mitten in +*dat*; **it's 20 cm ~** es ist 20 cm dick *or* stark; **~en** *vi* (*fog*) dichter werden ♦ *vt* (*sauce etc*) verdicken; **~ness** *n* Dicke *f*; Dichte *f*; Dickflüssigkeit *f*; **~set** *adj* untersetzt; **~skinned** *adj* dickhäutig

thief [θiːf] (*pl* **thieves**) *n* Dieb(in) *m(f)*

thieves [θiːvz] *npl of* **thief**

thieving [ˈθiːvɪŋ] *n* Stehlen *nt* ♦ *adj* diebisch

thigh [θaɪ] *n* Oberschenkel *m*

thimble [ˈθɪmbl] *n* Fingerhut *m*

thin [θɪn] *adj* dünn; (*person*) dünn, mager; (*excuse*) schwach ♦ *vt*: **to ~ (down)** (*sauce, paint*) verdünnen

thing [θɪŋ] *n* Ding *nt*; (*affair*) Sache *f*; **my ~s** meine Sachen *pl*; **the best ~ would be to ...** das Beste wäre, ...; **how are ~s?** wie gehts?

think [θɪŋk] (*pt, pp* **thought**) *vt, vi* denken; **what did you ~ of them?** was halten Sie von ihnen?; **to ~ about sth/sb** nachdenken über etw/jdn; **I'll ~ about it** ich überlege es mir; **to ~ of doing sth** vorhaben *or* beabsichtigen, etw zu tun; **I ~ so/not** ich glaube (schon)/glaube nicht; **to ~ well of sb** viel von jdm halten; **~ over** *vt* überdenken; **~ up** *vt* sich *dat* ausdenken

think tank *n* Expertengruppe *f*

thinly [ˈθɪnlɪ] *adv* dünn; (*disguised*) kaum

third [θəːd] *adj* dritte(r, s) ♦ *n* (*person*) Dritte(r) *mf*; (*part*) Drittel *nt*; **~ly** *adv* drittens; **~ party insurance** (*BRIT*) *n* Haftpflichtversicherung *f*; **~-rate** *adj* minderwertig; **T~ World** *n*: **the T~ World** die Dritte Welt *f*

thirst [θəːst] *n* (*also fig*) Durst *m*; **~y** *adj* (*person*) durstig; (*work*) durstig machend; **to be ~y** Durst haben

thirteen [θəːˈtiːn] *num* dreizehn

thirty [ˈθəːtɪ] *num* dreißig

this [ðɪs] adj (demonstrative: pl these) diese(r, s); **this evening** heute Abend; **this one** diese(r, s) (da)

♦ pron (demonstrative: pl these) dies, das; **who/what is this?** wer/was ist das?; **this is where I live** hier wohne ich; **this is what he said** das hat er gesagt; **this is Mr Brown** dies ist Mr Brown; (on telephone) hier ist Mr Brown

♦ adv (demonstrative): **this high/long** etc so groß/lang etc

thistle ['θɪsl] n Distel f

thorn [θɔːn] n Dorn m; **~y** adj dornig; (problem) schwierig

thorough ['θʌrə] adj gründlich; **~bred** n Vollblut nt ♦ adj reinrassig, Vollblut-; **~fare** n Straße f; **"no ~fare"** „Durchfahrt verboten"; **~ly** adv gründlich; (extremely) äußerst

those [ðəuz] pl pron die (da), jene ♦ adj die, jene

though [ðəu] conj obwohl ♦ adv trotzdem

thought [θɔːt] pt, pp of **think** ♦ n (idea) Gedanke m; (thinking) Denken nt, Denkvermögen nt; ♦ adj (thinking) gedankenvoll, nachdenklich; (kind) rücksichtsvoll, aufmerksam; **~less** adj gedankenlos, unbesonnen; (unkind) rücksichtslos

thousand ['θauzənd] num tausend; **two ~** zweitausend; **~s of** tausende or Tausende (von); **~th** adj tausendste(r, s)

thrash [θræʃ] vt verdreschen; (fig) (vernichtend) schlagen; **~ about** vi um sich schlagen; **~ out** vt ausdiskutieren

thread [θred] n Faden m, Garn nt; (TECH) Gewinde nt; (in story) Faden m ♦ vt (needle) einfädeln; **~bare** adj fadenscheinig

threat [θret] n Drohung f; (danger) Gefahr f; **~en** vt bedrohen ♦ vi drohen; **to ~en sb with sth** jdm etw androhen

three [θriː] num drei; **~-dimensional** adj dreidimensional; **~-piece suite** n dreiteilige Polstergarnitur f; **~-wheeler** n

Dreiradwagen m

thresh [θreʃ] vt, vi dreschen

threshold ['θreʃhəuld] n Schwelle f

threw [θruː] pt of **throw**

thrift [θrɪft] n Sparsamkeit f; **~y** adj sparsam

thrill [θrɪl] n Reiz m, Erregung f ♦ vt begeistern, packen; **to be ~ed with** (gift etc) sich unheimlich freuen über +acc; **~er** n Krimi m; **~ing** adj spannend; (news) aufregend

thrive [θraɪv] (pt thrived, pp thrived) vi: **to ~ (on)** gedeihen (bei); **thriving** ['θraɪvɪŋ] adj blühend

throat [θrəut] n Hals m, Kehle f; **to have a sore ~** Halsschmerzen haben

throb [θrɒb] vi klopfen, pochen

throes [θrəuz] npl: **in the ~ of** mitten in +dat

throne [θrəun] n Thron m; **on the ~** auf dem Thron

throng ['θrɒŋ] n (Menschen)schar f ♦ vt sich drängen in +dat

throttle ['θrɒtl] n Gashebel m ♦ vt erdrosseln

through [θruː] prep durch; (time) während +gen; (because of) aus, durch ♦ adv durch ♦ adj (ticket, train) durchgehend; (finished) fertig; **to put sb ~ (to)** jdn verbinden (mit); **to be ~** (TEL) eine Verbindung haben; (have finished) fertig sein; **no ~ way** (BRIT) Sackgasse f; **~out** [θruː'aut] prep (place) überall in +dat; (time) während +gen ♦ adv überall; die ganze Zeit

throw [θrəu] (pt threw, pp thrown) n Wurf m ♦ vt werfen; **to ~ a party** eine Party geben; **~ away** vt wegwerfen; (waste) verschenken; (money) verschwenden; **~ off** vt abwerfen; (pursuer) abschütteln; **~ out** vt hinauswerfen; (rubbish) wegwerfen; (plan) verwerfen; **~ up** vt, vi (vomit) speien; **~away** adj Wegwerf-; **~-in** n Einwurf m; **~n** pp of **throw**

thru [θruː] (US) = **through**

thrush [θrʌʃ] n Drossel f

thrust [θrʌst] (pt, pp thrust) vt, vi (push) stoßen

thud [θʌd] n dumpfe(r) (Auf)schlag m

thug [θʌg] n Schlägertyp m

thumb [θʌm] n Daumen m ♦ vt (book) durchblättern; **to ~ a lift** per Anhalter fahren (wollen); **~tack** (US) n Reißzwecke f

thump [θʌmp] n (blow) Schlag m; (noise) Bums m ♦ vi hämmern, pochen ♦ vt schlagen auf +acc

thunder ['θʌndəʳ] n Donner m ♦ vi donnern; (train etc): **to ~ past** vorbeidonnern ♦ vt brüllen; **~bolt** n Blitz nt; **~clap** n Donnerschlag m; **~storm** n Gewitter nt, Unwetter nt; **~y** adj gewitterschwül

Thursday ['θɜːzdɪ] n Donnerstag m

thus [ðʌs] adv (in this way) so; (therefore) somit, also, folglich

thwart [θwɔːt] vt vereiteln, durchkreuzen; (person) hindern

thyme [taɪm] n Thymian m

thyroid ['θaɪrɔɪd] n Schilddrüse f

tiara [tɪ'ɑːrə] n Diadem nt

tic [tɪk] n Tick m

tick [tɪk] n (sound) Ticken nt; (mark) Häkchen nt ♦ vi ticken ♦ vt abhaken; **in a ~** (BRIT: inf) sofort; **~ off** vt abhaken; (person) ausschimpfen; **~ over** vi (engine) im Leerlauf laufen; (fig) auf Sparflamme laufen

ticket ['tɪkɪt] n (for travel) Fahrkarte f; (for entrance) (Eintritts)karte f; (price ~) Preisschild nt; (luggage ~) (Gepäck)schein m; (raffle ~) Los nt; (parking ~) Strafzettel m; (in car park) Parkschein m; **~ collector** n Fahrkartenkontrolleur m; **~ inspector** n Fahrkartenkontrolleur m; **~ office** n (THEAT etc) Kasse f; (RAIL etc) Fahrkartenschalter m

tickle ['tɪkl] n Kitzeln nt ♦ vt kitzeln; (amuse) amüsieren; **ticklish** ['tɪklɪʃ] adj (also fig) kitzlig

tidal ['taɪdl] adj Flut-, Tide-; **~ wave** n Flutwelle f

tidbit ['tɪdbɪt] (US) n Leckerbissen m

tiddlywinks ['tɪdlɪwɪŋks] n Floh(hüpf)spiel nt

tide [taɪd] n Gezeiten pl; **high/low ~** Flut f/ Ebbe f

tidy ['taɪdɪ] adj ordentlich ♦ vt aufräumen, in Ordnung bringen

tie [taɪ] n (BRIT: neck) Krawatte f, Schlips m; (sth connecting) Band nt; (SPORT)

Unentschieden nt ♦ vt (fasten, restrict) binden ♦ vi (SPORT) unentschieden spielen; (in competition) punktgleich sein; **to ~ in a bow** zur Schleife binden; **to ~ a knot in sth** einen Knoten in etw acc machen; **~ down** vt festbinden; **to ~ sb down to** jdn binden an +acc; **~ up** vt (dog) anbinden; (parcel) verschnüren; (boat) festmachen; (person) fesseln; **to be ~d up** (busy) beschäftigt sein

tier [tɪəʳ] n Rang m; (of cake) Etage f

tiff [tɪf] n Krach m

tiger ['taɪgəʳ] n Tiger m

tight [taɪt] adj (close) eng, knapp; (schedule) gedrängt; (firm) fest; (control) streng; (stretched) stramm, (an)gespannt; (inf: drunk) blau, stramm ♦ adv (squeeze) fest; **~en** vt anziehen, anspannen; (restrictions) verschärfen ♦ vi sich spannen; **~-fisted** adj knauserig; **~ly** adv eng; fest; (stretched) straff; **~-rope** n Seil nt; **~s** npl (esp BRIT) Strumpfhose f

tile [taɪl] n (on roof) Dachziegel m; (on wall or floor) Fliese f; **~d** adj (roof) gedeckt, Ziegel-; (floor, wall) mit Fliesen belegt

till [tɪl] n Kasse f ♦ vt bestellen ♦ prep, conj = until

tiller ['tɪləʳ] n Ruderpinne f

tilt [tɪlt] vt kippen, neigen ♦ vi sich neigen

timber ['tɪmbəʳ] n (wood) Holz nt

time [taɪm] n Zeit f; (occasion) Mal nt; (rhythm) Takt m ♦ vt zur rechten Zeit tun, zeitlich einrichten; (SPORT) stoppen; **in 2 weeks' ~** in 2 Wochen; **a long ~** lange; **for the ~ being** vorläufig; **4 at a ~** zu jeweils 4; **from ~ to ~** gelegentlich; **to have a good ~** sich amüsieren; **in ~** (soon enough) rechtzeitig; (after some ~) mit der Zeit; (MUS) im Takt; **in no ~** im Handumdrehen; **any ~** jederzeit; **on ~** pünktlich, rechtzeitig; **five ~s 5** fünfmal 5; **what ~ is it?** wie viel Uhr ist es?, wie spät ist es?; **at ~s** manchmal; **~ bomb** n Zeitbombe f; **~less** adj (beauty) zeitlos; **~ limit** n Frist f; **~ly** adj rechtzeitig; günstig; **~ off** n freie Zeit f; **~r** n (timer switch: in kitchen) Schaltuhr f; **~ scale** n Zeitspanne f; **~-share** adj Timesharing-; **~ switch**

(BRIT) n Zeitschalter m; **~table** n Fahrplan m; (SCH) Stundenplan m; **~ zone** n Zeitzone f

timid ['tɪmɪd] adj ängstlich, schüchtern

timing ['taɪmɪŋ] n Wahl f des richtigen Zeitpunkts, Timing nt

timpani ['tɪmpənɪ] npl Kesselpauken pl

tin [tɪn] n (metal) Blech nt; (BRIT: can) Büchse f, Dose f; **~foil** n Stanniolpapier nt

tinge [tɪndʒ] n (colour) Färbung f; (fig) Anflug m ♦ vt färben; **~d with** mit einer Spur von

tingle ['tɪŋgl] n Prickeln nt ♦ vi prickeln

tinker ['tɪŋkər] n Kesselflicker m; **~ with** vt fus herumpfuschen an +dat

tinkle ['tɪŋkl] vi klingeln

tinned [tɪnd] (BRIT) adj (food) Dosen-, Büchsen-

tin opener [-əupnər] (BRIT) n Dosen- or Büchsenöffner m

tinsel ['tɪnsl] n Rauschgold nt

tint [tɪnt] n Farbton m; (slight colour) Anflug m; (hair) Tönung f; **~ed** adj getönt

tiny ['taɪnɪ] adj winzig

tip [tɪp] n (pointed end) Spitze f; (money) Trinkgeld nt; (hint) Wink m, Tipp m ♦ vt (slant) kippen; (hat) antippen; (~ over) umkippen; (waiter) ein Trinkgeld geben +dat; **~-off** n Hinweis m, Tipp m; **~ped** (BRIT) adj (cigarette) Filter-

tipsy ['tɪpsɪ] adj beschwipst

tiptoe ['tɪptəu] n: **on ~** auf Zehenspitzen

tiptop [tɪp'tɔp] adj: **in ~ condition** tipptopp, erstklassig

tire ['taɪər] n (US) = tyre ♦ vt, vi ermüden, müde machen/werden; **~d** adj müde; **to be ~d of sth** etw satt haben; **~less** adj unermüdlich; **~some** adj lästig

tiring ['taɪərɪŋ] adj ermüdend

tissue ['tɪʃuː] n Gewebe nt; (paper handkerchief) Papiertaschentuch nt; **~ paper** n Seidenpapier nt

tit [tɪt] n (bird) Meise f; **~ for tat** wie du mir, so ich dir

titbit ['tɪtbɪt] (US tidbit) n Leckerbissen m

titillate ['tɪtɪleɪt] vt kitzeln

title ['taɪtl] n Titel m; **~ deed** n Eigentumsurkunde f; **~ role** n Hauptrolle f

titter ['tɪtər] vi kichern

titular ['tɪtjulər] adj (in name only) nominell

TM abbr (= trademark) Wz

KEYWORD

to [tuː, tə] prep **1** (direction) zu, nach; **I go to France/school** ich gehe nach Frankreich/zur Schule; **to the left** nach links

2 (as far as) bis

3 (with expressions of time) vor; **a quarter to 5** Viertel vor 5

4 (for, of) für; **secretary to the director** Sekretärin des Direktors

5 (expressing indirect object): **to give sth to sb** jdm etw geben; **to talk to sb** mit jdm sprechen; **I sold it to a friend** ich habe es einem Freund verkauft

6 (in relation to) zu; **30 miles to the gallon** 30 Meilen pro Gallone

7 (purpose, result) zu; **to my surprise** zu meiner Überraschung

♦ with vb **1** (infin): **to go/eat** gehen/essen; **to want to do sth** etw tun wollen; **to try/start to do sth** versuchen/anfangen, etw zu tun; **he has a lot to lose** er hat viel zu verlieren

2 (with vb omitted): **I don't want to** ich will (es) nicht

3 (purpose, result) um; **I did it to help you** ich tat es, um dir zu helfen

4 (after adj etc): **ready to use** gebrauchsfertig; **too old/young to ...** zu alt/jung, um ... zu ...

♦ adv: **push/pull the door to** die Tür zuschieben/zuziehen

---

toad [təud] n Kröte f; **~stool** n Giftpilz m

toast [təust] n (bread) Toast m; (drinking) Trinkspruch m ♦ vt trinken auf +acc; (bread) toasten; (warm) wärmen; **~er** n Toaster m

tobacco [tə'bækəu] n Tabak m; **~nist** [tə'bækənɪst] n Tabakhändler m; **~nist's (shop)** n Tabakladen m

toboggan [tə'bɔgən] n (Rodel)schlitten m; **~ing** n Rodeln nt

today [tə'deɪ] adv heute; (at the present time) heutzutage

toddler ['tɔdləʳ] n Kleinkind nt
toddy ['tɔdɪ] n (Whisky)grog m
to-do [tə'duː] n Theater nt
toe [təu] n Zehe f; (of sock, shoe) Spitze f
♦ vt: **to ~ the line** (fig) sich einfügen; **~nail** n Zehennagel m
toffee ['tɔfɪ] n Sahnebonbon nt; **~ apple** (BRIT) n kandierte(r) Apfel m
together [tə'geðəʳ] adv zusammen; (at the same time) gleichzeitig; **~ with** zusammen mit; gleichzeitig mit
toil [tɔɪl] n harte Arbeit f, Plackerei f ♦ vi sich abmühen, sich plagen
toilet [tɔɪlət] n Toilette f ♦ cpd Toiletten-; **~ bag** n Waschbeutel m; **~ paper** n Toilettenpapier nt; **~ries** ['tɔɪlətrɪz] npl Toilettenartikel pl; **~ roll** n Rolle f Toilettenpapier; **~ water** n Toilettenwasser nt
token ['təukən] n Zeichen nt; (gift ~) Gutschein m; **book/record ~** (BRIT) Bücher-/Plattengutschein m
Tokyo ['təukjəu] n Tokio nt
told [təuld] pt, pp of **tell**
tolerable ['tɔlərəbl] adj (bearable) erträglich; (fairly good) leidlich
tolerant ['tɔlərnt] adj: **be ~ (of)** vertragen +acc
tolerate ['tɔləreɪt] vt dulden; (noise) ertragen
toll [təul] n Gebühr f ♦ vi (bell) läuten
tomato [tə'mɑːtəu] (pl **~es**) n Tomate f
tomb [tuːm] n Grab(mal) nt
tomboy ['tɔmbɔɪ] n Wildfang m
tombstone ['tuːmstəun] n Grabstein m
tomcat ['tɔmkæt] n Kater m
tomorrow [tə'mɔrəu] n Morgen nt ♦ adv morgen; **the day after ~** übermorgen; **~ morning** morgen früh; **a week ~** morgen in einer Woche
ton [tʌn] n Tonne f (BRIT = 1016kg; US = 907kg); **~s of** (inf) eine Unmenge von
tone [təun] n Ton m; **~ down** vt (criticism, demands) mäßigen; (colours) abtonen; **~ up** vt in Form bringen; **~-deaf** adj ohne musikalisches Gehör
tongs [tɔŋz] npl Zange f; (curling ~) Lockenstab m

tongue [tʌŋ] n Zunge f; (language) Sprache f; **with ~ in cheek** scherzhaft; **~-tied** adj stumm, sprachlos; **~ twister** n Zungenbrecher m
tonic ['tɔnɪk] n (drink) Tonic nt; (MED) Stärkungsmittel nt
tonight [tə'naɪt] adv heute Abend
tonsil ['tɔnsl] n Mandel f; **~litis** [tɔnsɪ'laɪtɪs] n Mandelentzündung f
too [tuː] adv zu; (also) auch; **~ bad!** Pech!; **~ many** zu viele
took [tuk] pt of **take**
tool [tuːl] n (also fig) Werkzeug nt; **~box** n Werkzeugkasten m
toot [tuːt] n Hupen nt ♦ vi tuten; (AUT) hupen
tooth [tuːθ] (pl **teeth**) n Zahn m; **~ache** n Zahnschmerzen pl, Zahnweh nt; **~brush** n Zahnbürste f; **~paste** n Zahnpasta f; **~pick** n Zahnstocher m
top [tɔp] n Spitze f; (of mountain) Gipfel m; (of tree) Wipfel m; (toy) Kreisel m; (~ gear) vierte(r)/fünfte(r) Gang m ♦ adj oberste(r, s) ♦ vt (list) an erster Stelle stehen auf +dat; **on ~ of** oben auf +dat; **from ~ to bottom** von oben bis unten; **~ off** (US) vt auffüllen; **~ up** vt auffüllen; **~ floor** n oberste(s) Stockwerk nt; **~ hat** n Zylinder m; **~-heavy** adj kopflastig
topic ['tɔpɪk] n Thema nt, Gesprächsgegenstand m; **~al** adj aktuell
top: ~less ['tɔplɪs] adj (bather etc) oben ohne; **~-level** ['tɔplevl] adj auf höchster Ebene; **~most** ['tɔpməust] adj oberste(r, s)
topple ['tɔpl] vt, vi stürzen, kippen
top-secret ['tɔp'siːkrɪt] adj streng geheim
topsy-turvy ['tɔpsɪ'tɜːvɪ] adv durcheinander ♦ adj auf den Kopf gestellt
torch [tɔːtʃ] n (BRIT: ELEC) Taschenlampe f; (with flame) Fackel f
tore [tɔːʳ] pt of **tear1**
torment [n 'tɔːment, vb tɔː'ment] n Qual f ♦ vt (distress) quälen
torn [tɔːn] pp of **tear1** ♦ adj hin- und hergerissen
torrent ['tɔrnt] n Sturzbach m; **~ial** [tɔ'renʃl] adj wolkenbruchartig

torrid ['tɒrɪd] adj heiß

tortoise ['tɔːtəs] n Schildkröte f; **~shell** ['tɔːtəʃel] n Schildpatt m

torture ['tɔːtʃər] n Folter f ♦ vt foltern

Tory ['tɔːrɪ] (BRIT) n (POL) Tory m ♦ adj Tory-, konservativ

toss [tɒs] vt schleudern; **to ~ a coin** or **to ~ up for sth** etw mit einer Münze entscheiden; **to ~ and turn** (in bed) sich hin und her werfen

tot [tɒt] n (small quantity) bisschen nt; (small child) Knirps m

total ['təutl] n Gesamtheit f; (money) Endsumme f ♦ adj Gesamt-, total ♦ vt (add up) zusammenzählen; (amount to) sich belaufen auf

totalitarian [təutælɪ'tɛərɪən] adj totalitär

totally ['təutəlɪ] adv total

totter ['tɒtər] vi wanken, schwanken

touch [tʌtʃ] n Berührung f; (sense of feeling) Tastsinn m ♦ vt (feel) berühren; (come against) leicht anstoßen; (emotionally) rühren; **a ~ of** (fig) eine Spur von; **to get in ~ with sb** sich mit jdm in Verbindung setzen; **to lose ~** (friends) Kontakt verlieren; **~ on** vt fus (topic) berühren, erwähnen; **~ up** vt (paint) auffrischen; **~-and-go** adj riskant, knapp; **~down** n Landen nt, Niedergehen nt; **~ed** adj (moved) gerührt; **~ing** adj rührend; **~line** n Seitenlinie f; **~sensitive screen** n (COMPUT) berührungsempfindlicher Bildschirm m; **~y** adj empfindlich, reizbar

tough [tʌf] adj zäh; (difficult) schwierig ♦ n Schläger(typ) m; **~en** vt zäh machen; (make strong) abhärten

toupee ['tuːpeɪ] n Toupet nt

tour ['tuər] n Tour f ♦ vi umherreisen; (THEAT) auf Tour sein; auf Tour gehen; **~ guide** n Reiseleiter(in) m(f)

tourism ['tuərɪzm] n Fremdenverkehr m, Tourismus m

tourist ['tuərɪst] n Tourist(in) m(f) ♦ cpd (class) Touristen-; **~ office** n Verkehrsamt nt

tournament ['tuənəmənt] n Turnier nt

tousled ['tauzld] adj zerzaust

tout [taut] vi: **to ~ for** auf Kundenfang gehen für ♦ n: **ticket ~** Kundenschlepper(in) m(f)

tow [təu] vt (ab)schleppen; **on** (BRIT) or **in** (US) **~** (AUT) im Schlepp

toward(s) [tə'wɔːd(z)] prep (with time) gegen; (in direction of) nach

towel ['tauəl] n Handtuch nt; **~ling** n (fabric) Frottee m or nt; **~ rack** (US) n Handtuchstange f; **~ rail** n Handtuchstange f

tower ['tauər] n Turm m; **~ block** (BRIT) n Hochhaus nt; **~ing** adj hochragend

town [taun] n Stadt f; **to go to ~** (fig) sich ins Zeug legen; **~ centre** n Stadtzentrum nt; **~ clerk** n Stadtdirektor m; **~ council** n Stadtrat m; **~ hall** n Rathaus nt; **~ plan** n Stadtplan m; **~ planning** n Stadtplanung f

towrope ['təurəup] n Abschlepptau nt

tow truck (US) n Abschleppwagen m

toxic ['tɒksɪk] adj giftig, Gift-

toy [tɔɪ] n Spielzeug nt; **~ with** vt fus spielen mit; **~shop** n Spielwarengeschäft nt

trace [treɪs] n Spur f ♦ vt (follow a course) nachspüren +dat; (find out) aufspüren; (copy) durchpausen; **tracing paper** n Pauspapier nt

track [træk] n (mark) Spur f; (path) Weg m; (racetrack) Rennbahn f; (RAIL) Gleis nt ♦ vt verfolgen; **to keep ~ of sb** jdn im Auge behalten; **~ down** vt aufspüren; **~suit** n Trainingsanzug m

tract [trækt] n (of land) Gebiet nt

traction ['trækʃən] n (power) Zugkraft f; (AUT: grip) Bodenhaftung f; (MED): **in ~** im Streckverband

tractor ['træktər] n Traktor m

trade [treɪd] n (commerce) Handel m; (business) Geschäft nt, Gewerbe nt; (people) Geschäftsleute pl; (skilled manual work) Handwerk nt ♦ vi: **to ~ (in)** handeln (mit) ♦ vt tauschen; **~ in** vt in Zahlung geben; **~ fair** n Messe nt; **~-in price** n Preis, zu dem etw in Zahlung genommen wird; **~mark** n Warenzeichen nt; **~ name** n Handelsbezeichnung f; **~r** n Händler m; **~sman** (irreg) n (shopkeeper) Geschäftsmann m; (workman) Handwerker *m*; (*delivery man*) Lieferant *m*; **~ union** *n* Gewerkschaft *f*; **~ unionist** *n* Gewerkschaftler(in) *m(f)*

trading ['treɪdɪŋ] *n* Handel *m*; **~ estate** (*BRIT*) *n* Industriegelände *nt*

tradition [trə'dɪʃən] *n* Tradition *f*; **~al** *adj* traditionell, herkömmlich

traffic ['træfɪk] *n* Verkehr *m*; (*esp in drugs*): **~ (in)** Handel *m* (mit) ♦ *vi*: **to ~ in** (*esp drugs*) handeln mit; **~ calming** *n* Verkehrsberuhigung *f*; **~ circle** (*US*) *n* Kreisverkehr *m*; **~ jam** *n* Verkehrsstauung *f*; **~ lights** *npl* Verkehrsampel *f*; **~ warden** *n* ≈ Verkehrspolizist *m* (*ohne amtliche Befugnisse*), Politesse *f* (*ohne amtliche Befugnisse*)

tragedy ['trædʒədɪ] *n* Tragödie *f*

tragic ['trædʒɪk] *adj* tragisch

trail [treɪl] *n* (*track*) Spur *f*; (*of smoke*) Rauchfahne *f*; (*of dust*) Staubwolke *f*; (*road*) Pfad *m*, Weg *m* ♦ *vt* (*animal*) verfolgen; (*person*) folgen +*dat*; (*drag*) schleppen ♦ *vi* (*hang loosely*) schleifen; (*plants*) sich ranken; (*be behind*) hinterherhinken; (*SPORT*) weit zurückliegen; (*walk*) zuckeln; **~ behind** *vi* zurückbleiben; **~er** *n* Anhänger *m*; (*US: caravan*) Wohnwagen *m*; (*for film*) Vorschau *f*; **~er truck** (*US*) *n* Sattelschlepper *m*

train [treɪn] *n* Zug *m*; (*of dress*) Schleppe *f*; (*series*) Folge *f* ♦ *vt* (*teach: person*) ausbilden; (*: animal*) abrichten; (*: mind*) schulen; (*SPORT*) trainieren; (*aim*) richten ♦ *vi* (*exercise*) trainieren; (*study*) ausgebildet werden; **~ of thought** Gedankengang *m*; **to ~ sth on** (*aim*) etw richten auf +*acc*; **~ed** *adj* (*eye*) geschult; (*person, voice*) ausgebildet; **~ee** *n* Lehrling *m*, Praktikant(in) *m(f)*; **~er** *n* (*SPORT*) Trainer *m*; Ausbilder *m*; **~ers** *npl* Turnschuhe *pl*; **~ing** *n* (*for occupation*) Ausbildung *f*; (*SPORT*) Training *nt*; **in ~ing** im Training; **~ing college** *n* pädagogische Hochschule *f*, Lehrerseminar *nt*; **~ing shoes** *npl* Turnschuhe *pl*

traipse [treɪps] *vi* latschen

trait [treɪt] *n* Zug *m*, Merkmal *nt*

traitor ['treɪtə'] *n* Verräter *m*

trajectory [trə'dʒektərɪ] *n* Flugbahn *f*

tram [træm] (*BRIT*) *n* (*also:* **~car**) Straßenbahn *f*

tramp [træmp] *n* Landstreicher *m* ♦ *vi* (*trudge*) stampfen, stapfen

trample ['træmpl] *vt* (nieder)trampeln ♦ *vi* (herum)trampeln; **to ~ (underfoot)** herumtrampeln auf +*dat*

trampoline ['træmpəliːn] *n* Trampolin *m*

tranquil ['træŋkwɪl] *adj* ruhig, friedlich; **~lity** [træŋ'kwɪlɪtɪ] (*US* **tranquility**) *n* Ruhe *f*; **~lizer** (*US* **tranquilizer**) *n* Beruhigungsmittel *nt*

transact [træn'zækt] *vt* abwickeln; **~ion** [træn'zækʃən] *n* Abwicklung *f*; (*piece of business*) Geschäft *nt*, Transaktion *f*

transcend [træn'send] *vt* übersteigen

transcription [træn'skrɪpʃən] *n* Transkription *f*; (*product*) Abschrift *f*

transfer [*n* 'trænsfə', *vb* træns'fɜː'] *n* (*~ring*) Übertragung *f*; (*of business*) Umzug *m*; (*being ~red*) Versetzung *f*; (*design*) Abziehbild *nt*; (*SPORT*) Transfer *m* ♦ *vt* (*business*) verlegen; (*person*) versetzen; (*prisoner*) überführen; (*drawing*) übertragen; (*money*) überweisen; **to ~ the charges** (*BRIT: TEL*) ein R-Gespräch führen; **~ desk** *n* (*AVIAT*) Transitschalter *m*

transform [træns'fɔːm] *vt* umwandeln; **~ation** [trænsfə'meɪʃən] *n* Umwandlung *f*, Verwandlung *f*

transfusion [træns'fjuːʒən] *n* Blutübertragung *f*, Transfusion *f*

transient ['trænziənt] *adj* kurz(lebig)

transistor [træn'zɪstə'] *n* (*ELEC*) Transistor *m*; (*RAD*) Transistorradio *nt*

transit ['trænzɪt] *n*: **in ~** unterwegs

transition [træn'zɪʃən] *n* Übergang *m*; **~al** *adj* Übergangs-

transit lounge *n* Warteraum *m*

translate [trænz'leɪt] *vt, vi* übersetzen; **translation** [trænz'leɪʃən] *n* Übersetzung *f*; **translator** [trænz'leɪtə'] *n* Übersetzer(in) *m(f)*

transmission [trænz'mɪʃən] *n* (*of information*) Übermittlung *f*; (*ELEC, MED, TV*) Übertragung *f*; (*AUT*) Getriebe *nt*

transmit [trænz'mɪt] vt (*message*) übermitteln; (*ELEC, MED, TV*) übertragen; **~ter** n Sender m

transparency [træns'pɛərnsɪ] n Durchsichtigkeit f; (*BRIT: PHOT*) Dia(positiv) nt

transparent [træns'pærnt] adj durchsichtig; (*fig*) offenkundig

transpire [træns'paɪəʳ] vi (*turn out*) sich herausstellen; (*happen*) passieren

transplant [vb træns'plɑːnt, n 'trænsplɑːnt] vt umpflanzen; (*MED, also fig: person*) verpflanzen ♦ n (*MED*) Transplantation f; (*organ*) Transplantat nt

transport [n 'trænspɔːt, vb træns'pɔːt] n Transport m, Beförderung f ♦ vt befördern; transportieren; **means of ~** Transportmittel nt; **~ation** [trænspɔː'teɪʃən] n Transport m, Beförderung f; (*means*) Beförderungsmittel nt; (*cost*) Transportkosten pl; **~ café** (*BRIT*) n Fernfahrerlokal nt

trap [træp] n Falle f; (*carriage*) zweirädrige(r) Einspänner m; (*inf: mouth*) Klappe f ♦ vt fangen; (*person*) in eine Falle locken; **~door** n Falltür f

trappings ['træpɪŋz] npl Aufmachung f

trash [træʃ] n (*rubbish*) Plunder m; (*nonsense*) Mist m; **~ can** (*US*) n Mülleimer m; **~y** (*inf*) adj minderwertig, wertlos; (*novel*) Schund-

traumatic [trɔː'mætɪk] adj traumatisch

travel ['trævl] n Reisen nt ♦ vi reisen ♦ vt (*distance*) zurücklegen; (*country*) bereisen; **~s** npl (*journeys*) Reisen pl; **~ agency** n Reisebüro nt; **~ agent** n Reisebürokaufmann(-frau) m(f); **~ler** (*US* **traveler**) n Reisende(r) mf; (*salesman*) Handlungsreisende(r) m(f); **~ler's cheque** (*US* **traveler's check**) n Reisescheck m; **~ling** (*US* **traveling**) n Reisen nt; **~sick** adj reisekrank; **~ sickness** n Reisekrankheit f

trawler ['trɔːləʳ] n (*NAUT, FISHING*) Fischdampfer m, Trawler m

tray [treɪ] n (*tea ~*) Tablett nt; (*for mail*) Ablage f

treacherous ['trɛtʃərəs] adj verräterisch; (*road*) tückisch

treachery ['trɛtʃərɪ] n Verrat m

treacle ['triːkl] n Sirup m, Melasse f

tread [trɛd] (*pt* **trod**, *pp* **trodden**) n Schritt m, Tritt m; (*of stair*) Stufe f; (*on tyre*) Profil nt ♦ vi treten; **~ on** vt fus treten auf +acc

treason ['triːzn] n Verrat m

treasure ['trɛʒəʳ] n Schatz m ♦ vt schätzen

treasurer ['trɛʒərəʳ] n Kassenverwalter m, Schatzmeister m

treasury ['trɛʒərɪ] n (*POL*) Finanzministerium nt

treat [triːt] n besondere Freude f ♦ vt (*deal with*) behandeln; **to ~ sb to sth** jdm etw spendieren

treatise ['triːtɪz] n Abhandlung f

treatment ['triːtmənt] n Behandlung f

treaty ['triːtɪ] n Vertrag m

treble ['trɛbl] adj dreifach ♦ vt verdreifachen; **~ clef** n Violinschlüssel m

tree [triː] n Baum m; **~ trunk** n Baumstamm m

trek [trɛk] n Treck m, Zug m; (*inf*) anstrengende(r) Weg m ♦ vi trecken

trellis ['trɛlɪs] n Gitter nt; (*for gardening*) Spalier nt

tremble ['trɛmbl] vi zittern; (*ground*) beben

tremendous [trɪ'mɛndəs] adj gewaltig, kolossal; (*inf: good*) prima

tremor ['trɛməʳ] n Zittern nt; (*of earth*) Beben nt

trench [trɛntʃ] n Graben m; (*MIL*) Schützengraben m

trend [trɛnd] n Tendenz f; **~y** (*inf*) adj modisch

trepidation [trɛpɪ'deɪʃən] n Beklommenheit f

trespass ['trɛspəs] vi: **to ~ on** widerrechtlich betreten; **"no ~ing"** „Betreten verboten"

trestle ['trɛsl] n Bock m; **~ table** n Klapptisch m

trial ['traɪəl] n (*JUR*) Prozess m; (*test*) Versuch m, Probe f; (*hardship*) Prüfung f; **by ~ and error** durch Ausprobieren; **~ period** n Probezeit f

triangle ['traɪæŋgl] n Dreieck nt; (*MUS*) Triangel f; **triangular** [traɪ'æŋgjuləʳ] adj dreieckig

tribal ['traɪbl] adj Stammes-

tribe [traɪb] n Stamm m; **~sman** (*irreg*) n

Stammesangehörige(r) m

tribulation [trɪbjuˈleɪʃən] n Not f, Mühsal f

tribunal [traɪˈbjuːnl] n Gericht nt; (*inquiry*) Untersuchungsausschuss m

tributary [ˈtrɪbjutərɪ] n Nebenfluss m

tribute [ˈtrɪbjuːt] n (*admiration*) Zeichen nt der Hochachtung; **to pay a ~ to sb/sth** jdm/einer Sache Tribut zollen

trick [trɪk] n Trick m; (*CARDS*) Stich m ♦ vt überlisten, beschwindeln; **to play a ~ on sb** jdm einen Streich spielen; **that should do the ~** daß müsste eigentlich klappen; **~ery** n Tricks pl

trickle [ˈtrɪkl] n Tröpfeln nt; (*small river*) Rinnsal nt ♦ vi tröpfeln; (*seep*) sickern

tricky [ˈtrɪkɪ] adj (*problem*) schwierig; (*situation*) kitzlig

tricycle [ˈtraɪsɪkl] n Dreirad nt

trifle [ˈtraɪfl] n Kleinigkeit f; (*COOK*) Trifle m ♦ adv: **a ~ ...** ein bisschen ...; **trifling** adj geringfügig

trigger [ˈtrɪgər] n Drücker m; **~ off** vt auslösen

trim [trɪm] adj gepflegt; (*figure*) schlank ♦ n (*gute*) Verfassung f; (*embellishment, on car*) Verzierung f ♦ vt (*clip*) schneiden; (*trees*) stutzen; (*decorate*) besetzen; (*sails*) trimmen; **~mings** npl (*decorations*) Verzierung f, Verzierungen pl; (*extras*) Zubehör nt

Trinity [ˈtrɪnɪtɪ] n: **the ~** die Dreieinigkeit f

trinket [ˈtrɪŋkɪt] n kleine(s) Schmuckstück nt

trip [trɪp] n (*kurze*) Reise f; (*outing*) Ausflug m; (*stumble*) Stolpern f ♦ vi (*stumble*) stolpern; **on a ~** auf Reisen; **~ up** vi stolpern; (*fig*) stolpern, einen Fehler machen ♦ vt zu Fall bringen; (*fig*) hereinlegen

tripe [traɪp] n (*food*) Kutteln pl; (*rubbish*) Mist m

triple [ˈtrɪpl] adj dreifach

triplets [ˈtrɪplɪts] npl Drillinge pl

triplicate [ˈtrɪplɪkət] n: **in ~** in dreifacher Ausfertigung

tripod [ˈtraɪpɔd] n (*PHOT*) Stativ nt

trite [traɪt] adj banal

triumph [ˈtraɪʌmf] n Triumph m ♦ vi: **to ~**

(*over*) triumphieren (über +acc); **~ant** [traɪˈʌmfənt] adj triumphierend

trivia [ˈtrɪvɪə] npl Trivialitäten pl

trivial [ˈtrɪvɪəl] adj gering(fügig), trivial

trod [trɔd] pt of **tread**; **~den** pp of **tread**

trolley [ˈtrɔlɪ] n Handwagen m; (*in shop*) Einkaufswagen m; (*for luggage*) Kofferkuli m; (*table*) Teewagen m; **~ bus** n Oberleitungsbus m, Obus m

trombone [trɔmˈbəun] n Posaune f

troop [truːp] n Schar f; (*MIL*) Trupp m; **~s** npl (*MIL*) Truppen pl; **~ in/out** vi hinein-/ hinausströmen; **~ing the colour** n (*ceremony*) Fahnenparade f

trophy [ˈtrəufɪ] n Trophäe f

tropic [ˈtrɔpɪk] n Wendekreis m; **~al** adj tropisch

trot [trɔt] n Trott m ♦ vi trotten; **on the ~** (*BRIT: fig: inf*) in einer Tour

trouble [ˈtrʌbl] n (*problems*) Ärger m; (*worry*) Sorge f; (*in country, industry*) Unruhen pl; (*effort*) Mühe f; (*MED*): **stomach ~** Magenbeschwerden pl ♦ vt (*disturb*) stören; **~s** npl (*POL etc*) Unruhen pl; **to ~ to do sth** sich bemühen, etw zu tun; **to be in ~** Probleme or Ärger haben; **to go to the ~ of doing sth** sich die Mühe machen, etw zu tun; **what's the ~?** was ist los?; (*to sick person*) wo fehlts?; **~d** adj (*person*) beunruhigt; (*country*) geplagt; **~-free** adj sorglos; **~maker** n Unruhestifter m; **~shooter** n Vermittler m; **~some** adj lästig, unangenehm; (*child*) schwierig

trough [trɔf] n Trog m; (*channel*) Rinne f, Kanal m; (*MET*) Tief nt

trousers [ˈtrauzəz] npl Hose f

trout [traut] n Forelle f

trowel [ˈtrauəl] n Kelle f

truant [ˈtruənt] n: **to play ~** (*BRIT*) (die Schule) schwänzen

truce [truːs] n Waffenstillstand m

truck [trʌk] n Lastwagen m; (*RAIL*) offene(r) Güterwagen m; **~ driver** n Lastwagenfahrer m; **~ farm** (*US*) n Gemüsegärtnerei f

trudge [trʌdʒ] vi sich (mühselig) dahinschleppen

true [truː] adj (exact) wahr; (genuine) echt; (friend) treu

truffle ['trʌfl] n Trüffel f or m

truly ['truːlɪ] adv wirklich; **yours ~** Ihr sehr ergebener

trump [trʌmp] n (CARDS) Trumpf m

trumpet ['trʌmpɪt] n Trompete f

truncheon ['trʌntʃən] n Gummiknüppel m

trundle ['trʌndl] vt schieben ♦ vi: **to ~ along** entlangrollen

trunk [trʌŋk] n (of tree) (Baum)stamm m; (ANAT) Rumpf m; (box) Truhe f, Überseekoffer m; (of elephant) Rüssel m; (US: AUT) Kofferraum m; **~s** npl (also: **swimming ~s**) Badehose f

truss [trʌs] vt (also: **~ up**) fesseln

trust [trʌst] n (confidence) Vertrauen nt; (for land etc) Treuhandvermögen nt ♦ vt (rely on) vertrauen +dat, sich verlassen auf +acc; (hope) hoffen; (entrust): **to ~ sth to sb** jdm etw anvertrauen; **~ed** adj treu; **~ee** [trʌs'tiː] n Vermögensverwalter m; **~ful** adj vertrauensvoll; **~ing** adj vertrauensvoll; **~worthy** adj vertrauenswürdig; (account) glaubwürdig

truth [truːθ] n Wahrheit f; **~ful** adj ehrlich

try [traɪ] n Versuch m ♦ vt (attempt) versuchen; (test) (aus)probieren; (JUR: person) unter Anklage stellen; (: case) verhandeln; (courage, patience) auf die Probe stellen ♦ vi (make effort) versuchen, sich bemühen; **to have a ~** versuchen; **to ~ to do sth** versuchen, etw zu tun; **~ on** vt (dress) anprobieren; (hat) aufprobieren; **~ out** vt ausprobieren; **~ing** adj schwierig

T-shirt ['tiːʃɜːt] n T-Shirt nt

T-square ['tiːskwɛər] n Reißschiene f

tub [tʌb] n Wanne f, Kübel m; (for margarine etc) Becher m

tubby ['tʌbɪ] adj rundlich

tube [tjuːb] n Röhre f, Rohr nt; (for toothpaste etc) Tube f; (underground) U-Bahn f; (AUT) Schlauch m

tuberculosis [tjubɜːkjuˈləʊsɪs] n Tuberkulose f

tube station n (in London) U-Bahnstation f;

tubing ['tjuːbɪŋ] n Schlauch m; **tubular** ['tjuːbjələr] adj röhrenförmig

TUC (BRIT) n abbr = **Trades Union Congress**

tuck [tʌk] n (fold) Falte f, Einschlag m ♦ vt (put) stecken; (gather) fälteln, einschlagen; **~ away** vt wegstecken; **~ in** vt hineinstecken; (blanket etc) feststecken; (person) zudecken ♦ vi (eat) hineinhauen, zulangen; **~ up** vt (child) warm zudecken; **~ shop** n Süßwarenladen m

Tuesday ['tjuːzdɪ] n Dienstag m

tuft [tʌft] n Büschel m

tug [tʌg] n (jerk) Zerren nt, Ruck m; (NAUT) Schleppdampfer m ♦ vt, vi zerren, ziehen; (boat) schleppen; **~ of war** n Tauziehen nt

tuition [tjuːˈɪʃən] n (BRIT) Unterricht m; (: private ~) Privatunterricht m; (US: school fees) Schulgeld nt

tulip ['tjuːlɪp] n Tulpe f

tumble ['tʌmbl] n (fall) Sturz m ♦ vi fallen, stürzen; **~ to** vt fus kapieren; **~down** adj baufällig; **~ dryer** (BRIT) n Trockner m; **~r** ['tʌmblər] n (glass) Trinkglas nt

tummy ['tʌmɪ] (inf) n Bauch m; **~ upset** n Magenverstimmung f

tumour ['tjuːmər] (US **tumor**) n Geschwulst f, Tumor m

tumultuous [tjuːˈmʌltjuəs] adj (welcome, applause etc) stürmisch

tuna ['tjuːnə] n T(h)unfisch m

tune [tjuːn] n Melodie f ♦ vt (MUS) stimmen; (AUT) richtig einstellen; **to sing in ~/out of ~** richtig/falsch singen; **to be out of ~ with** nicht harmonieren mit; **~ in** vi einschalten; **~ up** vi (MUS) stimmen; **~ful** adj melodisch; **~r** n (RAD) Tuner m; (person) (Instrumenten)stimmer m; **piano ~r** Klavierstimmer(in) m(f)

tunic ['tjuːnɪk] n Waffenrock m; (loose garment) lange Bluse f

tuning ['tjuːnɪŋ] n (RAD, AUT) Einstellen nt; (MUS) Stimmen nt; **~ fork** n Stimmgabel f

Tunisia [tjuːˈnɪzɪə] n Tunesien nt

tunnel ['tʌnl] n Tunnel m, Unterführung f ♦ vi einen Tunnel anlegen

turbulent [ˈtɜːbjulənt] adj stürmisch

tureen [təˈriːn] n Terrine f

turf [təːf] n Rasen m; (piece) Sode f ♦ vt mit Grassoden belegen; **~ out** (inf) vt rauswerfen

turgid [ˈtəːdʒɪd] adj geschwollen

Turk [təːk] n Türke m, Türkin f

Turkey [ˈtəːkɪ] n Türkei f

turkey [ˈtəːkɪ] n Puter m, Truthahn m

Turkish [ˈtəːkɪʃ] adj türkisch ♦ n (LING) Türkisch nt

turmoil [ˈtəːmɔɪl] n Aufruhr m, Tumult m

turn [təːn] n (rotation) (Um)drehung f; (performance) (Programm)nummer f; (MED) Schock m ♦ vt (rotate) drehen; (change position of) umdrehen, wenden; (page) umblättern; (transform): **to ~ sth into sth** etw in etw acc verwandeln; (direct) zuwenden ♦ vi (rotate) sich drehen; (change direction: in car) abbiegen; (: wind) drehen; (~ round) umdrehen, wenden; (become) werden; (leaves) sich verfärben; (milk) sauer werden; (weather) umschlagen; **to do sb a good ~** jdm etwas Gutes tun; **it's your ~** du bist dran or an der Reihe; **in ~, by ~s** abwechselnd; **to take ~s** sich abwechseln; **it gave me quite a ~** das hat mich schön erschreckt; **"no left ~"** (AUT) „Linksabbiegen verboten"; **~ away** vi sich abwenden; **~ back** vt umdrehen; (person) zurückschicken; (clock) zurückstellen ♦ vi umkehren; **~ down** vt (refuse) ablehnen; (fold down) umschlagen; **~ in** vi (go to bed) ins Bett gehen ♦ vt (fold inwards) einwärts biegen; **~ off** vi abbiegen ♦ vt ausschalten; (tap) zudrehen; (machine, electricity) abstellen; **~ on** vt (light) anschalten, einschalten; (tap) aufdrehen; (machine) anstellen; **~ out** vi (prove to be) sich erweisen; (people) sich entwickeln ♦ vt (light) ausschalten; (gas) abstellen; (produce) produzieren; **how did the cake ~ out?** wie ist der Kuchen geworden?; **~ over** vi (person) sich umdrehen ♦ vt (object) umdrehen, wenden; (page) umblättern; **~ round** vi (person, vehicle) sich herumdrehen; (rotate) sich drehen; **~ up** vi auftauchen ♦ vt (collar) hochklappen,

hochstellen; (nose) rümpfen; (increase: radio) lauter stellen; (: heat) höher drehen; **~ing** n (in road) Abzweigung f; **~ing point** n Wendepunkt m

turnip [ˈtəːnɪp] n Steckrübe f

turnout [ˈtəːnaut] n (Besucher)zahl f

turnover [ˈtəːnəuvər] n Umsatz m; (of staff) Wechsel m

turnpike [ˈtəːnpaɪk] (US) n gebührenpflichtige Straße f

turn: ~stile [ˈtəːnstaɪl] n Drehkreuz nt; **~table** [ˈtəːneɪbl] n (of record player) Plattenteller m; (RAIL) Drehscheibe f; **~-up** [ˈtəːnʌp] (BRIT) n (on trousers) Aufschlag m

turpentine [ˈtəːpəntaɪn] n Terpentin nt

turquoise [ˈtəːkwɔɪz] n (gem) Türkis m; (colour) Türkis nt ♦ adj türkisfarben

turret [ˈtʌrɪt] n Turm m

turtle [ˈtəːtl] n Schildkröte f; **~ neck (sweater)** n Pullover m mit Schildkrötkragen

tusk [tʌsk] n Stoßzahn m

tussle [ˈtʌsl] n Balgerei f

tutor [ˈtjuːtər] n (teacher) Privatlehrer m; (college instructor) Tutor m; **~ial** [tjuːˈtɔːrɪəl] n (UNIV) Kolloquium nt, Seminarübung f

tuxedo [tʌkˈsiːdəu] (US) n Smoking m

TV [tiːˈviː] n abbr (= television) TV nt

twang [twæŋ] n scharfe(r) Ton m; (of voice) Näseln nt

tweezers [ˈtwiːzəz] npl Pinzette f

twelfth [twelfθ] adj zwölfte(r, s)

twelve [twelv] num zwölf; **at ~ o'clock** (midday) um 12 Uhr; (midnight) um null Uhr

twentieth [ˈtwentɪɪθ] adj zwanzigste(r, s)

twenty [ˈtwentɪ] num zwanzig

twice [twaɪs] adv zweimal; **~ as much** doppelt so viel

twiddle [ˈtwɪdl] vt, vi: **to ~ (with) sth** an etw dat herumdrehen; **to ~ one's thumbs** (fig) Däumchen drehen

twig [twɪg] n dünne(r) Zweig m ♦ vt (inf) kapieren, merken

twilight [ˈtwaɪlaɪt] n Zwielicht nt

twin [twɪn] n Zwilling m ♦ adj Zwillings-; (very similar) Doppel- ♦ vt (towns) zu

Partnerstädten machen;**~-bedded room** *n* Zimmer *nt* mit zwei Einzelbetten;**~ beds** *npl* zwei (gleiche) Einzelbetten *pl*

twine [twaɪn] *n* Bindfaden *m* ♦ *vi (plants)* sich ranken

twinge [twɪndʒ] *n* stechende(r) Schmerz *m*, Stechen *nt*

twinkle ['twɪŋkl] *n* Funkeln *nt*, Blitzen *nt* ♦ *vi* funkeln

twinned *adj*: **to be ~ with** die Partnerstadt von ... sein

twirl [twəːl] *n* Wirbel *m* ♦ *vt, vi* (herum)wirbeln

twist [twɪst] *n (~ing)* Drehung *f*; *(bend)* Kurve *f* ♦ *vt (turn)* drehen; *(make crooked)* verbiegen; *(distort)* verdrehen ♦ *vi (wind)* sich drehen; *(curve)* sich winden

twit [twɪt] *(inf)* n Idiot *m*

twitch [twɪtʃ] *n* Zucken *nt* ♦ *vi* zucken

two [tuː] *num* zwei; **to put ~ and ~ together** seine Schlüsse ziehen;**~-door** *adj* zweitürig;**~-faced** *adj* falsch;**~-fold** *adj, adv* zweifach, doppelt; **to increase ~fold** verdoppeln;**~-piece** *adj* zweiteilig;**~-piece (suit)** *n* Zweiteiler *m*;**~-piece (swimsuit)** *n* zweiteilige(r) Badeanzug *m*; **~-seater** *n (plane, car)* Zweisitzer *m*; **~some** *n* Paar *nt*;**~-way** *adj (traffic)* Gegen-

tycoon [taɪ'kuːn] *n*: **(business) ~** (Industrie)magnat *m*

type [taɪp] *n* Typ *m*, Art *f*; *(PRINT)* Type *f* ♦ *vt, vi* Maschine schreiben, tippen;**~-cast** *adj (THEAT, TV)* auf eine Rolle festgelegt;**~face** *n* Schrift *f*;**~script** *n* maschinegeschriebene(r) Text *m*;**~writer** *n* Schreibmaschine *f*;**~written** *adj* maschinegeschrieben

typhoid ['taɪfɔɪd] *n* Typhus *m*

typical ['tɪpɪkl] *adj*: **~ (of)** typisch (für)

typify ['tɪpɪfaɪ] *vt* typisch sein für

typing ['taɪpɪŋ] *n* Maschineschreiben *nt*

typist ['taɪpɪst] *n* Maschinenschreiber(in) *m(f)*, Tippse *f (inf)*

tyrant ['taɪərnt] *n* Tyrann *m*

tyre ['taɪəʳ] *(US* **tire**) *n* Reifen *m*;**~ pressure** *n* Reifendruck *m*

U, u

U-bend ['juːbend] *n (in pipe)* U-Bogen *m*

udder ['ʌdəʳ] *n* Euter *nt*

UFO ['juːfəu] *n abbr (= unidentified flying object)* UFO *nt*

ugh [əːh] *excl* hu

ugliness ['ʌglɪnɪs] *n* Hässlichkeit *f*

ugly ['ʌglɪ] *adj* hässlich; *(bad)* böse, schlimm

UHT *abbr (= ultra heat treated)*: **UHT milk** H-Milch *f*

UK *n abbr* = **United Kingdom**

ulcer ['ʌlsəʳ] *n* Geschwür *nt*

Ulster ['ʌlstəʳ] *n* Ulster *nt*

ulterior [ʌl'tɪərɪəʳ] *adj*: **~ motive** Hintergedanke *m*

ultimate ['ʌltɪmət] *adj* äußerste(r, s), allerletzte(r, s);**~ly** *adv* schließlich, letzten Endes

ultrasound ['ʌltrəsaund] *n (MED)* Ultraschall *m*

umbilical cord [ʌm'bɪlɪkl-] *n* Nabelschnur *f*

umbrella [ʌm'brɛlə] *n* Schirm *m*

umpire ['ʌmpaɪəʳ] *n* Schiedsrichter *m* ♦ *vt, vi* schiedsrichtern

umpteenth [ʌmp'tiːnθ] *(inf) adj* zig; **for the ~ time** zum x-ten Mal

UN *n abbr* = **United Nations**

unable [ʌn'eɪbl] *adj*: **to be ~ to do sth** etw nicht tun können

unacceptable [ʌnək'sɛptəbl] *adj* unannehmbar, nicht akzeptabel

unaccompanied [ʌnə'kʌmpənɪd] *adj* ohne Begleitung

unaccountably [ʌnə'kauntəblɪ] *adv* unerklärlich

unaccustomed [ʌnə'kʌstəmd] *adj* nicht gewöhnt; *(unusual)* ungewohnt; **~ to** nicht gewöhnt an +acc

unanimous [juː'nænɪməs] *adj* einmütig; *(vote)* einstimmig;**~ly** *adv* einmütig; einstimmig

unarmed [ʌn'ɑːmd] *adj* unbewaffnet

unashamed [ʌnə'ʃeɪmd] *adj* schamlos

unassuming [ʌnə'sjuːmɪŋ] *adj* bescheiden

unattached [ʌnəˈtætʃt] *adj* ungebunden

unattended [ʌnəˈtendɪd] *adj* (*person*) unbeaufsichtigt; (*thing*) unbewacht

unauthorized [ʌnˈɔːθəraɪzd] *adj* unbefugt

unavoidable [ʌnəˈvɔɪdəbl] *adj* unvermeidlich

unaware [ʌnəˈweəʳ] *adj*: **to be ~ of sth** sich *dat* einer Sache *gen* nicht bewusst sein; **~s** *adv* unversehens

unbalanced [ʌnˈbælənst] *adj* unausgeglichen; (*mentally*) gestört

unbearable [ʌnˈbeərəbl] *adj* unerträglich

unbeatable [ʌnˈbiːtəbl] *adj* unschlagbar

unbeknown(st) [ʌnbɪˈnəun(st)] *adv*: **~ to me** ohne mein Wissen

unbelievable [ʌnbɪˈliːvəbl] *adj* unglaublich

unbend [ʌnˈbend] (*irreg: like* **bend**) *vt* gerade biegen ♦ *vi* aus sich herausgehen

unbias(s)ed [ʌnˈbaɪəst] *adj* unparteiisch

unborn [ʌnˈbɔːn] *adj* ungeboren

unbreakable [ʌnˈbreɪkəbl] *adj* unzerbrechlich

unbridled [ʌnˈbraɪdld] *adj* ungezügelt

unbroken [ʌnˈbrəukən] *adj* (*period*) ununterbrochen; (*spirit*) ungebrochen; (*record*) unübertroffen

unburden [ʌnˈbəːdn] *vt*: **to ~ o.s.** (jdm) sein Herz ausschütten

unbutton [ʌnˈbʌtn] *vt* aufknöpfen

uncalled-for [ʌnˈkɔːldfɔːʳ] *adj* unnötig

uncanny [ʌnˈkænɪ] *adj* unheimlich

unceasing [ʌnˈsiːsɪŋ] *adj* unaufhörlich

unceremonious [ʌnserɪˈməunɪəs] *adj* (*abrupt, rude*) brüsk; (*exit, departure*) überstürzt

uncertain [ʌnˈsəːtn] *adj* unsicher; (*doubtful*) ungewiss; (*unreliable*) unbeständig; (*vague*) undeutlich, vag(e); **~ty** *n* Ungewissheit *f*

unchanged [ʌnˈtʃeɪndʒd] *adj* unverändert

unchecked [ʌnˈtʃekt] *adj* ungeprüft; (*not stopped: advance*) ungehindert

uncivilized [ʌnˈsɪvɪlaɪzd] *adj* unzivilisiert

uncle [ˈʌŋkl] *n* Onkel *m*

uncomfortable [ʌnˈkʌmfətəbl] *adj* unbequem, ungemütlich

uncommon [ʌnˈkɔmən] *adj* ungewöhnlich; (*outstanding*) außergewöhnlich

uncompromising [ʌnˈkɔmprəmaɪzɪŋ] *adj* kompromisslos, unnachgiebig

unconcerned [ʌnkənˈsəːnd] *adj* unbekümmert; (*indifferent*) gleichgültig

unconditional [ʌnkənˈdɪʃənl] *adj* bedingungslos

unconscious [ʌnˈkɔnʃəs] *adj* (MED) bewusstlos; (*not meant*) unbeabsichtigt ♦ *n*: **the ~** das Unbewusste; **~ly** *adv* unbewusst

uncontrollable [ʌnkənˈtrəuləbl] *adj* unkontrollierbar, unbändig

unconventional [ʌnkənˈvenʃənl] *adj* unkonventionell

uncouth [ʌnˈkuːθ] *adj* grob

uncover [ʌnˈkʌvəʳ] *vt* aufdecken

undecided [ʌndɪˈsaɪdɪd] *adj* unschlüssig

undeniable [ʌndɪˈnaɪəbl] *adj* unleugbar

under [ˈʌndəʳ] *prep* unter ♦ *adv* darunter; **~ there** da drunter; **~ repair** in Reparatur

underage [ʌndərˈeɪdʒ] *adj* minderjährig

undercarriage [ˈʌndəkærɪdʒ] (BRIT) *n* (AVIAT) Fahrgestell *nt*

undercharge [ʌndəˈtʃɑːdʒ] *vt*: **to ~ sb** jdm zu wenig berechnen

undercoat [ˈʌndəkəut] *n* (*paint*) Grundierung *f*

undercover [ʌndəˈkʌvəʳ] *adj* Geheim-

undercurrent [ˈʌndəkʌrnt] *n* Unterströmung *f*

undercut [ʌndəˈkʌt] (*irreg: like* **cut**) *vt* unterbieten

underdeveloped [ˈʌndədɪˈveləpt] *adj* Entwicklungs-, unterentwickelt

underdog [ˈʌndədɔg] *n* Unterlegene(r) *mf*

underdone [ʌndəˈdʌn] *adj* (COOK) nicht gar, nicht durchgebraten

underestimate [ˈʌndərˈestɪmeɪt] *vt* unterschätzen

underexposed [ˈʌndərɪksˈpəuzd] *adj* unterbelichtet

underfoot [ʌndəˈfut] *adv* am Boden

undergo [ʌndəˈgəu] (*irreg: like* **go**) *vt* (*experience*) durchmachen; (*test, operation*) sich unterziehen +*dat*

undergraduate [ʌndəˈgrædjuɪt] *n* Student(in) *m(f)*

underground [ˈʌndəgraund] *n* U-Bahn *f*

♦ adj Untergrund-

undergrowth ['ʌndəgrəʊθ] n Gestrüpp nt, Unterholz nt

underhand(ed) [ʌndə'hænd(ɪd)] adj hinterhältig

underlie [ʌndə'laɪ] (irreg: like **lie**) vt zugrunde or zu Grunde liegen +dat

underline [ʌndə'laɪn] vt unterstreichen; (emphasize) betonen

underling ['ʌndəlɪŋ] n Handlanger m

undermine [ʌndə'maɪn] vt untergraben

underneath [ʌndə'niːθ] adv darunter ♦ prep unter

underpaid [ʌndə'peɪd] adj unterbezahlt

underpants ['ʌndəpænts] npl Unterhose f

underpass ['ʌndəpɑːs] (BRIT) n Unterführung f

underprivileged [ʌndə'prɪvɪlɪdʒd] adj benachteiligt, unterprivilegiert

underrate [ʌndə'reɪt] vt unterschätzen

undershirt ['ʌndəʃɜːt] (US) n Unterhemd nt

undershorts ['ʌndəʃɔːts] (US) npl Unterhose f

underside ['ʌndəsaɪd] n Unterseite f

underskirt ['ʌndəskɜːt] (BRIT) n Unterrock m

understand [ʌndə'stænd] (irreg: like **stand**) vt, vi verstehen; **I ~ that ...** ich habe gehört, dass ...; **am I to ~ that ...?** soll das (etwa) heißen, dass ...?; **what do you ~ by that?** was verstehen Sie darunter?; **it is understood that ...** es wurde vereinbart, dass ...; **to make o.s. understood** sich verständlich machen; **is that understood?** ist das klar?; **~able** adj verständlich; **~ing** n Verständnis nt ♦ adj verständnisvoll

understatement ['ʌndəsteɪtmənt] n (quality) Untertreibung f; **that's an ~!** das ist untertrieben!

understood [ʌndə'stud] pt, pp of **understand** ♦ adj klar; (implied) angenommen

understudy ['ʌndəstʌdɪ] n Ersatz(schau)spieler(in) m(f)

undertake [ʌndə'teɪk] (irreg: like **take**) vt unternehmen ♦ vi: **to ~ to do sth** sich verpflichten, etw zu tun

undertaker ['ʌndəteɪkər] n Leichenbestatter m

undertaking [ʌndə'teɪkɪŋ] n (enterprise) Unternehmen nt; (promise) Verpflichtung f

undertone ['ʌndətəʊn] n: **in an ~** mit gedämpfter Stimme

underwater [ʌndə'wɔːtər] adv unter Wasser ♦ adj Unterwasser-

underwear ['ʌndəweər] n Unterwäsche f

underworld ['ʌndəwɜːld] n (of crime) Unterwelt f

underwriter ['ʌndəraɪtər] n Assekurant m

undesirable [ʌndɪ'zaɪərəbl] adj unerwünscht

undies ['ʌndɪz] (inf) npl (Damen)unterwäsche f

undisputed ['ʌndɪs'pjuːtɪd] adj unbestritten

undo [ʌn'duː] (irreg: like **do**) vt (unfasten) öffnen, aufmachen; (work) zunichte machen; **~ing** n Verderben nt

undoubted [ʌn'daʊtɪd] adj unbezweifelt; **~ly** adv zweifellos, ohne Zweifel

undress [ʌn'dres] vt ausziehen ♦ vi sich ausziehen

undue [ʌn'djuː] adj übermäßig

undulating ['ʌndjuleɪtɪŋ] adj wellenförmig; (country) wellig

unduly [ʌn'djuːlɪ] adv übermäßig

unearth [ʌn'ɜːθ] vt (dig up) ausgraben; (discover) ans Licht bringen

unearthly [ʌn'ɜːθlɪ] adj (hour) nachtschlafen

uneasy [ʌn'iːzɪ] adj (worried) unruhig; (feeling) ungut

uneconomic(al) ['ʌniːkə'nɔmɪk(l)] adj unwirtschaftlich

uneducated [ʌn'edjukeɪtɪd] adj ungebildet

unemployed [ʌnɪm'plɔɪd] adj arbeitslos ♦ npl: **the ~** die Arbeitslosen pl

unemployment [ʌnɪm'plɔɪmənt] n Arbeitslosigkeit f

unending [ʌn'endɪŋ] adj endlos

unerring [ʌn'ɜːrɪŋ] adj unfehlbar

uneven [ʌn'iːvn] adj (surface) uneben; (quality) ungleichmäßig

unexpected [ʌnɪks'pektɪd] adj unerwartet; **~ly** adv unerwartet

unfailing [ʌn'feɪlɪŋ] adj nie versagend

unfair [ʌn'feər] adj ungerecht, unfair

unfaithful [ʌn'feɪθful] adj untreu

unfamiliar [ʌnfə'mɪlɪəʳ] adj ungewohnt; (person, subject) unbekannt; **to be ~ with** nicht kennen +acc, nicht vertraut sein mit

unfashionable [ʌn'fæʃnəbl] adj unmodern; (area etc) nicht in Mode

unfasten [ʌn'fɑːsn] vt öffnen, aufmachen

unfavourable [ʌn'feɪvrəbl] (US **unfavorable**) adj ungünstig

unfeeling [ʌn'fiːlɪŋ] adj gefühllos, kalt

unfinished [ʌn'fɪnɪʃt] adj unvollendet

unfit [ʌn'fɪt] adj ungeeignet; (in bad health) nicht fit; **~ for sth** zu or für etw ungeeignet

unfold [ʌn'fəʊld] vt entfalten; (paper) auseinander falten ♦ vi (develop) sich entfalten

unforeseen ['ʌnfɔː'siːn] adj unvorhergesehen

unforgettable [ʌnfə'getəbl] adj unvergesslich

unforgivable [ʌnfə'gɪvəbl] adj unverzeihlich

unfortunate [ʌn'fɔːtʃənət] adj unglücklich, bedauerlich; **~ly** adv leider

unfounded [ʌn'faʊndɪd] adj unbegründet

unfriendly [ʌn'frendlɪ] adj unfreundlich

ungainly [ʌn'geɪnlɪ] adj linkisch

ungodly [ʌn'gɒdlɪ] adj (hour) nachtschlafend; (row) heillos

ungrateful [ʌn'greɪtful] adj undankbar

unhappiness [ʌn'hæpɪnɪs] n Unglück nt, Unglückseligkeit f

unhappy [ʌn'hæpɪ] adj unglücklich; **~ with** (arrangements etc) unzufrieden mit

unharmed [ʌn'hɑːmd] adj wohlbehalten, unversehrt

UNHCR n abbr (= United Nations High Commission for Refugees) Flüchtlingshochkommissariat der Vereinten Nationen

unhealthy [ʌn'helθɪ] adj ungesund

unheard-of [ʌn'həːdɒv] adj unerhört

unhurt [ʌn'həːt] adj unverletzt

unidentified [ʌnaɪ'dentɪfaɪd] adj unbekannt, nicht identifiziert

uniform ['juːnɪfɔːm] n Uniform f ♦ adj einheitlich; **~ity** [juːnɪ'fɔːmɪtɪ] n Einheitlichkeit f

unify ['juːnɪfaɪ] vt vereinigen

unilateral [juːnɪ'lætərəl] adj einseitig

uninhabited [ʌnɪn'hæbɪtɪd] adj unbewohnt

unintentional [ʌnɪn'tenʃənəl] adj unabsichtlich

union ['juːnjən] n (uniting) Vereinigung f; (alliance) Bund m, Union f; (trade ~) Gewerkschaft f; **U~ Jack** n Union Jack m

unique [juː'niːk] adj einzig(artig)

UNISON ['juːnɪsn] n Gewerkschaft der Angestellten im öffentlichen Dienst

unison ['juːnɪsn] n Einstimmigkeit f; **in ~** einstimmig

unit ['juːnɪt] n Einheit f; **kitchen ~** Küchenelement nt

unite [juː'naɪt] vt vereinigen ♦ vi sich vereinigen; **~d** adj vereinigt; (together) vereint; **U~d Kingdom** n Vereinigte(s) Königreich nt; **U~d Nations (Organization)** n Vereinte Nationen pl; **U~d States (of America)** n Vereinigte Staaten pl (von Amerika)

unit trust (BRIT) n Treuhandgesellschaft f

unity ['juːnɪtɪ] n Einheit f; (agreement) Einigkeit f

universal [juːnɪ'vəːsl] adj allgemein

universe ['juːnɪvəːs] n (Welt)all nt

university [juːnɪ'vəːsɪtɪ] n Universität f

unjust [ʌn'dʒʌst] adj ungerecht

unkempt [ʌn'kempt] adj ungepflegt

unkind [ʌn'kaɪnd] adj unfreundlich

unknown [ʌn'nəʊn] adj: **~ (to sb)** (jdm) unbekannt

unlawful [ʌn'lɔːful] adj illegal

unleaded ['ʌn'ledɪd] adj bleifrei, unverbleit; **I use ~** ich fahre bleifrei

unleash [ʌn'liːʃ] vt entfesseln

unless [ʌn'les] conj wenn nicht, es sei denn; **~ he comes** es sei denn, er kommt; **~ otherwise stated** sofern nicht anders angegeben

unlike [ʌn'laɪk] adj unähnlich ♦ prep im Gegensatz zu

unlikely [ʌn'laɪklɪ] adj (not likely) unwahrscheinlich; (unexpected: combination etc) merkwürdig

unlimited [ʌn'lɪmɪtɪd] adj unbegrenzt

unlisted ['ʌn'lɪstɪd] (US) adj nicht im

Telefonbuch stehend

unload [ʌn'ləud] *vt* entladen

unlock [ʌn'lɔk] *vt* aufschließen

unlucky [ʌn'lʌkɪ] *adj* unglücklich; (*person*) unglückselig; **to be ~** Pech haben

unmarried [ʌn'mærɪd] *adj* unverheiratet, ledig

unmask [ʌn'mɑːsk] *vt* entlarven

unmistakable [ʌnmɪs'teɪkəbl] *adj* unverkennbar

unmitigated [ʌn'mɪtɪgeɪtɪd] *adj* ungemildert, ganz

unnatural [ʌn'nætʃrəl] *adj* unnatürlich

unnecessary [ʌn'nesəsərɪ] *adj* unnötig

unnoticed [ʌn'nəutɪst] *adj*: **to go ~** unbemerkt bleiben

UNO ['juːnəu] *n abbr* = **United Nations Organization**

unobtainable [ʌnəb'teɪnəbl] *adj*: **this number is ~** kein Anschluss unter dieser Nummer

unobtrusive [ʌnəb'truːsɪv] *adj* unauffällig

unofficial [ʌnə'fɪʃl] *adj* inoffiziell

unpack [ʌn'pæk] *vt, vi* auspacken

unparalleled [ʌn'pærəleld] *adj* beispiellos

unpleasant [ʌn'pleznt] *adj* unangenehm

unplug [ʌn'plʌg] *vt* den Stecker herausziehen von

unpopular [ʌn'pɔpjulə^r] *adj* (*person*) unbeliebt; (*decision etc*) unpopulär

unprecedented [ʌn'presɪdentɪd] *adj* beispiellos

unpredictable [ʌnprɪ'dɪktəbl] *adj* unvorhersehbar; (*weather, person*) unberechenbar

unprofessional [ʌnprə'feʃənl] *adj* unprofessionell

UNPROFOR *n abbr* (= *United Nations Protection Force*) UNPROFOR *f*

unqualified [ʌn'kwɔlɪfaɪd] *adj* (*success*) uneingeschränkt, voll; (*person*) unqualifiziert

unquestionably [ʌn'kwestʃənəblɪ] *adv* fraglos

unravel [ʌn'rævl] *vt* (*disentangle*) ausfasern, entwirren; (*solve*) lösen

unreal [ʌn'rɪəl] *adj* unwirklich

unrealistic ['ʌnrɪə'lɪstɪk] *adj* unrealistisch

unreasonable [ʌn'riːznəbl] *adj* unvernünftig; (*demand*) übertrieben

unrelated [ʌnrɪ'leɪtɪd] *adj* ohne Beziehung; (*family*) nicht verwandt

unrelenting [ʌnrɪ'lentɪŋ] *adj* unerbittlich

unreliable [ʌnrɪ'laɪəbl] *adj* unzuverlässig

unremitting [ʌnrɪ'mɪtɪŋ] *adj* (*efforts, attempts*) unermüdlich

unreservedly [ʌnrɪ'zɜːvɪdlɪ] *adv* offen; (*believe, trust*) uneingeschränkt; (*cry*) rückhaltlos

unrest [ʌn'rest] *n* (*discontent*) Unruhe *f*; (*fighting*) Unruhen *pl*

unroll [ʌn'rəul] *vt* aufrollen

unruly [ʌn'ruːlɪ] *adj* (*child*) undiszipliniert; schwer lenkbar

unsafe [ʌn'seɪf] *adj* nicht sicher

unsaid [ʌn'sed] *adj*: **to leave sth ~** etw ungesagt lassen

unsatisfactory ['ʌnsætɪs'fæktərɪ] *adj* unbefriedigend; unzulänglich

unsavoury [ʌn'seɪvərɪ] (*US* **unsavory**) *adj* (*fig*) widerwärtig

unscathed [ʌn'skeɪðd] *adj* unversehrt

unscrew [ʌn'skruː] *vt* aufschrauben

unscrupulous [ʌn'skruːpjuləs] *adj* skrupellos

unsettled [ʌn'setld] *adj* (*person*) rastlos; (*weather*) wechselhaft

unshaven [ʌn'ʃeɪvn] *adj* unrasiert

unsightly [ʌn'saɪtlɪ] *adj* unansehnlich

unskilled [ʌn'skɪld] *adj* ungelernt

unspeakable [ʌn'spiːkəbl] *adj* (*joy*) unsagbar; (*crime*) scheußlich

unstable [ʌn'steɪbl] *adj* instabil; (*mentally*) labil

unsteady [ʌn'stedɪ] *adj* unsicher

unstuck [ʌn'stʌk] *adj*: **to come ~** sich lösen; (*fig*) ins Wasser fallen

unsuccessful [ʌnsək'sesful] *adj* erfolglos

unsuitable [ʌn'suːtəbl] *adj* unpassend

unsure [ʌn'ʃuə^r] *adj* unsicher; **to be ~ of o.s.** unsicher sein

unsuspecting [ʌnsəs'pektɪŋ] *adj* nichts ahnend

unsympathetic ['ʌnsɪmpə'θetɪk] *adj* gefühllos; (*response*) abweisend; (*unlikeable*) unsympathisch

untapped [ʌnˈtæpt] *adj (resources)* ungenützt

unthinkable [ʌnˈθɪŋkəbl] *adj* unvorstellbar

untidy [ʌnˈtaɪdɪ] *adj* unordentlich

untie [ʌnˈtaɪ] *vt* aufschnüren

until [ənˈtɪl] *prep, conj* bis; **~ he comes** bis er kommt; **~ then** bis dann; **~ now** bis jetzt

untimely [ʌnˈtaɪmlɪ] *adj (death)* vorzeitig

untold [ʌnˈtəʊld] *adj* unermesslich

untoward [ʌntəˈwɔːd] *adj* widrig

untranslatable [ʌntrænzˈleɪtəbl] *adj* unübersetzbar

unused [ʌnˈjuːzd] *adj* unbenutzt

unusual [ʌnˈjuːʒʊəl] *adj* ungewöhnlich

unveil [ʌnˈveɪl] *vt* enthüllen

unwanted [ʌnˈwɒntɪd] *adj* unerwünscht

unwavering [ʌnˈweɪvərɪŋ] *adj* standhaft, unerschütterlich

unwelcome [ʌnˈwɛlkəm] *adj (at a bad time)* unwillkommen; *(unpleasant)* unerfreulich

unwell [ʌnˈwɛl] *adj*: **to feel** *or* **be ~** sich nicht wohl fühlen

unwieldy [ʌnˈwiːldɪ] *adj* sperrig

unwilling [ʌnˈwɪlɪŋ] *adj*: **to be ~ to do sth** nicht bereit sein, etw zu tun; **~ly** *adv* widerwillig

unwind [ʌnˈwaɪnd] *(irreg: like wind²) vt* abwickeln ♦ *vi (relax)* sich entspannen

unwise [ʌnˈwaɪz] *adj* unklug

unwitting [ʌnˈwɪtɪŋ] *adj* unwissentlich

unworkable [ʌnˈwəːkəbl] *adj (plan)* undurchführbar

unworthy [ʌnˈwəːðɪ] *adj (person)*: **~ (of sth)** (einer Sache *gen*) nicht wert

unwrap [ʌnˈræp] *vt* auspacken

unwritten [ʌnˈrɪtn] *adj* ungeschrieben

KEYWORD

up [ʌp] *prep*: **to be up sth** oben auf etw *dat* sein; **to go up sth** (auf) etw *acc* hinaufgehen; **go up that road** gehen Sie die Straße hinauf

♦ *adv* **1** *(upwards, higher)* oben; **put it up a bit higher** stell es etwas weiter nach oben; **up there** da oben, dort oben; **up above** hoch oben

2: **to be up** *(out of bed)* auf sein; *(prices, level)* gestiegen sein; *(building, tent)* stehen

3: **up to** *(as far as)* bis; **up to now** bis jetzt

4: **to be up to** *(depending on)*: **it's up to you** das hängt von dir ab; *(equal to)*: **he's not up to it** *(job, task etc)* er ist dem nicht gewachsen; *(inf: be doing: showing disapproval, suspicion)*: **what is he up to?** was führt er im Schilde?; **it's not up to me to decide** die Entscheidung liegt nicht bei mir; **his work is not up to the required standard** seine Arbeit entspricht nicht dem geforderten Niveau

♦ *n*: **ups and downs** *(in life, career)* Höhen und Tiefen *pl*

---

up-and-coming [ʌpəndˈkʌmɪŋ] *adj* aufstrebend

upbringing [ˈʌpbrɪŋɪŋ] *n* Erziehung *f*

update [ʌpˈdeɪt] *vt* auf den neuesten Stand bringen

upgrade [ʌpˈgreɪd] *vt* höher einstufen

upheaval [ʌpˈhiːvl] *n* Umbruch *m*

uphill [ˈʌpˈhɪl] *adj* ansteigend; *(fig)* mühsam ♦ *adv*: **to go ~** bergauf gehen/fahren

uphold [ʌpˈhəʊld] *(irreg: like hold) vt* unterstützen

upholstery [ʌpˈhəʊlstərɪ] *n* Polster *nt*; Polsterung *f*

upkeep [ˈʌpkiːp] *n* Instandhaltung *f*

upon [əˈpɒn] *prep* auf

upper [ˈʌpər] *n (on shoe)* Oberleder *nt* ♦ *adj* obere(r, s), höhere(r, s); **to have the ~ hand** die Oberhand haben; **~class** *adj* vornehm; **~most** *adj* oberste(r, s), höchste(r, s); **what was ~most in my mind** was mich in erster Linie beschäftigte; **~ sixth** *(BRIT: SCOL) n* Abschlussklasse *f*

upright [ˈʌpraɪt] *adj* aufrecht

uprising [ˈʌpraɪzɪŋ] *n* Aufstand *m*

uproar [ˈʌprɔːr] *n* Aufruhr *m*

uproot [ʌpˈruːt] *vt* ausreißen

upset [*n* ˈʌpsɛt, *vb, adj* ʌpˈsɛt] *(irreg: like set) n* Aufregung *f* ♦ *vt (overturn)* umwerfen; *(disturb)* aufregen, bestürzen; *(plans)* durcheinander bringen ♦ *adj (person)* aufgeregt; *(stomach)* verdorben

upshot ['ʌpʃɔt] n (End)ergebnis nt
upside-down ['ʌpsaɪd-] adv verkehrt herum
upstairs [ʌp'stɛəz] adv oben; (go) nach oben
♦ adj (room) obere(r, s), Ober- ♦ n obere(s)
Stockwerk nt
upstart ['ʌpstɑːt] n Emporkömmling m
upstream [ʌp'striːm] adv stromaufwärts
uptake ['ʌpteɪk] n: **to be quick on the ~**
schnell begreifen; **to be slow on the ~**
schwer von Begriff sein
uptight [ʌp'taɪt] (inf) adj (nervous) nervös;
(inhibited) verklemmt
up-to-date ['ʌptə'deɪt] adj (clothes) modisch,
modern; (information) neueste(r, s)
upturn ['ʌptəːn] n Aufschwung m
upward ['ʌpwəd] adj nach oben gerichtet;
~(s) adv aufwärts
uranium [juə'reɪnɪəm] n Uran nt
urban ['əːbən] adj städtisch, Stadt-; ~
clearway n Stadtautobahn f
urchin ['əːtʃɪn] n (boy) Schlingel m; (sea ~)
Seeigel m
urge [əːdʒ] n Drang m ♦ vt: **to ~ sb to do**
sth jdn (dazu) drängen, etw zu tun
urgency ['əːdʒənsɪ] n Dringlichkeit f
urgent ['əːdʒənt] adj dringend
urinal ['juərɪnl] n (public) Pissoir nt
urinate ['juərɪneɪt] vi urinieren
urine ['juərɪn] n Urin m, Harn m
urn [əːn] n Urne f; (tea ~) Teemaschine f
US n abbr = United States
us [ʌs] pron uns; see also **me**
USA n abbr = United States of America
usage ['juːzɪdʒ] n Gebrauch m; (esp LING)
Sprachgebrauch m
use [n juːs, vb juːz] n (employment) Gebrauch
m; (point) Zweck m ♦ vt gebrauchen; **in ~**
in Gebrauch; **out of ~** außer Gebrauch; **to**
be of ~ nützlich sein; **it's no ~** es hat
keinen Zweck; **what's the ~?** was solls?;
~d to (accustomed to) gewöhnt an +acc;
she ~d to live here (formerly) sie hat früher
mal hier gewohnt; **~ up** aufbrauchen,
verbrauchen; **~d** adj (car) Gebraucht-; **~ful**
adj nützlich; **~fulness** n Nützlichkeit f;
~less adj nutzlos, unnütz; **~r** n Benutzer
m; **~r-friendly** adj (computer)

benutzerfreundlich
usher ['ʌʃəʳ] n Platzanweiser m; **~ette**
[ʌʃə'rɛt] n Platzanweiserin f
usual ['juːʒuəl] adj gewöhnlich, üblich; **as ~**
wie üblich; **~ly** adv gewöhnlich
usurp [juː'zəːp] vt an sich reißen
utensil [juː'tensl] n Gerät nt; **kitchen ~s**
Küchengeräte pl
uterus ['juːtərəs] n Gebärmutter f
utilitarian [juːtɪlɪ'tɛərɪən] adj Nützlichkeits-
utility [juː'tɪlɪtɪ] n (usefulness) Nützlichkeit f;
(also: **public ~**) öffentliche(r)
Versorgungsbetrieb m; **~ room** n
Hauswirtschaftsraum m
utilize ['juːtɪlaɪz] vt benützen
utmost ['ʌtməust] adj äußerste(r, s) ♦ n: **to**
do one's ~ sein Möglichstes tun
utter ['ʌtəʳ] adj äußerste(r, s), höchste(r, s),
völlig ♦ vt äußern, aussprechen; **~ance** n
Äußerung f; **~ly** adv äußerst, absolut, völlig
U-turn ['juː'təːn] n (AUT) Kehrtwendung f

V, v

v. abbr = **verse; versus; volt**; (= vide) see
vacancy ['veɪkənsɪ] n (BRIT: job) offene Stelle
f; (room) freie(s) Zimmer nt; **"no**
vacancies" „belegt"
vacant ['veɪkənt] adj leer; (unoccupied) frei;
(house) leer stehend, unbewohnt; (stupid)
(gedanken)leer; **~ lot** (US) n unbebaute(s)
Grundstück nt
vacate [və'keɪt] vt (seat) frei machen; (room)
räumen
vacation [və'keɪʃən] n Ferien pl, Urlaub m;
~ist (US) n Ferienreisende(r) f(m)
vaccinate ['væksɪneɪt] vt impfen
vaccine ['væksiːn] n Impfstoff m
vacuum ['vækjum] n Vakuum nt; **~ bottle**
(US) n Thermosflasche f; **~ cleaner** n
Staubsauger m; **~ flask** (BRIT) n
Thermosflasche f; **~-packed** adj
vakuumversiegelt
vagina [və'dʒaɪnə] n Scheide f
vague [veɪg] adj vag(e); (absent-minded)
geistesabwesend; **~ly** adv unbestimmt,

vag(e)

vain [veɪn] *adj* eitel; (*attempt*) vergeblich; **in ~** vergebens, umsonst

valentine ['vælntaɪn] *n* (*also:* **~ card**) Valentinsgruß *m*; **V~'s Day** *n* Valentinstag *m*

valet ['vælɪt] *n* Kammerdiener *m*

valiant ['vælɪənt] *adj* tapfer

valid ['vælɪd] *adj* gültig; (*argument*) stichhaltig; (*objection*) berechtigt; **~ity** [və'lɪdɪtɪ] *n* Gültigkeit *f*

valley ['vælɪ] *n* Tal *nt*

valour ['vælə'] (*US* **valor**) *n* Tapferkeit *f*

valuable ['væljuəbl] *adj* wertvoll; (*time*) kostbar; **~s** *npl* Wertsachen *pl*

valuation [vælju'eɪʃən] *n* (*FIN*) Schätzung *f*; Beurteilung *f*

value ['vælju:] *n* Wert *m*; (*usefulness*) Nutzen *m* ♦ *vt* (*prize*) (hoch) schätzen, werthalten; (*estimate*) schätzen; **~ added tax** (*BRIT*) *n* Mehrwertsteuer *f*; **~d** *adj* (hoch) geschätzt

valve [vælv] *n* Ventil *nt*; (*BIOL*) Klappe *f*; (*RAD*) Röhre *f*

van [væn] *n* Lieferwagen *m*; (*BRIT: RAIL*) Waggon *m*

vandal ['vændl] *n* Rowdy *m*; **~ism** *n* mutwillige Beschädigung *f*; **~ize** *vt* mutwillig beschädigen

vanguard ['vænɡɑːd] *n* (*fig*) Spitze *f*

vanilla [və'nɪlə] *n* Vanille *f*; **~ ice cream** *n* Vanilleeis *nt*

vanish ['vænɪʃ] *vi* verschwinden

vanity ['vænɪtɪ] *n* Eitelkeit *f*; **~ case** *n* Schminkkoffer *m*

vantage ['vɑːntɪdʒ] *n*: **~ point** gute(r) Aussichtspunkt *m*

vapour ['veɪpə'] (*US* **vapor**) *n* (*mist*) Dunst *m*; (*gas*) Dampf *m*

variable ['veərɪəbl] *adj* wechselhaft, veränderlich; (*speed, height*) regulierbar

variance ['veərɪəns] *n*: **to be at ~ (with)** nicht übereinstimmen (mit)

variation [veərɪ'eɪʃən] *n* Variation *f*; (*in prices etc*) Schwankung *f*

varicose ['værɪkəus] *adj*: **~ veins** Krampfadern *pl*

varied ['veərɪd] *adj* unterschiedlich; (*life*) abwechslungsreich

variety [və'raɪətɪ] *n* (*difference*) Abwechslung *f*; (*varied collection*) Vielfalt *f*; (*COMM*) Auswahl *f*; (*sort*) Sorte *f*, Art *f*; **~ show** *n* Varietee *nt*, Varieté *nt*

various ['veərɪəs] *adj* verschieden; (*several*) mehrere

varnish ['vɑːnɪʃ] *n* Lack *m*; (*on pottery*) Glasur *f* ♦ *vt* lackieren

vary ['veərɪ] *vt* (*alter*) verändern; (*give variety to*) abwechslungsreicher gestalten ♦ *vi* sich (ver)ändern; (*prices*) schwanken; (*weather*) unterschiedlich sein

vase [vɑːz] *n* Vase *f*

Vaseline ['væsɪliːn] ® *n* Vaseline *f*

vast [vɑːst] *adj* weit, groß, riesig

VAT [væt] *n abbr* (= *value added tax*) MwSt *f*

vat [væt] *n* große(s) Fass *nt*

vault [vɔːlt] *n* (*of roof*) Gewölbe *nt*; (*tomb*) Gruft *f*; (*in bank*) Tresorraum *m*; (*leap*) Sprung *m* ♦ *vt* (*also:* **~ over**) überspringen

vaunted ['vɔːntɪd] *adj*: **much-~** viel gerühmt

VCR *n abbr* = **video cassette recorder**

VD *n abbr* = **venereal disease**

VDU *n abbr* = **visual display unit**

veal [viːl] *n* Kalbfleisch *nt*

veer [vɪə'] *vi* sich drehen; (*of car*) ausscheren

vegan ['viːɡən] *n* Vegan *m*, radikale(r) Vegetarier(in) *m(f)*

vegeburger ['vedʒɪbəːɡə'] *n* vegetarische Frikadelle *f*

vegetable ['vedʒtəbl] *n* Gemüse *nt* ♦ *adj* Gemüse-; **~s** *npl* (*CULIN*) Gemüse *nt*

vegetarian [vedʒɪ'teərɪən] *n* Vegetarier(in) *m(f)* ♦ *adj* vegetarisch

vegetate ['vedʒɪteɪt] *vi* (dahin)vegetieren

veggieburger ['vedʒɪbəːɡə'] *n* = **vegeburger**

vehement ['viːɪmənt] *adj* heftig

vehicle ['viːɪkl] *n* Fahrzeug *nt*; (*fig*) Mittel *nt*

veil [veɪl] *n* (*also fig*) Schleier *m* ♦ *vt* verschleiern

vein [veɪn] *n* Ader *f*; (*mood*) Stimmung *f*

velocity [vɪ'lɒsɪtɪ] *n* Geschwindigkeit *f*

velvet ['velvɪt] *n* Samt *m* ♦ *adj* Samt-

vendetta [ven'detə] *n* Fehde *f*; (*in family*)

Blutrache f
vending machine ['vendɪŋ-] n Automat m
vendor ['vendəʳ] n Verkäufer m
veneer [və'nɪəʳ] n Furnier(holz) nt; (fig) äußere(r) Anstrich m
venereal disease [vɪ'nɪərɪəl-] n Geschlechtskrankheit f
Venetian blind [vɪ'niːʃən-] n Jalousie f
vengeance ['vendʒəns] n Rache f; **with a ~** gewaltig
venison ['venɪsn] n Reh(fleisch) nt
venom ['venəm] n Gift nt
vent [vent] n Öffnung f; (in coat) Schlitz m; (fig) Ventil nt ♦ vt (emotion) abreagieren
ventilate ['ventɪleɪt] vt belüften; **ventilator** ['ventɪleɪtəʳ] n Ventilator m
ventriloquist [ven'trɪləkwɪst] n Bauchredner m
venture ['ventʃəʳ] n Unternehmung f, Projekt nt ♦ vt wagen; (life) aufs Spiel setzen ♦ vi sich wagen
venue ['venjuː] n Schauplatz m
verb [vəːb] n Zeitwort nt, Verb nt; **~al** adj (spoken) mündlich; (translation) wörtlich; **~ally** adv mündlich
verbatim [vəː'beɪtɪm] adv Wort für Wort ♦ adj wortwörtlich
verbose [vəː'bəus] adj wortreich
verdict ['vəːdɪkt] n Urteil nt
verge [vəːdʒ] n (BRIT) Rand m ♦ vi: **to ~ on** grenzen an +acc; **"soft ~s"** (BRIT: AUT) „Seitenstreifen nicht befahrbar"; **on the ~ of doing sth** im Begriff, etw zu tun
verify ['verɪfaɪ] vt (über)prüfen; (confirm) bestätigen; (theory) beweisen
veritable ['verɪtəbl] adj wirklich, echt
vermin ['vəːmɪn] npl Ungeziefer nt
vermouth ['vəːməθ] n Wermut m
versatile ['vəːsətaɪl] adj vielseitig
verse [vəːs] n (poetry) Poesie f, (stanza) Strophe f; (of Bible) Vers m; **in ~** in Versform
version ['vəːʃən] n Version f; (of car) Modell nt
versus ['vəːsəs] prep gegen
vertebrate ['vəːtɪbrɪt] adj Wirbel-
vertical ['vəːtɪkl] adj senkrecht

vertigo ['vəːtɪgəu] n Schwindel m
very ['verɪ] adv sehr ♦ adj (extreme) äußerste(r, s); **the ~ book which** genau das Buch, welches; **the ~ last ...** der/die/das allerletzte ...; **at the ~ least** allerwenigstens; **~ much** sehr
vessel ['vesl] n (ship) Schiff nt; (container) Gefäß nt
vest [vest] n (BRIT) Unterhemd nt; (US: waistcoat) Weste f
vested interests ['vestɪd-] npl finanzielle Beteiligung f; (people) finanziell Beteiligte pl; (fig) persönliche(s) Interesse nt
vestige ['vestɪdʒ] n Spur f
vestry ['vestrɪ] n Sakristei f
vet [vet] n abbr (= veterinary surgeon) Tierarzt m/-ärztin f
veteran ['vetərn] n Veteran(in) m(f)
veterinarian [vetrɪ'neərɪən] (US) n Tierarzt m/-ärztin f
veterinary ['vetrɪnərɪ] adj Veterinär-; **~ surgeon** (BRIT) n Tierarzt m/-ärztin f
veto ['viːtəu] (pl **~es**) n Veto nt ♦ vt sein Veto einlegen gegen
vex [veks] vt ärgern; **~ed** adj verärgert; **~ed question** umstrittene Frage f
VHF abbr (= very high frequency) UKW f
via ['vaɪə] prep über +acc
viable ['vaɪəbl] adj (plan) durchführbar; (company) rentabel
vibrant ['vaɪbrnt] adj (lively) lebhaft; (bright) leuchtend; (full of emotion: voice) bebend
vibrate [vaɪ'breɪt] vi zittern, beben; (machine, string) vibrieren; **vibration** [vaɪ'breɪʃən] n Schwingung f; (of machine) Vibrieren nt
vicar ['vɪkəʳ] n Pfarrer m; **~age** n Pfarrhaus nt
vice [vaɪs] n (evil) Laster nt; (TECH) Schraubstock m
vice-chairman [vaɪs'tʃeəmən] n stellvertretende(r) Vorsitzende(r) m
vice-president [vaɪs'prezɪdənt] n Vizepräsident m
vice squad n ≃ Sittenpolizei f
vice versa [vaɪsɪ'vəːsə] adv umgekehrt
vicinity [vɪ'sɪnɪtɪ] n Umgebung f; (closeness) Nähe f

vicious ['vɪʃəs] *adj* gemein, böse; **~ circle** *n* Teufelskreis *m*

victim ['vɪktɪm] *n* Opfer *nt*

victor ['vɪktə'] *n* Sieger *m*

Victorian [vɪk'tɔːrɪən] *adj* viktorianisch; *(fig)* (sitten)streng

victorious [vɪk'tɔːrɪəs] *adj* siegreich

victory ['vɪktərɪ] *n* Sieg *m*

video ['vɪdɪəʊ] *adj* Fernseh-, Bild- ♦ *n* (~ film) Video *nt*; *(also:* ~ **cassette)** Videokassette *f*; *(also:* ~ **cassette recorder)** Videorekorder *m*; **~ tape** *n* Videoband *nt*; **~ wall** *n* Videowand *m*

vie [vaɪ] *vi* wetteifern

Vienna [vɪ'enə] *n* Wien *nt*

Vietnam ['vjet'næm] *n* Vietnam *nt*; **~ese** *adj* vietnamesisch ♦ *n inv (person)* Vietnamese *m*, Vietnamesin *f*

view [vjuː] *n (sight)* Sicht *f*, Blick *m*; *(scene)* Aussicht *f*; *(opinion)* Ansicht *f*; *(intention)* Absicht *f* ♦ *vt (situation)* betrachten; *(house)* besichtigen; **to have sth in** ~ etw beabsichtigen; **on** ~ ausgestellt; **in** ~ **of** wegen +*gen*, angesichts +*gen*; **~er** *n (PHOT: small projector)* Gucki *m*; *(TV)* Fernsehzuschauer(in) *m(f)*; **~finder** *n* Sucher *m*; **~point** *n* Standpunkt *m*

vigil ['vɪdʒɪl] *n* (Nacht)wache *f*; **~ant** *adj* wachsam

vigorous ['vɪgərəs] *adj* kräftig; *(protest)* energisch, heftig

vile [vaɪl] *adj (mean)* gemein; *(foul)* abscheulich

villa ['vɪlə] *n* Villa *f*

village ['vɪlɪdʒ] *n* Dorf *nt*; **~r** *n* Dorfbewohner(in) *m(f)*

villain ['vɪlən] *n* Schurke *m*

vindicate ['vɪndɪkeɪt] *vt* rechtfertigen

vindictive [vɪn'dɪktɪv] *adj* nachtragend, rachsüchtig

vine [vaɪn] *n* Rebstock *m*, Rebe *f*

vinegar ['vɪnɪgə'] *n* Essig *m*

vineyard ['vɪnjɑːd] *n* Weinberg *m*

vintage ['vɪntɪdʒ] *n (of wine)* Jahrgang *m*; ~ **car** *n* Oldtimer *m (zwischen 1919 und 1930 gebaut)*; ~ **wine** *n* edle(r) Wein *m*

viola [vɪ'əʊlə] *n* Bratsche *f*

violate ['vaɪəleɪt] *vt (law)* übertreten; *(rights, rule, neutrality)* verletzen; *(sanctity, woman)* schänden; **violation** [vaɪə'leɪʃən] *n* Übertretung *f*; Verletzung *f*

violence ['vaɪələns] *n (force)* Heftigkeit *f*; *(brutality)* Gewalttätigkeit *f*

violent ['vaɪələnt] *adj (strong)* heftig; *(brutal)* gewalttätig, brutal; *(contrast)* krass; *(death)* gewaltsam

violet ['vaɪələt] *n* Veilchen *nt* ♦ *adj* veilchenblau, violett

violin [vaɪə'lɪn] *n* Geige *f*, Violine *f*; **~ist** *n* Geiger(in) *m(f)*

VIP *n abbr (= very important person)* VIP *m*

virgin ['vɜːdʒɪn] *n* Jungfrau *f* ♦ *adj* jungfräulich, unberührt; **~ity** [vɜː'dʒɪnɪtɪ] *n* Unschuld *f*

Virgo ['vɜːgəʊ] *n* Jungfrau *f*

virile ['vɪraɪl] *adj* männlich; **virility** [vɪ'rɪlɪtɪ] *n* Männlichkeit *f*

virtually ['vɜːtjʊəlɪ] *adv* praktisch, fast

virtual reality ['vɜːtjʊəl-] *n (COMPUT)* virtuelle Realität *f*

virtue ['vɜːtjuː] *n (moral goodness)* Tugend *f*; *(good quality)* Vorteil *m*, Vorzug *m*; **by** ~ **of** aufgrund or auf Grund +*gen*

virtuous ['vɜːtjʊəs] *adj* tugendhaft

virulent ['vɪrʊlənt] *adj (poisonous)* bösartig; *(bitter)* scharf, geharnischt

virus ['vaɪərəs] *n (also COMPUT)* Virus *m*

visa ['viːzə] *n* Visum *nt*

vis-à-vis [viːzə'viː] *prep* gegenüber

viscous ['vɪskəs] *adj* zähflüssig

visibility [vɪzɪ'bɪlɪtɪ] *n (MET)* Sicht(weite) *f*

visible ['vɪzəbl] *adj* sichtbar; **visibly** *adv* sichtlich

vision ['vɪʒən] *n (ability)* Sehvermögen *nt*; *(foresight)* Weitblick *m*; *(in dream, image)* Vision *f*

visit ['vɪzɪt] *n* Besuch *m* ♦ *vt* besuchen; *(town, country)* fahren nach; **~ing hours** *npl (in hospital etc)* Besuchszeiten *pl*; **~or** *n (in house)* Besucher(in) *m(f)*; *(in hotel)* Gast *m*; **~or centre** *n* Touristeninformation *f*

visor ['vaɪzə'] *n* Visier *nt*; *(on cap)* Schirm *m*; *(AUT)* Blende *f*

vista ['vɪstə] *n* Aussicht *f*

visual ['vɪzjuəl] *adj* Seh-, visuell; ~ **aid** *n* Anschauungsmaterial *nt*; ~ **display unit** *n* Bildschirm(gerät *nt*) *m*; ~**ize** *vt* sich +*dat* vorstellen; ~**ly-impaired** *adj* sehbehindert

vital ['vaɪtl] *adj* (*important*) unerlässlich; (*necessary for life*) Lebens-, lebenswichtig; (*lively*) vital; ~**ity** [vaɪ'tælɪtɪ] *n* Vitalität *f*; ~**ly** *adv*: ~**ly important** äußerst wichtig; ~ **statistics** *npl* (*fig*) Maße *pl*

vitamin ['vɪtəmɪn] *n* Vitamin *nt*

vivacious [vɪ'veɪʃəs] *adj* lebhaft

vivid ['vɪvɪd] *adj* (*graphic*) lebendig; (*memory*) lebhaft; (*bright*) leuchtend; ~**ly** *adv* lebendig; lebhaft; leuchtend

V-neck ['viːnɛk] *n* V-Ausschnitt *m*

vocabulary [vəu'kæbjuləri] *n* Wortschatz *m*, Vokabular *nt*

vocal ['vəukl] *adj* Vokal-, Gesang-; (*fig*) lautstark; ~ **cords** *npl* Stimmbänder *pl*

vocation [vəu'keɪʃən] *n* (*calling*) Berufung *f*; ~**al** *adj* Berufs-

vociferous [və'sɪfərəs] *adj* lautstark

vodka ['vɔdkə] *n* Wodka *m*

vogue [vəug] *n* Mode *f*

voice [vɔɪs] *n* Stimme *f*; (*fig*) Mitspracherecht *nt* ♦ *vt* äußern; ~ **mail** *n* (*TEL*) Voicemail *f*

void [vɔɪd] *n* Leere *f* ♦ *adj* (*invalid*) nichtig, ungültig; (*empty*): ~ **of** ohne, bar +*gen*; *see* **null**

volatile ['vɔlətaɪl] *adj* (*gas*) flüchtig; (*person*) impulsiv; (*situation*) brisant

volcano [vɔl'keɪnəu] *n* Vulkan *m*

volition [və'lɪʃən] *n* Wille *m*; **of one's own** ~ aus freiem Willen

volley ['vɔlɪ] *n* (*of guns*) Salve *f*; (*of stones*) Hagel *m*; (*tennis*) Flugball *m*; ~**ball** *n* Volleyball *m*

volt [vəult] *n* Volt *nt*; ~**age** *n* Spannung *f*

volume ['vɔljuːm] *n* (*book*) Band *m*; (*size*) Umfang *m*; (*space*) Rauminhalt *m*; (*of sound*) Lautstärke *f*

voluntarily ['vɔləntrɪlɪ] *adv* freiwillig

voluntary ['vɔləntərɪ] *adj* freiwillig

volunteer [vɔlən'tɪə] *n* Freiwillige(r) *mf* ♦ *vi* sich freiwillig melden; **to** ~ **to do sth** sich anbieten, etw zu tun

vomit ['vɔmɪt] *n* Erbrochene(s) *nt* ♦ *vt* spucken ♦ *vi* sich übergeben

vote [vəut] *n* Stimme *f*; (*ballot*) Abstimmung *f*; (*result*) Abstimmungsergebnis *nt*; (*franchise*) Wahlrecht *nt* ♦ *vt, vi* wählen; ~ **of thanks** *n* Dankesworte *pl*; ~**r** *n* Wähler(in) *m(f)*; ~**ting** ['vəutɪŋ] *n* Wahl *f*

voucher ['vautʃə] *n* Gutschein *m*

vouch for [vautʃ-] *vt* bürgen für

vow [vau] *n* Versprechen *nt*; (*REL*) Gelübde *nt* ♦ *vt* geloben

vowel ['vauəl] *n* Vokal *m*

voyage ['vɔɪɪdʒ] *n* Reise *f*

vulgar ['vʌlgə] *adj* (*rude*) vulgär; ~**ity** [vʌl'gærɪtɪ] *n* Vulgarität *f*

vulnerable ['vʌlnərəbl] *adj* (*easily injured*) verwundbar; (*sensitive*) verletzlich

vulture ['vʌltʃə] *n* Geier *m*

W, w

wad [wɔd] *n* (*bundle*) Bündel *nt*; (*of paper*) Stoß *m*; (*of money*) Packen *m*

waddle ['wɔdl] *vi* watscheln

wade [weɪd] *vi*: **to** ~ **through** waten durch

wafer ['weɪfə] *n* Waffel *f*; (*REL*) Hostie *f*; (*COMPUT*) Wafer *f*

waffle ['wɔfl] *n* Waffel *f*; (*inf: empty talk*) Geschwafel *nt* ♦ *vi* schwafeln

waft [wɔft] *vt, vi* wehen

wag [wæg] *vt* (*tail*) wedeln mit ♦ *vi* wedeln

wage [weɪdʒ] *n* (*also*: ~**s**) (Arbeits)lohn *m* ♦ *vt*: **to** ~ **war** Krieg führen; ~ **earner** *n* Lohnempfänger(in) *m(f)*; ~ **packet** *n* Lohntüte *f*

wager ['weɪdʒə] *n* Wette *f* ♦ *vt, vi* wetten

waggle ['wægl] *vi* wackeln

wag(g)on ['wægən] *n* (*horse-drawn*) Fuhrwerk *nt*; (*US: AUT*) Wagen *m*; (*BRIT: RAIL*) Wag(g)on *m*

wail [weɪl] *n* Wehgeschrei *nt* ♦ *vi* wehklagen, jammern

waist [weɪst] *n* Taille *f*; ~**coat** (*BRIT*) *n* Weste *f*; ~**line** *n* Taille *f*

wait [weɪt] *n* Wartezeit *f* ♦ *vi* warten; **to lie in** ~ **for sb** jdm auflauern; **I can't** ~ **to see**

him ich kanns kaum erwarten ihn zu sehen; **"no ~ing"** (BRIT: AUT) „Halteverbot"; **~ behind** vi zurückbleiben; **~ for** vt fus warten auf +acc; **~ on** vt fus bedienen; **~er** n Kellner m; **~ing list** n Warteliste f; **~ing room** n (MED) Wartezimmer nt; (RAIL) Wartesaal m; **~ress** n Kellnerin f

waive [weɪv] vt verzichten auf +acc

wake [weɪk] (pt **woke, waked**, pp **woken**) vt wecken ♦ vi (also: **~ up**) aufwachen ♦ n (NAUT) Kielwasser nt; (for dead) Totenwache f; **to ~ up to** (fig) sich bewusst werden +gen

waken ['weɪkn] vt aufwecken

Wales [weɪlz] n Wales nt

walk [wɔːk] n Spaziergang m; (gait) Gang m; (route) Weg m ♦ vi gehen; (stroll) spazieren gehen; (longer) wandern; **~s of life** Sphären pl; **a 10-minute ~** 10 Minuten zu Fuß; **to ~ out on sb** (inf) jdn sitzen lassen; **~er** n Spaziergänger m; (hiker) Wanderer m; **~ie-talkie** ['wɔːkɪ'tɔːkɪ] n tragbare(s) Sprechfunkgerät nt; **~ing** n Gehen nt; (hiking) Wandern nt ♦ adj Wander-; **~ing shoes** npl Wanderschuhe pl; **~ing stick** n Spazierstock m; **W~man** ['wɔːkmən] ® n Walkman m ®; **~out** n Streik m; **~over** (inf) n leichte(r) Sieg m; **~way** n Fußweg m

wall [wɔːl] n (inside) Wand f; (outside) Mauer f; **~ed** adj von Mauern umgeben

wallet ['wɒlɪt] n Brieftasche f

wallflower ['wɔːlflaʊəʳ] n Goldlack m; **to be a ~** (fig) ein Mauerblümchen sein

wallop ['wɒləp] (inf) vt schlagen, verprügeln

wallow ['wɒləʊ] vi sich wälzen

wallpaper ['wɔːlpeɪpəʳ] n Tapete f

walnut ['wɔːlnʌt] n Walnuss f

walrus ['wɔːlrəs] n Walross nt

waltz [wɔːlts] n Walzer m ♦ vi Walzer tanzen

wan [wɒn] adj bleich

wand [wɒnd] n (also: **magic ~**) Zauberstab m

wander ['wɒndəʳ] vi (roam) (herum)wandern; (fig) abschweifen

wane [weɪn] vi abnehmen; (fig) schwinden

wangle ['wæŋgl] (BRIT: inf) vt: **to ~ sth** etw richtig hindrehen

want [wɒnt] n (lack) Mangel m ♦ vt (need) brauchen; (desire) wollen; (lack) nicht haben; **~s** npl (needs) Bedürfnisse pl; **for ~ of** aus Mangel an +dat; mangels +gen; **to ~ to do sth** etw tun wollen; **to ~ sb to do sth** wollen, dass jd etw tut; **~ed** adj (criminal etc) gesucht; **"cook ~ed"** (in adverts) „Koch/Köchin gesucht"; **~ing** adj: **to be found ~ing** sich als unzulänglich erweisen

wanton ['wɒntn] adj mutwillig, zügellos

war [wɔːʳ] n Krieg m; **to make ~** Krieg führen

ward [wɔːd] n (in hospital) Station f; (of city) Bezirk m; (child) Mündel nt; **~ off** vt abwenden, abwehren

warden ['wɔːdn] n (guard) Wächter m, Aufseher m; (BRIT: in youth hostel) Herbergsvater m; (UNIV) Heimleiter m; (BRIT: also: **traffic ~**) ≃ Verkehrspolizist m, ≃ Politesse f

warder ['wɔːdəʳ] (BRIT) n Gefängniswärter m

wardrobe ['wɔːdrəʊb] n Kleiderschrank m; (clothes) Garderobe f

warehouse ['weəhaʊs] n Lagerhaus nt

wares [weəz] npl Ware f

warfare ['wɔːfeəʳ] n Krieg m; Kriegsführung f

warhead ['wɔːhed] n Sprengkopf m

warily ['weərɪlɪ] adv vorsichtig

warlike ['wɔːlaɪk] adj kriegerisch

warm [wɔːm] adj warm; (welcome) herzlich ♦ vt, vi wärmen; **I'm ~** mir ist warm; **it's ~** es ist warm; **~ up** vt aufwärmen ♦ vi warm werden; **~-hearted** adj warmherzig; **~ly** adv warm; herzlich; **~th** n Wärme f; Herzlichkeit f

warn [wɔːn] vt: **to ~ (of or against)** warnen (vor +dat); **~ing** n Warnung f; **without ~ing** unerwartet; **~ing light** n Warnlicht nt; **~ing triangle** n (AUT) Warndreieck nt

warp [wɔːp] vt verziehen; **~ed** adj wellig; (fig) pervers

warrant ['wɒrnt] n (for arrest) Haftbefehl m

warranty ['wɒrəntɪ] n Garantie f

warren ['wɒrən] n Labyrinth nt

Warsaw ['wɔːsɔː] n Warschau nt

warship ['wɔːʃɪp] n Kriegsschiff nt

wart [wɔːt] n Warze f

wartime ['wɔ:taɪm] n Krieg m

wary ['wɛərɪ] adj misstrauisch

was [wɒz] pt of **be**

wash [wɒʃ] n Wäsche f ♦ vt waschen; (dishes) abwaschen ♦ vi sich waschen; (do ~ing) waschen; **to have a ~** sich waschen; **~ away** vt abwaschen, wegspülen; **~ off** vt abwaschen; **~ up** vi (BRIT) spülen; (US) sich waschen; **~able** adj waschbar; **~basin** n Waschbecken nt; **~bowl** (US) n Waschbecken nt; **~cloth** (US) n (face cloth) Waschlappen m; **~er** n (TECH) Dichtungsring m; (machine) Waschmaschine f; **~ing** n Wäsche f; **~ing machine** n Waschmaschine f; **~ing powder** (BRIT) n Waschpulver nt; **~ing-up** n Abwasch m; **~ing-up liquid** n Spülmittel nt; **~out** (inf) n Reinfall m; (person) Niete f; **~room** n Waschraum m

wasn't ['wɒznt] = **was not**

wasp [wɒsp] n Wespe f

wastage ['weɪstɪdʒ] n Verlust m; **natural ~** Verschleiß m

waste [weɪst] n (wasting) Verschwendung f; (what is ~d) Abfall m ♦ adj (useless) überschüssig, Abfall- ♦ vt (object) verschwenden; (time, life) vergeuden ♦ vi: **to ~ away** verfallen, verkümmern; **~s** npl (land) Einöde f; **~ disposal unit** (BRIT) n Müllschlucker m; **~ful** adj verschwenderisch; (process) aufwändig, aufwendig; **~ ground** (BRIT) n unbebaute(s) Grundstück nt; **~land** n Ödland nt; **~paper basket** n Papierkorb m; **~ pipe** n Abflussrohr nt

watch [wɒtʃ] n Wache f; (for time) Uhr f ♦ vt ansehen; (observe) beobachten; (be careful of) aufpassen auf +acc; (guard) bewachen ♦ vi zusehen; **to be on the ~ (for sth)** (auf etw acc) aufpassen; **to ~ TV** fernsehen; **to ~ sb doing sth** jdm bei etw zuschauen; **~ out** vi Ausschau halten; (be careful) aufpassen; **~ out!** pass auf!; **~dog** n Wachhund m; (fig) Wächter m; **~ful** adj wachsam; **~maker** n Uhrmacher m; **~man** (irreg) n (also: **night ~man**) (Nacht)wächter m; **~ strap** n Uhrarmband nt

water ['wɔ:tər] n Wasser nt ♦ vt (be)gießen; (river) bewässern; (horses) tränken ♦ vi (eye) tränen; **~s** npl (of sea, river etc) Gewässer nt; **~ down** vt verwässern; **~ closet** (BRIT) n (Wasser)klosett nt; **~colour** (US **watercolor**) n (painting) Aquarell nt; (paint) Wasserfarbe f; **~cress** n (Brunnen)kresse f; **~fall** n Wasserfall m; **~ heater** n Heißwassergerät nt; **~ing can** n Gießkanne f; **~ level** n Wasserstand m; **~ lily** n Seerose f; **~line** n Wasserlinie f; **~logged** adj (ground) voll Wasser; **~ main** n Haupt(wasser)leitung f; **~mark** n Wasserzeichen nt; (on wall) Wasserstandsmarke f; **~melon** n Wassermelone f; **~ polo** n Wasserball(spiel) nt; **~proof** adj wasserdicht; **~shed** n Wasserscheide f; **~-skiing** n Wasserskilaufen nt; **~ tank** n Wassertank m; **~tight** adj wasserdicht; **~way** n Wasserweg m; **~works** npl Wasserwerk nt; **~y** adj wäss(e)rig

watt [wɒt] n Watt nt

wave [weɪv] n Welle f; (with hand) Winken nt ♦ vt (move to and fro) schwenken; (hand, flag) winken mit ♦ vi (person) winken; (flag) wehen; **~length** n (also fig) Wellenlänge f

waver ['weɪvər] vi schwanken

wavy ['weɪvɪ] adj wellig

wax [wæks] n Wachs nt; (sealing ~) Siegellack m; (in ear) Ohrenschmalz nt ♦ vt (floor) (ein)wachsen ♦ vi (moon) zunehmen; **~works** npl Wachsfigurenkabinett nt

way [weɪ] n Weg m; (method) Art und Weise f; (direction) Richtung f; (habit) Gewohnheit f; (distance) Entfernung f; (condition) Zustand m; **which ~? - this ~** welche Richtung? - hier entlang; **on the ~** (en route) unterwegs; **to be in the ~** im Weg sein; **to go out of one's ~ to do sth** sich besonders anstrengen, um etw zu tun; **to lose one's ~** sich verirren; **"give ~"** (BRIT: AUT) „Vorfahrt achten!"; **in a ~** in gewisser Weise; **by the ~** übrigens; **in some ~s** in gewisser Hinsicht; **"~ in"** (BRIT) „Eingang"; **"~ out"** (BRIT) „Ausgang"

waylay [weɪ'leɪ] (irreg: like **lay**) vt auflauern

+dat

wayward ['weɪwəd] adj eigensinnig

W.C. (BRIT) n WC nt

we [wiː] pl pron wir

weak [wiːk] adj schwach; **~en** vt schwächen ♦ vi schwächer werden; **~ling** n Schwächling m; **~ness** n Schwäche f

wealth [welθ] n Reichtum m; (abundance) Fülle f; **~y** adj reich

wean [wiːn] vt entwöhnen

weapon ['wepən] n Waffe f

wear [weəʳ] (pt **wore**, pp **worn**) n (clothing): **sports/baby ~** Sport-/Babykleidung f; (use) Verschleiß m ♦ vt (have on) tragen; (smile etc) haben; (use) abnutzen ♦ vi (last) halten; (become old) (sich) verschleißen; **evening ~** Abendkleidung f; **~ and tear** Verschleiß m; **~ away** vt verbrauchen ♦ vi schwinden; **~ down** vt (people) zermürben; **~ off** vi sich verlieren; **~ out** vt verschleißen; (person) erschöpfen

weary ['wɪərɪ] adj müde ♦ vt ermüden ♦ vi überdrüssig werden

weasel ['wiːzl] n Wiesel nt

weather ['weðəʳ] n Wetter nt ♦ vt verwittern lassen; (resist) überstehen; **under the ~** (fig: ill) angeschlagen (inf); **~-beaten** adj verwittert; **~cock** n Wetterhahn m; **~ forecast** n Wettervorhersage f; **~ vane** n Wetterfahne f

weave [wiːv] (pt **wove**, pp **woven**) vt weben; **~r** n Weber(in) m(f); **weaving** n (craft) Webkunst f

Web [web] n: **the ~** das Web

web n Netz nt; (membrane) Schwimmhaut f; **~ site** n (COMPUT) Website f, Webseite f

wed [wed] (pt, pp **wedded**) vt heiraten ♦ n: **the newly-~s** npl die Frischvermählten pl

we'd [wiːd] = **we had**; **we would**

wedding ['wedɪŋ] n Hochzeit f; **silver/golden ~ anniversary** Silberhochzeit f/goldene Hochzeit f; **~ day** n Hochzeitstag m; **~ dress** n Hochzeitskleid nt; **~ ring** n Trauring m, Ehering m

wedge [wedʒ] n Keil m; (of cheese etc) Stück nt ♦ vt (fasten) festklemmen; (pack tightly) einkeilen

Wednesday ['wednzdɪ] n Mittwoch m

wee [wiː] (SCOTTISH) adj klein, winzig

weed [wiːd] n Unkraut nt ♦ vt jäten; **~-killer** n Unkrautvertilgungsmittel nt

weedy ['wiːdɪ] adj (person) schmächtig

week [wiːk] n Woche f; **a ~ today/on Friday** heute/Freitag in einer Woche; **~day** n Wochentag m; **~end** n Wochenende nt; **~ly** adj wöchentlich; (wages, magazine) Wochen- ♦ adv wöchentlich

weep [wiːp] (pt, pp **wept**) vi weinen; **~ing willow** n Trauerweide f

weigh [weɪ] vt, vi wiegen; **to ~ anchor** den Anker lichten; **~ down** vt niederdrücken; **~ up** vt abschätzen

weight [weɪt] n Gewicht nt; **to lose/put on ~** abnehmen/zunehmen; **~ing** n (allowance) Zulage f; **~lifter** n Gewichtheber m; **~lifting** n Gewichtheben nt; **~y** adj (heavy) gewichtig; (important) schwerwiegend, schwer wiegend

weir [wɪəʳ] n (Stau)wehr nt

weird [wɪəd] adj seltsam

welcome ['welkəm] n Willkommen nt, Empfang m ♦ vt begrüßen; **thank you - you're ~!** danke - nichts zu danken

welder ['weldəʳ] n (person) Schweißer(in) m(f)

welding ['weldɪŋ] n Schweißen nt

welfare ['welfeəʳ] n Wohl nt; (social) Fürsorge f; **~ state** n Wohlfahrtsstaat m; **~ work** n Fürsorge f

well [wel] n Brunnen m; (oil ~) Quelle f ♦ adj (in good health) gesund ♦ adv gut ♦ excl nun!, na schön!; **I'm ~** es geht mir gut; **get ~ soon!** gute Besserung!; **as ~** auch; **as ~ as** sowohl als auch; **~ done!** gut gemacht!; **to do ~** (person) gut zurechtkommen; (business) gut gehen; **~ up** vi emporsteigen, (fig) aufsteigen

we'll [wiːl] = **we will**; **we shall**

well: **~-behaved** ['welbɪ'heɪvd] adj wohlerzogen; **~-being** n ['wel'biːɪŋ] n Wohl nt; **~-built** ['wel'bɪlt] adj kräftig gebaut; **~-deserved** ['weldɪ'zɜːvd] adj wohlverdient; **~-dressed** ['wel'drest] adj gut gekleidet; **~-heeled** ['wel'hiːld] (inf) adj (wealthy) gut

gepolstert
wellingtons ['welɪŋtənz] *npl* (*also:* **wellington boots**) Gummistiefel *pl*
well: ~-**known** ['wel'nəun] *adj* bekannt; ~-**mannered** ['wel'mænəd] *adj* wohlerzogen; ~-**meaning** ['wel'miːnɪŋ] *adj* (*person*) wohlmeinend; (*action*) gut gemeint; ~-**off** ['wel'ɔf] *adj* gut situiert; ~-**read** ['wel'red] *adj* (sehr) belesen; ~-**to-do** ['weltə'duː] *adj* wohlhabend; ~-**wisher** ['welwɪʃəʳ] *n* Gönner *m*
Welsh [welʃ] *adj* walisisch ♦ *n* (LING) Walisisch *nt*; **the ~** *npl* (*people*) die Waliser *pl*; ~ **Assembly** *n* walisische Versammlung *f*; ~**man/woman** (*irreg*) *n* Waliser(in) *m(f)*
went [went] *pt of* **go**
wept [wept] *pt, pp of* **weep**
were [wəːʳ] *pt pl of* **be**
we're [wɪəʳ] = **we are**
weren't [wəːnt] = **were not**
west [west] *n* Westen *m* ♦ *adj* West-, westlich ♦ *adv* westwärts, nach Westen; **the W~** der Westen; **W~ Country** (BRIT) *n*: **the W~ Country** der Südwesten Englands; ~**erly** *adj* westlich; ~**ern** *adj* westlich, West- ♦ *n* (CINE) Western *m*; **W~ Indian** *adj* westindisch ♦ *n* Westindier(in) *m(f)*; **W~ Indies** *npl* Westindische Inseln *pl*; ~**ward(s)** *adv* westwärts
wet [wet] *adj* nass; **to get ~** nass werden; "~ **paint**" „frisch gestrichen"; ~ **blanket** *n* (*fig*) Triefel *m*; ~ **suit** *n* Taucheranzug *m*
we've [wiːv] = **we have**
whack [wæk] *n* Schlag *m* ♦ *vt* schlagen
whale [weɪl] *n* Wal *m*
wharf [wɔːf] *n* Kai *m*
wharves [wɔːvz] *npl of* **wharf**

what [wɔt] *adj* 1 (*in questions*) welche(r, s), was für ein(e); **what size is it?** welche Größe ist das?
2 (*in exclamations*) was für ein(e); **what a mess!** was für ein Durcheinander!
♦ *pron* (*interrogative/relative*) was; **what are you doing?** was machst du gerade?; **what are you talking about?** wovon reden Sie?;

what is it called? wie heißt das?; **what about ...?** wie wärs mit ...?; **I saw what you did** ich habe gesehen, was du gemacht hast
♦ *excl* (*disbelieving*) wie, was; **what, no coffee!** wie, kein Kaffee?; **I've crashed the car - what!** ich hatte einen Autounfall - was!

whatever [wɔt'evəʳ] *adj*: ~ **book** welches Buch auch immer ♦ *pron*: **do ~ is necessary** tu, was (immer auch) nötig ist; ~ **happens** egal, was passiert; **nothing ~** überhaupt *or* absolut gar nichts; **do ~ you want** tu, was (immer) du (auch) möchtest; **no reason ~** *or* **whatsoever** überhaupt *or* absolut kein Grund
whatsoever [wɔtsəu'evəʳ] *adj see* **whatever**
wheat [wiːt] *n* Weizen *m*
wheedle ['wiːdl] *vt*: **to ~ sb into doing sth** jdn dazu überreden, etw zu tun; **to ~ sth out of sb** jdm etw abluchsen
wheel [wiːl] *n* Rad *nt*; (*steering ~*) Lenkrad *nt*; (*disc*) Scheibe *f* ♦ *vt* schieben; ~**barrow** *n* Schubkarren *m*; ~**chair** *n* Rollstuhl *m*; ~ **clamp** *n* (AUT) Parkkralle *f*
wheeze [wiːz] *vi* keuchen

when [wen] *adv* wann
♦ *conj* 1 (*at, during, after the time that*) wenn; (*in past*) als; **she was reading when I came in** sie las, als ich hereinkam; **be careful when you cross the road** seien Sie vorsichtig, wenn Sie über die Straße gehen
2 (*on, at which*) als; **on the day when I met him** an dem Tag, an dem ich ihn traf
3 (*whereas*) wo ... doch

whenever [wen'evəʳ] *adv* wann (auch) immer; (*every time that*) jedes Mal wenn ♦ *conj* (*any time*) wenn
where [weəʳ] *adv* (*place*) wo; (*direction*) wohin; ~ **from** woher; **this is ~ ...** hier ...; ~**abouts** ['weərəbauts] *adv* wo ♦ *n* Aufenthaltsort *m*; **nobody knows his ~abouts** niemand weiß, wo er ist; ~**as**

[wɛərˈæz] *conj* während, wo ... doch; **~by**
pron woran, wodurch, womit, wovon;
~upon *conj* worauf, wonach; (*at beginning
of sentence*) daraufhin; **~ver** [wɛərˈɛvər] *adv*
wo (immer)

wherewithal [ˈwɛəwɪðɔːl] *n* nötige
(Geld)mittel *pl*

whet [wɛt] *vt* (*appetite*) anregen

whether [ˈwɛðər] *conj* ob; **I don't know ~ to
accept or not** ich weiß nicht, ob ich es
annehmen soll oder nicht; **~ you go or not**
ob du gehst oder nicht; **it's doubtful/
unclear ~ ...** es ist zweifelhaft/nicht klar,
ob ...

KEYWORD

which [wɪtʃ] *adj* **1** (*interrogative: direct,
indirect*) welche(r, s); **which one?** welche(r,
s)?
2: in which case in diesem Fall; **by which
time** zu dieser Zeit
♦ *pron* **1** (*interrogative*) welche(r, s); (*of
people also*) wer
2 (*relative*) der/die/das; (*referring to people*)
was; **the apple which you ate/which is
on the table** der Apfel, den du gegessen
hast/der auf dem Tisch liegt; **he said he
saw her, which is true** er sagte, er habe
sie gesehen, was auch stimmt

whichever [wɪtʃˈɛvər] *adj* welche(r, s) auch
immer; (*no matter which*) ganz gleich
welche(r, s); **~ book you take** welches
Buch du auch nimmst; **~ car you prefer**
egal welches Auto du vorziehst

whiff [wɪf] *n* Hauch *m*

while [waɪl] *n* Weile *f* ♦ *conj* während; **for a
~** eine Zeit lang; **~ away** *vt* (*time*) sich *dat*
vertreiben

whim [wɪm] *n* Laune *f*

whimper [ˈwɪmpər] *n* Wimmern *nt* ♦ *vi*
wimmern

whimsical [ˈwɪmzɪkəl] *adj* launisch

whine [waɪn] *n* Gewinsel *nt*, Gejammer *nt*
♦ *vi* heulen, winseln

whip [wɪp] *n* Peitsche *f*; (*POL*) Fraktionsführer
m ♦ *vt* (*beat*) peitschen; (*snatch*) reißen;

~ped cream *n* Schlagsahne *f*

whip-round [ˈwɪpraund] (*BRIT: inf*) *n*
Geldsammlung *f*

whirl [wəːl] *n* Wirbel *m* ♦ *vt, vi*
(herum)wirbeln; **~pool** *n* Wirbel *m*; **~wind**
n Wirbelwind *m*

whirr [wəːr] *vi* schwirren, surren

whisk [wɪsk] *n* Schneebesen *m* ♦ *vt* (*cream
etc*) schlagen; **to ~ sb away** *or* **off** mit jdm
davon sausen

whisker [ˈwɪskər] *n*: **~s** (*of animal*) Barthaare
pl; (*of man*) Backenbart *m*

whisky [ˈwɪskɪ] (*US, IRISH* **whiskey**) *n* Whisky
m

whisper [ˈwɪspər] *n* Flüstern *nt* ♦ *vt, vi*
flüstern

whistle [ˈwɪsl] *n* Pfiff *m*; (*instrument*) Pfeife *f*
♦ *vt, vi* pfeifen

white [waɪt] *n* Weiß *nt*; (*of egg*) Eiweiß *nt*
♦ *adj* weiß; **~ coffee** (*BRIT*) *n* Kaffee *m* mit
Milch; **~-collar worker** *n* Angestellte(r) *m*;
~ elephant *n* (*fig*) Fehlinvestition *f*; **~ lie** *n*
Notlüge *f*; **~ paper** *n* (*POL*) Weißbuch *nt*;
~wash *n* (*paint*) Tünche *f*; (*fig*)
Ehrenrettung *f* ♦ *vt* weißen, tünchen; (*fig*)
rein waschen

whiting [ˈwaɪtɪŋ] *n* Weißfisch *m*

Whitsun [ˈwɪtsn] *n* Pfingsten *nt*

whittle [ˈwɪtl] *vt*: **to ~ away** *or* **down**
stutzen, verringern

whizz [wɪz] *vi*: **to ~ past** *or* **by** vorbeizischen,
vorbeischwirren; **~ kid** (*inf*) *n* Kanone *f*

KEYWORD

who [huː] *pron* **1** (*interrogative*) wer; (*acc*)
wen; (*dat*) wem; **who is it?, who's there?**
wer ist da?
2 (*relative*) der/die/das; **the woman/man
who spoke to me** die Frau/der Mann, die/
der mit mir sprach

whodu(n)nit [huːˈdʌnɪt] (*inf*) *n* Krimi *m*

whoever [huːˈɛvər] *pron* wer/wen/wem auch
immer; (*no matter who*) ganz gleich wer/
wen/wem

whole [həul] *adj* ganz ♦ *n* Ganze(s) *nt*; **the ~
of the town** die ganze Stadt; **on the ~** im

Großen und Ganzen; **as a ~** im Großen und Ganzen; **~food(s)** ['hɔːlfuːd(z)] *n(pl)* Vollwertkost *f*; **~hearted** [hɔːl'hɑːtɪd] *adj* rückhaltlos; **~heartedly** *adv* von ganzem Herzen; **~meal** *adj* (*bread, flour*) Vollkorn-; **~sale** *n* Großhandel *m* ♦ *adj* (*trade*) Großhandels-; (*destruction*) Massen-; **~saler** *n* Großhändler *m*; **~some** *adj* bekömmlich, gesund; **~wheat** *adj* = **wholemeal**

wholly ['hɔːlɪ] *adv* ganz, völlig

KEYWORD
---

whom [huːm] *pron* **1** (*interrogative: acc*) wen; (: *dat*) wem; **whom did you see?** wen haben Sie gesehen?; **to whom did you give it?** wem haben Sie es gegeben?
2 (*relative: acc*) den/die/das; (: *dat*) dem/der/dem; **the man whom I saw/to whom I spoke** der Mann, den ich sah/mit dem ich sprach

---

whooping cough ['huːpɪŋ-] *n* Keuchhusten *m*

whore [hɔːr] *n* Hure *f*

whose [huːz] *adj* (*possessive: interrogative*) wessen; (: *relative*) dessen; (*after f and pl*) deren ♦ *pron* wessen; **~ book is this?, ~ is this book?** wessen Buch ist dies?; **~ is this?** wem gehört das?

KEYWORD
---

why [waɪ] *adv* warum, weshalb
♦ *conj* warum, weshalb; **that's not why I'm here** ich bin nicht deswegen hier; **that's the reason why** deshalb
♦ *excl* (*expressing surprise, shock*) na so was; (*explaining*) also dann; **why, it's you!** na so was, du bist es!

---

wick [wɪk] *n* Docht *m*
wicked ['wɪkɪd] *adj* böse
wicker ['wɪkər] *n* (*also:* **~work**) Korbgeflecht *nt*
wicket ['wɪkɪt] *n* Tor *nt*, Dreistab *m*
wide [waɪd] *adj* breit; (*plain*) weit; (*in firing*) daneben ♦ *adv*: **to open ~** weit öffnen; **to shoot ~** danebenschießen; **~-angle lens** *n*

Weitwinkelobjektiv *nt*; **~awake** *adj* hellwach; **~ly** *adv* weit; (*known*) allgemein; **~n** *vt* erweitern; **~ open** *adj* weit geöffnet; **~spread** *adj* weitverbreitet, weit verbreitet

widow ['wɪdəu] *n* Witwe *f*; **~ed** *adj* verwitwet; **~er** *n* Witwer *m*

width [wɪdθ] *n* Breite *f*, Weite *f*

wield [wiːld] *vt* schwingen, handhaben

wife [waɪf] (*pl* **wives**) *n* (Ehe)frau *f*, Gattin *f*

wig [wɪg] *n* Perücke *f*

wiggle ['wɪgl] *n* Wackeln *nt* ♦ *vt* wackeln mit ♦ *vi* wackeln

wild [waɪld] *adj* wild; (*violent*) heftig; (*plan, idea*) verrückt; **~ly** *adv* wild, ungestüm; (*exaggerated*) irrsinnig; **~s** *npl*: **the ~s** die Wildnis *f*, Wüste *f*; **~-goose chase** *n* (*fig*) fruchtlose(s) Unternehmen *nt*; **~life** *n* Tierwelt *f*; **~ly** *adv* wild, ungestüm; (*exaggerated*) irrsinnig; **~s** *npl*: **the ~s** die Wildnis *f*

wilful ['wɪlful] (*US* **willful**) *adj* (*intended*) vorsätzlich; (*obstinate*) eigensinnig

---
KEYWORD
---

will [wɪl] *aux vb* **1** (*forms future tense*) werden; **I will finish it tomorrow** ich mache es morgen zu Ende
2 (*in conjectures, predictions*): **he will** *or* **he'll be there by now** er dürfte jetzt da sein; **that will be the postman** das wird der Postbote sein
3 (*in commands, requests, offers*): **will you be quiet!** sei endlich still!; **will you help me?** hilfst du mir?; **will you have a cup of tea?** trinken Sie eine Tasse Tee?; **I won't put up with it!** das lasse ich mir nicht gefallen!
♦ *vt* wollen
♦ *n* Wille *m*; (*JUR*) Testament *nt*

---

willing ['wɪlɪŋ] *adj* gewillt, bereit; **~ly** *adv* bereitwillig, gern; **~ness** *n* (Bereit)willigkeit *f*

willow ['wɪləu] *n* Weide *f*

willpower ['wɪl'pauər] *n* Willenskraft *f*

willy-nilly ['wɪlɪ'nɪlɪ] *adv* einfach so

wilt [wɪlt] *vi* (ver)welken

wily ['waɪlɪ] *adj* gerissen

win [wɪn] (*pt, pp* **won**) *n* Sieg *m* ♦ *vt, vi*

gewinnen; **to ~ sb over** or **round** jdn gewinnen, jdn dazu bringen

wince [wɪns] vi zusammenzucken

winch [wɪntʃ] n Winde f

wind[1] [wɪnd] n Wind m; (MED) Blähungen pl

wind[2] [waɪnd] (pt, pp **wound**) vt (rope) winden; (bandage) wickeln ♦ vi (turn) sich winden; **~ up** vt (clock) aufziehen; (debate) (ab)schließen

windfall ['wɪndfɔːl] n unverhoffte(r) Glücksfall m

winding ['waɪndɪŋ] adj (road) gewunden

wind instrument ['wɪnd-] n Blasinstrument nt

windmill ['wɪndmɪl] n Windmühle f

window ['wɪndəu] n Fenster nt; **~ box** n Blumenkasten m; **~ cleaner** n Fensterputzer m; **~ envelope** n Fensterbriefumschlag m; **~ ledge** n Fenstersims m; **~ pane** n Fensterscheibe f; **~-shopping** n Schaufensterbummel m; **to go ~-shopping** einen Schaufensterbummel machen; **~sill** n Fensterbank f

wind: ~pipe n Luftröhre f; **~ power** n Windenergie f; **~screen** (BRIT) n Windschutzscheibe f; **~screen washer** n Scheibenwaschanlage f; **~screen wiper** n Scheibenwischer m; **~shield** (US) n = **windscreen; ~swept** adj vom Wind gepeitscht; (person) zerzaust; **~y** adj windig

wine [waɪn] n Wein m; **~ bar** n Weinlokal nt; **~ cellar** n Weinkeller m; **~glass** n Weinglas nt; **~ list** n Weinkarte f; **~ merchant** n Weinhändler m; **~ tasting** n Weinprobe f; **~ waiter** n Weinkellner m

wing [wɪŋ] n Flügel m; (MIL) Gruppe f; **~s** npl (THEAT) Seitenkulisse f; **~er** n (SPORT) Flügelstürmer m

wink [wɪŋk] n Zwinkern nt ♦ vi zwinkern, blinzeln

winner ['wɪnər] n Gewinner m; (SPORT) Sieger m

winning ['wɪnɪŋ] adj (team) siegreich, Sieger-; (goal) entscheidend; **~ post** n Ziel nt; **~s** npl Gewinn m

winter ['wɪntər] n Winter m ♦ adj (clothes) Winter- ♦ vi überwintern; **~ sports** npl

Wintersport m; **wintry** ['wɪntrɪ] adj Winter-, winterlich

wipe [waɪp] n: **to give sth a ~** etw (ab)wischen ♦ vt wischen; **~ off** vt abwischen; **~ out** vt (debt) löschen; (destroy) auslöschen; **~ up** vt aufwischen

wire ['waɪər] n Draht m; (telegram) Telegramm nt ♦ vt telegrafieren; **to ~ sb** jdm telegrafieren; **~less** ['waɪəlɪs] (BRIT) n Radio(apparat m) nt

wiring ['waɪərɪŋ] n elektrische Leitungen pl

wiry ['waɪərɪ] adj drahtig

wisdom ['wɪzdəm] n Weisheit f; (of decision) Klugheit f; **~ tooth** n Weisheitszahn m

wise [waɪz] adj klug, weise ♦ suffix: **timewise** zeitlich gesehen

wisecrack ['waɪzkræk] n Witzelei f

wish [wɪʃ] n Wunsch m ♦ vt wünschen; **best ~es** (on birthday etc) alles Gute; **with best ~es** herzliche Grüße; **to ~ sb goodbye** jdn verabschieden; **he ~ed me well** er wünschte mir Glück; **to ~ to do sth** etw tun wollen; **~ for** vt fus sich dat wünschen; **~ful thinking** n Wunschdenken nt

wishy-washy ['wɪʃɪ'wɒʃɪ] (inf) adj (ideas, argument) verschwommen

wisp [wɪsp] n (Haar)strähne f; (of smoke) Wölkchen nt

wistful ['wɪstful] adj sehnsüchtig

wit [wɪt] n (also: **~s**) Verstand m no pl; (amusing ideas) Witz m; (person) Witzbold m

witch [wɪtʃ] n Hexe f; **~craft** n Hexerei f

┌─────────────┐
│ KEYWORD │
└─────────────┘

with [wɪð, wɪθ] prep **1** (accompanying, in the company of) mit; **we stayed with friends** wir übernachteten bei Freunden; **I'll be with you in a minute** einen Augenblick, ich bin sofort da; **I'm not with you** (I don't understand) das verstehe ich nicht; **to be with it** (inf: up-to-date) auf dem Laufenden sein; (: alert) (voll) da sein (inf)

2 (descriptive, indicating manner etc) mit; **the man with the grey hat** der Mann mit dem grauen Hut; **red with anger** rot vor Wut

withdraw [wɪθ'drɔː] (irreg: like draw) vt

zurückziehen; (*money*) abheben; (*remark*)
zurücknehmen ♦ *vi* sich zurückziehen; **~al**
n Zurückziehung *f*; Abheben *nt*;
Zurücknahme *f*; **~n** *adj* (*person*)
verschlossen

wither ['wɪðə^r] *vi* (ver)welken

withhold [wɪθ'həuld] (*irreg: like* hold) *vt*: **to
~ sth (from sb)** (jdm) etw vorenthalten

within [wɪð'ɪn] *prep* innerhalb +*gen* ♦ *adv*
innen; **~ sight of** in Sichtweite von; **~ the
week** innerhalb dieser Woche; **~ a mile of**
weniger als eine Meile von

without [wɪð'aut] *prep* ohne; **~ sleeping** *etc*
ohne zu schlafen *etc*

withstand [wɪθ'stænd] (*irreg: like* stand) *vt*
widerstehen +*dat*

witness ['wɪtnɪs] *n* Zeuge *m*, Zeugin *f* ♦ *vt*
(*see*) sehen, miterleben; (*document*)
beglaubigen; **~ box** *n* Zeugenstand *m*; **~
stand** (*US*) *n* Zeugenstand *m*

witticism ['wɪtɪsɪzəm] *n* witzige Bemerkung *f*

witty ['wɪtɪ] *adj* witzig, geistreich

wives [waɪvz] *pl of* **wife**

wk *abbr* = **week**

wobble ['wɔbl] *vi* wackeln

woe [wəu] *n* Kummer *m*

woke [wəuk] *pt of* **wake**

woken ['wəukn] *pp of* **wake**

wolf [wulf] (*pl* **wolves**) *n* Wolf *m*

woman ['wumən] (*pl* **women**) *n* Frau *f*; **~
doctor** *n* Ärztin *f*; **~ly** *adj* weiblich

womb [wu:m] *n* Gebärmutter *f*

women ['wɪmɪn] *npl of* **woman**; **~'s lib** (*inf*)
n Frauenrechtsbewegung *f*

won [wʌn] *pt, pp of* **win**

wonder ['wʌndə^r] *n* (*marvel*) Wunder *nt*;
(*surprise*) Staunen *nt*, Verwunderung *f* ♦ *vi*
sich wundern ♦ *vt*: **I ~ whether ...** ich frage
mich, ob ...; **it's no ~ that** es ist kein
Wunder, dass; **to ~ at** sich wundern über
+*acc*; **to ~ about** sich Gedanken machen
über +*acc*; **~ful** *adj* wunderbar, herrlich

won't [wəunt] = **will not**

woo [wu:] *vt* (*audience etc*) umwerben

wood [wud] *n* Holz *nt*; (*forest*) Wald *m*; **~
carving** *n* Holzschnitzerei *f*; **~ed** *adj*
bewaldet; **~en** *adj* (*also fig*) hölzern;

~pecker *n* Specht *m*; **~wind** *n*
Blasinstrumente *pl*; **~work** *n* Holzwerk *nt*;
(*craft*) Holzarbeiten *pl*; **~worm** *n* Holzwurm
m

wool [wul] *n* Wolle *f*; **to pull the ~ over
sb's eyes** (*fig*) jdm Sand in die Augen
streuen; **~len** (*US* **woolen**) *adj* Woll-; **~lens**
npl Wollsachen *pl*; **~ly** (*US* **wooly**) *adj*
wollig; (*fig*) schwammig

word [wə:d] *n* Wort *nt*; (*news*) Bescheid *m*
♦ *vt* formulieren; **in other ~s** anders
gesagt; **to break/keep one's ~** sein Wort
brechen/halten; **~ing** *n* Wortlaut *m*; **~
processing** *n* Textverarbeitung *f*; **~
processor** *n* Textverarbeitung *f*

wore [wɔ:^r] *pt of* **wear**

work [wə:k] *n* Arbeit *f*; (*ART, LITER*) Werk *nt*
♦ *vi* arbeiten; (*machine*) funktionieren;
(*medicine*) wirken; (*succeed*) klappen; **~s** *n sg*
(*BRIT: factory*) Fabrik *f*, Werk *nt* ♦ *npl* (*of
watch*) Werk *nt*; **to be out of ~** arbeitslos
sein; **in ~ing order** in betriebsfähigem
Zustand; **~ loose** *vi* sich lockern; **~ on** *vi*
weiterarbeiten ♦ *vt fus* arbeiten an +*dat*;
(*influence*) bearbeiten; **~ out** *vi* (*sum*)
aufgehen; (*plan*) klappen ♦ *vt* (*problem*)
lösen; (*plan*) ausarbeiten; **it ~s out at £100**
das gibt or macht £100; **~ up** *vt*: **to get
~ed up** sich aufregen; **~able** *adj* (*soil*)
bearbeitbar; (*plan*) ausführbar; **~aholic**
[wə:kə'hɔlɪk] *n* Arbeitssüchtige(r) *f(m)*; **~er** *n*
Arbeiter(in) *m(f)*; **~ experience** *n*
Praktikum *nt*; **~force** *n* Arbeiterschaft *f*;
~ing class *n* Arbeiterklasse *f*; **~ing-class**
adj Arbeiter-; **~man** (*irreg*) *n* Arbeiter *m*;
~manship *n* Arbeit *f*, Ausführung *f*;
~sheet *n* Arbeitsblatt *nt*; **~shop** *n*
Werkstatt *f*; **~ station** *n* Arbeitsplatz *m*; **~-
to-rule** (*BRIT*) *n* Dienst *m* nach Vorschrift

world [wə:ld] *n* Welt *f*; **to think the ~ of sb**
große Stücke auf jdn halten; **~ly** *adj*
weltlich, irdisch; **~-wide** *adj* weltweit

World-Wide Web ['wə:ld'waɪd-] *n* World
Wide Web *nt*

worm [wə:m] *n* Wurm *m*

worn [wɔ:n] *pp of* **wear** ♦ *adj* (*clothes*)
abgetragen; **~-out** *adj* (*object*) abgenutzt;

(*person*) völlig erschöpft

worried ['wʌrɪd] *adj* besorgt, beunruhigt

worry ['wʌrɪ] *n* Sorge *f* ♦ *vt* beunruhigen ♦ *vi* (*feel uneasy*) sich sorgen, sich *dat* Gedanken machen; **~ing** *adj* beunruhigend

worse [wɜːs] *adj* schlechter, schlimmer ♦ *adv* schlimmer, ärger ♦ *n* Schlimmere(s) *nt*, Schlechtere(s) *nt*; **a change for the ~** eine Verschlechterung; **~n** *vt* verschlimmern ♦ *vi* sich verschlechtern; **~ off** *adj* (*fig*) schlechter dran

worship ['wɜːʃɪp] *n* Verehrung *f* ♦ *vt* anbeten; **Your W~** (*BRIT: to mayor*) Herr/ Frau Bürgermeister; (: *to judge*) Euer Ehren

worst [wɜːst] *adj* schlimmste(r, s), schlechteste(r, s) ♦ *adv* am schlimmsten, am ärgsten ♦ *n* Schlimmste(s) *nt*, Ärgste(s) *nt*; **at ~** schlimmstenfalls

worth [wɜːθ] *n* Wert *m* ♦ *adj* wert; **it's ~ it** es lohnt sich; **to be ~ one's while (to do sth)** die Mühe wert sein, (*etw zu tun*); **~less** *adj* wertlos; (*person*) nichtsnutzig; **~while** *adj* lohnend, der Mühe wert; **~y** *adj* wert, würdig

---

KEYWORD

would [wʊd] *aux vb* **1** (*conditional tense*): **if you asked him he would do it** wenn du ihn fragtest, würde er es tun; **if you had asked him he would have done it** wenn du ihn gefragt hättest, hätte er es getan

2 (*in offers, invitations, requests*): **would you like a biscuit?** möchten Sie ein Plätzchen?; **would you ask him to come in?** würden Sie ihn bitte hereinbitten?

3 (*in indirect speech*): **I said I would do it** ich sagte, ich würde es tun

4 (*emphatic*): **it WOULD have to snow today!** es musste ja ausgerechnet heute schneien!

5 (*insistence*): **she wouldn't behave** sie wollte sich partout nicht anständig benehmen

6 (*conjecture*): **it would have been midnight** es mag ungefähr Mitternacht gewesen sein; **it would seem so** es sieht wohl so aus

7 (*indicating habit*): **he would go there on Mondays** er ging jeden Montag dorthin

---

would-be ['wʊdbiː] (*pej*) *adj* Möchtegern-

wouldn't ['wʊdnt] = **would not**

wound[1] [wuːnd] *n* (*also fig*) Wunde *f* ♦ *vt* verwunden, verletzen (*also fig*)

wound[2] [waʊnd] *pt, pp of* **wind**[2]

wove [wəʊv] *pt of* **weave**; **~n** *pp of* **weave**

wrangle ['ræŋgl] *n* Streit *m* ♦ *vi* sich zanken

wrap [ræp] *vt* einwickeln; **~ up** *vt* einwickeln; (*deal*) abschließen; **~per** *n* Umschlag *m*, Schutzhülle *f*; **~ping paper** *n* Einwickelpapier *nt*

wrath [rɒθ] *n* Zorn *m*

wreak [riːk] *vt* (*havoc*) anrichten; (*vengeance*) üben

wreath [riːθ] *n* Kranz *m*

wreck [rek] *n* (*ship*) Wrack *nt*; (*sth ruined*) Ruine *f* ♦ *vt* zerstören; **~age** *n* Trümmer *pl*

wren [ren] *n* Zaunkönig *m*

wrench [rentʃ] *n* (*spanner*) Schraubenschlüssel *m*; (*twist*) Ruck *m* ♦ *vt* reißen, zerren; **to ~ sth from sb** jdm etw entreißen *or* entwinden

wrestle ['resl] *vi*: **to ~ (with sb)** (mit jdm) ringen; **~r** *n* Ringer(in) *m(f)*; **wrestling** *n* Ringen *nt*

wretched ['retʃɪd] *adj* (*inf*) verflixt

wriggle ['rɪgl] *n* Schlängeln *nt* ♦ *vi* sich winden

wring [rɪŋ] (*pt, pp* **wrung**) *vt* wringen

wrinkle ['rɪŋkl] *n* Falte *f*, Runzel *f* ♦ *vt* runzeln ♦ *vi* sich runzeln; (*material*) knittern; **~d** *adj* faltig, schrumpelig

wrist [rɪst] *n* Handgelenk *nt*; **~watch** *n* Armbanduhr *f*

writ [rɪt] *n* gerichtliche(r) Befehl *m*

write [raɪt] (*pt* **wrote**, *pp* **written**) *vt, vi* schreiben; **~ down** *vt* aufschreiben; **~ off** *vt* (*dismiss*) abschreiben; **~ out** *vt* (*essay*) abschreiben; (*cheque*) ausstellen; **~ up** *vt* schreiben; **~-off** *n*: **it is a ~-off** das kann man abschreiben; **~r** *n* Schriftsteller *m*

writhe [raɪð] *vi* sich winden

writing ['raɪtɪŋ] *n* (*act*) Schreiben *nt*; (*handwriting*) (Hand)schrift *f*; **in ~** schriftlich;

~ **paper** n Schreibpapier nt
written ['rɪtn] pp of **write**
wrong [rɒŋ] adj (incorrect) falsch; (morally) unrecht ♦ n Unrecht nt ♦ vt Unrecht tun +dat; **he was ~ in doing that** es war nicht recht von ihm, das zu tun; **you are ~ about that, you've got it** ~ da hast du Unrecht; **to be in the ~** im Unrecht sein; **what's ~ with your leg?** was ist mit deinem Bein los?; **to go ~** (plan) schief gehen; (person) einen Fehler machen; **~ful** adj unrechtmäßig; **~ly** adv falsch; (accuse) zu Unrecht
wrong number n (TEL): **you've got the ~** Sie sind falsch verbunden
wrote [rəut] pt of **write**
wrought [rɔːt] adj: **~ iron** Schmiedeeisen nt
wrung [rʌŋ] pt, pp of **wring**
wry [raɪ] adj ironisch
wt. abbr = **weight**
WWW n abbr (= World Wide Web): **the ~** das WWW.

X, x

Xmas ['ɛksməs] n abbr = **Christmas**
X-ray ['ɛksreɪ] n Röntgenaufnahme f ♦ vt röntgen; **~~s** npl Röntgenstrahlen pl
xylophone ['zaɪləfəun] n Xylofon nt, Xylophon nt

Y, y

yacht [jɒt] n Jacht f; **~ing** n (Sport)segeln nt; **~sman** (irreg) n Sportsegler m
Yank [jæŋk] (inf) n Ami m
yap [jæp] vi (dog) kläffen
yard [jɑːd] n Hof m; (measure) (englische) Elle f, Yard nt (0,91 m); **~stick** n (fig) Maßstab m
yarn [jɑːn] n (thread) Garn nt; (story) (Seemanns)garn nt
yawn [jɔːn] n Gähnen nt ♦ vi gähnen; **~ing** adj (gap) gähnend
yd. abbr = **yard(s)**

yeah [jɛə] (inf) adv ja
year [jɪəʳ] n Jahr nt; **to be 8 ~s old** acht Jahre alt sein; **an eight-year-old child** ein achtjähriges Kind; **~ly** adj, adv jährlich
yearn [jɜːn] vi: **to ~ (for)** sich sehnen (nach); **~ing** n Verlangen nt, Sehnsucht f
yeast [jiːst] n Hefe f
yell [jɛl] n gellende(r) Schrei m ♦ vi laut schreien
yellow ['jɛləu] adj gelb ♦ n Gelb nt
yelp [jɛlp] n Gekläff nt ♦ vi kläffen
yes [jɛs] adv ja ♦ n Ja nt, Jawort nt; **to say ~** Ja or ja sagen; **to answer ~** mit Ja antworten
yesterday ['jɛstədɪ] adv gestern ♦ n Gestern nt; **~ morning/evening** gestern Morgen/Abend; **all day ~** gestern den ganzen Tag; **the day before ~** vorgestern
yet [jɛt] adv noch; (in question) schon; (up to now) bis jetzt ♦ conj doch, dennoch; **it is not finished ~** es ist noch nicht fertig; **the best ~** das bisher Beste; **as ~** bis jetzt; (in past) bis dahin
yew [juː] n Eibe f
yield [jiːld] n Ertrag m ♦ vt (result, crop) hervorbringen; (interest, profit) abwerfen; (concede) abtreten ♦ vi nachgeben; (MIL) sich ergeben; (US: AUT) „Vorfahrt gewähren"
YMCA n abbr (= Young Men's Christian Association) CVJM m
yob [jɒb] (BRIT: inf) n Halbstarke(r) f(m)
yoga ['jəugə] n Joga m
yog(h)urt ['jɔugət] n Jog(h)urt m
yoke [jəuk] n (also fig) Joch nt
yolk [jəuk] n Eidotter m, Eigelb nt

KEYWORD

you [juː] pron 1 (subj, in comparisons: familiar form: sg) du; (: pl) ihr; (in letters also) du, ihr; (: polite form) Sie; **you Germans** ihr Deutschen; **she's younger than you** sie ist jünger als du/Sie
2 (direct object, after prep +acc: familiar form: sg) dich; (: pl) euch; (in letters also) dich, euch; (: polite form) Sie; **I know you** ich kenne dich/euch/Sie

3 (*indirect object, after prep +dat: familiar form: sg*) dir; (*: pl*) euch; (*in letters also*) dir, euch; (*: polite form*) Ihnen; **I gave it to you** ich gab es dir/euch/Ihnen

4 (*impers: one: subj*) man; (*: direct object*) einen; (*: indirect object*) einem; **fresh air does you good** frische Luft tut gut

---

you'd [ju:d] = **you had; you would**

you'll [ju:l] = **you will; you shall**

young [jʌŋ] *adj* jung ♦ *npl*: **the ~** die Jungen *pl*; **~ster** *n* Junge *m*, junge(r) Bursche *m*, junge(s) Mädchen *nt*

your [jɔ:ʳ] *adj* (*familiar: sg*) dein; (*: pl*) euer, eure *pl*; (*polite*) Ihr; *see also* **my**

you're [juəʳ] = **you are**

yours [jɔ:z] *pron* (*familiar: sg*) deine(r, s); (*: pl*) eure(r, s); (*polite*) Ihre(r, s); *see also* **mine**[2]

yourself [jɔ:'sɛlf] *pron* (*emphatic*) selbst; (*familiar: sg: acc*) dich (selbst); (*: dat*) dir (selbst); (*: pl*) euch (selbst); (*polite*) sich (selbst); *see also* **oneself**; **yourselves** *pl pron* (*reflexive: familiar*) euch; (*: polite*) sich; (*emphatic*) selbst; *see also* **oneself**

youth [ju:θ] *n* Jugend *f*; (*young man*) junge(r) Mann *m*; **~s** *npl* (*young people*) Jugendliche *pl*; **~ club** *n* Jugendzentrum *nt*; **~ful** *adj* jugendlich; **~ hostel** *n* Jugendherberge *f*

you've [ju:v] = **you have**

YTS (*BRIT*) *n abbr* (= *Youth Training Scheme*) staatliches Förderprogramm für arbeitslose Jugendliche

Yugoslav ['ju:gəuslɑ:v] *adj* jugoslawisch ♦ *n* Jugoslawe *m*, Jugoslawin *f*; **~ia**

[ju:gəu'slɑ:vɪə] *n* Jugoslawien *nt*

yuppie ['jʌpɪ] (*inf*) *n* Yuppie *m* ♦ *adj* yuppiehaft, Yuppie-

YWCA *n abbr* (= *Young Women's Christian Association*) CVJF *m*

Z, z

zany ['zeɪnɪ] *adj* (*ideas, sense of humour*) verrückt

zap [zæp] *vt* (*COMPUT*) löschen

zeal [zi:l] *n* Eifer *m*; **~ous** ['zɛləs] *adj* eifrig

zebra ['zi:brə] *n* Zebra *nt*; **~ crossing** (*BRIT*) *n* Zebrastreifen *m*

zero ['zɪərəu] *n* Null *f*; (*on scale*) Nullpunkt *m*

zest [zɛst] *n* Begeisterung *f*

zigzag ['zɪgzæg] *n* Zickzack *m*

Zimbabwe [zɪm'bɑ:bwɪ] *n* Zimbabwe *nt*

Zimmer frame ['zɪmə-] *n* Laufgestell *nt*

zip [zɪp] *n* Reißverschluss *m* ♦ *vt* (*also:* **~ up**) den Reißverschluss zumachen +*gen*

zip code (*US*) *n* Postleitzahl *f*

zipper ['zɪpəʳ] (*US*) *n* Reißverschluss *m*

zit [zɪt] (*inf*) *n* Pickel *m*

zodiac ['zəudɪæk] *n* Tierkreis *m*

zombie ['zɔmbɪ] *n*: **like a ~** (*fig*) wie im Tran

zone [zəun] *n* (*also MIL*) Zone *f*, Gebiet *nt*; (*in town*) Bezirk *m*

zoo [zu:] *n* Zoo *m*

zoology [zu:'ɔlədʒɪ] *n* Zoologie *f*

zoom [zu:m] *vi*: **to ~ past** vorbeisausen; **~ lens** *n* Zoomobjektiv *nt*

zucchini [zu:'ki:nɪ] (*US*) *npl* Zucchini *pl*

GERMAN IRREGULAR VERBS

*with 'sein'

infinitive	present indicative (2nd, 3rd sg)	imperfect	past participle
aufschrecken*	schrickst auf, schrickt auf	schrak or schreckte auf	aufgeschreckt
ausbedingen	bedingst aus, bedingt aus	bedang or bedingte aus	ausbedungen
backen	bäckst, bäckt	backte or buk	gebacken
befehlen	befiehlst, befiehlt	befahl	befohlen
beginnen	beginnst, beginnt	begann	begonnen
beißen	beißt, beißt	biss	gebissen
bergen	birgst, birgt	barg	geborgen
bersten*	birst, birst	barst	geborsten
bescheißen*	bescheißt, bescheißt	beschiss	beschissen
bewegen	bewegst, bewegt	bewog	bewogen
biegen	biegst, biegt	bog	gebogen
bieten	bietest, bietet	bot	geboten
binden	bindest, bindet	band	gebunden
bitten	bittest, bittet	bat	gebeten
blasen	bläst, bläst	blies	geblasen
bleiben*	bleibst, bleibt	blieb	geblieben
braten	brätst, brät	briet	gebraten
brechen*	brichst, bricht	brach	gebrochen
brennen	brennst, brennt	brannte	gebrannt
bringen	bringst, bringt	brachte	gebracht
denken	denkst, denkt	dachte	gedacht
dreschen	drisch(e)st, drischt	drosch	gedroschen
dringen*	dringst, dringt	drang	gedrungen
dürfen	darfst, darf	durfte	gedurft
empfehlen	empfiehlst, empfiehlt	empfahl	empfohlen
erbleichen*	erbleichst, erbleicht	erbleichte	erblichen
erlöschen*	erlischst, erlischt	erlosch	erloschen
erschrecken*	erschrickst, erschrickt	erschrak	erschrocken
essen	isst, isst	aß	gegessen
fahren*	fährst, fährt	fuhr	gefahren
fallen*	fällst, fällt	fiel	gefallen

infinitive	present indicative (2nd, 3rd sg)	imperfect	past participle
fangen	fängst, fängt	fing	gefangen
fechten	fichtst, ficht	focht	gefochten
finden	findest, findet	fand	gefunden
flechten	flichtst, flicht	flocht	geflochten
fliegen*	fliegst, fliegt	flog	geflogen
fliehen*	fliehst, flieht	floh	geflohen
fließen*	fließt, fließt	floss	geflossen
fressen	frisst, frisst	fraß	gefressen
frieren	frierst, friert	fror	gefroren
gären*	gärst, gärt	gor	gegoren
gebären	gebierst, gebiert	gebar	geboren
geben	gibst, gibt	gab	gegeben
gedeihen*	gedeihst, gedeiht	gedieh	gediehen
gehen*	gehst, geht	ging	gegangen
gelingen*	——, gelingt	gelang	gelungen
gelten	giltst, gilt	galt	gegolten
genesen*	gene(se)st, genest	genas	genesen
genießen	genießt, genießt	genoss	genossen
geraten*	gerätst, gerät	geriet	geraten
geschehen*	——, geschieht	geschah	geschehen
gewinnen	gewinnst, gewinnt	gewann	gewonnen
gießen	gießt, gießt	goss	gegossen
gleichen	gleichst, gleicht	glich	geglichen
gleiten*	gleitest, gleitet	glitt	geglitten
glimmen	glimmst, glimmt	glomm	geglommen
graben	gräbst, gräbt	grub	gegraben
greifen	greifst, greift	griff	gegriffen
haben	hast, hat	hatte	gehabt
halten	hältst, hält	hielt	gehalten
hängen	hängst, hängt	hing	gehangen
hauen	haust, haut	haute	gehauen
heben	hebst, hebt	hob	gehoben
heißen	heißt, heißt	hieß	geheißen
helfen	hilfst, hilft	half	geholfen
kennen	kennst, kennt	kannte	gekannt
klimmen*	klimmst, klimmt	klomm	geklommen
klingen	klingst, klingt	klang	geklungen
kneifen	kneifst, kneift	kniff	gekniffen
kommen*	kommst, kommt	kam	gekommen
können	kannst, kann	konnte	gekonnt
kriechen*	kriechst, kriecht	kroch	gekrochen
laden	lädst, lädt	lud	geladen
lassen	lässt, lässt	ließ	gelassen
laufen*	läufst, läuft	lief	gelaufen
leiden	leidest, leidet	litt	gelitten

610

infinitive	present indicative (2nd, 3rd sg)	imperfect	past participle
leihen	leihst, leiht	lieh	geliehen
lesen	liest, liest	las	gelesen
liegen*	liegst, liegt	lag	gelegen
lügen	lügst, lügt	log	gelogen
mahlen	mahlst, mahlt	mahlte	gemahlen
meiden	meidest, meidet	mied	gemieden
melken	melkst, melkt	melkte	gemolken
messen	misst, misst	maß	gemessen
misslingen*	——, misslingt	misslang	misslungen
mögen	magst, mag	mochte	gemocht
müssen	musst, muss	musste	gemusst
nehmen	nimmst, nimmt	nahm	genommen
nennen	nennst, nennt	nannte	genannt
pfeifen	pfeifst, pfeift	pfiff	gepfiffen
preisen	preist, preist	pries	gepriesen
quellen*	quillst, quillt	quoll	gequollen
raten	rätst, rät	riet	geraten
reiben	reibst, reibt	rieb	gerieben
reißen*	reißt, reißt	riss	gerissen
reiten*	reitest, reitet	ritt	geritten
rennen*	rennst, rennt	rannte	gerannt
riechen*	riechst, riecht	roch	gerochen
ringen	ringst, ringt	rang	gerungen
rinnen*	rinnst, rinnt	rann	geronnen
rufen	rufst, ruft	rief	gerufen
salzen	salzt, salzt	salzte	gesalzen
saufen	säufst, säuft	soff	gesoffen
saugen	saugst, saugt	sog	gesogen
schaffen	schaffst, schafft	schuf	geschaffen
scheiden	scheidest, scheidet	schied	geschieden
scheinen	scheinst, scheint	schien	geschienen
schelten	schiltst, schilt	schalt	gescholten
scheren	scherst, schert	schor	geschoren
schieben	schiebst, schiebt	schob	geschoben
schießen	schießt, schießt	schoss	geschossen
schinden	schindest, schindet	schindete	geschunden
schlafen	schläfst, schläft	schlief	geschlafen
schlagen	schlägst, schlägt	schlug	geschlagen
schleichen*	schleichst, schleicht	schlich	geschlichen
schleifen	schleifst, schleift	schliff	geschliffen
schließen	schließt, schließt	schloss	geschlossen
schlingen	schlingst, schlingt	schlang	geschlungen

infinitive	present indicative (2nd, 3rd sg)	imperfect	past participle
schmeißen	schmeißt, schmeißt	schmiss	geschmissen
schmelzen*	schmilzt, schmilzt	schmolz	geschmolzen
schneiden	schneidest, schneidet	schnitt	geschnitten
schreiben	schreibst, schreibt	schrieb	geschrieben
schreien	schreist, schreit	schrie	geschrie(e)n
schreiten	schreitest, schreitet	schritt	geschritten
schweigen	schweigst, schweigt	schwieg	geschwiegen
schwellen*	schwillst, schwillt	schwoll	geschwollen
schwimmen*	schwimmst, schwimmt	schwamm	geschwommen
schwinden*	schwindest, schwindet	schwand	geschwunden
schwingen	schwingst, schwingt	schwang	geschwungen
schwören	schwörst, schwört	schwor	geschworen
sehen	siehst, sieht	sah	gesehen
sein*	bist, ist	war	gewesen
senden	sendest, sendet	sandte	gesandt
singen	singst, singt	sang	gesungen
sinken*	sinkst, sinkt	sank	gesunken
sinnen	sinnst, sinnt	sann	gesonnen
sitzen*	sitzt, sitzt	saß	gesessen
sollen	sollst, soll	sollte	gesollt
speien	speist, speit	spie	gespie(e)n
spinnen	spinnst, spinnt	spann	gesponnen
sprechen	sprichst, spricht	sprach	gesprochen
sprießen*	sprießt, sprießt	spross	gesprossen
springen*	springst, springt	sprang	gesprungen
stechen	stichst, sticht	stach	gestochen
stecken	steckst, steckt	steckte *or* stak	gesteckt
stehen	stehst, steht	stand	gestanden
stehlen	stiehlst, stiehlt	stahl	gestohlen
steigen*	steigst, steigt	stieg	gestiegen
sterben*	stirbst, stirbt	starb	gestorben
stinken	stinkst, stinkt	stank	gestunken
stoßen	stößt, stößt	stieß	gestoßen
streichen	streichst, streicht	strich	gestrichen
streiten*	streitest, streitet	stritt	gestritten
tragen	trägst, trägt	trug	getragen
treffen	triffst, trifft	traf	getroffen
treiben*	treibst, treibt	trieb	getrieben

infinitive	present indicative (2nd, 3rd sg)	imperfect	past participle
treten*	trittst, tritt	trat	getreten
trinken	trinkst, trinkt	trank	getrunken
trügen	trügst, trügt	trog	getrogen
tun	tust, tut	tat	getan
verderben	verdirbst, verdirbt	verdarb	verdorben
verdrießen	verdrießt, verdrießt	verdross	verdrossen
vergessen	vergisst, vergisst	vergaß	vergessen
verlieren	verlierst, verliert	verlor	verloren
verschleißen	verschleißt, verschleißt	verschliss	verschlissen
wachsen*	wächst, wächst	wuchs	gewachsen
weben	webst, webt	webte *or* wob	gewoben
wägen	wägst, wägt	wog	gewogen
waschen	wäschst, wäscht	wusch	gewaschen
weichen*	weichst, weicht	wich	gewichen
weisen	weist, weist	wies	gewiesen
wenden	wendest, wendet	wandte	gewandt
werben	wirbst, wirbt	warb	geworben
werden*	wirst, wird	wurde	geworden
werfen	wirfst, wirft	warf	geworfen
wiegen	wiegst, wiegt	wog	gewogen
winden	windest, windet	wand	gewunden
wissen	weißt, weiß	wusste	gewusst
wollen	willst, will	wollte	gewollt
wringen	wringst, wringt	wrang	gewrungen
zeihen	zeihst, zeiht	zieh	geziehen
ziehen*	ziehst, zieht	zog	gezogen
zwingen	zwingst, zwingt	zwang	gezwungen

GERMAN SPELLING CHANGES

In July 1996, all German-speaking countries signed a declaration concerning the reform of German spelling, with the result that the new spelling rules are now taught in all schools. To ensure that you have the most up-to-date information at your fingertips, the following list contains the old and new spellings of all German headwords and translations in this dictionary which are affected by the reform.

ALT/OLD	NEU/NEW	ALT/OLD	NEU/NEW
abend	**Abend**	aufsein	**auf sein**
Abfluß	**Abfluss**	aufwendig	**aufwendig**
Abflußrohr	**Abflussrohr**		or **aufwändig**
Abschluß	**Abschluss**	auseinanderbrechen	**auseinander brechen**
Abschlußexamen	**Abschlussexamen**	auseinanderbringen	**auseinander bringen**
Abschlußfeier	**Abschlussfeier**	auseinanderfallen	**auseinander fallen**
Abschlußklasse	**Abschlussklasse**	auseinanderfalten	**auseinander falten**
Abschlußprüfung	**Abschlussprüfung**	auseinandergehen	**auseinander gehen**
Abschuß	**Abschuss**	auseinanderhalten	**auseinander halten**
Abschußrampe	**Abschussrampe**	auseinandernehmen	**auseinander nehmen**
Abszeß	**Abszess**	auseinandersetzen	**auseinander setzen**
achtgeben	**Acht geben**	Ausfluß	**Ausfluss**
Adreßbuch	**Adressbuch**	Ausguß	**Ausguss**
Alleinerziehende(r)	**Alleinerziehende(r)**	Auslaß	**Auslass**
	or **allein Erziehende(r)**	Ausschluß	**Ausschluss**
alleinstehend	**allein stehend**	Ausschuß	**Ausschuss**
allgemeingültig	**allgemein gültig**	Ausschuß(artikel)	**Ausschuss(artikel)**
allzuoft	**allzu oft**	aussein	**aus sein**
allzuviel	**allzu viel**	außerstande	**außer Stande**
Alptraum	**Alptraum**	Autobiographie	**Autobiographie**
	or **Albtraum**		or **Autobiografie**
Amboß	**Amboss**	Baß	**Bass**
Amtsanschluß	**Amtsanschluss**	Baßstimme	**Bassstimme**
(Amts)mißbrauch	**(Amts)missbrauch**		or **Bass-Stimme**
andersdenkend	**anders denkend**	Ballettänzer(in)	**Balletttänzer(in)**
aneinandergeraten	**aneinander geraten**		or **Ballett-Tänzer(in)**
aneinanderreihen	**aneinander reihen**	beeinflußbar	**beeinflussbar**
Anlaß	**Anlass**	beiseitelegen	**beiseite legen**
anläßlich	**anlässlich**	bekanntgeben	**bekannt geben**
Anschluß	**Anschluss**	bekanntmachen	**bekannt machen**
Anschlußflug	**Anschlussflug**	Beschluß	**Beschluss**
As	**Ass**	Beschuß	**Beschuss**
aufeinanderfolgen	**aufeinander folgen**	bessergehen	**besser gehen**
aufeinanderfolgend	**aufeinander folgend**	Bettuch	**Betttuch**
aufeinanderlegen	**aufeinander legen**		or **Bett-Tuch**
aufeinanderprallen	**aufeinander prallen**	(Bevölkerungs)überschuß	
Aufschluß	**Aufschluss**		**(Bevölkerungs)überschuss**
aufschlußreich	**aufschlussreich**	bewußt	**bewusst**
aufsehenerregend	**Aufsehen erregend**	bewußtlos	**bewusstlos**

ALT/OLD	NEU/NEW	ALT/OLD	NEU/NEW
Bewußtlosigkeit	Bewusstlosigkeit	durchnumerieren	durchnummerieren
Bewußtsein	Bewusstsein	ehrfurchtgebietend	Ehrfurcht gebietend
bezug	Bezug	Einfluß	Einfluss
Bibliographie	Bibliographie	Einflußbereich	Einflussbereich
	or Bibliografie	einflußreich	einflussreich
Biographie	Biographie	einigemal	einige Mal
	or Biografie	einiggehen	einig gehen
Biß	Biss	Einlaß	Einlass
biß	biss	ekelerregend	Ekel erregend
bißchen	bisschen	Elsaß	Elsass
blaß	blass	Engpaß	Engpass
bläßlich	blässlich	Entschluß	Entschluss
bleibenlassen	bleiben lassen	entschlußfreudig	entschlussfreudig
Bluterguß	Bluterguss	Entschlußkraft	Entschlusskraft
Boß	Boss	epochemachend	Epoche machend
braungebrannt	braun gebrannt	Erdgeschoß	Erdgeschoss
breitmachen	breit machen	Erdnuß	Erdnuss
Brennessel	Brennnessel	Erdnußbutter	Erdnussbutter
	or Brenn-Nessel	erfolgversprechend	Erfolg versprechend
Büroschluß	Büroschluss	Erguß	Erguss
Butterfaß	Butterfass	Erlaß	Erlass
Cashewnuß	Cashewnuss	ernstgemeint	ernst gemeint
Chicorée	Chicorée	erstemal	erste Mal
	or Schikoree	Eß–	Ess–
Choreograph(in)	Choreograph(in)	erstenmal	ersten Mal
	or Choreograf(in)	eßbar	essbar
Computertomographie	Computertomographie	Eßbesteck	Essbesteck
	or Computertomografie	Eßecke	Essecke
dabeisein	dabei sein	Eßgeschirr	Essgeschirr
dafürkönnen	dafür können	Eßkastanie	Esskastanie
dahinterkommen	dahinter kommen	Eßlöffel	Esslöffel
darauffolgend	darauf folgend	Eßlöffel(voll)	Esslöffel (voll)
dasein	da sein	(Eß)stäbchen	(Ess)stäbchen
daß	dass		*or* (Ess-)Stäbchen
Dekolleté	Dekolleté	Eßtisch	Esstisch
	or Dekolletee	Eßwaren	Esswaren
Delphin	Delphin	Eßzimmer	Esszimmer
	or Delfin	Expreß	Express
dessenungeachtet	dessen ungeachtet	Expreß–	Express–
dichtbevölkert	dicht bevölkert	Expreßgut	Expressgut
diensthabend	Dienst habend	Expreßzug	Expresszug
differential	differential	Exzeß	Exzess
	or differenzial	Facette	Facette
Differentialrechnung	Differentialrechnung		*or* Fassette
	or Differenzialrechnung	Fährenanschluß	Fährenanschluss
Diktaphon	Diktaphon	Fairneß	Fairness
	or Diktafon	fallenlassen	fallen lassen
dreiviertel	drei Viertel	Faß	Fass
durcheinanderbringen	durcheinander bringen	faßbar	fassbar
durcheinanderreden	durcheinander reden	Fehlschuß	Fehlschuss
durcheinanderwerfen	durcheinander werfen	fernhalten	fern halten

ALT/OLD	NEU/NEW	ALT/OLD	NEU/NEW
fertigbringen	fertig bringen	gewiß	gewiss
fertigmachen	fertig machen	Gewißheit	Gewissheit
fertigstellen	fertig stellen	gewußt	gewusst
fertigwerden	fertig werden	glattrasiert	glatt rasiert
festangestellt	fest angestellt	glattstreichen	glatt streichen
Fitneß	Fitness	gleichbleibend	gleich bleibend
fleischfressend	Fleisch fressend	gleichgesinnt	gleich gesinnt
floß	floss	Glimmstengel	Glimmstängel
Fluß	Fluss	Grammophon	Grammophon
Fluß–	Fluss–		*or* Grammofon
flußabwärts	flussabwärts	(Grammophon)nadel	(Grammophon)nadel
Flußbarsch	Flussbarsch		*or* (Grammofon)nadel
Flußbett	Flussbett	Graphiker(in)	Graphiker(in)
Flußdiagramm	Flussdiagramm		*or* Grafiker(in)
flüssigmachen	flüssig machen	graphisch	graphisch
Flußufer	Flussufer		*or* grafisch
Fön ®	Fön	gräßlich	grässlich
	or Föhn ®	Greuel	Gräuel
fönen	föhnen	Greueltat	Gräueltat
Fönfrisur	Föhnfrisur	greulich	gräulich
Friedensschluß	Friedensschluss	Grundriß	Grundriss
Frischvermählte	frisch Vermählte	Guß	Guss
Frischvermählten	frisch Vermählten	Gußeisen	Gusseisen
frißt	frisst	gutaussehend	gut aussehend
fritieren	frittieren	gutgehen	gut gehen
Gebiß	Gebiss	gutgehend	gut gehend
Gebührenerlaß	Gebührenerlass	gutgemeint	gut gemeint
gefangen(gehalten)	gefangen (gehalten)	guttun	gut tun
gefangenhalten	gefangen halten	haftenbleiben	haften bleiben
gefangennehmen	gefangen nehmen	halboffen	halb offen
gefaßt	gefasst	haltmachen	Halt machen
geheimhalten	geheim halten	Hämorrhoiden	Hämorrhoiden
gehenlassen	gehen lassen		*or* Hämorriden
Gemeinschaftsanschluß		Handvoll	Hand voll
	Gemeinschaftsanschluss	hängenbleiben	hängen bleiben
Gemse	Gämse	hängenlassen	hängen lassen
gemußt	gemusst	hartgekocht	hart gekocht
genaugenommen	genau genommen	Haselnuß	Haselnuss
Genuß	Genuss	Haß	Hass
genüßlich	genüsslich	häßlich	hässlich
Genußmittel	Genussmittel	Häßlichkeit	Hässlichkeit
Geograph	Geograph	haushalten	haushalten
	or Geograf		*or* Haus halten
Geographie	Geographie	heiligsprechen	heilig sprechen
	or Geografie	Hexenschuß	Hexenschuss
geographisch	geographisch	hierbehalten	hier behalten
	or geografisch	hierbleiben	hier bleiben
geringachten	gering achten	hierlassen	hier lassen
Geschäftsschluß	Geschäftsschluss	hierzulande	hierzulande
Geschoß	Geschoss		*or* hier zu Lande
gewinnbringend	Gewinn bringend	hochachten	hoch achten

616

ALT/OLD	NEU/NEW	ALT/OLD	NEU/NEW
hochbegabt	hoch begabt	kompromißlos	kompromisslos
hochdotiert	hoch dotiert	Kompromißlösung	Kompromisslösung
hochentwickelt	hoch entwickelt	Kongreß	Kongress
(hoch)geschätzt	(hoch) geschätzt	Kongreßzentrum	Kongresszentrum
(hoch)schätzen	(hoch) schätzen	Kontrabaß	Kontrabass
(Honorar)vorschuß	(Honorar)vorschuss	kraß	krass
Imbiß	Imbiss	Kreppapier	Krepppapier
Imbißhalle	Imbisshalle		or Krepp-Papier
Imbißraum	Imbissraum	kriegführend	Krieg führend
Imbißstube	Imbissstube	krummnehmen	krumm nehmen
	or Imbiss-Stube	Kurzbiographie	Kurzbiographie
immerwährend	immer während		or Kurzbiografie
imstande	imstande	kurzhalten	kurz halten
	or im Stande	Kurzschluß	Kurzschluss
ineinandergreifen	ineinander greifen	Kuß	Kuss
ineinanderschieben	ineinander schieben	Ladenschluß	Ladenschluss
Intercity-Expreßzug	Intercity-Expresszug	Laufpaß	Laufpass
ißt	isst	leerlaufen	leer laufen
Jahresabschluß	Jahresabschluss	leerstehend	leer stehend
jedesmal	jedes Mal	leichtfallen	leicht fallen
Joghurt	Joghurt	leichtmachen	leicht machen
	or Jogurt	Lenkradschloß	Lenkradschloss
kahlgeschoren	kahl geschoren	letztemal	letzte Mal
kaltbleiben	kalt bleiben	liebgewinnen	lieb gewinnen
Kammuschel	Kammmuschel	liebhaben	lieb haben
	or Kamm-Muschel	liegenbleiben	liegen bleiben
Känguruh	Känguru	liegenlassen	liegen lassen
Karamel	Karamell	Litfaßsäule	Litfasssäule
Karamelbonbon	Karamellbonbon		or Litfass-Säule
Katarrh	Katarrh	Lithographie	Lithographie
	or Katarr		or Lithografie
Kellergeschoß	Kellergeschoss	Luftschloß	Luftschloss
kennenlernen	kennen lernen	maschineschreiben	Maschine schreiben
keß	kess	maßhalten	Maß halten
klarsehen	klar sehen	Megaphon	Megaphon
klarwerden	klar werden		or Megafon
klassenbewußt	klassenbewusst	Meldeschluß	Meldeschluss
Klassenbewußtsein	Klassenbewusstsein	meßbar	messbar
klatschnaß	klatschnass	Meßbecher	Messbecher
kleinhacken	klein hacken	Meßgerät	Messgerät
kleinschneiden	klein schneiden	Mikrophon	Mikrophon
klitschnaß	klitschnass		or Mikrofon
knapphalten	knapp halten	Miß–	Miss–
Kokosnuß	Kokosnuss	mißachten	missachten
Koloß	Koloss	Mißachtung	Missachtung
Kombinationsschloß	Kombinationsschloss	Mißbehagen	Missbehagen
Kommuniqué	Kommuniqué	Mißbildung	Missbildung
	or Kommunikee	mißbilligen	missbilligen
Kompaß	Kompass	Mißbilligung	Missbilligung
Kompromiß	Kompromiss	Mißbrauch	Missbrauch
kompromißbereit	kompromissbereit	mißbrauchen	missbrauchen

ALT/OLD	NEU/NEW	ALT/OLD	NEU/NEW
Mißerfolg	**Misserfolg**	Nebenanschluß	**Nebenanschluss**
Mißfallen	**Missfallen**	nebeneinanderlegen	**nebeneinander legen**
mißfallen	**missfallen**	nebeneinanderstellen	**nebeneinander stellen**
Mißgeburt	**Missgeburt**	Nebenfluß	**Nebenfluss**
Mißgeschick	**Missgeschick**	Necessaire	**Necessaire**
mißgestaltet	**missgestaltet**		or **Nessessär**
mißglücken	**missglücken**	Negligé	**Negligé**
mißgönnen	**missgönnen**		or **Negligee**
Mißgriff	**Missgriff**	Netzanschluß	**Netzanschluss**
Mißgunst	**Missgunst**	neuentdeckt	**neu entdeckt**
mißgünstig	**missgünstig**	nichtsahnend	**nichts ahnend**
mißhandeln	**misshandeln**	nichtssagend	**nichts sagend**
Mißhandlung	**Misshandlung**	Nonstop–	**Nonstop–**
Mißklang	**Missklang**		or **Non-Stop–**
Mißkredit	**Misskredit**	notleidend	**Not leidend**
mißlich	**misslich**	numerieren	**nummerieren**
mißlingen	**misslingen**	Nuß	**Nuss**
mißlungen	**misslungen**	Nußbaum	**Nussbaum**
Mißmut	**Missmut**	Nußknacker	**Nussknacker**
mißmutig	**missmutig**	Nußschale	**Nussschale**
mißraten	**missraten**		or **Nuss-Schale**
Mißstand	**Missstand**	obenerwähnt	**oben erwähnt**
	or **Miss-Stand**	obengenannt	**oben genannt**
Mißtrauen	**Misstrauen**	Obergeschoß	**Obergeschoss**
mißtrauen	**misstrauen**	offenbleiben	**offen bleiben**
Mißtrauensantrag	**Misstrauensantrag**	offenhalten	**offen halten**
Mißtrauensvotum	**Misstrauensvotum**	offenlassen	**offen lassen**
mißtrauisch	**misstrauisch**	offenstehen	**offen stehen**
Mißverhältnis	**Missverhältnis**	Ölmeßstab	**Ölmessstab**
Mißverständnis	**Missverständnis**		or **Ölmess-Stab**
mißverstehen	**missverstehen**	Orthographie	**Orthographie**
Mißwirtschaft	**Misswirtschaft**		or **Orthografie**
mittag	**Mittag**	orthographisch	**orthographisch**
Mop	**Mopp**		or **orthografisch**
Muß	**Muss**	paarmal	**paar Mal**
mußte	**musste**	Panther	**Panther**
nachhinein	**Nachhinein**		or **Panter**
Nachlaß	**Nachlass**	Paragraph	**Paragraph**
nahegehen	**nahe gehen**		or **Paragraf**
nahekommen	**nahe kommen**	Paranuß	**Paranuss**
nahelegen	**nahe legen**	Parlamentsbeschluß	**Parlamentsbeschluss**
naheliegen	**nahe liegen**	Paß	**Pass**
naheliegend	**nahe liegend**	Paß–	**Pass–**
näherkommen	**näher kommen**	Paßamt	**Passamt**
näherrücken	**näher rücken**	Paßbild	**Passbild**
nahestehen	**nahe stehen**	Paßkontrolle	**Passkontrolle**
nahestehend	**nahe stehend**	Paßstelle	**Passstelle**
nahetreten	**nahe treten**		or **Pass-Stelle**
naß	**nass**	Paßstraße	**Passstraße**
naßkalt	**nasskalt**		or **Pass-Straße**
Naßrasur	**Nassrasur**	patschnaß	**patschnass**

ALT/OLD	NEU/NEW	ALT/OLD	NEU/NEW
pflichtbewußt	**pflichtbewusst**	rotglühend	**rot glühend**
Phantasie	**Phantasie**	Rückschluß	**Rückschluss**
	or **Fantasie**	Rußland	**Russland**
Phantasie–	**Phantasie–**	Safe(r) Sex	**Safe(r) Sex**
	or **Fantasie–**		or **Safe(r)-sex**
phantasielos	**phantasielos**	Salzfaß	**Salzfass**
	or **fantasielos**	sauberhalten	**sauber halten**
phantasiereich	**phantasiereich**	Saxophon	**Saxophon**
	or **fantasiereich**		or **Saxofon**
phantasieren	**phantasieren**	Schattenriß	**Schattenriss**
	or **fantasieren**	schiefgehen	**schief gehen**
phantasievoll	**phantasievoll**	Schiffahrt	**Schifffahrt**
	or **fantasievoll**		or **Schiff–Fahrt**
phantastisch	**phantastisch**	Schiffahrtslinie	**Schifffahrtslinie**
	or **fantastisch**	Schlangenbiß	**Schlangenbiss**
platschnaß	**platschnass**	schlechtgehen	**schlecht gehen**
plazieren	**platzieren**	schlechtmachen	**schlecht machen**
Pornographie	**Pornographie**	Schlegel	**Schlägel**
	or **Pornografie**	Schloß	**Schloss**
pornographisch	**pornographisch**	schloß	**schloss**
	or **pornografisch**	Schluß	**Schluss**
Portemonnaie	**Portemonnaie**	Schluß–	**Schluss–**
	or **Portmonee**	(Schluß)folgerung	**(Schluss)folgerung**
Potential	**Potential**	Schlußlicht	**Schlusslicht**
	or **Potenzial**	Schlußrunde	**Schlussrunde**
potentiell	**potentiell**	Schlußrundenteilnehmer	
	or **potenziell**		**Schlussrundenteilnehmer**
preisbewußt	**preisbewusst**	Schlußstrich	**Schlussstrich**
Preßluft	**Pressluft**		or **Schluss–Strich**
Preßluftbohrer	**Pressluftbohrer**	Schlußverkauf	**Schlussverkauf**
Preßlufthammer	**Presslufthammer**	Schmiß	**Schmiss**
Prozeß	**Prozess**	Schnappschloß	**Schnappschloss**
Prüfungsausschuß	**Prüfungsausschuss**	Schnappschuß	**Schnappschuss**
radfahren	**Rad fahren**	Schnellimbiß	**Schnellimbiss**
(Raketen)abschuß	**(Raketen)abschuss**	schneuzen	**schnäuzen**
Rassenhaß	**Rassenhass**	schoß	**schoss**
rauh	**rau**	Schößling	**Schössling**
Rauhreif	**Raureif**	Schrittempo	**Schritttempo**
Raumschiffahrt	**Raumschifffahrt**		or **Schritt–Tempo**
	or **Raumschiff–Fahrt**	Schuß	**Schuss**
Rausschmiß	**Rausschmiss**	Schußbereich	**Schussbereich**
Rechnungsabschluß	**Rechnungsabschluss**	Schußlinie	**Schusslinie**
reinwaschen	**rein waschen**	Schußverletzung	**Schussverletzung**
Reisepaß	**Reisepass**	Schußwaffe	**Schusswaffe**
Reißverschluß	**Reißverschluss**	Schußweite	**Schussweite**
richtigstellen	**richtig stellen**	schwererziehbar	**schwer erziehbar**
Riß	**Riss**	schwerfallen	**schwer fallen**
Rolladen	**Rollladen**	schwermachen	**schwer machen**
	or **Roll–Laden**	schwernehmen	**schwer nehmen**
Roß	**Ross**	schwertun	**schwer tun**
Roßkastanie	**Rosskastanie**	schwerverdaulich	**schwer verdaulich**

ALT/OLD	NEU/NEW	ALT/OLD	NEU/NEW
schwerverletzt	schwer verletzt		or telegrafieren
Seismograph	Seismograph	Thunfisch	Thunfisch
	or Seismograf		or Tunfisch
selbständig	selbständig	tiefausgeschnitten	tief ausgeschnitten
	or selbstständig	tiefgehend	tief gehend
Selbständigkeit	Selbständigkeit	tiefgekühlt	tief gekühlt
	or Selbstständigkeit	tiefgreifend	tief greifend
selbstbewußt	selbstbewusst	tiefschürfend	tief schürfend
Selbstbewußtsein	Selbstbewusstsein	Tip	Tipp
selbstgemacht	selbst gemacht	topographisch	topographisch
selbstverständlich	selbst verständlich		or topografisch
selbstverwaltet	selbst verwaltet	totenblaß	totenblass
seßhaft	sesshaft	totgeboren	tot geboren
Showbusineß	Showbusiness	Trugschluß	Trugschluss
Sicherheitsschloß	Sicherheitsschloss	tschüs	tschüs
sitzenbleiben	sitzen bleiben		or tschüss
sitzenlassen	sitzen lassen	übelgelaunt	übel gelaunt
Skipaß	Skipass	übelnehmen	übel nehmen
sogenannt	so genannt	übelriechend	übel riechend
Sommerschlußverkauf		übelwollend	übel wollend
	Sommerschlussverkauf	Überdruß	Überdruss
sonstjemand	sonst jemand	übereinanderlegen	übereinander legen
sonstwo	sonst wo	Überfluß	Überfluss
sonstwoher	sonst woher	Überschuß	Überschuss
sonstwohin	sonst wohin	überschwenglich	überschwänglich
Spannbettuch	Spannbetttuch	übrigbleiben	übrig bleiben
	or Spannbett-Tuch	übriggeblieben	übrig geblieben
spazierenfahren	spazieren fahren	übriglassen	übrig lassen
spazierengehen	spazieren gehen	Umriß	Umriss
Sprößling	Sprössling	unbewußt	unbewusst
steckenbleiben	stecken bleiben	Unbewußte	Unbewusste
steckenlassen	stecken lassen	unerläßlich	unerlässlich
stehenbleiben	stehen bleiben	unermeßlich	unermesslich
stehenlassen	stehen lassen	unfaßbar	unfassbar
Stengel	Stängel	ungewiß	ungewiss
Stenographie	Stenographie	Ungewißheit	Ungewissheit
	or Stenografie	unmißverständlich	unmissverständlich
stenographieren	stenographieren	unpäßlich	unpässlich
	or stenografieren	unselbständig	unselbständig
Stenograph(in)	Stenograph(in)		or unselbstständig
	or Stenograf(in)	unterbewußt	unterbewusst
stereophonisch	stereophonisch	Unterbewußte	Unterbewusste
	or stereofonisch	Unterbewußtsein	Unterbewusstsein
Stewardeß	Stewardess	Untergeschoß	Untergeschoss
Stilleben	Stillleben	Untersuchungsausschuß	
	or Still-Leben		Untersuchungsausschuss
stillegen	stilllegen	unvergeßlich	unvergesslich
Streifschuß	Streifschuss	Varieté	Varieté
strenggenommen	streng genommen		or Varietee
Streß	Stress	verantwortungsbewußt	
telegraphieren	telegraphieren		verantwortungsbewusst

ALT/OLD	NEU/NEW	ALT/OLD	NEU/NEW
Verdruß	Verdruss	wiedergutzumachen	wieder gutzumachen
vergeßlich	vergesslich	wiederherstellen	wieder herstellen
Vergeßlichkeit	Vergesslichkeit	wiedersehen	wieder sehen
Vergißmeinnicht	Vergissmeinnicht	wiedervereinigen	wieder vereinigen
vergißt	vergisst	wiederverwenden	wieder verwenden
verhaßt	verhasst	wiederverwerten	wieder verwerten
Verlaß	Verlass	wieviel	wie viel
verläßlich	verlässlich	Wißbegier(de)	Wissbegier(de)
verlorengehen	verloren gehen	wißbegierig	wissbegierig
vermißt	vermisst	wohltun	wohl tun
Verschluß	Verschluss	wußte	wusste
vertrauenerweckend	Vertrauen erweckend	Xylophon	Xylophon
vielsagend	viel sagend		or Xylofon
vielversprechend	viel versprechend	Zahlenschloß	Zahlenschloss
(voll)fressen	(voll) fressen	zeitlang	Zeit lang
vollgepfropft	voll gepfropft	zielbewußt	zielbewusst
vollpfropfen	voll pfropfen	Zuckerguß	Zuckerguss
vollstopfen	voll stopfen	zufriedengeben	zufrieden geben
volltanken	voll tanken	zufriedenstellen	zufrieden stellen
vorgefaßt	vorgefasst	zufriedenstellend	zufrieden stellend
vorhinein	Vorhinein	zugrunde	zugrunde
	or zu Grunde		or zu Grunde
vorliebnehmen	vorlieb nehmen	zugunsten	zugunsten
Vorschuß	Vorschuss		or zu Gunsten
vorwärtsbewegen	vorwärts bewegen	zuleide	zuleide
vorwärtsdrängen	vorwärts drängen		or zu Leide
vorwärtsgehen	vorwärts gehen	zumute	zumute
vorwärtskommen	vorwärts kommen		or zu Mute
Waggon	Waggon	Zündschloß	Zündschloss
	or Wagon	Zungenkuß	Zungenkuss
Walnuß	Walnuss	zunutze	zunutze
Walroß	Walross		or zu Nutze
wasserabstoßend	Wasser abstoßend	Zusammenschluß	Zusammenschluss
wäßrig	wässrig	zuschulden	zuschulden
Weißrußland	Weißrussland		or zu Schulden
weitblickend	weitblickend	Zuschuß	Zuschuss
	or weit blickend	zustande	zustande
weitreichend	weitreichend		or zu Stande
	or weit reichend	zustande bringen	zustande bringen
weitverbreitet	weitverbreitet		or zu Stande bringen
	or weit verbreitet	zustande kommen	zustande kommen
wiederaufbauen	wieder aufbauen		or zu Stande kommen
wiederaufbereiten	wieder aufbereiten	zutage	zutage
wiederaufnehmen	wieder aufnehmen		or zu Tage
wiederbeleben	wieder beleben	zuviel	zu viel
wiedereinsetzen	wieder einsetzen	zuwege	zuwege
wiedererkennen	wieder erkennen		or zu Wege
wiedererwachen	wieder erwachen	zuwenig	zu wenig
wiedergutmachen	wieder gutmachen		